PRENTICE HALL
Quality Yearbook
1996/1997

Richard Barrett Clements
Editor

PRENTICE HALL
Englewood Cliffs, New Jersey 07632

Printed in the United States of America

10 9 8 7 6 5 4 3 2 1

ISSN 1087-125X

ISBN 0-13-249616-X

9 780132 496162

ATTENTION CORPORATIONS AND SCHOOLS

Prentice Hall books are available at quantity discounts with bulk purchase for educational, business, or sales promotional use. For information, please write to: Prentice Hall Career & Personal Development Special Sales, 113 Sylvan Avenue, Englewood Cliffs, NJ 07632. Please supply: title of book, ISBN number, quantity, how the book will be used, date needed.

PRENTICE HALL
Career & Personal Development
Englewood Cliffs, NJ 07632
A Simon & Schuster Company

On the World Wide Web at http://www.phdirect.com

Prentice Hall International (UK), Ltd., *London*
Prentice-Hall of Australia Pty, Limited, *Sydney*
Prentice-Hall Canada Inc., *Toronto*
Prentice-Hall Hispanoamericana, S.A., *Mexico*
Prentice-Hall of India Private Limited, *New Delhi*
Prentice-Hall of Japan, Inc., *Tokyo*
Simon & Schuster Asia Pte. Ltd., *Singapore*
Editora Prentice-Hall do Brasil, Ltda., *Rio de Janeiro*

ABOUT THE AUTHOR

Richard Barrett Clements is president of Solution Specialists, a firm specializing in management and quality assurance technologies for international competitiveness. He is the author of several books on the subjects of quality, computers, and management. This includes the best-sellers, *Handbook of Statistical Methods in Manufacturing* (Prentice Hall), *Quality Manager's Complete Guide to ISO 9000* (Prentice Hall), *Complete Guide to ISO 14000* (Prentice Hall), and the audio cassette tape "ISO 9000: Opportunity Within Confusion." He is best known for his pioneering work in using modern technology to create interactive user groups of companies sharing competitive experiences.

He is also one of the founders of the National ISO 9000 / ISO 14000 Support Group. This is a third-party, neutral organization dedicated to providing outreach support to companies seeking ISO 9000 and/or ISO 14000 registration. The Support Group has foreign offices in Dublin, Ireland and Sao Paolo, Brazil.

Currently, Mr. Clements is an ISO 9000 assessor registered with the Institute for Quality Assurance in England. He is a non-voting participant in Technical Committees 176 and 207, which are responsible for the creation and revision of the ISO 9000 and ISO 14000 standards, respectively.

Mr. Clements holds a Bachelors degree from Michigan State University and a Masters degree from the University of Chicago. He ia actively pursuing post-graduate studies. He is best known for his "generalist" approach to technology, the ability to express complex methods in terms of stories and simple analogies to make the methods easily understood by a wide audience. His writings have twice earned him the Golden Quill award from the American Society for Quality Control.

DEDICATION

To Wendy DeLange, tireless worker and primary reason this book was completed.

CONTENTS

SECTION One
BASIC KNOWLEDGE FOR THE QUALITY MANAGER

SECTION Two
QUALITY BY INDUSTRY

Section Three
QUALITY TECHNOLOGIES AND METHODS

Section Four
STANDARDS AND AWARDS

Section Five
THE STATE OF THE QUALITY PROFESSION

Section Six
CHECKLISTS

Appendices

INTRODUCTION

QUALITY—THE YEAR IN REVIEW

The beginning of 1996 sees a fundamental change in the profession of quality assurance. Deming is gone, Juran is retired, and ISO 9000 registrations are reaching the 100,000 mark worldwide. In brief, we are seeing philosophies being replaced by standardization. Gurus and their followers are being replaced by a movement toward uniformity and corporate dictates. Hammer's view of reengineering is confronting the ideal of total quality.

At the same time, the function of the quality manager—and most quality professionals—is changing. Only a dozen or so years ago, quality assurance personnel were primarily responsible for inspection and statistical control related activities. Today, the typical quality manager is also involved in problem-solving teams, productivity enhancement projects, and customer relations. This trend toward more responsibilities for the quality assurance department is expected to continue. Let us see why this is so.

WHY BUSINESS IS UNDERGOING A FUNDAMENTAL CHANGE

The end of the Cold War and the signing of treaties such as GATT, NAFTA, and the European Union has fundamentally changed the business structure of the world. Now the majority of countries are becoming capitalistic. Free and open trade is the goal of most nations. International standards for products, materials, and systems ease the complication of world trade. Low-cost transportation makes such trading possible. Low-interest rates promotes stability.

The result is a new business climate. In addition, corporations are reducing staff, reengineering systems, and diversifying responsibilities. For example, one of the top 10 corporations in the world has gone from a supplier quality assurance department with hundreds of employees to a single person now handling that function. Therefore, the tens of thousands of supplier companies involved with such corporations find that they now are examined by third parties.

At the same time, the interest in quality assurance is no longer associated with just the manufacturing field. Instead, service-based companies represent one of the fastest growing segments using quality assurance techniques. As you will see in this book, institutions such as finance, schools, governments, and the like are embracing techniques normally associated with manufacturing processes. This includes statistical process control, problem-solving teams, total quality management, and continuous improvement.

In the preparation of this book, I examined all quality assurance-related articles published over the past year in periodicals around the world. The majority of these articles dealth with non-manufacturing situations. This growing trend in the use of quality assurance techniques should be duly noted.

THE GROWTH OF STANDARDIZATION

Voluntary international standards and guidelines for management systems and product characteristics are growing in popularity. Much of this is due to the new world trading conditions and the restructuring of corporations. It also comes from a long held desire by smaller companies to have a single set of requirements for many customers.

Therefore, standards such as ISO 9000 and ISO 14000, as well as QS-9000, represent this movement toward standardization. Thus, quality managers must be aware of these standards even if they do not directly apply to his or her company. So many customers are now thinking of using these standards that virtually any company may find that they to have to conform.

THE NEW ROLE OF THE QUALITY PROFESSIONAL

Just a few years ago a quality professional would be expected to provide the quality assurance functions for a company. Today, that same individual is expected to contribute actively to the profitability of the company. The quality assurance function is being decentralized; with top management taking a more active role. The quality assurance professional is expected to participate on teams, work with reengineering efforts, cope with downsizing, advise the environmental staff, and deal with international standards.

To accomplish these new responsibilities, the quality manager and most other quality professionals need to learn new skills. This means attending training, practicing techniques, and keeping up-to-date with current literature. However, all of this has to be accomplished within the working schedule of the quality professional. Conflicts are inevitable.

Therefore, a whole new range of products and services are now becoming available to the quality manager. For example, this book is designed to allow you to review an entire year of critical literature in a short period of time. In addition, this book contains reference material to help you find the new resources needed to cope with the demands of your job. This includes the explosive growth of internet resources related to quality assurance. It also includes new technologies that allow you to organize your quality team more efficiently.

Technologies such as local area networks, e-mail, video conferencing, statistical software, decision making software, updated telephone services, and the like make it possible for the quality manager to control a larger number of people while increasing each person's productivity.

THE FUTURE

Predicting the future is always a tricky proposition. Any prediction beyond a year or two is hopeful conjecture. However, the next year promises additional growth in the trends described here. It also marks the full introduction of the ISO 14000 standard for environmental management systems. It if proves popular, it will represent another major change for the quality assurance department. Because it is based on the registration system established by ISO 9000, ISO 14000 will frequently involve the consulting of the person that implemented ISO 9000. In most cases, that will be you. This is why we included an entire section in this book on this topic.

In addition, you will note that some chapters do not at first appear to be related to the quality field. In many cases, articles discuss how to increase productivity, improve supplier relationships, legal issues, world trade situations, and the like. These are presented so that you can be aware of issues that can suddenly involve your job. The quality manager is no longer restricted just to "quality-related" issues.

The future should find that most professionals will have to learn new skills and technology just to keep up with the demands of their job. Most professionals today find that they have to accomplish more in less time with fewer resources. Only the well-prepared and informed manager will be able to cope with this situation.

Richard Barrett Clements

HOW TO USE THIS BOOK

The *Prentice Hall Quality Yearbook* was designed primarily to provide you with an overview of the best articles published during the year related to quality assurance. It was also designed to compile resource appendices to be used as daily reference tools. In other words, when you need to find an answer to a quality-related question this should be the first book you consult.

Therefore, the first time you look through this book you should scan the titles of articles in chapters that directly affect your responsibilities as a quality manager. You should also glance at the reference appendices at the back of the book so that you are familiar with the resources available.

Soon after getting this book you should read some of the articles related to your immediate concerns. This will bring you up to date with the newest information on topics of interest to you. Later, as new concerns arise you can consult this book to quickly get up to speed on the topic.

Finally, this book is designed to acquaint you with other voices in the quality field. As you read through this book you should note the sources of some of the information. You may find a periodical that supplies articles of interest to you. Or, you may read some samples from a newsletter to which you have always debated whether or not to subscribe. Either way, we have provided information on where each article originates and how to get further information from that publication.

HOW THIS BOOK WILL HELP YOU

The *Prentice Hall Quality Yearbook* is a multi-purpose book. Not only does it serve many functions, but it is interactive. At the end of this section is a list of contact information for asking questions of the authors and the editor. The resource appendices are filled with additional organizations you can contact to receive further information.

1. *Keep up to date.*

   The articles in this book represent information taken from the past year of publications. Therefore, only the newest information is available. Because quality assurance is a field in a state of change, this type of information will be invaluable for the quality manager wishing to stay on top of the situation.

2. *Find new sources of information you didn't know existed.*

   Because each article clearly identifies its source, you can find new sources of information to assist you in your job. The internet resources can point the way to a whole new world of information and discussions for the quality manager. Also, you will note that there are many more quality-related publications in the world than you thought possible. We found over 100 publications that have a strong quality assurance theme.

3. *Find answers quickly.*

   If you have a question this book doesn't quickly answer, there are many resources listed where you can get the information you need. There are national, trade, and professional organizations listed (see Appendix B). We tell you how to contact computer-based resources and support groups (see Appendix C). Do you want to talk to the author of an article? The phone numbers for the periodicals that published the particular article are also listed (see Appendix F).

4. *Become aware of the changing direction of the quality assurance field.*

As indicated in the introduction, the quality assurance field is changing. In this book you will find discussions of business process reengineering, productivity teams, group problem-solving, and other techniques that are more frequently involving the quality department. By reading the material you can prepare yourself and your department for participation.

5. *Begin to learn new skills.*

Many of the stories told in this book illustrate new techniques or new ways to use old techniques. These can help any quality manager to think of innovative ways to apply the right technique to a specific problem. The book can also alert you to any new techniques that seem to hold promise for your company. In such a case you can identify where you and your staff will need additional training to effectively use the technique.

6. *Keep your library in a small space.*

Most quality departments have a small library of reference works and trade journals. This book summarizes the best of the articles published over the past year, thus it gives you the information you need in very little shelf space. Each year another *Yearbook* will be published. Thus, you can quickly build up a considerable collection of important literature in just a few volumes.

FOR FURTHER QUESTIONS

To contact the editor of this book with any questions, please use the information below. If you find additional resources or have corrections about information presented in this book, your correspondence is welcomed. Specifically, if I have omitted a resource or someone has added a service or changed location, I would like to hear about it. Feel free to send a short message to any of the addresses below.

Updates of the information presented will also be posted to a computer bulletin board service (BBS), a world wide web home page, and a fax-on-demand service. All of these can the accessed at no charge. The world wide web page is accessible from any internet site around the world.

Richard Barrett Clements
Solution Specialists
9864 Cherry Valley
Suite C
Caledonia, MI 49302
USA

(616) 891-9114 voice / FAX
(616) 891-9433 BBS
(616) 891-0161 Fax on Demand (24 hours a day)

ACKNOWLEDGEMENTS

Naturally, the creation of a book of this size is beyond the capability of any individual. Therefore, I would like to thank the following people that made this yearbook possible, Ms. Sara Olberding of 17th Annual Spring Conference and Resource 1995 Proceedings, Ms. April Schumway of *ASQC Quality Management Journal*, Ms. Faith Kluntz of *BYTE*, Mr. Richard B. Clements of *Continuous Improvement*, Ms. Vicki J. Powers of *Continuous Journey*, Ms. Noelle Oertle of *Executive Excellence*, Mr. William C. Paulson of *F-D-C Reports*, Ms. Elaine McShulskis of *H R Magazine*, George Kershaw of *Journal of the Society for Software Quality*, Ellen R. Domb, Ph.D. of *Journal of the Society of Software Quality*, Mr. Peter R. Nelson of *Journal of Quality Technology*, Mr. James R. Koelsch of *Manufacturing Engineering*, Mr. John Falcioni of *Mechanical Engineering*, Ms. Susan Edgar of *Mortgage Banking*, Ms. Dawn Anfuso of *Personnel Journal*, Robin Yale Bergstrom of *Production*, Ms. Mary King of *Production and Inventory Management Journal*, Mr. Robert L. Karkoff of *Purchasing*, Mr. Gary Parr of *Quality*, Ms. Sandra J. Onorato of *Quality Assurance Bulletin*, Ms. Marion Harmon of *Quality Digest*, Amy Zuckerman of *Quality Digest*, Gary Blake, Ph.D. of *Quality Digest*, Ms. Sandra J. Onorato of *Quality Management*, Mr. Brad Stratton of *Quality Progress*, Ms. Sandra Onorato of *Quality Solutions*, Mr. Mark Morrow of *Quality Systems Update*, Ms. Kathryn Z. West of *Risk Management*, Mr. Robert W. Hall of *Target*, Ms. Kathy Velasco of *The Fabricator*, Mr. Dave Smith of *Ward's Auto World*. We also acknowledge the dedicated staff at Prentice Hall and Solution Specialists for the hundreds of hours of work they put into the production of this book. Finally, thank you to the Internet for making rapid worldwide communication on quality issues possible.

SECTION

One

BASIC KNOWLEDGE FOR THE QUALITY MANAGER

This section establishes the recent trends in quality assurance. It begins by looking at a classic description of one of the basic philosophies about quality. This will lay the groundwork for understanding the past and present attitudes within the quality-assurance field. Next it looks at news and legal issues. This will serve as a reminder that the quality-assurance profession is more than a collection of techniques wrapped in a philosophy.

The quality manager of today carries many responsibilities. The legal requirements of quality assurance have greatly increased over the past several years. New purchasing agreements and the use of national and international standards for products and management systems for quality assurance are more widely used. These contractual requirements can be the primary responsibility of the quality manager.

As you will see in later sections, the techniques and technologies related to quality assurance are presented against this background. Therefore, you should first study the background before you look at the primary activities in a quality department. You should also begin to see that the quality department is beginning to dissolve into other company functions.

TQC IS A THOUGHT REVOLUTION IN MANAGEMENT*
by Kaoru Ishikawa, translated by David J. Lu

If TQC is implemented company-wide, it can contribute to the improvement of a company's corporate health and character.

QC is one of the major objectives of the company. It is its new management philosophy.

Set your eyes on long-term profits and put quality first.

Destroy sectionalism.

TQC is management with facts.

TQC is management based on respect for humanity.

QC is a discipline that combines knowledge with action.

I. THOUGHT REVOLUTION

As discussed in Chapter 1, one of the reasons I began QC was: "The eight years that I spent in the nonacademic world after my graduation taught me that Japanese industry and society behaved very irrationally. I began to feel that by studying quality control, and by applying QC properly, the irrational behavior of industry and society could be corrected. In other words, I felt that the application of QC could accomplish revitalization of industry and effect a thought revolution in management."

To associate revitalization of industry with a thought revolution in management may sound somewhat excessive. But that expression represented the goal to which I aspired. Many companies had transformed themselves after applying QC. The manner in which they were transformed may be classified in the following six categories:

1. Quality first—not short-term profit first

2. Consumer orientation—not producer orientation. Think from the standpoint of the other party

3. The next process is your customer—breaking down the barrier of sectionalism

4. Using facts and data to make presentations — utilization of statistical methods

5. Respect for humanity as a management philosophy — full participatory management

6. Cross-function management

II. QUALITY FIRST

If a company follows the principle of "quality first," its profits will increase in the long-run. If a company pursues the goal of attaining a short-term profit, it will lose competitiveness in the international market, and will lose profit in the long-run.

Management that stresses "quality first" can gain customer confidence step by step, and the company's sales will increase gradually. In the long-run, profits will be substantial, and will permit the company to have stable management. If a company follows the principle of "profit first," it may obtain a quick profit, but it cannot sustain competitiveness for a long period of time.

These things are easier said than done. In practice, many companies are still operating on the basis of profit first. They may proclaim "quality first," but at the shop they are only interested in cutting cost. Some people still fear that raising quality means raising cost, which in turn will reduce profit. It is true that cost will rise temporarily when the quality of design is upgraded. However, the immediate trade-off can be found in the company's ability to satisfy the requirements of consumers and to meet competition in the world market.

*From the book: *What Is Total Quality Control? The Japanese Way.* By Kaoru Ishikawa as translated by David J. Lu © 1985. Used by permission of the publisher, Prentice Hall, Englewood Cliffs, NJ.

The additional advantages are not difficult to find. If the "quality of conformance" improves, defects become fewer and fewer, and the "go-straight-percentage" increases. There will be a substantial decline in the amount of scrap, in reworks, in adjustment, and in the inspection cost. This will bring about a very substantial cost saving, accompanied by higher productivity. Without this benefit, automation of the process becomes virtually impossible, and factories operated by robots become inconceivable. In fact, improvement in the quality of design is the first step toward higher sales and profits and lower cost.

This truth is made abundantly clear in Japan's competition with the United States in the markets for automobiles, color televisions, integrated circuits, and steel. Only recently have some Americans begun to realize this fact. In many areas, America is still governed by an old-fashioned capitalism. The owner, the chairman, or the directors are the ones who scout and hire a new president. The president thus chosen must show a quick profit or else may be fired. He has no time to think about long-term profit. He is forced to choose a short-term profit, and in so doing loses his match with the Japanese.

In the case of automobiles, American manufacturers did produce compact cars before 1970 to compete against the Japanese. However, the profit from a large-sized car came to from five to ten times that of a compact, so American manufacturers worked on their compact cars only half-heartedly. When the need arose, American consumers bought Japanese-made compacts irrespective of price because of their reliability and fuel efficiency.

In steel, in automobiles, and in integrated circuits, American companies have not been able to make the investments in equipment that they need in order to seek long-term profit. They have lagged behind in plant modernization. In addition, the Securities and Exchange Commission requires that reports be issued every three months. This relatively recent development has further contributed to the myopic views of American managers.

Some managers in the United States are simply tired of managing, so they sell their companies to enjoy their retirement. What is lacking is their concern for their social responsibility and the welfare of their employees. Society suffers from their unconcern and the companies are also affected because they cannot be expected to attain long-term profit.

Generally speaking, the higher the manager is on the corporate ladder, the longer must be the period used for evaluating his work. In the case of the president, marketing division head, and manager of the factory, evaluation must be based on their work extending over a period of three to five years. Without this safeguard, these people may seek only short-term profit, and neglect both quality and equipment investment. It is a sure way to lose long-term profit for the company.

III. CONSUMER AND NOT PRODUCER ORIENTATION

We have always taken the position that companies must manufacture products that the consumers want and are happy to buy. The aim of QC is to implement this basic approach. We have continuously stressed this since the inception of QC in 1949, so there is nothing new in this statement. In practice, however, unscrupulous people seem to find ways to counter this thought revolution. Pride and obstinacy may also be factors, but in any event, some companies plainly choose the path of producer orientation contrary to the consumer orientation that we suggest. This trend is especially noticeable in a seller's market, in a closed market that does not permit trade liberalization, and in a monopoly market. In such markets, producers make and sell products that they consider to be good without paying any attention to the requirements of consumers.

Example 1: It tastes good to me but not to the consumers.

A. The senior managing director is over 60 years old. He makes candy according to his own taste. The candy's primary market group is teenagers between the ages of 15 to 20. How can an old man of 60 know the taste of young men and women?

B. The shop had worked hard to produce margarine but its sales had remained poor. Market research, utilizing specially designed experiments and sensory testing, revealed that consumers did not like the taste.

In both of these instances, producers have considered their own taste paramount, disregarding the likes and dislikes of the consumers.

Example 2: We never expected that our customers would use our products that way.

This is an utterly irresponsible statement by those designers who do not try to know how consumers use their products.

Example 3:   One company received a large number of complaints about its electric wire without knowing how consumers were using it. How can a manufacturer provide quality assurance under such circumstances?

An electric wire factory manufactured electric wire according to company specifications. However, complaints kept coming in about the wire sold. An investigation uncovered unsatisfactory performance in the factory's wire-winding equipment, speed, after-treatment temperature, and insulation oil. The factory then made changes in company specifications.

A logical reaction to the consumer orientation approach is always to think in terms of another party's position. This means to listen to their opinions and to act in a way that will take their views into account. This principle also applies in international trade. For example, American car manufacturers have to lay off a large number of their workers due to sluggish sales. Most of the responsibility rests with management; it is really not the responsibility of Japan. However, if the United States is indeed suffering from the loss of trade, Japan must take America's position into consideration and extend helping hands to solve the problem, provided such an act does not violate the antitrust law.

IV. THE NEXT PROCESS IS YOUR CUSTOMER

The phrase "the next process is your customer" could be incorporated into the previous passage where we discussed consumer orientation. However, in a company where sectionalism is strong, this approach can be so important that I have decided to treat it separately.

I invented the phrase "the next process is your customer" while working with a steel mill from August 1950 to September of that year. Example 1 explains the situation.

Example 1: We were trying to work out a solution to the problem of reducing the number of defects and scratches in steel plate, and the following exchange took place:

Ishikawa: Why not call in the workers in the process next to yours and the one before yours to investigate?

Division Chief: Professor, do you mean to say we should call in our enemies?

Ishikawa: Wait a minute. The next process should be your customer. Why do you call them enemies? Every evening go to the plate mill that is your next process and ask, "Are those ingots we delivered today satisfactory?" That should create better relations.

Division Chief: Professor, we can never do that. If we go to the next process unannounced, they will think we are spying on them. They will immediately chase us out.

Example 2:   What is the proper role of the staff? Who is the customer of the staff?

Generally speaking, there are two tasks that the staff must perform. The first is to work as general staff. Staff members make plans and submit proposals to the president and the factory manager. The second task is that of the service staff. Staff members must consider the first line divisions, such as the design, purchasing, manufacturing, and marketing divisions, as the next process and serve them. I believe that a typical staff member should work thirty percent of the time as general staff, and seventy percent as service staff.

The trouble with most staff members is that they consider their work to be devoted one hundred percent to the general staff work, so they act as if they were members of the military General Staff. They act on the erroneous assumption that they should operate the entire company. They have no notion of serving line workers and divisions but rather give orders and constantly fight with the first line of company activities, divisions that should be the staff's customers. Conversely, line workers and divisions never listen to the staff. In war days, we used to speak of the acrimonious relations existing between the General Staff Headquarters and the Kwantung Army posted in Manchuria. The situation I have just described resembles it.

Within a company, the divisions of general affairs, personnel, accounting, production engineering, and quality control devote seventy percent of their time to serving their "customers," the line workers and divisions. Similarly, the staff must always consider what kind of service it can perform for the line divisions. The accounting division may erroneously feel that it is the only one engaged in profit and cost control, but the line divisions are actually the ones that are engaged in profit and cost control. The role of the accounting division is to provide data to these divisions to make their work of profit and cost control easier. That is the service they can perform effectively. My advice to people in line divisions and QC circle leaders is this: "Make the company staff work for you as much as possible."

Example 3:   Corning Glass Headquarters' organization (1958-1980).

I visited Corning Glass in 1958. Its organization chart for the headquarters had the term "service" printed everywhere. For example, there was a Service Accounting Department, a Service Engineering Department, a Service Quality Control Department, etc. The vice-president in charge of all of these departments had the title Service Vice-President. I asked why the term "service" was inserted as a prefix. The response was that unless the term "service" was placed there, people would forget that they were there to serve and would become rather arrogant.

Company-wide quality control cannot be complete without total acceptance of this kind of approach by all workers. Sectionalism has to be broken down, and the company has to be ventilated so that everyone can enjoy a breath of fresh air. Everyone must be able to talk to each other freely and frankly. That is the spirit of TQC.

One final thought on this issue. The customers, that is, workers in the next process, can make a request of the preceding process only if the request is reasonable and based on facts and data.

V. Presentation With Facts and Data: Use Of Statistical Methods

Facts are important and their importance must be clearly recognized. After this is done, try to express these facts with accurate data. The final step is to utilize statistical methods to analyze the data, which will enable you to make an estimate, pass judgment, and then take appropriate action.

QC is often called fact control, but people frequently ignore this. People do not look at the facts carefully, and the data they submit are not reliable. At times, they ignore the facts and rely on their own experience, sixth-sense, and gut feelings.

1. Facts—The first order of business is to look at the facts. A common fault among engineers is to have a preconceived notion in their minds and play with data to match it while ignoring the facts. To such engineers, my suggestion is to join the work process (e.g., assembly line) and quietly observe it for one week to ten days. Without knowing what is going on in the work process, engineers cannot adequately perform their duties.

2. Turning Facts Into Data—The next step is to translate facts into data. But the danger here is that the right data may be difficult to obtain. This is the reason I say, "If someone shows you data, consider them suspect. If someone shows you measuring instruments, consider them suspect, and if someone shows you chemical analysis, consider it suspect."

In brief, there are three ways of looking at this issue. They are:

- False data
- Mistaken data
- Inability to obtain data

A. *False data*

Unfortunately, there are many false data being used in industries and in society. I observed this problem in one factory. The factory manager said to me, "The trouble with our company is that whenever I tell my superiors the truth they become angry with me." That same factory manager lost his temper when a young engineer working for him told the truth!

False data are generated through this process.

Why is false data created? Often superiors are at fault.

1. The superior does not know how to think in statistical terms and does not have a sense for dispersion. So whenever the data vary a little, he thinks that something has gone wrong and becomes angry. Those who work under him are scolded although they do their job adequately. To protect themselves, they have to lie and write false reports.

2. When mistakes are made, anywhere from two-thirds to four-fifths of the blame lies with the superior or the superior's staff. Only one-third or one-fifth of the responsibility rests with those who work under him. But

usually, the subordinates are the ones who will be scolded. So they submit false data.

Unless the superior changes his or her way of thinking when situations similar to those in 1, and 2 arise, one can never expect total elimination of false data.

When workers make mistakes and funny data appear, the superior must not immediately report that to the upper level management or scold his/her subordinates. Instead, he/she must work with subordinates to prevent recurrence of the problem. If this is done, incidence of false data will diminish.

B. Mistaken data

Almost as soon as I began the work of quality control, I became aware that data were collected erroneously because the people engaged in it did not know proper methods. For example, they were not familiar with the sampling method and measuring method and collected data that were either wrong or useless. So I asked the Union of Japanese Scientists and Engineers to establish the Sampling Research Committee for them. This effort has been bearing fruit, but there are still some knotty problems in actual application.

Similarly, because definitions for defects, defectives, reworks, and adjustments are not clearly stated, mistaken data emerge in the number of defective products, percent defective, rework rate, adjustment rate, and the "go-straight-percentage."

C. Inability to obtain data, inability to measure

It is true that we have advanced technology, but there are many problems that defy measurement. With regard to quality, true quality characteristics cannot be measured for a large number of products. For example, the ease in driving and the comfort and style of a passenger car are quality characteristics that cannot really be measured.

We must study these problems to establish methods of measurement. But when that is impractical, we must inspect products by using the sensory testing method and then accumulate the results into statistical data.

3. Utilization of Data and Statistical Methods—Many books on SQC and QC devote a great number of pages to this subject, so here I shall try to be brief.

First, we must realize that by performing process analysis and quality analysis without

fanfare for a long period of time, we have been able to bring about progress in Japanese technology. Many people say that proper techniques have brought about progress in technology and control techniques have sustained it, but this is wrong. It does not make much sense to divide technique into proper techniques and control techniques. Western nations are better than the Japanese in this regard, for they are not very much concerned with this distinction.

My feeling is that the so-called control techniques are also proper techniques. By using whatever techniques are available to us we have been able to bring about improvement in quality, cost reduction, and efficiency. Process analysis and quality analysis have been done effectively through the application of QC. We have been able to export not just manufactured goods and hardware but also our technology and software.

The second point I wish to emphasize is this. If a manager does not utilize data and statistical methods, and relies only on his own experience, sixth sense, and gut feelings, he is admitting that his company does not possess high technology.

Improvement in the management's attitudes is an important byproduct of utilization of facts, data, and statistical methods.

VI. RESPECT FOR HUMANITY AS MANAGEMENT PHILOSOPHY

When the management decides on company-wide quality control, it must standardize all processes and procedures and then boldly delegate authority to subordinates. The fundamental principle of successful management is to allow subordinates to make full use of their abilities.

Industry belongs to society. Its basic goal is to engage in management with people in the center. Everyone who is connected with the company (consumers, employees and their families, shareholders, subcontractors, and employees in the affiliated distribution system) must be able to feel comfortable and happy with the company, and be able to make use of his/her capabilities and realize potential. Profit first is an old-fashioned idea that must be discarded.

The term humanity implies autonomy and spontaneity. People are different from animals or machines. They have their own wills, and do things voluntarily without being told to by others. They use their heads and are always thinking. Management based on humanity is a system of management that lets the unlimited potential of human beings blossom.

One of the basic ideas that motivates QC circle activities in the workplace is to create a "workplace where humanity is respected."

Top managers and middle managers must be bold enough to delegate as much authority as possible. That is the way to establish respect for humanity as your management philosophy. It is a management system in which all employees participate, from the top down and from the bottom up, and humanity is fully respected.

The Swedish people have observed the way we handle management. They termed it "industrial democracy." That says it all.

VII. CROSS-FUNCTION MANAGEMENT, CROSS-FUNCTION COMMITTEES

In 1960 I prepared a dual chart illustrating cross-function management by divisions and by functions. (See Exhibit 1 and Exhibit 2). This was adopted by the Toyota Motor Company. It has been modified and has been used at Toyota with

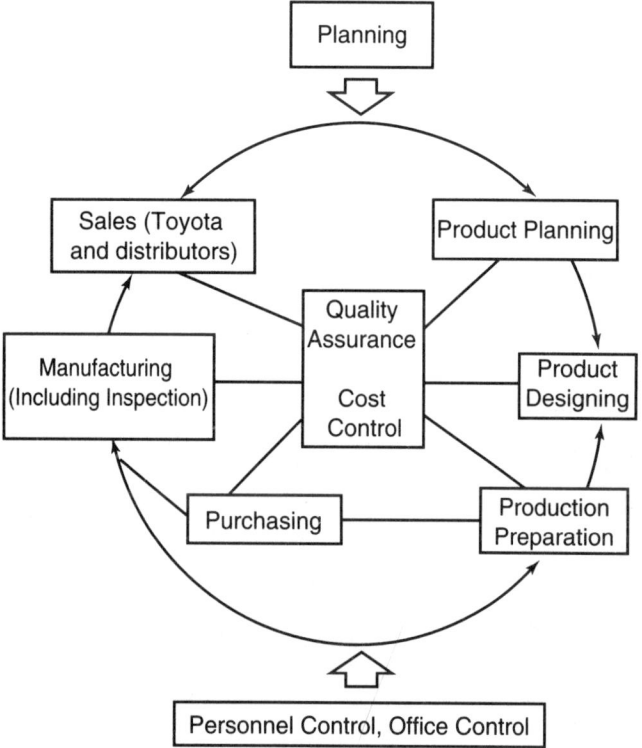

EXHIBIT 1.—CONCEPTS OF CROSS-FUNCTION MANAGEMENT–I

continued success. The full story is contained in an article written by Mr. Aoki of Toyota (*Statistical Quality Control*, February–April, 1981).

Japanese society is often described as a vertical society, and its industries share this structure. Industry has a strong top-to-bottom vertical bond while sectionalism hinders development of horizontal relations. For example, no matter how hard the division of quality assurance attempts to perform the function assigned to it, it cannot do so adequately within the existing organizational structure.

Cross-function management which has cross-function committees for support can provide the woof to help the company run crosswise, making possible the responsible development of quality assurance.

In textiles, the warp by itself remains a thread. Only when the woof is added, and when warp and woof are intertwined, will there be cloth. In a company, the analogy holds true. A vertical society resembling the warp is not an organization. It becomes a strong organization only when various functions such as quality assurance are intertwined with the warp as the table illustrates. Organizational management is possible only through the intertwining of the warp, which engages in management by divisions, and the woof, which engages in control by cross-function management.

When we speak of cross-function management, many topics immediately come to mind, including quality assurance, quantity control, cost (profit) control, new product development, control of subcontracting, sales control, and the list can go on and on. From the perspective of company goals, the main functions are the three functions of quality assurance, cost (profit) control, and quantity control. To these three may be added personnel control. All others are auxiliary functions defined by the steps to be taken or the means to be adopted.

In accordance with the functions to be managed, the company must establish cross-function committees. For example, a cross-function committee on quality assurance may be established. The chairman must be a senior managing director or a managing director who is in charge of that function. Committee members are selected from among those who hold the rank of director or above (if necessary, division heads may be included). The number should be around five. It is not desirable to select committee members only from among those who are directly connected with that specific function. Actually, it is better

CONCEPTS OF CROSS-FUNCTION MANAGEMENT—II						
Corporate Activities	Product Planning	Product Designing	Production Preparation	Purchasing	Manufacturing	Sales
Responsible Divisions	Technical Planning	Design	Production Planning	Purchase Control	Motomachi Factory	Domestic Sales
Functions	Product Planning	Testing	Production Engineering	Purchasing		Overseas Sales
Quality	◎	◎	◎	◎	○	◎
Cost	◎		◎	◎	○	○
Technology	○	◎		△	△	○
Production	△		◎	△	◎	○
Marketing	◎	○	△	△	○	◎
Personnel & Office	○	○	○		◎	○

(Right side label: Cross-Function Management)

Management by Division

EXHIBIT 2.—CONCEPTS OF CROSS-FUNCTION MANAGEMENT–II

to have one to two persons from nonrelated divisions as committee members. Each cross-function committee must maintain a secretariat within the division that handles the function under consideration, and appoint a secretary. The committee must be operated flexibly. When dealing with major functions, the committee must establish regularly scheduled monthly meetings which can engage in the audit of functions under study. The committee may also establish project teams under it.

The committee then allocates responsibilities and authority for quality assurance to all affected divisions in concrete terms. It creates a viable system of quality assurance and establishes applicable rules.

Every month the committee must study the conditions of quality assurance and determine if any claim has been registered against defective products. It must revise and redetermine the allocation of responsibilities periodically. At Toyota the monthly meeting of the cross-function committee does all of these things efficiently. (Please keep in mind that the company has had about ten years of experience in cross-function committees before reaching this stage.) The commit-

tee's meetings are formal ones. In contrast, the management conference above the committee makes reports but does not make policy decisions.

The committee, however, does not implement quality assurance. Nor does it assume direct, day-to-day responsibility for quality assurance. That task is performed by each of the line divisions in this "vertical society." The responsibility of the committee is to let the woof be woven into the warp to strengthen the entire organization. Examples of effective and ineffective uses of cross-function committees are given below.

Misunderstandings and Problems Connected with Cross-Function Committees

1. Some companies convene a meeting only when there are problems. They consider cross-function committees to be project teams and ad hoc in nature. That approach must be avoided. Committees must be established as standing committees and have regular meetings. They study the system

and provide the woof. Without them there can be no sound horizontal structure for the company.

2. Some people erroneously assume that once cross-function management is established, the company can dispense with control by division. Both are necessary.

3. Some people feel that all specialists and all affected divisions must be included in the committee. No, the cross-function committee is of a higher order than that.

4. Do not regard cross-function committees as your project teams. Let us assume that you have a cross-function committee for profit control and your profits have not reached an established goal. Does your committee establish quotas for the line divisions to reach certain profit goals? No, these are to be determined by the line divisions themselves (through their management by objectives).

5. Initially, company directors who are named committee members tend to represent only their sectional interests in their capacities as heads of the design division, accounting division, etc. This must not be allowed to happen. What they must strive for is to build a company-wide perspective from the outset.

6. Some people may genuinely believe in their devotion to the functions to which they are assigned, but continue to interpret everything that comes before the committee in terms of their own divisions. For example, a cross-function committee on quantity control must be concerned with the overall product amount for the entire company. However, a committee member from the production control division may not pay any attention to events in other divisions. Similarly, an accountant on a cross-function committee on cost control may forget the overall picture and only discuss accounting procedures.

7. The work of cross-function committees cannot go smoothly unless information is gathered routinely through all channels within the company.

8. Do not increase the number of cross-function committees excessively. When there are too many committees, they may engage in intercommittee disputes and create a situation very similar to interdivisional rivalries.

Another thing that has to be kept in mind is that there must be a thought revolution in the company in favor of cross-function management, otherwise the committees created for that purpose will remain committees in name only. In a company where the tendency for authority is to move from the top down, where the president exercises absolute power, the need for cross-function management is far more important than in other companies. Yet it is precisely in this kind of situation where it is most needed.

Effectiveness of Cross-Function Committees and Cross-Function Management

1. Company officers no longer think in terms of their narrow sectional interests but become true managers with broader perspectives. They become company directors worthy of the name. Their way of thinking becomes more flexible, and they tend to help one another more.

2. Quality assurance and quantity control are cross-functionally more effectively conducted on a company-wide basis.

3. Inspections are conducted across the divisions, so there is very little need to increase the number of divisions and sections.

4. Line workers also become conscious of cross-function management, which results in better communication between processes and divisions. Human relations among the workers are also enhanced.

5. It becomes much easier for those in the subordinate positions to submit proposals and suggestions.

VIII. COMPANY-WIDE QUALITY CONTROL AND IMPROVEMENT IN TECHNOLOGY

False notions about QC still abound in our society, in our industries, and among individuals. People claim that QC will stifle creativity and hinder improvement in technology. They also maintain that QC seeks only preservation of the status quo. These misunderstandings are caused by the word "control," which gives the impression that changes are not to be welcomed. Unfortunately, these people cannot perceive QC as a tool for bringing about a thought revolution.

Japanese intellectuals and journalists are beginning to appreciate the importance of QC, but only after it has been fully reported in mass media overseas. This is unfortunate, but I shall not complain. I prefer to let the results of our work speak for themselves. We must avoid the cacophony that usually accompanies journalism.

As QC activities have become widespread, group psychologists want to get a part of the action. There are theorists who create Theory X, Theory Y, and Theory Z and provide their critiques of our activities. My response to them has remained the same. "All of such theories are contained in our QC circle activities. We do not present them as theories, however, we simply practice them."

QC can be a theory, but at the same time it is a practical discipline. I urge people who are connected with QC not to become mere theorists or mere practitioners. They must become experts as both.

When I first became involved in QC, my aim was to help improve Japanese technology through QC and TQC. That was the thought behind the cause-and-effect diagram. In order to do process control, I became a strong supporter of process analysis, which then led me to on-line computer control. It was more than two decades ago that I engaged in quality analysis for newsprint rolls. We apply the same methods today, and through process analysis and quality analysis, causes and effects are becoming clearer. In other words, by engaging in QC effectively, one can establish a solid foundation for technology. Lately Japan has been experiencing an upsurge in its technology exports, although still remaining a net importer of technology. Perhaps through QC this situation can also be rectified.

I wish to close this chapter by repeating an old goal which I set for myself in engaging in QC, TQC and CWQC.

"As I perceive it, the goals of new quality control are to be as follows: First we must export good and inexpensive products in large quantities to make the Japanese economy stronger and to solidify the foundation of its industrial technology. Second, through quality control, we must enable Japan to export its industrial technology in order to solidify Japan's future economic base. And finally, as far as companies are concerned, they must reach the position where they can rationally divide their profits three ways, among consumers, employees, and shareholders, and as far as the nation is concerned, we must improve the living standards of our people."

1.2
QUALITY IN THE NEWS

PURITAN-BENNETT CLOSES TWO PLANTS*
by Paula Kurtzweil

A major U.S. manufacturer of ventilators and other medical devices was forced to shut two of its U.S. plants earlier this year, after agreeing to a corporate-wide injunction.

In a consent decree filed Jan. 13, 1994, Puritan-Bennett Corp. of Overland Park, Kan., agreed to a permanent injunction against itself and two of its principals, Burton A. Dole Jr., president and chief executive officer, and John H. Morrow III, vice president and chief operating officer. The injunction was filed in the U.S. District Court in Kansas. (See S.J. No. 21 in this issue's Summaries of Court Actions.)

The injunction forced Puritan-Bennett to shut plants in Boulder, Colo., and in Carlsbad, Calif. Its other U.S. manufacturing facilities are

---

*FDA Consumer (October 1994) is published by the Food & Drug Administration and is not copyrighted. Paula Kurtzweil is a member of the FDA's public affairs staff.

subject to closure if they do not comply with FDA regulations.

The action was the first corporate-wide injunction against a medical device manufacturer for violating good manufacturing practice (GMP) and Medical Device Reporting regulations. It followed 34 product recalls and two safety alerts undertaken by the company between 1985 and 1993. Many of the violations involved inadequate manufacturing specifications and processes.

"We believed that the violations were corporate-wide," said Bill Defibaugh, a consumer safety officer in FDA's Center for Devices and Radiological Health. "So we looked at the corporation as a whole, not the individual plants separately."

The corporate-wide regulatory approach toward noncomplying medical device firms that operate multiple facilities has since been used in similar actions against two other device manufacturers, National Medical Care Inc., Waltham, Mass., and Siemens Medical Systems, headquartered in Iselin, N.J. (See "Siemens Agrees to Correct Manufacturing Problems" in the September 1994 FDA Consumer.)

Puritan-Bennett makes resuscitators, ventilators for hospital and home use, and other respiratory therapy devices, as well as a blood gas monitoring system.

Resuscitators provide emergency respiratory support through a face mask. Ventilators control or assist the breathing of patients unable to breathe on their own, either permanently or for long periods. FDA considers the units "critical devices" because they support or sustain life.

In addition to the closed plants in Boulder and Carlsbad, Puritan-Bennett operates plants in Lenexa, Kan.; Wilmington and Marlborough, Mass.; and another in Carlsbad, Calif. The company also has plants in Mexico and Ireland, both of which ship finished devices to the company's U.S. plants. Distribution of these devices also is bound by the terms of the injunction, Defibaugh said.

Between 1985 and 1993, FDA conducted about 36 inspections of various Puritan-Bennett plants. Many of those inspections resulted in recalls of ventilators, airway delivery systems, and humidifiers. At least two of the recalls had to be repeated because the original recall failed to correct the problem.

Recalls resulted from such problems as defective circuits, fluid leaks, and software problems.

The company also issued two safety alerts. One followed the discovery of a potential burn problem with a pulse oximetry monitoring option used with the company's hospital ventilators. The other stemmed from a potential fire hazard due to possible development of high oxygen concentrations for various models of portable home-use ventilators.

According to Defibaugh, the company always responded to FDA's warnings and notices of adverse findings with a willingness to correct the problems. "They would correct some things and make promises to correct others," he said, "but then, upon reinspection, we would find some of the same GMP problems."

FDA sought the permanent injunction after a series of inspections between September and November 1993 revealed continuing significant GMP violations at the Colorado plant, which made portable home ventilators, and the Carlsbad facility that produced a blood gas monitoring system.

For example, FDA found that Puritan-Bennett failed to:

- ensure that a critical device did not leave the manufacturer for distribution until the appropriate employee checked all acceptance records and test results
- validate software programs by adequate and documented testing, when computers were used as part of an automated production or quality-assurance system
- maintain a device history record to show that a device was made according to the device master record
- receive, store and handle components used in manufacturing in a way that would prevent damage, mix-up, contamination, and other adverse effects and keep not-yet-accepted components separate from accepted components
- validate changes in the manufacturing process of a device
- provide complete information as required by FDA's Medical Device Reporting system.

Under the consent decree, the company may not reopen its two closed plants until the GMP violations are corrected, as determined by FDA. As of June 1994, the Carlsbad, Calif., plant had not reopened, and the firm has permanently discontinued manufacturing at the Colorado facility. FDA continues to monitor the company.

———————————————————■———————————————————

DRUG FIRM PRESIDENT AND OTHER OFFICIALS SENTENCED*
by Dixie Farley

"It was a business decision. If FDA says take the product off the market, take it off the market. So I'll lose a million dollars in sales. But look at all the money we made while I was selling it."
—Jay Marcus, former president of Halsey Drug Co., Inc., Brooklyn, in a tape-recorded conversation.

Marcus' "business decision" was to use an unapproved formula for a generic version of quinidine gluconate, a drug to treat irregular heartbeat. The product was one of numerous generics the firm manufactured illegally. In the end, Marcus got more than money from his business practices. He received a jail term and a fine.

Marcus and four other Halsey officials instructed employees to use unapproved formulas contained in what they called "phony cards." The employees were told to keep the cards in their pockets to hide their wrongdoing from FDA investigators. A federal investigation exposed the scam, the firm pleaded guilty to charges in an information, and a grand jury indicted the individuals.

The result: jail terms for the officials and a quarter-million-dollar fine for Halsey for conspiring to obstruct FDA's regulatory function and shipping adulterated, unapproved new drug products in interstate commerce. Halsey and four officials signed plea agreements; a fifth official stood trial and was convicted.

On June 17, 1994, Muhammad Uddin, former assistant vice-president of research and development, was sentenced to five months in prison, five months of home detention with electronic monitoring, and two years' supervised release. On Sept. 23, 1994, Hedviga (Heidi) Herman, former vice-president of manufacturing and the defendant who stood trial, was sentenced to 18 months in prison and two years' supervised release. On Oct. 14, 1994, Marcus was sentenced to 41 months in prison, and Amirul Islam, former vice president of technical services, to five months in prison and five months of home detention. At press time, Frederick Shainfeld,

former senior vice president of technical and regulatory affairs, hadn't yet been sentenced.

FDA first suspected a problem with Halsey when an agency reviewer found a discrepancy in one of Halsey's abbreviated new drug applications (ANDAs) to market a generic drug. The ANDA showed a drug batch with 75,000 tablets, while a Halsey letter showed the batch had 100,000.

When FDA's New York district office inspected Halsey in the spring of 1990, the agency found that the quantities of active drug ingredients listed as received were insufficient to make the quantities of finished product purported in batch records. The firm also had deficient good manufacturing practices (GMPs). Confronted with these findings, the firm withdrew two ANDAs, but did little else to correct its problems.

In June 1991, FDA referred the case to the Department of Justice's office of consumer litigation, which forwarded the referral to the U.S. Attorney for the District of Maryland. FDA agents of the special prosecutions staff, working with Assistant U.S. Attorney Christopher Mead and Susan Strawn of the office of consumer litigation, conducted the criminal investigation.

In October, FDA informed Halsey by letter of the agency's fraud policy and called for audits of the ANDAs. When an auditor hired by Halsey found continuing GMP problems, the firm withdrew seven more ANDAs.

FDA New York district investigators again inspected Halsey from Oct. 29, 1991, to March 23, 1992, and still found GMP problems. Despite many complaints to FDA about tablets with defects such as chipping, the investigators found no such problems noted in the firm's batch production records. The firm attributed the reported defects to rough handling after the products left Halsey. When FDA examined the firm's retained samples, they showed chipped tablets. Islam blamed Halsey's own packaging and warehouse personnel for throwing bottles around like a "football," says investigator James Liubicich.

On Sept. 2, 1992, an anonymous informant, a Halsey employee, called FDA, claiming the firm falsified batch records to show that drags were made according to approved ANDAs when, in fact, they were not.

In October, investigators Liubicich, Connie Gallagher, and Christina Ryan began a four-month inspection. While they couldn't prove the caller's allegations, their suspicions were raised. For example, experienced workers often seemed unfamiliar with written mixing instructions. Also, Liubicich says, "When excess powder came off the machine for compressing tablets, instead of discarding it, as GMPs require, the employees threw it back in the hopper for recompressing, a practice that could cause the problems being reported."

On Feb. 5, 1993, the informant—who had been fired—met with FDA's New York district office. He said Halsey used an unapproved formulation and manufacturing changes to make quinidine gluconate tablets. He gave FDA a Halsey formula "phony card," saying that supervisors would retrieve the cards and keep them in their pockets when FDA investigators were present. The investigators would be shown batch records prepared as if approved formulas were followed. He said that instead of discarding problem batches as required, employees usually reprocessed them by regranulating, adjusting moisture, or adding ingredients.

The district forwarded this information to the prosecutions staff. An investigation by the staff found the man had used a false name at the Feb. 5 meeting. Staff agents Melvin Szymanski and Wayne Mitchell, an FDA lawyer assigned to the staff at that time, discovered his real name, and the informant agreed to become a witness for the government.

In March 1993, Szymanski and Mitchell learned that a Halsey production supervisor, Marlon Farde, was an illegal alien from Trinidad. On March 3, along with two FBI agents, Szymanski and Mitchell approached Forde to cooperate with the government's investigation. If Forde would agree to fully cooperate, Assistant U.S. Attorney Mead promised he would not prosecute him and also offered to help him try to gain legal residency in the United States.

Forde agreed to wear a body wire to record conversations at Halsey.

The next day, as instructed, Forde told Herman that FDA agents approached him outside his house that morning and asked him about wrongdoing and "phony cards" at Halsey. She called Shainfeld into the room, had Forde say it again, and told him how he should lie to FDA, Szymanski says. "She asked, 'You gave me back all the phony cards before, right?' He said, 'Well, no I've still got some.' She said, 'Give them back to me immediately. You know you're supposed to come in my office when you make the product. You ask for the phony card, and I give it to you. And then as soon as you make it, you give it back.' "

Forde gave FDA copies of a "phony card." The next day he recorded conversations with Marcus, and the next week, with Uddin.

The district meanwhile was checking the informant's allegations on Feb. 5 about quinidine gluconate. On March 15, Shainfeld met with FDA and said he would stop making and selling the drug and begin a recall.

The next day, investigators Liubicich, Peter Abel, and John Cook, and analysts Gary Lehr and Kim Cruse-Thomas, began an inspection that would extend through May 1993. Liubicich insisted on seeing specific batch testing in Halsey's quality-assurance test room. He and Abel, with Islam, saw a woman test tablets and record information in a spiral notebook. Liubicich noticed similar notebooks on the lab bench behind her. Since Halsey let FDA review documents in plain view in the manufacturing area, Liubicich went over to take a look at the other notebooks.

"Lo and behold," he says, "I found records of reprocessing for the past 10 years. It was incredible, because no matter what we did before, Halsey kept us from getting proof of what was going on. Now here it was—documented batches, lot numbers, dates, what management said, who said it."

According to Liubicich, the employees said they kept the books because they wanted to be sure that if anything happened, they could say, "He told me this, or she told me this."

Mitchell and Szymanski bought two bottles of quinidine gluconate in Baltimore to establish the drug's sale in Maryland, where the staff tries its cases. "Tests showed they both contained the lubricants magnesium stearate and stearic acid, ingredients not listed in the approved ANDA," Mitchell says.

At the end of March, Mead informed the Halsey corporation about this evidence of fraud and the recorded conversations of its officers.

At FDA's request, on June 29, 1993, a complaint for seizure was filed against Halsey in the U.S. District Court, Eastern District of New York.

With respect to the criminal charges, on June 23, 1993, Halsey entered into the plea agreement with the U.S. Attorney's Office in Baltimore. The judge for the U.S. District Court, District of Maryland, accepted the agreement July 9. The agreement called for dismissing the five officials. Halsey's new management agreed, among other stipulations, to cooperate with the investigation, stop selling illegal products, and meet FDA manufacturing requirements. On July 12, 1993, the grand jury returned its indictment. On Nov. 19, 1993, Islam and Uddin signed plea agreements; on May 5, 1994, Shainfeld and Marcus signed plea agreements; and on June 2, 1994, Herman was convicted on four counts.

FDA received one report of a patient with arrhythmias who was hospitalized because Halsey's quinidine gluconate didn't work. With treatment, the patient recovered.

OXYGEN SUPPLIER CORRECTS PROBLEMS AFTER PRODUCT SEIZURE*
by Dori Stehlin

A Pennsylvania medical oxygen supplier is back in business after reconditioning oxygen seized last spring because the firm had failed to comply with FDA good manufacturing practice regulations.

Liquid bulk medicine oxygen and a storage vessel, valued at $10,000, were seized on May 17, 1994, at Butler Gas Products, Co., New Brighton, Pa., after two inspections and a warning letter had failed to bring the company into compliance.

Butler's one medical oxygen customer, Medic Rescue Health Care, supplies liquid oxygen for home use by people with respiratory difficulties or heart problems.

During a routine inspection of Butler June 14 through 16, 1993, Gladys Casper, an investigator with FDA's Pittsburgh office, found the firm had:

- no records to show that the equipment used to analyze the oxygen's purity had been calibrated for at least the last six months

- no certificate of analysis for the reference standard oxygen used to calibrate the analyzer

- no written procedures on how to fill oxygen tanks

- no supervisory review of batch production records for oxygen transferred into tanks

- no record of tests to ensure that liquid oxygen received from the supplier is of appropriate strength, purity and quality.

On July 14, FDA's Philadelphia district office, which oversees the Pittsburgh area, sent a warning letter to John T. Butler, president of the firm, at the company's headquarters in McKees Rocks, Pa. The firm replied on July 23, promising to correct all violations by Aug. 3.

However, when Casper returned to Butler on March 10, 1994, the firm had not corrected any of the violations cited in the warning letter.

"During my first inspection, the [firm's] headquarters office had faxed a copy of the filling procedures to this site, and they made me a copy," says Casper. "When I returned, I had my copy, but they had not kept theirs."

The most serious consequence of the violations, according to FDA compliance officer William Knipe, was that even if the firm was analyzing the oxygen it received, the analyses were worthless since the calibrations on the analyzer were based on gas of unknown purity.

"The oxygen may have been fine," says Knipe. "There aren't many contaminants [in liquid oxygen] unless it's not liquid oxygen in the first place. But you still need to demonstrate that the drug product is good through record keeping and analysis."

Because of the continuing violations, on May 17, at FDA's request, U.S. marshals seized the oxygen.

Butler filed a claim for the seized oxygen on May 23, and on June 16, signed a consent decree agreeing to recondition the oxygen and establish controls and procedures to ensure future compliance with good manufacturing practice regulations.

On June 29, FDA investigator Dan Tammariello, with the agency's Pittsburgh office, visited Butler. James S. Glessner, Butler's vice president for quality assurance, told Tammariello that all employees were being trained and tested on the firm's new written filling and testing procedures. Tammariello then watched as several employees calibrated the analyzer and tested oxygen for purity. All calibrations were performed correctly, and results of the analysis showed the oxygen in the tank to be at an acceptable level of 99.6 percent pure. He also found that all support documents were correct, up-to-date, and on site.

FDA received no reports of illness or injury among patients using Butler's oxygen.

SIEMENS AGREES TO CORRECT MANUFACTURING PROBLEMS*
by Marian Segal

Siemens Medical Systems, Inc., agreed last February to stop making a variety of medical devices until it complied with federal regulations for good manufacturing practices (GMPs).

The firm, based in Iselin, N.J., makes and distributes patient monitors, ultrasound equipment, radiation therapy devices, pacemakers, hearing aids, and other medical products. It also owns and operates a service and repair operation for its products. In addition, Siemens imports and distributes ventilators, pacemakers and ultrasound equipment made by subsidiaries of its German-based multinational parent company, Siemens Aktiengesellschaft (Siemens AG).

The consent decree of permanent injunction, entered March 23, 1994, in the U.S. District Court for the District of New Jersey, required Siemens and its president, Robert V. Dumke, to stop making and shipping medical devices at its plants in Concord, Calif., Danvers, Mass., and Issaquah, Wash., until it corrects manufacturing problems uncovered by numerous FDA inspections at those plants during 1993.

The consent decree also provided that:

• Siemens must correct problems at its facilities in Sylmar, Calif., and Piscataway, N.J., hire independent consultants, and certify within 60 days that these facilities comply with GMPs. These facilities were allowed to continue operating while correcting the problems.

• Siemens must stop importing and distributing medical devices made at two of Siemens AGs facilities in Solna, Sweden, and a related facility in Sweden until FDA verities problems at those facilities are corrected.

• Two other foreign facilities must correct manufacturing problems, and Siemens must certify that they comply with GMPs.

• Within 18 months of the consent decree, Siemens must certify that all other Siemens AG foreign facilities that make and export medical devices in the United States meet GMP regulations.

• The company must take steps to ensure that any device-related problems it becomes aware of through its nation-wide service and repair network are properly handled and investigated.

Other Siemens facilities in the United States not identified in the consent decree were allowed to remain open, but are also required to comply with the terms of the order.

"This was the most complex and extensive GMP action ever taken by the agency," says FDA

---

*FDA Consumer (September 1994) is published by the Food & Drug Administration and is not copyrighted. Marian Segal is a member of the FDA's public affairs staff.

attorney Mark Brown. "We were dealing with one of the biggest companies in the world, and the action extended not only to U.S. facilities, but to Siemens AG's foreign manufacturing operation, and to the service and repair network in this country."

Routine FDA inspections of Siemens facilities over the years had revealed repeated GMP violations and failure to correct them. A long history of deficiencies, device malfunctions, and recalls at several of the company's plants indicated to FDA a company-wide problem. Because of this, Brown says, in 1992, the agency decided to perform a comprehensive corporate-wide investigation.

The ensuing imspections showed that a number of the facilities had the same kinds of deficiencies, including:

• inadequate investigations of device and component failures

• failure to validate software revisions intended to correct defects

• inadequate quality assurance programs

The investigation included inspections of both domestic and foreign manufacturing facilities. The service and repair network was examined also, because information gathered at the plants suggested possible problems with procedures for reporting and evaluating service complaints.

"That was a particularly significant aspect of the investigation and enforcement action," says Brown, "because the design and operation of Sieman's service and repair network hindered the ability of the company to gather meaningful information about device failures or to judge the safety and efficacy of its devices.

"For example, in many cases, field service technicians weren't properly identifying certain problems as complaints, so they weren't submitting information up the line, and that information wasn't flowing back to the manufacturing facility. This prevented Siemens from recognizing numerous device mat-functions that required investigation."

Another major problem was the firm's failure to properly test, or validate, device software before releasing it. The software controls the operation of the device. Furthermore, Brown says, when software defects were recognized because the devices weren't functioning as intended, the revised software wasn't adequately tested to de-

termine whether the problem was corrected. "In fact," he says, "they even found instances in which the revised software introduced new, unanticipated defects."

Siemens' manufacturing violations resulted in faulty equipment that, in some cases, could have life-threatening consequences. The firm's Danvers, Mass., facility, for example, manufactures patient monitors that track critical functions such as infant and adult breathing, abnormal heart rhythms, and blood pressure. According to FDA inspection reports, the level of GMP compliance at Danvers has declined since 1988.

In one instance, in September of that year, the plant was informed that its electrocardiogram (EKG) monitors at a hospital nursing station were simultaneously displaying one patient's EKG wave form in two different locations, while the EKG of a second patient was not being displayed at all. More recent problems included reports that alarms for infant breathing monitors and heartrate monitors failed to sound. Those and other problems were attributed to defective software.

In August 1988, FDA sent Siemens' Concord, Calif., facility a warning letter citing GMP violations relating to defects in linear accelerators manufactured there. These devices, used to deliver radiation therapy to cancer patients, had defects that may have caused healthy tissue to be exposed to unintended doses of radiation. GMP violations continued at that plant until Siemens' president, Robert Dumke, closed it Oct. 29, 1993, which was the final day of FDA's last inspection of the facility. Dumke voluntarily agreed to stop manufacturing and distributing the linear accelerators after the investigators presented him with the inspection findings.

GMP violations at the firm's Issaquah, Wash., facility led to problems with the devices manufactured there as well. For example, ultrasound systems for assessing fetal growth, detecting tumors and their growth, and monitoring blood flow failed to provide a complete image.

Additional GMP deficiencies were uncovered at other of the firm's plants for manufacturing pacemakers and pace-maker leads, and hearing aids.

Between November 1992 and February 1993, FDA also inspected five foreign manufacturing facilities owned by Siemens AG, and one independent facility. All showed significant GMP violations, including inadequate complaint handling and investigation, inadequate device-failure investigation, inadequate software validation, and inadequate quality-assurance programs. FDA placed three of the facilities on automatic detention because of the severity of the problems.

After the U.S. inspections were completed in October 1993, Siemens agreed in negotiations with FDA to enter into a settlement that would enjoin several of its facilities, both domestic and foreign, from manufacturing and distributing its products. The Department of Justice brought the action to court, and Judge John W. Bissell signed the decree on Feb. 25, 1994. It was entered by the court on March 23.

When Siemens has provided the required certifications demonstrating the plants are in compliance, FDA will reinspect and determine whether the closed facilities can resume normal operations.

SUNTOUR GONE*

After years of losing market share, component maker Suntour/Sakae USA closed its doors Jan. 6. The company that once owned the largest chunk of the midprice component market was beaten to such key developments as index shifting in the late '80s, then encountered quality control problems in the '90s. By '93 they were spec'd on virtually no new bikes. Low-end (presumably mass-market) Suntour parts and Duotrack forks will continue to be made in Taiwan.

1.3
LEGAL ISSUES

BE INFORMED ABOUT PRODUCT LIABILITY*
by Randall Goodden

The population of this country is substantially more involved and preoccupied with initiating product liability lawsuits than any other country is the world, even though, in all probability, we manufacture the safest products. Product liability is an overwhelming field of activity that continues to grow as the media publicizes multimillion-dollar verdicts in favor of the plaintiffs.

In the Federal courts alone, between 1974 and 1988, product liability cases increased in number by 983%. But those thousands of cases brought to Federal court each year are a minority of the total picture. In the state court systems, there are roughly another 90,000 to 100,000 cases filed every year, and there is no end in sight.

The more safe and reliable a manufacturer tries to make a product through typical quality efforts, the more it seems that plaintiffs can still find the company negligent. Although most manufacturers may not currently be involved in a product liability case, one or two sudden cases could easily knock a good-sized company to its knees. The amount of effort it can take to gener-

---

ate a million dollars in profit does not compare to how easily it can be lost.

In 1993, a major insurance company studied 27 product liability cases involving its customers and found its losses had totalled almost $10 million. The company attributed its losses to:

- Inadequate or nonexistent consumer warnings (44%)
- Inadequate guarding (27%)
- Design defects (21%)
- Product defects (8%)

The types of companies involved in the suits were:

- Manufacturing companies (42%)
- Contractors (28%)
- Service industries (19%)
- Retail establishments (11%)

Most manufacturing company managers think that their involvement in product liability investigations and defense is not wanted by insurance companies and lawyers. Likewise, most insurance representatives and attorneys assume the manufacturer doesn't want to get involved. However, quality professionals who are educated and want to participant in the process find that their involvement is welcomed. When speaking at seminars on this subject, I find that defense attorneys are thrilled with the idea of manufacturers becoming involved.

EDUCATION IS CRITICAL

Product liability defense seminars for quality and engineering executives are being taught by legal research institutions and universities such as the University of Wisconsin-Madison, College of Engineering. The courses address how to assure the safety and reliability of newly designed products and how to improve many administrative aspects of the company's operation. Systems and procedures, record keeping, contractual agreements, and communications are covered.

Even more than the technical design of the product, manufacturers need to learn the requirements and expectations of the legal community prior to ever being dragged into a lawsuit. A knowledge of how the legal system works, from the initial incident investigation through interrogatories, depositions, and trials, is essential. The quality professional needs to learn the meaning of dangerous documents, strict liability, the elements of negligence, the various degrees of foreseeability, the duty to warn, and how product liability laws vary from state to state.

Getting involved in a product liability investigation is a major educational opportunity in itself. Working with insurance representatives, defense counsel, forensics investigators, and even counsel for the plaintiff, provides insight into another technical product dimension. The experience gained from this involvement will substantially improve the manufacturer's technical product quality program and effort, even if a case never occurs again.

The study of product liability creates new opportunities for corporate involvement and increases the profitability of the company in a financial area that goes unnoticed. It will launch new efforts within the manufacturing company that employees will understand and support, resulting in a higher level of product safety and reliability. This is a new frontier for quality.

WHY PRODUCT-LIABILITY AND MEDICAL-MALPRACTICE LAWSUITS ARE SO NUMEROUS IN THE UNITED STATES*
by Eugene L. Grant as told to Theodore E. Lang

Some time ago, I was talking with my friend, Ted Lang, about the increase of product-liability litigation in the United States. I commented that there are several reasons why the growth of such litigation has been more rapid in the United States than elsewhere. Three special aspects of the U.S. legal system have combined to encourage the many product-liability lawsuits and the related increases in monetary awards to plaintiffs. Most U.S. residents who are not lawyers are unaware that their legal system differs greatly from those of most other countries.

When I explained my ideas to Ted, he remarked that they should be published for non-lawyers who are concerned about product liability. He subsequently recorded our next discussion.

During the interview, it turned out that I needed to make many references to lawsuits about medical malpractice. As I see it, the same unique characteristics of the U.S. legal system that have caused the great increase in product-liability lawsuits have also caused a great increase in medical-malpractice lawsuits. Thus, product liability and medical malpractice have equal billing in the following interview.

—EUGENE L. GRANT

THE INTERVIEW

Lang: You're not a lawyer. How did you become interested in the difference between product-liability lawsuits in the United States and the rest of the world?

Grant: It started some years ago when I attended a meeting of the American Society for Engineering Education. At one of the many sessions, industrial-engineering professors were discussing the rapid growth of product-liability litigation in the United States. One of the Canadian members commented, "Lawsuits about product liability haven't increased in this manner in Canada. Canadian lawyers are not allowed to take lawsuits on a contingency-fee basis. In this respect, Canada is unlike the United States but is like most of the other countries in the world." It turned out that none of the American professors at the session had ever heard of this difference.

Lang: Is the allowance of contingency fees the only reason why product-liability lawsuits are more numerous and costly in the United States?

Grant: No. The allowance of the contingency fee is only one reason. A paper given by J.G. Cowell at the First European Seminar on Product Liability lists many differences between the laws of the United States and the laws of European countries that influence litigation about product liability.[1] In my opinion, two other differences listed by Cowell have interacted with the contingency-fee difference to cause more lawsuits and higher awards in the United States compared to abroad.

One difference is that the United States allows unlimited punitive damages to be awarded in addition to compensation for actual damages incurred, while most other countries do not. The other difference is that, in the United States, most cases involving product liability and medical malpractice are decided by juries, whereas in other countries, these types of cases are usually tried by judges without juries.

Over the years, I have talked to a number of people who have served as jurors on such cases. Usually, the plaintiff is an individual or group of individuals and the defendant is a corporation. Frequently, some jurors appear to be biased against the corporation and in favor of the individual. In jury deliberations, such jurors say: "The poor plaintiff certainly needs the money, and the corporate defendant can certainly afford to pay." In cases in which there are enough jurors with this opinion, the op-

---

*Reprinted with permission from *Quality Progress,* December 1994. Eugene L. Grant is currently enjoying retirement in Palo Alto, CA. Theodore E. Lang is the head of the Department of Civil Engineering at Montana State University in Bozeman.

portunity to award punitive damages sometimes leads to very high awards.

One of my friends was on a jury that awarded $3 million to a plaintiff in a product-liability suit. She commented to me that, although she thought this award was a bit high, it was easier to go along with the rest of the jury than to argue for a lower amount. Awards of millions of dollars seem to occur fairly often. Not too long ago, there was an award of $105 million in a product-liability cse.[2] In September 1994, there was an award of $5 billion in punitive damages in a highly publicized suit concerning an oil spill.[3]

Lang: What are the consequences of such high awards?

Grant: One consequence is that they tempt many trial lawyers to hunt for more lawsuits of that type. This temptation exists both in product and medical cases. It exists because the rules permit contingency-fee lawsuits. Such high awards are particularly tempting because they seem to occur at random—they are virtually unrelated to the relative merits of the various cases that come up for trial.

A second consequence is that, because of the randomness and unpredictability of such awards, insurance companies are inclined to settle many cases out of court rather than take the chance inherent in letting them go to trial. Naturally, the likelihood that cases will be settled out of court makes it more attractive than ever for trial lawyers to hunt for more cases on a contingency-fee basis because therein lies the chance to secure a very good fee with minimum work. Thus, over a period of time, there are more and more cases and higher and higher insurance costs. For example, the physician who paid, say, $70,000 a year for his or her medical-malpractice insurance a few years ago might now have to pay, say, $100,000.

Lang: In contingency-fee cases, how are winnings divided between the plaintiff and the plaintiff's lawyer?

Grant: It depends on the terms of the agreement between the parties. The most common agreement I have come across is 50% to each party. But in the December 1993 issue of FOCUS, however, the Strategic Development Staff of the National Center for Manufacturing Sciences estimates that 50% to 70% of the winnings in such cases go to the lawyers.[4]

Lang: When you talk to people about product-liability and medical-malpractice lawsuits, have you ever gotten the response: "I have never been involved in such lawsuits and never intend to be. They don't concern me."

Grant: Yes, occasionally. But the people who say that product liability or medical malpractice doesn't concern them don't realize what they are saying. In effect, they are saying that they don't care how much they pay for manufactured goods or health care services. They are also saying that they are indifferent to the United States' competitive position in world markets and its rate of technological progress.

Lang: That is quite a number of issues to be indifferent about. How do prices for manufactured products and health care services enter into the subject?

Grant: Usually, the ultimate effect of product-liability costs is an increase in the selling price of the manufactured product. Sometimes this might not be practical; the ultimate effect then becomes the discontinuance of the product or even the business.

Lang: Can you give any specific examples to illustrate such consequences of product-liability costs?

Grant: The December 1993 issue of FOCUS provides good examples of both types of consequences of product-liability costs.[5] In the U.S. automobiles industry, for example, the cost of product-liability defense claims averages about $500 per automobile sold. Presumably this cost influences the price of automobiles. The manufacture of football helmets is an example of discontinuance of a product or business. Twenty years ago, 20 companies manufactured football helmets in the United States. Since that time, 18 of these companies have discontinued making this product because of high product-liability costs.

Lang: You have been discussing the consequences of unlimited punitive damages in product-liability cases. Can a similar analysis be made in medical-malpractice cases?

Grant: Of course. Just as product-liability costs raise the price of products, medical-malpractice costs raise the price of health care services. The physician who must pay $100,000 a year for medical-malpractice insurance must either recover this amount in his or her fees or abandon the practice of medicine. Younger physicians usually raise their fees, which is an important contributor to the increasing cost of health care. Older physicians tend to go abruptly from full-time practice to full-time retirement because it is no longer economically feasible to taper off with a part-time practice. This is comparable to the manufacturer that abandons a product or goes out of business because of high product-liability costs.

Lang: I've heard the argument that one good consequence of the U.S. product-liability system is that it encourages safety improvements. Is this a valid argument?

Grant: Not necessarily. Sometimes the exact opposite is true. In some states, if a manufacturer brings out a new, safer version of a product, the new version might be used as evidence that all previous versions were unsafe. In this way, the U.S. product-liability system actually discourages safety improvements.

Lang: You mentioned that the product-liability system is adversely affecting the United States' competitive position in world markets and its rate of technological progress. How is this taking place?

Grant: The features of the U.S. legal system that promote product-liability litigation are very bad for the country as a whole. In effect, they cause U.S. companies to export jobs to foreign competitors. Moreover, they create obstacles to technological progress that prevent new jobs from being created here.

The Strategic Development Staff of the National Center for Manufacturing Sciences indicates that the price of product-liability insurance is 15 to 20 times higher in the United States than in Europe and Japan.[6] Higher product-liability costs make it harder for many U.S. companies to compete in international markets.

The uncertainty of product-liability costs for possible new products tends to slow down technological progress. Often, it is feasible to make accurate estimates of labor and material costs for a new product, but since there is no ceiling on punitive damages, there is no reliable way to estimate product-liability costs. In a recent Conference Board survey of chief executive officers of manufacturing companies, 39% reported that their companies had made decisions against coming out with a new product because of worries about product-liability lawsuits.[7]

Lang: Do you think there is a real chance to change the present legal system?

Grant: It won't be easy because a change would require legislation. There are two different obstacles to securing any needed legislation.

One obstacle is the widespread ignorance about this subject. Few nonlawyers are aware that the United States is practically alone in the world in allowing punitive damages and contingency-fee lawsuits. The public is also unaware that the country is unusual because it uses jury trials for product-liability and medical-malpractice lawsuits. I'm basing these statements on many conversations I have had with nonlawyers over the past 15 years. In contrast, all of the lawyers I have talked to during this period have known that these were special aspects of the U.S. legal system.

The other obstacle is quite different: Many legal professionals are active in politics. Many lawyers become members of state and federal legislative bodies, while others become state and federal executives.

Lang: If you were able to stipulate one change in the special features of the U.S. legal system, what would that change be?

Grant: In my opinion, the worst feature of the U.S. legal system is a jury's option to award punitive damages in any amount.

Lang: If punitive damages were to be continued but the amount limited, what should the amount be?

Grant: If punitive damages were limited to $10 million, for instance, very little change could be expected. There must be two kinds of award limitations, with the lower of the two figures setting the actual limit. One limit should be an actual amount, say $50,000; the other should be based on actual damages demonstrated to have occurred, say, double the actual damages.

Lang: Should the primary effort to make changes in U.S. laws be made at the federal or state level?

Grant: In principle, changes should be at the federal level. The special characteristics of the legal system that have been responsible for so many problems are nationwide, and the adverse consequences are nationwide. Moreover, any project that needs favorable action by 50 state legislatures and 50 state governors seems likely to take a very long time.

Lang: Does the fact that there are so many lawyers holding public office make it unreasonable to believe that the needed changes in U.S. laws will be secured?

Grant: That is a good question to which I believe no one yet knows the answer. Perhaps when gauging the attitude of the legal profession, you need to divide lawyers into two groups: trial lawyers who are engaged in product-liability and medical-malpractice litigation and all other lawyers. There is certainly no question about the prospective attitude of the trial lawyers. For obvious reasons, they will strongly oppose any change in the present system.

In guessing the attitude of the other lawyers, I think it is incorrect—as well as unfair to the legal profession—to make the simple assumption that nearly all lawyers will oppose any changes in these matters. Over the years, I have talked to a fair number of lawyers who have been critical of the present punitive damage system. Nevertheless, it is one thing to express such ideas in private conversation and quite another to advocate such changes in public, particularly if the ideas might be misconstrued as being disloyal to one's profession.

My hope is that a fair number of leading lawyers who favor change will join together and issue a statement indicating their position. This might make it acceptable for other lawyers who favor change to speak out—and, in some cases, vote—in favor of their convictions on this subject.

Lang: Do you personally plan to carry the torch for a change in U.S. law?

Grant: Considering that I'm 97, probably not. But a fair number of torchbearers will be needed before any changes in laws on these matters can take place.

Lang: Do you have any suggestions for prospective torchbearers?

Grant: I have one suggestion: Manufacturing professionals and medical professionals should make this a common cause. The reasons for U.S. product-liability and medical-malpractice crises are similar. It follows that the remedies should be similar, too.

Lang: Do you have any suggestions for others who have become convinced that the national laws need to be changed so that unlimited punitive damages are no longer possible?

Grant: Whenever possible, work on both ends of getting the law changed: try to convince the general public and try to convince U.S. legislators. Explain to your friends and neighbors that the laws on these matters are unique in the world and that their effect is to export a fair number of U.S. jobs to other countries. If you know any legislators, tell them in person; if not, write this message to your representatives in Congress.

REFERENCES

1. J.G. Cowell, "Product Liability: European Insurance Perspectives Reports," *First European Seminar on Product Liability,* Vol. 2, 1977, pp. 25-30.
2. A jury in Atlanta, GA, awarded this amount in a suit in which General Motors was a secondary defendant. This case was widely reported by newspapers across the nation.
3. An Alaskan jury awarded $5 billion in punitive damages against Exxon Corporation in September 1994. Although this did not involve product liability or medical malpractice, it is a striking illustration of the point that jury awards of punitive damages in the United States are not restrained by any upper limit. This case was widely reported by newspapers across the nation.
4. *FOCUS* is a monthly publication by the Strategic Development Staff of the National Center for Manufacturing Sciences in Ann Arbor, MI. The eight-page December 1993 issue of *FOCUS* is devoted entirely to product liability in the United States. For more information, call (313) 995-0300.
5. Ibid.
6. Ibid.
7. "Why Reforming Our Liability System Is Essential if America Is to Succeed in Overseas Markets," advertisement by the American International Group, *Newsweek,* Nov. 8, 1993, pp. 84-85.

SECTION

TWO

QUALITY BY INDUSTRY

The following articles discuss quality applications within specific industries. However, you should not restrict your reading just to your particular type of business. A manufacturing firm that provides engineering services to suppliers could benefit from studying quality assurance for service or supplier relationships. A bank could benefit from studying problem-solving techniques used in the chemical industry.

These are just a couple of examples of how reading about solutions to quality problems in different industries could prove useful for your company. Therefore, you will want to read through the articles related to your type of business. However, you will also want to scan the other articles for topics of interest.

Also, you should note that many of the techniques discussed in Section 3 (Quality Technologies and Methods) are taken from specific industries. Therefore, you should also scan these for more information about your type of company or the situation you are experiencing.

As mentioned in the introduction, quality assurance is a field undergoing rapid and sometimes radical change. This can be seen in the articles contained within this section. You will see the application of quality-assurance techniques developed for manufacturing applied to nonmanufacturing situations. In addition, you will read about quality professionals conducting nonquality-assurance activities.

This represents the changing role of the quality professional as part of the increasing flexibility of any professional in a world experiencing a dramatic change in the business environment. Especially, the rapid growth of world trade.

━━━━━━━━━━━━■━━━━━━━━━━━━

QUALITY AND PRODUCTION/INVENTORY:WHY IT'S SMART TO INTEGRATE THEM*

If your company's like many, it has separate but parallel systems for quality and production/inventory. Integrating those systems could bring many benefits, says Pamela Janson, a product market analyst with Systems Software Associates (Chicago, IL).

Exactly what are the benefits from tying the systems together? Janson points out three:

1. A common database for all departments. With such a database, quality professionals can look at the same information that people in Production, a laboratory, Materials Handling, or Inventory Control are looking at and can act on the same requirements. (For a rundown on the benefits of having an integrated data system, see the box on page 7.)

2. Automatic scheduling of quality activity requirements. "In the quality and inventory worlds, one activity should always trigger another," Janson says.

"For instance, when Inventory receives a shipment from a supplier, Quality should determine what quality activity should follow this. Perhaps Quality might schedule testing in this time slot. Or perhaps that supplier is certified, so you don't have to perform any testing."

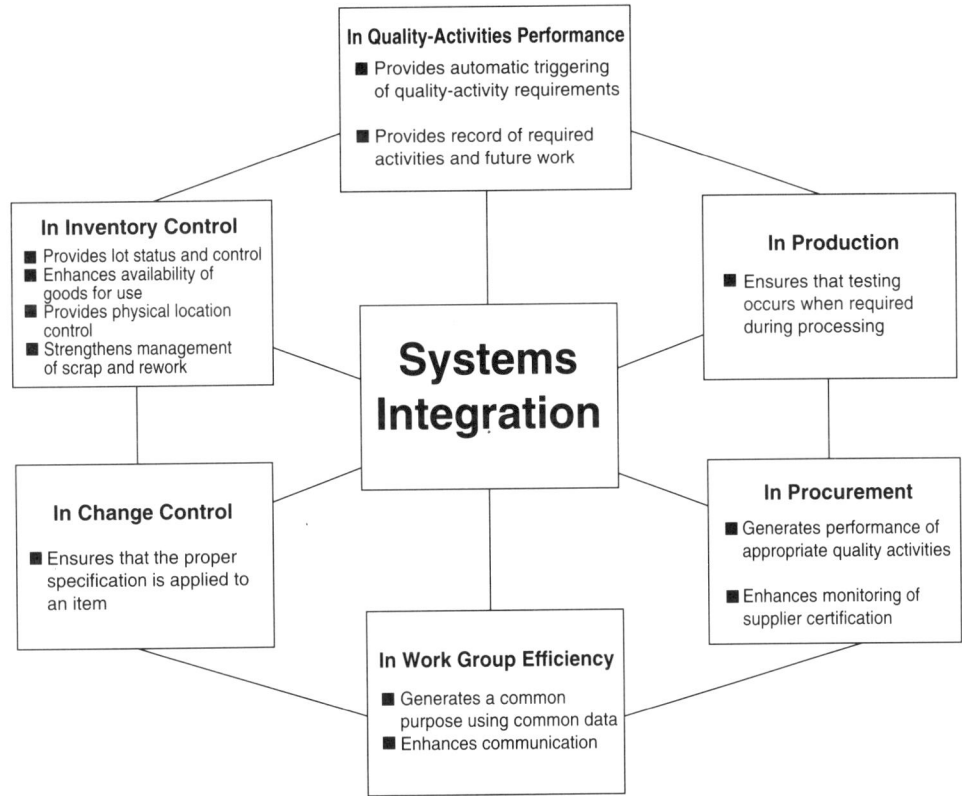

In Quality-Activities Performance
- Provides automatic triggering of quality-activity requirements
- Provides record of required activities and future work

In Inventory Control
- Provides lot status and control
- Enhances availability of goods for use
- Provides physical location control
- Strengthens management of scrap and rework

In Production
- Ensures that testing occurs when required during processing

Systems Integration

In Change Control
- Ensures that the proper specification is applied to an item

In Procurement
- Generates performance of appropriate quality activities
- Enhances monitoring of supplier certification

In Work Group Efficiency
- Generates a common purpose using common data
- Enhances communication

EXHIBIT 1.—WHAT SYSTEMS INTEGRATION CAN DO FOR YOUR COMPANY

* Copyrighted material. Reprinted with permission from Bureau of Business Practice, 24 Rope Ferry Road, Waterford, CT, 06386.

3. Automatic inventory statusing based on quality activities. The idea is to create a closed-loop data system where an inventory activity leads to a quality activity, and vice versa. Again, this is the aspect of one activity always triggering another.

Integration Affects Several Areas

In addition to these three general benefits of system integration, there are specific benefits in these areas:

- *quality activities*
- *inventory control*
- *production*
- *change control*
- *procurement*
- *work groups and teams*

Let's take a look at the specific effects system integration has on each of these areas:

Quality Activities Performance

Your quality activities are an important part of the production/procurement cycle. With system integration, that cycle should automatically trigger quality activity requirements.

Take advance resource planning for example. Looking at the information on your integrated data system, you'll be able to find out what Production expects to finish to fill orders received.

Being able to look at purchase orders will enable you to know when materials will be arriving. Using this information and your quality activity requirements, you'll be able to determine *when to assign the appropriate personnel to schedule and perform any necessary sampling or testing* and *how much time that sampling or testing will take.*

Inventory Control

An integrated system helps Inventory Control to

- Determine lot status and control. One of the most critical aspects of a quality management system is material. You need to be able to *trace back the quality information to a particular product lot should problems arise*

in the future; know when a lot was produced; know what components were used to produce that lot to determine what quality activities should occur.

- Determine location and availability of goods for use. A quick response is critical in the marketplace today. Inventory Control should be able to determine exactly where the goods furnished by suppliers are at all times through lot numbers or serial numbers. So as soon as something has passed quality testing (if testing is necessary), you'll want to allocate it for production or, if it's a finished product, get it out to your customers.

- Manage disposition of scrap and rework of materials. Quality Control must examine materials and decide which items must be scrapped, returned to the supplier, or sent back to Production for rework.

Production

An integrated system helps ensure that the right testing occurs when required during the processing. You can react sooner and perform functions faster if you know in advance what testing must be done and when it should be done.

Change Control

An integrated system assists in this area by ensuring that the proper specification is applied to an item and that the information gets on the database at once. For instance, let's say that your department adds a new quality sampling requirement or test. Inventory will know of the change immediately, and this virtually eliminates errors or oversights.

Procurement

Systems integration helps Procurement make sure that the right quality activities take place with a supplier. Also, if supplier certification is important to your firm, Procurement is responsible for certification and for entering supplier certification information on the data system.

Work Groups or Teams

An integrated data system offers your company a dependable communication channel with a single database. The result is more efficiency in work groups or teams. Energy and time won't be wasted on seeking information from various sources. For a chart of what systems integration can do for your company, see Exhibit 1 on page 2-3.

System Integration Increases Efficiency

Integrating your quality and production/inventory systems will increase your company's efficiency by providing a common database, by enabling automatic scheduling of quality activities, and by providing automatic inventory statusing on the basis of those quality activities. And that increase in efficiency will sharpen your firm's competitive edge—a top priority in today's business world.

———————————■———————————

PROCESS CONTROL'S NEW FACE*
by Mark Clarkson

Things are changing on the factory floor. In the beginning, there were PLCs (programmable logic controllers), metal boxes packed with jumper wires and chattering relays, and they were good. Well, pretty good. If you wired enough of these boxes in exactly the right way, setting the relay jumpers properly, you could program them to handle the types of quick, repetitive tasks involved in stamping airplane parts out of sheet aluminum or filling and capping bottles of root beer.

The user interface for one of these beasts was a large metal panel called an *enunciator panel*, covered with cryptic gauges and industrial-size buttons in primary colors. The programming language, if you could call it that, was *relay ladder logic*. It was implemented by physically yanking and rearranging jumper wires to govern the sequence in which relays were tripped by sensors and other relays. Over the years, the industry accrued a large base of electricians and production engineers who spoke relay ladder logic: even as microprocessors replaced the relays inside PLCs, relay ladder logic was still used to program them.

Then, as now, PLCs governed mostly discrete processes—the mechanical actions found in stamping parts, folding boxes, or running vending machines. To control more subtle analog processing, such as the distillation of huge vats of petrochemicals, there were DCSes (distributed control systems). Typically, these DCSes were operated from a single control room, isolated from the shop floor, and attended by a priest-like order of engineers and electricians. From this control room, lines snaked all over the plant, gathering information and sending orders.

The requirements on the factory floor are changing fast, says Gary George, director of marketing for Opto22, a maker of industrial-control systems for PCs. "People now want to talk to third-party devices like bar-code wands, intelligent scales, and gas analyzers—things that DCS and PLC weren't designed for. People want integration, and these older architectures are only going to take you so far. The real future of control is the computer."

A Matter of Trust

When small computers first began to appear on, or near, the shop floor, they were not trusted to do very much. Early computers were notorious for all kinds of failures. At first, all they were used for was to replace those big panels of buttons and dials on the shop floor with on-screen representations of buttons and dials. Even that represented some big cost savings.

"You'd be surprised," says George, "at the cost of building those enunciator panels—the materials themselves, plus the cost of someone putting in push buttons, pulling wires, and assembling the panels. Now all that stuff is done

* Reprinted with permission from *Byte* magazine, October 1994. Mark Clarkson is a freelance science writer based in Wichita, KS.

in software. Now, you use a touchscreen or a light pen." To change the process, continues George, "you only need to go in and create a new window or move a gauge from here to there. There are no rewiring costs." In the control industry, this is known as MMI (man-machine interface). Running MMI software is still the major function of PCs on the shop floor.

A PC running MMI software is probably not actually turning on pumps or opening and closing valves. According to George, traditional control elements, such as PLCs, still typically perform those tasks. What MMI offers is a new and better way of talking to those traditional control elements. If a valve opens, the computer may turn an icon red. If you click on a button, the computer tells the PLC to start or stop a process.

Even though the PLCs are still there, you can program them through the MMI. Today's programming languages are much easier to use than relay ladder logic. For example, Opto22's programming language is based on flowcharts. People understand flowcharts, says George. "They're intuitive. We go right from the flowchart into the controller. It eliminates a whole step in the programming."

Real Objects

MMIs have grown far beyond cartoon enunciator panels, although the emphasis on modeling physical hardware in the real world has remained. Today, a typical MMI display looks like a factory diagram drawn in Harvard Graphics, with colorful cartoon fluids pouring into cutaway vats or streams of widgets rolling down animated assembly lines. Lights wink on and off, numbers change, and gauges fluctuate.

The best MMIs are strongly object-oriented. You can move, duplicate, edit, and copy objects (e.g., gauges, vats, and conveyer belts) on the screen from application to application. When you copy or move objects, their characteristics and behavior go with them. If you copy a picture of an industrial cookie-dough mixer, you get the whole element (e.g., timers and animated beaters). If the second mixer differs from the first, you can edit only those characteristics that differ between the two.

The latest MMI software from Wonderware of Irvine, California, for example, lets you build libraries of complex, animated objects such as meters, valves, and pumps and configure them quickly in the shop environment. Dave Smith,

Wonderware's vice-president of marketing, says that an object that took you 20 to 30 minutes to configure before will now take only 20 to 30 seconds. If you have a meter with a scale of 0 to 100, and you need a scale of 500 to 5000, you simply click on the drop-down box, change the scale, and create a new object. This can save much time in programming the control system for 53 similar vats of acid or similar manufacturing stations at a dozen different locations in your plant.

"People on the factory floor," says Smith, "would like to follow the process as it really operates—to see tanks filling, valves opening, pumps pumping, and so forth. Instead of looking at numbers, they'd like to see a tank being filled and to see an alarm change color when it reaches capacity."

And that's the big difference between MMI and presentation graphics—objects in the MMI represent real objects in real time. MMI software is object-oriented in the most literal sense. For every animated vessel that is 58 percent full of cartoon petrochemicals, a real vessel exists that is 58 percent full of real petrochemicals.

Power for the People

Outfitted with slick new click-and-drag animated interfaces, industrial MMI is going places it's never been before—most significantly, out onto the factory floor. In the past, engineers and technicians programmed controllers. Today, thanks to sophisticated MMIs, many people on the shop floor who have never worked directly with computers are doing the programming themselves.

When dealing with such novice programmers, ease of use is a premium. "For the latest version of our MMI software," says Ralph Rio, manager of product marketing for Intellution, "the design objective was to enable a new user to go from opening the shrink-wrapped box to being truly productive within one hour. And we've done tests to make sure we achieved it."

Once users are comfortable with the new technology, companies begin to derive benefits they never expected. Companies shopping for automation-control software are initially interested in improving yields, reducing waste, or making processes more effective. They get those things, Rio says, but the real benefits come from empowering the workers. "Typically," he says, "the person on the production floor is not empowered at all. They're put in front of a machine and told to push a button every so often. They don't have the information needed to make high-quality decisions. By giving them information in a usable, digestible form, you empower them." Rio adds that this does more than make them feel good: it makes the companies they work for stronger.

He cites an example from an Intellution customer. "A guy on the plant floor—in his 50s, high-school education, not a computer jock at all—learned to use our software and started drawing his own screens, because he wanted to see the information a little differently. He found a relationship between things that were happening in the production process that no one had seen before. It turned into a $250,000-a-year cost savings for the manufacturer."

Windows Onto Factory Automation

From the beginning, Windows has been the platform of choice for PC-based industrial MMI. As a graphical operating environment, early versions left a lot to be desired. Still, says Smith, Windows had one important thing going for it: It didn't tie you to a specific brand of hardware.

Until five or six years ago, companies providing hardware and software for industrial-process control dealt in proprietary systems. Each system spoke its own particular language, and it was hard to incorporate other product lines. The manufacturer was often the only source for maintenance, service, parts, and programming. Once your company made the commitment to a particular line of products, you were stuck with them for a while.

The result was captive markets and high prices. Until recently, says Smith, control-system suppliers were paying $50,000 to $100,000 for a hard-wired graphics work-station. The PC has pretty much put an end to that by offering the industry something it's never had before: open architecture—a ubiquitous, open platform for developers of both hardware and software. Nowadays, there are scores of companies selling cards that plug into your PC to program, communicate with, or replace current control systems. A small but thriving software industry is growing around PC-based industrial control.

Even better, PCs are produced by the tens of millions all over the world. By investing in PCs, the industry, too, can reap the economies of scale, replacing those $50,000 graphics worksta-tions with $2000 PCs. If someone invents a faster parallel port or a bigger monitor, you just buy

one and plug it in. And Windows offered a relatively ubiquitous GUI for the PC.

In addition to graphics, Windows offers one other tool that has proved essential: DDE, which Windows applications use to pass data back and forth as they run. Software can use DDE to take data from other programs or, with the proper drivers, from hardware such as network cards, serial ports, and PLCs. Industrial-control programs send and receive their data via DDE.

"The beauty," says Smith, "is that customers can use those same DDE servers to move data into other Windows applications, such as Excel. They love the opportunity to do that." By wrapping DDE drivers and interfaces around other systems (e.g., VAXes), you can make their data available to the PC without having to do a full-scale port of your software to those other systems. To facilitate moving this data around, Wonderware wrote a network version of DDE, called Net DDE, which it subsequently licensed to Microsoft for use in Windows NT.

Speed Bumps Ahead

Anyone introducing new technology into an existing factory must be prepared to integrate it with an array of preexisting legacy hardware, both dedicated control systems and minicomputers — the latter consisting largely of DEC VAXes running VMS and Unix. "Corporate America," says Smith, "has a huge investment in these systems, not only in terms of the hardware but also in terms of the software written for those environments. They won't give that investment up easily."

Windows often serves as a universal client, letting users implement complex multiple-system solutions including PC, VAX, Unix, and DCS systems. The PC stands, like the robot C3PO in the movie *Star Wars*, as a translator between human and machine—and sometimes between humans and other humans—fluent in the myriad languages and dialect of the industrial-control machines. Factories can migrate toward less expensive distributed PCs at their own pace, without throwing away the millions invested in their older control systems.

Once you have linked these disparate systems together, they still require some sort of common language to talk to one another. SQL is the lingua franca of the database world. Given sufficient fluency in SQL, a program on your PC can access data from mainframes, minicomput-ers, and other PCs. Effective industrial-control software must speak SQL. On the PC side, ODBC (Open Database Connectivity), a nephew of SQL, is fast becoming important as well.

SCADA

Once you've started to implement a distributed system of PC clients and assorted hosts that are networked together and can speak to one another, the implications are enormous. Consider the lowly statistician toiling away in a cubicle, analyzing data. To gather the data, he or she may have walked down to the factory floor and taken samples off the line or may have taken it from periodic reports issued from the factory floor. In any event, the data is cold. The statistician is not seeing the process as it's happening now but rather as it was in the past—several hours or several days ago. Now he or she must enter the data into a statistical program and study the resulting graphs.

Consider the statistician's boss, who waits for the analyses. By the time he or she gets it, the data is colder still. Consider the contract process engineer, who works on the opposite coast, trying to fine-tune a process he or she's never seen running.

Now, give each of these people a PC plugged into the company network, with graphical software that shows the process running in real time. Let them redesign the screens, just like the industrial MMI users, to show the data they need the way they want it. Provide them with statistical control charts that update in real time. Add software that tracks inventory across the shop floor, that will show you where every component of a given order is and in what stage of completion at any given second. Make some of these PCs read-only, allowing certain people (e.g., accountants) to watch a process without being able to meddle with it. If people along the line speak different languages, say Spanish and English or German and French, then you should provide each user with data in the language of his or her choice. State-of-the-art software does all this.

Traditionally, this type of high-level software is known as SCADA (supervisory control and data acquisition). On the PC, the distinction between SCADA and MMI is ceasing to exist. Many vendors service both areas with a single, reconfigurable product.

Bigger, Better, Faster, and Safer

Windows may be a well-accepted graphical interface, but it has never been a paragon of stability. A general protection fault at the wrong time can crash your whole system, and a crash on the shop floor can be very costly. "People in the office may not like it when a piece of software burps," says Smith, "but they're more forgiving than the guy who's making a million dollars' worth of chocolate."

Also, industrial MMI is driven on real-time data, and Windows makes a lousy real-time environment. The smallest resolvable clock-tick is too large for finely timed processes. Even worse, Windows is a shared, multitasking environment that relies on every application behaving politely and not hogging resources. If a database takes an extra few seconds to close its files, other applications must wait in line. In the industrial-control environment, those seconds can mean disasters ranging from a ruined batch of cookies to a melting nuclear core; that's just not acceptable.

In the past, vendors of industrial-control software were forced to "fix" Windows to achieve the performance and reliability they need—writing patches and DLLs or hacking into Windows' multimedia drivers—or they had to use a less widely accepted operating system. But evolving operating environments and faster processors promise some relief. NT and the upcoming Chicago are slated to provide a more robust, fault-tolerant environment with true preemptive multitasking—something an industry weary of patching and tweaking sorely needs.

In addition, the new generation of microprocessors (e.g., Pentiums, Alphas, and PowerPCs) will make everything go faster in general. This will be a big boon to developers trying to make their products work successfully in real time.

As PCs become faster and more stable, they're winning the trust of the industry. Although there will probably always be two-box systems with dedicated PLCs controlling the machinery and PCs providing the interface to humans, more factories are giving over control of their manufacturing processes completely to PCs.

"We recommend that our customers use our software to actually control the line," says Intellution's Rio: "we're that confident. Our software runs in many mission-critical applications, including controlling nuclear power plants, so it's certainly safe to use it to make cookies."

Automated Process Control

Industrial-control software is showing up in areas far from the factory floor. Opto22 is wiring up the East German city of Leipzig (population 650,000) for the local water utility. The system has thousands of data points with multiple remote links and it's all handled with PCs.

Industrial MMI is being used in security and climate-control applications for museums, banks, and prisons, which might have thousands of sensors of all types. While a typical home-security system is fairly dumb, systems with thousands of components require considerably more intelligence—if for nothing else than dealing with the inevitable failures. "When you have thousands of sensors," says Rio of Intellution, "it's a lot more likely that one will go off accidentally. So the system might look for groupings of two or three alarms going off at once and *then* call the police," Rio adds.

Wonderware's software controls rides at Walt Disney World and monitors the worldwide flow of money for one Federal Reserve bank. "We realized a few years ago," says Wonderware's Dave Smith, "that this isn't about industrial MMI anymore. This is about getting real-time data from point A to point B, so you can make real-time decisions that affect your business."

OPTIMIZATION OF FINAL SCREENING STAGE PROVIDES ULTIMATE IN STOCK CLEANING*
by Hubert Gassman

Holes and other formation defects, sheet breaks, and coater breaks influence the efficiency of every paper machine. The causes for such problems—both known and unknown—are numerous, and such problems can determine whether a machine runs profitably or not.

The functions of thin-stock screening (or final screening) vary widely, both with the product being made and with the type of manufacturing processes. Final screening is a primary process for determining the quality of a specific grade, whether it is a free-sheet, wood containing, recycled-content printing/writing grade, or 100% recycled paper and paperboard.

For the first printing/writing grades, a sufficient amount of screening is almost guaranteed with current highly developed stock preparation systems. Therefore, the role of thin-stock screening can be defined as dispersion and fluidization of fibers, fillers, and additives in such a way that no deposition or spinning of material occurs. Furthermore, thin-stock screening separates contaminants that originate from the broke system, or it acts as a backup in case of contaminant overload in the stock-prep area.

The function of screening for the second group of grades is similar to the first, but has different priorities. First, final screening separates flexible debris, such as stickies, latex, and hot melts. Second, screening provides dispersion and fluidization of fibers, fillers, and additives so that no deposition or spinning occurs. Finally, screening separates contaminants that are added after thick-stock screening.

GREATER EFFICIENCIES

Today's excellent stock-prep systems can achieve up to 98% total cleaning efficiency. However, the remaining 2% of contaminants can and will have a severe impact on the paper-making process. This 2% or more can be handled in final screening as part of the thin-stock system.

Attention to this level of detail is very demanding on process equipment. For example, an average paper machine consumes 330 tpd of fiber. The stock flow to the stock-prep area contains about 3.5% mechanical contaminants. The cleaning efficiency is assumed at 90%. This re-

---

* Reprinted with permission from *Pulp & Paper*, September, 1995.

sults in a remaining contamination of 1.05 tpd to the paper machine headbox. Those numbers indicate the importance of final screening.

The following screen constructions are found in thin-stock screening applications:

1. Single-basket screens
   • Basket on perimeter
   • Rotor on inside of basket
   • Utilizes centrifugal forces
   • Feed now into the center of the basket.

2. Double-basket screens
   • Two screen baskets
   • Rotor passing between both baskets
   • Utilizes centrifugal forces for the outer basket
   • Utilizes centripedal forces for the inner basket
   • Feed flow into the center between both baskets.

3. Single-basket screen (suction principle)
   • Screen basket on perimeter
   • Rotor on inside of basket
   • Centripedal, suction effect from outside toward the center
   • Feed flow from perimeter
   • Design becoming outdated.

From a machine builder's perspective, single-basket screens as described in No. 1 above represent the optimal type of screen. The two most relevant components for screening results are the screen basket and the rotor. The most common operating problems with screens include the following:

Inefficient rejection of mechanical contaminants due to incorrect hole basket application

Wrong slot width (mostly too wide), non-optimized profile geometry, insufficient surface finish, or wrong screen basket design, even with installed slotted baskets

Insufficient rotor application and rotor wear.

Although they are widely used in the industry, double-basket screens as described in No. 2 pose a much greater operating difficulty than anticipated. According to the laws of physics, the outer basket is supplied with stock from internal rotor foils. The inner basket is supplied from outer rotor foils. That means centrifugal forces are being applied on stock traveling toward the

outer basket, and counteracting force (centripedal) is applied toward the stock flow trying to pass the inner basket.

At a constant rotating speed (circumferential speed), the centrifugal forces outweigh the opposing forces. The larger diameter outer rotor has an enhancing effect on the centrifugal forces applied. Therefore both baskets differ in their hydraulic load application, often reducing fiber-passing velocity to a minimum through the inner basket.

DEPOSIT PROBLEMS

Even baskets with hole sizes of 1.6 to 1.8 mm can generate deposits on the inner basket's feedside due to missing or incorrect profile geometry. The most severe case is a blinding over of the inner basket's feedside. The worst situation in regard to deposits is when those deposits are being generated on the basket's accept side. This situation arises when the fiber-passing velocity drops below a critical minimum. With an increase in velocity, those deposits will break loose, generate holes, and cause wetted breaks. Grade changes, as well as paper machine start-ups after long shutdowns, are often subject to these velocity changes.

This phenomenon is enhanced by an increase in flow resistance of a screen basket. Resistance to flow is changed through the conversion from hole baskets to slotted baskets or due to slot size reduction. Both screen types—double- and single-basket designs—are subject to this situation. Deposits are usually the most common operating problem.

All papermakers know of the possible causes for paper defects, primarily holes and breaks. The final screen can only reduce and/or eliminate possible causes generated prior to the screening function or causes generated from within the screen itself. To analyze the defects, it is helpful to pull screen baskets as soon as possible after a machine shutdown.

For the purpose of a break/hole analysis and its possible causes, the rinse/flush of the screens must be skipped. This ensures a true picture of the feed and accept side of the screen basket. Even at this point, it is very difficult to distinguish between deposits caused during operation or caused by a lack within the flush cycle.

SCREENING IMPROVEMENTS

Solutions to these problems are generally provided through a combination of steps, such as tuning the main components—rotor, basket, profile geometry, screen basket construction, wetted surface finishes, and passing velocity. The main rotor variables are rotor geometry and construction, foil geometry, impulses of rotor elements, surface properties. and rotor/basket clearance.

After a detailed analysis of the thin-stock system, recommendations for methods to improve runability are often possible. To achieve the desired results, the following process changes are either fully or partially required:

A required change is application of a screen basket that generates the optimum turbulence on the surface of the feed side to maximize the utilization of available open area and to eliminate deposits in order to minimize slot width.

Tendencies for spinning and depositing of material have to be eliminated through the surface and passing surface wall finishes. The application of milled baskets has been proven to be very successful.

A partially required process change is the alteration of an existing rotor or replacement with a newly optimized rotor to enhance the hydraulic load of one or both screen basket, to maintain a clean screen basket, and to save energy.

If all of these points are considered, evaluated, and properly calculated, then there is a good possibility that existing thin-stock screens can be converted to machines providing the new demands of highly advanced stock-prep systems.

QUALITY REQUIREMENTS FOR TEXTILES AND CLOTHING IN EUROPE*
by D. E. Morris and M. D. Crosby

The quality requirements for textiles and clothing sold on the European market are evolving rapidly, as competition in this sector increases and consumer concerns for environmental, health and safety factors gain momentum. A large number of developing countries supply these goods in various forms, whether as ready-made garments, textiles for specialized uses such as home furnishings or construction applications, or simply fabrics sold in general retail outlets. Exporters of such materials in developing countries should follow the changes underway closely, if they wish to maintain and expand their share in this lucrative trade. Some of the recent developments in the quality requirements for textiles and textile goods marketed in the European Union are discussed.

HEALTH AND SAFETY RULES

Health and safety legislation is, along with environmental measures, among the most important of the quality requirements for exporters of textiles and clothing in developing countries. Health and safety in specifications differ among the countries in the European Union (EU), particularly concerning the requirements on burning behavior of textiles in one form or other.

Textile Materials Used in Buildings

For textiles used in the construction industry, the main product affected by safety standards is floor coverings, which must meet the requirements of the EU's Construction Products

---

* A reprint of "Quality Requirements for Textiles and Clothing in Europe" by D.E. Morris and M.D. Crosby, published in *International Trade FORUM*, no. 2,1995, International Trade Centre UNCTAD/WTO, Geneva, Switzerland. D.E. Morris is an ITC consultant on the export marketing of textiles and textile products, who works with the International Rayon and Synthetic Fibres Committee in Brussels. M.D. Crosby is a management consultant, based in the United Kingdom, who contributed in particular concerning environmental issues.

directive and more particularly the test method for fire.

Under this directive, a construction product is defined as "any product which is produced for incorporation in a permanent manner in construction works including both buildings and civil engineering works." According to the directive, products of this type may be placed on the market only if they have characteristics that enable the works in which they are incorporated, assembled, applied or installed to satisfy essential requirements. Annex I of the directive lists these essential conditions, which fall under the following six areas: mechanical resistance and stability; safety in case of fire; hygiene, health and the environment; safety in use; protection against noise; and energy economy and heat retention.

Once such requirements, where applicable, have been fulfilled, the product can be given a "CE" (European Community) conformity mark. While this conformity mark does not imply any quality-assurance control, it indicates that the product complies with the relevant national standards transposing the harmonized standards, with a European technical approval or, if harmonized standards do not exist. with the national technical specifications. (The European technical approval is a favorable technical assessment of the fitness of a product for an intended use, based on fulfillment of the essential requirements for the building works in which the product is to be used. It may be granted to products for which there is neither a harmonized standard, a recognized national standard nor a mandate for a harmonized standard, and to products that differ significantly from harmonized or recognized national standards. However, in these cases a CE conformity mark is not given.)

Although the Construction Products directive was issued at the end of 1988, specifications for its application have not yet been harmonized. Consequently no attestations of conformity have been granted and no products labelled accordingly. One reason for the delay is the interpretation of what products are to be covered by the directive. In the case of textiles, for example, although floor coverings, curtains and drapes, wall coverings, upholstery fabrics and so on are within the scope of the directive, opinions differ on which products are "incorporated in a permanent manner." For instance wall-to-wall carpets that are glued or otherwise fixed to the floor meet this condition, but rugs do not. Concerning curtains, which themselves are not permanent but

are permanently fixed by means of curtain rails, there has yet to be agreement on whether or not they are covered by the directive. Upholstery fabrics for furniture pose a similar problem.

The Commission of the European Communities expects however to have the necessary formalities completed in the near future so that it can issue labels of conformity with the Construction Products directive this year. Common procedural rules for this directive were adopted in early 1994. What remains to be done is the publication of lists of certification bodies, inspection entities, testing laboratories and the products concerned—which are necessary to enable developing countries to comply with the agreed criteria when exporting such goods. Developing country exporters of textile products that are included in this directive will theoretically be able to obtain a CE conformity mark, provided the manufacturer adheres to the technical requirements and is able to provide an attestation of conformity.

Household Textiles

In the case of household textiles, or more particularly upholstered furniture and mattresses, as yet no EU legislation exists on safety requirements. National legislation is however in force in the United Kingdom and Ireland. Legislation has also been introduced in Italy for hotels, which includes items such as furniture, mattresses and floor coverings, and proposed in France. In the former case the new standards have been published, but in the latter case remain at the draft stage. In Ireland and the United Kingdom the legislation on safety requirements is based on the cigarette test and the match test. The first is an assessment of the ignitability of upholstered furniture using a smouldering cigarette; the second is a test of ignitability using a match flame, equivalent to 15 seconds of ignition. These test methods have been adopted for mattresses. As a result, for example, both Ireland and the United Kingdom have banned the use of mattresses of standard foam made from polyurethane.

At the EU level, although a proposed directive was published on upholstered furniture, it has been delayed because no reliable test methods have been found and the costs of such tests are relatively high. It is expected however that in the medium term a directive will be introduced to harmonize existing national legislation on upholstered furniture.

Tests have been developed for other household textiles, namely for curtains and drapes, and are being initiated for bed linen and duvets. Once these test procedures have been standardized, the European Commission will be in a position to introduce directives relating to the safety requirements of all household textiles.

Apparel

For garments, only the United Kingdom and Ireland have national legislation on safety requirements, and that relates to children's and ladies' nightwear. For children's nightwear, a flame retardancy test is an essential requirement. Women's nightwear must be labelled "flame retardant" or "keep away from fire." The Netherlands introduced legislation on 1 January of this year for nightwear. Nightwear has been defined as clothing used mainly for sleeping, including pajamas, night dresses and bathrobes and, as far as children's nightwear is concerned, has been defined by size categories. The requirements include vertical flame spread, surface flash and afterglow requirements. No flame retardants are to be used except those on a positive list. All nightwear must be labelled "keep away from fire."

At present the EU has accepted that legislation on flammability for nightwear is a matter for national governments. This stance may change if all states introduce widely differing legislation.

The EU has adopted legislation on personal protective equipment, which includes protective clothing. Personal protective clothing must satisfy basic health and safety requirements in terms of design, innocuousness, comfort and efficiency. It must be accompanied by relevant information supplied by the manufacturer. Additional requirements common to several types of such goods and specific to particular risks must also be met. A general requirement for protective clothing, for instance, is that it should be capable of signaling the user's presence visually. An example of a specific requirement is that clothing used as a buoyancy aid must not restrict the user's freedom of movement but must enable the person to swim, take action to escape from danger or rescue others.

If a product meets these basic requirements, a CE conformity mark can be issued, provided that the manufacturer produces a certificate attesting that the item placed on the market is in line with the directive. Suppliers outside the EU can apply for a conformity mark if their products meet all of the requirements. The complexity of the legislation may, however, make it cumbersome for developing country exporters to enter this particular market segment.

Although no legislation on apparel exists other than that described above, this situation is expected to change. In the medium term it is likely that once legislation on household textiles has been adopted, European legislators will turn their attention to apparel, not only with respect to burning behavior but also to the chemicals used in the production or cultivation of raw materials and the manufacture of the garment itself. For instance, it is likely that by the turn of the century certain chemicals will be banned in the dyeing and finishing processes for textiles, and the application of specific insecticides and pesticides currently commonly used in the production of textile raw materials will be forbidden. Indeed, in Germany new legislation has been brought in to protect health, and the importation of goods dyed with specific dyestuffs is being banned as of 1 July of this year. The present legislation applies to dyestuffs and not pigments.

ENVIRONMENTAL PROTECTION

Since the early 1980s, particularly in the industrialized countries, environmental considerations have assumed an increasing significance for suppliers and distributors. The Fifth European Community Programme on the Environment, adopted in early 1993 and entitled "Towards Sustainability, " has not only broadened the scope and direction of the issue but also provides for the development of a new range of instruments of environmental policy. Legislation to improve environmental data and public information on industrial activity and quality control has been launched. In addition, legislation is being drawn up in areas of relevance to the textile sector. Of these, the laws on eco-labelling. eco-auditing, waste management and recycling (including packaging and packaging waste) are the most significant.

Eco-labelling

The European Union's general eco-labelling scheme is set out in Council Regulation (EEC) 880/92, published on 23 March 1992. The scheme awards an eco-label to products with reduced adverse environmental impact. It is voluntary, is intended to be introduced gradually and gives manufacturers the right to decide whether or not to apply for the privilege of displaying the label. The criteria for the use of the label are to be defined for individual product groups. The regulation states that products imported into the European Union for which the award of an eco-label has been requested must at least meet the same criteria as products manufactured in the EU. As such criteria will be strict and compliance will require the application of the best available technologies, only a limited proportion of the products available will be eligible to carry the label. In the case of textiles, under an EU mandate, Denmark was required to undertake work on an eco-label for 100% cotton T-shirts and bed linen of polyester and cotton blends. The progress for developing the first criteria catalogue for a model case product group is not yet finished. Thus as yet no EU eco-labelling scheme exists for textiles.

Several EU countries have taken the initiative on their own of developing proposals for eco-labelling criteria for various product groups, some concerning textiles. The Netherlands and Sweden have also developed proposals for textiles. The European wool industry has carried out its own study of an eco-label for wool products.

Two different approaches are taken by the European textile industry on criteria for an eco-label. The first involves merely testing the final product. The product is accepted if it is not considered particularly damaging to the environment, i.e. the "non-nuisance" criterion applies. This approach is more suitable for developing countries than the second, which is based on a modified life-cycle analysis. The latter approach is particularly complex, as national authorities must assess each processing stage and the combined environmental effects of all inputs for the purpose of determining criteria for the eco-label. The number of variables that the analysis must take into consideration is huge.

Until the textile manufacturing industry in Europe takes a comprehensive stance on the complex issue of an eco-label for textiles, it is expected that the number of different eco-labels introduced will increase. Even if the EU itself develops an eco-label, it is to be expected that other schemes will exist in parallel, either nationally or sectorally.

Various national and private eco-labels are currently used in Europe. One of these is a label for textile products manufactured in Germany, called the "Oko-Tex-Standard 100," introduced by Gesamttextil. In the Netherlands, Stichting Miliuekeur has published criteria for a clothing and textile eco-label valid as of 1 January this year, which covers clothing and material for clothing.

The widening use of private and national eco-labels is making it increasingly difficult for consumers to differentiate between products. In some cases these labels are used solely as a marketing instrument and have little factual and technical substance.

In the face of the proliferation of eco-labelling schemes, the European Apparel and Textile Organization (Euratex), headquartered in Brussels, which supports a single European eco-label, prepared a comparative study on eco-labels in use in 1993 in order to coordinate the industry response and cooperate with the Danish competent body preparing a draft criteria catalogue.

Exporters of textiles and apparel in developing countries should follow these developments closely.

Eco-audit

Regarding the eco-audit scheme of the European Union, which is based on part of the overall EU action programme for the environment, the Commission published a regulation in June 1993 entitled "Allowing Voluntary Participation by Companies in the Industrial Sector in a Community Eco-Management and Audit Scheme." Unlike the eco-label arrangement, which is targeted at different product sectors, the management and audit scheme is company-site specific.

The eco-audit scheme is voluntary. Its objective is to promote the use of environmental auditing as a tool for the systematic and periodic evaluation of the environmental performance of certain industries, including the textile sector. Companies adhering to the provisions thus commit themselves to establishing and implementing an internal environmental management system.

Participation is open to companies operating a registered site or sites on which industrial activity is performed. For a site to be registered, the company must adopt an environmental policy, conduct an environmental review, introduce in the light of the review an environmental program, carry out an environmental audit, set objectives aimed at the continuous improvement of environmental performance, prepare an environmental statement and have the entire program verified and forwarded to a competent national body. Companies acquire the right to use one of the statements of participation given in an annex to the EU regulation for their registered sites, the graphic provided in the same annex and the registration number. The statement of participation cannot be used, however, on the products themselves or on their packaging.

The International Organization for Standardization through its Technical Committee TC207 Is developing a whole series of standards on environmental management systems (the ISO 14000 series). It is expected that by the end of 1996 most of these standards will be developed. The European Committee for Standardization (Comite europeen de normalisation) will then, under the normal procedure, take over these standards for Europe. A potential gap between those standards and the EU legislation within the Eco-Management and Audit Scheme may be controlled by guidelines. In the meantime, the existing U.K. standard BS 7750 will be widely used. The next five years will thus be a transition period in Europe with many gray areas to be resolved.

It is apparent that in the second half of the 1990s firms in Europe will have to undertake additional measures related to the conservation of the environment in response to growing general concern for environmental matters. Trading conditions will likewise become more and more sensitive to environmental considerations. Companies in developing countries intending to export to Europe will thus need to adapt accordingly to continue to compete successfully.

Management and Recycling of Nonhazardous Waste

Management and recycling of nonhazardous waste, including packaging and packaging waste, is becoming increasingly significant. In Europe the initial step towards reducing the environmental impact of packaging and packaging waste was in 1985. Germany was the first EU country to put a packaging waste ordinance into force, in 1990. The ordinance acknowledges the environmental impact of packaging, places a strong emphasis on recycling and insists on the principle that the polluter pays. Under the ordinance, collection systems are organized and each filler, distributor and retailer has a responsibility for taking back any packaging waste removed after the transport or purchase of the product.

The German ordinance subsequently became the basis of a proposed EU directive in 1992, later modified in October 1993. In March 1994, the Council of the European Union took a common position on adopting the directive on packaging and packaging waste, which was finally approved by the Council and the European Parliament on 20 December 1994 (94/62/EC). The targets set in the directive were that by 1999 between 50% and 65% by weight of packaging waste would be recovered and, within this target, between 25% and 45% by weight of the totality of packaging materials contained in packaging waste would be recycled, with a minimum of 15% by weight for each packaging material.

The directive could have consequences for the textile and clothing industries and the manufacture, merchandising and retailing of such products in Europe. It may affect the entry of textile goods into the European Union, raising questions of how packaging material, once it comes into the EU, is to be treated, and by whom, and who pays. Suppliers or importers will have to make arrangements with waste-handling companies within the EU or give a discount to customers who ensure that the waste is properly dealt with. Given the principle that the polluter pays, it may be that the disposal of packaging will have to be included in any contract between a developing country exporter and a European importer.

||||| 2.2
||||| SERVICE

---■---

HOW TO REALLY SATISFY YOUR CUSTOMERS*

Companies that keep customers satisfied are formidable competitors—that's a given. But what's a good recipe for generating that strong customer focus in your company? This expert offers one that blends a powerful new ingredient with your existing quality processes.

You can implement Total Quality Management and produce what you believe to be the best products or services in your market. But if you haven't integrated Customer Satisfaction Management (CSM) into your quality strategy, there's no guarantee that customers will want to buy what your company's selling.

That's why the Malcolm Baldrige National Quality Award assigns almost a third of its points to "Customer Focus and Satisfaction," notes Jean Otte, a Baldrige Award examiner and president of Customer Satisfaction Management Systems (Minneapolis). The Baldrige Award administrators recognize that the customer must be a key focus of any total-quality process for companies to achieve true success.

"One of the main problems companies have in managing customer satisfaction is that they haven't paid attention to who their customers really are and how they've changed," says Otte. A former corporate vice-president of quality management for National Car Rental, Otte has also held management positions at McDonald's, Gillette, and British Airways. She is also a former president of the Society of Consumer Affairs Professionals.

Many companies make the mistake of designing services and products on the basis of what they *think* customers want, without *asking them* what they really want. "Your company's customer base is different than it was 10 years ago, but you may still be targeting your original market. If you don't understand the needs of today's culturally diverse customers, you're not going to remain competitive," she warns.

According to Otte, Customer Satisfaction Management boils down to this five-factor formula:

1. *Determine who your customers are and what they want.*

2. *Produce a product or service that delivers what they want every time.*

3. *Make sure that everyone involved in designing, improving, delivering, or using the product or service is involved in the CSM process (including the customer).*

4. *Make sure that employees know what the services are supposed to do, and empower them to resolve any problems that come up in the production and delivery of the services.*

5. *Measure results to be certain that you're delivering what you promised the customer you'd deliver.*

Although this formula is relatively simple, companies often find that it's not so easy to put into practice, Otte concedes. These tips will help you integrate CSM into your quality management process.

START WITH TOP MANAGEMENT

CSM, like TQM, must begin with a commitment from senior management. Company leaders need to do more than just talk about the importance of customer satisfaction. They must continuously make their support for CSM visible to employees. This will encourage staffers to believe in the value of satisfying customers.

Once managers have made this type of commitment, their companies invariably reap rewards in terms of both profits and corporate image, notes Otte.

How can company leaders demonstrate their commitment to quality service through CSM? One way is by personally getting in touch with the customer. Otte reports that at the most successful quality-focused service companies, leaders make it a point to stay in close touch with customers. For example, CEOs have followed the lead of the late Sam Walton of Wal-Mart, who visited his company's stores and talked face to face with customers.

"If a senior manager for a credit card company has a problem with a card, I suggest that he or she call the company and go through the normal chain to get the situation resolved, to see what real customers have to go through," Otte advises.

"Senior managers should also try being their own 'mystery shoppers.' If the head of a service or retail chain goes anonymously into one of his or her operations and waits in line like everyone else, this CEO will find out much more about the customer's experience with the operation than he or she would if employees were told ahead of time to expect the visit."

GET MIDDLE MANAGEMENT BEHIND CSM TOO

Support from middle management is also critical to CSM success. The key to gaining this buy-in is ongoing training and education. Middle managers and supervisors need to learn how to manage in a total quality, customer-focused environment.

As employees are empowered to team up and make decisions that their bosses formerly made, some middle managers and supervisors may feel uncomfortable. "They may question their own role in CSM," Otte points out.

"They need to learn that their role is as vital as ever—just different. Now they must guide employees in making decisions and support those decisions. They learn that they still need to check on how employees are handling their new responsibilities. Managers need to be available to give guidance when employees are unsure how to handle a situation, and to help remove any roadblocks to quality service."

INVOLVE EMPLOYEES IN CSM

"Employees are the real key to managing customer satisfaction," Otte stresses. "They—not management—talk directly to customers and most affect whether those customers will be satisfied. Service employees can make or break your product or service; yet, traditionally, they are at the bottom of the hierarchical ladder and are the least paid and least trained."

So organizations that wish to achieve service excellence through CSM must ensure that their employees are qualified to make the right decisions regarding customer satisfaction. How can you make sure your firm's employees are fit for the task?

- *Foster customer awareness.* Let all employees know that they're in business to serve a customer—that it's truly the customer who signs their paychecks. All employees need to know how they directly or indirectly affect your customers, both internal (employees in other departments) and external (the purchasers and users of your company's products or services). Also, they should know that satisfying internal customers is just as important as satisfying external ones.

  "I like to talk to employees about the goal of giving 100 percent defect-free products and service every time," says Otte. "Most say. 'Impossible. People make mistakes. We're only human.' However, I suggest that they turn the tables and think of themselves as the customers. If they go into a bank with a $100 check, it's not acceptable to them to get $99. If they have surgery and the doctor removes only 99 percent of their appendix, that's not acceptable.

  "Show employees how much money the company loses when even one customer leaves, and how one dissatisfied customer can lead to more lost customers, lower revenues and, ultimately, loss of job security. Statistics like these teach employees how important it is to treat each and every customer well."

- *Involve employees in the design, delivery, and improvement of services.* One way to do this is with cross-functional quality or continuous improvement teams made up of the people who touch the service design and improvement processes. They can provide input during each step and identify possible problem areas so that these can be alleviated. Don't forget to include customers and suppliers in these processes, too. Ask for and consider any thoughts and suggestions they might have about the product or service from their standpoints.

- *Recognize employees for their customer satisfaction efforts.* Recognition by management and peers is essential. However, Otte likes to get customers involved in recognition efforts, too. "Having customers fill out a card or make a phone call that results in an employee getting an 'employee of the month' award helps people feel that they are being recognized by customers for the work they are doing," says Otte. "Customers appreciate and enjoy being able to single out and praise an employee who has provided good service."

- *Hire only those people who will effectively represent your company to the customer.* During the interview process, it's a good idea to pretest the ability of applicants to handle problems and placate disgruntled customers.

- *Give them the right kind of training.* This should go beyond basic "smiles" training. "When your customers' airplanes have been delayed two hours, the car rental company can't find their reservations, or the hotel doesn't have a room for them, smiling and telling them to have a nice day simply doesn't cut it," Otte observes. Employees need to be given the skills, ability, *and authority* to do whatever it takes to turn a situation around and keep those customers for your company. Recovering customers when problems occur is just as important to the CSM process as preventing problems.

MEASURE THE COST OF *NOT* USING CSM

How much future revenue is lost when dissatisfied customers take their business elsewhere? Many companies fail to measure this quality cost. However, an important part of CSM is measuring the real cost of *not* managing customer satisfaction.

"National Car Rental uses a measurement system that shows what customers rent, how often, and how much they spend," Otte explains.

"National also tracks when and under what circumstances its customers stop using its service. The data are then analyzed to show how much it cost to lose a customer who was worth x dollars to the company annually, plus what it had cost to get that new customer in the first place." The data also reveal how many people had complained about the same problem during a given month.

"Many companies are only now beginning to pay attention to these kinds of data. Statistics show that it costs five times more to gain a new customer than to keep one that you already have. Considering this, why not put more focus on managing the customer base you already have?" Otte asks. "If companies were to estimate conservatively that one fourth of their complaining customers won't use their services again and they start putting a dollar value to that, they would quickly realize that their losses due directly to customer dissatisfaction are absolutely staggering.

"A company that truly wants to participate in TQM needs to say, 'I'm going to do everything I can to keep each customer, because I know that a satisfied customer has a ripple effect, too.' There's nothing better than positive word-of-mouth advertising and nothing worse than negative word-of-mouth advertising."

Another area in which many companies fall short is in using the data they collect from and about their customers. "Often, when Baldrige examiners ask how companies use their data to support their ongoing improvement or to change the design of their product or service, the answers become hazy," Otte reports. "You can't just analyze data and leave it at that. You need to make the improvements that are indicated. Companies must be able to answer how they expect to achieve greater customer satisfaction in light of the data."

SET SATISFACTION GOALS

You need to set both short- and long-term customer-satisfaction goals. For example: *We want to improve our satisfaction levels 10 percent in two years. Here are the actions that will allow us to reach that goal.* Then, everyone needs to be held accountable for pushing forward reaching those goals.

"If every department were told to decrease costs by 2 percent each month for the next year, they would do it or be called in to explain why they fell short of the goal," Otte points out. "Customer Satisfaction Management needs that same commitment. People need to be held just as accountable for customer-satisfaction goals as they are for traditional areas of financial gains and losses. After all, whether or not customers are satisfied means financial gains and losses for any company."

Otte suggests that incentives be tied to reaching CSM goals. For instance, if one of your locations has exceptionally high customer-satisfaction levels, give these people some sort of reward. Ask them what they did to achieve those high satisfaction levels, and then teach these skills to the staffers at the other locations (or better yet, have the employees from the successful location do the training).

100 PERCENT GUARANTEED!

Companies that focus on customer satisfaction as part of TQM don't have to restrict their money-back guarantees—or explain what a money-back guarantee means, Otte suggests. "If you have to explain what your guarantee covers, you basically haven't got one. Simply put, a money-back guarantee should mean that if the customer is not satisfied by your product or service for any reason, you will replace it or give a full refund—no strings attached.

"If your company is truly focused on prevention, continuous improvement, recovery, and treating the employees who deliver the service well, you shouldn't have to worry about that guarantee, because there will be very few cases where customers will need to ask you to honor it."

KEEP IT SIMPLE*
by Horst Schulze

We need to make sure everyone wins from the decisions we make and the actions we take. When we added three positions in each hotel—a quality manager, a repeat-guest coordinator, and a training manager—several investors asked why we needed those positions; in fact, some insisted that we do away with them because at first we had no results to show, only agony and cost.

During the dark days, what pulled us through was vision—my vision and that of others around me—and the constant focus on that vision. I think that's the essence of leadership. Leadership doesn't go away. In fact, only leadership can pull you through the tough times. You can have a vision, be committed to the vision, and do things to get there. That's easy. But to keep focused on it, to keep people motivated behind it, and to not be sidetracked by excuses and by superficial effects is hard.

It would have been very easy for me to say, "We have 30 hotels. I have three optional em-

ployees in each hotel. I can dismiss 90 people tomorrow. That will save a few million dollars and show everybody what a hero I am." It was very tempting to do that during a recession.

But when you have a clear vision, you resist the temptation to sell out. You think, "What I will spend in four years on this effort, I will save in one month later, and from then on it's a benefit." I knew that. But it was still hard to explain to other people because they didn't want to listen to what might happen in three years. They wanted to know what would happen now.

At the top, we kept focused on our vision because the entire management team of about 10 people came here for a dream. We came here because this challenge was the only one left. And they're not only colleagues in this quest, they are dear friends.

The other day, one of my vice-presidents said, "You know, maybe the biggest accomplishment in our 10 years is that we're still good friends." He mentioned that I did what I had to

---

* Reprinted with permission from *Executive Excellence,* March 1995; for subscriptions call (800) 304-9782. Horst Schulze is president of the Ritz-Carlton Hotel Company. This article is adapted from an interview conducted for *Executive Excellence* magazine by Ritz Khadem in Atlanta in October 1994.

do—re-energize them, and keep re-energizing them. What was hard, however, was to re-energize myself every day. At one point, I put Post-it notes all around to remind myself not to give up—to do the right thing, not the convenient short-term thing or what seemed right to others, but to do the right thing for the long term and to be ethical about it.

We were trying to live by the values we teach, but it was difficult. People were often cynical. People were sending me articles from management magazines that argued, "Quality doesn't work." People were making fun of us in speeches, and newspapers were reporting that the Ritz-Carlton had problems.

IT CAN BE DONE ANYWHERE

At the same time, I was being told, "It can't be done in Florida; it can't be done in Atlanta; it can't be done in Australia, Spain, or Mexico." But that was a bunch of baloney. I told everybody, It can be done. And we proved it. In Australia our hotels just won a national mersy award—number one in service. We were inspected in Cancun, Mexico, for a national quality award. And our hotel in Spain won the European Quality Award.

Quality helps everybody—all the stakeholders. You should want your business to help your community and your industry. When you have all your stakeholders in mind, your decisions will benefit all concerned.

We conduct a survey every three months to identify what our customers want and expect. Today, for example, they want access to fax machines; they want speedy delivery; they want to keep in touch using the latest technology. So one aspect of continuous improvement is to be on top of the latest technology. But we've learned that most guests don't want fax machines in their rooms—but they want to have office capability in the hotel.

Service is not just about speed and technology. People want to feel well. It's all about people, about one-on-one contact with other human beings. And guests measure value and quality by those moments of human contact. The "moments of truth" are still the measure that most people use to evaluate service.

We sense that our guests want to have the product tailored to them. Customers want what they want in a hotel. If they want to be on a high

floor, they want to be on a high floor. If they want six pillows, they want six pillows. They want the service to be tailored and individualized to them, and they don't want to explain it all the time. They want to come in and have it their way. That expectation of a product tailor-made to the tastes of the individual is more and more the future in the service industry. Our customers want absolutely hassle-free service. That's why it's essential that we work defect-free. They want to go into a room and have everything working for them. They want a reliable product, on time, all the time, made to suit them.

CUSTOMERS, GUESTS, AND NON-GUESTS

I like to think in terms of guests, nonguests, and customers. Guests are the people who stay with us. Non-guests are people who haven't yet stayed with us. Customers are decision-makers. From our studies we know that the "customers" who have a meeting planned at one of our facilities have 42 different additional demands than the average guest has. So we must know how to deliver those products to them.

Our focus is to keep the customers and guests we have. In this area, we battle another tradition of the industry: to not care too much about losing customers if the competition loses even more. For example, if we lost 30,000 customers a year because of defects in our service, we were supposed to feel okay if the other guys lost 32,000. That's a horrible attitude. We said, "We need a process to ensure we keep our customers.

Every employee needs to understand how we keep customers." So we set a simple, clear, and precise objective: "We will keep every customer." We think if we can meet this first objective, we will meet the second—to win new customers—because to a great extent that objective is met by satisfying your customers to the point they become salespersons. The key to winning more customers is to first satisfy your current customers.

Until 10 years ago, we never knew what our customers and guests wanted because we never surveyed them. We thought we had the answers. Of course, once we found out what they wanted, we then had to evaluate how well we delivered what they wanted. We also analyzed our communications. We studied how to tell them that we have something better in ways they would understand.

FIVE-STEP IMPROVEMENT PROCESS

To improve the competence of our employees in the core skills that drive our business, we use a five-step process.

First, we have a selection process. It starts by not hiring people, but selecting people. At the beginning, we need to know if the person has the talent to become a competent and committed employee. So the first challenge is making sure that we have continuously improving employees who can meet the demands of our customers. Our selection process is designed to ensure that we have the right people. Careful selection costs more money on the front end, but it saves dramatically over time because it reduces turnover.

Second, we have an orientation process. When employees come into our organization and industry, we orient them to our values, vision, and mission. We don't just shove them into jobs. We orient them first to our values because they are at the core of who we are—and that won't change. They understand who we are, why we're different, what our vision is, what our mission is, and what our goals are. They must understand these things before we let them loose.

The third process is certification. New employees are taught what they need to know by the people who work in their various departments. After they've been taught, they have to pass a certification test, which tests their values and their knowledge. If they don't reach 100 percent, they have to start over until they reach 100 percent. Every hotel reports whether or not they're 100 percent certified. About 99% percent of our employees are certified. But we don't stop there. We measure everything. And managers are paid according to how they live up to their measurements. If their employees are not all certified, they do not get their bonus. They can only reach the highest pay rate once everyone is certified.

A fourth process is ongoing teaching or continuous learning. All employees in the company have to go through a learning process every day—not once a week or once a month, but every day for 15 minutes. This on-the-job training best fits our employees who have little formal education. We can't teach them in a classroom, because it's intimidating to them. So we have 15-minute teaching sessions. On every shift in every department, people get together, and the designated teacher for that day teaches the message of the day. The message comes from my office, and the same message goes to all hotels.

Whenever we detect a new need of the customer, for 10 consecutive days we teach employees how to meet that need. We pick one message every day, and we say, "We've had a number of complaints because we didn't have enough smiles" or "We aren't greeting our guests properly." At the same time in all departments in all of our hotels all over the world, the same thing is being taught.

Fifth, we have a reorientation process. Once a year our employees get reoriented to who we are, what we do, and why we do it. These involve every employee. We work on company-wide approaches to reaching objectives. The hotel managers get the objectives, but they work the hotel approach into the objective. Dishwashers get the same objectives, but they must decide how to accomplish their core objectives. So we are totally aligned—in objectives, strategic plan, mission statement—each hotel, every department, every employee.

When I first looked at our level of customer satisfaction, I came back totally depressed. I said, "I'll never reach this dream of zero defects." But I was wrong. We can reach it. It's no quick fix, but it's not that complicated either.

We need to find a way to look at our business the way our customers look at it, and not make quality improvement so complicated. We need to make quality simple to understand. I find this all so simple, and yet the quality people in this country are trying to make it so difficult. But what they're doing is frightening people away from quality. We have an obligation as a nation to be competitive. And we need to help make our industries more competitive.

I have mixed feelings about our situation. On one hand, I'm happy that we took early action, because it gives us such a competitive advantage. On the other hand, I'm sorry when I feel that way, because it's my industry. And it's my country. As a country we can't afford not to be competitive.

■

PRUDENTIAL MEASURES HR WITH A TOTAL-QUALITY YARDSTICK*
by Jennifer J. Laabs

In life, it's generally a good idea to practice what you preach. In business, it's not only a good idea, it can be crucial to your success.

Although Valhalla, New York-based Prudential Resources Management, a unit of The Prudential Insurance Co. of America, formally began a total-quality journey in 1991, that journey took a sharp and more focused turn a couple of years ago when the company revised its mission and tied that mission to the company's core values: Client Focus, Winning, Worthy of Trust and Respect for Each Other.

Because of the company's move toward quality objectives, the firm's culture had changed, but HR—and the systems it administered—had not. As a human-resources consultant, it was time for the company to practice what it preached. It was a goal that although clear—as it is for many companies—isn't always easy to reach. But it could offer large payoffs.

The company's revised mission is to be a world-class leader in providing relocation, real estate, human resources and related consulting services to individuals and institutions globally while generating a satisfactory retum. Above all, the company now strives to "delight its clients" and to do so with honesty, integrity and mutual respect, realizing that its greatest asset in achieving this mission is its employees. As a learning organization, the firm states that its employees' ongoing education and development is critical to its success.

After Prudential set its sights on total-quality improvements, the organization's Chairman and CEO, Matthew M. Luca, and President and COO, T. Stephen Gross, chartered an ongoing human relations assessment project (HRAP) team to be responsible for ensuring that all the company's human relations systems directly support the company's revised mission, vision and values.

"We recognized that in order to succeed, we needed to make sure that our human relations

---

EXHIBIT 1.—TEN HR OBJECTIVES

Prudential Resource Management's 10 HR Objectives

1. Foster open communication
2. Lead by example and assume personal responsibility
3. Understand clients' needs
4. Create an environment that's free from fear
5. Reward and recognize individuals and teams
6. Work toward continuous improvement
7. Encourage education and development
8. Emphasize teamwork and share successes
9. Encourage innovation, creativity and empowerment
10. Measure performance and make decisions based on fact

---

systems were aligned with our company's mission, vision and total-quality principles," explains Maria Stolfi, director of employee benefits and lead facilitator of the HRAP team. "When we say we [must] work toward continuous improvement, we [must also] give everybody the tools to do that." Some of the questions they began asking themselves were: Are our human relations systems supporting continuous improvement and total quality? Are our people getting rewarded and recognized according to our mission and values? Is their performance being managed on that basis? In many cases, the answer was *no*. It clearly was time for action.

THE HR TEAM TAKES STOCK OF HR SYSTEMS

According to their chairman's mandate, the company formed a cross-functional team of 10 associates (which is how Prudential refers to all its

---

* Reprinted with permission from the *Personnel Journal* (April 1995), a monthly magazine—by subscription only; $55 for one year, $93 for two years. In the US, call toll free (800) 444-6485. Jennifer J. Laabs is the senior writer at *Personnel Journal*.

employees) ranging in level from senior vice-president to lower-level employees.

Why give the task to a team instead of simply giving it to the HR department? "One of the things in our learning about total quality is the strength and the effectiveness of cross-functional teams and that's why we went that direction," says Thomas R. Jago, an internal communications officer and an HRAP team member. The firm had had success over the past few years in having cross-functional teams tackling multidimensional projects, so the company's senior management felt it should also give HR systems the same directive. Also, because there are only 10 individuals in the company's internal HR organization, it would be difficult to give sole responsibility for a project of this magnitude to so few people.

The team first looked at the HR services the company provided for its employees and categorized them into well-defined service units. They identified six broad human relations systems or services which the human resources function provides to the organization. These services included: performance management, reward and recognition, personnel policy, compensation and benefits, communication and career development.

After careful evaluation, the team ranked these systems, putting the performance-management system at the top of the list. They determined that these were the six areas where there were some concerns, where there was the greatest room for improvement and where they felt they could get some relatively quick results so that changes would have a positive impact on the organization.

The next step was to figure out how to systematically redesign each of these six systems so that they would be aligned with the company's new vision, mission and values. The team went about setting concrete objectives for measuring the six HR systems' impact on the organization. "We established a set of 10 objectives that we would base all of our human relations systems against," says Jago.

The goal of these 10 HR objectives, which included such areas as fostering open communication and leading by example (see Exhibit 1), was to recognize that the company's ongoing success is dependent on HR's ability to recognize and value each individual's unique differences and talents. The HRAP team envisioned that a work environment, supported by these 10 objectives, would allow each person the opportunity to reach his or her fullest potential, and therefore directly contribute to, and of course help improve the bottom line.

REALIGNING EMPLOYEES' PERFORMANCE GOALS WITH COMPANY GOALS

After establishing the 10 HR objectives, the HRAP team had to figure out what criteria to use in aligning the company's performance-management system with the 10 objectives. They had to determine: where the systems fell on the objectives continuum, where they should be and where the gaps were.

To figure all this out, the team gathered best-practice information from award-winning companies and consulted with leading experts through secondary-research sources. "We also did informal benchmarking by referring to publications that have written about other organizations and what they've done in performance management," Jago adds.

In addition, they evaluated a recent employee survey that had asked questions—many relating to performance management. From this, the HRAP group learned that the performance management system wasn't used consistently, it didn't stress ongoing and multilevel feedback and it didn't factor in team performance.

The team also spoke to other organizations on an informal basis to get an outside perspective. "We didn't actually go out and talk to other organizations because time was important to us," says Stolfi. The HRAP team also solicited feedback from the organization's senior management team about what changes they thought needed to he made. All those insights were incorporated into the evaluation process.

"Through our research of total quality, we *imagineered* what our HR systems would look like in terms of behaviors if they were aligned completely with all the [objectives]," Stolfi explains. "So we looked at all that data, came up with a common rating system and then conducted about 12 focus groups throughout our company of both management and nonmanagement groups," adds Stolfi.

Over the course of a month (late last summer), they met with about 20% of the company's employees in focus groups throughout the organization, facilitated by HRAP team members. The team's research lead them to the realization that employees wanted a more formal way to see how the work they do every day helps the company achieve its mission and quality vision.

PERFORMANCE MANAGEMENT TOPS THE LIST

The HRAP team's research suggested that the company's performance-management system was the first HR system that needed to be realigned with the company's new vision.

The system had flaws, both in design and in execution. The biggest flaws were that it didn't clearly tie individual objectives to company objectives and that it lacked clear evaluation standards. Although people could be rated on a scale of 1-5 (from "needs substantial improvement" to "outstanding"), in several areas such as client focus and technical ability, those performance dimensions needed further clarification. "The process that we had was pretty good if people were using it as it was intended," says Jago. "There were situations where people were doing quite well because employees' managers were very focused on it." But, in many eases, people weren't using the system as it was intended, often because they didn't receive training. Many weren't using it at all. "

Where we were falling short was that [the performance-management system] was not well-communicated and it was very unevenly implemented," says Jago. In fact, some employees weren't setting objectives at all so they couldn't be measured by any performance system. Often, managers were dictating objectives with little or no input from employees and employees weren't getting a lot of ongoing feedback throughout the year about how they were achieving whatever objectives were set.

The performance-management system underwent reconstruction. What emerged was a four-part improvement plan. The new plan calls for:

- *Systems improvements:* The plan requires feedback from three to five team members for each associate's performance evaluation. Everyone is reviewed—exempt and non-exempt—with a 360-degree feedback system. Also, managers are now responsible for coaching and counseling their direct reports on a scheduled basis.
- *Skills building:* A complaint of the old system was that managers, especially new managers, weren't trained on how to help employees set objectives and how to conduct performance evaluations. Within the last several months, 700 of the company's 1,000 employees have received training in how to set objectives for themselves or for their subordinates.
- *Education of the process and company expectations:* "People had been feeling lousy about the [old] process because they didn't know what the expectations were," says Stolfi. Employees are being educated about how to set their job objectives based on company objectives.
- *Management of the process:* There's now a cross-functional team that's responsible for managing the performance-management process—to make sure that there's continuous improvement and measurement of how the process itself is proceeding on a monthly or quarterly basis.

The new performance-management system now includes: setting performance objectives, ongoing communication and feedback between manager and associate, gathering associate input, client/project team input, performance review and compensation review. The biggest difference between the company's old system and the new one is that performance management is viewed as a shared, rather than a one-sided, top-down responsibility.

The new system was put into place for the company's 1995 planning purposes at the end of 1994. Every associate has developed 1995 objectives that are meant to track and be consistent with their manager's objectives and to support the company's four strategic objectives. Everyone will be evaluated at the end of the year based on the new system.

EVALUATING THE NEW PERFORMANCE-MANAGEMENT SYSTEM'S PROGRESS

Although the company is still in its first year of implementing the new performance management system, already the HRAP team has identified changes it will make to next year's plan.

It will be incorporating a section into the performance appraisal form to elicit feedback from clients—both internal clients, external clients and colleagues—similar to other feedback mechanisms the company has incorporated into areas of the business as a result of its quality objectives. Improvements such as these, in turn, help support the 10 HR objectives — communication being at the top of the list.

"One of the other things we're going to be doing [more] is putting a couple of questions on our E-mail system and having people zap back their answers," explains Stolfi. Before, they asked: "Were you setting objectives before, yes or no?" Now they'll ask: "Were your objectives set by January 15th?" Or, "Have you assessed to improve the process?" Adds Stolfi: "We're going to continually solicit more data. But there's a lot more work to be done."

IMPROVING FIVE OTHER HR SYSTEMS

Prudential Resources Management's HRAP team has started looking at revamping the next system on the list: reward and recognition. The realignment process for this system is taking the same course as the performance-management system did. "We're looking at where we are today, we're doing focus groups, we're looking at survey data and we're also doing a lot more internal work on the reward and recognition system," says Stolfi.

In tandem with this project, the company is further focusing on evaluating HR's approach to achieving total-quality objectives through: l) Discussions by the senior management group about where they perceive HR to be today; 2) Having an outside consulting firm conduct an assessment of how well the company is meeting its total-quality objectives; 3) Designing a formal matrix of the organizationally sponsored HR programs.

The firm's reward and recognition systems are a good place to start. "Right now, we're looking at the organizationally sponsored programs and identifying what we spend on the programs, how many people it affects and how they're utilized," explains Stolfi. "A lot of our regions have different programs they might do on their own." For instance, there might be 15 different types of reward and recognition programs used throughout the company, which include such variations-on-a-theme as base pay, benefits, incentive compensation, public thank you's and private thank you's.

"People are being asked to rank what personally motivates them," says Stolfi. "So we're going to take that data to determine if we're spending our money in the places that make sense for people." Says Jack Navarro, senior VP: "We've brought our client focus to a higher level, we've got tools to improve our processes and we're creating measurement systems for collecting data on client and associate satisfaction. Now we must focus on the human side of these initiatives."

Although the company is eager to tackle each of the remaining four HR systems that it has committed to aligning with the firm's mission, it doesn't want to hurry the process by laying out an overly ambitious schedule. In keeping with the company's commitment to continuous improvement, it plans to work on each remaining HR system until all have been revamped. But the process won't stop there. Because each system will have a cross-functional team as its monitor, each will continue to undergo tinkering. Such is the way of total quality.

MEASURING SUCCESS WITH A TOTAL QUALITY FILTER

For some organizations that decide to travel the total-quality road, results are immediate and measurable. Prudential Resources Management has found this to be true. Comparing its 1993 year-end results to l991 (the year the company began its total-quality journey), it has found that:

- The number of clients it serves has nearly doubled
- Overall client satisfaction increased almost 10%
- Associate productivity jumped 5%
- It increased its profits by 20%.

Why is Prudential's focus on tying quality objectives to HR systems so innovative? Sometimes, innovion is simply common sense put into action. However, common sense, as they say, often isn't common at all. "The key is that we're getting people involved and we're understanding that their contributions impact the organization," says Jago. Indeed, they have. "Last year we phased in more than $2.6 million in efficiency improvements, and it's because of this planning and focus that we've been able to do that," he adds.

Now, with numerous partnerships and more than 65 cross-functional quality planning and improvement teams throughout the company, total quality is well integrated into the fabric of the company. Practicing what you preach isn't always easy and may feel like *the road less traveled*. In the end, however, it very well may be the road most profitable.

■

QUALITY QUEST*
by Terry Hennessy

Rocked by 50% turnover rates, a shriveling work ethic and a shrinking pool of applicants, supermarket operators are scrambling to maintain quality service and products in bakeries and delis. Some have cut popular deli features, many have turned to self-service products and displays, and almost all are updating educational programs.

Three major national associations have been reaping the bonanza, churning out dozens of full-scale training programs. These training programs often include sophisticated videos and training manuals. But even with these new training options, many deli and bakery supervisors and executives remain pessimistic. "We hire people who are 18 years old, want to give them $5 an hour for 25 hours a week and then we wonder why they aren't staying," says Ginger Edwards, deli-bakery director for B&B Cash Grocery/U Save Supermarkets in Tampa, Fla.

Still, Edwards and others struggle to find and keep qualified bakery and deli employees as the economy grows—and the labor market shrinks. "It's a little worse right now because the economy is hot," says Peter Houstle, executive vice-president of the Retailer's Bakery-Deli Association (RBA) based in Laurel, Md. "They have to get more out of people because they aren't going to get more people. But they are better off using self-service than bad service. Good self-service can at least keep you up and running."

Keeping people is a tough challenge. Fully 50% of bakery and deli employees quit in the first seven months, according to a survey by the International Dairy-Deli-Bakery Association (IDDA), based in Madison, Wis.

The primary reason for the turnover, according to the survey? People didn't know how to accomplish the tasks they had been assigned.

Employers recognize the growing problem, as well. In Progressive Grocer's 1995 Bakery and Deli Update, grocers cited training and recruitment as the most serious problems in both delis and bakeries. Rating the severity of problems on a scale of 1 to 10 (with 10 being the most severe), supermarket operators rated recruiting for bakeries 7.9 and training 7.7. In delis, the ratings were even worse: 8.2 for training and 8.0 for recruiting.

Solutions have been elusive, with some retailers going to more self-serve products. others trying to bolster training and most trying pieces of both approaches.

Sometimes the solution is a matter of geography. "There are degrees of self-service," says May Kay O'Connor, director of education for IDDA. "There is a very heavy service orientation on the East Coast, a combination in the Midwest and more self-serve in the West."

However, no matter where stores are on the scale of self-service, the trend is clear: "Our analysis shows more bakeries and delis going to self-service," O'Connor says.

One company going this route is H. E. Butt, based in San Antonio, Texas. H.E. Butt created its City Kitchen three years ago in San Antonlo to provide quality prepackaged items for its delis and bakeries. "A big part of the reason our plant is in existence is the high turnover rate and so that we aren't in a constant training mode," says Bob Arnold, City Kitchen production supervisor.

"We are like a manufacturing center," he says. "The plant employs about 100 employees in both the deli and bakery, providing fresh products for the 38 stores our trucks can deliver to in a day. We centralized the labor and took the labor out of the stores as much as possible."

---

* Reprinted with permission from *Progressive Grocer,* May 1995.

The City Kitchen runs 24 hours a day. producing sliced packaged meats, sauces for pizzas, sauces for the Chinese kitchen, salads, dips, fresh pasta and Italian sauces, as well as bread and other bakery products to a growing number of HEB's 227 stores throughout Texas. Some of the items are finished and prepackaged, while some are components, with final assembly required at the stores.

Even at the City Kitchen, turnover has been a problem. Arnold says it's more difficult to find qualified people today than three years ago, when the plant opened. Today the company recruits at community colleges, advertises in newspapers and has shifted the major production schedule of the plant to days in an effort to give more employees desirable hours.

In Fort Collins, Colo., Steele's Markets is focusing on keeping good people at their baking center by cross-training and promotions. "We are building the bakers of tomorrow," says Barbara Harner, bakery director.

Harner's 40-person operation supplies baked goods to Steele's four stores and five bakeries in the Fort Collins area, generating about $43 million a year in sales. "We have continued to improve training," says Harner. "We started a couple of years ago, bringing people in through the packaging department in the lower-skilled area and promoting from within. We are taking people who seem to give us the work ethic we are looking for—if they catch on easily, we build and train, bringing them through the ranks."

The goal for Steele's is to cross-train promising bakers for three of four different positions, so that when someone leaves, it is easier to fill the job. With the right people—and intensive on-the-job training—Harner says she can fill even the most difficult positions in three to six months.

Training starts early. "We've been working with five high school kids in our bread baking program for the past two years," she says. "They've worked part time and during the summers and have moved on to higher skill levels. One is going into a full-time position in pastry. They find out that it can be a good job and rewarding."

Although Steele's does use some training videos, most of the learning comes in the form of on-the-job training. "It takes all our concentration just to get work done, which doesn't leave a lot of extra time for classroom training. We make our own icing, fillings, cream cheese," says Harner.

Houston-based Randalls Food Markets supplies video training tapes to all stores and uses classroom video training for all department heads, according to Carroll Brown, corporate vice president for food service operations. "But finding good people has become harder over the past few years; their loyalty is just not as good as it used to be," he says.

Like many other operators, Randalls has been forced to move to more self-service in its 125 stores. "There are two reasons," says Brown. "We can't find labor, and when labor gets short, the rates go up—and we can't afford it."

Randalls hasn't closed any of its delis or bakeries, but the company is relying more on prepackaged meats and cheeses. In addition, says Brown, Randalls is "taking a hard look at the way we have always done things as new stores open. We can't operate the same way in the future. None of us can survive like we did 10 years ago. The customers' needs are changing, and the labor force is changing, so you just have to find new ways to meet those demands."

In some cases, labor problems have caused supermarket operators to rethink many of their deli and bakery sections. For instance, B&B went from fresh to all frozen cakes because of the dearth of qualified bakery help. "It's harder to get people, and the work ethic is not good," Edwards says.

Raley's, West Sacramento, Calif., took more extreme measures. Labor cost and quality issues led the company to pull out such popular deli features as the Mexican Kitchen, pizzerias and salad bars. "Customers begged us not to pull them out, but we just couldn't compete with the fast-food restaurants," says Carolyn Phipps, deli director. "Our costs were just too high. We were paying union wages."

Turnover in the largely part-time delis is also a problem at Raley's. The rate has gone as high as 50% in California stores and 75 in Nevada, says Phipps. "Not everybody loves dealing with customers and being on the go all day," she says. "Not everybody is made that way. These are very physical jobs. People think it's just waiting on customers; they don't realize that they mop floors, handle raw chickens and are constantly cleaning."

Raley's uses a trickle-down method of training—giving managers a full range of formal training, which they, in turn, pass on to their largely part-time work force.

To deal with labor issues in the future, Phipps expects to see a mix of prepackaged and store-made deli products. "It's too costly to make all of those products, (especially] when outside manufacturers can produce them for 50 cents or 60 cents a pound and it costs us a few dollars (a pound] just for the labor," says Phipps. "But we are trying to stand our ground on some things. For example, we want our customers to have fresh-cut cheeses. If we have to go outside, we're afraid that little by little we will lose the ability to do it."

Like Raley's, Price Chopper Supermarket, based in Schenectady, N.Y., is both increasing training and going to more self-service—and it is beating the bushes for new people. "We do outside advertising and job fairs at community colleges," says Tom Brewer, vice-president of deli-bakery operations. "We actually try to tie ourselves to community colleges, letting them know that we have jobs."

Brewer says the company has always had trouble finding good people for the bakery. "There are still lots of people around, slicing bread and baking cakes, but everything is available to the customer as self-serve. Even in the deli, we have a lot more self-service than four years ago," he says. "Certainly there is much more sophisticated training in the deli because of health issues."

Brewer agrees that the underlying problem is that the staff is basically part time and young. "You are hiring youth," says Brewer, "the trick is to train people so that they love the business and decide to stay."

What will the future bring? Many executives are afraid that the future is bleak for full-service delis and bakeries, and service in general. "It scares me to death to think of what is coming down the road," says Edwards of B&B "I'm afraid of what customer service is going to be in two years."

CUSTOMER RETENTION: A NEGLECTED BUT NECESSARY PIECE OF THE QUALITY PUZZLE*

To help attract new customers and boost their market share, many companies introduce more aggressive marketing and sales programs. However, there's another step your company will need to take if it really wants to maintain a strong customer base and ensure future viability: *Retain the customers it already has.*

"The real issue is customer retention," says Carla Furlong, president of Furlong & Associates (Vancouver, British Columbia). She identifies three weaknesses many organizations have when it comes to customer retention:

1. *Lack of focus.* Few organizations have a specific and organized focus on customer retention," she points out. "They think that three other initiatives will suffice—*marketing, sales,* and *customer service.* However, *marketing* focuses on customer acquisition, but not really on retention," Furlong explains.

   "Most of the *sales* focus is transactional," she continues. "That is, it focuses on individual sales encounters rather than on building long-term relationships that support customer retention.

   And as far as *customer service* is concerned, "Service quality and customer service are not the same thing," Furlong points out. For example, service quality suggests that you treat the new customer who walks through the door with the same level of service quality with which you would treat a 20-year customer.

   However, this approach does not build customer *retention.*

   Research put out by the Conference Board of Canada shows that 7 out of 10 Canadian firms focusing on "service quality" alone are failing, she reports. Why? "The main reason is that 'service quality' can be fuzzy. It's not as *measurable* as customer retention is."

Simply understanding that you are not yet formally engaged in customer retention is the first and most important step to getting you started in the right direction.

2. *Neglecting to use key market information.* According to Furlong, few companies even have research information on their existing customers, and the information that others have is inaccurate or sketchy. "Companies just don't know their own customers and what is important to those customers," she observes.

3. *Paying inadequate attention to the "best" customers.* "Few companies focus enough attention to their largest customers," says Furlong. "Good business is not about being democratic; it's not about taking care of everyone equally. It's about providing sufficient resources to meet the needs of your largest customers."

Furthermore, according to Furlong, companies often don't even know who their best customers are. They often operate under erroneous assumptions. "One client of mine reported that most of their customers were large companies," she recalls. "I asked them to test that assumption by actually going through their records, something that they had never done before."

The results surprised the client: "They found that the 65 percent of their clients who generated the most business were 'mom and pop' operations," she says. "These customers had different needs than the large customers had."

STEPS TO CUSTOMER RETENTION

Furlong delineates some specific steps to get you started on the road to formal customer retention efforts:

■ **1. Identify your "best" customers.** Study your customer records to see who your largest customers are. Who buys the most? How often do they buy?

One way to identify your best customers is to create a "frequent customer" program (such as the airline industry's "frequent flyer" programs). "These programs allow your best customers to actually identify themselves," says Furlong.

■ **2. Offer special deals.** Once you've identified these customers, you can create some "relationship pricing"—offering special pricing to help retain these customers.

However, avoid discounting too deeply. There is a risk of actually losing money with your biggest and best customers. "For example, one of my clients found that its largest customer generated a lot of revenue," says Furlong. "However, research showed that my client was actually losing money on the customer because its demands were so picky."

Furlong's recommendation: Identify which customers are best for your bottom line, not which ones are necessarily largest in terms of revenue.

■ **3. Build a "predictive model" of customer retention.** Creating such a model includes taking these steps:

Heed Early Warning Signals

Create a process to detect early warning signs of discontent and possible defection. "One bank I know of analyzes all customer transactions by computer, which automatically flags accounts that have significant deviations from the norm, such as large drops in average balances," Furlong notes. These accounts are sent to an Account Retention Team for action.

Solicit Complaints and Take Them Seriously

However, don't necessarily base decisions on the nature of the complaints. Complaints simply mean that customers are dissatisfied. However, the specific things about which they complain may not be what is *really* bothering them. Here are some examples based on Furlong's research:

- *A copier equipment manufacturer found that customers regularly complained about paper jams.* However, further research indicated that everyone complains about paper jams, and that customers actually expect paper jams. What really concerns them is service responsiveness.

- *People in banks complain about long lines, but this will rarely cause them to change banks.* But having unresolved problems trying to get errors corrected *will* cause them to defect.

• *Most people complain about price, but this is rarely at the heart of the issue.* "Particularly in service businesses, price is not as important as it is in product businesses," Furlong suggests. "When people are upset, they complain about price because that's the only thing they can get their teeth into." (Price is a "tangible.") The real cause of concern is usually elsewhere.

Determine "Points of Contact"

There are certain points in your relationship with customers where they make decisions whether to stay with you or to search elsewhere for a service provider. Conduct research on the cycle of the company-customer relationship and identify the points of contact where interaction and relationship evaluation take place. These are the points at which customers defect, she says.

Create "Bonding Opportunities" at the Points of Contact

"An insurance company I'm familiar with uses a computer for market intelligence to generate 'red flag' reports and provide cross-selling cues," says Furlong. "For instance, when a client reaches age 55, the firm recommends retirement products to the client. Some people think that cross-selling is simply pushing more sales. Actually, it's a very effective customer-retention strategy."

Research shos that the more products/ services a customer has with a firm, the more likely he or she will remain with that firm. According to Furlong, in the financial services industry, for example, research shows that of clients who have

one product with the bank, 15% will still be there 5 years later

two products with the bank, 45% will still be there 5 years later

three or more products with the bank, 90% will still be there 5 years later.

■ **4. Utilize the predictive model of customer retention and defection** (what you have learned is important to customers) and be-

gin to work backwards, correlating this information with your company's existing processes.

For example, a Boston investment firm found that "inquiry responsiveness" was critical to customer retention. That is, when customers called with questions or problems, they either wanted them resolved during that call or expected a call back within 24 hours.

"Conventional wisdom suggested that the reason people left investment firms was because of the performance of their investment portfolios," observes Furlong. "This turned out not to be the case."

The firm then studied the processes that it had in place to make inquiry responsiveness happen, such as:

telephone protocol (how quickly telephones were answered, how long people were put on hold, etc.)

"bumping" (how many times customers had to be transferred to others to get their questions and problems resolved)

how detailed problems and questions were handled when the firm's personnel had to call customer's back.

The company completely reworked its processes to become more responsive to customers' real needs and desires.

■ **5. Prioritize process reorganization (or reengineering) efforts.** Identify the processes that need developing or reworking and apply these three criteria to determine your priority for addressing them.

Which processes have the greatest impact on customers?

Which processes are in the deepest trouble?

Which processes are the easiest to repair or replace?

Then, work through the processes one by one.

■ **6. As you begin to work on each existing process, identify what is wrong with it.** Then determine what the new process should do. How should it work?

For example, the credit/financing division of a computer company found that it took six days to reach decisions on customer-financing aplications. This severely stifled its ability to respond quickly to customer needs and to make sales.

To address the problem, two executives selected a customer request at random when it came in. Then, they walked this request through the process by hand—through all the steps that an application normally takes as it flows toward approval.

"All employees who worked within the process were instructed to immediately stop what they were doing and to handle his or her portion of the application for these two executives," explains Furlong. This exercise was designed to provide the executives with the information they needed to determine how long the actual work in the process took. Result: It actually took employees a total of only 90 minutes to process the application. "During the remainder of the six days,

the paperwork was sitting in in-baskets and out-baskets," she points out.

The result? The process was streamlined and wasted time was eliminated. Customer requests are now handled in a fraction of the time they previously took, and existing customers are more satisfied and willing to remain loyal to this bank.

Let's Hang on to What We've Got

Winning over new customers is certainly necessary to keep your business alive and growing. But while you're investing in dazzling new marketing plans and customer recruitment efforts, don't neglect the "old faithfuls" who've already come on board. Taking steps to keep these customers happy and satisfied is smart business indeed.

WHEN THEY'RE OUT OF "SITE," IS SERVICE QUALITY OUT OF MIND?*

If some of your company's employees work off site, it may be difficult to monitor their performance. How can you be sure that these staffers are maintaining your firm's high standards of service quality?

Try the five-step technique used by HCC, Inc.—Health Information Management Services (San Jose, CA), a provider of medical records copying services to hospitals nationwide. HCC has more than 900 employees, the majority of whom work in assigned client hospitals. These employees are HCC field representatives and handle all requests for copies of patients' medical records that come into the hospital from insurance companies, attorneys, physicians, and others.

Because client hospitals can contract with another copying service simply by giving HCC 30 days' notice, quality is of the utmost importance in retaining clients. HCC has two groups of clients—client hospitals and client requesters—and must be responsive to both groups' needs.

FIVE COMMONSENSE STEPS TO
QUALITY SERVICE

To ensure a quality response to both types of clients, HCC takes the following steps:

Hire Qualified People

Access to hospital records is based on several factors, so it's important that HCC hire managers who understand all aspects of the process. For example, in some states hospitals are required to copy records for authorized requesters, while in other states access is allowed, but copies may not be made.

For field management positions, HCC hires individuals with either a four-year Registered Record Administrator degree or a two-year Accredited Record Technician degree. Hires also should have previous experience as either a director or an assistant director of a medical records department.

Train Thoroughly

Field representatives undergo a four-week training program to help them understand how the company operates and their role in the flow of medical records. The program consists of 10 to 12 modules on such subjects as proper authorization for the release of medical records, reps' relationships with the hospitals where they're assigned, use of copy machines, appearance, and so on. After each module, employees are tested to determine whether they've absorbed the information.

Field managers also undergo formal training, learning the reps' job as well as management and interpersonal skills, such as communicating with clients and probing to understand individual client needs. Then their manager introduces them to the medical records staff at their assigned hospitals.

In addition to this training, HCC provides field reps' and managers' manuals, which are constantly being revised.

Match Reps to Customer Sites

Field representatives typically work at one hospital either full or part time, though some may service more than one facility. At the initial start-up with a hospital, HCC holds a protocol meeting with the medical records director to find out the hospital's needs, any rules or regulations that will apply to the field rep assigned to the hospital, and so on. Only then is a representative chosen for the assignment.

It's crucial to match a representative to that specific department. HCC makes sure that the person is aware of all the policies and procedures—including dress code—of the hospital and of the medical records department. The majority of the time there is a pretty good match, and the person blends right into the department.

Monitor Performance Carefully

Field reps' performance is monitored in two ways:

In the field. The average field representative copies 40 to 60 patient charts a day, each chart consisting of about 30 pages. The work is checked on site by the field manager and by a quality-control coordinator who makes unannounced visits on a regular basis.

The coordinator also fills out a checklist covering different aspects of the copying process, in-

cluding proper authorization for release of records, special authorization for records containing sensitive information, information requested versus information copied, and copy quality. Results go to the field rep's manager.

If any items are not covered properly or are done incorrectly, the manager reviews them with the representative. Managers usually handle 10 to 15 hospitals, although the number varies according to hospital size and the number of requests filled each month. Frequency of visits also varies according to the same criteria, and regular contact may include phone calls as well as in-person visits. Visits are more frequent if there are satisfaction issues to deal with. HCC field reps could be there every day until the hospital's medical records director is satisfied that the service they're getting is up to their level.

As the company has grown, more managers have been added to limit the number of clients each manager handles. Now, managers are able to spend more time at each client hospital to provide additional training, perform quality checks on field reps' work, and ensure that clients are satisfied with service. With more visits to hospitals, HCC can do more quality checks and make sure it is developing a sound relationship with the client—not an "over the phone" or "once in a while" relationship.

At a central location. HCC has six regional offices throughout the country, each with a quality assurance department staffed by individuals with experience in copying medical records. These people are given additional training for handling specific requests and are also responsible for checking each rep's work daily and filling out the same checklist the quality coordinator completes in the field. Results are summarized weekly and sent to each field rep's manager.

Quality Assurance does a random check on a portion of the work and a 100-percent check on the rest of it. If a new person is coming out of training. QA would check that person's work 100 percent of the time. A representative who's been established in the field and has a record of doing quality work is most likely to be randomly checked.

Involve Clients in Employee Evaluations

The hospitals at which HCC representatives work are asked questions about the performance of the company's employees, with topics including *punctuality, quality,* and *appearance.*

Other questions cover HCC's overall performance in terms of accuracy in copying records, responsiveness in answering questions, and other factors.

DON'T SHOOT IN THE DARK

For many companies whose employees work off site, the quality of their work is often a shot in the dark. The company *hopes* its people are doing well, but often finds out they're not only when a problem arises. At that point, however, it may be too late to salvage a relationship with a valuable customer.

By taking this proactive five-step approach, as HCC has done, you pinpoint and eliminate quality problems *before* they arise. And this allows your company to stay on good terms with *all* the customers at *all* the sites where its people work.

---■---

WANT TOP SERVICE QUALITY? TRY PUTTIN' ON THE RITZ*

It comes as no surprise that The Ritz-Carlton Hotel Company (Atlanta) is one of the three Malcolm Baldrige National Quality Award winners in the service category (1992). After all, the Hotel, long known for providing its customers luxurious service experiences, launched its quest for the ultimate service quality years before the Baldrige Award star was even a twinkle in Corporate America's eye.

In the early 1980s, setting its signts on being rated *the* premier hotel company by two major rating services (Mobil and AAA), the company took the first confident steps on the road to Total Quality Management. The Ritz-Carlton not only achieved the top ratings by Mobil and AAA but it actually became *the* company to benchmark for hotel service quality.

However, ever committed to quality, senior management emphasized that it wanted to *continue* to improve. It set its sights on meeting the demanding Baldrige Award criteria. What evolved in this quality quest was a comprehensive service-quality process that is thoroughly integrated into the company's marketing and business objectives.

YOUR "QUALITY STRUCTURE" MUST SUPPORT YOUR SERVICE OBJECTIVES

Quality has a formal structure at all levels of The Ritz-Carlton organization:

Corporate Level

Senior executives are members of a corporate steering committee, which does double duty as the senior quality-management team for the company.

The team meets weekly to review a number of issues related to quality, among them:

Product and service quality

Guest satisfaction

Market growth and development

Organizational indicators

Competitive status

Furthermore, executives in the company routinely devote approximately one fourth of

---

their time each year to quality-related issues. For example:

Face-to-face customer interaction. They meet one-on-one with guests and employees to discuss quality.

Setting quality goals. "The senior executives also develop quality-related objectives and action plans for each year's annual strategic plan," reports Susan Musselman, assistant to the corporate director of Quality. "Each quarter, they personally follow up to see how the plans are being implemented."

Quality training. Every time executives visit the Atlanta headquarters, Corporate Director of Quality Patrick Mene arranges quality training programs.

Property Level

Each individual hotel (property) also has a quality structure in place, which consists of the following elements:

A Quality Leader. This is usually a manager with operations and personnel experience and extensive TQM training. The Quality Leader's overall responsibility is to facilitate the quality process and make sure that everyone in the hotel remains focused on quality. As such, the Quality Leader is both a resource and an advocate. "The Quality Leader provides training, works on cycle-time reduction, and handles any other responsibility related to quality at the property level," Musselman explains.

Quality Teams. Each property also has cross-functional quality teams, each with a specific mission: to tackle the "vital few" problems identified through the strategic-planning process. These teams receive direction and assistance from the Quality Leader.

Department Level

A similar structure is in place at the departmental level. Each department in the property has a Quality Coach who is responsible for quality at the department level. "The Quality Leader meets weekly with all of the quality coaches to discuss issues and opportunities," Musselman reports.

EMPLOYEE INVOLVEMENT AND SERVICE

Front-line employees play a critical role in fulfilling The Ritz-Carlton's quality-service objec-

tives. Here's how these service providers are involved in the quality process:

- **Hiring.** The Ritz-Carlton has created a targeted selection process involving predictive instruments and other screening methods to help ensure that it very carefully selects applicants who will contribute to its high standards of service quality. The goal is a successful match between employee and position.

- **Training.** Training is so thorough at The Ritz-Carlton that each and every employee in the company receives certification in his or her position. This takes place in two phases:

  Phase 1: a comprehensive two-day orientation that focuses primarily on The Ritz-Carlton Gold Standards (see page 3) and the company's quality culture.

  Phase 2: extensive on-the-job training for 60 days. "The training is handled by experienced employees who have received training themselves," Musselman says. (Employee certification follows this 60-day training period.) In addition, all employees receive continuous training, including at least 126 hours of quality training that focuses on The Ritz-Carlton Gold Standards.

- **Managing.** At the beginning of each shift in each department, all employees participate in a "daily lineup." During this, the department manager and quality coach:

  Discuss the particular shift (specific issues; occupancy rate, any VIPs who are guests, etc.).

  Make sure that every employee is in proper attire and is groomed appropriately.

  Review one of the 20 Gold Standards.

  Talk about the day's "Commitment to Quality" topic (such as team building), which is distributed to all hotels from Musselman's office.

- **Appraising.** Performance appraisals are based on expectations that are explained during orientation, training, and certification. In essence, the appraisal process is a recertification process.

QUALITY FEEDBACK MECHANISMS ENSURE CONTINUOUS QUALITY IMPROVEMENT

While many companies operate in a vacuum when it comes to creating and implementing quality processes, The Ritz-Carlton is expending a great deal of time, expense, and energy generating detailed input from several key sources to make sure that:

100 percent of its customers will be satisfied and loyally use and recommend The Ritz-Carlton Hotel Company (complete customer retention).

Cycle time of key processes will be reduced 50 percent by 1996.

The company will achieve six sigma, a high level of quality designated by the ground-breaking Motorola, Inc., as, in a nutshell, 3.4 defects/ failures/errors per million uses of product or services.

In other words, the Hotel wants to make sure that it creates processes that help to ensure top-drawer service quality, that these processes are functioning effectively, and that all guests' ultimate expectations are fulfilled.

Here are The Ritz-Carlton's primary sources of input:

Guest Surveys. The hotels use Guest Comment Cards, focus groups, and third-party surveys to assess guest satisfaction. "We utilize the services of a third-party survey company to call recent guests and interview them on their stay with us," Musselman reports. This firm contacts approximately 25,000 guests per year.

Meeting Planner Surveys. The Hotel hires a second third-party survey firm to contact professional meeting planners who have recently held meetings at a Ritz-Carlton property. "Our goal is to be the best in the meeting planner market," Musselman points out.

Annual Employee Surveys. The Ritz-Carlton hires yet another third-party survey firm to survey its employees annually. This Annual Employee Satisfaction Survey contains over 150 questions. "We want to ascertain [internal customers'] levels of satisfaction," says Musselman. Employees complete their surveys confidentially and send them to a third party in Connecticut, where the results are tabulated and then shared with management at each hotel.

Semiannual Employee Surveys. This survey, called the Gold Standard Employee Satisfaction Survey, contains about 20 questions. "The procedure is similar to that of the annual survey, but the main goal here is to determine whether employee satisfaction levels are increasing or decreasing and why," Musselman explains.

Daily Quality Production Reports. These reports, compiled from several sources, serve as "early warning systems" for the hotel by identifying problems (guest complaints, system defects, system waste, etc.) that need to be solved. The reports are compiled primarily from three sources:

A guest complaint to a member of the hotel staff or management

Guest comment cards that are sent to the corporate office and routed back to the hotel

Employee comments (on an Internal Defect Report) based on experiences they have had that have prevented or hindered their efforts to provide quality service

The hotel's Quality Leader compiles the report each day. Each incident is reported in a specific category, such as

- Guest check-in
- Guest check-out
- Room service
- Billing

The hotels' quality leaders, teams, and coaches prioritize the problems and adopt action plans to prevent them from recurring. All reports are reviewed daily by the hotel executive committee," notes Musselman.

Computerized Guest Profiles

The Ritz-Carlton maintains a detailed computer database of the likes, dislikes, and special requests of almost a quarter of a million guests. This way, each time a guest makes a reservation, the staff will instantly know how best to serve him or her. For example:

- The guest likes a certain type of pillow.
- The guest prefers a certain type of wine.
- The guest likes to have reservations at a local theater.

Results of recent guest surveys confirm that The Ritz-Carlton Company's commitment to service quality is working. Approximately 95 percent of surveyed guests report that they experienced "a memorable visit." In addition, the Hotel has received almost 150 quality awards from the travel industry since 1991.

‖‖‖ 2.3
PUBLIC/GOVERNMENT

---■---

IS REINVENTING GOVERNMENT FOR REAL?*
by Marion Harmon

The government is broken and we intend to fix it," announced President Bill Clinton when he launched the National Performance Review. Those are fighting words, but do they really pack a punch? What started in March 1993 as a directive from the president to Vice-President Al Gore to reinvent the federal government has proven to be more than just a pipe dream. But while most people remember the image of Gore handing the president the 168-page NPR report in September 1993, amid forklifts piled with government manuals, the path of the federal government's reinvention effort since then remains somewhat of a mystery to the general public.

The vice-president's message to the president at the time: "This report represents the beginning of what must be, and—with your leadership—will be, a long-term commitment to change. The title of this report reflects our goals: moving from red tape to results to create a government that works better and costs less. . . . We present this report to you confident that it will provide an effective and innovative plan to make that vision a reality."

REFORM AT WORK

Four main management principles guide the reinvention effort: putting customers first, empowering employees, shifting from red tape to results, and cutting back to basics. Management experts would undoubtedly agree that these are excellent words to live by, but they also know that the translation into workable processes that improve products and services can be tough for even a company of 50 employees. How does a work force of 3 million stand a chance? By taking it one action item and one agency at a time.

The original timeline for the reinventing government effort was set at 10 years, a figure that the vice-president got from corporate executives who advised him on how long it takes to create culture change, according to Bob Stone, project director for the NPR. Stone reports that the reinvention effort is on track and has a good chance of reaching critical mass in three years.

"The reinvention process is taking place all over government in many ways," remarks Stone. "In tangible ways, like regulations being canceled, processes being simplified. And intangible ways, like people bringing a new attitude to their work. We haven't finished, but I think we planted the roots and it's sprouting all around."

The NPR is broken down into 835 specific action items affecting all major federal organizations. Of these action items, agencies report that 12 percent are complete and another 80 percent are in progress. In addition to the large agencies for which NPR prepared separate recommendations, there are about 100 other smaller agencies. Many of them have developed their own reinvention initiatives. For example, the Federal Communications Commission has re-

---

*Reprinted with permission from *Quality Digest.* © 1995 QCI International. Marion Harmon is managing editor of *Quality Digest.*

structured itself and is establishing its new cable division according to the NPR's basic principles. And the Pension Benefit Guaranty Corp. has initiated a customer-service program to identify people who did not even know they were customers. PBGC finds potential beneficiaries of defunct pension funds who didn't know they were due to receive payments.

David Osborne, a senior adviser to the vice-president during the NPR and chief author of the NPR report, says the reinvention effort has definitely gotten off to a good start and probably has achieved more than anybody expected. He observes that some departments seem to be doing better than others, and he points to two reforms that have had the most impact.

"While the NPR was going on, Congress passed the Government Performance and Results act, which we would have recommended had it not already passed," recalls Osborne. "That was a very significant reform requiring the federal government to begin measuring performance and moving in the direction of performance-based budgeting."

And Congress recently passed major legislation streamlining government procurement. The reform bill frees purchases of less than $2,500 from most restrictions and increases the federal government's reliance on commercially available products. Agencies will be able to buy what they need from such stores as Home Depot. This is a big deal, since small purchases account for 70 to 80 percent of government purchases.

"Many other things have been accomplished, either by Congress or through executive orders from the president," asserts Osborne. "For example, the president ordered every department to cut its internal regulations in half. Many of them have done that. He ordered those that deal directly with customers to begin surveying them and to develop customer-service standards. There has been downsizing of field service offices and flattening of organizations. The Department of Housing and Urban Development, for example, eliminated its regional offices."

Observers have been surprised by the NPR's achievements. The Brookings Institution is among them. "The NPR has produced impressive results—a genuine start on changing the culture of government," declares the influential Washington think tank. It credits the NPR with producing "more than almost anyone, including perhaps the reinventors themselves, believed possible. Even when the movement produced

sketchy results, the problems it attacked usually were the right ones."

However, the Washington group peppers its praise with specific concerns, namely the effort's preoccupation with savings over performance improvement and the lack of an explicit strategy for dealing with Congress.

"The tough thing now for the administration is to engage Republicans in downsizing without sacrificing the basic performance of government," states Donald F. Kettle, the University of Wisconsin at Madison professor who has followed the NPR for the Brookings Institution. "How do you create a government that costs even less but works well?"

RESULTS TO BANK ON

In kicking off Phase I of the reinvention, the vice-president aimed to save $108 billion and cut 252,000 civilian jobs, mostly managerial, within five years. The National Performance Review contains 384 major recommendations covering 3 million employees. Four days after Gore's presentation of the NPR, President Clinton issued his first three enabling Executive Orders. These mandated a plan for the 12-percent civilian work force cut, a 50-percent reduction in regulations in every department, and the development of customer-service initiatives throughout the government.

Perhaps the most spectacular achievements the NPR reports are the $63 billion in savings achieved so far (more than half of the five-year goal) and the work force cuts of more than 100,000 positions. Almost all of the savings came from personnel cuts, and the positions were eliminated through buyouts and other management techniques.

The "cost less" part aside, what is happening on the "work better" front? In his one-year status report, Gore declares that 90 percent of the NPR's proposals have moved forward—implemented by executive order or agency action, proposed in legislation and so forth. And following the vice-president's report, Congress passed major legislation streamlining government procurement. Other results Gore attributes to the effort:

- The president issued 22 directives and signed performance agreements with five Cabinet secretaries and leaders of two other agencies. The directives implement NPR recommendations on such subjects as customer service, agency streamlining, procurement, labor-management relations, intergovernmental cooperation, environmental justice for the disadvantaged and trade promotion. The performance agreements set specific goals to improve the quality and efficiency of service.

- For the first time, 150 agencies have set customer-service standards—1,500 of them. For example, Social Security promises to mail out cards within five working days, and if you need a social security number quickly, they will provide it in a day.

- Agencies are forming labor-management partnerships throughout the federal government. Departments and agencies have signed 32 partnership agreements with their unions.

- Agencies are slashing red tape. The Office of Personnel Management scrapped the 10,000-page Federal Personnel Manual. Labor, Veterans Affairs and other departments eliminated mounds of paper work associated with internal regulations, budget justifications and other requirements.

- Agencies are buying fewer "designer" goods and more off-the-shelf products. The Defense Department is aggressively eliminating military specifications in favor of commercial purchases, and the General Service Administration's commodity centers are working to give commercial descriptions to everything they buy and to stock commercial items.

- Agencies created 135 "reinvention labs" through which employees try new ways to conduct the people's business; already, some have improved customer service or cut costs. For example, the Small Business Administration reduced their standard loan application from a half-inch thick to a single sheet of paper.

PUTTING CUSTOMERS FIRST

What progress have individual agencies made in their transformation? Stone says one major accomplishment of the NPR is cutting red tape—simplifying government processes and bringing some common sense to them. This includes an overhaul of the procurement laws and regulations, and headquarters reductions and streamlining that have started across government. The other major accomplishment he stresses is a government-wide commitment to customer service. He points to individual accomplishments, such as the Small Business Administration promising to give an answer on loan applications within three days, to the Occupational Safety and Health Administration promising to ship business data within 24 hours or else ship it without charge.

Stone isn't your typical bureaucrat. Before becoming NPR project director, his focus as Deputy Assistant Secretary of Defense for Installations was to "staunch the flow of red tape" from Washington and allow base commanders to run their operations. He reduced a 400-page construction manual to four pages and cut 18 different sets of housing regulations to one. And in his old Defense Department biography, the first point under "major responsibilities" reads, "spreading a spirit of obsession with customer service."

"If we can really get the government committed and working on customer service, I think everything else will take care of itself," predicts Stone.

Of NPR's four main principles, the customer-service initiative has emerged as a major part of the culture change. Although the public often assumes that government doesn't care about its customers, especially its ultimate customers, the taxpayers, people who work with the NPR efforts say putting customers first is the main goal of reinventing government.

"The customer-service initiative is absolutely central to what the National Performance Review is trying to do," insists Greg Woods, a team leader on the NPR implementation task force responsible for the customer service and information technology teams. "It's not at all uncommon for us to talk about it as the most important thing that we'll do in the long haul."

In fact, one of Clinton's first executive orders after the NPR was released was "Setting Customer Service Standards." That executive order lays out the basics of a customer-service initiative for all federal agencies that deal with the public. It charges the government with becoming customer-driven and outlines specific actions for all executive departments and agencies, including: identify the customers served by the agency, survey customers to determine what services they want, post service standards and measure results against them, and survey front-line employees on barriers to, and ideas for, matching the best in business.

Woods, who is the primary author of the president's executive order on improving customer service, explains that the strong customer-service initiative is born from two initiatives that reinforced each other.

"One is the president and vice-president's ideas of putting people first, and that campaign theme was translated immediately when NPR began putting customers first as a way of delivering on that promise," explains Woods. "And the other thing that reinforces it is that ongoing quality efforts, which had already begun in government, were starting to develop and implement strong customer-service programs."

Some of the agencies have done a better job than others in the customer-service area, admits Woods, but all are in an ongoing improvement process of surveying their customers, getting inputs and publishing standards. The executive order outlined specific deadlines for reporting on surveys and publishing customer-service plans. As agencies cover more areas, more standards are coming out all the time.

BUILDING BETTER RELATIONSHIPS

The U.S. Customs Service's Miami operation has recently undergone a customer-service transformation. Historically there was an adversarial relationship between customs and the trade community there, according to Woods. But by going through a process of identifying who their customers are, they came to consider the trade community as a customer for some of the services they provide.

"They sat down and talked with that community about what they wanted," relates Woods. "They wanted speed; they didn't want their passengers to wait and flower shipments to wilt on the runway."

So Miami Customs set standards that would be acceptable to both sides in terms of performance. Those standards are published and well-understood, and they measure their performance against those on an ongoing basis.

"The adversarial relationship has been turned completely around," declares Woods. "It's much more of a partnership now. There are joint agreements on how long it'll take to process passengers, and they have set a standard that passengers will clear in five minutes or less."

Miami Customs has also automated to share passenger and cargo information, with some low-risk shipments actually being cleared before hitting port. And they share information with the airlines to target their resources on higher-risk areas.

"In return, customs has actually trained businesses to do some inspections, so that 40 percent of the drugs coming through that port are now detected by business," says Woods. "Business gets its passengers and cargo through more quickly, and the government does its job better with the assistance of business.

"If you talk to the business community down there, they'll tell you that this is the way government ought to work, in partnership, and that they really are raving fans of government."

While Miami Customs had already begun the process to improve service before the NPR initiatives, Woods says their efforts were reinforced by the NPR. Such success stories are used by agencies to encourage learning and produce a higher level of performance, but Woods stresses that practically every area needs more work.

"Our overall standard is to equal the best in business," asserts Woods. "We're certainly seeing examples of that within government, but we're looking to get there across the board. This is a multiyear effort, but the encouraging thing is that we're already seeing progress and getting customer feedback that things have changed."

The agencies perform their own surveys, a term the NPR uses broadly to encompass formal statistical surveys and also other customer-input tools such as focus groups and customer complaint systems. The NPR office runs workshops and conferences that expose them to experts, and they share with agencies through those workshops how other agencies and the private sector implement service improvements.

"Much of what we're building on came from the quality movement," explains Woods. "We're really counting on the quality leaders to continue generating ideas, maybe with more attention than ever paid to improving customer service."

AN AGENCY'S EVOLUTION

The Internal Revenue Service is no newcomer to the quality movement. It began localized quality improvement efforts as early as 1986. The agency maintains a strong labor-management partnership, and the Ogden IRS Service Center is the only civilian agency to win the President's Quality Award. They've worked in close partnership with the NPR, having had a senior IRS executive work directly on the initiative, according to Audrey Saari, National Director of Quality for the IRS. The senior staffer was able to influence the NPR based on some of the agency's experiences in quality and also brought back ideas gleaned from the interface with the NPR and various agency executives there.

The IRS's Total Quality Organization program has blended well with the NPR effort, and the four principles fit closely with the direction the IRS has set for itself, according to Saari. They work closely on improving processes with other agencies and the Federal Quality Institute, which the Clinton administration has charged with helping agencies access information, education and consultation on quality management.

"We have on an ongoing basis shared information with the Federal Quality Institute about our learning experiences and in return receive information on new ideas and techniques," reports Saari.

The IRS has drawn on ideas from other agencies and has received valuable advice from leaders in the private sector, adds Saari. Benchmarking, both informal and formal, has been a big driver of their TQO program.

"In 1991, we benchmarked against seven major companies on quality implementation," remembers Saari. "We have received significant advice from leaders in that field, such as Motorola and Xerox. Prior to that, we started with training from Joseph M. Juran, who had a very broad knowledge from the private sector. And we do a lot of informal benchmarking—sharing information about what works best."

Saari and a number of other IRS executives meet informally on a regular basis with various agencies to find out what they're doing, what successes they're having and what problems they're experiencing. In addition, they've also successfully created partnerships with state and local agencies, says Saari.

From automating tax returns to creating a new work environment for its 115,000 full-time employees, the IRS continues to move toward its goal of being a total quality organization.

"We're asking employees and managers of the organization to change their business practices, to become more focused on customers, to understand and reengineer their processes," emphasizes Saari. "So we're asking for dramatic changes, not only in the way we do business, but in our technology and organizational structure and many other areas."

TOOLS THAT REINVENT

Osborne, who co-wrote *Reinventing Government*, the best seller that was the model for the NPR, says he sees TQM as one of the key tools to reinvent an organization. But he adds that government needs other tools in addition to TQM. Because TQM was developed for private manufacturing businesses, certain assumptions were made that don't apply to government organizations, he notes.

"In the public sector, one of the biggest problems is that we're dealing with monopolies that have no particular incentive to get better. And while the bottom line is pretty clear in the private sector, the public sector has no bottom line, other than re-election, for elected officials who have only the most tenuous connection to actual service-delivery organizations. And so, you do need to measure process, but even more important, you need to measure results."

Another reason Osborne claims TQM doesn't cover all the bases is government's focus on operating systems—the budget, personnel and procurement systems. Such processes usually aren't a focus of TQM efforts, he contends.

"The government's focus needs to be broader; there are issues on the table that just aren't there in the private sector," charges Osborne. "Just using tools from the private sector will not be adequate."

Stone agrees that reinventing the government will mean culling various processes, such as reengineering, quality management and benchmarking. Different organizations will have different needs, he says.

"We have laid out the principles of the National Performance Review; they're pretty simple," observes Stone. "Accomplishing those four principles means using all the tools of the quality movement."

LEADING THE CHARGE

Strong leadership by the vice-president has been a key force in bringing the NPR along this far, says Osborne. Rather than sitting back and letting others do the work, Gore has surprised many by proving to be a staunch supporter of the reinvention effort.

"I think all of us were shocked by how effective a leader the vice-president was—how quickly he understood what reinventing government was about, how well he articulated the message and the vision, and how hard he worked to sell it, particularly to federal employees," remarks Osborne. "As an internal leader, the vice-president has been very, very effective. And then you get to the departmental level, and at that level, leadership has been mixed. Some of the Cabinet are quite strong on reinventing government and some of them aren't."

Those agencies that had already established quality-management programs before the NPR seem to be out in front. "Certain organizations like the IRS have been very successful in implementing some of these ideas," notes V. Daniel Hunt, president of Technology Research Corp. and author of *Quality Management for Government.* "At the same time, other organizations have not really implemented it at all. So there's a wide disparity in implementation of quality management in federal government."

Those organizations without some internal champion to effectively lead the charge tend to get bogged down in "Disneyland training programs" and management fads of the month, charges Hunt Small, anecdotal changes will continue to happen, but unless there is strong leadership, quality will pass to the next administration with minimal cost-benefit process changes, he predicts.

IMPROVING THE NPR

While various federal organizations have shown concrete improvements due to the effort, critics have blasted the NPR as a mere political ploy and recall previous change efforts, such as President Jimmy Carter's zero-based budgeting, which failed to live up to their promises. They point to serious deficiencies such as an emphasis on cutting costs over improving performance and the lack of a legislative strategy. And a senior NPR staffer acknowledged the fact that the downsizing was going to happen anyway as a result of budget cuts.

In its December 1994 Management Reform report on the NPR, the General Accounting Office states that some progress has been made in implementing many of the NPR recommendations since September 1993, but few have been fully implemented, and a number of measures will take years. The GAO reported that at least some action had been taken to implement 355 (93%) of the NPR's recommendations at the time they completed their analysis. Of these, 4 percent had been fully implemented, 37 percent had been partially implemented, 50 percent were acted upon in some manner (e.g., legislation was introduced or the agency was in the process of making suggested changes), and 6 percent were acted upon in a manner generally consistent with the recommendation's purposes, although not in the manner NPR suggested.

In December, Comptroller General Charles A. Bowsher, head of the GAO, pointed out that the first round of Gore's reinvention had not addressed several "high-risk" management issues in the government, according to a Jan. 30 *Washington Post* article. His list of troubled programs included the Farmers Home Administration's farm loans, defense weapons systems acquisition, defense contract pricing, Energy Department waste storage and disposal, Veterans Affairs loan programs and the Federal Aviation Administration's airline inspection program.

"We also remain concerned about whether agencies have the processes, systems and qualified staff needed to perform their current missions," Bowsher wrote.

He noted that the administration's original goal of cutting more than 250,000 federal jobs "was not the result of careful work-force planning" and that "some agencies have not ensured that critical skills needed for program performance and the prevention of mismanagement are not lost in their downsizing efforts."

The GAO reports that it still believes that NPR's success hinges on a legislative-executive partnership for action, atttention to agencies' capacities, and sustained political and career leadership. Stone agrees with that prognosis. In addition, the GAO generally agrees with the thrust of most of the recommendations and supports their continued implementation, and urges the executive branch and Congress to shift the focus of government management from an emphasis on inputs, outputs and processes to an emphasis on outcomes and results.

WHAT'S NEXT?

On Dec. 19, 1994, the president and vice-president launched Phase II of the NPR. Clinton described the next stage of reinvention as being aimed at "cutting things that can be cut." He has directed the vice-president to "review every single government program and department for further possible reductions" and to begin a review of the federal regulatory process.

While the administration originally considered completely eliminating five Cabinet agencies, Gore said he and the president believed that reform was preferable. But they will continue to examine all federal agencies and programs to deem whether their services are really necessary or can be done in a better way. Key areas they will be focusing on are privitization and devolution to state and local governments.

"We propose to stop doing things that government does not do very well and that do not need to be done by government," said Clinton.

The reinvention of the U.S. Government has only just begun, and no one knows for sure where it will lead. But one thing remains certain: The public will be the final judge of the promised transformation.

FEDERAL AGENCIES AGREE TO WORK TOWARD SINGLE QUALITY APPROVAL
FOR CONTRACTORS*

High-level management officials representing some of the federal government's largest purchasers have signed a Memorandum of Understanding (MOU) stating their intention to work toward common quality requirements for government contractors based on the ISO 9000 series standards.

The unprecedented initiative could lead to a formal agreement which ultimately would reduce costs for government contractors and promote the spread of ISO 9000 series standards, according to federal officials.

The one-page memorandum was signed by 10 agencies on April 24, including the Department of Defense (DoD), and the National Aeronautics and Space Administration (NASA)—both of which are already either encouraging or requiring contractors to meet ISO 9000 requirements on contracts, explained Carl H. Schneider, a NASA official who helped spearhead the effort.

Other agencies that signed the document are: the Army, Navy, Air Force, Defense Contract Management Command, Coast Guard, National Institute of Standards and Technology, National Oceanic and Atmospheric Administration and the Maritime Administration. Agencies expected to sign in the near future are the General Services Administration, Federal Aviation Administration and U.S. Marine Corps.

The document was drafted by the Government/Industry Quality Liaison Panel (GIQLP), a group of government and industry representatives that formed last year to promote the possibility of a government-wide quality standard for purchasing.

"These are the officials who can effectively commit resources for an agency," said Schneider of the signatories. "We're still debating whether we want to go to the heads of agencies, but we're very satisfied with this level."

Two of the most ardent supporters of the initiative are Fred Gregory, associate administrator for safety and mission assurance with NASA, and John A. Burt, director of test, systems, engineering and evaluation with DoD. Both men chaired the meeting at which the document was signed.

Schneider said a formal agreement would guarantee that an approved quality system at one contractor's facility would satisfy the quality requirements of all participating government agencies.

"It's really going to be a negotiated quality system at a contractor's facility that will satisfy all government contracts," he said. "The chal-

---

*Reprinted with permission from *Quality Systems Update,* published by IRWIN Professional Publishing, Fairfax, VA.

lenge is going to be designing a quality system within a contractor's facility that's acceptable to multigovernment customers."

Schneider said the next step is to select several government contractors that will voluntarily take part in a pilot program beginning this summer. The program is tentatively scheduled to run 12 to 18 months.

"Probably one of the most important criteria in the selection of a pilot contractor will be a contractor that has contacts with more than one government agency," he explained. "That's where we're going to see the greatest benefit I think."

The companies, which will be selected this summer, may be assessed against a model similar to the Big Three automakers' QS-9000 standard, which includes ISO 9001 in its entirety along with additional industry-specific requirements. "We're looking at QS-9000, which is ISO 9000 based but has additional requirements," Schneider said.

According to the MOU, participating government agencies agree to actively support the "mission, scope and objectives" of the GIQLP.

The document defines GIQLP's mission as to enable consistent satisfaction of customer expectations through a government and industry association partnership using world-class quality processes and practices to enhance international competitiveness.

As part of its scope, the GIQLP will encourage the participation of interested federal agencies and industry associations in the development and deployment of uniform quality management systems and advanced quality concepts, the document stated.

The organization has three main goals:

- To enable use of a single quality management system within a contractor's facility that satisfies each customer's requirements;

- To mutually recognize, share and utilize advanced quality concepts in the requirements definition, design, manufacture and acceptance of products; and

- To establish and implement effective and efficient oversight methods.

The rationale of basing such a standard on ISO 9000 stems from existing use of ISO 9000 in some government agencies, an increase in the number of government contractors that are voluntarily turning to ISO 9000 and the growing acceptance of the standards worldwide.

According to Schneider, technical adviser to the associate administrator for safety and mission assurance on quality initiatives with NASA, the single audit concept would minimize bureaucracy on contractors, promote better coordination among government agencies and ultimately reduce costs and improve product quality.

Industry representatives signed a similar document. Signatories included the Aerospace Industries Association, Electronics Industries Association, and the National Security Industrial Association.

Schneider said the signatories of the document appeared to have realistic expectations of the challenge in reaching a formal agreement. "I would characterize it as cautious optimism," he said.

TOTAL QUALITY MANAGEMENT IN K-12 EDUCATION: CINCINNATI PUBLIC SCHOOLS*
by Jennifer M. Wagner and J. Michael Brandt

BACKGROUND

September, 1991, the Cincinnati Public School district was publicly criticized for its fiscal irresponsibility evident by a $170 million state loan fund and its inability to balance the budget in more than four times in twenty years. It was also criticized for its declining achievement levels and

*Reprinted with permission from *Association for Quality and Participation 17th Annual Spring Conference and Resource Proceedings*, April 1995. Jennifer M. Wagner is the director of total quality management and J. Michael Brandt is the superintendent of Cincinnati Public Schools.

increasing drop-out rates. These criticisms were published in what has come to be known as the Buenger Report. This report was the result of a study of over 200 volunteers from our business community under the direction of Clement L. Buenger, Chairman of the Board of Fifth Third Bancorp. Their purpose was to evaluate the district's operations and recommend possible improvements. The results were shocking to many.

The Buenger report cited an inflated and complex bureaucracy and inefficient and outdated technology and procedures. The commission concluded *"the time has come for sweeping, fundamental change in the way CPS is managed and held accountable to the general public. The entire Cincinnati School System must be opened up and transformed from a top-down pyramid into an organization focused on individual schools and administered by professional managers who are given incentives—and the responsibility—to produce superior educational performance."* The new Superintendent, J. Michael Brandt, responded immediately. Over the last three years he has taken steps to implement many of the suggested recommendations including a drastic reorganization and a 60% reduction in force of the Central Administration in an effort to move toward site-based management in our schools. Brandt's management team after attending extensive training in Strategic Planning and Total Quality Management, realized that in order for this district to survive "we must fix ourselves" and saw the implementation of Total Quality Management principles as a means to continuously improve our systems, both educationally and operationally.

Late in 1991, Proctor & Gamble Company provided a temporary consultant to Cincinnati Public Schools to implement Total Quality Management using the Florida Power & Light model for continuous improvement, "The Quality Improvement Story."

The superintendent's cabinet brainstormed what they believed were "level two" intensity problems throughout the district to choose pilot projects. They chose 12 processes to learn the continuous improvement process and targeted a six-month time limit. Processes chosen included improving internal communications, discipline, the timely and proper placement of at-risk students, the textbook ordering process, in-school suspension, procedures, timeliness and accuracy of student information, timeliness and accuracy of financial reports and more.

We determined that twelve pilot teams were too many to support effectively and the complexity of the processes chosen were much more than anticipated. Team members were easily overwhelmed and discouraged when successes weren't quick to occur. They began to drop off teams and the energy level across the district began to wane. We also underestimated the cynicism of the individuals not initially chosen to participate in the pilot teams. They stood on the sidelines waiting for "the flavor of the month" to fail and were many times very vocal about their reservations.

When the consultant's time commitment ended (May 1993) and the teams' experiences were not what Superintendent Brandt had hoped for, he realized the district needed to show a sustained commitment from senior management. He decided to employ a full-time manager to direct the district's TQM efforts. In November 1994, the district hired Jennifer Wagner as Director of Total Quality Management to continue the implementation and development of our system of continuous improvement.

TRAINING

Through our consultant and using Proctor & Gamble resources, we initially trained approximately 60 employees on our new problem-solving model. We then trained twenty of those trainees to become internal facilitators. We have since developed our own training courses internally and host them through our staff development center. We are in the process of developing our own facilitator training courses to grow and sustain our capacity to form new TQ teams.

TEAM FACILITATING

Recognizing the newly trained facilitators would not be prepared to lead new teams through the 7-step problem-solving model having never experienced the TQ process, we paired our internal facilitators with external volunteers experienced in Total Quality Management. These volunteers came to us from local businesses and universities. They were to serve as coaches to the newly trained internal facilitators. We experienced two major problems with this concept. First, many of our volunteers reverted to using their TQM model rather than the Florida Power and Light model, which confused our team members and caused lengthy delays getting them back on track. Second, our internal facilitators became very dependent on the external volunteers and failed to develop their own skills. Consequently, when we lost all but one of our volunteers through corporate downsizing, reorganizations and maternity leaves, the affected teams began to lose focus and struggled to stay together. In the future, we decided, we would develop the skills of our employees experienced in TQM to serve as facilitators and trainers. The expected benefit is for those employees to begin to internalize this new problem-solving method which will assist in communicating and changing the district's culture.

STEERING COMMITTEE

Because of the delay between the consultant leaving and the hiring of the new director, the TQM steering committee was not formed until January, 1994. The current committee represents senior management from all functional areas of our school district, such as: Superintendent, Vice-President, Quality Improvement, Finance and Accounting, Human Resources, School Operations, Legal Counsel and Public Affairs. The committee's role is to charter new TQM teams to ensure district support and resource commitment and to review progress through team reporting. We began team reporting sporadically as the teams developed new recommendations; consequently the teams felt no sense of urgency or accountability for their progress or actions. Furthermore, senior management was not being kept informed of the actions being taken out in the field. To improve our team performance and communication system, we have restructured the steering committee meeting times and agendas to allow for regular team-progress reporting every 90 days. As the number of teams grows, the steering committee will expand to fulfill the teams' needs and members will rotate to give others an opportunity to serve in this leadership role.

TQM COMMUNICATION SYSTEM

Not only did we see the need for improved communications to the senior managers, we also saw a critical need to share successes to all of our em-

ployees and customers. We needed to improve the public opinion of Cincinnati Public Schools and we wanted to show our commitment to improving ourselves. A new TQM team called TQ^2, developed some awareness materials consisting of bulletin-board pieces, posters and tent cards for every employee in the district. TQ^2 also organized quarterly Quality Roundtables where teams present to each other, share experiences and learn new tools and techniques. Additionally, our public affairs department dedicated a column in our district newsletter to TQM tips and team stories. We plan to have some of our teams present to the Board of Education during public meetings to further communicate our successes.

EXTERNAL SUPPORT

As discussed above, we experienced a few problems with our external facilitators, but business partnerships, parents and universities can provide valuable assistance in the areas of TQM. They can serve as team members, assist with training needs and provide guidance on new procedures. Many parents use continuous improvement processes in the careers and are more than willing to share their expertise. We participate very heavily with quality networks, especially the Cincinnati Quality Education Network. The role we play there is that of a resource for school districts that are beginning their TQM journey. We have assisted in training, shared our experiences and resources, and supported new teams.

SUCCESS STORIES

We believe we are still in the infancy of Total Quality Management and educational reform, although we have experienced a few successes in improving our processes.

First, our Textbook team has been very successful. They were given the task to improve our district procedure for ordering textbooks. Through a survey of school principals, the team found that 50% of our students did not have all their textbooks on the first day of school. Further investigation revealed that in the 93/94 school year, 70% of the textbook requisitions contained errors, 90% of the schools missed the March deadline for submitting requisitions and the district overspent its replacement book budget by 50%. The root causes were identified as a lack of accountability, inadequate inventory control and the practice of hoarding books.

Recommended countermeasures to improve this process include:

- naming a textbook coordinator in every school to order and keep track of books;
- providing two days of training and a training manual for coordinators and principals;
- simplifying and streamlining the purchasing and delivery system so that books were delivered directly to schools instead of to a central warehouse;
- completing thorough physical inventories of current textbooks and maintaining them through a new computer package;
- placing "class sets" of textbooks in classrooms to be used as resources;
- instituting a "Help Desk" in the purchasing department.

The results were significant. Errors on requisitions for 94/95 went down to 30%. Schools submitting late requisitions (past the March deadline) went down to 30%. Overspending on the replacement book budget declined to 16%. Unfortunately, the data concerning the percent of students who did not have all their textbooks on the first day of school is unavailable at the time of this writing.

Another success story is with our District Clerical Quality Team. Members represent clerical staff from the three school levels (elementary, middle and high school) and central administration, as well as the clerical union. Their greatest area of concern was the lack of standardization in record-keeping procedures which caused many lost or misplaced student records. They found that every school had its own system of filing and updating. Further investigation revealed schools were filing documents not required by law. The team developed a list of required documents, redesigned the folder to better fit the size of documents inside and wrote standard procedures to implement district-wide.

THE FUTURE

We are now intensifying our efforts towards changing from a self-protecting, reactionary and self-serving culture to a customer-oriented school district and a data-driven team. We are expanding our training capacities by using our now experienced TQMers to train the newcomers. In the next two years, we plan to implement teaching teams where a group of teachers will be responsible for a child's development from entering a level (primary, intermediate, middle and high) to a successful exit of that level. Our new generation of teams are concentrating on processes cited in our "Warranty to Our Customers" developed in June of 1994. Finally, we plan to use the Malcolm Baldridge criteria to assess our progress and guide our future efforts.

CAN TQM IN PUBLIC EDUCATION SURVIVE WITHOUT COPRODUCTION?*
by Robert T. Chappell

Earning a Living: A Blueprint for High Performance, A SCANS *Report for America 2000* is the U.S. Department of Labor's contribution to educational reform following a decade-long stream of criticism of public elementary and secondary education.[1] SCANS—The Secretary's Commission for Achieving Necessary Skills—is the first document produced by the U.S. government that specifically details how public education should be changed to prepare students for the 21st-century workplace. The centerpiece of the *SCANS* report is "Workplace Know-How," a set of workplace competencies and foundation skills that all entry-level workers must possess in a high-perfomance workplace.

*Reprinted with permission from *Quality Progress*, July 1994. Robert T. Chappell is the assistant superintendent and a quality coordinator at Rappahannock County Public Schools in Sperryville, VA.

Graduates entering the workforce, according to *SCANS,* will be expected to have competencies in managing resources, managing information with computers, monitoring their own performance, improving systems, and selecting and applying technology. They will also need to have interpersonal competencies, such as the ability to work on teams and serve customers. Graduates will still need basic arithmetic and communication skills, but *SCANS* will also expect workers to have reasoning and problem-solving skills and personal qualities necessary for responsible self-management.

Among *SCANS'* recommendations is that U.S. schools "must be transformed into high-performance organizations," a trait that characterizes our most competitive companies. *SCANS* challenges school administrators to apply W. Edwards Deming's 14 points.[2] Educators, students, and parents should use total quality management (TQM) to coproduce quality educational services. If students use TQM to improve the quality of their school work, they should enter the work force with the workplace know-how identified in *SCANS,* which includes working on teams, serving customers, solving problems, monitoring and correcting performance, and improving systems.

PUBLIC SCHOOLS USE TQM

An increasing number of American public school districts are looking to TQM to improve services to their customers—the students. By 1993, more than 100 U.S. school districts had implemented some form of TQM.[3] The American Association of School Administrators formed a quality network in June 1991. More than 400 public school districts have representatives in the network.

There is great variation in the content and length of TQM training for educators. Some districts provide as little as a checklist on how their schools should operationalize Deming's 14 points. Some offer a partial-day, in-service training. And others provide several days of intensive quality training on customer service, team problem solving, and quality improvement.[4]

There is also considerable variation in the way TQM is implemented in school settings. In a study by William A. Hailey, Julie Horine, and Laura Rubach, it was found that of school districts using TQM, 80% use quality tools to improve administrative services, 50% use the tools

to improve teaching methods, and 50% use them to increase student achievement.[5] At least one district has mandated that all employees serve on problem-solving teams and quality improvement teams to improve instructional and support services.[6]

EVALUATING TQM IN SCHOOLS

TQM efforts in public education have not yet produced dramatic results. There have been no claims of massive increases in student achievement or decreases in student dropout rates. The Hailey, Horine, and Rubach study, however, cited positive results of TQM use by several school districts, such as reduced cycle time for special-education referrals, reduced student tardiness, reduced school safety problems, reduced need for remedial math instruction, improved student achievement, and reduced tax-collection cost.[7]

In 1990, a Virginia school district, Rappahannock County, began providing several days of TQM training for all teachers, bus drivers, secretaries, cafeteria workers, custodians, and administrators. This was made possible through a partnership grant with the Xerox Corporation and the Virginia Department of Education. Three years later, a study of the effects of TQM implementation in that district found that 89% of all school employees used aspects of the quality training in their work with students and parents; 72% thought administrators had increased efforts to meet employee needs; and 66% felt a greater sense of empowerment.[8] Nearly 80% of parents who responded to the survey said that school district employees had increased their efforts to meet the children's needs. Students also participated in a quality improvement team with bus drivers, parents, teachers, and administrators to reduce parents' dissatisfaction with district transportation services from 34% in 1991 to 11% in 1993.

A fair question to ask, however, is "How can we be certain that school districts that report implementing TQM are really using TQM?" Corporations might vary in their approaches to TQM, but those wishing to gain recognition for their quality efforts must submit to the stringent evaluation of the Malcolm Baldrige National Quality Award. Currently, there is no similar process to assess TQM efforts in public schools, but legislation that contains provisions for a Baldrige Award in education is currently

EXHIBIT 1.—COMPUTING A SCHOOL DISTRICT'S
MARKET SHARE

K-12 school district market share

A. Number of children ages 5-18 residing
within a district 25,000

B. Number of children in district in
private/parochial schools 1,250

C. Number of children in district receiving
home instruction 375

D. Number of children in district who have
dropped out 3,125

E. Number of children in district with long-term
suspensions/expelled............................. 250

Total not enrolled   5,000

Market-share formula:

$$\frac{A - (\text{sum of B, C, D, E})}{A} \times 100 = \text{market share}$$

$$\frac{25,000 - 5,000 \text{ (children not in school)}}{25,000}$$
$$\times 100 = 80\% \text{ of district's market served by district}$$

under consideration by the U.S. Congress (Senate Bill 4, House Bill 820).[9] If the Baldrige Award criteria are applied to education, there will be an objective process to evaluate whether applicant school districts are fashioning customer-driven services and procedures. Until a standardized evaluation process is developed, there can be no assurance that schools are really using TQM.

COST OF QUALITY

From a cost-of-quality perspective, superintendents and principals cannot point to increases in corporate profits as evidence that quality makes a difference. A school district's market share, however, might be an indicator of whether TQM is making a difference. Market share in K-12 public education can be measured as a percentage of the total resident-student population being served by a school district. Parents who think their children's needs are not being served by public schools might send their children to private schools or provide home instruction. Students who don't like school might drop out or purposely get expelled.

When a district's average daily membership decreases, its share of state revenues shrinks. Take, for example, a school district with 25,000 school-age children (5 to 18 years old) (see Exhibit 1). If the district receives $3,000 in state aid

for each student but 5,000 resident children are not enrolled in the district, the district loses out on $15 million (5,000 students multiplied by $3,000 each). The district's market share is 80% (20,000 of 25,000 students enrolled). If the district improves the quality of its educational services, its market share should, consequently, rise.

CUSTOMER SATISFACTION SURVEYS

To detect and correct causes of dissatisfaction, some school districts distribute customer satisfaction surveys (Exhibit 2). Surveys can show how well parents and students like the services provided by the school and can generate baseline data to help measure changes in attitudes toward school services. Surveys typically do not measure, however, the effectiveness of instruction.

Teachers often take the view: "No matter how much I improve the way I teach students, if they don't want to learn, I can't make them." Some students, on the other hand, say, "Why should I try? I don't want to be in school anyway." This debate points to a major issue of the schools' next-in-line customers, the students. Who is responsible for educational quality or improvement? Are teachers the only accountable parties or should the students be held equally accountable? And what about the responsibility of parents, principals, superintendents, and school boards?

THE CONCEPT OF COPRODUCTION

When TQM was gaining acceptance by U.S. corporations, academicians in public administration developed the concept of coproduction.[10] The theory of coproduction is based on the notion that the person providing the service and the next-in-line customer receiving the service share the responsibility for the quality and outcome of that service.

Gordon Whitaker describes coproduction in three service settings:

"Education or health care or crisis intervention have as their primary objective the transformation of the consumer. Others may benefit from a child's education or a worker's good health or the pacification of a husband or wife in a heated argument, but the primary beneficiaries are the clients themselves. In delivering ser-

EXHIBIT 2.—CUSTOMER-SATISFACTION SURVEY

Please answer the following questions using the scale below. Any comments that you wish to add may be placed at the end of the form.

	5 Strongly Agree	4 Agree	3 Neither	2 Disagree	1 Strongly Disagree
1. The academic program provided by the Rappahannock County Public Schools will prepare my child/children for the world of work in the 21st century.	❑	❑	❑	❑	❑
2. The various educational programs of the Rappahannock County Public Schools meet the needs of my children.	❑	❑	❑	❑	❑
3. There is open communication between our children's teachers, administrators, and the family.	❑	❑	❑	❑	❑
4. The cleanliness of the school buildings and grounds is acceptable.	❑	❑	❑	❑	❑
5. Discipline in the Rappahannock County Public Schools is fair and consistent.	❑	❑	❑	❑	❑
6. The major emphasis of the Rappahannock County Public Schools is a strong academic education of its students.	❑	❑	❑	❑	❑
7. Parents and students are dealt with by school personnel in a friendly and respectful manner.	❑	❑	❑	❑	❑
8. The transportation services that are offered by the Rappahannock County School Board are excellent.	❑	❑	❑	❑	❑
9. Everything considered, I am satisfied with the Rappahannock County Public Schools.	❑	❑	❑	❑	❑
10. Extracurricular offerings (athletics, clubs, and field trips) are adequate.	❑	❑	❑	❑	❑

11. Comments and suggestions: _____

_____

_____

Sample parent-satisfaction survey used by the Rappahannock County Schools, Sperryville, VA. Reprinted with permission.

vices, the agent helps the person being served to make the desired sorts of changes. Whether it is learning new ideas or skills, acquiring healthier habits, or changing one's outlook on family or society, only the individual served can accomplish the change. He or she is a vital coproducer of any vital transformation that occurs.[11]

No one in the school system can guarantee that every child will be taught well. There is too much variation in teaching styles and teacher preparation programs. Nor can educators issue a warranty that all students who get solid instruction will learn well. Students don't enter the classroom with equal interest or readiness for learning. What public education can do is work to improve the system. One way to improve the educational system is for educators, students, and parents to work together.

COPRODUCTION MODEL FOR TQM IN PUBLIC EDUCATION

Educators, students, and parents can and should learn to use the tools and strategies of TQM to coproduce quality educational services. The coproduction model for TQM is based on the premise that educators, students, and parents should receive training in TQM to help them learn to work together, solve problems, serve customers, monitor and correct performance, and improve systems.

These are the steps to follow to implement the coproduction model for TQM in a school district:

1. Get leadership from the top. If a coproduction model for TQM is to be implemented in an entire school system, the change should be led by the superintendent or deputy superintendent with the support of the school board.

2. Adopt a quality mission statement or policy. For example: "School district employees will strive to continuously improve services to students, parents, and fellow employees. Each employee will participate in team problem solving and quality-improvement efforts. Students will learn and use quality-improvement tools and strategies to help

them coproduce their education. Parents will be invited to learn and use quality improvement strategies to help them co-produce their children's education."

3. Select a TQM training program. Corporations might be willing to underwrite part of the cost of TQM training. Consider training all school employees, starting with volunteers. Invite parents to participate in training. Determine the appropriate grade levels and training content for students.

4. Organize a quality coordinating committee. This committee can:

   • Coordinate internal (employees) and external (students, parents, community, employers, and colleges) customer surveys.

   • Form quality teams composed of school employees, students, and parents to address problems and improve educational service quality.

   • Advise and assist quality teams on how to use the TQM process.

5. Institute a process for quality teams to measure, report on, display, and evaluate their results.

SUGGESTED TQM TRAINING TOPICS

Areas of TQM training that might be considered are:

• What is quality?

• What is a customer? Are parents and students the school's customers? When do teachers and parents become the students' customers? What are some methods to provide good customer service? How are customer requirements negotiated?

• What is continuous improvement? What are the steps and tools used in a data-oriented, team-based problem solving and quality improvement process? How are statistical tools, such as cause-and-effect diagrams, control charts, and Pareto charts, used in quality improvement? How can students use these to improve behavior and academic performance?

• What is coproduction? What are the roles and responsibilities of educators, students, and parents in improving educational ser-

vices and the educational system? How can brain storming, negotiation, and consensus be used to facilitate this partnership?

• What are the *SCANS* workplace competencies and foundation skills? How will TQM help students develop competence to work on teams, serve customers, solve problems, monitor and correct performance, and improve systems?

SHARED RESPONSIBILITY FOR RESULTS

The emphasis in the TQM coproduction model is based on shared responsibility for the quality of teaching and learning. The educational system must take the lead in designing and delivering quality and continuously improving instructional services that consider the needs of its customers. Parents have a responsibility to facilitate their children's learning through the provision of a calm, supportive environment. Parents should also demonstrate their commitment to improvement by supporting cost-effective school budget requests, serving on school quality improvement teams, and volunteering to help in the schools. Students are responsible for working hard, behaving appropriately, and continuously improving their work.

As students learn their roles in the coproduction model, they should become TQM literate. TQM training for public school students might provide the workplace know-how that *SCANS* expects of entry-level workers. If educators, parents, and students learn to work together to coproduce quality educational services, public schools and the U.S. work force might both reach the high performance level envisioned by *SCANS*.

REFERENCES

1. *Learning a Living: A Blueprint for High Performance. A SCANS Report for America 2000,* U.S. Department of Labor, 1992.
2. W. Edwards Deming, *Out of the Crisis* (Cambridge, MA: Massachusetts Institute of Technology, 1986).
3. William A. Hailey, Julie Horine, and Laura Rubach, "Transforming Schools," *Quality Progress,* October 1993, p. 23.
4. Robert T. Chappell, *The Effects of the Implementation of Total Quality Management on the Rappahannock County Virginia Schools,* doctoral dissertation registered with Dissertation Abstracts

International, Virginia Tech University, November 1993.

5. Hailey, Horine, and Rubach, "Transforming Schools."

6. Chappell, *The Effects of the Implementation of Total Quality Management on the Rappahannock County, Virginia Schools.*

7. Hailey, Horine, and Rubach, "Transforming Schools."

8. Chappell, *Implementation of Total Quality Management on the Rappahannock County, Virginia Schools.*

9. David M. Gangel, "Expansion of the Baldrige Award Eligibility to Education" *QED News,* October 1993.

10. Gordon Whitaker, "Co-Production: Citizen Participation in Service Delivery," *Public Administration Review.* May-June 1980, pp. 240-242.

11. Ibid.

IGNITING TOTAL QUALITY MANAGEMENT IN PUBLIC SCHOOLS*
by Robert H. Bender

"We have an awareness gap," the director of curriculum and instruction cautioned the Central Management Team (CMT) of the Crawford Central School District. He went on to remind them that comparatively few employees were knowledgeable about total quality management (TQM). The CMT was meeting to decide the next steps needed to incorporate TQM into the Crawford Central School District, which has approximately 5,000 students and 500 employees and is located in Meadville, PA, a small city surrounded by farmland about 70 miles north of Pittsburgh.

The CMT was discussing the conclusions in a study by Julie E. Horine of the University of Mississippi. Her report, "Public School Districts Implementing Total Quality Management: A National Survey," revealed some interesting findings. She disclosed that insufficient funding, a lack of training opportunities, and limited commitment of some staff members are often barriers to implementing TQM in school districts.[1]

The CMT concurred with the director of curriculum and instruction about the need to increase awareness of the potential applications of TQM on the part of administrators, teachers, and support staff. Moreover, team members recognized that the barriers of insufficient funding, lack of training opportunities, and limited commitment by some employees existed in their district.

QUALITY BACKGROUND

To understand the context of the CMT's concern about infusing TQM into the Crawford Central School District, some background information is needed. The district discovered the potential benefits of TQM when the superintendent was elected to the Meadville/Western Crawford County Chamber of Commerce Board of Directors. The chamber of commerce was instrumental in promoting the work of W. Edwards Deming.

Some board members met with a quality consultant who urged them to establish a council to provide some impetus toward implementing TQM. The result was the creation of the Crawford County Excellence Council. This council arranged for quality training and searched for opportunities to promote continuous improvement in organizations.

During the winter of 1989-90, Crawford Central School District sent its first team to learn about TQM. The emphasis of the training was on systems and the use of statistical and problem-solving tools. The first project—reducing the response time of repairs in classrooms and offices—was quite successful.

The CMT was subsequently trained in the use of hoshin planning tools. These tools were used in conjunction with processing large

*Reprinted with permission from *Quality Progress*, September 1994. Robert H. Bender is a consultant/trainer at North Star Development Services in Williamsburg, VA.

amounts of verbal data for short- and long-term planning.

The district then pursued three quality projects during the 1991-92 school year. These projects reduced the number of days it took goods and services to be ordered and received, psychological referrals to be submitted and decisions made about student placements, and requests for instructional computer repairs to be generated and machines restored to on-line service.

As the district approached the 1992-93 school year, no less than six quality projects were scheduled. These projects related to the amount of time students spent on instructional tasks, requests for substitute teachers, identification of students with special needs, the accounts receivable system, distribution of instructional software, and conservation of electricity.

Unfortunately, the barriers to implementing TQM revealed in Horine's report have doggedly persisted in the Crawford Central School District and have taxed the district in its quest for quality.

INSUFFICIENT FINANCIAL SUPPORT

School districts across the country struggle with shrinking funding bases. For example, Crawford Central received a minuscule annual increase and then no increase in subsidies from the Pennsylvania state government for the 1990-91 and 1991-92 school years, respectively. At the same time, contractual obligations and rising costs have squeezed the district's budget and left only morsels for developmental activity.

Adopting any degree of TQM requires some financial outlay. For example, trainers must be compensated and substitute teachers filling in for teaching staff who attend training and participate on quality teams must be paid. Training can be conducted on a shoestring, but for how long, and at what cost to quality?

LIMITED TRAINING OPPORTUNITIES

Limited training opportunities continue to hinder the infusion of TQM into the Crawford Central School District. The central issue is finding time for training when learning conditions are optimal while avoiding the disruption caused by pulling teachers from classrooms. Training during noninstructional time also generates additional

costs due to employees working beyond their contract hours. Clearly, limited training is directly related to the barrier of insufficient financial support.

Public education is people and time intensive. This fact is magnified when staff requires training and the public budget is shrinking. Moreover, quality consultants must be engaged and compensated at least until internal staff members are able to continue the training throughout the school district.

QUESTIONABLE EMPLOYEE COMMITMENT TO TQM

The matter of employee commitment to TQM is a subtle although no less consequential barrier. To close the awareness gap and strengthen the commitment to TQM, the superintendent traveled to each school and presented an overview of the continuous improvement concepts and their applications to school systems. In addition, quality concepts were featured in staff and community newsletters distributed by the school district. The underpinnings of these promotions were the ongoing quality projects involving about 30 staff members. Moreover, the CMT participated in extensive training, received ample written materials, and engaged in wide-ranging discussions regarding TQM applications.

The reaction to this quality campaign has been generally encouraging. Staff members have expressed everything from mild interest to enthusiastic support. These reactions are best understood in relation to the distinctions made between "enrollment," "commitment" and "compliance," by Peter Senge in his book, *The Fifth Discipline*.[2]

Senge defines enrollment as choosing to do something and doing whatever can be done within the "spirit of the law." He describes commitment in terms of wanting something and making it happen. By contrast, compliance is described as going along with a proposed vision or change and doing what is expected. Compliance involves some supportive behavior but falls short of enrollment and internalized commitment.

Crawford Central School District's response to the money and training barriers was to suggest a quid-pro-quo arrangement with local quality experts. The superintendent offered to contribute his training skills and group-process techniques to local organizations and individuals in exchange for securing expert assistance for district quality teams. This emphasis on mutual benefits resulted in the completion of three year-long quality projects with no cost for the external consultants involved.

Several additional positive elements were in effect that helped avoid the money and training barriers. For example, the Crawford County Excellence Council provided ongoing planning support. Paul Huber, president of Seco/Warwick., Inc., contributed funds to support the training of the quality team. Thomas Lang, president of Dad's Products Co., Inc., a local pet food manufacturer, provided district access to recognized national TQM consultants who provided advice to the superintendent regarding the district's quality efforts. Finally, some of the costs for materials were eliminated as a result of exchanges of plans, outlines, articles, and programs with other organizations.

Crawford Central School District is still grappling with the problem of time for TQM training. Although daytime training periods are scarce in school districts, some TQM sessions are planned to occur during Act 178 Days, the Pennsylvania-mandated provision for staff development in school systems. In partial response to the superintendent's appeal for staff to pursue quality initiatives, many teachers requested to receive initial training in TQM.

In regard to the third significant barrier—insufficient employee commitment—the Crawford Central School District is relying on patience and persistence. Although the opinions of staff members who are at least marginally exposed to TQM range from mild curiosity to unabashed enthusiasm, some are hesitant to pursue quality opportunities. The district is long on compliance but short on true commitment.

In the spirit of obtaining commitment to the vision, the superintendent and some of the district's staff members are attempting to model commitment, be honest about the benefits and problems of TQM, and let employees choose to declare their acceptance of these changes.

Progressively, Crawford Central is using many driving forces to encourage staff commitment. For example, the superintendent is a member of the Chief Executive Officers' (CEO) Roundtable, a group of five top managers of local organizations. The CEO Roundtable reviews the quality efforts of member organizations. It questions, advises, and supports member CEOs as they pursue quality opportunities. The CEO Roundtable meetings include top-line people and staff members who are continually exposed to TQM initiatives. This continued exposure and interaction can result in a shift from staff compliance with TQM initiatives to commitment to them.

Another example of an activity to build commitment to TQM was the fall 1992 Northwest Tri-County Intermediate Unit 2000 Initiative in northwestern Pennsylvania. Spearheaded by the Northwest Tri-County Intermediate Unit, a regional service agency of the Pennsylvania Department of Education, this initiative brought some 5,000 educators together to address continuous improvement opportunities in conjunction with Northcoast Quality Week in Erie, PA. The day's events included a keynote address, a panel discussion, and several workshops focusing on total quality in schools.

A key approach to developing employee commitment to quality is maximum and unremitting exposure to TQM concepts, knowledge, and applications. Employees are not compelled to pursue quality initiatives as a condition of employment. At the same time, the Crawford Central administration is committed to transforming the district into a constellation of subsystems that are unswervingly engaged in continuous improvement.

Crawford Central School District is experiencing the barriers identified in Horine's report, but it is responding by marshalling its resources, focusing on attainable objectives, and believing in a restructured and productive future for public education through TQM.

REFERENCES

1. Julie E. Horine. "Public School Districts Implementing Total Quality Management: A National Survey," The University of Mississippi, Oxford, MS, October 1991, p. 5.
2. Peter M. Senge, *The Fifth Discipline: The Art and Practice of the Learning Organization* (New York, NY: Doubleday, 1990), pp. 218–223.
3. Ibid.

2.4
HEALTH CARE

---■---

THE PATIENT-FOCUSED HOSPITAL: BRINGING ABOUT MASSIVE QUALITY IMPROVEMENT FAST*
by Sandy Panzer, Nancy Biettler, Dottie Kraus, and Kathy Lux

In the last two years at Theda Clark Regional Medical Center we have spent all of our efforts transforming and reengineering our inpatient delivery system. Traditional TQM programs in the hospital setting haven't brought about the type of improvements that are needed to reengineer decades of poorly designed systems within hospitals. We have taken an aggressive approach to what is well known as a patient-focused care redesign.

Booz-Allen Health Care consultants studied how hospital salary dollars are spent. In their time study analysis, they found that only 24% of personnel time was spent on caring for the patient and, of that 24%, only 16% is spent on direct medical, technical, and clinical services. The other 8% is spent on hotel services such as linens and cleaning. The rest, 76% of the time, is spent on nonvalue-added activities such as documenting medical information, documentating institutional information, transporting the patients or staff, coordinating among the many departments, and ready-for-action time. To sum up the findings, currently traditional hospitals have:

- structures that are too compartmentalized with many small units requiring separate managers and support staff

- jobs that are too specialized requiring coordination

- work that is too complex, process flows have too much variation

- too much time is spent doing process work, much of which is repeated

- too much ready-for-action time

For example, many of the services such as respiratory therapy or phlebotomy that come from centralized departments require a lot of scheduling, coordinating, and transporting just to perform the procedures. A routine respiratory therapy treatment requires a total of 33 minutes—but the processing time takes 18 minutes and the procedure only takes 15 minutes. So over half of the time that is spent doing this treatment is scheduling, coordinating and transporting because it is delivered from a centralized department. Our goal with reengineering was to decrease the complexity by defining new characteristics:

- hospital will be structured as multidisciplinary business units

- work is streamlined and takes place on the patient unit

- people work in self-directed teams

- process time is reduced

- job categories are more flexible

To implement Patient-Focused Care we went through four major phases. The first phase included work redesign. Three design teams were formed: Service, Administrative and Clinical. The teams flow-charted and redesigned over 200 processes to make them more customer focused. The criteria for redesign included: fewer handoffs, less paper work, fewer caregivers interacting with the patient, moving more services closer to the patient, less coordination required, less

---

* Reprinted with permission from *Association for Quality and Participation 17th Annual Spring Conference and Resource Proceedings,* April 1995. Sandy Panzer is the director of quality improvement, Nancy Biettler is a service associate, Dottie Kraus is an administrative associate, and Kathy Lux is a clinical associate at Theda Clark Regional Medical Center in Neenah, WI.

scheduling, and fewer phone calls. During the same time, we educated over 500 employees about the concept of Patient-Focused Care, work redesign and quality improvement in one and a half day seminars.

Phase Two was the restructuring phase. First, management was downsized. We eliminated 12 managers and six supervisors to make our management team more streamlined. Presently, there are only four layers between the staff person and the highest person in our corporate office. Next, we organized all of what we do into five patient care centers, Outpatient, Women-Infant-Children, Surgical-Ortho-Neuro-Rehab, Cardiac Medicine, and Behavioral Health. The concept was that these patient centers would be as self-contained as possible with all of the associates reporting to one or two managers within the center so that they would feel the accountability and the teamwork of working together.

Phase Three was patient-center design. Staff in the patient centers met to establish their mission and vision, then did a detailed analysis of tasks to decide who could do what and if volume would be high enough to be competent. New jobs were designed incorporating deployed functions from the Service, Administrative and Clinical teams. Centers then designed 24-hour accountable teams to take care of the patient, using the theory "do more for fewer patients, not do one thing for many patients."

Phase Four was the deployment of all the functions that we redesigned. We decided to do this by function, not by center, as many hospitals have. It is the fastest method, most cost-effective method, but it also is the more stressful method of deployment because you have the whole organization in chaos at one time.

We began our Service deployment in November of 1993 and completed it in February of 1994. The tasks in the service role include: housekeeping, stocking and receiving, user-level equipment maintenance, menu and meal tray passing, and assisting clinical associates with simple patient cares. Most of the reactions to this Service Associate (SA) deployment have been very positive. The patients have been very understanding and amazed at what a Service Associate can do for them. Patients like the idea that if they ask someone for a glass of water, the SA can get it for them immediately and not have to wait for it. The Clinical Team has also responded very positively to the Service Associate deployment and have felt that they are a valuable part of the team. Most of the Service Associates have

also reported increased self-esteem, as now they are dealing with patients, answering physicians' questions when appropriate, and contributing to the team.

Our second deployment was Administrative functions. It began in December of 1993, and was completed at the end of 1994. Those functions included in the deployment were transcribing orders, admitting and registration, insurance verification and precertification, medical records, general unit secretary functions, quality assessment data gathering, coding, utilization review, and discharge planning. Due to the varied skill level required to deliver these functions, we created two positions, Administrative Associate (AA) and Administrative Associate Analyst (AAA). The AAA position was most often filled by a Registered Nurse and included discharge planning, recertification, utilization review, coding and quality data gathering. The AA position performs admitting, precertification, medical records chart completion and basic unit secretary functions.

Although we continue to have CQI teams looking at unresolved issues that have resulted from administrative deployment, overall the change has produced positive results. Staff on the unit have an ownership of the functions that allows a continuity to the patient that was hard to achieve in the past.

Clinical services deployment is our current implementation. It includes Respiratory Therapy, Phlebotomy, EKG, basic Physical Therapy, basic Occupational Therapy, and bedside care. The simplest tasks deployed, Phlebotomy and EKG, were cross-trained among nonlicensed and licensed clinical people and are currently performed by our bedside teams. Respiratory Therapy cross-training, on the other hand, has been a more difficult deployment and the adjustment has been slower and longer. Respiratory Therapists were initially very skeptical, but now feel favorable about the outcome. They understand what's going on with the patient's care, and feel much more part of the team. They are learning some skills that they hadn't learned in their previous role and are feeling very proud of that. Currently we are training RNs, NAs, LPNs to do basic physical therapy and occupational therapy tasks, as well as training Physical Therapists and Occupational Therapists to perform basic bedside tasks while doing their therapy.

When we're finished with the design and implementation of patient-focused care, we have some aggressive goals and expected outcomes.

We hope to have improved patient, staff and physician satisfaction, a measurable cost reduction of 15-20% by the end of 1995, and improved clinical outcomes. It has been a challenging road to travel and we are about 80-90% through our plan for deployment. So far we have been able to claim our implementation a success since we have already achieved some financial reductions and improved staff and patient satisfaction. As we talk to staff, they usually say that they'd never go back, that things being closer to the patient makes it much easier for their care and patients are getting response much quicker.

Our next challenge and goals for 1995 include working toward developing teams, further CQI the issues that are yet unresolved with deployment, coming up with a better way to look at compensation for teams, and to assure fair compensation for new roles people have developed. In looking back, we realize that without major reengineering efforts we would never have been able to make the kind of impact we have made over this last year.

BIBLIOGRAPHY

Booz-Allen Health Care, Inc., *Activation Teams Design Guidelines*. Written for use at Theda Clark Regional Medical Center. September l6, 1992.

HEALTH-COST MANAGEMENT AND PHARMACY BENEFIT PLANS*
by Michael N. Cannizzaro

There is a new strategic partner on the frontier in the ongoing quest to reduce overall health care costs and improve the quality of care: the pharmacy benefits manager (PBM). Traditionally known for effectively managing the prescription drug benefit, which represents a relatively small yet growing portion of total health benefits expenditures, PBMs are rapidly evolving and will ultimately play a central role in managing and reducing overall health care costs.

The increasing prominence of PBMs stems from the health care community's growing realization that pharmaceuticals play a key role in managing overall health care and determining optimal treatment approaches, rather than simply being an ancillary consideration. Indeed, the tools, techniques and data that PBMs use each day will uniquely enable them to manage various disease states and improve overall health status, which ultimately will result in reduced total health care costs.

Why are PBMs in a unique position to achieve these cost reductions? First, PBMs have compiled vast databases of drug utilization and clinical outcomes information derived from their experience of managing the prescription drug benefits of millions of people. They are currently making rapid progress in analyzing the relationships between drug utilization and overall treatment protocols for many of the most costly and prevalent disease states, both chronic and acute. PBMs also have the ability to comprehensively monitor a patient's actual pharmaceutical and medical therapies, and the ultimate outcomes of those therapies. When this data is coupled with their clinical knowledge. PBMs can evaluate patient care against accepted treatment protocols, and identify the "best practices" that are most likely to result in improved outcomes and reduced costs.

DELIVERING COST/QUALITY CONTROL

The evolution of PBMs has occurred in logical, incremental steps. PBMs emerged in the late 1980s when benefit plan sponsors sought relief from spiraling prescription drug costs. At that time, both the price of branded drugs and overall pharmaceutical use were increasing, especially in health plans that covered large numbers of older workers and/or retirees. Additionally, statistics and clinical experience revealed that prescription drugs were—and still

---

* Reprinted with permission from *Risk Management* magazine, Vol. 42, No. 5, May 1995. Michael N. Cannazzaro is president of Caremark Prescription Service Division in Lincolnshire, IL.

are—often misprescribed, misused and under- or overutilized. The health and cost consequences of such misuse can be extreme. It was clear that the time had come for managed care strategies to be applied to the prescription drug benefit.

From the beginning, PBMs have provided expert management of the entire spectrum of drug benefit plans, both to reduce drug costs and to ensure safe and appropriate drug therapies. PBMs monitor and manage the safety and appropriateness of drug selection, prescription, dispensing, administration and reimbursement within a sponsor's benefit plan design parameters. Working in partnership with a benefit plan sponsor, PBMs typically analyze current plan design, usage and costs, and determine near- and longer-term objectives. They then recommend a plan strategy designed specifically for that organization's needs, taking into account such parameters as drug coverages, copayment levels, deductibles, refill limitations and plan maximums.

Depending on the needs of the plan sponsor, a PBM's services can range from basic prescription drug claims administration to innovative, leading-edge solutions that achieve maximum cost control. A good PBM will also provide a high level of ongoing management support services, including handling daily operational questions, resolving plan design and eligibility issues and communicating new program and service capabilities.

IMPROVING UTILIZATION

When PBMs originally came onto the scene, the "first tier" of services they offered reduced drug costs and ensured the appropriateness of prescribed drug therapies. Their positive impact on bottom lines and care quality proved their worth. Thus, the elements in this first tier of service are now considered to be essential cornerstones of any managed pharmaceutical plan strategy. These services include cost and quality-efficient drug distribution systems, standard drug utilization review, retrospective case management and physician profiling.

The first of these services is drug distribution systems. To reduce the cost of drugs and dispensing, PBMs typically provide a method—or a combination of methods—of prescription drug dispensing that best suits a plan sponsor's needs and benefit plan design. Retail pharmacy networks offer plan participants maximum convenience in filling prescriptions for acute conditions. Ideally, a PBM's retail network will provide broad nationwide coverage and utilize a sophisticated electronic on-line, real-time point-of-sale system to ensure that plan sponsors pay only for eligible patients and the drugs covered under their plans. Additionally, a traditional paper claims adjudication system should also be available for plan sponsors who prefer to have their employees pay for prescriptions at the time of purchase and file for reimbursement, or for instances in which participants must use out-of-network pharmacies.

Mail-service pharmacies give PBMs an even greater ability to control costs and quality. PBMs make high-volume pharmaceutical purchases, utilize a highly efficient drug-distribution system and reduce dispensing fees. Mail-service pharmacy is an ideal way to dispense maintenance prescription pharmaceuticals to patients covered under a participating drug benefit plan. Maintenance drugs include those used to treat chronic or long-term conditions, including heart disease and high blood pressure, pain, arthritis, diabetes and other maladies. Covered patients simply mail their prescription orders to the PBM, which screens each order to help ensure clinical safety, plan-design compliance and patient eligibility. Registered pharmacists fill all eligible orders and send them directly to the patient's home or office.

The PBM's computer system should automatically alert the mail service pharmacist when a generic equivalent to a prescribed drug is available. These generic drugs should then be employed whenever possible. Savings are also achieved through the reduction of billing expenses. Plan beneficiaries, save not only on out-of-pocket payments, but also enjoy the convenience and safety of having their medications delivered directly to their homes or offices. They also save time because there are no claim forms to fill out, and no waiting for reimbursement.

To ensure maximum safety and convenience for mail-service pharmacy patients, a PBM should provide a host of personal services that include toll-free telephone access to registered pharmacists and customer-service representatives. The services should also include a 24-hour emergency access to registered pharmacists; access to bilingual registered pharmacists and customer-service representatives; an around-the-clock, refill-by-phone system for medication orders; and, very importantly, drug-specific patient-counseling information for every prescription dispensed, with detailed instructions for proper drug use, possible interactions and side effects.

The second type of first-tier service is standard drug-utilization review, or DUR. Standard DUR is normally conducted for all plan sponsors—no matter what the benefit plan design—to protect and enhance the therapeutic value of the medications being dispensed. These safety checks, or "edits," are done prior to dispensing to ensure the highest level of safety for patients. Examples of DUR edits include: duplicate drug therapy; too early refill; drug dose check; low and high dose alert; duplicate prescription; drug-drug interactions; drug-disease conflict; drug-pregnancy/lactation conflict; drug-gender conflict; drug-age conflict and others. Additional edits that provide an even higher level of therapeutic evaluation are usually conducted through a PBM's case-management program.

Ideally, the PBM should be able to classify warnings generated by safety edits and notify— and require a response from—the dispensing pharmacist. Using an on-line system, the nature of a prescription problem can be very easily identified by the dispensing pharmacist. All standard DUR edits potentially can be classified in three categories: very severe, moderate and mild. A "'very severe" classification would actually stop the prescription from being dispensed. Beside safety edits, additional edits like "member ineligible" relate to plan design and administration, and provide an extra safeguard for controlling costs.

The third type of first-tier service provided by PBMs is retrospective case management. Through retrospective case management, a PBM evaluates each patient's historical drug usage profile to identify interventions that can improve the cost-effectiveness and quality of care in the future. Retrospective review of both retail and mail prescribing data identifies unsafe or inappropriate drug utilization based on trends, as well as prescribing choices that might prove inappropriate over the long term. Following evaluation, a PBM should suggest more cost- or clinically effective medication therapies to the prescribing physician, whose response should be encouraged and tracked when received. Overall changes in patient drug-use patterns are also subsequently measured and evaluated.

The objectives of retrospective case management include ensuring that patients receive appropriate drug therapy as measured against current clinically accepted prescribing standards, evaluating both retail and mail prescribing to optimize drug-therapy utilization and cost savings, performing clinical interventions to improve patient care in areas not resolved before a prescription is dispensed and enhancing the long-term appropriateness of physician prescribing decisions.

Physician profiling is the fourth type of first-tier service provided by PBMs. Physician profiling enables a plan sponsor to use physician prescribing history to improve and manage future physician prescribing. PBMs can evaluate a plan's historical data and then provide information on prescribing patterns and costs in several ways: by physician specialty, by practice group and by individual physician. They then work with the sponsor to optimize plan design and provider relationships.

INFLUENCING DRUG CHOICE

As these managed-pharmacy techniques became widely established in practice, PBMs embarked on the next step: to move beyond the management of drugs that had already been prescribed to guide the selection of those yet to be prescribed. With the objectives of further reducing drug expenditures and promoting therapeutically optimal prescribing practices, PBMs developed and introduced programs to proactively influence physician prescribing patterns and to enhance patient compliance.

Concurrent case management is one example of these "second-tier" programs. Physicians strive to provide their patients with the best possible care. There are many factors, however, that can complicate physicians' prescribing decisions. For example, some patients do not inform physicians about all of the medications they are receiving. In other cases, physicians are not aware of the most current clinically recommended prescribing guidelines for a particular disease or medication. Finally, physicians may not be informed about the relative costs of therapeutically equivalent medications.

A good PBM should be able to utilize automated clinical criteria and specially trained pharmacists to assist prescribing physicians in selecting the most appropriate medication for their patients prior to the dispensing of the medication. After a PBM's pharmacist consults with the physician via telephone or fax, the physician may agree to change the drug prescribed, adjust the drug dosage or alter the duration of therapy. Examples where a PBM pharmacist may perform an intervention include: excessive therapy duration; controlled substance abuse; therapeutic alternatives (to suggest those available at a lower cost); possible drug overuse and inappropriate therapy (when drug and/or dosage is not appropriate for the diagnosis).

Formularies are another type of second-tier service, and have become a key component in PBMs' clinical management programs. Formularies, which are lists of preferred, cost-effective prescription medications in commonly prescribed medical categories, give plan sponsors an extra measure of cost and quality control, promoting the use of less expensive drugs that offer equal or greater therapeutic value than other, more costly medications in the same category. Formularies generally encourage the use of generic medications when available and appropriate, since generics are the first choice in managing costs.

Plan sponsors may adopt one of several ways to implement a formulary, according to their objectives for controlling costs and influencing physician prescribing choices. An "open" formulary uses a voluntary approach to compliance, allowing plan participants to become familiar with the list of preferred drugs. An incented formulary, on the other hand, features co-payment incentives to encourage use of formulary drugs. Finally, the closed, or mandatory formulary, restricts patients to the use of formulary drugs only. In fact, an aggressive program of prescriber and patient education and communications helps to assure formulary compliance. This approach often includes personalized formulary reference guides as well as personal and written contacts.

Formulary reference profiles for physicians represent another second-tier service. To help physicians prescribe an effective and lower-cost drug for their patients covered under a PBM-managed drug benefit plan, PBMs should receive information about the PBM's formulary. This service is best accomplished with customized formulary guides featuring the name and address of each patient. These guides can be inserted directly into the patients' files, where they will serve as an ongoing reference for the physician.

The final type of second-tier service provided by PBMs are patient education/drug information programs. These programs play a key role in reducing prescription drug costs and increasing safety and compliance, There are several points at which a patient may receive important communications from a PBM regarding the drug therapy. For example, patients may receive a letter informing them of the physician's approval of a prescription change, a brochure on their medical condition and a question and answer brochure describing their new prescription. Regarding formulary use, patients should receive a letter introducing them to the formulary and its benefits, including a convenient formulary brochure they can take along to physician appointments. When a PBM performs concurrent drug utilization review, the patient may receive a letter that alerts them to possible drug interactions, long-term overall effects or any other concern that may warrant notification.

IMPROVING PATIENT OUTCOMES

Unquestionably, the most exciting development now taking shape—a movement that goes well beyond existing benefit management programs—is outcomes research and the advent of disease state management. This innovative, cooperative strategy will be of immense usefulness to patients, payors, physicians and the entire health care system. Patients will profit from these programs through the development of higher standards of treatment for high-cost, high-incidence diseases such as asthma, HIV/AIDS, heart disease, hypertension, depression and diabetes. Plan sponsors will also benefit through significant reductions of overall health care costs—inpatient, outpatient, physician and prescription drugs.

Under this new approach, the focus of PBMs has evolved from appropriate therapy to optimal therapy. Essentially, outcomes management represents an important paradigm shift for the health care community, when pharmaceuticals are viewed as a cost element, they, like all other cost elements, must be controlled by reducing acquisition costs and/or decreasing usage. But as prescription drugs become recognized as the viable, highly cost-effective alternative therapies they are, those considerations change. The new paradigm states that utilization of prescription drug therapy should increase, where appropriate, for two main reasons. First, the cost of pharmaceuticals is typically far less than the cost of many medical treatments, such as surgery. Second, increased drug utilization on an aggregate level reduces the total number of patients undergoing those more costly medical treatments.

Outcomes research brings some powerful tools and strategic linkages into play to achieve the goal of reduced costs and improved-care quality. Many PBMs have partnered with pharmaceutical manufacturers to share drug and medical data, conduct clinically based outcomes research to analyze the relationship between drug utilization and overall medical care and pinpoint the optimal treatment protocols. In this research, there are several vital questions to be answered. For example, what is the best way to treat certain diseases? Which treatments work, whicn do not and what is the overall cost? How can everyone work together to identify patients at risk, monitor them and then intervene at the appropriate time to better manage their therapy on an ongoing basis?

Here is an overview of how disease-state management works. It provides benefit plan participants who have certain chronic, targeted conditions with a total drug management program over time. For instance, a PBM may identify a patient with asthma whose medical data indicates that he or she is not being prescribed medications—or is not in compliance—within current, standardized treatment guidelines, such

as those approved by the National Institutes of Health. Under a disease-state management program, these patients and their physicians would be enrolled in a disease-management program, and counseled as to appropriate medication, dosage and usage. Patients and physicians who are already in compliance with the guidelines would receive alternative educational materials.

A PBM pharmacist then tracks patient compliance through follow-up counseling with both physician and patient. The PBM monitors the program outcomes, then reviews the medical data to determine the reductions in the health care costs associated with the patient's condition. Plan sponsors are then provided with updates on enrollments, physician participation, program costs and benefits.

Clearly, PBMs are well on their way to making a lasting contribution as health-cost managers in the ongoing effort to reduce overall health care costs and improve clinical outcomes. In the short term, outcomes and disease-state management will serve as an educational tool for physicians. Over the long term, these innovative strategies will effectively advance the health care community's ability to deliver coordinated, comprehensive and cost-effective care.

THE GOLD SHEET*
by Staff Writers

FDA LOOKING FOR BRIDGES WITH EU

The Food and Drug Administration views a "confidence-building" program as a necessary first step in developing a mutual recognition agreement with the European Union on good manufacturing practice (GMP) inspections for pharmaceuticals.

➤ At a March 31 industry and consumer exchange meeting sponsored jointly with the Animal and Plant Health Inspection Service (APHIS), FDA said it believes that a "confidence building" program could serve as a

potential bridge to an inspection agreement with the EU.

FDA International Affairs Staff Director Walter Batts noted that the agency and the EU concur that the possibility of an agreement covering drug and biologic GMPs is "well worth pursuing." Batts explained that an agreement providing for mutual reliance on inspection information "could be of great value to FDA in conserving its limited resources." He pointed out that the agency conducts "a significant number of inspections in the EU member states" and that

---

* Reprinted with permission from *F-D-C Reports*, Vol. 29, No. 5, May 1995. This report was written by staff writers.

"many pharmaceutical products produced [in Europe] are imported to the U.S."

➤ However, Batts stressed, the structure of the EU "presents significant complications"—particularly in coordinating the development and application of a single GMP standard across the different inspection and enforcement programs in each of the 15 member states.

The FDA official reported that the EU has expressed. "a keen interest" in an agreement that, would "essentially provide for the recognition of each side's current programs, with whatever current differences that exist." FDA, on the other hand, he said, while acknowledging the "potential value," of such an agreement, "believes that [mutual recognition] can only be accomplished if the entire regulatory program in the EU is equivalent to that of FDA," including standards, inspection procedures and enforcement.

A "confidence building program," Batts said, would provide the means of working toward that equivalence. From FDA's perspective, he explained, such a program would be a prerequisite for entering into an agreement "that allows for a reliance on the inspection information generated in an EU member state."

Noting that EU officials "have indicated a willingness to work together to build confidence in each other's programs," Batts suggested that "limited agreements could be achieved in the near term that might cover such issues as joint inspections, exchange of inspection reports and joint training activities."

Batts pointed out that "equivalence" in standards, inspection programs and enforcement procedures has served as FDA's yardstick in agreeing to "memorandums of understanding" (MOUs) with regulatory authorities in other countries related to good laboratory practices (GLPs) and GMPs.

While looking for equivalence as the foundation for these types of agreements, FDA is not insisting that programs be exactly the same, Batts stressed. "By equivalence, we do not mean necessarily that the regulatory systems are identical, but that they provide the same level of . . . health protection."

PDA Executive Director Edmund Fry suggested that FDA's requirement for equivalent enforcement procedures places a significant stumbling block in the way of international agreements. "I don't think FDA is going to find

anywhere in the world an equivalent enforcement procedure. . . . Nor do I think that it is absolutely necessary in order for FDA to make decisions on the acceptability of products from other countries," he asserted.

FDA MUST ADDRESS LEGAL CONSTRAINTS

Batts agreed that there should be "further dialogue" on whether equivalence "is necessary, or achievable." On the other hand, he pointed out, the "legal constraints" under which the agency operates require "that we exercise certain judgments, make certain decisions in a certain manner." Consequently, he explained, FDA believes that the "equivalence concept" has to be built into any agreement.

➤ "We are not looking for identical," the FDA official reiterated. "We have to make sure that in entering into any kind of agreement where we are accepting inspection results from other countries [that] there is a level playing field, and that the information we are given from other countries is the same kind of information that we would expect to get if were conducting the inspections ourselves."

In looking for equivalence in the enforcement component of a regulatory program, FDA Manufacturing and Product Quality Division Director Douglas Ellsworth noted that a key agency concern is the effective monitoring of industry corrective actions. When violations of FDA laws and standards for products being shipped to the U.S. occur in another country, there must be "some mechanism for assuring that corrective action takes place," Ellsworth stated.

FDA's position that a "confidence-building" program is a necessary first step before agreeing to an inspection recognition pact with the EU evolved from a fact-finding mission to Europe by former Mid-Atlantic Region Director Chard Davis in late 1993.

After meeting with European regulatory officials, Davis wrote a memorandum to top agency management in January 1994 addressing the problems involved in developing a mutual recognition type of agreement with the EU. He also suggested possible approaches the agency might take to help lay the groundwork for closer cooperation.

In his report, Davis pointed out a number of obstacles to a mutual recognition arrangement, such as: the lack of uniformity within the EU member states in their inspection programs; the lack of investigators to support the central EU regulatory agency; and the general lack of investigation manpower within individual member states, including the U.K., which has a relatively strong investigation program. Davis suggested that the EU would have to harmonize inspection programs within Europe before FDA could negotiate a formal inspection recognition agreement.

INFORMATION SHARING, CROSS-TRAINING PROPOSED

In line with the approach FDA has taken in developing MOUs in the past, Davis proposed that the agency focus on establishing a preliminary agreement with the EU that would include provisions for sharing inspection information and developing cross-training programs. The primary goal of such an agreement, he suggested, would be to cultivate a better understanding of U.S. inspection programs in Europe and thereby promote greater equivalence and uniformity.

➤ Under Davis' recommendation, FDA would continue to conduct foreign inspections at current levels.

The inspections would serve the dual purpose of evaluating plants as well as auditing local inspections to monitor the equivalency of the respective inspection programs. Such an agreement would leave FDA with full discretion to decide when it would do inspections in Europe and on what plants, while potentially helping to avoid the need for committing more resources abroad.

Important for any inspection agreement with the EU, Davis advised, would be to include a provision for sharing information on those plants found to have problems. For any kind of workable program, Davis stressed, there should be a way to identify problem plants and to prevent exports from those plants. He suggested that the issue had not received sufficient attention in MOU negotiations.

➤ The legal constraints on FDA also will have to be addressed in developing a regulatory agreement with the EU.

At the recent FDA/industry meeting, Batts pointed to three "key provisions that a mutual recognition-type MOU would need to include to be consistent with FDA's legal mandate and ensure its effectiveness": (1) the right to inspect as the agency deems necessary; (2) the ability to conduct periodic joint inspections to maintain continuing mutual confidence; and (3) the exchange of information on changes in laws, regulations and inspection programs.

In addition, FDA is concerned about the trade implications of an inspection agreement. The EU is tying "mutual recognition agreements" (MRAs) to market access, which significantly complicates the negotiation process for FDA.

At the FDA/APHIS-sponsored meeting in late March, Department of Commerce official Charles Ludolph explained the EU concept of the MRA as it applies to various regulated industries.

Under the general MRA concept, Ludolph explained, the EU authorities would officially designate a certified body in the U.S. to carry out conformity assessments to European standards and requirements. In return, the U.S. would "delegate to the Europeans the ability to conduct tests, inspections and perhaps product-certification or product-approval operations," as required by the FDA, the USDA and other U.S. regulatory agencies, on products to be delivered into the U.S.

➤ From the U.S. perspective Ludolph noted, "the talks therefore revolve around trying to define what is 'market access' in the European system, and how to make a full and effective comparison with the U.S. to define what is a balance of market access."

The U.S. also must make sure that it understands how the "evolutionary" EU system provides for the monitoring of manufacturers in the market given "both a European level of enforcement in Brussels and a national level of enforcement in each of the member states," Ludolph stressed. In addition, the U.S. is working on defining the potential scope of agreements in terms of what products and conformity assessment procedures should be addressed, the commerce official said.

The problems involved in applying the European MRA concept specifically to the drug inspection arena were highlighted by FDA Asociate Commissioner for Health Affairs Stuart

Nightingale at a Drug Information Association (DIA) meeting in mid-1994.

In his prepared remarks, Nightingale explained that "the MRA approach has brought the trade-related agencies, in addition to the technical and scientific agencies such as FDA and EPA, deeply into the bilateral negotiation process. FDA feels strongly, however, that the agreements that it negotiates are primarily technical and scientific, dealing with health and safety issues, notwithstanding the fact that they have trade implications." The agency "plans to proceed to negotiate them on that basis," Nightingale said.

➤ The EU sees MRAs as essentially trade agreements providing for mutual ease of market access and a balance of benefit between the parties involved, without necessarily being based on equivalence of systems.

By contrast, Nightingale explained, FDA inspection agreements or "memorandums of understanding" (MOUs) in the past have not provided for market access where preapproval is required, and have been based on equivalence of standards, inspections and enforcement. MOUs have not required that FDA accept the findings of the other government, and "should FDA have the need to visit the plant itself, such a possibility exists," the FDA official noted. MOUs also have been limited to the inspection component and there is no tie to any further agreement to accept data, for example, on other aspects of drug review.

EU WANTS AGREEMENTS TO COVER ALL MEMBER STATES

Further complicating the negotiation process is the EU position that agreements should apply throughout the member states. The problem first appeared for FDA when it informed the European Commission of the agency's desire to continue the various bilateral GLP agreements in place with EC members.

According to Nightingale, "FDA was told that the commission could negotiate with FDA to cover those countries and perhaps others, but that in the future, such agreements could not be negotiated bilaterally with individual EC countries. FDA was also told that the extant GLPs could remain in force while the agreements were

being negotiated." Since that time, the agency has been working with the EU to develop an MOU that would replace the country-level GLP MOUs, Nightingale explained. He noted that "significant progress is being made" toward that end.

➤ In addition, FDA and the EU have recently begun formal negotiations to explore the potential for closer cooperation in the GMP inspection arena. Representatives from the two organizations met in Brussels in early April to explain their respective GMP inspection programs as a first step in the negotiation process.

The meeting included presentations on the FDA and EU GMP regulatory structures as well as on individual EU member state programs. Industry's point of view was presented by the European Federation of Pharmaceutical Industry Manufacturers (EFPIA) and by the Pharmaceutical Research and Manufacturers of America (PhRMA).

Another meeting was held in Washington a week later to explore in more detail the issues involved in working out U.S./EU reciprocal arrangements in the GLP and GMP inspection areas. Attending the latter meeting were representatives of a variety of U.S. agencies, including the State Department, the U.S. Trade Representative (USTR), the Environmental Protection Agency (EPA), the National Institute of Standards and Technology (NIST), the Occupational Safety and Health Administration (OSHA), and the Commerce Department. Canadian representatives also participated at the meeting.

NAFTA, GATT PROD MRA NEGOTIATIONS

Trade agreements, such as NAFTA and GATT, which contain provisions for the removal of "technical barriers to trade," are prodding the U.S. and EU to look closer at the potential for harmonization of the inspection and other components of drug regulation.

The updated GATT treaty, which was ratified by Congress in late 1994, essentially requires the signatories to provide "national treatment" regarding their product-approval conformity-assessment processes. The term "national treatment" means that foreign governments, business or individuals should be treated in the areas covered by GATT as if they were a citizen or "national" concern of the country involved.

GATT allows nations to make an exception to protect health and safety standards. However, if a regulatory authority such as the EU is not able for reasons of health and safety to provide national treatment within their regulations, it is encouraged under GATT to engage in mutual recognition agreements where feasible.

In the drug approval area, the EU regulations do not provide full "national treatment" to non-Europeans regarding aspects of product certification, testing and inspection. Thus, the U.S. and other outside countries have begun to explore MRAs as a means of regaining a competitive footing for their industries.

➤ Also prompting increased attention to the international drug regulatory agreements is the establishment of a central EU agency, the European Medicines Evaluation Agency. The EMEA began operations in London in January 1995.

The centralized EU regulatory agency will have a "coordinator of inspection policy" but will not have inspectors assigned directly to it. In general, the individual EC countries will continue to have responsibility for conducting inspections relevant to drug products manufactured within their borders. The EC statutes call for the exchange of information between member states on inspection reports as well as on marketing authorizations.

Inspection procedures covering product applicants from non-EC countries have yet to be clearly defined. Under current EC policy, the EMEA may request a prelicensing inspection of a foreign manufacturing facility, which would normally be performed by the country designated as the site of import. However, given the limitations in resources and foreign inspection experience among member states, it is unclear how that approach will work in practice.

EU REG PROVIDES FOR BATCH TESTING OF IMPORTS

Of immediate concern to U.S. drug exporters to Europe is an EC regulation that calls for batch testing by a certified body within an EC member

state of drug imports from outside countries that do not have an inspection MRA with the EC.

Under the provision, the foreign manufacturer would bear the responsibility and expense for having the batch testing performed. The provision became effective in January. However, the requirement has not yet been adopted by any of the member states.

➤ Concern about the requirement for batch testing at the EU port of entry was voiced by U.S. industry representatives at the March 31 meeting with FDA on the MRA issue.

In a prepared statement delivered by PhRMA International Division Executive VP Richard Saul, the association maintained that "this obstacle to entry to the European marketplace poses practical and immediate concerns for our members." PhRMA cited, in particular: "a substantial cost burden associated with batch testing within the importing EU member state, especially when sterility must be demonstrated"; and "a risk of testing error, especially for complex products such as biologics." Such errors, PhRMA asserted, "could not only deny import but also precipitate a negative regulatory impact in other markets such as the U.S."

➤ Industry participants at the meeting maintained that the batch-testing requirement is being used by the EC as leverage on the U.S. industry to push forward the MRA negotiations.

"Several months ago when these discussions were in their start-up stage," Saul commented, "we were very forcefully approached by the [European] Commission and pointedly told that we were going to be in some sort of jeopardy if these talks did not move forward."

The concern to the association membership, Saul explained, is that "we find ourselves caught in the middle of two legitimate authorities who are trying to reconcile differences and create more understanding. But unfortunately, we believe that events are not necessarily going to wait until such time as an agreement is reached. In the meantime, this industry, its activities and the flow of products across the ocean are going to be jeopardized."

Commenting on the batch-testing provision, SmithKline Beecham Worldwide Regulatory Compliance Transnational Regulatory Affairs Director Thomas Honohan pointed out that some

EC members "simply are not prepared to do such testing." However, he added, "the U.K. Medicines Control Agency now is considering invoking that rule." According to Honohan, Smith-Kline is making plans for batch testing of new products that will be made in the U.S. and then sold in Europe "just in case" the rule is invoked.

INDUSTRY SUPPORTS FDA HARMONIZATION EFFORTS

In general, industry participants at the meeting expressed support for FDA's efforts to harmonize GMP compliance and drug approval activities with the EU. "At this time of scarce resources," PhRMA said, "the MRA negotiations appear to hold promise of achieving greater economies of scale without sacrificing current standards of quality assurance for all concerned."

PhRMA cautioned, however, that any inspection understanding reached between the U.S. and the EU should be premised on four basic principles: (1) "the need to ensure that the predetermined quality requirements for drug products are met;" (2) "that a common level of qualifications is met by all inspectors, FDA as well as those in the EU;" (3) "that harmonization of CGMP requirements is facilitated;" and (4) "that clear and uniform interpretations as to compliance are provided."

Baxter Healthcare Regulatory Affairs Director Richard Farb pointed out that his company—a drug, device and biologics manufacturer with 87 manufacturing plants around the world including 22 in Europe—has a large stake in the outcome of the harmonization negotiations. As such, "we are intimately involved and strongly endorse the FDA's activities to harmonize international technical requirements," Farb commented.

➤ Baxter agrees with the conclusion in the 1993 report of the FDA Task Force on International Harmonization that working with foreign governments and industry will only enhance the scientific knowledge base in the development of international standards, Farb said.

"Sharing the wealth of scientific knowledge around the world can do nothing but help to develop the best practices or standards or regulations or requirements wherever they apply," he

stated. For manufacturers such as Baxter, "that means that we can manufacture products the best way. We can design and develop in the best way and take advantage of economies of scale." Companies will be able to "get the best information," he added, "if we can facilitate harmonization with postmarketing surveillance and monitor the effects of our products across the globe in a common specific way."

HARMONIZED STANDARDS ARE PRIMARY INDUSTRY GOAL

The Baxter official echoed other industry participants at the meeting in emphasizing that, while "an MRA or MOU could be very important, . . . the greatest benefit of all of this activity is the development of common technical requirements." He urged FDA to make the harmonization of these technical requirements "a first priority" in negotiations with the EU and to continue to support International Conference on Harmonization (ICH) and International Standards Organization (ISO) activities.

➤ Farb suggested that FDA should consider closely the successful pattern of ISO negotiations in the medical device arena in pursuing harmonization of GMP enforcement for drugs.

The Baxter official noted that FDA's ISO Technical Committee and the "Global Harmonization Task Force" formed by the EU have been "extremely active" in the device area. "It might be a benefit to move toward harmonization of GMP requirements with the ISO 9000 model in other areas as well," he offered.

Farb reported that the Global Harmonization Task Force, with FDAs participation, is working on another ISO standard—ISO 10,013 —which provides procedures for notified bodies to use in conducting inspections. It is similar to the compliance program guidance manual that FDA uses to conduct inspections, he noted.

➤ A modification of the standard is being developed by a study group of the task force to apply specifically to medical devices. The aim is to develop harmonized guidelines for conducting medical device inspections throughout the world, Farb said.

To further this effort, the task force, which includes FDA representatives, was invited by Baxter to participate in an inspection of the firm's plant in Malta. The inspection was conducted by the German notified inspection body TUV to audit compliance with the EU medical device directives. The goal in including participation by the task force, Farb explained, was to expand its understanding of actual inspection processes and how they compare between regulatory authorities.

CONSISTENT INSPECTION POLICIES ENCOURAGED

The ultimate objective of the task force effort is to standardize the inspection process and reduce the number of inspections that are needed. Instead of winding up in a situation where there are multiple inspectors coming through a plant at one time, each with different approaches, "what we hope will happen," Farb says, "is that when FDA does an inspection, or TUV, or the Australians, or the Canadians, or Japan, that the other countries around the world will recognize those inspections."

➤ Addressing the prospect of FDA/EU harmonization in the drug-inspection arena, Merck Biolicensing Senior Director David Wonnacott said industry would "encourage a consistent inspection policy" as well as "reasonable and uniform interpretations of such policies by inspectors in the EU and the FDA."

Wonnacott stressed industry's need for an "open system" of GMP inspection policy and "clear guidance and open communication regarding these inspections." However, he cautioned, "that is a challenge. Even within the U.S. from district to district and inspector to inspector, having equivalence is a challenge. It takes time, effort and work."

FDA and industry officials agree that the type of painstaking negotiations that are necessary to develop closer U.S./EU accords in the drug GMP inspection area are likely to move slowly without an on-going formal structure supporting the process.

SmithKline's Honohan emphasized the point that "there needs to be an on-going process and

organization to deal with the evolution of . . . a mutual recognition agreement."

The existence of a forum to facilitate negotiations in the preclinical area, such as the Organization for Economic Cooperation and Development, has resulted in the development of "very good systems" for mutual recognition of GLPs, Honohan noted. However, in the drug GMP area, he said, "from what I can see here, we have no structure in effect looking into the future for supporting deliberations in a formal way between the FDA and EU." He pointed out that "the ICH has a defined life and it comes to an end."

➤ The recent turnover in field management and the departure of experienced agency veterans is another problem for the agency in addressing the challenges involved in international drug-inspection negotiations.

The European insistence that agreements need to apply throughout all member states is a particular sticking point in the negotiation process due to FDA's concern with the unevenness in the member-state programs—a concern reportedly shared by some of the EU members in implementing the system internally.

FDA REVIEWING DRUG INSPECTION MOUs

Highlighting these equivalency concerns is the FDA decision to reevaluate the drug inspection MOUs that have been in place with Canada, Sweden and Switzerland.

Under the MOUs, FDA has accepted the results of drug inspections conducted by the regulatory authorities of the three countries. However, in late 1992, the agency made the decision to review the agreements to make sure that the evolving standards for preapproval inspections and on-going GMP compliance were being strictly enforced. FDA officials were concerned, in particular, with the handling of the agreement by Switzerland, which has shown reluctance to facilitate the kind of inspection auditing process that FDA views as central to an MOU approach.

Richard Klug, who directs FDA's international inspections program, explained at a March meeting of the International Society of Pharmaceutical Engineers that the agency is currently not accepting inspection results from Sweden, Canada and Switzerland unless FDA investigators have participated jointly in the inspection process "and can determine that the inspection was conducted properly and that our requirements and specifications are being enforced."

The agency, he said, hopes to have completed the review "within this year or early next year." The objective is to "renew the MOUs, at least with those countries that can comply, and work with the others if they don't so that [FDA] can make use of the inspections by the foreign country's regulatory authority." Klug stressed that the agency "wants to attain equality in the coverage and felt this was the only way that could be done."

FDA STRENGTHENS FOREIGN PROGRAM

The reevaluation of the MOUs is one component of a larger FDA effort to beef-up its foreign product surveillance program ("The Gold Sheet" September 1993).

Over the past few years, the agency has been expanding its resource commitment to the foreign inspection program. That build-up reflects, in part, pressure eoming from Congress and industry to create a more level playing field for GMP enforcement. FDA's greater attention to overseas inspections also reflects the increased number of foreign manufacturers marketing in the U.S. and the strengthening of the agency's preapproval inspection operations, particularly in the bulk manufacturing area.

➤ In fiscal year 1993, FDA performed about 200 foreign drug inspections, including those related to bioresearch monitoring. Approximately 300 were performed in FY 1994, with an even larger jump slated for the current year. About 570 drug-related inspections are targeted for FY 1995. The current number includes more follow-up inspections for problem firms and more frequent routine visits.

Since 1992, the number of "full-time equivalent" or "person years" allocated to FDA foreign inspection work overall has risen from 8.1 in FY 1992 to 36 for FY 1995. During this time frame, foreign travel funding has increased proportionally from $450,000 to $2.48 mil. These figures, Klug explained at ISPE, are indicative of "the commitment the agency has made to have a more equal playing field between domestic and foreign inspections."

The agency has expanded the time planned for foreign inspections from 40 to 60 hours. Klug emphasized that this time module is only an average guideline and that investigators are advised to "spend whatever time is necessary to do a proper inspection." He noted that three FDA investigators recently spent 3-1/2 weeks to complete an inspection at one firm in the U.K.

FDA also has increased its use of investigator teams that include a laboratory analyst to perform foreign audits. Klug noted that "approximately 40% of our foreign inspections now require an investigator/analyst team."

As in domestic inspections, FDA has increased its focus on practices in foreign QC laboratories. The team approach. Klug explained, "has added a lot of cost to our foreign inspection program. But we are finding that it has really been good in terms of the results that we have found. The problems that were present in many of the foreign labs . . . are getting . . . corrected," he noted.

FDA WANTS TO REVIEW KEY DOCUMENTS IN U.S.

FDA has been asking foreign NDA/ANDA applicants and companies listed in applications to submit document packages for FDA field review prior to the preapproval inspection. This practice improves the efficiency of the inspection process, allowing the agency to "be more direct," Klug said. "If we see there are problems, we can ask for explanations, and then, based on . . . the document package, we can direct our attention to those areas that we still have questions about."

The presubmission of a document package also serves to confirm that the firm is actually ready for the inspection. Prior to asking for this preinspection document package, Klug explained, "we had found that, in many cases, firms were anxious for us to make the inspection, but when we got there they were not nearly ready." As a result, "we were wasting our time as well as theirs and, of course, the application was not approved."

➤ At a May 23 meeting of FDA's Central Atlantic States Association (CASA), Mid-Atlantic Region Technical Operations Group Manager Paul D'Eramo noted that the preinspection document review program is not working as smoothly as the agency would like due to the number of documents requested and the difficulty in getting them collected in time for the review.

However, the agency "is going to continue to work on that, because . . ., for efficiency reasons, we are going to have to do more of the work domestically before we go to do the foreign inspections," D'Eramo noted. FDA will be making the effort to have investigators visit the domestic application filing sites, or, in the case of generic products, agents or brokers, to review as many of the requested documents as possible, he explained.

FDA is paying closer attention to uncovering potential application discrepancies or fraud and will be "aggressive" in implementing the fraud integrity policy against foreign firms if problems are uncovered, Klug said. "We thought we had a few cases of that in the last year or two, but further investigation, in cooperation with the foreign regulatory authorities, did not show that to be true. However, we are looking at that," he said.

Other facets of FDA's effort to strengthen foreign surveillance are outlined in a late-1993 report prepared by former Mid-Atlantic Region Director Davis, entitled "Recommendations to Strengthen Surveillance and Enforcement Operations Associated with the Importation of Human Drugs." Cited in the report are specific measures for improving the documentation and/or scrutiny of ■ ■ inspections performed abroad ■ ■ foreign facilities ■ ■ U.S. trade representatives ■ ■ foreign drug master files ■ ■ foreign import samples ■ ■ and the existing inspection MOUs.

➤ Davis also recommended that FDA set up a certification system for FDA investigators to formally recognize their expertise in particular inspection areas.

The investigator certification concept is being explored by the agency as a means of tightening its training regimen for investigators and helping to ensure better consistency in the inspection process. It represents a response by FDA to the ISO-type certification systems being pursued in Europe.

Division of Human Resource Development Director Gary German is heading up the agency effort to develop a certification program. He indicated at the University of Georgia GMP conference in March that the agency is targeting a program in the medical device area as a first priority, with the intention of following up with programs for drugs, biologics and foods.

CERTIFICATION WOULD INCLUDE TRAINING, PERFORMANCE AUDITS

The certification program would operate as an add-on to FDA's standard six-month orientation regimen for investigators. The approach under consideration, German explained, would entail examinations to determine where the individual needs "to spend more time in obtaining training and experiences" as a first stage of the certification program.

Following additional technical training, the investigators would be subject to "performance audits." For example, German said, three inspections might be required "under the watchful eye of a performance auditor to assure that each inspection is done consistently" with other investigators in the agency. The final step would involve a certification exam. German indicated that the agency hopes to begin the quality auditing component of the program in the device area by the end of 1995.

Congressional concern with the equivalency of FDA's foreign and domestic drug inspection programs has continued despite the change in committee leadership following the November 1994 election.

Rep. Joe Barton (R-Tex.), who replaced John Dingell (D-Mich.) as chairman of the House Commerce/ Oversight Subcommittee, sent a letter to FDA Commissioner David Kessler on May 4 requesting information on FDA inspections of foreign drug plants to check on the equivalency issue.

Expressing concern that "inspections of foreign pharmaceutical plants may be significantly less thorough than those conducted at U.S. plants," Barton pointed out that "all the best research and well-designed clinical trials will not assure the effectiveness of the ultimate product if the manufacturing process does not meet reasonable current good manufacturing standards."

➤ The letter specifically requests that FDA provide "all unexpurgated written documents about foreign inspections" from the offices of Deputy Commissioner Mary Pendergast, Special Assistant for Investigations Jack Mitchell and Klug's international programs office. Barton also asked for "unex-purgated copies" of Davis' late 1993 and early 1994 memoranda on foreign inspections.

The Barton letter follows a similar request to FDA in August 1994 from then-committee chairman Dingell. Dingell had requested that FDA provide information about international agreements, documents pertaining to the foreign inspection program, the number of drug inspections in each EU country, the breakdown of inspections for bulk drugs and solid oral dosage form drugs, and a list of firms found violative and the resulting enforcement action.

WARNING LETTER USE EXPANDED TO FOREIGN FIRMS

In line with Davis' recomendations, one of the steps that the agency has taken to step up its enforcement efforts abroad is to begin to issue GMP warning letters to foreign firms ("The Gold Sheet" April 1995). FDA instituted the policy on October l, 1995. Since then, at least a dozen warning letters have been issued, mainly addressing bulk manufacturing concerns.

In the case of preapproval inspections, the foreign letters may include an indication that one of three enforcement measures is being taken: a withholding of the application involved; a withholding notification plus a threat of automatic product detentions; and a withhold with automatic detention.

Addressing the new policy at an NAPM meeting in mid-March, FDA compliance office staffer Maura Slattery said that the result, as intended, has been that FDA is "getting corrections much quicker and more complete." Sending the warning letters abroad ties in with FDA's "whole idea behind punitive actions," which is "to get voluntary corrections from the firm [and] . . . to indicate to the industry what types of things we are looking for and have people do it on their own," she said.

➤ Indicative of the reevaluation process to which the drug GMP inspection MOUs are being subjected by FDA are two warning letters received by Swiss-based firms. The warning letters were based on inspections performed jointly by FDA and Swiss inves-tigators in accord with the agency's MOU review program.

Ciba-Geigy received a warning letter in March based on an October 1994 joint inspection of the firm's facilities in Schweizerhalle and Stein, Switz. In February, Sandoz Pharma was issued a warning letter citing findings during inspections in June and November 1994 at the firm's plant in Basel, Switz. Both letters refer to both bulk and finished dosage form operations.

LAB PRACTICES IN FOCUS ABROAD

The two warning letters provide evidence of the FDA focus on laboratory practices. In Ciba-Geigy's case, the letter referenced the finding that the firm's dissolution testing equipment was not being calibrated using USP standard tablets. At Sandoz, FDA cited the failure of the firm to validate its lab computer systems.

➤ Other problem areas cited in common on the two letters involved procedures for blend validation and cleaning/cross-contamination controls.

Underscoring the increased attention FDA is giving to inspection follow-up at foreign facilities, the agency maintained that Sandoz' responses to FD-483 reports lacked "sufficient detail, explanations, or documentation to adequately address all of the deviations noted." FDA said "overall," it was "encouraged" by Sandoz' responses "in that many promises for corrections have been made." However, the agency stated, "we cannot conclude that adequate correction actions have been implemented until detailed information is provided for our review here in the Center for Drug Evaluation and Research [CDER], or reviewed by one of our investigators during a reinspection."

In Ciba-Geigy's case, FDA voiced a problem with the fact that "most of the text" in the firm's response was in German, which the agency was "not able to review." The letter notes that "investigators can review documents which are not in English during inspections because they have personnel from the firm available to translate as needed, but that is not possible" when CDER's compliance office is reviewing a written response. In the future, FDA advised, responses with all attachments should be translated into

English or else an English summary of the documents should be provided.

Warning letters also have been sent by FDA to EU-based firms since the new policy was initiated in October 1994. Berlin, Germany-based Schering AG and at least three Italian bulk manufacturers—Farmabios, Cosma, and Recordati—have been recipients.

TWO-THIRDS OF FOREIGN INSPECTIONS ARE IN EUROPE

Data for FY 1995 compiled by FDA's international programs staff through mid-May indicates that almost two-thirds (61%) of foreign drug inspections are being conducted in Europe. Inspections in the Far East comprised 22% of those conducted for the year, while 8% were conducted in Canada. Inspections in other countries made up 9% of the total.

➤ About 70% of the inspections performed abroad during this time frame were on bulk facilities and 30% on finished dosage form plants.

The inspections when classified by degree of seriousness of the findings showed a proportional breakdown: 68% of the total number of inspections given FDA's "official action indicated" (OAI) designation—meaning that follow-up enforcement action is warranted—were for bulk drugs compared to 32% for finished drugs. Bulk drug inspections comprised 66% of those classified as "voluntary action indicated" (VAI) vs. 34% for dosage forms.

About one in four (40 of 165) of the inspections evaluated for FY 1995 went rated OAI and about two thirds (103) were rated VAI. "No action" was indicated for 13% (22). About 88% of the foreign inspections conducted were preapproval audits. Among these, 45% involved NDAs and 41% ANDAs. Of the remainder, 9% covered veterinary drugs, 4% antibiotics and 1% generic veterinary products.

At the May 23 CASA meeting, Mid-Atlantic Region Assistant Director Joseph Phillips noted that the agency is beginning to break out the data on preapproval inspections performed abroad, including the reasons for turndowns, so that comparisons can be made with the domestic program. He expects the effort to produce results by the end of 1995.

The ICH system has proved very productive for the development of harmonized quality standards related to application filings. However, U.S. participants in the process are not confident that it offers an appropriate mechanism for harmonizing international GMP standards and inspection programs.

At a meeting in Washington at the end of March, ICH moved its guideline on "Impurities in New Drug Substances" into a Step 4 or "harmonized" status, meaning that a final draft was endorsed by the steering committee and returned to the three regions for promulgation. The impurities guideline is the third in the quality area to be finalized. Guidelines on "Validation of Analytical Methods" and on "Stability Testing of New Drug Substances and Products" also have been cleared ("The Gold Sheet" October 1994).

Moving forward for consultation by the regulatory bodies and public comment in the three regions (Step 2 status) at the March meeting were the ICH guidelines on genetic stability and general stability requirements for biotech products.

ICH also recently finalized a guideline covering good clinical practice (GCP) standards. However, the subject matter is related mainly to new drugs and is not enmeshed in the regulatory complexities involved with GMPs.

At the FDA public meeting on MRAs, Baxter official Farb voiced concern that international standards setting activities in the GMP area "should be open to public scrutiny and provide the opportunity for consideration of views by all parties concerned." While "the ICH activities are working very well," Farb said, Baxter is not a member of PhRMA and as a result, "we don't get to participate at the same level."

PDA director Fry concurred on the need for "maintaining a very open system in arriving at . . the end product" relating to inspection/GMP harmonization. Noting that ICH "has been pointed out as probably not the right forum to focus on harmonization of these technical requirements," Fry asserted that "some more open and more public method that allows input from all parties is called for."

➤ Nightingale commented at a May 23 meeting of the Food and Drug Law Institute that both industry and FDA see ICH as a resource-intensive process and are carefully evaluating its utility for harmonization in other areas such as GMP.

ICH "has changed the way the regulators deal with one another because of the very close working relationships that have developed . . . during this process," Nightingale noted. As a result, he said, "a lot more could be accomplished government to government even outside the ICH process *per se*. How much of this will be put back into the ICH process versus the government to government work . . . remains to be seen" He added that the issue "will be the subject of intense discussions" at the July steering committee meeting in Brussels and at the "ICH 3" conference in Japan in November.

A GOOK LOOK AT THE GOOD MANUFACTURING PRACTICES*

The phrase "good manufacturing practices" is more than just a generic way of saying "effective ways to carry out production." The Good Manufacturing Practices (GMPs) are actually regulations developed by the U.S. Food and Drug Administration in the 1970s for companies that manufacture medical devices, pharmaceuticals, and/or biological products.

With more and more companies in the United States becoming interested in achieving ISO 9000 registration, implementation of the GMPs is becoming more commonplace, as they go hand in hand with the ISO 9000 standards.

"The GMPs have covered most of what is required by ISO 9000 for quite a while," notes Richard Farb, director, Corporate Regulatory Affairs for Baxter Healthcare Corporation (Deerfield, IL). To date, Baxter has had 48 of its facilities worldwide registered to ISO 9000. "Since our industry isn't seeing any significant incremental requirements by seeking ISO 9000 registration, we're finding that we don't have to make many changes to achieve registration for our facilities," he notes.

Three GMPs

Farb explains that there are three GMPs:

PHARMACEUTICAL GMP

This GMP has 11 subparts, which are designed to ensure comprehensive quality processing.

Each subpart has between two and nine components that go into detail on each topic. The subparts are:

A. *General Provisions*
B. *Organization and Personnel*
C. *Buildings and Facilities*
D. *Equipment*
E. *Control of Components and Drug Product Containers and Closures*
F. *Production and Process Controls*
G. *Packaging and Labeling Control*
H. *Holding and Distribution*
I. *Laboratory Controls*
J. *Records and Reports*
K. *Returned and Salvaged Drug Products*

MEDICAL DEVICES GMP

"'This is the one that most closely reflects ISO 9000 guidelines," notes Farb. "This GMP is currently undergoing revision by the FDA." Among other things, the Medical Devices GMP requires the following:

- *A product master file* (a set of documents that defines how products are to be made)
- *Device history records* (records of the tests, control charts, etc., that were created during the production of the devices)
- *Statistical reviews*

---

* Copyrighted material. Reprinted with permission from Bureau of Business Practice, 24 Rope Ferry Road, Waterford, CT, 06386.

BIOLOGICAL GMP

This is a "custom fit" GMP, "usually a hybrid model between the pharmaceutical and medical devices GMP," Farb explains. "The elements of each are uniquely tailored to the specific biological."

The latest development related to GMPs is an initiative by health care companies worldwide to adopt uniform standards—"harmonizing" the GMPs from the various countries into a single, generally recognized set of GMPs. "Currently, most nations' GMPs are similar," Farb points out. "They merely need a little more commonality." This harmonization maybe achieved as part of a new ISO standard, ISO 46000, which will use ISO 9000 as its basis.

➤ If you'd like copies of the Good Manufacturing Practices, you can write to the Food and Drug Administration (FDA), Rockville, MD, 20857.

2.5
SMALL BUSINESS

DRAFT GUIDANCE FOR SMALL BUSINESS UNVEILED*

Responding to criticism that the ISO 9000 series requirements place an unfair burden on small companies, an international working group has drafted a proposed handbook to ease the implementation woes of such firms.

The working group, part of International Organization for Standardization Technical Committee 176, charged with maintaining the ISO 9000 family of standards, plans to publish the document next year.

The document, *Quality Systems Explained: A Guide to the Interpretation and Application of the ISO 9000 Standards for Small Business,* explains the purpose and benefits of quality system registration, and contains guidelines for selecting a consultant along with a detailed description of ISO 9000 requirements.

"If you are considering certification, your first step is to hold discussions with the certifying bodies to find out what is offered, what are the likely costs, the period for which the certification will apply and how often intermediate audits are carried out," the document states.

According to the handbook, companies should strive to have a system in place and running a few months prior to registration.

"This can save a lot of time and money. Certification bodies do not operate on the principle of what is going to happen," the handbook states. "They want to see what has happened. A few months of records demonstrating the operation of your quality system will be worth more than all the promises."

Along with one of the guidance standards, use of the document is intended to be a sufficient basis for installing a quality system.

The document also notes that companies have the option of implementing ISO 9000 requirements gradually rather than seeking third-party registration.

"Because most businesses will not have the financial or personnel resources to put all aspects of a quality system in place at the same time, a progressive approach is often used," according to the handbook.

2.6
SOFTWARE

MAXIMIZING QUALITY AND PRODUCTIVITY WITH AN OBJECT-ORIENTED ENVIRONMENT: METRICS*
by George Kershaw

Metrics should be defined before development begins. The criteria for measuring the goal accomplishment should be in the project plan. The staff should thoroughly understand these criteria, and how achievement will be measured.

The attributes of good software are identified. The importance of defining product goals and metrics are emphasized. This is followed by definition of the attributes of good software. These are: explicit structure, loose coupling, encapsulation, traceable and understandable.

The problems of getting useful metrics are quickly reviewed. The attributes of a good metric are identified. These are: measures conformance to product goals, is repeatable, used to evaluate staff. The types of metrics are identified—quantifiable, qualitative and pass/fail. Examples of ways to measure goal achievement are included.

> *An important step is to measure what a system does, then design improvements to make the system yield the best results.*
> —W. E. Deming

Metrics are assessed at all stages of product development. Metrics begin with the top-level specifications for a product and carry over to the lower level specifications.

An assessment of these on the specifications at one stage will carry over to later stages, and to the completed product. The magnitude of the carryover to the completed product corresponds to the level of specification at which assessment is made. For example, a specification that is not understandable at the top level will result in a far less understandable product than would result from a single, not understandable, low-level specification.

The problem is estimating the impact of these assessments. The assessments are qualitative—there are no "equations" to plug them in to.

Until better ways to assign values to metrics are found, judgment will be the driving factor in assessing metrics and estimating the impact.

WHAT IS A GOOD METRIC?

A good metric is useful, and predicts one or more attributes of the product under development. A good metric measures an important attribute of a product, and can be predicted by assessing product specifications as they develop. A good metric is used to evaluate staff performance.

A Good Metric Measures Conformance of a Product or its Development to a Product Goal

A quality product does the job and is manageable and testable. A quality product is delivered on time, and within budget.

Metrics are important contributors to success if the right metrics are used. The right metrics measure conformance to goals as the product moves through the devopment stages. For example:

Is the specified product the right product? Will it do the right job?

Are the operations specifications validated and testable?

* Reprinted with permission from *Society for Software Quality Journal*, August 1995. George Kershaw has an outstanding track record in the engineering and delivery of software products ranging from operating systems to major online applications.

Is the product correctly defined? Is it divided into manageable components?

Are component specifications verified and testable? Do the specifications conform to higher level specifications? Are specifications complete, consistent, and unambiguous? Can the product be tested?

Is the project ahead or behind schedule and budget?

Are resources required to complete development more or less than budgeted?

A Good Metric Is Repeatable—The Measure Assigned Is Objective. Two Independent Reviewers will Assign the Same Value

However, computer science is a soft science. Soft sciences envy the ability of hard sciences to quantify measures in a repeatable way—that is, different people would arrive at the same measurement values. Soft sciences have to make do with qualitative measures. This complicates the problem of assigning values to the metrics. They can't be plugged into "equations."

But important metrics are qualitative at best. Until better ways to assign values to metrics are found, judgment will be the driving factor in assessing metrics and estimating the impact.

TYPES OF METRICS

Quantifiable Metrics Quantifiable metrics have yard sticks that allow fine grain assessment of the subject being measured.

Further, this assessment is repeatable— i.e., two people making independent assessments will arrive at the same, or substantially the same value. Unfortunately, none of the important product goals can be quantified.

Qualitative Metrics Because measures should be repeatable, the qualitative measures of software engineering don't lend themselves to fine grained assessment (see Exhibit 1 and Exhibit 2).

The factors may be assessed at discrete levels or they may exist over a range. Ratings for factors with discrete levels are arrayed in a table with a metric value assigned for various values of the factors.

EXHIBIT 1.—EXAMPLE OF A QUALITATIVE METRIC—ASSESSING ENCAPSULATION LEVEL OF A PROCESS SCHEMA[1]

Encapsulation Level	Condition
Fully Encapsulated	All local data
Very Good	Shared data is minimized and is shared only with child processes of same parent.
Good	Shared data is minimized and is shared predominantly with child processes of same parent.
Fair	Shared data is minimized and is shared only with child processes of same grandparent.
Poor	Shared data is minimized and is shared predominantly with child processes of same grandparent.
Avoid	Shared data is minimized but is predominantly global.
Not Encapsulated	Mostly shared data that is global.

[1] A *schema* is the database of a process—the data manipulated by a process to produce the output interface data from its input interface data. A schema that is all local data is *fully encapsulated* with the process. One that is all shared data is *not encapsulated*. Mixtures of local and shared data are *partially encapsulated*.

EXHIBIT 2.—EXAMPLE OF A COMPOUND METRIC— ASSESSING ENCAPSULATION LEVEL OF A PROCESS

Encapsulation Level	Interfaces	Schema Encapsulation
Fully Encapsulated*	All External	Fully Encapsulated
Very Good	All External	Very Good
Good	All External	Good
Good	Mixed	Very Good or better
Fair	Mixed	Good or better
Fair	All Internal	Very Good or better
Poor	All Internal	Good or less
Not Encapsulated	All Internal	Not Encapsulated

There are two dimensions to process encapsulation—types of interfaces and schema encapsulation.
* A fully encapsulated process is a software object.

Pass/Fail Metrics A list of shortfalls is generated during the assessment. All shortfalls must be resolved before the reviewed item is considered complete.

Product management resolves differences between design and product assessment. Product management decides if work proceeds while shortfalls are resolved. Review of the lists of shortfalls produces a basis for assessment of staff performance.

THE PROJECT PLAN SHOULD INCLUDE THE CRITERIA FOR MEASURING GOAL ATTAINMENT

Product development goals should be defined before development begins. The criteria for measuring the goal accomplishment should be in the project plan. The staff should thoroughly understand these criteria, and how achievement will be measured. Each organization has to define metrics according to the goals for the organization and its products.

Staff training and other guidance are necessary to achieve repeatability. Management should test repeatability by having phase review materials assessed by other independent groups until a comfortable level of repeatability is achieved—e.g.; until different groups come up with the same short lists. Thereafter, repeat ability should be spot-checked by the quality-assurance function.

METRICS SHOULD BE USED TO EVALUATE STAFF

What you count, counts! The staff will adjust their behavior to attain high scores in the measures used.

- If they think lines of code are an important measure, they will produce lots of code.
- If they think thickness of specifications is important, they will produce lots of pages.
- If they know that performance evaluations are based on producing loosely-coupled, coherent processes, they will produce loosely-coupled, coherent processes.

The selection of measures strongly impacts project success. The important measures must be used no matter how difficult they are to get. Management has to avoid use of measures whose major attribute is that they are relatively easy to obtain.

EVOLVE METRICS

Getting metrics that the staff understands and that measure the important goals is an evolutionary process that has to be worked at. The staff has to be trained in the important goals and to work as teams in assessing metrics until there is consistency in the rating assigned.

Time should be made available during reviews to allow training and discussion of metrics. These should be used as a forum to evolve metrics until the organization is satisfied that the metrics satisfactorily measure goal achievement and the staff achieves consistency in the assignment of ratings. It is best to begin all metrics as Pass/Fail metrics adding ratings as they evolve.

SEARCHING FOR METRICS

Although the search for software metrics has continued since the early sixties, there aren't any satisfactory software metrics that quantify important aspects of software development.

Most work has been aimed at things that can be measured instead of ways to measure the important things.

Early work focused on the module level. Current work regards design metrics to be more important with coupling emerging as the most important consideration. But module level metrics continue to be worthwhile.

The criticism is that you don't measure until development has reached the coded module stage. But: better late than even later. Half of the development cycle—the test phase—and all of the maintenance cycle follow the coded module stage.

It's better to pause, simplify problem interfaces, and recode problem modules than to proceed with the integration of known problem modules and interfaces.

Of course, it's better to discover problems earlier. Thus the emphasis should be placed on design metrics which help improve the product design as it proceeds down the design levels.

ADD CHANGEABLE TO PRODUCT GOALS

Maintainability facilitates fault location and locates where changes need to be made to adapt a product to changing needs.

Half of the cost of a product occurs during the operations and maintenance phase of the product life cycle. Maintainability increases productivity and quality by facilitating error correction and by increasing the useful life span of a product.

Changeability is an extension of maintainability into development. The need to change during development will emerge as better design approaches become apparent. The need to change will continue as user's needs change during development as well as maintenance.

Whatever you do, it will eventually have to be changed. It will have to be changed because better design choices will become apparent or requirements will change. It will have to be changed to fix errors, to modify functionality or adapt to changes in the hardware/software environment during maintenance.

Design divides the problem into components, and the data which flows among them. Using changeability as a guide to design choice is an essential contributor to productivity and quality in software production and in product maintenance.

WHAT IS GOOD SOFTWARE?

The following software attributes are essential to meeting product-development goals:

- Explicit Structure
- Loose Coupling
- Encapsulation
- Traceable
- Understandable

The attributes are not independent—understandable products are more testable, etc. They are, however, important ways to view a product (see Exhibit 3).

These attributes apply to all product levels—to major components, to intermediate components and to modules. These attributes contribute to the manageable, testable and changeable goals as below. These attributes ap-

ply to all product levels—to major components, to intermediate components and to modules.

EXPLICIT STRUCTURE

Integral Structure

Integral structure is hierarchic from the processes at the top levels to modules at the lowest levels (see Exhibit 4.). Processes in an integral structure communicate through internal interfaces—interfaces that may be explicitly defined but are often implicitly defined. Implicitly defined interfaces are a major source of errors.

The data structure is usually a single-product schema in which all processes are embedded. All processes have direct access to all data. Two or more processes usually manipulate the same data.

Changes to data or the structure of data can ripple through the product and cause several processes to be changed. Errors can also ripple through the product because data is often manipulated by two or more processes. Making functional changes and adding new capability can also ripple through the product.

Conventional, top-down design approaches generate integral structure often with implicitly defined interfaces. Layered design improves integral structures by requiring explicitly defined interfaces.

No approach is totally integral. All structures will be discrete to the extent of calling the operating system, the DBMS and common routines.

Discrete Structure

Discrete structure avoids tightly integrated, hierarchic products. A discrete structure consists only of objects. Objects are abstract data

EXHIBIT 3.—SOFTWARE ATTRIBUTES ESSENTIAL
TO DEVELOPMENT GOALS

Attribute	Manageable	Testable	Changeable
Explicit Structure		X	X
Loose Coupling	X		X
Encapsulation	X	X	X
Traceable		X	X
Understandable	X	X	X

EXHIBIT 4.—INTEGRAL STRUCTURE

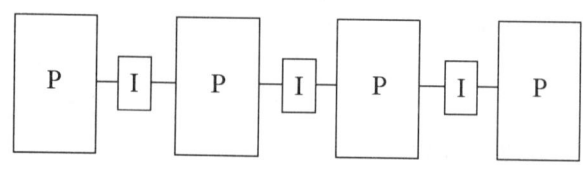

Internal interfaces generate integral structure

types (ADTs) on conventional platforms. Objects decentralize the product and avoid hierarchy (see Exhibit 5).

Components in a discrete structure are not directly coupled. Components communicate with each other only by external interfaces.

The bulk of the data structure is decentralized into component schemas. Changes to data or the schema of one component do not affect other components. Only the external interfaces remain in the product schema.

A component cannot manipulate the schema of another component. A component can manipulate only its own schema and the product schema. The product schema consists only of the message formats for calls to, and returns from, the external interfaces of other components. Locating and fixing errors, making changes and adding new capability are facilitated by discrete structure.

Other product processes are shielded from adverse effects of changes and new processes while the new processes are new and more fault prone.

Making product structure discrete provides resilience by lowering the risk of the effects of an error or change rippling through or crashing the product.

Comparing Integral and Discrete Structures

Integral and discrete structures are compared (see Exhibit 6).

EXHIBIT 6.—COMPARING INTEGRAL AND DISCRETE STRUCTURES

Feature	Integral	Discrete
Manageable	Maybe	Yes
Testable	Maybe	Usually
Encapsulation	No	Yes
Communication	Coupled	Messages
Process Schema	Usually Shared	Usually Local
Process Interfaces	Internal	External
Interface Definition	Usually Explicit	Usually Explicit
Effect of Errors and Changes	Diffused	Contained
Locating What to Fix or Change	Diffused	Contained
Resilience	Vulnerable	Stable
Reusable Components	No	Yes
Can Reuse Components	Yes	Yes

LOOSE COUPLING

Interfaces should be loosely coupled. Loose coupling reduces interaction between components, and reduces processing complexity. The components of a product should have loosely coupled interfaces (see Exhibit 7).

Similarly the components and their constituent processes should be broken into child processes that have loosely coupled interfaces. Operations that jump back and forth between

EXHIBIT 5.—DISCRETE STRUCTURE

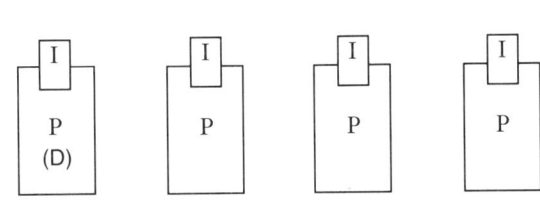

External interfaces generate discrete structure.
One process is a driver (D) that sequences the other processes to perform the layer functions

EXHIBIT 7.—DESIGN SHOULD MINIMIZE COUPLING BETWEEN PROCESSES

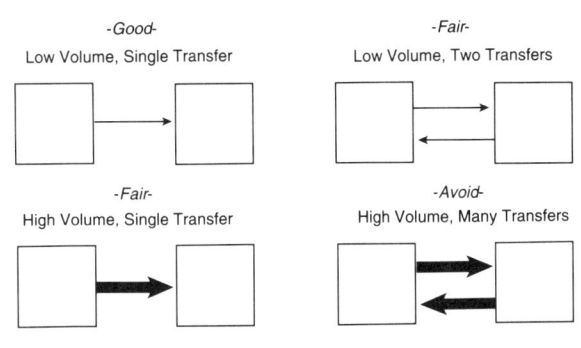

components generate tight coupling. Tightly coupled components are difficult to understand, to test and to change.

Loose coupling satisfies three objectives:

- Break work into packages that can be managed.
- Produce understandable work packages.
- Produce testable work packages.

Rating the Coupling of an Interface

The factors used here are Data Types, Data Volume and Data Flow.

Data Types refers to the number of different data elements flowing between the processes. Transfer of a table with several instances of three different data elements would be regarded as having three data types.

Data Volume refers to number of instances of the data types transferred. If the number differs among data types, the largest number is used.

Data Flow refers to the direction of data flow, the number of separate transfers and the protocol necessary to conduct a transfer.

Ratings for Data Types and Instances are selected according to the proximity of the interface value to the midpoints of the ranges for each

rating. The ranges overlap to avoid borderline disputes. The rating is selected which has its midpoint closest to the interface value (see Exhibit 8).

The Data Flow rating is selected according to which values of the three factors correspond most closely to the interface values.

Rating Interface Specifications

Interface specifications define coupling between processes. It's easier to rate the coupling between two components than the interface specification for each coupling. A complete, understandable interface specification is as important as looseness of coupling (see Exhibit 9).

Interface specifications are completely defined if:

- They identify all data in the interface.
- They define the protocol for transferring the data.
- The data is completely defined.

Inspection can rate the coupling between processes, but only judgment can assess understandability of the specifications. That is why testability review is important to assessing understandability.

EXHIBIT 8.—RATING THE COUPLING OF AN INTERFACE

Ratings For Data Types		Ratings For Instances	
Rating	**Number Of Types**	**Rating**	**Number Of Types**
Excellent	0-3	Excellent	0-5
Good	1-6	Good	1-10
Fair	3-9	Good	5-15
Poor	> 6	Poor	> 10

Ratings For Data Flow			
Rating	**Direction**	**Transfers**	**Protocol**
Excellent*	—	—	None
Good	One Way	One	Simple
Fair	One Way	Multiple	Simple
Poor	Two Way	Multiple	Simple
Awful	—	—	Complex

* An example of this is the calling of an external interface. There is no direct communication between the calling and the called process. This is usually a two-way interface with two transfers.

A second example would be where one process places the interface in data shared with another process and transfers control with no communication with the other process. This can only be a one way interface with one transfer.

EXHIBIT 9.—THREE INTERFACE EXAMPLES—I1, I2, I3

Factor	I1	Rating	I2	Rating	I3	Rating
Data Types	2	Excellent	5	Fair	7	Fair
Instances	7	Good	2	Excellent	22	Poor
Data Flow		Excellent		Poor		Awful
Direction		One Way		Two Way		Two Way
Transfers		One		Multiple		Two
Protocol		None		Simple		Complex

It's easier to rate the coupling between two processes than to assess the understandability of the interface specification for each coupling.

It's straightforward enough to check if the data entities have been identified, if their specifications exist, and if protocol for data transfer exists.

But are the data specifications and protocol understandable? Do people on both sides of an interface understand it the same way?

This is a further reason why coupling is important. The less the coupling, the less there is to be mutually understood on each side of an interface, and the less has to be understood by testers and maintainers.

A repository eases access by inspectors, and by those assigned to judge understandability.

ENCAPSULATION

Encapsulation divides a product into discrete parts that are easier to understand, easier to replace and easier to change.

It isolates a process and its local data from other components or processes—the process and its local data cannot be directly manipulated by other processes.

- If access to a process can be made only through explicitly defined interfaces, the functions are encapsulated.

- If the entire process schema is contained in the process—i.e., the schema data is all local to the process—the process encapsulates its schema.

- If part of the schema is in the process—some data is local and some is shared with other processes—the process partially encapsulates its schema.

- If all of the schema is shared with other processes, the schema is not encapsulated.

Rating Encapsulation. The preferred level is a process with only external interfaces and with the schema encapsulated within the process. Good is all external interface with schema partially encapsulated within the process. Other levels should be avoided.

TRACEABLE

What parts of the product have to be changed, what changes to test are required, test, and what documentation has been changed, have to be located. Changed software and documentation have to be reverified. Traceability between processes, interfaces, and data localizes problems and the parts of all documentation affected.

Traced functions and data are fundamental to validation, to verification, to test, to changeability, and to problem localization.

Traceability is important to:

- the user

- designer

- programmer

- tester

- quality assurance

- verification

- validation

- maintenance

All of the above must quickly locate parts of documentation affected by change, and must be confident documentation accurately reflects the product.

EXHIBIT 10.—RATING PROCESS ENCAPSULATION

Encapsulation Level	Interfaces	Schema Encapsulation*
Fully Encapsulated	All External	Fully Encapsulated
Very Good	All External	Very Good
Good	All External	Good
Good	Mixed	Very Good or better
Fair	Mixed	Good or better
Fair	All Internal	Very Good or better
Poor	All Internal	Good or less
Not Encapsulated	All Internal	Not Encapsulated

* See earlier discussion on page 5.

Functional traceability between processes permits review of the design for functionality and completeness:

Each functional requirement should trace to one or more items or functions in a design specification.

If there is no trace, the functional requirement is not reflected in the design, or the design addresses no specified need.

Each item or function defined in a process specification should trace to the functional requirement it satisfies.

Each item or function defined in a process specification should trace to one or more items in a lower order specification or to an item in source code.

Trace shows process, interface, and data relationships:

- Each data entity should trace to all data entities that incorporate it, and to all data entities that it incorporates.

- Each data entity should trace to the processes that set or use it.

- Each process should trace to all of data entities set or used by it.

- Each external interface should trace to all using processes.

Trace is assessed by inspection of functional trace tables, and of process—interface data trace tables furnished as part of the specifications. A repository can automatically provide these tables, and facilitate the inspection of trace relations.

Inspection does not attempt to produce measures of trace. Inspection generates action items for each trace deficiency discovered. The open action items are reviewed at the specification phase review, and a plan is established to remove each shortfall.

There is no reason to measure traceability. All shortfalls should be removed—preferably before the next phase.

Trace tables are established for each item in each layer process to the parent item in the parent process and to any source items in other specification trees.

Specifications should trace: from product requirements; through intermediate specifications to test specifications; to source code—and from source code back to product requirements. Trace tables are also established to all data specifica-

tions called by interface specifications (see Exhibit 11).

Rating Traceability. Traceability is a Pass/Fail attribute. All deficiencies must be removed prior to acceptance.

UNDERSTANDABLE

Understandability should be explicitly addressed in test reviews. The test reviews are probably the most systematic review for understandability.

Specifications should use simple declarative statements. Specifications for a product, its components and their constituent processes need to be understood by those assigned to design, code, test, and eventually maintain them.

Use External Specifications. Specifications should be divided into external and internal specifications. External specifications define what is to be done; internal specifications define how it will be done. For example:

"y = sin x" specifies what the relationship is between x and y;

"sin x is calculated by table lookup and interpolation" specifies how sin x is computed.

Only external specifications should be used for the bulk of a product's specifications. External specifications must avoid implementation details. Such details clutter an external specification and make it more difficult to understand.

Internal specifications should apply only to the lowest level processes or program modules.

EXHIBIT 11.—TRACE REQUIREMENTS

Functions of Specifications Must Trace to Functions in Other Trees
From Product Specifications to Source Code And Back

Operating Specifications	Component Specifications	Test Specifications	Source Code

Processes, Interfaces and Data Must Trace to Each Other
From Process to Interfaces to Data Aggregates to Data Elements and Back

Process	Interfaces	Data Aggregates	Data Elements

Trace is tedious to maintain without an online repository that traces between individual functions within specifications.

A component should be clear regarding what is done, and where in the component flow each function is performed. Operations that jump back and forth between components are difficult to understand. Clarity of process flow and cohesion help to produce understandability.

Clustered Logic. Process logic is usually embedded in the flow description of a process or in the code of a module. The logic is scattered throughout process-flow descriptions and module code. Scattered logic is prone to process loops and is difficult to change (see Exhibit 12).

Clustered logic localizes logical conditions and outcomes. This makes it easier to prevent extraneous paths and to add logical conditions for a new function.

Clustered logic is an effective, understandable way to assure that all logical outcomes are properly accounted for.

Clustered logic places the logic for the flow of software in one place usually near the beginning. Ideally there is one logical statement for each path.

Clustered logic can be used in component and process specifications and in the internal specifications, source code and PDL for modules. The last statement should generate an error return.

Decision Tables. Decision tables are an effective way to present logical flow to people unfamiliar with data processing jargon (see Exhibit 13).

Rating Understandability of Component Structure. This is a Pass/Fail attribute. All path definition should use decision tables or clustered logic. Any exceptions should be rewritten or be accompanied by a satisfactory explanation of why they are not put into decision table or clustered logic form. All deficiencies must be removed prior to acceptance.

REUSABILITY

The higher the level of encapsulation, the more suitable a component is for reuse. A component that is fully encapsulated is most reusable.

Discrete structure readily accommodates reusable components.

Integral structure can accommodate reusable components only by departing from pure integral structure—e.g.; reusable components are objects.

Sometimes only specifications and tests can be reused.

The software has to be reimplemented for the new environment.

*EXHIBIT 12.—*COMPARING EMBEDDED AND CLUSTERED LOGIC

	Embedded Logic		Clustered Logic
BEGIN	If A=10, do f1. If A<10, do f2, f3. Else, do ERROR.	BEGIN	If A=10 AND B=1, do f1, f2. If A=10 AND B=2, do f1,f3. If A<10, do f2, f3. Else, do ERROR.
f1	– – – – – – If B=1, do f2 If B=1, do f3 Else, do ERROR.	f1	– – – – – –
f2	– – – – – –	f2	– – – – – –
f3	– – – – – –	f3	– – – – – –
ERROR	– – – – – –	ERROR	– – – – – –

EXHIBIT 13.—DECISION TABLE EXAMPLE

Logical Conditions	If:	If:	If:	If:	If:	Else:
A=Yes	T(true)	T	T			—
A=No				T		—
B=Hostile						—
B=Friendly	T		T			—
B=Unknown		T				—
C < 5			T			—
0_C < 10				T		—
C_10					T	—
Executable Functions	**Do:**		**Do:**	**Do:**	**Do:**	**Do:**
F1	✔				✔	
F2	✔			✔		
F3			✔			
F4			✔	✔	✔	
F5			✔			
ERROR						✔

Logical conditions are listed in upper left column. Executable functions are listed in the lower left column.

The other upper columns show combinations of the logical conditions.

The other lower columns show the functions to be executed for each combination shown in the upper columns.

The entries in the columns represent the following logical equations:

(1) If (A=Yes AND B=Hostile) OR (A-Yes AND B=Unknown), execute F1, and then F2.
(2) If A=Yes AND B=Friendly AND C<5, execute F3, F4, F5.
(3) If A=No AND 0_C<10, execute F2, F4.
(4) If C_10, execute F1, F4.
(5) Else execute ERROR.

Each column shows one logical *AND* statement.

OR relations are listed in separate columns; e.g.; equation (1) above requires two columns:

Column 1: If (A=Yes AND B=Hostile), execute F1, and then F2.
Column 2: If (A=Yes AND B=Unknown), execute F1, and then F2.

Rating Reusability. Reusability is mostly a function of encapsulation level (see Exhibit 14).

SOFTWARE OBJECTS

Software objects satisfy all attributes of good software:

- Objects are fully encapsulated —a component comprised of objects has discrete structure and is loosely coupled.
- An object is reusable.

- Object procedures are associated one-to-one with the object's external interfaces. This enhances traceability and understandability.
- Traceability and understandability are further enhanced if the design of procedures also maximizes discrete structure, encapsulation and loose coupling.

Objects shield other components from complex data structures and complex derivations of data. Objects range from simple subroutines to

EXHIBIT 14.—RATING PROCESS REUSABILITY

Reusability	Encapsulation Level	Comments
Excellent	Fully Encapsulated	A Separate Executable Program is preferred.
Fair	Good	Has to be compiled and linked with using processes.
Marginal	Fair	Has to be compiled and linked with using processes. Shared data is an implicit interface among using processes. Risky.
Not Reusable	Poor or Not Encapsulated	Becomes tightly integrated with other processes.

EXHIBIT 15.—OBJECTS HAVE EXTERNAL INTERFACES

Interface ID	Input	Example	Output	Example
GET_ADDRESS	NAME	Doe	STREET CITY STATUS	10 Easy St. Boston, MA OK
NEW_ADDRESS	NAME STREET CITY	Jones 303 5th Ave. New York, NY	STATUS	OK
DELETE_ENTRY	NAME	Smith	STATUS	OK

extensive collections of related data operations. A database management system is an object.

Product components use external interfaces to call objects that perform the data operations such as storing, retrieving or deriving data. Each external interface of the object has an ID and data elements which specify the call and return messages of the interface.

The objects deal internally with the complexity of data files and the derivation of data outputs. These private operations are not available outside the object.

An early term for this is information hiding—i.e., objects hide data complexity from other programs. The current term is data abstraction.

A simple object would be a subroutine that returned the sine of an angle when entered with the angle. This would have a single external interface with an ID of SINE, one input data element, ANGLE, and one output data element SIN_ANGLE.

A multifunction example would be an array of instances of a set of data elements. Such an array could be a directory of names and addresses—an array of instances of the data elements NAME, STREET and CITY as in the table above.

Objects Provide Environmental Independence

Objects are a useful way to achieve data independence. The internal structure of the data entity can change but the user doesn't care as long as nothing changes in the external interfces (see Exhibit 15).

Objects are useful ways to buffer applications from changes to new database management systems, operating systems, etc.

If such a system is changed, only the objects have to be changed.

Rating Presence of Objects

This is a Pass/Fail attribute. All components or processes should be converted to objects. Exceptions should be justified by the reviewers.

END NOTE

Metrics should represent the goals of an organization for the development of products. The criteria for rating metrics present an alternate view of an organization's goals.

The metrics shown represent the values of the author. They are presented as a point of departure for metrics representing your organization's values.

The restructured metrics examples serve an important function —they present the organization's goals in a context that tells the staff what the organization values.

———————————————— ■ ————————————————

MAXIMIZING QUALITY AND PRODUCTIVITY WITH AN OBJECT-ORIENTED ENVIRNNMENT: PROTOTYPING*
by George Kershaw

Prototypes usually are required to develop validated specifications for user interfaces and operating cycles. The key to prototyping is a structure that readily accommodates change. Prototype development is compared to analytic development.

A prototype is a highly changeable development vehicle that should (1) have built-in quality and (2) avoid quick and dirty approaches. Software objects provide the best prototype structure.

SCOPE OF THIS ARTICLE

This article focuses on those aspects of the prototyping approach described in *Object-Oriented Product Design* (see panel at the end of the text, page 11) that impact the development cycle and product assurance. In this approach, prototypes are constructed using only software objects.

Operating cycles are fundamental to the approach. An operating cycle is the end-to-end sequence of events necessary to performing a mission of a product. There is one operating cycle for each mission. For example, a mission of an ATM would be the withdrawal of cash from a checking account.

The approach uses three types of software objects—cycle engines, display engines and stores. *Cycle engines* drive the operating cycles of a product. *Display engines* provide the user interaction. *Stores* do the data processing.

GETTING VALIDATED OPERATIONS SPECIFICATIONS

The hard job is turning the operating cycle descriptions generated by architectural design into validated operating cycle and display specifications. The user has to thoroughly understand the

impact of a proposed specification before true validation can happen.

A user can comprehend an operating cycle description but it is hard for a user to comprehend the details of a specification. This, and the need for analysts to better understand the problem, is the reason that prototyping is usually the most productive vehicle for attaining validated operating and display-cycle specifications.

CONTRASTING ANALYTIC DEVELOPMENT WITH PROTOTYPE DEVELOPMENT

Analytic development proceeds from operations specifications to component specifications to program design to component implementation in one pass.

Prototyping embeds a prototype cycle in the development cycle.

This blurs the distinction between operations design and component design. The theoretically nice progression from operations specifications to levels of component specification no longer applies.

If no prototyping is required, stores, cycle engines and display engines all follow the standard analytic development cycle.

Prototyping usually applies only to the cycle and display engines of an operating cycle. Stores can usually be developed analytically. The product development cycle will be a combination of: (1) analytic development for stores and some/no operating cycles, and (2) variations on prototype development for the remaining cycles.

Thus, there may be several development cycles for a product according to the prototyping needs of the product's operating cycles.

When an operating cycle is validated, its displays, display sequences and its operational sequence are validated. Thus, if an operating cycle requires prototyping, its operational sequence or

---

*Reprinted with permission from *Society for Software Quality Journal*, September 1995. George Kershaw has an outstanding track record in the engineering and delivery of software products ranging from operating systems to major online applications.

EXHIBIT 1.—IMPLEMENTATION OF AN OPERATING
CYCLE USING SOFTWARE OBJECTS

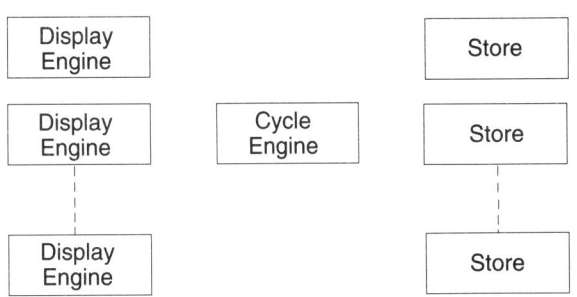

Software objects are accessed only through external interfaces.

Engines generally have one external interface. Stores usually have several external interfaces—one for each data operation.

The cycle engine drives the operating cycle to completion. It is initiated by another operating cycle.

A cycle engine calls display engines for user interaction and stores to perform the data processing for the operating cycle.

A prototype uses one cycle engine for each operating cycle. This allows independent development of operating cycles.

Engines and stores may be repackaged during component design.

some/all of its displays and display interactions or both are prototyped (see Exhibit 1).

EFFECT ON SPECIFICATIONS

Good design practice requires that at least the lowest level external specification and the internal specification for each engine be accurately maintained (see Exhibit 2). This is sufficient if functional trace is maintained from the operating cycle specification level and through component level external specifications to the lowest level of specifications and back. The trace allows efficient reverse engineering from low-level specifications to higher-level specifications.

The alternative is reverse engineering without the trace. This compounds the problem of verifying conformance of specifications. It is tedious and the tendency to skimp is high making reverse engineering a high-risk effort. It is al-

most impossible if, which is too often the case, not even the lowest level of specifications are accurately maintained.

A PROTOTYPE IS A HIGHLY CHANGEABLE DEVELOPMENT VEHICLE

A highly changeable development vehicle can be built from software objects. Because constraints that apply to the production model do not apply to the prototype, software objects can always be used in constructing a prototype.

Prototyping may also be quicker because other nonstructural design constraints are relaxed. For example:

- The prototype doesn't have to meet response time and space constraints.

- The prototype can be developed on a more flexible platform with more robust tools and a wider selection of reusable software available.

- Only moderate integration testing and no verification testing is necessary before incorporating components into a prototype.

BUILD QUALITY IN

Building a prototype is no excuse for abandoning good design practice. A prototype should be built using the same design practice as for a product. Quality should be built in:

- Initial operating and component specifications should be prepared.

- The prototype should be developed according to these specifications (see Exhibit 3).

These specifications should be maintained to reflect changes as the prototype evolves.

This way, iterating the prototype is under control—the prototype doesn't become unintelligible globs of spaghetti. Also, quality is built into the prototype and doesn't have to be "inspected in" after the prototype is built.

If the product platform is the same as the prototype platform, the prototype can be evolved

EXHIBIT 2.—COMPARING AN OPERATING CYCLE DESCRIPTION WITH ITS SPECIFICATION

Description	**Specification**
ATM—Withdraw From Checking Account	*ATM—Withdraw From Checking Account*
Customer selected "Withdraw From Checking" and entered an amount during Sign On cycle.	Input Interface:
	Amount, Account Number
ATM *gets* checking account balance.	Call *Withdraw From Checking* (store).
If balance is greater than amount entered, ATM dispenses cash, debits checking account and goes to Sign Off cycle.	(interface: input = Amount, Account Number; return = Action)
	If Action = OK, do A, X
	If Action = IF, do B, X
If balance is less than amount entered, ATM displays "Insufficient Funds" and goes to Sign Off cycle.	If Action = OM, do C, X
	If Action = IA, do D, X
	A Dispense cash
	Call *Confirm Transaction* (store)
	Print Receipt (display engine)
	B Call *Insufficient Funds* (display engine)
	C Call *Amoung Goes Over Daily Maximum* (display engine)
	D Call *Amount Not Multiple Of 20, Try Again* (display engine)
	X Go to Sign Off Cycle
	Output Interface: none

Only the cycle engine specification is shown. Specification of an operating cycle requires, in addition to the cycle engine specification: specifications for the two store interfaces and the four display engines.

In addition, attributes (e.g., Amount, Account and Action) require data specifications.

Although several operating cycles may each call a given store interface, the interface is independent of other interfaces of that store other than being colocated in the same store.

The need for new interfaces for stores and for changes to existing interfaces is coordinated in the operating cycle descriptions/specifications to assure coordination with all operating cycles affected.

---

into the product. This would produce a product with maximum changeability.

As prototyping is complete for each operating cycle:

- Either the operating cycle prototype or its operating specifications should be validated and be baselined—put under configuration management.

- If trace is maintained between specifications at all levels, it may be sufficient that only bottom levels of component specifications be strictly maintained. Trace often permits higher level specifications to be reverse engineered from lower level external specifications after validation with less effort than maintaining all specifications during prototyping. It also fits better with the "get on with it" attitude of most developers.

- Product assurance should verify that component specifications conform to the corresponding validated functions. The component specifications should then be baselined.

Any further changes to validated functions or their specifications should require engineering change orders.

Trace can be tedious to maintain. Use CASE tools that automatically establish and maintain trace between specification functions and between interfaces, data and functional specifications.

AVOID QUICK AND DIRTY APPROACHES

Some advocate building the prototype "quick and dirty" and reverse engineering for the specifications.

This can work but it is risky. It takes a lot of will power, strong product assurance, and penetrating reviews to accurately reverse engineer a functional prototype.

When a "quick and dirty" approach is used, it may create an initial prototype sooner. This is debatable. However, additional iteration of the

EXHIBIT 3.—COMPARING ANALYTIC AND
PROTOTYPE DEVELOPMENT

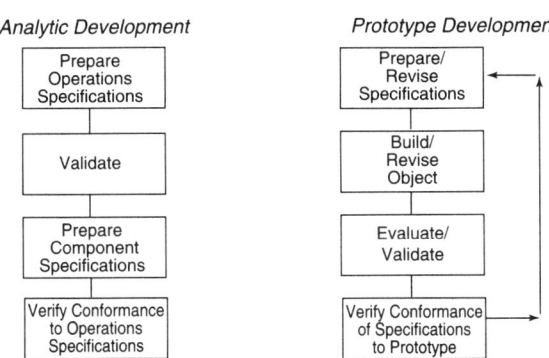

In analytic development, operations specifications are prepared and then validated by the user. Component specifications for objects are verified to conform to the operations specifications.

This is fine *if* operations specifications that can be validated by the user can be analytically derived. This is true of many product components—such as stores.

However, under some conditions—such as user interaction with displays—the user cannot validate a paper specification and prototyping is required.

Prototype development is iterative and specifications are verified for conformance to the prototype rather than to the validated operations specifications of analytic development.

Prototype development incorporates the prototype cycle:

- Initial specifications for the object to be prototyped are prepared; the object is built and its operation is evaluated.

- The specifications and object are revised; the revised object is evaluated.

- The cycle is iterated until the revised prototype operation is validated by the user.

The object's specifications are then verified for conformance to the operations of the object.

Prototyping may seem expensive but it is less expensive than proceeding with unvalidated operations specifications.

---

prototype will cost less if a "quick and dirty approach" is not used. This is not debatable.

STANDARDS FOR USER INTERFACES

Most prototyping is spent determining how to interact with users and exactly what the user wants to get back from the product.

It is important to maintain consistency between the way information is displayed to the user and the way interactions are defined among operating cycles.

The idea is to begin with a sample operating cycle from each user group. This is usually done as part of architectural design. These are later evolved into prototypes for all operating cycles for each user group during operations design.

Be sure to use display approaches that are deliverable on the product platform. Graphic interfaces are nice but can affect response time adversely. If response time is likely to be a problem, make it clear to users that a later tradeoff between graphic displays and response time mad be necessary.

Development should begin with a set of tentative common user access (CUA) standards to achieve consistency.

These standards establish initial standards for the appearance of displays and the interaction by which displays are navigated—how more information is requested about a display element.

A standard user interface such as Microsoft Windows could be the beginning point.

Developing the mock-ups and the prototype will evolve the standards. The evolving standards should be systematically reviewed to be sure adequate consistency is maintained.

CONSTRUCTION AND EVOLUTION OF A PROTOTYPE

Don't agonize—build. Expect to revise and revise again. Design a reasonable beginning point and build.

Begin with the sample operating cycles for different user groups. Add prototypes for all operating cycles for each user group one cycle at a time.

Review each cycle operation with the user. Revise until the user and you are both satisfied.

The prototype should make provision for recording user operations. This provides usage statistics to support discussions with users as to what should be included, how it should operate and how it should be tested.

DOCUMENTATION

Two or three levels of external component specification can be expected for the prototype's objects.

The modules are procedures or sub-procedures of the prototype objects. The module external specifications must be maintained in accordance with adopted design practices.

When an operating cycle is validated, the module specifications are verified to conform to the prototype operation of the cycle.

The module external specifications are the basis for reverse engineering. Each governing specification is then reverse engineered from the derived specifications moving up from the module specifications. The governing specifications are verified to conform with the derived specifications.

Higher level specifications need not be elaborate. They serve mainly to provide a road map from operating cycle and data specifications to the modules that actually do the work. When objects are the constituents, the road maps are straightforward.

The result of all this is validated operating cycle specifications and procedures that can be used in the product.

PROTOTYPE CYCLE

The prototype evolves as a basic cycle is iterated (see Exhibit 4). The prototype is constructed solely from objects —engines and stores. The objects can be developed independently if interfaces are maintained or carefully coordinated if changed. This applies only to external specifications of object interfaces. Procedures can be changed and stubs can be replaced by procedures without impact on other objects.

Thus, a complete product prototype is a loose confederation of operating cycle prototypes. Op-

EXHIBIT 4.—BASIC PROTOTYPE CYCLE

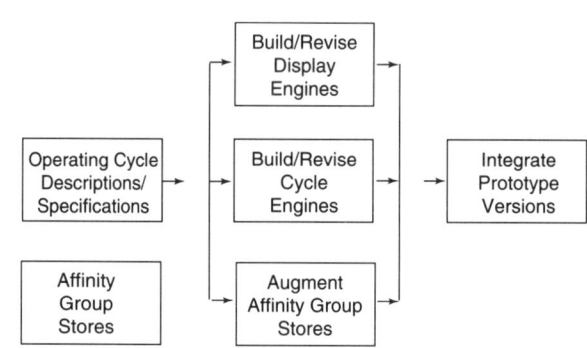

The cycle is iterated. An iteration revises engines according to findings of previous iterations and adds new engines for evaluation.

Effort for display engine, cycle engine and stores development is coordinated through the operating cycle descriptions/specifications.

Stores begin with stubbed interfaces—complete external interface specifications with stubs emulating procedures. Procedure implementation during prototyping is optional.

The above is an operating cycle prototype. There are also prototype cycles corresponding to display engines separately and to aggregates of operating cycles.

erating cycle prototypes consist of cycle engines, display engines and stores. Each of which may have been separately prototyped before being aggregated into the operating cycle prototypes. To run an operating cycle, only the cycle engine, called display engines and stores with called interfaces need be loaded.

If there is previously developed software—usually store interfaces or an entire store—it should be incorporated in early iterations of the prototype. It is critical that staff realizes that reused software is not to be changed. Its specifications are part of the operations design specifications.

Different people can run different operating cycles on different machines having the same development platform. Separate teams can work independently with each user group. Operations design specifications include operating cycle specifications, display specifications and store external interface specifications. Coordination is through the operating cycle descriptions/specifications which, when prototyping is finished, become the validated operating cycle specifications.

As an operating cycle is validated, its description/specification is baselined. What is actually being baselined? External specifications for interfaces and procedures (operating specifications), internal specifications for procedures (component specifications) and procedure code. Interfaces and procedures for one operating cycle are completely independent of those for another cycle so coordination with other cycles is unnecessary.

The prototype is iterated in small steps. Operating cycles are added a few, usually one, at a time. A cycle engine corresponds to each operating cycle. Each cycle is baselined as it is validated by baselining its cycle engine and its display engines.

Once baselined, a cycle engine is not changed unless a change is approved for its operating cycle. Display engines may be shared among operating cycles. If change to a display is required, the change has to be coordinated with each cycle using the display engine. This doesn't happen frequently and when it does, it rarely presents a problem.

Once the way a prototype is evolved has been assimilated, separate teams can work in parallel. At this point, evolution of the prototype can appear to be continuous. Take care to coordinate development of teams through the operating cycle descriptions/specifications. Things can get rapidly out of control!

PROTOTYPING END POINTS

There are several points at which exploitative development can be terminated. A development cycle variation corresponds to each stopping point. All product prototyping does not necessarily stop at the same point. Prototyping for some operating cycles may be halted at one point; other operating cycles may be halted at other points.

The product development cycle should include a variation for each point at which prototyping for product operating cycles ends (see Exhibit 5).

There are six places for terminating prototyping. These are not rigid end points. The stopping point may be between these places. The places, however, serve as reference points for describing the extent of prototyping.

While this is a reasonable sequence of events, it is by no means a required sequence:

- Mock-ups and slides shows are usually alternatives to display engine prototypes and, occasionally, operating cycle prototypes.

- Display engine prototypes are usually called by an operating cycle in order to demonstrate operations to the user but some display engines may be product-ready components implemented from operating specifications (validated by mock-ups and

EXHIBIT 5.—PROTOTYPING END POINTS

Point	Description	Purpose
1	Mock-ups and Slide Shows	Mock-ups of display appearance and contents. Slide shows simulate user interaction with displays.
2	Display Engine Prototype	Generates displays and user interaction for display sequences. A display engine prototype can be called by the cycle engine of an operating cycle prototype.
3	Operating Cycle Prototype	Generates displays and user interaction for a complete operating cycle. Calls display engines and store interfaces.
4	Aggregate Operating Cycle Prototype	Aggregates operating cycles to permit tests of interaction between operating cycles. Cycles may be aggregated into a complete product prototype.
5	Convert to Product Model	Converts aggregate operating cycle prototypes to corresponding product components. All store interfaces stubs are replaced by implemented interfaces.
6	Test Processor	Converts aggregate operating cycle prototypes to test processors for corresponding product components. All store interfaces stubs are replaced by implemented interfaces.

slide shows), or engines from a library of previously implemented software.

- It is difficult to have an aggregate operating cycle prototype without some individual operating cycle prototypes.

- A prototype converted to a product component would not also be a test processor.

A functional prototype that includes test facilities can be used as a test processor for the developed product. Such a prototype would be operated by a test driver in conjunction with the production model as a way to automate test data reduction.

The prototype would have to make provisions for test data insertion and recording.

Functions satisfying more stringent constraints than the production model may be required in this prototype. For example, higher accuracy in prototype functions may be required to adequately check the accuracy of the production model.

While some functions may have to satisfy more stringent accuracy constraints, the prototype does not have to satisfy response time and space constraints placed on the production model.

This allows the prototype to have discrete structure only. This, in turn, accounts for the easier to build, quicker to build and easier to change features of a prototype.

Such a prototype can be used in acceptance and verification test of the developed product.

The objects of the prototype can be used to verify corresponding functions of the developed product.

This does not presume the prototype to be an error-free test processor. If the test processor and the production model agree, both have functioned correctly. if they disagree, one or both are in error.

This is the reason test processes must be implemented independently of product processes.

Errors in the production model and the test processor are corrected as they are diagnosed.

END NOTE

A validated prototype can be built more quickly if the "quick and dirty" approach is avoided. Changeability is an important product attribute. Thus, the prototype should be converted to the product, or those parts of the product that are prototyped should be converted, unless design or test requirements prohibit it.

Changeability is so important to product maintenance that the case for relaxing design requirements should be presented to the user.

The product development cycle should be divided into separate development cycles according to the needs of developing the operating cycles.

The identification of which development cycle applies to each operating cycle should be determined during architectural design and presented in the product development plan.

2.7
AEROSPACE

AEROSPACE AND DEFENSE CONTRACTORS LEARN HOW TO MAKE THEIR BUSINESSES SOAR*
by Michael O'Guin

What leads to superior business performance in the aerospace and defense (A&D) in-

dustry? For example, why does one company consistently win more than 80% of the competitive

---

*Reprinted with permission from *Quality Progress*, June 1995. Michael O'Guin, formerly the manager at Price Waterhouse, resides in Trabuco Canyon, CA.

award dollars it bids on, while the rest of the industry averages less than 20%? To answer these questions, Price Waterhouse (PW) and a group of A&D contractors conducted a strategic benchmarking study of their industry. By comparing benchmarks and business practices among the participating companies, the study's analysis identified the characteristics and business practices that differentiate superior performers. The study's findings provide an understanding of the A&D industry and make a compelling case for what might be the true leverage points for any organization.

THE STRATEGIC BENCHMARKING STUDY

In 1991, AAI, a defense contractor, and PW formed the Best Practices 2000 alliance to conduct a three-year strategic benchmarking study. Twenty-four A&D divisions in the following companies participated in the alliance: AAI, Allied-Signal, Computing Devices International, E&S, E-Systems, General Electric, Grumman, IBM, Loral, McDonnell Douglas, Northrop, Paramax, Rockwell, Teledyne, Thiokol, TRW, and United Technologies.

To objectively compare the performance of each participant's key business processes, PW consultants sought to identify and define key performance indicators that are applicable to an A&D company. First, a design team identified the key business processes of an A&D company:

• Acquire business
• Manage programs
• Design products and processes
• Acquire material
• Build products
• Support products
• Manage resources
• Improve continuously
• Develop software
• Provide leadership

The study's designers conducted workshops with representatives of the participating companies to identify the performance measures for these key business processes. The design team, taking a total quality management approach, designed the study around satisfying internal and external customers. For each business process, the design team identified key customers, key outputs, and the performance metrics that measured the customers' satisfaction with the outputs. For example, one key output that the "acquire material" process receives from the "design products and processes" process is engineering drawings. Customers' satisfaction with this output can be measured by its timeliness (percent of engineering drawings released on time) and its stability (number of engineering changes per drawing).

Using this methodology, the design team developed a balanced, cross-functional set of 102 performance metrics covering the breadth of an A&D company. The metric set included:

• Program budget performance
• Percent of shop orders released on time
• Errors per 1,000 lines of software code
• Incoming material acceptance rate
• Changes per purchase order
• Rework and repair hours per 1,000 direct labor hours
• Quality training hours per employee
• On-time hardware and software deliveries

Next, the data were collected. Each participating company received data-collection forms and detailed definitions for each measure. To ensure uniform interpretation by all members, PW consultants conducted on-site data validations.

While at each company's site, the consultants interviewed process owners and key process experts. They scored each participant's business practices using more than 850 structured questions, which covered topics ranging from design-to-cost practices to program manager empowerment to the rigor of software corrective-action systems.

COMPARING THE PROCESSES OF DIFFERENT COMPANIES

Using these data, PW's Study Research Center constructed a database of more than 4,800 metrics and more than 20,000 business-practice responses. While the participants designed and manufactured products ranging from the F-15 aircraft's radar system to the space shuttle's main engines, there were surprisingly few measures skewed by the different technologies used. In addition, the business processes and the characteristics that satisfied customers varied little from one company to the next. For example, owners of manufacturing processes wanted to have their production material available on time; it did not matter whether they were assembling guidance systems or satellites.

This finding confirmed that a business-process perspective can be used to compare the performance of different businesses. As a result, process performance can be objectively compared across companies to identify those processes that are more successful at satisfying customers. This

analysis isolates the business-process characteristics and business practices that differentiate superior performers.

PW analyzed the database to identify the characteristics that differentiate the more profitable companies (i.e., the top five companies with the highest return on investment and cash flow to investment over the last three years). The analysis found striking consistency among the business processes of the more profitable A&D companies. The strength and consistency of the findings prove that superior process performance drives superior organizational performance. There are five characteristics that distinguish

EXHIBIT 1.—FIVE CHARACTERISTICS OF MORE PROFITABLE AEROSPACE AND DEFENSE COMPANIES

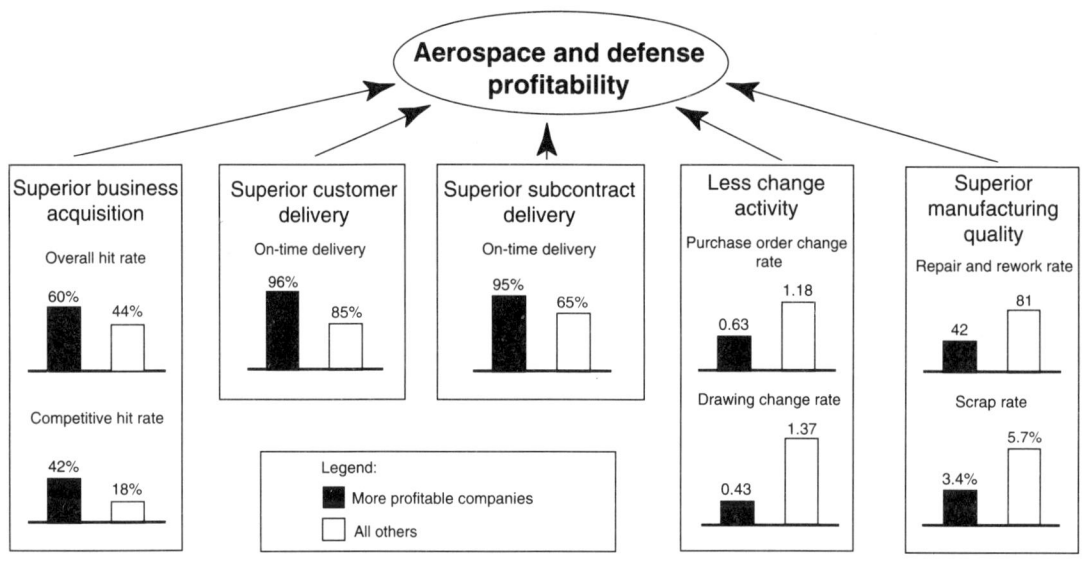

Notes

Overall hit rate: Total award dollars / total proposed dollars (includes competitive, follow-on, and add-on awards plus exercising options)

Competitive hit rate: Total competitive dollars / total competitive proposed dollars (includes only awards in which another company submitted a proposal)

On-time customer delivery: Number of on-time hardware and software deliveries to the customer / number of hardware and software deliveries scheduled

On-time subcontract delivery: Number of major subcontract line items received by the contractor on time / total number of subcontract line items scheduled

Purchase order change rate: Number of purchase order changes / total number of production material purchase orders placed

Drawing change rate: Number of engineering change notices / number of engineering drawings (development programs only)

Repair and rework rate: Number of repair and rework hours / 1,000 direct labor production hours

Scrap rate: Total scrap dollars / total production material dollars consumed

the more profitable companies from the rest (see Exhibit 1):

1. Superior business acquisition
2. Superior customer delivery performance
3. Superior subcontract delivery performance
4. Less change activity
5. Superior manufacturing quality

Surprisingly, the characteristics of "better performance to budget" and "superior material acquisition" did not differentiate the more profitable companies in this industry. In fact, the more profitable companies consistently performed worse on such material acquisition metrics as "line items received on time:" "incoming acceptance rates," and "dollars spent per supplier."

These data do not suggest that suppliers should be allowed to deliver more material late to increase profits. The results merely show that procuring material is not a key leverage point in the A&D industry. It also reveals that the more profitable companies do not excel at every process. They do, however, excel at the industry's five key leverage points. The following analyzes the top performers' business practices for each leverage point.

Superior Business Acquisition

In business acquisition, three companies significantly and consistently outperformed the rest of the participants (see Exhibit 2). Not surprisingly, the business practices of these three top performers are dramatically different from those of the rest of group. There are four practices that set them apart:

The more successful companies focus their strategic planning process on potential customer funding, customer needs, and technology trends many years in the future, and they compare their technical capabilities to those of their competitors to create a realistic assessment of the future market environment. The top performers formally track their competitors' technical strengths and weaknesses to win a significantly higher percentage of competitive proposals. They use dedicated intelligence staffs and possess a formal process for identifying, collecting, organizing, and analyzing customer and competitor information.

EXHIBIT 2.—THE HIT RATES OF THE THREE TOP PERFORMERS IN BUSINESS ACQUISITION COMPARED TO THE REST OF THE GROUP

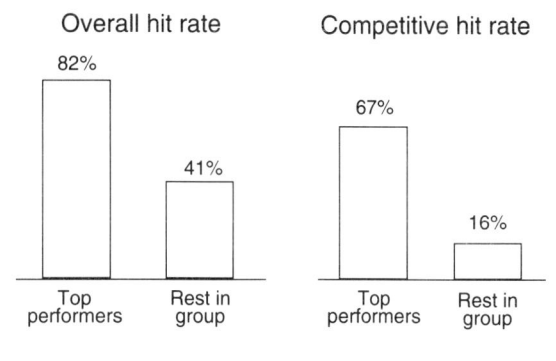

For example. when one top performer competes for a major award, a proposal team composed of program managers uses competitor files to write a mock executive summary of the competitor's proposal. The team then analyzes this summary to understand the competitor's strengths and weaknesses. It subsequently writes its own proposal to specifically play up the competitor's weaknesses and play down the competitor's strengths.

Another top contractor collects and organizes intelligence from all levels of the government—from the halls of Congress to Department of Defense labs. Its system is so disciplined that its capture team leaders usually know more about a program's status than the government counterparts do. This gives the company quite an advantage when it is trying to influence its customer's position.

The more successful companies rigorously review and reduce the number of award opportunities pursued. The study found that the key to making the acquisition process effective is carefully allocating and applying business-development, research-and-development, and other discretionary resources. The better performers clearly define a strategy that focuses them on winning only a limited selection of award opportunities. They poll and solicit information from all relevant customer representatives to qualify every opportunity. In this way, they develop a clear picture of their customers' true needs. They also learn how their customers' technical staff and key decision makers perceive the opportunity and the competition.

In ignorance, most award opportunities look viable. After discovering the dubious state of a customer's funding or the strength of a competitor's position, however, many opportunities look less attractive. Only with good field intelligence can management have the confidence to make a "no pursue" decision. As a result, the top performers do not squander their resources on programs that the customers will probably never fund or on programs they are unlikely to win.

The successful companies create formal teams, which they make responsible and accountable for winning specific future awards. The top performers never pursue opportunities haphazardly. When their managers decide to pursue an award opportunity, these companies consistently use a repeatable process to leverage all of their companies' marketing, sales, technical, and management resources on winning the selected business.

The process begins when a capture team is formed two years out to position the company and to start influencing the customer (compared to a year or less for the rest of the industry). The capture team identifies the key customer decision makers and their real wants. After developing the best solution, the team presells it to the customer. The team then listens to the customer's reaction and adjusts its win strategy accordingly by developing proof of the benefits and by correcting any perceived weaknesses.

As the award pursuit enters the proposal stage, the capture team, a dedicated core staff of proposal specialists, and other functional specialists come together to form a proposal team. Before any work begins on the written proposal, the core specialists first train the rest of the proposal team in proposal methodology. (The top three performers are also the top three users of proposal training.) The proposal process is carefully planned and organized to focus the writers on the important issues, such as addressing all requirements, dispelling technical concerns, and communicating the win strategy. From early on, management conducts frequent and thorough reviews of the proposal. This, coupled with the consistent approach and format, allows the proposal team to avoid rework.

As owners of the proposal process, the core staff conducts postproposal debriefings, looking for process improvements and lessons learned. Marketing management then uses these lessons to improve the qualification, capture planning, proposal, and training processes.

The successful companies devote significant resources to trying to influence their customers' priorities. This is accomplished by conducting customer-need studies and trade-off studies, lobbying Congress, and holding technical briefings and technology demonstrations.

The formal process of the top performers contrasts sharply with the haphazard approach employed by the rest of the industry. The poorer performers concentrate their strategic planning on financial analysis, giving only cursory attention to customer conditions and potential competitors' responses. These companies only informally collect field intelligence. They rarely trim the number of opportunities chased. Pet projects tie up resources, while "must win" programs go wanting. Capture planning starts late, is inconsistent, and is not tracked.

When the government's request for proposal arrives, the typical poor performer throws together a group of available personnel to write the proposal. The company lacks a core proposal staff and rarely provides any proposal training. As a result, writing the proposal is a chaotic experience. Management reviews the proposal for the first time late in the cycle. Typically, it then asks for a substantial rewrite, consuming the remaining time. After completing the proposal, management disbands the proposal team. The following month, management throws together yet another group, and it has to relearn the entire proposal process.

The poorer performers take the approach of proposing on as many award opportunities as possible. They seem to view submitting proposals as playing the lottery: the more tickets bought, the more opportunities to win. The data show, however, that these companies consistently underrun their sales forecasts, while the better performers, by staying focused, overrun theirs.

The lesson is clear: Successful companies are focused and develop a consistent, well-defined process. But, because competitive win rates are closely guarded secrets, the participants had little idea whether their performance was good or bad until this study. Not surprisingly, the data in Exhibit 3 shocked one division general manager. While his division was winning 21% of the competitive dollars it proposed, he discovered that the best-in-group companies were consistently winning more than 60%. He immediately established a team to improve his business-acquisition process.

EXHIBIT 3.—METRICS ALLOW MANAGEMENT TO OBJECTIVELY ASSESS PROCESS PERFORMANCE

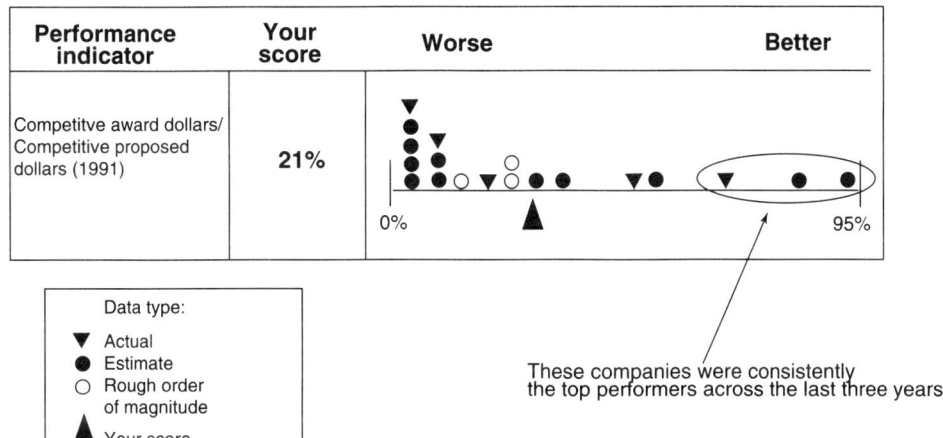

Superior Customer-Delivery Performance

Three of the four companies with the best customer-delivery performance over the last three years were also among the most profitable. There are three practices that set them apart:

The successful companies empower their program managers, who are responsible for ensuring cross-functional teamwork. These companies give their program managers authority over:

- Selecting and evaluating key personnel who work on their programs
- Selecting major subcontractors
- Finalizing product specifications
- Allocating program budgets

The study's results indicate that empowering program managers is more important for development programs than for mature production programs. This probably is due to the greater need for cross-functional cooperation on development programs than on mature production programs. The companies that empower their program managers are more likely to have program-manager development programs, such as mentoring, formal job rotation, and program-management training. At the other companies, program managers function principally as status reporters and have little real power.

The successful companies support their program managers with better information on bud-
gets, schedules, and material status. The information is better because it comes from well-disciplined systems, not because it comes from state-of-the-art systems. The program managers also use more comprehensive program schedules and set good internal milestones for long-lead procurement items and engineering drawings. These companies emphasize schedule adherence more than cost or productivity.

The successful companies emphasize formal risk management as part of program management. These companies have procedures to identify and assess key risk areas, to develop risk reduction action plans, and to track and update those plans throughout the life of the program. Across the rest of the group, risk management was haphazard at best. The most frequently heard comment on risk management was, "We write a good story about risk management in the proposal, but as soon as we get the award, we forget all about it."

Superior Subcontract Delivery Performance

The benchmarking study found that the more profitable companies and the ones with better customer delivery performance consistently receive their major subcontracts on time. A major subcontract is the purchase of the design and manufacture of a major subsystem. For example, for McDonnell Douglas. the manufacturer of the F-15 fighter, the F-15's fire control system is a major subcontract. Major subcontracts are critical components to the final product. They are highly valued, complex systems on which a significant portion of the final product's performance depends.

The study's results confirmed the obvious assumption that a company is much more likely to receive its subcontracted items on time if purchasing is given the subcontract request with sufficient lead time. In addition, those companies with superior subcontract delivery performance:

• Emphasize cross-functional involvement in selecting subcontractors

• Involve subcontractors in the design process and formally share technology with them

• Provide subcontract requests on time to subcontract administration

• Establish stronger partnerships

• Almost always require formal subcontract reviews

• Require subcontractors to develop formal risk management plans

• Formally measure and track subcontractor performance

• Manage subcontractors through the program-management organization rather than through procurement

The study's results also showed that if companies empower those responsible for negotiating and managing subcontracts, they will be more successful at managing subcontractors. When program-management organization is responsible for subcontracts, the subcontract managers have significantly more authority and control over resources. When procurement is responsible for subcontracts, the subcontract managers are, invariably, lower in the organizational structure and further removed from such resource owners as engineering and program management. Empowered subcontract managers can quickly respond to subcontractor problems with engineering assistance or renegotiate a contract to relieve troublesome requirements. Likewise, they can approve and allocate more money to a subcontractor to take advantage of unanticipated technology.

It is important to note that the characteristics identified by the data analysis are probably not all-inclusive. There were many indications that the study failed to isolate other factors that

were at work. For example, several companies confided that they had experienced problems giving program managers wide latitude over subcontractors. In these cases, it appeared that their program managers had little subcontract management experience. It appeared that the most successful companies have established career paths for program managers through subcontract management positions. This rotation explains why the more successful companies felt comfortable with, and were successful at empowering program managers with subcontract authority.

Finally, the benchmarking results found that material acquisition performance (buying piece parts) was not a critical factor in achieving superior profitability. The implications of this finding are crucial. Most A&D companies fail to differentiate subcontract management from procurement to any significant degree. While administratively these two processes are very similar, their complexity and potential effects are vastly different. Despite the growth of subcontracting over the last 15 years, few companies manage subcontractors consistently well. These findings indicate that the subcontract process provides an A&D company with one of its greatest opportunities to differentiate and improve its performance.

The scarcity of superior performers in the A&D industry probably results from the cross-functional nature of subcontracting. An interdisciplinary background is needed to be an effective subcontract manager. Few companies, however, develop people with this background. In addition, factors such as empowerment, program-management development, cross-functional involvement, and partnerships are difficult to identify and measure. Not coincidentally, these are the same characteristics that also differentiate companies with superior customer delivery performance.

Less Change Activity

The more profitable companies in the group exhibit less frequent change activity as measured by change orders per purchase order and by engineering change notices per engineering drawing. This is not a surprising finding, since frequent changes cause significant problems in any process. Changes result in rework, increased costs, and lower quality levels.

The top performers with fewer purchase order changes:

- Have highly functional systems for accounts payable, purchasing, and material planning. While many managers and technologists are enticed by new computer systems, only in material acquisition are significant benefits tied to superior computer systems. The study found that companies using closed-loop material requirements planning systems receive more material on time, have fewer purchased material rejections, and have fewer purchase order changes.

- Have formal supplier guidelines and perform thorough quality audits

- Provide suppliers with formal, structured performance feed back

- Emphasize supplier partnerships by developing and tracking partnership measures

These factors probably explain why these companies exhibit lower manufacturing scrap rates.

The top performers with fewer engineering changes per drawing:

- Have more cross-functional involvement in developing product requirements

- Make greater use of automated tools in developing product requirements

- Ensure greater involvement of reliability engineering in product design

- Make greater use of simulation, standard-parts databases, and solid modeling in design

- Place more emphasis on designing for ease of testing

- Use more concurrent engineering practices

These findings reveal two leverage points for improved design stability: developing good specifications up front and ensuring cross-functional involvement throughout the design process.

Superior Manufacturing Quality

The more profitable companies in the group exhibit superior manufacturing quality performance as measured by the number of repair and rework hours per 1,000 direct labor hours, the number of defects per 1,000 direct labor hours, and the cost of scrap compared to the cost of materials consumed.

The top performers in manufacturing quality:

- Emphasize and obtain good results from cross-training operators, forming natural work teams, and implementing employee and team recognition programs

- Have successfully implemented cycle-time reduction initiatives

- Use a cycle-counting program that almost never results in error

- Use up-to-date, clear, and well-illustrated work instructions

- Maintain clean, uncluttered, and well-lit manufacturing areas

- Emphasize the overall quality systems of their suppliers and subcontractors

The companies that successfully achieved significant quality improvements over the last three years had at least two characteristics in common: Senior management provided significant leadership on the importance of quality improvement, and the companies emphasized and conducted significant training in quality techniques (32 or more hours per employee).

At other companies senior executives expounded quality improvement, but they failed to back up their words with training investments. In other cases, corporate headquarters mandated substantial quality training. but divisional management believed in delegating quality leadership to lower-level managers. In both situations, the companies failed to achieve significant improvements.

LEADERSHIP IS A CRITICAL FACTOR

The strategic benchmarking study included an employee survey to assess each site's leadership. At each site, a cross-section of employees rated their senior managers on 70 questions. The survey covered such issues as creating values, communicating a vision, encouraging participation, providing commitment and involvement, and exhibiting leadership characteristics.

The study found that three of the five most profitable sites had general managers who demonstrated superior leadership. In addition, the business practices that differentiate the companies with the strongest leadership are almost

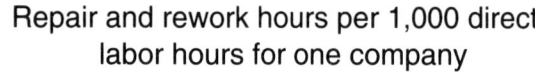

EXHIBIT 4.—A SIGNIFICANT IMPROVEMENT FOR
ONE COMPANY

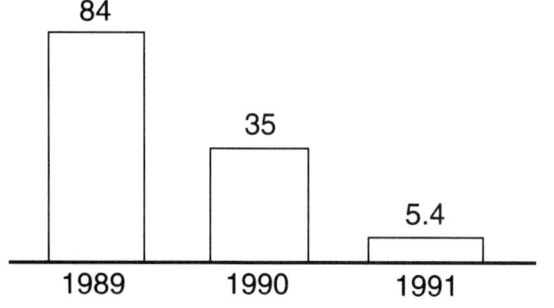

One company amply demonstrates the effect a leader can have on an organization. When touring one participant's factory, the consultants were struck by how clean, uncluttered, well lit, and well organized the factory was. The consultants did not realize that three years prior, the factory was frequently described as a pig sty. But in 1989, the company hired a new vice-president of production. He led manufacturing in a complete turnaround. The factory had reduced its repair and rework hours from 84 hours per 1,000 direct labor hours to five hours per 1,000 direct labor hours over three years (see Exhibit 4). This company had gone from the study's "worst in group" to "best in group" during the three years studied.

identical to those that differentiate the more profitable companies. These findings strongly suggest that a relationship exists between leadership and profitability.

In addition, the study found that companies with the strongest leadership:

- Emphasize strategic quality planning. They include quality goals in their strategic plans, involve many departments in quality planning, have a formal quality-planning methodology, and identify and prioritize business-improvement projects.

- Focus on the customer (internal and external)

- Promote quality awareness throughout their organizations. They develop formal quality missions and policies, develop and communicate quality goals, track performance in meeting those goals, have internal quality award and recognition systems, and have frequent senior management speeches on quality.

- Emphasize a goal-oriented organization. They track performance against business plans, allocate resources to quality improvement activities, provide incentives for improvement activities, link quality improvements to executive assessments, and link organizational goals to individual goals.

These findings validate the consultants' observation that participating companies with a strong leadership had a strong quality focus.

LESSONS APPLY TO ALL COMPANIES

The strength and consistency of the strategic benchmarking study's results validate that a group of companies can objectively compare and assess themselves using a process perspective. From this study, the A&D industry found that it has five key leverage points: superior business acquisition, superior customer delivery performance, superior subcontract delivery performance, less change activity, and superior manufacturing quality.

Equally important, the study found that the more profitable companies are not best at everything but instead differentiate themselves in these five key areas. The top performers recognize that they have finite resources, so they concentrate their resources on these leverage points. In addition, these companies did not achieve these results by developing a "silver bullet" of superior technology. They achieved these results by developing formal, consistent, disciplined, and repeatable processes.

Yet, the results found that achieving repeatable process performance depends on some subtle qualities. Despite this study's natural emphasis on quantitative measures and analysis, the study found that superior performance is driven by:

- Empowerment
- Partnerships
- A quality focus
- A process orientation
- Cross-functional teams

These characteristics appear to be the true leverage points for all businesses.

The final lesson is that leadership is required to create an improvement-driven organization. It is this key factor that enables the organization to improve its customer service and thereby position itself to generate profits.

NASA THROTTLES UP ON ISO 9000*

The National Aeronautics and Space Administration (NASA), which already has adopted ISO 9000 requirements for purchasing, now plans to require all of its own sites to become compliant with the international quality-assurance requirements.

"What we're saying here is 'if it's good enough for the contractors, it should be good enough for us too,'" explained Carl H. Schneider, technical adviser to the associate administrator for safety and mission assurance on quality initiatives with NASA.

In a March 31 memorandum to NASA's 10 field centers, the agency's headquarters directed all sites to develop an implementation plan for complying with ISO 9000 requirements. Third-party registration was not required.

"We do build spacecraft at some of our NASA centers and yet we weren't working to the same standards that we impose on our contractors," Schneider explained. The NASA centers are expected to be compliant with the standards by mid-1997. If so, NASA will become the first government agency to comply with ISO 9000 on a large scale.

Schneider said the White Sands Test Facility in New Mexico is in the process of attaining ISO 9000 registration as part of a joint effort with Allied Signal, its on-site engineering support contractor.

"They are teamed with a contractor so it's going to take both of them to pass the assessment," he said. "If they pass, as far as I know, that will be the first government/contractor as a joint-effort registered facility."

Though third-party registration is not mandated, Kennedy Space Center, one of the largest and best known NASA facilities, also is considering registration of its operations, according to Schneider.

NASA adopted ISO 9000 along with 13 supplementary requirements as the agency's preferred quality management standard in February 1994. Officials later dropped the supplementary requirements.

Schneider said the agency has not yet decided if third-party registration will become a contractual requirement. But the Johnson Space Center in Texas has made third-party registration mandatory on several contracts, including one for the shuttle program that combined five prior contracts.

That contract is for the shuttle orbiter, its main engines, solid rocket motors and launch support. It will affect operations at the Johnson and Kennedy facilities as well as the Marshall Space Flight Center in Alabama.

"The agency is starting to move out in this third-party area," Schneider explained. "Of course [the Department of Defense] and some of the other agencies are watching to see if what we're doing is smart."

Schneider said a number of NASA's contractors have voluntarily offered to adopt ISO 9000 in their operations. "To me that's a real indication that this whole concept has a lot of merit and we don't have to force the change process through intimidation or threat," he said.

"Companies are realizing that ISO 9000 makes a lot of sense and I think that they believe that NASA understands the real intent of going to ISO 9000," he added.

NASA also is participating in an effort to promote adoption of common quality requirements among federal agencies based on the ISO 9000 series standards.

---

*Reprinted with permission from *Quality Systems Update*, published by IRWIN Professional Publishing, Fairfax, VA.

||||| 2.8
AUTOMOTIVE

■

FINAL EXAMS*
by Tim Keenan

Say "automotive electronics" and what comes to mind? Usually it's high-profile antilock braking, traction control, air bag and engine management controllers. Or maybe vehicle navigation, adaptive cruise control or even sound systems and cellular phones. Some of the industry's most amazing and important electronics, however, take the form of low-profile testing equipment.

Industry challenges such as increasing quality, reliability and fuel mileage, reducing development cycles, costs and emissions — not to mention litigation—will not go away. They'll be even more challenging in the future. As components become more complex, the hardware used to assure their quality and reliability needs to keep pace.

No longer can an automaker merely run a car into a brick wall to make sure crash-test dummies stay in the vehicle. Today they need an instrumented crash wall like the one being installed at Ford Motor Co. in Dearborn, MI, by Kistler Instrument Corp. of Amherst, NY. Instrumentation includes 47 quartz piezoelectric multicomponent load cells that provide 141 output signals, which will give force data in three directions. The new wall will offer Ford engineers information about the distribution of forces during vehicle impacts.

Even the tried-and-true crash test sled is undergoing a high-tech transformation. The new HYGE Sled at Lear Seating Corp.'s remodeled advanced technology and test center uses a digital, high-resolution camera system developed jointly by Lear and Eastman Kodak Co. Digital images captured during tests are downloaded into an automated motion-analysis system that eliminates delays caused by film developing and enhances the quality and accuracy of analysis.

Kodak also is helping Textron Inc. design and test the effects of air-bag deployment on interior components. Using a pair of Kodak EktaPro HS motion analyzers, Textron records airbag release tests and views slow-motion replays to see how instrument panel and air-bag door designs perform. The Kodak device can record up to 4,500 full-frame images per second or up to 40,500 split-frame images per second with immediate slow-motion playback.

Advanced computers are even used to test seemingly low-tech components such as axles and driveshafts. Schenck Pegasus Corp. recently unveiled what it calls the industry's first axle and driveshaft road simulator. By merging a powertrain dynamometer and a servo-hydraulic axle test rig into one test machine, engineers will be able to perform overall verification tests of a full axle assembly in a laboratory setting.

The simulator's combined technology has the capability, says the company, of reproducing prerecorded dynamic service loads with eight channels of structural load inputs combined with three channels of torque control for the axles and driveshaft. All input signals are recorded simultaneously at a test track and reproduced in a lab.

Modine Manufacturing Co., which makes radiators and other heat-transfer components, also brings the road into the laboratory via electronics. While driving customer prototypes on test runs, data recorders give Modine engineers information on vehicle vibrations. The tape is brought to the lab, transferred onto a computer disk and played through the supplier's own test equipment. Because the system is computer-based it is capable of compressing the testing cycle, so periods of time when component stress doesn't happen— like waiting at stop signals—can be eliminated from the program, trimming up to 70% of the time needed to complete testing.

Reprinted with permission from *Ward's Auto World*, Volume 31, Number 8, © August 1995.

"This method has proved to be a very efficient way to test durability and ensure quality," says Andrew Schmidt, a Modine design engineer.

When Fasco Controls Corp. decided to extend its automotive component lines into high-performance solenoid valves, it ran headlong into the industry's mandates for 100% testing of function, flow and leakage, plus full statistical process control data available on demand. Fasco Project Manager Allen R. Clapper says besides requiring statistical control with documentation traceable to individual products by serial number or production runs by date code, OEMs now want a supplier's test equipment to physically take control of discrepant materials by automatically discarding rejects.

Chicago-based InterTech Development Co. (IDC) custom built for Fasco a 12-station dial (rotary turntable) type test stand allowing the supplier to test several parameters of air and brake-fluid pressures. Within a single seven-second station pause, IDC's mass-flow sensing technology gives direct volumetric measurement of flow rate or leakage accurate to 0.05 standard centimeters per minute. "While the computer automatically monitors each test against preset limits," Mr. Clapper explains, "our technicians study real-time displays to relate any suspect data back to individual components within the valve. This warns us about any upstream process or material variations they may need attention."

One of the biggest areas of concern for automakers in the '90s is noise, vibration and harshness. So naturally it is a big concern for suppliers. In addition to the HYGE Sled at the new Lear Seating test center, the company has installed equipment to test its products for NVH.

A computer-controlled multiaxis shaker table with 16-channel data-acquisition system simulates varying road conditions allowing the seat maker to test structural dynamics and seat comfort, evaluate squeaks and rattles and sound quality. In a typical test, an instrumented seat is bolted to the shaker table. Engineers use collected data to locate problem noises and refine seat designs.

"Because we have state-of-the-art test equipment in-house, we are able to better engineer the product, speed up developmental lead times and expedite product testing," says Art Vartanian, vice-president of advanced technology at Lear.

Electronics are even being used to test the thickness of automotive coatings. Fisher Technology Inc.'s Fisherscope X-Ray System XDV measures and analyzes dual and triple coatings, alloy coatings and electroless nickel coatings, all considered difficult to gauge.

While on-board electronics systems save lives and make driving a more pleasurable experience, the lesser-known automotive electronics make sure the entire vehicle does its job.

QUALITY IN TRANSPORTATION*

1. Generally speaking, transportation and quality are separate issues, Quality is the state of a product, transportation simply its movement. Or, transportation is a service, while the making of goods is a production.

2. Transportation is transportation. Get the goods from point A to B on this day for X number of dollars, and don't break anything. Period.

3. If you make a quality product, people will wait for it, and you can pretty much make

to order. So don't worry about transportation.

Sound familiar? They're typical comments from those who, frankly, just don't understand that quality has a place in service as well as in products. Whether it's widgets or LTL service, quality is quality: meeting the customer's requirements.

In transportation, as in other businesses, quality also has become a competitive issue. Some U.S. transport firms have seized the quality issue in an effort to distance themselves from their rivals. Companies that buy transport services know quality transport can literally make or break them.

Quality transportation does have a dimension, though, that most people don't talk about. Besides being all that you'd expect in terms of on-time delivery and lack of damage, quality in transport also means flexibility. A transport supplier has to be able to meet requirements—even as those requirements change.

MEASUREMENT

In fact, this ability to change with the requirements is what makes measuring quality performance in transportation so tricky. Quality measuring in transportation is in its infancy when compared to manufacturing, where SPC and the like have been around for years. There is barely a handful of transport companies that measure their services comparably to the way thousands of manufacturers measure their production processes.

Enter the transport-services buyer, who's prodding transport suppliers to rate themselves, or doing the measuring himself.

Motorola, for one, is on a drive to rate all its service buyers, transport included. Ken Stork, who runs Motorola's purchasing show, sees American service companies in the same position their compatriot manufacturers were in the 1960s and '70s. They're in good position now, but complacency could lead them down hardship road, as complacency led U.S. manufacturers down that road a decade ago.

In any case, there are basically two ways of going about measuring quality in transport. You can pay the supplier, more or less, to do it himself. Or you can do it yourself. Motorola is working on the former, 3M uses a combination of the two.

It's cheaper off the top to have the supplier measure himself for quality. But the dangers here are two-fold. One is, he'll likely just pass on the added cost of measurement. The second potential danger is that he'll slough off on the measuring to make it look good.

On the other hand, if the buyer does the measuring himself, there are added costs right away. The big advantage in this approach is that the buyer has total control over the measurement process.

Katharine Sullivan, Motorola's corporate manager of transportation and travel, says the decision on how to approach the measurement of transportation services hinges on what type of company is buying the services. She says that for a decentralized firm like Motorola, it makes the most sense to have the supplier do the measuring.

For highly centralized 3M, however, a combination—some supplier self-measurement, some vendor measurement by 3M—seems to be working well, says Phil Hovde, quality performance/administration manager.

3M started the program—Partners in Quality—in 1983, when it began contact negotiations wherein standards of performance—ratings—became part of the vendor-buyer lexicon. Motorola is now just approaching the negotiating stage.

After the setting of performance standards comes measurement of service, review of measurements, and, where necessary, corrective action. Hovde says the program was started as part of an overall quality-improvement push in all departments at 3M.

THE 3M PROGRAM

Vendors electronically send data in various formats to 3M. Items tracked include transit time, carrier response to request for movement, arrival date, billing accuracy, loss and damage, and shipping and receiving hours. Vendor and buyer already have agreed-to standards for many of the items, so it's easy to assess carriers.

The key to the program, Hovde says, has been transit times, which have improved drastically. Deliveries are now made on time 95% of the time, no small feat in dealing with truckload and LTL service.

Hovde also points out that what isn't measured is important as well. If you start measuring too many things, the program gets too complicated, and you get a lot of information that you don't need. For example, 3M decided not to measure parcel service—UPS, Federal Express, and the like—because it didn't want to get into the business of tracking letters across the country.

It's important to remember, however, that each company has to work out its own system. What's good for 3M, in other words, might not be good for you.

WHAT SUPPLIERS SAY

So, we've talked about quality through the eyes of buyers. What about the other side of the coin, the sellers? What do they have to say about quality in transportation? What are they doing about it?

What follow are comments from top officers in some of America's biggest transportation companies.:

L. Stanley Crane, the CEO at Conrail, says that because the railroad serves six of the top 10 U.S. markets and faces stiff competition from motor carriers: "To succeed, Conrail must offer a high-quality transportation product that is fast, reliable, economical, and competitive with other modes.

"The key to providing that service," Crane adds, "is an excellent physical plant. As railway maintenance, especially on track, signals, and structures, is extremely expensive, the goal is to have everything done right the first time with high-quality workmanship and supplies."

Hays T. Watkins, chairman and CEO of CSX Corp., reveals that a customer survey found its customers "were not satisfied with our service vis-a-vis our competitors." That, Watkins says, coupled with supplier conferences CSX attended plus cost-cutting, led the corporation to begin a quality process about a year ago.

As to what's been toughest about getting the process in place, Watkins says it's been "establishing management credibility with employees who have seen many other programs come and go.

"We expect the program," Watkins adds, "to help our customers, our employees, and our profitability. Customers will benefit from a new focus on meeting their requirements and improving communications. Our employees will benefit by having a greater opportunity to participate in their work and a greater ability to affect their work environment. Our profitability should reflect both greater revenue due to our enhanced ability to provide customers with the service they need and reduced costs as a result of eliminating the waste in the organization."

John C. Emery Jr., chairman and CEO Emery Air Freight, says his company recently began a quality program, in part because, a la CSX, a company survey found "our customers rank good consistent service above all else."

Emery adds that the quality program is significant because: "By setting our weighted criteria upon which each office is measured, the company focuses employees' attention and lets them know what the company sees as important. Now each office has some relative idea of its service performance and is not working in a vacuum."

J.T. Topping, executive vice-president of Roadway Express, says his company's quality push began as a pilot program in mid-1984 and became company-wide, through 61 quality teams, in January 1985.

"Our quality program was originally designed to produce input and ideas from front-line supervisors who are directly involved in prime areas where unquality can be eliminated," says Topping. "Additionally, requirements of customers were changing as they became involved in their own quality programs and we saw the need to be responsive to these changes."

Roadway established these goals for its quality teams: improve organizational productivity, improve employee satisfaction, develop employee capabilities through leadership and training, and improve communication by reducing frustration and conflicts.

R.L. Crandall, president and chairman of American Airlines, says his firm was prompted to make a quality push in part because of airline deregulation, which saw customer complaints and public scrutiny rise sharply. Crandall says the hardest part of the program "was to gain employee ownership."

FINAL QUESTION

The final question becomes whether the buyer and seller will work together toward the use of more widespread quality techniques in transport. As it appears now, if not working against one another toward quality, buyer and seller, must make more of an effort at partnership. That's the only way they'll achieve a measurable degree of quality.

Quality in transportation must become more standardized, so buyer and seller can understand one another in talking about quality. As the programs of the 3Ms and Motorolas spread, that might happen.

|||| 2.9
FINANCE AND BANKING

———————————————————■———————————————————

IS QUALITY CONTROL DEAD?*
by Joellen Abate-McEntire, Hakki C. Etem, Kim L. Sauter, and Rebecca B. Walzak

Nine years ago, responding to rising loan losses, Fannie Mae became the first agency investor to require mortgage sellers to implement quality-control programs. The direct cost of these programs to lenders has been substantial—both in actual dollars and in resources that otherwise could have been directed to production capacity or profitability. In light of this added burden on lenders, it's reasonable to ask whether these quality-control departments have contributed to lower loan losses and better loan quality, thus justifying their cost to the mortgage industry. Most lenders view their delinquency rates as indicative of loan quality. By this measure, the quality of loan originations for many lenders has generally declined since 1989, when Fannie Mae, Freddie Mac and FHA all required seller quality-control programs. Furthermore, early indicators suggest that the performance of the 1994 book of business is going to be poor and considerably worse than 1993 originations, according to a news report in National Mortgage News in May.

Delinquency trends, by themselves, appear not to validate the investment many lenders have made in quality control. However, to the extent quality control prevents bad or fraudulent loans from ever being made, that benefit would not show up in delinquency trends. But that particular benefit is difficult to measure.

As lenders struggle to reduce overhead in the face of declining volume and rising delinquencies, quality-control departments are getting close scrutiny. A technological innovation—automated underwriting—also could threaten the industry's commitment to quality control. Many observers expect that automated loan approval for a majority of loan applications, like that promised by Freddie Mac's Loan Prospector and Fannie Mae's Desktop Underwriter, will lead to a concurrent reduction in underwriting and quality-control staff and costs.

Given the difficulties in quantifying quality control's contribution to loan quality, and automated underwriting's promise of a cheaper, more effective way to underwrite loans, the future of quality control is in question. Is it possible that quality control, as we know it, is dead? This may seem a foregone conclusion to some, but it is wise to remember that appearances are frequently deceiving.

While conventional wisdom may lead us to believe delinquencies reflect loan quality, the fact is that overall performance trends do not reflect the efficacy of quality control. Furthermore, automated underwriting actually dictates the need for increased efforts to ensure quality. It must be acknowledged, however, that the need for quality is not being addressed by the practices in existence today. We must reach a better understanding of quality—what it is and how to achieve it.

This article presents a new perspective by analyzing current quality control requirements and comparing them to proven quality-management techniques. It then provides some alternatives, which if adopted by lenders, hold the promise of truly effective quality control.

———————————

*Reprinted with permission from *Mortgage Banking* magazine, (Volume 55, Number 11, August 1995, pp. 95-102), published by the Mortgage Bankers Association of America. Ellen Abate-McEntire is president of Abate and Associates in San Ramon, CA. Hakki C. Etem is president of Cogent Real Estate Economics in San Francisco, CA. Kim L. Sauter is assistant vice-president, quality assurance, of Commonwealth Mortgage Assurance Company in Philadelphia, PA. Rebecca B. Walzak is first vice-president, quality assurance, of Chemical Residential Mortgage Corporation in Jacksonville, FL.

QUALITY MANAGEMENT:

A Historical Perspective

Finding someone to define quality is not a difficult task these days. With all the books, seminars and articles being written about quality, everyone is eager to share a story, comment or philosophical approach. One thing is certain, quality in business is not a new concept. It has been around since commerce began. What has changed is the process for achieving it.

Historically, managing for quality began with the production of goods by individual craftsmen. At that time, customers relied on the workmanship and reputation of the craftsman to be assured of the product's quality. As goods began to be produced in large quantities, and the process for producing them became more complex, the idea of warranties developed. These warranties provided a quality guarantee.

Next came the concept of scientific management and the compartmentalizing of each piece of the production process so that each operated independently. To make sure that the products produced by such a system met the quality test, quality review also became a detached department whose focus was on product inspections. The job of this department was to separate the bad from the good, to reduce the number of defective products that were sent to the customers. These departments made no effort to eliminate the cause of the defective products or identify the processes that were failing to produce expected results, according to J.M. Juran in the book *Juran on Leadership for Quality: An Executive Handbook.*

Nevertheless, this was the approach prevalant in American corporations up through the 1970s. Then, in 1980, as Japanese products began to make a dent in American industry's reputation and profitability with a new level of quality, NBC broadcast a documentary on Japanese quality programs. This show crystallized these new ideas on quality and brought to a head the emerging new awareness of the need to once again change how we manage for quality. Edwards Deming and Joseph Juran emerged as experts in the development of quality management theory and prompted the development of a cadre of quality-improvement programs. The resulting successes in improved quality and increased profitability were widely publicized and further drove the pursuit of quality (see book by Mary Walton, *Deming Management at Work*).

These quality-management theorists tell us that a new understanding of the value and benefits that come from managing quality is necessary to achieve it. This approach involves understanding and defining quality, setting objectives to achieve it, evaluating progress toward those goals and making improvements on a continuous basis to meet the objectives established by the organization; in other words, planning, controlling and improving, according to Juran.

Quality Management in Mortgage Banking

Although never formalized in writing, quality in mortgage banking has traditionally been associated with loan performance. This connection between quality and performance was brought to light in part by the problems experienced by the savings and loan institutions. It was not unusual to find investigators during the savings and loan debacle attributing many of these institutions' problems to the lack of loan quality.

For its part, the secondary market was slow to act on establishing requirements to monitor loan quality. This was due largely to the belief that lenders would use compliance with these requirements "as a defense against indemnification requests or other disciplinary action, according to a 1989 article in *Mortgage Market Insight.*"

It was during this time, however, that individuals within the industry began to recognize the need for an emphasis on loan quality. Mortgage loan insurers were among the first to recognize that the mortgage market was overloaded with poor-quality loans and that this was not due to a deterioration in the borrowers' creditworthiness, but reflected a general lack of emphasis on quality loan origination and underwriting practices (see article in Mortgage Banking by Tames C. Miller, 1990, titled "Loan Quality Made in Heaven"). Finally, in 1986, Fannie Mae issued requirements for implementing quality control programs for its seller/servicers, and in 1989, Freddie Mac and FHA followed its lead.

The programs were designed as practical guidelines that mortgage lenders could readily implement with no undue burden, such as specialized staff or systems. The programs' intent was to ensure that loans met the requirements of Fannie Mae, Freddie Mac and FHA because these requirements were the basis on which performance expectations were built.

The programs were built around inspection processes that were heavily focused on making sure all the necessary documents that support the loan underwriting decision were included in the file. Loans that didn't meet the requirements were to be identified for the agency so it could decide whether to retain the loan. In addition, quality-control staffs were to identify any patterns or trends that came to light as part of these inspections and notify their management so changes could be made to prevent recurrence of problems. The final piece of the process was to reverify loan information through review appraisals, new credit reports and written reverification of borrowers' employment and assets.

All the agencies continued to monitor and revamp their quality-control requirements to make them more amenable to the industry's needs. In 1988, Fannie Mae expanded its guidelines to include statistical sampling, but most lenders chose to continue using the less-complex 10-percent sample program. It wasn't until dramatic volume increases drove lenders to find relief from the 10-percent sampling requirement that statistical sampling was given much attention. As more lenders became aware of the benefits of this sampling methodology, it became more widely accepted. Finally, in 1992, both Freddie Mac and FHA changed their requirements to include this type of sampling. As part of the lender approval and review process, better compliance with these requirements was expected and, as a result, better levels of loan performance. In addition, if lenders were found in noncompliance, actions could be taken to remedy their performance and improve their loan quality.

The Lenders' Perspective

Once the programs were established, it was left to the lenders to implement them. Most did so by developing a separate quality-control department whose responsibility was to conduct the reviews and report the findings to senior management. However, informal research revealed evidence that not all lenders endorsed or implemented these programs as required.

In a 1989 article in Mortgage Banking titled "Separating Fact from Fraud," author James Hagen stated, "Quality control is an area that many lenders take for granted and/or put on the back burner when other areas of the shop demand attention. Others have left quality control

to someone in their company who is responsible for a multitude of other tasks" Hagen added. "Many mortgage lenders choose to ignore quality control as additional unessential overhead. Still other lenders choose to do quality control in a half-hearted manner, taking comfort in the fact that they have set up a quality-control department, albeit in name only."

Despite the fact that some lenders were reluctant to commit the resources to quality control, the majority of lenders implemented the programs as required by the secondary market. In early 1994, the Mortgage Bankers Association of America's (MBA) Quality Assurance Committee conducted a survey of the industry's senior management to gather information on how these individuals felt about current quality-control programs. While the survey results demonstrated that 75 percent supported the concept of quality-control, only 33 percent indicated they had the time to review the reports prepared by their quality control staff. In addition, 40 percent of those surveyed felt that current agency requirements were actually impeding their ability to get the most from their reviews and wanted the requirements changed.

Very few respondents could place a dollar figure on the "cost per file" of quality control, but it is generally accepted by quality-control managers that a figure of $100 per file is reasonable, exclusive of the cost to review credit reports and appraisals.

Unfortunately, in the mortgage-lending industry, quality control has come to be viewed by many as an operational requirement and a cost with little-to-no measured feedback. Even less credence is given to the reports because the function is performed by individuals who may have fewer credentials and less experience than those they are reviewing, evaluating and reporting on. Overall, lenders appear to believe quality-control programs lack reliability, cost too much and provide few, if any, results that have a beneficial impact on the company, based on our experience in this field.

Secondary Market Perspective

Because the existing quality-control programs are the result of agency requirements, it is important to determine how the agencies view the effectiveness of their own requirements when put in practice. It appears agency representatives are skeptical about how these requirements are implemented and supported, as well as how effective they are in achieving the original objective.

Even though current requirements were developed by Fannie Mae, Freddie Mac and FHA, there is inherent confusion in the program parameters, which contributes to the lack of clearly defined focus in quality-control programs. Repeatedly the agencies state that the purpose of their programs is to review and evaluate the quality of the production process, yet many of the reviews required are due to the "high risk" associated with the performance of the products. This results in increased samples, reviews and reverifications. The fact that the results of these reviews must be reported within 90 days allows little time for any in-depth analysis that would indicate on-going quality variances.

Agency representatives also say that issues exist surrounding enforcement of the requirements. In reviewing the results of many of the lenders' programs, it is evident to representatives of Fannie, Freddie and FHA that some lenders consider it a necessary evil. These representatives have noted that compliance is to the letter of the requirements rather than to the spirit. This can be seen in management reports that emphasize the percentage of files reviewed to show that compliance to guidelines was achieved rather than percentages of variances consistent within the files reviewed. FHA, Fannie or Freddie can do little about lenders whose focus is to simply satisfy agency requirements, rather than improve the production quality of their operation. Although the agencies can retract a lender's approval to sell loans for failing to comply, they can have little impact on lenders that perform quality control in name only.

How effective existing quality-control programs have been in reducing loan delinquency also can be questioned. Overall delinquency trends do not reflect any strong or consistent impact that could not be explained by numerous other factors. Such things as loan mix, changing economic conditions and variable repayment rates most likely have a greater influence on portfolio delinquency rates than any quality control review—no matter how diligent.

Now both Fannie Mae and Freddie Mac are adding technology in the form of automated underwriting into the mix. There is little doubt that quality control will be affected by this new development. But the more important question to raise is, how will automated underwriting affect loan quality?

EMERGING TECHNOLOGIES AND QUALITY CONTROL

While technology has been an integral part of loan production and servicing operations for several years, the use of more sophisticated applications is just beginning to emerge for the loan underwriting process. Currently, both Fannie Mae and Freddie Mac have developed systems that will provide purchase decisions on loans evaluated by an automated underwriting system. While one is a rule-based system that applies a hierarchical set of underwriting criteria and the other uses a predictability model developed from performance reviews, both are designed to remove the individual underwriter subjectivity and provide the lender and agency with a loan that unquestionably meets their standards.

Once these loans are accepted by either of the two systems, all representations and warranties are waived with the exception of data integrity requirements. No waivers of reps and warranties are available for those loans that fail to meet the "accept" criteria under the automated underwriting system, but that are ultimately purchased by Fannie Mae or Freddie Mac.

Despite some agency claims that their systems are designed to accommodate all loans, many in the industry find it unlikely that one system would approve all loan applications. Atypical loan applications will still require manual underwriting approval, and for some lenders such loans can represent one-half or more of application volume.

Typical loans approved by automated underwriting are still subject to input errors, fraud and so forth, thus leaving a role for quality control. In addition, these competing secondary market investors have developed their systems with unique approval criteria. Since most lenders prefer to sell mortgages to several investors, implementing automated underwriting is likely to be complex and error prone.

Although neither agency has yet provided any formal documentation regarding changes to their quality-control requirements, it is unrealistic to believe none will be forthcoming. What the industry may well end up with is a program that requires additional types of reviews, such as for data integrity and increased sample sizes and/or criteria, with no corresponding reductions in existing requirements or any validation of the value added. While these new automated underwriting systems are expected to reduce concerns about guideline adherence, the changes associated with automated underwriting will only increase the current quality-control requirements, not address the need for truly effective quality control.

UNDERLYING CAUSES

From research done by the authors, including formal committee research, a review of the literature on quality control, and interviews with industry and agency representatives, it appears clear that neither the industry nor the agency investors are satisfied with the current state of quality control. There seems to be general agreement that the current approach to quality control lacks a clearly defined foundation, costs too much for the returns it produces and provides little value other than as a means to identify poor documentation integrity. But why is it that with all the quality management expertise around we have failed in our efforts? There are several underlying reasons for the situation the industry finds itself in today.

First, the current status of industry quality-control programs is the result of relying on conventional wisdom rather than mathematically validated facts. Conventional wisdom dictates there is a relationship between adherence to loan underwriting standards and loan performance. Thus, the way to manage performance risk is through ensuring adherence to these standards. However, if any relationship exists between these two areas, it has not been validated. Although no one denies there is probably some initial connection, the strength of that relationship and the duration have never been proven. Until that occurs, we cannot build any quality reliance on it.

Second, in addressing quality control, this industry has failed to recognize that we are dealing with two separate risks and that quality management is necessary for each. Both production and performance risks are inherent in this business. Production risk is the risk associated with failing to have processes in place that produce the product to the approved specifications, at the cost and within the time frame established by management. While it is identical for all loan types and is internally controlled, if not managed it will result in unnoticed technical and human errors, loan integrity problems and the po-

tential for a diminished reputation in the industry.

Performance risk is the risk associated with the nonperformance of loans and the potential underlying losses if this nonperformance results in foreclosure. The risks associated with performance vary by loan product and are influenced by external factors outside the organization's control. These variables, by definition, are not amenable to measurement through the testing of adherence to established standards and quality-control guidelines. No amount of feedback and corrective action will mitigate their adverse effect.

Relying on a quality-inspection process conducted by a detached quality department is another mistake that was made in designing the current system of mortgage quality control. The role assigned to this department clearly follows the pattern previously used by other American industries prior to the 1980s. Although quality-control departments are not distinctly charged to separate the bad from the good, agencies must be notified of any review results that show variances from underwriting standards, in other words, getting rid of the bad product.

Another feature in common with these earlier nonmortgage industry quality-control programs is the lack of identification of the underlying causes of product failure. While the agencies required reporting of trends and patterns, until very recently, the mathematical foundation necessary to do so with any validity was not an approved part of the program.

Finally, the process as it exists today does not require any definition of quality. It is, instead, a document-driven process that results in an internal audit approach, which ignores process and is easily dismissed by management because it provides no analysis from which action can be taken.

Based on this review it seems clear that the current approach to quality control in the mortgage industry is based on an erroneous foundation. Mortgage banking deserves better; quality control as we know it should be laid to rest. But the crucial question then becomes what should be put in its place.

APPLYING QUALITY THEORY

In reading any of the literature on quality management techniques, it becomes clear that the mortgage banking industry has simply brushed the surface of the potential benefits of implementing a total quality management plan—not simply quality control. Quality management theorists, Juran in particular, tell us that three managerial processes are required to achieve quality: planning, control and improvement. In this context, quality control is only one part of the quality-management discipline, and if unintegrated with the planning and improvement processes, it fails to accomplish the primary goal of quality management—the elimination of recurring deficiencies that result in inferior quality products.

The first step in implementing quality management is undoubtedly the most critical one and the one that typically appears to be overlooked by mortgage banking management. Because agency requirements are already in place and compliance is mandatory, it was easy for management to just "make them happen." However, if managers truly want quality in their production operations, then planning for it is crucial. Further, it must happen from within and be controlled by each individual company. This brings with it the challenge of introducing some fundamental changes into the dynamic, chaotic and uncertain realm of mortgage banking.

- The industry as a whole, as well as individual members of the industry, must define quality. Defining quality within the industry is critical to the success of a quality management program. We need to decide if a mortgage quality program is intended for production quality or performance quality or both. If we are to continue to connect quality to performance, the industry desperately needs a valid assessment of the contribution that quality control makes to improving loan performance, as well as a reconciliation of performance-quality and production quality relationships. It also requires that the agencies express a willingness to recognize that individual companies must define quality to meet their own corporate objectives. To achieve this, a universal definition for acceptable and defective loans is required. Agencies using the terminology "acceptable error rates" to evaluate a company's quality level when there is no clear consistent definition of what is meant by an "error" is counterproductive to developing a positive approach to quality management.
  If such terminology was instead replaced

with a common definition to which each company could attach a clearly defined statement of the company's quality objectives, it would be a much easier and more equitable way to measure performance. Of course, each company must then have in place a process for obtaining feedback (i.e., quality control) on its quality objectives that would provide consistent, reliable information upon which to make decisions. The flexibility this type of program provides also would allow lenders to pursue various markets they have not yet explored. By adjusting the definition and expected levels of quality, the industry may be able to open up new opportunities for borrowers and investors.

The responsibility that such flexibility carries with it requires that senior management be involved in the management of quality from start to finish. If the organization's culture limits effective feedback to the production department, little is gained by these reviews, no matter how salient. The involvement and support of senior management is recognized as critical to the success of any quality-management program, just as the process of trying to find a ready-made program instead of developing one internally is identified as an "obstacle to success," according to Dr. Edwards Deming, in Walton's book *Deming Management at Work*.

- There must be recognition of the difference between quality inspections and system analysis as well as the value of each. The current quality-control programs prescribed by the agency guides require a process that is based on a postclosing inspection to ensure that the loan specifications to meet eligibility requirements have been met. Then, in an effort to address any systemic issues that may arise, the agencies require the reporting of any trends or patterns to senior management.
  Based on the concepts indigenous to quality-management theory, this program has several major flaws. While it must be recognized that both types of reviews have value, the true value comes when each is used in such a way as to bring added benefit to the company. Therefore, the following changes are recommended:

- Shift the loan-inspection emphasis to preclosing reviews. A loan-inspection process that is designed to identify flaws in the loan file works best when it is in place prior to the loan closing. Identifying flaw after the loan has been funded so that it is not sent to an investor or is used to repurchase a flawed product is counterproductive to achieving an overall partnership with production in improving quality. Many companies have begun to move this process into a prefunding environment not only to reduce postclosing errors, but also to identify and eliminate fraudulent applications. This up-front process is the most effective way to address this growing problem, yet companies who have implemented this process have not been given recognition by the agencies for the overall value this review brings in achieving quality objectives.

- Recognize that effective quality management demands the use of statistical measurement and analysis. It must be recognized that the postclosing review process is a test of the company's production process and its quality to achieve the levels of quality it was designed to produce. The only way to do this type of test is by using mathematically sound measurement and analysis programs. Typically this is achieved by using statistical sampling programs. Without the ability to collect data and analyze it on a statistical basis, mortgage bankers are unable to obtain the information they need to correct problems.

  Currently many lenders are eager to take advantage of the reduced sample size generated by these programs, yet they fail to recognize that the true value is found in the ability to infer the findings to the entire population. As a result, they are failing to capitalize on some of the most important results of the review process. In addition, the current limitations on the sampling program (i.e., the 2-percent precision rate imposed by FHA that requires an increased sample size) add little value to the program and only make this program more complex than it need be, thereby inhibiting its use by some lenders.

- Add flexibility and consistency to the review process. The current review process focuses on ensuring that particular investor specifications are met. This approach is recognized by Deming as an obstacle to achieving quality. It fails to acknowledge that not only is there a wide variation in quality found in

products that meet specifications, but also specifications may not always be right. Because the industry already recognizes that independent variables influence loan performance, we tend not to rely entirely on compliance to specifications as a measure of quality. However, senior managers who are developing quality objectives for their organizations must have a clear understanding of the relationship—however tightly it is correlated—to establish quality objectives.

Another critical piece of the process that must be addressed by company plans is the methodology for collecting data in a consistent manner. A method for identifying and collecting data on variances found as part of the file reviews must be established. Without this consistent approach, collection and comparisons of monthly reviews is impossible. Imagine trying to compare two teams' seasons if one were a baseball team and one were a basketball team. This is what it would be like to compare two months' reviews if different variances were used to compile the results.

The industry also must learn to recognize random errors as opposed to systematic errors. Mistakes happen. If we continue to highlight each individual mistake rather than look for collections of errors, we will fail to identify process failures. Each company should establish a range of errors that are "acceptable" to them. This range of errors is what is commonly found in the reviews and indicates that the system is performing within the company's specifications. Individual errors then become irrelevant and, in fact, making corrections to address individual variations often leads to more variations. An added benefit to this approach is the lessening of the "fault-finding approach," which many underwriting staffs perceive to be the role of quality control.

- Ensure quality control is a "value-added" program by investing in quality. There is no doubt quality management costs money. Despite the once-popular book titled *Quality is Free*, supporters of quality management understand that an investment in quality costs money. This investment comes in two forms: One is the investment in the diagnostic process to discover the cause of poor quality, and two is the investment in the remedy to eliminate the cause. Yet as Joseph Juran wrote in his book *Juran on Leadership for Quality*, "The return on investment in quality improvement is among the highest available to managers."

• Recognize and support the need to evaluate the vendors and suppliers of data and documents that are integral to the production process. Although the reverification process is part of the existing program, many managers still do not effectively evaluate or manage the vendors and suppliers that provide elements of the loan package to them. In addition, the current reverification process adds significantly to the overall costs and adds minimal value to the postclosing review process.

The reverification process should be used as a systemic way to evaluate suppliers and vendors with clearly defined quality and error definitions. Percentages of these reverifications should be based on the company's vendor-quality standards, thereby allowing reverifications to be issued in a way that they would have the most impact and also provide the company with information needed to eliminate vendors and suppliers who fail to meet the quality requirements.

• Incorporate the data-integrity checks into quality-control plans as a value-added process for the system. Recognizing that data input is a critical part of the production process, even in today's environment, this review should be viewed as a necessary part of the loan quality-evaluation program. However, the focus should be on all loans, not just on those accepted by an automated underwriting program because the effect of bad data is equally serious for the originating entity. Agency requirements that isolate the loans accepted by their systems for this type of review hamper an overall statistical analysis of the company's data-input process.

• Support the education of quality-control staff and recognize their expertise in the company. Quality-management theorists view having a staff that is educated in and knowledgeable about quality-control processes and techniques as one of the most critical factors for companies that value quality management. However, the unfortunate fact is that many of the individuals running quality-control operations in the mortgage banking industry today have not been educated in quality-management theory and techniques.

While having an understanding of mortgage banking is necessary to manage the quality-control programs found in the industry currently, it is inadequate when charged with guiding the business in the development of its quality objectives. In addition, for a program to be truly effective, quality-management personnel must be included in strategic planning and technology development issues. While it is recognized that the ability to gain quality-management knowledge is relatively easy, gaining the mortgage-banking perspective cannot be accomplished outside the industry. MBA's Quality Assurance Committee is attempting to address these issues through conferences, newsletters and the possibility of a new Quality-Assurance Manager certification program.

• Focus on who is (are) the customer(s). Although a great deal of rhetoric is heard around any organization about quality and about taking care of the customer, the truth is this industry doesn't know who its customer is. The conflict between satisfying the borrower's requirements versus the investor's requirements—continually pits loan officers against underwriters and quality-control staff. Although lenders recognize that without borrowers there would be no need for their services, lenders must also accept the fact that without the secondary market, there would be limited funds for consumers to borrow. However, ignoring one over the other has proven an erroneous path, as legislative history and onerous reporting requirements will attest.

Certainly, making these changes would provide many advantages. The resulting process would provide an independent, unbiased review of production risk, early detection of possible misrepresentations, increased confidence in the accuracy of the data input and regular documented results that could be used to provide immediate improvement to processes and programs causing quality deficiencies. Once we understand that no amount of effective feedback and corrective action plans will mitigate the adverse effect of external forces on a lender's book of business, and we start focusing on defining and managing for quality in production and performance, we will begin to realize the true benefits of quality management. Only then will managers no longer be dependent on outside agencies to evaluate the quality of their products, and they will be able to reduce costs and the negative energy associated with a process based on outdated management practices.

MEASURING GAINSHARING RESULTS AT SECURITY PACIFIC: THE 17-PERCENT SOLUTION*
by Paul M. Jackson

INTRODUCTION

Questions Every Incentive Plan Designer Must Answer

While most American firms use incentives to motivate workers, there is anything but consensus about the most basic aspects of incentive plans. First, *what kind of plan will give the best results?* There are a number of plans to choose from, including those based upon individual piece-rates, profit sharing, and team performance, as well as combinations of these fundamental approaches.

How much incentive pay does it take to motivate workers? Put another way, assuming that incentive plans are adopted primarily to improve financial performance, *how much of the improvement in financial performance must be shared* in order to get the biggest bang for the buck?

Should workers be involved in the formulation of the plan? In setting the production standards? In modifying the incentive plan, once it has been in use for a period of time?

Once these decisions have been made and a plan has been operating for a period of time, *how do you really know how much you are saving?* Measuring improved financial performance is more than just calculating whether expenses went up or down, especially when the organization produces more than a few products in a changing, competitive environment. Downstream effects need to be considered as well as changes in the production volumes and product mix.

What about those nasty side effects attributed to the use of incentives? The use of incentives has been implicated in quality deterioration. Moreover, organizations with incentive plans often report that workers are unwilling to take on new tasks, since doing so will likely result in their not receiving the accustomed incentive pay. Incentive-paid workers are often less interested in contributing to operational improvements, since such changes impact their pocketbook; management is not likely to share the productivity savings from the investment in a new machine. On the other hand, management is likely to establish new production standards for use with the new machine, again creating uncertainty regarding incentive bonuses.

This article proposes a framework for determining the optimal incentive plan and then presents a case study on the use of shop-floor incentives. It provides clear insights regarding each of these important questions: What kind of plan is best for a given situation; how much incentive pay does it take to motivate workers; how can management know when a gain is a gain; and how can plans be designed to deal with incentive plan side effects.

OPTIMAL WORKFLOOR INCENTIVE PLANS

What is the best incentive plan to use? That depends upon the nature of the work and the environment in which the firm is operating.

Two factors are critical in determining the optimal incentive formula. First, can the output be traced to individuals? Second, does competition drive the firm to seek worker-generated process innovation? The recommendations stemming from the interplay of these two factors is diagramed in Exhibit 1. The specific advantages and disadvantages of each plan are summarized in Exhibit 2.

---

*Reprinted with permission from *Target*, Volume 11, Number 1, January/February 1995. Paul M. Jackson teaches management accounting at the University of Southern California (USC).

EXHIBIT 1.—PREDICTING ACCOUNTING-BASED INCENTIVE
CONTROLS

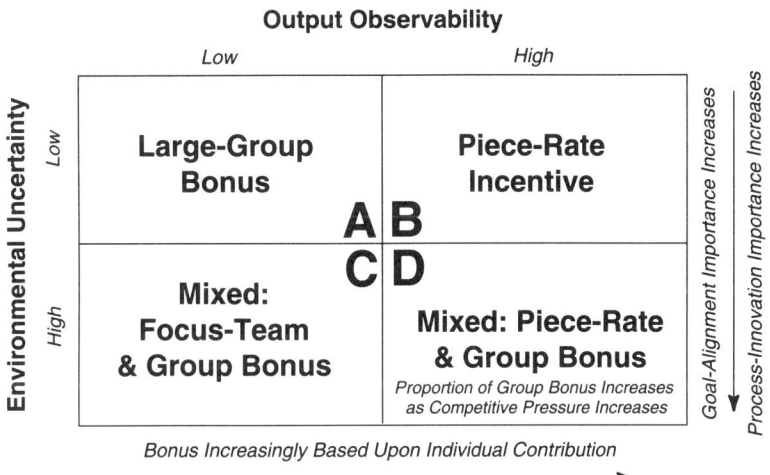

Recommendation for Incentive Plans
A) Incentive plan based upon organization-wide output measure(s).
B) Incentive plan based upon piece-rate measure(s)
C) Mixed incentive plan: measure(s) for focus team, combined with group bonus based upon organization-wide measure(s)
D) Mixed incentive plan: piece-rate measure(s), combined with group bonus based upon organization-wide measure(s).

OBSERVABILITY OF WORKER OUTPUT

When worker output is easily observable, then piece-rate plans have a considerable advantage. *Individual incentive components evoke the greatest increases in effort.* Firms must consider whether the benefits of an individual incentive component outweigh the disadvantages of such plans.

The financial and nonfinancial costs of piece-rate incentives can be high. Output must be tracked recorded, and analyzed at the individual level, and the expense to do this can be considerable. Moreover, the dysfunctional side effects must be anticipated and dealt with. Quality will suffer and unless defects are traced back to the responsible individual, the decrease in quality is likely to be significant.

Moreover, workers will be less willing to work in nonincented tasks and in those tasks which they perceive have higher required output standards. Worker innovation will suffer. Production workers will be resistant to processing changes, since such changes reduce the certainty of earning an incentive. Workers will not willingly perform unfamiliar tasks or accept changing work conditions unless they are offered even more compensation than they are already receiving.

These dysunctional side effects often reflect the lack of "goal alignment" between workers' incentives and firm goals. Under such circumstances, the worker has opportunities to improve his welfare that run counter to the needs of the firm. Goal-alignment problems occur when workers' goals are not the same as the firm's goals, or vice versa. For example, firms generally benefit from an increase in quality and a decrease in production costs. Workers under a piece-rate incentive (assuming no strict quality controls) benefit by working at maximum speed and not slowing down to minimize production mistakes. Firms can decrease the production cost by lowering the wage paid to labor. In each of these examples, goals are not aligned—the change in quality or cost benefits one party at the expense of the other party.

In summary, when the nature of the work tasks are such that worker output is very observable, firms have the most to gain from using in-

EXHIBIT 2.—ADVANTAGES AND DISADVANTAGES OF DIFFERENT INCENTIVE PLANS

Type of Incentive Based upon	Observability Requirement	Nature of Work	Advantages	Disadvantages
Piece-Rate Individual output	Output easily traceable	Highly routine	Evokes large increase in effort and output	Large overhead: —quality tracking —production by individual —loss of worker flexibility —"fairness"
Large Group Bonus Group performance	Cannot easily attribute	Routine or nonroutine	Increased profitability; increased worker flexibility; increased worker willingness to go along with firm goals. Pays for itself	Generally not very motivating; "free-rider problem," controllability problem
Mixed: Piece-Rate and Group Bonus Individual and group performance	Output traceable	Routine, but interdependencies okay	More effort evoked than with large-group plans; ameliorates some piece-rate problems	High overhead; piece-rate may dominate group incentive, leading to problems with quality, buffers, etc.
Mixed: Focus Team and Group Bonus Team and group performance	Many improvements traceable to a team	Nonroutine; innovation sought	Motivates teams; brings about rapid change and results	Large teams may have free-rider problems

dividual incentives. Individual incentives yield the highest increase in worker effort. However, they also have the greatest dysfunctional side effects. These side effects reflect the lack of alignment between workers' goals and firm goals.

ENVIRONMENTAL UNCERTAINTY: THE NEED FOR CHANGE

Individual piece-rate incentives have goal-alignment problems as their fundamental weakness. Piece-rate incentives work best when the firm only desires that the worker work as hard and fast as possible. In such situations, the optimal conversion process has been firmly established, and supervisors function as enforcers of inflexible procedures. In such situations, supervisors will look upon employee suggestions with disfavor. Supervisors are evaluated and rewarded for meeting production targets; the penalties for not meeting standard are not outweighed by the possible reward for improving productivity.

Putting all business press rhetoric aside, firms generally support this supervisor resistance to production-processing innovation—

unless competitive pressures compel the firm to seek processing improvements. Then competitive pressures come to bear upon those weaknesses brought about by the lack of goal alignment. The firm with a piece-rate incentive may find that its competitors have higher quality, more variety in their product line, faster turn-around time, more features, and shorter lead time. The firm with piece-rate incentives often finds itself less flexible and adaptive to competitive pressures, all things being equal.

Group incentives are one solution to this dilemma. Many advantages stem from group-based incentives. *Gainsharing plans*, for example, are group plans in which employees receive incentive payments only when the entire operation has experienced improved financial performance. Typically, in production operations, gainsharing plans are developed using a unit-cost formula: production is historically benchmarked and, perhaps, also benchmarked against significant competitors. In future periods, workers and their managers share in cost savings, often under a 50/50 sharing arrangement with the firm.

Gainsharing plans often induce *process improvements* rather than *increased levels of effort*. This is true because employees quickly realize that increased effort does not directly translate into a commensurately larger bonus for them; benefits are shared across the entire operation, and not everyone is willing to do their part in working harder. Nevertheless, gainsharing plans are believed to foster greater alignment of individual goals with firm goals in such areas as quality improvement, process change and operation flexibility—the very things that suffer under piece-rate incentives.

Gainsharing plans are distinct from profit sharing in that they are associated with an active and functioning employee-suggestion plan and are usually administered at the work-floor or plant level, rather than firm-wide. Gainsharing plans strive to preserve better line-of-sight between employee actions and bonuses than do profit-sharing plans. Gainsharing plans inherently have a mechanism and incentive for translating worker ideas into production-enhancing process improvements.

Many firms have created incentive-plan formulas that include both an individual piece-rate incentive and a group-based measure of performance. These so-called *"mixed" incentive plans* are contrived to obtain the higher productivity of individual piece-rate plans (stemming from increased effort) and the innovations and alignment of firm goals (quality, process improvements, and operation flexibility) that are associated with group-based plans. In practice, the individual component of such incentives seems to dominate over the group component, even when there is a 50-50 split between the individual and the group components of the bonus.

Team-based incentive plans are appropriate for situations where output is at best attributable to a small group of workers rather than a particular individual. One recent team innovation is the concept of *focus teams*. When rapid, successful change is sought, the formation of a focus team may be the best approach. The optimal incentive for a focus team would be a team bonus for meeting prespecified team milestones coupled with a group bonus tied to the improvement in work-group performance.

In summary, group incentive plans can be the optimal choice for firms facing competitive pressures. Group plans do not motivate as great an increase in individual effort as piece-rate plans. However, group plans do bring about alignment between the goals of the firm and the goals of individuals. Group plans do not have the negative side effects of individual plans. Moreover, group plans tend to foster innovation. Goal

alignment and process innovation can also be achieved by using a combination of group and individual plans ("mixed plans") when worker output is very observable and when increased effort is sought more than innovation.

INCENTIVES AT SECURITY PACIFIC

A Case Study in Piece-Rate and Mixed-Group Incentives

External Mail Services (EMS) was a large-scale mailing operation at Security Pacific. It was responsible for preparing bank statements, savings statements, and a host of other bank communications including overdraft notices, credit card bills and loan payment reminders, etc. EMS implemented a piece-rate incentive plan for the enclosing machine operators (about 23 full-time employees [FTE] across three shifts) early in 1989 and, nearly one year later in February 1990, a gainsharing-based incentive plan for the entire EMS staff.

The individual piece-rate plan adopted for the mail-enclosing "machine operators" was highly successful. The annual direct-labor savings were estimated to be $78,500 net of plan expenses. No employee layoffs were necessary; two employment requisitions were left vacant and five employees were redeployed to the mail-sorting function—for the first time, staff were available to use the "Jetstar" mail-sorting equipment. The Jetstar was a high-speed mail sorter that had been purchased six months earlier with the intent of obtaining a postage savings from presorting outgoing mail. Because of a lack of staff and the behind-processing circumstances, the Jetstar had remained idle ever since it was installed six months earlier.

The savings in direct labor was only a small part of the actual improvement, however. Average output per worker increased about 30 percent, making unnecessary the planned mail-enclosing equipment purchases of $1.05 million. Idle capacity increased to the extent that mail was processed only on the more recently purchased enclosing equipment, which revealed a mail mis-metering problem that had cost approximately $1 million annually in postage expense. There were some concerns regarding quality and preferential treatment in work assignments, however; these concerns were addressed directly by supervisors on an individual basis.

The machine-operator function met many of the requirements of an individual piece-rate incentive criteria of Exhibit 1. Workers performed highly-independent tasks; consequently their output was directly observable and was already being tracked as part of the normal production operation. The organization did receive pressure for process innovations that would lead to improved timeliness and, to a lesser extent, reduced direct labor expense. Process innovations were directly solicited from leads and workers by the EMS manager.

Quality-of-output issues were easily dealt with. Machine operator output became directly traceable with the introduction of an operator stamp; each piece of metered mail came to bear the stamp of the operator who produced it. Since the program affected only about 22 FTE operators, managing the program took only a few hours per week and required no incremental administrative personnel.

The piece-rate incentive plan had brought forth a tremendous increase in worker effort, as represented by the 30 percent productivity increase and idle machine capacity. The downside of piece-rate incentives was moderated by improved accountability (machine-applied operator stamp) and additional supervisor intervention. The operator piece-rate incentive plan was extremely popular and continued for one year until it was superseded by an EMS-wide group incentive in February, 1990.

PRESSURE TO ADOPT GROUP INCENTIVES

At the same time that the piece-rate incentive was implemented by EMS, group incentive plans were being innovated and developed under the direction of Mike Gerringer, division manager. They were adapted from a compensation consulting firm's presentation, which encompassed a modified gainsharing approach. Under the proposed group-incentive-plan framework, each individual worker would face a piece-rate incentive, but the amount of bonus received would be based upon overall organization financial improvement. That is, a production standard would be developed for every task (individual and/or group task); but the amount of incentive actually paid would be determined by operational savings for a given month.

This approach was not a traditional gainsharing plan at the worker level, since an indi-

vidual's incentive payout was based upon a worker's piece-rate performance. The managers and production leads (nonmanagers who performed many managerial tasks) did receive their incentives based strictly upon organization performance, however, which conforms to the usual gainsharing model. No formal suggestion plan was promoted as a part of the gainsharing incentive; however, an employee suggestion plan was already in place and workers throughout the division received awards on a monthly basis, ranging from $25 to several thousand dollars.

The goals of the incentive plans were:

- The lowest incentive was to be accessible to 80 percent of the permanent workforce

- Employees should know "at the end of the day" what incentive award they had earned

- Top incentive pay should be targeted to 30 percent of the workforce

- Incentive pay would be promoted as a 50/50 split with the company

- Fringe expense and other incidental savings would not be shared as part of the gainsharing plan

- Top incentive pay should be about 10 percent of base salary

- Piece-rate incentive payouts would be reduced if the operation did not obtain a labor savings; if unit cost was only 40 percent of the way between standard (past performance) and goal (direct labor unit cost if every one performed as well as the top 30 percent of the workforce), then only 40 percent of the incentive bonus would be paid

- The first three months would be funded at 33 percent even if no financial improvements were made

The plan took *considerable time to develop* because of the large number of individual tasks performed in EMS and the lack of reliable historical data. Data were collected over a two-month period to determine the distributional characteristics of each of 69 different tasks in EMS. Standards were developed for each task based upon average (median) performance. Goal rates were established as the performance level of the top 30 percent of observations for every task. In other words, the piece-rate standard for each of the 69 individual tasks was set to be the median rate per hour and the goal was set to be the rate per hour which 30 percent of the workers regularly exceeded and which 70 percent of the workers did not regularly exceed.

In July, the EMS management had "competitively benchmarked" the mailing operations against similar operations at the three largest California banks—Wells Fargo, First Interstate, and Bank of America. EMS production staff visited each of these bank's production operation and obtained information (by asking and by observing) that allowed them to measure how competitive EMS was in production efficiency, timeliness, and processing accuracy of major similar functions. They found that their unit-processing cost was half that of First Interstate and Wells Fargo bank, but that Bank of America's unit cost was about six percent lower than EMS. Wells Fargo was the most timely during the critical "month-end" business customer processing, but the remaining banks were about equivalent otherwise. With this information, EMS managers were relatively confident in setting a competitive unit production cost.

Considerable "what-if" analysis was done to determine the extent of savings that could be obtained at various levels of improvement, under different assumptions regarding the distribution of the improvements across employees and across tasks. This was done to ensure that labor savings could be obtained to fund the plan—that the plan was workable both from the perspective of employees and of Security Pacific. The data collection and analysis were performed by a production lead and a manager.

Nonmanagement employees did not directly participate in the development of the incentive plan, even though employee involvement is often cited as a prerequisite to building trust and to improving the implementation. Employee involvement would have been useful in the selection of the basic design. The ultimate plan was very complex, and had more employees participated at the design stage, it is likely that overall employee understanding of the plan would have increased. Nevertheless, employee trust did not seem to be an issue. Despite the complexity of the plan, it did evoke considerable increases in employee effort, whether measured by the change in production rates per hour or by the decrease in overall unit cost. While employees often commented that they did not understand the plan, many nonetheless quickly learned to game the plan by logging the maximum amount of

"nonincented time" which had the effect of inflating their piece-rate performance.

Employee involvement in other aspects of the plan development would not have been productive. Data collection was done by logging production where it had not been logged before. None of the regular production employees had the training and experience to develop the computer software. Resolving the difficult issues involved in converting a generic gainsharing/piece-rate concept into an implementable plan would not have been facilitated by having a committee of workers. Employee involvement would have both enhanced the implementation process and improved plan understanding and acceptance only if it had occurred during the initial, conceptual development phase.

Data collection began in earnest in August 1989 and a preliminary incentive plan was submitted at the end of November; additional management revisions were made to the plan between November 1989 and February 1990. The plan was in operation for one month in February and was halted due to management turnover and production-processing changes. The new management wanted a second validation of the original plan production standards, goal levels, and unit cost. The group-incentive plan was reinstituted, essentially unchanged, beginning in May 1990 and continued through the Bank of America/Security Pacific merger in 1992. The plan was ultimately discontinued during the first quarter of 1993.

Standardized forms were developed to track employee output for incented tasks and to collect additional data for tasks not yet under incentive. The incentive system had to incorporate considerable flexibility to deal with one particular form of complexity. Employees were assigned to tasks at the beginning of their shifts according to the production demands of the immediate situation (which varied considerably from day to day). On a given day, an employee could perform seven or more separate tasks, each for a duration of from ten minutes to several hours. Employees did not necessarily perform the same tasks from day to day. The plan needed to be sufficiently flexible to handle this aspect of job complexity.

For example, a typical manual-side production worker might handle ten or so registered mail items that came in that day, then move on to ordering reprints of five statements that had been damaged in the machine-enclosing process; then work on metering branch mail for several hours. The tasks which an individual manual worker performed on a given day depended upon the inflow on that day as well as work that had been left unfinished from the previous day, evening, or midnight shift. No manual-side worker did the same task every day for an entire month; most performed two or three different tasks each day.

A microcomputer software system was developed to capture individual employee work statistics and to calculate individual incentives on a weekly and monthly basis. Chris Duymich, the production lead who assisted in developing the incentive plan, was trained in the use of the software and later performed all aspects of the administration of the plan. These tasks included data entry, verification of input documents, bonus calculations, unit-cost calculations, bonus paysheet preparation, and answering worker inquiries regarding the specifics of a bonus award.

Concurrently, an SPC quality improvement effort was launched which involved measuring the extent of defects, understanding the causes of defects, establishing quality control levels, and training staff to sample and record production defects on each of three shifts. Defects were traced back to the responsible individual worker whenever possible. The penalty for a (detected) defect ranged from ten minutes to 150 minutes of production time added to the week's processing time, thereby reducing the weekly incentive award. Production leads and supervisors were likewise penalized for defects that occurred during their shifts.

ISSUES WITH UNIT COST BASED ON LABOR EXPENSE

Because the incentive plan was inherently based on the consultants' design, the expense portion of the unit-cost calculation only included labor costs; it comprised both the direct labor production cost and the overhead salaries of supervisors, production leads, and administrative staff. Compensation accounted for about 54 percent of total section expense ($1.63 million out of $3.05 million in 1990).

Postage expense (about $15 million annually) was not included in the EMS budget, which was a mixed blessing. Follow-up on an employee suggestion in 1989 revealed several systematic mis-meterings of postage. One of these mis-applications took place when processing was per-

formed on the older enclosing machines. Productivity improvements under the first piece-rate incentive plan made the processing of mail on the older machines unnecessary and resulted in an annual postage savings of nearly $1 million. However, the $1 million savings had gone unnoticed in the Retail Bank's overall expense budget! Had postage expense been a line item in the EMS budget (as it often is at other firms with large mailings), the postage savings could have funded incentive awards throughout the Brea facility.

Neither equipment maintenance nor depreciation were included in the unit-cost calculations. Productivity improvements in 1989 had made unnecessary planned equipment purchases of $1.05 million—saving an annual depreciation expense of $150,000. Proposals for in-house maintenance had been circulated which could have resulted in a savings of as much as $25,000 per year. Acting upon such proposals would not be rewarded under the new labor-based incentive plan.

The lesson is that *financial impacts can occur which are not necessarily included in the incentive formula*; they may impact another organization's budget. Relevant costs—both those directly controllable and those which might be influenceable—should be included whenever possible since workers will now be attuned to making improvements in areas affecting their bonus. Allowances should be made whenever there is an impact in another organization's budget.

THE IMPACT OF VOLUME CHANGES IN THE UNIT-COST FORMULA

The input mail-processing volume was essentially fixed, although the mix could have been changed with management attention. The relative volume of branch mail, large customer statements with checks, notices, etc. were determined by customer activity and were not directly controllable by EMS. However, management actions could have resulted in either work being sent to other bank-processing centers or in a change in the mix between slow and fast processing volumes.

EMS had high-speed and low-speed production operations. Processing was most efficient when mail was machine processed; a typical operator could handle 3000-5000 pieces of mail an hour. Processing was least efficient in the vari-

EXHIBIT 3.—IMPACT OF COST, VOLUME, AND MIX CHANGES AT EXTERNAL MAIL SERVICES

Costs/Volume Issues	Application	Explanation	Alternative Options
Input Cost on WIP	N/A at EMS	No transfer costs were used in the budgeting process.	This avoids complications but creates potential problems; reducing costs in one section of a tightly coupled operation may increase processing costs downstream.
Input Material Costs	N/A except for labor; temps; transferred employees	Only direct labor was relevant to the unit cost.	This formula failed to incent improvements in maintenance, equipment usage (through depreciation), and materials (here, primarily stationary and postage).
Capital Improvements	Generally N/A; only minor capital improvements were made for the most part	New postage-metering equipment and scales were purchased prior to the incentive plan; later, two new enclosing machines were also purchased. The meters and scales had a faster throughput, but this was deemed too minor to affect the plan.	Capital changes are generally considered to be "fair game" to change production standards; this could have been used as such an opportunity.
Seasonal Volume Changes	Applicable but not initially handled in the plan	January, October volumes increase by 50%; managers were encouraged to use variable staffing; later, three month rolling unit average cost was adopted to smooth fluctuations.	Explicit formula changes based upon production function could have been used. Longer-term moving average unit costs could also have been used; or standard volumes.
Variable Input Volume	Generally N/A	Most input volumes were slow to change, except for noted seasonal changes.	Input volume fluctuation potentially change the conversion mix; if so, a weighted average unit cost formula could be adopted, or a more complex production formula for the baseline (calculated) unit cost.
Variable Output Volume	Directly applicable: managers sought to increase Jetstar sorting	This in effect changed the mix balance from low to high-speed output, lowering the unit cost.	One correction would be to adopt a more complex unit cost formula that incorporated the percentage of each of the outputs; another would be to use a production function.

ous manual processes, where a worker could meter only a few hundred pieces of mail per hour.

With some lobbying, certain slow-paced mail processes such as "branch mail" could have been off-loaded to another processing center (Centralized Services Group). Moreover, a bank marketing promotion of "check safekeeping," wherein customer checks are microfilmed and not returned with bank statements, would also have been beneficial to EMS employees. This strategy would have had the effect of substituting slower-processed work with faster-processed work. How-

ever, no such actions were undertaken by the EMS management; the input volume and mix were treated as a given. The impact of cost, volume, and mix changes at EMS are summarized in Exhibit 3.

Note that the input mix could also have been changed by reducing rework within the unit. For example, efforts could be made to reduce machine-enclosing exceptions that, because of defects, required rework. Some efforts were made in this direction, but the impact upon section labor expense was negligible.

Several manual processes were significantly improved prior to the implementation of the group incentive plan. Many of these changes are detailed in an earlier article, "White Collar JIT at Security Pacific," *Target,* Spring 1991.

Increasing Output Volume Was the Main Focus of the Efforts of Management and Employees Under this Incentive Plan

Unit cost was most easily reduced by increasing output volume through increased processing on the Jetstar, a high-speed, high-volume mail-sorting machine. This was the single most controllable aspect of the unit cost formula—far easier than shifting low rate-per-hour tasks to other operations.

Jetstar sorting was initiated in February, 1989, using staff displaced by the machine operator piece-rate incentive. Jetstar volume increased from 9.3 million pieces to 18.6 million pieces in the year prior to the group incentive. Following the implementation of the gainsharing plan a year later, Jetstar volumes continued to skyrocket. Jetstar volumes increased an additional 11.1 million items during the first year of the plan—an increase of 59.8 percent. At the same time, the U.S. postal volumes increased 24.2 percent during 1989 (the year of the machine-side incentive) and only .6 percent during the first year of the group incentive. Exhibit 4 summarizes the U.S. Postal Volumes, Jetstar Volumes Compensation Expense, and Unit Costs.

Jetstar processing volume increases occurred despite the fact that the machine has only one processing speed and a single daily processing window that remained largely unchanged during the incentive period. Managers optimized Jetstar sort production by using better-trained operators and variable labor to increase output during process bottlenecks.

The experience of managers at Security Pacific is illuminating as a case study. Volume growth at Security Pacific was assumed to be predictable within the one-year budget horizon; managers were expected to hold budget growth to 2-4 percent despite forecast volume increases of 25-30 percent over 1988. (Acquisitions, which drove most of the volume growth, continued in 1990 but virtually ceased in 1991). Changing the incentive plan every year according to new volume forecasts runs the risk of violating procedural fairness and alienating workers, since it would be difficult and expensive to bring suffi-

cient numbers of workers into the budget negotiations.

Using a unit cost measure as the basis for incentive plans is more efficient than using total cost, given the fact that unit cost self-adjusts for volume changes. As volumes increase, compensation is allowed to increase, since the incentive is based upon the ratio of cost to volume. No new lengthy negotiations are required when input or output volume changes occur. Unit cost incentive formulas are analogous to flexible budgeting, wherein budgeted expenses are allowed to vary based on production output volumes.

For a monthly based gainsharing plan in a cost center, formula selection can be critical due to the month-to-month factors that tend to equalize across longer time horizons. For example, at EMS there were significant month-to-month seasonal effects. Postal volumes increased nearly 50 percent in January and October, due to year-end mailings and the contracted processing of property tax billings for L.A. County, respectively. Gainshare incentives could be lost through the over hiring of permanent workers and/or the late posting of the previous month's compensation expenses that were not supported by the increase in the previous month's seasonal volumes. The judicious use of variable staffing, training, and overtime was required to avoid cost overruns in February and November.

Because the unit cost fluctuated significantly from month to month with large bonuses awarded in one month and smaller bonuses awarded the next, EMS management adopted a change in the gainsharing portion of the formula beginning in October 1991. Thereafter, a three-month moving average unit cost was used to calculate the month's unit cost performance, which in turn determined the gainshare impact on the individual incentive award. This potentially reduced the opportunity for volume manipulations, although such manipulations were not a critical concern. The issue at the time was to reduce employee complaints regarding the fluctuation in bonus payments because of seasonal factors affecting unit cost.

THE EFFECTS OF THE GAINSHARING PROGRAM AT EMS

Employee Suggestions

An employee suggestion plan was implemented at EMS long before either incentive pro-

EXHIBIT 4—COSTS AND VOLUMES

U.S. Postal Volume

	Q1 May-July	Q2 Aug-Oct	Q3 Nov-Jan	Q4 Feb-April	Total
1989	4,153,424	4,968,316	5,113,386	4,474,000	56,127,380
1990	5,117,000	6,076,333	6,269,333	5,766,667	69,688,000
1991	5,475,000	6,000,333	6,412,667	5,491,000	70,137,000
1989-1990	23.2%	22.3%	22.6%	28.9%	24.2%
1990-1991	7.0%	-1.3%	2.3%	-4.8%	0.6%

Jetstar Mail-Sorting Volume

	Q1 May-July	Q2 Aug-Oct	Q3 Nov-Jan	Q4 Feb-April	Total
1989	640,000	720,000	750,750	1,003,633	9,349,115*
1990	1,532,643	1,368,801	1,387,045	1,923,228	18,635,151
1991	2,510,378	2,328,216	2,342,419	2,745,119	29,778,397
1989-1990	139.5%	90.1%	84.8%	91.6%	99.3%
1990-1991	63.8%	70.1%	68.9%	42.7%	59.8%

*estimates

Compensation Expense

	Q1 May-July	Q2 Aug-Oct	Q3 Nov-Jan	Q4 Feb-April	Total
1989	$119,260	$117,919	$130,999	$143,519	1,535,091
1990	$136,792	$156,978	$164,829	$160,144	1,856,229
1991	$154,119	$169,134	$156,845	$155,456	1,906,659
1989-1990	14.7%	33.1%	25.8%	11.6%	20.9%
1990-1991	12.7%	7.7%	-4.8%	-2.9%	2.7%

Unit Cost
(Labor Expense/Postal Volume + Jetstar Volume)

	Q1 May-July	Q2 Aug-Oct	Q3 Nov-Jan	Q4 Feb-April	Average
1989	0.0249	0.0207	0.0223	0.0262	0.02
1990	0.0206	0.0213	0.0217	0.0209	0.02
1991	0.0193	0.0203	0.0182	0.0189	0.02
1989-1990	-12.4%	2.4%	-0.4%	-21.7%	-8.0%
1990-1991	-6.2%	-4.6%	-16.1%	-9.5%	-9.1%

Note: The "quarters" refer to three-month time periods that have elapsed since the group incentive plan's inception.

gram had been adopted. It consisted of two basic formal plans. Under the first plan, employees at any level in the organization who performed "above and beyond" in the subjective opinion of a section manager could be given an "On The Spot" award consisting of a $25 gift certificate. This award was completely at the discretion of the section manager; in the case of EMS, supervisors were delegated the authority to give such

awards in early 1989. Prior to that time, three awards had been made to production workers in a 12-month period. During the next 12-month period, 13 awards were made. There were about seven suggestions for every award given during 1989.

Another formal employee suggestion plan, administered by the centralized human resources department, awarded cash prizes that

EXHIBIT 5.—PRODUCTIVITY IMPROVEMENT FROM GAINSHARING INCENTIVE

Comparing Manual Functions, Base 1989 Standard vs. 1991 Actual

Manual Functions	Nov '89 Original RPH Standard (A)	Nov '91 Production RPH (B)	RPH Improvement 1989-1991 [(B-A)/A]	FTE Reductions, Based on 1991 Production Volumes & Change in RPH
Jetstar Mail Sorting	1070	1763	64.76%	7.07**
File	3	5	76.21%	1.09**
Machine Errors	97	115	18.75%	1.06**
Clean	3	5	91.92%	1.01**
E-Scale	229	331	44.71%	0.98**
Stuffing Cyc 17	70	84	20.03%	0.65**
Branch Mail	774	1011	30.65%	0.53**
Stuffing	94	109	15.64%	0.39*
Setup Cyc 17	225	315	40.19%	0.35*
ARS	128	208	62.74%	0.34*
Postage 1 oz.	1894	2757	45.55%	0.33*
Mail Weigh	1872	2387	27.49%	0.33*
MARPS	210	2.42	15.19%	0.30*
Check-in	7	11	54.05%	0.25
Setup	356	515	44.62%	0.21
Clean Cyc 17	1.05	1.33	27.06%	0.21
Copy Center	399	541	36.31%	0.18
Large Wrap Cyc 17	17	28	68.66%	0.11
Tags	101	145	43.92%	0.10
APCS	492	1337	171.85%	0.09
Specials	24	28	16.38%	0.04
Registered Mail	48	63	45.83%	0.02
Specials Cyc 17	18	36	100.00%	0.01
Return Mail	117	123	5.15%	0.01
Hi Vol 00B	20	21	3.12%	0.00
Typing	33	34	2.09%	0.00
DNM Hi Vol	41	42	1.29%	0.00
Restores	46	46	0.51%	0.00
Errors 00B	34	26	−24.12%	0.00
Homebanking	347	137	−60.58%	0.00
Credit Union	174	135	−22.45%	−0.02
Postage 2 oz.	1534	1435	−6.43%	−0.03
File Cyc 17	160	1.49	−6.91%	−0.03
Foreigns	732	641	−12.42%	−0.03
Large Wrap	17	9	−44.11%	−0.04
Wire Transfers	188	159	−15.19%	−0.06
Postage 3 oz.	1240	1086	−12.41%	−0.12

Estimated FTE Reduction Attributable to Incentive = 15.32

DNM = Do not mail
Hi Vol OOB = High volume out-of-balance demand deposit cycle 17 accounts
Stuffing Cy 17 = Cycle 17 demand deposit statements
ARS = Account reconcilement service

**Saves in excess of .50 FTE, *Saves in excess of .25 FTE

amounted to 10 percent of the value of employee suggestions up to a limit of $10,000. Obtaining one of these awards required filling out considerable paperwork, an evaluation of the proposal by another section manager, and many delays. In one case, an employee made a suggestion that resulted in an annual savings in excess of $100,000. Unfortunately the employee was terminated for tardiness a few months before he was notified of human resources' disposition of his suggestion, which came about a year after he submitted the paperwork! Despite human resources' delay, EMS had acted immediately upon the suggestion and reaped the expense savings.

Throughout the gainsharing incentive period, employee suggestions were evaluated by one or more members of the management team—non-management personnel did not review employee suggestions. Any implementation of new ideas was at the discretion of production leads, supervisors, and the section manager. In 1990, the employee-involvement-oriented section manager was replaced with a more traditional control-oriented manager; this immediately resulted in fewer employee suggestions and process innovations. *When middle management is unreceptive to employee involvement, the resulting control-oriented environment can dominate the influence of incentive plans that are designed to increase worker-suggested process improvements.*

One counterexample does not rule out the possibility that incentive plan design can dominate over management attitude. If a larger proportion of employee pay had been at risk—for instance, if worker pay was wholly determined by the change in productivity—it is not unlikely that employees would have complained to the personnel department and that the middle manager would either have changed his approach or been replaced. Employee complaints to the personnel department on other issues had resulted in a change in management practice. Therefore it appears that an insufficient proportion of incentive pay was dependent upon successful process innovation. Retrospective analysis of the components of unit cost confirms that the increase in processing volumes, coupled with the increases in rates-per-hour (effort), were sufficient to allow employees to earn bonuses without much need for process innovations.

Nevertheless, many employee suggestions were implemented during the early portion of the incentive plan. Worktools were placed on every enclosing machine; the size of the check di-

viders was changed to increase the visibility of changes in accounts; the timing of some production runs was adjusted, and tasks were rotated among workers. While many of these suggestions improved the quality of the output, only the addition of worktools resulted in significantly measurable labor savings.

NON-FINANCIAL PERFORMANCE MEASURES

Several non-financial performance measures were used at EMS. These included quality indicators and production volume indicators. Production leads, supervisors, and managers used these on an immediate basis to regulate the daily operations of EMS. The financial measures, including unit cost, were primarily used at month-end to determine bonus payouts.

If gainsharing plans are not coupled with additional information sources (for example, non-financial operations measures) and training (changing the managers' and workers' production models to use the signals), it is likely that the group incentive plans will not have the effect desired. The group incentive plan may result in greater goal congruence between workers and managers and greater effort on the part of workers, but only a small rather than a large impact upon financial results. *Group plans without non-financial measures and training will likely result in just more of the same: more people working a little harder rather than smarter.* The financial indicators will score the results but may indicate the wrong actions to take. Incorporating superior measures that signal the cause of delay, excess, and unevenness[1] will improve gainsharing results, in the absence of improved employee or worker production models.

FINANCIAL SAVINGS

The use of a mixed individual incentive capped by a "gainshare" funding pool led to increased employee effort in nearly every production task. An internal memo analyzing the impact in the first month reports that the average increase in production volume per employee was 28 percent in the newly incented manual processes. A later analysis performed 18 months after the group incentive was installed showed that for 24 of 55 manual tasks, 50 percent or more of the employees working these tasks regularly achieved production rates that allowed them to be paid the maximum incentive bonus. Prior to the institution of the manual incentives, about 30 percent of employees in any task would have received a bonus.

Since relative volume and processing changes can make a unit-cost comparison misleading, a comprehensive comparison of the rates per hour for each production process in manual processes during 1989 and November, 1991 is given in Exhibit 5 and for machine-side processes in Exhibit 6.

This detailed comparison was made possible because of additional tracking that was initiated in the third quarter of 1991. The section manager, convinced that the incentive program was a boondoggle, wanted to raise production standards in order to reduce incentive pay, and sought justification by analyzing tasks at the individual level.

The production improvements resulting from the incentive plan are quite amazing. Average processing speeds increased for all but seven of 44 tasks on the manual side and for all but two of 19 tasks on the machine side. It is estimated that additional 20.33 FTE (15.3 manual and 5.03 machine side FTE) would be needed to process the November 1991 volumes if employees worked at the 1989 production rates (as estimated in Exhibits 5 and 6, respectively). If these workers had been paid at the average worker pay level, then the FTE-based estimate of (gross) incentive savings is $381,500.

Manual-side FTE actually decreased from 1989 to November, 1991, from 45.19 to 43.62 workers, despite the fact that manual volumes increased and Jetstar processing skyrocketed. In essence, the same number of people were doing considerably more work during the time that the incentive plan was in place.

The overall EMS annual savings are dramatic, as demonstrated in Exhibit 7. From the $381,500 in compensation savings, Security Pacific paid out $66,400 in incentives to EMS employees in calendar 1991. Yet based on the change in processing rates between plan installation and November, 1991, Security Pacific annually netted a total of $257,200 in annual labor savings. The compensation savings for Security Pacific from EMS amounts to 16.1 percent of calendar 1990 salary compensation. Security Pacific saved an additional $32,600 in presort vendor expenses through the operation of the Jetstar mail sorter (considering the machine to be a sunk cost). During the time of the group incentive from May

1990 to April 1992, annual total processing volumes increased 13.1 percent but annual total labor expense increased only 2.7 percent.

While the incentive plan did deliver considerable compensation savings to Security Pacific, the compensation savings were not shared on a 50/50 basis with the employees. As shown in Exhibit 7, employees received back only 17.41 percent of the (gross) compensation savings in bonuses. Direct labor overhead expense to track volumes, maintain software, and oversee the incentive plan consumed $57,892—nearly as much of the savings as were paid out in bonuses. Lead and manager time were also directed to oversee the statistical process control quality improvement effort.

The bulk of the gross compensation savings —67.4 percent—went directly to Security Pacific. Security Pacific also retained all of the savings from vendor presort charges obviated by Jetstar production—an estimated $32,600 in 1991 (May 1991-April 1992).

How did Security Pacific manage to snare the lion's share of the compensation savings? First, through the use of a sliding-scale payout. Workers who performed "at the goal" production level did receive 15 percent of their salary in bonus when the gainsharing savings were obtained. However, workers who performed half way between standard and goal received only a 5.2 percent salary bonus. The sliding scale payout was a mandated aspect of the Brea incentive plans; senior management from the outset did not intend to share cost savings 50/50 with employees.

Second, indirect savings from so-called "fringe" expenses were not shared. Employees were paid a bonus of up to 15 percent of their base pay; fringe elements such as medical benefits, taxes, training, and other employee-related compensation expenses were not included. Through these devices, Security Pacific management succeeded in retaining most of the compensation savings.

The detailed rates per hour by task are available because of a special study conducted in 1991, in which worker time and output was closely monitored for several months. Without this detailed tracking, we would be misled if we were to rely upon unit cost to determine organizational savings, after the relative quantities of slow- and fast-processed work had changed since the baseline was established. As shown in Exhibit 8, the unit-cost comparison here understates the FTE/RPH-based savings by 14 per-

EXHIBIT 6.—PRODUCTIVITY IMPROVEMENT FROM GAINSHARING INCENTIVE

Comparing Machine Functions, Base 1989 Standard vs. 1991 Actual

Machine Functions	Nov '89 Original RPH Standard (A)	Nov '91 Production RPH (B)	RPH	FTE Reductions, Based on 1991 Production Volumes & Change in RPH
Enclosures (W/Checks)	1240	1534	23.7%	1.60**
Zero Enclosures (No Chks)	3060	4023	31.5%	1.12**
Individual Retirement	1704	3673	115.6%	0.47*
NSF/XOD Notices	3174	4174	31.5%	0.45*
TDA Renewals	2938	4353	48.2%	0.25
Bank Services	1596	2265	41.9%	0.23
Overdraft Notice	2459	3448	40.2%	0.23
Small Business Ln	953	2020	111.9%	0.21
APCS	1242	2368	90.6%	0.18
Enclosures Cyc 17	880	950	8.0%	0.13
TDA Cyc 17	3862	4368	13.1%	0.06
Credit Line Increases	3732	5250	40.7%	0.06
High Volume	2033	2474	21.7%	0.03
Late Payment Remind	2030	2306	13.6%	0.02
Telephone Stop Payment	2943	3646	23.9%	0.01
Ready Teller Cancl	1700	1805	6.2%	0.00
Customer Profitability Stmt	1539	1447	−6.0%	−0.00
Time Deposit (TDA)	3862	3677	−4.8%	−0.01
High Volume Cyc 17	1222	718	−41.2%	−0.01
DesignLine Home Ln	2585	n/a		
Incentive Data Entry	not incented	274		
LA Cnty Folding	not incented	2370		
Retirement Checks	not incented	3558		
Tel Conf Letters	not incented	3146		
Thrift Plus	not incented	2920		
WCL	not incented	1064		
Wire Transfers	not incented	1978		
Non-incented Task	not incented	127		

Estimated FTE Reduction Attributable to Incentive = 5.03

**Save in excess of .50 FTE, *Save in excess of .25 FTE

The group-incentive machine-operator productivity improvement occurred on top of the piece-rate productivity gain!

cent. The analysis by rate per hour for each task, combined with the changes in volume, gives us the detail to understand exactly where incentive savings occurred and how great the total savings actually were.

The surprising thing is that *the section manager repeatedly attempted to discontinue the plan based on his perception that the savings were not signficant*. He never fully accepted the validity of

having Jetstar sorting volumes included as an output measure in the unit cost formula. Based on his definition of output, denominator volume changes should only reflect changes in mailing volumes. Overall mailing volume increased only 0.6 percent from 1990-1991 (May-April); labor costs for manual processes were flat (though manual volumes increased), and compensation increased slightly overall for the section. Conse-

EXHIBIT 7.—FTE-BASED ANALYSIS OF GAINSHARING SAVING

Based Upon a Comparison of 1989 and 1992 Production Rates* for 1991 Volumes

Savings From EMS Gainsharing Incentive Plan

Gross Salary Savings Based Upon Grade 12 Employees at Midpoint 15.30 manual employees @ $15,509 * 1.23 fringe (see Exhibit 5) 5.03 machine employees @ 15,509 * 1.23 fringe (see Exhibit 6)		$381,521
Incentive Plan Actual Bonus Payouts, 1991	$66,408	
Dedicated Administrative Lead	$30,709	
Dedicated Management Oversight Half-time Grade 45 Manager	$27,183	$124,300
NET SAVINGS (retained by Security Pacific)		$257,221

Dividing the Pie

Bonus Payout Percentage of Savings	($66,408/$381,521)	17.41%
Overhead as a Percentage of Savings	($57,892/$381,521)	15.17%
Security Pacific Portion of Savings	($257,221/$381,521)	67.42%

Additional Savings From Jetstar Processing, 1991

Presort Vendor Savings $.009 @ 28,109,000		$252,981
Compensation Expense 10.92 employees @ 15,509 * 1.23	($208,311)	
Jetstar Maintenance Expense	($12,000)	($220,311)
Net Vendor Savings From Jetstar Processing		$32,670

*Based upon calculations performed in Exhibits 5 and 6. FTE estimates for each task were obtained from an analysis of 1991 production statistics. The FTE needed to process 1991 production volumes based upon 1989 RPH were obtained by multiplying actual 1991 FTE for each task by the ratio of 1989 RPH/1991 RPH. This gave, for each task, the increase or decrease in FTE. The change in FTE was aggregated for machine-side and manual functions. The actual FTE for each task were obtained by special studies conducted in 1989 and 1991.

Note: This analysis may actually underestimate the savings. A Human Resources study of EMS compensation in 1989 showed that non-manager, non-lead workers averaged about 88% of the salary midpoint. Annual salary increases during this period ranged from 3%-5% and would have increased average salaries to about 96% of midpoint by 1991. Bonus payments raised average worker compensation to close to midpoint by 1991. Lower turnover was also a factor contributing to the higher average EMS worker earnings following the incentive plan implementation.

Regardless of what average worker wage is used, it is clear that 20.33 fewer production workers were needed during a time when labor costs were increasing.

quently, by his estimates, annual unit cost increased 2.3 percent from May 1990 to April 1992—there was essentially no improvement resulting from the incentive plan in 1991, though a slight improvement (3.2 percent) occurred in 1990 over 1989! The FTE-based approach to analyzing savings allows managers to see exactly where productivity improvements have resulted in cost savings. The approach is time consuming and expensive, and should only be done perhaps once every year to once every 18 months.

INCENTIVE PLAN CHANGES

Standards were added as new tasks were benchmarked; standards were also tightened following the fourth quarter 1991 incentive analysis. Most notable among the standard changes was the change to the Jetstar team standard, which was increased by 15.4 percent from 1070 to 1235 sorted mail pieces (output per worker hour). As noted earlier, EMS adopted a moving average unit cost in October 1991. The baseline unit cost

EXHIBIT 8.—MEASURING INCENTIVE SAVINGS: THE MISLEADING UNIT COST

Complex unit-cost-based estimates mislead whenever significant volume changes occur.

	Standard Unit Cost (A)	Actual Unit Cost (B)	Unit Cost Savings (A–B)	Monthly Volume (C)	Monthly Savings [(A–B) * C]
January	0.0224	0.0196	0.0028	8,956,659	$25,168
February	0.0224	0.0235	-0.0011	7,375,473	($8,334)
March	0.0224	0.0198	0.0026	8,080,983	$20,768
April	0.0224	0.0193	0.0031	7,613,228	$23,220
May	0.0224	0.0186	0.0038	8,170,134	$30,883
June	0.0224	0.0212	0.0012	7,666,345	$9,200
July	0.0224	0.0183	0.0041	8,119,655	$33,453
August	0.0224	0.0220	0.0004	7,626,240	$2,822
September	0.0224	0.0185	0.0039	7,491,798	$28,822
October	0.0224	0.0208	0.0016	9,867,611	$15,986
November	0.0224	0.0208	0.0016	7,584,601	$12,287
December	0.0224	0.0185	0.0039	8,125,437	$31,283

Net estimate based on unit cost: $225,579 *
Net estimate based on FTE & RPH: $257,221 **
Unit cost underestimated actual savings by 14%.

* The total of the monthly savings based upon monthly unit cost for 1991.
** Savings based upon FTE requirements, found by analyzing the change in RPH and volumes for each task (shown in Exhibits 5, 6, and 7).
The estimate based upon unit cost is inherently inaccurate whenever there are significant changes in the relative volumes of slow- or fast-production tasks. The analysis based upon FTE takes into account the relative changes in production volumes and RPH. However, collecting the data needed for the analysis is costly and should only be done infrequently.

remained fixed; the monthly unit cost was a three-month "rolling average" of the current month and the prior two months' actual unit cost. Other changes included the operationalization of penalties for tardiness and absences, which was implemented in the fourth quarter of 1990. Early in 1991, the implementation of quality standards changed in such a manner that exceeding quality standards was rewarded and falling below quality standards continued to be punished.

When Security Pacific merged with Bank of America in 1992, the incentive plan was gradually phased out. Bank of America had no incentive plan for back-office functions and no intention of adopting this innovation from Security Pacific. As customer accounts were converted to the Bank of America system, these accounts were processed at the Bank of America facility in downtown Los Angeles. Brea EMS continued processing Security Pacific accounts that had not converted. Finally, as the volume of Security Pacific customer accounts dropped off, the incentive plan was discontinued in 1993.

SUMMARY

The mixed gainsharing incentive model adopted at EMS was a success on several different indicators. It incorporated the highly motivational individual piece rates with a gainsharing bonus pool to limit incentive payments when no actual savings occurred—thereby protecting the firm from paying out incentive bonuses when no true savings were realized. While the plan was rather complicated in execution, it was designed so that 80 percent of workers received some incentive and was funded (at 33 percent) during the first three months to ensure employee acceptance. The plan was based on compensation savings and succeeded in generating reductions in compensation unit cost. The inclusion of a discretionary output volume in the unit cost (Jetstar mail sorting) had the additional benefit of focusing productivity improvements that generated non-labor expense savings; savings which were not shared with employees.

EXHIBIT 9.

Timeline		
Date	**Event**	**Impact**
February, 1989	Piece-rate incentive, Machine side only	Output per worker increases 30%; DL savings $78,500. Equipment purchases deferred: $1.05 million. Metering error discovered: saves $1 million annually. Jetstar mail sorter staffed with excess personnel
March, 1989	Gerringer requests group incentive plans	Units of Brea Bank Operations begin designing group incentive plans
July, 1989	EMS informally benchmarks three other banks	Determined that costs are in line with the most efficient competitor (Bank of America is 6% lower) and 50% lower than the cost of two other major CA banks
July-August, 1989	Establish production standards for group incentive	
Sept.-Dec., 1989	Develop group-based incentive plan, software	
February, 1990	Roll out initial plan	Immediate productivity improvement of 28% registered in manual tasks
March-April, 1990	Management turnover; Incentive plan deferred to May	Production levels drop to 80% of standard. Immediate reduction in employee suggestions result from style of new manager
October, 1991	Plan change: unit cost based on three-month average	Smoothed bonus awards across months
October-December, 1991	Special study measures production levels and time spent by each employee in each task	Study determines that for 24 of 55 manual tasks, 50% or more of workers achieve levels earning the maximum incentive
		Some production standards are increased; Jetstar standard increased 15%
		Data available to calculate production rates for each task for each employee
First Quarter, 1992	Merger with Bank of America approved	Volumes decrease as accounts and workers are transferred to Bank of America; incentive plan continues at Brea
First Quarter, 1993	Conversion of Security Pacific Accounts to Bank of America nearly complete	Bulk of mailing transferred to the Los Angeles, CA Bank of America processing center. Incentive plan discontinued, since Bank of America had no worker incentive plan for bank-processing centers

The piece-rate aspect of the plan, in combination with the discretionary Jetstar volume, had a distinct disadvantage. Unit-cost improvement could be attained by volume increases rather than through other production improvements. The incentive plan in itself did not appear to drive employee suggestions; these seemed to be more a function of the style of the section manager. Importantly, employee suggestions were not needed in order to achieve unit-cost improvement. Few worker innovations were made following the change in section manager.

Quality improvements were made through the use of a comprehensive SPC system that was incorporated into the incentive plan. Over time, employees were rewarded for exceeding quality standards as well as punished for failing to meet quality standards. In the first year of the incentive plan, the many employee suggestions resulted more in quality improvements rather than in cost savings.

Overall the plan achieved considerable compensation savings for the firm. While expense levels remained essentially flat, considerable volume increases were absorbed in some processes. The mix of volume did not remain constant over time; Jetstar production, a relatively "high speed" process increased considerably: from 16 percent of total volume in 1989 to 28 percent of total output volume by the end of 1991. This mix change was not explicitly addressed in the gainsharing unit-cost formula. Consequently, more incentives were paid out than otherwise would have been, had the mix remained constant or if some adjustment had been made for mix changes.

Nevertheless, the plan did not meet the "fairness" criteria as originally espoused by management: Company savings were not shared on a 50/50 basis with employees. Employees only received about l7 percent of the actual savings, based upon an analysis of the additional FTE needed to perform work in 1991 at 1989 production-rate averages. Finally, employees did not appear to have an equal opportunity to work in tasks which had the greatest inherent likelihood of earning an incentive.

‖‖‖ 2.10
‖‖‖ OTHER INDUSTRIES

———————————————■———————————————

THE U.S. SEMICONDUCTOR INDUSTRY'S WILD RIDE*
by Brad Stratton, editor

There might be no industrial roller coaster ride as wild as the U.S. semiconductor industry. Hurtling at a breakneck speed through the early 1980s, it was careening out of control by decade's end. What had been a three-quarters world market share in the 1970s and still a near 50% share for U.S. semiconductor makers in 1981 had dwindled to less than 40% by 1986.[1] Japan had taken over the No. 1 slot with about 46% of the market. Three years later, Japan pushed its share past 50%.[2]

This wasn't a momentary shock to the stomach like those given by an amusement park roller coaster—instead, these tracks were headed right into a brick wall. In 1987, the Semiconductor Industry Association projected that if current trends continued, the United States could have about a 25% share of the world semiconductor market by the mid-1990s.[3] The projection made the situation clear: The brick wall was going to be the end of the line for countless U.S. companies.

But why was this cause for alarm? Why was this industry different from others related to electronics—televisions, videocassette recorders, stereos—for which U.S. manufacturers had

already thrown in the towel? In part, the alarm was sounded because of the ubiquitousness of semiconductors. These tiny devices are the brains of larger parts that control such key U.S. products as computers, automobiles, and airplanes. And, in part, it was sounded because of the security implications of relying on other countries to develop semiconductors for sensitive weaponry. Something as relatively small as a Tomahawk cruise missile has 1,270 electronic component part types, while an F-16 fighter has 17,000.[4] The Department of Defense was so committed to keeping semiconductor manufacturing alive in the United States that it pledged $100 million annually for research in the field.

For the U.S. semiconductor industry to avoid the brick wall, someone or something would have to reroute the tracks.

ENTER SEMATECH

It is rarely possible to attribute the turnaround of any distressed industry or company to one change. This is the case with the semiconductor industry. But it is possible to attribute signifi-

*Reprinted with permission from *Quality Progress,* May 1995.

cant portions of the industry's turnaround to contributions that were in part coordinated by an organization called SEMATECH.

James Fallows, the Washington editor of *Atlantic Monthly* magazine, provides a detailed analysis of what happened in the worldwide semiconductor industry in his 1994 book *Looking at the Sun*. Fallows said that according to the people he worked with to develop the book, SEMATECH was certainly not the answer, but it was one of three conditions that influenced the industry.

"Clearly," he said, "the No. 1 influence was the quality efforts by the semiconductor companies themselves. They would not have reached the threshold of being able to compete internationally without this emphasis on quality."

The order and significance of the No. 2 and No. 3 conditions are not as clear, he said. But generally they were the pooling of resources through efforts made primarily by SEMATECH, and the 1986 Semiconductor Trade Arrangement signed by the United States and Japan.[5] "No one or two of these conditions would have been enough," he said.

Both the emphasis on quality and pooling of resources can be tracked in part to SEMATECH.

WHAT IS SEMATECH?

SEMATECH (SEmiconductor MAnufacturing TECHnology) is a consortium of U.S. semiconductor manufacturers that works with government and academia to sponsor and conduct research that will ensure the leadership in semiconductor manufacturing technology for the U.S. semiconductor industry.[6] Member organizations are Advanced Micro Devices, Inc., Sunnyvale, CA; AT&T, Berkeley Heights, NJ; Digital Equipment Corp., Maynard, MA; Hewlett-Packard Co., Palo Alto, CA; IBM Corp., Armonk, NY; Intel Corp., Santa Clara, CA; Motorola, Inc., Schaumburg, IL; National Semiconductor Corp., Santa Clara, CA; Rockwell International Corp., Newport Beach, CA; Texas Instruments Inc., Dallas, TX; and the U.S. Department of Defense through its Advanced Research Projects Agency. NCR Corp., Dayton, OH, was an original member of SEMATECH but has since merged with AT&T.

SEMATECH develops advanced semiconductor manufacturing processes, materials, and equipment and validates its research in a proofing facility that simulates its members' production lines. Research results are transferred to consortium members, with use them for commercial and military applications. The organization emphasizes manufacturing capability, not device design, and does not produce chips for sale.

The consortium has a reputable history today, but it is a history that almost didn't begin. SEMATECH was formed in 1987 but didn't find a facility or chief executive officer (CEO) until 1989. The facility was a former Data General site in Austin, TX. The first CEO, the highly respected Bob Noyce, who was the coinventor of the semiconductor and founder of Intel, died in June 1990. Six months passed before the second (and current) CEO was named: William Spencer, a research director for Xerox.

Funding for SEMATECH has always been the subject of controversy. The original annual budget of $200 million was to be evenly split between the government and member companies, the latter of which would make further contributions by assigning members of their staffs to full-time duty with SEMATECH. The Republican administrations of the 1980s, however, were not supportive of forming industrial policy for specific industries. In 1989, the proposed budget for SEMATECH was dropped from $100 million to zero by officials within the Bush administration. The recommendation was subsequently reversed because of the work of a bipartisan Congressional group.

While industrial policy was not in favor within the United States, it certainly was strong in the countries that were making huge improvements in the semiconductor industry during the 1980s. Fallows wrote, "When the American industry was doing everything right, according to American economic theory, it began to collapse. When European, Japanese, and Korean producers broke all the rules of American 'market rationality,' they started to rise. . . . Around the world, the growth and survival of semiconductor industries has not just been a matter of 'hacking it,' or fostering competition, or having very good schools—although each of these ingredients played a part. Every country that has waited for the industry to develop 'naturally' through the flux and play of market forces *is waiting still*."[7]

For the United States, it was time for new rules, and SEMATECH wrote the rule book.

SEMATECH'S SPECIFIC CONTRIBUTIONS

SEMATECH was not designed to make computer chips; it was designed to influence how others made chips. SEMATECH has done this in two ways, according to Phil Pierce, SEMATECH director of total quality. The first was conducting the research and development for leading-edge tools so U.S. semiconductor manufacturers could have access to the best and most capable tools at the right time. The second was to develop the supplier infrastructure so that the suppliers would be able to provide manufacturers with the right quality, reliability, capability, and volumes at the appropriate time.

Also, SEMATECH's overall practices are sensitive to the environment. This is especially noteworthy because of the semiconductor industry's poor environmental record in the 1970s and 1980s.

DEVELOPING TOOLS

Pierce said that in the semiconductor industry, there has been a constant drive toward improving the cost per electronic function that a semiconductor device delivers. He said a simple way to illustrate this point was to compare the cost of a television set in 1965 to one available today. The 1995 27-inch color television set has remote control, stereo sound, the capacity to receive more than 100 channels, and superior picture quality—*and it costs less* than its 1965 counterpart, which carried none of these features.

For the television—or any product relying on semiconductors—to be developed and sold this way, Pierce said the geometries of the semiconductor devices have had to shrink. By making the chips smaller, and the functions on the chip smaller, more functions could be packed on the chips and those functions could be closer together, increasing the speed with which a chip could complete a given activity.

Individual operating devices on current, state-of-the-art microchips are extremely small: 0.35 micron—or $\frac{1}{200}$th the width of a human hair. SEMATECH's 1993 annual report says that to comprehend something this small, imagine that the operating device is the size of a BB and the microchip is the size of a football field.

Needless to say, incredibly precise machines and manufacturing processes are needed to make such devices. SEMATECH makes dozens of con-tributions annually to these industry improvements. In 1994, SEMATECH not only assisted with the creation and refinement of machines for the industry, but also coordinated how these manufacturers and suppliers interacted through the oversight of benchmarking studies and workshops. The benchmarking studies ranged in scope from improving one company's component scrubber to studying the world's five best wire bonders to provide targets for a tool-development program.

EDUCATING AN INDUSTRY

To help make sure suppliers and manufacturers could clearly understand each other in matters related to quality, SEMATECH developed the Partnering for Total Quality process. The process was explained in nine guidebooks relating to quality improvement that were released between June 1990 and June 1992:

- Volume 1—*Partnering for Total Quality*
- Volume 2—*A Partnering Overview*
- Volume 3—*A Total Quality Overview*
- Volume 4—*A Partnering Guidebook*
- Volume 5—*A Total Quality Guidebook*
- Volume 6—*A Total Quality Tool Kit*
- Volume 7—*A Total Quality Training Guide*
- Volume 8—*Joint Assessment Guide*
- Volume 9—*Executive's Implementation Guide*

Volume 1 opened with a letter to the semiconductor industry signed by 18 key executives from SEMATECH and SEMATECH member companies. The letter summarized the industry's dire situation and stressed the importance of quality in its recovery:

"Eight years ago, the American semiconductor industry led the world in innovation, development, and introduction of new products and processes. Today, we are fighting for our survival in an environment where technological advancements have created an insatiable global demand for increasingly complex geometries, and economic pressures continue to squeeze profits.

"Many critical links in the industry supply chain are now dominated by foreign concerns. Sixty-two U.S. equipment and materials suppliers have disappeared during the last 2½ years. Some businesses failed, others merged with American companies; but, alarmingly, nearly half were acquired by foreign interests. We must move aggressively to protect our weakening infrastructure.

"We must evolve from adversarial business practices and develop a partnering culture based on open communication, integrity, mutual trust, and cooperation. We must realize that a break in any link of our domestic supply chain threatens the survival of every company in the domestic industry. We also need to focus our energies to achieve excellence and customer satisfaction in every activity of our organization—total quality.

"To that end, we declare the need for a transformation of our industry's culture and introduce the concepts of Partnering for Total Quality."[8]

The approach to quality described in the documents was based on the Malcolm Baldrige National Quality Award criteria and developed by two SEMATECH groups: the Supplier Relations Action Council Task Force and the Supplier Total Quality Task Force. Both had members from several semiconductor industry companies.

The documents in the nine-part series are not extremely detailed—partially by design. Many manufacturers and suppliers already had more detailed quality processes in place, so the document writers were clearly guarding against an organization feeling as if a particular approach was being dictated.

There were other areas, however, in which more specific quality-related information was shared with SEMATECH members in hopes of specifically influencing internal operations. Among these documents were:

Guidelines for Equipment Reliability, released in May 1992. These guidelines state that documents relating to reliability in general are plentiful, but this one is designed to provide a specific reference for the semiconductor industry. The guidebook describes the principles of a cost-effective reliability program, gives instructions on how to get started, and details several reliability tools, including failure-mode effects analysis, fault-free analysis, component failure analysis, and environmental stress screening. SEMATECH CEO Spencer stresses the impor-

tance of reliability in an opening statement within the document, saying research showed that reliability was the semiconductor industry's No. 1 problem for 10 straight years before dropping to sixth in the most recent study. "But, as with so much of this business today, reliability is a race without an end," wrote Spencer. "And the formula to improve reliability is to build it into every stage of development."

Design Practices for Higher Equipment Reliability Guidebook, released in 1993. It builds on the preceding document and focuses on system reliability for new products and upgrades of older products. To design in reliability, the guidebook suggests a six-step process: know reliability requirements, use proper parts properly, use proper design techniques, minimize effect of external factors, avoid failures through scheduled maintenance, and design reviews.

Cycle Time Improvement Guidebook, released in 1992. Written for senior executives, the guidebook defines five major components of cycle-time improvement—success factors, deployment process, implementation process, implementation tools, and measurements—and provides references for more information about the subject.

Equipment Change Control: A Guide for Customer Satisfaction, released in 1993. This starts with the intention of raising awareness (Do you really know the snowball effect of substituting one tiny part for another?) and builds to a structured system that tracks and reports any system change, no matter how seemingly trivial, to others in the manufacturing process.

Failure Reporting, Analysis, and Corrective Action System (FRACAS), released in 1993. FRACAS not only seeks to collect and record hardware and software failures, but also focuses on analyzing problems and improving the manufacturing process. The system is designed to fulfill ISO 9000 requirements. To assist FRACAS implementation SEMATECH developed FRACAS database management software. Use of the SEMATECH software is not mandated—similar commercial software is available—but the supplier and customer should use the same software.

In the generic and specific documents. SEMATECH stresses partnership repeatedly. In no area is this more evident than in dealing with suppliers.

STEERING SUPPLIERS TOWARD SELF-SUFFICIENCY

SEMATECH originally held training courses for any semiconductor industry company interested in learning more about improving quality. In 1991 and 1992, suppliers from the West and East Coasts that had attended SEMATECH training agreed to go beyond initial training. They formed discussion groups to help each other develop their total quality maturity as companies and as suppliers by continuing to learn from each other.[9] They are the West Coast Quality Forum (WCQF) and the Training Quality Management Boston Area Semiconductor Equipment (TQM BASE) Council. They started with six to eight companies each and now have about 30 companies each. A third group, made up of other eastern U.S. companies, primarily from Pennsylvania, is being spun off from TQM BASE. Called the Mid-Atlantic Council, it will have 10 members and should have 15 by the end of 1995. The third group was started, said Bob Stanion, SEMATECH supplier development manager, because these companies believed they were too far from Boston to actively participate.

Stanion said the timing of these groups was fortuitous because SEMATECH was re-examining its approach to training, which it believed wasn't cost-effective. "We were too far away from the people who needed the training," he said. The groups agreed to become the centers for training in their geographical areas, some of which is done in conjunction with community colleges.

WCQF and TQM BASE hold quarterly executive forums for member companies. During these forums, executives share benchmarking information and communicate with their customers. Stanion said SEMATECH officials are present to discuss current initiatives and emphasize developments that they think these suppliers and manufacturers should be interested in.

WCQF and TQM BASE also hold monthly meetings tht are geared toward midlevel managers and quality practitioners. Leo Berlinghieri, chairman of TQM BASE, said group members meet at a different company each month. (Berlinghieri works for MKS instruments, Andover, MA, which manufactures vacuum and flow gauges used in the semiconductor industry.) Meeting topics are an area of quality improvement that the company believes it does well, although it might be a combined presentation, as happened recently when three companies pre-

sented their approaches to ISO 9000 implementation. Meetings are usually held from 8 A.M. until noon, with an optional lunch allowed by a plant tour.

There has been some concern by members as to whether they should host meetings in which their competitors would participate, said Berlinghieri. But meeting content has been limited to nonproprietary information. "They realized they weren't sharing anything their competitors didn't already know," he said.

A useful segment of both the executive forums and monthly meetings, Berlinghieri said, has been the time set aside for networking. He said many separate meetings have been scheduled and held because of conversations that had taken place during networking breaks.

In summer 1994, SEMATECH rolled out an orientation guide and workbook designed to standardize audits of suppliers across the semiconductor industry. Called the Standardized Supplier Quality Assessment, Pierce said the three-module process is a hybrid of documents familiar to quality professionals:

- Module 1 addresses system quality and is structured to answer ISO 9001 requirements.

- Module 2 contains a set of common customer requirements that are fashioned after the Baldrige Award criteria, a section on business systems, and a section on organization capabilities.

- Module 3 is for software assessment and is based on Motorola's Quality System Review.

According to Pierce, nearly all semiconductor companies conduct some type of audit or assessment of suppliers. Suppliers are subjected to many audits that are nearly duplicate. "The belief was that we could do joint assessments using SEMATECH member-company people and SEMATECH supplier-development managers," he said.

"Instead of having four, five, or six assessments by companies, [suppliers] would have one." In practice, he said, it hasn't always been possible to do just one audit, but the overall number of audits has been reduced.

Pierce said a strength of the process is that it is designed for companies to first perform a self-assessment. SEMATECH representatives focus on validating the results. "The supplier has months to go through and address all the questions in that document, which provides examples of maturity levels," he said.

The process has been intimidating for some suppliers. "There has been some reluctance," said Pierce. "It looks like a lot of work because it is a thick document." (The orientation guide has 176 pages and the workbook has 146 pages.) "But once they have been through it, they agree that it has a lot of value and develop a continuous improvement program in the areas that they have identified as their business and quality systems' weaknesses. In fact, we now have suppliers requesting that we work [with their suppliers and their suppliers' suppliers] to deploy it further down the supply chain. . . . That's part of the supplier self-sufficient strategy."

Pierce's reference to going beyond suppliers' quality practices is significant. He said a problem within the semiconductor industry is that many of the suppliers are entrepreneurs that might have started with excellent product ideas but little more.

Stanion supported Pierce's position. "We find that the entrepreneurial technologial suppliers can do just so much," said Stanion. "If they are going to grow and be able to service the industry long term . . . they will have to change the way they do business. We help them make that change from a 50- to 100-person company to maybe a 300- to 500-person company."

"Or," said Pierce, "from a seven-person company to a 50-person company."

"Because," Stanion said, "people won't buy equipment from suppliers if they don't think they'll be there next year or three years from now."

From this assessment, Pierce said SEMATECH could then make recommendations for the supplier or potential supplier to improve not only its quality practices, but also perhaps its accounting or purchasing systems. "We would put in the statement of work for that project some specific milestones that we would like that supplier to meet as a part of doing this project with SEMATECH and its member companies," said Pierce.

ENVIRONMENTAL RESPONSIBILITY

Even though the semiconductor industry enjoys an ultraclean, high-tech image, it has more than its share of environmental problems.

"The extreme toxicity of making computer parts," according to *E / The Environmental Magazine*, "is one of the reasons why Silicon Valley, the region in central California where the majority of the companies that manufacture computer chips and boards are located, has the highest concentration of Superfund sites in the United States for an area its size.[10] According to Ted Smith of the Silicon Valley Toxics Coalition, 28 of the area's 29 Superfund sites are associated with high-technology electronics manufacture.

"And dozens more Superfund sites scattered throughout the country are tied to processes used to create electronic computer components. And those are just the largest messes—a recent report in the engineering journal *Spectrum* stated that 150 toxic leaks are being actively monitored in Silicon Valley alone."[11]

E / The Environmental Magazine credits SEMATECH with leading the industry toward investigating cleaner manufacturing alternatives. Indeed, during 1994, SEMATECH invested more than $20 million (about 10% of its overall operating budget in 46 projects related to the environment. John Q. Pope of the SEMATECH Communications Department states the organization's environmental responsibility in simple terms: "There is not a single SEMATECH project undertaken that does not have environmental safety and health considerations to it."

SEMATECH's approach toward the environment is put forth in a company fact sheet. The organization's philosophy on worker health and safety is, "No job is so important that it may be performed without regard for safety, health, and the environment." This philosophy is followed by an environmental program vision which states that SEMATECH seeks to "protect the health and safety of all, eliminate emissions, conserve natural resources, be good neighbors, and fully and openly cooperate with government." The strategy that incorporates that vision is as follows:

- Prevent the use of hazardous materials by designing for the environment.

- Replace hazardous materials and model the substitutes before using them in our factories.

- Reduce the use of hazardous materials.

- Recycle, treat, or dispose as a last resort.

This approach has led to the development of an environmental, safety, and health road map. It includes technological improvements, use of hazardous chemicals being reduced or phased out, and reduced emissions from specified chemicals.

The environmental focus by SEMATECH is mirrored in its daily activities, too. During 1994, the city of Austin honored SEMATECH with two awards, one for on-site recycling and the other for solid-waste management.

"We're establishing a road map that targets a semiconductor manufacturing process with zero environmental impact," said Frank Squires, SEMATECH chief administrative officer and recycling program sponsor. "Our recycling progress at all product levels can significantly contribute to achieving that goal."

THE WILD RIDE DOESN'T END

Quality improvement processes often are referred to as a race with no finish line. The wild roller coaster ride of the semiconductor industry is the same. Just because the U.S. semiconductor industry has recaptured the lead in key market segments doesn't mean that its advantage is guaranteed indefinitely. Several challenges are on the immediate horizon, among them:

Changing chip-pricing policies. Conventional logic in chip making has always been that prices go down as performance goes up. The 286 microprocessors of the early 1980s cost $360 each. By the early 1990s, the Pentium microprocessor cost $950, but its performance was 100 times faster.[12] But the cost of creating the fabrication facilities for increasingly complex microprocessors is skyrocketing; it stands at $1 billion per facility now and one estimate has that price reaching $2 billion by the year 2000.[13,14] Another report suggests that by the year 2000, the price could be $10 billion.[15] How such investments are recaptured could certainly change, with prices at least remaining stable rather than declining.

Changing chip-making processes. Instead of changing how chips are priced, the semiconductor industry is racing after making chips differently. Manufacturing processes are being reviewed and reworked. The most drastic proposal involves making chips one at a time in a $30 million facility instead of in groups of a few hundred at a time in the $1 billion facility. Texas Instruments is pioneering this technology, called

Microelectronics Manufacturing Science & Technology.[16]

X-Ray lithography. A by-product of the practice of making components increasingly smaller is the need to make the circuit between the components on the microchip smaller. X-ray lithography promises to allow circuit widths of one-tenth of what they are today. But even after several years of work and hundreds of millions of dollars in investments, the process is still not commercially viable. There are serious questions as to whether research in this area should be continued—even though Japanese companies are doing extensive research in the field, too.[17]

Dependence on personal computers (PCs). Much of the U.S. semiconductor market has thrived because of its strength (and Japan's relative weakness) in products related to PCs. What happens in new, wide-open markets, such as personal digital assistants, multimedia applications, and data superhighways, where neither the appropriate protocols nor the products have been established?

Trade policies and trade deficit with Japan. Fulfillment of the 1986 Semiconductor Trade Arrangement between the United States and Japan provoked negative reactions in Japan. Underlying that situation was the (quite real) fear that this could lead to similar arrangements in other industries, such as automobiles, agricultural products, and electronics.[18] No matter what your opinion of such policies, these approaches coupled with the multibillion-dollar trade deficit that the United States has with Japan each year promises political friction that could easily explode into trade wars. Semiconductor-filled products would certainly stop flowing between the two countries should such a war break out.

Embracing Japan into SEMATECH. In what would be a stunning policy change, SEMATECH is considering allowing Japanese companies to join. Reports in January 1994 issues of *Electronic Business Buyer* and *The Wall Street Journal* reported the various levels of cooperation that might be possible. While some of this cooperation would be in the areas of industry-wide environment, health, and safety practices, others could be complex combinations of U.S. companies sharing technology in return for Japan allowing further access to its markets.[19,20]

The Korean factor. As Japan has suffered through a financial crisis in the early 1990s, Korean semiconductor companies have made great capital investments and taken advantage of inexpensive labor to capture a sizable share of the memory-chip market. Korean companies are sure to branch out into other portions of the electronics market. Will Korean companies dominate all semiconductor markets? Perhaps, but only until the fledgling Chinese semiconductor companies overtake them in 10 to 20 years.[21]

No, the wild ride doesn't promise to end. But quality improvement practices have made a major contribution to the semiconductor industry through the work of the individual companies and the coordinating activities of SEMATECH, and this contribution has helped sustain the U.S. semiconductor industry. The wild ride is sure to continue with all of these elements as passengers.

REFERENCES

1. James Fallows, *Looking at the Sun* (New York, NY: Pantheon Books, 1994), pp. 31-36.
2. Robert Ristelhueber, "Setting Sun: The Slide of Japanese Semiconductors," *Electronic Business Buyer,* April 1, 1994.
3. *SEMATECH 1994 Accomplishments,* a report developed by SEMATECH in February 1995, Technology Transfer #94122666A-XFR, p. 7.
4. Ibid, pp. 52-53.
5. The 1986 Semiconductor Trade Agreement is an unusual beast, to say the least. Fallows, in *Looking at the Sun,* describes it as a quota bill that required Japanese companies to buy at least 20% of their semiconductors from non-Japanese companies (p. 64). But Japanese officials have contested the validity and spirit of the agreement—even though they met its requirements. Michael Zielenziger wrote the following in the May 2, 1993 edition of the *San Jose Mercury News:* " 'We were very upset and embarrassed that we reached the 20% figure,' Yasuo Tanabe, director for the North American trade policy planning of Japan's powerful Ministry of International Trade and Industry, said in an interview last week. 'It was very shocking for us. We never expected to reach that 20% figure—it was an accident. And now we are upset that we agreed to this goal in the first place.' "
6. "Facts About SEMATECH," a SEMATECH information sheet, February 1995.
7. Fallows, *Looking at the Sun,* pp. 63, 65.
8. *Partnering for Total Quality,* Volume 1, #90060275A-GEN (Austin, TX: SEMATECH, 1990), p. 2.
9. One could draw a parallel between these groups and the World War II-era training for quality professionals. That training—first starting at Stanford University in 1942 and 1943 and known as the Engineering, Science, and Management War Training program—led to the formation of regional quality control societies that united in 1946 as the American Society for Quality Control.
10. According to the *Environmental Protection Agency (EPA) Dictionary,* the Superfund is a program operated under legislative authority that funds and carries out EPA solid-waste emergency and long-term removal and remedial activities. These activities include establishing the National Priorities List, investigating sites for inclusion on the list, determining their priority, and conducting and/or supervising the cleanup and other remedial actions.
11. Kellyn S. Betts, "The Coming Green Computers," *E / The Environmental Magazine,* March/April 1994.
12. Otis Port, "Will We Keep Getting More Bits for the Buck?" *Business Week,* July 4, 1994.
13. Ibid.
14. Charles McCoy, "Lehi, Utah, Kayos Two Bigger Cities for a Highly Sought Micron Factory," *The Wall Street Journal,* March 14, 1995. This article suggests that $1 billion might not be enough today. The construction estimate for Micron Technology Corporation's new semiconductor plant is $1.3 billion.
15. Gary Stix, "The Wall: Chip Makers' Quest for Small May Be Hitting It," *Scientific American,* July 1994.
16. Ibid.
17. Leslie Helm, "Four Companies to Tackle New Chip Technology," *The Los Angeles Times,* Oct. 7, 1994.
18. Michael Zielenziger, "U.S. Trade Advances Breed Japanese Contempt," *San Jose Mercury News,* May 2, 1993.
19. J. Lineback, "SEMATECH Considering Access for Japanese Vendors," *Electronic Business Buyer,* Jan. 1, 1994.
20. Kyle Pope, Asra Q. Nomani, and David P. Hamilton, "Japan Suggests It May Want to Join U.S. Consortium of Chip Companies," *The Wall Street Journal,* Jan. 31, 1994.
21. David P. Hamilton and Steve Glain, "Silicon Duel: Koreans Move to Grab Memory Chip Market From the Japanese," *The Wall Street Journal,* March 14, 1995.

BIBLIOGRAPHY

Amirrezvani, Anita, "Coming Clean in the Semiconductor Industry," *PC World,* June 1, 1994.

Neff, Robert, "Facing Reality in Japan Trade," *Business Week,* Oct. 10, 1994.

Ristelhueber, Robert, "How Semiconductor Companies Design Products for Specific Applications," *Electronic Business Buyer*, June 1, 1994.

The TQM-BASE Council 1994 Annual Report, Andover, MD.

Walker, Tom, and Sandra Lowe, "Manufacturing and the Environment: A Matter of Regulation," *San Antonio Business Journal,* Dec. 23, 1994.

SECTION
Three

QUALITY TECHNOLOGIES AND METHODS

The line between traditional quality assurance methods and other responsibilities within an organization continues to become blurred. Take the case of the coordinate measuring machine. This began as a traditional inspection instrument to be used in a controlled environment within a laboratory to make critical measurements. Today, some coordinate measuring machines are being used by manufacturing personnel on the assembly line to confirm process controls.

Also, consider the example of business process reengineering. This is a method of restructuring an organization usually conducted by top management and outside consultants. Recently, the method is being adopted by quality-assurance managers to help them design a more efficient department.

Quality methods are spreading out across functions within organizations. At the same time, methods considered outside the responsibility of a quality professional in the past are now migrating into the quality department. Thus the clear distinction of a quality department is becoming less clear. This is reflected in this section on the methods typically used by quality professionals.

The section begins with a discussion of business process reengineering. This represents the philosophy of Hammer versus philosophies preached by people such as Deming. The past few years have seen a dramatic increase in corporations reducing the size of their operation while increasing the responsibilities of the surviving workers. This can fly in the face of the practices encouraged under total quality management. It is a delicate act to increase responsibilities, reduce the work force, and still encourage continuous improvement. As a quality manager, you should study the stories presented in this section as a lesson on how to achieve this delicate balancing act.

---■---

PROCESS REENGINEERING:
MAKE QUANTUM LEAPS IN QUALITY AND SERVICE*

Process reengineering is defined as *the fundamental rethinking and radical redesign of business processes to achieve dramatic improvement in a critical measure, such as cost, quality, or service.* "It is, basically, process reinvention, not incremental process improvement or process modification," explains Phillip D. Kruger, manager, Management Consulting for Grant Thornton (Minneapolis, MN). Each reengineering project focuses on business processes, which Kruger defines as "a combination of activities that has an input end and generates an output that is of value to the customer."

To really improve, companies must rethink all of their primary processes, says Nick McGaughey, managing director of Applied Information (Menlo Park, CA). The most effective way to accomplish this, he believes, is through process reengineering, which he defines as: "The fundamental analysis and radical redesign of an entire business process and the implementation of the changes required to achieve break-through improvements in critical measures of business performance—quality, cost, and time—that are important to customers."

REENGINEERING VERSUS TQM

Reengineering is the next logical improvement emphasis after TQM, McGaughey suggests. "TQM looks at the organization from a functional, vertical view.

Reengineering, however, looks at it from a process-oriented, horizontal view that crosses functions." In other words, TQM focuses on studying each function in a process and improving the quality of that function. Reengineering, on the other hand, focuses on trying to:

eliminate all the functions in the process that do not add value,

simplify the functions that remain, and

utilize technology to achieve dramatic process improvements.

"TQM provides 20 to 25 percent improvements. On the other hand, reengineering allows quantum improvements, on the order of 100 to 200 percent improvement," McGaughey points out.

REENGINEERING'S GUIDING PRINCIPLES

McGaughey delineates 10 guiding principles for reengineering critical processes. "Some of these are similar and common to TQM, but most of them are not," he observes.

1. Maintain a customer orientation.
2. Focus on outcomes and results.
3. Challenge the rules in terms of how you do business and how you relate to customers.
4. Empower employees.
5. Build in quality at the source.
6. Define end-to-end solutions (looking at the major business processes).
7. Set "stretch" targets and goals (for example, attempting to reduce the time involved in a process by 50 percent or more).
8. Eliminate nonvalue-added activities.
9. Compress time. (This is similar to Number 8, in that it involves eliminating nonvalue-added activities. However, it also focuses on *reducing the time required to complete value-added activities.*)

---

10. Use technology as an enabler.

Here are seven steps involved in process reengineering, according to Kruger:

- **Set your vision.** "Identify a high-level vision. Then, develop performance measures and evaluate what is occurring so that you can fit these into your strategic vision," he advises.

- **Select the process.** Identify the process that you want to reengineer. "Select the one that poses the most problems and that will ultimately give you the greatest results," he suggests.

- **Set up a cross-functional reengineering team to study and redesign the process.** Ideally, you want two types of people on this team:

  1. "Insiders" who are familiar with the process and work with it every day. Traditionally, Insiders will want to begin with the existing process and "redesign" it essentially the same, perhaps with a few modifications. Their rationale: "Once you've been here as long as I have, you'll know why we have to keep doing things this way."

  2. "Outsiders" who are not familiar with the process. They can be from another department or outside the company (for example, consultants). Outsiders, unlike Insiders, will probably want to start from scratch, with a "blank piece of paper." "They will continually ask such questions as: 'Why is this done?' 'What is the point of this step?' They tend to challenge the Insiders," notes Kruger.

- **Analyze the existing process.** Understand what the process's needs and outputs are. The best way to achieve this is by creating a process flow diagram. The diagram should show the primary steps in the process (activities) on one chart with the details of the steps (subactivities) shown on a separate chart. The team then studies the steps and the details in order to separate the nonvalue-added activities from the value-added activities. "Sometimes, in fact, simply laying out the process and creating flowcharts is quite an exercise in itself for the people involved," notes Kruger. It helps them in three ways:

They understand better what takes place in the process (instead of just seeing their individual portion of the process).

They begin to be able to identify the value-added and nonvalue-added parts of the process.

Their individual roles and responsibilities related to the process becomes much more clear.

- **Redesign the process.** "This may be the most difficult step," cautions Kruger. One way to approach redesigning the process involves benchmarking. "You don't necessarily want to copy what someone else is doing, but you can see what the best companies are doing and get a lot of good ideas," Kruger says.

- **Implement the new process.** Make certain that it is working effectively.

- **Sustain the changes.** "It requires a *cultural* change to make a new process work," Kruger points out. "So, you need to support it long enough for it to take hold on its own."

A Variation on the Theme

According to McGaughey, another approach to process reengineering is:

Phase I: *Start the effort by looking outside your company.* Focus on external customer requirements, conduct a competitive analysis of your market, and engage in benchmarking—both functional (with noncompetitive organizations) and competitive.

Phase II: *Next, look inside your organization at your existing processes,* and

- *Determine your process requirements based on the information you obtained in Phase I.*

- *Understand your current process* (via a focus group or process mapping).

- *Identify ways to streamline the process and reduce time and cost.*

- *Redesign the process and create associated process measurements.* (The latter helps you determine whether improvements are actually taking place.)

- *Implement the new process.*

To be successful with process reengineering, says McGaughey, you also need to

✔ *Analyze your business strategies and redesign critical business processes in ways that capitalize on state-of-the-art information technology.*

✔ *Design and change work and organizational structures; create cross-functional work teams; formulate new incentives, hiring, compensation, training, and other management systems.*

✔ *Design the information technology infrastructure in your company to support new business processes. Assess the technological readiness of your company. Help functional managers to reengineer their own functions.*

Regardless of which method you use to implement process reengineering, if you approach it carefully and methodically, you should expect to see significant improvements in quality, efficiency, and cost management. You might not realize 200 percent improvement with your first effort, but you should get the kind of promising results that will encourage your company to want to try reengineering other processes.

■

GETTING RESULTS THAT MATTER WITH REENGINEERING WITHOUT DESTRUCTION*
by Charlene Adair

"Guarantee"—"certainty"—"forever": these are words seldom used when describing the world today. Change is inevitable just to keep up. And to get ahead of the competition, change that is dramatic and fast is often required; reengineering is the most popular methodology applied today to change business processes dramatically. In recent conversations, people were asked to describe reengineering, and the following responses were common:

"Reengineering is a methodology to blow up the present business processes and start over with new ones."

"Oh, it's really nothing new—just a new term for process improvement."

"It's taken too long, and the results have not met our expectations."

"I don't want any part of it: putting in new software and systems creates too many problems."

"I'm not sure, but it scares me. My boss said that some of us would have to learn new skills and others might lose their job. I'm not sure that I'm ready."

"I think we've been doing it all along. Isn't it a lot like Total Quality?"

So, the word "reengineering" is causing a lot of confusion and yet everyone is talking about it. Almost all of the progressive companies today have something called "reengineering" going on, with mixed successes reported. The purpose of this article is to discuss the key drivers of change, how to determine if reengineering is the right approach for you, and how to ensure success from your change effort without destruction.

CHANGE DRIVERS

The first step in any change effort is to determine what needs to be changed and how much it should change; then, the most effective approach can be chosen to meet each need. The key drivers for change in any organization include: THE CUSTOMER, THE COMPANY VISION, THE BUSINESS IMPERATIVES, AND THE STRATEGY.

A critical starting point is to begin with the customer (this should include those customers you wish you had, too). Many companies that begin a change process which is internally focused

---

*Reprinted with permission from The Association for Quality and Participation, Cincinnati OH (513) 381-1959. From the *17th Annual Spring Conference and Resource Mart,* April 1995. Charlene Adair is a principal with The ChangeManagement Group in Boulder, CO.

improve the wrong things, spend a lot of money doing it, and eventually suffer in the marketplace. The company vision is a picture in the mind's eye of what is being created. Without this, employees can be very busy going in different directions, only to discover that they have pulled the company apart. Business imperatives are the two or three "must do" shorter-term things to keep the business moving successfully. Without business imperatives, companies have long lists of priorities that keep changing. Business strategy clarifies the mission of the company (why we exist/what business we're in) and how to accomplish all of the above. The strategy provides focus and specific actions to move the company toward the vision.

All companies are made up of core business processes. These are not functional areas, such as operations and finance, but instead processes that typically cut across functional lines. The most common are: the order-generation process, the product-development process, the order-fulfillment process, and the customer-service process. Change is most effective when thinking of it in terms of business processes, because that is the way work gets done within any company. Several important guidelines to get "Results that Matter" are:

- DON'T CHANGE IT MORE THAN YOU HAVE TO: save the big changes for the big needs.

- If big change is required, DO IT!

- Match the approach used with the need for change.

- ALWAYS consider "the human side."

How Do We Know If Reengineering Is the Right Choice?

Imagine that you own a chain of exclusive restaurants with business men and women as a target market. Your customers value quality, efficiency in service, and a friendly atmosphere. Your strategy is to maximize profits, which will be partially reinvested in growth. The opening of new restaurants must be a "repeatable" experience to maintain the consistency of value provided.

There are three primary business processes: greeting customers, cooking the food, and serving food to the customers. In your overall evalu-ation of the business (using the change drivers), you determine that the greeting process is pretty good. The "greeters" just need to "spruce up" their process and continue to look for improvements—they are known for their warmth and friendliness. The cooking process is basically sound, but needs a lot of improvement to provide consistent quality and timeliness. To accomplish this goal, the cooks identify some fairly significant changes to their process, such as a new layout of the kitchen, new scheduling procedures so orders are hot and coordinated when delivered to the customers, and some new utensils to measure the quality of the food.

On the other hand, the serving process is just not working. Customers wait too long for water, menu, order taking, getting food, and the bill. What your business customers want is more time to eat and talk and less time spent waiting and being interrupted. Even if more servers are hired, the menu is adjusted, and the server enters the order automatically, the problem will not be solved. You need a new process. Imagine entering the restaurant as a customer. The new process is that you are greeted and seated, you make selections from an electronic menu, your food arrives in no more than 10 minutes, and you pay automatically at your table. Servers are no longer assigned to tables, but are waiting to deliver the next food order as soon as it is completed (hot and consistent!). They add some additional friendliness and service (when needed) without adding the unwanted waits and interruptions.

Now let's apply this example to the change process. The greeting process just needed some "sprucing up," which most would term a continuous improvement process. This approach has often been linked to a Total Quality environment: everyone is making things better (which is a desirable foundation for all other change processes). For those processes that need major renovation, such as the cooking process, a different approach that includes specific chartering of cross-functional teams with breakthrough goals is required to get the change fast. The process redesign is deductive, utilizing specific flow and quality tools to achieve improvements that exceed 50% in a few months. The process is significantly improved, but still recognizable. It supports the existing strategy.

Reengineering is usually described as a "clean sheet of paper" approach. This approach may be required to create a new process that does not exist today or to dramatically change an existing one, like the serving example: If the old process can no longer meet requirements—even if it were ALL value-added—you will need to "build a new one." It is necessary to understand the inputs, outputs, controls, and constraints of the old process, but not every detail about it. Different improvement approaches will be required: more inductive and creative in nature. The leadership of the organization must drive this change. Skill requirements and organization structure may change significantly. Reengineered processes may actually create new capabilities that change the vision and strategy of the company. The transition to the new process can be exciting and compelling for employees if planned correctly.

Having the skills to "sort out" how much change and to what extent the change is needed is critical in planning any change effort. Using the change drivers and applying the right level of analysis will ensure that you are only applying more dramatic change approaches when they are really needed.

THREE DIMENSIONS OF SUCCESSFUL CHANGE

When three critical dimensions are considered equally during a change effort, the organizational health can actually be improved. Since the risk increases with the amount of change, including all three dimensions in a reengineering effort makes the difference between success and disappointment.

The operational, or process side is usually the focus of change efforts. This is the easiest to "get your hands around" and understand in detail—it appeals more to those of us who may take an engineering approach to processes and change. However, without the "people and climate" side, this approach can be destructive to the organizational health of the company. As the amount of change increases, more structural changes are inevitable on the organizational, business, and physical sides. For example, when a process is reengineered, it may very well include major organizational structure changes, such as organizing around processes instead of in functional areas. Business structure may move from being centralized to decentralized, and facilities may actually be required in different locations to support the reengineered process.

CONCLUSIONS

The outcomes of a change effort that is driven with the customer in mind and carefully addresses all of these dimensions should include the following:

- Core capabilities are built within the organization to change the next time.
- The people and climate of the organization are improved.
- Measurable big change happens fast.
- Your company will leap ahead of the competition.

So, set your sights high for change! Expect and get "Results That Matter" without destruction by using reengineering WHEN YOU NEED IT.

■
---

21 DAYS TO MAXIMIZE THE GAIN AND MINIMIZE THE PAIN OF REENGINEERING*
by Howard Deutsch and Maura Burke Weiner

Reengineering offers large gains, including cost reductions of 25 percent and more, decreases in cycle time of more than 50 percent, and large-scale improvements in quality and customer service. Unfortunately, the process of reengineering is often accompanied by major disruptions and pain to organizations and customers.

*Reprinted wth permission from *Continuous Journey,* April 1995. Howard Deutsch is president of Deutsch Consulting Services, Inc., in West Orange, NJ. Maura Burke Weiner is director of the Service Impact Group, based in Fairfax, VA.

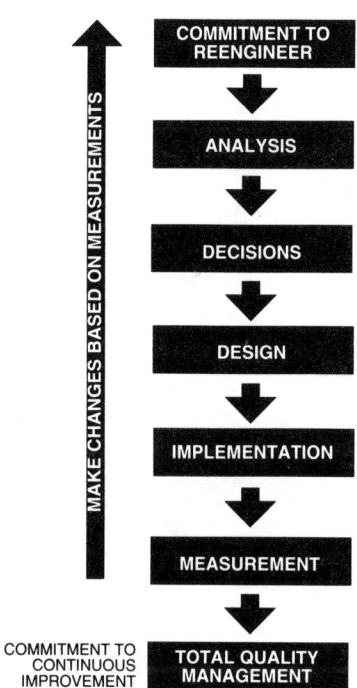

EXHIBIT 1.—THE BUSINESS REENGINEERING
PROCESS

Reengineering is "the radical redesign of business processes in order to achieve major gains in cost, time, quality, or service." While reengineering may often lead to reductions in staff, it is not downsizing, layoffs, or other stand-alone actions.

Let's start with a macro look:

- *In 1994, more than $30 billion was spent on reengineering projects.*

- *Two-thirds of all reengineering projects fail.*

- *More than 75 percent of all reengineering dollars are spent on technology.*

- *Multiple failed attempts at specific reengineering projects occur frequently.*

- *Reengineering is a bonanza for consulting firms.*

Despite these seemingly negative statistics, the potential rewards and paybacks from reengineering continue to generate new reengineering initiatives. Effective execution of the following six phases will greatly increase the chances for achieving success in your reengineering efforts: 1) commitment to reengineering, 2) analysis, 3) decisions, 4) design, 5) implementation, and 6) follow-up measurement/refinements (Exhibit 1).

The following 21 recommendations illustrate how to maximize the gain and minimize the pain of reengineering.

1. *Reengineered business processes should reflect the organization's written or implied mission, vision, and values.* Reengineering can be used as a catalyst to rethink an organization's mission, vision, and values. If there is a clear need for adapting a new set of guiding principles for either a particular business process or for the entire organization, this is the time to do so. Senior management must support and drive the organization's new direction.

2. *Business processes should be reengineered through the eyes of customers.* The majority of business processes flow across two or more functional units within organizations. Business processes also often include interaction with customers and vendors. Customers should not have to deal with inefficiencies, ineffective communications, and a myriad of problems that often occur at the boundaries between functional units within organizations and with their supporting vendors.

New processes should be designed so customers find them simple, convenient, and easy to use. The same is true of products produced by the reengineered processes. Every effort should be made to minimize cycle time, waiting time, and all other aspects of process time.

3. *Reengineering should include a broad overview of all business processes.* Reengineering projects often focus heavily on technology, but this narrow emphasis may not be what is best for the organization. Consulting firms often emphasize technological solutions because that is the area of their expertise and where big follow-on money can be found.

Review organizations and their processes from a broad perspective. Be sure to include a thorough analysis of information flow, organization structure, corporate culture, process ownership, and the selection and training of highly effective people to function within processes.

4. *Create a Business Performance Profile to balance and maximize the overall performance of business processes and the entire organization.* The Business Performance Profile (Exhibit 2) presents a model of the entire business performance cycle. Devised by Deutsch Consulting Services, Inc., the model offers a unique way of visualizing the importance of achieving balance in business processes. In using this method, rate the effectiveness of each aspect of the organiza-

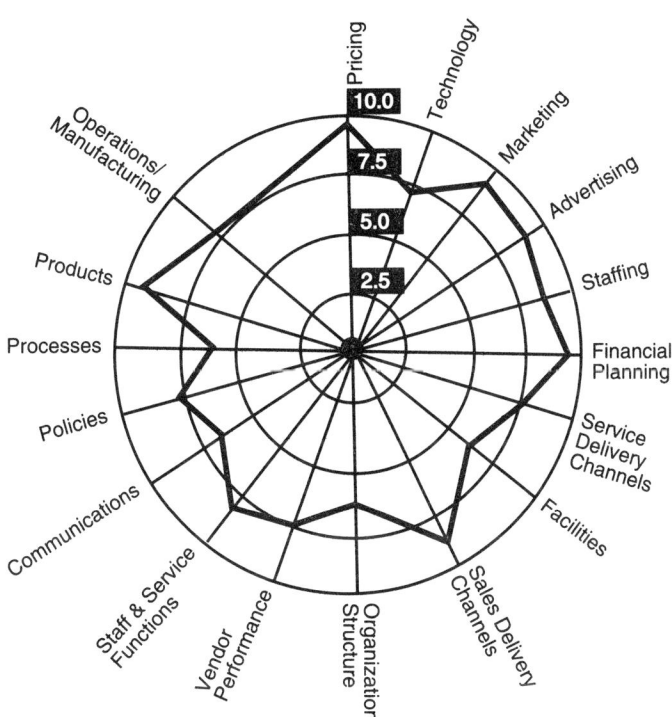

EXHIBIT 2.—PERFORMANCE PROFILE OF BUSINESS INPUTS

tion's business cycle by marking its respective axis on a scale of zero to 10 with 10 representing the best possible performance. Draw a line connecting your marks to see the overall performance profile of the business.

The goal of reengineering should be to optimize the performance of the business inputs to achieve the desired cost, quality, service, and timeliness results. Focus on all 17 business inputs, while also considering available capital, financial goals, customer requirements and expectations, and competitive knowledge. Using the guiding principles of the organization's vision, mission, and goals, leadership is required to transform the 17 inputs into highly effective outputs.

Ideally, the profile drawn will be large, indicating a high level of performance, and well-rounded, indicating balance of business efforts or results. Use the profile to establish priorities for improvement.

5. *Thoroughly understand current processes.* Contrary to the advice offered by some reengineering consultants, the analysis phase should include a thorough review of current practices. Be sure to get input from employees who manage and perform the various functions of current processes. The more one knows about current processes, the better able he will be to design new processes.

6. *Determine current customer-satisfaction levels and short- and long-term customer requirements and expectations.* Customer satisfaction should be a top priority. Talk with and survey customers and include the findings in new process designs.

7. *Benchmark best practice organizations prior to designing new processes.* Whatever business process organizations are reengineering, they need to identify others that perform these processes well and learn from several of them. In particular, other industries may be doing things in a way that could drastically change and improve the way to do business.

8. *Keep the size of the core reengineering team small.* Do not analyze and design by committee. The complexity and size of most processes does not require a large number of members on the core reengineering team. A small number of dedicated, knowledgeable, creative individuals is preferable (e.g., three to five people) to a significantly larger group. The core reengineering team can interview a wide range of people and bring in individuals on an "as needed" basis. An oversized reengineering team slows the process and spreads the tasks, making it harder to design new processes.

9. *Challenge the current paradigm and ask the difficult questions.* What if there was no management? What if everything was done with teams? What if we discard the policy manual and empower individuals to make all decisions based on common sense and customer needs? What if everything was outsourced? Who are the ideal people to work in this process and how can we get them? At what cost?

10. *Develop a high-level vision of the entire reengineered process before designing the details.* Typical considerations include:

- *Customer interfaces for sales, service, inquiries, and problem resolution,*
- *Vendor interfaces and requirements,*
- *Organizational/team structure,*
- *Process ownership,*
- *Policies,*
- *Use of technology,*
- *Service level standards, and*
- *Key performance measurements and how they will be collected and used.*

11. *Conduct a comprehensive review of the new process design before implementing the newly reengineered process.* Make sure the new process is very clearly defined and that the "right players" (i.e., people who perform the current process) review and critique it. This is the best time in the reengineering process to ensure that the new process makes sense. Changes made later on are much more costly and their negative impact on schedules, and possibly customers, are apt to be more significant.

12. *Establish realistic deadlines for reengineering projects.* This is particularly important for the analysis, decision, and design phases. Since organizations and their customers will be living with the results of the reengineering process for years to come, take the time to be thorough. Tight deadlines can significantly limit the success of reengineering projects.

13. *Select the right staff and train them well.* The best designed process in the world cannot compensate for ineffective staff. Hire the best people, provide comprehensive training, and set clear expectations for performance. Pay particular attention to customer contact staff—customers typically judge organizations based on the contact staff's performance.

14. *Define, communicate, and support the desired culture.* Most reengineering projects ignore the issue of corporate culture, often to the detriment of the reengineered process environ-

ment. In many instances, the corporate culture needs greater change than the business process. Should the culture emphasize sales and service or controls and audits? Should it be customer driven or policies oriented? Should the culture encourage or discourage risk? Should it favor teamwork or individual performance?

15. *Do not cut corners or make hasty compromises.* Many reengineering projects make major compromises that very significantly limit the potential success of reengineering. For example, never purchase software designed for other businesses. Otherwise, organizations will be designing processes around the strengths and weaknesses of other businesses, not their own.

16. *Use consultants to help reengineer.* Consultants can provide project guidance, reengineering process expertise, and project management support. They also can provide an objective perspective and make sure reengineering projects are properly scoped. Consultants often provide resources not available within organizations, including implementation support.

There are several cautions to keep in mind when using consultants on reengineering projects. Keep the consulting team small. If you are paying for experience, expertise, and the ability to make things happen, then make sure this is what you are getting. Insist the consultants clearly define their objectives, roles and approach, and hold them to it.

17. *"Anti-reengineering" efforts and battles over turf issues should not be tolerated.* Reengineering normally forces people to deal with large-scale change. This may include a loss of power and authority, and it could even result in loss of jobs. Be sensitive to concerns about the reengineering process, the approach, the results, and the reengineering team participants. However, do not tolerate behavior that will slow progress or otherwise hinder success of reengineering projects.

18. *Avoid setting arbitrary targets (e.g. 25 percent reduction in cost) at the outset of reengineering projects.* How can organizations possibly know what can be achieved until the analysis and design are completed?

Reengineering teams should be charged with quantifying the benefits during the analysis, decision, and design phases. Front-end targets often have the effect of demoralizing the team if they fall short of the goals. Targets can also cause teams to hold back from exceeding targets that may be too small.

19. *Provide strong leadership and visible support throughout the reengineering process.*

Senior management must inform the entire organization about the reengineering process. They should clearly communicate the general goals of the reengineering effort, how it is being done, and who is on the project team. General comments about the desired results and the potential impact on employees, customers, and the entire business organization should also be included. There can never be too much communication from the beginning of the reengineering process through to its completion.

20. *Designate a process owner or a process-ownership team to own each major business process.* Most business processes flow across functional organization lines, and many will continue to do so after reengineering.

Process owners should have clear ownership and authority for all aspects of the business process. Without that ownership and authority, reengineered processes relying on two or more functional units within the organization will fail to be responsive to the needs of the customers.

21. *Implement a total quality management (TQM) process throughout the organization, if one does not exist.* The TQM process, through its commitment to continuous improvement, will ensure that the newly reengineered business processes will be kept current with ever-changing market conditions. TQM is also an effective way to make adjustments and fix problems arising out of reengineering projects.

Competitive pressure and the potential benefits of reengineering provide a compelling argument to proceed with reengineering. Rather than posing the question, "Can I afford to reengineer?" organizations should be asking, "Can I afford not to reengineer?" With careful planning and attention, the chances for maximizing the gain and minimizing the pain of reengineering projects will be significantly increased.

WHEN DOING IT RIGHT THE FIRST TIME IS NOT ENOUGH*
by R.G. Boznak

Since the industrial revolution, management has targeted the processes of manufacturing and assembly as its means to extract greater business performance. This trend continued through the 1980s when manufacturers invested heavily in robotics and computer-aided design to improve productivity. General Motors alone spent $60 billion in this area.[1] Now, as we approach the 21st century, several additional themes are attracting management's attention. One theme is the quality revolution.

Today, the quality revolution's motto, do it right the first time, is embraced by most enlightened business leaders. There is also a potpourri of programs, such as reengineering, simultaneous engineering, design for assembly, electronic data exchange, just-in-time manufacturing, and executive information systems, that consumes much of management's attention and resources.

How well has management capitalized on these programs? Are they helping manufacturing businesses get back on a competitive track? The answers are all around. The automotive, electronics, and consumer products markets continue to erode. Corporate profits are down. Employee layoffs are so common that they no longer make the evening news. Many wealth-creating enterprises, such as IBM, are fighting for their economic lives.

This is not the picture of economic wellness. Why has this happened? The answer lies in the irony that, while most organizations strive to do it right, few are able to achieve the most basic step: defining what it is they want to do right.

---

*Reprinted with permission from *Quality Progress*, July 1994. R.G. Boznak is the president of Robinstone Tower, Inc., an executive consulting center in Bourne, TX.

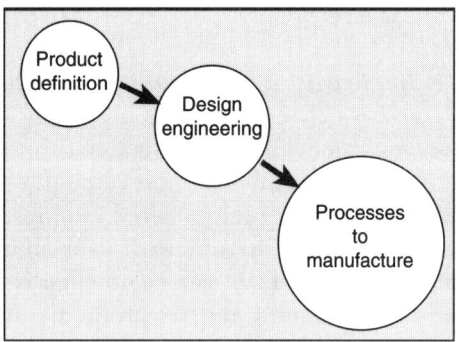

EXHIBIT 1.—NATURE OF WORK

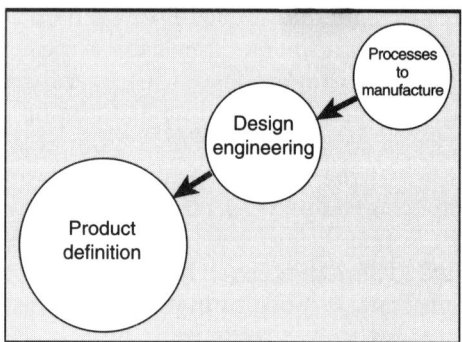

EXHIBIT 2.—NATURE OF PRODUCTIVITY
EMPOWERMENT

JUST DO IT

While Nike tells us to "just do it" in its commercials, what exactly are the "do" and the "it"? *Do* is the skills and processes required to develop a product, and *it* is the product.

Do has been the traditional focus of management. *Do* is the most visceral, visible, and seemingly important half of the new-product development equation. Therefore, organizational structures and functions are created to accomplish the *do*. Management of the *do* has been studied, processed, and proceduralized. Hundreds of books have been written about ways to execute the *do* better. Organizations even benchmark and measure how well they compare against the world-class *do*.

It, on the other hand, is the Rodney Dangerfield of product development. *It* gets no respect. Few companies recognize that the *it* must precede the *do*. Fewer companies have structures, functions, or processes to define, communicate, or manage their *its*. *It* is seldom the subject of a book or study. Nor is *it* often considered, benchmarked, or measured. A second reason most businesses have yet to discern the importance of *it* is because they cannot correctly visualize the nature of work or how their businesses really work (See Exhibit 1).

THE NATURE OF WORK

Nature-of-work advocates have long espoused the theory that where there are a lot of people and costs, there must also be many improvement opportunities. The theory is emotionally appealing and might offer some short-term benefits.

The theory, however, is merely a tactical approach to a holistic product-development issue.

This is because nature-of-work proponents have failed to discern a diametrically opposed phenomenon: the nature of productivity empowerment (Exhibit 2). In essence, the further downstream in the development process, the less influence a person or department can have on functional performance.

For example, production efficiency is highly dependent on the correctness of engineering designs, the timeliness of material support, and the accuracy and stability of marketing forecasts. Conversely, little attention has been directed to managing the productivity influencers at the front end of the business. As a result, management has misinterpreted the true nature of work for decades. Namely, how does one define the products an organization hopes to build?

As Exhibit 2 shows, nature-of-work promoters have failed to discern that efficiency of a product's development is directly influenced by the adequacy and integrity of its definition (or what it is that will be made). This argument is further substantiated by the product-development expenditure patterns of major industrial firms. An international study found that when companies increased their predevelopment emphasis, they increased the predictability of successful new-product commercialization by a 2-to-1 ratio.[2] (Note how this substantiates the nature of productivity empowerment.) A comparison of successes and failures illustrates how these critical front-end steps can separate winners from losers:

• Winners spent more than twice as many resources on predevelopment activities as did losers.

• Seventy-one percent of new-product development was delayed due to poor definition and understanding of customer require-ments.

- Changing product requirements induced more delays in product development than any other cause.

The reason for this is clear. Unless a product is adequately defined and controlled, communication and interpretation errors will be introduced within the remaining product-development processes. When this occurs, the integrity of the product and, more important, the stability of the processes required to produce it are undermined.

This phenomenon can be modeled by using the number, frequency, and periodicity of design change as the means of comparison. The fewer the number of changes, the greater the maturity and control of the definition. Conversely, the greater the number of changes, the less the definition is mature and controlled. This model sheds light on why most Western companies are finding it difficult to reduce costs, improve quality, and shorten cycle times.

TIMING OF PRODUCT DEFINITION

When the abilities of Western and Japanese manufacturers are contrasted (to define and control their product-development processes), the competitive implications of Japanese product-management effectiveness are immediately apparent. Using this logic, Exhibit 3 shows that Japanese manufacturers define their products much earlier than Western manufacturers.[3]

Conversely, the Western product-development model is represented by the philosophy of "we'll know it when we see it." Unfortunately, this cavalier viewpoint is still ingrained

in many manufacturing companies. A famous European carmaker typified this belief.[4] The development of its car emanated from a list of vehicle features. In turn, this list was used to specify the car's systems. Finally, detailed parts and components were derived and designed to achieve the systems' requirements.

The features list was the sun around which all developmental efforts revolved. Because of its strategic importance, the features list was held under direct control of the company's executive leadership. It was also a volatile document. For example, in 1986, the executive team approved nearly 600 features for its 1990 model-year car. Perhaps the team was too optimistic, because the closer it got to building the car ("Launch" in Exhibit 4), the more changes it made to the list.

In 1986 and 1987, 7% of the features were dropped. The pace of change accelerated in 1988 when 29% of the features were deleted before finally increasing to 32% immediately before manufacturing launch. These changes, however, masked the real problem. This is because the features list defined the car systems, which, in turn, defined the detailed parts design. One can only imagine what the addition and deletion of features had on the car's perceived value and marketability, the stability of the car's development processes, and the car's per-unit cost.

A significant advantage of early product definition and control is the creation of a plateau of stability (see Exhibit 5). This plateau provides stability to manufacturing operations, material procurement, and supplier partnering. The beneficial effects of stability on these downstream activities can be extraordinary.

The plateau's most critical consideration, however, might be its compressibility factor. The longer and greater its stability, the more a product's development cycle can be compressed with

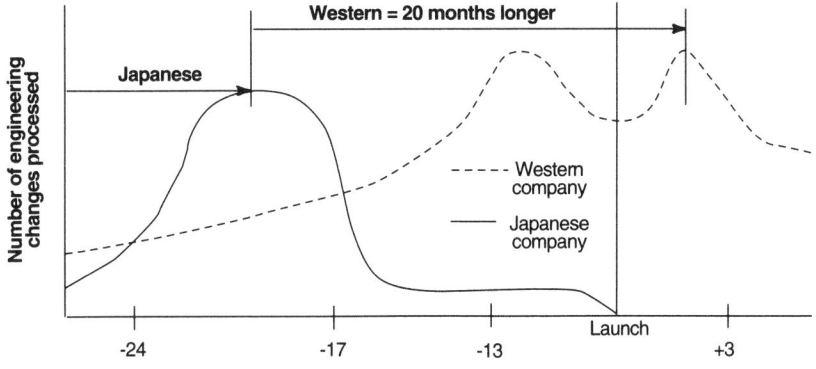

EXHIBIT 3.—TIMING OF PRODUCT-DEFINITION ACHIEVEMENT

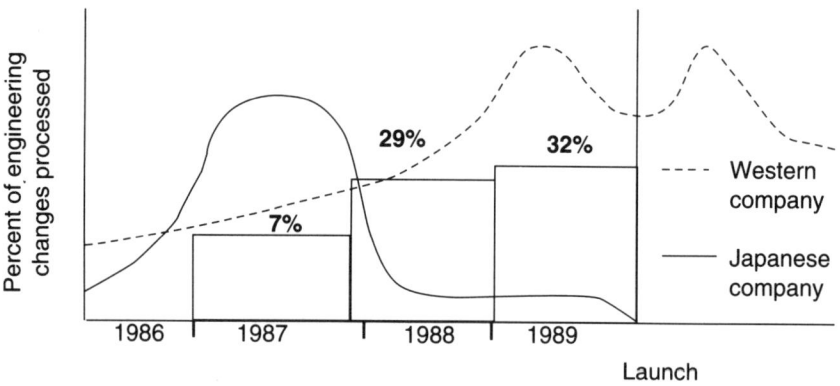

EXHIBIT 4.—CHANGES MADE TO FEATURES LIST

much less risk. Reducing a product's development cycle is a critical competitiveness factor for several reasons:

- The faster the response, the greater the threat to the competition. It requires the competitors' new product offerings to be on target and shortens their window of opportunity. Conversely, this same advantage can work in a competitor's favor.

- A company can more rapidly satisfy its customers' changing needs. This increases customer satisfaction and raises the barrier to market entry, both of which improve competitiveness.

- Cycle compression accelerates a product's time to volume. Time to volume is the elapsed time required to achieve a product's optimum manufacturing rate. Obviously, the faster manufacturing can achieve capacity, the faster the company can reap a product's differentiated gross-profit opportunities.

Reducing a product's development cycle is, however, difficult because of rework, design changes, process changes, and material shortages. For instance, a computer manufacturer made product-design changes late in the development cycle. This created planning conflicts, material shortages, and process adjustments. The combined effect of these actions caused production to fall. The shortfall represented a $55 million gross-profit opportunity loss.[5]

Given the increasing rates of product obsolescence, difficulties in maintaining product differentiation, and shrinking profit margins, a company must optimize its time-to-volume opportunities. Failure to achieve this critical success factor can mean the difference between business competitiveness and business mediocrity.

BEWARE THE CHAOS ZONE

The stability model in Exhibit 5 also reveals a significant barrier to achieving acceptable prod-

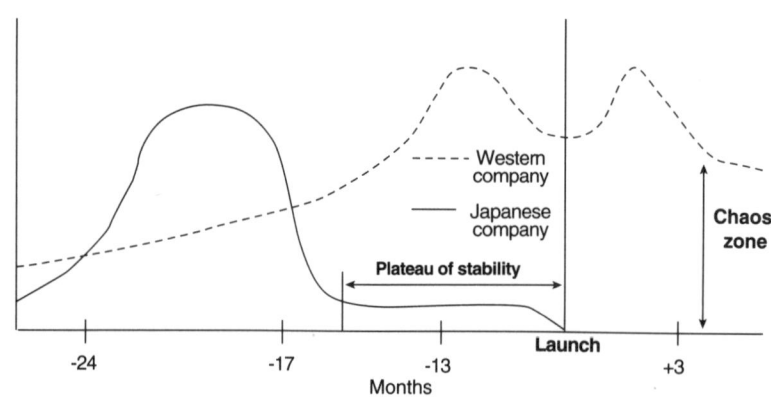

EXHIBIT 5.—CREATING PLATEAUS OF STABILITY

uct reliability, maintainability, and quality targets—the chaos zone. At best, improving product reliability, maintainability, or quality performance is difficult within a stable product-development environment. The closer a product gets to its manufacturing launch, however, the more changes tend to be made.

The potential quality, reliability, and maintainability impacts suggested by the model pose a few questions that demand answers. For example, if a company fits the chaos scenario and products are introduced on schedule:

- How are the changes that are generated during and after manufacturing accommodated?

- What is the difference between the first and last version of the most recently introduced new product?

- How do the company, support channels, and customers accommodate these product changes?

- How will the company become ISO 9000 certified?

Containing Product-Development Costs

Changes are direct contributors to unplanned product-development costs. Paul Strassman, former Xerox vice-president of systems applications, said an engineering change in three different companies required a chain of 53, 220, and 423 events, such as phone conversations, meetings, and memos, which cost the companies $1,000, $2,000, and $10,000 respectively.[6] "This expense represented only the cost of processing information rather than the total cost of the change itself." Administrative processing costs, from small firms to *FORTUNE* 500 companies, average $1,400 per change.[7]

A 1988 survey of international aerospace, defense, textiles, electronics, consumer products, construction, utility, ship repair, and foundry companies reported an average of 330 design changes per month.[8] The range of responses was from two to 1,000 monthly changes. What is the effect of this activity on product costs? The annual administrative processing cost alone could range from $3.4 million to $7.7 million, while 1,000 changes might easily result in a cost of $16.8 million.

The survey found that the cost of change experienced in these companies underscored their

difficulty in reducing product costs.[9] For example, the aerospace contractor's program changes exceeded $50 million; in retrospect, many of these costs were unnecessary. The European automaker's annual cost of change was more than $41 million. The computer manufacturer's case was more severe. The company's annual cost of change exceeded $21 million. This equated to more than 420,000 hours of nonvalue-added work and a loss of $55 million in gross-profit opportunity on one product. The computer maker's inability to manage its product-development processes put its $1.5 billion international business at risk because of noncompliance to ISO 9000.

Regrettably, these are not hypothetical numbers. They are examples that can be found in companies around the world. They reflect missed cost-reduction and profit-making opportunities that could have made these companies more successful.

Institutionalized Product-Development Inadequacies

Given the toll of reduced productivity and lost profits, it is difficult to understand why so many companies choose to institutionalize their flawed product-development processes rather than tackle them head on. For instance:

- An automotive manufacturer typically allots nearly 200 design-engineering man-years to optimize component designs, from the power train to the sun visor, after the vehicle has been fully prototyped.[10]

- A high-tech office equipment maker usually plans for five design iterations of a new product before it is released into manufacturing.[11]

- A defense manufacturer traditionally plans for a 300% rate of design change.[12]

- An aircraft maker habitually inflates its fabrication lead time by 50% to allow for anticipated and uncontrolled design changes.[13]

Achieving a Balance Between Do and It

Dollar, time, and opportunity costs of the magnitude noted here are unacceptable; they debilitate companies' competitiveness. They also imply that several actions must occur. First, people must understand how companies really work— more specifically, people must become students of effective product development. Second, people must develop ways to effectively define and control new products early in the development process. There must be a balance between do and it. "Right the first time" is only part of the solution. Management of the it is the missing key to greatness. Management of the it is the next revolution for industrial excellence.

REFERENCES

1. Leslie S. Hiraoka, "Paradigmatic Shifts in Automobile Manufacturing," *Engineering Management Journal,* June 1989, p. 14.
2. R.G. Cooper and E.J. Klienschmidt, "Resource Allocation in the New Product Development Process," *Industrial Marketing Management,* 1988, p. 260.
3. Chart used by permission. Lawrence P. Sullivan, "Quality Function Development," *Quality Progress,* June 1986.
4. R.G. Boznak, *Competitive Product Development* (Milwaukee, WI: Business One Irwin/Quality Press, 1993).
5. Ibid.
6. Ibid.
7. Ibid.
8. Ibid.
9. Ibid.
10. Ibid.
11. Ibid.
12. Ibid.
13. Ibid.

DOWNSIZING: HOW QUALITY IS AFFECTED AS COMPANIES SHRINK*
by Laura Rubach

Can quality survive in a time when companies are telling many of their employees that they are being let go due to corporate downsizing? At the same time, can the remaining employees maintain predownsizing quality levels?

Quality can survive if companies pay attention to their remaining employees. Many of these employees are fearful about losing their jobs, have decreased loyalty to their organizations, and feel guilty about retaining their jobs when co-workers have lost theirs. Before organizations and employees can move forward, senior management needs to be honest and sincere about what has happened in the organization and provide employees with information about where the organization is headed.

Organizations must make it clear that their employees are valuable and the organization is no better than its people. They must give employees interesting and important work, control over their work and careers, the freedom and resources to perform their work well, pay that reflects their contributions to the organization, and

the training they need to continue their employment.

This new contract of shared responsibility between employers and employees promises greater productivity, better quality, more flexibility, and higher profits. It might not be an overnight process, but quality in organizations can survive if downsizing is done right. If, after downsizing, an organization is created that can change and adapt, be flexible, and be responsive to the market, quality can survive. If the organization has properly redesigned its processes and structures, fewer employees will be able to perform more valuable work.

THE NEED FOR DOWNSIZING

As U.S. companies have become leaner and, it is hoped, more efficient, job security has virtually vanished. Over the past year, U.S. companies made almost 600,000 job cuts.[1] Global competition and the recent economic recession have ex-

*Reprinted with permission from *Quality Progress*, April 1995.

posed a serious weakness in U.S. organizations; namely, that many organizations had become overstaffed, cumbersome, slow, and inefficient.

To increase productivity, enhance competitiveness and contain costs, companies have re-examined the way their businesses are fundamentally organized and managed. A transition is being made from reacting to downturns in the economy to trying to improve internal efficiency. Instead of focusing on job redesign, working harder, and tightening rules and procedures, companies that are downsizing have become focused on bottom-up participation through redesigned work processes. Downsizing has been redefined as a productivity-improvement strategy rather than a last-ditch survival effort.

DOES DOWNSIZING HURT PRODUCTIVITY?

Organizational downsizing, focused on employee head counts and hierarchical levels, has been one of the major initiatives undertaken during the past decade to increase the productivity of American firms; often, however, it has not improved productivity. Some economists and industrial psychologists contend that downsizing can hurt companies more than help them because the wrong people, levels, or functions are removed; morale sinks; and contract or temporary workers wipe out much of the payroll savings from layoffs.[2] Many downsizings are also more expensive than they appear to be, leading to escalation rather than reduction of long-term costs.

"Overall, downsizing does not work. Studies have shown that one-half of the companies that have downsized have the same or lower level of productivity, and employees have low morale, distrust of management, and fear of future downsizing," said Jane Campanizzi-Mook, president of JCM Enterprises, a company that specializes in productivity and quality improvement for manufacturers, service firms, and government agencies and offers training services in reengineering.

Although it would seem natural that reducing overhead or cutting fat from an organization's balance sheet would lead to increased organizational productivity, it is not substantiated by the experience of many firms:

- A 1990 survey of 909 downsized U.S. firms conducted by Right Associates found that 74% of senior managers in downsized com-

panies thought that morale, trust, and productivity had suffered after downsizing.[3]

- The Society for Human Resource Management discovered that more than half of the 1,468 downsizing firms it surveyed indicated that productivity had deteriorated as a result of downsizing.[4]

- A survey conducted by the Wyatt consulting firm found that 71% of the firms involved in downsizing did so to increase productivity, but only 22% of those firms thought that goal had been accomplished.[5]

In a downsizing program that is implemented by upper management to cut costs, insufficient attention is usually paid to both the intended or unintended effects of downsizing on the productivity of individuals and work units. The question of whether aggregate cost savings should be disaggregated into subunit productivity gains—and if so, how—is seldom considered by downsizing strategists. This lack of attention to cross-level effects helps explain why organizational productivity typically suffers from downsizing. When an organization cuts costs but does not realize an overall productivity gain, the organization's ability to efficiently transform inputs into outputs has been seriously diminished.[6]

DON'T DOWNSIZE FOR THE SAKE OF DOWNSIZING

One explanation for the lack of productivity gains from downsizing is that organizations replace broad-based downsizing approaches with quick headcount reductions in the hope for immediate results. "In the short run, companies will save money by treating people as an expense and getting rid of them," said Ben Graham, president of The Ben Graham Corp., who has been working with companies at the operating level for more than 30 years. "At the risk of reduced quality and alienation of employees, profits may actually grow, temporarily, because companies can coast on their reputations for a while."

Although many U.S. organizations must undergo massive cost-restructuring programs because they are hierarchically and numerically bloated, excessive overhead is a symptom and not the problem. The overreaching problem is poor performance, characterized not only by poor productivity, but also by poor production and service quality, inferior product design, insensitivity to customer needs, lack of accountability among upper management, and lack of a global strategy.[7] Focusing on improving the short-term balance sheet by reducing overhead, without simultaneously addressing a broader range of issues, is shortsighted.

Organizations that take a cost-cutting approach to downsizing usually only see downsizing as a temporary, protective mechanism until normal working conditions return, or they view downsizing as an admission of weakness or failure. Managers in these organizations are so preoccupied with analyzing the causes of the problem that they don't see the need for aggressive remedies.

"Downsizing for the sake of downsizing and cutting costs just for the sake of cutting costs hurt long-term quality," said Campanizzi-Mook. "Many times, downsizing leads to more downsizing on a yearly basis because companies have to continually downsize to cut costs. Companies must look at improving their work objectives and key work processes and try to eliminate waste and steps that don't add value for the customer.

"Many companies downsize for short-term economic reasons; they don't look at the long-term effects. Companies that look at the long-term effects of downsizing do it for strategic reasons."

KEEPING QUALITY INTACT

"Quality can survive if downsizing is done right," explained Jennifer Howard, vice-president of Miller Howard Consulting Group, Inc., a firm specializing in organizational design. "The challenge is creating an organization that can change and adapt, be flexible, and be responsive to the market.

"A redesigned organizational structure can be implemented in a year to 18 months, but it will take a company about three to four years to operate unconsciously in this new way of life, because the new structure is still not the way the people feel and lead their lives. Employees shouldn't consciously be thinking that they are now doing their jobs in a quality way; they need to practice these principles as an unconscious

way of life so they are instinctively part of their patterns."

Howard compared the effort of internalizing quality to an unhealthy person who suddenly has to worry about eating right, exercising, and getting enough sleep. "This person can't just spend a few months doing these things and then go back to his or her old ways of doing things; it has to be forever a commitment," Howard said. "The company needs to integrate what it learned into work life, and it needs its employees to work as a team."

In the Right Associates survey of downsizing organizations, 75% said they downsized to improve the financial well-being of the organization, but only 32% said they downsized to add new business products. Moreover, less than half of the downsizing organizations revised or updated human resources, communications, reporting, administrative, or production systems in connection with downsizing.[8]

One dysfunctional consequence of this downsizing approach is that it could create a cynical reaction to the downsizing effort. People lose confidence in upper management because of its unwillingness to address long-term, systemic problems, and often there is resistance to the downsizing plan because it is seen as piecemeal and uncoordinated.

Early retirement incentives illustrate this problem. Many organizations found that this approach to reducing costs resulted in the wrong people leaving the organization.[9] The skills and experience levels of these employees were so vital to organizations' operations that organizations often ended up trying to hire these people back as consultants or recruiting new managers from outside the organization to replace the lost expertise.

"The short-term effect of downsizing is apt to be quite harmful to the organization due to the loss of the intuitive skills and knowledge that the veterans have acquired over the years," Graham said, "Intuitive skills are comparable to those of a cab driver who has learned the inner workings of a city and how to operate within it. People who have been with a company for many years also possess a similar intuitive knowledge of the inner workings of the company. This type of knowledge cannot be replaced with databases and electronic solutions."

PAY ATTENTION TO REMAINING EMPLOYEES

Often, companies that downsize pay more attention to the people who are leaving the company than those who are staying. Those who are leaving get elaborate early-retirement incentives, outplacement services, and personal counseling. Many executives overlook the negative effects of the downsizing process on the remaining work force because they erroneously assume that the relief of not getting a pink slip overshadows any negative feelings workers have about the consequences of the downsizing process.

Next to the death of a relative or friend, there's nothing more traumatic than losing a job.[10] Corporate cutbacks threaten the security and self-esteem of survivors and victims alike. They cause turmoil and shatter morale inside organizations. And they confirm the view that profits always come before people.

Downsizing causes incalculable stress to workers who fear losing their jobs, can't navigate new organization structures, or can't handle their new responsibilities. Job-related suicides are up, as is employee violence, which ranges from sabotage of computer systems to bloody rampages with assault weapons.[11]

Managers must attend to the emotional needs of employees before dealing with the cognitive issues. "No one is paying a lot of attention to the emotional side of downsizing, and this side shouldn't be ignored," said Howard. "The company must be open about what has happened in the company. If it isn't, it is as if a relative has died and no one wants to talk about it, although it is on everyone's mind.

"Quality can't survive unless the company is moving forward. Messages of what has happened in the organization and visions of where the organization is going need to come from senior management, and senior management needs to express these messages with sincerity."

Howard added that companies should develop teams for employees to talk about the loss of co-workers and how they feel to be the ones left. "Remaining employees need to talk to move forward, otherwise they will be dwelling on the loss of their fellow employees and wondering if they will be next," she said.

Remaining employees tend to feel insecure about their jobs and their psychological contract with the organization; they are anxious, fearful, mistrustful, and in crisis, even if they appear controlled or unemotional. Employees have traditionally assumed that if they were loyal to their organizations, showed up at work each day, performed their work competently, and contributed to the company's success, they would be rewarded with continued employment, pay increases, and some degree of job security. Downsizing destroys this psychological contract and, with it, the loyalty and commitment of employees to the organization. The traditional attributes of good employees—loyalty, hard work, and personal competence—no longer seem to count in the organization because individuals who displayed those traits lost their jobs.

"The company has a responsibility to those who remain," Campanizzi-Mook said. "Many people who are left will experience survival guilt, and many will have psychological problems. The organization should deal with these problems and be aware of the effects."

"Survivor guilt," or "layoff survivor sickness," is characterized by anger, depression, fear, and mistrust. Many have increased anxiety about losing their jobs; decreased loyalty and commitment to the organization and their jobs; guilty feelings about working overtime or receiving a paycheck when their former co-workers are out of work; a reduced desire to take risks; and a lack of spontaneity.

Layoff survivor sickness is toxic to both the human spirit and organizational survival. Many organizations that institute layoffs to cut costs and promote competitiveness often find themselves worse off than they were before because what they have gained is a depressed, anxious, and angry work force at a time when they need spirit and creativity.

"I have never seen so many people looking over their shoulders as I see today," Graham said. "People are distrustful. Even those who feel secure with the current downsizing efforts fear that their turn will come. As a result, this triggers job-protecting behaviors. People try to keep information to themselves instead of working openly with co-workers to develop better ways of getting things done. This is a serious blow to loyalty and teamwork, and it makes it very difficult to maintain the enthusiasm and pride that are needed for world-class performance. I see a lot of overworked, insecure employees, and this is bound to exact a serious toll."

Graham said surviving employees remember layoffs for a long time, and these are the employees who must eventually develop new intuitive skills to build quality performance. He added, "Companies need to appreciate that they will never be any better than their people. It is

Do Temporary Workers Reduce the Quality of the Company?

Many U.S. companies are shedding the jobs of full-time workers and using temporary employees to fill in the spaces and build in staffing flexibility. A quarter of those employed today do so on a temporary, part-time, or contract basis. The number of Americans working part-time has grown by 2.2 million since 1973, which, according to the Economic Policy Institute, is because many employees are being forced to take part-time jobs.[1]

Tomorrow's organization must turn a significant part of its work over to a contingent work force that can grow, shrink, and reshape itself as the situation demands. But many organizations should question whether they are ready to handle managing temporary and part-time employees, consultants, and contract workers.

The number of people working for temporary-employment services, such as Manpower and Kelly Services, has jumped 240% in the past 10 years, from 470,000 to 1.6 million. Temporary or part-time jobs accounted for roughly 20% of the 18 million jobs created since 1983. In fact, Manpower, the biggest of the approximately 7,000 U.S. temporary-employment organizations, is now also the nation's biggest private employer.[2]

These organizations are thriving because companies that continue to squeeze out inefficiencies rely on outsiders to fill positions at every level of the organization. Wherever possible, many are reducing fixed labor costs by drawing from a flexible staff that can be used when the workload is high, which eliminates the need to pay a nonproductive staff when the workload is low or nonexistent.

"All future companies will have outsourced employees and individual contractors," said Jane Campanizzi-Mook, president of JCM Enterprises, a company that specializes in productivity and quality improvement for manufacturers, service firms, and government agencies and offers training services in reengineering. "Therefore, companies need to provide awareness of their visions and goals, and will need to develop everyone, including temporary employees.

"Companies will need to perceive temporary employees as suppliers and work with them as if they are suppliers. If these employees properly meet the needs of the company, they will get more work with the company, just as a traditional supplier would."

What troubles some companies is that excessive reliance on temporary workers can drag productivity down, not up. Having many part-time workers doesn't create the loyalty and ownership of results that having full-time workers who are a regular part of the team does. Worse off are the growing numbers of people being forced into part-time jobs and self-employment.

Are temporary workers more of a headache than they are worth? In companies that employ large numbers of contingent workers, managing these workers well poses a challenge. In a typical U.S. corporation, benefits—Social Security and other mandatory employment taxes, health and life insurance, vacations and sick leave, pensions and bonuses—account for 30% of total labor costs. Therefore, hiring temporary and part-time employees should translate into big savings.

This is not necessarily true. Depending on their skill level, temporary workers sometimes command higher hourly wages than permanent workers. Good temporary firms, which have to recruit, screen, and pay employment taxes and benefits for their workers, also aren't inexpensive. The bill to corporate clients can run as much as 50% above a regular worker's hourly wage, though smart managers can whittle that premium to as low as 20% by striking deals with a few suppliers. Executives who try to save money simply by replacing workers with full-time temps or rehiring ex-employees as permanent consultants also risk incurring huge corporate and even personal tax liabilities.

In addition, companies are discovering that, like permanent employees, contingent workers need to be trained and managed. If they're not, excessive turnover and low productivity are the costly consequences.

Temporary employees also have their limits. Many companies need employees who are well trained, who understand the quality requirements of the job, and who will have loyalty for the organization; it is unreasonable to expect this of a temporary worker.

Will temporary workers be able to maintain companies' current level of quality service? Manpower is taking steps to ensure that its contract workers have more than just the technical skills needed to perform a job. The company has launched a massive quality training effort.

Manpower's "Putting Quality to Work" training program is based on customer research. Manpower found that companies are committed to improving service and demand the same commitment from temporary-help firms and their workers. Companies also expect temporary workers to have a customer focus.

"Businesses want our workers to understand how their jobs affect the company's product and reputation," said Melanie Holmes. Manpower's vice president of program development. "Our temporary employees are the front line of our organization and carry the responsibility of delivering service into our customers' environments."

The training, offered free of charge to Manpower's employees, consists of a series of eight programs that focus on service quality. Each program shows the right and wrong ways to handle on-the-job situations.

Holmes said, "Based on our research, two major themes appear throughout the training—providing exceptional service to a company's customers and providing the same exceptional service and support to co-workers. The skills we are giving our employees apply to all jobs. Knowing how to deliver quality service opens up opportunities for workers and gives them a competitive edge in the job market. More than 35% of Manpower's workers receive permanent jobs as a result of their assignments."

"Putting Quality to Work" is only one part of Manpower's total quality initiative. Since 1976, Manpower has used an extensive quality performance program to continually improve the services it provides by gathering information from customers and workers on their satisfaction. "This new training is the next step in our initiative to determine customers' needs and meet those needs," Holmes said.

References

1. Keith H Hammonds, Kevin Kelly, and Karen Thurston, "The New World of Work," *Business Week,* Oct. 17, 1994, pp. 76-87.
2. Jaclyn Fierman, "The Contingency Work Force," *FORTUNE,* Jan. 24, 1994, pp. 30-36.

amazing how easily managers lose track of the fact that their employees are far and away the best source of continuing improvement. They cannot prosper over time with alienated employees no matter how fancy the new technological opportunities may seem."

THE NEW EMPLOYMENT CONTRACT

Companies can no longer promise job security. The old psychological employment contract implied that employees who performed and fit into the organization's culture could count on a job until they retired or choose to leave. The new contract says that even the best performer or the most culturally adaptive person cannot count on long-term employment. This contract replaces loyalty to an organization with loyalty to one's work.

"With the globally competitive environment, companies will continue to be in a constant state of change, and more change is inherent. Therefore, since companies need more flexibility, no one is going to work for a company for 20 years," Campanizzi-Mook stressed.

"What companies valued in the past has changed," Howard said. "Loyalty to an organization isn't enough anymore. Employees must look for better ways of doing things, and this requires taking risks."

Today's employees must continually find ways to add value to the organization. In return, employees will have the right to demand interesting and important work, the freedom and resources to perform this work well, pay that reflects their contributions, and the experience and training needed to remain employable.

"Employees will have more responsibility," Campanizzi-Mook said. "They will need to know who their competitors are, why they are doing their jobs, why they are doing their jobs the way they are doing them, and the strategic vision of the company. Employees will have more and different types of responsibilities."

In companies that are flattening hierarchies and decentralizing decision making, workers are gaining greater control over what they do; self-direction has superseded the doctrine that workers do only what they're told. The new contract of shared responsibility promises benefits to both workers and employers in the form of greater productivity, better quality, more flexibility, and higher profits. It requires companies to relin-

quish much of the control they have held over employees, give authority to work teams, and provide individuals with opportunities for self-improvement. Companies will need to work harder to become attractive places to work, and employees will become more responsible for their work and careers.

Technology helps workers make decisions in organizations that encourage such responsibility. With computers, free access to information eliminates the need for traditional hierarchical management systems. "Employees are realizing that they can take risks and challenge their boss and not be punished," Howard said. "This is what will make the company better in the future."

The new contract between employer and employee also brings risks. For workers, the evolution of the workplace can mean giving up the security of a comfortable office, a permanent job, and a set income. Employers must understand that employees, like businesses, must be continually reinvented. Organizations have a responsibility to help workers sharpen existing skills or acquire new skills to keep pace with new technologies, even if such programs eventually lead employees to other companies.

"Companies want their employees to look for challenging work and do innovative things—not focus on climbing the corporate ladder and play political games," Howard said.

Campanizzi-Mook said, "Middle managers also have to radically change because, in the past, middle managers either were supervisors or conduits of information. The need for both activities has disappeared." Now, managers need to be multifaceted coaches, leaders in charge of getting things done, and developers of ideas and staff. "They also need to be more independent and able to make decisions and solve problems on their own," she said.

The big risk of downsizing is that it will do nothing to change the way people work; fewer employees will simply work harder. In companies that cut jobs without redesigning processes and structures, the remaining employees simply will take on more work, which could result in a staff that is overworked with a high potential for employee burnout.

But by redesigning processes and structures, fewer employees can perform more valuable work. "Companies need to change work objectives and corporate strategy, otherwise fewer people are left to do the same jobs, and quality is inevitably sacrificed," Campanizzi-Mook explained. "People who remain after the layoffs need to clearly see the links between the redesigned process and improved products and services to customers. Companies also need to provide the remaining employees who have redesigned jobs with enough time for training and development so they are not overwhelmed and can perform their redesigned jobs well."

DOWNSIZING IS THE KEY TO BEING COMPETITIVE IN THE FUTURE

U.S. corporations are beginning to position themselves for future growth. According to the American Management Association's (AMA) survey on downsizing in 713 U.S. corporations, two of every three U.S. companies now laying off employees are simultaneously hiring people. Nearly one in four companies reporting job cuts had no net change in total head counts, and the work force actually increased in 13% of the downsizing companies.[12] Rather than reducing head counts to cut costs, companies are downsizing for strategic reasons. They are getting rid of everything that fails to make them competitive, and expanding areas that add value. Companies have been hiring people who can help them enter new markets.

The AMA survey indicates that this restructuring often has little to do with economic conditions. Fewer than half of the downsizing companies (48.7%) attributed cutbacks to business downturns, vs. 65.7% a year earlier. Instead, more companies cited such reasons as "improved staff utilization" and "transfer of production or work." Therefore, companies are learning to do more with less by reorganizing work to be more efficient.[13]

That is a major reason why, for the first time in the eight years of the AMA survey, a majority of downsizing companies also are boosting profits. Some 50.6% of the companies that laid off employees from 1989 to 1994 had increases in operating income.[14]

Based on the survey's results, companies will continue to make cuts, but in each instance, the cuts will be less severe than in the past, because if companies keep making sizable job cuts, they will destroy morale and paralyze their companies.[15]

FIRMS WILL NEED TO CONTINUOUSLY DOWNSIZE IN THE FUTURE

AMA's survey found that cutting workers does improve profit and productivity. But the survey implies that repeated, low-level cutting after one major reduction might be the best approach. The results of this survey could encourage a growing tendency to make downsizing a permanent practice.[16]

The survey showed businesses that had trimmed their payrolls at least twice between 1989 and 1994 reported gains in operating profits and worker productivity. About 58% of these companies said their profits have increased since the cuts, while 44.3% saw improved productivity.[17] The recent change in philosophy about downsizing is evidenced also by the fact that nearly all of the *FORTUNE* 1000 firms engaged in downsizing between 1985 and 1990, and a majority indicated that they would engage in downsizing in the future.[18]

Some people disagree that organizations should and will engage in future downsizing. Graham said, "The rate at which layoffs have been occurring can't go on much longer. Downsizing in corporations will taper down; I predict there will be a big change after the year 2000. That event, the millennium, seems to be acting as a target date for a lot of very short-run goals, and the economy and politics are both being affected negatively. It will be nice when downsizing is behind us and we can get back to more long-term thinking."

Many others, however, indicate that, while U.S. workers might not like the idea of downsizing, it is here to stay because it is the only way firms are going to be globally competitive. Many companies are poorly managed, inefficient, and overstaffed; if they refuse to lay off people, they will likely incur bigger losses or fail. "Many people are uncomfortable with ambiguity. People still want closure and stability at work, even though stability and closure are something of the past." Howard said, "Employees must find rewards for their jobs in other ways. They must think about and focus on getting their work done well and not how they can climb the corporate ladder. Employees need to be focused on work and the customer and not on who their boss will be and where they will sit. This is a hard transition, but it is a healthy one because downsizing is never going to end."

REFERENCES

1. Michael J. Mandel, "Business Rolls the Dice," *Business Week,* Oct. 17, 1994, pp. 88-90.
2. Douglas H. Harris, editor, *Organizational Linkages* (Washington, DC: National Academy Press, 1994).
3. Ronald Henkoff, "Cost Cutting: How to Do It Right," *FORTUNE,* April 9, 1990, pp. 17-19.
4. Ibid.
5. A. Bennett, "Downsizing Doesn't Necessarily Bring an Upswing in Corporate Profitability," *The Wall Street Journal,* June 6, 1991, pp. B1-B4.
6. Harris, *Organizational Linkages.*
7. Ibid.
8. Ibid.
9. Donald F. Kettl, *Reinventing Government? Appraising the National Performance Review* (Washington, DC: The Brookings Institution, 1994).
10. John A. Byrne, "Why Downsizing Looks Different These Days," *Business Week,* Oct. 10, 1994, p. 43.
11. Stratford Sherman, "How Will We Live With the Tumult?" *FORTUNE,* Dec. 13, 1993, pp. 123-125.
12. Byrne, "Why Downsizing Looks Different These Days."
13. Ibid.
14. Ibid.
15. Joann S. Lublin, "Don't Stop Cutting Staff, Study Suggestions," *The Wall Street Journal,* Sept. 27, 1994.
16. Ibid.
17. Ibid.
18. Harris, *Organizational Linkages.*

BIBLIOGRAPHY

Auster, Bruce B., "The Causalities of Downsizing," *U.S. News & World Report,* Jan. 9, 1995, p. 31.
Bridges, William, "The End of the Job," *FORTUNE,* Sept. 19, 1994, pp. 62-74.
Byrne, John A., "The Pain of Downsizing," *Business Week,* May 9, 1994, pp. 60-69.
Dusharme, Dirk, "Avoid Employee Burnout," *Quality Digest,* October 1994, p. 6.
Fierman, Jaclyn, "The Contingency Work Force," *FORTUNE,* Jan. 24, 1994, pp. 30-36.
Hammonds, Keith H., Kevin Kelly, and Karen Thurston, "The New World of Work," *Business Week,* Oct. 17, 1994, pp. 76-87.
Henkoff, Ronald, "Getting Beyond Downsizing," *FORTUNE,* Jan. 10, 1994, pp. 58-64.
Morovec, Milan, "The Right Way to Rightsize: 10 Mistakes Companies Make in Downsizing," *Industry Week,* Sept. 5, 1994.
Noer, David M., *Healing the Wounds: Overcoming the Trauma of Layoffs and Revitalizing Downsized Organizations* (San Francisco, CA: Jossey-Bass Publishers, 1993).

3.2 TOTAL QUALITY

QUALITY AND THE THEORY OF CONSTRAINTS*
by H. William Dettmer

The quality philosophy is straightforward, the tools to achieve it are available, and most people accept the need to improve. So why are so many organizations struggling to achieve and sustain gains in quality?

The answer to this question is critical to corporate survival because quality alone is no longer a competitive weapon. It is the price of admission just to play the game. Quality has become a necessary condition, not a discriminator.

There are many reasons why companies struggle to achieve quality, but a major contributor is their inability to think and act in terms of systems rather than components. It seems simple, but consider total quality management (TQM), for example. TQM focuses on process control and process improvement. In most TQM applications, the emphasis is on improving individual components or processes, then "gluing" the results together. Interaction between pro-

*Reprinted with permission from *Quality Progress,* April 1995. H. William Dettmer is an adjunct professor of systems management at the University of Southern California in Los Angeles.

cesses is usually limited to consideration of the immediate upstream supplier and downstream customer. Synergetic effects of separate processes on the whole system are infrequently considered and almost never addressed.

W. Edwards Deming understood the need to maintain a systemic approach to continuous improvement. One of his four requirements for profound knowledge is appreciation of a system.[1] Unfortunately, many people don't really understand what Deming meant, even though they pay lip service to it. Because TQM focuses on improving processes, it doesn't address how to manage the system as a whole. The closest TQM seems to come to systemic guidance is the concept of concurrent engineering, which requires the cooperation of marketing, engineering, and production in product development. Effectively executed, concurrent engineering can do an excellent job of integrating the inputs of customers, designers, and producers.

But even concurrent engineering doesn't address the entire system. What about the finance, sales, supply, and distribution functions? They're all part of the system, too, and they have a major influence on corporate success.

THE THINKING PROCESS

What is essential to ultimate success is a thinking process that enables a company to appreciate the effect of local actions and decisions on overall system performance. Ideally, a systemic thinking process would provide a context in which to place all of the diverse elements of quality, management, and organizational behavior. Try to visualize the thinking process as the setting of a mosaic, which holds together and integrates all of the tiles, producing an overall picture that is larger than the individual tiles. Such a thinking process should provide a means of determining what to change in the system, what it should change to, and how to effect the change.

To some degree, all of the quality philosophies and tools address the issue of identifying what to change, although they usually address it at the local, or process level rather than the system level. Normally, little consideration is given to determining the overall effect of the change on the system as a whole, and virtually none to the collateral undesirable effects a change might have on other components or processes of the system. For example, how would a change in product X's production line affect company performance (the whole system) and the distribution or customer-service functions (other system components)? TQM doesn't answer this question, but a systemic thinking process does.

AN IMPORTANT BOOK

In 1986, a revolutionary book appeared in bookstores, corporate offices, and executive suites. Eliyahu M. Goldratt's *The Goal* has sold over 1 million copies during the last eight years with virtually no advertising or promotion.[2] The primary method of propagation has been readers passing on copies to their friends and colleagues. Managers read this book and order it by the case for distribution within their companies.

What makes this book so unusual? After all, it's just a book on production control. Or is it? *The Goal* is not a textbook or a how-to guide; it's written, by design, as a novel. Much as a fable or allegory teaches a higher lesson through the context of an everyday situation, *The Goal* presents a thinking process called the theory of constraints, in a way that readers can intuitively grasp. By following the story line, readers see the theory's logic clearly demonstrated and draw their own conclusions about its effectiveness and applicability.

The Goal's purpose is to introduce readers to the thinking process that provides the context for a new, continuous improvement approach. Its production control theme is merely one example, albeit a significant one, to which the thinking process can be applied. But, like an iceberg, only the tip of this thinking process shows above the waterline.

THE THEORY

So, what is the theory of constraints (TOC)? TOC facilitates the examination of assumptions underlying traditional rules, policies, and measures. It focuses on the few critical constraints that limit the success of a system. It provides the methodology to define what to change, what it should be changed to, and how to effect change to continuously improve the performance of an entire system. Moreover, TOC precludes suboptimization, ensuring that solutions to complex problems are effective at the system level.

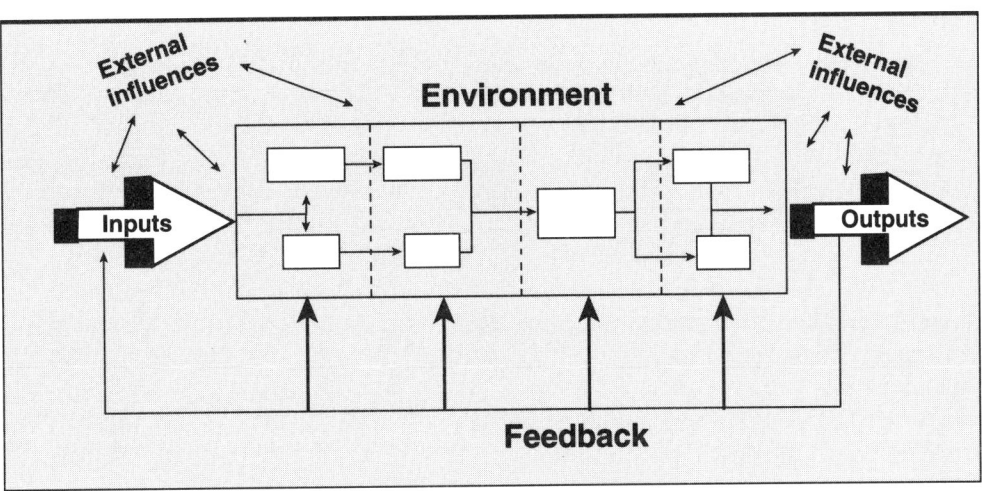

EXHIBIT 1.—GENERIC SYSTEM

Look at it another way. *Webster's New Universal Unabridged Dictionary* defines a system as "a set or arrangement of things so related or connected as to form a unity or organic whole."[3] Typically, in its simplest form, a system is depicted as an interrelated group of processes that receive inputs from the external environment, act on them in some way, and produce an output that is supposed to be of greater value than the sum of the inputs (see Exhibit 1). Systems thinking is based on three principles:

Systems principle No. 1: The performance of an entire system is affected by each of its components. In other words, every department influences the company's overall performance.

Systems principle No. 2: The parts of a system are interdependent. How one part affects the whole system depends, to some extent, on what at least one other part is doing.

Systems principle No. 3: If parts of a system are grouped together in any way, they form subgroups that are subject to the first two principles.

TOC goes a little further. Goldratt maintains that if the performance of each part of a system is individually maximized, the system as a whole will not behave as well as it could. Conversely, if a system is performing as well as it can, not more than one of its parts will be. If one considers this idea in the context of today's business world, it's somewhat revolutionary. Much effort and expense is devoted to maximizing efficiency at every level and in every sector of a company, without regard for the effect on the company's overall performance. In most cases, companies can't quantify what effect suboptimal decisions will have on the organization's overall performance, but they continue to make them anyway.

Consider an automobile, for example. Most are designed to achieve a specific objective, such as luxury, economy, or speed. As a complex system, an automobile has to integrate the performance of many components to achieve its objective. If the objective is economy, it's counterproductive to "improve" the system by installing racing cams in the engine, even if they're the best-performing cams to be had.

Likewise, inflating tires for maximum mileage efficiency certainly improves their service life. But an Indy car driver is more concerned with how the car handles than with the life of the tires. Overinflation might maximize tire life but compromise the overall performance of the car-driver system.

ANALYTICAL VS. SYSTEMS APPROACH

What is the usual approach to system improvement? The tendency is to use an analytical one. Companies reduce a large problem to a set of manageable problems, solve these component problems, and then reassemble them into a "system" solution. TQM typically takes this approach by dividing the system into processes, then optimizing the quality of each process. This, of course, is preferable to chasing symptoms or discrete variations in individual steps of a process, but it can create new problems if the role of the individual process is not considered in concert with the other processes it affects (systems principle No. 2).

TOC addresses the larger systemic picture. Rather than viewing the system in terms of discrete processes, TOC treats it as a chain or grid of interlinked chains. What determines the performance of a whole chain? The weakest link ultimately limits what the chain can do. Any effort to strengthen links other than the weakest one will do nothing to improve the chain's overall performance. Only after the weakest link has been reinforced will it be productive to concentrate on reinforcing other weak links.

TOC considers the weakest link to be the system constraint. By focusing exclusively on that constraint, any changes are immediately measurable in the system's output. Conversely, as long as the system constraint is not addressed, no effect on the global performance can be logically connected to actions or decisions elsewhere in the system. Once the single, overriding constraint is broken, some other weak link in the chain becomes the limiting constraint, which must subsequently be addressed.

TOC, like TQM, treats improvement as on ongoing process. But instead of focusing on localized improvements in all areas, it attacks the one constraint, or bottleneck, that limits overall system performance. By never losing sight of the system's performance, TOC maintains a systems, rather than an analytical approach.

THE FIVE FOCUSING STEPS

To ensure that emphasis remains at the system level rather than the component level, Goldratt has developed five steps to guide the improvement process:[1]

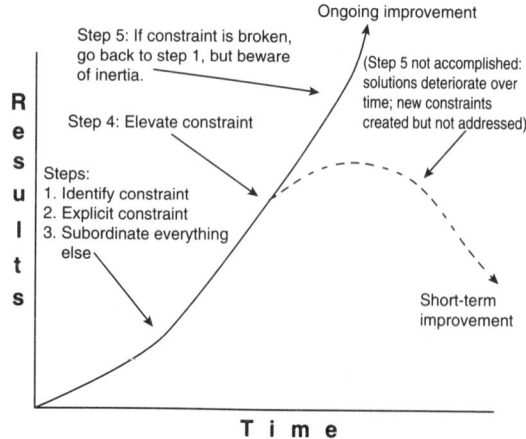

EXHIBIT 2.—SYSTEM IMPROVEMENT: SHORT TERM OR ONGOING?

"1. Identify the system's constraints [its weakest links]." There might be several weak links, but there is only one weakest link. This link should be the first target of improvement.

"2. Decide how to exploit the constraint." If the constraint is physical, make sure that no productivity is lost through inefficient use of the constraining resource. In other words, make the constraint, as it exists now, as effective as possible.

"3. Subordinate everything else to the above decision." Every other part of the system must be aligned and adjusted to support the maximum effectiveness of the constraint, even if this means "detuning" some nonconstraints.

"4. Elevate the system's constraint." If steps 2 and 3 don't relieve the constraint to the extent that it ceases to be the weakest link, more rigorous action is necessary, such as formulating strategies to increase throughput across the constraint (e.g., offloading work to other sources or acquiring more capability).

"5. If, in the previous steps, a constraint has been broken, go back to step 1, but do not allow inertia to cause a new constraint." This is the feedback loop that makes TOC a continuous process. Implicit in this step (and the reason so many organizations lose momentum in continuous improvement) is the caution to not become complacent. No solution is permanent. As the system's environment changes, a given solution will progressively deteriorate unless it is modified to account for those changes.

Moreover, changing a constraint usually changes the character of the system; it's not quite the same system it was before. Often the original system components don't interact in quite the same way because of system principle No. 2 described earlier. So, it's dangerous to believe that the improvement process can stop when the original constraint is broken (see Exhibit 2).

PHYSICAL VS. POLICY CONSTRAINTS

Throughout 12 years of developing and applying TOC, Goldratt has observed that very few constraints are physical (e.g., machines, people, facilities, or other tangible resources). By tracing undesirable effects to their root causes, Goldratt found that the vast majority of constraints are caused by policies—rules, training, or other measures—that might have once been effective solutions but are now obsolete.

For example, the large proportion of free-ways under repair (or needing repair) seems to be a physical constraint to the flow of traffic. But it's the federal acquisition policy mandating the award of contracts to the lowest bidder that has driven contractors to use lower-quality, shorter-life materials in an effort to keep costs down and remain competitive. Even if the physical constraint were removed (temporarily) by repairing all of the roads, the policy constraint would ensure a recurrence of the problem.

Why are policy constraints so much more insidious than physical constraints? Besides being less visible, policies set the rules for how things must be done. In so doing, they foreclose many lines of inquiry on possible solutions.

Most policies were put in place to solve a perceived problem. Contracts go to the lowest bidder because someone, at some time, saw a problem, such as: "We're paying too much for what we're getting." But the environment is continually changing, existing solutions are often not updated to keep pace, and few ongoing improvement processes are institutionalized to ensure that updates occur.

Herein lies a major strength of TOC. Direct observation and traditional TQM tools (such as statistical process control or design of experiments) work well at the process level, but they're ineffective in identifying policy constraints at the system level—constraints that can have the most dramatic effect on the entire system. In the TOC thinking process, Goldratt has provided a rigorous logical methodology that is well equipped to meet this challenge. Moreover, TOC provides a how-to vehicle for institutionalizing the process of continuous improvement, which is necessary to avoid having obsolete policies.

TRADITIONAL VS. SYSTEMS MEASUREMENTS

Traditional measurement systems are usually focused on improving local process efficiencies. A systems approach such as TOC requires a way to measure the effects of local decisions on global performance. Few traditional measurements offer this visibility.

TOC assesses the merit of local decisions by determining their effect on three dimensions of the system's performance in this order:

- *Throughput.* Throughput is the total sales revenues minus the total variable costs for producing a product or service.

- *Inventory.* Inventory is all of the money that a company invests in items it intends to sell.

- *Operating expense.* Operating expense is all of the money a company spends turning inventory into throughput.[5]

All management actions, at any level, should be measurable against one of these interdependent, system-level scales. A change in one will result in a related change in one or both of the others. When the overall system is improving, throughput increases while inventory and operating expenses decrease.

Two major outcomes of TOC's focus on throughput, inventory, and operating expense have been the virtual invalidation of traditional management cost accounting and a simultaneous improvement in competitive price advantage.[6] An important indirect benefit of TOC results from shedding the shackles of traditional cost accounting: Many companies are able to open doors to profitable new market segments.

TQM frequently drives people to measure everything. Organizations sometimes go "metric crazy." Many measurements are useless because nobody knows what to do with them. People often lose sight of the fact that the purpose of measurement is to gather data from which information can be derived. Information is the answer to a question asked about the system. TOC helps determine what questions should be asked and what important factors (constraints) should be measured to answer them.

Take the Pareto rule, for example, which is supposed to answer the question, "What should we work on first?" Conventional quality wisdom tells people to identify trouble spots, prioritize them by importance or value, draw a time/resource limit line below the most important problems, and start to work on the No. 1 priority. This is a good analytical approach, but consider this: What if priorities 1, 3, and 4 are caused by a less noticeable core problem ranked No. 8, which happens to be below the time/resource limit line? Perhaps a well-placed bullet into the heart of No. 8 will solve problems 1, 3, and 4, with no additional expenditure of resources. But without the system-level, cause-and-effect examination TOC affords, how would one ever know? Moreover, solving problems 1, 3, and 4 without addressing the core problem (No. 8) almost ensures that either similar problems will appear again or other undesirable effects will arise to replace those eliminated.

It should be emphasized that TOC does not replace TQM, statistical process control, design of experiments, teamwork, or other tools and philosophies. Rather, TOC integrates and focuses these toward the organization's goal. It provides the means to know when each of these process tools is necessary and appropriate to improve overall system performance. Remember, the sum of local optima is not the system optimum.

FOR PROFIT VS. NOT FOR PROFIT

A typical reservation about TOC sounds like this: "It might be fine for profit-making companies, but we're a not-for-profit organization. How can TOC apply to us, when we don't measure our throughput in terms of dollars?" Nonfinancial measures are always more difficult to deal with, but throughput need not always be expressed in dollars. Instead, a measure of the product or service delivered can be substituted.

For example, a university or high school could express throughput as a function of the number of students graduated compared with the number who initially enrolled. The goal might be to shorten the time needed to turn inventory (students) into throughput (graduates) while meeting the necessary condition of quality. Throughput could typically be increased by reducing the dropout rate.

Just because profit is not an organization's goal doesn't mean that TOC can't be applied. It might merely require an adjustment by defining the goal, throughput, and inventory in terms other than dollars. Money can be, however, a suitable starting surrogate if a nonfinancial measure cannot initially be well defined.

COMPANY STRUGGLING? TRY TOC

TOC is firmly rooted in common sense. It allows for a structured, orderly, logical representation of intuition. It provides three powerful capabilities that can turbocharge a TQM effort:

1. It provides a way to model an entire system and expose constraints to improved performance.

2. It provides a means for identifying what to change, what to change it to, and how to execute the change for maximum system effectiveness.

3. It provides a way to measure the effects of daily management decisions on the performance of an entire system.

The theory is only in its adolescence. As it evolves, new ways to apply it will surface. Until now, for example, TOC has been used primarily to identify and manage constraints in existing systems. The role TOC could play in the up-front design of constraints in new or emerging systems has yet to be examined.

If your company's TQM efforts have succeeded and continue to produce improvements, you might be thinking, "these ideas are valid but obvious. There's nothing new here." It might be obvious to those who have made continuous improvement succeed because, as Deming points out, a system perspective is essential. But since so many organizations are struggling with TQM, it must not be obvious to everyone. If your organization is having a tough time making continuous improvement efforts show up in the bottom line, consider using the theory of constraints to help keep your system and its goal in perspective and to focus TQM where it will do the most good.

REFERENCES

1. W. Edwards Deming, *The New Economics for Industry, Government, Education* (Boston, MA: Massachusetts Institute of Technology Center for Advanced Engineering Study, 1993).
2. Eliyahu M. Goldratt, *The Goal,* second edition (New York, NY: North River Press, Inc., 1992).
3. *Webster's New Universal Unabridged Dictionary* (New York, NY: Barnes and Noble Books, 1992).
4. Goldratt, *The Goal.*
5. John A Caspari, "Theory of Constraints" in *Management Accountant's Handbook,* fourth edition, edited by Donald E. Keller, James Bulloch, and Robert L. Shultis (New York, NY: John Wiley & Sons, 1993).
6. James T. Low, "Do We Really Need Product Costs? The Theory of Constraints Alternative," *Corporate Controller,* September/October 1992, p. 26.

BIBLIOGRAPHY

Deming, W. Edwards, *Out of the Crisis* (Boston, MA: Massachusetts Institute of Technology Center for Advanced Engineering Study, 1986).
Goldratt, Eliyahu M., *The Haystack Syndrome: Sifting Information Out of the Data Ocean* (New York: North River Press, Inc., 1990).

Goldratt, Eliyahu M., *What Is This Thing Called Theory of Constraints and How Should It Be Implemented? (New York, NY: North River Press, Inc., 1990).*

Goldratt, Eliyahu M., and Robert E. Fox, *The Race* (New York, NY: North River Press, Inc., 1986).

Hayes, Robert H., Steven C. Wheelwright, and Kim B. Clark, *Dynamic Manufacturing: Creating the Learning Organization* (New York, NY: The Free Press, 1988).

Senge, Peter M., *The Fifth Discipline: The Art and Practice of the Learning Organization* (New York, NY: Doubleday/Currency, 1990).

---◾---

DETERMINANTS OF QUALITY PERFORMANCE IN HIGH- AND LOW-QUALITY PLANTS*
by Barbara B. Flynn, Roger Schroeder, and Sadao Sakakibara

This article examines the differences in quality management practices between plants that achieve high, intermediate, and low levels of quality performance. Data from a survey of U.S. plants in the machinery, transportation components, and electronics industries were analyzed using multiple discriminant analysis. It was found that key practices included concurrent engineering, new-product quality, employee involvement, feedback, maintenance, labor skill level, selection for teamwork potential, process control, and supplier relationships. An interesting result was that the plants that achieved the best and poorest levels of quality performance used similar (strong) levels of these quality management practices, while those plants that achieved intermediate levels of quality performance used inferior quality management practices. It is believed that the intermediate-quality plants may be complacent, while the low-quality plants are striving to catch up and the high-quality plants seek continuous improvement.

What is it about high-quality firms that makes them different from other firms? Which quality management practices are most critical in achieving high-quality performance? This article will address these questions through the use of multiple discriminant analysis, a statistical technique that allows researchers to examine the differences between plants grouped according to their level of quality performance and to separate out the key practices that high-quality performance firms focus on, as well as the perhaps misguided focus of plants with low-quality performance.

Although there is a great deal of literature on quality management, the bulk of it falls into two groups, both of which fail to articulate the key practices associated with high-quality performance. First, there is a great deal of prescriptive literature, which describes in detail various quality management practices or examines the approach of a single organization in detail. While such articles are very useful in learning about the implementation of various practices, they fail to scientifically tie the use of such practices to performance or to demonstrate their ultimate utility. Second, most of the empirical studies are comparative in nature; for example, comparing quality management practices used in the United States and Japan. While there may be an implicit relationship with quality performance, these studies also fail to articulate the relationship between the use of specific quality management practices and quality performance.

This article begins with a description of the prescriptive literature on quality management practices, separating them into four primary dimensions. It then describes the details of the study, including the sample of plants and the methods used for gathering data about them. A nontechnical discussion of the results is followed by the conclusions. Technical details about the results are provided in Appendix B.

*Reprinted with permission from ASQC *Quality Management Journal*, Winter 1995. Barbara B. Flynn is an associate professor of operations management at Iowa State University. Roger G. Schroeder is a professor of operations management and co-director of the Quality Leadership Center at the Curtis L. Carlson School of Management at the University of Minnesota. Sadao Sakakibara is a visiting assistant professor of operations management at Keio University in Tokyo.

QUALITY MANAGEMENT PRACTICES

The practices that comprise effective quality management can be grouped into four primary dimensions: product design, transformation process, customer relationship, and supplier relationship. These are summarized in Exhibit 1, which models the process of producing a product. It begins with product design, which is believed to be supported by close relationships with customers and suppliers. Following product design is the process of transforming the product design, raw materials, technology, and labor into salable products. It portrays information management as the link between the process and the workforce. The transformation process is also believed to be dependent on strong relationships with customers and suppliers. A brief overview of the literature describing each of these dimensions follows.

Product Design

One of the primary tenets of quality management is to design quality *into* the product, rather than inspecting defects *out*. In fact, it has been estimated that poor product design may account for as much as 80 percent of all product defects (Fawcett 1989). Key approaches to effective product design include concurrent engineering, design for manufacturability, reliability engineering, and the use of design tools such as quality function deployment.

Concurrent engineering incorporates a team approach to product design, often including representatives from manufacturing, marketing, quality, suppliers, and customers, as well as product engineers (Hartley 1992). The input provided by these diverse parties helps to develop a product that meets the needs of customers and can be readily manufactured, using the desired materials. Although the approach may appear to be initially time-consuming, it may result in significantly fewer design changes once the product is being manufactured.

Reliability engineering considers the failure probabilities of each individual system and subsystem during the design process (Garvin 1983). All else being equal, the fewer parts in a product, or the higher their individual reliabilities, the lower its failure rate will be. While reliability may be achieved by product designers in isolation, manufacturability is enhanced by a concurrent engineering approach. Key activities

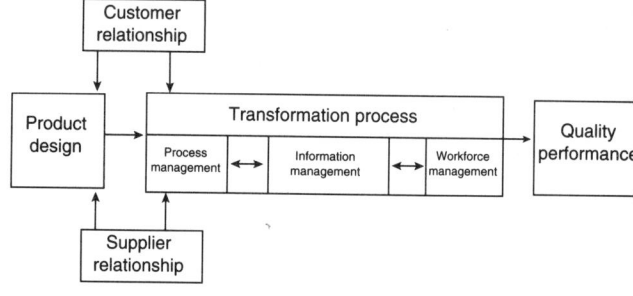

EXHIBIT 1.—MODEL OF DIMENSIONS OF QUALITY MANAGEMENT.

related to reliability engineering include prototyping and trial production runs (Juran 1978).

Transformation Process

During the transformation process, purchased materials and parts are transformed into products, following the product design. Key components of the transformation process include process management, workforce management, and information management.

Process Management. Process management focuses on keeping the transformation process running in a predictable and reliable fashion. This includes heavy reliance on preventive maintenance (Garvin 1984, 1983), as well as equipment run at less than capacity, thus reducing jams, breakdowns, and wear on machine parts and dies (Hayes 1981). Proprietary equipment may be developed in an effort to know as much as possible about the process (Wheelwright and Hayes 1985). Hayes (1981) notes that the cleanliness and organization of a workplace is important, quoting a Japanese manager, "If you clean up the factory floor, you tend to clean up the thought process of the people on it too" (p. 59).

Workforce Management. The workforce contributes to the manufacturing process through its skills, as well as its flexibility and motivation in using them. A number of elements contribute to effective workforce management. Training of the workforce is important in developing task-oriented skills, as well as skills in statistical process control, small-group problem solving, and communication (Garvin 1984). Recruitment and selection that focus on both task-oriented skills and ability to function as part of a team (Juran 1978) result in skilled and thinking employees. Egalitarian approaches, including relatively flat wage and salary scales and few management perks, minimize the distance between the levels in the organizational hierarchy, providing workers with the confidence to attack a problem, rather than defer to a supervisor. Compensation approaches, such as bonuses for quality production (Garvin 1984), group compensation plans, and skill-based pay (Ziskin 1986), reinforce employee flexibility, skills, and motivation.

Information Managment. Information management provides the link between the workforce and the process. Its goal is the provision of accurate and timely information in a way that makes it available to those who need it. Feedback of quality information provides the workforce with a means of maintaining and learning task-oriented behaviors (Ashford and Cummings 1984). For example, Garvin (1983) found that information on defects and failures was virtually nonexistent in companies with the lowest quality levels, resulting in design flaws that remained undetected and "epidemic" failures. Statistical process control is the primary means of providing direct laborers with feedback about the quality of their work. Feedback about the process, such as monitoring systems to check process flow and signal when jams occur, is also important (Hayes 1981). Finally, external feedback from supervisors is influential in improving performance (Shalley, Oldham, and Porac 1987).

Customers. Because customers are the ultimate judge of a plant's quality performance in the marketplace, they should be a key source of input into both the design and transformation processes. They serve two primary roles: providing input about their needs and wants to the product design process, and providing feedback about quality performance of the firm's products in the field. In order to stimulate the flow of these two important types of information, the establishment of two-way channels of communication between the firm and customers is critical. This can be done by encouraging customer input and feedback, making an effort to consult with customers on design and performance issues, and inviting customers to be a part of product design teams (Schonberger 1985).

Suppliers. The supplier relationship is important to both product design and the transformation process. Because purchased materials and parts are dominant sources of quality performance problems (Leonard and Sasser 1982),

selection of suppliers based on quality considerations encourages the provision of high-quality parts; in contrast, suppliers selected through the competitive bidding process have no incentive to improve quality once a contract has been awarded (Manoocherhri 1985). Companies with supplier relationships characterized by interdependence and cooperation establish links for systematically exchanging information. For example, supplier certification of qualification programs provides a means of conveying design teams' quality expectations to suppliers, as well as providing assurance about the quality of incoming materials and parts (Juran 1978).

RESEARCH METHOD

Hypotheses

This study examined two general hypotheses. The first deals primarily with the product design function. Supplier relationship and customer relationship are included in the testing of this hypothesis because they are believed to be important in supporting an effective product design process. The second hypothesis deals with the transformation process, and customer and supplier relationships, which are believed to be important in supporting it.

H1: Differences will exist among the high-, intermediate-, and low-quality performance groups, in terms of their product design, supplier relationship, and customer relationship practices.

H2: Differences will exist among the high-, intermediate-, and low-quality performance groups, in terms of their transformation process, supplier relationship, and customer relationship practices.

Instrument Development

Based on the dimensions of quality management described earlier, a set of 12 scales was developed. The content of these scales is described in Exhibit 2, and the complete scales are listed in Appendix A. Although no attempt was made to measure every possible aspect of each dimension, the scales were designed to provide breadth of coverage; there was at least one scale to correspond to each dimension of the framework.

EXHIBIT 2.—SCALE CONTENTS

DIMENSION	SCALE TITLE	CONTENT
Relationship with customers	Customer interaction	Frequency of verbal and face-to-face contact with customers, and customer feedback on quality and delivery performance
Relationship with suppliers	Supplier relationship	Establishment of long-term relationships with a small number of high-quality suppliers, and use of quality as the top supplier-selection criterion
Product design	New-product quality	Influence of quality considerations in the design and introduction of new products
	Concurrent engineering	Incorporation of manufacturing, quality, marketing, and direct labor personnel into the product design and redesign process
	Design characteristics	Design for manufacturability and reliability engineering
Transformation process: Process management	Cleanliness and organization	Implementation of measures to keep the plant neat and clean, putting all tools and fixtures in their proper places
	Maintenance	Use of good maintenance as a strategy for achieving quality and schedule compliance, setting aside a specific time for maintenance activities, and maintaining equipment in a state of readiness at all times
Transformation process: Information management	Process control	Use of statistical quality control, design of processes to be "foolproof," and analysis of customer requirements in the new-product design process
	Feedback	Posting of charts showing defect rates, schedule compliance, and machine breakdowns; verbal feedback about information from supervisors; and general information on plant productivity and quality performance
Transformation process: Workforce management	Employee involvement	Use of team problem solving and encouragement of employee involvement in the production process
	Labor skill level	Direct labor technical competence relative to industry, training and rewards for developing skills
	Selection for teamwork potential	Use of ability to work in a team, problem-solving ability, work values, and ethics as criteria in employee selection

Each scale consists of at least three items or statements about the use of various quality management practices. A typical item from the feedback scale is "Information on quality performance is readily available to employees." Respondents were asked to respond to each of the items by circling one of five choices: (1) strongly disagree; (2) disagree; (3) neither agree nor disagree; (4) agree; or (5) strongly agree. Although some of the items were negatively worded (such as "I am never told whether I am doing a good job"), the responses to those items were reverse coded in the analysis stage. Thus, higher values of the responses indicate "better" practices. In analyzing the responses, the point values of the responses to each item in the scale were averaged; thus, there is a single, average value that describes each plant's response to each scale.

The scales were assembled into seven questionnaires, each targeted at a different respondent, in order to tap into the best-informed sources. The assignment of scales to respondents is indicated in Exhibit 3. Every scale appeared on at least two of the questionnaires to help ensure reliability of the responses. The instrument was pretested at 12 plants located throughout the United States. Each pretest included a site visit, structured interviews with managers and workers, and administration of the pilot instrument. Revisions were made to the items, based on the comments of the pilot respondents.

Sample

The sample was constructed so that plant-level analysis could be conducted, because it is at the plant level that specific quality manage-

EXHIBIT 3.—DISTRIBUTION OF ORIGINAL SCALES WITHIN EACH PLANT

	Direct Laborers	Plant Manager	Quality Manager	Production and Inventory Manager	Supervisors	Process Engineer	Human Resources Manager
Feedback	10				3		
Process control			1			1	
Cleanliness and organization	10				3		
Maintenance					3	1	
New-product quality			1			1	
Concurrent engineering					1		1
Design characteristics							
Selection for teamwork potential							1
Labor skills	10				3		1
Employee involvement	10		1	1	3	1	
Supplier relationship			1	1			
Customer interaction			1	1	3		

ment practices are implemented. The sample was selected to be representative of a broad range of quality performance and quality management practices. In order to assure diversity, a three-by-three factorial sample design was used, with industry and plant type as the two factors. The three industries (machinery, electronics, and transportation components) were chosen because they are industries in transition, and a great deal of variability in quality performance and quality management practices was expected to be present. The three plant types were Japanese-owned (operating in the United States), world-class reputation (U.S.-owned), and traditional (U.S.-owned).

Approximately eight plants per cell were randomly selected from various lists of plants. The traditional plants were selected, within industry, from a plant-level manufacturing directory. The world-class-reputation plants were selected from within the appropriate industries in Schonberger's (1985) Honor Roll of world-class manufacturers and from discussions with industry experts. The Japanese plants were selected from a Japanese-language publication published by JETRO, the Japanese External Trade Orga-

nization. This procedure resulted in a diverse sample, randomly selected within strata.

Participation was solicited by telephone conversations with the plant managers from the selected plants. Participating plant managers appointed a plant research coordinator who served as the liaison between the respondents and the researchers. Sixty percent of the plants that were contacted ultimately participated in the study, providing a total sample size of 42 plants.

Measurement Analysis

Exhibit 4 contains a summary of the analysis of the instrument's reliability and validity, which was performed at the individual respondent level. Further detail on the measurement analysis and a complete listing of the scales is contained in Flynn, Schroeder, and Sakakibara (1994). Reliability was operationalized as internal consistency, measured by Cronbach's (1951) alpha. Following standard guidelines (Lord and Novick 1968; Nunnally 1978), the minimum acceptable alpha value was set at 0.60. Using intercorrelation matrices as a guide, items that did not strongly contribute to alpha and whose content was not critical were eliminated. Exhibit 4 shows that the final alpha values for the scales all exceeded 0.60, and that most did so by a substantial margin, indicating that the scales were internally consistent.

Construct validity measures the extent to which all items in a scale measure the same construct. It was established by within-scale factor analysis, which showed whether the items in a scale all loaded on a common factor. Table 3 shows that the eigenvalues for each of the scales all exceeded the minimum eigenvalue of 1.00 (Kim and Mueller 1978). Table 3 also shows the factor loadings by item. Factor loadings of at least ±0.40 indicate significance at the 0.03 level (Hair, Anderson, and Tatham 1987); thus, all of the items contributed significantly to the variance of their respective scales.

Analysis

All analysis was conducted at the plant level, with data from multiple respondents at the same plant collapsed into a plant average. Therefore, there was one composite response to each scale per plant.

Multiple discriminant analysis was used to analyze the differences between groups. Multiple discriminant analysis uses a linear combination of measurements for two or more independent variables to describe or predict the

behavior of a single categorical dependent variable (Hair, Anderson, and Tatham 1987). The dependent categorical, or grouping variable was the percent of parts passing final inspection without requiring rework, selected because it represents a good approximation of an important quality objective at the plant level, which is to reduce defects internal to the plant before final inspection. The groups were defined as high quality (98 percent or more parts passed final inspection without requiring rework), medium quality (88 percent to 97.99 percent parts passed final inspection without requiring rework), and low quality (less than 88 percent of the parts passed final inspection without requiring rework). Divisions between groups were selected with the goal of dividing the sample into approximately equal groups, facilitating interpretation of results. There were 12 independent variables, measured by scales corresponding to selected management practices.

In order to test whether fundamental differences existed among the plants in the three groups, analysis of variance was used to analyze the means of the groups on a number of characteristics. There were no differences between the groups at the 0.10 significance level or less on the following characteristics: sales value of production, net investment in plant and equipment, number of hourly personnel, number of salaried

EXHIBIT 4.—SUMMARY OF MEASUREMENT ANALYSIS

| Scale | Reliability | Validity | | | | | | |
| | Cronbach's Alpha | Eigen-Value | Factor Loading By Item | | | | | |
			1	2	3	4	5	6	7
Customer interaction	.6572	2.08	.80	.80	.89				
Supplier relationship	.7298	2.26	.75	.67	.76	.83			
New-product quality	.7231	2.44	.81	.77	.82	.72			
Concurrent engineering	.7878	2.70	.77	.79	.84	.88			
Design characteristics	.6010	2.13	.86	.82	.84				
Cleanliness and organization	.7616	3.59	.83	.93	.93	.56	.93		
Maintenance	.6169	1.92	.86	.71	.82				
Process control	.8459	2.41	.83	.92	.93				
Feedback	.7643	4.59	.78	.82	.66	.86	.89	.86	.79
Employee involvement	.7047	2.64	.49	.86	.93	.89			
Labor skill level	.6014	2.56	.77	.80	.75	.88			
Selection for teamwork potential	.7870	2.12	.84	.82	.86				

personnel, square feet used by the plant, year the plant was originally built, year of the most recent plant revitalization or modernization, type of production process, extent of product customization, percent of plant utilization, extent of process standardization, and degree of technology similarity throughout the plant. The plants were equivalent on these measures, increasing the ability to attribute differences in quality performance to differences in quality practices.

RESULTS

This section will provide a nontechnical overview of the results of the statistical analysis. The technical details are presented in Appendix B.

The results of multiple discriminant analysis indicate which independent variables are the best discriminators between groups. In this case, they indicate which practices best differentiate between the plants that reported achieving high, intermediate, and low levels of quality performance. Employee involvement was the best differentiator, followed (in order) by process control, new-product quality practices, concurrent engineering, feedback, maintenance, supplier relationship, labor skill level, and selection for teamwork potential. The practices that were relatively poor discriminators between the groups were customer interaction and design characteristics. The design characteristics scale measured design for manufacturability and reliability engineering considerations. Although these may have an impact on upstream quality performance, their use was not related to the percent of items that passed final inspection without requiring rework. The customer relationship scale was relatively poor, in terms of its reliability and validity, although it exceeded minimum guidelines. The authors believe that a better measure of customer relationship might provide a stronger discriminator between levels of quality performance.

Exhibit 5 indicates that the nature of the differences between the groups followed an interesting pattern. For the majority of the practices, both the plants that achieved high quality and those that achieved low quality reported using similar (strong) quality management practices. In contrast, the plants that achieved intermediate levels of performance reported using inferior practices. This is reflected in the V-shaped pattern in Exhibit 5.

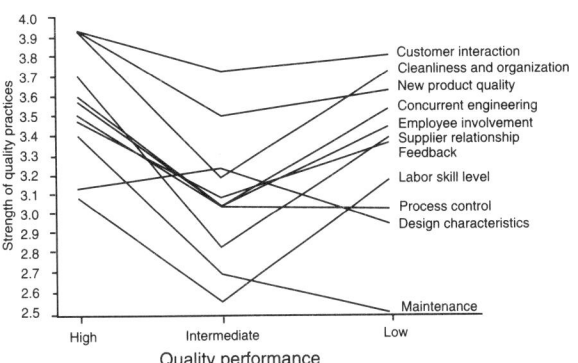

EXHIBIT 5.—GROUP MEANS FOR THE 12 SCALES

There are several possible explanations for this. First, it could be due to errors and variations in perceptions between plants. Depending on their frame of reference and experience in other organizations, the respondents may interpret the response choices in different ways. For example, respondents who have not visited a large number of other organizations may perceive that their own plants' quality management practices are better than do respondents from similar plants who have visited plants with extremely strong quality management practices.

A second possibility is that there could be bias in the sample. It is plausible that the plants that declined to participate in this study actually had systematically lower quality and were not pursuing any management practices to help improve it. Those that were classified as low, while the lowest in the group, may also be plants where decision makers have realized quality performance is low and have focused their efforts on improving it. Their incentive for participating in the study may have been the feedback that they received about their quality management practices, relative to plants with the highest quality in their industry. This is somewhat supported by the variability of the reported quality levels. All plants reported fairly good quality performance levels, compared with the performance they reported in other areas. The lowest reported levels of percent of items that passed final inspection without requiring rework were in the 75 percent to 80 percent range, while percent on-time delivery, for example, was as low as 25 percent for some plants. This may indicate some bias inherent in the sample. It may also indicate that U.S. industry, as a whole, has recognized that quality is a serious problem in the global competitive arena. In recent years, many industries have actively pursued quality improvement while perhaps devoting less attention to other dimensions

Section Three   Quality Technologies and Methods

of global competition. It is not surprising to find that quality performance was so highly rated overall; rather than indicating bias in the sample, it indicates the progress made by U.S. industry during the past decade.

The research suggests that the nonlinearity of quality management practices is due to a difference in orientation among the three groups. Respondents in the plants in the low-quality group are likely to be painfully aware of their relatively low quality level and its impact on competitive performance, and perhaps, on the survival of their livelihood. Therefore, they are making a concerted effort to improve quality, using many of the same management practices as the plants with the best quality performance. These practices and their expected impact on quality performance are well known, so it is not surprising that they would be known even to plants with the lowest quality levels. The research also suggests that plants in the intermediate quality group are somewhat more complacent, believing that their quality problem is "solved," or that they are competitive enough in terms of quality. On the other hand, the plants in the top quality group are striving to be the very best in their global industry, focusing on continuous improvement. They pursue these practices with a vigor equal to or better than the plants that currently achieve the worst quality, and consequently, they stand to benefit the most.

In addition, while the plants that have achieved the lowest quality report using similar practices as those that have achieved the best quality, they may not be using those practices in the same way. Barney (1986) describes this well-known phenomenon as "imperfect imitability." When decision makers emulate the management practices of other plants, they may focus on easily imitated practices, rather than the combination of practices that is really important to achieving the intended goal. The best plants are able to synthesize practices into the best means for achieving their goals in the culture of their organization. Those that imitate only selected practices, no matter how well they perform on those selected practices, will have inferior performance in terms of the intended goals. This offers support for the notion that it is the combination of quality management practices that is important, rather than the use of selected practices.

In terms of the tests of specific hypotheses, both hypotheses were supported. The most significant discriminant function in the test of the first hypothesis reflected the distinction between the plants that achieved intermediate levels of quality and the combination of the plants that achieved both high and low levels of quality, in terms of product design, customer, and supplier practices. The practices that best discriminated between these two groups were new-product quality and concurrent engineering. Using just the responses to these two scales, it was possible to correctly classify the plants into high-, intermediate-, and low-quality performance 74 percent of the time. Thus, the use of product design practices is, indeed, an important factor in discriminating between plants with different levels of quality performance. The new-product quality and concurrent engineering scales both focus on the direct incorporation of quality considerations during the product design process. Design characteristics, which focused on engineering considerations such as parts count reduction and design for manufacturability, however, did not contribute significantly to the quality performance differences between plants. Likewise, customer interaction and supplier relationship did not contribute significantly to the performance differences among the groups.

Thus, the incorporation of quality considerations during the product design process does have an impact on quality performance. Especially important are early incorporation of quality considerations and the use of a concurrent engineering approach, which includes input from a variety of areas, including customers, suppliers, manufacturing, marketing, and quality. The plants with the highest and lowest levels of quality performance used similar management practices related to new-product quality and concurrent engineering. The plants that achieved intermediate levels of quality performance used significantly lower levels of these quality management practices.

In the test of the second hypothesis, there were two significant discriminant functions. The first, which reflected the difference between the plants achieving intermediate levels of quality and the combination of the plants achieving high and low levels of quality, indicated that employee involvement, feedback, maintenance, labor skill level, and selection for teamwork potential were the best discriminators between the two groups. Employee involvement was the best discriminator in the entire analysis, by several orders of magnitude. This provides strong support for the importance of employees, both in terms of their ability to solve problems and in terms of their commitment to quality as a goal of the organization. An organizational culture that allows and encourages employees to contribute fully to quality performance and that focuses on quality as the primary goal of the organization is critical.

The test of the second hypothesis shows that the transformation process does indeed contribute to differences in quality performance. The five independent variables that contributed significantly to these differences included three related to workforce management (employee involvement, labor skill level, and selection for teamwork potential), and one each related to process management (maintenance) and information management (feedback). This demonstrates that differences in quality performance are due to differences in a variety of factors related to the transformation process. Plants that achieved high and low levels of quality performance used similar levels of management practices related to the transformation process. The plants that achieved intermediate levels of quality performance used lower levels of transformation process management practices.

The second significant discriminant function related to the transformation process reflected the difference between the plants that achieved the best levels of quality and the combination of those that achieved intermediate and low levels of quality. The best discriminators between these two groups were process control and supplier relationship. This discriminant function represented one dimension of the transformation process and one dimension of the supplier relationship. Thus, in addition to the factors listed earlier, the plants with the best quality performance also excelled in management practices related to process control and supplier relationship. Maintaining a good relationship with suppliers had a much stronger impact on the transformation process dimension than it did on the product design dimension. This is logical because of their direct involvement in supplying materials to the process. Maintaining close ties with suppliers helps ensure that this important input will be of appropriate quality. Although suppliers can provide important information about component capabilities during the product design phase, this information appears to be of somewhat less value in explaining performance differences than it was during the transformation process phase.

The two discriminant functions based on the transformation process had strong predictive power when combined. Using only the responses to the items in the employee involvement, feedback, maintenance, labor skill level, selection for teamwork potential, process control, and supplier relationship scales, it was possible to correctly classify 79 percent of the plants into high-, intermediate-, and low-quality performance categories.

A number of other findings were interesting. First, the results clearly showed that plants with the best quality used a variety of approaches related to workforce management, process management, and information management. This is consistent with the idea that a broad, integrated approach to quality management will result in the best quality.

The transformation process was shown to have an apparently greater impact on quality performance than the product design process. While this is intuitively appealing, it should be interpreted cautiously. The study tested many more dimensions of the transformation process than those of product design; thus, there were more opportunities for transformation process variables to be significant. Research that further articulates and tests the dimensions of product design may find that both are equally important, or that product design is more important, in terms of its impact on product quality.

Employee involvement emerged as the most significant independent variable (the best discriminator between the groups). Although the importance of employee involvement has been stressed in the literature, it is interesting that its impact is greater than the process management practices, some of which focus directly on quality. This supports the wealth of anecdotal evidence which suggests that, although some of the other practices are also important, it is the people that really make a difference. True employee involvement also helps create a competitive advantage because of its difficult replicability between organizations, unlike a technical process, a software package, or a set of practices. Key to developing employee involvement is the development of a quality culture that respects the potential contributions of all employees, provides employees with training and tools for problem solving, allows experimentation combined with accountability, and recognizes the success of employee involvement.

CONCLUSIONS

This study makes several important contributions to the literature. First, the research shows that all four dimensions of quality management (supplier relationship, customer relationship, product design, and the transformation process) are important to quality performance.

The most surprising finding of the study is that both the high- and low-performing groups, in terms of quality, tended to use more progressive quality management practices, while the intermediate group used less progressive quality management practices. One explanation for this was the desire of the high-performing group for continuous improvement of quality, while the low-performing group was attempting to catch up and the intermediate performers were complacent, believing that their quality performance was "good enough." This is an intriguing finding, which runs counter to the authors' previous thinking.

It is important to consider this study in terms of its limitations. The findings concerning practices are based on the respondents' perceptions of their own use of quality management approaches. Although the authors tried to identify the best respondents for the various types of information gathered, the accuracy of self-perceptions may be strongly influenced by the respondents' frame of reference and experience with quality management practices in other organizations. In addition, respondents in plants with high levels of quality may be inclined to believe that their quality management practices are also advanced. In this type of analysis, it may be difficult to determine the direction of causation, particularly for the variables that are more perceptual and less concrete. For example, does employee involvement really lead to better quality, or do better levels of quality lead to greater pride and involvement among employees?

Most of the previous research about quality management practices has been descriptive. This is one of the first studies that links quality management practices with quality performance. It lays the foundation for a number of directions for future research. The results of this study may be dependent on the operational definition of quality performance (the percentage of products that pass final inspection without requiring rework), which does not take into account upstream defects and rework. Other objective measures of quality performance should be considered in future studies. Future studies should consider a broader range of quality measures, including the development of effective means of measuring quality performance from the customers' viewpoint. The authors also suggest that future studies closely examine the relationship between quality management, just-in-time, and other factors. Another direction for future studies is to examine dynamic approaches in quality management: What is the effect of the length of time since various quality management approaches have been implemented? Finally, the specific form of the relationship between quality management practices and quality performance needs more study. If quality laggards as well as quality leaders are using similar quality management practices, then one can expect the laggards to catch up to the middle plants and eventually compete with the leaders.

APPENDIX A: SCALE LISTING

Relationship with customers

Customer interaction

1.*   We frequently are in close contact with our customers.

2.(R)* Our customers seldom visit our plant.

3.*   Our customers give us feedback on quality and delivery performance.

4.   A very important objective is to obtain satisfied customers.

5.   Our customers buy from us just-in-time to meet their needs.

Relationship with suppliers

Supplier relationship

1.*   We strive to establish long-term relationships with suppliers.

2.*   Our suppliers are actively involved in our new-product development process.

3.*   Quality is our number one criterion in selecting suppliers.

4.*   We rely on a small number of high-quality suppliers.

Product design

New product quality

1.* New product designs are thoroughly reviewed before the product is produced and sold.

2.* Customer requirements are thoroughly analyzed in the new-product design process.

3.(R)* Reducing the cost of new products is a more important priority than new-product quality.

4.(R)* Schedule concerns are more important than quality in the new-product development process.

Concurrent engineering

1.* Direct labor employees are involved to a great extent (on teams or consulted) before introducing new products or making product changes.

2.* Manufacturing engineers are involved to a great extent before the introduction of new products.

3.(R)* There is little involvement of manufacturing and quality people in the early design of products before they reach the plant.

4.* We work in teams with members from a variety of areas (marketing, manufacturing, and so on) to introduce new products.

5.(R) Routine product modifications are made by design engineering or the research and development lab, rather than manufacturing engineering.

Design characteristics

1. We make an effort in the design process to list only the specifications that are really needed.

2.* There is a strong customer focus in our design process.

3. The emphasis in part design is on minimizing the part count.

4.* We believe in the philosophy of loosely designed specifications.

5.(R) We are not concerned about the number of parts in an end item.

Transformation process:
Process management

Cleanliness and organization

1.* Our plant emphasizes putting all tools and fixtures in their place.

2.* We take pride in keeping our plant neat and clean.

3.* Our plant is kept clean at all times.

4.(R)* I often have trouble finding the tools I need.

5.(R)* Our plant is disorganized and dirty.

Maintenance

1.* Machine operators are in charge of their own routine maintenance.

2. Our equipment is in a high state of readiness for production at all times.

3.* Our maintenance department performs the major preventive maintenance tasks, such as complete tear-downs.

4. We dedicate a portion of every day solely to preventive maintenance.

5. We emphasize good maintenance as a strategy for achieving quality and schedule compliance.

6. We have a separate shift or part of a shift reserved each day for maintenance activities.

7.(R) We have a relatively high rate of downtime for repairs, compared with our industry.

Transformation process:
Information management

Feedback

1.* Charts showing defect rates are posted on the shop floor.

2.* Charts showing schedule compliance are posted on the shop floor.

3.* Charts plotting the frequency of machine breakdowns are posted on the shop floor.

4.(R)* I am never told whether I am doing a good job.

5.* Information on quality performance is readily available to employees.

6.* Information on productivity is readily available to employees.

7.(R)*   My manager never comments about the quality of my work.

Process control

1.*   Processes in our plant are designed to be "fool-proof."

2.*   A large percent of the equipment or processes on the shop floor are currently under statistical quality control.

3.*   We make extensive use of statistical techniques to reduce variance in processes.

4.   We have standardized process instructions that are given to personnel.

5.   We use inspection for quality control.

6.   We use statistical process control in many of our office processes.

7.(R)   Our employees are never allowed to inspect their own work; we use trained quality inspectors.

Transformation process:
Workforce management

Employee involvement

1.*   Our plant is organized into permanent production teams.

2.*   During problem-solving sessions, we make an effort to get all team members' opinions and ideas before making a decision.

3.*   Our plant forms teams to solve problems.

4.*   In the past three years, many problems have been solved through small-group sessions.

5.(R)   When I have a problem with my job, my supervisor tries to solve it.

6.(R)   Problems are usually solved by supervisors.

7.(R)   When I have a problem on the job, I try to solve it myself.

Labor skill level

1.   Direct labor undergoes training to perform multiple tasks in the production process.

2.   Plant employees are rewarded for learning new skills.

3.(R)   Our plant has a low skill level, compared with our industry.

4.   Direct labor technical competence is high in this plant.

Selection for teamwork potential

1.*   We use ability to work in a team as a criterion in employee selection.

2.*   We use problem-solving ability as a criterion in selecting employees.

3.*   We use work values and ethics as criteria in employee selection.

4.   We use knowledge and skill level as criteria in selecting employees.

*Items retained in the final version of the scales. Items without stars were removed from the final version of the scales and should not be used.

Items indicated by an (R) were reverse scaled; accordingly, they were reverse coded during data entry to correspond to the connection that higher values indicate better practices.

Appendix B: Technical Discussion of Results

Technical discussion of the results will begin by examining the statistical significance of each of the discriminant functions. It will then move to discussing the validity of the significant discriminant functions, using classification matrices to evaluate their predictive accuracy. Finally, the significant and valid discriminant functions will be interpreted, in terms of the independent variables (quality management practices) that contributed most to discriminating between the groups.

Significance of Discriminant Functions

The process of constructing discriminant functions began with the selection of independent variables to be included in the analysis of each hypothesis. Including all possible independent variables would very likely result in nonsignificant discriminant functions and provision of very little information. Thus, the initial step in the analysis used univariate analysis of variance as a guide in selecting independent variables for inclusion in the discriminant functions. Because this was used only as a guideline for the selection of independent variables for further testing, a relatively generous significance level (0.10) was used as the criterion. Results of this analysis are contained in Exhibit 6. Nonsignificant independent variables were evaluated in terms of their overall contribution to the research (Hair, Anderson, and Tatham 1987). The authors adopted the decision rule to include at least one independent variable representing each dimension of the framework, even if the best choice was not statistically significant. For example, in constructing the solution for the first hypothesis, "design characteristics" was eliminated from further consideration, since concurrent engineering and new-product quality were both significant and represented the same dimension. Customer interaction, however, was not eliminated, although it was not statistically significant, because it was the sole representative of its dimension.

Exhibit 6 lists the means of the independent variables (these means were shown graphically in Exhibit 5). Higher values of the scales correspond to "better" quality management practices, as defined by the literature review. It is interesting to note that the group with the intermediate-quality performance typically used the worst quality management practices. For seven of the independent variables, the groups with both the best and worst quality performance used similar quality management practices. The process control and supplier relationship scales, on the other hand, distinguished between the three groups as expected, while the remaining three scales did not account for a significant difference between the groups at the 0.10 level.

Exhibit 7 lists information related to the statistical significance of the discriminant functions by hypothesis. By definition, there are two discriminant functions for each hypothesis, since there were three a priori groups. The first discriminant function explains the largest amount of difference between the group and the remaining two, combined. The second discriminant function, orthogonal to the first, explains the largest amount of residual variance, after the variance for the first function has been removed.

The canonical correlation coefficients indicate each function's importance. Squared, they indicate the percent of variance explained. Thus, the discriminant functions account for between 14.49 percent and 49.21 percent of the variance in the dependent variables. The Wilks' lambda statistic is a measure of the difference between groups; the greater the difference between groups, the smaller the value of lambda. The chi-square statistic describes a function's ability to

EXHIBIT 6.—GROUP MEANS

Independent Variables	Group Means			Statistical Significance	
	High Quality	Intermediate Quality	Low Quality	F Value	Level of Significance
Customer interaction	3.92	3.71	3.81	0.431	.6536
Supplier relationship	3.58	3.06	3.02	2.939	.0678
New-product quality	3.89	3.14	3.41	4.565	.0183
Concurrent engineering	3.68	2.84	3.40	4.101	.0263
Design characteristics	3.15	3.20	2.95	0.616	.5465
Maintenance	3.10	2.56	3.08	3.712	.0359
Cleanliness and organization	3.92	3.55	3.63	2.296	.1176
Feedback	3.52	3.10	3.46	4.048	.0274
Process control	3.41	2.73	2.47	5.117	.0120
Employee involvement	3.59	3.07	3.52	9.120	.0008
Labor skill level	3.47	3.16	3.38	2.685	.0841
Selection for teamwork potential	3.90	3.20	3.67	2.507	.0979

EXHIBIT 7.—ANALYSIS OF DISCRIMINANT FUNCTIONS

Hypothesis	Function	Canonical Correlation	Variance Explained	Wilks' Lambda	Chi-Square	Level Of Significance
H1: Differences will exist among the high-, intermediate-, and low-quality performance groups, in terms of their product design, supplier relationship, and customer relationship practices.	1A	.7015	49.21%	.4343	24.19	.0071
	1B	.3807	14.49%	.8550	4.54	.3376
H2: Differences will exist among the high-, imtermediate-, and low-quality performance groups, in terms of their transformation process, supplier relationship, and customer relationship practices.	2A	.6921	47.90%	.5131	31.57	.0114
	2B	.6254	39.11%	.6089	13.64	.0579

discriminate between groups, and was the overall measure of the statistical significance of the discriminant functions. Using a criterion level of 0.05, Exhibit 7 shows that the first discriminant function for each hypothesis test was statistically significant.

Exhibit 8 uses group centroids to determine where the significant differences lie. For the tests of both hypotheses, the statistically significant difference fell between the combination of the high- and low-quality performance groups and the intermediate-quality performance group. Thus, the plants that achieved both the best and worst quality performance used similar (better) quality management practices. The plants with intermediate-quality performance used significantly different (inferior) quality management practices. The second discriminant function for H2 was borderline significant (0.0579). This function profiled the factors that were important in discriminating between plants with high-quality performance and those with intermediate- or low-quality performance, combined.

EXHIBIT 8.—GROUP CENTROIDS

Function	Comparison	High	Intermediate	Low
1A	High and low versus intermediate	0.8422	−1.3136	0.1989
2A	High and low versus intermediate	0.3795	−1.3394	0.7691
2B	High versus intermediate and low	0.8981	−0.0384	−1.0265

Validity of the Functions

Although the chi-square test analyzes the statistical significance of a discriminant function, it may be a relatively poor indicator of a function's ability to actually discriminate between groups. With sufficiently large sample sizes, the functions could be statistically significant, while group centroids were virtually identical. Because of this, classification matrices are commonly used to determine the predictive ability (validity) of discriminant functions. Exhibit 9 contains the classification matrices for both hypotheses.

The hit ratio (percent of cases correctly classified) reveals how well the discriminant functions classified observations. Hit ratios are interpreted using the Maximum Chance Criterion, which is based on the sample size of the largest a priori group. If the hit ratio does not exceed the proportion of observations in the largest group, then the discriminant function has not helped to predict group membership (chance assignment could do as well or better). Because of the relatively small sample, it was not possible to use a separate sample of plants for developing the discriminant functions. Thus, because the observations being classified are the same as those used to calculate the discriminant functions, there is likely to be an upward bias in the hit ratios. Hair, Anderson, and Tatham (1987) recommend that, in a case such as this, hit ratios should be at least 25 percent greater than the Maximum Chance Criterion. The criterion value of 46.5 percent (38% × 1.25) for both null hypotheses was used here. Because both of the hit ratios exceeded the criterion, it was concluded that both discriminant functions were valid.

EXHIBIT 9.—VALIDITY OF DISCRIMINANT FUNCTIONS

A Priori Group	Number Of Cases	Percent Of Cases	Predicted Group Membership			Percent Correctly Classified
			High	Intermediate	Low	
H1: Differences will exist among the high-, intermediate-, and low-quality performance groups, in terms of their product design, supplier relationships, and customer relationship practices.						
High quality	13	38%	9 (69.2%)	2 (15.4%)	2 (15.4%)	
Intermediate quality	10	29%	1 (10.0%)	9 (90.0%)	0 (0.0%)	73.53%
Low quality	11	32%	4 (36.4%)	0 (0.0%)	7 (63.6%)	
H2: Differences will exist among the high-, intermediate-, and low-quality performance groups, in terms of their transformation process, supplier relationship, and customer relationship practices.						
High quality	13	38%	12 (92.3%)	1 (7.7%)	0 (0.0%)	
Intermediate quality	10	29%	3 (30.0%)	6 (60.0%)	1 (10.0%)	79.41%
Low quality	11	32%	4 (36.4%)	3 (27.3%)	4 (36.4%)	

Interpretation of Discriminant functions

Specific independent variables were analyzed using rotated discriminant loadings (structure correlations), which measure the simple linear correlation between each independent variable and the discriminant function. They reflect the variance that each independent variable shares with the function. Exhibit 10 provides the discriminant loadings for both hypotheses. In each case, the first group of independent variables (above the dashed line) was more highly related to the first discriminant function (A), while the second group of independent variables was more highly related to the second discriminant function (B), which was not statistically significant in either case. They are listed in order of decreasing magnitude within each of the groups. Discriminant loadings of at least 0.30 are considered to contribute significantly to the discriminant function. The sign of the discriminant loadings indicates whether the variable makes a positive or negative contribution to the composite discriminant function.

EXHIBIT 10.—ROTATED DISCRIMINANT LOADINGS

Independent Variable	Function A	Function B
H1: Differences will exist among the high-, intermediate-, and low-quality performance groups, in terms of their product design, supplier relationship, and customer relationship practices.		
New-product quality	.6833	.4717
Concurrent engineering	.5673	.0517
Customer interaction	.1992	.0787
Supplier relationship	.5461	.7115[†]
Design characteristics	.0562	.4294[†]
H2: Differences will exist among the high-, intermediate-, and low-quality performance groups, in terms of their transformation process, supplier relationship, and customer relationship practices.		
Employee involvement	.8312	.2889
Feedback	.5533	.1922
Maintenance	.5367	.1258
Labor skill level	.4337	.2296
Selection for teamwork potential	.4113	.2440
Process control	.1540	.6862
Supplier relationship	.2046	.5009

[†]This discriminant function was not statistically significant.

REFERENCES

Ashford, S. L., and L. L. Cummings. 1984. Feedback as an individual resource: Personal strategies of creating information. *Organizational Behavior and Human Performance* 32:370–398.

Barney, J. B. 1986. Organizational culture: Can it be a source of sustained competitive advantage? *Academy of Management Review* 11, no. 3:656–665.

Cronbach, L. J. 1951. Coefficient alpha and the internal structure of tests. *Psychometrika* 16:297–334.

Fawcett, S. I. 1989. The Japanese challenge: A note on the emergency of Japanese competitiveness. *Operations Management Review* 7:46–52.

Flynn, B. B., R. G. Schroeder, and S. Sakakibara. 1994. A framework for quality-management research and an associated measurement instrument. *Journal of Operations Management* 11:339–366.

Garvin, D. A. 1983. Quality on the line. *Harvard Business Review* 61:64–75.

_____ . 1984. Japanese quality management. *Columbia Journal of World Business* 19, no. 3:3–12.

Hair, J. F., R. E. Anderson, and R. L. Tatham. 1987. *Multivariate statistical analysis*. New York: Macmillan.

Hartley, J. R. 1992. *Concurrent engineering*. Cambridge, Mass.: Productivity Press.

Hayes, R. H. 1981. Why Japanese factories work. *Harvard Business Review* 59, no. 4:56–66.

Juran, J. M. 1978. Japanese and western quality—A contrast. *Quality Progress* (December): 10–18.

Kim, J. Q., and C. W. Mueller. 1978. *Factor analysis: Statistical methods and practical issues*. Newbury Park, Calif.: Sage Publications.

Leonard, F. S., and W. E. Sasser. 1982. The incline of quality. *Harvard Business Review* 60:163–171.

Lord, F. M., and M. R. Novick. 1968. *Statistical theories of mental test scores*. Reading, Mass.: Addison-Wesley.

Manoochehri, G. H. 1985. Building quality into the product. *Business* (September): 47–50.

Nunnally, J. C. 1978. *Psychometric theory*. New York: McGraw-Hill.

Schonberger, R. 1985. *World class manufacturing*. New York: Free Press.

Shalley, C., G. Oldham, and J. Porac. 1987. Effects of goal difficulty, goal setting method and expected external evaluation on intrinsic motivation. *Academy of Management Journal* 30:553–566.

Wheelwright, S. C., and R. H. Hayes. 1985. Competing through manufacturing. *Harvard Business Review* 59:57–64.

Ziskin, I. V. 1986. Knowledge-based pay: A strategic analysis. *Compensation and Benefits Review* 19:56–66.

HOW TO CONSTRUCT A BASIC QUALITY MANUAL*
by William R. Hamilton

When was the last time someone in your company updated the corporate quality manual? Does the current version meet the ISO 9000 series standards? Does your quality staff proudly present it and use it as a general guide for external customer audits? If not, why not? Could it use some changes or maybe even a face-lift? Why isn't anybody doing that? You might be familiar with some of these excuses: "It takes too much time," "I don't know where to start," or "I've got higher priorities."

A quality manual is a communication tool. It provides a concise, adequately detailed description of quality procedures, policies, and management hierarchy. A well-written quality manual will benefit both the company's external customers and internal departments.

Customers will benefit from the single-source reference on company documentation and general procedures. This can be a major plus when a customer representative reviews company operations during an on-site visit. The representative (or auditor) can quickly request the specific documents and procedural examples he or she needs to help qualify a potential supplier just from scanning the manual.

Departments (e.g., marketing and sales, production, and corporate management) can use the manual as a reference on general quality procedures and policies. As a measure of good practice, everyone in the company should be familiar with the quality manual topics.

For a small to midsize company, a quality manual can be constructed relatively quickly and easily. Large companies with more than 5,000 employees might have a more elaborate approval loop. In either case, an intelligent move is to see how other companies have constructed their quality manuals. No one technique will work for every company, but this shouldn't discourage you. Adequate planning and foresight, driven by high motivation, will make this project a reality.

If you must sell the project to your supervisor, it is helpful to point out the benefits of having an updated, practical quality manual:

1. You need an updated quality manual for ISO 9000 registration. If your company plans to become registered under the ISO 9000 standards, one of the first requirements is to submit the corporate quality manual. The manual is scrutinized for completeness and is used as a base to determine what changes your company will need to make to qualify for ISO 9000 registration.

---

*Reprinted with permission from *Quality Progress,* April 1995. William R. Hamilton is a miocroelectronics systems engineer at the Semiconductor Division of Raytheon Co. in Mountain View, CA.

2. Satisfying an external customer's audit requirements can be accomplished through effectively presenting your company's quality systems via a well-constructed quality manual. Be aware that no matter how well a quality manual is composed, it will not by itself secure a favorable grade from the customer. It will, however, be an advantage. The less effort an auditor spends obtaining descriptions of your company's working quality systems, the better the grade.

3. The quality manual represents the company's quality consciousness. It encompasses the ideal practices of everyone in the company, from top executives to manufacturing personnel. A powerfully written manual can impress your customers. As they read about your company's efforts to ensure high-quality performance, they will be more confident in your company's products or services.

Once you have sold the idea of a new quality manual to your supervisor and his or her manager, you have to carefully plan how you will accomplish the task. Exhibit 1 contains an example of a process that can be followed. Do not rush the quality manual project; give yourself plenty of time to accomplish the various tasks involved. Allow about three months for each of the planning, management negotiation, and final revision stages. The entire project should take about a year.

The following is a more in-depth look at some of the steps in constructing a basic quality manual.

Step 1: Review others' quality manuals

You should review about six quality manuals to see the various types in existence. These manuals can be from any type of company; you should, however, obtain several from companies that are in the same industry as your company. (Ideally, you should review your competitors' quality manuals, but this isn't always possible.) You can check your company's procurement department for quality manuals issued from suppliers. Likewise, you can ask customers for copies of their manuals.

Read the quality manuals, noting what you like and dislike about each one. Consider such matters as:

• Is it easy to read?

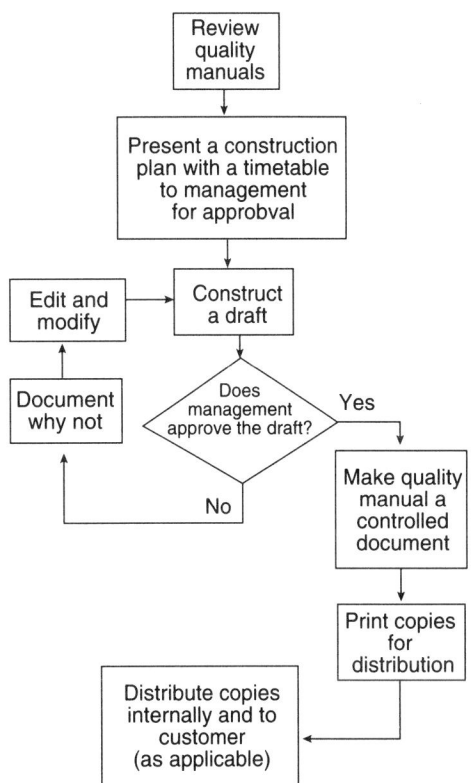

EXHIBIT 1.—FLOWCHART FOR CONSULTING A BASIC QUALITY MANUAL

• What information is included?

• Can you look up any quality subject quickly?

• Is its appearance appealing?

• Does the manual flow logically from one subject to the next?

• How frequently did the company revise its manual?

• What was memorable about the company's manual?

• Do you understand that company's quality policies and organization?

This exercise will provide you with a list of important items to include and poor practices to avoid in your manual.

If your company is constructing a manual for a specific purpose (e.g., ISO 9000 registration), you should also check to see whether guides have been published. For example, if you want to customize your quality manual to meet ISO 9000 requirements, there are two sources that can help: *ISO 9000 Handbook of Quality Standards and Compliance* and *The ISO 9000 Book:*

A Global Competitor's Guide to Compliance & Certification.[1,2]

Step 2: Prepare a construction plan

After reviewing various quality manuals, the next step is to prepare a plan for constructing your manual and getting management's approval of that plan. Here is one of many ways that this can be accomplished:

Before you type the manual's first word, develop a proposal that includes the manual's outline, content description, and benefits. Distribute this information, in memo form, to the quality department. Schedule a meeting to discuss each individual's edits and ideas.

Repeat this activity for each department in the company. You do not need to give the memo to every employee in each department, but you should obtain opinions from key contributing individuals, with "key" meaning seasoned individuals who are very familiar with the company's internal working systems.

After consolidating everyone's opinions and edits, revise your proposal and send it to each department manager. Collect the managers' thoughts and revisit the manual's construction plan. By now, you should have a solid design for the quality manual.

Next, present the quality manual design and a concise memo to the company's vice presidents and chief executive officer (CEO). Include a brief section describing how the present design evolved. If you cannot gather all of the company officers in a meeting to review the manual, visit them individually to solicit their advice and comments. Do the same for the CEO, but make him or her last and be sure to obtain his or her written approval of the plan.

Finally, when the quality manual design is approved, issue a memo describing the approved plan to top management and to each person from whom you received feedback.

Step 3: Construct the manual

As a rule of thumb, a quality manual should contain the following characteristics:

1. The quality manual should be firmly bound and appealing to the eye, since the customer's first impression of the manual will be of its appearance. The cover should make you want to open it and read what's inside. The cover should include the company's name and the words "quality manual."

    A graphic design can also be included. For example, a semiconductor manufacturer might have a large screened picture of a wafer with printed circuits, surrounded by statistical process-control charts, bell curves, fishbone diagrams, and silhouettes of people. Be creative.

    The cover must be durable. It can be made of vinyl, laminated cardboard, or another sturdy material.

    If the cover is appealing and sturdy, you're moving in the right direction.

2. All text in the manual should be high resolution (laser-printer quality) and in an easy-to-read font and type size, such as Courier in 10-point size. In addition, text should be printed on only one side of each page. Using a word processor with a spell checker and grammar checker is recommended. You will be reworking or updating this manual repeatedly. With a word processor, changes are easily made.

3. The quality manual should contain a table of contents that includes subjects listed by numbered sections and their respective page numbers.

4. The manual is a corporate specification, so it must include the following information on every page: specification number, title of the document, page number, total number of pages, revision level, and company name. Including the company logo or emblem on each page looks impressive.

5. The quality manual should include the corporate quality policy. Your company likely has such a policy. You should contact the vice president or director of quality to obtain the most recent, approved version. Remember, this policy must be endorsed by the CEO.

    If a quality policy has not been developed, you need to create one. Draft a policy and obtain management's approval of it. The policy shouldn't be more than a few sentences stating the company's quality vision, such as, "It is the first intent of every employee to provide unparalleled quality services and supply defect-free products to all of our valued customers." Once you obtain approval from the vice president and directorate levels, obtain the CEO's approval signature on official company letterhead.

6. The quality manual must display the CEO's signature because it represents the level of authority at which the manual received approval. If the signature is only from a vice president or director, the manual will lack authority. The CEO's signature also indicates that quality is practiced and upheld at all management levels, including top management. Do not take shortcuts on this crucial step.

7. The quality manual should contain a preface describing the manual's purpose. The preface can also list the government and commercial standards with which the company complies. Keep it short and to the point. For example, it could state: "This is Widgets Inc.'s corporate quality manual. The following provides a systematic overview of quality systems implemented and management's responsibility to those systems. This document also provides references to company-specific documentation for needed details not found herein. This quality manual complies with the following government and commercial standards: . . . ."

8. The quality manual should contain a list of corporate reference documents. Undoubtedly, you will reference all kinds of corporate documentation. In this section, compile the list of corporate documents used to create your manual. It should be tabular, listing the document number and title. The specifictions required for your manual will depend on the document's main body.

9. The quality manual should contain an introduction to the manual's main body. This introduction should include short descriptions of:

   • The company, including its products, services, and corporate headquarters' address

   • The company's quality philosophy and how it is perceived by employees

   • How the company manages its quality system. This could include describing the quality department's responsibilities, the role of teams and committees, and so forth.

   • The company's quality plan. Describe the quality plan, who generates it, and how often it is updated.

   • Quality training programs. Briefly describe the training offered to employees.

10. The quality manual should have a comprehensive but concise main body that outlines the company's general procedures and practices. Auditors pay special attention to this section. It is imperative that the main body include all or most topics that your customers look for in quality specifications and requirements. It should read smoothly from section to section. If this sounds like a tough job, you're right. It is! This is where you will be spending most of your efforts.

    Every quality manual differs in its body. Be flexible and willing to include ideals that are impressive and unique to your organization. Create an outline of topics to include in the body text. The approved construction plan (step 2) will provide a good place to start. Sample outlines are available in *Juran's Quality Control Handbook* and in military standard MIL-Q-9858A.[3,4]

    Once the topics are listed, determine the official corporate documents that apply to each. Do not perform this step alone; solicit the assistance of the quality department's senior manager. Once the documents are determined, confirm them with key members in manufacturing areas.

    Now you can begin to actually write the main body of text. Each topic should contain:

    • Objective statements. These statements, taken from appropriate corporate documents, generally outline the topic.

    • Critical requirements. Critical requirements are statements that refer to specific procedures used in the promotion of a particular topic.

    Objective statements and critical requirements for various quality topics are discussed in *Quality Planning and Analysis*.[5] There are additional examples of quality management topics in *TQM: Management Processes for Quality Operations*.[6]

    As an example, consider the topic of training. The objective statements should explain why your company trains its employees. In other words, what is the purpose of the training activities? Do not include specifics, such as "All employees receive eight hours of quality training from the outside contractor, Professional Quality Associates. This program includes control charts, fishbone diagrams, Pareto charts. . . ." This is too specific and will cause numerous revisions in your manual. A better statement is, "To facilitate the companywide awareness of quality methods, each employee shall participate in the approved corporate quality training program."

The critical requirements should then reference where one could find the specific topics regarding the mentioned training plan. They should also address responsibility issues, such as: What departments are in charge of training? What are their responsibilities? How are records maintained?

To format the main body, use a legal outline, which is an outlining system that uses ordered periods and numbers to identify paragraphs indicating what section within a document they pertain to. Here is an example:

3 Training
   3.1 Policies
      3.1.1 It is the responsibility of each department to ensure that adequate training is provided to individuals within that department so that they can perform their designated duties.
      3.1.2 Individuals not having adequate training to perform a particular operation will not be allowed to perform that operation.

It is a good practice to have at least two subtopics for each topic. The manual will thus be easier to follow and reference. You should maintain enough printed material on each page without making the document seem crowded. It should be easy to read and understand.

11. The quality manual should have a corporate organization chart. A computer with organization chart software will make this task easier. Create an easy-to-follow chart that does not include names or titles. Names continually change and sometimes so do the titles. It's obvious to see why you should not be specific here. Keep this chart general and describe only the highest levels.

12. The quality manual should contain a quality organization chart. The same procedures listed in the corporate organization chart (No. 11) apply here. The quality organization and the corporate organization charts are separate to allow more detail in the quality organization chart—after all, this is a quality manual. Describe the quality department at all levels, including teams, groups, leaders, and divisions. Leave enough space to allow the auditors to write in the names of current quality figures while auditing. This will make their job a little easier, and every little bit counts.

13. The quality manual should include a cross-reference of corporate documentation to government and ISO 9000 standards. Use this section to list what corporate documents you used to address relevant standards. Present this information in columns or tables. The auditor will probably be following an outline of a government or ISO 9000 standard. Listing the corporate documents will limit the search, since the auditor simply has to ask for the documents while scanning through the manual. The idea here is to have a powerful company document that quickly identifies other key documentation for anyone who needs it.

14. The quality manual should include a glossary of quality terms and acronyms. Different companies and industries use different terminology. List all company- and industry-specific terms, using no more than two sentences to define each one. For acronyms, identify what each letter stands for and include a brief definition. A fast and effective means of completing this task is to have the spell-check function of your word processor provide a list of unrecognized words found in the document.

Step 4: Obtain management's approval

Like most corporate documents, you will need the quality manual approved by various management levels. Undoubtedly, there will be changes as you move through the company approval list. If you were thorough in collecting feedback (step 2), however, the changes should be minor. Again, present the final package to the CEO last.

Schedule a personal meeting with the CEO to discuss any final changes. You must get his or her approval for the manual to be successful.

Skipping CEO approval damages the manual's integrity.

A business necessity

Every company's quality manual will be unique. Your new manual will be an improvement over the old one. While creating the manual, you will probably discover flaws in your organization's quality systems. This brings another important advantage to constructing a quality manual: You will discover where and to what degree your company has quality weaknesses—weaknesses that your customers might have already discovered.

A quality manual reflects a company's commitment to quality and customer satisfaction. A complete, concise quality manual is an important selling tool to potential customers. It indicates how well the company plans, implements, and improves its quality procedures and processes. With standards such as ISO 9000 becoming a driving force in the global marketplace, a

well-designed quality manual is a business necessity.

REFERENCES

1. Bureau of Business Practice, *ISO 9000 Handbook of Quality Standards and Compliance* (Englewood Cliffs, NJ: Prentice Hall, 1992), p. 134.
2. John T. Rabbitt and Peter A. Bergh. *The ISO 9000 Book: A Global Competitor's Guide to Compliance & Certification* (White Plains, NY: Quality Resources, 1993).
3. J.M. Juran, editor, and Frank M. Gyrna Jr., associate editor, *Juran's Quality Control Handbook*, fourth edition (New York, NY: McGraw-Hill Book Co., 1988), pp. 6.40-6.45.
4. Military Standard MIL-Q-9858A "Quality Program Requirements."
5. J.M. Juran and Frank M. Gryna Jr., *Quality Planning and Analysis*, second edition (New York, NY: McGraw-Hill Book Co., 1980).
6. Richard S. Johnson, *TQM: Management Processes for Quality Operations* (Milwaukee, WI: ASQC Quality Press, 1993).

‖‖‖ 3.3   TOTAL QUALITY MANAGEMENT

———————————■———————————

QUALITY TRAVELS AT THE SPEED OF CHANGE*
by Howard Skolak, CMC

Benchmarking and reengineering are not total quality management (TQM). But they are two tools that can help develop a total quality culture.

There is confusion around the relationship of TQM and tools, such as problem solving tools, self-directed work teams, empowerment, ISO 9000, and Statistical Process Control (SPC). Are the tools used in place of, or to accomplish TQM? Is total quality a way of running the business or is it a tool to improve the business? There is a tendency for firms to place a short-term emphasis on projects such as employee involvement, teams, results, and rewards, and believe that they have implemented total quality.

Tools and techniques, however, rank dead last in terms of relative importance to a total quality effort. "TQM is at least 80 percent concept and probably only 20 percent tools and techniques," said Bill Ginnodo, executive director of QPMA, in *Industry Week*. "It's far more important to deal with leadership, training, and empowerment—the conceptual issues that will get people in sync with the effort."

Benchmarking is a tool that can be used to identify the processes that need to be reengineered. Through the benchmarking process, a firm will study how other firms, including competitors, handle everything from product development to marketing.

*Reprinted with permission from *Continuous Journey*, January 1995. Howard Skolak is president of Howard C. Skolak, Inc., a consulting firm that specializes in helping manufacturing people improve profits and increase sales.

Dr. Michael Hammer, co-author of *Reengineering the Corporation,* defines reengineering as the radical design of a business process for dramatic improvement. He further states that it is not for the faint of heart. It requires companies to shatter their assumptions about how they do business and implement wholesale change in their business processes.

In contrast, the TQM philosophy is to proceed on an effort that will continually change the way the business is run. This change will be in response to the needs of all the business elements, including the customers, suppliers, employees, and stockholders. During this neverending journey, adequate tools and techniques will be used to insure progress and direction are maintained.

Improvement through change is the end result of both total quality and reengineering. One significant difference between the two is the speed at which this change is expected to occur. Most of us will more readily accept change if we understand why it is required and if it can occur at a reasonable pace. Like the infant with a wet diaper, people must feel the need for a change.

Unfortunately, this need for change usually results from a major downturn in business or request from a major customer. There are, of course, some successful firms who feel they must change to remain competitive. A total quality focus would be an appropriate response under all of the above conditions.

Taco Bell used reengineering to dramatically alter the concept of its business and significantly increase the volume of its sales. It went from a modestly successful fast-food restaurant, concerned with preparing food, to a food provider focused on serving customers. Its typical restaurant went from 70 percent kitchen and 30 percent dining area to 30 percent kitchen and 70 percent dining area. Its sales volume increased by a factor of six.

In addition to the need, employees must develop confidence that the changes will not seriously threaten job security. Individuals must be able to make mistakes without fear of major consequences and realize that not changing could be more of a threat than changing. Employees must move into this unknown atmosphere of change. This is very difficult, because most people have a fear of the unknown. An organization can reduce this fear of the unknown by developing a clear vision of who it is, where it is going, and how it plans to get there.

A tendency also exists to underestimate the degree of commitment and the time required to travel toward the total quality culture. Firms frequently meet a "wall" along the continuous journey. This wall results when the investment of time, energy, and dollars is questioned. Comparing this "up front" investment to a major machine tool is difficult because the initial results are not as easy to predict or measure.

The following points from a Conference Board study by Kathryn Troy and Lawrence Schein, released February 1994, illustrate the commitment that total quality requires:

- Companies implementing total quality need at least four years to persuade their employees to buy into the philosophy and eight to 10 years to fully establish total quality principles.

- That kind of patience is not the norm in the boardrooms of corporate America, according to the study, which is based on more than five years of research on hundreds of U.S. companies.

- "Look at Motorola," she said. "It was seven or eight years into its quality effort before it won the Malcolm Baldrige Award in 1987."

It is also critical to thoroughly understand the desired results of current business processes before considering to make a change. Current business processes can be documented by an old technique called flow process diagramming. This exercise is performed by the operating team to produce a better understanding of the business process, identify improvement opportunities, encourage teamwork, employee involvement, and teach the use of other tools and techniques.

BUILDING A FIRM FOUNDATION

The TQM culture must be supported by three strong and level pillars anchored in a firm foundation.

The foundation of today's total quality culture is the same as that required of any successful business. The firm must provide a product or service that customers will purchase at a price that will permit the firm to make a profit and remain in business. This foundation must support three pillars as follows:

PILLAR #1

This pillar focuses on improving customer perception of the product and service, not on beating the competition or gaining market share. (If the three U.S. automobile manufacturers would have focused on responding to their customers and expanding the market, rather than trying to gain market share, they may not have all lost market share to the Japanese.)

PILLAR #2

This pillar emphasizes educating, training, and leading employees to greater involvement in the business process.

PILLAR #3

This pillar assists employees with tools and techniques to systematically address major issues. These tools and techniques include teams, flow-charting, benchmarking, reengineering, brainstorming, Pareto analysis, cause-and-effect diagrams, ISO 9000, Malcolm Baldrige National Quality Award, and Statistical Process Control (SPC).

LOOKING IN DETAIL

The first pillar, the customer's perception of the product or service, can be influenced more by the treatment the customer receives from employees than by the functional value of the actual product or service. This is supported by a survey conducted by the Forum Corporation on companies in the manufacturing and service industries. Survey results indicated that two-thirds of the people surveyed switched to a new product or service because of the way they were treated (or ignored), rather than by the value of the product or service.

Richard Melman, founder of the successful Chicago restaurant, Lettuce Entertain You Enterprises, believes his servers are one of the key assets to the business because they are the "restaurant" in the customer's eyes. The perception of a good restaurant is not based only on the taste and temperature of the food served. The server can significantly adjust the customer's perception of his restaurant experience.

To comply with the second pillar, executives and managers should be spending the major part of their time leading the workforce along a path that will insure the current vision is understood and being pursued. Managers, therefore, will not have the time, or the knowledge, to make the "shop floor" decisions. Those are left to the people who are closest to the action and understand how the actions support the company vision.

To increase employee involvement, there must be an atmosphere that encourages employees to take on responsibility without the fear of failure. Employees must also have the necessary knowledge, training, and skill that will give them the confidence to make decisions based on the team's analysis of the problem. Executives and managers should help their employees by developing the vision and atmosphere that will lead to the desired culture change.

Many companies attempting to embrace the total quality concept are expecting to use the tools described in the third pillar, without the proper education, training, and atmosphere. This is like the Russian farmer who was beating his first tractor with a whip because it had stalled.

Another major stumbling block is placing too much emphasis on a particular tool. If the major emphasis is on benchmarking, people may find themselves playing catch-up. The goal should be to get outside of the "paradigm" by doing a better job of responding to customer's (and desired non-customer's) perception of product and service. This is enforced by the following quote from Peter Drucker in *The Wall Street Journal:* "In fact, the most probable assumption is that no currently working business will be valid 10 years hence—at least not without major modifications."

The same might also be said for reengineering, which improves a business process. Organizations must be careful not to spend too much time and effort improving the business process for something with a decreasing demand (hula hoops, carburetors, etc.).

The basic concern must be that the atmosphere exists to support and encourage the cultural change process. The foundation must support the pillars that are, in turn, strong enough and level enough to adequately support the culture.

The Ford Motor Company provides an example of a successful application of total quality improvement. From 1978 to 1980, Ford's U.S.

market share dropped from 23.5 to 17.2 percent. Then Chairman Donald Peterson was quoted as saying, "If we aren't customer-driven, our cars won't be either." With the help of Dr. Deming, they began implementing a new strategy that is now history.

A firm will not successfully achieve the benefits of total quality without first recognizing a need and then establishing the foundation for the continuous change. This is a slow and deliberate process that requires a commitment and persistence. There is no short cut in the continuous journey toward the total quality culture.

ADAPTATION OF TRADITIONAL HUMAN RESOURCES PROCESSES FOR TOTAL QUALITY ENVIRONMENTS*
by Robert D. Costigan

The worldwide total quality (TQ) movement, which emphasizes quality, continuous improvement, empowerment, and teamwork, is redefining the context in which workers behave in organizations. Traditional human resources (HR) processes appear to be more compatible with the bureaucratic organization than with the TQ organization. For instance, some of these HR processes tend to be static rather than dynamic, and oriented to the individual rather than the team. This article addresses the concern of how HR processes, such as job analysis, recruitment, selection, training, performance appraisal, and discipline, should adapt to support the cultural changes occurring in TQ organizations. Implications and directions for future research are also considered.

INTRODUCTION

Nadler and Tushman's (1980) congruence model says that organizational effectiveness is contingent upon how well the organization's subsystems fit together as a whole. The human resources (HR) subsystem of the 1970s and 1980s organization typically stressed job analysis, work samples, technical training, top-down appraisals, and progressive discipline. The traditional HR subsystem seems to be incongruent with the total quality (TQ) philosophy because the HR subsystem was originally designed for the bureaucratic organization. Allowing total quality organizations (TQOs) to function with a traditional HR subsystem is analogous to pouring new wine into old skins. Thus, HR departments in TQOs are scrambling to redefine themselves in the context of TQ.

TQ themes such as continuous improvement, quality, personal growth, self-direction, empowerment, teamwork, and leadership need to be integrated into all organizational subsystems, including HR. The remaining sections of this article will be spent redefining traditional HR processes, such as job analysis, recruitment, selection, training, performance appraisal, and discipline, to make them compatible with TQ themes. First, the prevailing cultural themes operating in TQOs will be briefly reviewed.

W. Edwards Deming, a leader of the worldwide TQ movement, developed 14 points and 7 deadly diseases that have radically altered the look of modern-day organizations (Walton 1990). Deming was highly critical of merit pay, individual bonuses, ranking employees on the basis of overall performance, and management by objectives (Deming 1993; Walton 1986, 1990). Deming believed that ranking and merit pay single individuals out as poor performers and ultimately rob them of their dignity. Merit pay and individual bonuses fuel employees' extrinsic motivation—that is, motivation that comes from external sources such as the boss—but do very little for increasing intrinsic motivation—that is, motivation that comes from liking to perform the job. The organization's assumption that poorly

---

*Reprinted with permission from ASQC *Quality Management Journal*, Spring 1995. Robert D. Costigan is an assistant professor of management at St. John Fisher College (Rochester, NY).

performing workers are responsible for an organization's lack of profitability is, in his view, terribly misguided (Deming 1975). A fundamental attribution error is oftentimes committed when things go awry, with employees being blamed instead of possible breakdowns in the system.

"Full participation and personal growth" is often used to describe the kind of working environment that TQ workers enjoy. Alderfer's (1972) concept of growth need or Hackman and Oldham's (1976) growth need strength (GNS) is closely related to the intrinsic motivation concept. Persons with high GNS or high intrinsic motivation, working in an enriched environment, have a positive regard for improving the way they perform their work (Hackman and Oldham 1976). They take the initiative on their own to analyze and change work processes. These employees thrive on the organization's push for continuous improvement (Waldman 1994). They strive for excellence, not for extrinsic awards, but because they feel personal gratification in providing customers with high-quality products and services in a timely fashion and at a low cost.

Management's role in organizations that value continuous improvement is to manage change, meaning that processes need to change and so do the workers (Imai 1986). TQOs ask all levels of employees to become thinking employees, continuously searching for ways to improve the work being done (Deming 1993). Workers at all echelons in TQOs are merging thinking and doing in their work (Senge 1994). Smart employees who work exceedingly hard are desired.

The leadership imperative of upper-level management in TQOs is to be a catalyst for change, articulating a philosophy of management that is no longer driven by control but driven to meet customers' requirements (Anderson, Rungtusanathan, and Schroeder 1994). Upper-level management is to rid the organization of bureaucratic impediments that, at times, originate in the "policing" activities of quality departments (Senge 1994). Leaders of self-directed teams (SDTs) are to be more facilitative than directive. These leaders are to communicate a clear vision, act on the basis of principle rather than personal gain, empower team members, and listen and ask relevant questions. Leadership within SDTs is the responsibility of each team member. Individual team members assume responsibility for the improvement of one or more of the team's processes (Brower 1994).

Paralleling Trist, Susman, and Brown's (1977) work in the area of sociotechnical sys-

tems theory, SDTs have emerged as a powerful force in the TQ movement. SDTs usually have 5-20 rank-and-file workers who are entrusted with the authority and responsibility of overseeing a complete set of work processes (Brower 1994). In time, these teams evolve to a point where they can function without formal supervision. SDTs are capable of studying and improving their processes, conducting effective meetings, and managing conflict effectively. Skill development in each of these areas, as well as knowledge of statistics, quality techniques, (for example, cause-and-effect diagrams, flowcharts), and basic computer education, are focal for SDT members (Yeatts, Hipskind, and Barnes 1994). TQOs rely on extensive training and coaching to remove any gaps in these skill and knowledge areas. Once the initial phase of this development process is completed, decisions concerning quality, customer service, and so on can be based on accumulated data, as well as the collective wisdom of SDTs, rather than on hunches and simplifying heuristics (Walton 1986).

In sum, continuous improvement, SDTs, empowerment, leadership, personal growth, and quality are themes that strongly characterize TQOs. Recommendations for redefining HR processes, such as job analysis, recruitment, selection, training, performance appraisal, and discipline in the light of these themes will now be presented.

JOB ANALYSIS

Job analysis, as traditionally understood, is a process of systematically collecting detailed information, such as tasks, knowledge, skills, and abilities, about a particular job. In the bureaucratic organization, job analysis is the foundation for recruitment, selection, training, performance appraisal, and compensation processes. These HR activities cannot properly proceed without a detailed picture of the job. Existing job analysis methods seem to be incongruent with the needs of TQOs. For instance, the cornerstone of two popular job analysis methods, functional job analysis and task inventory procedure, is the listing of relevant task statements for each job in the organization and then rating each task with appropriate scales (for example, the relative importance of each task). These task statements and ratings are then used for different HR purposes, such as classifying jobs and assigning pay. Jobs with a fixed bundle of tasks and a fixed set of qualifications, however, may be a thing of the past. Job content in TQOs is fluid, not static; broadly defined, not narrowly defined; and team oriented, not focused toward the individual worker. Knowledge, skills, abilities, and other characteristics (KSAOs) necessary to perform yesterday's, and some of today's jobs may reflect the KSAOs of an obsolescent specialist (Aaron 1994). In some cases, such a specialist may be too rigid and closed-minded for the TQ work setting.

TQOs have some serious choices to make when it comes to the issue of job analysis.

1. Sanchez et al. (1993) suggested that existing methods could be modified by incorporating TQ themes, such as quality, customer service, and continuous improvement. Each task assigned to a worker could be rated not only on scales, such as frequency and importance, but also on TQ scales, such as customer focus, quality, and continuous improvement. For instance, the extent to which each task involves a customer perspective could be assessed.

2. Instead of highly specific task statements, TQOs could focus attention on broad duty statements providing increased flexibility (Sanchez et al. 1993). A list of general duties and corresponding KSAOs would then be constructed to reflect the work necessary to meet the needs of customers.

3. TQOs could move away from the job analysis concept and toward team analysis and organization analysis. The unit of analysis would no longer be specific activities in a particular job but would be the work assigned to the team. In this way, the team members have the responsibility for performing all of the processes involved in providing a final product or service to customers. Instead of a job description and job specification—that is, a list of KSAOs relevant to a job—a team description and team specification would be produced via team analysis.

Key characteristics of the organization's mission, vision, and culture should also play a role in shaping HR activities. Therefore, a systematic process of identifying key values articulated in the organization's mission and vision statements, as well as values in the organization's in-

formal culture, can be used to specify KSAOs necessary to work effectively across jobs in the organization. This process, referred to as organization analysis (Offermann and Gowing 1993), produces an organization description; that is, a summary of the organization's mission, vision, and culture from the employee perspective and the KSAOs necessary to work effectively in this culture.

Lawler's (1994) notion of moving from job-based to competency-based organizations corresponds to organization analysis. A competency-based orientation focuses on the individual's capabilities and accomplishments instead of job requirements, allowing for increased flexibility. For instance, the competency-based organization selects individuals who fit the characteristics of the organization and not a specific job.

RECRUITMENT

Recruitment Sources

Most organizations have not scrutinized the effectiveness of their recruitment sources. By default, newspaper advertisements, employment agencies, and internal recruitment are used to attract applications for position openings. After reviewing the recruiting source literature. Wanous and Colella (1989) concluded that different recruitment sources yield different voluntary turnover rates. The results of Conard and Ashworth's (1986) meta-analysis (an analysis of the results of previous studies) revealed that the voluntary turnover rate of employees recruited via employee referral was 24.9 percent and 29.8 percent lower than employment agencies and newspaper ads, respectively. The turnover rate of walk-ins was 19.4 percent and 24.6 percent lower than employees recruited through employment agencies and newspaper ads, respectively. Across occupations, recruitment sources such as employee referral and walk-ins produce the lowest voluntary turnover rates (Wanous 1992).

Breaugh (1981) found that the quality of job performance, measured with supervisory ratings, was higher when research scientists at a midwestern chemical company were initially recruited at a professional convention, through a professional journal ad, or as a walk-in instead of through college recruitment. That is, the mean performance ratings on a five-point quality dimension were 4.15 for scientists recruited at a convention or with a journal ad, 3.94 with walk-ins, and 3.33 with college placement. Considering the sample, this relationship between recruitment sources and quality of job performance makes a great deal of sense.

Heeding Deming's call for data-driven decision making in TQOs, it is recommended that recruitment data in TQOs be analyzed to discover whether certain recruitment sources yield low voluntary turnover and high performance, not only on the quality dimension but also on other TQ dimensions such as adaptability, leadership, and continuous improvement. Following Caldwell and Spivey's (1983) suggestion, this analysis should be done separately for each minority group to develop a high-caliber yet diverse TQ workforce.

Realistic Organization Previews

A realistic job preview (RJP) is a recruitment strategy that provides a realistic picture of the job to applicants (Wanous 1992). Applicants are given accurate job information, which means both positive and negative aspects of the job are shared. One intent of the RJP is to reduce the new hire's initial level of job dissatisfaction. RJPs should theoretically reduce the organization's voluntary turnover rate because there are better matches between the qualifications of the new hires and the requirements of the jobs. Wanous (1992) proposed a model that incorporates four mediating variables. These are met expectations, coping ability, air of honesty, and self-selection. Theoretically, RJPs "vaccinate" applicants with a small dose of the job, lessening the ill effects of unmet expectations. Met expectations are then hypothesized to lead to increased coping ability, increased appreciation of the organization for being honest, and increased number of applicants who decide not to pursue the job opening (that is, self-selection).

As the name implies, RJPs focus on specific jobs. Since jobs in TQOs tend to be fluid as well as broadly defined, RJPs appear less useful than would a realistic organizational preview (ROP). ROPs provide applicants with accurate information about the organization's culture and climate (Breaugh 1983). Applicants are exposed to the following:

1. Prevailing corporate values; for example, valuing the customer

2. Performance norms; for example, high quality of performance

3. HR strategies unique to TQOs; for example, self-directed teams

4. Appropriate behaviors; for example, cross-functional integration

Similar to RJPs, ROPs are intended to reduce the shock that new hires may encounter in TQ environments and ultimately lead to an improved person-organization fit (Bowen and Lawler 1992). It should be noted that organizations providing RJPs and ROPs are viewed more positively by applicants; according to Wanous and Colella (1989), applicants perceive RJPs and ROPs as the organization's way of showing care and concern. They believe that this care and concern experienced by applicants will in time produce increased commitment to the organization.

Consistent with the call for empowerment in TQOs, employees can be a part of the design and implementation of ROPs. The content of the ROPs could, in part, be developed with input from team members. They might be able to provide applicants with both an organization and work perspective that HR people could not. As for implementation of ROPs, team members could informally meet with applicants to provide realistic organization information. RJP researchers (Breaugh and Billings 1988; Popovich and Wanous 1982) have encouraged the use of job incumbents to deliver RJP information to applicants. Incumbents are perceived by applicants to be trustworthy and knowledgeable sources. Two-way communication in the form of questions and answers between incumbents and applicants is also encouraged.

SELECTION

Some organizations attempt to increase validity (the ability to predict applicant job performance) by utilizing work sample tests. Work samples give applicants the chance to perform the job to determine their suitability for the opening. These tests are content valid, meaning that the content of the test approximates the content of the job. "Seeing is believing" is a saying that applies to work samples. Seeing good performance on the test is believing that applicants will perform well on the job. Since the work assigned to employees in TQOs changes frequently, work samples that are highly specific to a set of tasks in a job may not be suitable. In short, the person-job fit concept is giving way to the person-organization fit concept in TQOs (Bowen, Ledford, and Nathan 1991; Waldman 1994).

Aaron's (1994) KSAOs of a generalist, which are not job-specific but organization-specific, appear compatible with the needs of TQOs. Examples of these KSAOs include clear thinking, adaptability, ability to work in a team environment, leadership, noble character, ability to communicate effectively, and conscientiousness. Considering the speed with which work will change in TQ environments, KSAOs of the generalist, rather than the KSAOs of an obsolescent specialist, may make greater sense. KSAOs appropriate for enhancing the person-TQO fit, such as quick learning, high GNS, and ability to relate effectively with others, are not easily assessable with work samples since there would likely be a low correspondence between test content and work content. By default, other selection devices such as biographical data (biodata), structured interviews, personality tests, and cognitive ability tests may be more appropriate for TQ environments.

Quick Learners

Hunter and Hunter's (1984) review of selection processes provides a strong clue to the assessment of one's ability to learn quickly. They reported that cognitive ability tests measuring numerical ability, verbal reasoning, verbal comprehension, and similar skills have an excellent record in predicting performance across many kinds of entry-level jobs. Specifically, Hunter and Hunter (1984) looked at 425 validation studies and found a mean corrected validity of 0.53. This was corrected for both unreliability in the criterion and range restriction. This validity coefficient of 0.53 is the correlation between cognitive ability test scores and performance scores. Considering that validity coefficients can range from −1 to +1, this particular validity coefficient is impressive relative to other workplace predictors. There is, however, a downside to these tests. Cognitive test scores for some minority groups are historically lower than scores for nonminority groups. Organizational goals of increasing workforce diversity and increasing the cognitive abilities of the workforce may, at times, be at odds (Hunter and Hunter 1984).

In Mayfield's (1964) review of the interviewing literature, he concluded that interviewers are

particularly adept at assessing applicant intelligence. In a reanalysis of Hunter and Hunter's (1984) data, Huffcutt and Arthur (1994) found that the more structured interviews, versus the less structured, produced a mean corrected validity of 0.56. This validity is comparable to the validity of the cognitive ability tests. Hence, structured interviews appear to be another way of predicting performance in TQOs as well as identifying quick learners.

GNS

Biodata items are excellent workplace predictors of performance, especially when they are verifiable and historical (Gatewood and Field 1990). Schneider and Schmitt (1986) reported biodata validates ranging from 0.25 to a high of 0.50. Likewise, Hunter and Hunter's (1984) review revealed a mean corrected validity for 12 biodata studies to be an impressive 0.37. Feuer and Lee's (1988) biodata items, such as, "I find it enjoyable to constantly learn new things about my job," may indicate the applicant's GNS and fit for a continuous learning environment.

Ulrich and Trumbo (1965) concluded that the structured interview may be effective in predicting the applicant's motivation. Consistent with TQ's theme of empowerment, team members could be entrusted with the responsibility of constructing and conducting these interviews (Blackburn and Rosen 1993). That is, designing valid, structured interview questions and then interviewing candidates for the team's openings can be effectively accomplished by team members, with appropriate training. The results of Wiesner and Cronshaw's (1988) meta-analysis provided strong evidence for the effectiveness of team interviews. They reported that structured team interviews using a consensus decision-making approach produced a mean corrected validity of 0.64.

The results of Barrick and Mount's (1991) meta-analysis suggest that personality tests assessing the trait of conscientiousness are surprisingly good predictors of performance across job categories. In their sample of 12,893 managers, salespersons, professionals, police officers, and skilled/semiskilled workers, the estimated true score correlation between conscientiousness scores and performance was a statistically significant but modest 0.23. Instruments used to measure applicant conscientiousness include, among others, Personal Characteristics Inventory and Hogan Personality Inventory. There appears to be a relationship between the personality trait of conscientiousness and one's need to grow professionally, that is, GNS. This may be true since Digman's (1989) research indicated that the conscientiousness construct not only reflects dependability but also achievement orientation, perseverance, and intrinsic motivation. Utilizing a reliable personality test measuring conscientiousness with other selection strategies, such as cognitive ability tests and structured interviews, may prove effective in predicting performance in TQOs.

Interpersonal Skills

Interpersonal skills keenly needed in TQOs are as follows:

1. Ability to work effectively in a team environment

2. Ability to communicate effectively with diverse groups, which also means relating cross-functionally

3. Ability to relate effectively with customers

4. Ability to lead

Structured interviews, such as situational interviews, have long been considered the method of choice when it comes to assessing the applicant's level of interpersonal skills (Ulrich and Trumbo 1965). McDaniel et al.'s (1994) meta-analysis, which included 946 interviews, revealed a mean corrected validity of situational interviews to be an effective 0.50. For instance, interview questions that ask the applicant, "How would you deal with an angry customer who shouted profanities at you?" may be effective in predicting performance. The content of each hypothetical question might reflect the theme expressed in a team or organization KSAO.

Again, biodata teams, embedded perhaps in the application form, may assist with the prediction of employee performance on work teams. Wagner and Moch's (1986) individualism-collectivism scale (for example, "I prefer to work with others in a work group rather than to work alone") might be helpful in assessing the applicant's desire to work in a team environment. Items in Feuer and Lee's (1988) inventory (for example, "I believe it's important for hourly workers and managers to work together") might play the same role as Wagner and Moch's (1986) scale. Russell et al. (1990) offer some biodata

items that may predict teamwork, such as, "How often have you set aside personal differences in order to get the job done?" Biodata items in the Russell et al. (1990) study were developed with life-history essays written by job incumbents. Biodata items in their study effectively predicted performance as well as peer ratings of leadership.

TRAINING

Needs Assessment

A prevalent theme in TQOs is lifelong employee learning (Senge 1994). Not only do TQOs expect lifelong learning, but high GNS workers also expect it. Continual employee learning will become a way of organizational life. In line with TQ's empowerment notion, Goff, Sheckley, and Hastings (1994) suggested that TQ workers should become self-directed in their learning. That is, they should be responsible for assessing their own learning needs and initiating action to meet those needs. When employees notice performance slippage or foresee a need for a specific knowledge base or skill, they would initiate corrective action and find suitable training. Self-directed learning should increase employees' acceptance of training content as well as commitment to transfer the training from the classroom to the work setting. This is a positive transfer. Self-directed learning in many ways is no different from the old notion of technical training, except that employees, not supervisors, are responsible for needs assessment. Fellow team members could also be responsible for assessing employee training needs. Research, such as that by Fox, Ben-Nahum, and Yinon (1989) and Kane and Lawler (1978), has shown that peer assessments are generally reliable and valid, especially in noncompetitive work environments.

Training Methods

Considering the emphasis of hiring highly motivated workers in TQOs, training methods suited to adult learners may be especially effective. Methods that are active, trainee-centered, and team-centered, such as case discussion and behavior modeling, seem appropriate for these continuous learning environments. Such methods complement the more traditional training methods, such as classroom and lecture, best suited for instructing trainees on other TQ concepts, such as cause-and-effect diagrams and Pareto charts.

Mentor programs are typically reserved for the development of managers. These programs allow organizations to meet several needs: meaningful work, career development, and employee acculturation. With personal growth and empowerment as prominent TQ themes, informal mentoring programs that dip into the lower echelon of TQOs may pay off. Creating a mentoring climate that gives rank-and-file workers an opportunity, if they wish, to enhance the meaningfulness of their work, to develop in their careers, and to grow in their understanding of the organization's culture, appears to nicely fit the quality philosophy.

The informal mentorship concept advocated here is distinguished from formal mentorships. Spontaneous mentoring relationships are encouraged in the informal mentoring program, whereas formal mentoring programs are highly structured and managed by the organization (Chao, Walz, and Gardner 1992). These researchers found that protégés in informal mentorships received more career-related support from their mentors than did protégés in formal mentorships. They also reported that protégés in informal mentorships experienced significantly higher job satisfaction as well as organizational socialization than did nonmentored individuals. Thus, the informally mentored protégés learned information necessary to adjust to their role. Since the manager's role in TQOs is evolving into a coaching role, perhaps rank-and-file employees could choose leaders and managers in other departments to be informal mentors.

Evaluation of TQ Training

In the past, corporate training programs have either not been evaluated or have been ineffectively evaluated. At best, the reactions of participants to the training may have been collected and the judgment of the training program's effectiveness based solely on the results of these surveys. Long ago, Kirkpatrick (1959) advised that four criteria be used in the evaluation process.

1. Participant reaction
2. Learning that has occurred because of the training
3. On-the-job behavior changes

4. Positive organization outcomes

Kirkpatrick's last two criteria are considered the best because they indicate whether or not the newly learned skills or knowledge have been transferred to the work setting. Simply put, training is deemed successful when positive on-the-job behavior changes are noted in the latest performance appraisal and when favorable organization outcomes, measured in an objective way, are also noted after training. Considering the money that is being spent on TQ training, the recent push for treating quality programs as investment decisions [for example, Greising's (1994) return on quality], and Deming's call for more data-based decision making, it makes sense to use these criteria—with an appropriate research design—to evaluate the effectiveness of TQ training. Both behavior and outcome criteria could incorporate relevant TQ themes, such as customer service, quality, teamwork, and cost reductions, to ensure that the training effects are consistent with the overall strategy of TQOs.

After receiving training, employees could be empowered to develop appropriate TQ-related criteria to evaluate the training. With such participation, employees would become thoroughly familiar with training objectives and the corresponding measures used to assess whether these objectives have been met. Their acceptance of, and commitment to achieving training objectives should increase. The likelihood that the newly learned skill or knowledge is actually transferred to the work setting should be greater as a result. The training content provides employees with shortcuts and strategies to perform exceedingly well against these criteria. Admittedly, it may be difficult to evaluate the effectiveness of training content when trainees are allowed to develop relevant criteria; but this can easily be resolved with an appropriate research design.

PERFORMANCE APPRAISAL

In Deming's view, many traditional appraisal strategies generate humiliation, fear, self-defense, and competition. His disdain for management by objectives (MBO), which emphasizes end results over processes, is extensively reported (Deming 1993). The likelihood of process inefficiencies, a short-term managerial perspective, and unethical conduct is increased when upper-level management is most concerned with the achievement of objectives and the bottom line. Deming contended that performance should not be evaluated for the purpose of dispensing rewards and punishments but for feedback and continuous self-improvement. With this new direction for appraisals in TQOs, supervisors and workers alike could be allowed to participate in the development of the performance appraisal system. Increased employee acceptance of the appraisal process should occur with such participation.

Appraisal Formats

Organizations have shown marginal interest in knowing their raters' preferences for different rating formats. Since the performance appraisal process in TQOs is attempting to foster self-improvement and not the attainment of monetary rewards, it should be a user-friendly system. User-friendliness should be broadened to include not only the format preferences of managers but also the preferences of those being evaluated. The appraisal format that is best suited to meet the varied needs of both managers and employees should be adopted. The one stipulation that TQOs could make is that the TQ themes of quality, customer service, and teamwork permeate the items in the preferred format.

Moving one step further, TQOs should consider allowing both managerial and nonmanagerial personnel the opportunity to coproduce the format. Utilizing a multitrait-multimethod approach to assessing validity and error, Friedman and Cornelius (1976) found that raters who constructed either traditional graphic rating scales or Smith and Kendall's (1963) behaviorally anchored rating scales rated with less halo error and more convergent validity (interrater agreement) than did raters who were uninvolved in the scale-construction process. Friedman and Cornelius attributed the improved psychometric quality of ratings to the involved raters' increased understanding of the rating instrument and a better understanding of the job. The benefits attained through this empowerment process (that is, involvement in scale construction) should offset the amount of time and expense involved.

Diary keeping (Balzer 1986; Bernardin and Walter 1977) may be a useful appraisal strategy in TQOs. Both raters and ratees could be taught to keep diaries on their own performance as well

as the performance of others. Ongoing accounts of performance, rich with behavioral detail, could provide sound feedback and help with the self-improvement process. Diaries might be formatted along the lines of TQ themes—quality, teamwork, cost consciousness, and customer service—and brief daily entries would then be placed in appropriate TQ categories. Information from the diary would be the basis for the more formal appraisal, improving, it is hoped, the quality of these ratings. In support of diary keeping's effectiveness, DeNisi, Robbins, and Cafferty (1989) found that performance ratings were more accurate when raters kept diaries than when raters did not keep diaries. Similarly, Bernardin and Walter (1977) reported less leniency, less halo error, and greater interrater agreement when diaries were kept, versus when they were not kept.

Appraisal Training

Performance appraisal researchers have thoroughly evaluated the effectiveness of different rater training programs, such as rater error training, frame-of-reference training, and observation training. In his literature review of rater training programs, Smith (1986) concluded that the more involved participants are in the training program, through discussion, practice, and feedback, the greater the rating accuracy and the lower the leniency error. Training programs that provide raters with a common understanding of the job, of the scales to be used, and a frame of reference of what good, bad, and average performance are, have fared the best in increasing rating accuracy (Smith 1986). In a recent rater training study, Stamoulis and Hauenstein (1993) found that frame-of-reference training, which provides raters with a common understanding of what good, bad, and average performance are, increased raters' differential accuracy relative to a control group not receiving training.

Organizations have not, however, considered the orientation and training needs of the employees who are being evaluated. It is commonly accepted that self-ratings produce leniency error (Harris and Schaubroeck 1988; Thornton 1980). TQ employees are frequently being asked to rate themselves (self-ratings) and rate each other (peer ratings), but little effort is made to orient and train them to observe performance from a common frame of reference. Raters in TQOs, which include managerial and nonmanagerial workers, could be given clear behavioral examples depicting excellent performance in a TQ environment (for example, an employee suggesting a cost-saving idea or helping team members catch up with assignments). Such training should enhance the quality of their ratings as well as increase their acceptance of, and commitment to the appraisal process.

Sources of Ratings

The best way to provide performance feedback to TQ workers is with 360-degree appraisal feedback (Nowack 1993). Feedback is gathered from "all around" workers. Multiple raters from different organizational perspectives, such as bosses, the workers themselves, co-workers, subordinates, internal customers, and external customers, complete the ratings on all TQ employees. Averages are computed for each employee on each performance dimension and item. These averages can then be charted over time to ascertain whether workers are showing signs of continuous progress. Nowack (1993) referred to charting one's performance progress as *ipsative scoring*. The strength of 360-degree appraisals is having a number of raters from different levels of the organizational hierarchy, as well as raters outside the organization, such as external customers, evaluate workers. With so many raters, the biases of the few idiosyncratic raters have a less dramatic effect on the quality of the ratings.

DISCIPLINE

The progressive-discipline system has historically been used by supervisors to deal with problem employees. Under this system, supervisors hope to cure the low performers' problems by progressively levying more severe penalties when the particular problems persist. These penalties include oral warnings, written warnings, three-day suspensions without pay, and termination. This system treats problem employees in a childlike way, creating an adversarial relationship between supervisors and employees (Grote 1994). With such a discipline system, fear and failure are emphasized, producing a workplace that is contrary to Deming's ideal.

Since self-direction is a theme in TQOs, an alternative system—discipline without punishment—might be better. Unlike the progressive-discipline system, poor performers in the discipline-without-punishment system take personal responsibility for correcting their own

problems (Campbell, Fleming, and Grote 1985; Sherman and Lucia 1992; Grote 1994). They are treated in an adultlike manner by the organization, in the hope that self-discipline, rather than supervisory discipline, will eventually correct substandard performance. Punishment is not emphasized with this approach. Supervisors handle poor performers in a less confrontational manner, coaching rather than forcing behavioral change. They provide reminders instead of warnings and may direct the problem workers to an employee assistance program (EAP), when available. EAPs provide employees with personal counseling in a variety of areas, such as drug and alcohol abuse and family and financial counseling. Undoubtedly, the most controversial aspect of the discipline-without-punishment system is the paid decision-making leave. According to Grote (1994), this one-day paid leave gives problem employees time to reevaluate their future with the company. It also demonstrates the organization's sincerity in wanting to retain these employees. Campbell, Fleming, and Grote (1985) offered anecdotal evidence for the effectiveness of discipline without punishment. At one company, the change to this positive approach from a progressive-discipline approach produced (1) fewer successful unemployment compensation claims after termination; (2) less absenteeism; (3) fewer grievances; and (4) fewer arbitration hearings. In short, discipline without punishment appears to be more in line with the coaching role of managers in TQOs than is the progressive-discipline approach.

CONCLUSION

TQ themes of quality, empowerment, continuous improvement, leadership, personal growth, and teamwork should affect the look of HR processes in quality-minded organizations. The purpose of this article is not to suggest a radical shift in thinking of the HR concept but to suggest modifications in HR processes to make them compatible with TQ themes. Specific modifications and recommendations presented thus far will now be summarized.

First, existing job analysis methods appear to be out of sync with the HR needs of TQOs. These methods, such as functional job analysis and task inventory procedure, appear too job-centered and static. In this article, three alternatives were suggested: (1) incorporate TQ themes into existing methods; (2) use broader duty statements; and (3) focus on teams and/or the organization instead of the job. Another possibility is to ignore the job analysis concept completely. Some of these options are not without risk, especially from a legal perspective. Both the *Americans with Disabilities Act* of 1990 and the *Uniform Guidelines on Employee Selection Procedures* of 1978 emphasize the importance of having job-related selection processes. It is uncertain whether the U.S. Equal Employment Opportunity Commission and the courts will view organization analysis with complete favor.

Second, evaluating the effectiveness of recruitment sources with TQ criteria, as well as adopting ROPs, are recruitment strategies thought to be consistent with the needs of TQOs. Both recommendations involve few costs and have potential in certain key outcome areas.

Third, selection in TQOs tends toward person-organization fit over person-job fit. Therefore, alternative selection processes, such as biodata, that can assess person-organization fit were proposed instead of work sample tests that, by definition, assess the applicant's fit for a specific job.

GNS is an important concept for the enriched work environment within TQOs. If the ideal of continuous employee learning and continuous process improvement is to happen, the makeup of the TQ workforce should consist of high GNS-type individuals. GNS is not only important from a selection perspective but also from other HR perspectives. Training, performance appraisal, and discipline systems have been redefined in this article on the assumption that the TQ workforce consists primarily of high GNS-type people. The success of training's self-directed learning, appraisal's continuous improvement, and even discipline without punishment depends on a workforce that is ready and willing to grow professionally.

Fourth, training programs in traditional, bureaucratic organizations are initiated and evaluated in a top-down fashion. For example, a supervisor identifies a subordinate's training need via the performance appraisal. In this article, how TQ themes of self-direction and empowerment can be integrated into the different phases of training were discussed. Trainees in TQOs might be responsible for assessment of their own training needs as well as for the development of relevant behavioral and outcome criteria to evaluate the effectiveness of the training.

Fifth, it was suggested that empowerment play an integral role in the shaping of performance appraisals. When the purpose of the appraisal changes from an award-dispensing mechanism to a feedback mechanism for the sake of continuous improvement, it makes sense to allow managers and nonmanagers to coproduce the appraisal system (for example, scale construction) and then, with appropriate training, to implement the redesigned system (that is, self- and peer ratings).

FUTURE RESEARCH

On the basis of these five recommendations, directions for future research will now be considered. First, as a replacement for job analysis, new data collection methods that focus on the work to be done, on the team and in the organization, should be developed. These work analysis methods should be able to quickly identify the team's responsibilities, the organization's mission and culture, and appropriate KSAOs for both the team and the organization. These psychometrically sound methods should also be suitable for the various HR needs of the organization, such as compensation and selection.

Second, continued work in evaluating the effectiveness of alternative recruitment sources, in light of TQ values, should be fruitful. With the arrival of employee leasing and contract workers as sources of labor, scrutinizing their effectiveness is encouraged.

Third, the positive effects of ROPs, such as higher self-selection, higher job satisfaction, and lower voluntary turnover, may prove to be more powerful than the effects of RJPs. Recruiting individuals for the TQ organization rather than a specific job may be an abstract process. Applicants' preconceived notions of the job may generally be more accurate and realistic, thereby limiting the potential benefits of RJPs. On the other hand, applicants' preconceived notions of the organization's work environment may be less clear, thereby enhancing the potential of ROPs. Future research should consider whether ROPs produce more powerful effects, such as higher self-selection, higher job satisfaction, and lower voluntary turnover, than do RJPs.

Fourth, since ROPs and recruitment sources, such as employee referral and walk-ins, are primarily intended to reduce voluntary turnover, it may be of interest to assess the relationship between voluntary turnover in TQOs and a lagged measure of customer satisfaction/customer retention. If, in fact, there is a strong inverse relationship, TQOs would then have an incentive to reduce voluntary turnover to a healthy level.

Fifth, selection strategies developed specially for TQOs should be validated. That is, demonstrating the relationship between these predictors and relevant TQ performance criteria, such as quality of performance, is strongly suggested. Developing biodata items and GNS instruments that are valid across TQ environments would also be constructive research.

Another research issue to consider is the effectiveness of the personality trait of conscientiousness in predicting group performance in TQOs. Recall that the validity of personality tests measuring this trait was statistically significant but modest (that is, 0.23) in predicting individual performance. Hiring more conscientious employees for SDTs should be crucial to the success of these teams. Highly conscientious team members who exert maximum effort to team affairs may enhance group performance, whereas team members low in this trait may look more often for opportunities to loaf, at the expense of the group's performance. Employee conscientiousness may be less crucial in bureaucratic, non-team environments because supervisors' controlling activities reinforce employees' individual performance obligations.

Seventh, adopting a selection strategy that stresses the person-organization fit, not the person-job fit, may invite more bias into the selection process. Simply put, deciding an applicant's fit to the organization may be less defined and involve more inferences than deciding the applicant's fit to a specific job. If given leeway, decision makers may idiosyncratically interpret each applicant's organizational fit—that is, the right chemistry. Research should consider this possibility and demonstrate whether or not the person-organization fit approach produces more bias than does the person-job fit approach.

Eighth, researchers investigating the effectiveness of traditional training programs have continually expressed concern for the lack of positive transfer of content learned in the training setting to the job setting. Does self-assessment of training needs improve positive transfer relative to the more traditional needs assessment approaches? Does trainee involvement in the development of evaluation criteria improve positive transfer relative to the more traditional evaluation approaches?

Ninth, performance appraisal researchers should consider the effects of empowerment in a number of appraisal domains. Specifically, empowerment—that is, allowing managers and nonmanagers an opportunity to select or even construct the appraisal system—may lead to improved appraisals in TQOs—that is, increased reliability and validity. Also, just as important, empowerment leads to increased worker acceptance of, and commitment to, the appraisal process. This deserves formal investigation. Furthermore, employee perception of procedural justice might be enhanced because of employee involvement in the appraisal process. Procedural justice concerns the fairness of the process by which personnel decisions are made within organizations (Folger and Greenberg 1985). One of Folger and Greenberg's six rules for attaining procedural justice is the Representativeness Rule, which means that the process addresses the concerns of all affected employees. Co-opting TQ workers with appraisal strategies that solicit their input (for example, scale construction) should not only improve the quality of self- and peer ratings but also, in the eyes of the ratee, increase the perceived fairness of the appraisal process (that is, procedural justice). Job satisfaction and organizational commitment may be increased when ratees perceive the appraisal process to be procedurally just (Folger, Konovsky, and Cropanzano 1992). These appraisal issues are worthy of investigation.

Tenth, the effectiveness of discipline without punishment should be formally evaluated. Determining whether the discipline-without-punishment system is perceived as more just by workers—that is, with higher procedural justice—than the progressive-discipline system should be examined. The two disciplinary systems could also be contrasted on measures of absenteeism, grievances, arbitration hearings, unemployment compensation claims after termination, job satisfaction, and organizational commitment.

To end on a rather sober note, TQOs that experience success with continuous process improvement (Imai 1986) or reengineering work (Hammer 1990) may, in time, produce a surplus of workers. Paradoxically, problem-solving teams that have been effective in identifying and eliminating processes not adding value to customers may be working themselves out of a job. The temptation will be to downsize, which seems incompatible with the TQ philosophy. Deming (1993) was of the opinion that TQ workers should enjoy an environment that is free from fear and threats. Downsizing or layoffs may only undermine the cultural changes transpiring in TQOs. Based on the response of 27 MBA students holding midlevel managerial positions (18 of which had personal experience with downsizing), Roth (1993) reported that communication patterns within the organization change when downsizing occurs. To protect themselves, workers in downsized organizations begin to hoard information and often tend to lay personal claim to any successes that the work group experiences (Roth 1993). Instead of working for the good of the team and organization, self-interests may reemerge as the driving force behind workers' behavior. Once this occurs, effective team problem solving may be hard to recapture. Furthermore, if the performance appraisal system is used to identify surplus workers, the underlying purpose of the appraisal is no longer continuous personal improvement but the ranking of workers on the basis of performance. Instead of maintaining cooperation in the appraisal process, defensiveness on the part of ratees will resurface. With downsizing, self-ratings and peer ratings—and perhaps even customer ratings—may no longer be viable because of the reemergence of political behavior into the process. A strong component of the TQ training process is self-directed learning; needs assessment may become more political with downsizing. Why would employees want to "shoot themselves in the foot" by admitting serious deficiencies? In short, it appears that TQOs have much more to lose with unnecessary downsizing and layoffs than to gain. Irreparable harm may occur if downsizing and layoffs are used injudiciously in such environments.

REFERENCES

Aaron, H. 1994. The obsolescent specialist. *The Wall Street Journal*, 16 May.

Alderfer, C. P. 1972. *Existence, relatedness, and growth*. New York: Free Press.

Anderson, J. C., M. Rungtusanathan, and R. G. Schroeder. 1994. A theory of quality management underlying the Deming management model. *Academy of Management Review* 19 (July): 472–509.

Balzer, W. K. 1986. Biases in the recording of performance-related information: The effects of initial impression and centrality of the appraisal task. *Organizational Behavior and Human Decision Processes* 37 (June): 329–347.

Barrick, M. R., and M. K. Mount. 1991. The big five personality dimensions and job performance: A meta analysis. *Personnel Psychology* 44 (spring): 1–26.

Bernardin, H. J., and C. S. Walter. 1977. Effects of rater training and diary keeping on psychometric error in ratings. *Journal of Applied Psychology* 62 (February): 64–69.

Blackburn, R., and B. Rosen. 1993. Total quality and human resources management: Lessons learned from Baldrige Award-winning companies. *Academy of Management Executive* 7 (August) 49–66.

Bowen, D. E., and E. E. Lawler III. 1992. Total quality-oriented human resources management. *Organizational Dynamics* (spring): 29–41.

Bowen, D. E., G. E. Ledford, and B. R. Nathan. 1991. Hiring for the organization, not the job. *The Executive* 5 (November): 35–51.

Breaugh, J. A. 1981. Relationship between recruiting sources and employee performance, absenteeism, and work attitudes. *Academy of Management Journal* 24, (March): 142–147.

———. 1983. Realistic job preview: A critical appraisal and future research directions. *Academy of Management Review* 8 (October): 612–619.

Breaugh, J. A., and R. S. Billings. 1988. The realistic job preview: Five key elements and their importance in research and practice. *Journal of Business and Psychology* 2:291–305.

Brower, M. J. 1994. Implementing TQM with self-directed teams. In *Readings in total quality management,* edited by H. Costin. New York: Dryden.

Caldwell, D. F., and W. A. Spivey. 1983. The relationship between recruiting source and employee success: An analysis by race. *Personnel Psychology* 36 (spring): 67–72.

Campbell, D. N., R. L. Fleming, and R. C. Grote, 1985. Discipline without punishment—At last. *Harvard Business Review* 63 (July-August): 162–176.

Chao, G. T., P. M. Walz, and P. D. Gardner. 1992. Formal and informal mentorships: A comparison of mentoring functions and contrast with nonmentored counterparts. *Personnel Psychology* 45 (autumn); 619–636.

Conrad, M. A., and D. S. Ashworth. 1986. Recruiting source effectiveness: A meta-analysis and reexamination of two rival hypotheses. Paper presented at the first annual meeting of the Society of Industrial/Organizational Psychology, 10–11 April, Chicago, Illinois.

Deming, W. E. 1975. On some statistical aids toward economic production. *Interfaces* 5 (August): 1–15.

———. 1993. *The new economics*. Cambridge, Mass.: MIT.

DeNisi, A., T. Robbins, and T. P. Cafferty. 1989. Organization of information used for performance appraisals: Role of diary keeping. *Journal of Applied Psychology* 74 (February): 124–129.

Digman, J. M. 1989. Five robust trait dimensions: Development, stability, and utility. *Journal of Personality* 57 (June): 195–214.

Feuer, D., and C. Lee. 1988. The kaizen connection. *Training* (May): 23–35.

Folger, R., and J. Greenberg. 1985. Procedural justice: An interpretative analysis of personnel systems. In Vol. 3 of *Research in personnel and human resources management,* edited by K. R. Rowland and G. Ferris. Greenwich, Conn.: JAI Press.

Folger, R., M. A. Konovsky, and R. Cropanzano. 1992. A due-process metaphor for performance appraisal. In Vol. 14 of *Research in Organizational Behavior,* edited by B. M. Staw and L. L. Cummings. Greenwich, Conn.: JAI Press.

Fox, S., Z. Beh-Nahum, and Y. Yinon. 1989. Perceived similarity and accuracy of peer ratings. *Journal of Applied Psychology* 74 (October): 781–786.

Friedman, B. A., and E. T. Cornelius. 1976. Effects of rater participation in scale construction on the psychometric characteristics of two rating scale formats. *Journal of Applied Psychology* 61 (April): 210–216.

Gatewood, R. D., and H. S. Feild. 1990. *Human resource selection.* 2d ed. New York: Dryden.

Goff, B. A., B. G. Schekley, and S. L. Hastings. 1994. Lessons for a learning organization. In *Readings in total quality management,* edited by H. Costin. New York: Dryden.

Greising, D. 1994. Quality: How to make it pay. *Business Week,* 8 August, 54–59.

Grote, D. 1994. Discipline without punishment. *The Wall Street Journal,* 23 May.

Hackman, J. R., and G. R. Oldham. 1976. Motivation through the design of work: Test of a theory. *Organizational Behavior and Human Performance* 16 (August): 250–279.

Hammer, M. 1990. Reengineering work: Don't automate, obliterate. *Harvard Business Review* 68 (July-August): 104–112.

Harris, M. M., and J. Schaubroeck. 1988. A meta-analysis of self-supervisor, self-peer, and peer-supervisor ratings. *Personnel Psychology* 41 (spring): 43–62.

Huffcutt, A. I., and W. Arthur Jr. 1994. Hunter and Hunter (1984) revisited: Interview validity for entry-level jobs. *Journal of Applied Psychology* 79 (April): 184–190.

Hunter, J. E., and R. F. Hunter. 1984. Validity and utility of alternative predictors of job performance. *Psychological Bulletin* 96 (January): 72–98.

Imai, M. 1986. *Kaizen.* New York: McGraw-Hill.

Kane, J. S., and E. E. Lawler III. 1978. Methods of peer assessment. *Psychological Bulletin* 85 (May): 555–586.

Kirkpatrick, D. L. 1959. Techniques for evaluating training programs. *Journal of the American Society of Training Directors* 13:3–9.

Lawler, E. E. III. 1994. From job-based to competency-based organizations. *Journal of Organizational Behavior* 15 (January): 3–15.

Mayfield, E. C. 1964. The selection interview: A re-evaluation of published research. *Personnel Psychology* 17 (autumn): 239–260.

McDaniel, M. A., D. L. Whetzel, F. L. Schmidt, and S. D. Maurer. 1994. The validity of employment interviews: A comprehensive review and meta-analysis. *Journal of Applied Psychology* 79 (August): 599–616.

Nadler, D. A., and M. L. Tushman. 1980. Frameworks for organizational behavior. In *Managing organizations: Reading and cases,* edited by D. A. Nadler, M. L. Tushman, and N. G. Harvany. Toronto: Little, Brown, and Company.

Nowack, K. M. 1993. 360-degree feedback: The whole story. *Training and Development* (January): 69–72.

Offerman, L. R., and M. K. Gowing. 1993. Personnel selection in the future: The impact of changing demographics and the nature of work. In *Personnel selection in organizations,* edited by N. Schmitt and W. C. Bowman. San Francisco: Jossey-Bass.

Popovich, P., and J. P. Wanous. 1982. The realistic job preview as a persuasive communication. *Academy of Management Review* 7 (October): 570–578.

Roth, W. 1993. The dangerous ploy of downsizing. *Business Forum* (fall): 5–7.

Russell, C. J., J. Mattson, S. E. Devlin, and D. Atwater. 1990. Predictive validity of biodata items generated from retrospective life experience essays. *Journal of Applied Psychology* 75 (October): 569–580.

Sanchez, J. I., D. M. Fernandez, W. Korbin, and J. Valdes. 1993. Reshaping job analysis to meet emerging business needs. Paper presented at the meeting of the Academy of Management, 8–11 August, Atlanta, Georgia.

Schneider, B., and N. Schmitt. 1986. *Staffing organizations.* 2d ed. Glenview, Ill.: Scott, Foresman.

Senge, P. 1994. Building learning organizations. In *Readings in total quality management,* edited by H. Costin. New York: Dryden.

Sherman, M., and A. Lucia. 1992. Positive discipline and labor arbitration. *Arbitration Journal* (June): 56–58.

Smith, D. E. 1986. Training programs for performance appraisal: A review. *Academy of Management Review* 11 (January): 22–40.

Smith, P. C. and L. M. Kendall. 1963. Retranslation of expectations: An approach to the construction of unambiguous anchors for rating scales. *Journal of Applied Psychology* 47 (April): 149–155.

Stamoulis, D. T., and N. Hauenstein. 1993. Rater training and rater accuracy: Training for dimensional accuracy versus training for rate differentiation. *Journal of Applied Psychology* 78 (December): 994–1003.

Thornton, G. C. 1980. Psychometric properties of self-appraisals of job performance. *Personnel Psychology* 33 (summer): 263–271.

Trist, E. L., G. I. Susman, and G. R. Brown. 1977. An experiment in autonomous working in an American underground coal mine. *Human Relations* 30:201–236.

Ulrich, L., and D. Trumbo. 1965. The selection interview since 1949. *Psychological Bulletin* 63 (February): 100–116.

Wagner, J. A., and M. K. Moch. 1986. Individualism-collectivism: Concept and measure. *Group and Organization Studies* 11 (September): 280–304.

Waldman, D. A. 1994. The contributions of total quality management to a theory of work performance. *Academy of Management Review* 19 (July): 510–536.

Walton, M. 1986. *The Deming management method.* New York: Perigree.

———. 1990. *Deming management at work.* New York: Putnam.

Wanous, J. P. 1992. *Organizational entry: Recruitment, selection, orientation, and socialization of newcomers.* Reading, Mass.: Addison-Wesley.

Wanous, J. P., and A. Colella. 1989. Organizational entry research: Current status and future directions. In *Research in personnel and human resources management,* edited by K. R. Rowland and G. R. Ferris. Greenwich, Conn.: JAI Press.

Wiesner, W. H., and S. F. Cronshaw. 1988. The moderating impact of interview format and degree of structure on the validity of the employment interview. *Journal of Occupational Psychology* 61:275–290.

Yeatts, D. E., M. Hipskind, and D. Barnes. 1994. Lessons learned from self-managed work teams. *Business Horizons* 37 (July-August): 11–18.

PENTON PUBLISHING: USING TEAMS FOR STRATEGIC IMPROVEMENTS*
by Vicki J. Powers

Penton Publishing remembers life before total quality—and does not want to experience *that* again. Otherwise, it might not be in business.

"We wouldn't have been able to survive the media recession in the early '90s if it wasn't for total quality," said CEO Sal Marino, with 43 years of service at Penton. "I certainly don't feel smart enough to run this organization on my own. You must expose issues to others in the company who can make a contribution."

Martino and Dan Rumella, president, have given Penton over to employees by empowering them to make decisions. They have flattened the organization and moved employees closer to the customer to solve customer needs. Penton became involved in total quality to focus on customer satisfaction.

"Total quality makes our employees feel they are a greater part of the organization, and they can see a tangible result from their efforts," Marino said. "It's more efficient, cost-effective, and satisfies the customer in ways he doesn't expect. It really works."

A NEW BEGINNING

In January 1991, Penton announced its focus on total quality and moved Jim McDermott from group publisher to vice president, total quality assurance. As a 30-year Penton veteran, McDermott knew it would require a significant culture shift within the company.

"In many respects, the writers and artists had never looked at their work as part of a process," McDermott said. "When you start out with 30+ magazines, you have lots of entrepreneurial business units. We began to pull together and look at things from the same perspective, all on behalf of our end customer. We began to change the way we operate."

Marino said Penton knew about total quality and would write about it in its publications. But soon it realizes the best way to tell readers about it was to do it themselves. At the same time, those companies who were embracing total quality said they would prefer to do business with those who were quality-oriented.

*Reprinted with permission from *Continuous Journey,* January 1995.

"These are our customers," Marino said. "We need to practice what we preach."

In the beginning, employees attended quality awareness training through Penton's Quality College. This introduced them to total quality and described what it meant to employees, customers, and the organization. This began to set the base for a common language. From there, Penton introduced team building and problem solving, and all employees went through a two-day program, with one day added for team facilitation.

Penton also started a leadership training program, which addressed the issue of leading organizations under the TQM process. It discussed the specific skills required to move the organization in a strategic fashion.

TEAMING FOR SUCCESS

As a fairly large company, Penton tended to be democratic in the way it ran its business before total quality. Once it made its new commitment, Penton turned to cross-functional teams as a way to solve various problems. It also started a suggestion program called Quality Recommendation (QR), which encouraged employees to offer their good ideas. According to Marino, "if it's worth doing, we'll start a team."

One team, for example, worked on decreasing paper costs. This team thought it would be wise if the company could offer a variety of paper to the various magazines, but restrict the selection to six or eight rather than unlimited. This would give each publication the freedom to pick its own paper quality and weight, without requiring Penton to supply hundreds of different kinds. Today, each publication buys paper that best fits the specifictions of the press, and Penton has saved $1 million in paper costs.

Another team focused on the high costs of overtime. Penton spent $1.7 million per year on overtime. Forcing overtime on employees was a result of the publisher missing a closing date, which created a backlog at the printing plant. These employees created a system to flag closing dates to ensure they were met. This reducd overtime to $700,000 that year—a $500,000 savings.

"If we hadn't let our rank-and-file employees offer suggestions, it wouldn't have been solved," Marino said. "By opening a can of worms to look at the problem, we were able to find an answer."

One six-month team focused on reducing the production cycle and costs. More than 100 recommendations came out of this team, and Penton is now building a course on the topic for all levels of exployees—from the publisher to the editor and production manager. Penton expects to save another several million dollars in this area.

Another significant improvement focused on ad pages that were sold in the various publications. Marino said he never knew on a daily basis how many pages were bought. As a result of a team, they came up with a suggestion for an on-line billing system.

"Within a couple of months, I will know what business is in each of the profit centers," Marino said. "This will increase efficiency and offer projections based on fact, not fiction. Others can tap into the data source, as well. One simple idea has created a whole wealth of new potential."

THE NEW FACE OF PENTON

All of these team examples have experienced bottom-line results. But Marino emphasizes that total quality is also changing the personality of the company. One employee suggested a casual dress day on Fridays. After a vote in the company, Penton defined "casual day" as any day an employee won't be interfacing with a customer.

"This action has helped morale," Marino said. "We have a very casual atmosphere, yet people are producing more and more.

"Penton is unique, because most total quality organizations are manufacturing companies," he continued. "We had total quality at the press division before the publishing division. In the idea business, it's often harder to come up with measurements."

Although total quality is a focus on the customer, Penton has certainly not forgotten its employees. With the creation of an incentive system in 1994, the Million Dollar Challenge, Marino challenged employees to drive up revenue. If Penton hits the target, 1,000 employees minus management will each get $1,000. In 1995, Penton has a new incentive to improve profits by 90 percent. Marino believes recognition makes a quality effort work, and organizations must recognize success.

Penton has seen its own challenges with total quality however. In the beginning, Marino said a lot of "doubting Thomases" were talking quality, but not practicing it. Managers were saying one thing, and supervisors were saying another.

"It has taken three years to get through this," said Marino. "You must stick with total quality and not listen to the naysayers. You will always find some evangelists and some doubting Thomases. But it takes total quality missionaries, because the natives are constantly restless."

McDermott also agrees that Penton has seen great success with its total quality focus. The company is far more efficient in its processes than before, and he believes they have weathered it fairly well.

"Organizations don't change overnight—you're building new values and creating a mission." McDermott said. "We don't sit back and say, 'Look how good we are.' You don't give up on it. The key is enough people make a commitment to make it happen."

REDSTONE HOTELS, INC.: MAKING QUALITY WORTHWHILE*
by Laurie W. Payne

When Greg Clark stepped into the housekeeping department of the Westchase Hilton & Towers he couldn't believe his eyes. Standing before him was a large huddle of very anxious housekeepers, all straining their eyes to see a clipboard one fellow co-worker held tightly in her hands. He listened intently and suddenly realized that the housekeepers were reviewing survey results detailing guest satisfaction from the previous day.

"It was wonderful seeing everyone eager to view the results and talking with each other about them," said Clark, executive vice-president, Redstone Hotels, Inc. "We had been doing the survey for some time, but didn't realize the quantum improvement in the guest experience until we began sharing the guests' feedback with people who were actually doing the work.

"Once we started showing people the results of the survey, they started making changes on their own," said Clark. "It shows you the power that pride has over individuals. People are committed to the success of our company."

Clark said jobs and tasks may vary between individuals but their importance to the company and customer is equal.

"The scores were a direct reflection of team performance . . . and they all wanted to succeed."

Redstone nurtures the entrepreneurial spirit in everyone—whether it be the general manager, valet attendant, kitchen steward, or front desk clerk. The philosophy is this: all people in the workplace will perform *better* when the individual is treated with dignity; jobs and tasks are valued equally; and opportunity for advancement is available to everyone. An unusual synergy is created among the staff—a rich pool of highly-respected, empowered team players. Conversations on dignity, empowerment, and self-worth are spoken daily at Redstone properties.

In December 1992, Redstone Hotels, Inc. expanded its portfolio to include four properties—The Westchase Hilton, Houston: and the Hyatt Regency, Austin; and The Houstonian Hotel & Club, Houston.

Soon after purchasing The Houstonian, Redstone began a multi-million dollar renovation not only in its physical appearance but also within its internal culture. Using its own approach to total quality management, Redstone started this culture change, which Clark knew would present many challenges.

When asked what makes Redstone different from other hospitality management companies, Clark answered, "people and their importance to the organization. Redstone is very uncompromising on this subject.

"We try to provide the proper tools, training, environment, and freedom for success," he continued. "It is the dedication and spirit of the

Reprinted with permission from *Continuous Journey,* January 1995.

people that makes our properties special . . . and it is the magic that will keep Redstone successful."

Redstone's management teams was formed five years ago on the basic principles of dignity; value of workmanship; the need for opportunity; and an equal balance between employees, customers, and owner.

A BETTER ATTITUDE

Clark estimated that people spend one-third of their time at work, so he believes Redstone Hotels has a moral obligation to make the work experience a positive one. Redstone Hotels' msssion is "making peoples' lives better through business."

Clark said that Redstone's biggest challenge is to overcome generations of negative conditioning that began with the onset of the Industrial Revolution—an era that saw vast improvement in productivity at the unfortunate expense of skilled workers.

"Society is accepting of the 'low man on the totem poll' attitude that undervalues workers and their various tasks. People are conditioned to believe the more prestigious the title, the higher the value and importance," Clark said.

"This negative and damaging attitude is prevalent in our culture. Remember the comic strips about Dagwood, Fred Flintstone, George Jetson, and Beetle Bailey?" Clark asked. "These demonstrate the on-going distasteful attitude toward the worker. Although amusing at times, it is unfortunate that these comics further reinforced our negative image of the worker."

Not at Redstone Hotels. Clark's team works to break down these beliefs and incorporate a higher value in each person. The Houston-based management company surveys its staff on a bi-annual basis to gain insight into their experience as a Redstone team member. According to Clark, surveys have given the organization a tool to help identify and overcome those negative attitudes.

"We must treat people with respect and dignity. It is as simple as that. If you come and go with friendly greetings, if you show interest in the work people are doing, it will make a great difference. It will produce greater market penetration and higher profits. Your guests will want to come back, and the workforce will want to stay," he said.

Redstone's approach to TQM gets results. Employee turnover is less than half of the industry average. More than 50 percent of Houstonian Hotel guests repeat their stay and 95 percent report a willingness to return.

At the Westchase Hilton, market share has risen an impressive 50 percent under the ownership and management of Redstone Hotels. When Redstone purchased the property in 1989, the Westchase Hilton had a performance rating in the lower 25 percent. Today, it ranks in the top four of all Hilton hotels. All this has resulted in an amazing 400 percent increase in profitability.

"It is very satisfying to read comments from guests who 'hate to travel but would come back to the Westchase Hilton anytime;' or that 'The Houstonian is my home away from home.' It really makes you proud," said Clark.

In fact, a recent guest of Redstone Hotel's newest property left an impressive comment: "Clearly, The Houstonian is focused on excellence. As a Malcolm Baldrige Examiner, I recognize all elements of quality in hotel management. You deliver the best. Your people are outstanding. You have become a 'best practice' example in all my speeches."

Comments such as this strengthen Clark's belief that Redstone Hotels has something special to offer customers and employees.

DON'T GIVE UP

Some companies experience failure when implementing TQM. There are many reasons for this, but Clark believes it comes from a lack of commitment to the process and the work force.

"The foundation of TQM must be based on a mutual relationship of trust, respect, and dedication between the company and workforce. If not, TQM will not be successful," Clark said.

"You have to realize it is a slow and continuous process, and you must stick with it," he added. "At the Houstonian, we have been working with this process for two years now. Although vastly improved, much is yet to be accomplished.

"Our total quality management is about a fundamental belief that the work a person does is important. If you share with the team the problems within the system, you can both work toward the same goal," Clark said.

"When I saw the housekeepers looking at that report, I knew our company had achieved a new and lasting commitment from the people within Redstone. Future success was in our hand," Clark said. "It is an image that really sticks out in my mind. It is something I will never forget."

———————————————◼———————————————

THE IAMS COMPANY: BUILDING QUALITY FROM DAY ONE*
by Vicki J. Powers

The customers of The Iams Company are not the pet owners who purchase food. Its ultimate customers are the cats and dogs who eat it. How do you ensure these nonvocal customers are happy? By practicing total quality from day one.

Nearly 50 years ago, Paul Iams founded The Iams Company based on values of creating high quality, highly nutritious pet food. His concern was the well-being and nutrition of cats and dogs. And he instilled in Iams' culture that quality is the responsibility of everyone.

"When Paul Iams started the company, quality was key to him. He wanted high quality ingredients, and sometimes would even make them himself," Jeff Milne said, director of total quality. "He stressed quality to employees and proved it was not 'lip service.' It's even written as part of the Iams Beliefs: 'Quality is the cornerstone of our business and the number one responsibility of all employees, suppliers, and customers.'"

To help employees keep "quality on the brain," Iams created three specific courses through its training program, Iams University. "Iams Way" serves as a refresher course to reemphasize the culture and remind employees that only high quality products can leave the door. In the last 12 months, employees have attended two new courses, "Making a Difference" and "Partnerships for Improvement." These discuss how employees can make a difference in the company and describe how teamwork can get bigger results.

A FOCUSED VISION

Each year Iams conducts a planning session to review its mission, vision, and philosophy. First, executives meet off-site to ask, "Is this still where we want the company to be?" Then every employee has an opportunity to give feedback on these ideas, which are taken back to the president and owner.

"Six issues might be the focus in each division, which focus on the company objectives," Milne said. "As a result, departments and divisions are tied to meet the corporate objectives. It's part of the quality process. Everyone knows where we're trying to go."

Milne continues to emphasize that total quality is not a formal effort at Iams. He said the company was established based on total quality, and it's an ongoing way to do business. And it has experienced results. In the last three years, Iams has doubled its number of employees and *more* than doubled its sales. It has introduced 14 new products in the last two years—all of which have been successful. On example is its cat food. The dry cat food was selling adequately, but Iams decided to branch out into can cat food. Today, it is the number one premium can cat food in the country.

"The unique part about Iams' approach to total quality is that everyone believes it," Milne said. "It's not something you post on the wall. It's something employees feel inside. When everyone believes it, everyone supports it and pitches in to help."

IMPROVEMENT OPPORTUNITIES

Just like any other company, Iams also has experienced its share of problems. Two years ago, Iams received many customer complaints regarding the seal on its pet food bags. The bags would not stay closed during shipment, and food would spill at the retail outlets. Iams realized one of its plants was performing better than the other two plants, so Milne facilitated a team of Quality Assurance managers, engineers, and line operators to study the problem.

---

*Reprinted with permission from *Continuous Journey,* January 1995.

"We decided to do some internal best practice and benchmarking to examine the plant that had better success in this area," Milne said. "We did root cause analysis and observed the line to determine the exact cause of the problem—was it the glue, the equipment?"

The team put together a plan and within 18 months it experienced a dramatic improvement. The new process reduced customer complaints by 75 percent.

Iams also nurtures its relationship with customers and suppliers. There is always an open invitation to distributors and key retail accounts to attend Iams university courses, such as "How to Set Up Retail Accounts." Milne believes Iams goes further than any company he knows in regard to "training" its customers. This setting also allows Iams to try ideas out in class and receive feedback from customers.

Iams also attends dog and cat shows to educate owners and trainers, because the organization believes it's imperative to reach that audience. Veterinary schools are another opportunity Iams takes advantage of to inform students about proper animal nutrition.

With its vendors, Iams offers a two-year certification program to help ensure Iams can meet the quality its customers expect.

"We do business with our vendor for one year before we begin the certification process," Milne said. "We want it to be a win-win situation for everybody."

Iams conducts a vendor profile on each vendor to determine if it is able to grow with Iams. The vendor also fills out a self-survey regarding its equipment, on-time delivery, service, and other essentials. Iams then performs a vendor analysis by conducting a site survey on them and discussing the self-survey. Iams works closely with its vendors during the two-year process by providing training and helping them purchase equipment.

Iams also pays special attention to the 200 cats and dogs in its kennel. Although it's not unique for a pet food company to own a kennel, Iams went one step further by building the kennel at twice the government regulations.

"All of our animals are handled every day as if they were pets," Milne said. "A key part of the animal handler's job is to spend time with the animals and give them lots of attention. Since we use them to test our products, we want them to eat as if they're actually hungry for meals."

Why does total quality work at Iams? Because it's in the culture of the company, according to Milne.

"During each quarterly meeting of our company, the owner always mentions quality," he said. "By reinforcing it every three months, it eventually soaks in. Total quality means doing what you can to get better."

TQM AND ISO 9000 CHINESE STYLE*
by Lawrence P. Creedon

The quality of goods produced and services offered by the Chinese concerns not only China but also customers and investors in the United States.

The basic issue is that while China is by volume the world's third-largest economy, it does not as yet approximate that position in the quality of the goods and services it produces. However, the country's goal, as stated by the China Quality Assurance Association, is to make the label *Made in China* recognized worldwide as a symbol of quality.

Regardless of the quality of products made in China, China is the 10th-largest trading nation in the world, with a volume of $200 billion annually. The United States is its third-largest trading partner, and it is the sixth-largest customer for U.S. goods. Bilateral trade between the two nations reached $35.4 billion in 1994, according to the March 6, 1995 *China Daily*.

*Reprinted with permission from *Quality Digest*, July 1995. © 1995 QCI International. Lawrence P. Creedon is managing director of Pacific Rim Trade and Business Consultants in Reston, VA, and an assistant professor at Jersey City StateCollege.

Since 1980, when China embarked on its current wave of economic reform (the most ambitious since the Opium Wars of 1840–42), Americans have invested $4.4 billion in China, and there is no end in sight. A sampling of 1994 U.S. initiatives makes the point. Salomon Brothers Inc., one of the world's top five investment banking firms, opened its first China office in Beijing. Fleishman-Hillard, the international public relations firm, embarked on a first-ever joint venture with China. General Motors announced that it would conduct its first international tests of its all-electric car, the Impact, in China. And, after the United States and Japan, China has become the world's third-largest user of cellular phones.

In a self-congratulatory tone, Chinese officials have declared that urban Chinese homes are becoming "castles of comfort." As if to provide evidence to support such a dramatic and, by U.S. standards, vastly overstated claim, Amway has moved into the Chinese domestic market. In its initial promotion in two Chinese cities, Amway attached 30,000 potential affiliates.

With such an impressive array of marketplace accomplishments in a short period of 15 years, the Chinese would seem to be masters of TQM strategies and boast a bounty in ISO 9000 certifications. Not so!

TQM and ISO 9000 are concepts and practices that for the most part remain embryonic in China. However, that also is undergoing change as China propels itself forward in its second long march (the first was a military effort led by Mao Tse-tung and contributed to the communist takeover in 1949). The second march is economic and aimed at freeing the nation from its controlled economy by building a socialist market economy featuring Chinese characteristics.

TQM REMAINS UNKNOWN

In China, the concept of quality is heralded everywhere. Statistics alluding to the ever-increasing quality of products are readily available from government agencies charged with monitoring quality. Yet, the process of TQM as understood in the United States and Japan remains unknown. And less than 200 enterprises out of a total 8 million nationwide are ISO 9000-certified.

In terms that ring familiar to Americans, the Chinese Quality Assurance Association has stated "Quality is the hallmark of a country's economic and cultural condition. The improvement of quality plays a vital role in the development and prosperity of the country." (*China Daily,* Sept. 29, 1994)

The Chinese understand the relationship between poor quality and losing money. A major focus of the reform movement is to reverse the tide of red ink that flows from state-owned enterprises. The government's goal is to privatize industry but not to duplicate Western practices. Rather, they intend to develop a socialist economy with Chinese characteristics. For example, the private ownership of property as understood in the United States is not envisioned in China. Rather, long-term leasing is their approach.

In a never-ending assault on the limitations of state-owned enterprises, the Chinese government requires enterprises to convert from state ownership to Chinese forms of private ownership. A 1994 government report recognizes that as recent as 1991, close to 70 percent of the state-owned enterprises that were losing money could blame government red tape, bureaucracy and interference. In a dramatic reversal, the government now says that more than 80 percent of firms in the red must look in the mirror and blame themselves. In so doing, management surfaces as the whipping boy.

Citing many examples, the government report reflects on areas that are compatible with TQM strategies. It concludes that improved management would effectively bring in profits. Management improvement means appointing more competent managers and directors without government interference, revamping management systems, devising better accounting systems, increasing emphasis on the market's role and improving technology.

The report concludes that most state-owned firms had not adequately tackled overstaffing. It is common for government-owned firms to be overstaffed by one-third. In some factories, managerial staff equal the number of workers. Labor, wage and personnel reforms lag behind. And insurance of any kind for employees is not common. As a result, pensions and welfare payments slash at profits.

Unlike the United States, Chinese enterprises must provide worker housing, schools, hospitals and marketplaces. Each work unit is an independent community, almost totally dependent upon the enterprise for the necessities of life. Obviously the system drains resources, including management skill and efficiency.

At least one-half of the money losers are victims of outmoded equipment and technology. Others lack contemporary accounting controls as well as quality controls of the most rudimentary nature.

In an effort to cope with the shortcomings, the report recommends that the first and most basic solution is to become market-oriented. The second measure is to transform management. The third is to divide enterprises into smaller and more independent units where different management strategies may emerge. And the fourth measure is to replace incompetent managers with better leadership.

In the final analysis, if a state-owned enterprise cannot get its own house in order, then the solution is to allow it to go bankrupt. In the past several years, this has been more than an idle threat, and many enterprises have closed their doors. Currently, two-thirds of all state-owned enterprises operate at a loss, according to the Jan. 13, 1994, *China Daily*. For example, the majority of the country's 130 automobile plants operate in the red. The government's goal is to encourage eight to 10 plants to become stronger and, finally, to reshuffle all those that remain into three competitive giants by the year 2010.

PURSUING QUALITY

All too frequently, the pursuit of quality in China has remained tied to the out-moded, end-of-the-production-process inspection practices associated with pre-TQM and pre-ISO 9000 approaches to quality. Government agencies as well as semi-official watchdog organizations conduct the inspections. These groups canvas the country annually, assessing quality and reporting their findings publicly.

For example, in 1993, government inspectors from the Bureau of State Technical Supervision inspected 8,150 enterprises and collected data on 10,000 products. The conclusion was that while 90 percent of the products from large state enterprises met state standards (not to be confused with internationally recognized quality standards), more than 60 percent of those from small township enterprises failed.

Neither the government agencies nor the watchdog organizations are bashful about calling attention, and forcefully so, to enterprises they find guilty of producing shoddy products. In a six-month period in 1993, the government uncovered close to 4,000 cases of forged products, according to the Oct. 15, 1993, *China Daily*.

Two recent examples turned the spotlight on the production of soft drinks and the manufacture of steel reinforcement bars. Samples of soft drinks were taken from 1,300 manufacturers, and only 37 percent of the samples satisfied state standards. The steel reinforcement bars were in worse shape—close to 5,000 manufacturers were sampled, and only 20 percent met state requirements.

The reason for the shoddy quality was cited by the government agency as the thirst for profits by the individual enterprise as well as aging, inadequate equipment and outmoded technology.

CONSUMER WATCHDOGS

For the past several years, journalists have toured China acting as quality watchdogs by visiting factories and writing about what they observed. The journalists got involved as the result of consumers complaining that domestic products such as TV sets and refrigerators did not work and that shoes fell apart shortly after purchase.

The journalists came to the same conclusion as the government inspectors and leveled the responsibility with locally managed factories in rural areas. But rather than recommend government reprisals against the offenders, the journalists cautioned that consumers must serve as their own quality watchdogs and refuse to buy shoddy products.

Adding to the dilemma has been the emergence of fake inspection teams roving the country. Bogus teams enter a rural area, pose as media personalities, conduct an inspection tour, find discrepancies and then blackmail the managers into paying them in return for worthless quality certifications (*China Daily*, Jan. 6, 1994).

In an effort to curb abuses in this area, the Chinese government has introduced a commodity accountability system and enacted consumer advocacy laws. The system applies only to state-owned stores; private enterprises are not affected. It introduces the previously unheard of concept of warranties as well as other taken-for-granted Western practices. It obliges shops to put price tags on goods and provides a system for handling consumer complaints about substandard goods. Now stores must offer to repair or exchange the product and pay compensation if necessary. Large cities hold Consumer Days, when the government sets up sidewalk stands to explain to shoppers their rights.

TOWARD ISO 9000

Quality assessment Chinese style began in 1981. The focus then, and to a large extent now, was on adherence to state-determined standards. Quality did not mean "fit for customer use" as the term is understood in the United States. Rather, it meant conformance to state standards as measured by the all-important government-conducted inspection held at the end of the production process.

ISO 9000 first appeared in China in 1992. Thirteen Chinese enterprises won ISO 9000 certification in 1993. By 1994, the number rose to 151, and the goal for 1995 is to add 200 more. In government circles, ISO 9000 is promoted as a passport to international business and world trade.

In tooling up to manage ISO 9000 certification, the Chinese government has established six third-party independent assessment centers. (Independent must be understood in the context of anything in China that is truly independent of government regulation). The centers are located in areas of heavy commerce such as Shanghai and Beijing, as well as Guangdong Province. Forty percent of China's exports channel through Guangdong, and the province is within commuter distance from Hong Kong. Chinese enterprises that have gained ISO 9000 certification include those dealing with oil and gas, diesel engines, automobiles, housing, an optical fiber and cable company, and a brewery.

According to the Conformity Assessment Office of the State Technology Supervision Administration, since 1992 the government has sponsored the training and certification of 160 ISO 9000 auditors. However, the number seems high for such a limited number of certifications. In fact, the number has raised the eyebrows of some mainland Chinese businessmen. In their opinion, it may indicate some degree of featherbedding and attempts by the government to control the certification process by controlling the auditors.

TRADEMARK PROTECTION

The thrust of China's quest for quality can be encapsulated in the Renowned Trademark Protection Organization. Founded in 1992 in response to senior leader Deng Xiaoping's national quality inspection tour, the organization has about 100 members. In official language, Renowned Trademarks are treasures of the country, and any damage to these trademarks will result in serious consequences.

A trademark is defined as a name for one or a group of products. In its declaration of purpose, the organization states: "No matter how many goods [sic] he has done, a person without a name won't be known by the public. And no matter what quality it possesses, a product, if without its own trademark, won't be remembered by the customers." (*China Daily,* July 21, 1993)

In layman's language, a renowned trademark enterprise is one that is committed to the pursuit of quality assurance standards as understood by ISO 9000. A Chinese renowned trademark enterprise might be compared to a Baldridge Award-class company in the United States or a Deming Prize-class company in Japan.

In addressing the issue of quality, the Renowned Trademark Protection Organization states: "A market economy is a system of competition among individual participants. What is the key to winning such competition? The most basic, most effective, most direct and most long-lasting means to win competition is quality— quality of products, services, engineering and work.

"Quality today is no longer limited to the traditional definition of inexpensive and durable items and beautiful outlooks. The extensive modern quality concept consists of various internal and external indexes of varieties, styles and services. Its core element is how much a product can satisfy the market and the consumers.

"It has been quality that we rely on to become famous enterprises with renowned trademarks. There, we will make full use of the advantages to compete on the domestic market and pull up China's economic and product levels and to compete on the world market to bring about profits and fame for the country. In this respect, we, enterprises with renowned trademarks, should ask ourselves: If we don't do this, who will?" (*China Daily*, July 21, 1993)

Certainly the above statement is compatible with the positions of American quality gurus such as the late W. Edwards Deming, Joseph M. Juran and Philip B. Crosby. The reference to modern quality concepts as consisting of various internal and external indexes of varieties, styles and services reflects on the focus of ISO 9000. And the appeal "If we don't do this, who will?" is reminiscent of the 1981 PBS documentary that is largely credited with starting the move in the United States toward TQM.

The title of that documentary is: *If Japan Can, Why Can't We?*

The hard reality is that for China, the march toward quality as understood in terms of TQM and ISO 9000 standards has just begun. The march will be a long one. However, the Chinese are quick to point out that they are accustomed to long marches, setting long-term goals and deferring personal rewards in quest of a greater common good.

TQM & ADA: PROVIDING QUALITY SERVICE TO ALL YOUR CUSTOMERS*

Any discussion of issues that strongly affect the way U.S. businesses operate today invariably points to two significant developments. The first is the implementation of Total Quality Management (TQM) as a way to run a better company, produce top-drawer products and services, and stay competitive in a challenging marketplace. The second is the commitment to uphold civil rights for people with disabilities, driven by the Americans with Disabilities Act (ADA).

Although these two issues might seem unrelated, they can be tied together to improve the quality of service given to external and internal customers. And this is the ideal time for you to be thinking about linking these concepts: National Quality Month, National Customer Service Week, and National Disability Employment Awareness Month *all* fall in October!

Understanding how to make the connection can help you guide your company in providing better services *and* in complying with the law. This information can also aid you in making better decisions on accommodating staffers. You need to know how "TQM + ADA" can enhance the way you manage personnel with special needs.

WHAT DOES THE ADA SAY?

You've no doubt read about TQM, but you may not be quite as familiar with the provisions of the ADA. So before we discuss the ways in which the two can be tied together, let's take a closer look at the ADA.

The ADA is a civil rights bill that guarantees people with disabilities the same types of rights held by women and ethnic minorities. Signed into law on July 26, 1990, the Act prohibits discrimination against people with disabilities in employment, transportation, public accommodation, communications, and activities of state and local governments.

Modifications to the ADA in July 1992 made the employment provisions more specific: It is now illegal for organizations that employ 25 or more people to discriminate in certain sectors against qualified candidates with disabilities. Those sectors include hiring, firing, salaries, benefits, training, and career advancement.

In a letter to the ADA employment summit held in December 1992 by the President's Committee on Employment of People with Disabilities, President Clinton expressed his support for the Act by saying, "In a competitive global economy, our country doesn't have a single person to waste—opportunity must be open to everyone. I am strongly committed to full implementation and enforcement of the ADA, because I believe our entire nation will share in the economic and social benefits that will result from full participation of Americans with disabilities in our society."

---

*Copyrighted material. Reprinted with permission from the Bureau of Business Practice, 24 Rope Ferry Road, Waterford, CT, 06386.

VALUABLE EXTERNAL CUSTOMERS

"People with disabilities are your external customers, and it is to your profit to accommodate them," says Dale S. Brown, program manager, President's Committee on Employment of People with Disabilities (Washington, DC). She points out that many businesses are now addressing special needs. For instance:

- *Broadway theaters are using audio loops and other technologies to accommodate people with hearing impairments.*

- *Disney World is providing motorized wheelchairs for its visitors to rent.*

- *AT&T has devised modifications to enable special-needs customers to use its telephones with greater ease.* AT&T has also set up an internal task force that regularly reviews its products and services for accessibility and use by people with disabilities. This group and others also make suggestions for new and improved products and services to meet a variety of needs.

Brown believes that, despite the efforts of these and other caring and committed companies, the bulk of U.S. businesses don't fully recognize people with disabilities as an important part of their customer base.

VALUABLE INTERNAL CUSTOMERS

Companies shouldn't just consider the *external* customer needs of people with disabilities. These people have proven to be assets to many companies' staffs, and should therefore also be regarded as *internal* customers whose needs are to be accommodated in every way feasible. Statistics gleaned from employer surveys back this up (see box below).

People with disabilities *want* to work. And their drive and commitment make for conscientious, quality-minded staffers. "According to one Harris poll, two out of three people with disabilities say that they want to work. This is the highest percentage of any minority group," Brown points out.

"However, quite a bit of money is lost by companies whose managers feel that employees can't do the job any longer when they become disabled. Even if the employees want to work, the companies put them on disability, and this knocks them out of the labor force. This is a debit on the company's book and a great loss of human potential." And it's not a *quality* way to manage a business and the people who help make it run.

One of the issues Total Quality Management addresses is employee *empowerment*, Brown notes. The theory is that the person doing the job should have the best knowledge of how it should be done to achieve a quality result. "This is also true for people with disabilities," she says. "If employees become disabled but would still like to work, companies should empower those employees to help devise ways they can still do their jobs effectively."

ACCOMMODATING INTERNAL CUSTOMERS

One of the key phrases in the ADA is *reasonable accommodation*. This relates closely to the TQM principle of satisfying the internal customer. To return to work, or to be hired in the first place, people with disabilities may have particular needs that must be met so that they can perform their jobs effectively. So employers must accommodate the special needs of qualified applicants or employees (unless it would cause undue hardship for them to do so).

An accommodation might be as simple as putting down blocks to raise a desk so that a person's wheelchair would fit under it. Or it might be adding a "Brailler" to a computer used by a blind person. It might be a matter of having people speak more loudly or slowly, or using a paper and pencil when talking with a person with a hearing impairment. The best way to find out what will help is simply to *ask the person involved*.

Brown considers accommodation to be more than a legal issue. It also refers to the process of matching up the communication style, work environment, and performance expectations of the company with the needs of employees with disabilities to make sure that they can produce quality service.

JOB ACCOMMODATION NETWORK

To gauge what types of accommodations can best assist internal customers with disabilities, Brown recommends calling the President's Committee on Employment of People with Disabilities' Job Accommodation Network (JAN). "This is a free telephone consulting system that's open to anyone in the United States," she explains. "It's funded by the government and is totally confidential." The number is (800) 526-7234.

"You can call whether you're an employee or an employer, or if you're starting up a TQM program and an ADA program and want some ideas for developing an effective system. The Network staff is very customer focused and will give you one or more options for accommodations," says Brown.

WHAT IT TAKES TO CREATE QUALITY

"Accommodating people with disabilities—whether they're *external* customers buying your products and services or *internal* customers helping make your company run—is an important part of what it takes to create quality," Brown stresses.

Doing everything possible to provide quality service to these critical customers makes smart business sense, too. "As President Clinton said, we don't have a single person to waste. If we want to become globally competitive, we need to make the most of every talent that we have. So ignoring people with disabilities is just not an option anymore. Through Total Quality Management, we now have the tools we need to do a better job of accommodating people with disabilities," Brown concludes.

The ADA gives U.S. businesses an excellent opportunity to improve the quality of service they provide to their customers. By tying the ADA together with TQM principles, your company can help ensure that it complies with the law and delights *all* of its external and internal customers.

3.4 QUALITY TRANSFORMATION

---■---

TRANSFORMATION THINKING: INSPIRING AND HARNESSING CHANGE FOR THE 21ST CENTURY*
by Tim Richardson

In 1981, Branch Banking & Trust of Wilson, North Carolina, held assets of $1.4 billion. Ten years later their asset base had grown to almost $7 billion. Why? In a turbulent decade of financial industry failures and scandals, how did BB&T's asset base increase by a factor of five?

Reflexite Corporation is a rust-belt factory with a difference. In the five years between 1986 and 1991, sales for this technology-based company that competes head-on with 3M doubled and doubled again while profits went up sixfold. Why? Why has Reflexite done so well when the plant next door, the now defunct New Britain Machine, sits empty?

In 1983, Springfield Remanufacturing Company, a remanufacture of engines, had a stock value of ten cents and a debt level 89 times its asset base! Today the stock value is close to $20 per share and the company has reduced its debt ratio by over 4000%! How did this low-technology company with no patents or proprietary products create wealth at a faster rate than almost all of the "glamour" stocks?

While there are probably dozens of reasons why each of the above companies have dramatically outperformed their industries and peers, the following comments by their respective leaders gives us some insight:

---

*Reprinted with permission from The Association for Quality and Participation, Cincinnati OH (513) 381-1959. From the *17th Annual Spring Conference and Resource Mart*, April 1995. Tim Richardson is with Total Development Resources, Inc.

John Allison, Chairman & CEO of Branch Banking & Trust: BB&T's biggest challenge is to provide room for all of our people to grow.

Ceil Ursprung, President of Reflexite: If you give workers some power, they will repay the company a thousand times over in performance.

Jack Stack, CEO of Springfield Remanufacturing Company: When you appeal to the highest level of thinking, you get the highest level of performance.

What's going on here? Are these "captains of industry" really focusing on staff growth, worker power, and levels of thinking? Yes, and these are only three examples in a growing field of transformed organizations. More leaders are recognizing the importance of the human element in organizations . . . and are beginning to do more than give the concept "lip-service."

We've talked about our "human resources" for decades and invested a great deal of time and effort trying to find the secret to motivation and organizational success. Most paths seem to lead toward a management style that is participative and democratic but we're not sure why. It seems like a good idea and it's more fun than chaining people to their desks but is it really more effective? And, if it is, why is it more effective?

George Land suggests a simple answer: It's the only way to keep people alive. It is a biological imperative that we grow or die. If we aren't growing, we're dying. An organization can be simplistically defined as a group of people trying to do something together. Therefore, the only way an organization can sustain growth is if its members are growing.

Growth is defined as the process that occurs when we reach out to our environment, take in nutritional materials and to reformulate them until they become part of our selves. The cell does this by ingesting its environment and transforming it into cells that match its own genetic pattern. Mentally we do it by absorbing our cultural environment and using that material to think, communicate, socialize, invent, create, build, destroy, mate and act in a thousand different ways. Growth is a requirement of life. Long past the time when our physical growth ceases, our need for mental growth continues. There is no such thing as a viable status quo.

The Three Types of Growth

In order to create an environment that fosters the growth that leads to long-term success and prosperity, we need to understand the three types of growth:

Expansion—an increase in size without basic change of nature. All organisms go through this stage of getting bigger, reaching their mature size. A giant redwood may grow to 400 feet while a petunia reaches only a few inches.

Extension—an organism extends itself by reproducing or joining with similar others. At some point in its growth cycle, an apple tree stops getting bigger and begins to produce apples; a child reaches adult size and passes into puberty. All surviving organisms find a way to biologically reproduce themselves. We also extend ourselves by connecting with friends, family and the organizations. We choose people and groups that are like ourselves in some way and these groups become an extension of our self.

Transformation—an organism willingly allows itself to be changed, often dramatically, through interaction with another organism and a mutual exchange of information. A simple example of transformation is the cow and the cowbird. The cow naturally attracts flies, mosquitoes and other insects that provide a feast for the cowbird. A roving meal for the bird and a free pest control for the cow.

It's impossible to know today what changes occurred due to the cow-cowbird transformation but imagination conjures up a picture of an irritable, fly-bitten cow and a frantic, hungry bird. They discover each other and become content and fat ever after.

The "melting pot" of America is another example of the transformation form of growth. People arriving from different cultures, religions and political persuasions change and are changed by being thrown together in the same environment. The more "politically correct" metaphor of a tossed salad where people maintain their identity intact and just mingle together doesn't offer the same growth possibilities. In the same fashion, transformation teachers learn from their students as well as teaching them. Participants on legendary "teams"—from sports teams to the early space mission to the Macintosh computer team— report a sense of being changed by the experience as well as being change agents for their projects.

Another way to look at these types of growth is to compare them to three stages of maturity or world view:

Me/Mine—In the expansion stage the infant is only interested in itself. The child's job is expanding physically and mentally . . . making a bigger footprint in the world. Only disease or a malfunction in the physical or mental make-up prevents us from completing this growth stage and moving into the next stage.

Our Gang/Our Turf—At puberty, growth moves into extension . . . a search for connection by reproduction or finding others who are similar to us. This "teenager" state is ruled by peers and hormones and is seductive. It seems more comfortable than venturing beyond the familiar turf into the unknown arena of the next stage. Gangs, pregnant teens, racism, sexism and wars are some of the negative effects of getting stuck at this stage.

The Global Us/World System—The third phase of growth comes as we begin to value diversity and the mutual benefit that comes from sharing, appreciating and using the wide variety of information available to us. In this stage we recognize the need to find new sources of information beyond those on our own turf. When we find these new sources of information, we begin to become more than we were (although still within the boundaries of our genetic potential) as we incorporate the diverse information offered by others. Transformation requires a letting go of previous assumptions and comfort levels. It is a disruptive, chaotic stage . . . a time when the caterpillar crawls out on a limb, wraps itself in a dark cocoon and hopes for the best. People need all the help and support they can get at this stage.

While these types of growth and stages provide a nice, neat breakdown for discussion, in actuality growth is not a simple, straight-forward process. All three types of growth are jumbled up in everyone and all three forms are critically important. This is not a personality typing model where someone winds up saying, "Oh, I'm a Transformer . . . you're just an Expander." These are forms of growth that we each experience and each type needs to be fostered a great deal more than we currently do.

THE HUMAN ANIMAL

Somewhere in our evolution or divine intervention we made a transformation. This evolution-ary leap added a wrinkle to our DNA . . . one that permitted creativity. Not only permitted it, but made it a mandatory part of our growth process. Never before, in the world as we know it, was an organism granted the charter of making fundamental changes in its environment. While beavers might dam a creek, man was given the tools to dam great rivers and harness their power to light up the night. It was as if someone gave us the keys to the kingdom and said, "Ok, see what you can do with it." You might believe that the use of creativity is a test—if we handle this drive and grow well enough, maybe we will make another evolutionary leap. It may be that the rapid change we're experiencing right now is the pot heating up getting ready to explode into a new realm. The result might be a new being that is as different from us as we are from the dog asleep on our hearth. Then, again, maybe not.

As our DNA pulled us into this new form of growth, we required increasing amounts of information. The need to create made us look in new places for answers to the problems that surrounded us. And, the information we found showed us even more new places to look and other new ways to change our environment which again created new problems and further sources of information and additional ways to change the environment . . . and so on.

Following the pull of our newly found creativity, we learned to exchange information with others and incorporate their learnings while at the same time sharing our learnings with them. Everyone benefited . . . families, tribes, organizations, and communities.

CREATIVITY: POSITIVE OR NEGATIVE?

The growth process relates directly to our drive to create. Too often we talk about creativity as if it were a quality that we were either given or denied. It is not a talent or a personality quirk, it's the fundamental fact of human nature. The growth process involves taking in material or information from our environment and then we do something with it. We transform it into something new. If it's food we're absorbing, we create new cells. If it's information, we use it to create ballet, books or bridges . . . or bombs

Creativity is not linked to one type of growth—it's simply the way we translate who we are into external reality. Once creativity was added to our bag of tricks, it became available to us at every stage our growth. A child may put information together in a way to create a game as 8-year-old Joshua White did when he invented Dino-mite, a board game about dinosaurs. A different child might use his creativity to eliminate a frustration by killing his fustrator, as did a recent 12-year-old who shot a loved and respected store owner for a bicycle. A teenager might combine concern about his world with a new music style and come up with rap. Or a fanatical leader obsessed with protecting his turf could be very destructively creative about waging war.

Creativity is neither positive nor negative ... it is a neutral tool for charging our environment. A bulldozer can be used to clear a space for a new health facility, level an old growth forest or destroy a church. A bulldozer is a bulldozer ... creativity is creativity. How we use it is our choice.

The choices we make depend on our stage of growth and weather our growth process is being frustrated or encouraged. A person with a supportive background who receives the nourishment necessary for growth will naturally grow into the synthesis stage. On the other hand, an acorn might be bursting with life but if it happens to land in the middle of a four-lane highway, it's probably not going to fulfill it's potential. Here is a brief description of how to nourish each "stage" of growth:

Expansion—basic physical needs must be met: food, shelter, clothing, security. Mental expansion comes from free availability of materials and experiences. This is the "dry sponge" stage. The environment should be rich with information that stimulates all the senses. When parents place a brightly colored mobile over a baby's crib they are increasing the nutritional growth value of that infant's environment. When people attend training programs, the information level of their environment is increased.

Sensory stimulants such as music, color, texture, tastes, shapes. Books, games, toys, magazines, animals, field trips, training sessions, nature hikes and other experiences.

Barriers: poverty disease, inadequate education system, warfare, sterile environments, monotonous routines, low self-esteem.

Extension—needs for affiliation and connection must be met through interaction with other people and identification with groups and organizations.

Nourishers: Social events, group projects, plays, readings, recitals, dances and meetings, common eating areas, central water coolers, accessible conference rooms, newsletters, e-mail, telephones, faxes, organization t-shirts, buttons, bumper stickers, stationery, business cards, uniforms, membership cards—t-shirts, hats, buttons, bumper stickers, stationery, business cards, uniforms, etc.

Barriers: chain of command communication structure, excessive rules or bureaucracy, rigid organizational charts, favoritism or cronyism, walls or barriers between people, enforced silence or excessive noise levels that prevent interaction.

Transformation—need for self-actualization and service must be met through an increased level of exchange of information between diverse groups.

Nourishers: Interaction between diverse groups, field trips, job exchanges, cross training, cross-functional teams, tolerance of mistakes, support for risk taking.

Barriers: Bigotry in any form, pyramidal hierarchies, restrictions in communication flow, lack of organizational direction and vision, harsh punishment of mistakes.

Gary Beyer, vice-president of International Survey Research in Chicago states that in 1990, attitude surveys of over 6,000 managers and 25,000 employees, feedback about employee performance was rated as one of the most important factors in job satisfaction. The simplified model of growth says there are three steps to the process:

1. Searching for and finding material or information for growth.

2. Using the material or information for growth activity.

3. Receiving feedback from the environment about the effects of the growth activity.

Simplified even further, this is the Plan-Do-Check cycle. Hundreds of years were spent doing without much planning, then we developed a bunch of business schools to help us learn to plan. But we still haven't made enough progress on checking. Most of us would really like to know how we're doing (if someone could tell us in a nice way, of course) but we resist like mad telling other people how they're doing. Even when we were shown how to do one-minute reprimands and praisings, we found it hard to do. Most of the magic from the total quality management programs comes from the emphasis on checking. Frequent and regular data gathering and measurement provides a steady stream of feedback.

The process of growth involves finding nutrition or information, doing something with it, and then seeing how the environment reacts. If something positive happens, we know that what we did was a good thing and we can do it again or build on it in our future learnings. If something negative happens, we know we need to make an adjustment. If nothing happens, our learning is interrupted.

In the growth process, negative feedback is actually better than no feedback because it provides information about our actions. In most organizations, however, the environment provides little feedback. Even when there is a relatively high level of vocal "strokes" of the "nice job" variety, there is usually little real feedback. In order for the feedback to be effective, it needs to have the following qualities:

Real time—feedback must be received as soon as possible after the action. What normally happens is plan-do-...........................-check, by which time everyone has forgotten what it is we're checking.

On-going—it must be part of an on-going process so the person has a chance to make revisions, a chance to "redo" and improve—the growth cycle becomes plan-do-check—plan-redo-check-etc. What we often call feedback is actually a grade. Turn in a project, get an A or an F, pass or fail, win or lose. No chance for rework, no chance to try again. Informative feedback fosters the passion for learning; grades kill it.

Meaningful—the response must contain information. "Good job," or "You screwed up the count again," don't provide enough information to adjust actions. Meaningful feedback is specific: I really like the way you organized the shelves so it's easier to reach the faster-moving items. . . . It looks like the count is off—did you check the supply room and the holding area?

Accountable—feedback should guide behavior relative to the goals and objectives of the group or organization. Your arrangement of the shelves is going to help us reach our goal of same-day shipments. . . . Double checking in-

voices has cut our billing errors but it's taking twice as long to get them in the mail . . . can we find a way to speed up the process without losing accuracy?

ENCOURAGING INNOVATION

For the past decade there has been a lot of discussion about Japanese vs. American productivity. The Japanese invented the word for continuous improvement (kaisen) and we acted like we were somewhat handicapped in the worker motivation category. According to this belief, they had people who worked hard and did all that quality stuff and we just had people who wanted to punch the time clock, collect their checks and go home. One of the statistics used to support this hypothesis was the staggering numbers of suggestions-per-employee that Toyota and other Japanese firms experience versus our rather pathetic record.

The key lies in the implementation. Japanese firms implement 95 percent of the suggestions received. American firms implement 5 percent of their employee-suggestions. Why would anyone make a suggestion if there was a 20 to 1 chance that it wouldn't be implemented?

One firm had an official suggestion policy (it was in the Employee Handbook) and nice wooden boxes in three or four locations around the building. The boxes were locked and when tried to check for new suggestions, it was discovered that the keys had been lost years ago! How many hapless employees had naively stuffed their ideas into that locked abyss and then anxiously awaited some feedback? How many times would the average, idea-filled employee offer his suggestions to those official-looking boxes before he figured out that there was a gap between policy and reality?

Not all American companies are lax in responding to suggestions. IBM acknowledges all suggestions and estimates that employee suggestions saved the company over $300 million in the four-year period from 1978-82. Total Quality programs have been extremely effective at raising the awareness of the potential benefits of suggestion programs and the importance of recognizing and implementing suggestions in companies across the nation.

One example is Reflexite, where CEO, Cecil Ursprung, charged Matt Guyer, manufacturing manager, with developing a feedback loop where suggestions didn't get lost, one that didn't duplicate the existing structure for getting things done in the company. Guyer brought representatives together from various departments for a day to reinvent a suggestion program. The resulting program was the Employee-Assistance Request System (EARS). But this wasn't just another passing program. Every employee attended classes to learn the steps and skills necessary to identify and solve problems. The EARS process gives them a way to identify problems, document them and plot and evaluate potential causes. It also provides them with a process to determine costs and benefits of solving the problem.

Within 24-hours of receiving a suggestion, the EARS coordinator assigns an action coordinator who immediately contacts the originator. Together, they fill out as much of the form as possible, work through the problem-solving steps and decide if they will need a team. They develop a solution and determine a follow-up date to verify that the solution is working. Two weeks after that, the EARS form is distributed to top management, who visit the EARS originator and discuss the project. Shortly thereafter the originator receives a certificate of appreciation.

"EARS works," explains Guyer, "by making people who identify problems step back and quantify the magnitude of the problem and its impact on the entire company before offering a solution. That allows them not only to offer better solutions but also to understand why some problems are given a higher priority than others."

When the growth drive is not fustrated, people want to improve their environment; they want to make products better; they want to offer better customer service; they want to have a more pleasant working environment; they want to cut costs. Without proper feedback, however, they aren't sure which direction they're going. Feedback is how they know they're on track or off. What employees object to most is simply not knowing.

Probably the number one word in management literature today is change. We've heard it described a hundred different ways and all of them boil down to fast and chaotic.

The real debate about change though is whether people hate it or love it. We seem to love the part of change that gives us a chance to grow and explore new avenues. We love buying new cars, exploring exotic vacation spots, wearing new clothes, and having the latest electronic gadgets. We hate the part that threatens our security. We hate wondering whether we'll have a job once the smoke clears, not knowing whether or not we'll be able to "make it" in the new environment, and not knowing if we'll have friends in the new group. What we really hate is the uncertainty of the change . . . the feeling of having no control.

The breakup of AT&T has been described as one of the most significant planned organizational changes of the twentieth century. The breakup created a high level of stress among employees who had a "job for life." Suddenly, they were "Ma Bell's orphans," abandoned by the company that had traditionally provided career-long caring and support.

Susan J. Ashford, associate professor of organizational behavior in the School of Business Administration at the University of Michigan, studies the AT&T break-up to gain information about the effectiveness of various strategies used for coping with stress during this change.

One of Ashford's findings reinforced previous studies that cited uncertainty as the prime cause of change-related stress. Most transitions are accompanied by uncertainty about procedures and the impact to daily routines and careers. Employees are uncertain about terminations, transfers, new supervisors, new policies, and possible new demands. Will they be able to meet the new demands? Will they prosper under the new conditions? Feelings of competency are suddenly disrupted and employees lose their sense of control.

Employees who can maintain a sense of competency and feelings of control, at least partially, seem to suffer less stress than those who do not experience those feelings. Self-esteem buffers the employee from the ravages of the uncertainty associated with change. Ashford's studies also found that employees who have a relatively high tolerance for ambiguity experience less stress.

THE POWER OF "CHATTING"

One surprising result of Ashford's study was that some commonly used "change techniques" actually increased stress and the one that relieved stress the most was simply "chatting." She looked at techniques such as perceiving the change as challenge, ignoring the situation, trying to find out more about change, asking for feedback and expressing feelings. The techniques that tended to mask feelings, such as looking at the challenge (called "putting on a happy face"), didn't work. The method that most often succeeded was open expression of feelings... "chatting" about the change and sharing fears and concerns. Openly discussing concerns helped reduce the stress prior to the transition and was shown to have lowered stress levels for six months following the change.

This study indicates that the most important thing a manager can do in a transition period is allow employees to express their feelings. It seems to be even more important than providing them with information about the change although that is a critical second step. Establishing a climate where employees can "chat" freely and vent their concerns greatly reduces stress and smoothes the transition even when the situation remains the same. Employees need to share their worries and concerns and know that those concerns are taken seriously. Without official permission to share their concerns, employees usually feel that they have to appear positive in order to get management approval. When they can express their feelings openly, the stress of maintaining a "front" is removed. Even if management can't remove the concerns, the employees feel that they were listened to and given consideration.

BUILDING WALLS

Marvin Weisbord begins his outstanding book *Productive Workplaces* with a story from his past. It was in the mid-60s and he was working in the printing/direct mail business his father had founded. Weisbord was fairly typical of managers during that time—everything he knew about management came from doing rather than books or workshops. When he became interested in the possibility of using incentives to increase production, a friend of his introduced him to McGregor's *Human Side of Enterprise* (the management Theory X/Theory Y book).

Weisbord immediately recognized that he wanted to be a "Theory Y" Manager but when he looked around him he saw "Theory X" stuff: "time clocks, narrow work rules, jobs so subdivided anyone would be bored, grown people treated like children, never let in on decisions, given no consequential information about the business or even their own work, expected to deliver for management and not to reason why, all in return for

a $5 raise every six months, a turkey at Christmas, and a chance, if they didn't die of boredom in the meantime, to become supervisors."

Weisbord decided to change his style of management. One of the first requests he received was for a wall down the center of the large order processing area. The billing people and the order entry people didn't like each other and the supervisors thought it would end the fighting if they couldn't see each other. In keeping with this new Theory Y management style, Weisbord built them a wall.

Order processing was organized on a typical functional basis with no cross training. Anytime someone was absent, that person's function went undone and progress was halted; since turnover and absenteeism were high, the department was often backlogged. Weisbord's first action was to reorganize the department into work teams, each handling a block of customers with each person on the team able to handle all the tasks required by the team. The new teams were formed including one person from each of the former functions and instructed to teach each other their jobs. Supervisors become floating coaches.

The first result was chaos. Problems came up that people didn't know how to handle ... problems that had always been handled by supervisors or higher management. A weekly meeting was instituted to work through all the problems. Weisbord describes the meetings, "The meetings dragged on interminably. I could not believe that such a little business could generate such a long list of problems, or that so many people knew so little about what they were doing—including me. I realized with a pang that the supervisors, now eliminated, had for years been making every decision. Every one, that is, except those (and I suddenly was appalled by the number) that they used to delegate upward—to me."

After four of those "interminable" meetings, Weisbord decided that this experiment in work redesign was a failure. There were too many problems and the weekly meetings were taking too much time. He decided to announce the end of the experiment at the fifth meeting. As the meeting opened, in an attempt to delay his announcement, he asked for problems. An embarrassed silence followed.

Finally, one woman said, "We don't have any this week." Sensing Weisbord's surprise they told him they knew how to handle all the problems from the other meetings! For Weisbord, the light dawned and he realized that the meetings he had thought a waste of time had actually been learning experiences for the team members.

Perhaps the biggest lesson from his first experiment in participative management came a week later when the teams called an ad hoc meeting and told him they wanted the wall taken down. When he asked why, they replied, "We don't need it anymore; we like talking to each other."

Weisbord summarizes his experience:

In a learning organization, of course, you don't need walls. When everybody has a chance to learn, grow, and achieve, when mistakes become okay, when a lot of people get in on the action there is a great deal more control in the system—self-control. It's the strongest kind, but it can't be bought, legislated, or behavioral-scienced in.

It's an ironic twist that the goal of almost all management systems—control—is only really achieved by turning control over to someone else. The harder we clamp down as managers, the more human nature oozes out from under. Take away the clamp and provide a guiding beacon and the ooze self-organizes and marches off in unison toward the goal. While the concept is simple and true, the implementation is complex enough to provide challenges for a lifetime.

AN UGLY DUCKING BECOMES A SWAN:
AN ORGANIZATION BECOMES CUSTOMER FOCUSED THROUGH LISTENING*
by Ruth Ebert Asercion and Vickie Myer

INTRODUCTION

The story we're about to tell is true and the names have not been changed to protect the innocent because BCS Richland, Inc. (BCSR), a subsidiary of the Boeing Company, is proud of its metamorphosis from the ugly duckling of computer support to the shining swan-like star of the Help Desk industry. The transformation occurred in the midst of an all but antiquated computer technology environment, rapid technology changes, low employee morale, and high amount of customer frustration.

BCSR, located at the Hanford site in the southern corner of Washington State, provides information resource management and computer support to the Department of Energy (DOE) complex located at the site. The primary mission of DOE is environmental restoration and waste clean-up.

End User Support (EUS), an organization within BUSR, is tasked with all aspects of microcomputer support, both hardware and software. EUS efficiently and effectively supports approximately 12,000 computer users across the entire 560 square mile site. With a small staff of 50 consultants and technicians, EUS provides support to a diverse customer base that includes engineers and scientists, as well as financial personnel, managers, and clerical support. But it wasn't always this way. BCSR management recognized it and empowered the EUS staff to make the necessary changes. Here's how they did it.

HISTORY OF BCSR HELP DESK

"The Ugly Duckling" of the Past

The EUS organization has not always been the smooth and effective organization it is today—in fact, it was an "ugly duckling!" In 1989, EUS provided computer support in an outdated environment with awkward processes.

Support was provided with three different End User Computing centers (EUC) across the Hanford Site using three different phone numbers to support 8,000 customers with a pen and paper tracking system. Field consultants rotated shifts to answer phone calls from customers and when a problem couldn't be resolved was then transferred to a consultant in the field by phone, page or slip of paper.

---

*Reprinted with permission from The Association for Quality and Participation, Cincinnati, OH (513) 381-1959. From the *17th Annual Spring Conference and Resource Mart*, April 1995. Ruth Ebert Asercion and Vickie Myer are with Boeing Computer Services, Inc., in Richland, WA.

A steady increase of customers to support, ever-changing technology, low employee morale and high customer frustrations all made it necessary to implement drastic changes.

"The Swan" of Today

Today, customers now see the EUS organization as one team who provides microcomputer support through a central point of contact. Where customers previously had to call one of three different numbers they now can call one phone number for the Help Desk. The Help Desk ties together the EUS organization and is made up of Customer Technical Support (CTS) which provides phone support, three field support End User Computing centers (EUC), PC Hardware Maintenance and Computer Aided Drafting (CAD) support groups. All of these groups work together as a finely tuned team to provide computer support in a timely and effective way to the customer. Support to the entire Hanford Site is provided by 50 consultants and technicians from these groups.

CTS is the front end to the Help Desk. It is here that all phone calls for computer problems are made. CTS consultants receive between 10,000 to 12,000 calls per month. Consultants at the Help Desk are able to answer 50-60 percent of the computer questions and problems over the phone. All calls are logged and recorded through an automated ticket tracking system. This tracking system allows for history and trending reports which are used to evaluate and improve processes. When a customer's request cannot be answered over the phone, the tracking ticket is forwarded to either a field EUC or CAD consultant for software problems or a PC technician for hardware problems.

A customer service oriented attitude is evident in the mission statement which was developed by both managers and employees:

> "Support the Hanford Site Mission by providing timely, high quality computing support services that aligns technology and our support with the customer's business needs."

Rewards of the Journey

In March of 1994, the BCSR End User Support organization was awarded the Help Desk Institute's 1994 International Help Desk Team Excellence Award. This award was presented to representatives of the team during the Help Desk Institute's 5th Annual International Help Desk Conference. The award criteria was based on all aspects of customer services, strategic quality planning, management processes and the Help Desk's professional image.

Customer Satisfaction

The question is often asked how did this change happen. How did a highly effective customer service organization develop out of a primitive environment which thought it was meeting all of their customer's needs? The answer is simple, they stopped and started listening to the customers! The customers in this case were not only the computer users who needed a quick and responsive resolution to their problems, but also internal customers like the field consultants and technicians. By listening to the needs of both internal and external customers, the Help Desk was conceived, developed and implemented.

It's an Attitude!   A phrase often heard in the EUS organization is "How can we help our customers?" Managers have tasked consultants and technicians with an end-to-end responsibility toward the customer and are empowered to accomplish this responsibility. If the customer has a problem, it is followed through until it is resolved to the customer's expectations. Often this requires much interfacing and teaming with other organizations within the company. This isn't just something written into the job description: It is an overall attitude.

Daily Conversations   Consultants and technicians begin by listening to customers when they are either on the phone or at their computer helping to solve a problem. These daily conversations are very insightful. Customers are very candid and consultants provide an environment to allow them to speak freely. The information received during daily conversations provides the opportunity to take care of the problem directly, providing the customer with information that will aid them in problem solving the problem or in a few cases, elevates the problem to a supervisor or manager. The management team allows consultants and technicians to take any necessary steps to properly help the customer.

Surveys   Random electronic surveys are sent to customers after an EUS consultant or technician provides a service. Survey questions ask how well the customer's expectations were met in regard to the whole service, i.e.; timeliness, explanation of solution and overall quality. Completed surveys are then compiled and a copy sent to the respective consultant or technician. Consultants are able to track their performance and follow up with a customer whose expectations were not met. This has become a powerful tool in improving service and listening to the customer.

Metrics   Statistics from the automatic call distribution (ACD) phone system and the automated tracking system provide monthly reports which provide a basis from which metrics are built. The statistics also provide a tool for analysis of EUS volume of work, performance in resolving all priorities of work and consistence in answering phone calls. The statistics and metrics are posted every month and all members of the EUS organization see them. Each team member has an opportunity to analyze the date and is encouraged to ask questions and make recommendations to improve service.

Computer User Profile   Every year, the EUS organization conducts a user profile. A cross-section of the computer user base is sent a questionnaire regarding the use of their microcomputer and software. This data is compiled into a computer user profile which shows what software they use, how well it is meeting their needs and how important the software is to their productivity.

Customer Focus Groups & One-on-One Meetings   Customer focus group meetings are an opportunity for department leads and managers to meet and listen to key customers. These meetings allow EUS to listen to customer perceptions and expectations of service. One-on-one meetings are held periodically to provide a customer a more personal opportunity to give feedback. Constructive feedback is often easier to share in this way.

Proactive Approach   The EUS consultants and technicians are daily on the "front lines" putting out "fires". As consultants and technicians tackle assignments and support calls, they are also looking for proactive approaches to taking care of a problem, before it actually becomes a problem. Everyone in the EUS organization is charged with and given the opportunity to improve daily processes.

THE TEAM

The "Empowered" Team

The environment within EUS is that of the "empowered" team. As described previously, we have 50 consultants and technicians and other support personnel who service approximately 12,000 computer users over a geographical area which covers approximately 560 square miles. Teaming in this environment is extremely critical. There are six main teams which cover both geographical and technical areas. The geographical teams are generally referred to as Centers. In addition to the main teams there are often subteams within a given geographical area. The geographical area is constantly changing and growing so these subteams adapt accordingly.

Some of the main advantages to having a team environment are:

customer and work-driven quality

sharing of technical expertise for resolution of customer problem

formation of teams to address process improvement in specific areas needing improvement

empowered teams having the ability to make a decision to immediately resolve a problem

the ability to cover one another's geographical area when there is a consultant or technician shortage due to vacation or illness

helping each other out with back-logs or special assignments

development of leadership skills

development of decision-making and team building skills

The Cross-Functional Team

The support provided to the Hanford computer user entails a mix of hardware and software support, network technology and network applications. These products are developed and maintained by organizations other than EUS, but are often supported by the EUS. Consequently, it is vital to the customer that EUS work with these organizations from design through implementation of new products to guarantee the least amount of impact not only to the customer but also to the support provided by EUS. All of this is accomplished through team efforts. By having a representative from EUS on the various teams that are involved in the development and maintenance of these products, we can provide the input necessary for successful introduction of these products.

For ongoing support and process improvement of existing products the same method is utilized. These teaming efforts provide better communication across organizations, a better product to the customer and a vehicle to improve existing processes.

Teams in the Hiring Process

Teams are utilized in the hiring of new consultants, technicians, managers and team leads.

Two teams are involved in the process for hiring new consultants. Both teams have representatives from each of the EUS Centers. One is comprised of managers and the other comprised of consultants. Each team independently goes through all the resumes submitted and reaches consensus on the applicants that they want to interview. The two teams then combine their consensus results and form a list of all possible candidates. Candidates are then interviewed by both teams. Each team independently reaches consensus on which candidates best meet the job qualifications. Qualifications are based first on customer service skills, then technical expertise. The results of the two teams are then combined in a joint effort. This teaming effort where teams interview and hire new consultants has met with great success in getting the right mix of consultants within the EUS.

A similar approach is used in hiring managers and team leads. However, the process varies in that the candidates are first interviewed by the management team and then once they have determined the most likely candidates, a team interview is conducted by the full team for which the manager or lead position is available.

Team Training

EUS consultant training is a top priority. Each consultant is encouraged to acquire any necessary technical, self-development or customer service training they feel necessary to properly perform their duties. In addition, BCSR provides tuition assistance for those employees who would like to further their formal college training.

To address the need for continuous technical training requirements, a team of consultants was formed to develop an innovative training program for consultants. The team conducted a survey to determine what was working and what wasn't. By doing so the team was able to find out what the specific needs and requirements were as perceived by the consultants. The name they chose for the team is SHARING OUR KNOWLEDGE, now commonly known as the SOK team.

The SOK team proceeded to design a technical training program which utilizes the expertise of consultants and other technical organizations within BCSR. This innovative approach to training, the SOK program, is not only the most efficient way to share knowledge among associates within BCSR, but is also the most cost-effective. The SOK program provides ongoing training for products used by the customer and also provides just-in-time training for the introduction of new products.

The SOK team also developed a new-hire training program which was developed through conducting a survey of all consultants asking them the best way to conduct new-hire training. The program consists of a six-week mix of classroom and on-the-job training. The training is conducted by consultants who present every aspect of computing unique to the Hanford Site.

Providing computer training for the introduction of new site-wide software product also comes under the auspices of the SOK team. The training for new software is done just-in-time.

The Team Image

EUS teams are highly motivated and constantly strive to maintain a high level of quality in services provided. Excellence in customer service is first and foremost in the minds of all EUS consultants and technicians. Each individual personally strives to provide the customer with immediate and quality solutions to computer problems. This may involve teaming with other consultants and technicians to achieve a quality end result.

In addition, consultants and technicians productively use time when they are not working with customers by increasing their knowledge base and technical expertise through training, testing and learning new and existing products. EUS consultants and technicians are proud of their skills and the service they provide their customers.

Recognition

The team environment within EUS provides for both informal and formal recognition. It is recognized by EUS that some of the most effective forms of recognition cost nothing; a simple thank you or a pat on the back for a job well done. Praise and thanks among team members is a day-to-day occurrence.

EUS also supports recognition with an individual award where team members can nominate another team member who has shown exceptional leadership and/or outstanding customer service. The SUPER award, Support Users with Pride, Excellence and Reliability, is awarded each quarter to an outstanding team member. The company also has several recognition programs which EUS utilizes.

CONTINUOUS QUALITY IMPROVEMENT

You might think that the End User Support (EUS) organization would want to rest on its laurels, having won the 1994 Team Excellence Award as best in industry from the Help Desk Institute. Nothing could be further from the truth.

Numerous improvements have been accomplished since then that play a significant role in continuing to provide even better quality support. Process improvement activities are focused on evaluating how to constantly improve services which best meet the customer's business and computer needs.

All continuous improvement efforts are in line with the EUS strategic direction of creating an environment where computer users can be more self-sufficient. Teams are used to focus on these activities—not only within EUS but across other organizations within BCSR.

Improved Services

Through process improvement, EUS was able to reduce the cycle time for providing network account services for computer users from ten working days to just minutes from time of initial call. This enables customers to receive same day service for most of their network services.

This was the result of two years of ongoing efforts by several cross-functional teams. Hurdles that were overcome included: no process owner,

power struggles, little management leadership, lack of communication and knowledge of process components, and hardware/software incompatibilities. As part of a massive realignment of the company, all components of the process were brought under one organization, a result of direct input from this team. Team members changed during this time and with more management support the goals and vision also changed. This also eliminated many of the hurdles that the team had been faced with previously. It still took another six months of ongoing team efforts to iron out the details and implement the new process. The service now known as HLAN Account Services was implemented the first of October.

Empowering the User

Another significant accomplishment, as a result of continuous quality improvement efforts, is the implementation of the HLAN User Help-n-Hints (HUH) Windows application. HUH contains information on several network applications and standard software products and provides computer users the opportunity to find their own answers to common questions. This is an important component of the strategic direction EUS is pursuing in helping computer users become more self-sufficient.

In further support of this strategic direction, EUS is also developing a DOS and Windows version of a customer-initiated software installation program. This will enable customers to install their own standard applications without having to receive a visit from an EUC consultant. The installation reduces the cycle time up to 10 working days for a field visit.

In efforts to be even more responsive to computer users experiencing difficulties, a new remote workstation utility is being implemented to allow support staff to access customers, workstations, to resolve these problems, upon customer's approval. This will enable EUS to provide immediate resolution to numerous problems that would normally be sent to the field for resolution at a later date.

Teamwork Is the Key

The EUS organization has accomplished these tasks while continuing to meet all service-level targets. It is through the integrated team efforts of phone consultants, field-support consultants and technicians working together that such ambitious undertakings have been made possible.

In conclusion, "An Ugly Duckling Becomes a Swan" by listening to the customer, both internal and external, and working together in a team environment which continuously strives to improve customer satisfaction.

CHANGING FASTER BY LEVERAGING THE VOICE OF THE CUSTOMER*
by William Band

Businesses across North America are struggling to transform their organization cultures and work processes to become "high-performing," customer-value creating enterprises. Most will not be able to change fast enough to reach the levels of achievement they hope for.

You can overcome this problem by attending to the "hidden" step in the transformation process. This means using the Voice of the Customer not only to *inform* organization change efforts, but also to *energize* and *align* them as well.

THE "HIDDEN STEP"

Thanks to efforts like "Customer Focus" or "Customer First" or "Customer Delight," organizations today are devoting considerable time and effort to *listening* to their customers more effectively.

Of course, listening to customers is one thing. Translating what you hear into *operational improvements* is quite another. Still, in recent years organizations have also devoted themselves to making such improvements, whether under the banner of "Total Quality," or "Process Reengineering," or "Cycle Time Reduction."

So, on the whole, organizations are getting better at *understanding* what customers value and at *operationalizing* around customers' wants and needs. However, they are still dissatisfied with their ability to keep pace with change: "We are understanding and operationalizing faster than ever before. But the Voice of the Customer changes so fast we can't keep up. The faster we move, the farther we fall behind."

As shown in Exhibit 1, many companies are feeling the *pain* of lost market share and eroding profit margins because the rate of change in customer expectations is increasing faster than their ability to respond.

What's needed to remedy this problem? You first must discern the root cause. There is a "hidden step" that most often goes unrecognized, and because it is unattended to, slows down the changes necessary to remain competitive. The hidden step, as illustrated in Exhibit 2, is situated *in between* Understanding and Operationalizing. This step is *Internalizing* the Voice of the Customer.

Think about where time gets used up in your company's response to a rapidly evolving marketplace. The time is consumed in three places:

- Knowing what to do
- Deciding to do it
- Doing it

Or said another way, in *Understanding* customer wants, in *Internalizing* the need to do

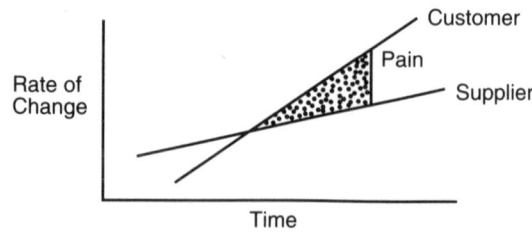

EXHIBIT 1.—FALLING BEHIND CUSTOMERS

---

*Reprinted with permission from The Association for Quality and Participation, Cincinnati, OH (513) 381-1959. From the *17th Annual Spring Conference and Resource Mart*, April 1995. William Band is vice-president of Rath & Strong, Inc., management consultants.

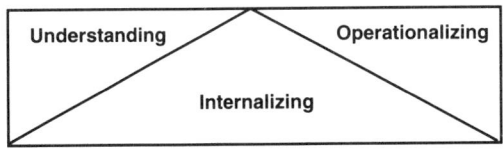

EXHIBIT 2.—INTERNALIZING THE VOICE
OF THE CUSTOMER

something about them, and in *Operationalizing* (taking action on) those wants. This has always been the case. Why does it take so long?

Perhaps your company doe market research (the Understanding phase). The results from that research then fall into the great corporate maw, are digested, and a decision to act will eventually emerge (Internalizing). Then, you put your newly acquired process reengineering skills to work and respond with new products and services (Operationalizing), and the cycle is complete.

Some problems with this approach are clear. First of all, everything is done *serially*. But experience tells us that there are always opportunities to shave off cycle time by doing as many activities as you can *concurrently*.

Second, the process is performed in a segmented, compartmentalized way. Sales and Marketing "own" the customer and are, in effect, responsible for Understanding. The Operationalizing phase is owned by, coincidentally, the Operations function. As for Internalizing, it is *not even recognized* as an explicit step, much less owned by anyone in particular.

In other words, people need to know what customers have said. They have to understand what they have heard. They have to believe that the customer's voice is being interpreted in a valid way. They have to achieve consensus as to what actions are necessary. In certain circumstances, some people—especially those who do not have direct customer contact—might need to be convinced that the Voice of the Customer has any bearing on their work in the first place.

The process of internalization does not take place overnight; it requires time and effort. As organizations get better and better at understanding and operationalizing, the *speed* of internalization of the Voice of the Customer becomes more important. It can become a key source of competitive advantage.

THE LEVERAGE IS IN THE LINKAGES

Top-rated tennis players learn early in their training that strong individual strokes are not enough to win. You must also develop your footwork and learn to put together sequences of winning moves. It is this *uniting* of skills that give you the wherewithal to overwhelm your opponent.

In the same way, top executives must learn to master a combination of critical competencies to gain leverage for enabling rapid enterprise-wide change. In particular, the Voice of the Customer is an underutilized resource for speeding up this process.

As a case in point, listen to the words of a vice president of a manufacturing company that had an enviable reputation for being on the leading edge of management practices. Committed to becoming a "high-performing enterprise," the company often hosted visits from other organizations seeking insight about the best new ways to manage.

"We've been working with our new management philosophy for nearly a decade," he said. "We see our enterprise as a *system* comprising several key elements. Each part of our system is a point of leverage that drives our business results."

"First, *connecting with customers* is highly important. We have enshrined our commitment to improving customer value in our mission statement."

"Second, we have ongoing initiatives to improve our *work processes*; decreasing cycle time is a religion in this company."

"Third, we work hard to improve and enrich our *organizational culture* to take advantage of the best ideas from everyone, regardless of rank or function. We use team-based management practices wherever practical."

"Finally, we know that *effective leadership*, at all levels, is critical to success. We work intensely to give our people the training and on-the-job experience they need to enrich their leadership skills."

Without question, the success of the company was enviable. Even with such a record, however, they were missing out on attaining even higher levels of performance. They neglected to look for the hidden opportunities for leverage *in between* the four areas of competency described.

As shown in Exhibit 3, there are three links between customers, processes, culture, and leadership that are high-potential leverage points. The Voice of the Customer can help speed up organization change in *three* ways.

• *It can **inform**.* The Voice of the Customer can help you make better informed decisions about the best work processes to "reengineer." This is the most common use of the customer information.

For example, an industrial products supplier was faced with trying to decide how to redesign its business practices to improve its standing with customers. Three options seemed attractive: offer customers faster standard delivery times, new financing options, or more product configurations.

"We thought speedy delivery would be the best way to go," reported the company's general manager. The company asked customers for their opinion. "Our customers said faster delivery would be nice, but new financing options would be *great*. So we knew exactly where to focus our efforts."

• *It can **energize**.* The issue isn't just about being informed; it's making something happen with the information you have. The Voice of the Customer can provide the energy boost that's needed.

Take the case of a leading manufacturer of electronic devices. For years, customers had been asking for a "small" wireless model. For just as long, the company's response had been, "We already offer a 'small' wireless product." Then one day a customer stood up in front of a group of the company's senior executives and said, "No. I mean *small*, like *this!*" Whereupon he pointed to the nail on his finger—about 1/3 the size of the

company's existing "small" model—to illustrate his point.

After hearing (and seeing) what the customer *really* wanted, everyone got excited and a commitment was made to quickly develop the new product. The company successfully introduced a "mini-model" that was a roaring success.

The key lies in just who heard the customer's voice. It wasn't just people from sales and marketing and customer service. It was also people from manufacturing, personnel, and the corporate staff. The company had established mechanisms so that a broader range of people heard what the customer had to say—directly and unambiguously—and they were moved to overcome institutional inertia and take action.

• *It can **align**.* The right people must hear The Voice of the Customer, or the organization will be slow to respond. The "right people" are those with the power to act on customers' suggestions.

For example, one company made sure important customer information was available to the most influential individuals in the business. They organized customer forums and panels that exposed senior executives to customer concerns. They conducted customer surveys, and the findings were widely communicated throughout the company. Senior leaders also made visits to customer sites.

When an accountant in the company attended a series of customer interviews, she had an inspiration for a way to improve forecasting which would increase customer service and lower costs. One of her colleagues observed "She didn't wait around looking for approval or permission. She just went and tested out her idea. It worked, so we implemented it. She had the confidence to do it because she knew that we're all moving in the same direction . . . that we're all aligned around what we've been hearing from customers."

THREE USEFUL TOOLS

How can you take advantage of all three ways of using the Voice to the Customer to spur rapid

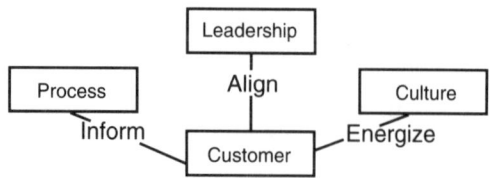

EXHIBIT 3.—THREE LEVERAGE POINTS

Customer Value Criteria	CORE PROCESS							
	New Product/ Service Development	Supplier Management	Order Acquisition	Order Fulfillment	Invoicing and Cash Collection	Financial Resources Acquisition and Management	Human Resources Acquisition and Management	Competitive Strategy Development
Quality								
•								
•								
•								
Service								
•								
•								
•								
Cost/Price								
•								
•								
•								
Time								
•								
•								
•								
Total Score								

Scoring: Low Impact = 1   Medium Impact = 2   High Impact = 3

EXHIBIT 4.—VALUE DEPLOYMENT MATRIX

change? There are three tools that make the task easier.

Value Deployment Matrix

Great strides are being made in the techniques for understanding what customers value. Similarly, enterprises are learning new skills to redesign work processes in order to operationalize value improvement. A potential pitfall is not knowing what impact specific business processes have on specific customer perceptions. The Value Deployment Matrix (VDM), shown in Exhibit 4, can *inform* you about the business processes most important to delivering value.

The VDM is an adaption of the matrices used in Quality Function Deployment (QFD). Product design teams use QFD matrices to systematically think through the connection between customer requirements and the specific features that need to be designed into a product to meet those expectations.

Theoretically, it's rather simple to complete a VDM. Its true power lies in the kind of information you have to gather, and the insight gained by a senior executive team as they work through the interrelationships in the data. The three steps to creating a VDM are:

• *Determine what customers value.* To complete the "Y-axis" of the matrix, you must understake dialog and research with customers to determine the specific criteria they use to judge the value of doing business with your organization.

Organize the "value attributes" into categories, reflecting the four ways of creating customer value: 1) increasing quality, 2) increasing service, 3) reducing cost, 4) reducing cycle time. You should also ascertain the relative importance of each value attribute.

• *Define the organization's core business processes.* To complete the "X-axis" of the matrix, you must define your "core business processes." Every organization comprises a handful of core processes. Each core process consists of a set of interrelated activities, decisions, information, and material flow. Core processes are the means through which value is actually created for customers. Core processes cut across functional, geographic, business-unit, and even company boundaries.

Many companies have never thought of themselves as comprising a collection of cross-functional processes. The traditional view defines an organization in terms of departmental functions. For example, a manufacturer might have four essential business processes: new product and process design, customer-order-to-delivery, materials management, and estimating and contracting.

Defining processes is important so you can identify the best focal points for creating value. For example, a Ford Motor Company survey showed that 75 percent of a product's costs are fixed by decisions made in the product design process, not in production. Yet, most companies do not work to improve the way products are designed. In other words, little attention is paid to a process that has the greatest effect on cost and creates the most utility for users.

• *Determine the relative impact of each core process on customer value perception.* The objective of business process improvement is to eliminate work that adds cost but does not add value to the product (or service); or, anything that negatively affects product quality or that adds time to the process. Obviously, it is important to target the right processes for improvement.

To accomplish this, use the VDM to "score" each process relative to each customer value attribute. Low Impact is scored as a "1"; Medium Impact as a "2"; and High Impact as a "3." By summing the scores in each column, you will identify the processes most critical to delivering customer value.

Constructing a VDM stimulates discussion and debate that helps top management teams to reach consensus on the most important priorities for high-value performance. For example, a construction materials company was trying to stem a tide of lost customers caused by aggressive competitors who were slashing prices. The company responded to this threat with an intensive "service improvement" initiative. A great effort was made to improve the company's hiring and training processes to produce employees who were "nicer" to customers.

However, after they had completed a VDM, senior executives realized the best way to improve buyer loyalty was to increase speed of delivery and offer more creative credit options. Research revealed courteous treatment was, of course, desired by customers. But, courtesy was of little value if product was not available when needed, or if the terms of sale were too strict. As a result, the company refused its attention on these latter high-value benefits.

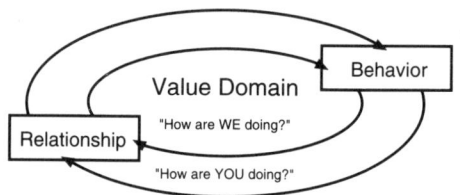

EXHIBIT 5.—VALUE CONVERSATIONS

Value Conversations

Engaging customers in "value conversations" is an effective way to *energize* a company for change. A value conversation is a specialized kind of interview designed to uncover *unarticulated* customer needs rather than just to gather data about current performance. And, it exposes more people in your organization to customers in a way that enables a critical mass of "customer thinkers" to emerge within the company.

Value Conversations are conducted by cross-functional teams of employees who make personal contact with buyers in person or by telephone. It is important that all parts of the company be represented on the teams. Most people in an organization don't have direct contact with customers, but what they do on the job can have a profound effect on customer satisfaction. Value Conversations help employees to get a better "feel" for what customers truly value.

Each team needs special training in how to effectively interact with customers during the Value Conversations. Then, interviews are scheduled to include a representative sample of customers.

One of the aims of a value conversation is to change the nature of the relationship between buyer and supplier so that, working *together*, new opportunities for creating value can be discovered. The relationship between buyer and supplier can be viewed as the "Value Domain": the "space" where value as created. The goal of Value Conversations are to expand the Value Domain, to enlarge the opportunity for mutual problem solving. As illustrated in Exhibit 5, the questions used during a Value Conversation are different from standard "customer satisfaction" types of survey questions. The aim is to better understand what it feels like to be a customer. Why?

Because, when you boil it down, a typical customer satisfaction survey asks one basic type of question:

"How are *we* doing?"

In other words, we typically ask the customer how well we are performing compared to a list of predetermined criteria which presumably define customer satisfaction. If there is one thing we can be sure of, it's that customers don't care how we're doing. They care about how *they're* doing. It's not wrong to ask "How are *we* doing?" It's just not enough. Asking the companion question, "How are *you* doing?" is essential for a number of reasons:

- *It leads more directly to an understanding of customers' true wants and needs.* For example, every hotel room you've ever been in has some sort of "How are *we* doing?" survey card on the dresser. It asks guests to relate things like the friendliness and efficiency of the check-in process, or the temperature of the meal ordered from room service. While those things are important to know, they're not top-of-mind to hotel guests who, when they check in, are more apt to be thinking something along the lines of, "The flight into town was brutal. I've had a long day. I'm exhausted. I've still got important business to do tonight to prepare for tomorrow. I don't want any hassles."

  Would it be useful for hotel employees to have a powerful, visceral understanding of their guests' state of mind when they serve them or design new services? It would seem so. How do you create such empathy for customers? By asking them, "How are *you* doing?"

- *You're more apt to come up with breakthrough ideas.* Customers can only speak from their own frame of reference. So while customers can tell you whether the check-in process at the hotel was friendly and efficient, the question, "Why do you need a check-in process at all?" is not likely to come up. You are more likely led to think about such radical notions if you engage in a fundamentally different line of inquiry, asking questions designed to get at "How are *you* doing?"

- *It creates a more positive, inspiring climate within your organization.* When you ask, "How are *we* doing?", the focus inevitably winds up being on avoiding problems and not making mistakes—this is rather negative and enervating to the organization. But

when you ask, "How are *you* doing?" the implication is that you are gathering important data that will be used to help make informed choices about how you can apply your special expertise to make something positive happen. That's a much better platform on which to build change efforts.

- *Satisfying customers doesn't build customer loyalty, although dissatisfying customers can cost it.* While it's true that "all things being equal," customers will stay with the supplier that satisfies them, that qualifier is a very restrictive one.

Given the pace of change these days, things are rarely equal. The focus, therefore, should be not only on how you did, but also on what you will be *doing next*. The objective should be to create memorable (positive) experiences for customers and not just to avoid dissatisfying them. That calls for knowing your customers in a different way, and that calls for asking "How are *you* doing?"

Influence Leverage Map

The third tool, the Influence Leverage Map, is used to *align* the personal priorities of leaders to the changing realities of the marketplace.

It's one of the inescapable facts of organizational life that businesses are not democracies. Certain individuals, because of their roles and position, have more influence in decision making and have greater control of resources than others. Others, by virtue of their tenure, expertise, and personality, can wield great informal power. Even the lowest rung employee has the power to thwart change by selectively ignoring orders from above.

The Voice of the Customer can be a powerful force for transformation. It can help the individuals in an organization see the *need for change*: threats to the business, or untapped opportunities for growth. However, if the most influential people in your enterprise are not *aware* of threats and opportunities, the needed responses will be slow in coming. A key tactic for speeding change is to ensure that the customer's voice reaches the ears of influential people.

The Influence Leverage Map, shown in Exhibit 6, is a simple way for identifying the people with the most formal and informal influence in

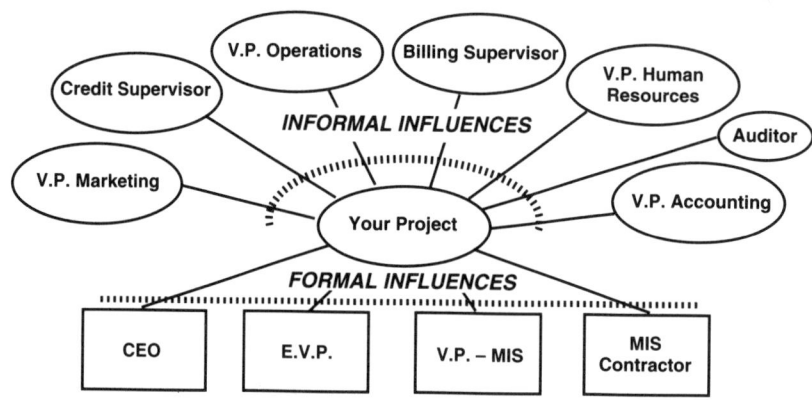

*EXHIBIT 6.—*INFLUENCE LEVERAGE MAP

your organization. The Map is a "stakeholder analysis" because your purpose is to identify the people who have a stake in change or the status quo. A little time spent thinking about the patterns of influence will make it apparent where the leverage points for change exist within the social system of the company.

When the mapping is complete, you can move on to the next two steps: 1) anticipate the likely attitude of each individual toward change: positive or negative, 2) dig deeper and ask yourself *why* they hold these attitudes—what are the consequences to them of change? Answering these questions may require some "detective work," talking to the individuals involved, probing colleagues, observing behavior. Once complete, you will have a picture of where to "broadcast" the Voice of the Customer.

For example, the employees at one company endured the complaints of customers about the unreliability of the equipment they manufactured. Front-line workers were unsuccessful in getting top management to make the investment in new equipment needed to remedy the problem.

The workers constructed an Influence Leverage Map to try to find a solution to their dilemma. Their analysis helped them to understand that middle managers were sympathetic to

the need to spend the money, but the power to release the funds was held only by the top executive of the company. The middle managers themselves said they didn't know how to effectively prod the President to make the investment.

As result of these new insights, front-line workers suggested a plan for working with middle managers to solve the problem. They asked some of the managers to organize a series of customers visits to the manufacturing facility. They then asked the President to make "courtesy" appearances when customers arrived on-site. The organizers had a special motive for doing so. The meetings gave customers the opportunity to express their concerns directly to the chief decision maker. After hearing the complaints first-hand, the President quickly released the funds needed to resolve the issue.

To keep up with today's rapidly changing marketplace, your enterprise must find ways to adapt ever more quickly. The key to success is how fast the organization "internalizes" the need for change. Using the tools described above, your company can gain increased leverage from the Voice of the Customer. The result? Not only will you be better *informed*, but your organization will be better *energized* and *aligned* as well.

QUALITY SUCCESS STORIES IN SAN ANTONIO INDUSTRY*
by Rafael G. Moras, Ph.D., P.E., Constantino Moras Sánchez, and Roger G. Ford, Ph.D., P.E.

In this article, we will discuss the results of a survey of manufacturing companies located in San Antonio, Texas. The purpose of the survey was to investigate the degree of application and success of total quality management (TQM) and Just-in-Time (JIT) principles and techniques. Our goal is to enable interested readers to relate some of the accomplishments realized by the companies in the survey to their own manufacturing plants, and devise ways to improve productivity at their location.

PROCEDURE

A two-page questionnaire was mailed to plant managers of 279 manufacturing companies located in San Antonio. The questionnaire contained twenty questions worded carefully to avoid ambiguity. Ninety-three questionnaires were returned, for a response rate of 33%. This response rate compares favorably with those experienced by others conducting similar surveys; in particular, Cheng [1], 20%; Barton [2], 33%; Im and Lee [3], 36%; and Rao [4], 22%.

EXHIBIT 1.—INDUSTRY CATEGORY OF RESPONDENTS

Type of Industry	Number of Respondents
Food	9
Defense	8
Aerospace	7
Electrical or electronic	7
Plastics	7
Beverage	5
Chemical	5
Clothing	5
Automobile	4
Other	36

RESULTS

The respondents were asked to indicate the type of products manufactured at their plant. Many respondents reported belonging to the food, defense-related, aerospace, electrical-electronic, or plastic industries. Other companies produced drinks, chemicals, clothing items, or automobile parts. The remaining responses were quite varied and are summarized in Exhibit 1. Other types of industry include flag, construction, steel, newspaper, printing, furniture, aircraft, brick, tractors, diesel engine, optical, textile, cosmetics, bottled water, woodwork, containers, envelopes, limestone, heating and air conditioning, semiconductor, vinyl, petroleum, and telecommunications.

There was considerable variation in the age of the companies participating in the survey. The oldest company had been in business for 117 years, while others had started operations less than one year before this study was conducted.

Seventy-two of the 93 respondents claimed to be using some form of TQM or JIT. They were asked which of the following techniques were being applied:

A. Kanban
B. Lot-size reduction
C. Plant layout modifications
D. Vendor programs
E. Maintenance programs
F. Setup-time reduction
G. Standardization
H. Cross-training
I. Simultaneous engineering
J. Visual administration (managing by observation)
K. Synchronous manufacturing
L. Work cells
M. Total employee involvement
N. Statistical quality control
O. Total quality management

*Reprinted with permission from The American Production and Inventory Control Society, *Production and Inventory Management Journal,* Fourth Quarter, 1994. Rafael G. Moras, PhD, PE is a member of the department of engineering at St. Mary's University in San Antonio, TX. Constantino Moras Sánchez, is a member of the Center for Research and Graduate Studies at Orizaba Technological Institute, in Orizaba, Ver, Mexico. Roger G. Ford, PhD, PE, is a member of the department of engineering at St. Mary's University in San Antonio, TX.

EXHIBIT 2.—PRINCIPLES AND TECHNIQUES USED BY THE RESPONDENTS

Technique or Principle	Respondent																		
	1	2	3	4	5	6	7	8	9	10	11	12	13	14	15	16	17	18	19
A	X						X					X					X		
B	X		X														X		
C	X				X	X				X		X	X	X		X	X	X	X
D	X				X	X				X		X	X	X		X	X		X
E	X				X	X				X		X		X	X		X	X	X
F	X		X							X	X	X	X	X			X		
G	X	X			X	X				X		X	X	X		X	X	X	X
H	X	X		X	X	X				X		X	X	X		X	X	X	X
I	X		X		X	X	X	X	X	X	X	X	X	X	X	X	X	X	X
J	X	X	X			X							X				X		
K			X									X					X		X
L	X		X							X			X				X		
M	X		X	X								X					X		
N	X	X			X		X	X	X	X		X	X	X		X	X	X	X
O	X		X	X		X	X		X	X	X	X	X	X		X	X		
P	X	X			X			X			X	X	X	X	X		X	X	X
Q	X							X		X	X		X	X		X	X	X	X
R	X			X		X	X	X	X			X		X		X	X		
S	X		X										X				X		
T	X				X		X	X				X		X	X		X		X

Technique or Principle	Respondent																			
	20	21	22	23	24	25	26	27	28	29	30	31	32	33	34	35	36	37	38	39
A											X	X						X		
B							X	X			X	X					X	X	X	
C	X	X				X	X				X	X	X		X	X	X	X	X	
D	X		X				X				X	X			X	X	X	X		X
E	X						X	X	X		X		X			X	X	X		X
F				X			X	X	X		X	X			X	X				
G					X		X	X	X		X		X		X	X	X		X	
H	X	X		X			X	X	X			X	X	X	X	X	X	X	X	
I	X	X	X				X	X		X	X	X	X	X	X	X	X	X	X	X
J	X	X										X			X					
K																				
L	X													X	X					
M	X							X			X	X							X	
N	X						X	X		X		X		X	X	X	X	X		X
O	X								X		X	X								X
P	X						X				X	X							X	X
Q	X	X					X	X			X	X				X		X	X	X
R	X								X		X	X						X	X	X
S							X					X		X	X	X	X			
T	X					X						X						X	X	X

EXHIBIT 2.—(continued)

Technique or Principle	40	41	42	43	44	45	46	47	48	49	50	51	52	53	54	55	56	57	58
A																			
B											X	X							
C				X						X		X		X	X	X			X
D				X					X			X	X	X	X	X			X
E	X	X	X	X		X	X			X	X	X	X	X	X	X			X
F											X	X							X
G				X		X				X	X	X	X	X	X	X			
H	X	X		X		X	X		X	X		X	X	X			X	X	
I	X		X	X		X	X	X	X			X	X	X			X	X	X
J	X												X	X		X			X
K			X																
L	X																		
M	X																X		
N	X	X	X	X		X		X				X	X		X	X			
O							X				X	X		X		X			
P			X	X			X	X						X	X			X	
Q						X	X					X		X			X		
R		X		X			X				X	X					X	X	
S				X	X				X					X	X				
T					X									X					

Technique or Principle	59	60	61	62	63	64	65	66	67	68	69	70	71	72	No. Companies Applying
A															7
B	X											X			14
C	X					X						X	X		34
D		X	X		X	X					X	X		X	34
E	X	X			X	X			X						39
F	X				X	X					X		X	X	25
G	X	X	X		X					X	X	X			36
H	X	X			X	X		X					X	X	46
I	X							X				X			49
J						X					X		X		17
K						X						X			8
L	X														10
M	X				X									X	15
N		X			X				X	X	X		X		41
O	X	X	X						X						27
P		X							X			X			30
Q		X			X	X			X	X	X		X		32
R									X						28
S	X	X	X		X	X						X	X	X	21
T		X										X			19

P. Problem solving teams
Q. Statistical process control
R. Any type of quality program
S. Lead-time reduction
T. Deming, Juran, Crosby principles

Some of these techniques or principles are generally considered to fall under the total quality management umbrella (i.e., SQC, SPC, the philosophies of Deming, Juran, and Crosby, quality programs, problem-solving teams). Some others are typically listed as components of Just-in-Time (i.e., reduction of setup and lead times, kanban). Moreover, some techniques may be classified as elements of both JIT or TQM (i.e., lot-size reduction, vendor programs, cross-training). What is most important is that they are all productivity improvement techniques.

The techniques or principles implemented by each company are presented in Exhibit 2 by letter designation.

A random code number was assigned to each company to ensure complete confidentiality. While the maximum number of techniques applied by any company was 20, the minimum was one. More than 50% of the respondents indicated that they had adopted a quality program, cross-training, total employee involvement, or maintenance programs. Many others had implemented vendor programs, modified their plant layout, standardized processes and parts, or formed problem-solving teams. Only a few respondents had implemented synchronized manufacturing, simultaneous engineering or kanban. Four respondents did not indicate any specific techniques. The number of companies applying each technique is depicted in the histogram shown in Exhibit 3.

A related question explored the results of the application of TQM/JIT. Specific inquiries were made concerning the following categories:

A. Higher productivity
B. Reduced production costs
C. Shorter cycle times
D. Lower inventory levels
E. Shorter lead times
F. Higher inventory turnover ratio
G. Fewer line stoppages
H. Higher quality

The respondents were given two options to express the relative change in each category: either (1) provide an exact figure (in the form of a percentage change) or (2) indicate improvement with a check mark. Exhibit 5, on page 3-100 summarizes the results experienced by each company by letter designation. Increased quality and reduced production costs were the most important benefits of TQM/JIT. Other reported benefits were increased productivity, lower inventory levels, and a higher inventory turnover ratio. Lead times and cycle times were shortened by many companies. Only five companies—29, 50, 62, and 66—failed to obtain any results. Company 66 stated that the main reason for their lack of results was the fact that they had started JIT implementation only a few weeks prior to answering the questionnaire. The number of companies experiencing each result is shown in Exhibit 4.

The respondents applying TQM/JIT were asked if, in their opinion, there was a need for TQM/JIT education. Forty-two of the respondents reported that education or training was needed in their plant at all levels. Six companies reported that this type of education was not needed at all. The remaining 24 respondents stated that education was needed only at certain managerial levels (i.e., executive, labor force, management, or supervisory).

ANALYSIS OF RESULTS

The results of many successful productivity improvement efforts are often only reported internally. There is the possibility that in some of the returned questionnaires, only the most significant results were reported; other techniques could have been implemented without being mentioned. However, this study provided several major findings. An analysis of the responses reveals that:

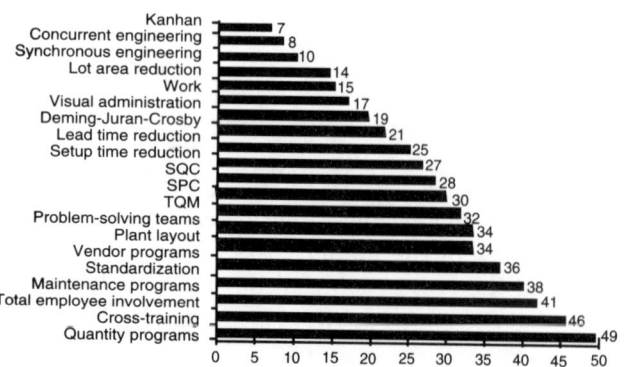

EXHIBIT 3.—NUMBER OF COMPANIES APPLYING
EACH TECHNIQUE

1. The implementation of JIT or TQM appears to be a flexible process. Only one company (17) had applied all the techniques or principles mentioned in the questionnaire. The rest of the firms were applying only a selected number of techniques, and some companies exclusively implemented one technique. Given the great variety of applications, it would be impractical to provide a strict procedure for TQM/JIT implementation. Each manufacturing environment is unique, and the problem solver is usually confronted with many alternatives.

2. It is significant to note the high percentage of respondents indicating the implementation of quality programs (49 out of 72–68%), cross-training (46 out of 72–64%), total employee involvement (41 out of 72–57%), and maintenance programs (39 out of 72–54%).

3. The application of TQM or JIT techniques usually produces benefits. Sixty-eight of the companies with TQM or JIT programs had realized improvements in at least one of the categories mentioned in the questionnaire. It is not necessary to apply all the techniques and principles usually mentioned in the literature to successfully implement TQM or JIT.

4. No particular technique or principle appears to be a requirement for successful implementation of TQM/JIT. For instance, some companies in the survey that did not have a vendor program applied JIT by reducing their setup times or by modifying their plant layout. A manager should not use the lack of a particular technique as an excuse to delay a productivity improvement effort identifiable as TQM or JIT.

5. Ideally, a manufacturing system should run smoothly, with zero defects and zero inventory. However, although productivity may improve considerably as a result of the implementation of TQM and/or JIT, the ideal targets may never be achieved.

6. A comparison of Exhibits 2 and 4 seems to suggest a correlation between the total number of TQM/JIT techniques and the perceived benefits reported by a company. It appears that the more techniques a company uses, the greater the benefit to the company.

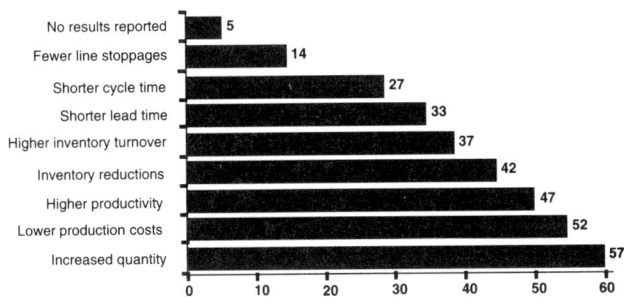

EXHIBIT 4.—NUMBER OF COMPANIES EXPERIENCING RESULT

CONCLUDING REMARKS

While this study dealt exclusively with San Antonio industry, the conclusions should be universally applicable. The companies responding to the questionnaire belong to different types of industries and vary both in size and annual sales. Their level of technology is varied as well. While some companies producing electronic products can be considered to be high tech, many others are definitely labor intensive. Managers interested in improving quality and productivity should take the results reported here as a strong indicator that TQM and JIT are utilized extensively (as the literature would indicate) and can be applied in every type of industry.

The reportedly high usage of quality programs, being the most widely used of all the techniques, at 68%, reinforces the generally accepted fact that quality is foremost in the minds of those manufacturing products for consumer use. Competition is requiring virtually everyone to be concerned about quality.

Because of the increasing labor costs, cross-training is a crucial factor in maximizing utility of existing employees. The second highest utilized technique in our survey, at 64%, was cross-training. In addition, retaining good employees is very important because of the high cost of training new employees and the loss of efficiency in production usually experienced during the training process. Total employee involvement was the third most popular technique in the survey, at 57%, indicating the perceived need to keep employees informed in order to raise their morale, thus increasing retention rates.

Because of the higher costs of doing business and the realization that downtime is both costly to the bottom line as well as disruptive to production schedules, maintenance programs were found to be the fourth most utilized of the techniques in the survey at 54%. The practice of

EXHIBIT 5.—RESULTS OBTAINED BY EACH COMPANY

Respondent

Result	1	2	3	4	5	6	7	8	9	10	11	12	13	14	15	16	17	18	19
A	X	X		X	X	X		X		X	X	X	X	X	X	X	X	X	X
B	X	X		X	X	X	X	X		X		X	X	X	X	X	X	X	X
C	X	X					X			X			X	X		X	X		X
D	X	X	X		X	X	X			X	X	X	X	X		X	X		
E	X	X	X		X		X				X	X	X				X		
F	X	X	X		X	X				X		X	X			X	X		X
G		X												X				X	
H	X	X		X	X	X	X	X	X	X	X	X	X	X	X	X	X	X	X

Respondent

Result	20	21	22	23	24	25	26	27	28	29	30	31	32	33	34	35	36	37	38	39
A	X			X		X	5	X	X		X	X	X		10	X	X		X	X
B	X			X		X	10	X	X		X	X			10	X	X	X	X	X
C								X			X	X			10	X	X	X		
D	X	X				X	15	X					X	X	50	X		X	X	X
E	X				X		5	X			X	X		X	25	X				
F		X					10	X					X	X	50	X		X	X	X
G											X				X					
H	X	X	X	X		X	20		X		X	X	X		25	X	X	X	X	X

Respondent

Result	40	41	42	43	44	45	46	47	48	49	50	51	52	53	54	55	56	57	58
A	X	X	20			X							X	X	X		20		X
B	X	X	10			X	X	X	X	X		X	X	X	X	X			X
C	X		2					X					X			X	X		
D	X		15	X	X					X		X	X	X		X	X		
E	X	X	20	X	X		X						X	X					
F	X		50	X	X		X			X		X	X				X		X
G							X	X	X					X		X			
H	X	X	X	15		X	X	X				X	X		X	X	X	X	X

Respondent

Result	59	60	61	62	63	64	65	66	67	68	69	70	71	72	No. of Companies Obtaining Result
A	X		X						X	X	X	X	X	X	47
B	X	X			10				X	X	X	X	X		52
C	X	X			10					X				X	27
D	X	X				X			X	X	X		X		42
E	X				5					X	X	X	X	X	33
F	X					X			X	X	X		X		37
G	X									X		X	X		14
H	X	X	X		5				X	X		X	X	X	57

keeping machines in good working order delays new machine purchases and reduces downtime during production cycles.

There are usually two alternatives available to improve productivity. The first option is to enhance the control of production resources. This enhanced control is essential regardless of the level of technology used by the plant. The second approach (which is not always beneficial) consists of increased use of advanced technologies and manufacturing processes. Proper understanding of the technologies and techniques precludes the implementation of anything new. These results can serve as a benchmarking information source for interested manufacturing managers to compare their in-place productivity improvement techniques with those used by the companies surveyed.

REFERENCES

1. Cheng, T. "The Just-in-Time Production: A Survey of Its Development and Perception in the Hong Kong Electronic Industry," *Omega* 16, no. 1 (1988): 25–32.

2. Barton, M. F., S. Agarwal, and L. M. Rockwell, Jr. "Meeting the Challenge of Management Concepts." *Management Accounting* (September 1988): 49–53.

3. Im, J. H., and S. M. Lee. "Implementation of Just-in-Time Systems in U.S. Manufacturing Firms." *International Journal of Operations and Production Management* 9, no. 1: 5–14.

4. Rao, A. "Manufacturing Systems—Changing to Support JIT." *Production and Inventory Management Journal* 30, no. 2 (1989): 18–21.

STILL LEADERSHIP*
by Tom Peters

"All of the 'Great' management ideas and gurus have failed us. Meanwhile, companies large and small have been inventing an approach to making money that is as radical as it is simple. For many of us it will quickly become the only way to run a business." With those immodest words on the cover, the June issue of Inc. purportedly demolishes all fads . . . and, surprise, introduces its very own wannabe fad! It's "open-book management" time, sports fans.

"My dad can beat up your dad." And "my fad's better'n your fad." That's the way it feels. Business folks are rightfully confused by the maelstrom of change. Consulting fee growth is going through the roof; gurus are sprouting up like mushrooms after a summer downpour; and the torrent of fads rushes through corporate America like the Mississippi on a rampage.

Consider: Total Quality Management, re-engineering, the flat organization, the virtual corporation, customer-isking, the learning organization, third-wave management, empowerment, teams for all seasons and all reasons, and now, thanks to Inc., open-book management. What in the hell is a manager supposed to make of it? Is it all hype?

A friend who runs a successful nonprofit (and is an unbashed consultant baiter/hater) thinks it is. "Leadership," she says, "that's it. Give me, for example, a rotten school system, a decrepit schoolhouse, a school-budget crisis but a great principal, and you've got a good-to-great school. Give me a 'great' system, great facility, etc. but a rotten principal, and you've got a poor-to-awful school."

She's not alone. Jim O'Toole of the Aspen Institute says the same thing in a scholarly way in Leading Change. Most/almost all of the "salvation-through-quality, re-engineering, etc." programs fail; the only constant that correlates with organizational success is over-the-top leadership.

My own take is as follows. There is usually gold in them thar hills of fad, even if most "programs" do fail; leadership is a sine qua non for standout performance; there are indeed some constants; and a new, if still inchoate, paradigm (if we must use that damnable word) is emerging.

Gold in fad hills. The date is 1980: Japan Inc. is kicking Detroit's butt. The date is 1995: Detroit is more or less roaring back, and the yen at 85 yen-to-the-dollar is far from the whole story. Net: America had no quality tradition. Fad or not, high program failure rate or not, the "quality thing" is real, firmly embedded in the American managerial psyche and has improved national competitiveness.

*Reprinted with permission from *FORBES ASAP Magazine* © Forbes Inc., 1995.

Deming's 14 steps, Crosby's "quality is free," the "MBN-QAC" (or Malcolm Baldrige National Quality Award Criteria) etc. are not the point. And who cares if 90% of balloon-launched programs don't amount to a hill of beans? The best are showing the way. The tide is rising. And laundromat owners as well as jet-engine makers now speak the language of quality, however haltingly.

The date is 1985: Thanks to Mike Milken and international competition, our corporate giants are forced to get lean and flat. How do you manage these newly shaped buggers? Late 1995: The answer is . . . re-engineering.

Sure, re-engineering can be a cover for mindless middle-management genocide, but the essential idea stands. Repeat of TQM: Most re-engineering programs fail. The hype nauseates. But . . . the tide is rising, true-believer stars are showing the way and we are learning to manage "horizontally."

The quality/re-engineering "fad" stories are repeated chapter and verse for virtual organizations, empowerment and so on: a lot of smoke, numerous fires, a handful of bonfires and a slowly rising tide. In fact, most of the grand fads are rooted in good sense. Peter Drucker's mid-'50s management by objectives, though perverted into bureaucratic gobbledygook, was perfect for the disorganized times (post-World War II; firms getting huge, growing fast . . . without a coherent management framework). Message: Just because it's faddish, just because it's hyped and then poorly executed most of the time, don't write it off.

It's leadership, meathead. I agree with psychologist James Hillman: Leaders are more or less born, not made (most recently stated in his book Kinds of Power). Leadership training can lead to awareness, but some folks have the touch, a lot don't. If the "got its" aren't born to it, they certainly are well on their way to it by age 10. And I believe, as do Jim O'Toole and my consultant-hating pal from the nonprofit world, that inspired leadership can turn sows' ears (rotten circumstances) into silk purses (great schools, great factories, etc.).

Witness, again, the quality "revolution." Exemplar companies, such as Milliken & Co., have all the charts, all the graphs, use the language. But the magic factor is, pure and simple, "Rushmorean leadership," to steal a phrase from O'Toole. Roger Milliken at Milliken & Co. lives, sleeps, eats, breathes, sweats quality. Go to Germany, as I did a couple of years ago to study stel-

lar middle-sized companies (members of the Mittelstand), and you'll get it. No quality circles, No statistical process-control charts. But talk, even for a few minutes, with Siegfried Meister, boss of the high-end stove-maker Rational, and you will really begin to understand what it means when quality is in the genes. The passion is there. The integrity is there. In a word, leadership!

Truth is, there's truth to be had. I'm convinced, after watching and working in organizations for three decades, that there are five constants that mark success sustainers:

Decentralization. A lot of the In Search of Excellence companies let me down. But the three I loved most when Bob Waterman and I did the research for the book in 1979 still inspire me; namely Hewlett-Packard, Johnson & Johnson, 3M. Their businesses are different. All are participants in intense global horse races. But, year in and year out, they deliver . . . and reinvent. The common core: an amazingly high level of entrepreneurship in monster-sized institutions. You can get decentralization very wrong (often decentralization on paper isn't decentralization in reality), but granting astonishing degrees of unit autonomy, encouraging entrepreneurship and more or less letting the chips fall where they may tends to be the No. 1 key to sustained vitality.

Empowerment. No word has been so overused, and thence abused, in the last few years. Nonetheless, giving everyone a piece of the action, fiscally and psychologically, and letting them by and large do their own thing . . . well, that is the ticket.

I was highly amused when the Harvard Business Review (May-June 1995) featured an article by star business researchers Christopher Bartlett and Sumantra Ghoshal, titled "Changing the Role of Top Management: Beyond Systems to People." It turns out that these two scholars have discovered human beings. Good for them. And good for corporations that are getting it. Again, the empowerment "thing" can be screwed up to a fare-thee-well, but immeasurable energy is unleashed when it's done right.

A passion for product. Button-down strategy researcher Michael Porter sounds more like Elmer Gantry when he says, "You almost have to be a true believer to be competitive. . . . Of the hundreds and hundreds of world-class companies from around the world that I studied, an enormous proportion were . . . run by some maniac who had spent the last 20 years of his life on a crusade to produce the best product."

I have discovered there are two sorts of corporate bosses: those who are gung-ho about management per se, and those who are obsessed with the product or service they deliver. Talk with the former for an hour, and you may still have no idea what they make. Hang around the others for 15 seconds, and you'll be regaled (like it or not, and it can get old for the innocent bystander) by tale after tale of the product, how it's being improved and changed, why it's great, etc.

Great systems. Okay, so I just trashed Bartlett and Ghoshal for having belatedly discovered that people are more important than systems. I believe that, but there's still lots of room for great systems. Pittsburgh-based K. Barchetti Shops has won accolades as an awesome retailer, and boss Katherine Barchetti's secret is totally aimed-at-the-customer systems (and the most sophisticated application of information technology I've seen in a small firm). Research by Mc-Kinsey & Co.'s Global Institute suggests that methods of organization (such as the Japanese automakers' lean production system) contribute more to national productivity than any other factor. Bottom line: Svelte, focused systems are priceless.

Paranoia. "Only the paranoid survive," claims ever-paranoid Intel chief Andy Grove in an oft-quoted (and deservedly so) line. "The new code of conduct," Dartmouth business school professor Rich D'Avent writes in *Hypercompetition*, "is an active strategy of disrupting the status quo to create a series of unsustainable advantages."

Today's' winners, and especially tomorrow's, will have a penchant for disruption, a love of disorder—and even a willingness to throw baby parts (e.g., cherished "core competencies") out with the bathwater . . . again and again.

Something big is going down. Canadian researcher Henry Mintzberg, by far the most underrated management "guru" around, chides us for our arrogance. Every generation, he says, claims the old days were simple, while today is fraught with peril and unprecedented change. There's some truth to Mintzberg's rap. In a sense, the five verities cited above are for the ages: decentralize, empower people, love that product, etc.

Nonetheless, it is a spanking new world. The information-systems/information-technology revolution is real, and still in its infancy! One result: My five constants have been the trademark of big-time winners (3M, HP, Johnson & Johnson, et al.): now they are the minimum survival requirements for running info-tech-rich, dispersed "empires" in which no one works for a particular company (the virtual corp. gig) . . . which is going to be everybody's game, or else. Going global at birth will also become commonplace . . . for the one-person professional-service firm run out of the spare bedroom as well as for the big guys.

So listen to the fads (with two, not only one, grains of salt). Insist on demonstrated leadership potential in every new hire. Understand that some things (radical decentralization and paranoia, for instance) are eternal. And believe Bob Dylan when he says the times they are a-changing'. And a-changing' damn near everything.

3.5
TEAMWORK

---◼---

SUCCESS STRATEGIES FOR CROSS-FUNCTIONAL TEAMS*
by Glenn M. Parker

To coin a phrase, "No cross-functional team is an island." Although so much of the research and thinking about teams has focused on their internal dynamics, experts are only now com-

*Reprinted with permission from The Association for Quality and Participation, Cincinnati, OH (513) 381-1959. From the *17th Annual Spring Conference and Resouce Mart*, April 1995. Glenn M. Parker is president of Glenn M. Parker Associates.

ing to realize the importance of external relations, or what some call "managing the outside" (Hastings, Bixby & Chaudhry-Lawton, 1987). The importance of building bridges for cross-functional teams should, by now, be obvious. Cross-functional teams are linked in many ways to many different people and organizations and, in fact, dependent on others for their success. Some of these people may know your work and be supporters, some may have worked with you in the past and be potential barriers, and others may not be aware of your work and may need to be convinced of its value.

If this whole thrust toward the proliferation of cross-functional teams is to be successful, there must be an emphasis on what is sometimes called boundary management. Boundary management is the process by which a team manages its "borders" and the information and resource flow with its key stakeholders. The flow may be vertical (senior management) or horizontal (functional departments). As you might suspect the flow is interactive in the sense that it concerns how the team both sends and receives information or resources to and from these stakeholders. While all of this makes sense, does it work? A recent study of cross-functional new product teams seems to indicate that effective boundary management can make a real difference: ". . . high-perfoming product development teams carry out more external activity than low-performing teams. . . . High performers interacted more frequently with manufacturing, marketing, R&D, and top division management during all phases of activity. Members of high-performing teams did not simply react to communications from others; they were more likely to be the initiators of communication with outsiders than those individuals on low-performing teams" (Ancona & Caldwell, 1990, p. 28).

As others have noted cross-functional teams differ from functional teams in the required emphasis on effective boundary management. The unique nature of the cross-functional team makes it essential that cross-functional teams develop positive relationships with key stakeholders in the organization.

> The interdisciplinary work team differs from homogeneous groups in two major repects. First, it is an open rather than a closed system. A group's experiece is often owed to some agent outside the group's boundaries who places requirements on the group in an unpredictable sequence. In performing its role, the group must import resources and export products across its boundaries to appropriate portions of the environment. In addition to the sociopsychological boundary that separates the group from its environment, other boundaries are more salient than in laboratory groups. Production schedules and commitments to outside agents emphasize temporal bounds [McCorcle, 1982, pp. 293-294].

McCorcle also points out that the cross-functional team must maintain an appropriate balance between external relations and internal team development. For a cross-functional team this drive toward interaction with the outside world coupled with the equally strong drive toward positive internal dynamics can provide the team with certain tension points. Properly managed this tension can be helpful when it requires the team to look at two competing and important success factors.

THE KEY STAKEHOLDERS

For most cross-functional teams there are a consistent group of important stakeholders. The number of stakeholders and their names will vary by organization. Therefore, each team must do its own stakeholder analysis and develop a plan to effectively manage the boundary.

Functional Department Managers

The managers of the members of the cross-functional are often in a make-or-break role in regard to the success of the team. They can freely give the resource—their employee—or they can keep the person on a tight leash. For the team to be successful, the functional department managers must:

- Understand the purpose and priorities of the cross-functional team.

- Allow and even encourage the team member to complete team assignments.

- Clarify the team member's authority as the department's representative on the team. And then allow the team member to exercise that authority.

- Regularly communicate with the team member about the work of the team.

- Periodically communicate with the team leader about the team's progress and the work of the team member.

Obtain feedback from the team leader about the team member's performance.

Customers and Clients

Since no team should exist without a customer for its output, the interactions with customers are critical to the success of the team. The team's efforts have to be directed by data from customers. In some cases teams have varying levels of customers with varying levels of needs and data. These customers, of course, can be internal or external. The team needs on-going information on customer needs and requirements. On some teams specific team members are designated as the client liaison person with reponsibility for on-going contact with the customer. Often the person responsible is the project manager but it can also be the product manager, client interface manager, or systems analyst. One of my clients, an automobile industry supplier, has designated customer representatives who are reponsible for communication and plant visits with their automobile assembly customers.

Having a single point of contact is an efficient and often effective way of working with clients because it (1) makes it easier for the client to give their feedback, (2) allows the team to designate, train and develop one person skilled in client interface, and (3) eliminates the confusion which occur on teams where many team members are talking to the same client. Some teams have reduced the stakeholder communication problem by having customers serve as members of the cross-functional team. They attend all meetings and provide their input throughout the process.

Senior Management

One of the key internal stakeholders is senior management or, more specifically, the senior manager who sponsored the cross-functional team. It is critical that the team keep management informed about the progress of the team, successes, potential problems, especially problems with clients, resource needs, and changes in the time-table. Geri Weber, a leader and member of many cross-functional teams at Bell Communications Research, recommends that the team, and particularly the team leader, take responsibility for establishing a structure for ensuring systematic feedback to management, even in those cases where no formal structure currently exists (Interview with the author, January, 1993).

Senior management does not like surprises such as complaints from customers, delays in the project timetable, and unforeseen, last-minute problems. One cross-functional team in a major pharmaceutical company spent a great deal of time preparing their plan and developing their internal communication processes, but neglected to "sell" their concept sufficiently to senior management. The team and the concept, despite much good work and good intentions, was killed. In another company, a team prepared a careful market analysis of a potential product, but their boss refused to fund the continuation of the project. The team agreed they had not brought him in early enough to gain his support.

In some situations senior management is an on-going member of the team. This can prove beneficial to the team. At Motorola's plant in Austin, Texas, a senior manager serves as team sponsor who helps the team get the resources it needs (Kumar & Gupta, 1991). In this case, resources can mean anything from an expert the team needs to help solve a problem to the procurement of a piece of equipment.

Support Groups and Service Departments

At various stages in the life cycle of a cross-functional team there is a need for assistance from other groups in the organization. The effective team builds and maintains positive relationships with these groups because their support is often in the form of tangible aid.

CROSS-FUNCTIONAL TEAM NEEDS

Information

For the on-going empowered teams there is a constant need for acurate and current information required for daily decision making. Project teams, of various levels of empowerment, usually have a great need for information at the outset of a project. They need customer and market data about the potential need for the product, system or service. Quality action teams need data about the nature and extent of the problem. All cross-functional teams have to draw data from the political winds in the organization to see if there is support for the team's project.

Resources

At some point the team will need some "stuff." Types of resources teams often need from support and service groups include:

- *People*—this can range from experts to offer advice and do real work to extra hands to pitch in and get the work done.
- *Product*—this can mean anything from the production of a prototype or the supply of test samples for a field trial.
- *Research*—this may involve statistical studies, laboratory experiments, focus groups or field tests.

Support

Something of an intangible, support groups can truly support the team by stepping up to the help needed by the team. They can provide the help in an easy, no-hassle manner. They can do the work in a professional and timely fashion. On the other hand, if the team has to fight to get the support it needs, to get work done quickly, to get it done correctly, then the whole process breaks down.

Awareness of Impact

Cross-functional teams need to be aware of the impact of their work on other groups in the organization. For example, the team may come up with a wonderful new procedure which reduces the time it takes to get the job done. However, the new procedure may cause problems for another group. At one plant, a team on the C shift came up with a way to speed up the process by eliminating the set-up work for the next job. Their time improved but the A shift was left with extra work. Effective teamwork requires collaboration among teams.

BRIDGE-BUILDING BARRIERS

Despite all the good reasons for effective inter-team relationships, groups in organizations often do not work well together. Cross-functional teams do not manage their boundaries well, do not get the support they need, do not get the resources they require and, as a result, fail. There

are methods for achieving positive external relations by cross-functional teams, but the first place to start is to look at the causes of breakdowns in the process.

Stereotyping

Yes, plain old fashion prejudice. Team members come to a relationship with preconceived ideas about how certain groups behave. These stereotypes stand in the way of building positive relationship bridges. Think about the stakeholder groups we identified—how are they perceived by cross-functional teams in your organization?

Here are some typical stereotypes about these stakeholders. Feel free to add some perceptions of your own.

1. *Senior Management.* "All they care about is the bottom line." "They don't know what it's like out here in the real world." "When's the last time they talked to a real customer?"

   Add your own:

2. *Functional Department Managers.* "All they care about is meeting their personal objectives." "They see this cross-functional teamwork stuff as an annoyance." "For them the cross-functional team is something they give to but get nothing back in return."

   Add your own:

3. *Customers and clients.* "All they want is more for less." "They never tell us their needs up front, but sure do have a lot of comments on the finished product."

   Add your own:

4. *Support Groups.* "Ask those market research people for some help and they dump a stack of useless data on you." "You know how those lawyers are, they'll find all the reasons why you shouldn't do it." "Ever try getting a *fast* answer out of an engineer?"

   Add your own:

5. *Other Internal Units.* "All they care about is making it easier for themselves." "They never did anything for us, why should we do

anything to help them?"

Add your own:

Competition

Groups in organizations are in competition. There is nothing wrong with some healthy competition between teams in an organization. Competition to be the best team, to get to the market faster, to solve a complex problem, to bring in the most sales are all examples of positive competitive goals. But if our team tries to achieve a goal at your expense by, for example, not sharing resources or information, we get negative competition. And unhealthy competition can stand in the way of healthy collaboration which is key to successful cross-functional teamwork.
Teams compete for all sorts of things:

* Recognition for their efforts.
* Budget to continue or expand their project.
* Tangible rewards and compensation.
* Opportunities to work on the high visibility and interesting projects.
* Use of internal resources.

Differentiation

Depending upon the degree of certainty in the environment, groups in an organization need to be differentiated (Lawrence & Lorsch, 1967). As groups become more differentiated in their work styles, practices and orientations, the challenge of integrating them increases. While this differentiation helps units in an organization pull together to get the work done, it can be a barrier when they have to work collaboratively with another group or, in this case, with a cross-functional team. Tension exists due to the need to maintain the differentiation while supporting the drive for the necessary integration of their efforts.

BRIDGE-BUILDING STRATEGIES

Cross-functional teams need to recognize the importance of managing the outside. Beyond recognition is the necessity of taking action—planning to work effectively with the key stakeholders. Certain actions can help.

Identify Your Key Stakeholders

Begin by making a list of the people and groups you need to ensure your team is successful. Include in the list the things you need from these stakeholders. Consider a list of people and groups who have something to gain and something to lose from the work of your team. For example, if you come up with some cost saving or quality improvements, will some people stand to lose their job as a result?

Look for Commonalities

Look beyond what you need from them, to see what you can do for them. In what ways do the other groups need your ideas, help or other resources? The net result of this analysis should be a set of *common* objectives—outcomes you both share. Is there an umbrella you can both get under?

Communicate Information

Find ways to tell others about your team. Use reports, meeting minutes, newsletters, company publications and other written methods to communicate with your key stakeholders. In most cases verbal communication still works best. Look for opportunities to make formal presentations, have informal chats at lunch, in the hallways, at the copy machine and other places where you can report to groups of managers, customers and others in the organization. For example, each team member representing a functional department should have the on-going responsibility of keeping his or her manager informed and "sold" on the team's project. Some teams also ask key stakeholders to come to team meetings to hear first-hand how the team is doing.

Select Boundary Managers

The best cross-functional teams carefully select the team members who will handle the key interfaces. They do not assume that the team leader will do all of this work. They think—what needs to be done and who is the best person to do it? For example, we need some help from the computer center. Who has worked successfully with them in the past? We need to get budget approval for some additional field studies, let's ask Arlene to talk with them because she used to work over there. And one of our customers has a complaint about the product, why not ask Ming to handle it since she helped develop the prototype.

Identify Potential Barriers

An important aspect of relationship building with key stakeholders is looking at potential barriers. For example,

- Any past problems which need to be resolved or overcome?
- Are you in competition with this group?
- Do they stand to lose as a result of your team's project?
- Do they support the concept of cross-functional teamwork?
- Do you respect them?

Once the team has identified the actual barriers, they can begin to prepare a plan for overcoming the barriers and achieving successful stakeholder relationships.

Be Credible

All of these strategies work only if you are believable, only if other people can depend on you and your word. Assess your team. Do other people trust you? Can they count on you . . . to deliver on promises . . . to tell the truth? In developing positive relationships with key stakeholders:

- Don't ask for more than you need.
- Don't promise more than you plan to deliver.
- Don't set a due date you can't possibly deliver.
- Don't exaggerate project benefits or results.

Prepare an Analysis and a Plan

You can use the form on the next page as a planning tool for building bridges to key stakeholders for your cross-functional team. If you identify several stakeholders, you can divide the task by asking subgroups to each do an analysis of one of the stakeholders.

BUILDING BRIDGES WORKSHEET

1. Identify a person, department, or other team you need to help your team be successful.
2. What **specific** types of help do you need from them?
3. What kinds of assistance or input do they need from your team?
4. Identify common objectives you share with them.
5. What potential barriers may prevent the two of you from working together effectively?
6. How can you overcome these barriers?
7. Which member of your team would be the best person to work with the other team?
8. What specific steps will you take to develop a positive relationship with the other team?

BIBLIOGRAPHY

Ancona, D.G., and Caldwell, D. "Improving the Performance of New Product Teams." *Research-Technology Management*, Mar.-Apr., 1990, pp. 25-29.

Hastings, C., Bixby, P., and Chaudhry-Lawton, R. *The Superteam Solution.* San Diego, Calif.: University Associates, 1987.

Kumar, S., and Gupta, Y.P. "Cross-Functional Teams Improve Manufacturing at Motorola's Austin Plant." *Industrial Engineering*, May 1991, pp. 32-36.

Lawrence, P. R., and Lorsch, J.W. *Organization and Environment: Managing Differentiation and Integration.* Boston: Harvard Business School, 1967.

McCorcle, M.D. "Critical Issues in the Functioning of Interdisciplinary Groups," *Small Group Behavior*, Aug. 1982, 13(3), 291-310.

This article is based on the author's book, *Cross-Functional Teams: Working with Allies, Enemies and Other Strangers*, San Francisco: Jossey-Bass, 1994.

■

WHY? BECAUSE WE LIKE YOU!*
by Gillian Flynn

Just Imagine a group of 50 professionals strapping on mouse ears for a training meeting and you get the idea of how St. Francis, Wisconson-based Wixon/Fontarome combines business with pleasure.

At the end of a particularly busy fall quarter, President J.H. "Bud" Morgan, knew it was time for the spice and seasonings company to put together its quality plan for the new year. "We thought we could take our top management people and go to Hilton Head and have wonder dinners and play golf," says Morgan. "We could take a week and break down all kinds of programs on quality and mission statements. Only one problem. It's all the people in the company that make quality. It's not management dictating—it's every single person at this company wanting quality."

So rather than sequester an elite group of high-rung people, the company decided to elicit all 150 employees' input. To combine quality training with rewards for a job well done, Morgan decided to take his hard-working employees on a field trip—to Walt Disney World. "We thought: How can we impress everyone about quality? Let's do something that only one other company in the history of Disney World has done—and that is take everybody in the company down there for a weekend devoted to looking around Disney World, which is (an organization) as big on quality as there is," says Morgan. "It's clean, it's modern; the people are always pleasant; it's progressive; it's always changing and challenging."

To make the trip more manageable, groups of 50 employees went down over several weekends in March and February. Each employee received two airline tickets—one for the worker and one for a spouse or friend—along with $300 in spending cash. Over the weekend, the groups conducted several training meetings and discussed the various quality characteristics that make Disney so successful. Then they asked themselves how to transfer that attitude to Wixon.

But the weekend was as much about relaxation and fun as it was about fiscal improvements. Most of the employees' time was spent exploring The Magic Kingdom, EPCOT Center and The Disney/MGM Studios. For 21% of employees, the trip was their first on an airplane; for 69% it was their first time to Disney World.

"We love having a good time as we're running our business," says Morgan. "There's nothing in the rule book that says you can't enjoy going to work every day." The idea isn't a cheap one: Morgan estimates the cost at more than $250,000. But the payoff is big. The company's generous attitude—exemplified by the Disney trip—has helped it maintain a less than 1% turnover rate, with 14 years of uninterrupted growth in sales and profits. And morale is at an all-time high. Says Morgan: "It's been the most wonderful thing that's ever happened to the company."

*Reprinted with permission from *Personnel Journal*, April 1995, as an excerpt from the "For Your Information Column." *Personnel Journal* is published monthly at a subscription rate of $55 per year, $93 for two years in the US. All other countries, $95 per year. Please call (800) 444-6485.

—————————————————■—————————————————

INTERNAL SABOTAGE IMPEDES QUALITY INITIATIVES*
by Linda Morris

Many companies are currently pursuing quality initiatives and using teams. In fact, representatives of nearly three-quarters of the 1,000 companies recently surveyed by Achieve International, the strategic consulting division of Zenger-Miller, said that their firms were doing so.

But more than a third of those companies reported sabotage or internal resistance to their initiatives. Middle managers received the greatest blame for impeding both quality and team efforts, at 75 percent and 70 percent, respectively.

The survey. The survey was conducted independently for Zenger-Miller by the American Institute for Research. It went to 4,500 potential respondents, 75 percent of whom worked in human resources and quality departments. Almost half (44 percent) of the respondents worked in service industries, and 56 percent in product-based industries. Overall, the survey garnered a 22 percent response rate.

Researchers Linda Moran, Jerry Hogeveen, Jan Latham, and Darlene Russ-Eft summarized the findings in a white paper titled "Winning Competitive Advantage: A Blended Strategy Works Best."

According to Moran, the research confirms that executive and middle-manager resistance and even sabotage can significantly influence the success of a company's quality, team, and process-management strategies. Such strategies are crucial techniques for achieving global competitive advantage, so Moran recommended specific interventions early on, to wear down the pockets of resistance. She said that such interventions can work, whether resistance involves individual personalities, the protection of turf, or a lack of buy-in.

What works. In addition to overcoming internal resistance, most of the companies that avoided pitfalls and achieved success through their quality initiatives shared one principle: A blended approach works best.

The companies that reported the highest success rates with their quality efforts were those that adopted simultaneous quality, team, and process-management initiatives — and formally included those initiatives in their business plans.

The survey identified the following quality-initiative success factors:

* inclusion of quality initiatives in the business plan

* executive support

* management belief in the importance of quality efforts

* coordination of quality programs with a team structure

* beginning quality initiatives before beginning teams.

Talking to the boss. In addition to gathering statistics on the current state of corporate quality initiatives, the study also included qualitative research. Researchers asked participants what single piece of advice they would give their CEOs if they could. Most responses fell into the following five categories:

* "Give us direction." (Concentrate on mission, vision, and strategic planning.)

* "Relinquish control and empower people." (Get to know and trust employees; encourage their input.)

* "Walk the talk." (Close the credibility gap by providing commitment through action.)

* "Invest in high-quality people, and train them." (Support programs to provide new skills for employees, executives, and middle managers.)

* "Focus on the customer." (Base desicions on customer requirements.)

Other survey highlights. Additional statistical information gathered through the survey included the top five expected benefits from quality and team initiatives, the five most important

*Reprinted from *Training & Developement*. Copyright (January 1995), the American Society for Training and Development. Reprinted with permission. All rights.

factors for managing strategic processes, and the five most important skills for managing strategic processes.

For a copy of "Winning Competitive Advantage: A Blended Strategy Works Best," contact Susan Muttart, Zenger-Miller, 1735 Technology Drive, 6th Floor, San Jose, CA 95110-1313; 408/ 452-1244.

3.6
STATISTICAL PROCESS CONTROL

STATISTICAL PROCESS CONTROL (SPC): A SOLID INVESTMENT IN QUALITY*

Quality control efforts have always been a strong focus at Precision Castparts Corp. (Portland, OR), an investment casting foundry that manufactures parts for jet engines and aircraft. "Our system has evolved from a combination of common sense, economics and an overall company attitude and commitment made by the company's founder and passed on by management," says Ellen Hinds, quality assurance manager for Precision's Large Parts Campus. "That attitude says that we will be the best in the world."

In the many steps of the complex parts manufacturing process, operators make molds for and cast very complicated configurations with fine features and keep dimensional tolerances at a very tight level.

"In the past, we didn't use statistical process control," says Hinds. "We looked at the systems affecting the process—in our case, people, methods, material, and machines—and would consider that a process was wherever we had an input and an output. We would then place process control parameters on the elements of that process.

"Overall, a process control procedure would tell you that controlling raw materials, following good instructions, and operating between here and there would generate good quality product."

The system worked well enough, but with time, the company wanted to produce even better results at lower prices. Management knew from experience that SPC could help. In addi-

tion, more and more customers were asking for SPC.

So, Precision decided to formally convert the entire company to SPC in mid-1993. The implementation is expected to take another one to three years to complete. The company is taking the first SPC steps in the front-end processes like wax, investing, and casting. These will be followed by finishing and inspection operations.

"Adopting statistical process control was like finding ways to control your car between the lanes as opposed to putting a speed limit on the highway," says Hinds. Using these control limits, we can actually control our process by taking data from the process itself and incorporating the feedback to improve it."

OPERATOR CONTROL IS KEY

The cornerstone of Precision's process control effort is operator control at the source of the characteristic being generated. Process data are available to operators so that they can immediately see what the characteristic is. For instance, operators can tell from the dimensions of a wax pattern after it is molded whether their process is in control.

Operators plot data that indicate when a process is operating correctly. Any naturally occurring random process will have a normal distribution of parts above and below the average.

"In our operation, if we have seven consecutive points above or below the average and the points are trending up or down, we conclude that our process is beginning to shift." says Hinds. "When operators see these indicators, they know they have a process that's on the verge of going out of control. In addition, if a point is outside the control limits, they see a process that's already out of control."

Each operator uses a "cookbook," where the individual is led through a set of such questions as

Do you see this?

If this happens, does that happen?

Are raw materials correct?

Are process parameters being kept?

Depending on the answers, the cookbook suggests ways that operators might fix the process. Operators also perform a couple of verification runs.

OPERATORS CAN SHUT DOWN PRODUCTION

If the process is still out of control, operators shut it down. "In the past, we might have said 'This isn't quite right here but we'll fix it later on and make up for it in cost, extra inspection, and rework,'" says Hinds. "Now we stop and fix it before continuing. Shutting down production has its time and money costs, but we know that if we're making good quality products each step of the way, we won't have to make up for earlier errors further downstream."

After shutting down, operators immediately call a response team of experts assigned to them. A typical response team might include:

- a supervisor
- an engineering manager
- the quality manager
- a maintenance representative
- a parts engineer

"Since response-team members have training in that scientific discipline, they may be able to offer suggestions for techniques that operators aren't aware of," says Hinds. "In some cases, we make a management decision to shut down until "a" and "b" happens. In others, we decide

that a particular out-of-control point won't affect the process in that specific area.

"Generally, we find out a way to fix whatever's wrong, and the operator is included in the decision," Hinds continues. "We make sure investigations are thorough enough to address what caused the problem so that it isn't repeated."

As another guide, each area at Precision has established a process control matrix in which processes are rated according to process capability, which has a mathematical symbol of CPK. A CPK of 1.33 or greater means that you have a process using SPC. That CPK also represents a ratio where upper and lower control limits are in relation to specification limits. So with that CPK, you're probably not going to have anything out of control. Precision's goal is to have all processes with a CPK of 2.0 or greater.

CHALLENGES WERE STIFF

When initiating process control, the company faced some stiff challenges. "The more we would work process control, the more each main process would break down into multiple practices or 'microprocesses,'" says Hinds. "For instance, in terms of wax, we'd have to look at areas including temperatures, pressure, molding, and storage in holding tanks. In the beginning, we didn't know which was affecting variability, but if the wax was the same again and again, our castings wouldn't be the same."

Initially, process control involves choosing the most critical areas and characterizing that part of the process. "We take a lot of data and find out that at 'x' temperature, the wax comes out one way, and at 'y' temperature, it comes out another way—or that if the temperature varied from 'a' to 'b,' it didn't make any difference,' says Hinds.

"Finding this out takes time, money, and commitment," she continues. "It also means experimenting. If your data have a lot of scatter and you're getting both good and bad product, you don't know if you should limit it toward the top or the bottom. It's possible to limit variability toward the wrong side."

Once you figure out how to limit variability, however, you gain control of the process. "Then, you're no longer a victim of random occurrences causing variability," says Hinds. "Even if you've had a failure, you learn how to correct it."

SPC Required Cultural Change

To ease the transition to SPC, management went to bat to effect the cultural change necessary at the company. Managers and supervisors went to their people and asked such questions as:

How can we do this better?

What do you think contributes to variability?

How do you control the chemistry in the metals?

"We'd tell people 'That's a good idea. Now what do we do?'" says Hinds. "Motivation to do this has to come from the top or you won't get the money or time needed. However, just telling people to do something new isn't enough either. There has to be coaching, training, and technical resources to change attitudes and increase awareness."

Training Is on Group Basis

Precision carries out its training in a group atmosphere. Part of the training is about statistics and identifying the tools used in characterizing the process. In addition, the training concerns getting the message across to operators that they won't lose their jobs or be penalized if they shut down an out-of-control process. "Training also expresses that all the changes will not happen overnight, and that trial and error are involved," says Hinds.

SPC Brings Benefits

The benefits of SPC and its resulting limitations on variability are already beginning to show at Precision. For instance, in the past, engineers would make changes and improvements, and then they would have to wait until the end of the production cycle to see the effects of those changes.

In another scenario, engineers would develop a manufacturing process that would produce good results at first. Later, however, if the parts failed in some way, they would have to be changed again. As a result, development took longer. More product had to be reworked.

With statistical process control,

Engineers see what works or doesn't work immediately.

Product development time is cut.

Engineers can spend more time developing new product.

Customers receive the desired quality, and Precision meets those quality expectations consistently.

The company can afford to offer customers lower prices because rework is much less.

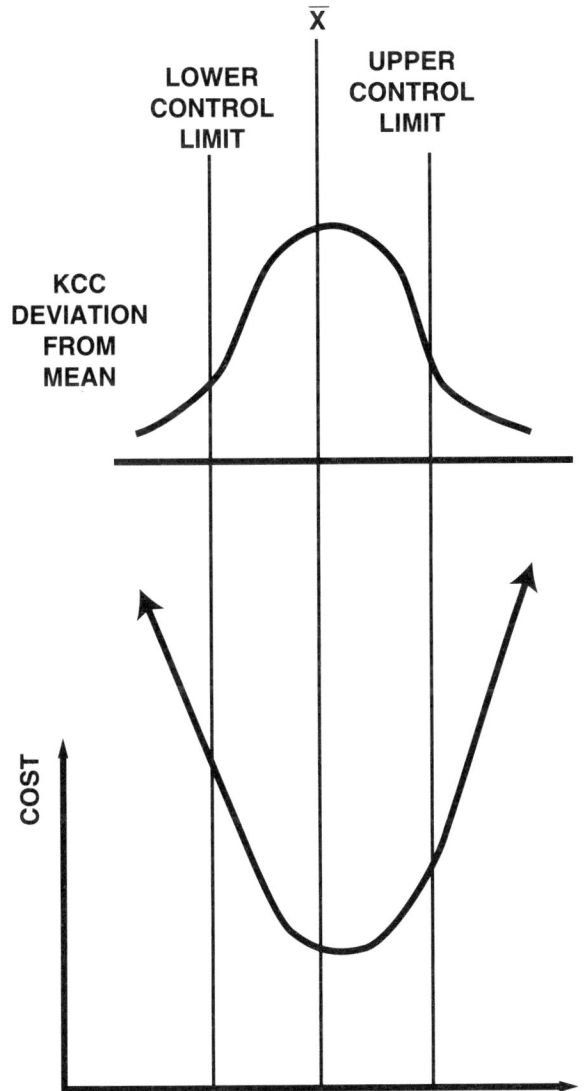

EXHIBIT 1.—RELATIONSHIP BETWEEN THE COST TO PRODUCE A PRODUCT VERSUS KCC DEVIATION FROM AIM

(For chart that shows how the deviation of key control characteristics affects production cost of a product, see page 4.)

Despite these early advances through SPC, however, Precision is pushing ahead to hone the process even further. Each area checks its process-control limits, analyzes them to see if they're adequate and, in some cases, compresses the control limits because of what the data show.

"Even when we're in statistical process control, we're always looking for ways to limit variability more," says Hinds.

What's the key to Precision's implementation of SPC? Hinds characterizes it this way: "Process control takes hard work, persistence, and amendment. It can't be a program or a project. It has to be the way you're doing things from one end of the organization to the other."

SPC ON THE LINE*
by John J. Kendrick

To have a successful SPC program, data must be analyzed and acted on. Feedback from corrective actions enable more refinements and the cycle begins again. During this process, data must be shared by the shop floor, engineering, quality control, and management. The faster data are circulated, the sooner it can be acted on. This is why software developers are closely watching as statistical methods move from off-line office-based SQC to on-line production-based SPC.

As industries increase their use of SPC, new measurement systems and hardware are emerging. Interfaces for multichannel coprocessors, for example, are allowing high-speed direct data input from 100 different devices to 100 different data files. Many SPC programs accept data from most measuring devices, and users can access it through spreadsheet programs such as Excel or Lotus 1-2-3 and copy control charts directly into word processing programs.

MONITORING SUPPLIERS

The United Technologies Automotive facility in Tampa, FL (UTA/Tampa) supplies electronic modules to the automotive industry. The facility makes the keyless entry module for Ford Motor Co., the electronic turn signal/hazard module for Cadillac, four different electronic modules for Honda of America, and electronic modules for BMW.

UTA/Tampa recognized its image as a quality automotive electronics manufacturer was in jeopardy if decisions were made on subjective, unproved information. This led Joe Kurial, manager, to initiate PC-based decision making using SPC Express software from Major Micro Systems Inc (Troy, MI).

Now the focus is not on meeting specs, but on how well components and products perform within spec. The plant requires suppliers to provide SPC analysis, and it evaluates their performance by using computer reports.

"After introducing our vendor SPC program, suppliers became aware of the importance of statistically controlling their own processes and conforming to our requirements," says Tim Roth, quality control vendor representative. "Now vendors are in line with our SPC-derived zero defects program, so they can concentrate on specific quality issues rather than merely meeting a standard acceptable quality level."

The software was first used for incoming inspection of resistors, where resistance values were evaluated against specified limits provided by design engineering and the customer. Then C_{pk} was computed from a sampling of resistance readings.

This initial effort showed SPC could be used with other components and various component operating parameters. UTA/Tampa and its suppliers, for example, analyze parameters such as capacitance and leakage of capacitors, voltage and leakage current of Zener diodes, and gain and leakage current of signal transistors.

---

*Reprinted with permission from *Quality,* Volume 34, No. 1, January 1995. John J. Kendrick is a senior editor with *Quality.*

The most extensive SPC use is in final testing of electronic modules, which involves monitoring the output of 10-20 parameters per module. In the past, C_{pk} was evaluated on certain parameters as needed. On-line continuous measuring was necessary for effective feedback and process control.

Initial attempts with the SPC application in the final test area were burdened with time-consuming data entry. A built-in user expansion feature solved the problem. A Gespac computer was linked to a PC running SPC Express and a program developed to speed the entire process. The resulting system permits one-key operation that organizes the incoming data and transfers it between the two computer systems.

Using the two-computer system, the SPC software archives data and prints histograms. An analysis of all modules tested during a production shift is done in less than an hour.

Stockwell Mfg (Grand Rapids, MI) has been using the same SPC software for over five years. Howard LaCroix, QA manager, helped computerize the company's automated gaging, analysis, and reporting of quality control information.

Stockwell is running 50 screw machines, 20 hours a day. LaCroix installed a network of 18 workstations, with each shop-floor computer monitoring the output of four screw machines. They measure 6 pieces per hour from each machine with one sample per spindle.

"The software can choose which spindle samples should be used in capability studies," says LaCroix. "This allows doing a more thorough machine analysis on a spindle-by-spindle basis."

Inspections are done by machine operators and roving inspectors. As operators gage samples, they see color, real-time process control charts without touching the computer's keyboard. All measurements are taken from digital electronic gages. Characteristics measured include OD, ID, cut-off length, thread pitch, and chamfer angles.

"Our quality improved due to process changes and the ability to make adjustments quickly, resulting in more consistent pieces and reduced scrap," says LaCroix. "I can track our 50 machines from my office."

NET BENEFITS

The benefits of running SPC software on a network include improved data handling and security, and faster resolution of process problems. "In a total quality environment," says Paul A. Keller, CQE, technical services director, Quality America Inc (Tucson, AZ), "users find disseminating information reinforces work team cooperation and understanding among diverse groups. Networking SPC is a powerful way of enabling people to communicate. When SPC software is in an easy-to-use format, users will do creative things with it."

Quality analysis is moving closer to production, and SPC networks speed process feedback. The people that need the data no longer are burdened with passing paper around the plant. They can access data from wherever they are in the factory and don't have to wait for charts.

Paul Mychalowych, vice president, DataNet Technologies Inc (Troy, MI), advises planning ahead if you intend to migrate from standalone to a networked system—purchase a computer with at least a 486 processor, 8MB RAM (or more) and a large hard disk (1GB). Also, have NE2000 compatible cards installed when purchasing the standalone. "An SPC network file server, however, requires more power, speed, and capacity," he says. "I recommend a Pentium-based PC with 32 MB of RAM and 1GB hard drive because the server must function as the central storage unit for all users in the plant; running Windows SPC software and storing data in an SQL database such as Oracle, Sybase or Microsoft Sequel Server, or other ODBC compliant databases requires the increased capacity; and future Windows versions (Windows '95, Chicago, NT) will require it.

"Choose a stable, proven network software product and card. While newer products often have desirable features, glitches can outweigh the advantages. The card should support the Ethernet frame type standard 802.3, and Novell NE2000."

Your plant layout ultimately will dictate the cable and hardware required. Have a certified network engineer plan the total system up front and then install everything in stages. Properly ground network cable terminator and computers to prevent problems.

"Protect each workstation on the network and the file server with an uninterruptible power supply" adds Mychalowych. "If possible, use special software and hardware on the server that senses when power is lost and automatically brings the server down."

To prevent catastrophes, operators should only have login access to SPC data for read/write purposes and no delete capability. Only allow operators access to the workstations they will be using, and running a regularly scheduled automatic or manual backup program using a digital audio tape (DAT)2-5GB cartridge will protect valuable programs and data on a timely basis.

Use gage station carts or stands with nonconductive surfaces to prevent damaging electrostatic discharge between the cart, computer, and electronic gage. To prevent damaging screen distortion caused by magnetic induction, operate electronic gages 3-4 ft from the monitor.

DataNet's WinSPC Network Manager is an on-line network monitor that displays up to 300 different processes or characteristics on a single screen in a Windows environment. Jergens Inc (Cleveland, OH), Bergstrom Mfg (Rockford, IL), and Kismet Products Inc (Plainsville, OH) are all using DataNet WinSPC network systems successfully in their manufacturing operations.

WINDOWS TO SPC

Brady Div., Medtronic (Fridley, MN), makes pacemakers for heart patients. The functionality of a pacemaker is critical, so the manufacturing process is closely regulated and quality control is stringent.

Quality manager Guy Bristol established five steps for buying a SPC system: It must generate real-time data; provide easy-to-use data; reduce distraction on the production floor; store data for traceability; and be acceptable on a world-wide basis. Bristol then added a need for a relational database to the list.

He tested 14 SPC products by having plant managers and operators run standard data acquisition tasks. Once this process was started, it became apparent that real-time data acquisition and ease-of-use were the key requirements.

But real-time data—or the ability to collect information on-line as products are produced—is just one critical component in an SPC system. "Data alone will not help if it's difficult to acquire and interpret," notes Bristol. "We realized

only a GUI-based system like Windows or Macintosh would do."

He chose Applied Stats SPC and data acquisition software from Applied Statistics Inc (St Paul, MN). "It offers real-time data acquisition combined with a robust graphical user interface," he says. Bristol also concluded that an SQL database had no purpose in an SPC application on the factory floor due to workstation performance.

The workstations installed at Brady have been in use for three years. According to Bristol, process related scrap is less than 6 ppm. Brady's processes have been brought under documented control, and it now can focus on vendor-related defects.

In another example, Micro Motion Inc (Boulder, CO), a manufacturer of mass flow meters, is using Quality America's SPC-PC IV for engineering, manufacturing, and administrative applications and is planning to increase the number of SPC workstations. Future plans include using the software's wireless data entry and real-time charting features.

With real-time SPC in Windows, the company quickly tracks and detects process shifts. Shop-floor personnel watch control charts as data come in, observe control limits as they are automatically updated, and get charts instantaneously so operators have immediate process feedback.

"With real-time capabilities we catch out-of-control situations before the next part is started," says John Spangler, process quality engineer. "This helps reduce scrap and rework, and allows for quicker corrective action."

Micro Motion is also using the advanced networking capabilities of SPC-PC IV. The program enables concurrent set up of a supervisory station for monitoring processes. With this feature, data can be entered at one workstation, either manually or in realtime, and the file and accompanying charts are updated automatically at the shop-floor and supervisory workstations. The software sends alert messages notifying of any user-defined condition such as a violation of a control limit, spec limit, or C_{pk} value. Dialog between the operator and the supervisor can also be sent (*Figure 1*), clarifying the situation and documenting special causes.

The software also can annotate special causes directly onto the chart and store that information with the data, allowing easy analysis. By networking, the supervisor can check for alert messages, determine if everything is running smoothly, and communicate with the operator, all without leaving the office.

CONNECTIVITY

SPC software is an essential tool that helps companies meet tight tolerances and minimize errors and scrapped parts. But total quality management (TQM) requires an approach that integrates SPC with other applications on enterprise-wide networks, running manufacturing execution systems (MES) or customer-oriented manufacturing systems (COMS). Such a production automation system may be referred to as a manufacturing information control system (MICS) and provide all workers with access to all necessary information.

Curtis-Wright Flight Systems (Fairfield, NJ) makes advanced aerospace components such as hydro-mechanical and electro-mechanical flight actuation systems. In its active pursuit of the paperless factory, it has learned about the interrelationship of SPC, TQM, and a MICS.

Like many manufacturers, the company acquired a hodgepodge of application systems running on a mixture of hardware and operating systems. SPC data was written down and entered manually via keyboard. Initially a cultural shift to TQM created an awareness of open communication of manufacturing information. This prompted manufacturing to investigate distributed numerical control (DNC) to communicate part programs directly to machine tools and eliminate punched paper tape. Further refinement led to a MICS approach, using CIMNET Folders MICS from JNL Industries (Robesonia, PA). The functions included in the MICS are DNC, SPC, file management, labor and job tracking, and machine monitoring.

Will Kleemeier, SPC coordinator/manufacturing engineer, implemented the SPC portion of Folders because of his interest in short run SPC. "Run sizes in product development are about 40 pieces, but can go as high as 500," says Kleemeier. "As part of our TQM effort, we continually analyze production to improve performance. With short runs, we combine key characteristic data from several different runs and analyze the impact of other variables on the data. A relational database gives us access to that kind of data associativity, through multiple electronic folders based on specific operations. Short run analysis for developmental processes is valuable

because we can optimize a process before going into production."

Over time, an extensive history of operating capabilities for different variables, such as machines, tooling, operators, and process techniques can be established. "We segment data and analyze trends for similar characteristics for different runs—the system shows which came from which. By isolating variables and testing different characteristics, we predict results much faster," says Kleemeier. "We use this information to determine machine capability and track part performance.

Additionally, measurement data, job, part, or operation numbers; time; machine operator; and four user-defined fields can be stored in the system, enabling recombining and analyzing them, using any of a number of charts and statistics. "We go back and look at the values using different types of statistics, including C_p, C_r, C_{pk}, comparison studies, and regression analysis. By combining dissimilar characteristics, tolerances, and varying sampling plans, we can isolate assignable causes of variation and make changes to improve the process," says Kleemeier.

An obstacle to upgrading an existing automation environment is the preservation of data and systems. At Curtis-Wright the design department was using Unigraphics for CAD/CAM on HP Unix workstations, or Apple Quadra PCs running X-terminal emulators. "CIMNET Folders was able to work in the HP Unix operating system," says Joseph Vinhais, JNL's SPC manager, "and on the Windows-based PCs on the shop floor. None of the existing systems needed to be modified."

Familiarity with SPC minimized the training needed by Curtis-Wright Camden's operators on the new system. "The operators quickly learned to use the system modules because of its simplified graphic user interface," says Kleemeier. SPC instructions, measurements, and messages are part of a user-definable template that was set up by Kleemeier and other manufacturing engineers.

As part of the criteria for choosing a MICS, Curtis-Wright wanted a system that could communicate through standard protocols with other open system components. The system's application programming interface enables reading in standard database files such as FoxPro, dBase, Access, Paradox or others and multiple system platforms. The company is establishing electronic data interchange with its suppliers. In addition to the standard electronic document transfers, Kleemeier is adding SPC data files to the process. "We get SPC values from our suppliers as part of their paperwork. We specify the characteristics to measure, and they provide us with the data along with the parts. With the relational database functionality, we can create an electronic folder for a supplier's part and insert the SPC data. We can use files directly from suppliers who use the software, or we can modify the format. Our plan is for files to be submitted as a common database or spreadsheet format. We can then analyze it just as we do with our parts. Suppliers who give us paper documents such as histograms and X-bar charts, will eventually give us those documents as electronic files. We expect this to save a tremendous amount of data entry time, and provide the results almost immediately.

"We know Folders has a lot of potential we haven't used yet," says Kleemeier, "and we are creating procedures to get the most out of it. Originally, NC programmers built the folders, but now many workers contribute files to a folder. We add SPC specification templates, and design adds part drawings. Expanding the use of the real-time nature of the system to examine operation's current status and automatic updating of work queues and machine schedules based on integration with our MRP system will further improve performance. MICS is making our application for ISO 9000 certification easy through quick, accurate communication of required procedures to each workcenter. Our objective is to become a paperless factory."

SPC and all manufacturing applications have been developed to solve specific production problems. "Falling technology costs will enable putting a computer in every machine operator's workspace, and networks will interconnect them into a company-wide automation system," says Vinhais. "Machine operators will perform essential functions that provide manufacturing information to everybody in production. Gathering SPC data is an important function in a paperless factory. Using it effectively is fundamental for TQM and ISO 9000 certification."

REAL-TIME QUALITY

Automated Technology Associates (Indianapolis, IN) also offers users a quality management system for real-time SPC monitoring of factory floor processes. Called Real-Time Quality Management (RQM), it provides automated data analysis and interpretation, and alarming only on detected process changes. Status screens enable viewing the current state of processes and investigating alarm conditions. The open architecture design allows direct interface or integration with most plant-floor devices and software systems. It offers client/server capabilities to support the need for distributed access to data collection and information on the factory floor.

The RQM data-driven logic (DDL) function is an application of the concept of "stored procedures and triggers." It allows automating calculated test points, short run SPC, data compression and summarization, and other calculation and data-management activities. "Although DDL is a command interpreter, it runs at speeds comparable to compiled code," says John Layden, ATA president, "offering comprehensive statistical capability."

Heidtman Steel Products Inc (Toledo, OH) uses RQM in tandem with ATA's quality tracking system (QTS), making their performance more comprehensive in controlling product quality operations. RQM continuously monitors SPC data as an order is being processed, while QTS is measuring product quality. Applying the system at its Erie, PA, facility increased capacity by 17% without a capital increase, a value of approximately $1 million per year.

THE NEW SPC NET EFFECT*
by Jerry Wolak

Statistical process control isn't new, but its application is. When Walter Shewhart at Bell Labs invented manual plotting of control charts in the '20s, how could he have envisioned the decision making pace of today's production operations. "By the time you collect data and draw and analyze charts, thousands of bad parts can accumulate," says Paul A Keller, CQE, technical services director, Quality America Inc (Tucson, AZ). "Quality engineers can't languish while calculating and analyzing control charts any longer. Information simply must be available to decision makers whenever they need it."

Too often, however, nothing is done with process data because it is cumbersome and time consuming to deal with. In operations using computer-based, but isolated, data collectors, somebody must harvest the data—walk around and download it from individual PCs on the shop floor—and take it to a central location where someone else does off-line analysis. "That's sneaker net," says Dave Lagerstrom, software manager, Allen-Bradley/DataMyte (Minnetonka, MN), "using Nike power to get data back and forth. It's slow and expensive. Today, quality managers want shop-floor data at their desks, as do plant managers, purchasing agents, and marketing staff. The only way to make that feasible is through networking."

The benefits of running SPC on a network include improved data handling and security, and faster resolution of process problems. "Shop-floor operators will have access to more information," says Keller, "customers can get capability reports on supplier processes, and other areas of the plant can use the data to improve tangential processes. Making machine operators, quality engineers, and production managers aware of out-of-control situations is the single most meaningful benefit."

Networking is rarely driven by SPC. Typically, SPC is one of many applications, such as shop-floor execution software and MRP, that motivate a manufacturing facility to install a network.

"Financial systems started off as single-user systems and then became networked," comments Mike Campbell, CEO, Powerway—Integrated Technologies Inc (Indianapolis, IN). "Windows for Work Groups is an example. The same is happening in manufacturing systems. In a total quality environment, users are finding disseminating information reinforces work team cooperation and understanding among diverse groups. Networking SPC is a powerful way of enabling people to communicate."

"One networked SPC user didn't know who else wanted the information—other than the shop floor and quality assurance," adds Evan Miller, president, Hertzler Systems (Goshen, IN). "Nevertheless, the company knew it was valuable. If SPC software providers make it available in an easy-to-use format, users will do creative things with it. That's a real practical view of how quality information should be handled.

"As large organizations shed mini and mainframe computers and smaller companies search for ways to connect isolated PCs, they are converging on the middle ground—local area networks. A SPC network provides a central repository—a file server—where data reside and can be accessed by managers from any PC on the network. Managers can rapidly access data and make decisions about out-of-control conditions quickly. They no longer need to peer over the shoulders of operators."

Putting SPC on a network requires adequate security to prevent data from being compromised. Additionally, operators must be trained in SPC so they know when the process is out of control. Operators must be able to make decisions or at least know when to alert the quality engineer. From a machine operator's standpoint, it doesn't matter whether a program is on a network or on a stand-alone system. The biggest hurdle for shop-floor workers is understanding what to do with SPC (see sidebar "Don't Network Bad Data").

"Users are moving quality analysis closer to production," says Campbell. "SPC networks are key enablers, speeding process feedback. The

---

*Reprinted with permission from *Quality*, Volume 33, No. 8, August 1994. Jerry Wolak is a managing editor with *Quality*.

people that need the data no longer are burdened with having to pass paper around the plant. They can access that data from wherever they are in the factory and don't have to wait for charts.

"Manufacturing engineers that oversee multiple processes take on an enormous data burden that can consume all of their available time. With a network, an operator can keep an engineer advised of process problems only when something significant happens."

Networking SPC also provides economies through hardware sharing. A network doesn't require a printer at each workstation to generate hard copy. If you have 20 users on the network, each data collection station or network PC can then print from a central printer.

We've assembled a sampling of case examples to give you a look at how networked SPC is changing quality on the shop floor.

CASE 1: ELECTRONICS ASSEMBLY

Plexus Co (Neehah, WI) makes printed circuit boards (PCBs) for computers, medical, automotive, and communication equipment. Most PCB assembly requires high-rate processing in automated cells that must be fine tuned. The company has been using networked SPC since '90, but just recently installed QI Analyst network SPC software from SPSS (Chicago).

"Our boards are made so quickly that seemingly simple problems can cause scrapping thousands of parts in a short time," says Joe Simo, manager of data collection and SPC services. "On our solder paste line, for example, tooling may slowly wear out. Knowing its yield tells us when to do maintenance to bring it back in line. If we can count defects, we can control the process. To determine the line's capability, we measure temperature, pressure, and solder-paste height and input these parameters into the SPC system.

"After the boards get through the manufacturing process, we test them electrically to verify all components are present and functioning properly. We must flush out all bad boards because we can't send bad product to our customers.

"On some boards," he continues, "we place over 5000 components. If yields on chip resistors, capacitors, or integrated circuits come in at 99.9%, then one out of every 1000 components is bad. Considering we use about 5 million components a day, that's a lot of variability in the products we buy."

"Some of our customers demand access to our process capability and data tracking. They want yield charts and parts per million charts. Our networked SPC system provides all of this."

CASE 2: AUTO MOTIVE

Bailey Corp (Seabrook, NH), supplier to Ford and General Motors, makes bumpers and side panels to the tune of $20 million annually. "We use networked SPC throughout the plant—in receiving, on the paint lines, and in manufacturing," says Candy Dow, quality analyst. "We measure all the parts we make."

About a year ago, the company switched from semiautomatic SPC. The biggest problem in the transition involved the inspectors. They had never used computers and needed training in SPC and how to use the network.

Before networking its SPC, Bailey was buying 15 separate copies of SPC software every year just to stay current. Also, the quality department found that standalone SPC suffered from security problems. "We experienced disk errors and lost data," says Dow. "Without the network, we had no data security. Anybody could change whatever they wanted, whenever they wanted."

Bailey chose to network SQCpack PLUS from PQ Systems (Dayton, OH). The installation includes 15 workstations at a cost of about $16,000, including all hardware, the SPC software and Novell network software.

"Benefits from the systems were immediate," notes Dow. "Everybody on the network can access data, I can analyze data and get it to customers faster, and our manufacturing engineers can deal with shop-floor problems rapidly."

CASE 3: DETECTS GAGE PROBLEMS

Fleetguard Inc, a division of Cummins Engine, is our third example. The company supplies filtration products to customers such as John Deere, Case, and Navistar. It has been using SPC for about 5 years, collecting data and charting X-bar and R, P, U, X and R, and moving range charts. Initially this was done manually, but because it was labor intensive, the company installed networked SPC software from Hertzler Systems. "We went from paper to a network in 3 months, and we have continued to add stations to the system," says Steve Horswell, quality equipment engineer. "We now have 22 operational workstations on the net—15 in the shop and 7 in offices."

The network has made possible tracking of product characteristics such as perpendicularity of threads, part concentricity, porosity of filter media, burst strength of paper, and collapse strength. Attribute data are collected with the system, including machinery downtime, rework, and absenteeism. "Much of what we are doing with the SPC network cannot be done with paper charts without investing tons of effort," notes Horswell. "A major benefit from using the network is we found our measurement tools were inadequate. If you are looking to reduce variation, much of the data collected will tell you your gages aren't being used the right way or you are using a gage in the wrong application."

CASE 4: WIRELESS NET

Our final example comes from General Automation (Skokie, IL), a high-tech screw-machine shop specializing in small-turned products for the aerospace, automotive, electrical, medical, and hydraulic-pneumatic manufacturing industries. The company is combining SPC data-collection equipment from GageTalker Corp (Bellevue, WA) with a Motorola Altair Plus II radio transmission system.

"Our screw machines are very stable, but when starting a new job, we need intensive SPC data collection to ensure process integrity," explains Max Starr, president. "We wanted a way to collect data on new jobs in various locations and get that data to our shop-floor network without hardwiring workstations for those temporary applications."

"Instead of dedicating a separate SPC workstation for each start-up job," adds Al Podolak, quality assurance director, "we combined the Motorola transmitters with two GageTalker III data-collection workstations that we could wheel anywhere in the factory. With the free-standing workstations, operators can easily move within the facility and have SPC capabilities at their fingertips. The independent workstations are also used to monitor infrequently performed jobs and other secondary operations." According to Chip Manning, GageTalker SPC specialist, even if the transmission doesn't go through immediately, the data are held in the workstation until the network link is reestablished.

General Automation is using 30 GageTalker III data-collection workstations linked on an Ethernet local area network (LAN). The data collection units are fully Ethernet compliant, so the company could use off-the-shelf Motorola components to add radio transmission capabilities to the LAN. SPC data are transmitted to a master receiver connected to the LAN.

"Using the data-collection workstations on a wireless network allows doing a capability study and heavy SPC on a job without requiring the operator to walk parts to one of our permanent stations," says Podolak. "When the process stabilizes and the operators are familiar with the new setup, we decrease our sampling rates and use one of the permanently wired data collectors."

Wireless networks are ideal for difficult to cable areas and temporary start-up jobs where you don't want hard cabling. They eliminate the need to drop cabling to every potential data-collection station.

MAKING THE BEST USE OF CHARTS IN DATA ANALYSIS*
by Barbara A. Cleary, Ph.D.

A shop floor supervisor tells of a recurring nightmare he has had about being in a room where the wallpaper peels itself from the walls and falls in disorganized heaps around him.

*Reprinted with permission from *The Fabricator*, copyright 1995 by the Croydon Group, Ltd. Barbara A. Cleary, Ph.D., is Corporate Vice-President of PQ Systems, Inc., in Dayton, OH.

Trying to put it all back, he struggles with the strips of paper but realizes that he has no idea where each one goes in relation to the others. He awakens, with the memory of the piles of paper surrounding him and his own confusion about restoring order to the room still fresh in his consciousness.

The supervisor's dream may reflect your own nightmares about the mountains of charts and graphs that surround you in your work area. You may find yourself drowning in charts and data, and still starved for real information.

Statistical process control (SPC) is a way of preventing errors or defects in the fabrication process by monitoring that process carefully and collecting data on all aspects of it. By contrast, traditional manufacturing processes have emphasized detection of errors rather than prevention.

Detection is generally accomplished through inspection at the end of a process to "weed out" good results from defective ones. Inspection for defects involves visual examination and the judgment of an inspector about the quality of the finished product. Preventing errors by carefully controlling processes will reduce costs by eliminating scrap, waste, and the need for rework in a process.

Computers have enhanced the use of SPC and facilitated real-time charting capability. SPC software programs are available that will not only "crunch the numbers" by calculating such statistics as control limits, moving ranges, and standard deviations, but can also display and print several charts on a single page, generate alarms when processes are out of control, and compute data in a variety of formats, including attributes and variables charts, histograms, scatter diagrams, Pareto charts, and others.

With its ability to gather more data with greater frequency and higher accuracy, computer technology represents a boost to traditional methods of gathering and analyzing data and using it to improve quality.

Using SPC to improve processes without the right "glue" to hold it together, however, can actually deteriorate into meaningless paper work that is not only not helpful, but can actually get in the way of doing good work.

How can you make sense of the data and interpret the charts in such a way that they will actually help to improve the process? Control charts, fundamental to process analysis and control, will help you to make decisions about how and when to change a process to improve its output.

We are all familiar with the finger-to-the-wind approach to changing things: "Let's just adjust this pressure dial slightly, lower the temperature for this process a little, and see what happens." This random approach results in waste, higher costs, and poor quality of output.

Without accurate data, the dangers lie in making changes before understanding what really needs to be done to improve the process or ignoring changes in processes until it is too late to change them ("Let's just wait and see if the situation corrects itself.").

Though sometimes seen as arcane or mysterious, statistics can make process improvement more of a science and less of an art. A few fundamentals can be applied to gathering data and charting it in such a way that it will begin to be directly useful in analyzing and making improvements in processes.

GATHERING DATA

Interpreting charts is a matter of recognizing patterns and asking the right questions. If, for example, a control chart demonstrates that a stamping machine overheats at the same time every day, you might ask, "What factors come into play at that time of day to contribute to the overheating?" Without data about the time of day, that question might never be asked.

Seeing the pattern the same time every day will help you to formulate questions about the process and then pursue solutions. If the same pattern is observed every week on Fridays between 3:00 and 5:00 P.M., for example, far more information is provided than if you have no idea when the overheating episodes had occurred, just knew that it seemed to happen every so often.

Figures 1 and 2 demonstrate how data can be collected and charted to provide information about fabricating processes. Once the data is charted, patterns can be clearly identified, and the stability of the system can be analyzed.

For example, measure the temperature of the machine every 15 minutes for a week to have enough data for accurate analysis. If pH levels of a chemical used in a coating process are measured, it must be clear when and where the measurements are made.

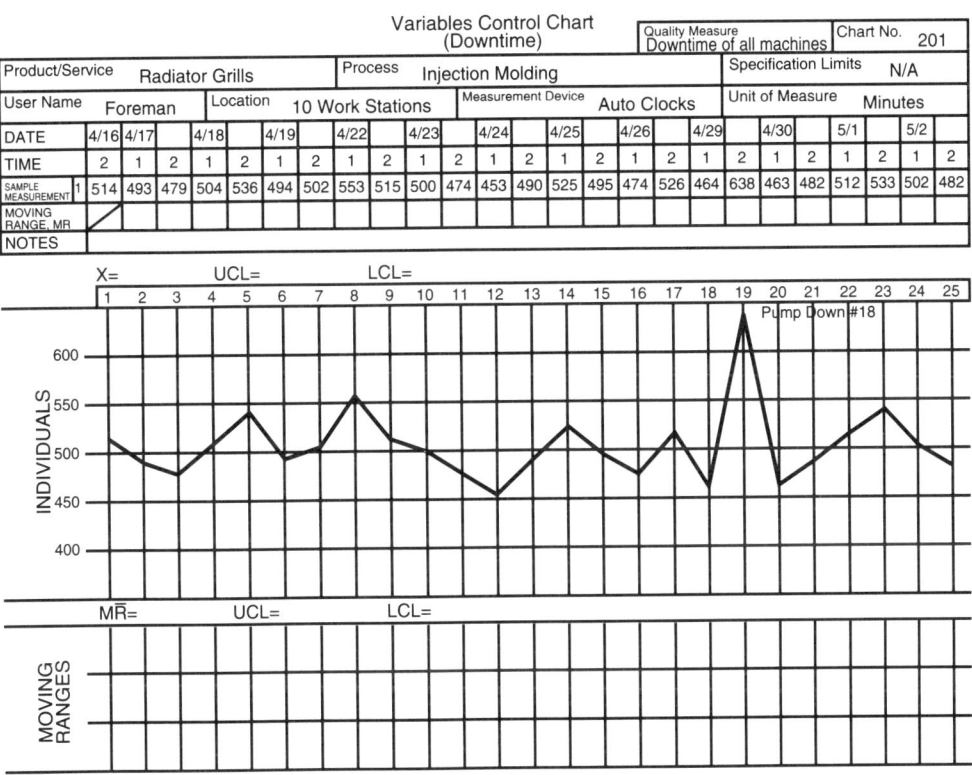

Variables Control Chart (Downtime)																					Quality Measure Downtime of all machines				Chart No. 201	
Product/Service Radiator Grills							Process Injection Molding											Specification Limits N/A								
User Name Foreman			Location 10 Work Stations					Measurement Device Auto Clocks						Unit of Measure Minutes										
DATE	4/16	4/17		4/18		4/19		4/22		4/23		4/24		4/25		4/26		4/29		4/30		5/1		5/2	
TIME	2	1	2	1	2	1	2	1	2	1	2	1	2	1	2	1	2	1	2	1	2	1	2	1	2
SAMPLE MEASUREMENT 1	514	493	479	504	536	494	502	553	515	500	474	453	490	525	495	474	526	464	638	463	482	512	533	502	482
MOVING RANGE, MR																									
NOTES																									

EXHIBIT 1.—DATA HAS BEEN PLOTTED ON A VARIABLES CONTROL CHART, WITH A PROCESS NOTE TO INDICATE WHAT MAY BE A SPECIAL CAUSE OF VARIATION

Note that control limits have not yet been calculated, although at this point there are enough data points to do this calculation. The data itself, not an external source, sets control limits.

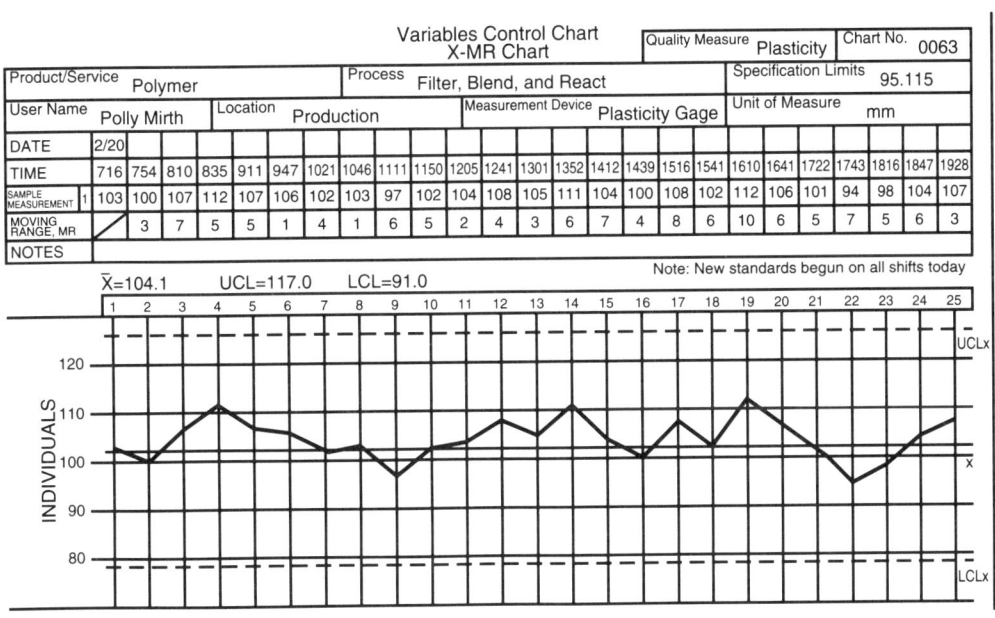

Variables Control Chart X-MR Chart																								Quality Measure Plasticity	Chart No. 0063
Product/Service Polymer						Process Filter, Blend, and React													Specification Limits 95.115						
User Name Polly Mirth			Location Production					Measurement Device Plasticity Gage						Unit of Measure mm										
DATE	2/20																								
TIME	716	754	810	835	911	947	1021	1046	1111	1150	1205	1241	1301	1352	1412	1439	1516	1541	1610	1641	1722	1743	1816	1847	1928
SAMPLE MEASUREMENT 1	103	100	107	112	107	106	102	103	97	102	104	108	105	111	104	100	108	102	112	106	101	94	98	104	107
MOVING RANGE, MR		3	7	5	5	1	4	1	6	5	2	4	3	6	7	4	8	6	10	6	5	7	5	6	3
NOTES																		Note: New standards begun on all shifts today							

$\bar{X}=104.1$ $UCL=117.0$ $LCL=91.0$

EXHIBIT 2.—THIS IS A VARIABLES CONTROL CHART FOR A FILTER, BLEND, AND REACT PROCESS FOR A POLYMER. THE DATA INDICATES THAT THE PROCESS IS STABLE

If the measurements are taken from different batches (without identifying them) or under different circumstances (morning, afternoon, inconsistent collection methods, etc.), it would be meaningless to try to adjust the pH levels that are being produced.

START SMALL

If you are just beginning your data analysis efforts, try the approach out on a small problem or a specific aspect of a job. If you try to analyze several problems at a time, you may find that the improvement theory you generate is far too complex to be successful.

A team that examines clogging in a spray mechanism may focus only on the paint viscosity and gather its data accordingly. If the same team tries to examine viscosity of paint, size of spray holes in the mechanism, temperature of the paint, and operator technique simultaneously, it may find itself frustrated and its efforts unproductive.

Collect data on one aspect, and proceed in a methodical way to apply tools of analysis to that aspect of the process. Remember that if you try to take all the steps that make up a journey at once, you will probably fall down.

LOOK AT INDICATORS OF UNSTABLE CONDITIONS

Statistically determined control limits (not specification limits established by engineers, but limits created by the data itself) provide a way to determine the stability of a system.

Among the indicator flags that suggest instability are:

1. A point that lies outside the control limits.

2. A run of seven or more consecutive points that seem to lie in a line above or below the average.

3. Nonrandom patterns of data that are too close to the average, too far from the average, or appears in a regular cycle (see Exhibit 3).

ADDRESS SOURCES OF INSTABILITY

The first analysis that must be made relates to the source of instability in a system.

It may be that the sample size was too small to make an accurate observation—for example, measuring an inside dimension of only one critical part rather than five consecutive parts. Or, perhaps some regular, periodic change is occurring in the system, such as a better-trained welding crew on a particular shift each day. Maybe

the instability was caused by a one-time failure of a timing mechanism in a heat-treating process.

Once the causes have been determined, ask whether these causes are creating opportunities for improvement or representing problems for your business.

If they have created a positive condition, such as a best-ever reading on a stamping machine, investigate to see what created this situation and make it part of the process. If the causes created a bad outcome, such as an unusually high number of die marks on sheet metal process, address the ways in which you can alter that situation.

You have examined causes of instability (those that are out of control) and have addressed them. All data points fall within the statistically determined control limits. Now what?

ANALYZE CHART INFORMATION

Sometimes, after examining the charted data, teams working on a process are surprised to find that the process is actually stable, or in control. One team felt that the cadmium plating mixture in a metal coating process was often unbalanced. After collecting data, team members were surprised to find that each data point actually fell within the control limits.

They knew that they would not have to work on the stability of the system but could concentrate on reducing variability among the data points, improving the predicted capability of the process.

The goal is not just to create a stable system but to generate improvement. Temperature measurements taken at appropriate intervals may all fall within the control limits and still be unacceptably high or low to the customer. A joining process that "almost fits" may reflect a stable process, but it is clear that it will not produce acceptable results.

In addition, not all out-of-control conditions indicate trouble. In charting machine output, you may find that seven consecutive points are above the average. In this case, the pattern suggests a positive development if the goal is to increase machine output. Responding to the pattern by altering the process so the output remains at the formerly stable level would defeat the long-range objective.

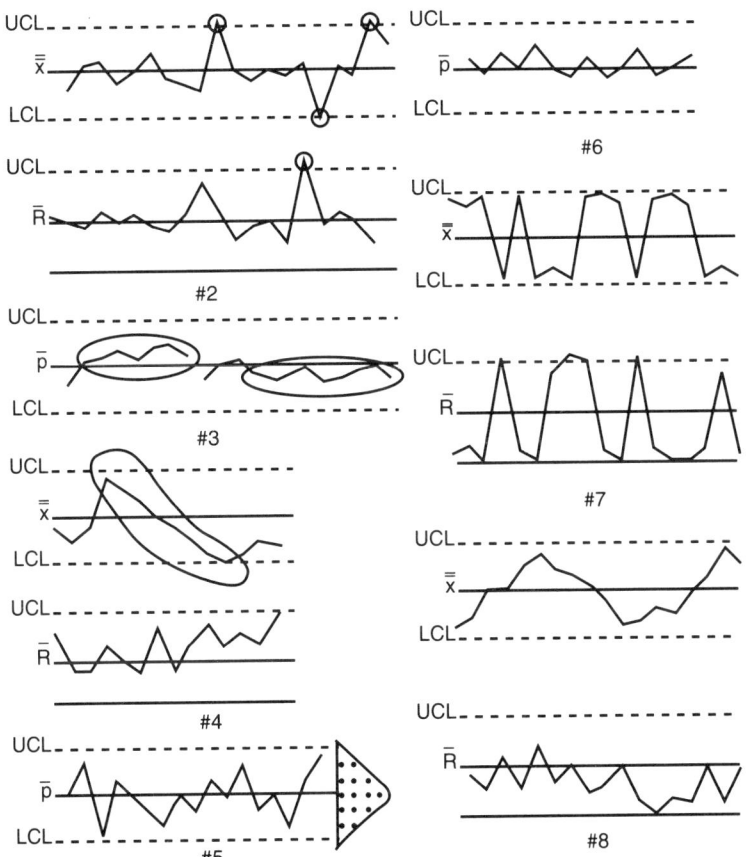

EXHIBIT 3.—THIS SHOWS RECOGNIZABLE PATTERNS INDICATING OUT-OF-CONTROL CONDITIONS. They are as follows:

#2: Points lying outside the control limits;

#3: Seven points in a row either above or below the center line;

#4: Any nonrandom patterns (repeating patterns);

#5: If data patterns are random, you could expect all data points to fall into a normal distribution if the chart could be "titled" on its side;

#6: Data points are all too close to the average;

#7: Data points are all too far from the average;

#8: Data rises and falls in a rhythmic pattern.

Analysis of charts lies at the heart of the improvement process. As you become more familiar with the visual clues and patterns that a control chart provides, even a first-glance analysis may reveal useful information. Additional statistical analysis will help to ensure predictability in the system.

REDUCE VARIABILITY IN THE PROCESS

By reducing variation, you can enhance the predictability of systems—the key to consistently high quality. Knowing that the application of a laser beam in a welding process will be consistent time after time will help ensure that the process can be approached in the same way by different welders at different times of day with different welding equipment still produce consistent product quality.

Reducing variation means that analysis is never really done. Charts may suggest inconsistencies in an anodizing process from shift to shift. Further analysis may pinpoint those inconsistencies to a particular batch of the coating solution, a specific day of the week, or even a particular technique. This information will help the analyst diminish the inconsistencies by giving attention to the area where they occur rather than changing the entire process.

This attention may involve tracking the process further upstream (to the makeup of the anodizing solution), pursuing cause-and-effect analysis related to when the inconsistencies occur, or providing training to ensure standard techniques are used by all operators.

GET RID OF THE "WALLPAPER"

If you find that you are creating charts simply to hang in your work area to make your work group look good or to impress your boss or visitors, throw them out.

This use of charts is counterproductive for a number of reasons. It gives an impression that you are working to improve processes and solve problems, when in fact you and the other members of your work team may be doing things in the same old ways, week after week and month after month.

It also reinforces your own loss of power to control those procedures; unused charts hang as reminders that you really do not know what is going on, since you are not taking advantage of the information that the charts may provide. Charting for its own sake is not a useful activity.

The time that it takes to create charts manually is significant; do not allow your team to waste this investment. Even if you are using the power of the personal computer and an SPC software program, remember that the output should not be produced for its own sake but only to improve the analytical process. Charts may not have to be printed at all; they can be accessible on a shared network basis among those who need to see the data.

CONTINUE TO REFINE YOUR ANALYSIS

If improvements to both stability and variability have been made, but the process is still not good enough to satisfy your own quality standards or those of your customer, you may want to continue the analysis in the following ways:

1. Study the measurement system for consistency and accuracy.

2. Study the raw materials. Do they consistently meet your requirements?

3. Study the training of operators to determine variation in their approaches to the process.

Analyzing a process with SPC can improve the process itself. Among the benefits of accurate and consistent application of SPC are enhanced competitiveness, greater levels of productivity, and improved quality of products. Companies worldwide have undertaken training for their employees to ensure the understanding of SPC and improvement of processes.

Recognized as a fundamental aspect of ISO 9000 certification and of continuous improvement of organizations, SPC is becoming as widely used in some industries as inventory control and other established practices.

SPC can be less beneficial to a company when the long-term results or improvements that are achieved cost far more than the resources required to bring about those results.

Barbara A. Cleary, Ph.D., is Corporate Vice President of PQ Systems, Inc., Dayton, Ohio.

STATISTICAL PROCESS CONTROL OF MULTIPLE STREAM PROCESSES*
by Robert R. Mortell and George C. Runger

Statistical process control methods for a process with multiple streams are developed and compared to traditional solutions. New methods maintain the simplicity of the group control chart while improving on traditional limitations. A model that allows correlation between the streams is described and a simple control strategy is recommended. Performance comparisons are provided.

* Reprinted with permission from *Journal of Quality Technology*, January 1995. Robert R. Mortell is an engineer with the Port Authority of New York and New Jersey. Dr. George C. Runger is an assistant professor of management sciences and statistics at the University of Maryland in College Park.

INTRODUCTION

Consider the process of filling shampoo bottles. The inputs to this process consist of a large vat of shampoo and a continuous stream of empty shampoo bottles. If a 24-head filling machine is used to fill the shampoo bottles, it is reasonable to assume that the shampoo and empty bottles are distributed among the 24 heads randomly. These heads constitute the 24 streams. The company wants to know if too much or too little shampoo is placed in a bottle. This situation can occur if bottles of the wrong size enter the system, the viscosity of the shampoo is incorrect, or a filling head malfunctions, possibly due to a clog. Problems with the bottle size or the viscosity of the shampoo can affect the product from all 24 heads, but a clogged head only affects the output from that one stream. It is important to detect both an assignable cause that results in all heads shifting out of control and an assignable cause in which one (or a few) head(s) shifts out of control.

The automated bottle filling operation described above, in which 24 bottles are filled simultaneously by one machine, is an example of a manufacturing process consisting of a number of identical product streams. At regular time intervals, a sample is taken from each stream and measured. Simple methods for determining when a problem occurs in this type of process are described in this paper.

To monitor the bottle filling process, 24 individual control charts can be maintained simultaneously. An out-of-control condition is signaled whenever either the filling head malfunctions or the process inputs change. Rather than maintaining 24 individual charts, one would prefer to monitor the process using fewer charts. The disadvantages from multiple comparisons are also important. As the number of charts increases, the opportunities for false alarms also increase. Furthermore, if the variability of the product is large over time, relative to the differences among streams, the ability of individual charts to detect an assignable cause affecting one stream is poor.

In our work, statistical process control methods that use the range (across streams) of subgroup means at a sample time are described and compared to traditional methods of controlling multiple stream processes. Advantages of our approach include simplicity and performance. Furthermore, our approach is not affected by correlations between individual product streams at a given time caused by a drifting overall process mean.

Using the range, one can separate assignable causes that affect all streams from those that affect only one stream. Isolating assignable causes helps to identify problems that can then be quickly eliminated. It is important for a control scheme to provide as much information as possible relating to the root cause of a problem. Our approach maintains the separation that is an important advantage of the group control chart, and this separation is the primary motivation for our strategy. Typically, quality analysts for multiple stream processes need to understand the differences between streams before they can effectively eliminate the variability over time. That is, for a filling operation, it is common to begin process improvement by first obtaining a consistent performance from all filling heads. This is facilitated by a control chart that is sensitive to head-to-head differences. It is more difficult to improve these processes without some separation between assignable causes that affect all streams from those that affect specific streams. For example, generating a control chart that is based on the average measurement from all the streams at a particular time is clearly not helpful for identifying stream-to-stream differences. In order to prioritize and implement practical improvement projects, it is important to generate a signal that is sensitive to an assignable cause that impacts a specific stream, regardless of the overall process performance.

Current methods for monitoring processes with multiple streams are discussed in the next section, and this is followed by a section that discusses new approaches. In a subsequent section, the methods used to evaluate the new and traditional control schemes are discussed, and performance results are provided. Based on the performance evaluation, recommendations are provided in the last section.

REVIEW OF CURRENT METHODS

Montgomery (1991, Sec. 8.3) discusses a control scheme for monitoring multiple stream processes that is often referred to as a *group control chart*. Also, see Nelson (1986). This control scheme has two primary objectives: (1) to detect a shift in the mean of all of the product streams; and (2) to detect a shift in the mean of an individual product stream. Two decision rules are used in a group control chart to detect assignable causes of type (1) or (2).

To detect a shift in the mean of all of the streams, the following approach is used. After taking a sample from each of the streams, the maximum and minimum sample means are plotted. If both of these points are within a set of control limits, then clearly the means from all other streams are also within these control limits. On this control chart, the control limits are based on the standard deviation of the subgroup mean from only one product stream. This standard deviation is often estimated from the average range across all subgroups. That is, the average ranges of the subgroups from each stream are averaged to estimate the process standard deviation. The part of a group control chart that signals whenever a maximum or minimum sample mean exceeds these control limits is referred to as the *singular control scheme*.

To detect a shift in an individual stream, the group control chart identifies the maximum and minimum sample means from the streams. For example, if the sample mean of the amount dispensed from a specific head is greater than the sample means of the amounts dispensed from all of the other heads for a specified number of consecutive samples, then it is assumed that individual head has gone out of statistical control. Specifically, assume that head #4 dispenses an average of 7.7 ounces of shampoo in each of the last six inspected samples, but all of the other heads dispense less than head #4 in each of the last six samples. Because head #4 consistently dispenses more shampoo than any of the other heads, it is likely that head #4 is malfunctioning.

The part of a group control chart that signals whenever the mean of a particular stream is an extreme in r consecutive samples is referred to as the *runs control scheme*. The average run length (ARL) of the runs control scheme for an in-control process is often calculated using the following formula from Nelson (1986) and Montgomery (1991):

$$\text{ARL1} = \frac{s^r - 1}{s - 1} \qquad (1)$$

where s is the number of product streams and r is the number of consecutive times that a particular stream is the maximum (or minimum) value. The notation "ARL1" indicates that (1) is a one-sided result in the sense that the ARL is for the event that a stream is the maximum (or minimum) in r consecutive samples.

An alternative criterion for the runs control scheme is the two-sided event that the mean of a stream is *either* a maximum or a minimum in r consecutive samples. The ARL of a runs control scheme using the two-sided criterion is denoted as ARL2. Values of ARL2 are provided in Exhibit 1, and a derivation is provided in the Appendix. The two-sided ARL2s have not previously appeared in the literature. The results in Table 1 indicate that when ARL1 is large, ARL2 is very nearly one-half of ARL1. Throughout this paper, our definition of a runs control scheme assumes the two-sided criterion. If there are only two product streams, stream A yielding the maximum value results in stream B yielding the minimum value, and vice versa. In this case, ARL1 = ARL2.

Multiple Stream Process Model

Measurement k from stream j at time t will be denoted by Y_{tjk} for $t = 1, 2, \ldots; j = 1, 2, \ldots, s$; and $k = 1, 2, \ldots, n$. For simplicity, we use summation notation such that when a subscript is omitted it implies the variables are averaged over the omitted subscript. Then, let the subgroup mean from stream j at time t be denoted as Y_{tj}, for $j = 1, 2, \ldots, s$ and $t = 1, 2, \ldots$. In many applications of group control charts, the subgroup size of the sample selected from each stream is one. Because of the number of streams, it is often difficult to use a larger subgroup size. However, our analysis assumes an arbitrary (but equal) subgroup of size n from each stream.

Consider the model for Y_{tjk},

$$Y_{tjk} = \mu + A_t + e_{tjk} \qquad (2)$$

where μ denotes the process mean; A_t denotes a normally distributed random variable with mean 0 and variance σ_a^2, that represents the difference of the process mean over all streams at time t from μ; and e_{tjk}, for $j = 1, 2, \ldots, s$ denotes independent, normally distributed random variables, each with mean 0 and variance σ^2, that represent the differences of the k measurements from stream j from the process mean over all streams at time t. We assume the e_{tjk}'s are independent of the A_t's. The subgroup mean from stream j at time t is

$$Y_{tj} = \mu + A_t + e_{tj}.$$

Consequently, $\sigma_a^2 + \sigma^2 / n$ is the variability of each subgroup mean.

EXHIBIT 1.—AVERAGE RUN LENGTH FOR IN-CONTROL RUNS
CONTROL CHART, TWO-SIDED CASE

Number of Streams, s	Consecutive Samples, r					
	2	3	4	5	6	7
2	3.0	7.0	15.0	31.0	63.0	127.0
3	3.0	8.2	22.8	65.0	189.1	557.5
4	3.4	12.0	44.9	174.1	687.7	2738.0
5	3.9	16.9	80.2	393.7	1957.5	9771.6
6	4.3	22.9	131.6	780.5	4669.6	27999.0
7	4.8	29.9	202.0	1403.4	9807.8	
8	5.3	37.8	295.5	2343.3	18728.0	
9	5.8	46.8	412.0	3693.2		
10	6.3	56.8	557.4	5558.2		
15	8.8	121.8	1809.9	27123.0		
20	11.3	211.8	4212.3			
30	16.3	466.8	13967.0			
50	26.3	1276.8				
100	51.3	5051.8				

The quantity A_t can be interpreted as representing characteristics of the product and equipment at time t that are common to all streams, such as viscosity, and e_{tjk} can be interpreted as representing deviations of the jth stream from the common characteristics, such as pressure differences and valve performance differences.

We will not assume that the A_t's are independent, although if the interval between subgroups is large relative to the time constant of the process, an assumption of independence is reasonable. Conversely, one of the advantages of our model is the provision for correlations between the observations at time t, $Y_{t1}, \ldots, Y_{ts}$, due to the common term A_t, even if the A_t's are independent. The performance of the control chart described below is not affected by correlations among the A_t's.

Typically, a group control chart model assumes all Y_{tj} are independent. For example, if the streams consist of 20 machine tools used for cutting operations, small time constants might imply that all the observations are independent. Our model incorporates the complete independence of all data as a special case where A_t is identically 0 (that is, using $\sigma_a^2 = 0$).

A shift of all product streams at time T can be represented in our model as a shift in the mean of A_t, for $t \geq T$, whereas a shift in one product stream, say j, at time T can be represented as a shift in the mean of e_{tj}, for $t \geq T$.

We are particularly interested in the case in which σ_a^2 is large relative to σ^2. In our experience, this case best represents filling (and coating operations) in which the process mean drifts over time and the variability of these drifts is large relative to the variability between outputs from different streams at a particular sampling time. For another example, whenever several automated mesurement tools are used simultaneously, the observations from the tools can be represented as a multiple stream process, and it is not unusual that the product variability over time is large relative to variability between the tools at a particular time. The application that motivated this research was the control of dozens of measurement tools, operating simultaneously. A representative time plot of this important special case is shown in Exhibit 2. Two streams are shown in Exhibit 2, and the variability over time is much greater than the differences between streams. At sample number 20, an assignable cause affects the output from one stream and there is separation between the streams that can be detected by an appropriate control chart.

If σ_a^2 is large relative to σ^2, an individual control chart for each stream is ineffective in detecting a shift in a single stream of magnitude σ (in addition to being tedious to maintain). This is because the control limits for Y_{tj}, for each j, need to include the variability of A_t, σ_a^2. The control limits for Y_{tj} are $\mu \pm 3 (\sigma_a^2 + \sigma^2 / n)^{1/2}$, and these variance components are estimated from the available data. A shift in a single stream, that is, a shift in the mean of e_{tj}, is difficult (nearly impossible) for this control chart to detect when σ_a^2 is large relative to σ^2. Consequently, in this case, the singular part of a group control chart its quite ineffective. For example, consider a simple case in which $n = 1$,

$\sigma_a = 4$, and $\sigma = 1$. Then the control limits for Y_{tj}, for each j, are $\mu \pm 3 (\sigma_a^2 + \frac{\sigma^2}{n})^{1/2} = \mu \pm 12.37$. A shift in the mean of e_{tj} of magnitude $\sigma = 1$ is equivalent to a shift in the mean of Y_{tj} of magnitude 1 and is poorly detected. In Figure 1, the assignable cause that occurs at time 20 is very difficult for the singular control chart of any stream to detect.

However, this is the case for which the runs control scheme is most useful. The runs component of the traditional group control chart is constructed to be insensitive to the variability in A_t. By plotting the maximum and minimum subgroup means of the streams and identifying trends, the streams are compared to each other. Changes in A_t over time do not affect the ability of the runs control scheme to detect a shift in a single stream. The development and use of the classical runs scheme indicates the importance of the case in which σ_a^2 is large relative to σ^2.

Limitations of the Runs Control Scheme

Because the singular scheme of a group control chart is ineffective in the important case that σ_a^2 is large relative to σ^2, the out-of-control ARL of a group control chart is nearly equal to ARL2, the ARL of the runs component. In the runs control scheme, r and s must be integers greater than one. As the number of product streams increases, one can see from Table 1 that the number of reasonable in control ARLs available for the runs scheme decreases rapidly. Consequently, specifying that the in-control ARL of a

runs scheme must exceed, say 370, can result in an actual in-control ARL much larger than 370. The important impact of such a large in-control ARL is the poor detection of an out-of-control shift.

As can be seen, the discreteness of the in-control ARL can be a major drawback when using this control scheme. For example, consider a manufacturing process with 15 product streams and a target in-control ARL of approximately 370. The runs control scheme can only offer ARLs of either 122, which is less than half the desired ARL, or 1810 which is five times the acceptable in-control ARL. Choosing the parameters associated with the lower ARL results in too many false alarms. On the other hand, using the parameters associated with the higher ARL results in many more samples being taken before an actual out-of-control situation is detected. Furthermore, because the singular part of a group control chart is ineffective when σ_a^2 is large relative to σ^2, changing the parameters of the singular scheme do not correct this fundamental disadvantage of the runs component of a group control chart. For these reasons, the ability to specify an arbitrary in-control ARL is a major asset for process control.

In addition to the possibilities of exactly one of the streams shifting or all streams shifting simultaneously, two or more of the streams can shift at nearly the same time. On a 24-head filling machine, three or four heads can clog at the same time due to some impurity in the shampoo. The runs control scheme might not detect this type of out-of-control condition or the clog of

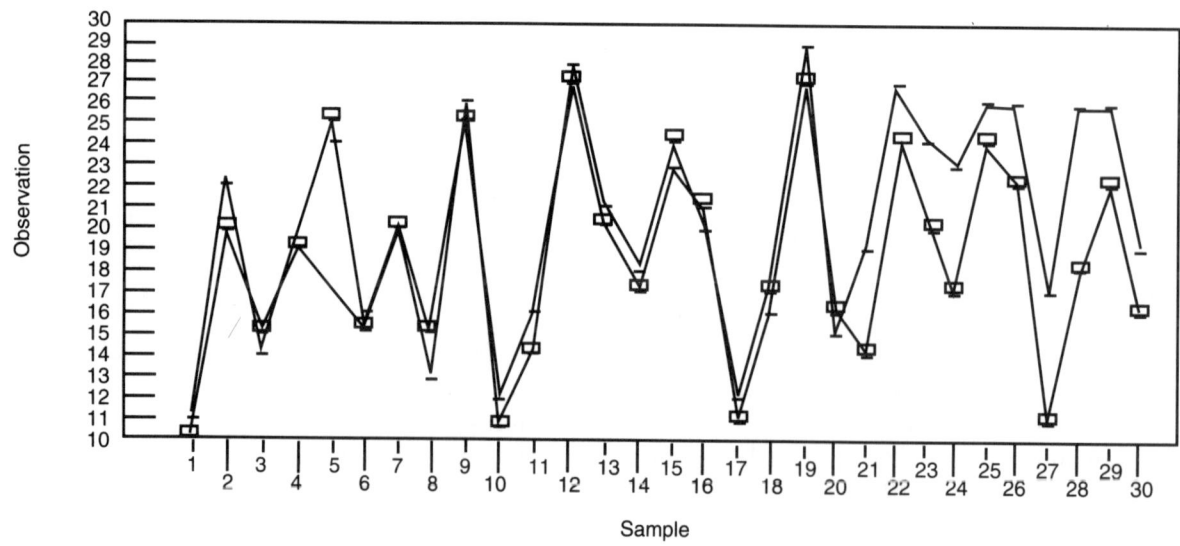

EXHIBIT 2.—PLOT OF DATA FROM TWO STREAMS WITH A SHIFT AT SAMPLE 20

a single head. If the mean of only one stream shifts upward, it is most likely that from then on, that stream has the maximum value. If two streams shift upward the same amount, most likely one of these two streams has the maximum value. However, the two streams are equally likely to obtain the maximum value. The runs scheme is only sensitive to one stream consistently obtaining the maximum value; it does not check for the maximum alternating between two streams. The performance of the runs scheme for this type of assignable cause is evaluated below.

NEW METHODOLOGY

Like a group control chart, the new method has two basic features: (1) a control scheme that monitors a change in all product streams; and (2) a control scheme that monitors a change in one stream relative to the others.

To detect changes common to all streams, a variation on the basic Shewhart chart is used. Rather than using the subgroup mean from one product stream as the control variable, the new method uses the average of the subgroup means across all of the product streams at a sample time. That is, the plotted statistic is Y_t.

This can result in narrower control limits than the singular scheme of the classical group control chart for the same in-control ARL. Clearly, averaging across streams builds the sample size and improves the ability of this chart to detect an assignable cause that shifts the mean of all streams simultaneously. The performance of this chart is sensitive to autocorrelation in A_t, as is the singular scheme of the classical group control chart. Typically, autocorrelation generates additional false alarms, and methods described by Montgomery and Mastrangelo (1991) can be useful.

To detect a change in one stream relative to the others, a simple control scheme that is effective when σ_a^2 is large relative to σ^2 and improves upon the disadvantages of the runs scheme is needed. The basic control charting methods, Shewhart, CUSUM, and EWMA, do not have the discreteness problem inherent in the design of a runs scheme. However, running a Shewhart, CUSUM, or EWMA chart on each stream has the same disadvantage as the singular scheme; the large variability of A_t prevents quick detection of a shift in one stream. To detect an individual

stream malfunctioning when σ_a^2 is large, a chart that is sensitive to the difference of one stream from the others is useful.

One approach is to subtract the average value of all of the streams from the value of each individual stream, at every sample time. This is sometimes referred to an analysis of the residuals (Ott and Snee, 1973). Using a residual as the control variable on a control chart for each stream eliminates the variability of process drifts common to all streams. Consequently, the residuals are insensitive to autocorrelation in A_t. Furthermore, one can now more easily determine whether a process shift is the result of an assignable cause that shifts all streams or one that shifts only a few streams, because the residual chart is insensitive to the former and sensitive to the latter.

The analysis of residuals can also be developed from a multivariate approach to multiple stream control. Let $\mathbf{V}_t$ denote the vector of averages from the s streams at time t, that is $\mathbf{V}_t = (Y_{t1}, Y_{t2}, \ldots, Y_{ts})'$. The vector $\mathbf{V}_t$ can be considered a multivariate response from the process at time t. Let $\mathbf{I}$ denote the $s \times s$ identity matrix and let $\mathbf{J}$ be the $s \times s$ matrix with all entries equal to one. Then, the covariance matrix of $\mathbf{V}_t$ is $(\sigma^2/n)\mathbf{I} + \sigma_a^2\mathbf{J}$.

Recommendations from the multivariate control chart literature can be applied to the model (2) to develop a control scheme that is sensitive to the shift of one stream. It is shown in the Appendix that to detect a shift in stream j the general, multivariate control variable recommended by Pignatiello and Runger (1990) reduces, in the case of model (2), to

$$X_{tj} = \frac{Y_{tj} - Y_t}{\sigma^2/n} + \frac{Y_t}{\sigma_2/n + s\sigma_a^2}. \qquad (3)$$

The resulting control variable is a linear combination of the average of all streams at time t and the difference of the jth stream from the average at time t. From (3), if σ_a^2 is large relative to σ^2, X_{tj} is approximately proportional to $Y_{tj} - Y_t$. The difference between Y_{tj} and Y_t is used to eliminate the variability of A_t from the control variable. Because the effect of A_t is reduced, control charts on X_{tj} can be more effective in monitoring a shift in an individual stream than using a control chart based on Y_{tj}.

To detect a change in all streams (a shift in the mean of A_t), the control variable recommended by Pignatiello and Runger (1990) for the model in (2) is the average over all streams Y_t.

This result matches intuition and has already been suggested as the approach for detecting an assignable cause that shifts all streams.

The monitoring of X_{tj} requires a chart for each stream and is not as simple as the runs procedure of the traditional group control chart. If a process consists of 24 streams, an analysis of the residuals requires 24 control charts. If, rather than the residuals, the range of the stream subgroup means at time t is used as the control variable, one chart can be used to monitor all streams. Essentially, the minimum subgroup mean across all streams at time t is subtracted from the maximum subgroup mean across all streams at time t and this difference is then controlled by either a Shewhart, CUSUM, or EWMA chart. That is, the control variable is

$$R_t = \max_j Y_{tj} - \min_j Y_{tj}.$$

Because R_t is used rather than the actual values, only changes in one stream with respect to the others, not changes in the process as a whole, are monitored by this method. Similarly to the X_{tj}'s and a runs scheme, the use of the range removes the variability of the A_t from the control variable. When the variability of A_t is large, this will be an important benefit. When the subgroup size from each stream is n, R_t is the range of the s subgroup means from each stream at time t.

In the context of the shampoo bottle filling example, assume shampoo is passed through the filling head for a specified period of time depending only on the size of the bottle. If the shampoo becomes too watery, the lower viscosity allows a higher flow rate. Therefore, all of the heads dispense too much shampoo. Assume that for a certain sample, when the shampoo has its normal viscosity, heads #6 and #4 dispense the most and least shampoo, respectively. If the viscosity decreases, both heads dispense more shampoo; however, the difference between the amount dispensed by head #6 and head #4 remains approximately unchanged. On the other hand, if any head becomes worn and dispenses too much shampoo, that head almost always produces the maximum measurement, and because the means of the other streams remain unchanged, the value of the range increases substantially.

An alternative to use R_t as the control variable is to subtract the average value of all streams from the value of the stream with the maximum measurement. This is largest of the residuals. By plotting this residual, that can arise from a different stream each time a sample is taken, one can monitor a positive shift in any one stream with respect to all of the others. Clearly, the residuals of all other streams are less than the maximum. Therefore, if this maximum residual is in control, all of the other streams are in control with respect to the upper control limit. Similarly, a minimum residual can be compared to a lower control limit in order to detect one stream shifting lower than the others. Therefore, it is unnecessary to plot the residuals of all the streams. Plotting the maximum (and minimum) residual is suggested as a way to reduce some of the variability inherent in the range. Both methods are compared further below.

PERFORMANCE EVALUATION

Evaluation Method

Simulations and an analytical analysis were used to compare several alternative control schemes for detecting the shift in one (or a few) streams in a multiple stream process. All the schemes compared are based on control variables that eliminate the impact of large variability in A_t. Therefore, the schemes are most useful in the case that σ_a^2 is large relative to σ^2. In this case, the performance of the singular scheme of the classical group control chart is poor and the performance of the group control chart is evaluated only on the basis of the runs scheme.

Shewhart, CUSUM, and EWMA schemes using R_t as the control variable are compared to the Runs scheme. The maximum residual is also used as the control variable for a one-sided CUSUM scheme. Processes containing 2, 3, 5, 10, and 20 product streams are analyzed. Three weighting factors, 0.1, 0.3, and 0.5, are used for the EWMA control scheme. Because the in-control ARLs of the runs scheme are restricted, our first analysis chooses control limits for the other schemes to match selected choices of the in-control ARL of the runs scheme. Our second analysis specifies a particular in-control ARL and chooses the value for r in the runs schemes that is nearest to the specified in-control ARL. Because our goal is only to consider the relative performance of the schemes under study, an in-control ARL of 200 is specified as an easy to evaluate target. As always, the best choice of in-control ARL depends on the application.

At each sample time, one observation is generated for each stream. The observations are independent and normally distributed with mean

0 and standard deviation 1. Because A_t has no effect on these schemes, independent observations can be used to evaluate the performance of these schemes and the conclusions still apply to applications in which the A_t are autocorrelated. The single observation from stream s at time t represents the standardized sub-group mean 0 and standard deviation 1. The control limits, described below, are chosen to obtain a specified ARL for the in-control process. The mean of one or more streams is shifted to simulate an out of control process. The out-of-control ARLs are found for shifts in the mean of the standard normal observations of 0.5, 1, 1.5, and 2 standard deviations. These shifts are interpreted as multiples of the standard deviation σ/n.

Successive trials are simulated until the length of a 95% confidence interval for the ARL is less than 10% of the estimated ARL. Therefore, the precision of each estimated ARL in Exhibits 3 through 8 is plus or minus 5%.

A two-sided runs scheme is used and the value of r is chosen from Table 1. For a process with only two product streams, the out-of-control ARL can be found analytically by calculating the probability that the range from two normal distributions with different means exceeds a control limit. If the process contains more than two streams, the out-of-control ARL is simulated.

A traditional Shewhart chart using R_t as the control variable is used. One value is generated for each stream at time t and the range between these values is calculated to obtain R_t.

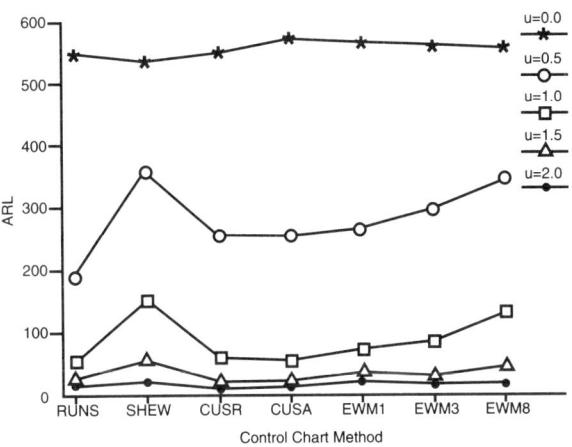

EXHIBIT 4.—COMPARISON OF CONTROL CHART ARLS WITH STREAMS = 3

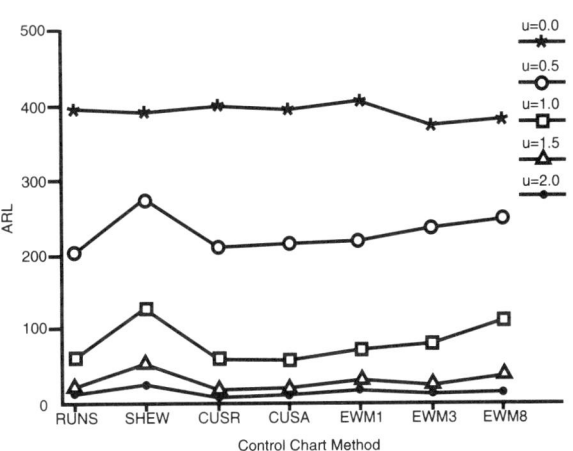

EXHIBIT 5.—COMPARISON OF CONTROL CHART ARLS WITH STREAMS = 5

For analyses in which an in-control ARL of 200 is specified, control limits for the Shewhart chart are found using tables of the range from Pearson and Hartley (1976). Simulation is used to find control limits when the in-control ARL is not 200. After the control limits are determined, the out-of-control performance is simulated.

Several EWMA charts using R_t as the control variable are evaluated. The EWMA variable, S_t, is found from the formula $S_t = aR_t + (1 - a) S_{t-1}$, where a is a weighting factor between 0 and 1, and $S_0 = 0$. Charts using three different weighting factors, 0.1, 0.3, and 0.8, are evaluated. The control limit for each acceptable in-control ARL is determined by simulating the in-

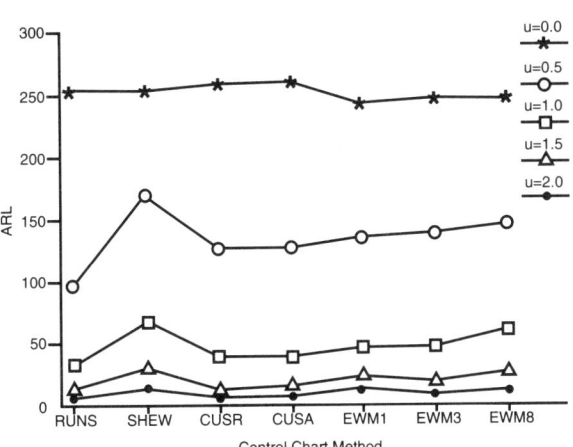

EXHIBIT 3.—COMPARISON OF CONTROL CHART ARLS WITH STREAMS = 2

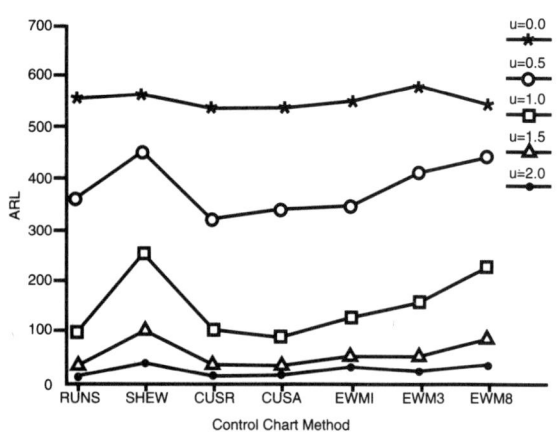

EXHIBIT 6.—COMPARISON OF CONTROL CHART
ARLS WITH STREAMS = 10

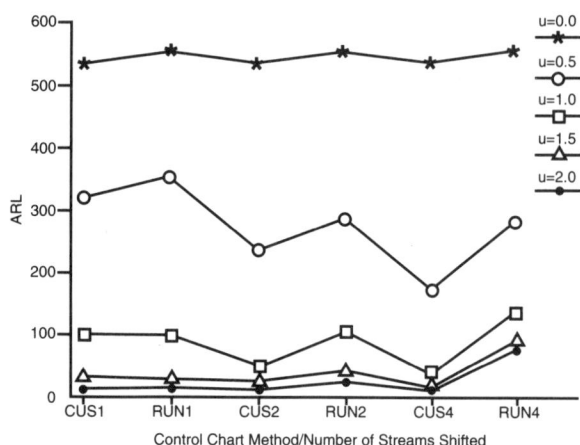

EXHIBIT 8.—COMPARISON OF CONTROL CHART
ARLS WHEN MULTIPLE STREAMS SHIFT FOR
TOTAL STREAMS = 10

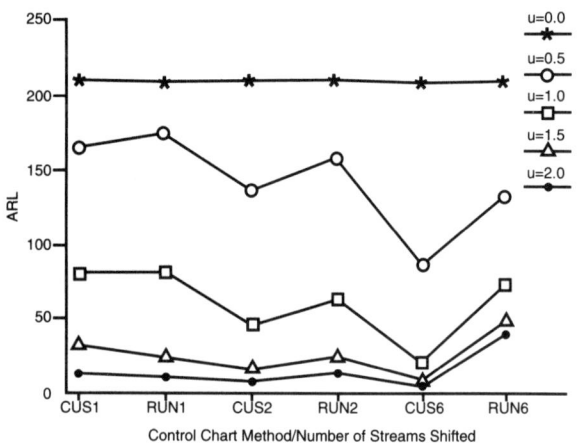

EXHIBIT 7.—COMPARISON OF CONTROL CHART
ARLS WHEN MULTIPLE STREAMS SHIFT FOR
TOTAL STREAMS = 20

control process. The out-of-control processes are simulated to determine the ARLs.

Two CUSUM schemes are investigated. The first one uses R_t as the control variable, and the second one uses the maximum residual as the control variable. The second CUSUM is investigated to determine if damping out the variability in the minimum stream improves performance. The first CUSUM is calculated as follows: $S_t = \max(0, S_{t-1} + R_t - k)$, where $S_0 = 0$, and k is a constant. For these simulations, k is set equal to the expected value of R_t when one stream shifts one standard deviation from the mean of the other streams. This value for k is relatively easy to calculate. Also, preliminary simulations found that this choice of k provided the best performance among choices such as k equal to 0.5 or 2 times the selection above. The second CUSUM is calculated similarly, with the maxi-

mum residual replacing R_t. The second CUSUM is used to detect the mean of a stream shifting up. A two-sided control procedure can be implemented by supplementing the CUSUM of the maximum residual with a simultaneous CUSUM of the minimum residual. However, we show below that the maximum residual is not more effective than using R_t. Consequently, a two-sided, residual CUSUM is not analyzed.

The simulation programs were written in Quick-BASIC (1988) and executed on an IBM PS/2 personal computer. Pseudo-random normal variables were generated by the Sine-Cosine method of Box and Muller (see Ahrens and Dieter, 1972).

Single Stream Shifting

First, the control limit for each scheme is chosen such that the in-control ARL is equal to that used for the runs scheme. This ensures that the runs scheme is not penalized for not allowing arbitrary in-control ARLs. For each method, one stream is shifted from a mean of 0 to a mean of 0.5, 1, 1.5, or 2.

Exhibits 3 through 6 provide graphical comparisons of the ARLs for the different methods for 2, 3, 5, and 10 streams, respectively. These methods are denoted CUSA, CUSR, EWM1, EWM3, EWM8, RUNS, and SHEW corresponding to a CUSUM chart using the maximum residual as the control variable, a CUSUM chart using R_t as the control variable, an EWMA chart based on R_t with the weighting factor equal to 0.1, 0.3, and 0.8, the runs scheme, and a Shewhart chart using R_t the control variable, respectively. The plot for $\mu = 0.0$ at the top of each figure provides the in-control ARL.

Among the cases considered, the Shewhart chart based on R_t performs worst until the shift is equal to at least two standard deviations. For this reason, the Shewhart chart is not recommended when small shifts are anticipated. Also, the EWMA charts never exceed the performance of either the CUSUM or runs chart. However, the value of the weighting factor used by the EWMA plays a key role in the performance of this control scheme. In general, a relatively small weighting factor is better for small shifts while a large weighting factor is better for large shifts. Overall, a weighting factor of 0.3 might be an acceptable compromise. Although the simulation data shows that an alternative method can always perform as well as an EWMA, a better choice for the weighting factor might make the EWMA a viable candidate for detecting the shift of one stream with respect to the others.

Little difference is observed between the two CUSUM methods studied. Using the maximum residual offers no real improvement over simply using the range of stream values. Because the range requires fewer calculations, with no loss of performance, it is recommended that the range be used as the response for the CUSUM method.

The CUSUM and runs schemes perform better than the alternatives. Between these two, the better choice depends on the number of product streams and the size of the shift in one of the streams. When the process consists of only two or three streams, the runs scheme is better for a small shift, generally less than 1.0. The CUSUM scheme is better for larger shifts when the process consists of only a few streams. Both methods perform equivalently for 5 product streams, but with 10 product streams the situation is reversed. With many product streams, the CUSUM method outperforms the runs method for small shifts in one stream. As the shift in one product stream increases to $\mu = 2$, the run method performs better. Even with 20 product streams, the CUSUM method is better for small shifts in one stream while the runs method is better for large shifts.

The difference in the in-control ARLs chosen for Exhibit 3 through 6 demonstrate the discreteness of the possible in-control ARLs for the runs scheme. The above comparison between the runs and CUSUM methods assumes that both methods have the same in-control ARL. This is essentially a worst case scenario for the CUSUM method since control limits can be found for any

in-control ARL. For example, suppose a process has 10 streams. Control limits for the CUSUM method can provide an arbitrary in-control ARL exactly, but the runs method is restricted to in-control ARLs of either approximately 57 or 557, when $r = 3$ or 4, respectively. When both the runs and CUSUM methods have an in-control ARL of 557, a shift in the mean of one product stream equal to 1.5 standard deviations results in the CUSUM method requiring an average of 31 samples to observe the out-of-control condition, while the runs method requires an average of 27 samples. However, if false alarms once every 200 plotted points can be tolerated, then a CUSUM method with an in-control ARL of 200 could be used, and it only requires an average of 22 samples to detect the out-of-control condition.

As the number of streams increases, one can see from Exhibit 1 that the number of in-control ARLs for the runs scheme that would be considered in practice decreases rapidly. Consequently, specifying that the in-control ARL of a runs scheme must exceed, say 200, can result in an actual in-control ARL much larger than 200. The important impact of such a large in-control ARL is the poor detection of an out-of-control shift. The CUSUM scheme is far more versatile when a large number of streams are being monitored.

Multiple Streams Shifting

It is possible that more than one product stream shifts before an out-of-control situation is signaled. As the number of out-of-control streams increase, the ARL of the runs scheme can increase. The runs scheme is only sensitive to one stream consistently obtaining the maximum value; it does not check for the maximum alternating between two streams. Exhibits 7 and 8 provide simulation results showing the effect of shifts in multiple streams on a runs control scheme.

In Exhibits 7 and 8, RUN1, RUN2, RUN4, and RUN6 refer to runs charts with 1, 2, 4, or 6 streams shifting, respectively, and CUS1, CUS2, CUS4, and CUS6 refer to CUSUM charts based on R_t as the control variable with 1, 2, 4, or 6 streams shifting, respectively. The in-control ARL is given by the top plot of each figure. The CUSUM method detects the out-of-control condition more quickly than the runs method as more streams shift out of control. The out-of-control ARL for the runs method can increase as the number of shifted streams increases, especially when the shift is large. Even when only two streams shift, the CUSUM method outperforms the runs method.

Conclusions

Processes with multiple, identical product streams, such as a multiple head filling machine, can be monitored using many different control chart methods (Ott and Snee, 1973). The most suitable method depends on the number of product streams and the expected size of the shifts in the streams. The method described here requires only two charts to monitor the entire process, is simple and, consequently, is likely to be implemented and maintained.

For processes with a large number of streams, using a pair of control charts is suggested. The first chart, used to monitor shifts common to all product streams, can be a Shewhart chart with the control variable at sample t being the average of all of the measurements across all of the streams. Clearly, this scheme can have tighter control limits and better performance than the singular scheme in a traditional group control chart when a shift common to all streams occurs. The second control chart, used to monitor a change in one stream with respect to the others, can be a CUSUM chart with the response variable equal to R_t. This range eliminates the variability arising from A_t to improve ARL performance, while maintaining the simplicity of using a single control chart. For a large number of product streams, the runs control scheme is likely to respond poorly if either the shift is small or if more than one product stream shifts. Furthermore, depending on the number of streams and the desired in-control ARL, the actual in-control ARL for the runs scheme may be far greater than necessary resulting in longer out-of-control ARLs.

The CUSUM method requires two control parameters, the control limit and the constant k. A reasonable choice for k is the expected value of R_t when the mean of a single stream shifts by one standard deviation. If this design strategy is selected, simulation can be used to find this expected range. It should be noted that this is not necessarily an optimal k value. Lucas (1976) discusses the choice of k in the construction of CUSUM schemes and further work might improve the performance of the CUSUM by using a better value for k. This choice for k would tune the CUSUM to be most sensitive to a shift by one stream of one standard deviation. However, many other choices for k would provide acceptable performance.

Also, a transformation of the distribution of R_t to normality can be used to design a CUSUM based on typical guidelines for normally distributed data. For example, software packages that automate the fit of data to a distributional family and adjust for the appropriate control limits are available commercially.

The control limit for a CUSUM control chart is usually chosen to meet an in-control average run length objective. Consequently, a CUSUM based on R_t can be developed from the distribution of a studentized range. Alternatively, a transformation to normality can again be used. Another method for tuning the control chart is to modify parameters by processing historical data and judging the results. This use of an empirical reference distribution is useful for the design of any control chart.

Our approach to control charting multiple stream processes is actually more general. We do not require that a sample be chosen from every stream at each sample time. Nothing in the construction of the charts is changed if one calculates the mean and range at a sample time from just a subset of the process streams. In fact, the charts can be operated as described even if the subsets are chosen randomly at each sample time. We only require that the number of streams sampled at each sample time is constant. The Runs scheme assumes that all streams are measured at each sample time. This is an important benefit of our methods as the number of streams increase and it requires greater resources to sample from each stream at each sample time. In practice, for many filling operations it is common that only a subset of streams are measured at each sample time.

Appendix

Derivation of Control Variables

The control variables used for the model in (2) are briefly developed in this section.

Given a multivariate observation vector, denoted as Z, with identity covariance matrix, to detect a shift in the mean of Z from the vector 0 to the vector δ, Pignatiello and Runger (1990) recommend that a multivariate control scheme be based on the length of the projection of Z onto the subspace spanned by δ. That is, the recommended control variable is proportional to $\delta'Z$.

In the model in (2), the covariance matrix of the vector V_t, denoted as Σ, is $(\sigma^2/n)\, I + \sigma_2^a\, J$, where J is an $s \times s$ matrix of all ones. A shift of one product stream is equivalent to a shift in the mean of V_t from μ to the vector $\mu + d$, where d has all zero components except for the component corresponding to the stream that shifts. To apply the result of Pignatiello and Runger (1990), V_t and d are transformed to $Z_t = \Sigma^{-0.5}(V_t - \mu)$ and $\delta = \Sigma^{-0.5}\, d$, respectively. Therefore, the recommended control variable is $d'\Sigma^{-1}(V_t - \mu)$.

From the form for Σ, the eigenvalues of Σ are found to be σ^2/n, with multiplicity $s - 1$, and $\sigma^2/n + s\sigma_2^2$, with multiplicity one. Therefore, it can be shown that

$$\Sigma^{-1} = \frac{nI}{\sigma^2} - \frac{\sigma_a^2\, J}{[(\sigma^2/n)(\sigma^2/n + s\sigma_a^2)]}$$

After algebraic simplification, the control variable in (3) is obtained.

A similar approach can be used to show that the recommended control variable for detecting a shift in the mean of A_t that affects all streams is Y_t.

Derivation of ARL2

The derivation of the ARL for the two-sided runs scheme, ARL2, is provided next. Given values of the parameters r and s, a Markov chain with r^2 states is constructed. Each state is represented as a pair of integers, (x, y), in which x denotes the number of consecutive samples in which the same stream has produced the maximum subgroup, $x = 1, 2, \ldots, r$, and y denotes the number of consecutive samples in which the same stream has produced the minimum subgroup, $y = 1, 2, \ldots, r$. Whenever $x = r$ or $y = r$, the two-sided Runs schemes signals. Therefore, the $(r - 1)^2$ states for which $1 \le x \le r - 1$ and $1 \le y \le r - 1$ are transient states, and any state with $x = r$ or $y = r$ is an absorbing state. When the process is in control, there are only four distinct (nonzero) transition probabilities between the states,

$Pr((x,y) \to (1,1)) = (s^2 - 3s + 3)/(s(s - 1))$
$Pr((x,y) \to (1, y + 1)) = (s - 2)/(s(s - 1))$
$Pr((x,y) \to (x + 1,1)) = (s - 2)/(s(s - 1))$
$Pr((x,y) \to (x + 1, y + 1)) = 1/(s(s - 1))$

Let P denote the matrix of transition probabilities of the transient states. Since there are only four distinct, nonzero transition probabilities, P contains much repetitive pattern. Because the first sample from each stream is used to enter the state $(1, 1)$, ARL2 equals one plus the mean time until absorption of the chain. Therefore, ARL2 $= 1 + b'(I - P)^{-1}\, 1$, and where 1 and b are $(r - 1)^2 \times 1$ vectors. See Brook and Evans (1972). The components of 1 are all one. The component of b corresponding to the state $(1, 1)$ equals one and the other components of b are zero. This expression is evaluated numerically for the values of r and s in Table 1.

References

Ahrens, J. J. and Dieter, U. (1972). "Computer Methods for Sampling From the Exponential and Normal Distributions." *Communications of the ACM* 15, pp. 873–882.

Brook, D. and Evans, D. A. (1972). "An Approach to the Probability Distribution of CUSUM Run Length." *Biometrika* 59, pp. 539–549.

Lucas, J. M. (1976). "The Design and Use of Cumulative Sum Quality Control Schemes," *Journal of Quality Technology* 8, pp. 1–11.

Montgomery, D. C. (1991). *Introduction to Statistical Quality Control,* 2nd ed. John Wiley & Sons, New York, NY.

Montgomery, D. C. and Mastrangelo, C. M. (1991). "Some Statistical Process Control Methods for Autocorrelated Data." *Journal of Quality Technology* 23, pp. 179–193.

Nelson, L. S. (1986). "Control Chart for Multiple Stream Processes." *Journal of Quality Technology* 18, pp. 255–256.

Ott, E. R. and Snee, R. D. (1973). "Identifying Useful Differences in a Multiple-Head Machine." *Journal of Quality Technology* 5, pp. 47–57.

Pearson, E. S. and Hartley, H. O. (1976). *Biometrika Tables for Statisticians 1.* Biometrika Trust, London.

Pignatiello, J. J. Jr. and Runger, G. C. (1990). "Comparisons of Multivariate CUSUM Charts." *Journal of Quality Technology* 22, pp. 173–186.

QuickBASIC (1988). Version 4.5, Microsoft, Bellevue, WA.

Key Words: *Average Run Length, Cumulative Sum Control Charts, Exponentially Weighted Moving Average, Group Control Charts, Shewhart Control Charts.*

■

$\overline{X}$ AND R CONTROL CHARTS FOR SKEWED POPULATIONS*
by D. S. Bai and I. S. Choi

This paper proposes a heuristic method based on a weighted variance concept of setting up control limits of $\overline{X}$ and R charts for skewed populations. It provides asymmetric control limits in accordance with the direction and degree of skewness estimated from the sample data, by using different variances in computing upper and lower control limits. For symmetric populations, however, these control limits are equivalent to those of Shewhart control charts. The new heuristic control charts are compared by Monte Carlo simulation with Shewhart charts and the geometric control charts of Ferrell. When the underlying population is Weibull or Burr's, the heuristic charts are found to perform better than Shewhart or geometric charts as the skewness increases.

INTRODUCTION

Shewhart $\overline{X}$ and R control charts are based on the assumption that the distribution of the quality characteristic is normal or approximately normal. When $\overline{X}$ and R charts having 3σ limits and a sample size of five are employed for a process that is normally distributed, the probabilities of a point falling outside the limits when the process is in control are 0.0027 and 0.0046, respectively.

In many situations, however, we may have reason to doubt the validity of the normality assumption. For example, the distributions of measurements from chemical processes or cutting tool wear processes, and of observations on lifetimes in accelerated life test samples are often skewed. Burr (1967), Shilling and Nelson (1976), Balakrishnan and Kocherlakota (1986), and Chan, Hapuarachchi, and Macpherson (1988) have examined the effect of non-normality on $\overline{X}$ and R charts. For skewed populations, Type I risk probabilities grow larger as the skewness increases. The trouble arises from the discrepancy between the variability pattern of the asymmetric distribution and the normality assumed in placing control limits on Shewhart $\overline{X}$ and R charts. For highly skewed populations, one possible solution is to increase sample sizes. This is, however, often expensive. Therefore, a method which provides asymmetric control limits in accordance with the actual variability pattern of the population is desirable.

Some authors assumed the underlying distribution and derived exact probability limits for control charts satisfying the desired Type I risk. Ferrell (1958) proposed geometric midrange and geometric range charts for a lognormal population in place of Shewhart $\overline{X}$ and R charts. Nelson (1979) obtained control limits of median, range, scale, and location charts for the Weibull distribution. In some instances, it is possible to transform the nonnormal variate into the normal and use the Shewhart method to determine control limits. Also, one can fit a theoretical frequency curve such as the Gram-Charlier or Pearson system, and obtain asymmetric control limits satisfying the desired probability. However, these approaches can be complicated, and most quality engineers would probably prefer to use the standard approach based on the normality assumption if the effect of non-normality is not serious.

Heuristic approaches to the skewness problem have also been considered. Cowden (1957) proposed a split distribution method which provides asymmetric control limits when the underlying population is skewed. He divided the asymmetric distribution into two parts at its mode and treated each part as a half of a distinct normal, each having the same mean but different standard deviations. Cowden, however, did not report any computational results to support the method and did not provide control charts for standard deviations or ranges. Choobineh and Ballard (1987) proposed a weighted variance (WV) method based on the semivariance approximation of Choobineh and Branting (1986). Their

* Reprinted with permission from *Journal of Quality Technology*, April 1995. D. S. Bai is a professor in the Department of Industrial Engineering at Korea Advance Institute of Science and Technology in Daejon Korea. I. S. Choi is a graduate student in the Department of Industrial Engineering at the same institution.

method provides asymmetric control limits of $\overline{X}$ and R charts for skewed distributions based on the standard deviation of sample means and ranges (between sample variation), rather than the mean of sample standard deviations or sample ranges (within sample variation), for constructing $\overline{X}$ and R charts. The process standard deviation, however, should be estimated from within sample variation, not from the between sample variation. See Abel (1989) for a discussion on this point.

In this paper, we propose a simple heuristic method of constructing $\overline{X}$ and R control charts using the WV method with no assumptions on the population. This method provides asymmetric control limits in accordance with the direction and degree of skewness estimated from the sample data by using different variances in computing upper and lower control limits for skewed populations. The charts reduce to Shewhart charts for symmetric populations. In the next section we review the WV method. A heuristic method of setting up control limits of $\overline{X}$ and R charts based on the WV follows. An example illustrating the use of the proposed method is given. $\overline{X}$ and R chart constants for skewed populations are then obtained. The performances of the proposed charts are compared with the Shewhart charts and the geometric charts of Ferrell. Finally, a comparison with the exact method is given.

THE WV METHOD

The WV method is based on the idea that a skewed distribution can be split into two segments at its mean and each segment is used for creating a new symmetric distribution. The two new distributions created from the original skewed distribution have the same mean but different standard deviations. The WV method uses these two distributions for setting up the limits of the control chart. That is, one of the two distributions is used for computing the standard deviation for the upper control limit (UCL), while the other is used for the lower control limit (LCL). If the population is skewed to the right, then the distance of the UCL from the process mean is larger than that of the LCL. Similarly, if the pop-

ulation is skewed to the left, then the distance of the LCL from the process mean is larger than that of the UCL. For a symmetric population, however, the distances of the UCL and the LCL from the process mean are the same, and the chart based on the WV method reduces to Shewhart chart.

The WV method, like the Shewhart method, uses the standard deviation to set the limits of the control chart. However, it differs from the Shewhart method in that the standard deviation is multiplied by two different factors. One factor is used for the UCL, while the other is used for the LCL. Let P_x be the probability that random variable X will be less than or equal to its mean μ_x. Then the UCL factor is $\sqrt{2P_X}$, and the LCL factor is $\sqrt{2(1 - P_X)}$. See Chobineh and Ballard (1987) for a derivation of these factors.

The control limits of the $\overline{X}$ chart based on the WV method are

$$\text{UCL}_{\overline{X}} = \mu_X + 3\frac{\sigma x}{\sqrt{n}}\sqrt{2P_X} \qquad (1a)$$

$$\text{LCL}_{\overline{X}} = \mu_X - 3\frac{\sigma x}{\sqrt{n}}\sqrt{2(1 - P_X)} \qquad (1b)$$

where σ_X is the standard deviation of X. Similarly, the control limits of the R chart are

$$\text{UCL}_R = \mu_R + 3\sigma_R\sqrt{2P_X} \qquad (2a)$$

$$\text{LCL}_R = \left[\mu_R - 3\sigma_R\sqrt{2(1 - P_X)}\right]^+ \qquad (2b)$$

where μ_R and σ_R are the mean and standard deviation of the range R of a sample of size n, and $[a]^+$ denotes max$[0, a]$. If P_X and process parameters μ_X, σ_X, μ_R, and σ_R are known, equations (1) and (2) could be used as control limits for $\overline{X}$ and R charts based on the WV method. If the underlying population is symmetric, then $P_X = 0.5$. That is, the charts reduce to Shewhart $\overline{X}$ and R charts. However, if the underlying population is skewed to the right, then P_X is greater than 0.5, and the distance of the UCL from the center line (CL) is larger than that of the LCL. Similarly, if the underlying population is skewed to the left, then P_X is less than 0.5 and the distance of the LCL from the CL is larger than that of the UCL.

The WV method is based on an adjustment to the distribution of X, but it has been found empirically that when applied to the distribution of

$\overline{X}$, it works better than the standard method for small and moderate values of n.

$\overline{X}$ AND R CHARTS BASED ON THE WV METHOD

To use the $\overline{X}$ and R charts based on the WV method in practice, P_X and the process parameters must be estimated. Since P_X is the probability that X will be less than or equal to μ_X, P_X can be estimated by using the number of observations less than or equal to $\overline{\overline{X}}$,

$$\hat{P}_X = \frac{\sum_{i=1}^{k} \sum_{j=1}^{n} \delta(\overline{\overline{X}} - X_{ij})}{n \times k} \tag{3}$$

where k and n are the number of samples and the number of observations in a sample, respectively, and $\delta(x) = 1$ for $x \geq 0$ or $= 0$ for $x < 0$. The performance of P_X is discussed later.

Generally, μ_X and μ_R are estimated by the grand mean $\overline{\overline{X}}$ and the mean of sample ranges $\overline{R}$, respectively. Shewhart $\overline{X}$ and R charts use the constants d_2 and d_3 in estimating the process standard deviation and the standard deviation of the range in calculating control limits (i.e., $\hat{\sigma}_X = \overline{R} / d_2$ and $\hat{\sigma}_R = d_3 \times (\overline{R} / d_2)$). These constants, however, have been obtained under the normality assumption. Therefore, when the underlying population is skewed, constants reflecting the degree of skewness are desirable.

Let d_2' and d_3' be the constants for the given skewed population corresponding to constants d_2 and d_3 for the normal distribution. Values of d_2' and d_3' are calculated later for given n and P_X. The control limits of $\overline{X}$ chart based on the WV method are

$$\text{UCL}_{\overline{X}} = \overline{\overline{X}} + \frac{3\,\overline{R}}{d_2'\sqrt{n}} \sqrt{2\hat{P}_X} = \overline{\overline{X}} + W_U\,\overline{R}$$

$$\text{LCL}_{\overline{X}} = \overline{\overline{X}} - \frac{3\,\overline{R}}{d_2'\sqrt{n}} \sqrt{2(1 - \hat{P}_X)} = \overline{\overline{X}} - W_L\,\overline{R}.$$

Exhibit 1 gives $\overline{X}$ chart constants W_U and W_L of the WV method for selected combinations of n and P_X. These values are calculated later. W_U for the case of $P_X \leq 0.5$ are the same as W_L for $1 - P_X$ in Exhibit 1, and vice versa. If $n = 5$,

EXHIBIT 1.—$\overline{X}$ CHART CONSTANTS OF THE WV METHOD

P_X	$n = 2$	3	4	5	6	7	8	9	10	15	20	25
					(a) W_L							
0.50	1.88	1.02	0.73	0.58	0.48	0.42	0.37	0.34	0.31	0.22	0.18	0.15
0.52	1.86	1.01	0.72	0.57	0.48	0.41	0.37	0.33	0.30	0.22	0.18	0.15
0.54	1.83	0.99	0.71	0.56	0.47	0.41	0.36	0.33	0.30	0.22	0.18	0.15
0.56	1.81	0.98	0.70	0.56	0.47	0.40	0.36	0.32	0.30	0.21	0.17	0.14
0.58	1.82	0.97	0.70	0.56	0.46	0.40	0.35	0.32	0.30	0.21	0.17	0.14
0.60	1.84	0.99	0.71	0.56	0.46	0.40	0.35	0.32	0.29	0.21	0.17	0.14
0.62	1.85	1.00	0.71	0.56	0.46	0.40	0.35	0.32	0.29	0.21	0.17	0.13
0.64	1.89	1.02	0.72	0.57	0.47	0.40	0.35	0.32	0.29	0.20	0.16	0.13
0.66	1.96	1.08	0.75	0.58	0.48	0.42	0.37	0.32	0.29	0.20	0.16	0.13
0.68	2.04	1.09	0.77	0.61	0.49	0.42	0.37	0.32	0.29	0.20	0.16	0.13
0.70	2.13	1.17	0.81	0.65	0.50	0.43	0.36	0.32	0.29	0.20	0.15	0.13
					(b) W_U							
0.50	1.88	1.02	0.73	0.58	0.48	0.42	0.37	0.34	0.31	0.22	0.18	0.15
0.52	1.93	1.05	0.75	0.59	0.50	0.43	0.38	0.34	0.32	0.23	0.18	0.16
0.54	1.97	1.08	0.77	0.61	0.51	0.44	0.39	0.35	0.32	0.23	0.19	0.16
0.56	2.04	1.11	0.79	0.63	0.52	0.45	0.40	0.37	0.33	0.24	0.19	0.16
0.58	2.14	1.14	0.82	0.65	0.54	0.47	0.42	0.38	0.35	0.25	0.20	0.17
0.60	2.26	1.22	0.86	0.68	0.56	0.49	0.43	0.39	0.36	0.25	0.20	0.17
0.62	2.36	1.28	0.91	0.71	0.59	0.51	0.45	0.41	0.37	0.26	0.21	0.17
0.64	2.53	1.36	0.96	0.76	0.63	0.54	0.47	0.43	0.39	0.27	0.21	0.18
0.66	2.74	1.49	1.04	0.81	0.67	0.58	0.51	0.45	0.41	0.28	0.22	0.18
0.68	2.98	1.59	1.12	0.88	0.71	0.61	0.54	0.47	0.42	0.29	0.23	0.19
0.70	3.26	1.78	1.23	0.99	0.72	0.62	0.55	0.50	0.44	0.30	0.24	0.19

for example, $W_U = 0.71$, and $W_L = 0.56$ for $P_X = 0.62$; and $W_U = 0.56$ and $W_L = 0.71$ for $P_X = 0.38$.

If P_X is estimated from the sample data, then appropriate constants can be chosen according to n and $\hat{P}_X$. For example, when setting up $\overline{X}$ chart for $n = 5$, if $\hat{P}_X = 0.567$, then either $W_U = 0.63$ and $W_L = 0.56$ or interpolated values $W_U = 0.64$ and $W_L = 0.56$ can be used.

Exhibit 1 shows that if $P_X = 0.5$, the $\overline{X}$ chart constants of the WV method are equal to those of the Shewhart method, and the distance of the UCL from the CL increases as P_X increases. In the case of $P_X \leq 0.5$, the distance of the LCL from the CL increases as P_X decreases. Exhibit 1 also indicates that the $\overline{X}$ chart constants of the WV method are quite robust relative to skewness for a large sample size.

The control limits of the R chart based on the WV method are

$$\text{UCL}_R = \overline{R}\left[1 + 3\frac{d'_3}{d'_2}\sqrt{2\hat{P}_x}\right] = V_U\overline{R}$$

$$\text{LCL}_R = \overline{R}\left[1 - 3\frac{d'_3}{d'_2}\sqrt{2(1 - \hat{P}_x)}\right]^+ = V_L\overline{R}.$$

Exhibit 2 gives R chart constants V_U and V_L of the WV method for selected combinations of n and P_X. These values are calculated later.

If $\hat{P}_X$ is calculated from the sample data, then appropriate constants can be selected according to n and $\hat{P}_X$. For example, when setting up the R chart for $n = 7$, if $\hat{P}_X = 0.432$, then either $V_U = 2.04$ and $V_L = 0.00$ or interpolated values $V_U = 2.06$ and $V_L = 0.00$ can be used.

AN ILLUSTRATIVE EXAMPLE

We illustrate our procedure with the chemical process data of Cowden (1957). These data are 30 successive random samples of five measurements each, representing the concentrations of the residue resulting from a chemical process which is in control. The frequency curve of these data shows the highly positive skewed character of the distribution. $\overline{\overline{X}} = 18.45$, $\overline{R} = 40.37$, and 103 observations fall below $\overline{\overline{X}}$. Thus $\hat{P}_X = 0.687$ from (3), and $W_L = 0.61$, $W_U = 0.88$, $V_L = 0.00$, and $V_U = 4.02$ from Exhibits 1 and 2. The control limits of $\overline{X}$ and R charts of the WV and Shewhart methods are:

The WV method—

$$\text{UCL}_{\overline{X}} = \overline{\overline{X}} + W_U\overline{R}$$
$$= 18.45 + 0.88 \times 40.37 = 53.98$$

$$\text{LCL}_{\overline{X}} = \overline{\overline{X}} - W_L\overline{R}$$
$$= 18.45 - 0.61 \times 40.37 = -6.18 \Rightarrow 0.00$$

$$\text{UCL}_R = V_U\overline{R}$$
$$= 4.15 \times 40.37 = 162.29$$

$$\text{LCL}_R = V_L\overline{R}$$
$$= 0.00$$

The Shewhart method—

$$\text{UCL}_{\overline{X}} = \overline{\overline{X}} + A_2\overline{R}$$
$$= 18.45 + 0.58 \times 40.37 = 41.86$$

$$\text{LCL}_{\overline{X}} = \overline{\overline{X}} - A_2\overline{R}$$
$$= 18.45 - 0.58 \times 40.37 = -4.96 \Rightarrow 0.00$$

$$\text{UCL}_R = D_4\overline{R}$$
$$= 2.11 \times 40.37 = 85.18$$

$$\text{LCL}_R = D_3\overline{R}$$
$$= 0.00$$

The results show that the distance of the UCL from the CL of the WV method is larger than that of the Shewhart method. Exhibit 3 represents the resulting $\overline{X}$ and R charts of the WV and Shewhart methods.

We note that all of the points fall within the control limits of the proposed $\overline{X}$ and R charts indicating that the process is in control, whereas two and three points are above the UCL in the Shewhart $\overline{X}$ and R charts, respectively, signaling a 'false alarm'.

The WV method is more useful than Shewhart method when the underlying population is skewed. If the underlying population is symmetric, the use of the proposed method can be cumbersome relative to the standard method. To use the WV method in practice, therefore, it is important to determine whether the underlying distribution of a process is skewed or not. In addition, when examining process data for skewness, the process should be in control. For example, if a data set of 30 samples from a normal distribution had a few samples in which the mean is shifted upward, it might give a fale impression that the distribution is skewed. Therefore, one should attempt to check that the apparent skewness is due to a skewed distribution rather than to an out-of-control process. For a discussion on tests of normality, see, for example, Bradley (1977) and Ramsey and Ramsey (1990).

EXHIBIT 2.—R CHART CONSTANTS OF THE WV METHOD

P_x	$n = 2$	3	4	5	6	7	8	9	10	15	20	25
					(a) V_L							
0.30	0.00	0.00	0.00	0.00	0.00	0.00	0.00	0.00	0.00	0.00	0.00	0.00
0.32	0.00	0.00	0.00	0.00	0.00	0.00	0.00	0.00	0.00	0.00	0.00	0.00
0.34	0.00	0.00	0.00	0.00	0.00	0.00	0.00	0.00	0.00	0.00	0.00	0.00
0.36	0.00	0.00	0.00	0.00	0.00	0.00	0.00	0.00	0.00	0.00	0.00	0.00
0.38	0.00	0.00	0.00	0.00	0.00	0.00	0.00	0.00	0.00	0.00	0.00	0.00
0.40	0.00	0.00	0.00	0.00	0.00	0.00	0.00	0.00	0.00	0.00	0.00	0.02
0.42	0.00	0.00	0.00	0.00	0.00	0.00	0.00	0.00	0.00	0.01	0.06	0.12
0.44	0.00	0.00	0.00	0.00	0.00	0.00	0.00	0.00	0.01	0.12	0.20	0.25
0.46	0.00	0.00	0.00	0.00	0.00	0.00	0.03	0.03	0.10	0.24	0.31	0.37
0.48	0.00	0.00	0.00	0.00	0.00	0.05	0.10	0.13	0.18	0.30	0.38	0.43
0.50	0.00	0.00	0.00	0.00	0.00	0.08	0.14	0.18	0.22	0.35	0.42	0.46
0.52	0.00	0.00	0.00	0.00	0.00	0.08	0.14	0.17	0.21	0.33	0.41	0.45
0.54	0.00	0.00	0.00	0.00	0.00	0.04	0.10	0.12	0.17	0.30	0.37	0.41
0.56	0.00	0.00	0.00	0.00	0.00	0.00	0.02	0.03	0.07	0.22	0.29	0.34
0.58	0.00	0.00	0.00	0.00	0.00	0.00	0.00	0.00	0.02	0.15	0.20	0.25
0.60	0.00	0.00	0.00	0.00	0.00	0.00	0.00	0.00	0.00	0.06	0.08	0.13
0.62	0.00	0.00	0.00	0.00	0.00	0.00	0.00	0.00	0.00	0.00	0.01	0.03
0.64	0.00	0.00	0.00	0.00	0.00	0.00	0.00	0.00	0.00	0.00	0.00	0.00
0.66	0.00	0.00	0.00	0.00	0.00	0.00	0.00	0.00	0.00	0.00	0.00	0.00
0.68	0.00	0.00	0.00	0.00	0.00	0.00	0.00	0.00	0.00	0.00	0.00	0.00
0.70	0.00	0.00	0.00	0.00	0.00	0.00	0.00	0.00	0.00	0.00	0.00	0.00
					(b) V_U							
0.30	4.47	3.89	3.58	3.52	3.10	2.97	2.95	2.84	2.71	2.60	2.52	2.43
0.32	4.24	3.49	3.25	3.16	2.91	2.79	2.75	2.66	2.57	2.49	2.38	2.31
0.34	4.03	3.27	3.01	2.81	2.72	2.64	2.57	2.54	2.45	2.37	2.24	2.20
0.36	3.79	3.07	2.82	2.63	2.52	2.44	2.38	2.35	2.33	2.24	2.14	2.07
0.38	3.58	2.94	2.67	2.51	2.40	2.32	2.27	2.23	2.19	2.08	2.04	1.97
0.40	3.49	2.82	2.53	2.39	2.27	2.21	2.15	2.12	2.09	1.94	1.92	1.87
0.42	3.37	2.67	2.43	2.29	2.18	2.10	2.04	2.02	1.98	1.85	1.80	1.75
0.44	3.28	2.62	2.32	2.23	2.12	2.04	1.99	1.96	1.93	1.78	1.71	1.66
0.46	3.26	2.59	2.30	2.15	2.04	1.96	1.90	1.86	1.83	1.70	1.63	1.59
0.48	3.25	2.58	2.28	2.13	2.00	1.92	1.86	1.82	1.79	1.67	1.60	1.55
0.50	3.25	2.58	2.28	2.11	2.00	1.92	1.86	1.82	1.78	1.65	1.59	1.54
0.52	3.34	2.64	2.33	2.18	2.04	1.96	1.90	1.86	1.82	1.70	1.62	1.57
0.54	3.43	2.72	2.41	2.25	2.12	2.04	1.97	1.94	1.90	1.76	1.69	1.63
0.56	3.58	2.83	2.49	2.38	2.26	2.18	2.11	2.09	2.05	1.88	1.80	1.75
0.58	3.79	2.96	2.67	2.52	2.38	2.30	2.23	2.19	2.16	2.00	1.94	1.88
0.60	4.06	3.23	2.87	2.70	2.56	2.48	2.41	2.37	2.33	2.15	2.12	2.06
0.62	4.30	3.48	3.14	2.93	2.79	2.69	2.62	2.58	2.52	2.39	2.33	2.25
0.64	4.72	3.76	3.43	3.18	3.03	2.92	2.84	2.80	2.77	2.65	2.52	2.43
0.66	5.23	4.16	3.80	3.52	3.39	3.28	3.19	3.15	3.12	2.90	2.73	2.67
0.68	5.71	4.64	4.27	4.02	3.99	3.62	3.56	3.42	3.39	3.17	3.02	2.91
0.70	6.10	5.41	4.94	4.66	4.21	4.01	3.97	3.81	3.71	3.44	3.32	3.18

CONTROL CHART CONSTANTS FOR SKEWED POPULATIONS

Since the proposed control charts, like Shewhart charts, use the control chart constants to set the limits of the control chart, determination of these constants is required. Constants d_2 and d_3, popularly used in Shewhart charts when the underlying population is normal, are the mean and the standard deviation of the relative range R / σ_X in a sample of size n. Constants d_2' and d_3' for non-normal populations such as Weibull, lognormal, Burr's, etc., are similarly defined as the mean and standard deviation of the relative range. These values can be computed via numerical integration once the distribution is specified.

In order to compute the control chart constants for skewed populations, d_2' and d_3' for several skewed populations are compared. Weibull, lognormal, and Burr's distributions are chosen because they represent a wide variety of shapes as parameters change.

The cumulative distribution function (CDF) of the Weibull distribution is

$$F(t) = 1 - exp[-(\lambda t)^\beta], \qquad t > 0$$

where λ and β are the scale and shape parameters, respectively. Then P_X of the Weibull distribution is

$$P_X = 1 - \exp\left[-(\Gamma(1 + 1/\beta))^\beta\right] \qquad (4)$$

where $\Gamma(.)$ is the gamma function. That is, P_X of the Weibull distribution depends on the shape parameter β only. Therefore, the value of β satisfying a given P_X can be obtained uniquely using numerical integration. Also, the skewness α_3 and kurtosis α_4 depend on β only, and α_3 and α_4 of the Weibull distribution can also be obtained uniquely for a given P_X.

The CDF of a lognormal distribution is

$$F(t) = \phi\left[\frac{\log t - \zeta}{\sigma}\right], \qquad t > 0$$

where $\Phi(.)$ denotes the standard normal distribution function, and ζ and σ are the location and scale parameters ($\sigma > 0$), respectively. Then P_X of the lognormal distribution is

$$P_X = \phi(\sigma/2)$$

and σ, α_3, and α_4 are unique for a given value of P_X.

The CDF of Burr's distribution is

$$F(t) = 1 - (1 + t^c)^{-k}, \qquad t > 0$$

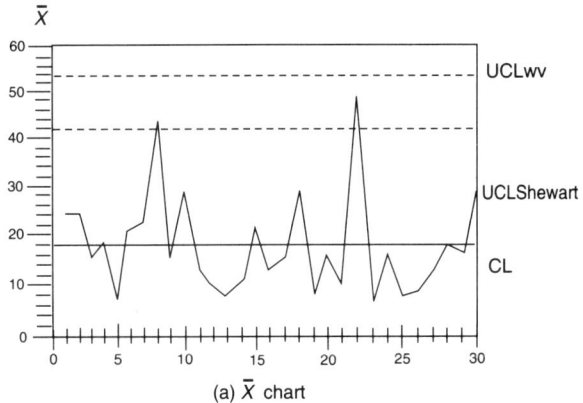

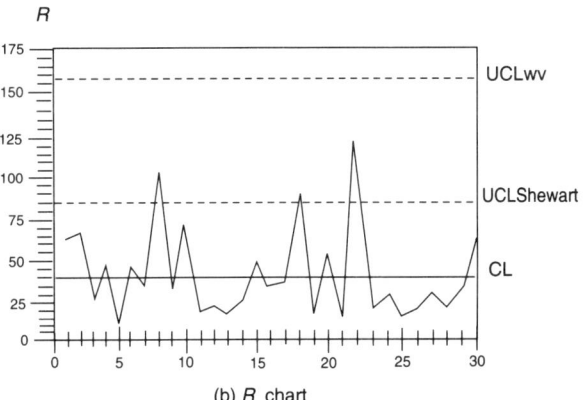

EXHIBIT 3.—$\overline{X}$ AND R CHARTS OF THE WV AND SHEWHART METHODS FOR THE CHEMICAL PROCESS DATA.

EXHIBIT 4.—SELECTED VALUES OF (C,K) AND (A_3, A_4) CORRESPONDING TO $P_X = 0.60$, $C \leq 10$, $K \leq 10$ AND $CK > 4$

(c,k)	(α_3, α_4)
(1.86, 3.00)	(2.20, 16.31)
(1.74, 3.60)	(2.02, 12.77)
(1.67, 4.10)	(1.93, 11.21)
(1.59, 4.90)	(1.83, 9.79)
(1.53, 5.80)	(1.75, 8.87)
(1.46, 7.50)	(1.67, 7.92)
(1.44, 8.20)	(1.65, 7.69)
(1.43, 8.60)	(1.64, 7.58)
(1.42, 9.10)	(1.62, 7.45)
(1.41, 9.60)	(1.61, 7.34)

where c and k are parameters (c, $k \geq 1$). Burr's distribution can be shown to approach the Weibull distribution as k increases, and α_3 and α_4 of Burr's distribution exist if $ck > 3$ and $ck > 4$, respectively. See Burr and Cislak (1968). Unlike the case of the Weibull or lognormal distributions, P_X of Burr's distribution depends upon two parameters c and k. Therefore, (c, k) cannot be obtained uniquely for a given value of P_X. For the comparison of d_2' and d_3' for Weibull, lognormal, and Burr's distributions, we consider the largest value of k is similar to the Weibull distribution. Since the value of P_X decreases as c increases while k is fixed and values of $c \le 10$ cover practically meaningful range of $0.5 \le P_X \le 0.7$, we also consider the largest value of c to be 10. Thus, (c, k) for a specified P_X can be found numerically within the ranges of $c \le 10$, $k \le 10$, and $ck > 4$, and (α_3, α_4) corresponding to (c, k) can be calculated. For example, Exhibit 4 presents some of the (c, k) and (α_3, α_4) combinations corresponding to $P_X = 0.60$.

Three of these combinations—the two extreme and intermediate values of (α_3, α_4) combinations—are selected to compare d_2' and d_3' values according to (α_3, α_4) satisfying a specified P_X. For example, $(c, k) = (1.86, 3.00)$, $(1.41, 9.60)$, $(1.41, 9.60)$, and $(1.53, 5.80)$ or $(1.46, 7.50)$ are used when $P_X = 0.60$.

Exhibit 5 gives d_2' and d_3' for the Weibull, lognormal, and three of Burr's distributions for $n = 5$ and selected values of P_X, and shows that α_3 and α_4 of the five populations are different for a given P_X, but d_2' and d_3' values are alike. Similar patterns were observed for $n = 2, 3, 4, 6, 7, 8, 9, 10, 15, 20, 25$. Therefore, it may be reasonable to use the means of these five values as the representative values of the constants. Admittedly such an approach in calculating the constants d_2' and d_3' is heuristic, but the values given would be an improvement over d_2' and d_3' for the normal distribution.

Values of d_2' and d_3' incorporated in Exhibits 1 and 2 are the eaverages of d_2' and d_3' respectively, of the Weibull, lognormal, and three of Burr's distributions for each P_X. For example, if $P_X = 0.62$ and $n = 5$, then $d_2' = (1.12 + 2.08 + 2.07$

EXHIBIT 5.—D_2' AND D_3' OF THE FIVE POPULATIONS FOR $N = 5$ AND SELECTED VALUES OF P_X

P_X		Weibull	Lognormal	Burr's		
0.50	(α_3, α_4)	(0.01, 2.71)	(0.00, 3.00)	(0.08, 3.62)	(0.06, 2.99)	(0.05, 2.89)
	d_2'	2.33	2.33	2.32	2.33	2.33
	d_3'	0.86	0.87	0.87	0.86	0.85
0.52	(α_3, α_4)	(0.31, 2.81)	(0.30, 3.16)	(0.45, 4.09)	(0.40, 3.50)	(0.34, 3.04)
	d_2'	2.32	2.32	2.30	2.31	2.32
	d_3'	0.86	0.88	0.94	0.90	0.86
0.54	(α_3, α_4)	(0.58, 3.15)	(0.61, 3.37)	(0.85, 5.36)	(0.74, 4.31)	(0.63, 3.48)
	d_2'	2.31	2.30	2.28	2.29	2.30
	d_3'	0.88	0.91	0.99	0.94	0.89
0.56	(α_3, α_4)	(0.85, 3.73)	(0.96, 4.67)	(1.51, 11.02)	(1.20, 6.53)	(0.93, 4.25)
	d_2'	2.27	2.26	2.22	2.25	2.27
	d_3'	0.91	0.97	1.05	1.02	0.94
0.58	(α_3, α_4)	(1.13, 4.60)	(1.34, 6.34)	(2.09, 19.34)	(1.60, 9.21)	(1.25, 5.46)
	d_2'	2.23	2.22	2.17	2.22	2.22
	d_3'	0.98	1.05	1.13	1.05	1.01
0.60	(α_3, α_4)	(1.43, 5.82)	(1.78, 9.01)	(2.27, 18.01)	(1.83, 9.79)	(1.61, 7.34)
	d_2'	2.19	2.16	2.13	2.15	2.18
	d_3'	1.06	1.13	1.18	1.14	1.09
0.62	(α_3, α_4)	(1.77, 7.58)	(2.32, 13.91)	(2.44, 16.83)	(2.22, 12.76)	(2.02, 10.07)
	d_2'	2.12	2.08	2.07	2.09	2.10
	d_3'	1.16	1.23	1.24	1.22	1.19
0.64	(α_3, α_4)	(2.15, 10.07)	(3.00, 22.34)	(3.05, 25.86)	(2.72, 18.22)	(2.52, 14.70)
	d_2'	2.04	1.99	1.99	2.01	2.03
	d_3'	1.22	1.32	1.33	1.31	1.29
0.66	(α_3, α_4)	(2.60, 13.69)	(3.92, 42.12)	(3.66, 36.08)	(3.57, 33.27)	(3.50, 31.24)
	d_2'	1.89	1.89	1.91	1.90	1.89
	d_3'	1.33	1.42	1.42	1.41	1.37
0.68	(α_3, α_4)	(3.12, 18.99)	(5.20, 77.80)	(7.94, *)	(17.70, *)	(33.00, *)
	d_2'	1.80	1.77	1.84	1.78	1.75
	d_3'	1.47	1.54	1.57	1.56	1.49
0.70	(α_3, α_4)	(3.76, 27.21)	(7.05, 160.7)	(77.40, *)	(*, *)	(*, *)
	d_2'	1.69	1.65	1.63	1.54	1.48
	d_3'	1.57	1.60	1.67	1.68	1.71

*: nonexistent

+ 2.09 + 2.10)/5 = 2.09 and $d_3' = (1.16 + 1.23 + 1.24 + 1.24 + 1.22 + 1.19)/5 = 1.21$. If the underlying population is skewed to the left, then P_X is less than 0.5. When $P_X < 0.5$, d_2', and d_3' values corresponding to $1 - P_X$ can be used. For example, if $P_X = 0.38$ and $n = 5$, then we use $d_2' = 2.09$ and $d_3' = 1.21$, corresponding to $P_X = 1 - 0.38 = 0.62$.

PERFORMANCE OF THE PROPOSED CONTROL CHARTS

Performance of $\hat{P}_X$

To investigate the performance of $\hat{P}_X$, the bias and mean square error (MSE) of $\hat{P}_X$ for a Weibull distribution were estimated by Monte Carlo simulation. 100,000 $\hat{P}_X$ values, each of which was based on $n \times k = 5 \times 30$ Weibull random variates generated using IMSL (1987) subroutine, were computed, and deviations and squared deviations of $\hat{P}_X$ from P_X were averaged to obtain (estimated) bias and MSE, where the value of P_X was computed from equation (4). The results for $\beta = 0.5(0.5)5.0$ are given in Table 5. In general, the (estimated) bias and MSE of $\hat{P}_X$ are found to be very small and tend to decrease as P_X approaches to 0.5. Exhibit 6 shows that $\hat{P}_X$ is a very good estimator of P_X in terms of bias and MSE.

Monte Carlo Simulation

The probability of Type I risk of the WV method was compared, using Monte Carlo simulation, with those of the Shewhart and Ferrell methods where the underlying distribution is Weibull or Burr's. These distributions were cho-

EXHIBIT 6.—BIAS AND MSE OF $\hat{P}_X$ IN THE WEIBULL DISTRIBUTION

β	P_X	Bias ($\times 10^{-3}$)	MSE ($\times 10^{-4}$)
0.5	0.757	−3.428	8.503
1.0	0.632	−1.155	6.485
1.5	0.576	−0.481	5.950
2.0	0.544	−0.346	5.811
2.5	0.524	−0.067	5.781
3.0	0.509	−0.040	5.753
3.5	0.499	−0.019	5.752
4.0	0.491	0.225	5.838
4.5	0.484	0.221	5.859
5.0	0.479	0.441	5.900

sen because they can represent a wide variety of shapes, from highly skewed to nearly symmetric. For the Weibull distribution, a scale parameter of 1.0 was chosen for convenience since skewness depends on the shape parameter only. The geometric chart of Ferrell uses statistics η and ρ in place of $\bar{X}$ and R for the Shewhart method. The geometric midrange η and geometric range ρ are

$$\eta = \sqrt{X_{(1)} \cdot X_{(n)}}$$

$$\rho = X_{(n)}/X_{(1)}$$

where $X_{(n)}$ and $X_{(1)}$ are the maximum and minimum of a sample of size n, respectively. Let weif(β) denote the Weibull distribution with shape parameter β and scale parameter 1, and burf (c, k) denote Burr's distribution with parameters c and k.

The simulation consists of two segments. The steps of each segment are described below.

Segment 1: Control chart selection

1.1 Generate n i.i.d. weif(β) or burf (c, k) variates using IMSL (1987) subroutines.

1.2 Repeat step 1.1, 30 times.

1.3 Compute the control limits for the WV, Ferrell, and Shewhart methods.

Segment 2: Control chart operation

2.1 Generate n i.i.d. weif(β) or burf (c, k) variates using the procedure of step 1.1.

2.2 Compute the sample statistics $\bar{X}$ and R for the WV and Shewhart methods, and η and ρ for the Ferrell method.

2.3 Record whether the sample statistics are within the control limits of step 1.3 or not for each method.

2.4 Repeat steps 2.1 through 2.3, 100 times, and estimate Type I risk for the limits of step 1.3.

2.5 Repeat steps 1.1 through 2.4, 10,000 times, and obtain an average Type I risk for each method.

The two segments can be repeated for given values of n and β in weif(β), or n and (c, k) in burf (c, k).

The Results

Type I risks of the WV, Shewhart, and Ferrell methods estimated by the Monte Carlo simu-

EXHIBIT 7.—TYPE I RISKS OF THE THREE CONTROL CHARTS FOR SELECTED COMBINATIONS OF N AND β IN WEIF (β)

β α_3	n	WV Method		Shewhart Method		Ferrell Method	
		$\bar{X}$ Chart	R Chart	$\bar{X}$ Chart	R Chart	η Chart	ρ Chart
3.50 0.03	2	.0029	.0074	.0031	.0076	.0215	.0330
	5	.0028	.0052	.0029	.0053	.0259	.0328
	7	.0028	.0051	.0028	.0051	.0284	.0317
	10	.0028	.0048	.0028	.0048	.0338	.0304
2.00 0.63	2	.0042	.0089	.0059	.0133	.0221	.0333
	5	.0029	.0055	.0044	.0084	.0261	.0330
	7	.0029	.0053	.0039	.0086	.0300	.0320
	10	.0028	.0050	.0032	.0074	.0340	.0305
1.50 1.07	2	.0063	.0104	.0101	.0217	.0223	.0338
	5	.0035	.0062	.0069	.0173	.0267	.0331
	7	.0031	.0059	.0061	.0210	.0301	.0324
	10	.0029	.0060	.0045	.0192	.0342	.0310
1.20 1.51	2	.0081	.0124	.0183	.0325	.0223	.0343
	5	.0049	.0074	.0115	.0335	.0268	.0335
	7	.0036	.0070	.0097	.0354	.0302	.0327
	10	.0029	.0061	.0067	.0376	.0342	.0316
1.00 2.00	2	.0097	.0136	.0252	.0417	.0224	.0348
	5	.0058	.0091	.0174	.0518	.0270	.0341
	7	.0043	.0082	.0126	.0547	.0305	.0339
	10	.0030	.0074	.0083	.0603	.0350	.0324
0.85 2.56	2	.0115	.0149	.0337	.0535	.0225	.0352
	5	.0069	.0097	.0234	.0625	.0272	.0341
	7	.0046	.0088	.0189	.0727	.0310	.0338
	10	.0030	.0083	.0101	.0748	.0358	.0327
0.75 3.12	2	.0127	.0159	.0380	.0602	.0227	.0352
	5	.0078	.0100	.0300	.0748	.0275	.0343
	7	.0050	.0093	.0228	.0805	.0325	.0340
	10	.0032	.0087	.0120	.0893	.0373	.0335

lation are given in Exhibit 7 for selected combinations of n and β in weif(β) and in Exhibit 8 for selected combinations of n and (c, k) in burf(c, k). The values of β and (c, k) in Exhibits 7 and 8 are selected so that a wide range of populations from nearly symmetric to highly skewed can be represented, and α_3 corresponding to β and (c, k) are calculated. The three methods are compared in terms of α_3 in Figures 2 and 3 when the underlying population is weif(β) and burf(c, k), respectively.

Exhibits 7 and 8 and Exhibits 9 and 10 together show that:

1. the WV and Shewhart methods are comparable when the population is approximately symmetric,

2. $\bar{X}$ and R charts of the WV method provide Type I risks mostly less than 0.010 and 0.015, respectively, and perform signifi-

cantly better than Shewhart method as α_3 increases,

3. the difference in Type I risks of the WV and Shewhart methods is more pronounced in the R chart than in the $\bar{X}$ chart, and

4. Type I risks of the WV method are consistently less than those of the Ferrell method.

COMPARISON WITH EXACT METHOD

The proposed heuristic method is useful for the case where the underlying population is not fully known. If one knows the form of the underlying distribution, then exact probability limits for control charts satisfying the desired Type I risk can be derived. In this section, performance of the proposed method is compared with the exact and Shewhart methods for the case where the

EXHIBIT 8.—TYPE I RISKS OF THE THREE CONTROL CHARTS FOR SELECTED COMBINATIONS OF N AND (C, K) IN BURF(C, K)

(c, k) α_3	n	WV Method		Shewhart Method		Ferrell Method	
		$\bar{X}$ Chart	R Chart	$\bar{X}$ Chart	R Chart	η Chart	ρ Chart
(7, 3) 0.00	2	.0043	.0060	.0044	.0062	.0164	.0284
	5	.0039	.0061	.0039	.0061	.0203	.0255
	7	.0037	.0066	.0037	.0067	.0231	.0268
	10	.0032	.0071	.0032	.0071	.0288	.0301
(3, 6) 0.48	2	.0048	.0061	.0063	.0094	.0179	.0300
	5	.0041	.0062	.0049	.0086	.0217	.0269
	7	.0039	.0067	.0043	.0097	.0268	.0284
	10	.0032	.0074	.0037	.0102	.0304	.0310
(2, 7) 1.01	2	.0069	.0070	.0112	.0154	.0185	.0305
	5	.0048	.0072	.0076	.0174	.0223	.0285
	7	.0042	.0075	.0062	.0195	.0275	.0299
	10	.0033	.0080	.0045	.0225	.0317	.0334
(3, 2) 1.59	2	.0086	.0084	.0144	.0248	.0175	.0298
	5	.0066	.0080	.0105	.0305	.0219	.0279
	7	.0053	.0082	.0097	.0387	.0270	.0287
	10	.0035	.0091	.0058	.0419	.0311	.0321
(2, 3) 1.91	2	.0102	.0105	.0167	.0299	.0177	.0304
	5	.0072	.0117	.0130	.0384	.0220	.0284
	7	.0060	.0126	.0114	.0463	.0271	.0301
	10	.0040	.0128	.0071	.0509	.0303	.0342
(5, 1) 2.49	2	.0118	.0131	.0186	.0389	.0185	.0299
	5	.0079	.0146	.0147	.0456	.0226	.0283
	7	.0071	.0153	.0130	.0547	.0282	.0287
	10	.0047	.0149	.0086	.0618	.0314	.0330
(1.2, 5) 3.04	2	.0134	.0127	.0288	.0481	.0193	.0324
	5	.0099	.0138	.0227	.0542	.0233	.0305
	7	.0080	.0154	.0184	.0693	.0290	.0331
	10	.0056	.0136	.0102	.0805	.0315	.0347

underlying distribution is exponential with known parameter λ (Weibull with $\beta = 1$). In this case exact calculation is possible because $2n\bar{X}/\lambda$ has a chi squared distribution with $2n$ degrees of freedom.

The exact probability limits for the $\bar{X}$ chart satisfying the desired Type I risk α are then

$$UCL_{exact} = \frac{X^2_{(2n, \, 1-\alpha/2)}}{2n}\lambda$$

$$LCL_{exact} = \frac{X^2_{(2n, \, \alpha/2)}}{2n}\lambda$$

where $X^2_{(2n, \, \alpha/2)}$ is the $\alpha/2^{th}$ quantile of the chi squared distribution with $2n$ degrees of freedom. The control limits for Shewhart $\bar{X}$ chart with Type I risk α are

$$UCL_{Shewhart} = \left(1 + \frac{z_{\alpha/2}}{\sqrt{n}}\right)\lambda$$

$$LCL_{Shewhart} = \left(1 - \frac{z_{\alpha/2}}{\sqrt{n}}\right)\lambda$$

where $z_{\alpha/2}$ is the $\alpha/2^{th}$ quantile of the standard normal distribution. Since P_X of the exponential distribution is 0.6321, the limits for the proposed $\bar{X}$ chart are

$$UCL_{wv} = \left[1 + \frac{z_{\alpha/2}}{\sqrt{n}}\sqrt{2(0.6321)}\right]\lambda$$

$$LCL_{wv} = \left[1 - \frac{z_{\alpha/2}}{\sqrt{n}}\sqrt{2(1 - 0.6321)}\right]\lambda$$

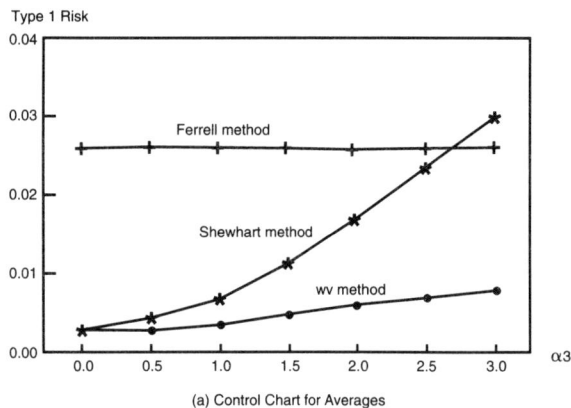

(a) Control Chart for Averages

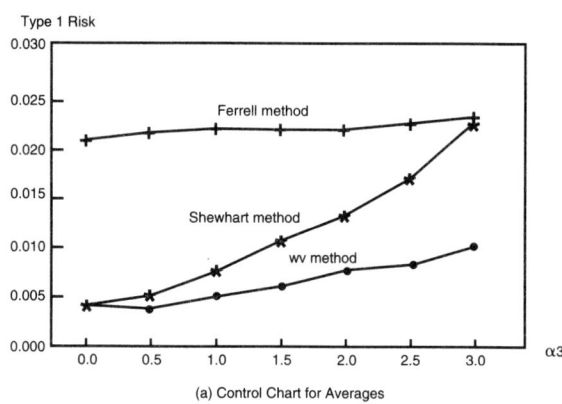

(a) Control Chart for Averages

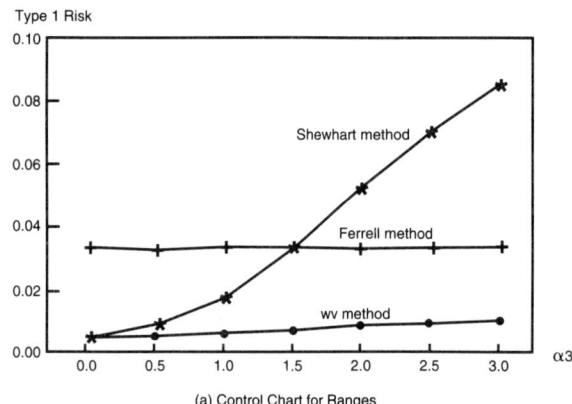

(a) Control Chart for Ranges

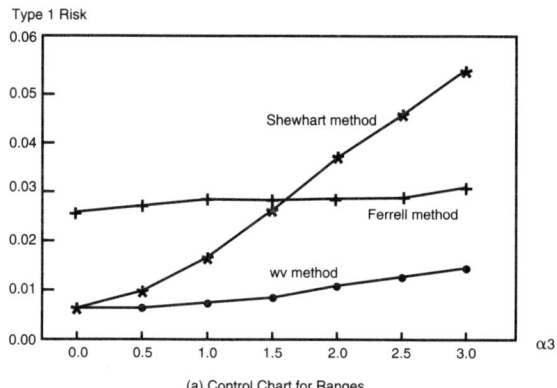

(a) Control Chart for Ranges

EXHIBIT 9.—TYPE I RISKS OF THE THREE CONTROL
CHARTS VERSUS A_3 IN WEIF (β) FOR $N = 5$

EXHIBIT 10.—TYPE I RISKS OF THE THREE
CONTROL CHARTS VERSUS A_3 IN BURF(C,K)
FOR $N = 5$

Exhibit 11 gives the $\overline{X}$ chart limits and Type I risk probabilities for three methods for $n = 1, 2, 3, 5, 7, 10, 15, 20, 25$ when the underlying distribution is exponential with $\lambda = 1$. α_L and α_U in Exhibit 11 denote Type I risk probabilities generated in the lower and upper tails, respectively. The control limits of Exhibit 11 indicate that the WV method underadjusts for skewness in the exponential distribution when the sample size n is small. As the sample size increases, the limits of the WV method approach those of the exact method. The Shewhart method, however, does not adjust for skewness. The Type I risk probabilities in Table 8 also illustrates that the proposed method does not work as well for $n = 1$ or 2 as it does for intermediate or large n, and is naturally somewhat inferior to the exact method when the underlying distribution is exactly known. However, the use of the proposed method leads to an improvement over the Shewhart method. Note that due to the skewness of the underlying exponential distribution $\alpha = \alpha_L + \alpha_U \approx \alpha_U$ for the Shewhart and the proposed methods, whereas $\alpha_L = \alpha_U = 0.00135$ for the exact method.

CONCLUSION

We have proposed a simple heuristic method based on the WV of constructing $\overline{X}$ and R control charts without assumptions on the underlying distribution. The proposed charts provide asymmetric control limits for skewed populations and reduce to Shewhart charts for symmetric populations.

Our simulation study on the Type I risk indicates that the WV and Shewhart methods are comparable for approximately symmetric populations, and that considerable improvement over the Shewhart charts and geometric charts of Ferrell can be achieved when the underlying populations are skewed.

In many applications, $\overline{X}$ and R charts are applied without full knowledge of the form of the distribution of the quality characteristic. Indeed, the distribution of a process cannot be determined until the process is in a state of control. Thus there are times when a control chart is used prior to determining the distribution of the underlying process. The method presented in

EXHIBIT 11.—CONTROL LIMITS AND TYPE I RISKS OF $\overline{X}$ CHARTS WHEN THE UNDERLYING DISTRIBUTION IS EXPONENTIAL

n	Exact Control Limits ($\alpha_L = \alpha_U = 0.00135$)	Shewhart Method			WV Method		
		Control Limits	α_L	α_U	Control Limits	α_L	α_U
1	(0.001, 6.607)	(0.000, 4.000)	.0000	.0183	(0.000, 4.373)	.0000	.0126
2	(0.026, 4.450)	(0.000, 3.121)	.0000	.0141	(0.000, 3.385)	.0000	.0089
3	(0.070, 3.623)	(0.000, 2.372)	.0000	.0118	(0.000, 2.947)	.0000	.0071
5	(0.158, 2.878)	(0.000, 2.342)	.0000	.0093	(0.000, 2.508)	.0000	.0052
7	(0.229, 2.517)	(0.000, 2.114)	.0000	.0079	(0.027, 2.275)	.0000	.0042
10	(0.308, 2.217)	(0.051, 1.949)	.0000	.0067	(0.186, 2.067)	.0000	.0034
15	(0.400, 1.954)	(0.225, 1.775)	.0000	.0056	(0.336, 1.871)	.0003	.0026
20	(0.460, 1.805)	(0.329, 1.671)	.0000	.0049	(0.425, 1.754)	.0005	.0022
25	(0.510, 1.708)	(0.400, 1.600)	.0001	.0045	(0.485, 1.675)	.0008	.0020
30	(0.540, 1.638)	(0.452, 1.548)	.0001	.0042	(0.530, 1.616)	.0010	.0018

this paper will be particularly effective in such a case. That is, the method allows one to use control charts earlier in the product life cycle.

ACKNOWLEDGMENT

We are grateful to the referees for their comments and suggestions which led to substantial improvements in the contents and presentation.

REFERENCES

Abel, V. (1989). "Comment on: Control-Limits of QC Charts for Skewed Distributions Using Weighted Variance." *IEEE Transactions on Reliability* 38, p. 265.

Balakrishnan, N. and Kocherlakota, S. (1986). "Effects of Non-normality on $\overline{X}$ Charts: Single Assignable Cause Model." *Sankya* B 48, pp. 439-444.

Bradley, J. V. (1977). "A Common Situation Conducive to Bizarre Distribution Shapes." *The American Statistician* 31, pp. 147-150.

Burr, I. W. (1967). "The Effect on Non-normality on Constants for $\overline{X}$ and R charts." *Industrial Quality Control* 24, pp. 563-569.

Burr, I. W. and Cislak, P. J. (1968). "On a General System of Distributions: I. Its Curve-Shape Characteristics, II. The Sample Median." *Journal of the American Statistical Association* 63, pp. 627-635.

Chan, L. K.; Hapuarachchi, K. P.; and Macpherson, B. D. (1988). "Robustness of $\overline{X}$ and R Charts." *IEEE Transactions on Reliability* 37, pp. 117-123.

Choobineh, F. and Ballard, J. L. (1987). "Control-Limits of QC Charts for Skewed Distributions Using Weighted Variance." *IEEE Transactions on Reliability* 36, pp. 473-477.

Choobineh, F. and Branting, D. (1986). "A Simple Approximation for Semivariance." *European Journal of Operational Research* 27, pp. 364-370.

Cowden, D. J. (1957). *Statistical Methods in Quality Control*. Prentice Hall, Englewood Cliffs, NJ.

Ferrell, E. B. (1958). "Control Charts for Log-normal Universe." *Industrial Quality Control* 15, pp. 4-6.

IMSL Library (1987). *Reference Manual*. International Mathematical and Statistical Libraries, Inc., Houston, TX.

Nelson, P. R. (1979). "Control Charts for Weibull Processes with Standards Given." *IEEE Transactions on Reliability* 28, pp. 283-287.

Ramsey, P. P. and Ramsey, P. H. (1990). "Simple Tests of Normality in Small Samples." *Journal of Quality Technology* 22, pp. 299-309.

Schilling, E. G. and Nelson, P. R. (1976). "The Effect of Non-normality on the Control Limits of $\overline{X}$ Charts." *Journal of Quality Technology* 8, pp. 183-188.

Key Words: *Consumer Risk, Control Limits, Monte Carlo Simulation, Shewhart Control Limits, Skewed Distributions, $\overline{X}$ Control Chart.*

||||| 3.7
COST OF QUALITY

---■---

THE COSTS OF QUALITY*

Doing it wrong the first time is industry's biggest single quality expense. Quality consultant Phil Crosby estimates costs of bringing goods back into line with customer requirements can range as high as 40% of sales for many firms, with the industry average running close to 25%. In effect, firms, are spending a quarter of their income patching up their own mistakes. With so many firms carrying such a major non-productive expense on their backs, it's no wonder U.S. industry has been having such a hard time staying competitive with such quality-conscious nations as Germany and Japan. But more and more U.S. firms are learning they can cut operating costs significantly—and boost their profit margins at the same time—by tightening quality standards and cutting the cost of conformance sharply.

Crosby notes that the first step toward implementing a quality program is to let management know how much they're already spending on conformance to quality requirements— either as specified by customers or as defined by warranties. This usually amounts to 25% of sales or more, although Crosby thinks many firms could get by nicely with a cost of quality of only 2.5% or so. Once these costs—and potential savings—are detailed, he notes, you're certain to get management's attention to the quality issue. "All you really need is enough information to show your management that reducing the cost of quality is in fact an opportunity to increase profits," he says.

It's no wonder U.S. industry has been having such a hard time staying competitive.

And since about 30% of the total costs of quality are the direct result of defects in parts and materials from suppliers, the purchasing department is virtually guaranteed a prominent role in any quality program. If your total costs of conformance average 25% of sales, an effec-

tive zero-defect supplier program, for example, could boost corporate profits by 6% or more as a result.

What cost? Quality costs usually break down into three groups: Prevention costs, evaluation or appraisal costs, and failure costs.

PREVENTION COSTS

In a perfect world, prevention costs—as well as all other costs of quality—wouldn't exist. But with a good prevention program, most other costs of conformance to quality should disappear. And prevention costs themselves should shrink dramatically. Prevention costs include: design review; supplier evaluation, education and certification; product qualification; employee training; quality control engineering; quality process controls; preventive maintenance.

EVALUATION COSTS

If you don't trust your supplier to consistently provide zero-defect goods, the final cost of those goods will rise substantially between the receiving room and final assembly. Testing of incoming goods is only one of those added costs. Other expenses: supplier surveillance; inspection of product in process; cost of products damaged by test processes; purchasing and maintenance cost of test equipment; overhead for testing procedures; process control, data collection, and record keeping; product acceptance; and packaging inspection.

Evaluation costs rise as quality fails. In a perfect world—one where suppliers are responsible for pretesting and for total quality control of their own products—evaluation costs can ap-

---

*Reprinted with permission from *Purchasing Magazine,* 1991. Copyright by Cahners Publishing Company.

proach zero. In fact, it's in reducing evaluation costs that many purchasing departments have made a name for themselves within their own companies.

FAILURE COSTS

Failure costs can develop either inside the company while the product is in production or storage, or outside the company after delivery. Internal failure costs include value lost through scrapping, rework costs, reinspection of repairs, and reduced value of products sold as seconds. The biggest cost of external failures is not quantifiable: loss of customer good will. Failure of a purchased product in the field can create major costs of purchases, especially if the product is used as an input for manufacture. Failure can therefore lose a company significantly more in sales than the actual cost of failed goods. Other costs of external failure: replacement of defective goods; field repair costs; overhead costs for field maintenance; cost of receiving and processing complaints; liability costs due to product hazards, or loss of production time; additional scrap; and repairs to repairs.

There is a direct relation between the expenditures on prevention and appraisal and the costs of failure (see Exhibit 1). But one cost—the cost of lost sales due to customer perception of low quality products—can make the financial tradeoff of prevention vs failure irrelevant to a firm. Says Richard T. Weber, quality control man-

ager for Genicom Corp. in Waynesboro, Va.: "More and more firms are deciding that their optimum cost point is at a very low level of defective units, possibly close to zero defects, because of the high cost of lost sales." In addition, he notes, recent innovations in automated equipment and statistical controls are giving process engineers the tools they need to measure and implement zero-defect programs.

Doing it wrong the first time is industry's biggest quality expense.

COSTLY LOW COSTS

Everybody has a favorite story of the buyer who opted for low cost and ended up paying twice again as parts continued to fail in production. But most purchasing departments actually have institutionalized this buy-cheaper mentality when they only accept anything less than zero-defect supplies. The solution, says Ross Johnson, management professor at James Madison University, is to institute a vendor quality strategy—and stick to it. "The vendor quality strategy must be based on cost versus quality and its impact on the firm's business." Some of the costs of quality directly attributable to accepting even a small percentage of shoddy materials from suppliers: cost of extra inventories and resulting overhead generated both in anticipation of defects and by holding the defective material itself; cost of rework due to bad materials; cost of scrap; cost of production delays; inspection cost for incoming

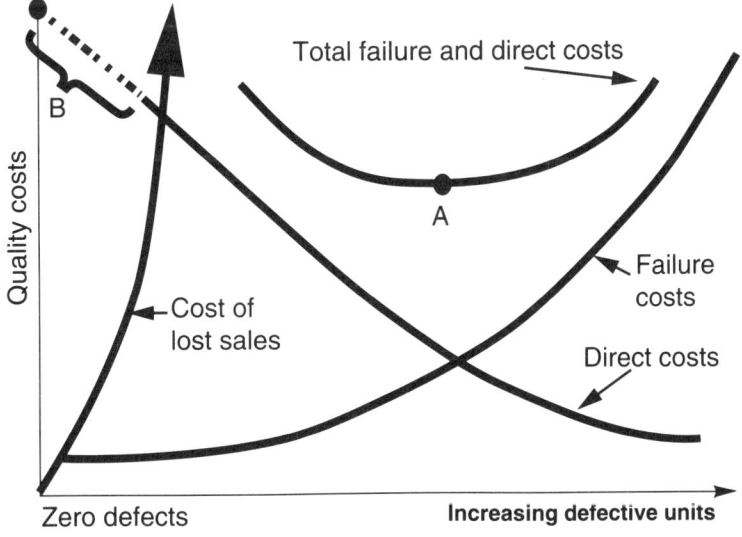

EXHIBIT 1.—COST OF QUALITY TRADEOFFS

material; supplier evaluation costs including surveys, supplier visits; overhead costs to handle and return defective goods and to process defect claims and reissue purchase orders; cost of business lost due to defective suppliers; and cost to maintain records on supplier performance. As these costs have increased, more and more managers are trying to push them back onto suppliers themselves.

CARROTS AND STICKS

Firms use several strategies to convince suppliers to provide 100% acceptable products on a consistent basis. These include both carrots and sticks. The most popular carrot: exclusive contract award. Many big manufacturing firms spend more than $1-billion per year on supplies

and materials. Promising a supplier a sizable chunk of that buy can make miracles happen almost overnight. That's the biggest carrot. Others include: premium payments for achieving prearranged quality goals; top vendor awards, with accompanying play in the business press; and letters of praise to supplier management.

Sticks are also valuable tools to let suppliers know management is serious about incoming quality. The biggest threat to a supplier: cancellation of contract. This is happening more and more frequently in U.S. industry these days. Buyers can no longer accept anything short of zero defects when corporate financial management has decided to boost profits by improving vendor quality. Competitive pressures mean more and more alternative suppliers exist who can promise—and—produce quality goods.

USING QUALITY COSTS TO DRIVE PROCESS REENGINEERING*
by Jim Robison and Rick Harrington

In today's business environment, many customers require their suppliers to have a formal quality system in place. Quality systems such as ISO 9000 require documentation of your company's quality-management system, which reflects the way you operate with defined documented business processes.

Efficiently managing these processes not only supports ISO 9000 requirements but can result in significant bottom-line savings. Process reengineering activities can eliminate nonvalue-added process steps when focused and measured using quality costs as part of reengineering efforts. Quality costs include the American Society for Quality Control internationally accepted elements of external failure, internal failure, appraisal and prevention.

External failure can be defined as any nonvalue-added activity that impacts the paying customer. Common examples as mentioned in the Malcolm Baldrige National Quality Award criteria include customer-satisfaction indexes

such as complaints, returns, defections (i.e., lost customers due to poor performance) and customer-appeasement costs.

Internal failure can be defined as those nonvalue-added activities that are transparent to the paying customer, often called "waste generators," yet are real to an organization's bottom line. Examples mentioned in the Baldrige criteria under Information and Analysis include problems, defects, rework, reprocessing and activities that have to be done but should not be required.

Appraisal costs are those resources spent to ensure conformance to requirements. Baldrige criteria under Information and Analysis, Process Management and the Business Results categories can measure appraisal activities such as reviews, inspections, tests and assessments.

Prevention costs are the vital investments required to ensure that failure is prevented from entering a business process. Often small in comparison to an organization's failure expenditures,

*Reprinted with permission from *Quality Digest,* May, 1995, © 1995 QCI International. Jim Robinson is vice chairman of the ASQC Quality Cast Committee. Rick Harrington is president and chief executive officer of The Harrington Group in Orlando.

prevention dollars spent are at the apex of root-cause elimination. Examples as encompassed in the Baldrige criteria include the investments to train and implement continuous-improvement projects.

You can streamline your organization by re-engineering your business processes to eliminate nonvalue-added activities (or imbedded waste, called failure). An efficient organization realizes maximum output using minimal resources.

PROCESS MANAGEMENT

Process-management concepts have become popular with those involved in continuous-improvement activities and can be defined to varying degrees. Process management can be defined as a systems approach to achieving continuous process improvement and improved conformance to requirements. Process management requires that you take the necessary actions to ensure that a process is continuously managed, measured, supported and improved.

A process can be defined as a series of steps that transforms inputs (from suppliers) into outputs (to customers). To have an efficient process, your transformation steps must be value-added and contain no waste or failure. Failure components can be identified using a quality-cost analysis and be reduced (or eliminated) by using process-management techniques such as process reengineering.

FINE-TUNING PROCESSES

Process reengineering can be defined as changing the way a process is managed, maximizing the use of value-added resources while minimizing the nonvalue-added (or failure) activities. This results in optimum process efficiency and output.

Process reengineering should be part of process-management techniques because processes are:

- The grouping of tasks required to meet customer requirements.

- Required to produce an organization's products and services.

- Required to maintain an organization's technological edge.

- Boundaries limiting how effective workers can perform.

Combining the concept of quality costs with process-management techniques creates a powerful quality-management tool to focus process-reengineering efforts to specific "opportunities." Successfully applying this tool provides an important indicator of the efficiency of a business process as measured in dollars.

The better you know your customer requirements, the better you can reengineer or fine-tune your processes to efficiently produce what your customers want. The cost of quality is how you spend your time and resources to accomplish this—or the failure to do so. A "before" and "after" quality-cost analysis will show management the savings achieved by investing in prevention resources to change or reengineer a selected process.

DRIVING PROCESS REENGINEERING

How can we use quality costs to drive process-reengineering activities? Management and financial professionals often ask this question. The following methodology provides a road map for how a quality-cost analysis can drive process reengineering activities:

Step 1: Volunteer or select a project leader.
- Typically, a quality professional will plan for and propose that the company undertake this process. Usually the quality professional already understands the concept of process management and has some background in quality-cost principles.
- Obtain training for the project leader on quality-cost principles. A refresher course can help re-open the thought process and generate new ideas. (Note: Contact the ASQC Quality Cost Committee for more help).

Step 2: Get top-management support.
- Invite six to 10 people who comprise the quality, finance and other major process areas such as operations and service to an awareness meeting. You may invite sales/marketing, product, program management and engineering staff members if applicable to your business. Select at least one or two top managers who will support this project and make resources available to per-

form (as a minimum) the cost-of-quality baseline assessment.

• Work in advance with finance to obtain some real numbers on your quality costs to show to this group. Focus first on external and internal failure components, followed by appraisal and prevention costs.

• Show this group where other companies have implemented a quality-cost process and quality systems such as ISO 9000. Stress that process reengineering was implemented using a quality-cost focus resulting in bottom-line savings.

Step 3: Establish a cost-of-quality implementation team.

• After your awareness meeting, assess who, by function, has the conviction and excitement to work on your cost-of-quality implementation team. Keep the team small (about three to five people is good). You must have strong representation from finance and quality.

• Educate this team on quality-cost principles and implementation techniques.

Step 4: Conduct a cost-of-quality general ledger baseline assessment.

• Working with finance, obtain annual (or six-month ending) itemized general ledger financial statements that show (at least) itemized expense accounts. Using this listing of line items showing dollars spent, identify high-dollar accounts (i.e., >$20,000) and assess for the cost elements of internal failure (IF), external failure (EF), appraisal (A) and prevention (P).

You will have to interview those people familiar with the line items to determine how charges are made into specific accounts. For example, if you are assessing your customer-service organization, you should ask experts in that department what percent of their time they spend with IF, EF, A and P-type activities. A worksheet can be designed to record assessment interviews and create backup for future reference.

• To simplify, look for whole accounts first, followed by partial accounts.

Whole Accounts: Where 100 percent of the line item is F, A or P. Examples include scrap (IF), returns (EF), auditing/inspection (A) and training (P).

Partial Accounts: Where X percent of the line item is F, A or P. Examples include labor, operating expense, cost of goods sold and other accounts (where a partial percentage of the line item is cost-of-quality).

Some accounts may have no quality-cost association at all. You need not force-fit every line item into one of the four quality-cost elements. Be careful that you don't get caught in the fine detail, otherwise you could spend too much time conducting this assessment. The idea is to separate the vital few from the trivial many. A typical assessment should not take more than 40 hours maximum and usually doesn't contain more than 25 to 50 line items when complete.

Step 5: Analyze general ledger items with high-failure dollars.

• Summarize and do a Pareto analysis on line items by failure dollars using the quality-cost elements you recorded during your general ledger assessment interviews. You will find this to be an eye-opening experience, especially when looking at some key labor accounts.

• Load this information into a cost-of-quality software package for tracking and trending analysis. This will help you focus by line item and cost center to process areas that need to be further analyzed for possible process redesign.

Several cost-effective cost-of-quality software packages cost as little as $300. This small investment can save significant time and makes future "before and after" measurements much easier.

Step 6: Assign cross-functional teams to analyze by process area.

• Using the results from the cost-of-quality assessment, form cross-functional process teams to analyze the general ledger line items that have practical opportunity for failure-cost reduction. Use failure dollars to focus on key opportunities by cross-functional process area (e.g., customer complaints, accounts receivable, order administration or service delivery).

• Develop problem statements based on the general ledger line items selected. You may have to add a few of the line items together because many general ledger costs are summarized as vertical cost roll-ups, not as horizontal or cross-functional process-cost roll-ups. Keep in mind your purpose—to use a quality-cost analysis to better quantify process-reengineering activities.

Step 7: Create process maps for targeted process improvements.

• A process map shows the sequence of tasks and activity relationships that convert process inputs into outputs. Process mapping helps better define process requirements, including inputs/outputs, resources, performance objectives, documentation and process "uncertainties." Typically, these process uncertainties cause process waste and inefficiency, which you now have identified using a quality-cost analysis.

• Using the problem statements formed in Step 6, create process maps for the targeted processes. Document the "as is" condition, drawing process inputs and outputs. List the current "resources allocated" (People by competency level, equipment/tools, etc.) and current "performance objectives" (quantity, quality, time and cost standards). Collect copies of any existing documentation that describes (or attempts to document) how to perform the process. After review, look for any "as is" process uncertainties. For example, is the process producing any unneeded outputs, missing any inputs or generating any nonvalue-added steps? These process changes can be made by process-reengineering activities.

Step 8: Formulate cause diagrams and change recommendations.

• Once you analyze the "as is" condition, you will find it helpful to create a cause-and-effect diagram, listing the problem statement (as defined in Step 6) and the possible causes for this problem. This step can provide valuable insight into the areas of manpower, methods, machines, materials and environmental/safety, providing input on how the process can be reengineered to eliminate waste and improve efficiency.

• Using input from the cause-and-effect diagram, you now can diagram the "should be" process map, highlighting the necessary changes that are required to improve or reengineer the process.

Step 9: Calculate cost and savings if process is reengineered.

• Like any improvement, process change or reengineering requires an investment. Using a quality-cost perspective, this prevention investment, when correctly applied to the root cause of the problem, will decrease (or eliminate) process failure.

• Calculate how much the reengineering (or prevention) activity will cost, including time (multiply by dollars/hour) and out-of-pocket expenses. Then estimate the achievable failure-cost reduction for a 12-month period if the process is reengineered. By dividing the "failure cost reduction" by the "needed-prevention investment," you can calculate a cost-benefit ratio. The payback period can also be calculated by using the inverse of the cost-benefit ratio.

• Ratios such as these allow you to make better financial justifications as to why process-reengineering activities should be implemented.

Consult a good accounting textbook for other financial relationships that may benefit you.

Step 10: Present proposal, reengineer processes and monitor.

• Summarize the potential cost-benefit that your quality-cost analysis has shown. Present an action plan to management and a timeline to accomplish process-reengineering activities. Stress that you now have the techniques to better measure quality-improvement expenditures.

• Gain management support of the proposed reengineering activities and begin the change process. Make sure to include ongoing process measurements, including quality costs. Change and update documentation to reflect any new ways. Train and inform those involved and establish process ownership.

• Monitor and manage process changes monthly by reviewing the established measurements. Fine-tune any additional process enhancements to maximize efficiency. By doing so, you have ensured that your reengineered processes are continuously managed, measured and improved.

CONCLUSIONS

The methodology described in this article is intended to provide a focus to process-improvement teams, managers and others who are involved in quality improvement. It will provide a financial report that can be used for focusing process-reengineering efforts. It helps focus and rationalize which process areas have the highest return on investment, return on assets, return on equity and other financial justifications that are important to your organization.

Reengineering business processes using a quality-cost analysis can be a powerful approach to obtain significant savings by eliminating waste and reengineering inefficient processes. A quality-cost analysis will drive process-reengineering activities to better focus process changes to the right area.

REFERENCES

1. *ASQC Quality Cost Committee.* Principles of Quality Costs, *2nd Edition, (Milwaukee, ASQC Quality Press, 1986).*
2. *Harrington, Rick,* New COQ Software. *The Harrington Group Inc. (Orlando, Florida, 1993).*
3. *Robison, Jim,* COQ Implementation in Service Organizations, *(Annual Quality Congress, 1993).*

———————————————— ■ ————————————————

COMMON PRINCIPLES OF QUALITY MANAGEMENT AND DEVELOPMENT ECONOMICS*
by Spencer B. Graves

Three principles seem to be basic for quality management and economic growth in rich and poor countries. (1) Improvements in quality of life are built on improvements in work methods. (2) Improvements occur most often where they are expected, supported, and rewarded. (3) Continual improvements are necessary just to stay even. In this article, these three principles are illustrated and tied to literature in both quality management and the economics of development and growth.

INTRODUCTION

W. Edwards Deming (1986) wrote, "Need any country be poor? . . . If Japan be an example, then it is possible that any country with enough people and with good management, making products suited to their talents and to the market, need not be poor" (pp. 5–6). This quote suggests a connection between development economics and managing for quality and productivity improvement. An understanding of this connection can be useful, especially now as public sector agencies throughout the world begin to focus on improving quality and productivity. This article summarizes this connection in three basic themes, or principles, that seem to underlie both quality management and development economics.

1. Modern quality of life is built on goods and services whose relatively high quality and low cost are due to improvements, adopted over years, in the work methods used to produce them.

2. Improvements occur most often where they are expected, supported, and rewarded.

3. Continual improvements are necessary just to stay even.

QUALITY OF LIFE IS BUILT ON IMPROVED WORK METHODS

Consider a modern 0.5 mm mechanical pencil. Mechanical pencils were sold 30 years ago, but those early versions were hard to load and use; their leads were thick and broke easily; and they were generally more expensive than mechanical pencils today. Because of improvements in work methods adopted by the pencil manufacturers, distributors, and sellers, users can spend more of their time thinking about what marks to put on paper and less time getting the wherewithal to make those marks. This is a material improvement in their quality of life, based on nothing the users have done.

IMPROVED WORK METHODS

This example illustrates the basic mechanics of economic growth and technological development; namely, that innovators, entrepreneurs, and employees change work methods to improve quality or productivity. Some of these changes introduce new machinery; others simply reorganize existing tasks to reduce quality problems, increase productivity, or produce new goods or services that make others more comfortable or more productive. The economist Vernon (1989) essentially describes this process—without mentioning quality—while ascribing the reasons for differences in the rate of industrialization in different countries primarily to the second of the three principles discussed here.

One leading organization in the history of quality management is the Japan Productivity Center, which was founded in 1955 by people who saw that a high standard of living could only be achieved with high productivity (Japan Productivity Center 1989). Since Japanese productivity then was low, rapid achievement of a high

*Reprinted with permission from *ASQC Management Journal,* Volume 2, Issue 2, Winter 1995. Spencer B. Graves is a principal with Spencer Graves Associates in San Jose, CA.

standard of living required a high rate of growth in productivity. This meant that many people would have to adopt new, more productive work methods.

This sentiment is echoed by Drucker (1993), "People can only get paid in accordance with their productivity. . . . If productivity does not go up, let alone if it declines, higher *real* incomes cannot be paid" (p. 84). In his 1930s publications R. Buckminster Fuller (1981) "identified this progressive doing-more-with-less as *ephemeralization*. . . . [T]he *combination of accelerating acceleration* [in the rate of improvement in productivity and standard of living] *and ephemeralization* has now elevated 60 percent of humanity from its year-1900 99-percent poverty level into realization of an everyday standard of living supperior to that enjoyed by any kings, tycoons, or other power-commanding humans prior to the twentieth century" (p. 133).

In the quality management literature, it is common to read phrases such as "quality is the key to productivity" (Lambert 1993, 4). This and similar phrases are a convenient shorthand that make no sense without understanding the basic mechanics of quality and productivity improvements. An analysis of defects and variations in quality often identifies sources of process complexity (Fuller 1985), the study of which, in many cases, stimulates ideas for changes in work methods that increase both quality and productivity. Conversely, changes in work methods that are not focused through the lens of quality problems often have negative side effects that are greater than the problems they attempt to resolve.

This principle applies to the legislative process. Many changes in law and public administration have negligible or negative impact on the issues they attempt to address and on the general quality of life for citizens. Genuine improvements are likely only when such changes are based on honest, effective research. This will be discussed in a later section. In general, quality is often the key that unlocks the door to productivity, but people pass through the door by changing work methods.

QUALITY OF LIFE AND THE REAL AND MONETARY ECONOMIES

To elaborate on the relationship between quality of life and improvements in work methods, some definitions are needed.

Improvement—A change that delivers increased value to customers relative to the total cost to society.

Quality—The value added to customers' lives relative to the alternatives.

In these definitions, the "real economy" includes all goods and services of value that people produce for themselves and others, as opposed to the "monetary economy," which is only those goods and services traded in ways that are counted for macroeconomic measures, such as gross domestic product (GDP). When, for example, a mother takes a job in the monetary economy, any accompanying degradation in the quality of her life and that of her children is part of the real economy but not the monetary economy (Henderson 1991). In some cases, the new job of a previously unemployed mother might not be an improvement for the purposes of this article, although the new job increases GDP.

Quality of life is not yet a clearly defined scientific concept. Szalai (1980) notes that it includes people's physical well-being, health, welfare, and prosperity, as well as their subjective perceptions of how things are going for them. Slottje et al. (1991), Inkeles (1994), and Scheuch (1994) compare and contrast a variety of indicators of health, literacy, human rights, and economic activity in discussing alternative measures of quality of life, without advocating a single definitive measure.

The purpose here is to simply note that the impact of improvements in quality and productivity—properly interpreted—is not confined to the monetary economy, but contributes to helping people live better emotionally, spiritually, and materially. One possible exception to the asserted dependence of quality of life on improvements in work methods should be noted: A large cultural effect has been noted in quality of life as measured by people's responses to surveys on happiness and well-being, Inkeles (1994) notes that the French and Italians are consistently below the European average in reported happiness and satisfaction with life in general, while the Brazilians "seem impervious to the reality of their objective situation" (p. 63). These response patterns may change over time in ways unrelated to changes in work methods; however, life expectancy, infant mortality rates, literacy rates, and people's ability to control their own destiny are unlikely to change unless some individuals or groups change the way they approach paid or volunteer work.

The remainder of this section is devoted to additional illustrations of the differences between the real and monetary economies. One category of differences has been studied by economists using the term *externalities*. These are costs to society that are not included in the price to the consumer and are, therefore, external to the purchase decision (Case 1986; Slitor 1976). A common example is pollution. Some companies sell products at a low price because they pollute air and water without compensating people harmed by the pollution. Such business practices may increase the quality of life for a few, such as stockholders and employees unaffected by the pollution; however, the quality of life for society as a whole may be diminished. Since these costs are not reflected in the purchase price, consumers are pushed into decisions that may be bad for the quality of life for society as a whole.

An example of externalities was given by the U.S. Secretary of Health and Human Services (Sullivan 1990; Harwood et al. 1984), who reported that the United States lost roughly $117 billion in 1983 due to the consumption of approximately $60 billion in alcoholic beverages (Bunch and Simon 1985). The losses included increased health problems, traffic accidents, and reduced productivity known to be associated with excessive alcohol consumption. The $117 billion was a cost to society not included in the price to consumers. To the extent that this number is accurate, on average, a dollar of alcoholic beverage consumed translates into roughly $2 (117/60) of harm to other parts of society.

U.S. society does not currently require the consumers and producers of alcoholic beverages to compensate the victims and their families for the alcohol-induced portion of damage from traffic accidents, nor does it require that employers be compensated for loss of productivity on the job due to alcohol consumption. Some consumers who currently pay $5 for a bottle of wine would be something else if they had to pay the "total cost" of $15 [$5 + (2 × $5)]. Some economists (Anderson and Leal, 1991) have recommended that externalities be "internalized" into the market transaction; for example, through a tax on alcoholic beverages proportional to the best available data on the externalities.

Theoretically, it might be possible for quality of life to improve based on changes in private, recreational behavior but not on work methods. This could happen, for example, if there were a spontaneous reduction in alcohol consumption corresponding to the result of internalizing the externalities. A spontaneous change like this, however, is unlikely. If alcohol consumption were to decline, it would more likely result from a combined effort by researchers, philanthropic organizations, and citizens who convince their elected representatives to change the law in some way that results in a change in the work behavior of public employees.

The definition of improvement at the beginning of this section refers to delivering increased value to customers. Thus, the end user is not the only customer. Ishikawa (1985) said, "The next process is your customer." In many cases, process improvements can improve the quality of work life for people employed in the next step in the process, as well as the quality of life for end users.

IMPROVEMENTS OCCUR MOST OFTEN WHERE THEY ARE EXPECTED, SUPPORTED, AND REWARDED

People who work for someone else generally focus on what they think the boss will reward them for doing. People who are self-employed tend to focus on what they think their customers will reward them for doing. Efforts to improve quality and productivity for the long term get attention only to the extent people perceive they will benefit from such efforts. As a result, improvements, whether major innovations or small changes, tend to occur most often where they are expected, supported, and rewarded. This statement summarizes many of the principles of managing for quality and productivity improvement, as enunciated by Deming (1986), Ishikawa (1985), and Juran (1964).

The economist Vernon (1989) notes that

> Some of the most critical factors in the successful transfer and application of technology are internal to the receiver of the technology: internal to the country in terms of the economic and regulatory environment, internal to the firm in terms of the capacities, incentives and attitudes of managers and technicians, and internal to the industrial structure of the country. (pp. 36–37)

Vernon says the Industrial Revolution began in Great Britain because, "Unlike most other national environments, the British environment of the 19th century contained relatively few threats to those who improved and applied existing inventions, whether from business competitors, labor or the government itself" (p. 6). Vernon also notes that inventors in Russia and France had steam engines before or concurrent with their invention by James Watt, but only Watt commercialized the idea. The French invention "was officially suppressed," and the excessive power of veto groups, including the czar, may have contributed to the disappearance of the Russian steam engine (p. 19).

Government in the United States today provides obstacles to change and improvement. Virtually anyone starting a business in the United States must get licenses and permits from a number of different agencies. A manager reported that his small chemical company was required to have a business license, a permit for hazardous material storage, a permit to have an air pressure tank, a permit from the Occupational Safety and Health Administration to have a liquefied petroleum gas tank, a compressed gas permit, a hazardous waste permit from the Environmental Protection Agency, and a resale number, among others. Reed (1993) lists 229 statutes, ordinances, executive orders, and governmental agencies regulating the environmental impact of business activities in Santa Clara County and the city of San Jose, California; 53 of these are federal, 165 are state, and 11 are local.

This extensive paper jungle limits change and improvement because it can be difficult and expensive just to learn the rules. An organization called Joint Venture: Silicon Valley has a number of projects under way to improve local economic growth (Joint Venture: Silicon Valley 1992, 1993). One project is applying quality management concepts to streamline the regulatory process without sacrificing the local quality of life. The long-term vision is one-stop shopping for licensing and permits, whereby applicants could go to one central location for permits involving many different governmental agencies, and a person could get a ruling on most applications within minutes without leaving that central office.

Uncertainties regarding possible future changes in law and regulation are themselves obstacles to change. Anderson and Leal (1991) described a rancher who converted 25 percent of his land into marshes for wildlife and paid a surprisingly high price for his efforts. He said, "My lands have been zoned. I am being regulated for wetlands that weren't there before I created

them. Like most of my neighbors I can save myself from financial disaster only by some creative land management, but the state legislature has cut out most of my options" (p. 73). Other ranchers were reluctant to build similar wildlife habitats for fear that the government would take them away. "It's just plain easier and a lot safer to sterilize the land," they said.

This problem is not restricted to the United States. According to this theory, the underdeveloped world is poor because governments and other veto groups present too many obstacles to improvement. The Institute for Liberty and Democracy in Lima, Peru, estimated that roughly two-thirds of the Peruvian population and one-third of its gross national product are involved in the "informal sector" of the economy (de Soto 1989). These people work in illegal businesses or live in illegal settlements and typically pay bribes to stay there. Virtually the entire public transportation system of Lima is "informal;" these are bus or taxi operators who do not have the licenses required by law. Because of their precarious situations, they cannot afford to be too successful for fear they may be jailed and their property confiscated. Chickering and Salahdine (1991) describe similar problems in other countries.

The actions of governments play a major role in determining the extent to which improvements are expected, supported, and rewarded. The rest of this section discusses applications of quality management principles in government under each of these three headings.

Expecting Improvements: PDCA in the Legislative Process

Part of expecting improvements is employing a methodology that explicitly looks for improvements. This could be achieved by applying the plan-do-check-act (PDCA) improvement cycle in the legislative process (Graves 1992a). This would mean that virtually every piece of legislation would include a clear statement of purpose (plan), appropriate provisions for measuring its effectiveness (check) during implementation (do), and a schedule for hearings on the results (act to improve), as preparation for deciding whether and how the program should be extended (planning the next cycle). Appropriate collection and use of data would address the concerns of the spectrum of political opinion in a way that would elevate the debate, leading to improved regulations that were simultaneously more effective, more efficient, and easier to understand and follow.

This is not a new idea. Dupuit (1844) called for honest evaluation of public works 150 years ago, and considerable experience has been accumulated in this area since World War II (Rossi and Freeman 1989). The Governmental Accounting Standards Board (1994; Hatry et al. 1990) now recommends that data be compiled and reported on the accomplishments of governmental agencies as well as on the money spent. Several governments now have legislative mandates in this area, including the U.S. federal government and Washington state, to name only two (Sonntag 1993). While these legislative mandates seem to be a step in the right direction, they are still relatively new, and there remains substantial opportunities for improvement in how they are applied.

Governmental programs are generally specified in terms of the objectives to be pursued and the means to be used in pursuing those objectives. Most of the political debate is over means, and disagreements over objectives are rare. Dasgupta (1993) said,

> Divergences in people's opinions about how the world "works" assume importance in political debate long before differences in ethical views manifest themselves. I have yet to meet anyone who does not wish to see unemployment reduced, or destitution a thing of the past. I have also heard many disagreements on what are the most effective means of bringing them about. (p. 6)

Fisher, Ury, and Patton (1991) note that in negotiations, it is often easier to get agreement on the decision criteria than on the issue under negotiation. By extrapolation, this suggests that it might often be easier to get agreement on criteria to evaluate how well alternative programs work than to get agreement on a program to address specific objections.

This suggests that a political discussion be summarized in the format of Exhibit 1. If Dasgupta (1993) is correct, it should be relatively easy to get agreement on the objectives for a given piece of legislation. With the assistance of respected researchers in the subject matter, it should also be relatively easy to get consensus on evaluation criteria. Alternative proposals over how to achieve the objectives could then be packaged in a way that several options could be tried

EXHIBIT 1.—A TEMPLATE FOR NEGOTIATING IMPROVEMENTS IN GOVERNMENT

	Agreement	Disagreement
Objectives		
Evaluation criteria		
Means		
Lessons from history		

simultaneously and the results used to guide the selection of future governmental policies.

This template should also include a summary of differing perceptions of the relevant history of the issue. In some cases, this may come fairly early in the process as good strategic planning exercises begin with a review of the past (Kouzes and Posner 1987); act is often the best place to start the PDCA cycle. This is part of the current process, a product of the legislative hearings that are held on many issues.

Some evaluations of the type suggested here have already been performed. Collections of papers edited by Boruch and Wothke (1985) and Bloom, Cordray, and Light (1988) describe experiments involving randomized assignment of welfare recipients to alternative programs; randomization of the decision of whether to arrest the offender in domestic violence cases; randomizing the selection of treatment for depression; randomizing the collections effort to pursue delinquent tax accounts; and randomizing the selection of alternative mediation efforts in civil trials.

Unfortunately, such experiments are still the exception. Without them, the terms of the political debate have remained virtually unchanged for decades. The arguments heard today regarding welfare, for example, are similar to the arguments 400 years ago when the Elizabethan Poor Laws of 1601 were adopted (Day 1989). Even in the cases in which quality evaluation efforts have been performed, they are still too often overlooked or ignored (McLaughlin et al. 1988). Schweinhart and Weikart (1980) and Berrueta-Clement et al. (1984; Barnett 1992) compared children from the Perry Preschool program, a 1962–65 Head Start program, with a control group. At age 19, 31 percent of the Perry Preschool group had an arrest record versus 51 percent for the control group; 50 percent were employed versus 32 percent of controls; and 18 percent were on welfare versus 32 percent for controls. There were 1.3 arrests per participant versus 2.3 for controls. (These differences were all statistically significant at the 0.05 level.) People still debate a variety of issues surrounding Head Start, including whether 20 percent or 100 percent of eligible children will be covered, at $2600 or $4000 per child (Rovner 1990). These questions could be answered by careful study of the results of past programs, extending Schweinhart and Weikart (1980) and Berrueta-Clement et al. (1984). These previous evaluations indicate that progress can be made against the problems of crime and poverty.

In a sense, virtually all government programs are experiments, but they are rarely described as such. They should be managed in a way that will help citizens learn how to improve them in the future. The current reinventing government movement (Osborne and Gaebler 1992; Gore 1993) takes important steps toward applying PDCA in government, but has not yet transformed the legislative process as previously suggested.

The press could help by being systematic about the following:

1. Researching relevant history

2. Organizing its reports to clearly expose issues such as those in Exhibit 1

3. Asking questions like, "How do you know that?" "What is the history of this issue?" and "How will the effectiveness of this proposal be evaluated?"

4. Informing its audiences when the plans for a program seem inconsistent with the record of experience or the evaluation plan seems inadequate

A June 1994 edition of an award-winning television news program featured a discussion of President Clinton's Welfare Reform Proposal. Most of the time was taken with claims and refutations of what the new program would or would not accomplish; there was no substantive discussion of what has been learned from the past 50 years of evaluations of welfare programs. As a viewer, this author often has difficulty keeping all the details of a complex discussion mentally organized. This program might be enhanced by considering the suggestions just made and summarizing some of the results in appropriate visual aids.

Elected representatives must respond to large campaign contributors (Etzioni 1984; Stern

1988), but any movement in the direction of greater clarity of purpose and accountability in government can be expected to improve the quality of governance and quality of life for all.

Supporting Improvements: Education

One major principle of quality management is investing in educating and training the workforce. The importance of education for economic development has been stressed in recent World Bank reports. Tilak (1989) relates that "education, age, and sectoral distribution of population explained more than half of the differences in income levels between the United States and a group of 28 countries" (p. 13) and "investment in human capital in general, and in education in particular, may be more conducive to economic growth than investment in physical capital" (p. 19). (Also see Levine and Renelt 1992.) Porter (1990) claimed, "Education and training constitute perhaps the single greatest long-term leverage point available to all levels of government in upgrading industry" (p. 638).

Quality professionals might suggest that education in quality management may contribute more to economic development than courses in traditional subjects. Everyone might make better use of the resources they have if (1) they are all trained in improvement tools, and (2) managers and leaders of all kinds are trained and supported in creating a social environment supportive of quality and productivity improvement. This could impact the success of individual organizations and real economic growth of communities and nations.

Rewarded: Three Conditions of Productivity Growth

In 1955, the Japan Productivity Center promulgated "three conditions of productivity growth" (Japan Productivity Center 1989, 22, 33). They are

1. Stable employment

2. Equitable allocation and distribution of gains of productivity growth

3. Consultation between labor and management

These three points can be compared with the results of surveys of U.S. and Japanese workers. Grayson and O'Dell (1988; Yankelovich and Im-

EXHIBIT 2.—JAPAN PRODUCTIVITY CENTER AND ECONOMIC GROWTH

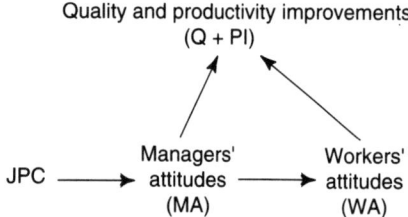

Quality and productivity improvements
(Q + PI)

JPC → Managers' attitudes (MA) → Workers' attitudes (WA)

JPC—*The Japan Productivity Center* and its "three conditions of productivity growth" had a major impact on the subsequent thoughts and attitudes of Japanese managers. This hypothesis is supported by Hashimoto (1990), who said that "many unique features of Japanese labor markets became widespread only after the mid-1950s. Cultural and traditional factors alone, therefore, cannot explain their existence" (pp. 245-294).

MA—The change in Japanese *managers' attitudes* led to the differences in worker's attitudes (WA) between the United States and Japan found in the surveys by Grayson and O'Dell (1988) and Yankelovich and Immerwahr (1983).

Q + PI—The difference in attitudes between the United States and Japan explain some of the differences in the rates of *improvement in quality and productivity.*

merwahr 1983) reported that "only 13 percent [of U.S. workers] believe they would personally benefit from producing more effectively [while] 93 percent [of Japanese workers] believe that they will benefit from improvements in their employers' performance" (pp. 26–27). While differences in attitudes between the United States and Japan may not be as stark as these surveys suggest, it seems unlikely that this difference could be totally an artifact of survey methodology or is a thing of the past. If substantial differences exist, could they *not* impact economic growth? This question suggests three hypotheses that sound plausible but have not been proven (see Exhibit 2).

Labor's distrust of management in the United States is reflected in restrictive work rules in union contracts that limit change and improvement. Labor fought for those rules after watching layoffs that resulted from productivity improvements. The three conditions of productivity growth of the Japan Productivity Center carry a message for both management and labor: Each group should offer these conditions to the other in exchange for collaboration in improving productivity and customer satisfaction to generate wealth that would not exist without the collaboration.

This discussion raises the issue of the impact of quality management on the economic growth of Japan since World War II. An analysis of World Bank data on economic growth in 101 countries is reported by Levine and Renelt (1992). They fit several regression models, of which the following was the one they preferred.

$$GYP = -0.83 - 0.35\ GDP - 0.38\ GPO$$
$$(-0.93)\ (-2.50)\qquad (-1.73)$$
$$+\ 3.17\ SEC + 17.5\ INV + e$$
$$(2.46)\qquad (6.53)$$

where

GYP = growth in real per capita GDP 1960–1989

GDP = real GDP per capital in 1960, in thousands of 1980 international dollars (Summers and Heston 1988)

GPO = growth of population 1960–1989 (World Bank Social Indicators)

SEC = secondary school enrollment rate in 1960, as a percent of age group

INV = investment share of GDP (1960–1989)

e = residual due to misspecification or lack of comparability between countries in variables in this model (R^2 = 46 percent)

The numbers in parentheses are t-statistics. This equation says that the rate of economic growth (GYP) increases with investments in human and physical capital (SEC and INV) and decreases with the size of the country's current per capita income (GDP). Levine and Renelt (1992) include GDP, SEC, and INV in their preferred model because these variables were statistically significant over a broad range of choices for other variables in the model. They included GPO because their understanding of economic theory made it impossible to believe that the population growth rate would not have an impact on the rate of growth in per capita income.

This author obtained levine and Renelt's data, which by then included 109 countries, and got comparable results with several models of this nature. Japan's growth was 0.1 standard deviation below the regression line for this model. Other models were fit using different measures of education, some without GPO and including measures of quality of governance. In each case, Japan's growth exceeded the model by less than one standard deviation and R^2 was between 40 percent and 50 percent. *Japan's economic performance, at least in this analysis, is consistent with standard econometric theory.* This analysis should establish conclusively that Deming and/or Japanese total quality control was not the sole reason for the Japanese economic miracle, as had been suggested by various quality experts. As a minimum, Japan's high rate of investment must also be considered.

Economists have offered different explanations for Japan's recent economic history (Minami 1986; Kosai 1986; six books cited by Banks 1993). Factors identified include democratization of capital and politics via legalizing labor unions, trust busting, land reform, and Japan's democratic constitution. Quality management is rarely mentioned.

There is still a way that quality management may have contributed to the growth of Japan since World War II, namely by catalyzing an increase in the rate of investment in human and physical capital. The increased investment would contribute to economic growth as predicted by the regression equation cited. During periods of high economic growth, more wealth is produced every year than before and some of that excess is invested (Baumol, Blackman, and Wolff 1989). This contributes to even higher rates of economic growth and may also increase the difficulties of identifying and evaluating the many factors that contribute to the growth.

The macroeconomic data clearly show that quality management was not the sole reason for the Japanese economic miracle, but leave open the possibility that quality management might have made important contributions. Readers are left with Ishikawa's (1985) comment that Japan's quality control "activities . . . [are] not *the* reason, but *one* of the important reasons for" the great success of Japanese industry (p. 5).

Rewarded: Savings and Investment

Economists have long proclaimed the need for capital investments to achieve economic growth (Denison 1985, Table 8.3; Abramowitz 1989). This argument is often used to justify special tax rates for capital gains and interest income (Porter 1990). Two rarely mentioned points in this area may be obvious to people familiar with quality management.

- Savings and investment should be expected, supported, and rewarded by the national political and economic environment. Govern-

ment tax policies are only part of this issue. Bureaucracy and the power of bribes are also important factors. Bulow and Rogoff (1990) suggest that the Third World debt crisis of the 1980s was, in essence, Third World money circulated through First World banks. The desire of Third World governments to attract the return of this money is similar to the problem that employers face in creating an environment in which their workers will believe that improving quality and productivity will benefit them (Graves 1992b, 1993). Both require a change in mind-set at the top, supported by continual data collection to monitor the impact of policy changes and guide the bureaucracy in a direction supportive of growth.

- Investments in physical capital will produce little return if the workforce cannot be trained to use the new equipment (Blinder 1990). General Motors lost several billion dollars in the early 1990s in part because it did not train its workers to use the robotics purchased during the 1980s (Taylor 1992). But training is not a one-shot affair. workers who know how to improve quality and productivity can often teach themselves to make equipment and production processes perform better than the vendors and managers originally expected. Quality management ideas, including training and support for the use of tools for quality and productivity improvement, may increase the rate of return on physical capital.

Minami (1986) notes that during most of their period of industrialization beginning in the mid-nineteenth century, Japan and Germany were net capital exporters, although other nations achieved industrialization using imported capital. Many less-developed countries, in contrast, are mired in foreign debt, unable to grow because local governmental policies motivate substantial capital flight (Bulow and Rogoff 1990). This analysis led Graves (1991) to conclude that development can be self-financed; no country needs foreign capital.

CONTINUAL IMPROVEMENTS ARE NECESSARY JUST TO STAY EVEN

Continual improvement is often cited as a fundamental tenet of quality management. At a macroeconomic level, differences in the rate of improvement underlie the current enormous negative trade balance that the United States has with Japan. The relatively slow rate of improvement in the United States over the past 30 years has led to the current situation that customers all over the world more often choose Japanese to U.S. products. If customers today in Latin America, Africa, Europe, and Asia more often chose U.S. over Japanese products, as they did 30 years ago when the United States led the world in quality and productivity, few people in the United States would care about the U.S.–Japanese trade balance. The difficulties in selling U.S. goods in Japan would concern only a handful of researchers. It would not be an item of discussion between the U.S. president and the Japanese prime minister. It would not be discussed in the popular press. It is an issue today because the rate of improvement in the United States has appreciably lagged behind that of Japan.

Continual improvement has economic implications that might be called the *Third World commodity trap*. Over time, knowledge about how to do anything useful becomes ever more widely available, which leads to increases in the availability of products or services to meet any given need. As competition increases, existing products or services must either come down in price or go up in value. The Third World, producing commodities, has been forced to accept ever lower prices for its increasingly abundant commodities.

The escape from the Third World commodity trap can be found through quality and productivity improvement and market segmentation. The businesses of two brothers, both dairy farmers and acquaintances of the author, illustrate this. Around 1962, they helped found the Dairy Herd Improvement Association. In 1986, they described how they regularly measured the milk production of each cow and kept the data on computer. This helped the brothers figure out which cows and which dairy management policies were most productive. In not quite 25 years, they had tripled the milk production of the average cow. Most of their competition had done the same. As a result, one brother left the dairy business, unprofitable at only triple the productivity of 25 years earlier.

The brother who stayed in the dairy business is doing great. Milk for him is only a sideline: He also sells pedigreed animals to other dairy farmers. He has a highly specialized product for a narrow but adequate market. He makes a comfortable profit based on continual improvement to maintain leadership in his chosen market segment. Market segmentation does not ensure high profit; it is only a tool to help businesses focus on the high-profit customers (Stalk, Evans, and Schulman 1992; Stalk and Webber 1993; Duboff 1992).

The brother who left the dairy business still has an egg delivery business started by his father 50 years ago. He has a steady clientele who like the idea of farm-fresh eggs delivered to their doors. He has no chickens, only delivery. He has a specialized, segmented market, quality service; and good profit.

These dairy and egg examples suggest a vision of a world populated with organizations continually developing products and services of ever higher value (quality) and profitability for precisely segmented markets. Continually improving organizations may provide a continually improving standard of living for an increasing share of the world's population.

SUMMARY

There are similarities between the theories of quality management and development economics. This article described three principles as central to both.

1. Improved quality of life is built on improved work mthods.

2. Improvements occur most often where they are expected, supported, and rewarded.

3. Continual improvements are necessary just to stay even.

There appears to be one idea, more than others, that has yet to see the application it deserves: application of the PDCA improvement cycle in the legislative process to improve government from the top to support change and improvement.

ACKNOWLEDGMENTS

The author wishes to thank Elizabeth Coleman, Bob McQueen, David Passarell, Betsy Wolf-Graves, W. Lee Hansen, Bruce Ankenman, the reports committee at the Center for Quality and

Productivity Improvement at the University of Wisconsin-Madison, and anonymous referees for valuable comments on earlier versions of this article. The second basic principle discussed is sometimes called "Harmer's Law" after Chet Harmer, who enunciated it when he was controller for the Direct Marketing Division of Hewlett-Packard Company. The preparation of this article was supported in part by a grant from the Alfred P. Sloan Foundation.

REFERENCES

Abramowitz, M. 1989. *Thinking about growth*. New York: Cambridge University Press.

Anderson, T. L., and D. R. Leal. 1991. *Free market evironmentalism*. San Francisco: Pacific Research Institute for Public Policy.

Banks, D. 1993. Is industrial statistics out of control? *Statistical Science* 8, no. 4:356–409.

Barnett, W. S. 1992. Benefits of compensatory preschool education. *Journal of Human Resources* 27, no. 2:279–312.

Baumol, W. J., S. A. B. Blackman, and E. N. Wolff. 1989. *Productivity and American leadership*. Cambridge, Mass.: MIT Press.

Berrueta-Clement, J. R., L. J. Schweinhart, W. S. Barnett, A. S. Epstein, and D. P. Weikart. 1984. *Changed lives: The effects of the Perry preschool program on youths through age 19*. Ypsilanti, Mich.: High/Scope Press.

Blinder, A. S., ed. 1990. *Paying for productivity*. Washington, D.C.: Brookings Institution.

Bloom, H. S., D. S. Cordray, and R. J. Light. 1988. *Lessons from selected program and policy areas*. San Francisco: Jossey-Bass.

Boruch, R. F., and W. Wothke, eds. 1985. *Randomization and field experimentation*. San Francisco: Jossey-Bass.

Bulow, J., and K. Rogoff. 1990. Cleaning up Third World debt without getting taken to the cleaners. *Journal of Economic Perspectives* 4, no. 1:31–42.

Bunch, K., and G. Simon. 1985. *Total food consumption, prices, and expenditures 1964–1984*. Washington, D.C.: USDA Economic Research Service, Statistical Bulletin No. 736.

Case, K. E. 1986. *Economics and tax policy*. Boston: Oelgeschlager, Gunn & Hain.

Chickering, A. L., and M. Salahdine, eds. 1991. *The silent revolution: The informal sectors in five Asian and near eastern countries*. San Francisco: International Center for Economic Growth.

Dasgupta, P. 1993. *An inquiry into well-being and destitution*. Oxford, England: Oxford University Press.

Day, P. J. 1989. *A new history of social welfare*. Englewood Cliffs, N.J.: Prentice Hall.

Deming, W. E. 1986. *Out of the crisis*. Boston: MIT Center for Advanced Engineering Study.

Denison, E. F. 1985. *Trends in American economic growth, 1929–1982*. Washington, D.C.: Brookings Institution.

de Soto, H. 1989. *The other path*. New York: Harper & Row.

Drucker, P. F. 1993. *Post-capitalist society*. New York: Harper Business.

Duboff, R. S. 1992. Marketing to maximize profitbility. *Journal of Business Strategy* (November/December): 10–13.

Dupuit, Jules. 1844. De la mesure de l'utilité des travaux public. *Annales des Ponts et Chausées*, 2nd ser., 8. English translation appeared in *International economic papers*, no. 2, edited by A. T. Peacock, F. A. Lutz, R. Turvey, and E. Henderson (New York: Macmillan).

Etzioni, A. 1984. *Capital corruption: The new attack on American democracy*. San Diego: Harcourt Brace Jovanovich.

Fisher, R., W. Ury, and B. Patton. 1991. *Getting to yes*. 2d ed. Boston: Houghton Mifflin.

Fuller, F. T. 1985. Eliminating complexity from work. *National Productivity Review* 4, no. 4:327–344.

Fuller, R. B. 1981. *Critical path*. New York: St. Martin's Press.

Gore, A. 1993. *Creating a government that works better and costs less*. New York: Random House.

Governmental Accounting Standards Board. 1994. *Service efforts and accomplishments reporting, GASB concepts statement no. 2*. Norwalk, Conn.: Governmental Accounting Standards Board.

Graves, S. B. 1991. ¿Quién necesita del capital extranjero? (Who needs foreign capital?) *Encuentro con Calidad* (February–April): 13–21.

_____. 1992a. A political platform for quality improvement. In 1992 *ASQC quality congress transactions*. Milwaukee: American Society for Quality Control.

_____. 1992b. Compensation systems and other human resources policies to promote quality and productivity improvement. *International Productivity Journal* (summer): 17–30.

_____. 1993. *Compensation and employment security*. Report no. 104. Madison, Wisc.: University of Wisconsin Center for Quality and Productivity Improvement.

Grayson, C. J., and D. O'Dell. 1988. *American business: A two-minute warning*. New York: Free Press.

Harwood, H. J., D. M. Napolitano, P. L. Kristiansen, and J. J. Collins. 1984. *Economic costs to society of alcohol and drug abuse and mental illness*. Research Triangle Park, N.C.: Research Triangle Institute.

Hashimoto, M. 1990. Employment and wage systems in Japan and their implications for productivity. In *Paying for productivity*, edited by A. S. Blinder. Washington, D.C.: Brookings Institution.

Hatry, H. P., J. R. Fountain Jr., J. M. Sullivan, and L. Kremer. 1990. *Service efforts and accomplishments reporting: Its time has come.* Norwalk, Conn.: Governmental Accounting Standards Board.

Henderson, H. 1991. *Paradigms in progress: Life beyond economics.* Indianapolis: Knowledge Systems.

Inkeles, A. 1994. Industrialization, modernization, and the quality of life. In *Ecology, society, and the quality of social life,* edited by W. V. D'Antionio, M. Sasaki, and Y. Yonebayashi, New Brunswick, N.J.: Transaction Publishers.

Ishikawa, K. 1985. *What is total quality control? The Japanese way.* Englewood Cliffs, N.J.: Prentice Hall.

Japanese Productivity Center. 1989. *New paradigm of productivity movement in Japan.* Tokyo: Asian Productivity Organization.

Joint Venture: Silicon Valley. 1992. *Silicon Valley regulatory climate: Opportunity briefing paper* (October). Palo Alto, Calif.: SRI International.

_____. 1993. *Network news* (fall). San Jose, Calif.: Joint Venture: Silicon Valley.

Juran, J. M. 1964. *Managerial breakthrough.* New York: McGraw-Hill.

Kosai, Y. 1986. *The era of high-speed growth.* Tokyo: University of Tokyo Press.

Kouzes, J. M., and B. Z. Posner. 1987. *The leadership challenge.* San Francisco: Jossey-Bass.

Lambert, I. T. G. 1993. *Out of the crisis with George, Mises, and Deming.* Wiltshire, England: British Deming Association.

Levine, R., and D. Renelt. 1992. A sensitivity analysis of cross-country growth regressions. *American Economic Review* 82, no. 4:942–963.

McLaughlin, J. A., L. J. Weber, R. W. Covert, and R. B. Ingle. 1988. *Evaluation utilization.* San Francisco: Jossey-Bass.

Minami, R. 1986. *The economic development of Japan: A quantitative study.* New York: St. Martin's Press.

Osborne, D., and T. Gaebler. 1992. *Reinventing government.* Reading, Mass.: Addison-Wesley.

Porter, M. 1990. *The competitive advantage of nations.* New York: Free Press.

Reed, C., ed. 1993. *Environmental laws and regulators.* San Jose, Calif.: Law Offices of Reed, Elliott, Creech, and Roth.

Rossi, P. H., and H. E. Freeman. 1989. *Evaluation: A systematic approach.* Newbury Park, Calif.: Sage.

Rovner, J. 1990. Head start is a program everyone wants to help. *Congressional Quarterly weekly Report,* 21 April, 1191–1195.

Scheuch, E. K. 1994. The puzzle of quality of life. In *Ecology, society, and the quality of social life,* edited by W. V. D'Antionio, M. Sasaki, and Y. Yonebayashi. New Brunswick, N.J.: Transaction Publishers.

Schweinhart, L. J., and D. P. Weikart. 1980. *Young children grow up: The effects of the Perry preschool program on youths through age 15.* Ypsilanti, Mich.: High/Scope Press.

Slitor, R. E. 1976. Pollution taxes. In *Taxation and development,* edited by N. T. Wano. New York: Praeger.

Slottje, D. J., G. W. Scully, J. G. Hirschberg, and K. J. Hayes. 1991. *Measuring the quality of life across countries.* Boulder, Colo.: Westview Press.

Sonntag, B. 1993. *Advocating accountability.* Olympia, Wash.: State Auditor's Office.

Stalk, G., Jr., P. Evans, and L. E. Shulman. 1992. Competing on capabilities: The new rules of corporate strategy. *Harvard Business Review* (March/April): 57–69.

Stalk, G., Jr., and A. M. Webber. 1993. Japan's dark side of time. *Harvard Business Review* (July/August): 93–102.

Stern, P. M. 1988. *The best Congress money can buy.* New York: Pantheon Books.

Sullivan, L. W. 1990. *Alcohol and health.* Washington, D.C.: U.S. Department of Health and Human Services.

Summers, R., and A. Heston. 1988. A new set of international comparisons of real product and price level estimates for 130 countries, 1950–1985. *Review of Income and Wealth* 34 (March): 1–25.

Szalai, A. 1980. The meaning of comparative research on the quality of life. In *The quality of life,* edited by A. Szalai, and F. M. Andrews. Beverly Hills, Calif.: Sage.

Taylor, A., III. 1992. Can GM remodel itself? *FORTUNE,* 13 January, 26–34.

Tilak, J. B. G. 1989. *Education and its relation to economic growth, poverty, and income distribution.* Washington, D.C.: World Bank.

Vernon, R. 1989. *Technological development.* Washington, D.C.: World Bank.

Yankelovich, D., and J. Immerwahr. 1983. *Putting the work ethic to work.* New York: Public Agenda Foundation.

3.8
STATISTICAL METHODS

———————————■———————————

UNDERSTANDING CANONICAL ANALYSIS*
by Donald G. Watts

Canonical analysis is hard to explain because it involves the difficult concepts of eigenvalue and eigenvector. In this note, I describe an approach that I have found to be effective in overcoming these difficulties which uses the new concept of an Eigen*angle* to explain eignanalysis.

INTRODUCTION

Users of response surface methodology are often bewildered by one of the most important parts of the method—canonical analysis—which is commonly viewed as a complicated and highly mathematical process that, *if it could only be understood*, would be a neat thing to be able to do.

To understand canoncial analysis, it is necessary to know its purpose. Accordingly, I offer the following:

> The purpose of canonical analysis is to allow one to appreciate a thing in a meaningful, informative, and truly enlightening way.

A nonstandard example of canonical analysis is provided by Brian Joiner who, when trying to help students decide whether to use a binomial distribution or a Poisson distribution, advises "If you can count what happens *and what doesn't*, use the binomial; if you can count *only what happens*, use the Poisson."

As an example of a standard canonical analysis, suppose we have a function

$$y = 67 + 9x - 16x^2 \qquad (1)$$

What does this curve look like? It is possible to find out by substituting values of x into the equation, calculating the values of y, and then plotting the pairs; but a more powerful procedure is to perform a *canonical anaylsis*. In this situation, the canonical analysis exploits the fact that by completing the square, any quadratic function

$$y(x) = \beta_0 + \beta_1 x + \beta_2 x^2 \qquad (2)$$

can be written in the form

$$y(x) = \alpha_0 + \alpha_2(x - \alpha_1)^2 \qquad (3)$$

where the parameters α_1, α_0, and α_2 have the meaningful interpretations of the *location* of the extreme, of $y(x)$, the *value* at the extreme, and the *rate of deviation* of $y(x)$ from it's extreme. It is thus possible to envision the curve without recourse to calculating and plotting any points!

The correspondence between the parameters α and β can be obtained by expanding equation (3) and equating the coefficients of the powers x with those in equation (2). For equation (1), the canonical form becomes

$$y(x) = 68.3 - 16(x - 0.28)^2 \qquad (4)$$

From equation (4), we 'see' that at $x = 0.28$, $y(x)$ has an extreme value of 68.3, and that this extreme is a maxium (since $\alpha_2 < 0$), that the 'rate of deviation' at the maxium is -16 units, so there is a steep drop as x deviates from 0.28.

Unfortunately, completing the square does not provide all the illumination needed to understand the behavior of a quadratic function in higher dimensions—one must also use eigenanalysis, which often hinders understanding of canonical analysis. Accordingly, in this paper I offer a simple geometric interpretation of eigenvectors based on the concept of an *eigenangle*.

---

*Reprinted with permission from *Journal of Quality Technology*, Volume 27, Number 1, January 1995. Donald G. Watts is a professor emeritus in statistics at Queen's University in Kingston, Ontario.

EIGENANALYSIS

Completing the square is generalizable to higher dimensions. For example, suppose we have a K-dimensional quadratic,

$$
\begin{aligned}
y(x) &= \beta_0 + \beta_1 x_1 + \cdots + \beta_K x_K \\
&\quad + \beta_{11} x_1^2 + \cdots + \beta_{KK} x_K^2 \\
&\quad + 2\beta_{12} x_1 x_2 + \cdots + 2\beta_{K-1, K} x_{K-1} x_K \\
&= \beta_0 + x^T \beta + x^T B x \qquad (5)
\end{aligned}
$$

where $x^T = (x_1, ..., x_K)$, $\beta^T = (\beta_1, ..., \beta_K)$, and

$$
B = \begin{bmatrix}
\beta_{11} & \beta_{12} & \cdots & \beta_{1K} \\
\beta_{12} & \beta_{22} & \cdots & \beta_{2K} \\
\vdots & \vdots & \ddots & \vdots \\
\beta_{1K} & \beta_{2K} & \cdots & \beta_{KK}
\end{bmatrix} \qquad (6)
$$

is symmetric. Completing the squares gives

$$
y(x) = \alpha_0 + (x - \alpha_1)^T B (x - \alpha_1) \qquad (7)
$$

but this reveals only part of the story: the value, α_0, and the location α_1, of the extreme. We are still in the dark as to the nature of the surface described by the equation.

How can we simplify equation (5) so that the behavior of the surface is revealed simply and unequivocally? The answer is by finding a different set of factors, or equivalently, a more illuminating set of coordinate axes *before* completing the square. This is accomplished via eigenanalysis.

A NUMERICAL EXAMPLE

To explain, we begin with the case $K = 2$, so

$$
y(x) = \beta_0 + \beta_1 x_1 + \beta_2 x_2 + \beta_{11} x_1^2 + 2\beta_{12} x_1 x_2 + \beta_{22} x_2^2 \qquad (8)
$$

and, to make things specific, suppose we want to determine what kind of surface is specified by

$$
y(x) = 6.0 + 1.3 x_1 - 1.7 x_2 + 2.2 x_1^2 + 2.8 x_1 x_2 + 3.0 x_2^2 \qquad (9)
$$

We now focus temporarily on the quadratic portion

$$
q(x) = 2.2 x_1^2 + 2.8 x_1 x_2 + 3.0 x_2^2 \qquad (10)
$$

and consider a point with coordinates (x_1, x_2) on the curve $q(x) = \text{constant} = K^2$.

If we rotate the axes by angle θ, what are the coordinates u_1 and u_2 of that point in the new axis system? Referring to Exhibit 1 and writing the point in terms of a radius, r, an angle, δ, and

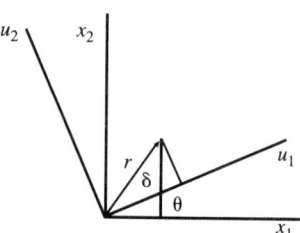

EXHIBIT 1.—A POINT ON A CONTOUR IN TWO COORDINATE SYSTEMS

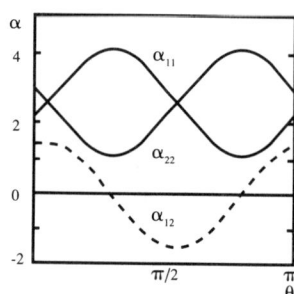

EXHIBIT 2.—THE COEFFICIENTS OF u_1^2, $u1u2$, AND $u2;2$ AS A FUNCTION OF θ

the axis rotation angle, θ, in the new coordinate system we have $u_1 = r \cos \delta$, $u_2 = r \sin \delta$, and so

$$
\begin{aligned}
x_1 &= r \cos(\theta + \delta) \\
&= r [\cos \theta \cos \delta - \sin \theta \sin \delta] \\
&= u_1 \cos \theta - u_2 \sin \theta \\
x_2 &= r \sin(\theta + \delta) \\
&= u_1 \sin \theta + u_2 \cos \theta \qquad (11)
\end{aligned}
$$

Then the curve

$$
k^2 = 2.2 x_1^2 + 2.8 x_1 x_2 + 3.0 x_2^2 \qquad (12)
$$

becomes, after substituting for x_1 and x_2 in terms of u_1 and u_2 and gathering terms in u_1^2, $u_1 u_2$, and u_2^2,

$$
\begin{aligned}
k^2 &= [2.2 \cos^2 \theta + 2.8 \sin \theta \cos \theta + 3.0 \sin^2 \theta] u_1^2 \\
&\quad + [(-2.2 + 3.0) \sin \theta \cos \theta + 2.8(\cos^2 \theta - \sin^2 \theta)] u_1 u_2 \\
&\quad + [2.2 \sin^2 \theta - 2.8 \sin \theta \cos \theta + 3.0 \cos^2 \theta] u_2^2 \qquad (13)
\end{aligned}
$$

As the angle θ is varied from 0 to π, the coefficients of the u_1^2, $u_1 u_2$ and u_2^2 terms behave as shown in Exhibit 2.

At the special angle θ^*, (and $\theta^* + \pi/2$, $\theta^* + 2\pi/2$, ...) the coefficient of the cross-term $u_1 u_2$ is zero! We refer to θ^* as the *eigenangle*, since it is the angle which *eliminates the cross-term* and gives the simplified equation

$$
4.06 u_1^2 + 1.14 u_2^2 = k^2 \qquad (14)
$$

(The task of finding eigenangles, or rather, the compound rotation matrix when there are more than two eigenangles, is discussed later.)

This rotation to new coordinates allows us to 'see' the behavior of the surface without plotting it:

1. Because the coefficients are of the same sign, each curve is an ellipse.

2. The ellipse intersects the u_1 axis at $\pm k / \sqrt{4.06}$ and the u_2 axis at $\pm k / \sqrt{1.14}$ and so is long in the u_2 direction and narrow in the u_1 direction.

3. The extreme value of the quadratic *surface* $q(\mathbf{u})$ is 0 and this extreme occurs at $\mathbf{u} = \mathbf{0}$.

4. The extreme is a minimum since the coefficients of u_1 and u_2 are positive.

5. A perpendicular slice through the quadratic surface produces a parabola.

6. The quadratic surface rises steeply in the u_1 direction and more gradually in the u_2 direction.

7. The surface is a regular "bowl," narrow in the u_1 direction and wide in the u_2 direction.

Eigenangles in Two Dimensions

To develop the theory of eigenanalysis, we simply note from equation (11) that the coordinates $\mathbf{x}$ and $\mathbf{u}$ are related by

$$x = R(\theta)u \qquad (15)$$

$$u = R^{-1}(\theta)x = R^T(\theta)x \qquad (16)$$

where

$$R(\theta) = \begin{bmatrix} \cos\theta & -\sin\theta \\ \sin\theta & \cos\theta \end{bmatrix} \qquad (17)$$

is the rotation matrix which converts from the $\mathbf{u}$ to the $\mathbf{x}$ factors. Then the equation for the quadratic portion becomes

$$q(x) = x^T B x = u^T A(\theta) u \qquad (18)$$

where

$$A(\theta) = R^T(\theta) B R(\theta)$$
$$= \begin{bmatrix} \alpha_{11}(\theta) & \alpha_{12}(\theta) \\ \alpha_{12}(\theta) & \alpha_{22}(\theta) \end{bmatrix}$$
$$\alpha_{11}(\theta) = \bar{\beta} + \gamma \sin(2\theta + \omega)$$
$$\alpha_{22}(\theta) = \bar{\beta} - \gamma \sin(2\theta + \omega)$$
$$\alpha_{12}(\theta) = \gamma \cos(2\theta + \omega)$$

$$\bar{\beta} = \frac{\beta_{11} + \beta_{22}}{2}$$

$$\gamma^2 = \left(\frac{\beta_{11} - \beta_{22}}{2}\right)^2 + \beta_{12}^2$$

$$\omega = \arctan\left(\frac{\beta_{11} - \beta_{22}}{2\beta_{12}}\right).$$

For the special (*eigen*)angle $\theta^* = \pi/4 - \omega/2$, the term $\alpha_{12}(\theta^*) = 0$. The remaining coefficients are called the *eigenvalues* of the matrix $\mathbf{B}$ and the special rotation matrix $\mathbf{R}(\theta^*)$ is called the *eigenvector* matrix.

Note that although there is only one eigenangle, there are two eigenvectors, and the two vectors are completely specified by the single eigenangle.

Eigenangles in Higher Dimensions

It turns out that the case $K = 2$ is special; for all other values there are exactly K eigenangles, K eigenvalues, and K eigenvectors.

To illustrate, for $K = 3$, suppose there is a surface of a quadratic function in $\mathbf{x} = (x_1, x_2, x_3)^T$ which can be rendered intelligible by rotating to new coordinate axes. Each rotation will generate a new set of coordinates, say, $\mathbf{x} \rightarrow \mathbf{w} \rightarrow \mathbf{v} \rightarrow \mathbf{u}$. It takes one rotation, say $\mathbf{R}_3(\theta_3)$ around the x_3 axis. The next rotation, $\mathbf{R}_2(\theta_2)$ about the w_2 makes the v_1 axis lie along one principal axis of the quadratic surface, and finally, a rotation $\mathbf{R}_1(\theta_1)$ about the v_1 axis brings the remaining two axes u_2 and u_3 into coincidence with the other two principal axes of the surface. Then, since $\mathbf{R}^T = \mathbf{R}^{-1}$, $\mathbf{u} = \mathbf{R}^T\mathbf{x}$, where $\mathbf{R} = \mathbf{R}_3\mathbf{R}_2\mathbf{R}_1$, is the compound rotation matrix. The special compound rotation matrix is the eigenvector matrix.

A physical situation corresponding to this can be imagined with an ellipsoid (say a football slightly flattened along its long axis to make it non-circular in cross-section) suspended at an oblique angle relative to a set of coordinate axes (East-West, North-South, and Up-Down). The first rotation, about the Up-Down axis, brings the East-West axis into alignment below the long axis of the football. The second rotation, about the (rotated) North-South axis, brings the East-West axis into coincidence with the long axis of the football. The final rotation, about the (rotated) East-West axis, brings the North-South axis and the Up-Down axis into coincidence with the axes of the flattened football.

The component rotation matrices are always in the form of the matrix (17) embedded in an appropriately dimensioned identity matrix. For the four-dimensional case with rotation about the x_2 axis from x_3 to x_4, for example

$$R_2 = \begin{bmatrix} 1 & 0 & 0 & 0 \\ 0 & 1 & 0 & 0 \\ 0 & 0 & \cos\theta_2 & -\sin\theta_2 \\ 0 & 0 & \sin\theta_2 & \cos\theta_2 \end{bmatrix} \quad (19)$$

Note that the eigenvector matrix is unique but the eigen*angles* are not because different rotation orders can be used. In fact, we never determine the actual eigenangles, we only determine the resultant eigenvector matrix **R**!

CANONICAL ANALYSIS

Having established that eigenanalysis can be interpreted meaningfully as a rotation from the original coordinate system to a new coordinate system in which the new coordinate axes are coincident with the principal of the quadratic surface, conceptually we can use the following steps to generate the canonical form of a general quadratic function

$$y(x) = \beta_0 + x^T\beta + x^T Bx. \quad (20)$$

1. Rotate to new axes using

$$u = R^T(\theta)x \quad (21)$$

to generate new linear coefficients

$$\alpha(\theta) = R(\theta)^T\beta \quad (22)$$

and new quadratic coefficients

$$A(\theta) = R^T(\theta)BR(\theta) \quad (23)$$

so that the quadratic in equation (20) transforms to

$$y(u) = \beta_0 + u^T\alpha(\theta) + u^T A(\theta)u. \quad (24)$$

Select *eigenangles* θ^* which eliminate the diagonal terms in **A**, and therefore the cross-terms $u_1u_2, \ldots$, in equation (24), to give

$$y(u) = \beta_0 + \alpha_1^* u_1 + \cdots + \alpha_k^* u_k + \alpha_{11}^* u_1^2 + \cdots + \alpha_{KK}^* u_K^2. \quad (25)$$

Note that in pratice, the eigenvalues and the eigenvector matrix are calculated directly, so we proceed immediately from equation (20) to equation (25).

2. Complete squares to eliminate the terms in $u_1, u_2, \ldots$, using

$$X_k = u_k + \Delta_k \quad (26)$$

where

$$\Delta_k = \frac{\alpha_k^*}{2\alpha_{kk}^*}. \quad (27)$$

This corresponds to a *translation* from the rotated coordinates **u** to the canonical coordinates

$$X = u + \Delta \quad (28)$$

and gives the canonical equation

$$y(X) = \alpha_0 + \alpha_{11}^* X_1^2 + \cdots + \alpha_{KK}^* X_K^2 \quad (29)$$

with the constant term adjusted for the translation,

$$\alpha_0 = \beta_0 - \frac{1}{4}\left[\left|\frac{\alpha_1^{*2}}{\alpha_{11}^*}\right| + \cdots + \left|\frac{\alpha_K^{*2}}{\alpha_{KK}^*}\right|\right]. \quad (30)$$

3. Interpet the canonical equation (29) in terms of the canonical factors **X**. (See, e.g., Box and Draper (1987) for excellent discussion and figures for cases $K = 2$ and $K = 3$.)

4. Translate the salient features of the canonical equation in terms of the original design factors **x** for use by the experimenter, using (21) and (28) to give

$$x = R(X - \Delta). \quad (31)$$

For the example, in equation (9),

$$y(x) = 6.0 + (x_1, x_2)\begin{pmatrix} 1.3 \\ -1.7 \end{pmatrix} + (x_1, x_2)\begin{bmatrix} 2.2 & 1.4 \\ 1.4 & 3.0 \end{bmatrix}\begin{pmatrix} x_1 \\ x_2 \end{pmatrix}$$

the steps are as follows:

1. Rotate to new axes using eigenangles (Eqn. 21):

$$u = R^T(\theta^*)x = \begin{bmatrix} 0.602 & -0.798 \\ 0.798 & 0.602 \end{bmatrix}x.$$

Generate the new linear coefficients (Eqn. 22):

$$\alpha^* = R^T(\theta^*)\beta = \begin{pmatrix} 2.140 \\ 0.014 \end{pmatrix}$$

and the new quadratic coefficients (Eqn. 23):

$$A^* = R^T(\theta^*)BR(\theta^*) = \begin{bmatrix} 4.056 & 0 \\ 0 & 1.144 \end{bmatrix}.$$

2. Determine the translation components (Eqn. 27):

$$\Delta = \begin{vmatrix} 2.140 / 2(4.056) \\ 0.014 / 2(1.144) \end{vmatrix} = \begin{pmatrix} 0.264 \\ 0.006 \end{pmatrix}.$$

3. Adjust the constant term (Eqn. 30):

$$\alpha_0 = 6.0 - \frac{1}{4}\left[\left(\frac{2.140^2}{4.056}\right) + \left(\frac{0.014^2}{1.144}\right)\right] = 5.72.$$

4. State the canonical equation (Eqn. 29):

$$y(X) = 5.72 + 4.06X_1^2 + 1.14X_2^2.$$

5. Interpret the canonical equation in terms of the canonical factors $\mathbf{X}$:

   The surface is a 'bowl' with a minimum of 5.7. The bowl rises about 4 times more steeply in the X_1 direction than in the X_2 direction.

6. Translate the salient features of the surface in terms of the design factors $\mathbf{x}$ (Eqn. 31):

   The minimum of the bowl occurs at $\mathbf{x} = -\mathbf{R}\Delta = (-0.154, -0.214)^T$, which is near the origin $\mathbf{x} = \mathbf{0}$ of the design factor space. The surface rises steeply along $-0.798x_1 + 0.602x_2 = -0.006$ and gradually along $0.602x_1 - 0.798x_2 = -0.264$.

DISCUSSION

The motivation behind eigenangles is to give a geometric interpretation to an algebraic result, and, therefore, to explain eigenvectors and eigenvalues. The *eigenvectors* are the combined rotation matrices which bring the original coordinate axes into coincidence with the 'canonical' axes of the quadratic portion of the response surface; the eigenvectors allow us to relate the canonical axis factors to the original design factors. The *eigenvalues* are the coefficients in the equation for the quadratic portion when expressed in terms of the 'canonical' axis factors; the eigenvalues describe the rate of deviation of the surface from its extreme in the most meaningful way, and so allow us to appreciate the behavior of a response surface in an informative and truly enlightening way.

ACKNOWLEDGMENTS

I would like to thank my colleague, Professor W. Woodside for helpful comments. Support for this research came from the Natural Sciences and Engineering Research Council of Canada.

REFERENCES

Box, G. E. P. and Draper, N. R. (1987). *Empirical Model Building and Response Surfaces.* John Wiley & Sons, New York, NY.

3.9
DESIGN OF EXPERIMENTS

————————————————— ■ —————————————————

PINCH ROLLER SYSTEM OPTIMIZATION: A COMPARISON BETWEEN TRADITIONAL DOE AND TAGUCHI METHODS*
by Jean Agostinelli and Daniel Hannon

A case study was done to attempt to optimize the pinch roller sub-system in a color printing system. The printing system designers wished to determine optimal parameter settings to minimize mis-registration. For this case study, a Taguchi analysis was compared to a more traditional design of experiments approach. Traditional experimental analysis and Taguchi methods were employed using the same raw data set.

The Taguchi experiment consisted of performing a static, Smaller-the-better analysis with an L27 array. Analysis of the mean values of a partial factorial experimental array was the technique used to perform the traditional analysis. In addition to comparing results, this paper includes time and cost comparisons between the two methods.

This paper covers both the Taguchi and traditional analysis and results, followed by a comparison of the two methods.

- *Company:*
  Eastman Kodak Company, Digital and
  Applied Imaging, ESPC
  Engineering Services
  901 Elmgrove Road
  Rochester, New York 14653-5817

- *Principal Author:*
  Jean Agostinelli, Manager, Electrical
  Design Engineering Center, Engineering
  Services

- *Co-author:*
  Dan Hannon

- *Objective:*
  The objective of the study was to perform parameter design of a color printer, pinch roller subsystem to minimize mis-registration between colors.

- *Description:*
  The Taguchi experiment was a static, Smaller-the-better experiment using an L27 array. There were three, three level control parameters, and two, two level control parameters. Interactions between all three of the three level factors. A traditional partial factorial experiment was performed, and the results compared.

- *Cost:*
  The most substantial cost associated with the experiment was the data gathering process. Time required to gather the data was estimated at one hour per experimental run. At a labor cost of $50 per hour, the Taguchi experiment "cost" $1350. The traditional partial factorial experiment "cost" $3000.

- *Time Expended:*
  As with cost, time expended was affected primarily by the number of experiments performed. The most time consuming part of the process was data gathering, which took approximately 27 hours for the Taguchi experiment, and 60 hours for the partial factorial analysis. In both cases, a few hours was required to perform data analysis.

- *Quality Improvement:* The purpose of this design was to do parameter design for a new product, therefore no good quality improvement data is available.

June 3, 1994

INTRODUCTION

An experiment was designed to study the pinch roller subsystem in a multipass printing system. The purpose of this experiment was to determine if new pinch roller materials and design modifications could improve registration performance when printing with faster line times and rewind speeds. Plans were in place to perform a traditional designed experiment to study this problem. It was decided to analyze the problem using both a traditional experimental approach, and Taguchi Methods.

TRADITIONAL EXPERIMENT

A traditional design of experiments approach was used to analyze the pinch roller sub-system design to determine optimal parameter settings which minimized mis-registration, and allowed for faster line times and rewind speeds.

Experimental Array and Data Acquisition

This experiment was performed using a research fixture designed for studying the pinch roller subsystem. In this experiment, a full factorial design was used for one 3 level factor, pinch roller pressure (pinch load), two 2 level factors (line time and rewind speed), and two 2 level factors with center point (pinch roller core diameter and pinch roller durometer). The technique of using two 2 level factors with a center point was used to save time and expense by reducing the number of experimental runs required. This is illustrated in Exhibit 1, Experimental Combinations of Core Diameter and Durometer. Run combinations between core diameter and durometer that were used are marked with an X. It was felt that enough was known about the interaction of these two factors that a full 3×3 factorial was not necessary to map the design space being investigated. The number of experimental runs required to gather data for this experiment was 60.

The experimental design was generated using a software program called DESRA. DESRA utilizes SAS code to generate the experimental design as well as conduct regression analysis and generate plots and graphs.

The response to be optimized in this example was mis-registration in a multi-pass print-

EXHIBIT 1.—EXPERIMENTAL COMBINATIONS OF CORE DIAMETER AND DUROMETER

| | | Core | | |
		0.59	0.656	0.716
Durometer	20	X		X
	50		X	
	80	X		X

ing system. To measure mis-registration, a line was printed on the paper by the printing system, and the line width was measured under a microscope. In this experiment, only one replicate of each treatment combination was run due to the excessive time required to measure each print. Each print was measured in both the horizontal and vertical (intrack and cross track) directions at each corner of the print (8 measurements per print total). These measurements were acquired using a microscope, and the value recorded was the difference between the theoretical line width and the actual line width measured. Perfect registration would show a registration response of 0.0″. The registration response modeled was an average of the corner measurements for each print.

Experimental Analysis

It was planned that analysis for each experimental run would be performed using each of the eight data points acquired from a test print. Very little signal was generated in the cross track (vertical) direction, therefore the data analyzed for this experiment was limited to the intrack (horizontal) registration data only. (Note that the average registration measured for the cross track direction was approximately 0.003″, and very little of the variability of the data could be accounted for in a model.)

Analysis of the data using DESRA and a General Linear Model Procedure in SAS indicated there were four factors that were highly significant for intrack registration. The model generated in DESRA was able to account for a large amount of the variability in the data. (R^2 = 0.82). Additional analysis of the data in SAS indicated whether there was statistically a significant difference in the mean registration values for each level of the factors at Alpha = 0.05 (95% confidence interval).

Durometer. The durometer of the pinch roller was the most significant factor affecting registration in this experiment (see Exhibit 2). Analysis indicated that the 80 durometer roller had a mean registration measurement of 0.023″ and was significantly worse than the 50 and 20 durometer measurements of 0.013″ and 0.014″. Statistically, the measurements with the durometer set to either 50 or 20 were the same, therefore either of these settings would be equally preferable over a setting of 80.

Pinch Load. The load applied to the pinch roller was the next most significant factor affecting registration in this experiment (see Exhibit 3). At pinch loads of 5 lbs., the mean registration was significantly worse (0.022″) than at pinch loads of 10 and 15 lbs. where the registration was statistically the same, with measurements of 0.015″ and 0.016″ respectively. A pinch load setting of either 10 lbs. or 15 lbs. minimized mis-registration.

Rewind Speed. Increasing the rewind speed of the fixture caused the registration measurement to increase (see Exhibit 4). At a fast rewind speed, the mean registration measured was 0.020″, while at the slower rewind speed, the mean registration measurement was significantly better at 0.015″.

Line Time. As the line time of the fixture increased, so did the registration measurement (see Exhibit 5). At a fast line time, the mean registration measured was 0.019″ while at the slower line time the mean registration measurement was significantly better at 0.015″.

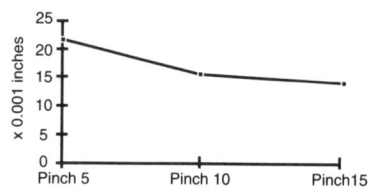

EXHIBIT 3.—EFFECT OF PINCH LOAD

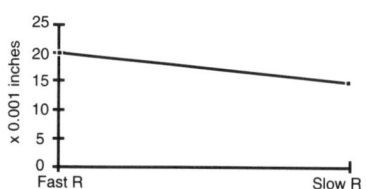

EXHIBIT 4.—EFFECT OF REWIND SPEED

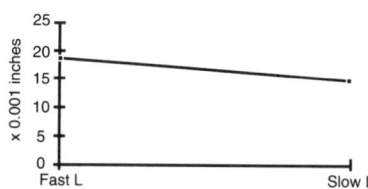

EXHIBIT 5.—EFFECT OF LINE TIME

Other Factors. Other factors such as core diameter, pinch load confounded with itself, durometer pinch load interaction, and durometer rewind speed interaction were statistically significant, however, the majority of the variability in the registration data could be accounted for with the first four terms.

Note that the average response of four registration measurements (one in each corner) for each print was modeled in this experiment. Further analysis could be done on all four of these measurements to determine how registration varies within a print.

Traditional Experimental Conclusions

Optimal settings based upon this experiment are a durometer of 20 or 50, a pinch load of 10 lbs. or 15 lbs., slow rewind speed, and slow

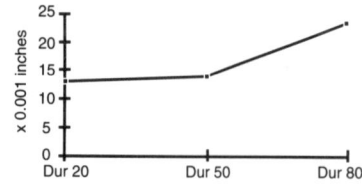

EXHIBIT 2.—EFFECT OF DUROMETER

line time. With respect to optimizing misregistration, the core diameter doesn't matter.

TAGUCHI EXPERIMENT

Taguchi Experimental Design

A static, smaller-the-better treatment was used for the Taguchi analysis. When employing Taguchi Methods to analyze this design, the measurement procedure was identical to that used for the traditional analysis. As with the traditional analysis, ideal (minimum) line width was subtracted from the raw data measurements, therefore the target value was 0.0″.

The control factors, identified during the design of the traditional experiment were durometer, core diameter, pinch pressure, line time and rewind speed. Durometer, core diameter, and pinch pressure were treated as 3 level parameters, and line time and rewind speed were treated as 2 level parameters. Note that for this experiment, core diameter and durometer were each treated as independent 3 level parameters, which was not the case with the traditional analysis.

Ideally, in order to effectively study the noise, multiple prints would need to be measured while varying donors, paper, and atmospheric conditions. Due to the cost and time limitations imposed upon the design team undertaking this analysis, it was decided that for each experiment, one print would be made. Both the horizontal and vertical line width was to be measured at four locations on each print, yielding 8 measurements per experiment. In order to maintain consistency with the traditional experiment, for each run, only the 4 intrack (horizontal) measurements were used.

The P diagram representative of the Taguchi experiment is shown in Exhibit 6.

Experimental Array. Two orthogonal arrays were considered for this experiment. Potential interactions were suspected between durometer, core diameter, and pinch pressure. This was taken into consideration when selecting the orthogonal array.

The smallest array that could accommodate all parameters is an L18. One interaction could be studied with this array, however the interaction that could be studied is between a 2 level parameter and a 3 level parameter. Since the three potentially interacting parameters were 3 level

P Diagram

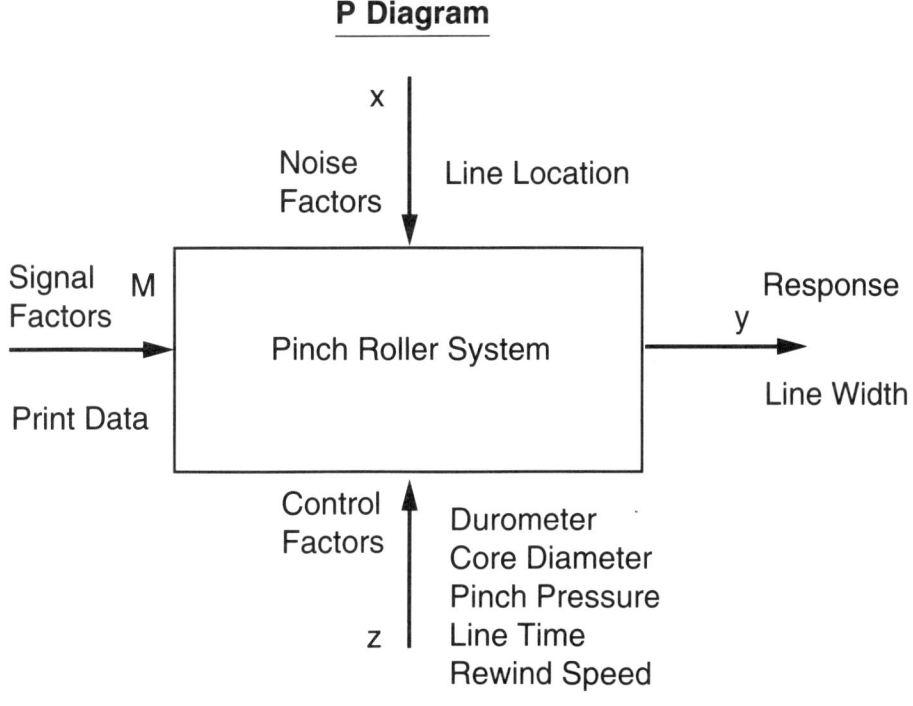

EXHIBIT 6.—P DIAGRAM

parameters, none of the potential interactions of interest could be examined.

An L27 (3^{13}) array was chosen to allow for the examination of all parameters of interest, plus the interactions between core diameter, durometer, and pinch load. The L27 array, reflecting the actual experimental design is shown in Exhibit 7. Note that the actual data collection process incorporated taking data on 72 total run combinations. Twelve provided data exclusively to fill the Taguchi array. The remaining 60 runs were required for the traditional analysis, 15 of which were also used for the Taguchi analysis.

Taguchi Experimental Results

SNR Evaluation.   The type of response for this case study was smaller-the-better. The SNR was calculated using the standard smaller-the-better SNR equation:

$$\text{SNR} = \theta = 10\log_{10}\frac{1}{n}\sum_{i=1}^{n}y_i^2$$

The SNR's for the different parameter levels of core diameter, durometer, pinch load, print time and rewind time were calculated and are plotted in Exhibit 8.

Interaction data was calculated, and evaluated prior to choosing optimal parameter levels. This is plotted in Exhibit 9.

Taguchi Experimental Conclusions. The Taguchi based conclusions were drawn by examining the graphs in the previous section entitled Taguchi SNR Plots, Exhibit 8, and Taguchi Interaction Plots, Exhibit 9. First the Parameter SNR Plots were examined, then the effects of the interactions were considered. Parameter significance was determined by examining the maximum excursion of the signal to noise ratio (SNR).

EXHIBIT 7.—L27 EXPERIMENTAL ARRAY

Param	1	2	3	4	5	6	7	8	9	10	11	12	13
Exp#	Roller Dia.	Roller Duro.	1×2	1×2	Pinch	1×5	1×5	2×5	Print Time	Rew. Time	2×5	E	E
1	0.59	20			5				fast	slow			
2	0.59	20			10				slow	fast			
3	0.59	20			15				slow	fast			
4	0.59	50			5				slow	fast			
5	0.59	50			10				slow	fast			
6	0.59	50			15				fast	slow			
7	0.59	80			5				slow	fast			
8	0.59	80			10				fast	slow			
9	0.59	80			15				slow	fast			
10	0.66	20			5				slow	fast			
11	0.66	20			10				slow	slow			
12	0.66	20			15				fast	fast			
13	0.66	50			5				slow	slow			
14	0.66	50			10				fast	fast			
15	0.66	50			15				slow	fast			
16	0.66	80			5				fast	fast			
17	0.66	80			10				slow	fast			
18	0.66	80			15				slow	slow			
19	0.72	20			5				slow	fast			
20	0.72	20			10				fast	fast			
21	0.72	20			15				slow	slow			
22	0.72	50			5				fast	fast			
23	0.72	50			10				slow	slow			
24	0.72	50			15				slow	fast			
25	0.72	80			5				slow	slow			
26	0.72	80			10				slow	fast			
27	0.72	80			15				fast	fast			

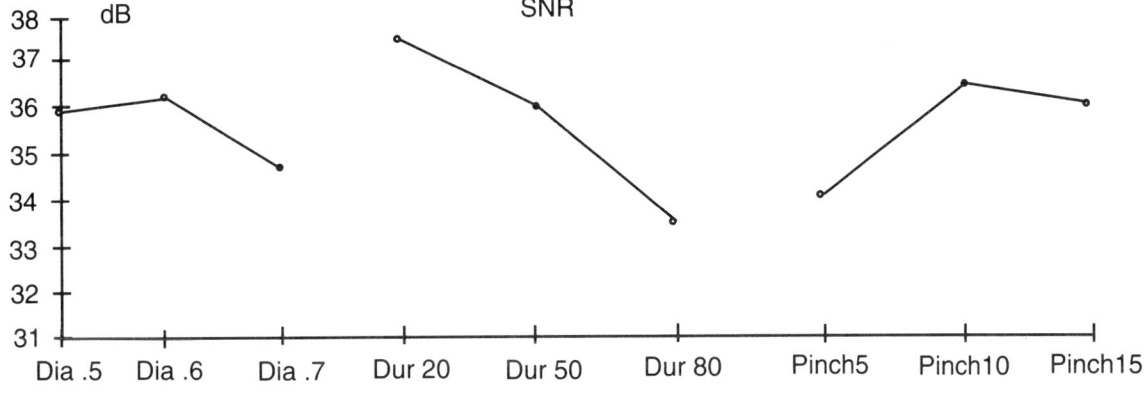

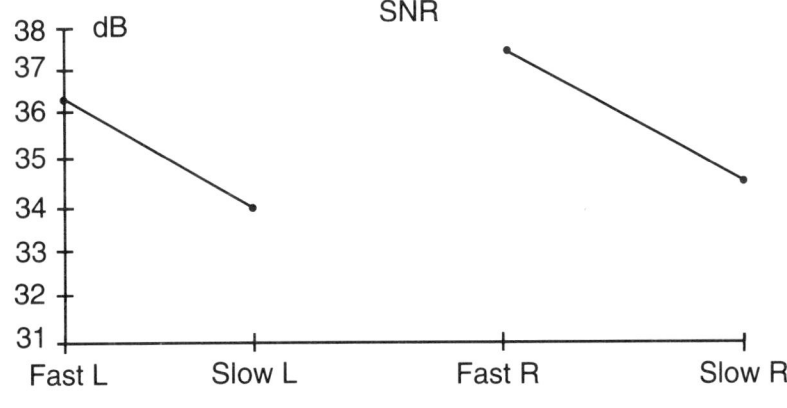

EXHIBIT 8.—TAGUCHI SNR PLOTS

Durometer. Durometer was the most significant factor, with a maximum variation in SNR of 3.74 dB. A durometer of 20 appears to be clearly preferable.

Rewind time. The maximum variation for rewind time was 2.78 dB, making rewind time the second most significant factor. The slower rewind time exhibited the better performance.

Line time. A slower line time was preferable. Line time, with a maximum variation of 2.20 dB was the third most significant factor.

Pinch load. The pinch load parameter exhibited maximum variation of 2.06 dB. Although a pinch load of 10 lbs. yielded a slightly higher SNR than a pinch load of 15 lbs., there was little variation between a pinch load of 5 lbs. and 10 lbs.

Core diameter. Core diameter with a maximum variation of 1.4 dB exhibited the minimum SNR variation. There was little difference between a core diameter of 0.590 and 0.656.

Based upon the Parameter SNR Plots in Exhibit 8, the optimal core diameter is 0.656, although not much improvement was seen over core diameter of 0.590. A durometer of 20 showed clearly better performance than a durometer of 50 or 80. A pinch pressure of 10 lbs. appears optimal, however the performance varies little from a pinch pressure of 15 lbs. Slow line speeds and rewind times were clearly preferable. The parameter SNR Plots indicated that optimal performance occurred with a core diameter of 0.590, durometer of 20, pinch pressure of 10 lbs., a slow line speed, and a slow rewind time.

Interactions. Exhibit 9, Taguchi Interaction Plots show the interactions between durometer and core diameter, pinch pressure and core diameter, and pinch pressure and durometer.

Durometer/diameter interaction. The durometer/diameter plot indicates a slight inter-

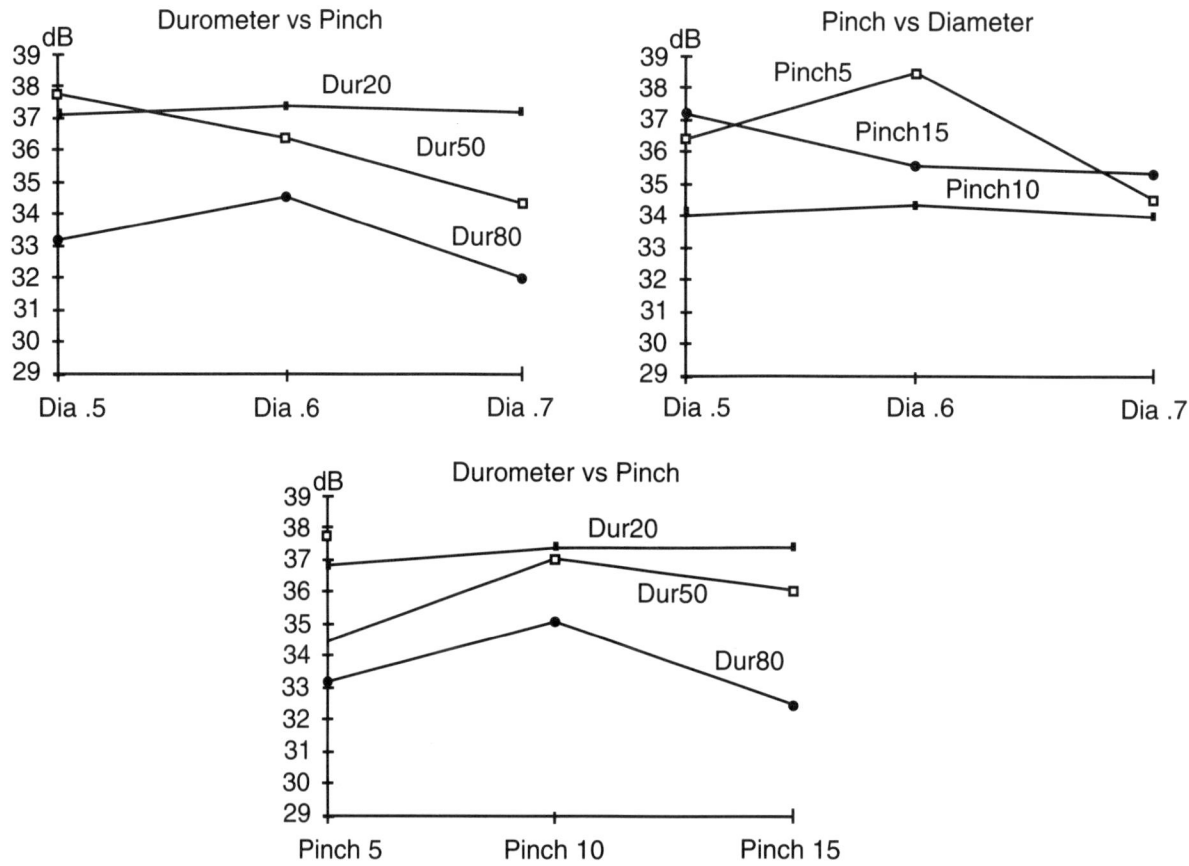

EXHIBIT 9.—TAGUCHI INTERACTION PLOTS

action. The combination of durometer of 20, and core diameter of 0.656 appears optimal according to the interaction plot. This agrees with the conclusions drawn from the SNR Plot of Exhibit 8.

Pinch Pressure/core diameter interaction. Pinch pressure and core diameter exhibit a small interaction according to Exhibit 9. According to this plot, the optimal combination of pinch pressure and diameter was a pinch pressure of 10 lbs., and a core diameter of 0.656. Based upon this information, selecting a pinch pressure of 10 lbs. and a core diameter of 0.656 would be preferable.

Durometer/pinch pressure interaction. Pinch pressure and durometer exhibit little interaction. The optimal choice based upon the parameter SNR plots of pinch pressure equal to 10 lbs., and a durometer of 20 do not differ significantly in SNR from the optimal choice according to this plot of a pinch pressure of 15 lbs. and durometer of 20.

The Taguchi based conclusions, considering both SNR and interactions are that optimal performance can be realized with a core diameter of 0.656, a durometer of 20, pinch pressure of 10 lbs., a slow line speed, and a slow rewind time. Note that these are the same conclusions drawn without examining interactions.

Confirmation Run. The optimal Taguchi settings of a core diameter of 0.656, durometer of 20, pinch pressure of 10 lbs., and slow line times and rewind speeds correspond with experiment #11 in the L27 Taguchi array. The SNR associated with experiment #11 was 41.82 dB, the maximum SNR observed for all 27 experiments. The average SNR, (SNRave) of all the runs was 35.475 dB. An improvement of 6.34 dB above the average was realized with this configuration. The predicted optimal SNR based upon the optimal settings listed above was calculated as follows:

$$snr_{opt} = \eta_{opt} = m + \sum_{n=1}^{N} (m_{n,opt} - m) = 41.20 dB.$$

The average SNR, and optimal predicted and measured SNR's are listed in Exhibit 10.

Both the predicted optimal and measured optimal SNR was approximately 6 dB above the average SNR.

SUMMARY AND CONCLUSIONS

A comparison of the experimental conclusions based upon traditional methods (DESRA) and Taguchi methods is shown in Exhibit 11. Exhibit 12 lists the parameters in order of significance according to both the traditional and Taguchi analysis.

Although there are minor differences in the conclusions, there is generally agreement between both the Taguchi and traditional analysis. Conclusions based upon using Taguchi Methods are also optimal settings according to the traditional analysis.

The factor significance varies slightly between the two methods. Both methods lead to the same conclusion about the most and least significant factors (durometer and core diameter). For the Taguchi analysis, the total variation in maximum SNR for rewind time, line time and pinch load is only 0.72 dB.

The traditional DESRA analysis provides additional data about the statistical significance of the conclusions, although ANOVA analysis could have been done on the Taguchi data to provide similar information.

The Taguchi analysis conclusions and traditional analysis conclusions are in agreement. In order to select one technique over the other, two major factors need to be considered: time required to perform the analysis, and the depth of understanding of the process or product that is required.

The time required to perform the data analysis for both the Taguchi and traditional analysis is comparable, and is insignificant compared to the time required for data gathering. For this experiment, the time required to gather the data was approximately one hour per experiment. Twenty-seven experiments were required to generate the Taguchi data, and 60 experiments were

EXHIBIT 10.—CONFIRMATION RUN SNR DATA

Average SNR	35.475 dB
Optimal Predicted SNR	41.20 dB
Optimal Measured SNR	41.82 dB

EXHIBIT 11.—TRADITIONAL AND TAGUCHI EXPERIMENTAL CONCLUSIONS

	Traditional	Taguchi
Line Speed	slow	slow
Rewind Time	slow	slow
Pinch Pressure	10 or 15	10
Core Diameter	Don't Care	0.656
Durometer	20 or 50	20

EXHIBIT 12.—PARAMETER SIGNIFICANCE (PARAMETERS ARE LISTED IN ORDER OF SIGNIFICANCE)

Traditional	Taguchi
Durometer	Durometer
Pinch Load	Rewind Time
Rewind Speed	Line Time
Line Time	Pinch Load
Core Diameter	Core Diameter

required to perform the traditional analysis. Expressed another way, the time required to gather the data for the Taguchi experiment was only 45% of the time required to gather data for the traditional experiment. Fewer materials were consumed for the Taguchi analysis, however the materials cost was insignificant compared with the time, and labor costs involved in generating data. If labor costs are assumed to be $50 per hour, the cost to generate the Taguchi data was $1,350. Based upon the same assumptions, the data gathering for a traditional analysis was $3,000. It should also be noted that it may have been possible to draw the same conclusions using an L18 array which would have cut the experimental cost and time even further.

In conclusion, if the desire is to perform a one-time optimization of a product or process, Taguchi methods provide a very time and cost efficient, easy-to-understand approach. If the goal is to understand a product or process that cannot be easily modeled, the additional information that could be gathered using more lengthy traditional design of experiments techniques may prove to be more valuable. For this experiment, Taguchi methods led to the same conclusions as the traditional experiment in less than half the time, for less than half the cost.

ACKNOWLEDGMENTS

Thanks to Daniel Maslanka and Robert Moore of Eastman Kodak Company for their assistance with these experiments.

———————————————————■———————————————————

CHALLENGING A TAGUCHI METHOD PARADIGM—REDUCING LENGTH OF STAY IN A HOSPITAL EMERGENCY ROOM*
by Kelly Eager, P.E., and Sandy Macfarlane

ABSTRACT

This paper describes what the authors believe is a new application of Taguchi Methods. This study challenges the paradigm that Taguchi Methods do not apply to a service or social science. We used a simple Taguchi approach to optimize the process of a hospital emergency room. Results show a reduction in average patient length of stay (LOS) of 25% without major capital investment for an expanded facility. Confirmation runs showed excellent repeatability. The ideal function demonstrated expected but non-exponential results. The greatest challenge was helping the team accept and implement the results, thus improving quality without larger staffs, facilities, and budgets. This study suggests that Taguchi Methods can be used to optimize processes outside the product development arena.

1. INTRODUCTION

We followed the classical Taguchi approach for a smaller-is-better analysis, following the case presented by Quinlan[1] to design the test program. We used analytical methods presented by Taguchi[2] to select the orthogonal array, complete the analysis, plan and complete the confirmation, and justify results.

2. THE EMERGENCY ROOM

This experiment tested the process of a hospital emergency room (ER). This ER provides medical treatment for urgent illness or injury of common to many serious conditions. This ER does not treat severe conditions such as severe head injuries, burns, and cardiac conditions, particularly for pediatric patients. These severe cases require stabilizing the patient and transferring them to a larger, regional hospital.

When a patient appears at the ER, a nurse rates the severity of their condition on a scale of 1 to 7, from routine to severe. The unit of measure for this scale is *acuity*. An acuity of 1 could be a routine suture removal while an acuity of 7 represents a severe life threatening condition. Guidelines used to establish a patient's acuity, typical to most Emergency Rooms, are provided in Exhibit 1.

At the onset of this study, ER staff supported a major ER expansion estimated to cost several million dollars. The American College for Emergency Physicians (ACEP) recommends one ER bed per 2000–3000 annual patient visits[3]. At 33,000 annual visits, this hospital *should* have at least 11 beds. This ER has 7 beds in 7 private examining rooms and 2 beds in the corridors for suture removal and other low acuity procedures.

Previous attempts to improve the quality of ER service included one-factor-at-a-time analysis. ER staff considered several different and independent steps of their process. These single studies did not consider the many related factors affecting any single important criteria or quality characteristic. While addressing important issues, the improvements were not approached in a systematic way.

3. THE QUALITY CHARACTERISTIC, LENGTH OF STAY (LOS)

The quality characteristic was time spent by a patient in the ER. We define this patient time or length of stay (LOS) as the difference, in minutes, between arrival and departure. In ER terms, this equates to time of an initial assessment of the patient's condition upon of arrival

EXHIBIT 1.—ACUITY DESCRIPTIONS

Acuity Level	Description & Typical Cases
1	**Minimal Patient Care:** Suture removal, blood pressure check, etc.
2	**Brief Patient Care:** Minimal assessment, prescription or over the counter drugs. Typically employee exams, flu shots, URI, rechecks of problems.
3	**Limited Patient Care:** Urgent problems with ancillary diagnostic tests. Typically small lacerations, infections, minor burns, hypertension, cardiac monitoring, foreign body removal, etc.
4	**Intermediate Patient Care:** Emergent problems that require rapid care to avoid further degradation of condition. Typically allergic reactions, foreign body removal from eyes, spine immobilization, hypertension with IV treatment, cardiac monitoring with chest pain, lacerations of face, chest, abdomen, some drug overdoses.
5	**Prolonged Patient Care:** Emergent problems of a complex or dangerous type that require continuous or repeated care. Typically sexual assault, emergency surgeries, multiple/large lacerations, overdoses, amputations, burns up to 40% of body, etc.
6	**Extensive Patient Care:** Highest level of care for emergent problems that could result in cardiac or respiratory arrest. Typically chest/head trauma, drug overdoses with unconsciousness, gunshot wounds, burns over 40% of body, shock, major fractures, etc.
7	**Life Saving Patient Care:** Patient will die without immediate care. Typically comatose patients, violent patients, "Code Blue" patients, deliveries, etc.

(also called *triage*) and discharge, before departure.

A cross functional team selected the quality characteristic from several problem categories. This team represented health care, administrative, and business functions. The team obtained the opinions of several customer groups including

- patients (patient relations coordinator)
- ER staff (nurses, doctors, and technicians)
- internal suppliers (registration, floor nurses, lab, X-ray, pharmacy, and respiratory therapy)

The team chose LOS from brainstorm and consensus building sessions. They identified 75 problems, some duplicating others, then grouped them into 8 major categories. The team developed 7 criteria by which to compare and rank the problem categories, then selected "ED Patient Flow" and LOS for its strong relationship with the criteria. Exhibit 2 demonstrates this comparison.

Length of stay drives ER volume and volume drives revenue. Regarding volume as a function of LOS, patients routinely decide where to receive treatment after asking ER staff how long is the wait. Some exit as quickly as they enter at the sight of a full to capacity waiting room. Regarding revenue as a function of volume, many hospital ERs are currently reimbursed on a volume basis so revenue is directly related to volume. Given the strong demand for ER services, particularly at certain, known, busy times, reducing LOS can increase volume and thus revenue.

4. DESCRIPTION OF THE PROCESS

The following list describes the ER process:

1. Triage (initial assessment) for acuity.
2. Hospital registration or call family physician if requested.
3. Wait for, then move to, an examining room.
4. Thorough assessment of patient condition, patient history.
5. Physician examination.
6. Order X-ray, lab work, and/or respiratory therapy.
7. Wait for analysis and results.
8. Determine cause and treatment (or order more studies).
9. Discharge or admission to in-patient care.

Prior to the study, ER staff were especially sensitive to patient wait time (steps 1–3), as a

Criteria	Strong (9) ◉ Moderate (3) ◯ Weak (1) △	Decreases Quality of Medical Care/Outcome	Delays Treatment	Decreases Customer Satisfaction	Decreases Staff Satisfaction	Decreases Efficiency	Inhibits Physician Support	Decreases Effectiveness Between Departments	Total
Problem									**Total**
Communication/Service		◯		◯		△	△	△	9
ED Space		◯	◉	◯	◉	◉	◯	△	37
Appearance				△	△				2
ED Patient Flow		◯	◉	◉	◉	◉	◯	◉	51
Mission/Other Services				△	◯		◯	◉	16
Staffing		◯	◉	◯	◉	◯	◯	◉	39
Forms			△		◉	◯	△	◉	23
Clinical Issues		◉		△	◯		◯		16

EXHIBIT 2.—PROBLEM AREAS VS. CRITERIA

fraction of LOS, during busy times. The entire process contributes to LOS, even after the patient is in an examining room. Focusing on wait time, ER physicians brought patients into the ER to wait so they would see the level of activity and appreciate the reason for their wait.

Other efforts included frequent calls to in-house services that typically delay ER treatment

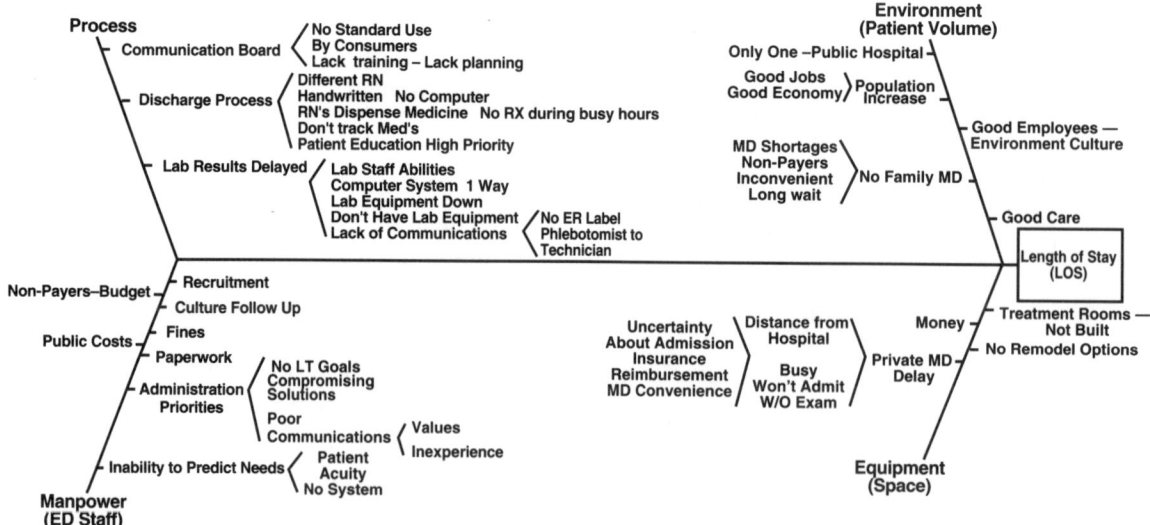

EXHIBIT 3.—CAUSE & EFFECT DIAGRAM

(steps 6–7). In hopes of reducing the delay, ER staff placed calls to the lab or X-ray technicians to increase visibility of ER work. Often, these calls had the opposite effect, reducing responsiveness of the auxiliary or ancillary services. Instead of performing an analysis, ancillary staff were answering the phone or duplicating work because several calls about one request were often thought to reflect several different requests.

5. USING CAUSE AND EFFECT ANALYSIS TO IDENTIFY CONTROL AND NOISE FACTORS

We used cause and effect diagrams to generate a list of potential test factors. Exhibit 3 is an abbreviated version of the actual C-E diagram.

We formed a second cross functional team to generate an independent C-E diagram. This redundancy reduced the chance of overlooking a factor that might contribute to the quality characteristic. The second team identified one factor that the other team overlooked. It was tested and ultimately ranked third in overall importance.

From the C-E diagram, the team chose the factors that most significantly influence LOS. These control factors are listed below, as they were tested. Level 1 reflects existing practice and Level 2 reflects the tested improvement. In a hospital setting, one cannot test a reduction in service or the failure of the system as you can in product applications. Exhibit 4 summarizes the control and noise factors and their two level settings.

• *Number of ED beds.* Based on the ACEP recommendation, we added 5 beds, for the duration of the experiment, set up temporarily in offices and other space adjacent to the ER. The total of 12 beds was tested against the existing number of 7 beds.

EXHIBIT 4.—CONTROL AND NOISE FACTORS

	Type	Experiment Factors	L 1	L 2	
Control Factors					
A	LIB	Number of ED beds	7	12	
B	LIB	Number of Nurses on Staff	Existing	+1	Each Shift (7am–7pm; 7pm–7am)
C	LIB	Number of Health Unit Coordinators on Staff	1	+1	Add 2nd position (10am–4pm; 4pm–10pm)
D	LIB	Number of Doctors on Staff	1	+1	Add 2nd MD (10am–10pm)
E	LIB	Pharmacy Hours of in-house coverage	Existing	Rx Open Added Hours (10pm–1am)	
F	LIB	ED Coordinator/Leader	None	Add Position	
G	NIB	Auto/Holding—No admit charge to Patient if discharged	None	Implement (Internist/Cardiologist, General Surgeon, Orthopedic Surgeon, and Family Physicians)	
H	LIB	Dedicated X-Ray services (Room and Technician)	None	Add dedicated position (10am–10pm)	
I	LIB	Number of Nurses dedicated to primary care	None	Dedicate 4–6 to P.C. (12:30–7:30pm)	
J	NIB	Dedicated Laboratory services (Phlebotomist and Technician)	None	Add two dedicated positions (10am–10pm)	
K	LIB	Private Triage Space	Existing	Change one room to private triage. (Convert office to exam room to maintain total number of beds)	
Noise Factors					
L	NIB	ED Staff and ancillary staff availability	Existing	Standby for "automatic" replacement should staff be absent for any reason Unable to Test	
M	SIB	Day of the week (volume of patients)	Sun–Mon	Tues–Sat Unable to Test	
N	SIB	Acuity		Tested	
O	NIB	ED Physician (Relative Differences)	Type A	Type B Unable to Test	

- *Number of nurses on staff.* Two positions were added, on 12-hour shifts, for one additional nurse, 24 hours/day. Matching the experiment time of 7am–7am, the additional nurses worked 7am–7pm and 7pm–7am.

- *Number of Health Unit Coordinators.* The Health Unit Coordinator (HUC) is also called a ward clerk in some hospitals. This person handles administrative functions that are too numerous to list. A second HUC was added from 10am–10pm.

- *Number of Doctors on Staff.* A second physician was added during the hours 10am–10pm.

- *Pharmacy hours of in-house coverage.* When the pharmacy closes at 10pm, all patients discharged after that hour must get medications from the discharging nurse. The nurse must go to the pharmacy and check-out the medication, adding time to ER process. The pharmacy hours were extended to 1am.

- *ED Coordinator / Leader.* Existing conditions allow for nurses to work independently on patients as appropriate with no one providing a coordinating role. We tested a new role for the senior staff nurse of coordinating the work of others without being directly involved in that work.

- *Auto / Hold.* Private and specialty physicians were asked to agree by phone with the ER-MD recommendation to admit or discharge a patient. If they did not, the ER physician could "hold" the patient on an inpatient floor, until the outside physician made his/her own examination and determined the patient's disposition. Existing practice is to keep the patient in the ER, tying up an ER bed for, sometimes, hours, waiting for the specialty physician.

- *Dedicated X-Ray services.* We tested the use of an X-Ray room and technician solely for the use of ER patients.

- *Number of Nurses dedicated to Primary Care.* Here we tested the practice of one nurse treating a patient from triage to discharge. Existing practice was to hand off between two or more nurses during one patient's visit. We were testing the impact of repeating certain steps of process due to that hand-off.

- *Dedicated Laboratory Services.* We tested the dedicated service of a laboratory technician who runs the sample for analysis and of a phlebotemist who draws the sample from the patient. This was tested against existing practice of serving all hospital inpatients and out-patients on a first come, first served basis.

- *Private Triage Space.* The lack of private triage, the existing condition, was tested against a dedicated examining room for private triage. The rationale was elimination of duplicated work because the initial triage was repeated when the patient was in the exam room.

A number of noise factors were present during testing. One was easily measured, patient acuity.

Other noise factors were difficult to measure or to test against. These noise factors could influence output but it was difficult to effectively measure their impact on results. The factors are listed and the actions we could take to reduce their effect are mentioned.

- *Efficiency / productivity of individual staff members, including physicians, nurses, and technicians.* The staff discussed this and understood its potential impact on results. They agreed to follow consistent practices on the experiment days.

- *Staff absenteeism and willingness to participate in the test program.* Staff volunteered to work extra hours for the experiment.

EXHIBIT 5.—ORTHOGONAL ARRAY AND TEST ARRANGEMENT

Exp No.	A 1	B 2	C 3	D 4	E 5	F 6	G 7	H 8	I 9	J 10	K 11	Day	Date	A Add'l Rooms	B Add'l RNs	C Add'l HUC	D Add'l MD	E Rx Hours	F ED Coord	G Auto Hold	H Dedicated X-Ray	I Rn Prim	J Dedicated Lab	K Private Triage	Exp No.
	ORTHOGONAL ARRAY																								
1	1	1	1	1	1	1	1	1	1	1	1	Sun.	3-Oct	No	No	No	No	No	No	No	No	No	No	No	1
2	1	1	1	1	1	2	2	2	2	2	2	Mon.	4-Oct	No	No	No	No	No	Yes	Yes	Yes	Yes	Yes	Yes	2
3	1	1	2	2	2	1	1	1	2	2	2	Sun.	10-Oct	No	No	Yes	Yes	Yes	No	No	No	Yes	Yes	Yes	3
4	1	2	1	2	2	1	2	2	1	1	2	Mon.	11-Oct	No	Yes	No	Yes	Yes	No	Yes	Yes	No	No	Yes	4
5	1	2	2	1	2	2	1	2	1	2	1	Sun.	17-Oct	No	Yes	Yes	No	Yes	Yes	No	Yes	No	Yes	No	5
6	1	2	2	2	1	2	2	1	2	1	1	Mon.	18-Oct	No	Yes	Yes	Yes	No	Yes	Yes	No	Yes	No	No	6
7	2	1	2	2	1	1	2	2	1	2	1	Sun.	24-Oct	Yes	No	Yes	Yes	No	No	Yes	Yes	No	Yes	No	7
8	2	1	2	1	2	2	2	1	1	1	2	Mon.	25-Oct	Yes	No	Yes	No	Yes	Yes	Yes	No	No	No	Yes	8
9	2	1	1	2	2	2	1	2	2	1	1	Sun.	31-Oct	Yes	No	No	Yes	Yes	Yes	No	Yes	Yes	No	No	9
10	2	2	2	2	1	1	1	2	2	1	2	Mon.	1-Nov	Yes	Yes	Yes	Yes	No	No	No	Yes	Yes	No	Yes	10
11	2	2	1	1	1	2	1	1	1	2	2	Sun.	7-Nov	Yes	Yes	No	No	No	Yes	No	No	No	Yes	Yes	11
12	2	2	1	1	2	1	2	1	2	2	1	Mon.	8-Nov	Yes	Yes	No	No	Yes	No	Yes	No	Yes	Yes	No	12

- *Patient load as a function of time.* All experiments were run on Sunday and Monday, historically and equally the busiest days of the week.

- *Acuity as a function of time.* Many high acuity patients received at once could greatly increase the wait time for low acuity patients.

6. ORTHOGONAL ARRAY AND TEST PROGRAM

We selected an $L_{12}(2^{11})$ orthogonal array for three primary reasons. It accommodated the most important control factors, its 12 tests were manageable and affordable, and it was resistant to interactions. Exhibit 5 demonstrates this array and test plan.

The twelve tests were run for twenty-four hours, 7 AM to 7 AM over twelve days of ER operation, Sunday and Monday for 6 consecutive weeks in October and November, 1993. Patient load ranged between 67 and 107 for the 12 tests with the full range of acuity, 1–7.

7. RESULTS

Exhibit 6 presents the results, showing signal to noise ratio, number of patients, average LOS, and standard deviation for the twelve tests. The large number of data points prevents presentation of all data in this format.

Exhibit 7 shows the factor ranking and recommended operating philosophy. The number of patient beds, Factor A, was not significant and

thus became an economic factor, discouraging capital expansion. The most significant control factor was number of physicians. We tested the difference between one doctor 24 hours/day (existing condition) and two doctors for the 12 hours, 10 AM–10 PM.

8. FURTHER ANALYSIS

More detailed analysis includes the same 4 parameters for acuities 1, 2, 3, 4, and 5–7, as shown on Exhibit 8. Factor importance varies with acuity for reasons provided in Exhibit 8.

We also completed an analysis of the ideal function. Our initial assumption was that average patient LOS would exponentially increase with acuity. This proved true for low acuity (1–4) but not for high (5–7). At higher acuities, average LOS decreased, relative to low acuity. Many factors accelerate discharge of high acuity patients. Among them are nurse to patient ratio of at least 4:1, increased responsiveness of specialty physicians, immediate discharge (to surgery, for example), or patient death.

These results suggest the greatest opportunity for improvement comes in the lower acuity category, 1–4. Exhibit 9 demonstrates average LOS as a function of acuity.

Patient load by acuity also supports improving process flow for low acuity business. Acuities 1–4, as a group, represent 85% of this facility's patient load. Only 15% of ER patients are in the high acuity range of 5–7 and thus true emergen-

EXHIBIT 6.—TEST RESULTS

Test Number	π (Count)	MSD (min²)	S/N Ratio (dB)	Mean (Minutes)	Standard Deviation (Minutes)
1	77	11418	−40.58	92	66
2	84	7046	−38.48	73	31
3	97	5449	−37.36	63	26
4	90	5993	−37.78	63	19
5	68	5352	−37.29	62	34
6	85	3872	−35.88	53	24
7	84	4348	−36.38	56	19
8	78	7543	−38.78	75	41
9	88	7731	−38.88	72	38
10	107	12753	−41.06	102	43
11	80	4830	−36.84	58	13
12	67	5259	−37.21	61	34

cies. The hospital ER has become a surrogate physician's office.

CONFIRMATION

We ran confirmation studies during mid–late January 1994. The team elected to complete four confirmation runs based on factor ranking.

1. Existing Conditions (Level 1 for all factors)
2. The top three factors at their optimum setting, the remaining factors at their existing (Level 1) conditions
3. The top four factors at their optimum setting, the remaining factors at their existing (Level 1) conditions
4. The top five factors at their optimum setting, the remaining factors at their existing (Level 1) conditions

Average patient LOS using existing conditions was 92 minutes, with a SIB S/N ratio of −40.58, while the confirmed LOS implementing the top three factors was 69 minutes and the S/N ratio was −38.37. This provides a 25% reduction in LOS from the top 3 factors alone. The predictive calculation for the first confirmation run is shown in Exhibit 10.

The predicted and actual results for the confirmation runs matched very closely. Exhibit 11 shows the average LOS and the standard deviation using initial settings and the confirmation results.

EXHIBIT 7.—RESULTS AND RECOMMENDATIONS

Factor Influence	Optimum Settings	Factor Weighting (S/N Δ)	Recommendation
STRONGEST Factors (Major Impact):			
1. Number of MDs	Add one M.D. (10AM–10PM)	1.71	Add one M.D. (10AM–10PM)
2. Dedicated Lab	Add Dedicated ER Lab Staff	1.56	Add Dedicated ER Lab Staff (10AM-10PM)
3. Auto Admit/Hold	Change to Auto Admit/Hold Procedure	1.25	Change to Auto Admit/Hold Procedure
Medium Factors (Little Impact):			
4. Number of RNs	Add Two Nurses	0.74	No Change consider change if results not repeatable
5. ED Coordinator	Add ED Coordinator/Leader	0.70	No Change consider change if results not repeatable
6. Private Triage	No Change	0.68	No Change
7. Dedicated XRAY	No Change	0.54	No Change
8. Number of HUC	Add One Health Unit Coordinator	0.50	No Change
Weak Factors (No Impact):			
9. RX Hours	Increase RX Hours	0.32	No Change
10. Number of Rooms	No Change	0.30	No Change
11. Number of RNs—Primary Care	No Change	0.21	No Change

*EXHIBIT 8.—*RESULTS ANALYZED BY ACUITY

| | S/N Based on Overall Analysis (Not by Acuity) | | S/N Calculated Using Individual Acuities | | | | | | | | | | | |
| | | | Acuity 1 | | Acuity 2 | | Acuity 3 | | Acuity 4 | | Acuity 5–7 | | |
Factor	Optimum	Bank	Optimum	Bank	Optimum	Bank	Optimum	Bank	Optimum	Bank	Optimum	Bank	Notes
Rooms	A1	10	A1	3	A1	11	A1	4	A1	7	A1	6	Always better to have fewer rooms. Poor arrangement? Spent more time per patient because so many different rooms?
# RNs	B2	4	B1	11	B2	6	B2	5	B2	2	B1	9	Generally better to add nurses, strong on Acuity 4
HUC	C2	8	C2	7	C2	10	C2	8	C2	4	C1	4	Generally weak, stronger at higher acuities
# MDs	D2	1	D1	5	D2	1	D2	1	D2	9	D2	3	Very Strong Factor—more MDs speed LOS—added MD slows flow at acuity 1
RX Hrs	E2	9	E1	6	E2	8	E2	6	E2	10	E2	7	Weak—lack of Rx support in two tests may impact results
ED Crd	F2	5	F2	4	F2	7	F1	10	F2	3	F2	8	Weak—Helps at acuities 1 & 4
Auto/H	G2	3	G2	8	G2	5	G2	3	G1	8	G2	1	Very Strong Factor, notably at higher acuities
Xray	H1	7	H1	10	H1	3	H1	9	H2	1	H2	2	Strong at higher acuities, otherwise no change is preferable
RN Prim	I1	11	I2	9	I1	9	I2	7	I1	5	I1	5	Weak—Better to use level 1
Lab	J2	2	J2	1	J2	2	J2	2	J2	11	J2	10	Strong—notably at lower acuities, lower LOS with dedicated lab
Trge.	K1	6	K1	2	K1	4	K2	11	K1	6	K1	11	Faster without private triage—physical arrangement likely slowed LOS
n	1000		43		313		495		111		38		
%	100%		4%		31%		50%		11%		4%		

10. IMPLEMENTATION

Implementation in some form (either formal or informal) is in place or soon will be for the top 6 factors. Implementation to date of these factors is described in order of priority.

A. Add a second ER Doctor, 10 AM–10 PM

The ER physicians have a contract with the hospital that specifies payment structure in exchange for their services. It does not encourage them to add another doctor, even temporarily, regardless of how long patients are waiting. While the experiment tested the addition of a doctor, the ER physicians agreed to add a Physician's Assistant (PA) for the hours tested, four days per week, Friday through Monday. While less qualified than an ER-MD, a PA can do more than an ER-RN, particularly at low acuities.

B. Add an ER dedicated lab technician, 10 AM–10 PM

Without adding a full time equivalent technician, the lab director rearranged his staff to meet the intent of recommendations from the study. Moving a day shift tech to the evening shift (2 PM to midnight) he provided 2 technicians, 7 days a week, during the busy times in the ER. On Saturday and Sunday, one of evening shift technicians work noon to 10 PM to ease the busy mid-day load. The day shift was back filled with a part time staff for the summer. The lab director is considering options to keep those day+ hours covered into the Fall.

C. Auto/Hold of Patients awaiting a private or specialty physician

The ER staff did not implement formal procedures to accelerate discharge of patients waiting for an outside physician. What has happened since the experiment is an informal implementation of the concept tested by level two of this factor. Two changes are taking place:

1. Outside physicians, aware of the experiment and its emphasis on their timeliness, are more responsive to ER physicians.

2. ER physicians are more aware of the ER process flow and, thus, the impact of patients who are simply awaiting another physician's arrival.

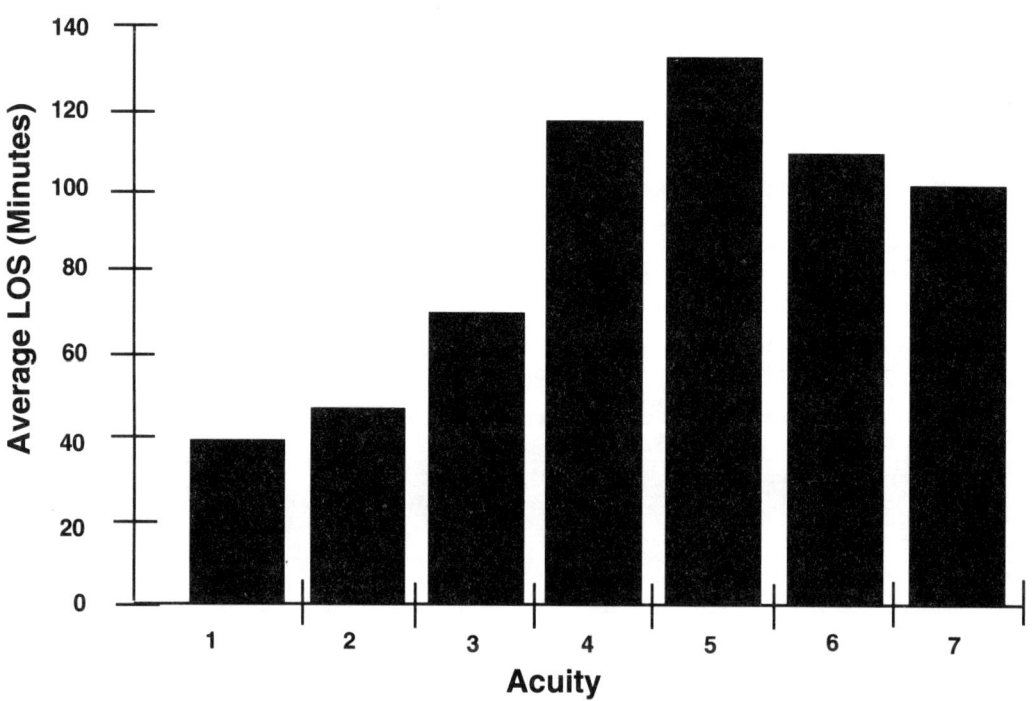

EXHIBIT 9.—AVERAGE ER LOS SORTED BY ACUITY

D. Add one nurse to both, 12-hour, day and night shifts

Following the same logic of the physicians adding a PA instead of an MD, the task force considered adding an LPN or EMT instead of an ER-RN. The nursing staff was not open to hir-

ing either, even though they would cost less to employ and are capable of handling most low acuity patient care. Staff concerns are too numerous to list completely. An abbreviated list of the primary concerns follows.

EXHIBIT 10.—PROJECTED S/N RATIO FOR CONFIRMATION TEST

Method:

• Use Average S/N from original array
• Calculate influence of changing three most influential variables

S/N for "Base Case" = –40.58

Average S/N for original array = –38.04

Most influential factors are D, J, and G (change each to setting #2)
  D2 = –37.19
  J2 = –37.26
  G2 = –37.42

Projected S/N for Confirmation Run:

  = –40.58 + (–37.19 – (–38.04)) + (–37.26 – (–38.04)) + (–37.42 – (–38.04))

  = –38.33

EXHIBIT 11.—CONFIRMATION RESULTS

Test #	π (Count)	MSD (Min²)	S/N Ratio (dB)	Mean (Minutes)	Standard Deviation (Minutes)
Original 1	77	11418	–40.58	92	66
2 (3 Factors)	83	6868	–38.37	69	41
3 (4 Factors)	86	7502	–38.75	73	35
4 (5 Factors)	80	5231	–37.19	60	20

Comparison to Projection (Signal to Noise Ratios –38.33 vs. –38.37):
• Projected/Actual = 0.9989
• Δ = 0.11% (1/1000)

Average LOS Improvement:
• 92 minutes vs. 69 minutes (23 minutes faster, 25% Time Improvement)
• 38% Reduction in Variability

1. RN responsible for LPN care due to liability and license concerns (RN licensure/credential issue)

2. Physicians may "overextend" the LPN

3. Trying to break apart the ER to save money

4. Downgrade the ER, lose jobs

The task force could not agree on the RN/LPN/EMT staff issue so a temporary solution was implemented. A part time nurse was added during the hours 3PM–3AM for the busiest four days of the week, Friday through Monday.

The long term position, taken by the hospital administrator, is to build a separate, stand alone, "urgent care" facility to compete with private enterprises in the low acuity patient business. Rather than use its own ER staff to run the facility, the hospital hired a health care management organization. The management group and ER staff are discussing options to share future, low acuity business and/or staff.

E. ER Coordinator

Training of the highest ranking ER-RNs is ongoing to improve their communication and supervision skills. The ER coordinator must remove themselves from the day-to-day treatment of patients and coordinate and direct the activity of all other ER and ancillary staff involved in treating ER patients.

F. Private Triage

While private triage did not reduce LOS measurably, it is an important factor for other reasons, namely confidentiality. Currently a patient must discuss their condition and the RN must examine the patient over a desk in plain view of the waiting room. Private triage provides a private space for the triage process.

With the staff's hope of a facility expansion deferred, at least for the short term, the ER team considered remodel options for private triage. Their work is complete and the private triage remodel is underway.

11. SUMMARY AND CONCLUSIONS

- The results were a surprise to everyone on the team. The biggest surprises were the first and last factors, number of ER physicians and number of ER beds, respectively. Initially, surprise was translated into disbe-

lief and resistance to change. Over time, however, change has occurred and results of those changes are being measured at the time of this writing.

- With the addition of an urgent care center to the hospital campus, these results may be used to design that facility's process. The similarity between the ER and urgent care center are the predominant low acuity patient load.

- Larger facility and staff are not always the answer. Results suggest that the guidelines provided by the American College of Emergency Physicians, for number of ER beds, are not directly applicable to all hospital ERs in all locations, and given all possible factors influencing ER efficiency.

- This hospital deferred a significant capital expansion. While number of patient beds is not an important factor now, increased capacity from reduced average LOS and increased volume may ultimately raise the importance ranking for number of patient beds.

- The hospital took a step toward influencing private physicians to consider their impact to the hospital's bottom line. And, internally, the ER staff increased their awareness of the impact of certain factors to total LOS, looking beyond the time a patient spends in the waiting room.

- An improvement to this study may be to redesign the existing process, generating a new concept of how to deliver emergency services, then optimize the newer, presumably better process.

- A recommendation to the hospital is to complete the final analysis of the implementation. Once the most important factors are fully implemented, a time study should be done to, again, verify the results and also demonstrate the increase in patient volume that should result from the reduced average LOS. Additional revenue, as a result, could also be estimated.

REFERENCES

1. Quinlan, J. 1985, "Product Improvement by Application of Taguchi Methods," *Transactions of the 1985 Taguchi Symposium.*

2. Taguchi, G. 1986, *Introduction to Quality Engineering*, Tokyo: Asia Productivity Organization.

3. Riggs, L. 1993, *Emergency Department Design,* Dallas, TX: American College of Emergency Physicians.

ACKNOWLEDGMENTS

The authors thank James Kowalick, Ph.D., P.E., of the Renaissance Leadership Institute for his guidance, advice, warnings, and willingness to answer questions. Completion of this study would have been difficult without his support.

3.10
INSPECTION

MEASUREMENT PUT TO THE TEST*
by Gail Stout

Beth Cone—a manufacturing engineer specializing in metrology at Caterpillar (Pontiac, IL)—believes strongly in GR&R. "When I buy automated gaging or gaging that pushes technology," she says, "I always do a study. GR&R also helps justify repairing or replacing gages. It's a great analysis tool."

Cone recommends using *Measurement Systems Analysis (MSA)*—a reference manual produced by Chrysler, GM, and Ford in collaboration with the Automotive Industry Action Group (Ann Arbor, MI) and the American Society for Quality Control (Milwaukee, WI)—as a GR&R guide. Although other books cover the topic, this one has wide acceptance from software suppliers, equipment vendors, and gage users alike. The US auto industry developed it to level the supplier playing field.

Quality engineers use the *MSA* manual to evaluate GR&R results so they can determine if a measurement device is acceptable for an application. Acceptance depends on a percentage of the part tolerance, or the manufacturing production process variability consumed by measurement system variation. If, for example, there is less than 10% error, the gage works well. If there is a 10–30% error, the gage may be acceptable based on the importance of the application, cost of repair, or gage price. More than 30% variation is unacceptable.

Cone explains how she uses GR&R to select a gage for a specific application: "I send the same five workpieces to several suppliers to run a GR&R—three operators running three measurements on five parts, totaling 45 runs—and compare results. For running the studies, I accept the vendor's technicians as operators. If a vendor can't bring its own equipment to a 10% level when measuring my parts, how can I? I don't worry about having three different operators for automatic gaging systems."

After a supplier's successful five-piece study qualifies a gage for consideration, Cone may decide to buy it. She uses a machine runoff, a full 10-piece study—three operators, three tests on 10 parts, totaling 90 runs—done on the supplier's floor as a final test.

"We send out a Manufacturing Quality Requirement," she notes, "a company form that in essence says, 'Here's a part print, the features we want, and the GR&R percent required for each feature.' If a measurement device makes the five-piece cut, it usually passes the 10-piece study as well."

Tom Remington, metrology lab manager at industrial distributor Machinery Systems Inc (Menomonee Falls, WI) handles many GR&Rs as a condition of sale. "Know what you're asking for" he advises. "It's easy to get caught up in definitions. A GR&R doesn't determine accuracy, but

*Reprinted with permission from *Quality,* Volume 33, No. 9, September 1994. Gail Stout is a senior editor with *Quality.*

it is involved. Accuracy is a quantitative measure of the degree of conformance to a recognized standard such as ANSI B89.1.12M-1990 for coordinate measuring machines."

Sometimes a GR&R will be more than 30% for a reason other than gage error. In a recent study done on a View Engineering (Simi Valley, CA) Voyager vision-based measurement system, correcting a fixture improved the result from a dismal 83% of tolerance to an acceptable 3.83%. As required by the study, parts were removed and replaced three times by three different operators. The feature of interest was a slot in the side of a cylindrical part. Attempts to measure the slot value varied greatly with each placement of the part. Finally, an operator determined that a slight rotation of the part caused a large variation in the measurement value. Redesigning the fixture to allow more precise part indexing with each placement reduced the variation.

REPEATABLE, REPRODUCIBLE

GR&R measures a gage's ability to produce the same result when sequentially sensing the same part under the same measuring conditions. And—here's the connection—if a gage is accurate, it should take readings consistently when performing under identical conditions. That's repeatability. Reproducibility is the ability to reproduce measured values on similarly manufactured parts by various operators under similar conditions.

"The user and gaging system supplier must agree on the GR&R criteria," notes Remington. "The user must make the supplier aware of accuracy, environmental specifications for the test, and have trained operators on hand to run the study.

Woodward Governor Co (Stevens Point, WI) uses the 3-3-10 rule—three operators, three measurements, 10 parts—for all its GR&R studies. "When buying new gages," says Richard Napper, SPC coordinator, "we might do a GR&R to see what their capabilities are, which is especially significant for big ticket items. We're evaluating buying a new CMM, for example, by doing a GR&R comparison on three candidate systems."

Woodward Governor makes fuel controls for the aircraft industry. Representative features of parts the CMM will check include linear positional tolerances, tight angles, and hole-to-hole

true position on large castings. The candidate CMMs have more accuracy than those in-house, and cost more, GR&R is important here because the company will base many manufacturing decisions on feedback the new CMM will provide.

"Metrology vendors check their CMMs in a perfect environment," says Napper. "We want a GR&R before and after installation. We will do an initial study in the vendor's quality lab, then on our shop floor," a systematic approach similar to what Cone does at Caterpillar. Such things as probe lobbing, ability to prove normal to the part surface, stylus length, continuous scanning requirements, or the need to change probes can affect the GR&R result for a CMM. And, as mentioned earlier, fixturing is important. A fixture should allow for precise indexing of the part with each placement, and clamps must not distort the part.

Napper routinely initiates many GR&R studies that cover the thousands of gages Woodward Governor already has on the shop floor. He can't study every OD micrometer in the factory, but a GR&R on one in excellent condition will give him a general idea of the capability to expect from that type of gage. This helps him understand which gages of that type are acceptable with what tolerances.

MOBIL GAGING

At Mobil Chemical Co (Canandaigua, NY) many measurements require custom gaging. The company makes polystyrene containers for fast food restaurants and clear OPS plastic containers for baked goods. GR&R improved product quality dramatically.

Torsten Rhode, Mobil's quality and productivity manager says, "Since 1990, we require a GR&R on every new gage." Gages are certified by the vendor, Quality Measurement Systems (Macedon, NY), and then Mobil repeats the GR&R at its plant. Generally, a GR&R under 10% is acceptable.

When Rhode helps design a new container, he conducts a fitness-for-use survey, talking to hundreds of users to determine what is important. For example, a customer might want to hear a click when the container top is closed. Depending on what the customer needs, Mobil and QMS design a gage. "Without a good GR&R," notes Rhode, "we have no assurance we can deliver what the customer wants.

"Before 1990, we were in trouble with our OPS container product line. We decided to reintroduce the line, designing containers using the fitness-for-use philosophy. We developed a test for each critical parameter that couldn't be designed in. The affect of GR&R was tremendous. We're a top quality supplier now."

A SWIPE AT QUALITY

Michael Colicci, manager of engineered products, Federal Products Co (Providence, RI), qualifies gage performance with GR&Rs and other statistical studies. "Many variables influence gaging results," he notes "We use the acronym SWIPE to recall them: Standard, Workpiece, Instrument, Personnel, and Environment."

- *Standard*: Even gage blocks certified by the National Institute of Standards and Technology have a level of uncertainty. Master rings or discs used in production are two or three steps removed from certified gage blocks, so every time the gage is compared, there is a degree of variability.

- *Workpiece*: "These vary," says Colicci, "which is why we want to measure them. Several are involved in a single GR&R study. If one of these measures are at an extreme of the tolerance range and the others are dead center, you've introduced a broad variation range. No part is perfectly round or flat. Unless each operator gages each part at the same location during every trial, GR&R will not isolate the variability."

- *Instrument*: The gage consists of several components, all of which contribute to uncertainty. According to Colicci, these include the sensitive contact and motion-transfer mechanism, the fixture, and the readout or indicator. Readout resolution and mechanism repeatability must be appropriately matched.

- *Personnel*: Variation comes with operator influence. Each user cleans and positions the part with a different degree of care and reads the indicator dial from a different angle with variable accuracy.

- *Environment*: This is extremely influential and often ignored. Temperature variations in the room, workpiece, gage, and master all influence measurement, as can dirt and vibration.

Caterpillar's Cone also follows SWIPE for eliminating variation. "We had a CMM that performed to manufacturer specifications, but at a 50% GR&R. The inspectors and skilled tradespeople got together and began eliminating sources of variation: dirt, vibration, and environmental conditions. Working down the SWIPE list, they eliminated the major measurement variation sources and eventually brought the GR&R to an acceptable 17%."

MORE RIGOROUS VIEW

Jim Maunder, an engineer at Motorola's (Austin, TX) manufacturing and engineering department, uses the Semiconductor Manufacturing Technology consortia's (SEMATECH) *Gage Capability and Designed Experiment* analysis of variance (ANOVA), basing his GR&Rs on this statistical method. His perspective is from the electronics world. Even though he is measuring skew and co-planarity of leads, Maunder still does GR&Rs to check how repeatable and reproducible measurements are on video microscopes. Even though the ANOVA method can estimate variances well and can extract more information than the widely accepted auto industry method, some similar issues pop up.

"Watch out for freaks—measurements that are way out of line," Maunder warns. "Find what the probable cause is and re-do the measurement. A piece of dirt can ruin a study. Also, be careful about what you use for the denominator when calculating a percent GR&R. And plan your experiment carefully. Use parts in the study that are representative rather than perfect."

PROBLEMS SURFACE

Not all measurement instruments respond well to GR&Rs. According to Roger Morton, senior vice president and general manager, Rank Taylor Hobson (Rolling Meadows, IL), GR&R seldom provides acceptable results when conducted on instruments designed to measure surface texture. "The first complication lies in the instrument," he says. "Instrument variables affecting measurement variation include accuracy, linearity, stability, and repeatability."

The accuracy of a surface texture measuring instrument can only be assessed by measuring a master standard with a valid traceable certificate of calibration and comparing the result with the value of the standard. For instruments designed to measure surface texture, you can conduct a simple check against a variety of commercially available master standards. Linearity can also be checked by progressive height changes measured from gage blocks or an accurately inclined straight surface.

Problems start with stability, which is significantly harder to determine. Instrument design (such as the materials used, instrument configuration, and the measurement loop length) affects stability. The environment affects the equipment.

"As with stability," adds Morton, "repeatability is often difficult to measure correctly and that's why most companies want GR&R testing. By the very nature of surfaces, though, results can be misleading by suggesting an instrument has poor repeatability when in actuality, adverse repeatability can be due to fixturing and part variations."

Parameters used in measurement can also adversely affect variability. Averaging parameters such as Ra (arithmetical mean of the absolute values of profile departures within the measuring length) and Rq (root-mean-square parameter corresponding to Ra) provide a measure of stability. These data are less susceptible to environmental conditions. They're averaged over the entire measurement length.

Parameters such as Rt (distance between the highest peak and its corresponding lowest valley within the measuring length), Rp (distance between the highest peak and the mean line within the measuring length), and Rv (distance between the lowest valley and the mean line within the measuring length) are very unstable because they measure one particular feature of the surface. Also, each of these parameters is susceptible to dirt and dust.

This principle also applies to filter selection. Eliminating shorter wave-lengths from the roughness data or analyzing the data over a small band-width provides a more stable result.

According to Morton, reducing operator variability relies on many factors. First, the operator must strictly adhere to the measurement procedure. Programmable software techniques can help here. Second, any variation in component location will affect the measurement result, thus affecting repeatability.

Accurate, repeatable metrology measurement requires stable, precise component set up.

Fixturing can overcome this to an extent, but factors such as differences in clamping load will produce variations in component distortion and hence potentially affect results.

Dirt, vibration, and temperature changes are especially troublesome when measuring surface texture. "Because operators conduct surface texture measurement at the micron level," says Morton, "measurements can be easily affected by dirt particles. If operators use parameters such as Rt, measurement results can vary substantially. This isn't instrument error, since the instrument measures the surface correctly. It simply sees dust and dirt as part of the surface.

"No matter how well damped the instrument is," he continues, "a stylus on the end of a pivoted beam will act as a vibration detector. Additionally, temperature changes in the work environment produce minor variations in the surface of the component, thus affecting the measured result. While the effects of temperature may be minimal on the micro-texture of a surface, large temperature variations affect the fixturing and the instrument."

The work surface represents the biggest variable. Problems with measuring surface texture, as distinct from dimension or other form measurement, lie in the fact that surface roughness is not uniform. It has many irregularities on a micro-level.

The only way to assess instrument variation separately from other factors is to measure the same component from the exact starting point, over the exact traverse length, using the same parameter and filter settings. Because the surface is always somewhat random, any starting point variation affects the result.

"This is where GR&R studies of surface measurement equipment fail," comments Morton. "It is nearly impossible to begin each traverse of the stylus at the same starting point (down to the submicron level)." Irregularities and randomness in surface texture will appear as variations in measurement.

Though running a GR&R on a precise surface texture measurement instrument is difficult, it is possible. Instead of repeating the traverse by starting and stopping at the same exact points, Dean Dawson, Rank Taylor Hobson product specialist, suggests determining a range within the measurement length sufficient to do the necessary filters and parameter calculations. "Designate a start and stop point within the data," he says. "If the measuring system has optical encoders on the traverse position, you can achieve repeating the start point of the data to about 0.1 μm, which is much better than physically positioning the start point of the stylus." See the sidebar "Surface Study Strategy."

BUILT-IN ASSISTANCE

New developments in data collection and software are relieving much of the tedium and cost associated with ongoing in-house GR&R studies. For instance, Quality Measurement Systems developed the Genesis 1000 series of data collectors available with GR&R built-in. An operator can collect data directly from the gage or key-in measurements. Taking data directly from the gage eliminates another possible source of error. Genesis 1000 has automatic gage-to-gage recognition and begins data collection without operator set up. The unit can read up to 32 gages simultaneously.

"We've been producing custom gages for 15 years," says David Rucinski, QMS vice president. "Early on we recognized the requirement to include performance criteria as part of custom gage proposals. Users needed to know what they could expect from the gage, and we needed protection from unrealistic expectations. Initially, we developed a PC program for GR&R; however, manually entering data introduced an error source. With the new data collectors, as the gage takes the reading, results get collected automatically."

Applied Statistics Inc (St Paul, MN) has GR&R as part of its Windows-based Applied Stats software. When the operator selects the gage capability module, the program will walk you through choices and tell you what to do. The software is based on the average and range method taken from the auto industry's *MSA* manual.

"In the early years it was a nightmare to do GR&Rs," recalls Peter Belsito, vice-president of engineering. "You wanted a simple, quick answer, but the majority of time was spent deciding how to get data in the right format so the software package could analyze it. Today it's easy."

Fischer Technology Inc (Windsor, CT), normally associated with coating thickness measurement equipment, offers a standalone GR&R software package as well. Its DeltaSoft/Gage R&R program is also based on auto industry requirements. Test data can be entered automatically using a serial connection to the gage studied. Data and calculations appear on screen, or as hard copy.

IQS (Cleveland, OH) recently made an early version of its GR&R Study/Calibration Management software available for free downloading from its electronic bulletin board. It offers a complete Windows graphical user interface, ability to do a GR&R study with a single operator, and automatic data input from measuring devices and customizable reports.

Gages degrade in performance, just like any other tool, so now many gage manufacturers are building in GR&R capability. A change in the GR&R value signals something has happened to the equipment and can tell you when to repair or replace a gage. This month, Ram Optical Instrumentation Inc (Huntington Beach, CA) introduced embedded GR&R in its three-axis, non-contact video measuring machines. Having GR&R in the gaging equipment's software makes self-test easier for users. Now operators can run a GR&R for every video measurement application.

THE EVALUATION OF A MEASUREMENT SYSTEM*
by Marilyn K. Hart, Ph.D., and Robert F. Hart, Ph.D.

The perceived variation of a manufacturing process includes both the true but unknown product variation and the variation (lack of repeatability) within the measurement system. When

*Reprinted with permission from The American Production and Inventory Control Society, *Production and Inventory Management Journal*, Fourth Quarter, 1994. Marilyn K. Hart, Ph.D., is a full professor and Robert F. Hart, Ph.D., is a distinguished visiting professor in the College of Business Administration, University of Wisconsin, Oshkosh.

a manufacturing process is "not capable" of meeting the specification tolerance limits, a measurement study is needed to determine whether the improvement efforts should be made on the *manufacturing* process or on the *measurement* process.

In this article, a second reason for a measurement system evaluation will be addressed: the need to *document* that its quality is satisfactory for the purpose intended. In the pursuit of a quality system within the ISO 9000 standards, it is required that the supplier "ensure that the inspection, measuring, and test equipment be capable of the accuracy and precision necessary." [1, p. 5]

It is the purpose of this article to present improved methods for evaluating the precision of a measurement system which have evolved through extensive applications by the authors but which have not yet been introduced into the literature. The foundation for the present work is in the Western Electric (now AT&T) handbook [6], Hart and Hart [3], and the Technicomp videotape series on measurement systems analysis [5]. The methods presented here are more thorough, yet simpler than those previously available.

In this article, the suggested procedures are illustrated using a case study from GageTalker Corporation in Bellevue, Washington, in which a voltmeter is used for the measurement of the output voltage for a digital gage interface device. The study was one of many studies made while preparing for ISO 9000 registration and is in accordance with the GageTalker Corporation Quality Assurance Manual:

> We control, calibrate and maintain our inspection, measuring and test equipment. . . in a manner which ensures that measurement uncertainty is known and is consistent with the required measurement capability.

PRELIMINARIES

An essential part of the evaluation of a measurement system is the verification that the measurement system is in a state of statistical control. Only then is the measurement system stable and predictable, and only then do the bias and the precision of the system have meaning. The precision of the measurement system refers to the spread of a set of replicate independent measurements made on the characteristic. Precision is often referred to as the repeatability of the measurement process.

The bias of a system is the average of independent repeated measurements minus the "true" value for that measurement. It may be difficult to establish the true value (called an accepted reference value, or ARV). The ARVs should come from a "higher authority," by using a better gage under more controlled conditions. Details of establishing an ARV and calculating bias are beyond the scope of this article and may be found in works such as that of Propst [4]. If the average of the measurements equals the ARV, the measurement system is said to be "unbiased." Following the American Society for Testing Materials (ASTM) [2], the word "accurate" should be avoided. It has multiple definitions which can lead to confusion. (For instance, in the ISO 9000 context, accurate is intended to mean unbiased. In other contexts, accurate may be used to mean precise and unbiased.)

To determine if the measurement system precision is suitable for the purpose intended, it must be realized that there may be two primary purposes for measuring the product:

• The simple acceptance (or rejection) of the product

• Improvement of the production process

The measurements in the case study were used for product acceptance, so only those criteria will be illustrated. The procedure used to verify that the measurement process is acceptable for improvement of the production process will be given without illustration.

CRITERIA FOR A GOOD MEASUREMENT SYSTEM

To evaluate the precision of a measurement system, three characteristics must be checked: the increment of measurement, statistical control, and the standard deviation of the measurement system (σ_m).

INCREMENT OF MEASUREMENT

The increment of measurement must be fine enough for the purpose intended. (This is to avoid the problem of measuring precision ball bearings with a yardstick.)

For product acceptance, it is suggested here that the measurement increment must be smaller than $\frac{1}{6}$ of the specification range. For the voltmeter application, the specification tolerance limits are 5.00 ± 0.25 volts. The increment of measurement is 0.001 volts, which is less than the maximum acceptable increment of .500/6 = .083 volts.

For process improvement, the increment of measurement must be smaller than the standard deviation of the combined variability of the manufacturing and measurement process, σ_c. The value of σ_c is often estimated by

$$\sigma_c = \overline{R}/d_2 \qquad (1)$$

using a conventional $\overline{X}$ and R chart that is in statistical control. The value $\overline{R}/d_2$ is typically thought of as the variability of the product, but really is the combined variability of both the manufactured product and the measurement system. σ_c may also be estimated by $\overline{MR}/d_2$ (from an X and MR chart), by the standard deviation of all of the X values, etc.

STATISTICAL CONTROL OF THE MEASUREMENT SYSTEM

It is essential for the measurement system to be in statistical control. Following the Western Electric [6] procedure, two *independent* measurements would be made by the same operator on each of 50 pieces of a product. The authors' experience has shown that 40 pieces are sufficient, and that is the number used here. The 80 observations in Table 1 are duplicate voltage measurements in volts from 40 pieces of product.

When the 80 measurements are complete, they are arrayed as 40 subgroups (pieces) of size two (duplicate measurements on each piece). The usual practice has been to make a Shewhart $\overline{X}$ and R chart on the 40 subgroups, but the authors' experience has shown that it is preferable to make only the R chart. The ranges reflect only the measurement variation and, if the R chart is in control, provide the needed estimate of the standard deviation of the measurement process, σ_M. The deletion of the $\overline{X}$ chart is a significant improvement since it is very difficult to interpret, and the information it provides can be found by the calculation of ME%, discussed later.

Before proceeding with the control chart analysis, the data must be checked for any evidence of within-subgroup patterns, i.e., the first observation of a pair must not be systematically higher (or lower) than the second. This step is essential but has not previously been identified in the literature. A simple way to accomplish this check is to circle or underline the higher of the two measurements in each of the 40 pairs.

Ignoring tied pairs, let A be the number of untied pairs and B be the number of pairs where the first reading is the higher of the two. The data set is then assumed to be free of within-subgroup patterns if B falls within the limits

EXHIBIT 1.—DATA FOR MEASUREMENT SYSTEM STUDY

Measurement						Piece Number					
		1	2	3	4	5	6	7	8	9	10
	1	4.961	4.964	4.970	4.966	5.963	4.967	4.965	4.967	4.963	4.963
	2	4.962	4.965	4.965	4.962	4.963	4.967	4.965	4.963	4.968	4.964
	R	0.001	0.001	0.005	0.00,1	0.000	0.000	0.000	0.004	0.005	0.001
		11	12	13	14	15	16	17	18	19	20
	1	4.965	4.966	4.968	4.969	4.966	4.967	4.968	4.968	4.962	4.966
	2	4.966	4.964	4.967	4.967	4.963	4.967	4.968	4.969	4.961	4.964
	R	0.001	0.002	0.001	0.002	0.003	0.000	0.000	0.001	0.001	0.002
		21	22	23	24	25	26	27	28	29	30
	1	4.964	4.962	4.967	4.966	4.963	4.965	4.968	4.965	4.962	4.961
	2	4.965	4.961	4.969	4.964	4.962	4.964	4.964	4.963	4.965	4.962
	R	0.001	0.001	0.002	0.002	0.001	0.001	0.004	0.002	0.003	0.001
		31	32	33	34	35	36	37	38	39	40
	1	4.962	4.968	4.967	4.962	4.964	4.959	4.963	4.963	4.964	4.969
	2	4.961	4.968	4.967	4.967	4.963	4.960	4.964	4.967	4.964	4.969
	R	0.001	0.000	0.000	0.005	0.001	0.001	0.001	0.004	0.000	0.000

$[.5A \pm \sqrt{A}]$. (See derivation in the Appendix.) In this example, A = 31 so the limits are [10, 21]. If B were to fall outside of these limits, one would assume that some "assignable cause" was responsible for the systematic variation.

In Exhibit 1, the higher value in each subgroup is underlined. Seventeen of the 31 unpaired first measurements are seen to be "high." Since the data are free from within-subgroup patterns, the R chart may be made.

The R chart for the 40 subgroups of size two is shown in Figure 1. Three-sigma control limits are calculated for the R chart in the usual way for n = 2:

$$UCL(R) = 3.27\overline{R} \qquad (2)$$

$$LCL(R) = 0 \qquad (3)$$

where $\overline{R}$ is the average of the ranges from all the subgroups. In this case, $\overline{R} = 0.001625$, so UCL(R) = 0.0053.

Because ranges are quite badly skewed to the right, occasional points above the three-sigma limits can be expected. With 40 subgroups the measurement system may be accepted as in statistical control unless three or more points on the range chart exceed the three-sigma limit. In Exhibit 2, no points on the range chart are above the three-sigma limit, so it is accepted that the measurement process is "in control."

PRECISION: STANDARD DEVIATION OF THE MEASUREMENT SYSTEM, σ_M

When the range chart exhibits statistical control, its precision may be quantified by the standard deviation of the measurement system, σ_M, which may be estimated by

$$\sigma_M = \overline{R}/d_2 = \overline{R}/1.13. \qquad (4)$$

In this case, $\sigma_M = 0.001625/1.13 = 0.00144$ volts. σ_M must be evaluated to see if it is small enough to give acceptable precision.

For the purpose at hand, product acceptance, $6\sigma_M$, must be less than 20% of the specification tolerance range [5]. In this case, $6\sigma_M$ is only 1.7% of the tolerance range. The measurement system precision is acceptable; it can satisfactorily discriminate between good and bad product.

If the measurements were being made for improvement of the production process, σ_M would be required to be small compared to σ_C. Defining ME% as the proportion of the combined variance (σ_C^2) attributable to the measurement process:

$$ME\% = 100\frac{\sigma_M^2}{\sigma_c^2}\% \qquad (5)$$

From experience in industry, it is suggested here that ME% be less than 25% for a satisfactorily precise measurement process. This requirement is more lenient than has previously been found in the literature, but has proven to be both adequate and realistic in a large number of applications. A mathematical discussion in the Appendix compares σ_C and σ_M.

OTHER STUDIES

The output voltage was only one of many studies done at GageTalker to comply with ISO 9000 system requirements. A measurement system includes the operator, the gage, the product being measured, the environment, and when in time the product is measured. The study of the measurement system for the diameters of steel cylinders showed evidence of lack of control from the R chart, indicating a need to improve the stability of that measurement system. An R chart used

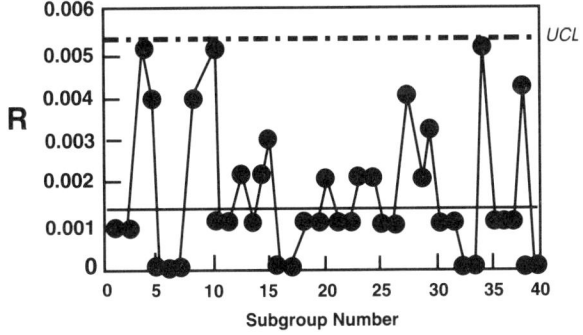

EXHIBIT 2.—R CHART

on an ongoing basis would help prevent such outages in the future. However, the measurement system for the cylinder length was quite satisfactory. Each measurement system must be evaluated separately.

LIMITATIONS

In reviewing this method, some limitations are evident:

1. Bias must be evaluated by appropriate calibration procedures; no evaluation of bias is included in this study.

2. There will be cases where it is not economically feasible to have 40 product samples available for duplicate measurements.

3. Product measurements may be destructive, in which case duplicate measurements would not be obtainable.

However, for most manufacturing processes, the procedure recommended here will be applicable, and for these processes this simple procedure for evaluation of the measurement process may be quite valuable. One final point needs to be emphasized. It is not enough to evaluate a measurement system at only one point in time because it may be anticipated that it will deteriorate with time. The above procedure makes it practical to evaluate independent duplicate observations on an ongoing basis. For example, once a week one piece of product could be independently measured twice and the range plotted on the R chart. This would provide a continuously updated evaluation of the measurement system at very little cost. In summary, a flowchart of the steps for evaluating measurement system precision is given in Exhibit 3.

CONCLUSION

Measurement processes must be checked on an ongoing basis for statistical control with satisfactory precision and bias. A check on the data for within-subgroup patterns and a simple range (R) control chart made on independent duplicate measurements on each of 40 pieces of product provides a simple, but effective method for evaluating the measurement process for control and precision. Repeat measurements made on an on-

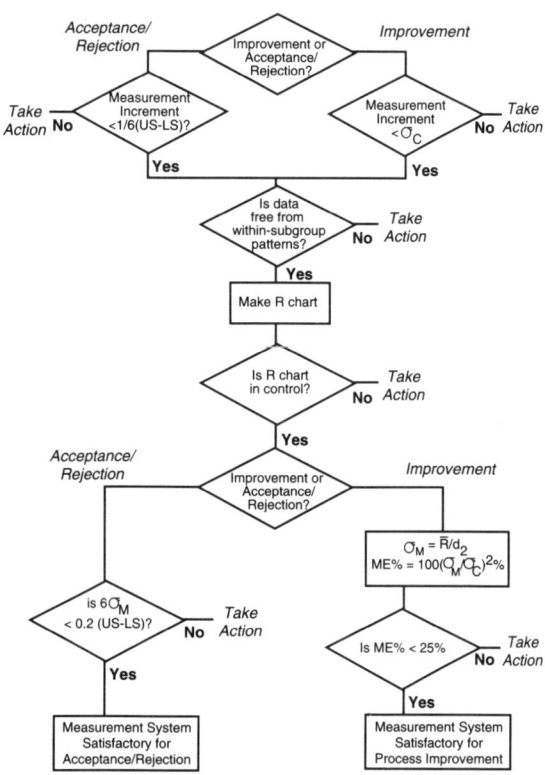

EXHIBIT 3.—FLOWCHART FOR EVALUATING MEASUREMENT SYSTEM PRECISION

going basis will then provide a continuous evaluation method. A separate evaluation of measurement bias is needed.

ACKNOWLEDGMENTS

The authors wish to thank Eric Berg, president; Thomas Coleman, technical support engineer; Richard Holm, vice-president; and Annie Twiss from GageTalker Corporation for the contribution of their measurement studies.

APPENDIX

Derivation of Limits

Let $\bar{p} = 0.5$ = the expected proportion of highs in the first set of readings and n = the number of pairs of observations without ties. The expected number of highs in the first set of readings is $n\bar{p} = 0.5n$. The 2σ np control limits are

EXHIBIT 4.—TWO KINDS OF R CHARTS

Conventional	Measurement Error
1 observation/piece	n observations/piece
n pieces/subgroup	1 piece/subgroup
k subgroups	k subgroups
for example, k = 25,	(k = 40, n = 2 in this
n = 4	paper)
If in control:	If in control:
$\overline{R}/d2 = \sigma c = \sigma$(combined)	$\overline{R}/d2 = (\sigma_M =$
	σ(measurement)

$$\overline{np} \pm 2\sigma_{np} = 0.5n \pm 2\sqrt{0.5n(1-0.5)} = 0.5n \pm \sqrt{n}$$

Mathematical Discussion

Note the differences between conventional R charts and measurement error R charts and between σ_c and σ_M. These differences are shown in Exhibit 4. Under conditions typically met in industry, the addition of variances will hold, i.e.,

$$\sigma_c{}^2 = \sigma_P{}^2 + \sigma_M{}^2 \qquad (7)$$

where σ_P is the standard deviation of pure product (with zero measurement error).

REFERENCES

1. American National Standards Institute. *Quality Systems-Model for Quality Assurance in Design/Development, Production, Installation, and Servicing,* ANSI/ASQC Q91-1987. Milwaukee, WI: American Society for Quality Control, 1987.
2. American Society for Testing Materials. *Standard Practice for Use of the Terms Precision and Bias in ASTM Test Methods,* ASTM E1 77-86. Philadelphia, PA: ASTM, 1986.
3. Hart, R. F., and M. Hart. "Is That Measurement Valid?" *Chemical Processing* (October 1988): 28-32.
4. Propst A. "Verification of a Shop Floor Measurement System." *Quality Engineering* 2, no. 1 (1989-1990): 1-12.
5. Technicomp. *Measurement Systems Analysis Series—Application Guide.* Technicomp, Inc., 1987.
6. Western Electric. *Statistical Quality Control Handbook.* Newark, NJ: Western Electric Company, Inc., 1956.

CALIBRATING ARTIFACTS*
By Leo O'Connor

Modern production standards and the demands for high quality and traceability have prompted private gear manufacturers to seek a calibration service more credible than that offered by private companies. As a result, gear engineers working in industry, government, and universities have formed the Gear Metrology Consortium to offer a calibration service that is traceable to the National Institute of Standards and Technology (NIST), in Gaithersburg, Md. The service, called the Deployment of a National Infrastructure for Gear Metrology program, will be administered by the American Society of Mechanical Engineers. Such a service has not been available in the United States for nearly a decade.

For gear manufacturers seeking ISO 9001 certification—and wanting to compete more effectively overseas—it is important that their products are traceable to NIST standards and the international standard of length. In many cases, it is gear customers, such as automotive manufacturers, who are asking for credible levels of gear calibration.

The first stage of the new initiative is expected to take effect this fall at the Y-12 nuclear weapons plant in Oak Ridge, Tenn. The plant, part of the Department of Energy-operated Oak Ridge Center for Manufacturing Technology, will begin a service to calibrate an involute master, or artifact, with a 4.5-inch-diameter base circle. Artifacts are gears or gear elements used to calibrate gear inspection equipment. An involute artifact has a profile of one side of an involute gear tooth.

Artifact calibration is available through private industry. But artifact makers, such as Fellows Corp., in Springfield, Vt., have had to calibrate by comparing their products with old artifacts calibrated by NIST. In 1986, NIST de-

*Reprinted with permission from *Mechanical Engineering* magazine, a publication of the American Society of Mechanical Engineers, Volume 117, Number 9, September 1995.

cided that its instruments were too old and unreliable to continue calibrating artifacts.

To develop the new service, NIST and Oak Ridge are working closely with Pennsylvania State University, in University Park, the American Gear Manufacturers Association, in Alexandria, Va., and ASME. The program is receiving funds from the Technology Reinvestment Plan (TRP), a federal program created to help transfer military technology and its infrastructure to civilian use. TRP is providing $3 million over a three-year period, which started in 1994, and the Gear Metrology Consortium is contributing $4.8 million in matching finds.

COMPLEX GEOMETRIES

The idea for a new gear calibration service took hold at a workshop sponsored by NIST in August 1992. To determine which areas of industry needed greater measurement support and services, NIST and Oak Ridge conducted a second workshop in March 1993 and asked gear manufacturers about the type of services they required, as well as the urgency of the services. After the workshop, the ASME Committee on Gear Metrology was formed for administering the gear calibration program.

Because of their complex geometries, gears are among the most difficult components to calibrate. The new calibration service will use gear-quality inspection methods and procedures and a statement of measurement uncertainty developed by NIST and Oak Ridge.

The gear calibration centers—Y-12 and NIST—will present progress reports to the gear industry at committee meetings held every few months. Engineers working in the gear industry will offer suggestions as to how the program might be improved or modified.

NIST identified the Y-12 nuclear weapons plant as the most suitable facility to conduct gear calibration services. The plant, managed by Lockheed Martin Energy Systems, is stocked with state-of-the-art measuring equipment previously used in building nuclear weapons. The plant has several microprocessor-controlled coordinate-measuring machines, including both Leitz and Moore machines, capable of submicron accuracy. Both machine types operate on QUINDOS software, produced by Leitz.

For its part, Penn State is conducting research into the new gear standards that need to be established. The university is also developing training courses to teach gear inspection methods.

To calibrate an involute artifact, engineers at the Y-12 plant mount it on a computerized coordinate-measuring machine with a three-dimensional analog probe head. The gear artifact is mounted on a ground shaft, and the assembly is then mounted on V-blocks fitted to the coordinate measuring machine.

The centerline of the shaft is established by probing the cones machined inside the ends of the shaft so that the shaft can be set up for manufacture. The coordinate measuring machine also probes the profiled surface of the involute, and engineers can then determine the amount of deviation from theoretical dimensions.

To verify the accuracy of the machine's measurements, engineers at Y-12 used a traditional method in which the artifact is calibrated on a three-axis manual coordinate-measuring machine with a rotating table. First, the machine probes a precision-ground ball that sits at the center of the table to verify that the table is set up accurately. The shaft and involute profile are mounted vertically on the table and secured in a fixture so that the shaft's center axis is perpendicular to the table. The involute profile is then probed while the table is rotated.

Measurements of the machine's linear motion are compared with measurements of its rotary motion. The machine's linear slides give a precise (within +10 microinches) measurement of length. The rotating table gives an accurate measurement of rotation (within one arc second). Gear industry engineers were impressed by the striking correlation between the measurements made by the traditional manual machine and the more advanced computerized machine, said Howard Harary, a physicist at NIST.

EXTENDING THE SERVICE

Within a year, Oak Ridge plans to extend the service to include the calibration of lead and pin masters used to calibrate inspection equipment for parallel-axis gears. Eventually, the Gear Metrology Consortium hopes to provide calibration services for master gears, which are used to inspect production gears. Manufacturers that supply gears to the automotive industry use gear inspection machines called roll checkers, on which a master gear is rotated in mesh with a production gear. The movements of the production gear are then monitored to determine its quality.

Oak Ridge engineers expect the involute artifact service will provide measurements of 127 points along the involute profile, using journals and centers as references. The service will likely provide a 2 sigma uncertainty of +/–40 micro-inches on the profile, so 95 out of 100 measurements will fall within the band of uncertainty. This compares favorably with the standards offered by British and German national laboratories.

With the new service, private companies now have available a high-level gear calibration service to check involute artifacts, said Bill Rasnick, a metrology engineer at Oak Ridge. "Part of our mission is to help companies improve their own calibration laboratories," Rasnick said. "The idea is to get the metrology infrastructure back in place so that the quality of gears and gear manufacturing processes will improve throughout the United States."

---■---

MORE POINTS MEAN BETTER INFORMATION IN MEASURING*
by Robin Yale Bergstrom

Russ Shelton, president, Electronic Measuring Devices, Inc. (Flanders, NJ), a manufacturer of metrology equipment, thinks that some companies are unintentionally, or unknowingly, taking an insufficient number of points when measuring workpieces to get a true understanding of what they have.

Shelton points out that tests he ran as long ago as 1988 indicate one needs a minimum of 100 to 200 data points per square inch to really know a surface. The tests involved half a dozen one-inch square pieces of aluminum, all with varying surface features (see box), from which were taken 2,500 to 2,700 data points of information per sample using analog technology.

The gist: "If you're willing to live with an uncertainty of 10% of surface form information," Shelton says, "you only need to take 200 data points per square inch. If you can live with 25% uncertainty, you need only 100 data points per square inch." Shelton maintains the fact is, however, today's general measurement practice is to take only 10-20 data points per square inch.

So "few" points, Shelton suggests, is probably fine when tolerances are on the order of, say, 0.003 to 0.004 in. But when tolerances are reduced to tie micron level (0.00001), such as in aerospace, medical and some automotive applications, for example, the need for more and more data is imperative to demonstrate part, component, surface, or feature integrity. And why is

this a problem? Because, Shelton suggests, any time a part, component, or surface undergoes a manufacturing process—grinding, milling, turning, heat treating, and such—accurate measurement becomes increasingly difficult.

"Nobody's going to take 200 data points per square inch on an engine block, for example," Shelton says. "There's got to be a better way. Our experiment simply points out that today's measurement processes and real-world physics don't allow things to be as simple as we'd like to think."

Shelton's solution, of course: More points.

THE EXPERIMENT

Philosophy and practice. Russ Shelton, president, Electronic Measuring Devices, Inc. explains:

"I once spent two days with a room full of really conscientious and knowledgeable people trying to define the meaning of a plane. It seemed that the real problem was simple—not enough data is being used to define the geometric elements which we all measure, and because of that, there is a lot of guesswork and uncertainty surrounding the calculations involving data. To prove or disprove this hypothesis, a colleague and I did the following experiment:

We made up six sample planes, each about one inch square. All were lapped aluminum.

---

*Reprinted with permission from *Production*, Volume 107, No. 9, September 1995.

One was flat; one was concave; one was convex; once was hit with a hammer to create a discontinuity; one was randomly gouged with a Dremel grinder; and the last was milled so that one corner was a bit lower than the rest of the surface.

Further, we created a mathematically "perfect" piece to be sure that the evaluation process we intended to use would actually work.

Each of the physical parts was scanned in a grid such that we ended up with about 2,500 evenly spaced data points per square inch.

The time required to collect the data from each piece was about 10 minutes, and after we finished we felt for all practical purposes we knew all there was to know about the surfaces of these pieces. Results. The results were these: depending on the specific sample, it took between 80 and 357 points (average—191) per square inch to achieve a 90% certainty of form, and between 48 and 227 points (average—102) per square inch to achieve a 75% certainty of form."

TAKING THE ZAP OUT OF ESD*
by John J. Kendrick

ESD destroys. "Electrostatic discharge through microscopic conductive paths in an electronic device causes a heat spike that will damage the gates or insulative parts of an electronic component," says Ed Weggeland, VP engineering, Richmond Technology Inc (Redlands, CA), a supplier specializing in devices for controlling ESD. "A large enough discharge will destroy the component, otherwise it might just wound it. This will produce a latent failure that usually isn't exposed by component or board testing. What will happen is mysterious field failure, which could be a critical problem."

A principle source of ESD in the factory is the human body—a capacitor with conductive leads, not always controlled, not always grounded. Electrostatic potential also can build up on automatic handling equipment, set-up jigs, and other tools. A printed circuit board (PCB) may be inductively charged by a nearby stationary field then discharged to ground causing damage.

"Growing use of surface-mount technology (SMT) in electronics manufacturing," says Weggeland, "increases vulnerability to EDS damage because there is less space on PCB sections where sensitive components are located. Reduced capacitance exacerbates the problem by allowing higher voltages for a given ESD energy pulse."

Failure threshold studies of electronic components show failure depends on such varied factors as whether the discharge is direct (resistive), capacitive, or inductive. The particulars of the ESD event, such as the rise time, duration, band frequency, energy content, and even polarity of the stray transient all have varying influence on ultimate product reliability.

STATIC-CONTROL STRATEGY

In his book, *ESD Program Management: A Realistic Approach to Continuous Measurable Improvement in Static Control*, G. Theodore Dangelmayer, senior engineer, AT&T Network Systems (Andover, MA) advocates integrating ESD program management into every aspect of electronics manufacturing—from product design to customer acceptance.

One reason ESD prevention is cost-effective is the requirements vary with device sensitivity. Older, less sensitive applications require minimum precautions at minimum cost. Requirements for ultrasensitive devices specify extensive precautions. Requirements are based on an area sensitivity classification system that lists five classes of sensitivity:

---

*Reprinted with permission from *Quality*, Volume 33, No. 9, September 1994. John J. Kendrick is a senior editor with *Quality*.

- Class 0 areas contain devices with ESD thresholds ranging from 0–199 v.
- Class I areas range from 200–499 v.
- Class II areas range from 500–1999 v.
- Class III areas range from 2000 v and up.
- Class IV areas do not contain devices sensitive to ESD damage.

Classify each area in an electronics manufacturing facility according to the most sensitive device handled in that area. Consequently, PCB assemblies are classified according to their most sensitive component. For example, a device with an ESD threshold of 100 v would be produced in a Class 0 area, and all other devices in that area would be handled by the same Class 0 requirements. A device with a minimum threshold of 10,000 v would be produced in a Class III environment. Operations that involve hardware only, where there are no ESD-sensitive components, such as backplane wiring or faceplate assembly, would take place in a Class IV area.

"Area of classification simplifies training and communications within a plant," notes Weggeland. "It allows engineering greater protection into the handling of sensitive devices without requiring employees to learn more complicated handling requirements." For instance, a Class III area does not require a dissipative work surface, whereas a Class II area does. Devices handled in the Class II area are better protected, yet employees in both areas use the work surface in the same manner.

It is the work surface that provides the added protection, and not a change in procedure. An employee can enter any area regardless of the sensitivity classification, use the facilities in that area, and know he is complying with proper procedures.

Class III precautions are basic: grounding employees, training, certifying the facility, properly transporting the product in carts, and packaging, which are minimum precautions. When a tote box is used in a Class I area, it must be static dissipative, whereas in a Class II area it is not.

Three basic rules apply to ESD control regardless of area classification: Assume all electronic (solid-state) components and assemblies are sensitive to ESD damage; never touch a sensitive component or assembly unless it is properly grounded; and never transport, store, or handle sensitive components or assemblies except in a static-safe environment. A static-safe environment involves controlling static charge generation, eliminating charges, wherever they exist, and having a common grounding philosophy. This is essential where all conductors in the workplace are grounded, including people, table mats, floor mats, tote trays, wrist straps, and heelstraps. Workers must always use grounded wrist straps or conductive footwear in conjunction with grounded conductive flooring.

DAMAGE CONTROL

According to industrial market researcher Frost & Sullivan (New York, NY), almost two-thirds of electronics manufacturing facilities responding to a recent survey plan to expand ESD programs. To control ESD damage potential, ground all conductors, eliminate all insulators, make all exposed surfaces antistatic, and install ionizers either at or above workstations or over work areas where known static problems exist such as when nongroundable conductors or insulative materials required for production are present.

You also must have competent packaging outside of the static control areas to protect against abrasion, dust, EMI, humidity, solvents, static build-up, as well as static discharges. Electronics packaging transparency is an important part of a static control strategy because it permits identification and inspection of a PC board without removing it from its protective wrap.

Use wrist straps, heel grounders, static dissipative work surfaces, and target area ionizers. Contain all ESD sensitive parts in certified ESD-safe packaging.

Rigid reusable containers are replacing disposable plastic bag and cardboard container combinations. Some bags use copper foil as a conductive layer. If grounding the worker as he moves around the facility is required, complete footwear can be mandated, but heel or toe guards serve the same purpose. Floor treatments—tile or carpet, conductive coatings, and wax—also are available.

To help document an ESD event, pinpointing where it occurred, you can attach a static detection device to a component to track it through production to final use. There steps will keep static potentials within the system near zero.

■

MAINSTREAMING NONDESTRUCTIVE TESTING*
by Gail Stout

Shrinking defense spending and airline industry restructuring is changing the thrust of nondestructive test applications from flaw detection to providing feedback for process control. Technology changes abound, adding user-friendly computerized functions in most equipment. Because of this, US implementation of nondestructive test technology will grow from $406.5 million in 1992 to $512 million in 1997, a 4% compound annual rate, projects industrial market researcher Frost & Sullivan (Mountain View, CA). Eddy current will grow the fastest, followed by ultrasonic, acoustic emission, and radioscopic methods.

According to the report, *The US Market for Non-Destructive Test Equipment*, artificial intelligence, especially expert systems, will enhance ultrasonic and acoustic emission technologies by easing decision making. Equipment is available in IBM-compatible formats using additional backplane plug-in boards rather than adding standalone equipment. James Nash, eddy current manager, MQS Inspection Inc (Elk Grove Village, IL), says using computers allows NDT inspectors to add more information to a database leading to an in-depth, representative look.

"NDT technology is changing rapidly," adds Don Commare, manager, analytical inspection services, Sonoscan (Bensenville, IL). "In the past, it focused on aerospace, military, and high-reliability industries. Now it's leaning more toward process control, crossing many industry segments. Manufacturers aren't looking for flaws as much as where manufacturing practices are not in tolerance."

SOUND INNOVATION

One example comes from the food packaging industry. To save on grocery refrigeration, especially in developing countries, manufacturers are producing shelf-stable prepared foods. The food industry retorts the package in a high-temperature environment to kill bacteria. A customer simply buys the shelved packaged dinner, keeps it in an unrefrigerated cupboard until needed, then microwave zaps it at mealtime. Seal or seam integrity of the package is critical to protect its contents from bacteria after retorting. Sonoscan is working with the FDA, using a C-mode scanning acoustic microscope (SAM) to verify seam integrity.

Another new application for C-SAM is examining the seals of small pouches used for disposable contact lenses. Foil coverings do not interfere since these are dense, acoustically transmissive (conductive) materials.

In space propulsion, replacing steel with silicon-nitride ceramic bearings in pumps and turbines presents an inspection challenge. Says Commare, "We designed an inspection technique in conjunction with Pratt & Whitney (West Palm Beach, FL) that uses our ultrasonic system to inspect hybrid roller bearings. The first scheduled flight with ceramic roller bearings inspected with ultrasonics will be in 1995."

Operators precisely machine the hybrid ceramic bearings, which don't require lubricants, withstand higher temperatures, and last longer. Ultrasonics tests for volumetric flaws (voids), subsurface flaws (anomalies), and surface flaws (cracks).

Acoustic microscopes use a 10-150 mHz transducer to pulse a focused ultrasonic beam into the sample at a point perpendicular to the specimen's surface. A reflection generates from a change in material properties and bounces back to the transducer. The reflection's image is captured in real time.

A new nondestructive imaging technique from Sonoscan, Virtual Cross-Sectioning, can tell a user when physical sectioning is needed and where to section, which promises to improve semiconductor manufacturing throughput. Virtual cross-sectioning is an outgrowth of acoustic microimaging that permits nondestructive cross-sectioning of light-opaque parts to reveal internal features in seconds. With it, an operator draws horizontal lines in the planar CRT image to define one to three vertical slices. Cross-

*Reprinted with permission from *Quality*, Volume 33, No. 11, November 1994. Gail Stout is a senior editor with *Quality*.

section views through these slices are them imaged automatically.

In other ultrasonic developments, Lockheed Fort Worth Co (Fort Worth, TX), LK Tool (Brighton, MI), and Wesdyne (Concord, CA) invented the LK UT90, an ultrasonic scanner for product inspection. Previously, collecting pulse-echo data (PE) on complex compound shapes of composite aircraft parts was impractical. It's easier now because the LK UT90 integrates ultrasonic data acquisition with coordinate measuring machine (CMM) technology.

The LK UT90 is a large, 10-axis twin-column, horizontal quill water-squirter machine. Its granite and air-bearing construction, together with carbon-fiber spindle, eliminates hysteresis and friction. This NDT innovation works well on large workpiece inspection unsuitable for immersion in the typical ultrasonic bath. It handles through-transmission scanning, independent or simultaneous PE scanning, or a combination of both.

The motion-control system dynamically matches each axis and uses scanning software that automatically learns part shapes and compensates for dimensional variations. The scanner works with CMM accuracy and has a linear speed up to 20 ips.

In a portable format, Panametrics' (Waltham, MA) Epoch III breaks all records for compactness in a digital ultrasonic flaw detector. The company makes Epoch III's splash-proof housing of impact resistant Lexan and seals the keypad to prevent contamination. Though rugged, it weighs only 2.6 lbs, light enough for holding and operating in one hand when using the remote battery pack. The unit has practical features for flaw detection and thickness measurements: standard echo-to-echo thickness measurement, standard rf waveform display, a distance amplitude correction curve option selectable in ASME and JIS formats, and minimum depth alarm. Its datalogger stores and retrieves up to 300 screen images or 3000 thickness readings.

Portable ultrasonic flaw detectors, such as the Epoch III, look for echoes from hidden internal cracks, voids, or other material variances. An ultrasonic pulse travels through a solid, homogeneous material such as a pressure vessel wall until it encounters a boundary such as another wall or a crack (ultrasonic waves don't travel through air). Though portable units are designed for large or remote inspection of aircraft, tubes, or tanks, ultrasonic flaw detection can be used for continuous on-line testing of cast, forged, or extruded parts—billets, pipes, bar stock, or rolls, for example.

PENETRATING ADVANCEMENTS

A new image system technology uses a focused beam of high-energy neutrons to see defects in engines under operating conditions. Unlike other imaging methods, such as x-ray, that see through objects, neutrons can penetrate metals but can't travel through hydrogen-containing materials. Thus, an operator can see water and lubricating oil going through an engine as it works, spotting otherwise undetectable defects. Researchers at Oxford Instruments (United Kingdom), Rolls-Royce, and Birmingham University in the English Midlands designed the neutron-based imaging system for use in the auto, aerospace, and materials industries.

Formerly, neutron analysis was impractical because the necessary high-energy neutrons were not available except from expensive sources such as nuclear reactors and cyclotrons. Oxford Instruments generates neutrons in a cyclotron using electromagnets made of a low-temperature superconductor rather than iron. Their high-tech cyclotron consumes 30 to 40 kw of power when producing neutrons, compared with 100 kw for a standard iron-magnet based cyclotron, thus making the technology feasible for production applications.

New equipment from CMI International (Elk Grove Village, IL) uses x-ray fluorescence to measure coating and plating thicknesses. Operators can measure costly materials, such as titanium-nitride deposited over steel, with the XRX deep-well system. It can measure coatings on parts as large as 12" × 12" × 6". The XRX has motorized table positioning, built-in SPC capability, and runs in a Windows software environment. The system can measure multilayers on any base.

David Wall, quality manager, Hohman Plating Co (Dayton, OH), uses the XRX x-ray system to check plated tin thickness on an aluminum automotive part. "It has a long focal distance that allows measuring into a recess," he says. "I first focus with a laser, calibrate, then run parts through, measuring coating thickness inside the hole or a well. The x-ray activates the part's electrons, creating back fluorescence that the instrument reads. Changes in energy varies with coating density. The system then calculates the coating thickness."

Before the XRX, Wall would cut the part four times to expose the inside well surface, then run the x-ray fluorescence analysis. The XRX saves time because it's programmable, measuring points on multiple parts and handling more than one part type with minor operator intervention.

In other x-ray advances, Smartscan from Scientific Measurement Systems (Austin, TX) operates in a digital radiographic mode (a less-expensive alternative to conventional x-ray film) in real-time radiography, and can include the additional capabilities of computed tomography (CT) and digital laminography. The system can be used for flaw detection, dimensional analysis, reverse engineering, and other nondestructive imaging applications. Smartscan inspects turbine blades, ceramics, sealed systems, and automotive casings for flaws.

An x-ray computed tomography image can be used to generate a computer aided design (CAD) model for rapid prototyping. If you have a part, but drawings aren't available, CT x-ray imaging can use the existing part to reduce, enlarge, or simply reproduce that object. Smartscan examines an object both internally and externally and projects it in stereo. Not only can you find a flaw, but you can reconstruct the entire part geometry.

Tosoh SMD Inc (Grove City, OH) is applying a new twist to NDT procedures for determining crystallographic orientation and grain size in sputtering targets used in semiconductor manufacturing. The company uses x-ray diffraction to verify crystal orientation and ultrasonic testing to determining grain size.

Crystal texture and target grain size improve thin film uniformity and can affect the electrical impedance of the plasma during sputter deposition. Tosoh integrated NDT into the manufacturing process to ensure every target is consistent, and crystal texture and grain size are optimized.

"In the past, grain size or crystal orientation had to be done destructively," says Steve

Bardus, manager, semiconductor planar systems at Tosoh. "By using a standard Caldata Systems (Newbury Park, CA) ultrasonic system, we created a calibration curve correlating ultrasonic echo intensity with grain-size results measured by destructive means. Now, we can determine grain size data directly from ultrasonic results. "To measure crystal orientation," he continues, "we used an x-ray diffractometer, an off-the-shelf product by Rigaku USA (Danvers, MA). We changed it so an entire target, not just a sample, would be accepted for examination. Now we can use these techniques on a production process and apply true SPC on product characteristics, rather than do destructive spot testing."

CURRENT THINKING

"Our MIZ-40 RFT (remote field technology) is a new development in eddy current," reports Fred Coffman, manufacturing manager, Zetec Inc (Issaquah, WA). "Standard eddy current doesn't work on ferrous materials; however, this new unit can inspect both ferrous and nonferrous materials for flaws such as cracks, corrosion, pitting, steam erosion, and vibrational wear." The MIZ-40 RFT is a microprocessor-based instrument with touch screen display, and uses ASME standards to analyze system sensitivity, phase spread, signal-to-noise ratio, signal repeatability, and flaw discrimination.

Doug Calender, general manager at Verner & James (Belleview, WA), travels to customer sites worldwide to handle eddy-current, ultrasonic, magnetic-particle, and liquid-penetrant inspections. He does remote field testing of ferrous materials such as petroleum refining tubes, so the portability of the MIZ-40 RFT is important. "It's a 69-lb piece of checked luggage on wheels that goes with me on the plane," says Calender. "We've done inspections in heat exchanger tubing and in the petrochemical industry. We can inspect ferrous materials using its wide frequency range, even in harsh environments."

THE COMPOSITE CHALLENGE*
by Jerry Wolak

Composite work materials are a unique inspection challenge. Delaminations, voids, and inclusions—faults difficult to detect using conventional optical and tactile inspection equipment—can't hide from new-generation nondestructive-based technologies. Ultrasonics, for example, provide a powerful way to nondestructively characterize parts made from fiber glass, graphite fiber-reinforced plastics, or carbon-carbon composites.

"The reflection, transmission, refraction, diffraction, interference, and scattering of ultrasound," says MC Bhardwaj, president, Ultran Laboratories (Boalsburg, PA), "provides surface and internal structure images; accurately detects discontinuities; and can help evaluate microstructure, density, porosity, and elastic and mechanical properties. Material composition and microstructure variations affect ultrasonic parameters—incident frequency, bandwidth, pulse shape and its size in time domain.

"While a 1 mHz frequency may be adequate for analyzing a 20 mm coarse-grained fused SiO_2, it is too small for interrogating a 1 mm dense SiC test object. The wavelength at 1 mHz is about 4.0 mm for fused SiO_2 and about 12 mm for dense SiC. Ultrasound frequency, pulse width, and other parameters must be matched to the response characteristics of the composite under test," notes Bhardwaj.

"While developing acoustic parameters for a composite work material," Bhardwaj continues, "you must consider its physical dimensions, particularly the thickness ultrasound must traverse and frequency-dependence of ultrasound attenuation."

Traditional ultrasound methods require coupling the instrument sensor to the test specimen by applying a thin layer of water, oil, grease, or glycerine between the transducer and target surface; however, when test materials are fragile, porous, or liquid-sensitive (superconductors, ceramic electrolytes, salt-based compositions, green materials, etc) liquid coupling is not desirable. The need for wet coupling is obviated by the development of dry coupling longitudinal and shear wave devices ranging in frequency from less than 100 kHz to more than 20 mHz. What makes dry coupling possible is the replacement of the conventional transducer impedance matching layers with a solid, compliant, acoustically transparent transitional layer in front of the active piezo-electric element.

A DIFFERENT SOUND

A general term for high-frequency ultrasonic inspection, acoustic microscopy comes in three distinct types: the scanning laser acoustic microscope (SLAM), the scanning acoustic microscope (SAM), and the C-mode scanning acoustic microscope (C-SAM). All use ultrasound to produce an image.

In a study that examined graphite/epoxy laminate composites, Stanford University and Sonoscan Inc (Bensenville, IL) asked how do these composites fail when subjected to an impact? Specifically, what is the quantitative relationship between impact energy and internal damage? Because of their complex structure, multilayer composites had previously been hard to study.

Samples of 15-layer hot-pressed quasi-isotropic graphite-epoxy laminate were clamped in a fixture and subjected to low-velocity ballistic impact. Respective impact energies of 8.36 and 13.25 joules were computed based on measured data in the tests. Horizontal fiber orientation of the layers was 0°, 90°, and 0°.

"Acoustic microscopy inspection detected changes in internal structure and internal defects," says Sonoscan's R&D director, Albert Wey, PhD. "In this instance, we used a reflection-mode acoustic microscope, which uses a scanning head to alternately beam ultrasound into the sample and receive the return echoes."

The researchers observed that when hit, the composite material began bending downward. Bending and accompanying stress were more pronounced in the lower part of the sample, away

*Reprinted with permission from *Quality*, Volume 33, No. 10, October 1994. Jerry Wolak is a managing editor with *Quality*.

from the impact. Stress was relieved two ways: by microcracking within each layer and by delamination between layers. Acoustic imaging showed the area of delamination between layers became larger and penetrated deeper into the sample. Delamination areas closely followed the areas of microcracking.

Delamination between layers was greatest when layers were at 90° to each other. Microcracking and delamination continued downward through the composite until all stress was relieved.

The ultrasonic inspection confirmed theories about how composites fail under load. It suggests the internal damage (measured as the total area of microcracking among the layers, 10.36 and 15.22 cm^2, respectively in this case) was proportional to the impact energy. If the impact energy is doubled, for example, the area of damage is doubled.

X-Ray Vision

Another technology used to inspect composites is radiography, which detects object features of varying thickness or density compared with surrounding material. Radiographs can be viewed in film or even in real time. Using film, high-resolution x-ray images are recorded and magnified for detailed study, but angular distortion can hamper accurate dimensional analysis of images.

Although x-ray systems can see internal faults such as voids and open joints, it is difficult to interpret these images. In real-time radiography, an image is magnified by having the object close to the x-ray source while magnifying the x-ray shadow.

In 3-D x-ray, the limitations of conventional systems are overcome by multiple-angle radiography and combining various reconstruction techniques. This technique provides 3-D information by moving the x-ray source and leaving the object and detectors stationary. Two images can be super-imposed by overlaying multiple images and reconstructing the shape with appropriate offset distances using a computer to create a tomograph. The technique, computer axial tomography, has out-of-focus features along the edges of the superimposed planes, causing data obscurity.

X-ray laminography creates cross-sectional images. A part for inspection is placed between the x-ray source and detector, moving in a synchronous parallel motion. The board remains stationary. An image of points is projected and appears stationary in the plane of interest while points outside are blurred. This yields a cross-sectional image that deals with a specific plane of interest. The plane is in focus while other planes are not. In operation, several planes are examined to build a 3-D database.

Reverse geometry x-ray, a technique developed by Digiray Corp (San Ramon, CA), uses a large raster scanning source placed adjacent to the test specimen. One or two small point detectors are placed at a distance to register primary radiation, and a computer processes the detector signal every microsecond to generate a display on a video screen. The system produces a high-resolution 1-million-pixel image with high-contrast sensitivity.

DISMANTLING THE QUALITY LAB*
by Robert Eade

There are a few grease stains on the once-pristine lab coats of quality professionals. Not because they're sloppy or careless, but because they're spending less time in the lab and more time on the production floor. As companies seek new ways to improve their products and cut costs, they are finding ways to make many functions traditionally found in the quality lab an actual part of the production process. Along with this shift comes a host of issues related to machine

*Reprinted with permission from *Quality*, Volume 34, No. 9, September 1995. Robert Eade is a freelance writer based in Waterbury, CT.

and instrumentation ruggedness and operator training.

"The line between the quality department and the manufacturing department is blurring," said Arthur Weller, manager of quality assurance for Giddings & Lewis, a machine tool builder in Fond du Lac, WI. "The thrust now is to get the quality function to the people who need it, the people who are making the product."

It's now a new idea. As far back as the early 1920s, Rockwell hardness testers were used to check bearing races as they were produced. Eddy current and magnetic particle inspection equipment have long been common on the shop floor. However, the movement is accelerating as companies realize the costs they incur by producing in one location and inspecting in another. The most significant cost is continuing to produce scrap until lab results become available.

Evolving process

Aris Melissaratos, vice president of science, technology and quality for Westinghouse Corp., Pittsburgh, sees this trend as part of the ongoing evolution of the manufacturing process. "First there was final inspection, which was after the fact, after non-quality parts had been produced. The next step is having the machine operator do the inspection, trying to catch errors as close to the point of manufacture as possible.

"The final phase is building a corrective capability right into the equipment and being able to detect a potential problem and correct it before it becomes a real problem. We're seeing that happening already in many places," he said.

"Technology is driving everything, and technology requires precision. Products are becoming smaller all the time. Miniaturization offers more performance in a smaller space, but the smaller the product, the more precise the manufacturing process has to be. It's important that metrology be built into the machine tool and other production equipment. For that reason, I think that quality and manufacturing will eventually become a single department," Melissaratos said.

Charles Carter, vice president of technology for the Association for Manufacturing Technology, McLean, VA, said, "The quality focus is changing. I see it disappearing in its classic form—with a cadre of inspectors roaming around the factory. In more and more companies the ma-

chine operators are taking over the quality function. You often hear that 'you don't inspect quality into a product, you build it in,' and that happens where the product is being produced.

"The two keys to success are hardening the metrology equipment for use in the manufacturing environment and making it user-friendly so that people can quickly learn to use it," he added.

Carter stressed that the quality lab won't disappear; it will merely change on purpose. "With machine operators assuming a greater role, calibration of metrology equipment becomes even more critical," he said. "This will be perhaps the prime responsibility of the lab, keeping the instruments in calibration and relating them back to some suitable metrology standard. The shop floor people can't be expected to handle that."

Quality task force

One company making the move from the lab to the floor is Cummins Engine Co., Inc. Columbus, IN. Said Jerry Wright, manufacturing technology advisor, "Manufacturing managers are becoming more aware of how metrology impacts on what they do. What we're seeing is something like a new task force being created with the barriers between the two departments coming down.

"We've got a Zeiss coordinate measuring machine on the floor and we're looking at adding more. We use a magnetic particle [system] to inspect forging quality and we use ultrasonic inspection in the piston manufacturing operation. The strategy is definitely to blend machining and inspection together, with no final inspection. I personally prefer to have the quality control equipment on the shop floor," said Wright.

Elektro-Physik USA, Arlington Heights, IL, sells a variety of surface testing instruments, including coating thickness testers and wall thickness gages. Asked how his customers are now using the equipment, Dennis Houseweart, sales manager, said, "The walls are coming down. More and more, our customers use our gages on-line. In some cases, they store the readings in memory and then download them to the lab, so the two areas still work hand in hand. ISO 9000 calls for inspection gages right in the production area. The key to doing this is to design the units to be portable and to be easy to use."

Houseweart feels that the driving force behind the movement to on-site inspection is the need to eliminate the continued production of bad parts. "Say you can take a few samples to the lab for testing and they're no good. While you're gone, defective parts are still being turned out. In the coating business, and in lots of other businesses, this can be very costly. If you're faced with a batch of defective coatings, once they have dried the only thing you can do is strip them down and start over again. That's why on-line inspection has become so important."

LAB STILL IMPORTANT

The current trend, according to Richard Whipple, executive vice president of Kingsbury Corp., a machinery manufacturer in Keene, NH, is to think of quality control as a two-pronged effort. "The first is inspection at the point of manufacture. Our machine operators are now responsible for the quality of what they produce. We no longer have final inspection.

"The second is to use the lab for authenticating quality, for checking critical or key characteristics. A part may only have one such characteristic but it's essential to the customer and has to be documented. We mark these characteristics with a circled "K" on the drawings and each one goes to the lab for inspection. So there are two sides to the quality issue, the shop floor and the lab," Whipple said.

Robert Christensen, vice president of quality and operations for Fischer Technology, Inc., Windsor, CT, a supplier of various measurement systems, said. "The quality lab is as important as it ever was. Even though management now wants inspection to be as close to the point of manufacture as possible, it also wants a record of the inspection results.

"Inspection instruments are becoming more portable and they have an increased storage and downloading capacity so that more testing can be done in the production area. Where that's not possible, we use the lab," he said.

Christensen added that many types of inspection instruments have become easier to operate, making their use on the shop floor more practical. "Simplicity of operation is essential. Our equipment is calibrated by part number. All the operator has to do is press a button. We have customer facilities where about 150 people all use a single instrument. A complex piece of equipment wouldn't work at all."

COLOR BY THE NUMBERS

By adopting portable instruments, manufacturers can improve their quality procedures and perform checks more efficiently. A prime example is production-floor color quality control. One wrought-iron furniture maker uses a portable spectrophotometer from BYK Gardner, Silver Spring, MD, to do on-the-spot checks during its seven-step furniture coating process. The portable unit correlates coating results after the seven-step process with the laboratory instrument used for original paint formulation. The aim is not only to arrive at the right final color, but to check that each coating layer is applied correctly.

A high volume of visual quality checks can also point out the need for portable instruments. "When you're doing 400 evaluations a week, as some of our customers are, you find that even trained people perform visual checks inconsistently," said Raymond Horn, product manager for BYK Gardner color products. "Our portable liquid-color instrument establishes consistency from operator to operator because the samples are viewed and illuminated the same way every time. The instruments are also repeatable and consistent from unit to unit."

BATTLING THE ELEMENTS

Rank Taylor Hobson, Rolling Meadows, IL, makes a variety of instruments for measuring roundness and surface finish. "Our equipment is used primarily in the lab," said Roger Morton, senior vice president and general manager, "but we're seeing increasing application on the shop floor. Our instruments resolve down to a millionth of an inch so impurities in the environment can present a real problem. We try to get around that by protecting the electronics and using self-cleaning mechanisms that clean the part before inspection. We also try to design customized systems that interface with specific workpieces."

Coordinate measuring machines, however, are a different matter. Chris Grow, marketing manager for CMM supplier Carl Zeiss, Minneapolis, MN, supports the need for "from the ground up" design of CMMs for the shop floor. "Among other parameters, the sensor technology must retain its sensitivity yet be rugged enough for a shop environment," he said. He added that scale design and selection of the right type of enclosure for the environment are also important.

Gregory D. Lee, national sales manager for Zeiss, added, "Where we might have used enclosures and air-conditioning a few years ago to protect our CMMs, now we're using advanced materials technology to try to limit the effect of fluctuating temperatures and environmental contamination."

SHOP FLOOR HAZARDS

David Genest, director of corporate communications for Brown & Sharpe, North Kingstown, RI, said that the CMM electronics also have to be modified for shop floor use. "They have to be isolated from noise, electric radiation, heat, moisture, humidity and other factors which can affect measurements. They also have to be protected from shock and vibration. The biggest threat is getting hit by something, like a shop vehicle. Some people go so far as to put Jersey barriers around the equipment," he said.

TRAINING OPERATORS

Moving metrology out onto the shop floor means that machine operators have to upgrade their skills. This seldom presents a problem. As Francis pointed out, "With electronic hand tools, there's a very small learning curve and the operators adapt to the equipment very quickly."

Weller said that major pieces of metrology equipment, such as CMMs, are regarded as another piece of equipment inserted into the production line. The people who use the CMMs are not expected to perform as professional quality technicians, but as machine operators controlling the quality of the work they produce.

"Machine operators are not inspectors," Weller lsaid. "We don't teach them every single nuance of the equipment. We teach them just what they need to know to do their jobs.

"The test results are all compuerized and downloaded, so that takes the human error out of the inspection. The key to success and operator satisfaction is keeping everything as simple and as automated as possible."

In general, the operators at Giddings & Lewis check only a few dimensions, with inspection instructions printed directly on the routings. More difficult readings, such as measuring for parallelism and the relationship between bores, are left to skilled, roaming quality personnel.

EQUIPMENT DESIGN THE KEY

Training machine operators to run shop-floor inspection devices will become even easier as the equipment becomes more sophisticated. "The expertise has to be in the gage," said Genest. "Operators have no time, and in many instances no desire, to learn the ins and outs of complicated instruments. In a shop environment, the operator interface with the equipment has to be simple and totally user-friendly, even though the equpment is very high-tech and powerful."

Lee says the software strategy at Zeiss is "to adapt equipment software to the needs and expectations of operators. Today's operators, who use several different pieces of computerized equipment on the shop floor, are used to a Windows screen and feel comfortable with it."

LOOKING AHEAD

In the near future, two contradictory forces will be operating in the field of quality assurance. On the one hand, the drive to bring more Q.A. functions to the point of production will accelerate, particularly as eqiupment that is currently labbound becomes shop-hardened and simpler to operate.

At the same time, the growing movement in industry towards micro-manufacturing will make the quality lab, with its trained technicians and ultra-high precision equipment, more important than ever. It's difficult to visualize microscopes and other delicate systems operating properly out on the shop floor, especially given the micro-tolerances that have become commonplace in many industries.

Will the quality department ever disappear entirely? Will it merge with manufacturing into a single entity as many have predicted? Genest doesn't think so.

"They might merge for a time," he said, "but it could be that in 10 years or so Q.A. could become a separate function again. Things have a tendency to come full circle. Years ago, Honda decided it would abolish titles and fancy offices. Everybody would be the same from the president on down. They promptly lost their competitive edge.

Now they have titles and offices and job descriptions again and are doing quite well.

"Today manufacturing is responsible for its own destiny as it relates to quality. But it's in the nature of people to get lazy. That means they'll eventually start producing more scrap and then somebody will say, 'We'd better start checking to see what's going on.' And that will mean the return of inspectors and of the quality department." said Genest.

Morton said that new developments will no doubt come rapidly over the next five years or so as the technology database deepens. However, he feels the quality lab will continue to occupy a position of importance.

"There will always be machines and processes developed where the need for absolute measurement accuracy is still required," he added. "Such measurements must be made in an environment where the many variables are kept as constant as possible. For this reason, laboratory instruments will never disappear."

■

THREAD GAGING UNRAVELED*
by John J. Kendrick

Several years ago, the US military found most of its threaded fasteners did not meet specification, triggering cries to tighten tolerances, change gaging methods, and cultivate best manufacturing methods. To this day, there is no single method to ensure screw threads are in spec. Fastener manufacturers, gagemakers, and governing agencies debate this controversy, citing poor metrology and misunderstanding of equipment performance and thread specifications as reasons for out-of-spec threads.

"Gaging threads can get complicated," says John Twining, chief metrologist, SPS Technologies Inc (Jenkintown, PA). "There are many options. Some thread gages are simple, only showing if a screw is over or undersized. Others are complex, capable of checking multiple variables. As requirements for fastener accuracy increase, so does the need for sophisticated gaging."

FULL MEASURE

Cutting a thread on a part introduces a major diameter, minor diameter, and pitch diameter, all of which must be measured. In addition to taper and out-of-roundness variations, you also must gage lead and flank angle, helical path, and root fillet if required by the application.

Thread gaging involves comparing thread dimensions with a calibrated standard. Some gages—ring and snap gages, for example—only give a feel for fit. Indicating gages show how much the screw varies in size from the standard master thread plug used to set the gage.

A screw thread has two sizes: The maximum material or functional size (requiring go/no-go checks for conformance to specifications) and minimum material or pitch diameter (PD) size. Both must be within the specified tolerance to ensure dimensional conformance.

Functional size—the measured value of the maximum material size of either internal or external scrw threads—includes variations in lead angle (including uniformity of helix), flank angle, taper, and roundness.

PD size is the diameter of the cylinder that passes through the thread profile of an internal or external screw thread to make the widths of the thread ridge and thread groove equal on both sides of the thread and parallel to the axis. It is used as the design reference for all mathematical calculations for tensile and shear strength

---

*Reprinted with permission from *Quality*, Volume 33, No. 9, September 1994. John J. Kendrick is a senior editor with *Quality*.

and fatigue. It also is the size control datum for manufacturing process control.

SPC ADVANTAGE

The evolution of acceptance standards and specifications, as well as rising customer expectations, are forcing a reassessment of fastener quality, resulting in the growing acceptance of statistical process control (SPC). There is nothing on the horizon that offers as many long-term competitive advantages while improving both efficiency and accountability. "Despite considerable effort and well-documented successes, the full potential of SPC as a competitive weapon has yet to be realized," says Stanley Johnson, president, Johnson Gage Co (Bloomfield, CT). "Too often, using statistical techniques to improve a process is a Band-Aid, a short-term commitment to satisfy a temporary problem. Few use it as a way to radically improve manufacturing."

"Modern indicating gages made SPC a reality," adds Ralph Veale, National Institute of Science and Technology (Gaithersburg, MD). NIST investigated the efficacy of indicating gages used to measure the PD and functional size of threaded fasteners. Three external systems and four internal systems, representing four manufacturers, were used in the test, and 27 external and 11 internal threads were measured. Some of the samples were purposely produced with form errors near and beyond product tolerances.

All the indicating gages gave consistent readings for PD, except when the form of the test specimens deviated significantly from nominal. In general, the greater the deviation, the greater the error in the indicator reading. When form errors were outside product tolerances, test data also showed that instruments from different manufacturers gave different results and didn't always match the values obtained by alternate methods.

GAGING CHOICES

Thread gaging systems are differentiated by the inspection systems necessary to achieve required dimensional conformance. They are Systems 21, 22, and 23 per Federal Standard H28/20A (see sidebar).

Fixed-limit (go-no go, System 21) thread gages are inexpensive and easy to use, but wear quickly. They cannot determine dimensional conformance at the minimum material size; however, they do provide a check for assembly. "These gages must be used with devices or gages for measuring minimum material to determine dimensional conformance beyond just assembly," says Bruce Dupont, thread gaging specialist, The LS Starrett Co (Athol, MA).

Several design contact types are used to measure minimum material. "Per ANSI/ASME B1.3M," notes Dupont, "cone & vee design measures the actual pitch diameter. Other designs, such as thread measuring wires, cone, radius, and B & C Not Go are used to measure thread groove and boundary thread flank, respectively.

"Specifically," he continues, "cone & vee is the best design for measuring pitch diameter of product screw threads. Thread measuring wires are typically used to measure and calibrate thread gage masters where variations in thread form are minimal. Because wires rest in the grooves of thread flanks, the groove diameter is averaged over more than one pitch. This is unlike a cone & vee arrangement, which makes no contact on adjacent thread flanks and contacts over the pitch of a thread."

According to Dupont, disputes arise when using different gage contact designs. The discrepancies between these various designs cause incompatible measurements such as geometric differences of gage contact, design, or measurement uncertainty.

"Pitch micrometers are generally used for measuring minimum material size," says Dupont, "but do not provide any protection at the assembly maximum material size. ANSI/ASME B1.3M recommends modifying pitch micrometer contacts to approximate a cone & vee arrangement to measure diameter."

Thread comparators when set up for both assembly size (functional size) and pitch diameter can provide an easy, accurate way to determine complete dimensional conformance, as well as actual size data for SPC and differential gaging analysis. This variables/indicating (System 22) gaging eliminates operator feel and subjectivity.

Depending on the manufacturing process, several comparator rolls or segment configurations are available to measure parts. For example, single-point OD threading would typically be gaged using a hand held (portable) roll/roll (multi-rib/cone & vee) gage system. Flat-die rolled fasteners would use a bench (segment/ roll) full form/cone & vee gage system. Receiving inspection would typically use a segment/ roll gage because the segment, being full form, envelops the workpiece. This emulates a Go ring gage.

"Roundness, taper, lead, flank angle errors, and a 120°/180° geometry are factors to consider in these examples," comments Dupont. "Choices for this type of gaging include multi-rib rolls, full form segments and cone & vee rolls." Consult a thread gaging specialist when determining the best gaging for an application.

Comparator suppliers offer a great benefit to manufacturers. Measurements taken for both functional diameter and pitch diameter can determine thread form quality. "The difference between the two measurements is thread form errors," says Dupont, "which is called the *differential* and is valuable in the setup and manufacturing process. Differential gaging is used to position a setup with the screw thread tolerance to maximize tool life, plating allowances, and the process. Differential Gaging is the basis for compliance with System 23, the gaging system used for safety critical applications."

RING OF TRUTH

The ring gage is one of the oldest, most widely used devices for determining the size limits of external threads. It determines if a part will assemble in a thread of a given size. It engages several threads on the bolt and provides a functional check on PD.

A new concept in external thread gaging comes form Multi Gaging Systems (Danvers, MA). This design offers multiple thread ring gages in one tri-roll adjustable ring gage. A ring body houses three annular pitch rollers.

"The pitch rollers accommodate different size ring bodies that provide interchangeability of various pitch rollers," says David Wright, MGS chief engineer. "An example is in the #10 through 5/8" ring bodies, where the diameter of the pitch rollers is the same. There are 10 different pitch rollers that fall within this range. The 1/4" ring body, for example, will accommodate the 20 pitch rollers for course thread, 28 for fine thread, and 32 for extra fine thread. If you also make 5/16" or 3/8" threaded products, you can interchange

the pitch rollers into either size ring for gaging the proper pitch and class of fit."

GAGING GAGES

Pratt & Whitney (Plainville, CT) offers a laser-based instrument for measuring thread gages. This direct-reading instrument can measure both internal and external dimensions up to 14" (356 mm) to an accuracy of 2 millionths of an inch (0.05) microns).

It uses four accessories for measuring thread gages: an adjustable force system, finger positioner, flat anvils, and thread measuring wires. The adjustable force system provides the range of pressures (2 - 48 oz) required to meet thread measuring specifications. The finger positioner provides the means to apply the pressure. The flat anvils are the gaging fingers contacting the measuring wires that contact the thread gage. The flat anvils are lapped parallel to a tolerance of 8 millionths. The accuracy of the overall measurement of a thread gage, however, is not as much limited by the laser as by anvil parallelism and accuracy of the thread wires.

In the laser-based system, the light wavelength provides a high resolution, linear, stable reference for dimensional measurement. The instrument effectively couples the light wavelength to the part to be measured by using a laser interferometer to detect linear motion of probes that contact the part. The system uses patented laser parts in line with the measurement axis to minimize Abbe error. The probes and associated optics are guided along low friction air slides by precision force systems to minimize instrument error.

TAPPED OUT

Thread checking challenges CMM technology as a result of ANSI Y14.5M-1982's stipulation that a screw thread's position is defined by the axis of its pitch cylinder. "If you probe the thread crest, at best you can only inspect the location of the thread's minor diameter," says Walter Stites, manager, production services, AccraTronics Seals Corp (Burbank, CA). He is a member of the ANSI/ASME subcommittee support group.

"A roll-type tap should form a burr-free minor diameter, relatively coaxial to the pitch cylinder," Stites continues. "A milled thread, generated in a bored hole, should do about as well, assuming a rigid machine and no shifting of the part between the boring and milling stages.

"A cutting tap, however, is usually held in a floating head, and once started in a hole, can follow a line quite different from the axis of the drilled hole. Yet it is the tap, not the hole, that establishes the all-important pitch cylinder. A burr on the thread crest creates a false minor diameter that is particularly misleading."

Tapped holes controlled with positional tolerance per ANSI Y14.5M-1982 must be checked to specified datums. That means the part must either be fixtured on those datums and the fixture probed, or the datum surfaces must be probed directly in the same setup as the tapped holes themselves. Since a positional tolerance applies to the full depth of the thread, it is usually insufficient to check position at a single depth. Instead, the pitch cylinder axis should be determined, especially for deeper threads or projected tolerance zones.

"These same obstacles hinder all other inspection methods," notes Stites. "Surface plate techniques often preclude setup on the specified datums. Measurements are usually based on the minor diameter and only at a single depth. Visual methods—comparator or vision-type CMMs—suffer from the same problems and usually check position only at the entrance of the hole."

According to Stites, these limitations can be overcome with functional gages, but most such gages "cheat" on ANSI Y14.5 by employing either an undersize thread gaging member (having slight helix angle error) or a projected tolerance zone where none is specified on the part drawing. "Functional gages require long lead times, are usually expensive to design and build, and can't provide data for use with SPC," he says.

"For these reasons, manufacturers risk relying on the consistency of the matching process to control tapped hole positions. As assembly tolerances become tighter and customers become more able to check incoming parts, however, that risk is no longer acceptable. With proper techniques and supplemental tooling, a CMM can check most internal threads as reliably as a functional gage, and provide variable data too."

Effective CMM use starts with the probe. Rigid "hard probes," traditionally used with CMMs for tapped holes, are a poor choice because they can't contact the pitch cylinder and can only be used manually, subject to operator

"feel." The tapered or spherical varieties only check the position of the hole's chamfer or burr on the first thread.

Cylindrical hard probes require perfect physical alignment of the hole to the machine and then only check the location of the minor diameter, often broaching or reforming that diameter as they slide in. In most cases, tapered and cylindrical probes can neither probe the datum surfaces, nor be "qualified" (using a reference sphere), allowing the datum surfaces to be contacted with a different probe first.

"Touch-trigger probes are more accurate than hard probes," comments Stites, "and because they allow changing the stylus and requalifying, they offer more technique choices. A touch-trigger probe with an ordinary ruby-ball stylus can check most features on a part in a single setup, including tapped holes, but it needs some outside help in the form of special thread members. These gages, available from many different manufacturers, are specifically designed for checking tapped hole locations."

The most accurate method for checking a tapped hold location with a CMM is to first use a touch-trigger probe to contact the part's datum surfaces and use the CMM's leveling and alignment functions to establish the datum reference frame. Then, install a special thread member in the hole, change the stylus, and probe the thread member.

Since many thread members are available, choosing the right one is crucial. Look for a member that will orient and locate itself on the actual flanks of the thread, simulating the pitch cylinder, preferably over the thread's full depth (avoid types with flanges on the face outside the hole, overcoming the orientation of the thread).

A good example is the family of Center Line Flex-Plugs from Southern Gage (Erin, TN). A 0.250" or larger Flex-Plug has a thread precision-ground to the no-go PD and then slit in two directions, allowing it to collapse enough to go into the tapped hole. Smaller Flex-Plugs cannot be slit, but instead are tapered from the go to the no-go PD. Bogh types start freely in a proper-size thread and gradually "snug-up" as they are screwed in, mating almost perfectly with the actual thread flanks.

Once the member is installed, its shank is probed as a cylinder to determine its axis, or (depending on the type of member and probe stylus used) a face perpendicular to the axis and its shank or hole are probed to construct the axis. The intersection of the axis and the part face is determined and its position is checked. Then a second intersection is determined and checked at the minimum thread depth. If a projected tolerance zone is called out, the second point should be at the specified projected height above the part surface instead. In this way, with as few as six or seven touches and a few seconds of computing, most CMMs can check the thread location at both ends of the tolerance zone. Special thread members also can be probed either manually or automatically in conjunction with inspection of other part features, either in-process or in final inspection.

Thread members provide no PD data. This deficiency, however, will never cause acceptance of a bad thread.

CALIBRATION COMMENTS

According to Stites, calibration should also be a consideration—don't depend on the manufacturer's specs. Verify runout of in-house gages to maintain their reliability. When using special thread members, study part inspection data carefully. A member with excessive runout will make a well-positioned thread look bad. This is most apparent when a group of gages are repeatedly and randomly installed in a pattern of holes and probed. An eccentric member will create the appearance of a "bad hole" that shifts around at random.

"A savvy CMM programmer can make an automatic machine move its probe in a helical path, attempting always to touch on the thread crest 360° around," Stites reports. "At best, check the position of the thread minor diameter this way, but there is no guarantee each touch will hit squarely on the thread crest or even in the same relative spot of the crest. If the thread has burrs, this method won't work. An easier scheme would be to install the largest possible (straight) gage pin in the minor diameter, probe the pin, and project the axis to two intersection points."

Renishaw (Schaumburg, IL) and others make a cylindrical stylus for touch-trigger probes intended to contact the thread minor diameter. Satisfactory results depend on alignment (parallelism) of the probe to the hole, and the absence of burrs on the thread. Many CMMs can't qualify such a stylus, so it would have to be used to contact the datum surfaces as well.

"The CMM with a touch-trigger probe and a special thread member offers the easiest, fastest, least expensive, most accurate way to check tapped hole locations," concludes Stites. "This combination even surpasses a functional gage when coordinate data are needed for SPC."

3.11
SUPPLIER QUALITY

———————————■———————————

QUALITY SUPPLIERS: THE SEARCH GOES ON BY PURCHASING*

Forget quick fixes when it comes to improving purchased goods' and services' quality. Our survey of purchasing execs, and interviews with those on the leading edge of reliability programs, show that:

- There can't be any letup in getting the need for steady quality improvement across to vendor firms. And the continuing drumbeat must be audible to everybody in suppliers' ranks—from CEOs to blue-collar workers—not just to sales reps.

- A new brand of vendor rating plays a key role in the overall effort. Its purpose isn't just supplier flagellation, but finding the root causes of quality problems. And there's no blinking when the buying firm turns out to

---

*Reprinted with permission from *Purchasing Magazine*, copyright by Cahners Publishing Company.

be the culprit, because of unmakeable specs, impossible tolerances, or faulty buyer-owned tooling. Instead the emphasis is on solving problems for good.

Design and manufacturing engineering, along with quality assurance, have just as big a technical role in the ongoing effort as they do in initial sourcing for quality.

For the record, no fewer than 85% of your peers have beefed up their vendor rating efforts in the past couple of years. As the chart (p. 3-219) shows, quality is the number-one facet of performance being rated. It scores 9.6 on a 1-10 scale, making it first among equals with other attributes: delivery, cost reduction help, etc. But don't expect overnight results if you're just about to crank up a quality improvement program with your sources.

IT TAKES TIME

"We're now seeing the fruits of efforts that we started back in 1986," says Robert J. Bretz, director of purchasing and distribution for Pitney Bowes Corp., Stamford, Conn. "We had 652 parts certified as of September, 1987, against a goal for that year of 400."

However, says Bretz, who is also chairman of NAPM's business survey committee, it took a little while after the summer of '86 when Pitney Bowes undertook a five-year plan to improve suppliers' quality, for the incoming reject rate to trend down. Reason: vendors had become accustomed to a situation where their goods were often accepted on a waivering-in basis.

"It seemed as though everybody in the place has a little hammer or pliers to fix things up," he jokes. So, when purchasing determined to stop that, and decreed that incoming inspection was going to measure strictly against specs, the reject rate went up. Then vendors yelped. So the big job became convincing suppliers that Pitney Bowes was deadly serious about quality.

"It's missionary work," says Bretz. "We have to constantly remind suppliers that extra quality does not cost us or them anything. It demands improved communications to get the message across, and it's one that has to be directed at all levels within suppliers firms."

Getting that message across is a multi-pronged effort at Pitney Bowes. For one thing, the contract schedules printed out by computer reiterate whatever quality specs apply to the part in question. For another, there's a monthly report card on quality based on lots accepted. As of about six months ago, the report card is now sent to the president of each supplier.

Early each year, also, Bretz gets together with two of his aids: manager of supplier quality assurance John Quartarone, and manager of components purchasing James Lown. Aim of the huddle: to divide the country into regions, and set up vendor visit schedules for themselves, Quartarone's quality engineers, and Lown's buyers. "And when we go," says Lown, "we take along our TV camera."

Having the camera enables the survey team to tape operations out on the supplier's shop floor. Later, back at Pitney Bowes, design and manufacturing engineers can view the tapes via VCR, and witness things such as type of equipment being used by the supplier, and the line operation's actions in feeding and running it, and his or her steps in shutting it down if parts drift off-spec.

The TV taping also gives the Pitney Bowes team a chance to interact with the supplier's line workers. And that often provides a valuable insight into the vendor's overall quality attitude. "A truly committed company is talking quality to all its workers," says Quartarone. "When workers start talking quality and SPC to you, and show you how they plot their measurements, then the company darn well has a system."

"And an overall quality system is what we want them to have," adds Lown. "We don't want them to have a special setup just for us. We want quality to be a way of life with them."

Inevitably, there has been some fall-off in the vendor list. "We have had a few casualties," says Bretz. "Some companies talk the quality line, but don't walk it." Or, as Lown puts it: "An awful lot of top managers out there only give it lip service. So you have to go out there and look and explore what they're doing."

At Pitney Bowes, suppliers are also brought in, not only for explanations but for assistance. The company has held several vendor days, with themes such as "partners in progress." It has also trained no less than 63 suppliers in SPC. Since suppliers are asked to bring an "application project" (one of their parts) when they come for SPC training, that gives Pitney Bowes' design and manufacturing engineering a chance to brainstorm quality improvements too.

Out of such mutual sessions, and other interactions among purchasing, engineering, and suppliers, have come a number of more reliable ways of doing things. A few quick examples:

• Broken core pins were a chronic problem on a die casting. It was decided to retool the part, and produce 48 holes with one stroke. The tool was approved after monitoring 13 characteristics by x-r charting. The acceptance level on the part went from 85% as of July '86 to 100% as of October '87.

When a supplier suggested that structural foamed part might be used, engineering okayed that idea and found that a total of six components could be replaced with two foam units. Machining errors have been eliminated.

• A washer and spacer supplier couldn't hold tolerances after plating on 1010 steel. There was too much springback. A change to stainless eliminated the need for plating, and made blanking truer. Result: 100% acceptable and certified parts.

"It isn't easy to find world-class suppliers," says John Quartarone, but Pitney Bowes is clearly well on the way. For one thing, it now has a roster of "preferred suppliers." These are the quality-oriented sources that are going to get new Pitney Bowes business as needs arise. And pointing out the existence of the preferred list—and what a good thing it is to be on it—is one of the basic quality measures that Bretz and his staff hammer home to incumbents.

SOURCING IS STRATEGIC

A similar long-term program to identify and use "strategic suppliers" is under way at Texas Instruments, says Paul K. Moffat, vice-president of material for TI's materials and controls group, Attleboro, Mass. Moffat was NAPM president 1985-86, and logged about 10 years as a quality control manager back in the '50s.

"Prior to 1983," Moffat says, "we had been tolerating a parts supplier quality level of less than 95% acceptance. We knew a thorough analysis of the root cause was in order." When the study was made, however, it uncovered a couple of quirks:

For one thing, different suppliers in the same industry were interpreting TI's specs and instructions in varying ways.

For another, the tooling in suppliers' shops (whose cost was shared with TI) wasn't always capable of producing parts to spec.

"But regardless of whose fault it was," says Moffat, "we at TI had the responsibility to bring our suppliers up to the required quality level to serve our ultimate customers. We really needed to make it easier for our suppliers to do business with TI, and invest in the necessary resources to do this in a spirit of partnership."

With that in mind, purchasing told suppliers that they would no longer be measured just on total lot acceptance. Under a new approach, inspection was going to classify defects and rejects into two categories: "S-faults" and "T-faults." S-faults are those attributable to the supplier; T-faults are those where TI is at fault.

In addition to the T and S classification system (which continues today), TI developed a supplier questionnaire to probe vendor capabilities in three areas: communication, interaction (early involvement in design), and support (engineering and tooling). One aim was to help TI sourcing teams—buyers, engineers, quality staffers and sometimes planners—decide where to place their emphasis with particular suppliers.

When the questionnaires came back from the suppliers, TI decided to interview 25-30 of them to define quality issues and assign an order of importance to them.

"In parallel with this," says Moffat, "we carried out an educational program to develop suppliers' understanding of SPC and other quality improvement techniques. The buyers played a leadership role in all of this. After all, we look to them as responsible for their suppliers' quality."

Out of those original meetings came decisions to: (1) review and rewrite TI's engineering drawing standards specifications, and (2) audit all tools used by suppliers to produce goods for TI.

"We asked a core group of strategic suppliers to work with us on developing the new engineering standards spec," says Moffat. "We wound up changing things like what constitutes a burr, or a scratch, or a clean surface. Descriptions of all of these were standardized. Dimensional references were clarified, too, and the definitions of what constitutes a major, minor, or critical dimension." (see Exhibit 1).

Suppliers' inputs and critiques during the redrafting were "very helpful," says Moffat, although the rewrite took a full nine months. Then, with engineering approval from TI's four business groups, there was a big push to get the new

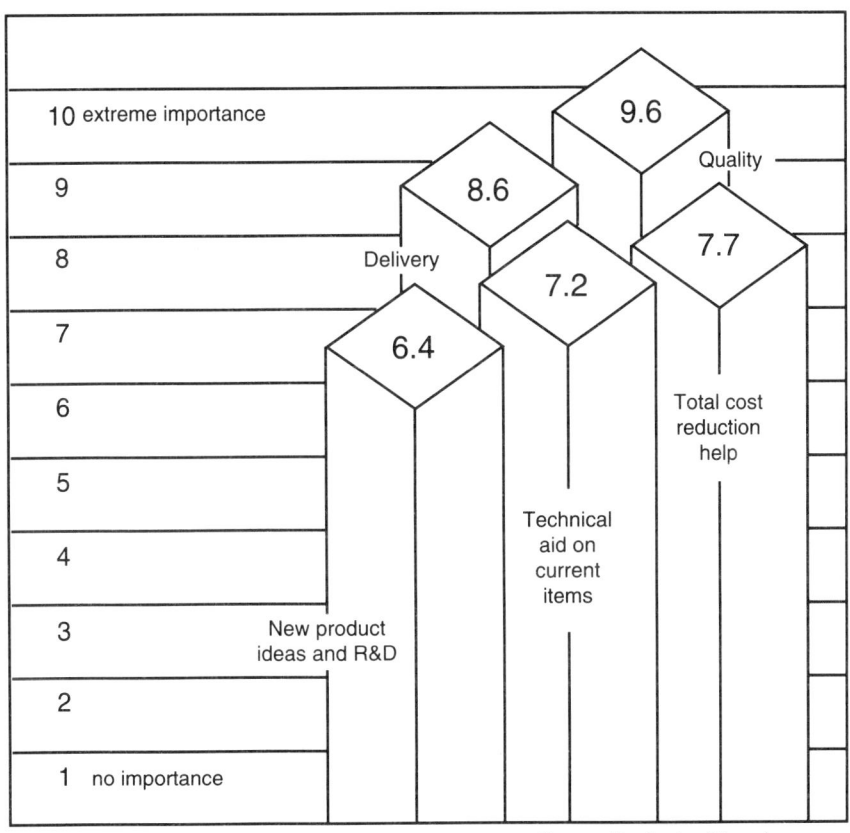

Source: Purchasing Magazine survey

EXHIBIT 1.—WHAT'S IMPORTANT IN SUPPLIER PERFORMANCE?

interpretation spec to all suppliers. That came after all vendors had about two or three months to study it, at which time management and technical reps were invited in for a one-day seminar where final questions were fielded face-to-face.

The tooling upgrade is a longer-term project, according to Moffat. However, TI has already invested several million dollars in upgrading supplier-held tooling to meet SPC demands. Buyers have clarified supplier's responsibilities for tool maintenance, and guaranteed tool life has become part of purchasing's contracts.

At the same time, a 13-step certification process has started, so that parts from new or upgraded tools can be certified for use directly in TI's manufacturing line (dock-to-stock).

The net result of the program overall so far, says Moffat, is excellent. Some 60% of the T-faults have been eliminated. Suppliers have made only about a 30% improvement, but they are working against a stiffer standard. (Some T-faults, in other words, have turned into S-faults temporarily.)

But, emphasizes Moffat, TI's quality acceptance rating has moved up into the high 90s. "We can now consider conversion to measuring our suppliers on the basis of defects per million. Even more important, we have had almost zero supplier-related defects show up in our manufacturing or customer processes."

The bottom line? "Only continuous improvement can lead to assured quality."

WORKING WITH QC

A double-barreled program is similarly leading to improved supplier quality at Beckman Industrial, a subsidiary of Emerson Electric Co., in Fullerton, Calif. A vendor excellence program set up by purchasing manager Chris Beck brings suppliers in to discuss some of the nuances of trickier commodities such as plastic molded and machined parts. And vendor quality assurance manager Wayne Heard has wedded vendor rating to a corrective action program that (like Texas Instruments') identifies the cause of supplier's quality miscues.

"Under the vendor excellence program," says Beck, who started it in 1983, "suppliers of moldings and some machining come in every other week. We do it selectively, mostly in plastic injection molding, because the nature of the process means a lot of subjective judgments. I've even had one supplier tell me, 'Give me any molded part, and I can find a reason for rejecting it!'"

There's a germ of truth in that comment, notes Beck. That's why there's a degree of formality to the meetings with vendors. "We keep minutes and assign action items for follow-up. The key is having regular meetings, so people don't go off and become preoccupied with doing something else."

Recently, for example, Beckman was having problems with a small (1/4-in × 1/4-in) molded part serving as a contact slider for a trimmer potentiometer. (The firm's line is resistive products like pots and networks, and hybrid circuits.) The part was hanging up in the bowl of the vibratory feeder in a semi-automated assembly operation.

To discuss the matter at a vendor excellence meeting, the president of the supplier firm brought in his plant manager and QC manager. And Beck arranged for Beckman's operations manager and assembly supervisor to attend.

"We showed them what it means when they don't ship good parts to us," notes Beck. "Our manager and supervisor explained how far behind schedule it was putting us, and how long it would take us to catch up. Then we arranged for the supplier personnel to talk to our setup man, who has 20 years experience, and the part is back on spec now."

Most of the suppliers in the vendor excellence program are local, but the vendor rating plan started by Heard, who joined Beckman last February, covers distant sources too. The rating system is based on a formula where lots accepted are multiplied by samples accepted, and the result is divided by lots inspected times samples rejected.

"The only time they get 100 is when they ship 100% good parts," says Heard. "That's why we have the number of samples included in the formula's numerator and denominator. Otherwise, there'd be no penalty for cases where some parts aren't to print, but we accept the lot."

On the other hand, the corrective action status reports that Heard produces each week indicate whether the supplier, or Beckman, is the cause of miscues. And the split is running about 50/50 right now.

"If you rate a supplier, you have the responsibility to rate him accurately," says Head. "When we notify a supplier of a rejection under our corrective action plan, there's a space for him to fill in and return. If he's on top of things, and a problem is our fault, we expect him to sound off about it."

The payoff, according to PM Beck: Last April, supplier rejects were running 10.5%. In November, they were down to 4.5%. "Our goal right now is 1%," says Beck. There has been some falloff in the number of vendors, and there's now an approved supplier list that reflects the joint opinions of purchasing, quality, and engineering.

STRESSING SPC

A multi-disciplinary approach to supplier quality is also very much in evidence at OTC division of Sealed Power Corp., Owatonna, Minn., with emphasis on vendor certification and SPC. Purchasing manager Mike Ellingsen gives an example:

"We were at a cold heading firm in Ohio. We wanted to be sure we knew what they were doing, and that they understood our needs. So we had a team: the buyer, a design engineer, a manufacturing engineer, and a procurement quality engineer. No one person can keep it all in his head. You can lug blueprints around all day, but it's not the same as face-to-face discussions."

Engineer Ken Jacobson, designer of the part in question, agrees completely. "The supplier had a knowledgeable tooling person at the meeting. We were able to iron out tolerances and tooling. The supplier could punch and thread, so we weren't limited in using his processes. We were even able to use some of his suggestions about fixtures in our in-house operations.

"What we're mainly interested in," Jacobson continues, "is using the right process. Purchasing is good in finding the best source, so we leave that up to them. But there's a real quality payoff when we (technical specialists from each side) can talk in person. That half-hour session with the vendor probably saved 15 or 20 times as much in calling back and forth to discuss samples."

QTC's overall interest in supplier quality is quickly evidenced by a silver-covered booklet titled "Supplier Quality Program," and carrying the subtitle "Pulling Together for Quality." Co-signed by Ellingsen and quality/productivity manager Jerry Ensminger, the booklet's preface reads in part:

"As business partners, we have joined forces toward a common objective. That objective is to serve our customers with a quality product which is 'fit for use'. . . To back up this commitment, we have extended to our customers a lifetime warranty against material and workmanship defects. This is how serious we are about quality. . . Only through a team effort, can we mutually succeed."

As a practical matter, says Ellingsen, SPC is just about a must for OTC suppliers. "We're most interested in those firms that are on SPC and are aiming at our using total quality control. We will rarely work with someone who doesn't have it. We just can't make parts consistently without it."

There are eight buyers at OTC, working with 85 or so engineers, and many of them have experience as machinists or quality assurance staffers. They are "high in mechanical aptitude," says Ellingsen. "They have to be. If you don't understand the print, you're a dead duck! Plus, we don't switch commodities that often."

As at Beckman Industrial, rejection of a supplier's goods triggers a non-conforming material action request, which goes to the supplier. A part on the form is for the vendor's corrective action report. "We won't close the books until he comes back with what he's going to do to correct things," says Ellingsen, "and that doesn't mean just, 'I talked to Joe and he'll take care of it.' Then we track the incident to see if there is a reccurrence."

All told, there are about 28,000 computer-controlled parts at OTC. But there's a lot more to controlling suppliers' quality than just counting or recounting mistakes. "Mutual respect between the two companies must be a given," declares Ellingsen, "or there's no communications and no consistency. We will dedicate quality engineers to their sites if they need help. We have brought their quality people in for two or three-day sessions. Or, perhaps, we may supply checking fixtures to help them provide quality to us."

TEARING DOWN FOR TESTS

An alliance between purchasing and quality control, with lots of emphasis on product tear-downs and testing, is helping the Maytag Co. maintain its reputation for top quality. Sure, everybody at the Iowa company is concerned about quality; director of purchases Dean M. Ward and QC manager Gerry Weaver naturally assume co-quarterback roles.

"Quality has always been important here," notes Ward, "and we want to be sure we're dealing with suppliers who are committed to excellence, and have the financial and process controls to give us consistent quality."

One of the methods for assuring that, which has been used for a number of years at Maytag, is to take apart units returned from the field, and disassemble them in a joint diagnostic scrutiny with parts suppliers.

"We collect units over a three to six-month period," says Weaver. "Most of the studies involve timers, or motors or switches. We might find that a follower is bent, or cam is warped, or there's a broken tooth on a gear. Our design engineers and quality people make the disassembly along with the supplier's technical people. The end result might be design change, or the supplier's getting a new piece of equipment or tool to make the part even better."

According to Weaver, the tear-downs are physically done at either Maytag or the supplier's site. "We try to alternate the site with each supplier," he says. Wherever the disassembly is performed, however, results are followed up by a team that typically includes purchasing (Ward or a purchasing agent or buyer), Weaver, the manager of production engineering, and the vice-president of manufacturing.

"We listen to what they have to say," stresses Ward. "Quite often, the supplier group we're talking with includes the president as well as manufacturing, quality, and engineering executives. Plant people such as foremen also are represented, usually.

"During such a visit to a supplier plan," Ward continues, "we normally visit the people in the plant too, such as machine operators. A tour through any plant will tell you a lot about the company's attitude toward quality. Is it clean? Is everybody working safely? What quality-improvement measures are in place—including ways to stop rejects before they leave the plant?

By the same token, says Ward, a number of suppliers have sponsored tours of the Maytag plant for their production-line workers—to give

3-222   Section Three   Quality Technologies and Methods

them a sense of their customer's commitment to (and need for) consistent quality.

THE BIG PICTURE

At NCR Corp., suppliers' contributions to improved quality are seen as part of an overall program known as "supply line management." As pointed out by director of corporate purchasing James H. Currier, vendors are important stakeholders in the firm. And Joseph Bookataub, director of manufacturing for NCR's San Diego plant, spells it out now:

"Purchasing is an integral part of selecting a supplier base that will work with us in the early stages of new product development, to help us design to optimum quality and cost.

"We started a supplier analysis program about nine months ago," continues Bookataub, whose plant is part of NCR's general purpose systems division, and produces mainframe and minicomputers. "We have reduced the vendor base from 400 to 190, and that has enabled us to spend more time with each supplier. We've even had cases where engineering simply specified the requirements, and the vendors did the design without prints or drawings."

"We want designs to be manufacturable and testable," stresses Bookataub. "One of our goals is to get from concept to customer's hardware in under 12 months. It wouldn't be possible without early supplier involvement."

It also helps, says Bookataub, that a buyer is assigned to a group of 12-15 engineers working on advanced manufacturing operations. The engineers report to Bookataub, and the buyer reports to Thomas R. Leitake, manager of purchased materials management, who also reports to Bookataub. That assures that advanced products are kept in mind during all sourcing.

Until last summer, Leitake was quality control manager at NCR's Orlando, Fla. plant, and he notes now that there will be additional narrowing down of the vendor base. "We expect to be down to 125 by the fourth quarter of 1990. We are already scheduling review sessions where we share our quality and other expectations with suppliers."

An important part of the process, says Leitake, is defining NCR's and suppliers' responsibilities. To that end, he recently rewrote the terms on the company's standard contract form (which is now known as a supply line agreement) and arranged for the legal department's scrutiny and okay.

The new-look contract now includes the supplier's pledge to quality improvement, with space for ppm targets to be inserted. The need for regular review sessions is noted. The supplier subscribes to early supplier involvement and commitment (ESIC). Ditto for leadtime management efforts, related to actual manufacturing cycles; and joint value analysis efforts, with start-up dates insertable.

"Our responsibility," says Leitake, "includes setting up long-term deals, and providing accurate long-term forecasts. We also have to give vendors the opportunities for early involvement. It's only when you have mutually acceptable specs that there's a true win/win relationship."

Like most big companies, NCR's purchasing is basically decentralized to the plant level. But there's still a lot going on at HQ to share good supply line management ideas.

Recently, for example, corporate purchasing sponsored a keyboard sourcing conference attended by people from seven plants. "The conference brought together test engineers, designers, and those involved with procurement," says John Caltabiano, source development engineer in corporate purchasing. "Our objective was to work together toward developing a consistent manner of identifying keyboard technologies, analyzing the purchasing process, sourcing the best suppliers, and involving those suppliers early in the product development process to insure greater success."

Corporate purchasing's Dan Ostendorf, for his part, recently wrote an excellent outline of what supply line management is all about, for NCR's internal purchasing newsletter. While copies last, you can get one by writing Ostendorf at WHQ-1E, NCR Corp., 1700 S. Patterson Blvd., Dayton, Ohio 45479.

BEING REALISTIC ABOUT SUPPLIER QUALITY*

When Michael Harding was hired by a Fortune 500 corporation in the early 1980s to assist in the company's supplier certification process, he knew that some problems existed.

"I learned quickly that the traditional certification procedure of visiting supplier facilities was next to useless," reports Harding, now president of Michael Harding Associates (Bristol, VT).

Harding says that companies using the traditional approach to work with suppliers on quality improvements are very likely to run into such problems as these:

- You might not have a clear understanding of your quality requirements. "Certifying suppliers requires that you have a clear understanding of your quality requirements—commodity by commodity, component by component," Harding states. "This isn't always the case."

- You are expected to evaluate processes of which you have limited knowledge. "For example, I worked for a computer manufacturer," he says. "We knew computers, but what did we know about ion deposition on microthin wafers? In essence, we were passing judgment on suppliers who had been working with their processes for decades."

- You may mistakenly assume that your own quality system is in shape and not inadvertently adding problems. "It's possible to get good product from suppliers but end up with quality problems because of deficiencies in your own quality processes," he explains.

- Certification is erroneously based on historical performance and data. "There is no assurance that the future will look like the past. Yet certification assumes that the supplier will continue to perform in the same manner."

- Suppliers may not respond to you because you're one of many customers, "If you are one of 50 or more customers evaluating a given supplier, why should that supplier listen to you?," Harding asks. Suppliers generally pay attention to the customer with the most money."

- The process of evaluating, auditing, and certifying suppliers is costly. You do little more than move the incoming inspection process back to the supplier's facility. "The net result is that you incur additional expense by taking the inspection process to the supplier's location," he adds.

TRADITIONAL PROCESSES CAN WORK UNDER CERTAIN CIRCUMSTANCES

Are traditional evaluation and certification programs ever effective? Harding believes they can be if three elements are in place:

1. You are a very large company and/or represent a significant portion of the supplier's business.

2. You have the resources and willingness to provide suppliers with quality improvement, training, and other support.

3. You have adequate quality processes in place in your own facility.

If your company doesn't have all these factors in place, Harding recommends an alternative—an eight-step process designed to achieve the kind of supplier quality improvement you need. "This eight-step process enforces the concept of continuous improvement by placing the burden of proof on the right people," he explains.

EIGHT-STEP PROCESS PROVIDES ALTERNATIVE ROUTE

STEP 1: Create a clear definition of what you want and need relative to quality—in specific terms. "Don't ask for something unless you know

---

what it is and unless you actually need it," he states.

Quantify these needs by setting quality targets for each commodity. These can be expressed in parts per million (PPM), six sigma, and so forth.

STEP 2: State what kind of proof you will accept that suppliers are achieving these requirements. For instance, will you accept

✔ *copies of control charts?*

✔ *certificates of compliance?*

✔ *certificates of analysis (for chemicals)?*

✔ *other documentation?*

STEP 3: Come to agreement on the supplier's plan for improvement. "Regardless of the quality system the supplier selects, make sure that he or she has a plan to maintain and improve quality," says Harding. "The idea is not necessarily to change the supplier's system, unless it is totally inadequate. Rather, you want to ask, 'What is your plan for getting better over time?' "

Then, along with the supplier, track the supplier's improvements in quality over a specified period of time. For example, ask the supplier to provide you with evidence of improvements (reduction in PPM from 700 to 400, for example) on a quarterly basis. Example: PPMs reduced from 700 to 400.

STEP 4: Determine the supplier's cost of quality. This includes direct costs and hidden costs. "A lot of companies don't know their cost of quality," states Harding. "They think it is nothing more than the salaries in the quality department." Direct costs include:

✔ *the quality department,*

✔ *inspection,*

✔ *rework,*

✔ *scrap, and*

✔ *warranty repairs.*

Hidden costs include:

✔ *added inventory,*

✔ *obsolescence,*

✔ *late delivery,*

✔ *delayed customer payments, and*

✔ *lost sales.*

"The total figure can be as high as 35 percent of the cost of the sale," reports Harding. "However, as quality improves, this costs decreases."

STEP 5: Insist that the supplier move quality from the quality department to the production floor. "Quality occurs at the point of action," he explains. "No amount of inspection or policing will improve it. So don't look for people in white lab coats performing after-the-fact testing. Look for what's happening on the floor, at the point of manufacture. Are control charts in sight? Are cause-effect diagramming and problem-solving taking place?"

A well-trained workforce, then, is the best way to guarantee quality. "A supplier's training budget will tell you just how serious they are about improving product and process quality," notes Harding.

✔ *For a manufacturing firm, look for a training budget for line employees equal to at least 3 percent of payroll.*

✔ *For a service firm, look for a training budget for line employees equal to at least 5 percent of payroll.*

STEP 6: Determine the supplier's manufacturing cycle time and its plan to improve that cycle time. "Cycle time is the true indicator of cost, quality, and delivery," explains Harding.

In the United States the ratio of cycle time to actual value-added time averages 300 to 1. That is, it takes most companies 300 hours to add one hour of value to a product. The remaining 299 hours are order entry, scheduling, queue time, rework, handling, and other non-value-added tasks.

In one company with which Harding is familiar, the ratio is 13,700 to 1. "They have a quoted lead time of eight days, but their value-added time only totals 37 seconds," he states.

Ask your supplier to reduce his ratio to 10 to 1. "This will force him to focus on non-value-added tasks and make the necessary improvements," he explains. Only when processes are predictable can a supplier reduce his ratio to

✔ *10 to 1 for discrete manufacturing or*

✔ *10 to 1.5 or 1 for process manufacturing.*

STEP 7: Become familiar with your supplier's plan to make your incoming inspection department obsolete. "Incoming inspection is a costly and unnecessary overhead," he explains.

STEP 8: Require the supplier to notify you before any significant processes change. Examples of changes: ownership, quality management, equipment, and anything else that will materially affect your product.

"You need to know about these changes before they occur so that you can discuss their impact and anticipate any problems that might arise as a result of the changes," Harding states.

Harding offers a final recommendation when it comes to offering supplier certification: Make the certification temporary. "Some suppliers work hard to get the plaque so that they can hang it on their wall to impress other customers and visitors," he observes. "However, they don't improve after receiving certification. If you're going to give certification plaques to suppliers, have those plaques 'expire' about "every six months," he concludes.

NO REWARDS FOR PLAIN VANILLA*
by Peter Bradley

Transportation providers have a special niche in the pursuit of quality. They provide the tangible links between suppliers and buyers, between manufacturers and customers in the supply chain.

So winning recognition as a top transportation supplier means fundamentally strengthening those links.

"We want carriers focused on our mutual customers," says Tim Houghton, director of corporate transportation for Baxter Healthcare.

Achieving that, in the eyes of buyers, requires carriers to reach beyond the traditional measures of on time and intact at the right price. Basic service excellence is no longer a differentiator; it's the ante in an increasingly competitive game. Says Phillip Rine, who manages transportation for Aristech Chemical Corp., "I'm not interested in plain vanilla. I want carriers who can offer a whole bag of services and do it well."

The Baxter case exemplifies how many companies evaluate their carriers. For example, the company has identified five attributes that it looks for in its carriers:

- Financial stability.
- Consistency of transit time.
- Value-added service focus.
- Broad geographic scope.
- Market competitive pricing.

Baxter, which spends about $300 million a year on transportation, selects and manages carriers through three councils: a national purchasing council for express and long haul less-than-truckload carriage; a volume purchasing council for truckload, intermodal and boxcar serviceproviders; and five regional councils that assess regional LTL carriers.

Becoming a Baxter transportation supplier is only the beginning. What distinguishes the top suppliers is their ability to work with Baxter to continuously evolve their service.

Says Houghton, describing Baxter's transportation excellence program, "The idea is to improve relationships. If we can do that, we can enhance the quality of service to our mutual customers."

And what do the customers want? Jerry Arthur, who was vice president of supplier management for Baxter and is now vice president of supply, told carriers gathered at the company's first logistics/carrier symposium last fall that customers were under pressure to reduce costs. He told the carriers that manufacturers and distributors had to cut end-user costs by reducing unit prices, logistics costs, administrative costs, inventory costs, and usage costs. "Together, we must take cost out and increase the value of the supply chain."

At that symposium, Baxter recognized its top carriers with a series of awards. It named Federal Express its carrier of the year. It cited

---

several others for what it calls its Business Partner Award: APL Distribution Services, Crouse Cartage Co., Roadway Package System, Schneider National/Schneider Dedicated, and TNT Bestway. Another eight carriers received Baxter's Transportation Excellence Award: Crowley American Transport, CSX Intermodal, LEP, Ozark Motor Lines, Saia Motor Freight, Southeastern Freight Lines, Sunflower, and Wilson Trucking Corp.

Houghton lists major factors he considers inherent in building quality relationships with carriers.

- *Open and timely communications.* Baxter meets with each of its carriers at least once a quarter, and with major carriers once a month.

- *Quality processes.* Baxter looks for carriers that communicate and apply nationwide performance measures to gauge quality.

- *Environment.* Carriers should have ingrained a "defect-free" culture.

- *Performance measures.* Document performance for the benefit of both the carrier and Baxter management.

- *Costs.* The partnership must move toward reducing total pipeline costs. "The focus is not on transactional costs," says Houghton.

- *Technology.* Baxter wants carriers that are on the leading edge of transportation technology. The company will even take part in carriers' beta tests of new efforts.

- *World class.* The company wants the best in the business.

Baxter has a number of specific measures of carrier performance. Most are familiar enough: On-time pickup and delivery, notification of late pickups, pre-notification of late deliveries, damage-free transit, timely and accurate freight billing, and responsiveness of sales representatives.

In one respect, the measures of the sales reps indicate the way the roles of carriers are changing. Baxter expects carrier reps not only to be accessible and flexible, but to bring consultative skills to the table as well. They are expected to help solve problems.

Other measures are specific to the mode. In the truckload sector, for example, where equipment availability is a major issue, Baxter looks for lane-by-lane commitments for equipment.

All the measures aim at one thing: "One of the challenges we have as these relationships develop and mature is to continually raise the bar and assure our mutual customers have enhanced levels of service," says Houghton. "We're looking for consistency. That's the key to driving inventory out of the replenishment pipeline."

CPI BUYERS WANT MORE THAN QUALITY*
by Kevin R. Fitzgerald

Quality awards are becoming a common tool for recognizing and rewarding superior supplier performance in the chemical/process industries (CPI). However, purchasing professionals should bear in mind that quality awards are only as good as the rating systems on which they are based and the extent to which they encourage suppliers to continuously improve total quality systems.

Purchasing departments in the CPI that have formal, quantitative supplier-rating systems in place are a minority. More common are companies that either use qualitative systems or are just beginning to create supplier rating systems.

Of course, the criteria for rating suppliers often varies from one company to the next. Purchasing at a commodity chemicals manufacturer might emphasize low-cost production processes, while buyers at a specialty chemicals producer may place a supplier's technological innovation as the most important factor. Regardless of the

---

relative importance different criteria may have, purchasers can learn from the supplier rating benchmarks set by their peers in the CPI.

Two Good Examples

At Miles Inc., the Pittsburgh-based operating arm of German chemical giant Bayer AG, purchasing selects annual winners of the "MILEStone" award for top-performing suppliers in several procurement categories. The award is based on Miles's comprehensive supplier-rating system, which takes into account virtually all factors that might affect profitability, the quality of Miles's final products, or the ability of Miles to remain competitive in its markets. The program began four years ago with raw material suppliers. Today, it encompasses every important product and service.

"Strategic" suppliers to Miles are monitored twice each year, and each strategic supplier receives a mid-year "report card." All appropriate suppliers are rated in three general categories: quality, delivery, and service. Determination of MILEStone award winners is coordinated between corporate and plant purchasing. To qualify for a MILEStone, a supplier must meet a predetermined dollar volume of business with Miles, supply a minimum of two Miles plant sites, and achieve high ratings: 99% in quality, 98% in delivery, and 97% in service. For strategic raw material suppliers in 1993, seven suppliers met these criteria and were eligible for the MILEStone award.

Final ratings are weighted, with quality comprising 50%; delivery, 35%; and service, 15%. MILEStone awards for raw material suppliers were given to Shell Chemical in 1992 and PPG in 1993.

A key focus of Mile's program is on removing cost from the procurement and manufacturing processes. With some key suppliers, Miles shares cost savings.

The MILEStone award program has produced many benefits for both Miles and its suppliers, according to Dr. Helmut Porkert, senior VP of materials management. In addition to recognizing superior supplier performance, the award helps Miles meet the supplier audit requirements of its major customers. It results in more concise requirements to suppliers and stimulates discussion within the supplier's organization.

"Suppliers appreciate the input we give them," says Porkert. "Pointing out their weaknesses helps suppliers correct them and improve their relationships with all their customers, not just Miles."

Indeed, identifying deficiencies that are "hidden" in the supplier's operations or corporate culture can be invaluable to the supplier. These types of weaknesses often are difficult or even impossible for the supplier itself to recognize.

Purchasing at DowBrands, the consumer product division of Dow Chemical Co., recognizes top-performing suppliers in 13 different product categories each year. In 1993, Shell Chemical bested 24 other chemical manufacturing suppliers to receive the award. Van Waters & Rogers won the 1993 award for chemical distributors.

DowBrands also gives out supplier awards for labels, sprayer components, folded cartons, aerosols, bottles, plastic resins, corrugated, fragrances, dyes and brighteners, specialty packaging, and end molds. The supplier award program has been in place for several years.

Like the system at Miles, DowBrands uses a final rating system that is weighted by category: 30% for quality, 30% for cost effectiveness, 20% for service, 10% for service/receiving issues, and 10% for various support activities.

The awards program has benefited both DowBrands and its key suppliers, says Bob Harris, purchasing director for packaging materials. "We're working closer with suppliers than ever before," he says. "Everything is more open. Our suppliers have seen that this process benefits them, too, because they can use what they learn in other parts of their business."

Exorcising Costs

Many purchasing departments in the CPI are partnering with suppliers in efforts to identify and eliminate unnecessary costs. In more sophisticated programs, cost savings are shared between supplier and customer.

This approach to sharing of cost savings has been adopted at Miles, which uses the carrot of financial return to encourage key suppliers to aggressively seek out and eliminate cost from the supply chain, *wherever it may exist.*

DowBrands also strives to encourage suppliers to find and eliminate cost from the supply chain. "If an action doesn't add value," says Bob Harris, "why do it?"

From the supplier viewpoint, Shell Chemical attributes part of its success as a supplier to working with its customers in similar efforts to remove unnecessary costs from the supplier/customer interface.

THE BEST REWARD

Purchasing attempts, with obvious logic, to reward award-winning suppliers with more business. This approach not only gives suppliers incentive to perform better, but it increases the volume of business that purchasing does with its best suppliers.

But all purchasing pros should remember that quality awards, whether they be the "supplier of the year" type or attainment of a preestablished level such as "certified" supplier or "partner," should not be viewed as an endpoint. By definition, there is no finish line in the continuous improvement process. Suppliers that stand out from the pack understand this, and will continue to work with purchasing to form closer relationships, which will be flexible enough to change as future conditions warrant.

3.12
AUDITING

---■---

INTERNAL AUDITS HELP YOU MEASURE
WHERE YOU ARE AND WHERE YOU WANT TO GO*

You can't enhance the quality of your operation and the services it provides without knowing where you stand today. Assessing the current state of affairs gives you a baseline upon which to build your goals and strategy for improvement.

Internal audits are an excellent tool for helping your company determine how it's doing in terms of meeting quality standards, and where it needs to go. And often, internal audits aren't just something that "would be nice to do"—they can be required by your customers as part of doing business with you. In addition, companies that are implementing initiatives such as ISO 9000 must conduct internal audits on an ongoing basis to ensure continuous improvement and continued compliance with the standards.

FOLLOW THE BOY SCOUT MOTTO

The key to effective internal quality audits is *preparation*. How your company prepares for an audit is often more important than how the audit is conducted.

How can you prepare effectively for internal audits? *Develop a checklist*. This is the most important prerequisite. The checklist is a series of questions that the auditor (usually the quality leader or a trained person within the company who is not directly involved in the function being audited) follows while conducting the quality assessment.

Why is a checklist so essential? "The questions serve as a general guide to what the auditor is seeking throughout the audit process," says

Frank Morrison, president of Morrison and Associates, a Glen Ellyn, Illinois-based consultant in quality affairs. "They help the auditor effectively evaluate the aspect of the business, procedure, or system being assessed."

Each audit requires a checklist that is customized to the type of company and the business element that's being examined, Morrison stresses. With a customized list, you'll be better able to serve the main purpose of audits—to discover and correct errors, failures, and weaknesses. A more general checklist, he notes, will not effectively help you accomplish this.

Two Key Types of Audit Checklists

Morrison divides audit checklists into two categories:

The SITOOCAATEC Audit Checklist

Morrison translates this lengthy, self-named, tongue-in-cheek acronym into Sit In The Office Over Coffee And Audit The Entire Company in a yes/no situation. This is a status-only checklist that is designed to say whether your company is meeting both external and internal customer requirements, whether its performance is satisfactory or unsatisfactory.

This type of audit is often used because it emphasizes filing an audit report as quickly as possible at the lowest possible cost. However, because it is not particularly specific, it does not observe, record, or recognize any deficiencies. "I've sat through a number of audits of this type," says Morrison. "You can say yes or no and come off with a shining example of what your company is doing, whether or not it's true. I believe that this kind of audit does your management a disservice because the results can easily mislead them."

Corrective Action-Oriented Audit Checklist

This also requires a question-and-answer type approach, but one that goes much deeper than the SITOOCAATEC approach by eliciting information on problem areas. The strategy: Take requirements of the standards you're auditing to and restate them as open-ended questions, thereby precluding a simple yes or no answer.

This approach enables the auditor to get as much detail as possible about the function being audited. As a result, the auditor can detail the corrective actions needed to clear up deficiencies.

Guidelines to an Effective Checklist

What's the best way to fashion an effective quality audit checklist? Morrison offers these suggestions:

• *Become very familiar with the standards you're auditing to.* Your key responsibility during the audit is to gauge how well the process you're auditing measures up to the standard. The standard may be requirements supplied by your customers, ISO 9000 standards, the Malcolm Baldrige National Quality Award criteria, a company policy, or a government compliance regulation. You are, in effect, taking a photograph of what is happening in your company at that moment as compared with the standard.

• *State each requirement of the standard requirement in the form of an open-ended question.* This way, they can't be answered with a simple yes or no. By doing this, you get a true measure of how well each individual requirement is met.

Using open-ended questions has other advantages, too. "In the past," Morrison says, "I went in with the feeling that I knew the best way to achieve compliance with the standard. I very quickly learned that there is more than one way to meet the requirement. Asking open-ended questions will allow you to explore the different ways a task can be done. It will prevent you from coming up with a deficiency because someone is not doing something in a way you think it should be done."

• *Document the compliance level and include proof of the compliance or non-compliance.* Everything you do during the audit should be put in writing and supported by factual evidence. Explain exactly how the requirements were met or not met. Be sure to indicate in your recorded answers the compliance level against each requirement of the standard.

• *Reference the document, system, and/or authority that requires the compliance.* "Very often, after you have finished your audit and returned to your office, you forget where you were when you said that 'this was terrible' or 'that was great,' " says Morrison. "Therefore, it's helpful to reference each question to the standard by page or section. This helps anyone reading the report to find the citation that led you to rule that something was compliant or noncompliant. It's also helpful to note the location where you made the observation."

• *In the requirements-met section, record information that allows the evaluation of new methods that can improve the system or process.* You may find that your company has procedures or policies that cannot be followed as written. These cases are often solved by "workarounds" created by innovative employees who find ways to meet the requirements of the policy in a different manner than written.

Explore this avenue if you run across it and note it with the idea of improving the written policy or procedure. Delineate what is actually done as opposed to what the written policy says is done.

• *Allow for a provision that says that your company met the standard but wishes to exceed the standard.* "Very often, a standard is a minimum requirement," Morrison explains. "Your company may wish to exceed that standard, so the standard must be adapted to fit within the company's policies and strategic plans. "In such cases, the audit checklist should show that you met the standard but felt that just meeting it was not good enough. Remember that the purpose of your audit is to improve the entire system within your organization."

EARN AN "A" FOR AUDITING

Implementing these guidelines will put you well on the road to success with internal quality audits. Auditing to specific standards, using open-ended questions, documenting your observations, and referencing compliance sources will pave the way not only to a smooth audit but also to an upgrading of all your company's processes and services.

HOW TO LAY THE GROUNDWORK FOR A SUPERIOR INTERNAL QUALITY AUDIT*

The most important step in planning for an internal quality audit is to develop a checklist. The checklist is a series of questions that the auditor follows while conducting a quality audit.

Why is a checklist so essential? "The question serve as a general guide to what the auditor is seeking throughout the audit process," says Frank Morrison, president of Morrison and Associates, a Glen Ellyn, Illinois-based consultant in quality and regulatory affairs. "They should trigger the auditor's thought processes and help the auditor effectively evaluate the aspect of the business or the procedure or system being assessed."

Morrison stresses that each audit requires a checklist that is customized to the type of company and the business element that's being examined. With a customized list, you'll be better able to serve the main purpose of audits—to dis-

cover and correct errors, failures, and weaknesses. A more general checklist, he notes, will not effectively help you accomplish this.

TWO KEY TYPES OF AUDIT CHECKLISTS

Morrison divides audit checklists into two classifications:

The SITOOCAATEC Audit Checklist

Morrison translates this lengthy self-named tongue-in-cheek acronym into *Sit In The Office Over Coffee And Audit The Entire Company* in a yes/no situation. This is a status-only checklist that is designed to say whether your company

---

meets requirements, whether its performance is satisfactory or unsatisfactory. This type of audit does not observe, or record, or recognize any deficiencies.

However, this type of audit is often used because many auditors are charged with auditing various systems or suppliers within a very short time frame.

This type of checklist emphasizes filing an audit report as quickly as possible at the lowest possible cost. Much less emphasis is placed on the status of such matters as supplier relations. "I've sat through a number of audits of this type," says Morrison, "and you can say yes or no and come off with a shining example of what your company is doing, whether or not it's true. I believe that this kind of audit does your management a disservice because the results can easily mislead them."

Corrective Action-Oriented Audit Checklist

This also requires a question-and-answer type approach, but one that goes much deeper than the SITOOCAATEC approach by eliciting information on problem areas. The strategy: Take requirements of the standards you're auditing to and restate them as open-ended questions, thereby precluding a simple yes or no answer.

This approach enables the auditor to get as much detail as possible about the function being audited.

GUIDELINES TO AN EFFECTIVE CHECKLIST

What's the best way to fashion an effective quality audit checklist? Morrison offers these suggestions:

• Become very familiar with the standards you're auditing to. Your key responsibility during the audit is to gauge how well the process you're auditing measures up to the standard. The standard may concern ISO 9000, the Baldrige award, criteria, a company policy, or a government compliance regulation. You are, in effect, taking a photograph of what is happening in your company at that moment as compared with that standard.

• State each requirement of the standard requirement in the form of an open-ended question. This way, they can't be answered with a simple yes or no. By doing this, you get a true measure of how well each individual requirement is met.

Asking open-ended questions also will allow you to explore the different ways a task can be done. It will prevent you from coming up with a deficiency because someone is not doing something in a way *you* think it should be done.

• Document the compliance level and include proof of the compliance or noncompliance. Explain exactly how the requirements were met or not met. Be sure to indicate in your recorded answers the compliance level against each requirement of the standard.

• Reference the document, system, and/or authority that requires the compliance. "Very often, after you have left the site, you forget where you were when you said that *this* was terrible or *that* was great," says Morrison. "Therefore, it's helpful to reference each question to the standard by page or section. This helps anyone reading the report to find the citation that led you to rule that something was compliant or noncompliant."

• In the requirements-met section, record information that allows the evaluation of new methods that can improve the system or process. You may find that your company has procedures or policies that cannot be followed as written. These cases are often solved by workarounds created by innovative employees who find ways to meet the requirements of the policy in a different manner than written.

• Allow for a provision that says that your company met the standard but wishes to exceed the standard. "In such cases, the audit checklist should show that you met the standard but felt that *just meeting it* was not good enough. Remember that the purpose of your audit is to improve the entire system within your organization."

A SYSTEMATIC APPROACH TO QUALITY ASSURANCE AUDITING*
by Rafik H. Bishara and Michael L. Wyrick

Quality Assurance (QA) auditing is a systematic examination of representative aspects of quality systems within an organization, its suppliers, and third-party operations. Eli Lilly and Company, a pharmaceutical company, has applied QA audits to enhance continuous quality improvement.

The purpose of a QA audit is to ensure understanding of corporate philosophies and adherence to organizational and regulatory requirements. Although auditing is not mentioned in the Food and Drug Administration's good manufacturing practice (GMP) for finished pharmaceuticals,[1] it is specifically mentioned in the GMP for medical devices.[2] Section 820.20(b) of the regulation states that "planned and periodic audits of the quality assurance program shall be implemented to verify compliance with the quality assurance program." Requirements for a written audit procedure, documentation of audit results, and review of the audit report by management are also sited.

An audit cycle has been developed to facilitate the auditee/auditor partnership. During this cycle, QA auditors talk with the auditees throughout every phase of the audit process because educational exchange, in which the auditors learn about the auditees' quality systems and auditees learn what areas require quality improvements, is fundamental to the success of the audit.

The Eli Lilly audit cycle clarifies responsibilities, standardizes the audit process, and encourages the interaction between auditors and auditees. This audit cycle, which is similar to the plan-do-check-act cycle, is based on five steps: preparing, conducting, writing/reviewing, reporting, and following up (see Exhibit 1).[3] The audit process Eli Lilly follows when conducting internal GMP audits is presented in Exhibit 2.

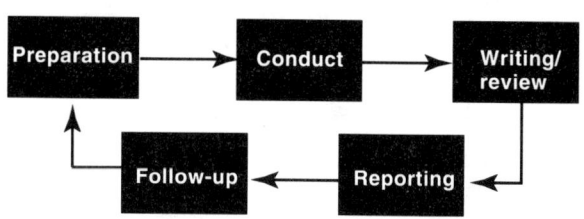

EXHIBIT 1.—THE FIVE STEPS OF THE QUALITY ASSURANCE AUDIT CYCLE

PREPARATION

Preparing GMP audits consists of developing the following:

- *An audit plan.* The QA organization annually creates risk/exposure profiles of all auditable units.[4] An auditable unit is a manufacturing or manufacturing-support operation that could affect product safety, identity, strength, purity, or quality. Creating a quality profile involves assessing various risk factors (the probability of a hazard) and exposure factors (the business value or the materiality, such as economics and image, to the company). Examples of risk factors include the probability of a regulatory action, QA inspection history, quality systems, documentation, equipment, process validation, and quality plan. Examples of exposure factors include product portfolio, company image, and need for products. Each company must determine its own factors and continuously revise or delete what is not appropriate. In the process of developing a profile, each factor is assessed as being high, medium, or low; a numerical value is assigned; and a total score for each auditable unit is calculated. The totals of the risk/exposure scores are plotted to determine the

*Reprinted with permission from *Quality Progress*, December 1994. Rafik H. Bishara is the manager of quality assurance projects at Eli Lilly and Company in Indianapolis IN. Michael L. Wyrick is the project leader of computer validation compliance at Eli Lilly and Company in Indianapolis IN.

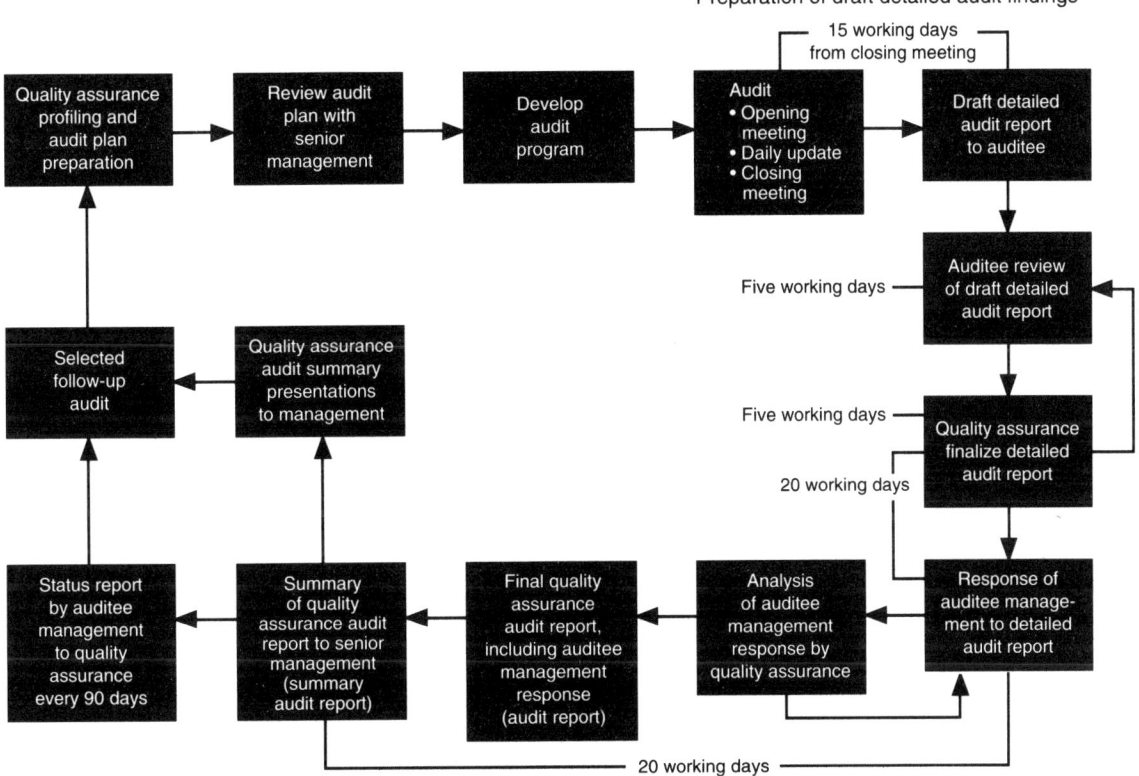

EXHIBIT 2.—QUALITY ASSURANCE AUDIT CYCLE

priorities of the audit plan for the following year. Auditable units with a high-risk and high-exposure profile receive immediate attention. QA management reviews the audit plan with senior corporate quality management.

- *An audit program.* Representatives from the manufacturing area to be audited, quality control management, and other appropriate management are contacted to develop the audit program. The audit to be performed (general, focused, or follow-up), the scope of the audit, the dates when the audit will be held, and the primary contact for the audit team are determined at this time.

CONDUCTING THE AUDIT

The audit process is significantly influenced by how auditors conduct it and how it is perceived by the auditees. Successful audits happen when communication barriers are broken down so that opportunities for enhancements can be shared openly, ideas can be shared, and an auditor/auditee partnership can be formed. During the

audit, the auditors should take a balanced approach that reports both good points and points for improvement.

The audit consists of three phases:

Opening meeting. At the beginning of the audit, the audit team, which consists of one or more people led by a corporate QA member called the lead auditor, meets with the auditees and their management to review the scope and schedule of the audit, verify the auditee liaison, identify the recipient(s) of the audit findings report, identify primary contacts during the audit, and review any other matters that might expedite the audit process. Clarification of the audit process at the opening meeting is a very important step toward getting the audit started on a positive note. The auditors' clear definition of the audit objectives and the comprehensive information supplied by the auditees will provide a solid foundation for enhancing the efficiency of the audit process. A tour of the facilities at this stage will help the auditors gain an overall understanding of operations.

Fieldwork, examination, and daily update. Next, the auditors observe, examine, document, and interview the auditees. Paper or computerized checklists can help auditors make sure that they have covered essential areas and items of interest. The audit plan provides boundaries for the auditors, but the auditors have an obligation to "follow the thread" when they identify improvement opportunities.

The audit team meets daily to discuss audit findings before sharing them with area personnel and the auditee liaison. Periodic review meetings can also be held to inform auditee management of any significant audit findings that will be presented at the closing meeting. Having no surprises at the closing meeting is one of the golden rules of auditing.

Closing meeting. On completion of the audit, the audit team presents the audit findings, which are to be documented in the audit report to the auditees and their management. It is important that both parties understand the significance of the audit observations (specific audit findings that are grouped to support and clarify any key audit findings) and the overall impact of the audit. Time commitments and responsibilities for the written review and report are also discussed.

WRITTEN REVIEW

The auditors prepare a draft detailed audit report (DDAR) that includes the audit observations. The DDAR is distributed to the auditees' management within 15 working days after the closing meeting. Within five working days after receipt of the DDAR, the auditee management issues a written response to the QA manager and lead auditor acknowledging the accuracy of the audit findings and/or adding any comments it might have. On completion of the QA review process, the detailed audit report is published within five working days. Within 20 working days after receiving the final detailed audit report, auditee management issues a written response and action plan for resolving each key audit finding (a departure from corporate and/or regulatory requirements or accepted technical practices). These reports are treated as privileged and confidential documents.

THE AUDIT REPORT

Within 20 working days of the receipt of the auditee management's response and action plan,

the audit team analyzes the responses and resolves any open issues. The audit report—consisting of key audit findings, site management's response, and an action plan—is circulated to appropriate management. This report is generally not more than 30 pages long. A summary audit report, generally not more than three pages long, is also prepared at this time for senior management. The auditees will issue status reports to the QA department every 90 days until all action plan items have been completed.

On completion of the action plan for all key audit findings, the auditee management issues a memorandum to QA management and the lead auditor stating that all actions have been implemented. When applicable, a follow-up audit can be performed to verify the successful implementation of the auditee action plan.

TIME FRAMES FOR COMPLETION

As indicated in Exhibit 2, several steps of the audit cycle have a predetermined time for completion. The completion of the other activities, however, depends on the type and scope of the audit and on the available resources. For example, a general comprehensive audit could require one to two weeks, and a focused audit could require one to three days. To stay on schedule, the audit team might have one to four auditors. Preparing the profile and audit plan might take a couple of working days. This is followed by a two-hour presentation to senior management. The average time required for developing the audit program is four to eight hours. The number of audit observations and the seriousness of the findings determine the length of time required to develop, implement, and complete the action plan. To ensure proper communication and timely completion of the plan, the auditees provide periodic status updates to the auditors until the action plan has been completed.

SYSTEMATIC AUDIT APPROACH

This QA audit cycle has proven to be an excellent vehicle to establish better understanding, cooperation, and partnership between the QA function and its customers. A benefit of using this systematic audit approach is that auditees receive unbiased facts for management decisions. The improved communication and partnership between the auditors and auditees result in the identification of areas for improvement. The focused audit facilitates the identification of specific areas for enhancements (such as equipment validation or process capabilities) that should be expeditiously corrected. Other benefits include the assurance of having standard operating procedures and proper staff training.

Although a systematic audit process is time and resource intensive, correcting the findings will improve quality, enhance the fitness of the product, and avoid delays in launching new products or recalls of marketed products. The systematic audit process has also changed the perception of the auditor as an internal adversary, cop, or error finder to a team player, consultant, and problem solver.[5]

This model should be used to manage internal QA audits and to work with customers to develop tools for continuous self-audits. Implementing a successful self-audit program diminishes the number and significance of audit observations documented in future QA audits. It could also reduce the number of required future audits.

REFERENCES

1. Food and Drug Administration, "Current Good Manufacturing Practice for Finished Pharmaceuticals," CFR 211.
2. Food and Drug Administration, "Current Good Manufacturing Practice for Medical Devices," CFR 820.20(b).
3. W. Edwards Deming, *Out of the Crisis* (Cambridge, MA: Massachusetts Institute of Technology, Center for Advanced Engineering Study, 1992), p. 88, Chapter 8, and Chapter 15.

4. Rafik H. Bishara, D.G. Schott, and G.M. Tush, "Quality Assurance Profiling: Prioritizing Audits," *Pharmaceutical Technology*, Vol. 17, No. 4, 1993, pp. 92-100.
5. L.B. Sawyer, *Elements of Management: Oriented Auditing* (Altamonte Springs, FL: The Institute of Internal Auditors, Inc., 1983), Chapter 1 and Chapter 8.

BIBLIOGRAPHY

Cates, M., and M.F. DeMane, "The Meaning of Quality," *Medical Device and Diagnostic Industry*, Vol. 15, No. 2, 1993.

The Ernest & Young Quality Improvement Consulting Group, *Total Quality: An Executive's Guide for the 1990s* (Homewood, IL: Dow Jones-Irwin, 1990).

Feigenbaum, Armand V., *Total Quality Control* (New York, NY: McGraw-Hill Book Company, 1983).

Juran, Joseph M., *Quality Control Handbook* (New York, NY: McGraw-Hill Book Company, 1974).

Sawyer, L.B., *Elements of Management: Oriented Auditing* (Altamonte Springs, FL: The Institute of Internal Auditors, Inc., 1983).

Sayle, A.J., *Management Audits: The Assessment of Quality Management Systems* (Hampshire, England: A.J. Sayle Ltd., 1991).

Sheng, S.K., "The Bare Essentials for Internal Auditing," *Medical Device and Diagnostic Industry*, Vol. 15, No. 4, 1993.

Suntag, Charles, *Inspection and Inspection Management* (Milwaukee, WI: ASQC Quality Press, 1993).

ACKNOWLEDGMENT

The authors appreciate the help of Susan E. Crowe and Pat Lottes in preparing this article.

LONG-AWAITED AUDITOR AGREEMENT REACHED*

Thirteen of the world's largest ISO 9000 auditor certification bodies have reached agreement on a stringent new international auditor certification program that will eliminate the need for multiple certifications.

Under the agreement signed in Australia last month, ISO 9000 auditors soon will be able to seek certification to one of two newly-created international grades—IATCA auditor and IATCA senior auditor. The agreement was reached

*Reprinted with permission from *Quality Systems Update*, published by IRWIN Professional Publishing, Fairfax, VA. August 1995.

through the International Auditor and Training Certification Association (IATCA) for which the grades are named.

ISO 9000 registrars, now forced to pay multiple auditor certification fees, stand to gain the most from the agreement. But it was not immediately known whether the reduced operating costs would be passed on to clients in the form of lower auditing costs.

Once certified, auditors theoretically will be able to work anywhere in the world where a participating auditor certification organization is located or recognized including Australia, Brazil, China, France, India, Japan, Korea, New Zealand, Malaysia, Singapore, Southern Africa, Taipei, United Kingdom and the United States.

The agreement also will provide for recognition of ISO 9000 auditor training course providers accredited by participating organizations and could possibly be extended to cover the certification of auditors for ISO 14001 registrations.

John Hulbert, executive director of the Joint Accreditation System of Australia and New Zealand (JAS-ANZ), which was one of the signatories, said that operational details of the agreement are still being worked out, but that the first international auditor certifications should be available in mid 1996.

"The criteria which candidates themselves will have to meet have been agreed to. There is still a need to fine tune the details of how candidates will be evaluated under the uniform program," Hulbert said.

He also said officials agreed in principle that existing auditor certifications granted under conditions that meet IATCA criteria will be transferable to the relevant IATCA grade, but details of how the transfers will be accomplished have yet to be worked out.

Unlike most existing certification programs, the international program will require candidates for IATCA auditor certification to conduct at least 30 days of auditing under the supervision of a certified IATCA auditor, including at least two, two-day audits.

In addition, the candidate will have to meet minimum education and work experience criteria and have successfully completed an approved auditor training course.

The audit experience conducted under supervision must cover all aspects of a complete quality management system audit, such as ISO 9000 and be performed in accordance with ISO 10011.

For certification as an IATCA senior auditor, the candidate must carry out at least five full audits acting as a leader of an audit team, each under the supervision of an experienced certified IATCA senior auditor.

"An IATCA auditor would demonstrate competence in auditing all elements of an ISO 9000 standard," Hulbert explained. "An IATCA senior auditor would have demonstrated competence over and above what was required for certification as an IATCA auditor with the additional requirements aimed at demonstrating competence at managing an audit team covering all functions of an audit."

The international certification requirements, which will be administered by existing auditor certification bodies, will not replace national auditor certification requirements for the foreseeable future.

Officials deliberately avoided using the terms lead auditor or lead assessor in the international grades to avoid marketplace confusion. In the past, many people have confused certification as lead assessor and lead auditor with the person designated by the registrar to oversee an audit.

Hulbert said the international approach to auditor certification will be one of mentoring.

"You will be able to guide a person through, given them background and knowledge based on your experience and then certify that they have that background and experience and are applying it in an appropriate manner," Hulbert said.

"Some programs at the moment give a certification based on verified claims of experience but not necessarily having that experience witnessed by any competent auditor," he said.

It was not immediately known how the international agreement would be implemented in the United States or what the planned fee structure would be.

George Lofgren, president of the Registrar Accreditation Board (RAB), which operates auditor certification and course accreditation programs in the United States, participated in the agreement but was not available for comment as of press time.

Alan Marash, another US representative who attended the Cairns, Australia meeting, said the new international certifications would probably raise the competence level of ISO 9000 auditors.

"The agreement between the nations has raised the level of auditor qualification and provides us with additional assurances as to the actual auditor qualifications which ultimately provides a higher level of confidence on the part of the customer of the supplier's quality system," said Marash, vice president of Stat-A-Matrix, an ISO 9000 course provider that has attained multiple accreditations of its training courses.

According to Hulbert, participating organizations hope to finalize the operational details of the agreement by the beginning of next year. He said they will then undergo a yet-to-be determined peer review process and must sign a formal multilateral recognition agreement before the first international auditor certifications are issued.

An agreement recognizing auditor certification has been in place since March 1994 between RAB, the UK's Institute of Quality Assurance (IQA) the Quality Society of Australasia, which operates an auditor certification program in Australia and New Zealand, and JAS-ANZ. Hulbert said the prior agreement also will remain in place.

‖‖‖‖ 3.13
COORDINATE MEASURING MACHINES

SIZING UP NON-CONTACT MEASUREMENTS*
by Quality Staff

All non-contact gaging systems use some form of radiant energy to probe objects. The energy used can be in the form of light, ultrasonics, x-rays, or electron beams, depending on the properties that need to be measured and the accuracies required.

There are four basic methods of non-contact measurement:

- Air gaging
- Capacitance
- Diffraction
- Focus follow

Each of these has advantages and disadvantages and provides different kinds of measurements. The air-gaging method measures the flow rate of air between a workpiece and a custom-made air nozzle. Although this method is low-cost, robust, and quick and simple to operate, it has limitations. Among these are the need for special nozzles for curved surfaces and being severely influenced by surface defects such as scratches and burrs. Even for smooth surfaces, it is difficult to accurately measure the flow of air.

The capacitance method measures the electrical capacitance between a workpiece and a transducer head. As the object approaches the sensor, the capacitance between the two increases. Capacitance sensors have limited range compared with ultrasonics, but much higher resolution.

The biggest disadvantage is that many other factors affect capacitance, such as the material composition of the object. Because of this, the accuracy of a capacitance sensor often is much worse than its resolution.

The diffraction method measures the distribution of light and the intensity of diffracted light. This method only works on a small range of surfaces and needs special lenses to measure curved or formed components. However, diffraction provides fast analysis, is simple to operate, has few moving parts, and has the potential to be used on a machine tool.

In the focus follow method, a moving lens is used to focus a spot of light on the sample surface, while the lens movement is measured. There are, however, inherent disadvantages with this approach. If a surface has high slopes, insufficient light is reflected back into the focusing

*Reprinted with permission from *Quality*, Volume 34, No. 3, March 1995.

lens, causing the system to follow inaccurately. Also, since there is no contact, there is no force to move contaminants such as dirt, oil, or finger-prints away from the surface, resulting in those contaminents being measured as part of the surface. In addition, when oxide layers are present the focusing lens will oscillate between the top and the bottom of the oxide layer, thus providing a rough appearance. Due to the effects of diffraction, a focus follow measurement will give rise to an overshoot when measuring over a sharp edge.

Despite these innate disadvantages, focus follow provides very similar results to stylus instruments and uses the same parameter definitions. It also can be retrofitted to many existing surface finish instruments.

SENSING WITH LIGHT

Some instruments that use the focus-follow method use laser sensors in a variety of ways. "Interferometers work very much like ultrasonic sensors, but they emit and detect light rather than sound waves," explained Jeff Jelkio, vice president of research, CyberOptics Corp., Minneapolis. "As a result, they can operate over very long distances while maintaining high accuracy. Some high-end CMMs use laser interferometers as encoders.

"Laser triangulation is probably the most common type of laser sensor. These sensors emit a beam of light and view that beam's reflection at an angle. In this way, the object's distance can be measured just as larger distances are measured by surveyors. Sensors of this type are available with a wide range of accuracies."

The focus-follow method has seen continued development, with efforts being made to reduce the spot size of the laser beam, typically from 5 to 1 mm. "This gives greater correlation with stylus-based instruments," commented Roger Morton, senior vice president and general manager, Rank Taylor Hobson Inc., Rolling Meadows, IL. "Efforts have also been made to reduce the size of the complete gage. Size factors restrict the instrument's ability to penetrate bores. In the phase measuring area, developments have concentrated on increasing the spatial resolution, which is dictated by the charge-coupled device (CCD) array size. This has been 256×256 points, while the latest developments are now increasing that to $1,024 \times 1,024$," said Morton.

Today, however, 512×512 is considered the norm. The greater the data density, the greater the data processing requirements. But the use of 256×256 does not give sufficient spatial resolution to accurately measure surface finishes on high-quality parts," Morton said.

NON-CONTACT: WHEN AND WHY

Why would a manufacturer prefer a non-contact method of measurement over a contact method? And under what circumstances? According to Nabeel Sufi, manager, inspection products, Phase Shift Technology Inc., Tucson, "Contact vs. non-contact is typically based on access, surface damage, instrument wear, measurement time, and frequency considerations. Non-contact measurements are, in general, faster than contact measurements and less prone to wear during measurement. On the other hand, the environmental conditions are typically greater for non-contact approach."

Each type of measurement has pros and cons, according to Sufi. Contact methods generally are more rugged, simpler, and therefore cheaper. However, contact methods may damage surfaces, lack resolution and accuracy, and generally are slower. Non-contact methods, on the other hand, are faster, provide higher resolutions and accuracies, are less prone to wear, and don't damage product surfaces. While they currently are more expensive, technology advances are changing this.

THERE ARE FINER DISTINCTIONS

There basically are three reasons to use non-contact gaging, according to CyberOptics' Jelkio. "First, the object you need to measure may be 'untouchable,' " he said. "CyberOptics does much of its business in the electronics industry and many of the materials that must be measured are liquids or pastes (solder paste, resistive inks, and adhesives). Contact methods simply don't work if the object is deformable.

"Second, in high-volume applications, contact gages may wear quickly," Jelkio continued. "This requires frequent replacement or recalibration. Non-contact gages eliminate this. One of our customers previously used a contact gage that they had to replace every six months. It was easy for them to justify a more expensive contact gage.

"Third, in some applications, non-contact gaging can be used to obtain shorter inspection times than contact methods," he said. "This is because the sensor can be scanned over the object surface to make many measurements.

None of these three circumstances should be written in stone. It is probably best for a process engineer to erase the line between contact and non-contact gages, keep them all in his toolkit, and select the sensor most appropriate for each measurement."

"The crucial difference between the two should not be ignored," explained Robert Smythe, director, marketing and sales, Zygo Corp., Middlefield, CT. "Non-contact is nondestructive and noninvasive," he said. "Many applications today are sensitive to contact. Contact techniques tend to be slow compared with non-contact optical measurements."

It should be noted that hardness or softness of the product to be measured is not always a criterion for deciding between the two methods. A manufacturer may turn to a non-contact stylus when a mechanical pickup damages or deforms the surface of a product, according to Nick Grant, product specialist, Mahr Corp., Cincinnati. "This is the case with soft materials, such as rubber, plastics, aluminum, copper, and tin," he commented. "But manufacturers of very hard materials, such as ceramics and diamond, also may turn to non-contact measuring to eliminate increased wear on a conventional diamond stylus." Also, manufacturers of highly polished materials, such as copier rollers, would use a non-contact method to avoid scratching the surface, which can affect part performance.

"With non-contact systems, there is no mechanical filtering, which occurs during tracing, so a better representation of surfaces can be obtained," said Grant. "With most contact probes, the operator is required to manually lower the probe until it is in the center of its range. Often, when an operator is careless, the probe could be lowered into the surface past its range. This can damage both the probe and the product surface. With non-contact measurements, the risk of damaging the stylus or the surface is eliminated," he added.

BEYOND THE BASICS

There are, of course, other types of non-contact measuring methodologies. Typically, solid-state methods such as diffraction and phase measuring interferometry (PMI) incorporate benefits of very fast analysis over an area, said Rank Taylor Hobson's Morton.

One example of a PMI product comes from Wyko Corp., Tucson. "One method for obtaining extremely accurate, high-resolution surface measurements uses PMI and vertical scanning interference microscopy," said Wyko president James Wyant. "The phase measuring mode makes it possible to measure smooth surfaces with a vertical resolution as low as 0.1 nanometers (nm). The vertical scanning mode provides a measurement range to 500 mm."

This combination of technologies lets the user select a measurement mode that is optimized to the surface characteristics of the sample. Instruments combining PMI and vertical scanning interference microscopy provide rapid three-dimensional (3-D) measurements of surface roughness with sub-nanometer vertical resolution. These instruments can measure a range of samples such as paper, metal, ceramics, glass, and plastic without damaging the surface.

However, all optical microscope systems typically have a small field-of-view and a lateral resolution that is limited by the pixel spacing and optical spatial resolution. The best visible-light optical microscopes cannot resolve lateral features smaller than approximately 0.3 mm.

THE THIRD DIMENSION

Three-dimensional measurements are so advanced that they may represent a separate case from other non-contact methods. "Manufacturers use non-contact 3-D surface measuring methods for several reasons," said Dan Cohen of Michigan Metrology, Detroit. "First, they want to rapidly measure multiple (>200) two-dimensional (2-D) profiles in two orthogonal directions (for example, across the lay and with the lay). By averaging the multiple profiles, more statistically significant information is available than with a conventional 2-D surface measurement technique. Second, 3-D non-contact systems allow the user to rapidly 'see' and measure the surface. This is an improvement over photographing the surface and then using a stylus to measure the roughness. Third, 3-D systems can characterize surfaces that are 3-D in nature, such as shot-peened or laser-etched surfaces. Fourth, these non-contact techniques are minimally affected by debris on the surface that may interfere with stylus or scanning measurements, since each point is measured."

There are additional advantages. "Noncontact optical measuring systems such as our RST Plus can simultaneously measure the entire image area without damaging the surface," commented Tami Balter, sales application development manager, Wyko Corp. "It works well on soft surfaces such as thin metallic foils, plastic films, and unbaked resists that are easily damaged by the force of a stylus. It also measures kinetic devices such as micromachined accelerometers and springs that would deflect or deform under the weight of a stylus."

MORE SYSTEMS

There are, of course, other systems on the market. Two from Zygo Corp. apply two basic data acquisition techniques to interferometric optical systems to measure surface structure. The New-View 100 and Maxim GP microscope products measure surface structure (shape and roughness) and analyze the data with sophisticated analysis software. The two basic data acquisition techniques are PMI for the Maxim GP and scanning white light interferometry (SWLI) for the New View 100.

"PMI is very accurate (0.1 nm Rq) and very fast (<3 sec./measurement for 64,000 data points), yet it is limited to surfaces with step heights less than 0.15 nm and surfaces smoother than 2 min. Ra," explained Zygo's Bob Smythe. "PMI can be extended to measure surfaces with up to 10-nm step heights, but the throughput is greatly decreased and the surfaces measured still must be <2 min. Ra. SWLI is slightly less accurate than PMI at 0.3 nm Ra and slower (15 sec./typical measurement) with a very large measurement range of 100 nm. Further, SWLI is not limited to 2-min.-Ra. surfaces, but can measure extremely rough surfaces such as papers, fibers, and 64-min.-Ra surfaces," added Smythe.

A combination of interferometric techniques, high-performance CCD imagers, digital-signal-processor (DSP) based video digitizers, and robust algorithms has given rise to a family of instruments from Phase Shift Technology Inc., Tucson, that provides non-contact measurement of shape, flatness, and finish. For example, the MicroXAM is a surface mapping microscope that can measure surface finish of a few angstroms up to 16 nm. Due to it's non-contact nature and 3-D representations of surface microstructure, the instrument is used to quantify surface topography, finish, and texture by various industries, including metals, ceramics, printing plate, and semiconductor.

Another phase shift technology product, OptiFlat XAM measures flatness over surfaces as large as 90 × 70 in. within a few seconds. The strip flatness in rolled materials is an important process parameter that typically is monitored for compliance to customer specifications. At rolling mills in the U.S. and Europe, OptiFlat XAM is being used to monitor the strip flatness at crucial stages in the rolling process. As a process control tool, OptiFlat XAM allows users to locate and eliminate the sources of variability in their process.

In-process gaging is provided by another Phase Shift product, TaperTester, which is a specialized instrument that measures the taper angle and length of thin film sliders used by the hard disk manufacturing industry. In combination with an automated part indexing system, TaperTester can measure more than 1,500 sliders within an hour.

Two products from Mahr Corp. operate on the "Dynamic Focusing" measuring principle. The RM600 3-D system is designed for quality inspection in a laboratory environment. The system consists of a laser probe, a sensor interface, power supply, evaluation unit using the DOS operating system, high-resolution monitor, and an X/Y table that allows construction of 3-D topographical images.

Mahr Corp.'s Nick Grant explained the Dynamic Focusing method used by these instruments. "A laser diode built into the probe's casing serves as the light source," he explained. "The light initially passes through a collimator, where it is brought into a parallel beam and then guided by a prism to the micro-objective. Another prism directs the light onto the surface to be inspected. The objective focuses the beam onto a 1-mm dot on the surface. The light is reflected back through the same path and directed by a beam splitter to the detector.

"The detector is part of a control loop. By means of a powerful linear motor, it readjusts the measuring arm continuously, so the laser stays in focus on the surface. As the probe is guided across the surface, the measuring lever follows the surface profile. As in a conventional pick-up, an inductive path measuring system converts the motion of the measuring lever into an electronic signal," Grant added.

Wafer Film Resistivity

"Traditional contact techniques measure film resistivity on monitor wafers," explained Tom Stroebel, resistivity product manager, Tencor Instruments, Prometrix Div., Santa Clara, CA. "To obtain contact measurements, the system contacts and damages the monitor wafer surface. Test monitor wafers are expensive and may not fully represent the metal film processing variables."

Tencor Instruments' OmniMap NC 110 directly measures sheet resistance in the blanket metal layers on product wafers without contacting the surface. Actual product wafer measurements ensure accurate characterization and control of the deposition process and allow for higher frequency of process monitoring, thereby reducing the risk of misprocessed wafers. When asked about the potential for cost savings on the inspection of wafers, Stroebel commented, "Contact measurement systems require the use of test monitor wafers. Monitor wafers require the expense of silicon substrates, chemicals, labor, and the loss of equipment utilization time.

Tencor Instruments' OmniMap NC 110 system actually measures film sheet resistance directly on product wafers. Process control can be monitored without the cost and inconvenience of test wafers, thus allowing fab operations to dramatically reduce processing costs.

According to Stroebel, "a fab that has 2,500 wafer starts per week could save well over $1 million/year by directly monitoring product wafers and eliminating monitor wafers. At 10,000 wafer starts per week, the savings could reach $5 million per year."

■

PRECISION MEASURING FLEXES ITS MUSCLES*
by Quality Staff

Today, more than ever before, manufacturers have the most extensive selection of flexible precision measuring options according to many quality control industry experts. But this is only half the story. Flexible inspection will remain a growing trend that will revolutionize manufacturing in the U.S.

SOON TO COME

Sounding the charge to the future, Dr. Thomas Lettieri, manager of the Advanced Technology Program (ATP) of the National Institute of Standards and Technology (NIST) (Gaithersburg, MD) manages a $8,761,000 research project to develop a high-speed, noncontact gaging system that will operate up to 100 times faster than currently available systems. If the project achieves its goal, the U.S. precision machining industry can save as much as $1 billion per year through increased productivity.

This research, called Rapid Agile Metrology for Manufacturing (RAMM) is directed and funded by a consortium of U.S. companies, education centers, agencies, and ATP. The consortium includes Chrysler Corp., Eaton Corp., General Electric Aircraft Engines, GE Corp. R&D, and TRW Inc. The system integrator for the team is Giddings and Lewis, Sheffield Div. where the prototype system will be built and tested. NIST will manage system calibration. Other members of the consortium include the Cleveland Advanced Manufacturing Program (CAMP), the NASA Lewis Research Center, USAF Wright Laboratory, Industrial Technology Institute, the

*Reprinted with permission from *Quality*, Volume 34, No. 2, February 1995.

University of Cincinnati, and Central State University, among others. The Ohio Aerospace Institute will act as facilitator for the consortium. In a way, Ohio Aerospace is the coach of this team, and NIST's ATP serves as the referee. Taxpayers also are research partners since $4,267,000 or 49% of this project will be paid by ATP.

Lettierei believes RAMM will be a winner for U.S. manufacturing. "I am not certain we will reach 100% of the goal," he says, "but we will achieve substantial improvements in faster, more flexible data gathering and processing so that the U.S. can stay competitive in global markets and save hundreds of millions of dollars per year. Other countries are not going to be standing around waiting for us. U.S. and foreign companies have been making steady progress toward faster and more flexible gaging, but this group effort should give the U.S. a faster path to the next level of performance."

BUT WHAT EXACTLY ARE THEY MAKING?

ATP is not into product development. That part of the project will progress naturally from the research. "We are looking at systems and the process from a practical point-of-view, attempting to apply technology to reach our stated goals," Lettieri notes. ATP is looking at a flexible system not only in application compatibility but also in its operation. The system could use a host of technologies, such as white light, laser, photographic, and moiré.

Lettieri stresses that contact gages will not be a part of this new system. "By the year 2000, there will be two basic technologies," he says. "Noncontact systems will give manufacturing flexibility and speed but sacrifice accuracy when compared with contact gages, which will continue to be more accurate than noncontact systems." RAMM will not eliminate the need for high-precision contact gages. Instead it will be ideal for use in rough environments such as the shop floor. As processes speed up, online inspections can be made accurately without slowing down manufacturing, improving productivity, or reducing workpiece costs.

Targeted applications of RAMM are the automotive and aerospace industries since they are directly involved in the research. But Lettieri stresses that defense, white goods, and many other manufacturing sectors also will benefit.

WHAT IS HERE NOW?

Although companies involved in making flexible measuring systems focus on different technologies, there is a common theme among them. In the past dozen years, computers and software have advanced the capabilities of flexible quality control systems dramatically.

WHITE LIGHT SYSTEMS

An integration of computes and software with data gathering technology is evident in the Profile Series from TESA Measurement Systems (Novi, MI), a Brown & Sharpe Co. "The Profile Series is an automated, programmable series of instruments," says Claes G. Maxe, president of TESA, "designed to use white light for measuring a variety of round or turned parts." TESA instruments project parallel beams of collimated white light over a workpiece and capture its form on a bank of light-sensing diodes. The Profile's noncontact measuring system gathers accurate data faster than traditional contact gages. But true machine capability can be appreciated through its computer and software options.

The series' ability to create part programs on or off line gives operators the flexibility to switch from one workpiece to another in seconds. It can be linked to machine tools to provide feedback or connect to a shop-floor data-collection network. The software also provides SPC, charts, and process capability reports. "This technology contributes to the system's functionality, but it is the computer and software options that provide system flexibility," says Maxe.

MOIRÉ SYSTEMS

Another technological method, the CADEYES system, for gathering data comes from MEDAR, Inc (Farmington Hills, MI). "We use a 3-D noncontact inspection system that combines a state-of-the-art video camera and computer technology with moiré interferometry," says Dr. Leonard H. Bieman, director of Vision Engineering at Medar, "for fast and accurate data acquisition of surface geometry." The system uses two line-grids on a workpiece, producing a black-and-white pattern. A data rich 3-D digital image is extracted from the shape of this pattern. Data are obtained in areas instead of line profiles, thus increasing its operational throughput. Through high-speed processing, CADEYES acquires images consisting of 250,000 data points in seconds. It enables programmers to write customized applications, similar to part programs using Microsoft Visual Basic software.

A desktop unit was developed to gage small precision parts such as cutting tools. Measuring machine cutting tools can accurately define the geometry of the small features that are critical to cutting performance. Measurements quantify variations of cutting tool geometry and wear patterns and are used to improve machining quality and define tool replacement cycles. Other applications include measuring and inspecting surfaces with critical specifications and fine-detail reverse engineering for precision die and mold making.

CAPACITIVE SYSTEMS

ADE Technologies, Inc. (Newton, MA) promotes its patented capacitive noncontact dimensional gaging systems. Application flexibility comes from the systems technology, software, and optional sensors. Capacitive gaging uses an electric field generated between a capacitive sensor and the part to be measured. This technology is used in the company's 3700 SpinCheck system, offering graphic characterization of spindle runout and evaluating dynamic error motions of precision rotating parts. The system PC and software give operators the flexibility to inspect various characteristics. High-speed data acquisition and powerful graphics capability provide time- and frequency-based analysis of complex rotational motions in applications that include measuring spindles, bearing and motor runout, surface flatness, and metallic and ceramic sheet thickness.

VISION SYSTEMS

View Engineering, Inc., Metrology Products Group (Simi Valley, CA) makes use of high-accuracy, noncontact vision systems for 2- and 3-D measurements for metrology applications. The system gathers data via a high-resolution solid-state camera and combines it with the output of X, Y, and Z stage scales for position information. It is similar to a contact CMM but View's technology is a true noncontact system. Some

models also use edge, surface, and programmable Ranchi Grid autofocusing, offering accurate Z-axis measurement on smooth surfaces.

As with other noncontact inspection instrumentation, the software offers a large selection of measurement options and statistical functions. Some systems take full advantage of Microsoft Windows, allowing easy-to-operate automatic, semi-automatic, or manual control. Operators can create measuring routines to measure part families. And a graphic feature window provides CAD compatibility and a teach mode assists operators when creating and storing complex routines.

INTERFEROMETRY SYSTEMS

Combining phase measuring interferometry and optical microscopy, Zygo Corp. (Middlefield, CT) created a flexible noncontact surface profiler called the Maxim GP. The "GP" stands for general purpose and the system is designed to offer operators many choices with the basic unit, leaving room for expansion if needed. In broad terms, interferometry splits light into two beams. One beam of light goes to an internal reference surface within the system. The other beam goes to the workpiece. After reflection, the beams of light recombine inside the interferometer and produce a light and dark fringe pattern. Examining this pattern and also using a precision translation stage with a camera, a computer generated image of a 3-D profile is constructed from the data. This system can inspect surfaces, such as ball bearings, read/write heads, or polymer film.

INSPECTION AND CONTROL SYSTEMS

Providing a window and a control system, the GC492 gaging and control console from AirTronics (Elgin, IL) adds greater flexibility to in-process gaging. The system is a computerized, touch-screen gaging console offering a full range of statistical information. In-process gaging is controlled via a closed-loop feedback system via a RS-242C or RS-422C interface. Four discrete LVDT inputs can be used to gage preprocess, in-process, post-process, and master on a single machine. The console can control up to four separate machines.

The G2500 Ultra Gage from K.J. Law Engineers Inc. (Novi, MI) is an intuitive graphical interface that is similar to the AirTronic's GC492 gaging and machine control system. With the PC-based UltraGage there is no need for the user to search for commands in various menus or to back out of a program to access other commands.

An out-of-control flag, for example, will prompt the operator with an SPC icon. When se-

lected, the system will display an X-bar and R chart. To further examine the information on these charts, the user need only touch a point on the chart and more information about the selected subgroup is provided. To resume gaging, the operator simply pushes a large yellow gage button and the inspection continues.

THE IMPORTANCE OF FOLLOWING GD&T SPECIFICATIONS*
by Collin Wearring and Dennis P. Karl

Geometric dimensioning and tolerancing (GD&T) is an engineering product definition standard that geometrically describes design intent. It also provides the documentation base for the design of quality and production systems. Used for communication between product engineers and manufacturing engineers, it promotes a uniform interpretation of a component's production requirements.

Using GD&T, the allowable limits of variation during the design, fabrication, and evaluation processes are specified using a standard syntax for describing the proper positioning sequence for accepting the component. Used properly, GD&T coordinates these activities effectively and reduces the influence of variation on final assembly. Ignoring GD&T creates inaccuracies in the inspection process, which can generate a misleading impression of the process capability of a fabrication activity.

GD&T symbols are used in an engineering drawing to communicate the required functionality of the component by design. These symbols are also used by the inspection department to describe how to position the component during inspection and the allowable dimensional variation for individual features. The combination of GD&T symbols applied to a component is referred to as its GD&T specification.

To illustrate the negative effects of ignoring GD&T specifications, a computer simulation of the fabrication and inspection of a simple block with four holes was performed. A computer program that models 3-D component geometry and

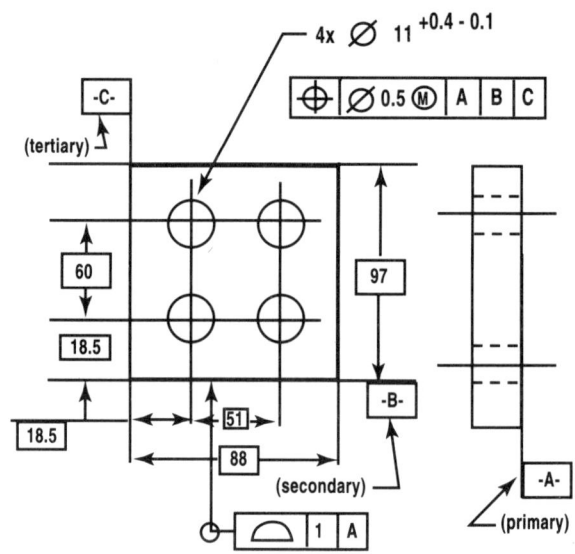

EXHIBIT 1.—PART DRAWING (SPECIFIED DATUM FEATURES)

uses Monte Carlo random-number simulation to assign tolerances to each component was used to construct the fabrication and inspection processes. During the simulation, each component was manufactured, inspected, and assembled using the specified datum features and positioning sequences. This process was repeated for thousands of assemblies, each with unique components generated by the Monte Carlo process. Results of these simulations were summarized and statistically analyzed to predict variation and nonconformance.

---

*Reprinted with permission from *Quality Progress*, February 1995. Collin Wearring is a product manager at Variation Systems Analysis in St. Claire Shores, MI. Dennis P. Karl is president of Karl Engineering Service, Inc., in Jackson, MI.

THE SIMULATION PROCEDURE

Using the simulation model, 5,000 blocks were fabricated within the specifications on the part drawing in Exhibit 1. Each hole was created with a process capability (C_{pk}) of 1 for its location relative to the datum features. An increase in the positional tolerance was allocated based on a hole's deviation from its maximum material condition.

Results from the 1,000-, 2,000-, 3,000-, 4,000-, and 5,000-block simulations were reviewed. The difference between estimates of the mean and standard deviation for 4,000 simulations and 5,000 simulations was less than 1%. Based on these results, the convergence of model results was deemed adequate and the sample size of 5,000 was chosen for the analysis.

The simulation model represents variation in the block external dimensions and hole positions using normal distributions centered on the target (nominal) dimensions of the part. Each simulation creates a unique block, selected from a normal population, whose 3-sigma value equals the design specification for the part. In this situation, approximately 99.73% of each parameter (dimension) will lie within the tolerance specification.

The drawing that incorporates GD&T specifies the datum features used for positioning the component and their order of precedence for component inspection. The drawing also expresses the allowable variation for the features (holes) of the part being controlled to the datum reference frame established by the datum feature.

In this case, the specifications stated that the form of the part must be held within a profile tolerance of 1mm, and the axis of each hole was restricted to a cylindrical zone of diameter 0.5mm with respect to the datum reference frame (Cartesian Coordinate System) defined by the datum features. The computer simulation model was created using the simplifying assumptions that the axis of each hole was perpendicular to the primary datum reference plane (shown as A in Exhibit 1) and that there was no variation of form for the primary datum feature of the component. To simplify the study, manufacturing and assembly fixtures were created at their nominal geometry with no deviation in form.

The blocks were inspected by loading them into an inspection gauge with rails contacting the datum features (see Exhibit 2). Pins (sized to the virtual condition) were inserted through the holes into the component. A block passed inspection if all four pins were inserted without inter-

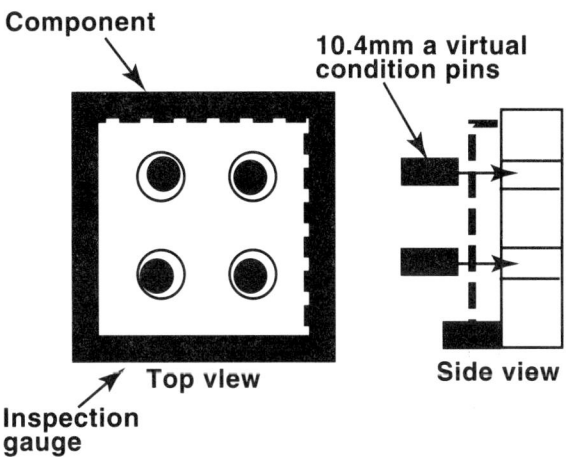

EXHIBIT 2.—INSPECTION GAUGE AND COMPONENT

ference. If any hole failed to pass, the block was rejected. In addition to tracking the number of blocks that passed the inspection process, each individual hole was recorded.

The blocks were inspected for the following assembly scenarios: proper features and positioning sequence, proper features and improper positioning sequence, and improper features and positioning sequence (see Exhibit 3).

A LOOK AT THE RESULTS

The results are shown in Exhibit 4. Simulation results indicate that the percentage of parts passing the inspection gauge was approximately 99% when following the GD&T specifications, but it dropped to approximately 20% when both improper features and improper positioning sequence were used (about 80% of good parts were rejected). All results are measurements from the same parts, the only difference being the positioning features and sequence used during inspection.

C_{pk} values for the clearance measurement were calculated using a single-sided design limit. The design limit for the measurement was an interference of the pin with the edge of the hole. The output distributions (measurement of the clearance in the functional gauge) were nonnormal distributions.

Inspection results for each hole show that using the proper GD&T features and positioning strategy produced results that mirror the process capability of fabrication. Each hole had

Proper features and positioning sequence

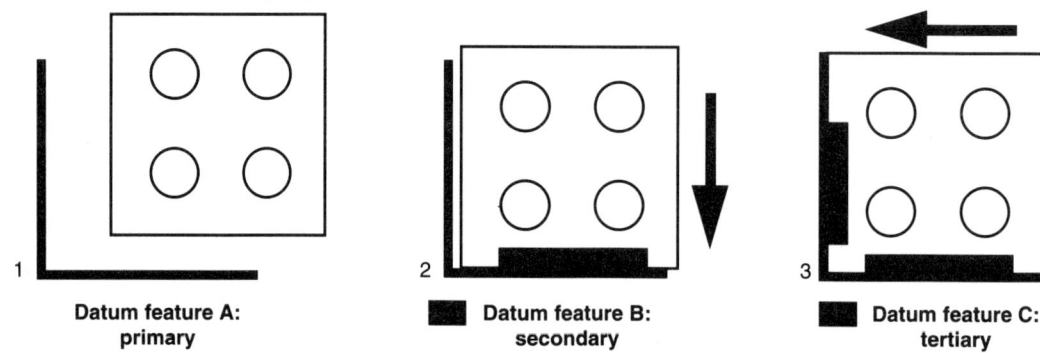

Datum feature A: primary   ■ **Datum feature B:** secondary   ■ **Datum feature C:** tertiary

Blocks are staged in the gauge using the proper datum feature sequencing per the geometric dimensioning and tolerancing (GD&T) drawing (same as fabrication fixture).

Proper features and improper positioning sequence

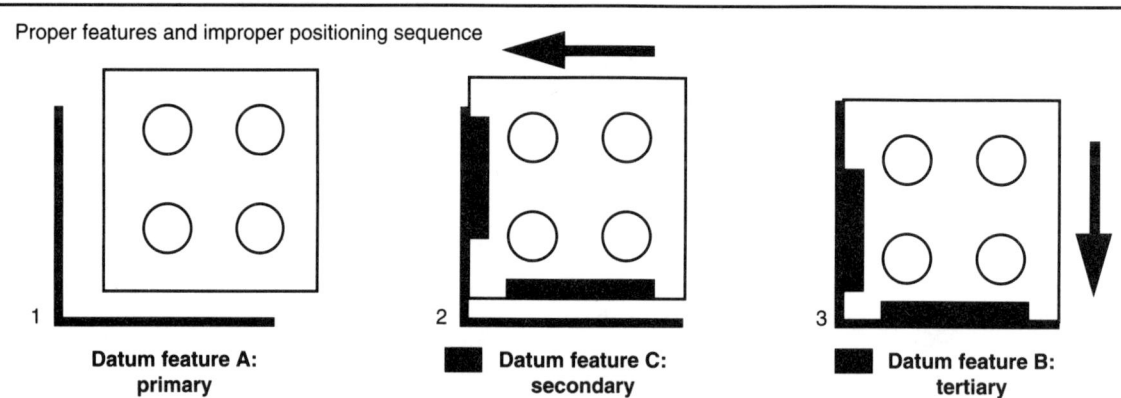

Datum feature A: primary   ■ **Datum feature C:** secondary   ■ **Datum feature B:** tertiary

Blocks are staged in the gauge using the proper datum feature C as secondary, and B as tertiary (reverse order from manufacturing and drawing specification).

Improper GD&T and positioning sequence

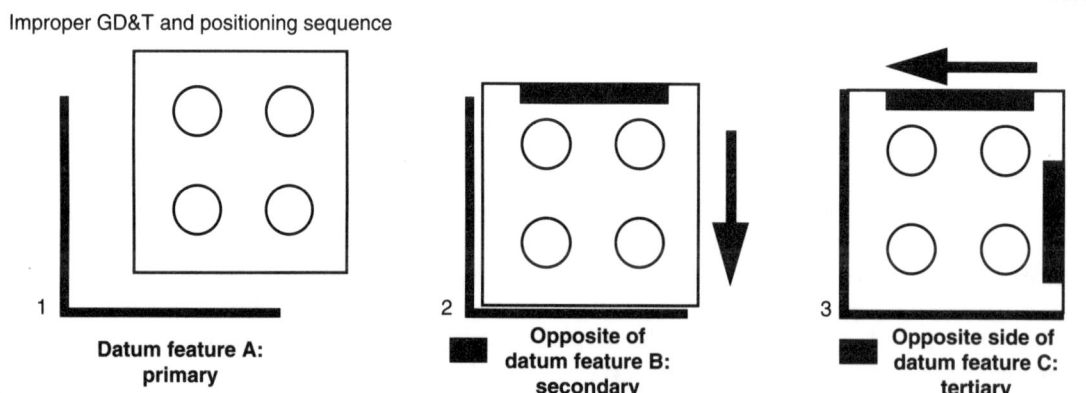

Datum feature A: primary   ■ **Opposite of datum feature B:** secondary   ■ **Opposite side of datum feature C:** tertiary

Blocks are staged in the gauge using opposing sides of datum features B and C.

EXHIBIT 3.—BLOCK STAGING AND INSPECTION SCENARIOS

a measured process capability of approximately 1, the same as that of the fabrication process. Process capability was reduced when improper (different) features and/or sequencing were used.

Building on these results, a second related study was conducted to identify the effects of controlling the form of datum features; in other words, what effect increasing or decreasing the profile tolerance would have on the acceptance of parts passing through the gauge.

Using the blocks from the first study, the profile tolerances on datum features A, B, and C were revised from 1mm to 1.5mm, 0.5mm, and 0.3mm, creating three new scenarios for each datum feature. The hole position tolerance (0.5mm) remained the same. Five thousand parts with a C_{pk} of 1 were fabricated (through software simulation) to product drawing specifications. The software block simulated the inspection in the same manner as the first study.

Increasing the form tolerances on the datum features (introducing more variation) decreases the number of parts passing during an improper inspection process; conversely, decreasing the form tolerances on the datum features increases the number of parts passing. (For results, see Exhibit 5.) The results also showed that when the blocks were inspected with datum features staged in their proper order, the change in profile tolerance had no effect on the percentage of parts passing.

Following GD&T Procedures Can Lead to Savings

Ignoring GD&T procedures for the manufacture and inspection of parts significantly increases the effect variation has on final assembly. The simple fabrication/inspection examples given here demonstrate:

- Ignoring GD&T specifications during the fabrication and inspection of components might cause rejection of good parts because the inspection process cannot accurately identify an acceptable component.

- Using improper positioning strategies during inspection obscures the fabrication process. The measurement information will provide a misleading view of the process.

- Computer modeling is an effective technique to quantify the influence of dimensional variation on inspection and assembly opera-

EXHIBIT 4.—INSPECTION RESULTS

Test 1: proper features and positioning sequence

	Hole number	Out of specification	C_{pk} value
99% of the blocks pass the gauge.	1	0.25%	1
	2	0.19%	1
	3	0.32%	1
	4	0.21%	1

Test 2: proper features and improper positioning sequence

	Hole number	Out of specification	C_{pk} value
53.1% of the blocks pass the gauge.	1	22.8%	0.011
	2	26.0%	0.14
	3	27.4%	0.12
	4	22.4%	0.13

Test 3: improper features and positioning sequence

	Hole number	Out of specification	C_{pk} value
20.6% of the blocks pass the gauge.	1	55.1%	0
	2	55.5%	0
	3	54.7%	0
	4	55.4%	0

EXHIBIT 5.—RESULTS FOR DIFFERENT PROFILE TOLERANCES
on Datum Features

Profile tolerance	Test 1—percentage pass	Test 2—percentage pass	Test 3—percentage pass
1.5mm	99%	38.3%	7.9%
1.0mm	99%	54.6%	20.6%
0.5mm	99%	83.2%	62.7%
0.3mm	99%	94.8%	88.2%

tions during the design phase of the product life cycle.

Following GD&T procedures can lead to substantial savings in process time and operations costs by ensuring the accurate identification of acceptable components, providing a more accurate view of the fabrication process, and reducing the influence of the datum feature form tolerances.

BIBLIOGRAPHY

ANSI Y14.5M, "Dimensioning and Tolerancing Standard," 1982.

"GDT Gets Everyone Working on Design Quality," *Quality Assurance Bulletin*, No. 1315.

"VSA-3D: Analysis Reference," Variation Systems Analysis, Inc., St. Clair Shores, MI.

Wearring, Colin, and Gary Cola, "Identifying Sources of Build Variation Using VSA Audit," SAE Technical Paper, No. 911644.

Wearring, Colin, and Chris Slon, "Process Capability Measurements for Complex Assemblies," SAE Technical Paper, No. 911641.

3.14
PROBLEM SOLVING

■

7 NEW TOOLS: THE INGREDIENTS FOR SUCCESSFUL PROBLEM SOLVING*
by Ellen R. Domb, Ph.D.

Why more tools? Don't teams have enough to learn with flowcharts, brainstorming, nominal group technique, scatter plots, X-bar charts, Pareto charts and run charts? What about histograms? Cause-and-effect diagrams? Force field analysis?

We've all learned from others and taught each other a lot of tools for analyzing processes, finding improvement opportunities, making improvements, maintaining the improved processes and, in the best of circumstances, continuously improving the processes. That's the good news.

But teams and whole organizations bog down in the improvement process. People frequently fail to manage the process of improvement and don't apply what they have learned about improving the processes, products and services of the organization to the organization. They also often attempt to apply quality improvement tools to creating new processes, products and services in situations without sufficient data.

The seven management and planning tools can help you and your team through both situations. Look to these tools when you need to:

- Stimulate, then organize, your group's creativity.

- Build consensus.

- Analyze relationships.

- Formulate and carry out action plans.

The seven management and planning tools are not new. People have developed them individually, for a variety of applications, during the past 60 years. They've been used in many strategic planning and operations research contexts. Michael Brassard's book *The Memory Jogger Plus+* (GOAL/QPC, 1989) includes an excellent short history of how the seven tools came to be used together. The tools migrated from all around the world to Japan. They then came back to the rest of the world as a suite of tools for the improvement of management and planning. Shigeru Mizuno's book *Management for Quality Improvement: The 7 New QC Tools* (Productivity Press, 1988) describes the tools in the form used in Japan. This article describes each tool and shows how to apply them to your management and planning challenges.

AFFINITY DIAGRAM

This tool allows teams to creatively generate many ideas and then organize them. The team either generates ideas through brainstorming or starts with ideas generated by others (customers, suppliers, researchers, etc.). As with other forms of brainstorming, the team members agree on the issue and post it where everyone can see it while brainstorming. They write the ideas on cards (3"x5" Post-it notes are also popular) and post them on the walls. Seeing others' ideas frequently stimulates new concepts.

The team then sorts the cards, finding patterns and affinities among ideas, and creates new concepts as the patterns emerge. Most instructors recommend that members sort silently so that the team reaches consensus by seeing the affinity groups form without the influence of discussion. During the sorting, the emerging affinity groups frequently stimulate new ideas. New cards get added as the sort progresses, sometimes changing the entire pattern.

When the pattern stabilizes, the team creates a header card for each affinity group. This is a word or phrase that links the group of ideas on the cards to the original issue. The test of a good header card: If all the idea cards fell off the wall, would the header card tell us what was there? In some groups, writing the header card may take as long as the idea generation and sorting, and is the most creative part of the process.

There is active research in the use of the affinity chart especially in quality function deployment applications. If the team sorts ideas about customer needs according to customers, frequently different patterns emerge than those seen by product or service development teams. Try it both ways and then combine your insights.

INTERRELATIONSHIP DIGRAPH

Teams use this technique to explore complex situations by looking at relationships between pairs of elements. The team develops consesus on the cause-and-effect relationship between the elements by asking, "Does this cause (or strongly influence) that about each pair of items on the list?" At the end, they look at those with many "cause" attributes as the best place to start work since the results will change if the causing agents change.

Take the ideas that you think may be related (10 to 40 is typical), place them on cards on the wall, and proceed to ask the question of each pair. If the answer is "yes." that "A" causes "B," then draw an arrow from A to B. If "no," draw nothing. If "B" causes "A," draw the arrow from B to A. Seem simple? You've managed to get the team to agree on what "A" really means, on what

"B" really means and whether they are independent. (Do I hear echoes of "clear operational definitions" from introductory quality classes?)

Eventually, you can look at the wall and see that items with many outgoing arrows cause things to happen, items with incoming arrows result from other things and those with both are complex. This frequently helps a team make a preliminary choice of where to concentrate their efforts.

TREE DIAGRAM

This tool systematically breaks down a goal into detailed tasks in order to better accomplish that goal. Teams frequently use it to track results and evaluate the effectiveness of planning. If you perform all the tasks, have you accomplished the goal? Or have you just performed the tasks?

An alternative use of the tree diagram is to explore all the options available to solve a problem or accomplish a goal. The trunk of the tree is the goal, branches are major options, twigs are elements of the options, leaves are all the different ways to accomplish the options. Trunk, branches, twigs, leaves, caterpillars crawling on the leaves, fuzz on the caterpillars, bacteria on the fuzz! Knowing when to stop can be the key to effective use of the tree diagram.

PRIORITIZATION MATRIX

This method helps teams compare and narrow down options based on weighted criteria. If your team has just done a tree diagram of all the possible ways you could achieve a goal, the prioritization matrix can help you select which of the options to put into action.

If you agree on the criteria and their weights (e.g., doing something that helps customers get good service is important, but is it twice as important as holding down overtime expenditures?), use one of the simple forms. If you can't agree on the weights for the criteria, apply each criteria to each option, then combine the results to develop the team solution.

Sounds complicated, but it helps develop genuine consensus; the team becomes so involved in the process, they forget which ideas were whose.

Use〳Tool	Creativity	Analysis	Consensus	Action
Affinity Chart	◎		◎	△
Interrelationship Digraph		◎	●	
Tree Diagram		●		●
Prioritization Matrix			◎	
Matrix Diagram		◎	●	●
Process Decision Program Chart	●	●	●	●
Activity Network Diagram			●	◎

Key:	Always ◎	Frequently ●	Occasionally △

Note: The symbols shown (◎ ● △) are becoming common in North America and Japan for showing many kinds of relationships. Numbers or words can also be used, but many groups find it easier to recognize patterns when the chart is filled in with symbols.

EXHIBIT 1.— USES OF THE SEVEN MANAGEMENT AND PLANNING TOOLS

MATRIX DIAGRAM

These diagrams allow teams to describe relationships of lists or items in lists. Just as the control chart is not one tool, the matrix diagram can mean any of several formats. We're all familiar with the financial spreadsheet, which is a matrix describing the relationship of tasks to months, with the amount to be spent in each cell as the relationship symbol. Exhibit 1 shows the relationship between the seven management and planning tools and the needs of people who plan and manage work.

Product and service design teams use quality function deployment as a method of keeping the voice of the customer visible throughout the design and development process. There are several formal ways to present QFD, but all involve using matrixes to explore the relationships between the customers' needs and the technological issues in development. Examining the matrix for empty rows or empty columns provides a simple but powerful tool. Empty rows mean customer needs have no relationship to the product or service characteristics, and empty columns mean that characteristics are included that the customer doesn't need.

PROCESS DECISION PROGRAM CHART

Teams use this tool for contingency planning. It helps them identify what could go wrong so they can plan how to prevent or correct the problem. The PDPC looks a lot like a tree diagram, but the question that generates the next layer of "twigs" or "leaves" changes at each level (see Exhibit 2). If your team has many options in the "what can we do to prevent or fix this" level, you might need a prioritization matrix to decide how to fill in the bottom layer.

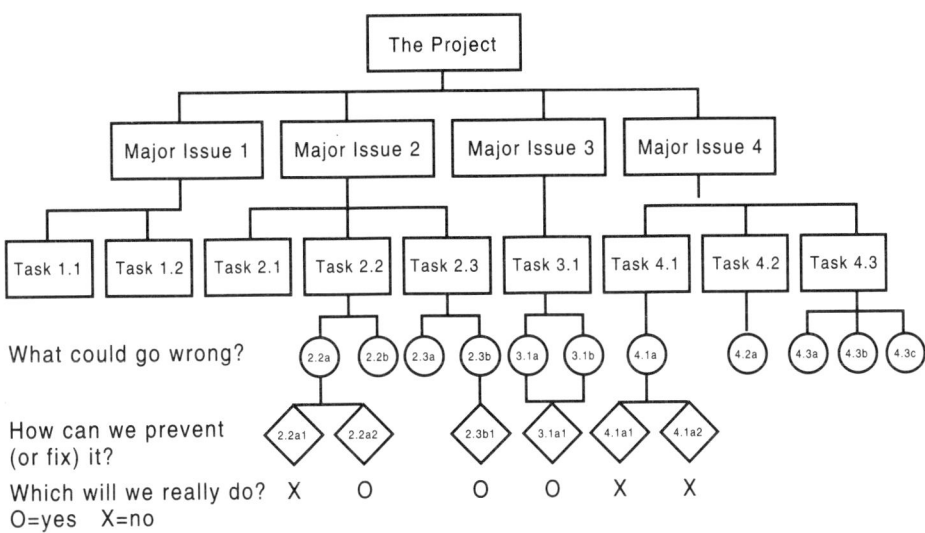

EXHIBIT 2.—PROCESS DECISION PROGRAM CHART

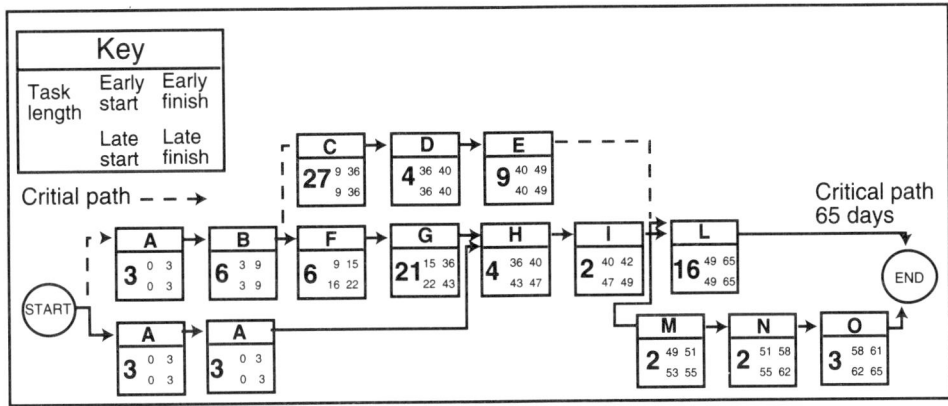

EXHIBIT 3.—ACTIVITY NETWORK DIAGRAM

ACTIVITY NETWORK DIAGRAM

This diagram allows detailed planning, tracking and managing of action plans. It graphically shows total completion time, the necessary sequence of tasks, those tasks members can do simultaneously and the critical tasks they should monitor. In the example in Exhibit 3, if task D is two days late, the whole project will be two days late, since D is on the critical path (the path with no way of being shorter). But task K can start any time between day seven (the earliest day that it can get what it needs from task J) and day 33, and still get its output to task H in time to keep the project on schedule. With this kind of visibility, the team can adjust its resources, understand its opportunities and manage the flow of work.

COMBINING THE TOOLS

As soon as you start to use the tools, you'll discover that they repeat and may be most powerful when used together. A new project might start with various kinds of brainstorming, which generates so many opportunities that an affinity chart is the natural way to look for patterns and create actionable categories of ideas. But if you suspect that some of the concepts are related, try an interrelationship digraph to test your suspicion.

Build a tree diagram to understand everything you must do to act on the driving causes you discovered in the interrelationship digraph, and you might end up with far too many tasks to do (Or you may not think of any and start with another affinity chart to generate tasks.) Use a

What are the issues for a state quality award?

Emphasize quality improvement statewide	Select judges and examiners to get good feedback to applicants	Governor should publicy, visibly promote quality for all CA organizations & agencies
Encourage applicants' lots	From prior year award organizations	Governor presents awards
Stress value of feedback	Experience in a variety of business, gov't, education	Keep Governor's role symbolic
Publicize year-round, not just award day	Use Baldrige judge/ examination criteria	All state agencies should apply award criteria
Get a variety of companies to apply	Demonstrated knowlege	Governor's office starts quality transformation
Get government agency applicants	Big Q, not little "q"	Awards should be part of high-level plan to bring business back to CA
Publicize cases	Avoid appearance and reality of political selection	Model Baldrige/US Gov't relationship
Award everybody		Governor gives award high profile
Get help from members as local speakers	Membership provides policy, money and promotion	
Collaborate with university business schools	Membership selects board	Winners will be role models
Avoid win-lose attitude	Involve community	Previous winners active
Publicize all catagories	Members explain award process	Model cooperation vs. competition
Publicize all applicants are winners	Members are polled on policy matters	Symposia, news, media, town meetings...
	Members contribute & find sources of money	Provide examiners
	Members involve their organizations	

EXHIBIT 4.—PART OF THE AFFINITY DIAGRAM FROM THE CCQS MEETING

prioritization matrix to help select your course of action and a matrix of tasks vs. resources vs. people to translate that choice into action.

The task team creates its process decision program chart to look for contingencies. This helps them plan the tasks that will prevent problems. Then use the activity network diagram to understand the system of tasks that will accomplish their goal and show them their options in scheduling the work. Exhibits 4 and 5 show some of the thinking that has been done by the California Council for Quality and Service in orga-

nizing the administration of the U.S. Senate Productivity Awards and the Eureka Award.

Exhibit 4 shows a piece of one of three affinity diagrams done by 70 people at the organization meeting. After some consideration and some more brainstorming, they decided to change the affinity groups "Winners will be role models" and "Emphasize quality improvement statewide" to one larger group, with four subgroups.

The issues relating to identifying, selecting and training examiners became very complex, and the board needed to narrow down the op-

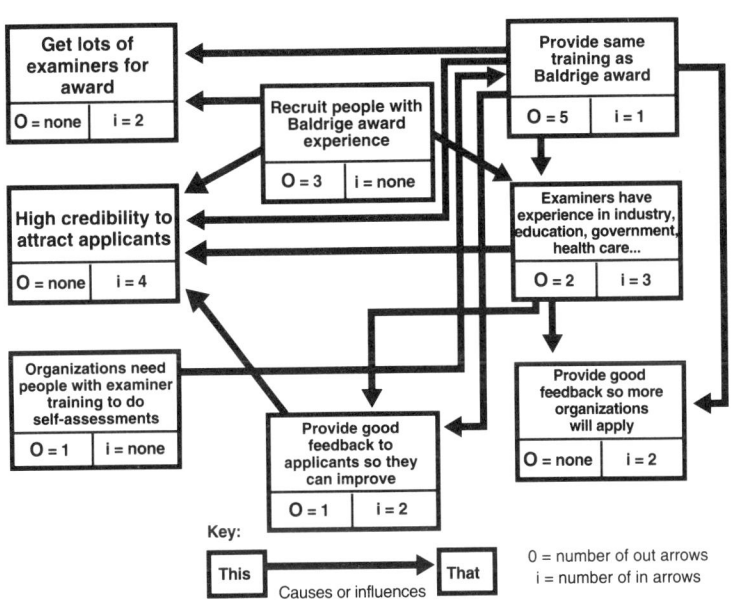

EXHIBIT 5.—INTERRELATIONSHIP DIGRAPH FOR "DEVELOPING EXAMINERS"

tions. They strongly suspected that many of the issues were related, so they tried using the interrelationship digraph to see if they could isolate the few issues that cause the rest to happen. Exhibit 5 shows the results.

It quickly became clear that providing the same training as the Baldrige Award for the California Eureka Award and the U.S. Senate Productivity Award and recruiting experienced Baldrige examiners would "cause or influence" most of the desired results for the award process. It also would provide a necessary service for self-improvement for those companies that wanted people trained as examiners, whether they applied or not. Consequently, both actions became priorities for the CCQS.

They then produced a tree diagram for "Provide training"—this is a logical diagram, not a flowchart or an activity network diagram. It doesn't show which actions happen before or after other actions. Instead, the tree helps the team be creative about all the issues and break each major issue into tasks they should perform.

What about *your* projects? Do you really need more tools?

All the quality-improvement tools interact in real projects. Pareto charts and prioritization matrixes help you choose the "vital few." The fishbone diagram is a specialized form of the affinity chart, with the header cards preassigned (people, processes, materials, machines).

Expand your team's capability to plan and manage complex situations by adding the seven management and planning tools to your quality tool kit.

PROBLEM-SOLVING: METHOD AND TOOLS TO GUIDE THE PROCESS*
by Barbara J. Streibel

INTRODUCTION

Lee and Noreen work in the financial services department of a large company. One of their key responsibilities is processing travel reimbursement checks and they work as fast as they can because they know their co-workers like to get reimbursed quickly. Recently, they made some

*Reprinted with permission from The Association for Quality and Participation, Cincinnati, OH (513) 381-1959. From the *17th Annual Spring Conference and Resource Mart*, April 1995. Barbara J. Striebel is with Joiner Associates Inc.

changes within their department that helped eliminate delays caused by having outdated accounting codes in their computer database. They also sent around a memo to all staff explaining how to fill out the reimbursement request forms correctly. Yet despite these changes, people all over the company still complain about how long it takes to get reimbursement checks.

What would you do if you were in Lee and Noreen's shoes? You're trying your best to have your work flow smoothly and quickly, but haven't been able to make enough improvement to satisfy your "customers."

Situations like these are common in the workplace. Every day, people make changes that they think are improvements. But often these changes fall short of expectations and the problems either continue unchanged or else reappear at a later date. The failure of supposed "solutions" is what happens often when the changes do not attack the root causes of a problem or when one of many competing ideas about how to solve a problem is chosen almost at random. In both cases, using a structured problem-solving method can help achieve the desired results, especially when combined with basic data collection tools. Many problem-solving methods exist. This article follows the experiences of Lee and Noreen to examine a detailed problem-solving approach called the 7 Step Method and shows how basic data collection and analysis can help uncover and eliminate deeply rooted problems.

THE JOINER 7 STEP METHOD

The keys to effective problem solving are

- being clear about what you want to accomplish;

- establishing a deep understanding of the problem;

- making sure solutions are linked to causes that were verified with data;

- monitoring and adapting the changes.

These key elements are captured in the Joiner 7 Step Method, shown in Exhibit 1. The flowchart shows the name of each step, the main outcome or goal expected from that step, and the questions that serve as a guide for achieving that goal. It is just one version of a popular data-based problem-solving method. Following the

steps helps people establish clear links between cause and effect, which helps to ensure that the underlying causes of a problem will be exposed and that solutions will be targeted at those deep causes.

Step 1: Project

In Step 1, the goal is to define the project's purpose and scope—what problem or opportunity is being addressed, why it is important, and how much progress or improvement is expected. This helps people focus their attention, set boundaries for what will and will not be addressed in the improvement effort, and develop common expectations about what can be accomplished.

Step 2: Current Situation

This step is critical for the overall success of an improvement effort, yet it is commonly overlooked or done at a cursory level. The goal is to develop a deep understanding of the current situation, using data collection and analysis as the primary source of knowledge (not just opinion and theory!). If this step is done well, the remaining steps often go quickly and smoothly; if done poorly, people often get frustrated in later steps. By the end of Step 2, people should have a good idea of when the problem appears, under what circumstances it is likely to occur, and so on.

Step 3: Cause Analysis

In Step 3, the knowledge gained in Step 2 is translated into theories about causes, then data is collected to refine and verify those theories.

Step 4: Solutions

Having collected data to confirm which possible causes of a problem are in fact at fault, this step guides people to try out planned solutions on a small scale before attempting full-scale implementation of any changes.

Step 5: Results

Step 5 provides a needed check to make sure the chosen solutions actually accomplish what they were intended to accomplish and gives people a chance to make refinements. Equally importantly, it directs people to evaluate not only the outcome but the *methods* used in implement-

EXHIBIT 1.—THE JOINER 7 STEP METHOD

7 Step Method for Improvement

Step	1. Project	2. Current Situation	3. Cause Analysis	4. Solutions	5. Results	6. Standard-ization	7. Future Plans
Goal	To define the projects's purpose and scope	To further focus the improvement effort by gathering data on the current situation	To identify and verify deep causes with data; to pave the way for effective solutions	To develop, try out, and implement solutions that address deep causes	To evaluate both the solutions and the plans used to implement them	To maintain the gains by standardizing work methods or products	To anticipate future improvements and to preserve the lessons from this effort
Questions to be answered	• What is the project's purpose? What problems or "gap" are you addressing? • What impact will closing this gap have on customers? • What other reasons exist for addressing this gap? • How will you know if things are better? • What is your plan for this project?	• What is the history? • Can the problem or situation be depicted in a sketch or flowchart? • What happens when the problem appears? What are the symptoms? • Where do symptoms appear? Where don't they appear? • When do symptoms appear? When don't they appear? • Who is involved? Who isn't?	• What are the possible causes of the symptoms? Which of these are verified with data? • What are possible deeper causes of the verified causes? • How does the verification of causes affect decisions about who should be working on this effort?	• What solutions could address the deep causes? • What criteria are useful for comparing potential solutions? • What are the pros and cons of each solution? How do they relate to the gaps and causes? • Which solutions seem best? Which will you select for testing? • How will you try them on a small scale? What data will you collect? • Which trial solution turned out to be most effective? • What are the plans for implementing it full scale?	• How well do results meet the targets? • How well was the plan executed? What can this tell you about planning for improvement?	• What is the new standard method or product? • How will all employees who do this work be trained? • What's in place to assure the gains are maintained? To prevent backsliding? • How will methods, procedures, and results be monitored? How will anyone know if things are working the way they should work? • What means are in place to foster ongoing improvement?	• What remaining needs were not addressed by this project? • What are your recommendations for investigating these remaining needs? • What did you learn from this project? How can these lessons be communicated? • How will the documentation be completed? What happens to it when it's finished? • How will this project be brought to a close? How will you celebrate?

ing the changes. Such knowledge is invaluable in raising people's overall knowledge about how to make effective changes.

Step 6: Standardization

Standardization is usually ignored, partly because many people associate the word "standards" with mindless, robotic control over work practices. These dangers are real only when standardization is done incorrectly. In fact, the goal of this step is to make work more meaningful and productive by

- involving employees in updating the processes and methods needed to carry out the proven changes

- having people pool their resources and skills to ensure a more consistent outcome

- providing means to constantly monitor and update the changes as needed.

Simply put, the changes are not imposed on employees and then forgotten. Everyone doing the work gets involved in incorporating the changes into work methods and looking for further improvements.

Step 7: Future Plans

In almost all improvement efforts, people uncover related problems that are outside the range of their project or find that they cannot achieve all of their goal at once. It is the responsibility of the people making the improvements to document exactly what they did and did not accomplish and capture ideas for further improvement efforts. An organization interested in ongoing improvement should make sure this knowledge is captured and incorporated into the pool of issues that need attention.

CASE STUDY

Here are some highlights from Lee and Noreen's first experience with the 7 Step Method, showing how it helped them shorten the time needed to issue reimbursement checks. Typical of first

attempts, they did not follow the method in exact detail, but by adhering to the basic logic of the sequence of steps, using several simple data tools, and focusing on the overall goal, they were able to make significant progress.

Step 1: Project

One of the first things Lee and Noreen did was to talk with their customers, the people in the organization who requested reimbursement checks. These people told them it took too long to get the checks. Noreen and Lee collected their first data to help them understand exactly what was going on with their process. In this case, they realized they could show the magnitude of the problem by creating a frequency plot comparing the actual turnaround times of this process to the customer's target of 5 working days (see Exhibit 2). Each dot on this plot represents the time it took one reimbursement check to be processed.

This chart showed Noreen and Lee that they had a ways to go to meet their customers' expectations. In the current process, some reimbursements took two working weeks or longer to complete. This could easily mean it would take three to four weeks for their customers to get the

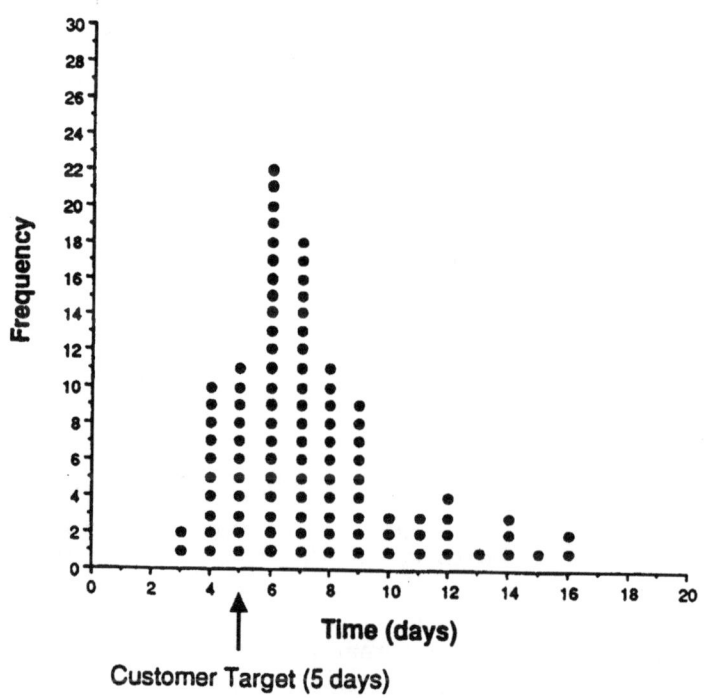

In this chart, each dot represents the turnaround time for one reimbursement check. The arrow indicates that customers would like a turnaround time of 5 days. More than half the checks take longer than 5 days, showing Lee and Noreen that they have a lot of improvement to achieve.

EXHIBIT 2.—FREQUENCY PLOT OF TURNAROUND TIME

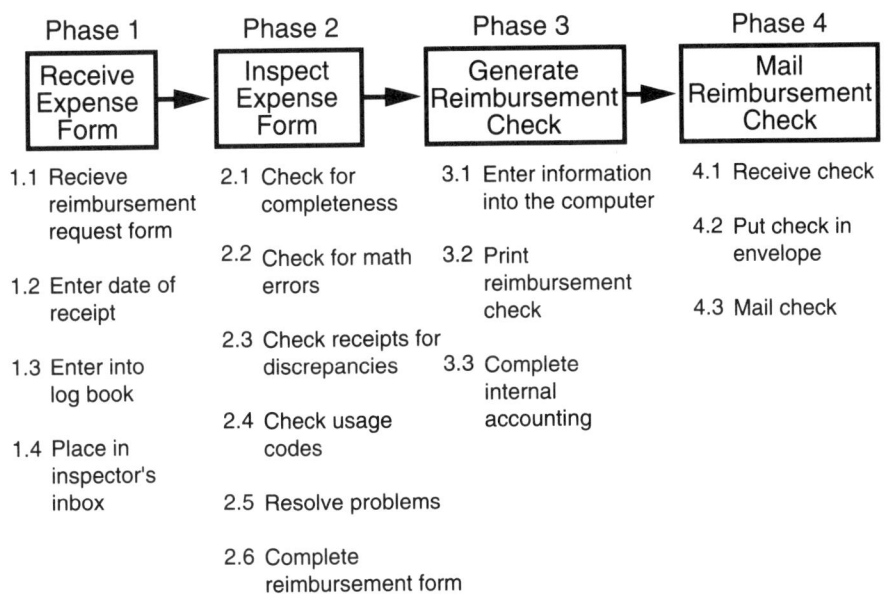

EXHIBIT 3.—FLOWCHART OF REIMBURSEMENT PROCESS

checks (because the mail system would add several days onto the requests at each end). Creating plots like these early in an improvement effort helps in creating a baseline for comparing the effects of changes down the road.

Step 2: Current Situation

Understanding the "current situation" means knowing what happens in the process as it operates today. The frequency plot shown in Figure B is one way to represent what is currently happening with the process. Lee and Noreen also created a flowchart to get a picture of the process and a control chart to show the capability of process.

A flowchart is a picture of the sequence of steps in a process. Different steps or actions are represented by boxes or other symbols. Each box represents a different step in the process. The boxes can be arranged in various ways to highlight time sequence, various levels of detail, handoffs between people or departments, and rework loops. Exhibit 3 shows a simple flowchart of the reimbursement process, starting from when Lee and Noreen receive a request form and ending when the check is sent to the employee. A basic flowchart like this is a valuable reference tool throughout an improvement effort. It helps ensure that everyone shares a common understanding of how the process works. The only data needed to create a flowchart is people's knowledge about how they perform their jobs.

Often the simple act of creating a flowchart exposes places where work is done differently from day to day or from person to person, thus revealing opportunities for immediate improvement.

A control chart, like the one shown in Exhibit 4, uses data from the process to establish what that process is capable of achieving. In the example shown, for instance, the center line shows that the average turnaround time for reimbursement checks is a little over 7 working days. The other lines on the chart, called control limits, show the range of variation that can be expected in turnaround times. In this case, Lee and Noreen can expect the turnaround times to vary anywhere between 0 and 17 days as a normal part of the process.

One other tool that is often used in Step 2 is a Pareto chart, which is a specialized bar chart showing the relative frequency or impact of different parts of a problem. In a Pareto chart, the problem with the biggest bar is always placed furthest left, with the smaller bars arranged in descending order to the right. This makes it obvious right away which aspects of a problem should be given the most attention. Lee and Noreen ended up creating two Pareto charts, as shown in Exhibit 5. They got data on *the kinds of errors* that appear, and *what impact* those errors had on turnaround time. The charts show that although problems with missing receipts did not occur as frequently as problems with miscoding of expenses (see the chart on the left), it took much longer to correct the missing receipt

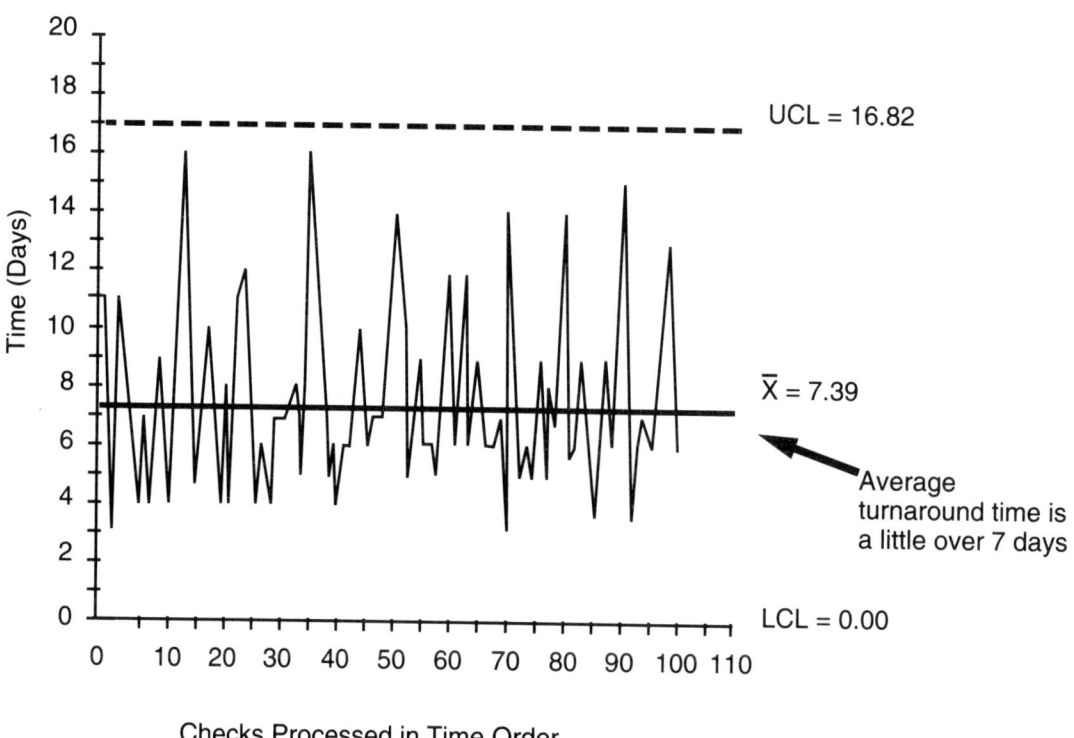

EXHIBIT 4.—CONTROL CHART OF TIME TO PROCESS REIMBURSEMENT CHECKS

problems than any other kind of problem.

Step 3: Cause Analysis

By the end of Step 2, Lee and Noreen knew that they would have the biggest impact on overall turnaround time if they tackled the problem of missing receipts first. Achieving this level of detailed knowledge about the problem provides the kind of focus that usually makes cause analysis much easier than it might otherwise be. Exhibit 6 shows a cause-and-effect diagram that captures their thinking about why people might not include receipts when turning in their reimbursement request forms. A cause-and-effect diagram helps people organize their thinking about potential causes of a problem. The head of the diagram is a brief description or title of the problem. The main "bones" or shafts off the central line represent major types of potential causes. Added bones represent more and more specific causes that may be contributing to each major type of cause. Lee and Noreen thought of four potential causes of missing receipts: People may (1) Lose them; (2) Not get them in the first place; (3) Have the receipts but forget to attach them to the form; (4) Not know when receipts are needed. For each of the main causes, Lee and Noreen then asked themselves why that particular problem might appear. For instance, they asked why people would lose the receipts, or why they wouldn't get them in the first place. The result is a simple cause-and-effect diagram, with only a few "bones" indicating possible causes. By talking with many people who used the reimbursement process, Noreen and Lee discovered that the two main reasons why people did not include receipts were because they (1) didn't know a receipt was necessary, or (2) lost the receipts they did get.

Step 4: Solutions

To counteract the two main causes verified in Step 3, Noreen and Lee developed a two-part solution. First, they created a quick checklist to help people know when a receipt was needed (see Exhibit 7) and they held a training session in one department to make sure everyone there who used the reimbursement process understood the guidelines and the importance of including receipts with their forms.

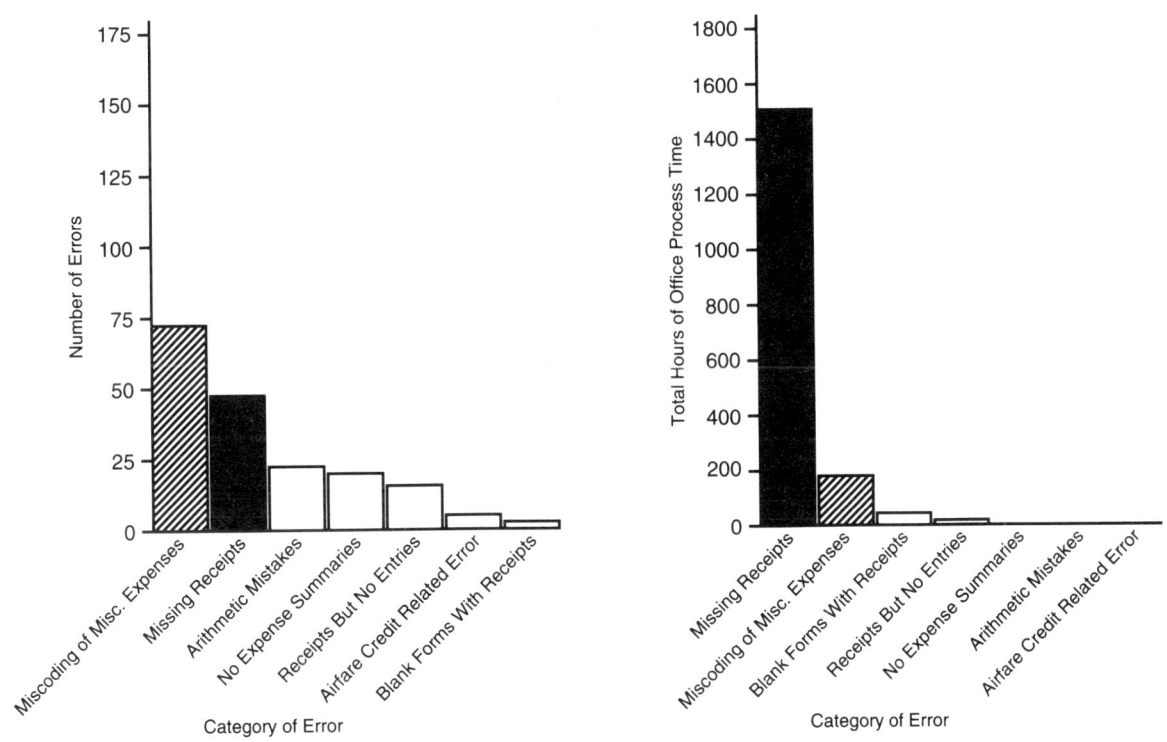

EXHIBIT 5.—PARETO CHARTS ON TYPES OF REIMBURSEMENT ERRORS

The Pareto chart on the left shows that problems with "missing receipts" did not occur as often as problems with miscoding expenses. However, the chart on the right shows that correcting the missing receipt problems took much longer than any other kind.

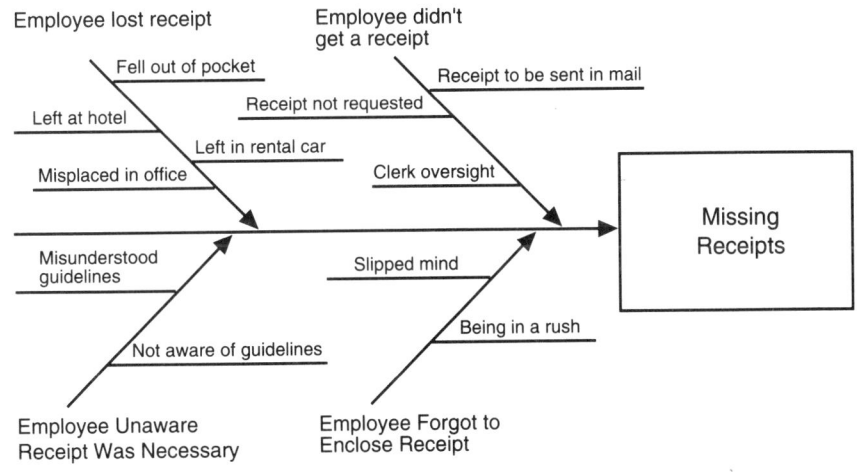

EXHIBIT 6.—CAUSE-AND-EFFECT DIAGRAM ON CAUSES OF MISSING RECEIPTS

Steps 5 and 6: Results, Standardization

The last three steps went quickly for Lee and Noreen. The results (Step 5) of the test of the checklist and training in one department revealed several ways to improve both, and also led them to have the checklist printed on an envelope that people could carry with them. After

```
┌─────────────────────────┐
│    Required Receipt      │
│       Checklist          │
├─────────────────────────┤
│  ✔ Airplane ticket receipt │
│  ✔ Hotel receipt         │
│  ✔ Rental car receipt    │
│  ✔ All meal receipts     │
│  ✔ Other Receipts over   │
│    $25                   │
└─────────────────────────┘
```

EXHIBIT 7.—CHECKLIST FOR REQUIRED RECEIPTS

This simple checklist is printed on envelopes that employees carry with them when they travel on business or will be incurring business-related expenses.

making these refinements, Noreen and Lee took the training, checklist, and envelope to other departments throughout the company, and provided regular feedback when people did or did not use the new standard forms (Step 6: Standardization). These changes allowed them to reduce the number of forms with missing receipts by 86%. The amount of progress they made on their overall goal to reduce turnaround time is shown in Exhibit 8, another frequency plot that shows the before and after results. Obviously Noreen and Lee have more work to do achieving the overall goal of issuing reimbursement checks within five days, but they have made significant progress.

Step 7: Future Plans

Noreen and Lee want to keep working on the reimbursement process, hoping to find more ways to make it simpler for people to track and code expenses, and for they themselves to process the checks. They summarized the results of this project and submitted it to their manager, along with recommendations for further areas of investigation ("miscoding of expenses," for example was a problem that ocurred frequently and that might need attention).

SUMMARY

The Joiner 7 Step Method is a problem-solving method that can be applied to a wide variety of business problems. Following the steps in sequence and using some simple data collection and analysis tools helps people pinpoint the causes of a problem and address those problems at their source.

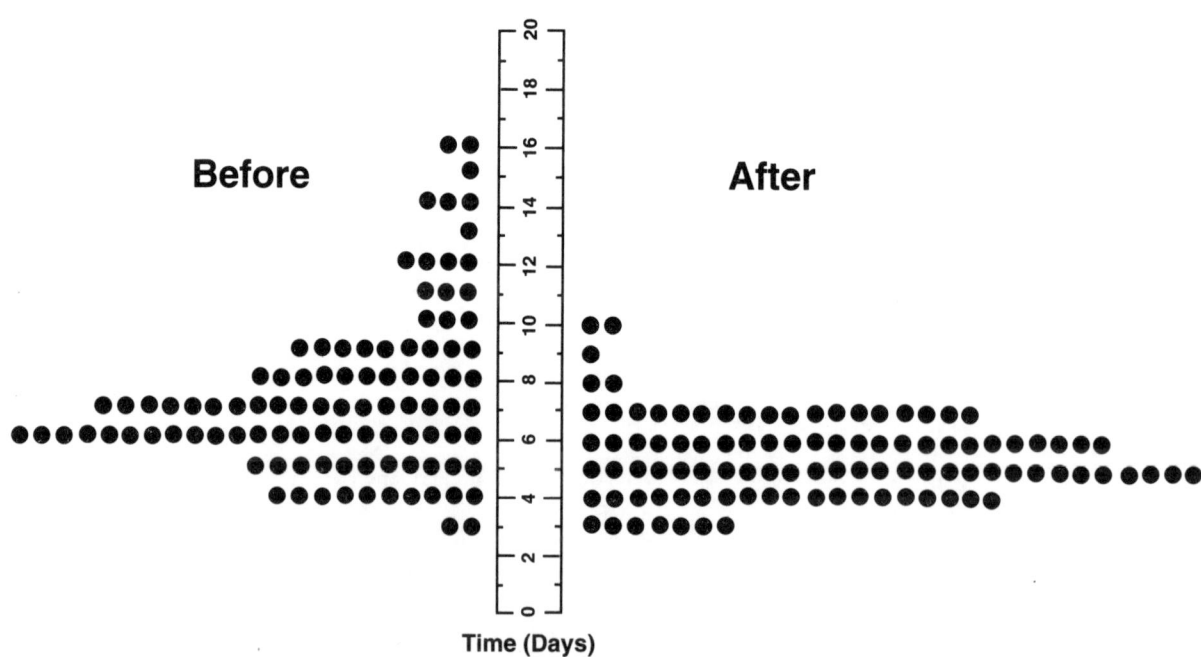

EXHIBIT 8.—FREQUENCY PLOTS OF TIME TO PROCESS CHECKS BEFORE AND AFTER CHANGES

BIBLIOGRAPHY

Brassard, Michael. *The Memory Jogger II*. Methuen, MA: GOAL/QPC, 1994.

Joiner Associates Inc. *The Joiner 7 Step Method*. Madison, WI: Joiner Associates Inc, 1990.

Joiner Associates Inc. *Introduction to the Tools*. (Part of the Navigator™ Series). Madison, WI: Joiner Associates Inc, 1994.

Ishikawa, Kaoru. *Guide to Quality Control*. Tokyo: Asian Productivity Organization, 1982.

Kume, Hitoshi. *Statistical Methods for Quality Improvement*. Tokyo: The Association for Overseas Technical Scholarship, 1985.

Scholtes, Peter R. and other Joiner Associates Inc. *The Team Handbook: How to Use Teams to Improve Quality*. Madison, WI: Joiner Associates Inc, 1988.

QUALITY TRAINING THAT SPARKLES HELPS THEM DO IT RIGHT THE FIRST TIME*

Your employees can do their jobs right the first time only if they've had effective quality training. Whether you're outlining the techniques of statistical process control or describing the route to ISO 9000 registration, a lot rides on how—and how well—you convey the information.

As with all training programs, the two biggest barriers to learning are monotony and its consequence—boredom. Overcoming that deadly duo calls for training that will make participants sit up and take notice.

HOW TO PUT PIZZAZ INTO YOUR QUALITY TRAINING

One person who really knows how to grab an audience is Larry Washburn, a TQM trainer and practitioner from Evergreen, Colorado. "Words, flip charts, and audiovisual aids are not enough," says Washburn, who brims with ideas for offbeat but effective training methods. He advises that if you want your instructions to sink in, go beyond routine techniques. Here are three methods he advises using to make training both entertaining and educational:

Participation

Role-playing and *games* are two good examples of participation.

- *Role-playing* may be especially helpful for production team members who have trouble dealing with quality inspectors. Consider using a joint role-playing session or a scene from a "play" illustrating a typical example of a confrontation.

  Ask an operator to represent an inspector and an inspector to represent the production person, and have them play out their assigned parts without a script. The operator will have to think up reasons the inspector is right and the inspector will have to think up reasons the operator is right. Each will develop a better understanding of the other's point of view. Then have them switch roles.

- *"People love to play games,"* says Washburn, "so I use common games like tennis or baseball to explore quality concepts. I also emulate the Deming technique of using marbles and a funnel to illustrate the futility of overcontrolling a process."

Washburn is referring to what's called the "Nelson Funnel Technique," named after the 1987 winner of the American Deming prize. In the technique, you repeatedly drop a marble through a funnel mounted on a stand with its nozzle a few inches off the floor. Your aim is to hit an X placed on a carpet. You then mark how far the marble stops from the target. Repeated attempts to move the funnel to make successive drops get closer to the target actually make the situation worse than leaving the funnel in a fixed position. The technique illustrates that adjusting or interfering with a stable system can do more harm than good.

Songs and Rhymes

Washburn, a jazz pianist, often uses his musical talent to brighten his presentations. One of his most effective techniques is modifying familiar songs to blend them into the context of what he's teaching. Most of the songs are lighthearted parodies, which draw laughter—and interest—from his audience.

Such takeoffs on songs go much further in driving instructional points home than would a dry recitation. In addition to the unusual twists of the songs themselves, the rhymes in the lyrics serve as an excellent memory aid—for both instructor and participants alike.

Metaphors

Metaphors—figures of speech in which words or phrases normally used to describe one thing are applied to another to imply comparison—are another good training tool. For instance, Washburn once made a TQM presentation in which he related a variety of TQM concepts to fishing. Since most of the audience understood and enjoyed fishing, the interest was immediate and lasting.

"When using metaphors, pick something that holds the audience's interest," he advises. "Then, relate large parts of the presentation to that activity. The more passionate the audience is about the activity used in the metaphor, the more helpful the activity is as a tool to enhance learning."

Involvement Leads to Learning

Washburn sums up his training philosophy this was: "Encourage people to think like a Gary Larson (The Far Side©) cartoon," he says, indicating that a bit of the bizarre can do much to liven up instructional sessions by evoking a laugh or two. "This approach helps to get people involved. The more people participate, the more their level of interest—and the more they learn."

3.15
BENCHMARKING

MEASURE FOR MEASURE*
by Anne Graham

A benchmarking circle, made up of a half dozen or so association magazine staffs, can provide a systematic way to learn more from others, not only in terms of evaluating a finished product but in understanding how it was created, how problems were solved, and what organizational structures complement these procedures. Benchmarking can foster a spirit of openness and cooperation among participants. This sense of support can be especially meaningful to association staffs. A prerequisite for successful benchmarking in association environments is buy-in from association leadership. It is important to have all circle members contribute questions to the initial benchmarking survey.

Benchmarking, in essence, is simply measuring a competitor's product according to certain criteria in order to improve your own product. Every association staff person who thumbs through the competition's latest issue is, in essence, benchmarking. Evaluating other publications and lifting or adapting choice elements is an obvious and essential aspect of magazine publishing.

Many major commercial publishers use sophisticated, complex measurements in their

*Reprinted with permission from *Folio*, Volume 24, Number 14, September 1995. © 1995 Cowles Business Media. Anne Graham is executive of *Internal Auditor*, published by the Institute of Internal Auditors, Altamonte Springs, FL.

benchmarking efforts, but these are probably relevant only to the largest association staffs. But the underlying concept, appropriately adapted, can be of immense value to association staffs of any size. "Benchmarking isn't brain surgery," says Robert Boxwell Jr., author of Benchmarking for Competitive Advantage. "It's plain and simple learning from others. Identify [magazines you would like to benchmark against], study them, and improve based on what you have learned."

A benchmarking circle, made up of a half dozen or so association magazine staffs, is a good way to make that idea a reality. Such a circle can provide a systematic way to learn even more from others, not only in terms of evaluating a finished product—the association magazine—but in understanding how it was created, how problems were solved, and what organizational structures complement these processes.

Benchmarking may actually be a much more open, straightforward and useful process for association staffs than for others in the industry, partly because legalities and competitive risks that might worry commercial publishers aren't likely to be a major concern for association titles. Though association staffs must still be cautious about any "dancing with the enemy" issues, benchmarking can foster a spirit of openness and cooperation among participants. This sense of support can be especially meaningful to association staffs, who often feel an inherent sense of isolation in environments where the business of magazines is not always well understood. In fact, a key benchmarking area could focus on how staffs deal with some of these challenges.

Another positive aspect of the benchmarking process is that there is no mandate for the meetings to conform to any predetermined format, and no need to quantify findings. Although someone has to act as the initiator, the rules of the game can be as loose or as structured as participants wish.

GETTING STARTED

A prerequisite for successful benchmarking in association environments is buy-in from association leadership. This is a key step, because the organization may already be benchmarking in other areas. Thus, magazine benchmarking might simply be a matter of broadening these other efforts by pulling in the publication's dimension.

While association approval to proceed is being acquired, you should identify potential benchmarking partners. There are no formulas regarding the size of the group, but six seems to be a manageable number. If there are no "natural" alliances already established by your association, you may want to establish your own criteria—such as similarities in size, style or types of audiences. Identifying "best practices" is one of the fundamental precepts, and you may well want to seek out periodicals you admire and can learn from. Above all, each participant must have something to offer the others.

Prospective team members should be contacted by letter or memo, rather than by phone. Both the concept and the objectives need to be explained. Examples of the questions to be considered should be included, and the benefits should be described. Participants may need time to study the idea and to discuss it with their own organizational leadership. Others may elect to join on a "contingency basis," to see how the project plays out before making a commitment.

Your staff can feel comfortable in offering to design the initial benchmarking survey, and to compile the results and circulate them to everyone, because these processes don't have to be time consuming. The benchmarking instrument can be a simple questionnaire. Questions might focus on one issue or on several: how international circulation is handled; how the editorial mission statement was developed; staff size and structure; how manuscripts are solicited; what kinds of graphics software are used; or in-house versus outside advertising reps, for example.

It is important to have all circle members contribute questions. All participants can agree to withhold any information that might be compromising.

Deadlines for returning the questionnaires should be honored. Compile and circulate the results to everyone by an agreed-upon date. Once you have refined a computer format for reporting results, it can be used again and again.

EXPAND YOUR CONTACTS

After circle members have received your report, partners may want to pursue one-on-one contacts. For example, one association staff, noting that a problem they are wrestling with has been conquered by another, may want more direct information. Partners may also want to discuss future topics and explore other possibilities for exchanging information, such as conference calls or joint meetings.

Benchmarking surveys can be used on a regular or "as needed" basis. The responsibility for developing the topics and the questionnaires can rotate so that everyone has a chance to participate. It is conceivable that these benchmarking circles might be altered as some association titles change their focus or direction. New partners might join the group as others move on to new alliances.

Benchmarking can help association staffs to improve their processes and products, visualize their unique publishing issues in different ways, and forge valuable systems of support.

■

THE STATE OF BENCHMARKING*
by Robert C. Camp and Bjorn Anderson

Interest in benchmarking has virtually exploded since 1979 when Xerox first introduced it. Today, benchmarking, as a tool, is widely used. It has spread geographically to large parts of the world and proliferated in a variety of manufacturing and service businesses, including health care, government, and education organizations.

Along with the increased use of benchmarking, some changes in its practice have occurred. The focus of benchmarking studies has gradually shifted. In early studies, the focus tended to be on performance measures, competitors, and ambitious targets. Recent studies have examined how noncompetitors and industrial outsiders learn to improve business processes. Comparison of performance measures has developed into learning about best practices.[1] In fact, some authors have used the term *benchlearning*.[2]

There also has been a trend to use benchmarking in a more coherent fashion and to more closely link it to an organization's strategy. Some large organizations have established formal benchmarking efforts.

ASSESSING AND PROJECTING

To understand the current state of benchmarking and attempt to project its future developments, a survey was conducted among a cross-section of organizations.[3] The survey questions and respondents were purposely structured to gain insight into emerging benchmarking developments. Among these were capture, sharing, and dissemination of best practices and the influence of technology—including computers, databases, and networks—on benchmarking.

A two-page questionnaire was designed and mailed to a sample of 59 organizations known to be active in benchmarking. The sample was composed to display large differences among the businesses in terms of size and type of industry. Included in the 59 organizations were both large, medium, and small companies, ranging from manufacturing and service industries to health care and government institutions.

Thirty-nine percent responded to the survey. Of the 23 returned questionnaires, five were excluded from the analysis for not being properly completed. Of the remaining 18 questionnaires, 12 were from manufacturing companies, five from service groups, and one from a government institution.

Survey respondents were asked about the current and future use of benchmarking. Questions covered areas such as the existence of a formal benchmarking effort, benchmarking training, mechanisms for transfer of best practices, and the use of PCs, software, and on-line services for benchmarking.

The questions were selected and sequenced to first ask about the current and easy-to-implement procedures and then question the future and difficult-to-implement benchmarking practices. Questions were grouped into eight topics, and respondents were asked to rate the im-

---

*Reprinted with permission from *Contiuous Journey*, Volume 4, Number 3, Summer 1995. Robert C. Camp is with The Quality Network. Bjorn Anderson is with Rochester Institute of Technology.

portance of the issues raised in the topic. A 10-point scale was used for this purpose, where 1 represented the least important and 10 represented the most important.

Furthermore, the questionnaire instructed the respondents to force rank the topics from 1 (high priority) to 8 (low priority). This exercise was included to reflect where additional benchmarking efforts and resources were likely to be spent or believed to be worthwhile.

To illustrate the differences between the importance rating and the priority force ranking, consider the following example. The questions covering benchmarking training are rated 9 for highly important to an organization; but benchmarking training, as a topic, was ranked only 6—that is, having a rather low priority. Such an outcome would probably mean that respondents regarded training as essential for benchmarking success. From the low ranking, however, it can be interpreted that training is already sufficiently covered and would not receive any further resources.

OVERALL FINDINGS

The eight topics were sorted according to ascending mean importance rating. This resulted in the chart shown in Exhibit 1. All eight topics rated fairly high—the lowest being 5.6 on a scale from 1 to 10. The highest rated item scored 7.8. Thus, the difference between high and low was a mere 2.2 points. Some of this evenness could probably

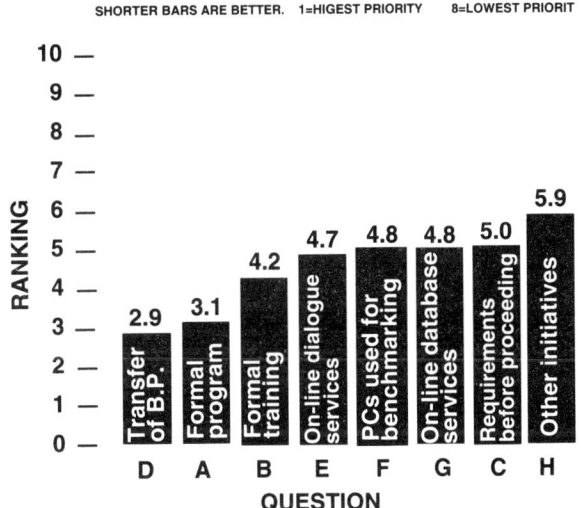

EXHIBIT 2.—FORCED RANKING OF THE SURVEY QUESTIONS

be attributed to the fact that such rating scales are rarely fully utilized.

An equivalent chart, displaying the mean ranking of each topic, is shown in Exhibit 2. Compared to the importance ratings, a higher degree of discrimination was found in the ranking data. The highest ranked item scored 2.9, and the lowest scored 5.9. This was expected, however, as the questions had to be forced ranked.

Formal Benchmarking Effort

Looking closely at the importance ratings, two issues stand out on the high-importance end. The existence of a formal benchmarking effort was perceived as essential. This issue also was ranked high, which was a little surprising, as about three-fourths of the organizations said a formal program had already been established. On the other hand, many of these were said to have been just recently formed, which might explain why it is an area considered likely to receive additional resources.

Transfer of Best Practices

The other highly rated topic addressed mechanisms for transferring best practices revealed through benchmarking. About 75 percent of the respondents indicated a need for a formal process in this area. This question also elicited the strongest wording in the entire questionnaire, including terms like *tremendous need* and *one of the top priorities of the organization*. The issue ranked highest, 2.9, which probably repre-

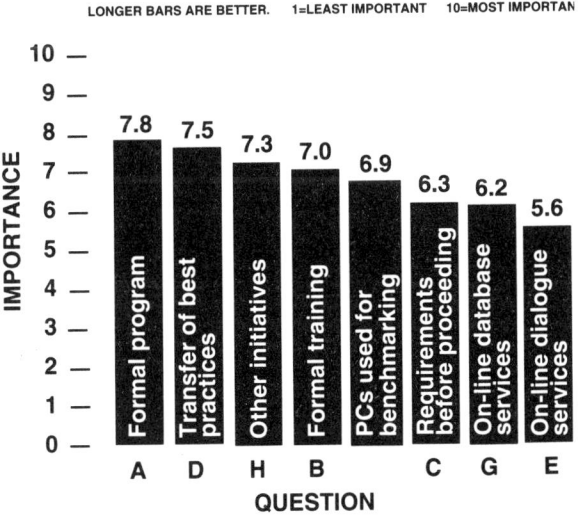

EXHIBIT 1.—IMPORTANCE RATINGS FOR THE SURVEY QUESTIONS

sents one of the most significant findings in the survey. Developing a process and mechanisms for transferring best practices is an area of high concern. Some work has been done to address the issue, such as Grabriel Szulanski's *Transfer of Best Practices Project* from INSEAD—The European School of Business Administration, but there is clearly a need for further development.

Other initiatives ranked as moderately important topics, including quality management (TQM), business process management, benchmarking training, and the use of networked PCs for benchmarking.

Issues on the low end of the importance rating included requirements before proceeding with benchmarking and the use of on-line database and dialogue services. These, however, were ranked higher than the respective importance ratings. These services were said to be used infrequently and of medium usefulness, which might explain the low importance. The higher ranking might reflect an expected increase in the use and benefits of such services as they are further improved and extended.

FINDINGS FOR THE INDIVIDUAL QUESTIONS

The following observations were made after reviewing the survey answers, question-by-question, and the ranking order.

Transfer of Best Practices

As noted, an overwhelming majority of the respondents indicated a compelling need for establishing a formal process for the transfer of best practices. This is to avoid duplication and replicate best practices globally. It's viewed as a top priority that has not been seriously addressed.

No respondent claimed to have solved the problem, however. Mechanisms that organizations currently use include informal exchange during meetings and other networking activities, Lotus Notes, newsletters, and stored documents. As this is a priority issue that many organizations indicated they would put resources into, this is an area within benchmarking that is likely to be further developed during the next few years. This belief also is substantiated by the fact that academia has taken an interest in the issue.[4]

Formal Benchmarking Efforts

With regard to formal benchmarking efforts, again as much as 75 percent claimed to have formed them, albeit some just recently. For those without a formal effort, benchmarking activity was reported to be sporadic, part of a larger initiative, and used when needed, often as a fact-finding tool. In the organizations where formal efforts had been established, some sort of central competency functioned as a driving force. Tasks completed by such a competency included benchmarking training, search for and maintenance on best practices, and implementation of incoming benchmarking requests. The high ranking might indicate that the practice of formal efforts will be further developed, thus more strongly linking benchmarking to strategy and other improvement efforts in the organizations.

Training

Most of the respondents claimed to have established formal benchmarking training programs. Two major types of training included manager awareness training and benchmarking team training. Most of the training was of two days' duration and given on a just-in-time basis. About half of the organizations had developed training course material in-house, while the rest mainly relied on external consultants for training delivery.

On-Line Services

Another medium-ranked question pertained to the use of on-line, internet-type services for internal or external dialogue on best practices. Only four respondents reported not using any such services, 13 accessed the International Benchmarking Clearinghouse Network, nine used The Benchmarking Exchange, while five had access to other internal or external services. Many organizations, however, pointed out that these services were used very infrequently. The relative high ranking of this issue could indicate an expected increase in the use of such services, perhaps as a consequence of an increased need to find benchmarking partners for various business processes.

The next question in order of ranking covered the use of networked PCs for benchmarking. A predominant finding reveled most organizations had a high number of PCs connected to both internal and external networks. About half were using some groupware software, mainly Lotus Notes, but some were using Mosaic and E-mail systems. Furthermore, approximately two-thirds were, in some capacity, using these items for benchmarking—mainly for information sharing and dialogue handling, information requests and responses, and outside information searches.

When asked about the use of on-line databases, only one-fourth of the respondents answered they were not using any such services. The predominant use included the International Benchmarking Clearinghouse database and The Benchmarking Exchange, mainly for contacts, partnering, and data searches. Many people have expressed doubts about the benefits of such best practice databases, and the low ranking seemed to confirm that this is not an area of high importance to benchmarkers.

Other Requirements Before Benchmarking

The second-to-last ranked issue dealt with requirements, other than benchmarking training, that had to be satisfied before proceeding with benchmarking. The major emphasis was that the process in question had been mapped, that the benchmarking team was trained, and that a management sponsor was present. Also, some emphasis was put on confidentiality agreements and the existence of a project plan. Training in information research and project management also were among the requirements. There was some mention of the need for information searches, cycle time analysis, and survey design. The low ranking probably reflects that resources already have been committed to this area, and no further developments have been predicted.

SUMMARY AND CONCLUSIONS

The most significant conclusion of the survey found the mechanisms for the transfer of best practices within an organization is truly a high-priority issue. Large organizations seem to have experienced major problems in disseminating best practices found in benchmarking studies to other areas of the organization. Such problems limit the outcome of benchmarking and result in a less-effective use of resources put into benchmarking studies and a loss of opportunity for the adoption of best practices throughout the organization. This is obviously an area for further work and research.

The use of computers in benchmarking, both for information sharing internally and externally, and for partnering and searching for best practices, seems to be growing. On the other hand, direct contact with other companies and firsthand observation of best practices still seem to be the preferred methods. Some development within this area does, though, seem to be expected.

Formal efforts for benchmarking in general, and for benchmarking training specifically, were also highly important areas likely to be further developed. These might be signals that benchmarking is about to be increasingly institutionalized and become an intregal part of business.

REFERENCES

1. *The development of benchmarking, from competitive benchmarking focused on performance measures to functional and generic benchmarking focused on business processes, has been described by several authors. For example, see Gregory H. Watson,* Strategic Benchmarking: How to Rate Your Company's Performance Against the World's Best *(New York: John Wiley & Sons, 1993) and Mohamed Zairi and Paul Leonard,* Pratical Benchmarking: A Complete Guide *(London: Chapman & Hall, 1994).*
2. *Bengt Karlof and Svante Ostblom,* Benchmarking: A Signpost to Excellence in Quality and Productivity *(New York: John Wiley & Sons, 1993).*
3. *Robert C. Camp developed this survey, which was conducted from March through May 1995.*
4. *Gabriel Szulansli,* Transfer of Best Practices Project: Executive Summary of the Findings *(Houston: INSEAD—The European Institute of Business Administration/American Productivity & Quality Center, 1994).*

||||| 3.16
CONTINUOUS IMPROVEMENT

---------------------------------■---------------------------------

HIGHER LEVELS OF CONTINUOUS IMPROVEMENT*

Introducing Total Quality Management (TQM) in bite-sized chunks rather than all at once builds quality awareness that gathers momentum. As this case study shows, that momentum can propel a company to the top rung of productivity and profit.

In the mid-1980s, Gilbarco (Greensboro, NC) faced some tough challenges. The company had:

✔ high scrap rates

✔ delivery problems

✔ high inventory levels (but also excessive stockouts)

✔ high absenteeism, excessive overtime, and low morale

Gilbarco not only met those challenges but also left them far behind. How did the firm do it? "Mainly through Total Quality Management—and in phases," says Ralph Alexander, quality manager.

PROCESS STARTED IN PRODUCTION

The first phase of the company's continuous improvement initiative was labeled CRISP (Continuous Rapid Improvement System of Production). CRISP, which was limited to continuous improvement efforts in the manufacturing area, focused efforts on:

- Work Cells

- Just-in-time (JIT) manufacturing

- Statistical Process Control (SPC)

- Total Preventive Maintenance (TPM)

- Design for Manufacturing and Assembly (DFMA)

- Self-Directed Work Teams (SDWTs)

"We initiated a lot of improvements in the manufacturing process, in inventory, and with suppliers," reports Alexander. Examples included better inventory control, reduced setup times, and better inspection.

Along with the changes in processes came improved training. Employees in the SDWTs received training in the new strategies as well as in interpersonal skills. Overall, each employee received

24 hours of interpersonal skills training.

18 hours of quality training.

10 hours of JIT training.

The second phase of the improvement strategy was dubbed [4 X 94]—so named for the company's goal of achieving a quality level of 4 errors or fewer per million opportunities by the end of 1994.

[4 X 94] also took the quality improvement effort beyond the "four walls" of manufacturing and introduced it to the company at large. Added to the goals at that time were

- Quality in every functional area

- Common goals and clear direction from management

- Employee involvement and empowerment

- Continuous quality training

All of this came about as a result of a new commitment to total customer satisfaction, again

---

emphasizing the significance of expanding the improvement process beyond just manufacturing.

[4 × 94] quickly evolved into a full-blown TQM effort. "In fact, TQM is now our driving force," states Alexander.

One of the most important elements of TQM at Gilbarco has been an even greater emphasis on and expansion of training. This training focuses on

people behavior,

teamwork,

problem-solving principles, and

process improvement principles.

Two elements of the TQM process deal with ways to keep the continuous improvement process fresh in the minds of all employees. These are the *Hall of Measures* and *the employee recognition programs.* Here's a more detailed look at these two elements:

Hall of Measures

This is a huge display board in a hallway that showcases measurements in these six areas:

Customer satisfaction. The company hires a third-party firm to survey its customers annually. To ensure that the survey is on target, the third-party firm goes to special lengths. "They even ask our customers what questions they want to be asked!" notes Alexander. (The 1993 results posted an impressive 4.0 satisfaction level on a five-point scale.)

People measures. This measures how well the company treats its employees and how satisfied its employees are. Currently, the company measures this factor in four ways:

Employee morale.

Quality of communication to employees.

These two measures are taken with a single survey. Initially done quarterly in order to build a database, the survey is now conducted annually.

Training. This is measured in the number of hours of training that employees receive.

Safety. This is measured by time without lost-time accidents, among other factors.

➤ ***Product quality (pre-shipment quality).***

➤ ***Cost.***

➤ ***Schedule.***

➤ ***Reliability (field quality).***

Employee Recognition Programs

There are two specific employee recognition programs in place at Gilbarco.

In one program, called PRAISE, individual employees can receive recognition for outstanding individual contributions. Such contributions can involve exceptional performance on the job, community service, significant safety and/or quality efforts. Employees are nominated in the following ways:

Employees can nominate their peers or themselves.

Supervisors can nominate employees.

A coordinator and selection team receives and reviews the nominees and selects two to six winners per quarter. Winner can select prizes (worth between $40 and $60) from a catalog.

Each year, the selection team reviews all quarterly winners and selects an Employee of the Year who receives a more substantial prize *and* a lifetime reserved parking spot. (It should be noted that even management does not have reserved parking spots at Gilbarco.)

In the other program—*Teamwork Selection Awards*—committees composed of representatives from a number of departments review team projects and select quarterly team winners, which receive plaques and companywide publicity.

Quarterly winners then compete for Team of the Year awards.

Results Are Impressive

Improvements over the years have been impressive.

• *Manufacturing space decreased 125,000 square feet. This allowed the company to consolidate some departments into one building, saving the cost of a separate facility.*

• *Setup times decreased by up to 90 percent.*

- *Manufacturing cycle time decreased by 80 percent.*
- *Total "cost of quality" decreased by 83 percent.*
- *Inventory decreased by 44 percent.*
- *Absenteeism decreased by 40 percent.*
- *Per employee production more than doubled.*
- *Scrap and rework decreased from $1 million per year to under $100,000 per year.*
- *Product availability improved from 99.5 percent to 99.8 percent. (This is the percentage of time the customer expects a product to be available for use compared to the time it is available for use.)*
- *Defects in final assembly decreased from 600 ppm to 200 ppm.*
- *Line fallout (what gets rejected in the line) decreased from 1,800 ppm to well under 200 ppm and approaching zero.*

The bottom line is exemplary. "Today, business is booming," emphasizes Alexander. "We finished 1993 with record production and profit, and 1994 is turning out to be even bigger and better. Marketshare is increasing, and incoming orders continue at record levels."

Keys to Success

To what does Alexander attribute these phenomenal results? He cites four critical factors:

- **Leadership.** "Our success has only been possible as a result of senior management's commitment and involvement," he states.

- **Empowerment.** The second element has been management's commitment to empowering employees and getting them involved in making improvements.

- **Midmanagement Involvement.** Many companies forget to address the needs and concerns of this group. Without their support, success can only be limited at best.

- **Commitment.** "In the late 1980s, we had a significant business downturn in our industry," reports Alexander. "However, management remained committed to spending time and resources in our improvement efforts, in spite of the economic hardships at the time."

Taking TQM to Suppliers

Gilbarco doesn't hide its TQM efforts, and it has started another phase. "We are beginning to provide free training to anyone and everyone in the Gilbarco supply chain of products," he states. This includes key suppliers, distributors, and other authorized service contractors.

"This is a three-day 'train the trainer' program," he explains. "They will then have access to the programs and tools they need to implement TQM."

The rationale? "To most of our customers, our distributors and service contractors *are* Gilbarco," he replies. "Many of our customers never even see us."

3.17 FLOWCHARTING

MAPPING ADMINISTRATIVE PROCESSES: A TOOL FOR TOTAL QUALITY TEAMS*
by Gary Saunders

For decades, process maps have helped individuals understand complex systems. As

the computer became a greater force in society, computer programming needs grew geo-

---

*Reprinted with permission from *Quality Digest*, August 1995. © 1QCI International 1995. Gary Saunders is a professor of accountancy and holder of the Miller Distinguished Chair at Marshall University in Huntington, WV.

metrically, and process maps supported that growth.

A process map (or flowchart) is literally a picture showing each step in a process, and it can take many forms under different names. Barry Cushing and Marshall Romney[1] group flowcharts into three broad categories: systems, program and document. Other authors have referred to flowcharts as maps,[2] process flowcharts[3] and deployment flowcharts.[4] Whatever the name used or the process considered, process maps probably are the most underutilized tool of total quality teams.

Process maps are useful for designing new processes and depicting existing ones for improvement. They also are invaluable for training new employees. As total quality teams increase their focus on improving the processes in support areas, the importance of process maps to that effort cannot be overstated. If improvements are made in a process that is not understood, it is a result of happenstance and not by design. Deming would call this "tampering." Meaningful improvement only comes with a thorough understanding of a process, and process maps are key to understanding processes.

As total quality efforts broaden from physical production processes to administrative service areas, the challenges became more formidable. Employees must be convinced that the service they perform is a product and that they have customers for that product, even when they're internal to the organization. Many refer to internal customers as stakeholders. Once they recognize their customers, they must commit to serving their customers better by continuously improving service. And in order to improve a service, they must understand the processes involved in producing it; enter process maps.

An organization should prepare process maps for all service processes, but, in reality, few organizations have done this. Their preparation requires a significant time commitment, and many executives remain unconvinced of their value. That attitude should change as they endeavor to meet ISO 9000 documentation requirements. Total quality personnel at a medium-sized Midwestern university were convinced of the value of process maps and decided to devote the effort necessary to prepare them for some of the basic administrative processes. This article describes the experience of that university's to-

tal quality team in producing high-quality process maps of a number of its administrative processes at a very reasonable cost.

OBTAINING AFFORDABLE PROCESS MAPS

One total quality team, the Process Simplification and Paperwork Reduction Team, formed to recommend improvements in selected administrative processes. Through brainstorming, the team developed a prioritized list of processes for consideration. That list included, among others, the employment process, the procurement process and the drop-add process for students.

The total quality team decided that for them to understand the processes under consideration and to develop recommendations, they would need both process decision maps and document maps. According to Diane Pattison, "process flowcharts are a simple way to begin to understand and communicate how a process actually works." A process map depicts the major steps in a process, including all decisions (in a yes-no format) and the actions that each decision triggers. It does not identify the individuals making the decisions or the relationships between those individuals. The process map illustrates the sequence of logical operations performed in completing a process in an organization.

Max Laudeman[5] says that "a document flowchart permits a reader to better visualize complex procedures and thus facilitates the identification of both redundant features and processing steps where controls are inadequate." This is accomplished, at least in part, because document flowcharts graphically portray the movement of documents through the organization's different departments and functions for a particular process or transaction. They trace the flow of a document from its creation to its destruction, or permanent storage location. They provide a broad view of the formal communications network in an organization and permit a reader to better visualize complex procedures. This, in turn facilitates the identification of nonvalue-added operations and those operations where controls are inadequate. Nonvalue-added operations can then be eliminated and those resources shifted to provide more for customers without additional resources.

Mapping Symbols

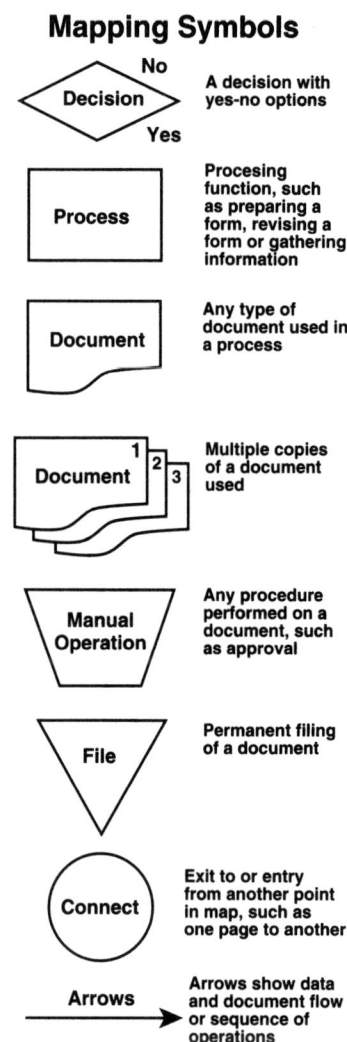

EXHIBIT 1.—MAPPING SYMBOLS

One major obstacle to mapping administrative processes is the knowledge and effort it requires. Individuals most familiar with the processes do not normally possess the requisite knowledge or have the time to map them. Training one or more individuals in each functional area to prepare maps for processes in their area is probably quite inefficient. The university's total quality team selected a talented graduate student[6] to prepare all process maps, which therefore allowed them to invest in training only one person. Learning the basics of preparing process maps was made easier by selecting a relatively small number of symbols to use. Exhibit 1 shows the symbols used in preparing process decision and document maps for the total quality team. During the student's final semester, the team selected another graduate student to train with him as a replacement.

Before beginning the actual mapping, the team developed a sequential list of steps to guide the process and facilitate training replacements. These steps are:

1. Obtain a thorough understanding of the basic steps in the process.

2. Identify all of the decisions required in each step of the process.

3. Identify the documents used in each step of the process.

4. Interview individuals who work most closely with the process to develop an in-depth understanding of the process.

5. Sketch the map on paper and then draw it on the computer.

6. Distribute the map to the individuals interviewed for their study and validation of its accuracy.

7. Revise the map based on a consensus of the feedback obtained from individuals working with the process.

8. Distribute copies of the map to members of the total quality team and obtain their feedback.

9. Revise the map based on feedback from members of the total quality team.

10. Present the completed map to the total quality team for their use in formulating recommendations.

Exhibit 2 shows these steps in a process decision map. In completing steps 1, 2 and 3, the individuals preparing the map will obtain copies of relevant documents and discuss the process with people who are process customers but have not been central to the process design. These are the "forgotten customers" for whom the process was established.

For example, when considering the faculty employment process, discussions may begin with departmental secretaries and proceed through the dean's office to the academic vice president's office. Beginning at the lower levels in the hierarchy and proceeding upward will provide interesting viewpoints on how the process actually works. As you move up in the administration, closer to the policy makers, you will tend to receive the story of how the process should work. These insights can prove invaluable to the total quality team.

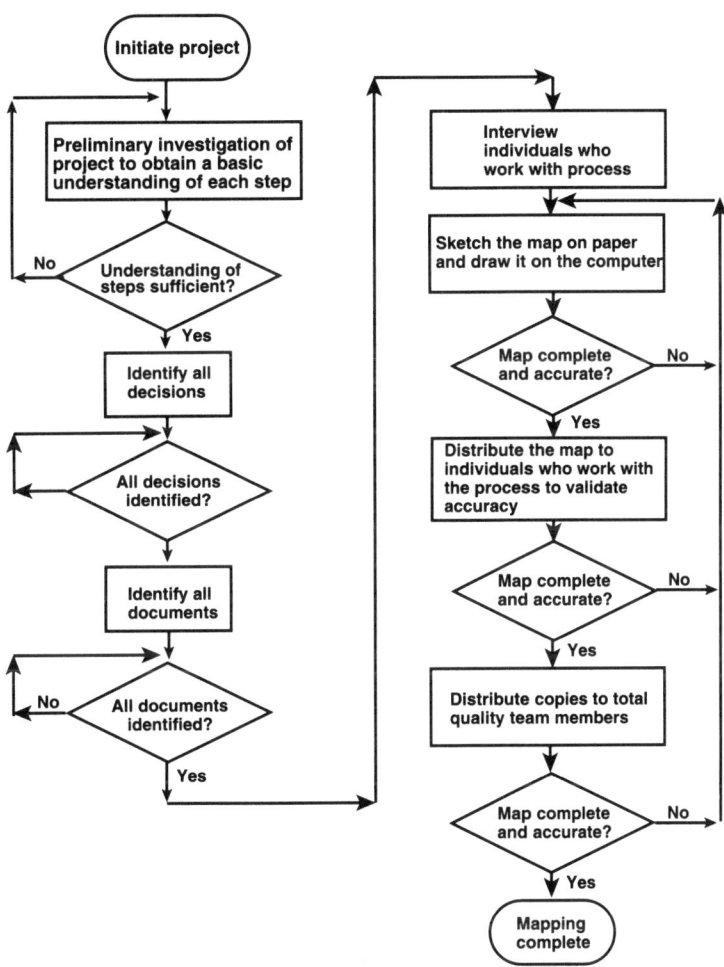

EXHIBIT 2.—MAP OF MAPPING PROCESS

Step 4 requires you to identify someone in the area having responsibility for the process under consideration. For the employment process, this will usually be the personnel department, or one with a comparable name. This department will be most familiar with legal requirements and most involved in the process design or modification. Not only can you gain a thorough understanding of how and why the process is designed to work from these individuals, but their support of any recommended modifications will be almost a necessity for improvements to occur. Discussions with individuals should result in a thorough understanding or the step-by-step procedure to be followed in the process, including what offices or individuals must approve each decision, the flow of documents and where each copy of completed documents is filed.

As shown in step 5, the map can be sketched by hand using a flowchart-symbols template available at most university bookstores. Also, the

Goal/QPC *Memory Jogger* and *Memory Jogger II* are useful aids in preparing maps. When a map is first prepared, using a flowchart template, pencil and paper can facilitate understanding of the process. When using a computer for drawing process or document maps, a variety of software programs are available.

After completing the map, schedule additional interviews with those individuals (step 6) who provided input in step 4. If possible, they should study the map very carefully to ensure accuracy. If they cannot find the time to review the map, they can usually assign that responsibility to another individual in the area. Based on feedback, the map can be modified (step 7) and returned to the relevant persons for additional study. This process of ensuring accuracy may require more than one revision and may take several weeks to complete, but the map should be as accurate a depiction of the process as possible when completed.

After verifying the map's accuracy, you can duplicate and distribute it to total quality team members for their comments. Frequently, team members will have experience or insights that may add to a better understanding of the process. They may have a comment to add to the map or may note a discrepancy. After making any revisions based on team member feedback, the map can be presented to the team (step 10) for its use in formulating recommendations to improve the process.

This 10-step procedure has been used successfully on about six different processes at the university, and a third graduate assistant is now being trained to prepare additional maps for the total quality team. The total quality team and the administration are pleased with the quality and economy of the mapping efforts.

GENERATING TEAM RECOMMENDATIONS

While maps have been prepared for a number of total quality team projects, including the employment process, a subprocess of the employment process—the personnel action request process—illustrates the benefits of mapping. Five documents are used in the university's employment process: the staff personnel recruitment authorization, the position information questionnaire, the PAR, and the WV-11 and I-9 forms. Not surprisingly, the forms repeat much of the same information. A PAR must be processed when the status of an employee, or potential employee, changes. Commonly, the process begins when an individual has been recruited for a position and ends when the individual shows up as an employee in the organization's records. However, if a current employee's payroll status changes (e.g., a change in pay rate, overtime work for an hourly employee or summer teaching for faculty), a PAR must be processed.

Using the 10-step procedure, a decision process map and a document map were prepared (see Exhibits 3 and 4).

After maps of the recruitment process were completed, they were presented to the total quality team. Members were given time to study them for accuracy and to identify any forms or setups that could be omitted or shortened. Any necessary changes to the maps were made, and team discussion centered on potential improvements.

After carefully studying the maps and holding team discussions, the total quality team de-

cided to first address the processes that were completely within the university and, therefore, under the control of university administrators. Falling under that category, the PAR process was one of the first considered. The team realized that for continuing employees, practically all of the information on the form was repeated each time a PAR was prepared for that employee. They believed that by eliminating or greatly reducing the effort of completing PARs, the process would significantly improve. Note that the first area identified as offering the greatest potential savings did not fall directly in the area under study, the recruitment process, but in the routine completion of PARs relative to continuing employees or repeating part-time instructors.

In order to more fully develop a recommendation to submit to the administration, the team decided to form a subcommittee to develop and test a model for computerizing the PAR form. The subcommittee included several total quality team members, the computer center director and a key payroll employee who approved all payroll vouchers.

They developed a tentative computerized network model for testing. With the model, an individual initiating a PAR could retrieve most of the data for past and present university employees from a database and could avoid reentering much of the data required on PAR. The form would be approved or rejected electronically at each administrative level. If an administrator failed to act upon the PAR (neither approved nor rejected) within an established time frame, approval would be assumed and the form would move forward.

Of course, an administrator who failed to act might reopen the issue later, but nearly 100 percent of the forms are approved. Ordinarily, a PAR is rejected because of data errors, and these would be virtually eliminated with electronic processing. However, this model was never fully developed because of a shortage of computer-programming assistance.

Undaunted, the quality team considered other alternatives. Some subcommittee members agreed to work with others in the university to eliminate the PAR by sending a list containing all relevant data through the existing process. The list would include only existing employees and rehires (e.g., part-time faculty previously employed) and would be transmitted via the computer network. This option is scheduled for implementation in one academic college and, after eliminating the problems, expanded cam-

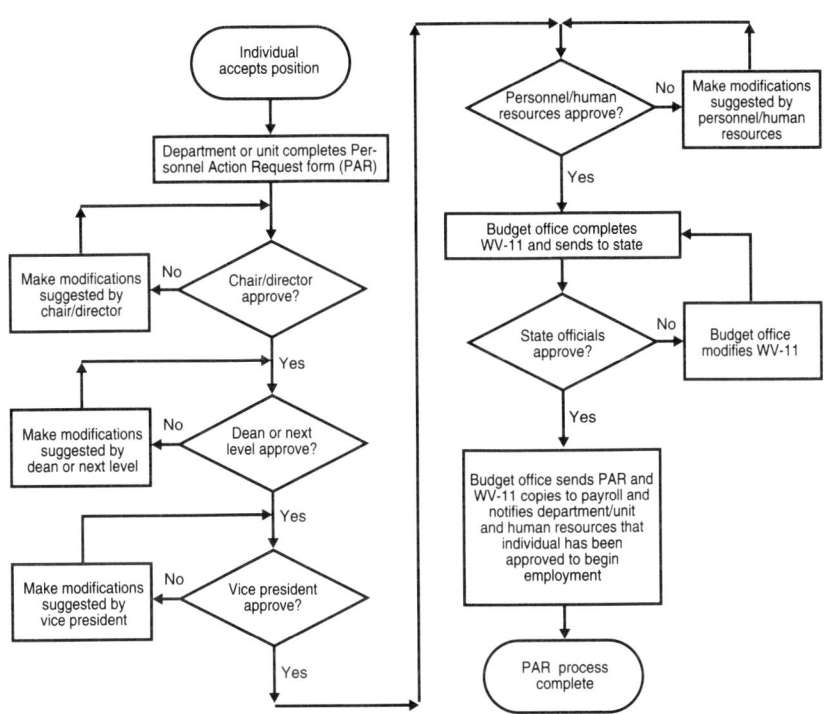

EXHIBIT 3.—PAR DECISION PROCESS MAP

puswide. The team discussed other improvements but could not implement them without changing state requirements—an option not available to the team in the short term.

MAPS ARE WORTH THE EFFORT

Most total quality team members had little previous knowledge of how the hiring process actually worked or how much paperwork was involved and where it went. Before studying the process and document maps, most thought the process was relatively simple and that improving it would not be very complicated. The maps helped dispel these ideas and showed how the process worked and where the paperwork moved. By seeing the process details depicted in the maps, team members could more easily understand why the process takes so long to complete and could focus on steps where employees performed nonvalue-added or redundant work. The maps also made formulating recommendations much easier.

If all employees were aware of the steps required in administrative processes, they might better understand why the processes take so long to complete. Then they might stop complaining about the processes and work to improve them

in conjunction with total quality teams. Consistent with this premise, some administrators have decided to include some process and document maps prepared as part of this project with organizational charts and other materials that will be distributed to employees.

The most negative factor in mapping administrative processes is lost time. Some processes are very complicated, which makes the maps difficult and time-consuming to complete. In addition to the time required to draw the maps, information must be obtained from several different sources. Probably the biggest difficulty encountered in preparing the maps for this study was arranging time to speak with the different administrators about how the process works. With most of them, meetings had to be made weeks in advance, and often they would cancel the meetings because of seemingly more pressing issues. While this added to the time required in gathering the information, most administrators were very cooperative.

Overall, the mapping of administrative processes described in this article has been a success. According to Laudeman, maps "present interrelationships more clearly than is possible in a narrative description." That may be important in today's society, where people are more used to learning by looking at a picture or model than by

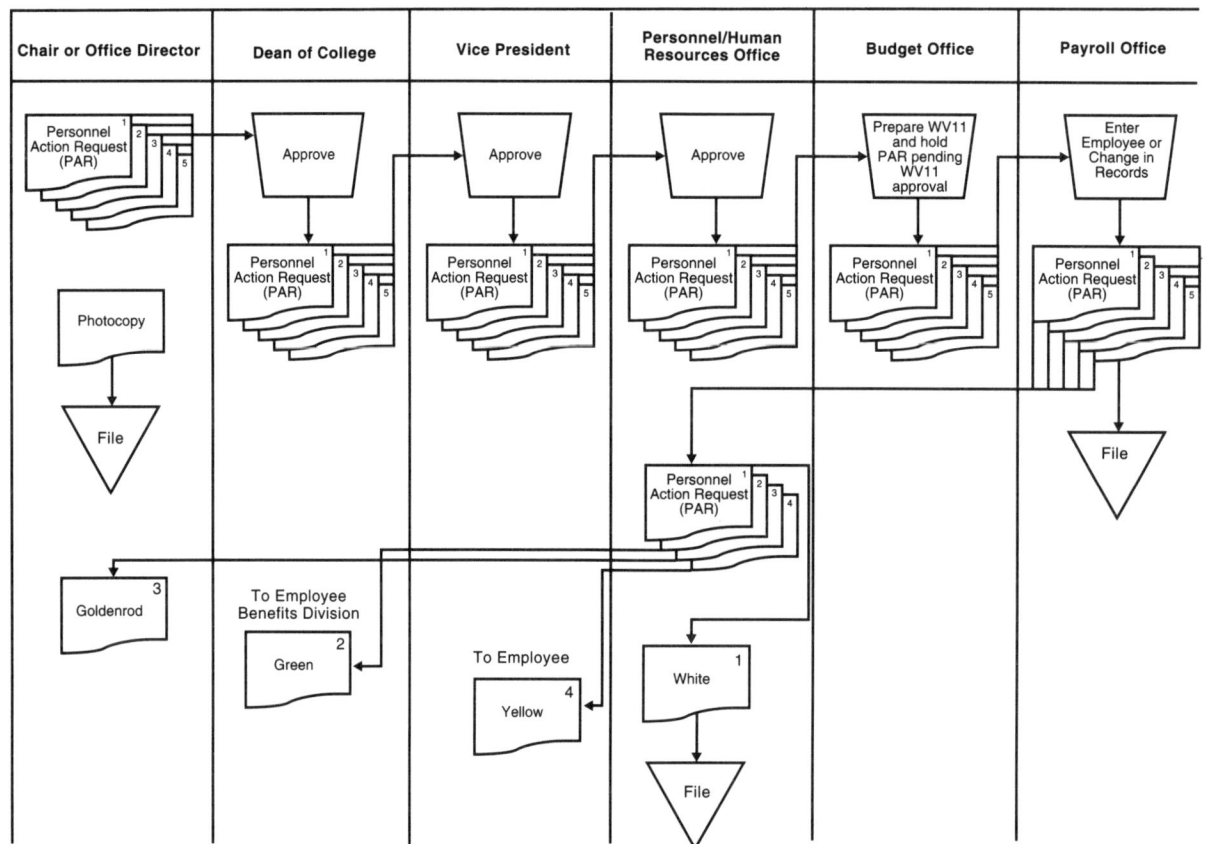

*EXHIBIT 4.—*PAR DOCUMENT MAP

reading. Michael Bauer says: "The map does not have to be a graphic; but, a picture is worth a thousand words and is sometimes more communicative than text. A graphic is also sometimes less open to human interpretation than text is."

Graduate students produced high-quality maps at a nominal cost and proved invaluable to the total quality team's work. When recommendations are prepared for submission to the administration, process and document maps can serve as strong supporting evidence for them.

REFERENCES

1. *Cushing, Barry E. and Romney, Marshall B.,* Accounting Information Systems and Business Organizations, *1987, pp. 161–162.*

2. *Bauer, Michael W., "The Very Beginning of Analysis and Development: The Map,"* Journal of Systems Management, *December 1992, pp. 37–40.*

3. *Pattison, Diane D., Caltrider, James M. and Lutze, Robert, "Continuous Process Improvement at Brooktree,"* Management Accounting, *February 1993, pp. 49–52.*

4. *"TQM Tools and Techniques,"* TQM in Higher Education, *July 1993, pp. 4–5.*

5. *Laudeman, Max, "Document Flowcharts for Internal Control."* Journal of Systems Management, *March 1980, pp. 22–30.*

6. *The talented graduate student is John Burdette, and the author wishes to recognize his initiative and ability. His efforts were a major factor in the success of this project.*

PROCESS MAPPING TRIMS CYCLE TIME*
by D. Keith Denton

At Owens-Corning, cycle time not only drives business, it drives customer satisfaction. Cycle time extends from the moment customers place an order to the moment the company receives payment for that order.

The reason Owens-Corning decided to focus on reducing cycle time is simple. As the company concentrated on speed, it began eliminating things that were not adding value to customers. As Corning eliminated inefficiencies, it began to reduce cost and improve quality.

PROCESS MAPPING

Often speed comes from something as simple as finding out what you are actually doing. Owens-Corning CEO and Chairman, Glen Hiner used one business unit's confirmation success rate to illustrate this point. The unit was able to confirm its customers' orders on a first-time basis, with no errors, only about 25 percent of the time. That service level was unacceptable, so the unit mapped out its Process to see where the obstacles and barriers were. By having a graphical picture of what was going on, it was possible to make some simple changes that radically improved the process—and customer satisfaction.

One simple change—installing an 800 number for the fax machine—increased fax orders by 65 percent. Because fax orders are 95 percent accurate, this simple change increased overall accuracy by 50 percent. Transactions are faster too. In the past, transactions averaged 90 minutes; now they average five minutes with a maximum of thirty minutes.

Cycle time reduction at Owens-Corning centers on what it calls the three R's—responsiveness, results acceleration and resource effectiveness:

1. Responsiveness—meeting your customers' final needs within their time requirements using current resources. The objective is not to create expensive capital investments that outweigh benefits, but to make maximum use of what already exists.

2. Results acceleration—speeding up current performance to take full advantage of current resources.

3. Resource effectiveness—minimizing resources while being responsive and accelerating results. Creating resource effectiveness is more likely if you remove barriers and non-value-added steps.

It is easier to identify barriers to speed in organizations built around customer transactions—products or services that flow horizontally. When organizations are vertical—information moves through accounting, finance, marketing, production function and other support areas—it is more difficult. Work is performed in piecemeal format. Everyone contributes, but the overall objective can get lost in the chain-of-command details.

AT&T recognized the danger of concentrating too much on the chain of command rather than on its customers. As a result, AT&T flattened its organization so it could get to its customers easier. The goal is to never have more than two layers between the customer and "the answer." Horizontal organizations and those focused on processes, not functions, do tend to be faster.

USING THE TEAM APPROACH

Asea Brown Boveri (ABB), like Owens-Corning, has had great success at gaining speed through process mapping. ABB is a global electrical engineering company that was formed in 1988 through the merger of the Swedish ASEA and the Swiss BBC. Employing more than 200,000 people, ABB's business interest includes a wide

*Reprinted with permission from *HR Magazine* (February 1995), published by the Society for Human Resources Management, Alexandria, VA. D. Keith Denton is professor, distinguished scholar of Southwest Missouri State University in Springfield, MO.

range of products primarily related to the generation, transmission, distribution and efficient use of electricity.

Since summer 1990, ABB has been involved in a comprehensive program of change called T50. The "T" stands for time and the "50" refers to ABB's goal to reduce all cycle times by 50 percent. The company's success is due in part to using team management, improving the competencies of its employees, focusing on decentralization, improving supplier relationships, extensive benchmarking and process mapping.

ABB Switchgear in Ludvika, one of ABB's many companies, builds transformers. It was suffering from a defect rate that ran as high as 30 percent. To combat this problem, a team was formed to map out possible sources of defects. It was able to narrow the cause of these defects to three areas: machines used in the process, shortcomings in initial materials, and problems in an area called wire snapping.

By closely examining these areas, the team discovered that one of the three machines was responsible for half the defects. The other two machines were causing many of the remaining defects.

The technique used, process mapping, enabled the group to solve many of the defect problems. The group, convinced of the utility of this procedure, began to set aside one hour of working time each week to solve problems. Defects in production have largely been eliminated, the number of operators has been reduced from 12 to eight, and the volume has increased by 10 percent.

Another one of ABB's companies, ABB Treasury Center in Stockholm, assists other business units with loan investment of liquid funds and currency transactions. The faster the reports are produced, the better the service. The company was able to gain speed through simple mapping where it examined the routines, discussed them, and made suggestions for improvements. It improved the computer support for the forms that need to be filled out. The time required to produce balance sheets of the various activities was reduced from seven to three working days.

FAST CUSTOMER SERVICE

Owens-Corning, like ABB, has been able to use what it calls time mapping to speed up its customer service. One Owens-Corning operation had an order process system in place to ensure that both Owens-Corning and some of its customers were in compliance with the tax regulations in various states. Confusion and disagreement were not uncommon during this verification process. All of this created a "Customer Payment Variance," which meant that customers' bills were not getting paid and, in turn, they were becoming annoyed.

The solution to the problem was to develop a time map to see how the process flowed. The map clearly showed the problem. The company began to eliminate multi-steps and so-called "touch times" that did not add value. Eventually, two departments were completely moved out of the process. In the end, Owens-Corning was able to reduce cycle time for handling claims from 120 days to three days! Their first-time success rate has risen from 1 percent to 90 percent.

CLARIFYING EXPECTATIONS

Owens-Corning created cross-functional teams composed of people from the Americas, Europe and Asia. The objective was to "qualify" all of the company's global sources of glass fiber so it had a consistent quality that met its customers' demands in North America. The goal was to adapt the American product to different manufacturing hardware that existed in other worldwide locations.

A key to the whole process was the team's ability to work closely with its customers to develop a clear understanding of the customers' expectations. A greater understanding of these expectations enabled Owens-Corning to re-engineer a product that could be qualified and released to manufacturing in three and a half months versus the nine to 12 months that it normally had been taking.

ABB's facility in Finpang manufactures gas and steam turbines and heat pumps. ABB developed a systematic procedure for clarifying expectations that it calls customer radar. This card survey procedure matches cards to different types of service. There are cards for spare parts service, another for planned service. The difference between customer radar and the typical customer survey is that with customer radar each service transaction is followed up at the time service is delivered.

COMPETENCIES

Employee development is a big part of ABB's empowerment activities. For instance, at one of ABB's locations employees were given responsibility for maintaining and servicing an area. With each new empowerment came training to make employees competent. As they were given training, they gained power.

Now the employees plan all the work themselves and are given the authority to quote prices for their services without instructions from management. They report on work performed and provide to their customer directly on site so their ideas and experience can be directly available to their customers.

ABB Motors in VasterAs manufactures 110,000 electric motors each year. As part of the company's change efforts, employees in groups were allowed to decide the appearance and location of production lines. This necessitated a massive training effort to develop competency among these employees. All production team members received between 800 to 2,500 hours of training, enabling each of them to handle up to six different tasks. The result was greater flexibility and speed. Now 85 percent of ABB's motors are supplied in one to 10 days. Before the cross-training, it took an average of 47 days to do the same thing.

At ABB, competence development is a far-reaching concept. For instance, at its VasterAs location, ABB developed competence matrices identifying what competencies each working group needs to cope with new tasks. It identifies what competencies employees already have and what development is planned. Each individual has his or her competence plan reviewed in talks between managers and employees. The goal is to set aside 150 hours per employee, per year for competence development. The training includes areas such as job rotation, benchmarking, training on the job, participation in technical development or theoretical education.

SUMMARY

Speed comes from eliminating simplifying, or combining processes, people, products and services. The first choice should be elimination. Owens-Corning eliminated the top layer of its executive management to bring the company closer to the customer, enhance flexibility, simplify decision-making and improve the flow of information. In the process, the speed at which work was done improved. Everything being equal, elimination creates speed.

Simplification should be considered next. Owens-Corning tried to simplify the way work is done by creating work units with more autonomy and more accountability for the profit and loss statement. Simplifying the way work is done helps improve productivity and increase speed.

The last choice should be to combine. Forming a team by combining people, decision-making ability or knowledge can help to increase speed. But although team management is good for ownership and good for empowerment, you should only form a team if you cannot eliminate a need for the decision or simplify it so that an individual can make it.

To begin, simply focus on cycle time. Anything that keeps you from being good, fast and cheap for your customer should be eliminated. Look for those non-value-added steps or multisteps in the process. You can map out the process to find them. You may discover you can eliminate a problem by improving the competencies of workers, increasing their accountability or responsibility, or improving supplier relationships.

REFERENCES

Hiner, Glen H., "Corporate Change to Face the Challenges of Global Competition." Presented at Cadina Del Exito 1994, An Executive Meeting Hosted by Vitro, S. A., February 11, 1994.

Stead, Jerre, "Creating Customer Focus Through People Power," Third Annual Tri-State Telecommunications Association Seminar Series and Trade Show. Cincinnati, Ohio, April 13, 1994.

Stead, Jerre, "The Power Of People In Transforming Organizations." IEEE-USA Conference, Fort Worth, Texas, April 14, 1994.

T50 ABB Swedens Customer Focus Program (an internal document).

|||||| 3.18
PREVENTIVE MAINTENANCE

JAPAN'S NEW ADVANTAGE: TOTAL PRODUCTIVE MAINTENANCE*
by David Turbide

How can a company harness the tremendous power of work teams? Is there a way to encourage production workers to become more involved in quality for the benefit of the company and themselves? The answer to these questions is simple: total productive maintenance (TPM). TPM involves workers taking ownership of their work areas and equipment. In practice, this means that production workers become responsible for routine production-equipment maintenance, including lubrication, adjustments, and minor repairs.

In several Japanese companies I visited, TPM has become a rallying cry for wide-ranging quality improvements. For example, several years ago at Yamato Kogyo, a motorcycle control-cable maker (for Yamaha and other motorcycle manufacturers), business was slow, profits were disappearing, and worker enthusiasm was waning. A previous improvement program got off to an encouraging start but stalled in the second year after modest results. Something had to be done, and it had to be done quickly.

Yamaha convinced Yamato management to use TPM to get Yamato production workers more involved and enthusiastic about quality. Yamato management explained to its workers the problems it faced and how TPM could solve those problems. Five years after Yamato began its TPM program, the firm had improved its productivity by 130%, cut accidents by 90%, reduced defects by 95%, and increased the suggestion rate from 1.3 per employee per month to more than five

suggestions per employee per month. Profits recovered, and Yamato received a TPM Award from Yamaha.

WHAT IS TPM, AND HOW CAN IT BE IMPLEMENTED?

The idea behind TPM is to have production workers take responsibility for the care and routine maintenance of their equipment and work space. Instead of an attitude of "I operate the machines, and someone else fixes them," the approach becomes "I'm responsible for my own equipment." This goes beyond cleaning and oiling. Wherever possible, workers take over simple repairs and more-involved maintenance duties. There is still a maintenance department, but it exists to train production workers, serve as backup for the workers, handle the more-demanding maintenance tasks, and maintain the parts and supplies stock.

Implementing a TPM program starts with training equipment operators so that they are prepared to assume their new duties. The next step is to clean up the work areas. To avoid equipment failure, maintenance activity should be preventive. Preventive maintenance includes watching for early signs of wear, misadjustments, or problems that might be developing. It helps if the area is clean and neatly organized

*Reprinted with permission from *Quality Progress*, March 1995. David A. Turbide is a management consultant with Production Solutions, Inc., in Beverly, MA.

and the floor painted a light color (the better to see oil spatters, errant chips, and loose parts).

There are bound to be improvements needed to help keep the area clean. Typically, splatter guards, hoods, chip collectors, cable conduits, tool racks, and other accessories are installed at this stage.

Workers are intimately involved in the TPM process. They are organized into teams of five to eight people, and the teams develop improvements and implement them on their own, if possible. Yamato regularly held all-company, end-of-the week meetings that often lasted through the night to develop and review rolling 90-day plans, build enthusiasm, discuss progress, and share ideas.

Yamato's TPM program extended beyond equipment maintenance. Work areas were reorganized for convenient access to tools and materials, and cross-functional teams were developed to provide mutual support. Ultimately, improvement suggestions helped increase efficiency and safety. Worker morale soared.

Due to the program's success, Yamato has become a TPM showcase. Charts, graphs, and posters cover the walls, and awards decorate each department. Visitors to the company will notice white Plexiglas signs hanging overhead with colored stickers that mark achievements: A copper sticker signifies that a basis for improvement has been established, silver means that the goal is in sight, and gold signals that the goal has been achieved.

WHY TPM WORKS

TPM's success stems from its focus on identifying a problem's cause and not merely its effects. Clean-up efforts and intimate worker involvement can lead to the early detection of situations that could result in machines malfunctioning or producing substandard parts. TPM is similar to statistical process control: The goal is prevention rather than correction.

Like Yamato, Somic Ishikawa received an award for its TPM effort, this one from the Japan Institute for Plant Maintenance. In Somic's case, the challenges that led to TPM implementation included difficulty in keeping up with rapid product changes, intense competition, a need to improve quality, price pressure, and too many defects for too long at the new product start-up stage.

Somic makes suspension and steering parts for most of the Japanese automotive companies. This highly competitive industry is extremely cost and quality sensitive. To survive in this market, Somic saw the need to simultaneously outperform its competition and reduce its costs. Somic's TPM program had four phases that led to productivity and quality improvements with reduced costs:

Phase 1. The first activity included organizing small teams to initiate the program by cleaning up the facilities and developing daily maintenance tasks for the workers. The first phase's focus was reducing equipment failures and identifying and reducing primary causes of defects.

Phase 2. The second activity (production preparation) addressed design for manufacturing, improving machine and die design, and establishing a better production management system. In describing this phase, Somic officials pointed to a redesign process for one product that resulted in a 17% reduction in cost, a significant reduction in weight (an important factor to the automotive-industry customer), and significant quality improvements. Perhaps the story's most significant aspect is that Somic proposed the changes to the customer, not the other way around. In Japan, many contracts are written so that the supplier is encouraged (or required) to reduce costs and improve quality every year. A significant redesign initiated at the supplier level must be approved by the customer. Cost savings resulting from supplier-initiated improvements are typically shared between supplier and customer.

During my Somic tour, a number of employee-suggested improvements were highlighted. Typical of these was a set of milling machine fixtures that for a changeover required removing three bolts, swapping the fixture, and replacing and tightening the three bolts. In the fixture's improved version, the modified fixture base remained attached to the machine while the detachable top portion was simply slid out and the replacement slipped into the same slot. This improvement was suggested by the machine operator, validated and designed by engineering, and installed for a significant reduction in changeover time.

In another example, an employee suggested that a rack of hand tools be moved from the right side of a work area to another position directly in front of the work area. Not only did this change save time whenever a tool was needed, but it also reduced muscular strain for the worker and reduced the potential for injury and tool damage. This minor change, along with thousands of similar suggestions, has helped transform the somic workplace.

Phases 3 and 4. The third and fourth activities directed automation improvements in the plant and office. Plant automation is directed at improved productivity and quality. Office automation is an area to which Japanese companies have not paid much attention in the past.

The results of TPM at Somic include a 75% reduction in defects, a significant reduction in defects during the start-up phase of new products (a major concern in a fast-changing industry), 50% higher productivity, 95% reduction in unexpected equipment breakdowns, and reduced manpower requirements, despite a significant increase in business volume.

TPM UNIFIES THE WORK FORCE

At Yamato and Somic, TPM provided a mechanism for focusing the work force's energy and creativity. TPM relies on employee teams to initiate and implement changes, most of which come from worker suggestions. The famous Japanese kaizen suggestion-based continuous improve-

ment process is leveraged in an organized TPM program and directed toward specific strategic targets, such as reduced defects, reduced equipment failures, increased productivity, and cost-reduction goals.

At both companies, specific challenges led to the initiation of TPM programs. But there is much to be gained from TPM, and it shouldn't take a crisis to get it started. The first and most obvious potential benefit is a reduction in machine downtime due to proper routine care. In today's lean-and-mean, just-in-time world, machine breakdowns can be deadly.

Second, making the workers responsible and more involved in the machinery's operation should lead to less abuse and accidental damage. Because they understand the equipment better, the workers will be motivated to take better care of it. This increased involvement, along with management's willingness to listen, can lead to a high volume of improvement suggestions that can improve productivity, raise morale, and positively influence quality. A side benefit is that many TPM improvements don't require large investments. It is often the little things and the small changes that, when added together, generate significant results.

3.19
TRAINING

---■---

COOKIES AND QUALITY*
by Jeffery Marx and Sherri Kimery

Our firm launched its total-quality-management initiative with a companywide training session. To encourage staff to participate fully, the training and development staff decided to take advantage of employees' shared sweet tooth.

We created the "Cookie Store" as part of the training. We placed six trays of cookies on a table at the front of the classroom. In front of each tray we hung a poster that listed the cost of a cookie from that particular tray (costs ranged from 10 cents to 75 cents per cookie) and the days and

---

times that participants could sample the cookies on that particular tray.

We asked each participant to choose "the quality cookie" from the selection provided based on three indicators: taste, cost and availability. Then we divided the group into teams and asked each team to rate the cookies and select one as tops in quality.

We tabulated the individual and team responses and created Pareto charts. Because staff were invited to eat cookies throughout the day, we also were able to chart consumption of each kind of cookie.

We found the choices made by both individuals and teams varied widely. Also, every group suggested different indicators of quality. We used the group's activities as a springboard for discussing the need to evaluate products and services from the customer's point of view.

Participants said they appreciated the hands-on experience. Later, we shared this training strategy with a citywide Quality User's Group in Memphis, Tennessee; several other firms plan to use the technique with their own staffs.

SECTION

Four

STANDARDS
AND
AWARDS

In the following section, three standards are emphasized. They are ISO 9000, QS-9000, and ISO 14000. These are, respectively, the voluntary standards for a management system of quality assurance, the management system of quality assurance for automotive suppliers, and the model for an environmental management system.

Although they seem to be three separate standards they are, in fact, three standards on a course of convergence. The ISO 9000 family of standards is scheduled for a massive revision in 1999. The plan is to expand the standard to begin to include health and safety issues and to expand its now minimal environmental concerns. In addition, ISO 14000 will also expand into health and safety concerns. The automotive industry has already hinted that it will start to require ISO 14000 compliance among some of its suppliers. This requirement or parts of it could show up in future editions of QS-9000.

At the same time, groups in the international community want a voluntary standard for general management of a company—including financial management. The idea is to eventually produce a single standard for all management aspects of a company. Therefore, because this is the trend, every quality manager should carefully study the three standards highlighted. If your company does not already have to conform to one of these standards, chances are that essentially at least one of these standards will eventually affect your operations.

As for quality awards, they continue to grow in numbers and types. However, some of the more famous awards are losing favor. Take the example of the Malcolm Baldrige National Quality Award. For the past few years, the number of companies applying has steadily dropped. There are several causes for this. One is the growing popularity of ISO 9000, which has a demonstrated economic benefit and is fairly easy to obtain. Another is the number of corporations reducing pursuits of prizes and awards.

This is not to say that quality awards do not have benefits for companies. As a quality manager, you should study the stories of how companies won their awards. The effort they exerted represents what is necessary to achieve a large project goal. Therefore, many valuable lessons are here to be learned.

QS-9000: FINDING COMMON GROUND*
by Jean V. Owen

The new quality standard for auto suppliers and the truck suppliers who got on the QS-9000 bandwagon with them—Freightliner, Kenworth, Mack Trucks, Navistar International, Peterbilt, and Volvo/GM Heavy Truck—will save all parties concerned a lot of time and money. It's more logical, less contradictory, simpler, and clearer. What's more, it carries ISO 9000's global recognition with it.

"Suppliers tell us that separate standards cause waste because they do the same thing three different ways," says Dennis Atkinson, rewards and recognition manager, Ford Automotive Operations (Dearborn, MI). "Because QS-9000 is based on ISO 9000, the common denominator in quality, it's readily transferable to other industries, and we expect to see it replacing a lot of individual quality systems."

Radley Smith, who was Ford's representative on the standards committee and is now a registrar at KPMG Quality Registrar (Detroit), says the Big Three group recognized in the summer of 1993 that ISO 9001:1994 Sec. 4, which covers everything from design through servicing, represented their individual quality systems better than anything they could concoct. "We decided that Not Invented Here did not apply," he says. "The ISO document said it all."

Chrysler's manager of supplier quality planning, Russ Jacobs, who was on the standards committee, says suppliers who've done the old SQA survey satisfactorily may find different documentation requirements but nothing new or difficult otherwise.

ONE BIG HEADACHE?

Despite Big Three assurances, some suppliers continue to wonder whether they face one more set of quality requirements on top of the old ones.

Five documents go with the standard and the QSA manual: Advanced Product Quality Planning and Control Plan, Measurement Systems Analysis Manual, Statistical Process Control Manual, Production Part Approval Process, and Potential Failure Mode and Effects Analysis, Add Sec. III of the standard itself, with OEM-specific requirements.

Though Chrysler mostly focuses on the use of the company's shield, diamond, and pentagon, GM and Ford's documents cover everything from accreditation of supplier test facilities and packaging of production parts to problem reporting and resolution. "What GM and Ford did," says one supplier, "is simply add all their processes to the standard."

Gregg Bish, a quality engineer and QS-9000 coordinator at Standard Products Co's Lexington Div. (Lexington, KY), welcomes the link to ISO as strengthening his company's products in Europe but fears the new standard makes audits harder to pass. "Under the old system," says Bish, "you could present evidence that you'd taken some action in every case. The OEM's auditors would measure the effectiveness of your effort and, because the score was variable, might reduce it somewhat while still qualifying you. Now we have an attribute score: you do it, or you don't. If the third-party auditor finds one nonconformance, you may not get registered."

What will surprise many companies, says Bob Kozak, who does QS-9000 audits for Entela Inc. (Grand Rapids, MI), is the detailed systems approach. "The old requirements didn't pay much attention to purchasing, maintenance, order entry, or production control. They focused on engineering and manufacturing quality. ISO brings even safety and environmental departments into the audit picture. Departmental procedures or quality manuals have to be kept up to date. None of the old quality systems required these full sys-

---

*Reprinted with permission from *Manufacturing Engineering*, April 1995. Jean V. Owen is a senior editor at *Manufacturing Engineering*.

tems audits, and a lot of suppliers will be shocked."

Apart from audit headaches, Chrysler and GM suppliers must now pay the bills for QS-9000 registration and periodic quality audits, and though Ford continues to do its own audits, the company will require third-party registration soon.

DOWN THE SUPPLY CHAIN

Looming ahead is another hurdle that can really escalate costs—suppliers' suppliers. Because the automakers say most problems with raw materials and subcomponents come from subcontractors, not Tier I suppliers, they want to push responsibility for Tier II and III quality systems onto the Tier I group. What's good for one must be good for all, and the Big Three standards group in January. "First-tier suppliers must use QS-9000 to develop the fundamental quality system requirements of their subcontractors."

Ford suppliers must complete their self-assessments by June 30; third-party registration can be substituted if complete by the deadline. Ford's Atkinson estimates that the process won't take longer than the survey mandated by the Q101 process. At General Motors, new suppliers must get third-party registration by January 1, 1996; current suppliers have one more year—December 31, 1997. Chrysler suppliers must do their QSAs by June 5 and their third-party registration by July 31, 1997.

Here's a rundown on how the new standard meshes with ISO 9000, some tips for buyers of registration services, and suggestions on priorities.

UNDER ISO's BIG TENT

A look at the standard makes the linkage between ISO 9001:Sec. 4 clear (QS-9000 even uses the ISO numbering). Registration to QS-9000 gives a company automatic ISO 9001 registration. Edward Lawson, vice president, quality assurance, Aetna Industries (Center Line, MI), a supplier of stampings and assemblies to Chrysler, GM, and other automakers, has been through both processes. Aetna (opening photo) got ISO 9000 registration in November 1993, QS-9000 registration a year later. "The ISO experience," he says, "was more effective than anything I've ever seen in getting an organization to focus on quality management as a way of improving. Going to QS-9000 meant having a registrar examine the additional steps it requires."

"ISO 9000 is descriptive," he says. "It identifies the elements in a good quality management system, puts a process of assessing compliance to those elements in place, and then leaves it to the company to figure out how to do it. Then the Big Three added a lot of 'supplier shall' commands and made QS-9000 prescriptive, like their old quality systems."

It's easy to spot the "shalls." ISO 9001 has 144, QS-9000 has 244. If the supplier does not follow all the "shalls," it must prove that its system "is equal to or better than QS-9000 criteria." Supplier systems often fall down on the issue of proof.

FIRST STEPS

Before a company can be considered for registration, it must take three steps, says Perry Johnson, an ISO 9000 consultant and trainer in Southfield, MI. First, it must have a quality system in place that meets the QS-9000 requirements; second, it must prove it—that means creating a quality manual that addresses every QS-9000 requirement; third, it must have operated its quality system for three to six months.

Start with a hard look at your quality manual. Sorting out a sack full of procedure documents isn't as hard as it might seem, says Entela's Kozak, because ISO takes a functional approach in which every functional area has an operating procedure. People tend to forget certain sacred areas. "We often find a company's QA department doing audits based on the manufacturing floor. Then we ask: 'Who's auditing QA?' We ask: 'Who's auditing engineering?' People tell us, 'Nobody audits QA, and nobody messes with engineering.' An audit ensures that someone will."

The next step is setting up and training a plant steering committee responsible for delivering the elements of the program on time and for disseminating information throughout the organization. The committee can pick local area representatives who will compile the data on the procedures in place, guide the third-party auditors around the plant, and generally serve as the eyes and ears of the QS-9000 coordinator.

You now have an organizational chart to handle the first two sections of QS-9000. The QS-9000 coordinator, who is independent of the quality group, conducts ongoing management-level audits of the quality system. The internal audit process verifies two things: that the manual reflects what you're really doing, and that you're ready for registration, almost ready, or not ready.

Many companies overlook this step, says KPMG's Smith, but internal audits can be extremely valuable. Kozak of Entela also stresses their importance. "We auditors aren't the police force," he says. "Companies pick up their own problems through audits of their whole system."

PICKING A REGISTRAR

Some ground rules: check the Registrar Accreditation Board's approved list for the name of the registrar you are considering. Only about a dozen companies have made it thus far, though many are in the process. The registrar must follow a Code of Practice written by the Big Three (see Appendix B to the standard) that sets forth the services you can expect and the documentation registrars must produce. The registrar should be ready to show you its QS-9000 certificate if asked.

Check the resumes of the registrar's auditors to verify their knowledge of your business. Then talk to some of their customers. Remember that proactive registrars go beyond identifying acceptable quality systems: they identify opportunities for more efficient practices that optimize resources and save their clients money.

PAYING THE BILL

Many small and medium-sized suppliers who fear the cost of training, consultants, employee hours, and registration fees will find intense competition driving down the cost of implementation and registration. Smith of KPMG says everything depends on auditor days. A small supplier (20-40 people) might require only one day at $1400 to do an audit; a three-year contract, covering the cost of registration and the mandatory surveillance audits, might be $10,000—$15,000. A 5000-employee plant might keep three $1400-a-day auditors busy for a week.

Treat a registrar contract like any other supplier contract—cautiously. Negotiate everything, say those who've been there. Try to get every-thing included in the per-diem fee, including travel and overhead charges. If you can't, know what the extras are.

WHAT ABOUT SOFTWARE?

"An electronically based documentation system is not a requirement," says Smith of KPMG. "A shop of 20-40 employees needs QS-9000 software about as much as it needs electronic mail." Paper and pencil or a Lotus spreadsheet will do fine. On the other hand, companies unfamiliar with quality manuals or lacking a manual that supports QS-9000 can find generic software to produce an implementation blueprint that can easily be customized. Beware the standard boilerplate that fits you into an uncomfortable format and takes you longer to customize than it would to handle the job manually.

Lexington's Bish estimated that doing the research, checking to see that all the standard requirements are met, and writing a new quality manual for his 275-employee plant would take four to six weeks. Assessor and Document Writer 9000/Automotive software from Powerway (Indianapolis) let him produce a quality manual in a week instead of six. It created a network repository and control of approved documents, so staff can track compliance status as internal audits proceed.

The best solution for American Sunroof Co.'s Columbus, OH, plant, where Cynthia Zollo-Davis is coordinating standards efforts, was software from IQS (Cleveland). She likes it because users can pick the software modules they need from a list of 13. ASC is using all 13 software packages; Zollo-Davis also recommends Powerway software.

THE THIRD-PARTY DEBATE

Third-party registration is a very hot button these days. Companies like Cummins, Motorola, Hewlett-Packard, Timken Bearings, Eaton Corp., and others with plants all over the world were alarmed to hear that third-party registration would be required in each plant. Some took the issue to the ISO authorities in Europe, pointing to the meaninglessness of the process for a company going through it for the 20th or 30th time. Instead, these companies suggest a single third-party audit of the corporate quality system and internal audit procedure. After corporate registration, a corporate registrar could register individual sites. Nothing has been decided so far, and the issue remains on the boil.

Lawson doesn't have those problems; Aetna's plants are all in Michigan. Though he dislikes the prescriptive approach in general, he sees third-party audits as a vast improvement over the customer audits of the old days, which had a Catch-22 quality. "When a customer makes business decisions about your company based on audit observations, there's a strong incentive for you to dress things up. Kidding the third-party registrar not only devalues the registration you paid for but also ensures that your product or service won't benefit from the registrar's analy-

sis." What's more, he says, second-party auditors vary wildly in knowledge, ability, and training, whereas registrars' auditors must pass the Big Three's written test and then pass a witness audit—an audit performed before an observer from the certification board.

For many Tier I suppliers the cost of QS-9000 compliance may well turn out to be far smaller than the benefits. "The QS-9000 standard says some familiar and true things," says Bish. "You can't fix a product once it's made, so make it right the first time; if you say you do something, prove it, and then prove it's doing you some good; standardization enhances profitability."

■

MORE HELP WITH QS 9000—FMEAS*
by Richard B. Clements

Unlike the generic, open interpretation of ISO 9001, QS 9000 gets very specific about what a supplier should do to conform. This includes mandating particular methods to assist with conforming to the standard. Statistical process control (SPC) is one good example of a method that helps with statistical methods, process control, and other related elements of ISO 9001. Another method is Failure Mode and Effects Analysis (FMEA).

The AIAG released a guideline standard for this method called Potential Failure Mode and Effects Analysis. It serves as a reference manual and as a way to keep the use of FMEAs uniform within the auto industry.

Two Types of FMEA and Their Purposes

FMEA is a kind of brain-storming, stream of conscienceness method used to examine what might happen to a product or a process. Two types of FMEA exists. The first is called a Product FMEA because it looks at potential failure points within a product. The second is called a Process FMEA because it examines the potential failure points

within a process. Both manufacturing and service process can be used as part of a process FMEA study.

The overall nature of FMEA is to brainstorm out a list of potential failure points and then examine the likelihood of them happening versus the potential effect they would cause. This allows you to convert your internal thinking about a process or product into a tangible table of possibilities. Then you can sort your potential failure by the risk they present and take corrective actions based on objective information.

Example One—Product FMEA Conducted on a Global Positioning Unit

A FMEA is really the documentation of the thought process an engineering team goes through in developing a new product. First, the overall product is broken down into its components and significant parts. For each of these, potential failure points are identified by a design team. It is critical the design team be made of people with expertise in several fields, such as engineering, regulations, manufacturing, quality, and so on.

---

*Reprinted with permission of *Continuous Improvement*, April 1995. Richard B. Clements is president of Solution Specialists.

A specific example would be a global positioning unit (GPU). A GPU is a small radio receiver and computer that typically is smaller than a cigar box. The radio receiver portion of the unit picks up the signals of at least three earth-orbiting satellites designed to provide positioning data to the unit. The information is fed to a computer that tracks time very accurately and calculates the units position on earth in three axis to within a meter or two.

In an automobile, such a unit could constantly tell a driver his position and other information, such as how to reach a particular destination. In recreational applications, a hand-held version of the unit can tell a hiker her position and the direction and distance back to common reference points, such as the previous day's campsite. Altogether, the GPU is a very interesting device. However, it has many potentials for failure. We will examine only one in detail.

A good FMEA should begin with a list of what the customer wants the product to do and what the product should not do. This list can be derived from methods such as customer surveys and quality function deployment (QFD). Added to this should be a diagram of the actual product. This helps the team to focus on the needs of the product and to visualize the interrelationships between components.

FMEA forms are provided in the AIAG reference manual. For each item in the design, fill in the following information:

• item name and intention

• potential failure modes

• potential effect of the failure

• severity and classification of the failure

• potential causes of the failure

• likelihood of the failure occurring

• list the current design controls

• likelihood that current design controls will detect the failure

• calculated risk

• recommended actions to prevent failures

• who will carry out the recommended actions

• new calculation of risk after corrective actions are taken.

This is a dynamic process and the FMEA form is constantly updated during the design process as new information is received.

Let's return to our example. One item to be considered is the source of electrical input. Assume we are designing a hand-held unit. The source of power is a rechargeable battery rated for 12 volts DC.

Begin by listing the item as "12 volt DC rechargeable battery." Under this we would list its design intentions, such as delivering between 10 volts and 13.5 volts DC to the GPU at all times, that it be rechargeable at least 100 times, and that it deliver the right amount of power for at least eight hours with the unit in operation.

Next we would list potential failure mode. For example, if the battery gave out less than 10 volts DC, it is believed this would lead to a potential failure in performance. We would normally list all items and all potential failures. For the sake of this illustration, we will follow through on just this one potential failure.

Now we list the potential effects of the failure, in other words, what the customer might experience. In our example, the screen may fade, the data calculations become unstable, or the unit might fail to receive any signals from the satellites. In short, the end-use customer finds himself lost with no data on his location. This potential failure's severity would be ranked as high, or 8, on a scale from one to ten. Thus the classification of the battery system is "critical."

Next, list out the potential causes of the failure. In our case, it could be from a number of sources, such as a defective battery, a battery with too many recharges, a defective charger, cold temperatures, moisture in the circuitry, and so on. Let's focus on just the defective battery and the moisture on the circuits. Using a one-to-ten scale, we rank a defective battery at 4 (about 1 in 2000 chance) and moisture seepage into the unit at 2 (about 1 in 150,000). The AIAG reference manual has the criteria listed for making these determinations.

At this point we list the current design controls in place to prevent the potential failure. This includes inspection methods, design features, design verification, and design validation activities. Once listed, rate the detection capability of current design controls. In our example, we may find our sealed unit that is tested at the plant is very likely to detect a problem, so it gets a 1 rating. The random testing of batteries installed into units gets a detection rating of 3, because it is less likely to detect a problem.

Using simple multiplication we create what is called a Risk Priority Number. You take the ratings for severity, occurrence, and detection and multiply them together. For example, the defective battery creates a severity rating of 8, an occurrence rating of 4, and a detection rating of 3. This creates an RPN of 96. The moisture problem gets an RPN of 16. Thus, by using RPNs we can rank order the potential failures into a priority ranking. In our case, the defective battery would be addressed before the moisture problem.

Now we can brainstorm and list our corrective actions. Focusing on the defective battery problem, the unit might be redesigned to have a low battery warning displayed to give the end user time to switch to a fresh battery. We might also make the rechargeable battery holder removable so that alternative power source can be attached, such as a solar cell, conventional battery pack, or a second rechargeable cell. Although the severity of the potential failure would remain high, the likelihood of occurrence would drop along with the likelihood of detection.

The redesign would be listed and a person assigned the task of assuring the action is completed and tested. Once completed, note when the action occurred. You would also recalculate your RPN to measure the effectiveness of the action. In our example, the occurrence and detection ratings drop to 1 and 1. The RPN also drops to 8.

In this way, go down the list of RPN ranked potential failures and do your best to reduce their occurrence and/or increase your ability to detect when they occur before the product is shipped. The earlier this detection occurs, in general, the less the cost of the corrective actions.

Example Two—Process FMEA for Plastic Injection

Although the FMEA form for a process FMEA looks like the Design FMEA form, the actual implementation differs. For one thing, a process FMEA must take into account both process functions and the design characteristics of the product being manufactured or the service being delivered.

Let's take the example of a plastic injection machine producing 16 plastic keyboard buttons with each cycle. The buttons are used to assemble a machine control keyboard. Each button will have strict dimensional and weight tolerance to meet, along with appearance criterion.

To conduct a process FMEA, begin with a process flow chart. In this way, the engineering team can visualize the process. A risk assessment of the process should also be conducted. The AIAG manual has an appendix on how to perform this task.

The plastic injection process involves the loading of resin, the heating of the resin, the loading of a mold, the injection of resin into the mold, the removal of finished parts, and the occasional cleaning of the mold. We will focus on the actual molding cycle of the button where the mold closes, resin is injected, the mold stays shut an additional 30 seconds to allow the button to harden, the mold opens, and operator pulls out the finished buttons and separates them.

The molding cycle is listed as a process function. Examine potential failure modes. One is the failure of the resin to properly "set" in the mold. The result is missing material, cracks, flow lines, or misshaped parts. Just like a product FMEA, we would list out the effects of these failures and rate their severity. We would also list out the potential causes, such as too much regrind, too much moisture in the resin, too low a barrel temperature, and so on. Each of these are rated by their likelihood to occur.

Then the current process controls are listed. This might include machine controllers, set-up sheets, SPC, visual inspections, designed experiments, or other such process controls. Each process control is rated for its ability to detect the potential failure. You have the same three numbers available for calculating the RPN. Once calculated, the potential failure can be rank ordered as before. This will give you a list of priorities to address.

Now create a list of recommended actions to be taken to reduce the potential failure. For example, a designed experiment might be conducted to create a new set-up sheet with machine settings that makes the process robust against the potential failures. Also, inspection of resins for moisture content and establishing the amount of regrind allowed into the process can also be effective. As before, a particular individual is assigned to make sure the action is carried out and notes the date of completion.

Once completed, recalculate the RPN to determine the effectiveness of your actions. In this way, a process FMEA can be an excellent tool of continuous improvement and preventive actions.

HOW NON-AUTOMOTIVE COMPANIES CAN BENEFIT FROM FMEA

The overall intention of FMEA is to prevent problems before they occur. FMEA is a group effort that happens before the production of products. In that way, FMEA represents one of the best tools available for demonstrating continuous improvement in both product and processes. For example, it would be easy to use a FMEA to examine an existing process procedure that doesn't work well and design a better process. It would be even better to use FMEA to develop all of your new processes.

Because the automotive industry has become very specific about the type of methods a supplier should use, non-automotive companies also benefit. If you work outside the automotive industry and are trying to implement ISO 9000, the QS 9000 program can help. If you are uncertain about using techniques like FMEA as part of your design process, then obtain the AIAG reference manual and have the whole system, including forms and instructions, in your hands. This will save you valuable development time and will facilitate training.

---■---

ADVANCED PRODUCT QUALITY PLANNING (INCLUDING CONTROL PLANS)*
by Richard B. Clements

This is the third in a series of articles on the reference standards developed by the Automotive Industry Action group (AIAG) that can assist any company seeking ISO 9000 registration, specifically companies seeking QS 9000 registration.

The AIAG has produced a series of reference standards for the automotive industry that have been universally adopted by the Big Three, Chrysler, Ford, and General Motors. We have already looked at FMEAs and PPAPs. The reference standard "Advanced Product Quality Planning and Control Plan" represents one of the more ambitious attempts to standardize a practice within an industry.

Advanced quality planning (AQP) is a long and complex method of assuring the quality of production before production begins. A key component of this is the creation of a quality control plan. The 1994 edition of ISO 9000 calls for the use of quality control plans within several areas of the requirements. The standard from AIAG can prove very helpful for getting any company up to speed on meeting the control plan requirement. It can also help the automotive supplier or other company seeking to initiate an AQP system.

INSIDE THE STANDARD

This standard applies to any company with a recognized design function for the product being produced. The standard assumes that cross-functional teams will work on the AQP tasks. It is assumed that either a product or service can be submitted to the processes described in the standard. The standard also grants automotive suppliers the rights to copy and use the forms contained within.

The central purpose of AQP activity is to promote clear and effective communication between a customer corporation and its suppliers. The main topic of this communication is the quality requirements of the product or service and how the supplier plans to assure these requirements are fulfilled.

The AQP process begins with top management commitment. Then team leaders and their teams are selected. If necessary, training is given on the methods to be used. Other organizational tasks are performed to establish the procedures to be used and to identify the customers to be satisfied.

The first step of the AQP team is to create a timing chart. This chart shows each phase of

*Reprinted with permission from *Continuous Improvement,* May 1995. Richard B. Clements is president of Solution Specialists, Alto, MI.

product development and implementation. Typically it is broken into the following sections:

- concept initiation
- approval of program
- prototype
- pilot run
- launch.

The actual activities involved in AQP follow the familiar Plan-Do-Check-Action sequence of continuous improvement. At all stages of the AQP process, feedback is sought out to confirm the project is on target in terms of both time and meeting the requirements of the customer.

This means that project management methods should be used with a well-defined set of "status reports" being generated. It also means simultaneous engineering should be used so that development activities are occurring concurrently and striving for common goals.

THE ROAD TO AQP

The AIAG standard describes the steps taken in a common AQP exercise. It is comprised of several activities, each containing many tasks. Some of these occur concurrently. It is important to be properly trained or experienced in AQP before you lead such an effort. The steps are:

1. Plan and Define the Program. This is basically gathering up the requirements of the customer, creating a list of design outputs, and drawing up the overall plan of attack for a particular component. Methods used to gather up information on customer requirements include warranty information, quality data, market research, personal experiences, business plans, marketing objectives, benchmarking, brainstorming assumptions, reliability studies, customer's contractual requirements, and other similar source of information. This information is used to create a preliminary bill of material, list of quality goals, process flow chart, product assurance plan, and a list of special characteristics. All or some of these may be modified by later activities.

2. Product Design and Development. Here the team tries to finalize the design features and characteristics. Design reviews and verifications now take place. A prototype is typically produced and tested. Issues such as the design for manufacturability, design FMEA, and feasibility studies take place. Produced are the engineering drawings, specifications, list of tools to be used, and the special characteristics to be verified.

3. Process Design and Development. Now armed with a list of requirements and the specifications of the product, a team can design the process to produce a quality product at a cost-to-yield value. Tasks include the completion of a process FMEA, packaging standards, quality review system, process flow chart, floor plan layout, characteristic matrix, pre-launch control plan, process instructions, capability studies, measurement equipment control plan, and other analysis as needed.

4. Product and Process Validation. At this point, a trial run of the proposed process should be possible. From this trial run, an evaluation must be made for the capability of a full production run in meeting customer requirements. The information will also be used to finalize the control plan and process flow chart. Methods such as PPAP, production validation, packaging evaluation, quality planning sign-offs, and measurement system adequacy are all addressed.

5. Feedback and Corrective Action. Once the first four steps are completed, you should be ready for initiating regular production. Now switch your efforts over to activities such as assuring continuous monitoring of special characteristics using SPC. You should also confirm the production is meeting all customer requirements and your planning was sufficient to produce the expected results. From this point on, your focus changes to customer satisfaction, delivery, service, and continuous improvement.

As you can see, AQP is no small effort. Typically, several teams are involved and the activities can take months to complete. Yet, for all of the tasks required, you do get paid back by two very big returns on your investment. The first is that the customer is most likely to be satisfied. The second is that you will make the product right the first time. As we have stated before, a part made right the first time that satisfies the needs of a customer is usually the most cost effective method of production.

Quality Plans

The second section of the AIAG standard reviews the method of creating control plans. It does so in great detail with specific instructions on the steps to take. To assist you, it includes blank forms and completed examples. Standardizing the control plan form makes it possible for an automotive supplier to prepare a single plan acceptable to multiple customers.

We have previously discussed the method of preparing a control plan. For review purposes, remember these key points.

- Create a process flow chart to visualize the production sequence.
- Select verification points in the process that match any special characteristics.
- When possible, make sure verification activities can add value to the product.
- Add reaction plans for when verification finds nonconformances.
- Make the control plan a living document that can be modified and improved at any time.

If necessary, you can use methods such as designed experiments, cause and effect charts, fault tree analysis, and the like to clarify where verification is necessary. In the case of designed experiments, it is sometimes possible to also determine the level of variation you can expect. Another use for a designed experiment is to design a process that is robust against identified sources of variation.

More Goodies Contained in the AIAG Standard

The back material in the AIAG standard is packed with additional useful information. For example, Appendix A contains checklist for the product quality planning activities. These help guide any team to a complete and thorough review. The back material also includes additional descriptions of possible analytic methodologies, more blank forms, descriptions of special characteristics symbols used in the automotive industry, and glossaries of terms.

Conclusion

Taken as a whole, the AIAG standard for AQP represents an excellent reference manual for any company interested in first-time success in the launch of a new product. ISO 9000 seeking companies will find the methodology presented will easily meet the design control requirements of the standard. In addition, it will also help with contract review, process control, and other production related requirements. Therefore, the AIAG standard is beneficial to both automotive and ISO 9000 companies.

MANAGEMENT RESPONSIBILITY AND THE QUALITY SYSTEM FOR QS-9000*
by Richard B. Clements

"This article begins a series of discussions on the requirements in Section One of QS-9000, the automotive guideline for supplier quality. As we shall see, Section One of QS-9000 begins by using all of Section 4.0 of ISO 9001 and then adds some automotive specific requirements. We will examine each of the elements and how to comply with their requirements. Companies outside of the automotive industry will benefit from this discussion by observing how specific customer requirements can be easily incorporated into the ISO 9000 system."

Elements 4.1 and 4.2 of QS-9000 deal with management responsibility and the quality plan used at a company. These are the two elements companies fail most often. Also, you should note that all of Section One of QS-9000 makes heavy

*Reprinted with permission from *Continuous Improvement,* July 1995. Richard B. Clements is president of Solution Specialists, Alto, MI.

use of ISO 9001: 1994, Section 4.0. Therefore, other ISO standards can be used as guidelines.

The Key Word Is "Management"

Remember, QS-9000, especially Section One, is a standard on the management system of quality assurance. As such, the QS-9000 standard begins by assuming your company has a consistent, well-documented system of quality assurance that is understood by all employees. A lead assessor is interested in finding out if every person in your organization knows their job and how that job affects the quality of the product.

Therefore, if you read elements 4.1 and 4.2, they ask for the following:

- a written quality policy related to business goals and understood by all employees
- an established quality organization
- regular management review of the system
- written quality procedures
- effective use of procedures
- verification and process/product inspection system
- well-defined roles within the system
- continuous improvement of the system
- criteria of acceptability
- quality records
- an organizational chart showing lines of responsibility
- a QS-9000 representative from an executive level
- a written business plan
- statistical monitoring of business trends against objectives
- a method for determining customer satisfaction
- written quality plans
- written quality records
- use of advanced product quality planning process (APQP) using cross-functional teams
- feasibility reviews
- use of failure mode and effects analysis (FMEA)
- use of production part approval process (PPAP).

As usual, ISO 9004-1 and ISO 9000-2 expand these elements by providing guidelines for implementation. These particular elements, ISO 9004-1, sections 4.0 and 5.0, make it exceptionally clear that meeting management and quality system requirements is not an easy task.

To begin with, ISO 9004-1 makes it clear that only the top manager at a site is ultimately responsible for quality, not the quality manager. It is then this top manager's responsibility to assure the company's quality policies are understood by all employees.

What You Need to Do

As for documentation, the first step is to develop you general, company-wide quality policy. Not one of those "motherhood" policy statements you see at the front of a company's sales literature. The QS-9000 standard requires a real policy that identifies specific goals and methods. For example,

"Our policy is for management to provide the training and leadership to all employees in the art of continuous improvement to constantly seek improved quality at reduced costs that still exceed the expectations of our customers."

See how this type of policy is more specific and to the point than the following.

"The AXC company supports the concept of quality and the importance of maintaining customer satisfaction."

Once this company-wide policy is in place, you can begin to assemble your QS-9000-related documents. The first should be a detailed, company-wide quality plan containing objectives, goals, time lines, and responsibilities based on your company's business plan.

Any plan should be broken down into the specific objectives, such as the objective of training all workers in the use of continuous improvement techniques. This is where you specify what particular training will be delivered to which people. You also list who is responsible for implementing the training, and when it should be done. For other parts of this detailed quality plan, you should also address the issue of costs, reliability, manufacturability, the meeting of customer needs, and other important considerations.

The Quality System

With a well-thought out quality plan, you now focus on implementation of your quality system. This is where you write the Level I documents for each of the elements of the QS-9000, Section One. In addition, procedures must be written or updated to match the quality plan's intentions.

When developing a quality system, you are developing your Level I, II, and III documents. These should always be written to conform to the type of business you conduct. Remember, the idea behind QS-9000 is that you have a quality system that makes sense for the type of business you are in. It is inappropriate to place more layers of bureaucracy on your company just to meet the QS-9000 requirements.

When writing your documentation to meet the other elements of QS-9000, keep in the back of your mind these ideas:

- you need to meet your contractual requirements

- you need to understand and meet customer needs

- specific people have to be made responsible for each element

- the emphasis is on problem prevention.

Element 4.2 is actually the requirement for writing procedures for all the other requirements in QS-9000. The closest procedure for this particular section would be your method of writing and approving new procedures and policies. However, the lack of a specific Level II document for this requirement does not save you from danger. Instead, any other element that is found out of conformance with QS-9000 is also a violation of the element 4.2 requirement for a consistent and conforming quality system.

To conform to element 4.2, you must conform to all other elements of the QS-9000.

What About Management?

Element 4.1 requires a different set of documents. The first to consider developing is an organizational chart of your company showing lines of responsibility under the quality system. If you don't know these lines, then now is a good time to find out. If any job titles are not connected to the quality system, now is the time to develop those links.

To evaluate element 4.1, assessors look at how well top management has identified who is responsible for each element of the standard. This is why we have been telling you to list the job title of the person responsible for each element in your Level I documents. Lines of responsibility and communication need to be well defined.

In addition, the assessors look at your system of identifying current and potential quality problems. They are particularly interested in your history of corrective action and preventive measures. A good company will have a documented history of reacting quickly to problems and also spending time looking for and eliminating potential problems.

For your top managers, this comes back to the need for regular internal audits of your quality system. The top managers should review the system and work toward continuous improvement of the system. These audits need to be formal and well-documented. They should also include documented corrective actions with followup until the close of the file.

Your management must also assure adequate resources and well-trained personnel are provided for every function within the quality system. This includes the need for appropriate equipment for test, measurement, and verification.

Finally, the company-wide quality plan should lead directly to written work instructions for every employee. At a minimum, any quality-related activity must have written instructions that include a list of the equipment and resources needed to complete the activity. This includes the obvious tasks of testing, inspection, and auditing. However, it also includes less obvious tasks such as preventive maintenance, design review, keeping communication records, housekeeping, supplier evaluation, and so on.

The quality control plans are developed for each product, service, or family of products your company offers. These were discussed in detail in our story on advance product quality planning (May 1995).

Also, a business plan for your company is necessary. It should look closely at your position in the marketplace and how you plan to be a top leader in your niche. Although QS-9000 states this is not audited, it is hard for an auditor to examine your system without making reference to this document. Questions such as "How did you come to write your quality policy?" will lead back to the business plan.

You should also have a regular system of monitoring the performance of your company. The measurements should be based on the objectives and goals laid out in your business plan.

You can envision a wall of charts showing how much market share you have, the price per unit, the level of nonconformance, and so on. Each should be headed for its stated target and beyond. Management has to leave behind a written record of reviewing this data, the internal audits, and other related activities. They should also show, in writing, they reacted to the reviews with changes to the system. Regular management review minutes should be kept.

There is also the issue of measuring customer satisfaction. This is not always an easy task. Your primary customers will be the OEMs or a tier-one supplier. You must interview them, and your staff, to see what makes the customer happy. Is it no rejects, on-time delivery, attached process information, or all of these items?

Finally, you must use cross-functional teams to deploy techniques such as FMEA, APQP, PPAP, and problem-solving. Each of these have

been addressed in previous articles, and they represent a major expansion of the QS-9000 requirements. It is these techniques that make QS-9000 lose its well-defined border of compliance. With ISO 9001, there are ends to each requirement. With QS-9000, once you get into a technique like APQP, you open a can of related methods. Methods like designed experiments, team building, problem-solving tools, risk assessment, value analysis, and the like.

Summary

Elements 4.1 and 4.2 lay the foundation for the conformance of your company to all elements of QS-9000. If you begin with a solid policy and back it up with detailed plans that can be quickly adjusted to meet changing market needs, then writing your Level I, II, and III documents for all QS-9000 elements becomes much easier.

QS-9000 COMPANIES SHARE SUCCESS STORIES*

The first ISO 9000 certificates have been issued under the Big Three automakers' QS-9000 standard and the initial reaction from suppliers that have gone through the process: an overwhelming thumbs up.

Several suppliers that were among the first companies to attain QS-9000 registration told *QSU* they did not find the process to be any more difficult than meeting former Big Three requirements and undergoing an ISO 9000 audit.

"If you are an automotive parts supplier today, you have to meet the quality requirements that are spelled out by the company," explained Lowell Jacobs, director of quality operating systems at Prince Corporation of Holland, Michigan.

"They have done nothing more than take those quality system requirements and put them into an ISO format. To me it's amazing that people are so scared of it."

QS-9000 late last year was imposed on approximately 13,000 first-tier suppliers that produce components that ultimately become a permanent part of the cars and trucks manufactured

by the Big Three in North America. The document contains ISO 9001 in its entirety along with additional industry-specific requirements.

Jacobs, whose company manufactures automotive trim and other components for the Big Three, said his company found the industry-specific requirements contained in QS-9000 to be complementary to ISO 9000.

"ISO describes those elements that are necessary in a good quality system," he observed. "Then along came the car companies and they took that description and added to it some specific requirements. They have prescribed what systems you need to use in certain areas."

The biggest internal challenge for Prince was documenting procedures, according to Jacobs. "We essentially had no [written] procedures," he said. Now, "as new engineers come in, we have a Bible to train them with and no longer do they just bump along trying to pick it up."

Jacobs said his company also struggled over the question of how QS-9000 must be passed down to the company's suppliers.

---

*Reprinted by permission of Quality Systems Update, published by IRWIN Professional Publishing, Fairfax, VA.

"Our suppliers have to be at least expected to understand the QS-9000 requirements," he explained. "It means when you go in to do an assessment or an evaluation that you have built into your assessment those essential elements of QS-9000."

In general, Jacobs said, most Big Three suppliers can expect more frequent audits under the third-party system.

"Typically the audits were not done on a regular basis because of [a lack of] resources," he said. "The resources were applied to . . . suppliers that were having a little more difficulty than others."

Ed Lawson, vice president of quality assurance with Aetna Industries Inc. of Center Line, Michigan, another QS-9000 registered company, agreed that suppliers should have no difficulty attaining QS-9000 registration if they are compliant with ISO 9000 requirements and one of the old Big Three quality requirements.

"The step from ISO 9000 registration to QS-9000 registration was relatively minor," explained Lawson. "As an automotive supplier, none of the requirements contained in QS-9000 were new requirements."

Lawson, whose company manufactures automotive stampings, roll formings and welded modular assemblies, said the move from second-party to third-party auditors may be one of the greatest benefits of QS-9000.

He suggests that suppliers try to get the most out of their third-party audits rather than viewing compliance as a necessary part of doing business. "If you're going to derive benefit [from the process] it should be real," he said.

John Yeung, quality manager of Polywheels Manufacturing Ltd. of Ontario, Canada, which manufactures heat shields and which also received QS-9000 registration, said the third-party auditors seemed to have a broader focus than most second-party auditors he had worked with in the past.

"They just concentrate on their products," he said of the second-party auditors he has observed. "They pay less attention to other products that we make."

In contrast, he said, third-party auditors look at all the product lines. "They have to spend more time in our facility," he explained. "They have to look at every product that we make."

Yeung also said he believes that QS-9000 will help suppliers be more competitive. "One of the requirements for the QS-9000 is continuous improvement," he said. "I think that will be beneficial to any company that is doing it."

Terrie L. McDaniel, quality manager of the Robinson Gasket Plant of the Dana Corporation-Victor Products Division in Robinson, Illinois, said her company's registration to QS-9000 was complicated by the fact that company officials had not been exposed to ISO 9000 requirements in the past.

"For us, there was a lot that we had to catch up on because of the fact that about 90 percent of the QS-9000 is ISO 9000," she explained. "It was a different philosophy for us because they ask you for so much documentation."

McDaniel said one of the biggest challenges was documenting the company's efforts with respect to continuous improvement.

"They're looking really hard at what you're doing in the plant to continually improve," said McDaniel, whose company manufactures soft gaskets and service kits for the Big Three.

"I think that's going to be tough on smaller companies that don't have the resources to do it."

Even so, McDaniel said, companies that successfully implement QS-9000 should be better positioned to do business in the global economy.

"We feel that in the long run it's going to save us money and I think our product is going to be better," she said.

|||||| 4.2
|||||| ISO 9000

■

THE FUTURE OF ISO 9000*
by Amy Zuckerman

Claude Hetu is mighty relieved that his Ontario forging company can switch from ISO 9000 to QS-9000 registration with ease and at no extra cost.

On the other hand, Robert Peuperbaugh, president of a small Michigan cutting-tool company, finds the emergence of the Big Three's QS-9000 quality program "frustrating" at best.

What Hetu and Peuperbaugh, both auto industry suppliers, are reacting to is the hybridization of the ISO 9000 international quality management program.

Multinationals like the Big Three have created a industry-specific version of ISO 9000 called QS-9000. Major truck manufacturers like Freightliner, Mack, Navistar, Paccar and Volvo/GM have adopted QS-9000. Other industries, specifically steel and metal tooling, are reportedly spinning off their own versions of QS-9000.

But the changes on the ISO 9000 and related quality fronts don't stop with the automotive, steel or metal-tooling industries. In electronics, both Motorola and Hewlett-Packard are waging a worldwide campaign for reform of the ISO 9000 registration system. Mobil Oil's quality staff has raised alarms publicly that international standards development is becoming increasingly political, with some multinationals apparently hitting at their competition through the International Organization for Standardization technical committees. And McDonnell Douglas has questioned using ISO 9000 in lieu of military specifications.

Curt Reimann, director for quality programs at the government-sponsored Malcolm Baldrige National Quality Award, says the 1995 Baldrige Criteria are further than ever from the ISO 9000 approach. The intent, he says, is not to purposely differentiate the Baldrige from ISO 9000 but to offer companies what the Baldrige committee believes they need to create a full quality process. This includes more emphasis on strategic business issues, high performance and business results.

The European Union, in the meantime, is moving ahead with plans to create its own European quality program that will be based more on a Baldrige than an ISO 9000 approach. ISO 9000 methodology will be included in the EU plan, but the ISO 9000 certificates may be abolished or downplayed. EU officials expect to have a proposal before the European Commission sometime this spring.

There are ongoing efforts within the ISO to better administer the standard on a worldwide basis. The ISO recently authorized a memorandum of understanding to the International Accreditation Forum giving that organization the green light to create international rules binding accreditation bodies.

These are only a handful of the developments worldwide in the international standards arena. Since the ratification of the General Agreement on Tariffs and Trade, new programs and mandates come to the fore almost daily. For example, the Japanese plan to make ISO 9000 registration mandatory for all software manufacturers planning to do business in Japan.

Of more immediate concern to American small-businesspeople is how to cope with developments on the automotive, electronics and European fronts. The following summarizes what is taking place:

---

*Reprinted with permission from *Quality Digest,* May 1995. © 1995 QCI International. Amy Zuckerman is the author of *ISO 9000 Made Easy: A Cost-Saving Guide to Documentation and Registration* (AMACOM Books, 1995).

ISO 9000 vs. QS-9000

In September, the Big Three unveiled their first-ever common quality program, QS-9000. The program utilizes an ISO 9000 quality assurance base coupled with industry-specific guidelines drawn from the auto industry's former quality programs: GM's North American Operations Targets for Excellence, Ford's Q-101 Quality System Standard, Chrysler's Supplier Quality Assurance Manual and GM Europe's General Quality Standard for Purchased Materials.

General Motors was the first to mandate QS-9000 for its North American suppliers, Chrysler followed suit, and only Ford is holding back until QS-9000 is more established. General Motors and Chrysler have plans to introduce QS-9000 to their European suppliers this winter and to the worldwide operations down the line. Ford is also looking into introducing QS-9000 to its European suppliers.

Because QS-9000 is still very much in its infancy, the rules governing the program are in constant flux. So much flux, in fact, that the editor of a major automotive trade magazine has trouble keeping QS-9000 stories current. Any auto supplier or related industry supplier should be aware of a number of factors when pursuing QS-9000:

*   New GM North American suppliers have until Jan. 1, 1996, to comply with QS-9000, while long-time suppliers have a deadline of Dec. 31, 1997. Chrysler suppliers have until July 31, 1997, to earn QS-9000 certificates.

*   ISO 9000 certificates, alone, will not be accepted.

*   The Big Three are pursuing acceptance for QS-9000 outside of the United States. To date, Great Britain and the Netherlands have given their approval. Blanket European acceptance of the certificates (in lieu of ISO 9000 certificates) is expected.

*   ISO 9000 registrars must earn the Big Three Code of Practice of Quality Systems Registrars to issue QS-9000 certificates. Training of registrars is ongoing, and Big Three representatives have been in Europe scouting reinforcements. Only registrars that have earned the Code of Practice can issue QS-9000 certificates.

*   So-called hybrid or transplant companies—specifically Honda North American

and Nissan North American—are not adopting QS-9000 for their suppliers.

Electronics

In a joint effort, Motorola and Hewlett-Packard have gathered the support of 37 major electronics companies worldwide to push streamlining of the ISO 9000 registration process. Companies include AT&T, Xerox, Digital Equipment, Microsoft, Matsushita Electric Corp. of America, Philips Electronics, Whirlpool, Bausch & Lomb, Stala Oy (Finland) and many others.

Richard Buetow, quality chief at Motorola, explains that his company and Hewlett-Packard have formed "a marriage of convenience" to push for creating a new system that would cut back on the amount of work ISO 9000 registrars perform in a major corporation. The companies that have signed the so-called "supplier's declaration of conformity" are seeking approval from the European Union, the ISO and other major international standards institutions to eliminate plant-by-plant ISO 9000 registration. They want one-stop registration based on internal manufacturer certification.

Although loathe to criticize the Big Three's efforts, Buetow says he is concerned with the decision to continue with an altered version of the ISO 9000 registrar system. Because so many electronics companies supply the Big Three, he says they will have to earn QS-9000—and work within that registrar system—at the very time so many electronics giants are trying to alter it, he says.

Europe

In a series of reports issued throughout 1994, EU standards officials announced their intent to downplay the for-profit aspect of European quality and re-emphasize the quality process. To this end, they intend to reinforce the fairly new European Quality Award. If all goes as planned, national accreditation bodies will operate under the jurisdiction of Jacques McMillan, chief of the Senior Standards Policy Group for Directorate-General III for Industry. They will no longer operate for profit or compete with each other.

In a fall interview in Brussels and in subsequent interviews, McMillan and quality associate Antonio Silva Mendes insist the EU does not intend to "kill" ISO 9000. Their concern has been the rampant commercialization of the international quality program and the fact that many

European companies have complained that ISO 9000 hasn't lived up to its advertising hype as a quality tool. McMillan and Mendes consider the standard a good quality base but not adequate as a total quality process.

"A lot of people thought we were trying to kill ISO 9000," says McMillan. "Now people are understanding the message. We're not trying to kill it; we're trying to save it.

"One problem industry faces is that they shouldn't do things that don't give them added value. They shouldn't pay for things that don't give added value. I get into fights with certifiers and consultants who have found a good market [in ISO 9000]. But if industry pays for services that provide no added value, then that's not a good quality market."

Because of such issues, McMillan has found multinationals "fed up with having to face different [ISO 9000] regimes from different organizations. Insofar as their internal audits are as good as any others, they're not prepared to play ball with the [ISO 9000] registrars."

ISO Officials React

Although QS-9000 has the ISO's support and EU officials' backing, there are those in the ISO 9000 "community" watching the hybridization of the international standards program with some concern. These experts include Willen Deken, deputy director of the Dutch Council for Certification (RvC); Reg Shaughnessy, international chairman of the ISO TC-176 committee that creates the ISO 9000 series; and Peter Ford, secretary of TC-176.

They all concur that ISO 9000 is, and should be, a living and evolving standard that meets industry needs. On the other hand, they worry that the trend toward a more industry-specific approach may lead to ISO 9000 dissolving as an international standard.

Of QS-9000, Deken said the RvC was "glad to follow their rules" if the U.S. car companies wanted to add industry-specific guidelines to an ISO 9000 base. But he also worried that the industry-specific approach would "splinter the [ISO 9000] program. That will mean higher costs. But it's up to the market to decide."

Shaugnessy, who is based in Toronto, admits there is "pressure worldwide" to make the ISO 9000 series more "industry-specific and more prescriptive." However, he feels "the standard's strength has been to hold the line at a minimum number of practices. If decentralization contin-

ues, it will undermine the international [approach]."

Shaugnessy's not as concerned about QS-9000 as long as they retain third-party auditing. "QS-9000 is more product-specific," he says. "But they've built in [that aspect] as supplementary. If the supplementary were to become dominant, that would take away from a generic system."

Citing the example of medical devices—an industry with very specific product needs and requirements—he says TC-176 has struggled to keep this grouping under the ISO 9000 standards umbrella. If this industry and others start forming separate versions of ISO 9000, he argues, we would be back to the same pre-ISO 9000 picture. "There's no question that if we decentralize, we've lost it," Shaughnessy explains.

On the other hand, Shaughnessy says it will take solid leadership to keep ISO 9000 centralized. He points out that ISO Secretary General Larry Eicher has assigned Christian Fabre to oversee the ISO system. "He's there to do the job effectively," says Shaughnessy.

As things now stand, member countries advise the Geneva-based ISO about their preferences vis-à-vis the standards series. These issues come before the ISO council, and amendments and revisions eventually eke their way into the world. For instance, it took seven years for the 1994 revisions to be made public, with many more revisions to the standards series in the works. This laborious process has not always suited industry groups, hence the creation of QS-9000 and possible QS-9000 spin-offs.

Shaughnessy says he does see the need for more emphasis on employee involvement—a total quality management approach—to be included in the ISO 9000 process. However, he does not see the standards "going the way of the awards for excellence."

As for revisions to the actual standard, Peter Ford of TC-176 says there is an ongoing effort to harmonize the vocabulary document—what he calls 8402. There will be more "support technology," including development of standards for auditing and how to write a manual.

Ford is witnessing increased sales in the 9004-1 (formerly 9004) document, the support document that explains the ISO 9000 process. "That's a significant shift," he says, explaining that 9004 used to be 5 percent to 10 percent of series sales. "Now 9004-1 sales are almost equal to 9001."

Like Deken and Shaughnessy, Ford hopes the answer won't amount to the dismantling of the ISO 9000 system. "There's a difference between using the standard as a base and translating it into the vernacular," he explains. "If we lose the global aspects, maybe we've created more of a monster than an asset."

Some Prefer a C hange

Motorola's Buetow, a long-time critic of ISO 9000, says his company is a firm believer that one's future should be determined by the marketplace, not by some bureaucratic process. "The bureaucratic process gets life because people get scared that if they don't have it, they don't do business," he explains. "People have used the word 'blackmail' [in reference to companies being coerced into earning ISO 9000 certificates]."

Quality expert Pat Townsend considers ISO 9000 the baby of old-line quality types with slide rules in hand, who are mostly interested in conformance to specifications. "They've taken good, simple tools like statistical process control—which mainly involves the ability to do arithmetic—and made them mysterious, mechanical and expensive," he says.

These so-called old-liners were left out in the cold by the quality revolution of the 1980s, which went far beyond simple conformance to spec, says Townsend. "When ISO 9000 came down the pike, these guys saw it as a safe refuge from the far-reaching and really interesting quality efforts that had left them behind." he explains. "Suddenly there was a new, numbers-driven bandwagon that looked a lot like their old, familiar bandwagon."

As far as Townsend is concerned, ISO 9000 would not have been created if the Europeans didn't need a means of slowing down the Japanese and American quality juggernaut.

"The Europeans, who were lagging behind Japan and the United States in the quality movement, saw ISO 9000 as a way to catch up with their global competitors," Townsend explains. "It buys them some time to get their products into the world market and establish product standards. And—though this may not have been the intent—in effect, it imposes barriers on North Americans and Asians seeking entry into the European market."

In terms of the future, Townsend has long predicted the eventual disintegration of ISO 9000 as currently constructed. He agrees with Buetow's now-famous criticism that ISO 9000 as a quality process breeds consistency, not quality. That, in effect, someone can create cement life

preservers and still earn an ISO 9000 certificate if the manufacturing process is a consistent one.

Industry Reaction

With these ongoing—and sometimes contradictory— messages emanating from multinationals and some standards institutions, it's no wonder that business owners are sometimes left scratching their heads.

Robert Peuperbaugh, president of the 30-employee Joint Production Technology in Macomb, Michigan—a manufacturer of specialized cutting tools—feels caught in the middle between ISO 9000 and QS-9000. Highly frustrated that after his company earned Ford's original quality certificate Q-101, and then the successor Q-1, the Big Three, and Ford in particular, are again "changing everything."

"We're floundering because there's no real guide [to QS-9000]," explains Peuperbaugh. On the other hand, he says he's been "too busy to worry about it."

At Gananoque Steel Forging in Gananoque, Ontario, Canada, company president Claude Hetu is encouraging his 177 employees to complete QS-9000 registration by the end of 1996. Hetu says Gananoque Steel Forging is lucky to have embarked on ISO 9000 preliminaries—mainly preparing documentation of work procedures—without getting so far along in the registration process that a switch over to QS-9000 would prove costly.

Many companies, especially companies unrelated to the Big Three, believe in ISO 9000 and will continue to pursue the quality process no matter what the European Union or multinationals decide. One such company is Yankee Environmental in Turners Falls, Massachusetts, an eight-employee manufacturer of computerized environmental instruments.

Yankee General Manager Mark Beaubien, who has worked on streamlining ISO 9000 documentation methodology, says the company's primary interest in ISO 9000 "is to do it for our own quality. We believe in it. We're an instrument company, so quality is very important to us."

And at Simplex Technologies in Portsmouth, New Hampshire, where about 700 employees manufacture cables for the telecommunications industry and the U.S. government, Quality Manager Russell Miles believes that their ISO 9000 certification only improved a solid documentation system the company maintained for many

years of meeting military and customer specifications.

"We're very pleased with our quality system," says Miles. "We have to make sure our procedures are ISO and military compliant, but
that's not a big deal for this company."

---■---

THE 1999 REVISIONS OF ISO 9000*
by Richard Clements

*Technical committee 176 has released the
specification for the 1999 revisions to the ISO
9000 family of standards. The greatest effect will
be the elimination of ISO 9002 and ISO 9003.
Also significant is the further incorporation of
health, safety, and environmental requirements.*

The ISO 9000 family of standards was first
released in 1987. It has been agreed these standards should be revised and updated every five
years. However, it was 1994 before the first revision was released. Technical committee 176 is
responsible for the task of revising and updating this set of standards. They have set a target
date of 1999 for the next revisions.

We have received the specifications for this
next set of revisions. Even though revisions are
years away, the nature of the proposed changes
require companies to begin considering what future impact these changes will have.

The Standards Being Revised

Most ISO 9000 related standards are constantly being revised. However, the core standards, ISO 9000-1, ISO 9001, ISO 9002, ISO
9003, and ISO 9004-1, are always revised as a
set. They also represent the most important standards to be revised within the family. This is because they are the actual standard to which you
get registered and the most basic guideline standards.

Also being revised is Vision 2000, the planning paper that originally drew up the general
plan on how ISO 9000 would be developed and
implemented as an international standard. This
revision will support the general revision of the
ISO 9000 standard. It will also lay the groundwork for future revisions of the ISO 9000 standard and its registration scheme for the next
century.

The Proposed Changes to ISO 9000-1

The recurring theme throughout the specifications for revision is that the users of ISO
9000 are not totally satisfied. Dissatisfaction is
along two major themes. The first general complaint is that small and medium-size companies
feel the standard is intended for larger corporations. This includes the pressing for a great deal
of documentation where it doesn't make much
sense for a smaller company.

The second complaint is the standard is really written for manufacturing. Service, software, process material, and job-shops feel it is
too difficult to adjust the standard to their type
of business. All of these concerns will be addressed in the 1999 revisions.

This can be seen in the proposed revision to
ISO 9000. This guideline standard is a general
discussion of the principles of a management
system for quality assurance. The discussion will
be changed in the proposed revision to a discussion more generic and applicable to any business. For example,

- encourage continuous improvement
- increased ability to meet the expectation of
  customers
- extending discussion of the concept of stakeholders
- use of self-evaluation as part of continuous
  improvement
- use of quality management principles to improve the performance of the company

---

*Reprinted with permission from *Continuous Improvement,* September 1995. Richard B. Clements is president of Solution
Specialists in Alto, MI.

- allow the incorporation of quality award criteria (i.e. Malcolm Baldrige)

- point out the need for other management standards for other areas of concern (i.e. the environment).

At the same time, the current form and structure of ISO 9000-1 will be retained. Look more for changes in the discussion then for changes in the topic headings.

The new ISO 9000-1 will also recognize the secondary players in the ISO 9000 drama. This includes government bodies, consultants, the community at large, and private individuals. It will lay the groundwork for making the connection to ISO 14000 and a yet unwritten standard for health and safety.

The revised standard will also provide informational and directional guidance to the use of the ISO 9000 family of standards. This will include the value, role, and function of each standard. The proposed title of the revised standard is "Quality Management Standard—Introduction to the Concepts and Guidelines for Application of the Standards."

A central goal of this revision is to position ISO 9000 in the field of generic management. ISO 9000 will be more closely associated with the general methods of managing any company. For example, financial management will be considered. You may find your one system of management will cover the concerns of finance, quality, health, safety, and the environment. All of these concerns will eventually have related ISO standards. Each goal of these different topics should be eventually incorporated into your level 1 policy statements.

Another key concept which already exists in ISO 9000-1, but which will receive special attention and emphasis in the revision, is the plan-do-check-act (PDCA) problem solving system. It will be pointed out that PDCA will be the recurring structure of an ISO 9000 system.

In addition, the language of the standard will be clarified using common business terms. Extensive use of illustration within the standard is being encouraged. The key illustration will be the interrelationships between standards in the ISO 9000 family. It will be emphasized that the standard can be used for small and medium size companies, any economic sector, and every type of product. Direct relation to the use of an environmental management system is

called out. Also the relationship to total quality management is established.

The general headings being proposed include:

1. scope
2. normative references
3. definitions
4. key concepts
5. directional guide and informational guide for the ISO 9000 family
6. roles of documentation and information
7. quality management system situation
8. selection and use of international standards for quality management and internal quality assure
9. selection and use of international standards for external quality

THE NEW ISO 9001—THE DEATH OF ISO 9002 AND ISO 9003

In the ongoing attempt to alleviate the confusion over which core standard to use for registration, the use of three registration standards will be eliminated. ISO 9002 and ISO 9003 will be rolled into ISO 9001. At the same time, ISO 9001 will be dramatically changed in its content and fluency.

A major criticism of ISO 9001 was that it emphasized system compliance rather than assuring the quality of your products. The new ISO 9001 will change emphasis to the use of best practices to improve corporate performance, achieve excellence in quality, and meet customer expectations. ISO 9000-2 and ISO 9004-1 will no longer be emphasized as alternative standards to model your management system for quality assurance.

ISO 9001, ISO 9002, and ISO 9003 will be combined into a single and more flexible standard. It will allow the company to select the appropriate functions for achieving customer satisfaction. At the same time, it will address all categories of product, including services. It will use a logical structure of linked processes that are consistent with any business operation. It will use a simple format usable by both small and large companies. The emphasis will be on business activities directly affecting product quality. The amount of documentation required will vary according to the needs of the company.

The new ISO 9001 will also encourage the use of objective measurements of effectiveness and process improvement. It will also expand the requirement for customer interfaces. The structure of the revised standard will more easily accommodate alignment with other systems such as the environmental management system.

The proposed title for the new ISO 9001 is "Quality Management System—Requirements for Quality Assurance."

The revised standard will allow a company to design a management system for quality assurance that addresses only intended products which you have identified. This will allow job-shop type environments and other exceptional cases to find more flexibility within the standard. A company will have to identify the minimum quality assurance requirement for each of its generic product categories.

The good news is a serious attempt will be made to keep the new standard consistent with the 1994 revision. Therefore, you don't have to worry about completely changing your management system for quality assurance if you are already registered. Instead, you will have to evaluate whether you went too far in your original implementation of ISO 9000. If you did, then the 1999 revision will allow you to revise your management system into a smaller and more sensible form.

The actual structure of the proposed revised ISO 9001 might look something like this:

1. Executive management
    - policy
    - objectives
    - management representative
    - management review

2. Process management
    2.1 Human resource
    - performance
    - education
    - training
    2.2 Customer relations
    - customer needs and expectations
    - review of agreement
    - interface requirement
    2.3 Product realization

- design and development
- purchasing
- control of processes
- handling and delivery

3. Measurement
    - process
    - product
    - system
    - customer
    - measurement support

4. Preventive action
    - evaluation of result
    - corrective action and process improvement

By looking at the major topics, you can see the PDCA cycle. Executive management represents planning. Process management represents actually doing something. Measurement represents checking the work you have just completed. Preventive action represents acting on the result of checking.

This structure for the standard emphasizes the following:

- understanding and meeting customer expectations
- adding value to your processes above and beyond your documentation of procedures
- measuring actual process performance
- looking at the effectiveness of processes and procedures
- feedback on process performance
- setting objective criteria for evaluating the effectiveness of your quality system
- identify and analyze critical processes within your company that have to be controlled
- identify critical activities related to product quality.

Some of the requirements of ISO 9001 being expanded in the 1999 revision include training, the work environment, contract review, meeting customer requirement, measurement performance, and preventive action. Many of the system elements suggested as enhancements to ISO 9001 suggested by this newsletter in the past will now become requirements. This is especially true for the training requirement. Expect more emphasis on training as a management resource.

THE NEW ISO 9004

For the revision of ISO 9004-1, the most interesting change will be a return to the designation ISO 9004. This is part of the strategy to make ISO 9004 a broader and more applicable guideline standard. The proposed title is "Quality Management Systems—For Effective Management Systems." As you can see from the title, the objective is to make ISO 9004 a general guideline for any management system.

Just like the rest of the proposed revision to the ISO 9000 family of standards, ISO 9004 will be written in a way that those who make important decisions within their organization can both read and use the standard to achieve the best results possible. ISO 9004 is intended as guidance for quality management including analysis, planning, implementation, integration, and evolution of quality system element with a focus on customer satisfaction. Customers are seen as both internal and external to your company.

The revised ISO 9004 will include quality system elements defined in ISO 9001. It will also absorb many of the existing guideline standards such as ISO 9004-2 and ISO 9004-3. It will include cross-references to the family of ISO 9000 standards. The revised ISO 9004 will harmonize with ISO 9000-2, the guideline on how to apply ISO 9001.

The revision will include the following:

- quality management system elements
- improved linkage to business management systems
- appropriate linkage to ISO 9001

- be based on quality management principles
- business process model applications for service, software, hardware, and processed materials
- mechanisms for establishing degrees of excellence
- expended quality management content.

In short, ISO 9004 will discuss what should be considered by management but not how to do it. The new emphasis will be on obtaining results from processes instead of requiring documented procedures. It will also encourage process performance measurement and a system of feedback to encourage improvement results. Value-adding activities will be encouraged.

SUMMARY

As you can see, the proposed new ISO 9004 will be a powerful document indeed. It will begin to catch up with an all purpose standard such as QS-9000. Also, it will move closer to the ideals of total quality management. At the same time, it will leave open the possibility of using award criteria such as those from Malcolm Baldrige. It also moves much closer to the general practice of management. This should bring new people from your company into the ISO 9000 process—particularly the finance department and the strategic planners.

However, this is still four years away and many committee meetings from reality. We can only hope the final 1999 revision to the ISO 9000 family of standards is successful. If successful, it means fewer standards and more easy-to-use and understandable standards for industry. It also means any business can now use the ISO 9000 standard.

———————————————■———————————————

SELLING REGULATED PRODUCTS IN EUROPE*

While European product directives continue to come on line, US companies do not yet appear to be taking full advantage of the single market concept.

The reason, say European market experts, is confusion over the approval process and an absence of European-approved notified bodies on this side of the Atlantic.

Fewer than a dozen ISO 9000 registrars operating in the United States are believed to have the necessary qualifications to conduct certifications in support of CE marking. In theory, the CE mark allows companies to market their products throughout the member countries of the European Union.

The greatest demand is among manufacturers of medical devices, according to several US representatives of notified bodies. The medical devices directive, which affects the majority of medical device manufacturers took effect last month. Companies will have until 1998 to comply.

Another directive for active implantable medical devices also took effect in January of 1993 with companies having until last month to comply. A third directive for in-vitro diagnostic devices was still awaiting approval as of press time. All three directives give manufacturers the option of using ISO 9000 quality systems as a component of compliance.

"Medical is the hot thing in the notified body area," acknowledged Martin Langer, manager of ISO 9000 registration services with TUV Rheinland of North America, which offers notified body services in the US through its parent company's medical technology division.

Depending on the product, Langer said, the costs of demonstrating compliance with European directives exceeds a typical ISO 9000 registration. "The price can sometimes even double [that of an] ISO 9000 registration," he said. "It depends also on how many products you have."

Ann Preece, products directives manager with Lloyd's Register Quality Assurance Ltd., another ISO 9000 registrar that offers notified body services in the US, said companies that select an ISO 9000 registrar that is not a notified body, run the risk of paying for the same service twice.

"It's different from an ISO 9000 audit in that we are going to audit you against the essential requirements of the directive," she said. If a company is already registered to ISO 9000 "I'd say the chances are that it's going to be a reduced audit. We may not require the same amount of time that we would if we went into a company that didn't have any approval, but each company has to be looked at."

Langer said it is important for companies to understand that ISO 9000 registration in itself does not satisfy European directives. "ISO 9000 can be part of the whole CE marking process," he said. "Additional product specific requirements usually apply."

REGULATED PRODUCTS

Construction Products

This directive applies to any product intended to be a permanent part of a new construction.

Products must be such that works in which they are incorporated satisfy the essential requirements with regard to mechanical strength and stability, safety in case of fire, hygiene, health and the environment, safety in use, protection against noise and energy economy and heat retention for an economically reasonable working life.

The European standardization bodies are responsible for harmonizing standards for construction products.

The directive took effect on June 27, 1991. However, substantial technical work remains to be completed before most manufacturers will be able to certify that products comply with the provisions of the directive. New products for which

*Reprinted with permission from *Quality Systems Update,* February 1995, published by IRWIN Professional Publishing, Fairfax, VA.

standards have not been identified can be submitted for a European Technical Approval (ETA).

Telecommunications Terminal Equipment

This directive requires that certain types of terminal equipment satisfy "essential requirements" before being placed on the market.

It obligates member countries to withdraw exclusive rights enjoyed by their telecommunications administrations for import, marketing, installation and maintenance of terminal equipment.

The essential requirements are described in various common technical regulations are not covered by this directive. In such cases, manufacturers may continue to comply with national requirements for each country in which they plan to market their products.

Essential requirements focus on aspects such as user safety, protection of the network from harm, interworking with network equipment and electromagnetic compatibility. Some products, which are multifunctional, may be subject to more than one essential requirement and related common technical regulation (CTR).

Manufacturers have a choice of demonstrating compliance through one of three ways: Two of the three require type examination by a notified body and the third requires the manufacturer to operate a quality system approved by a notified body to be compliant with the ISO 9001 external quality assurance standard. Approval with an ISO 9002 system requires that manufacturers undergo a type examination by a notified body.

Once a manufacturer has demonstrated compliance it gains the right to affix a CE mark to its product. Other marks also may be applicable depending on whether the equipment is intended for network connection.

The directive was published in the *Official Journal* in 1991 and was to take effect in 1992. However, implementation of the directive has been delayed pending adoption of CTRs.

Furniture Flammability

This directive affects all upholstered furniture, related articles and constituent products.

Upholstered furniture is defined as furniture containing more or less compressible material, such as chairs, settees, divans, mattresses and beds which contain an upholstered element. Related articles are defined as mattresses, pillows, and removable cushions constituting upholstered furniture. Constituent products are defined as polyurethane foams, latex foams, and so on.

The directive does not cover upholstered furniture, related articles and constituent products that are intended to be placed in a public or private means of transportation including caravans, mobile homes and boats even if they are used as dwellings.

The aim is to obtain zero reaction to sources of ignition, the scale and/or intensity of which increase according to the nature of the risks involved.

All affected products must meet essential safety and health requirements before being placed on the market. To be deemed compliant, companies must undergo a type-examination procedure under which a notified body verifies and declares that a representative sample of the production concerned meets the requirements of the directive.

The approval process also includes quality system approval by a notified body to the ISO 9002 series standard.

Manufacturers that comply may affix a CE mark on their products. Theoretically, they will then have the right to market their products throughout the member nations of the European Union.

The directive was originally scheduled to take effect on January 1, 1993 but implementation has been delayed.

Measuring and Testing Instruments

This directive outlines the requirements for legal metrological control of measuring instruments.

Measuring instruments are defined as a device or set of devices to be used alone or in association with other equipment for the determination of the value of a measurable quantity and/or the value of the quantity, parameter or characteristic related to or derived from the measured quantity.

Companies that are deemed to be in compliance with the directive are given the right to affix a CE mark on their products. This directive is still in the proposal stage.

Cableways Equipment

This directive affects cableway installations designed to carry passengers.

It includes capital equipment made up of several components designed, manufactured, assembled and put into service with the object of providing an operational service to carry the general public.

Affected equipment includes funicular vehicles mounted on wheels and supported on a track or road; cable cars where two cabins are lifted by one or more carrier cables and traction is provided by one or more tow cables; gondolas combining on the same cable, or group of cables, and dual lifting and traction functions. Their movement is continuous and unidirectional; chair lifts, usually with fixed mountings; and drag lifts which usually constitute the basic equipment at ski resorts.

Under this directive equipment manufacturers are required to eliminate or, if this is not possible, reduce hazards as far as possible by means of design and construction features which prevent them from occurring; to define and implement all necessary measures to protect against hazards which cannot be eliminated by the design and construction features; and to inform persons concerned about the precautions which should be taken to avoid the hazards which could not be completely eliminated.

Manufacturers that comply with the directive earn the right to affix a CE mark on their equipment.

The directive was still in the proposal stage as of press time.

Articles of Precious Metals

This directive affects finished or unfinished precious metals.

An article of precious metal is defined as any item of jewelry, goldsmith's ware or watchmaker's ware and any other object made entirely or in part from a precious metal.

Articles comprising various precious metals is any item of jewelry, goldsmith's ware or watchmaker's ware and any other object made entirely or in part from precious metals. Mixed articles are those that comprise parts of precious metal and parts of base metal or other substances.

Companies have the option of undergoing a procedure for conformity based on a system of product quality assurance; following a procedure for conformity; or submitting the articles for verification.

In general, articles must bear a fineness mark, or must be accompanied by an EU certificate of conformity.

Products must be marked with a fineness mark, a registered sponsor's mark, together with the letter "e" and where required have a European certificate of conformity. Companies must seek approval from a notified body.

This directive was still in the proposal stage as of press time.

Amusement Park and Fairground Equipment

This directive covers amusement rides and related structures.

Under the directive, equipment must be so constructed that it is fitted for its function, and can be adjusted and maintained without putting persons at risk when these operations are carried out under the conditions foreseen by the manufacturer.

The directive covers risks due to materials and products, risks due to darkness, risks due to lack of strength, risks due to accidental contact with the equipment, risks due to access circulation and exits, risks due to fire, risks due to handling of the equipment as well as a number of other areas.

This directive was still in the proposal stage as of press time.

GLOBAL SYSTEM CLEARS FINAL ADMINISTRATIVE HURDLE; OPERATIONAL DETAILS PENDING*

After months of discussion, the International Organization for Standardization (ISO) has given final approval to a proposal that would promote the global acceptance of ISO 9000 registration certificate.

In a resolution approved last month in Geneva, the ISO Council directed officials to proceed with the execution of the quality System Assessment Recognition (QSAR) program but left unresolved the operational details of the program.

It was not clear as of press time if a controversial provision allowing ISO 9000 registrars to bypass traditional accreditation programs would be integrated into the program.

The council invited the International Accreditation Forum (IAF), a group of ISO 9000 accreditation bodies from around the world, to participate in developing the operational details.

The proposal calls for ISO and International Electrotechnical Commission (IEC) to recognize ISO 9000 registrations performed by accredited registrars whose accreditations have been issued by participating organizations. While the program would initially be limited to ISO 9000 registrations, it could later be expanded to other areas such as ISO 14001 registration.

"The conclusive definition of what it is ISO wants IAF to do is not yet refined," explained IAF Chairman Reuben Autery.

George Willingmyre, vice president of the American National Standards Institute (ANSI) for Washington operations, said the IAF will offer to perform the peer review evaluations, a key element of QSAR.

"IAF could perform that function very efficiently since it consists of the national accreditation bodies," he said.

Last year, the IAF went on record as supporting the QSAR proposal in principle, but the group has since raised objections to the estimated $25,000 annual cost to participate, and

the potential conflict of interest that would arise for some ISO and IEC member bodies that also offer ISO 9000 registration services.

The peer reviews will involve teams drawn from one or more ISO 9000 accreditation bodies for competence using defined criteria.

In theory, the proposal would equalize all ISO 9000 registration certificates issued by registrars that are accredited by a participating accreditation body. This would give companies more flexibility in selecting their ISO 9000 registrar.

The Independent International Organization for Certification (IIOC), an international group of registrars, have said it will oppose any provision that allows registrars to evaluate other registrars for acceptance into the program. Such a provision only would pertain to countries where there are no recognized accreditation bodies.

In anticipation of the IAF's expanded role within QSAR, the group's members have taken steps to formalize its organizational structure through a memorandum of understanding among participating bodies.

"The IAF will have formal members, so to speak, and the members will subscribe to the terms of the memorandum of understanding," Willingmyre said. "The memorandum of understanding calls for working together and harmonizing procedures encouraging regional mutual recognition agreements."

George Lofgren, president of the Registrar Accreditation Board (RAB), which operates the American National Accreditation Program for Registrars of Quality Systems along with ANSI, said a small steering group of ISO and IAF officials were planning to meet to map out the IAF's role.

A spokesman for the International Organization for Standardization (ISO) in Geneva said invitations to participate in the program are expected to be sent to accreditation bodies during

*Reprinted with permission from *Quality Systems Update,* July 1995, published by IRWIN Professional Publishing, Fairfax, VA.

the fourth quarter. He added that a minimum of 10 accreditation bodies will be required before the program begins operation.

The IAF represents 18 of the world's 30 known accreditation bodies of ISO 9000 registrars.

■

NEW EUROPEAN APPROACH*
by Amy Zuckerman

On the hill overlooking the Grand Place in Brussels lies a maze of streets and back alleys housing European Union offices.

There are no signs to these offices, just street numbers. Locating 200 Rue de la Loi, the office of Directorate-General III for Industry, takes some persistence.

Locating Jacques McMillan proves far simpler. For McMillan, chief of the Senior Standards Policy Group for DG III, is one of the more accessible bureaucrats around.

But don't let McMillan's accessibility—let alone his wit and charm—fool you. A small, energetic man of half-British and half-French descent, McMillan is arguably one of the most knowledgeable standards experts in the world, having drafted and implemented in Europe the "Global Approach" to testing and certification in 1991.

McMillan is also one of the most powerful men in the industrialized world. Representatives of government standards agencies come courting McMillan. Multinationals come courting McMillan. Journalists come courting McMillan. The reason is that McMillan, who began service with the European Commission in 1974 as a trade-barrier specialist, now heads up the policy-making arm of EU standards. If McMillan wields a big stick, it's because standards in Europe are a government matter. The communications McMillan and his standards group draft may very well become EU directives, EU law.

And he is determined to shake up the European quality community, which he feels has become far too reliant on the ISO 9000 certification model and not enough concerned with making European companies truly competitive worldwide. In the winter of 1994, McMillan and his colleague Antonio Silva Mendes shocked the

ISO 9000 community with a report calling for creation of a new European quality policy that would diminish the certification (registration in the United States) aspect of the ISO 9000 process. McMillan, who rarely minces words, openly condemned the rampant commercialization of ISO 9000.

Throughout the last year, he has continued to criticize any approach to quality that is quick and dirty, one that goes for a certificate rather than emphasizing the process. McMillan insists he has no intention of killing the ISO 9000 standards series. He has no intention, either, of boosting ISO 9000 certification in Europe. McMillan and Mendes consider the standard a good quality base, but inadequate as a total quality tool.

On June 6, his group released the final draft of "A European Quality Promotion Policy." The 50-page report calls for reinforcing the fairly new European Quality Award, which takes a Malcolm Baldrige approach. If all goes as planned, national accreditation bodies will operate under EU jurisdiction. They will no longer operate for profit or compete with each other. The EU also wants to strengthen a "harmonized European system for qualification of quality professionals, managers and auditors." According to the final draft report, which will not be considered for implementation until the end of this year, the proliferation of ISO 9000 certificates "throughout the world reveals to us that there is no relation between the number of certified companies and the competitiveness of the national economies. . .

"It is clear that if this 'boom' [in ISO 9000 certification] is beneficial for the distribution and promotion of quality, then it should be equally apparent that it has also involved some negative aspects linked to an excessively rigid use of

---

*Reprinted with permission from *Quality Digest*, August 1995. Amy Zuckerman operates an international market research company in Amherst, MA.

standards, in particular a sometimes exaggerated recourse to certification. . . ."

EU officials recommend the "use of these standards as a reference frame for the quality systems (and did not make the certification of the quality system obligatory, as was misinterpreted by many)."

What does this report mean for the future of ISO 9000? McMillan is far too cagey to make any definite prognostications. He says he's not even certain whether his standards group wil push for an EC vote or let the report stand as a recommendation. The first sign of any movement on this subject will be in November when the European Council of Industries meets. McMillan expects the report will be on the agenda for discussion, not action.

"The debate taking place now will shape the future," predicts McMillan. "We're getting favorable feedback from industry, member states, national administrations and most who've read the paper."

As for ISO 9000, McMillan says: "In practical terms, we can't do anything about it. All we're trying to do in the marketplace is send the message to think of quality first. We can't tell the certifiers to go home, throw their pens away and change jobs.

"But we're trying to pass down the message to certifiers, manufacturers and customers repeatedly asking for ISO 9000 when they don't need it to think twice. If someone has earned a certificate in six months, they're thinking wrong. We're not saying certification is bad, but it's not necessarily indispensable in certain cases."

Whether words alone will stop the ISO 9000 juggernaut still remains to be seen. In the meantime, the report doesn't address the issue of EU directives that mandate European ISO 9000 equivalents for manufacturers of telecommunications equipment, pacemakers and other industries that McMillan has still to identify.

For example, the directive regarding "terminal equipment" relating to telecommunications was issued on April 29, 1991, and mandates EN 29001 and EN 29002 (ISO 9000 equivalents) as part of the requirement for passing an "EC-type examination." Without the appropriate certificates or proof of conformity with these standards, the directive allows member EU states to "take all appropriate measures to withdraw such products from the market, or to prohibit or restrict their being placed on the market."

U.S.-based electronics companies want to see McMillan go beyond criticizing ISO 9000 certification. They want McMillan and the EC to lift the directives that tacitly make the standards law in Europe. And if the standards are law, as these companies insist, then ISO 9000 can be considered a possible European trade barrier.

"We've never forced anyone into doing ISO 9000," insists McMillan. "That's rubbish. They have a choice of ISO 9000 or product certification in most cases. It's rare that the Council forces ISO 9000 as a mandate."

Even so, the EU directives call for companies doing business in Europe to have in place a quality system that meets or exceeds the ISO 9000 requirements. Outside of Germany, there reportedly is no guidance document outlining how a manufacturer's declaration would substitute for ISO 9000 certification. That means it's pretty much ISO 9000 in Europe for some industries or don't do business there.

Never one to be deterred, let alone back down in the face of confrontation, McMillan concedes that "there may not be a market option in some cases. I'm not too perturbed about that. If in some cases we've overshot the mark, we'll rethink it."

McMillan, who clearly gets a kick out of tweaking noses or even pushing noses out of joint, doesn't promise a timetable for the rethinking process. Tune in some time in the next few months for continued debate on this topic.

————————————————■————————————————

GLOBAL OUTLOOK—CANADA*
by William O. Jarvis

In 1994, Canada exported more than $220 billion worth of merchandise and services, 80% of which went to the United States. As Canada moves toward diversifying its trade portfolio, particularly in the Pacific Rim, Europe and Latin America, compatibility of quality standards becomes more vital. While there are no rules for succeeding in the international marketplace, quality assurance is always a selling feature.

The most respected series of quality standards is ISO certification, established by the Geneva-based International Organization for Standardization. ISO is a series of quality assurance guidelines identifying the steps a company should follow for its business activities. When a company has met these guidelines and can show that its staff understands and follows these procedures, it is awarded certification. The average time it takes to achieve registration is 18 months.

Although the certification process is costly and time consuming, ISO companies have discovered the benefits far outweigh the investment. A survey of 620 companies, performed by Quality Systems Update and Deloitte & Touche, found that ISO companies enjoyed a competitive edge by differentiating themselves from noncertified companies. By offering quality assurance, these companies improved the level of customer satisfaction and, in many cases, increased market share. The internal advantages are just as impressive: better documentation, greater quality awareness, positive cultural change and increased productivity.

There's no question that ISO is the wave of the future, and for business it will be a necessity. Already adopted by more than 70 countries, these international generic quality standards have given certified companies the competitive advantage since ISO-certified companies want to do business with other ISO firms. When a company knows its suppliers are using the same high-quality standards, there is an increased level of comfort.

The bottom line is that almost every industrialized national has adopted ISO as its quality systems standard. For companies looking to expand their markets, it's prudent to remember that ISO is not only a passport to increased business at home, but it also pays dividends abroad.

————————————————■————————————————

WHAT YOU NEED TO KNOW
ABOUT CHOOSING AN ISO 9000 CONSULTANT AND REGISTRAR*

If your company's been thinking about becoming registered to ISO 9000, lend an ear to Ed Mahoney.

Mahoney is director of quality assurance at Bailey Controls Company (Wickliffe, OH), one of the first companies in the United States to become registered to the standards.

"We began to rewrite our quality program around ISO 9000 requirements in January 1990 and received registration in December 1990," says Mahoney.

Acquiring the registration in just 11 months was no small feat for a company with several thousand employees and 15 plants. Even more impressive is the fact that the company accomplished its results *without* a consultant.

Should your firm hire a consultant to guide it along the ISO 9000 registration road? And how

———————————

———————————

should you choose a registrar? Mahoney offers this advice:

ON CONSULTANTS

"When we were ready to pursue ISO, we interviewed several consultants," reports Mahoney. "U.S. consultants had very little to offer at the time, because ISO was still so new in this country."

Undaunted, Mahoney interviewed some consultants in Europe. Indeed, many of them had sufficient ISO 9000 experience. "But the problem was that they wanted us to run our company to fit *their* individual models," he states. "We weren't interested, because we felt we knew how to run our business better than anyone else. If we had to fit our business to some consultant's quality program, we'd quickly go bankrupt."

Mahoney feels that the same problem occurs stateside today. "Instead of helping you take your business system and deciding if it meets ISO 9000 standards, many consultants try to get you to run your business in a completely different way by forcing bureaucracy and other functions that simply are not required by the standards," he points out.

Does this mean that Mahoney is against the idea of using consultants? Not at all. He believes that some consultants *could* be helpful in a company's quest for ISO 9000 registration.

"First, the only type of consultant I'd hire for ISO 9000," he explains, "is one who had been the quality manager of a successful company that has already received ISO registration.

"Until a person has registered a firm, has personally lived with the results, *and* has seen the firm continue to make a profit, I don't believe he or she has the experience necessary to tell anyone else how to do it. In other words, select a consultant who's already walked the walk."

Second, the consultant you select should assess your *existing* quality system and determine what needs to change or improve to meet ISO requirements.

"Such a consultant can be helpful for organizations that don't have the necessary in-house expertise. In my experience, however, there are few such consultants like this in existence today," observes Mahoney.

ON REGISTRARS

Mahoney was as thorough in his search for a registrar as he was in his search for a consultant. However, since a registrar is necessary for ISO registration and a consultant is not, he did end up selecting a registrar.

"We 'shopped' a lot," he states. "I visited registrars in the UK, France, Canada, and the United States, and ultimately, I found one in Canada that met our needs very well."

Based on his experience, here is what Mahoney recommends when selecting a registrar. Select one who

- Understands your specific business needs and has the capabilities and willingness to meet those needs. "We realized that we would be aligned with our registrar for a long time, so we wanted to consider the arrangement a partnership," he explains.

- Is recognized internationally and within your specific industry. While there are many excellent registrars with impeccable credentials, not all of them have equal visibility and status within all industries.

  To help your decision-making process in such a situation, Mahoney recommends *asking yourself* this question: "When I give a customer or prospect my ISO 9000 registration, is the listed registrar well-enough known to that customer and in that customer's market for the customer to say, 'We'll accept this registration' "?

- Has specific experience with your type of business. "For example we manufacture electronic circuit boards," continues Mahoney. "As such, we wanted to deal with a registrar that had a background in such fields as chemistry, plating, and electronics. We also wanted a registrar that had engineering background, because we are also a design firm."

- Will enter into a trusting relationship with your company. While you certainly need a contract, you want to be able to work with the registrar on an informal basis. "If you have to write every little bit of service into a contract, you're probably dealing with the wrong registrar," states Mahoney.

Here are other pointers on working with a registrar:

- Bring the registrar into your ISO 9000 process early. "For example, if you write your quality manual and find out later that the registrar won't accept it, you've wasted a lot of time and money. Talk about everything early in the process. Tell your registrar what you plan to do; then make him or her a partner in the process." Not all registrars are willing to do this, according to Mahoney, but many of them are.

- Determine what kinds of services the registrar will provide *after* registration. There are two considerations Mahoney feels are important in this area. If possible, hire a registrar that has an advisory service that keeps us abreast of all changes in quality standards, in their quality system, and in their auditors," he states.

- *Is willing to help your firm enter new markets based on its business needs.* "For example, we recently began doing business with a customer in Pakistan who was not familiar with our registrar," Mahoney explains. "Our registrar was willing to begin working with a recognized Pakistani registrar to get our registration accepted by that customer."

Bailey Controls' registrar provides both of these services free of charge.

CHOOSING IS A BIG TASK

There are a great number of ISO 9000 consultants and registrars out there today. However, using Mahoney's advice and pointers will make it easier for your company to zero in specifically on what you want in both categories. In making the right choices, you'll be able to orchestrate a smooth and effective journey to ISO 9000 registration for your firm.

ISO 9000 NOW MORE USER-FRIENDLY FOR SERVICE COMPANIES*

The ISO 9000 quality standards have taken the world by storm since their publication in 1987. The standards were developed by an international technical committee (TC 176)—which included U.S. members—operating under the auspices of the International Organization for Standardization (Geneva, Switzerland). This committee is still actively working on the ongoing development and continuous improvement of the ISO 9000 standards, which provide an excellent blueprint for an effective quality management and assurance system.

The ISO 9000 standards have been adopted by more than 80 countries. And many foreign customers are demanding that their suppliers become "registered" to ISO 9000. This means that the suppliers have set up a quality system that is in complete alignment with the provisions of ISO 9000 and that they have been audited by a third-party "registrar" who has certified that the company indeed conforms to the ISO 9000 standards.

ISO 9000 was primarily designed for the manufacturing sector and has been having the greatest impact in that area (well over 4,000 manufacturing companies have been registered in the United States to date). However, some service-sector companies are also implementing ISO 9000, either because they supply services to manufacturers who must comply with the standards to meet the demands of their customers, or as a way to improve quality.

Any service company interested in ISO 9000 will be glad to know that the latest version of the standards, published in July 1994, is now more applicable to service companies, says Donald W. Marquardt, president, Donald W. Marquardt and Associates (Wilmington, DE). Marquardt has been leader of the U.S. delegation and chair of the U.S. technical advisory group for TC 176.

---

*Copyrighted material. Reprinted with permission of the Bureau of Business Practice, 24 Rope Ferry Road, Waterford, CT 06386.

Here are some of the aspects of the standards that service companies will find most important, according to Marquardt.

EXPECTATIONS OF CUSTOMERS ARE PARAMOUNT

The new ISO 9000 standards, called the "Phase 1 revision," put more emphasis on a service organization's meeting the needs and expectations of its customers, says Marquardt. This is paramount to the registrars whose auditors must determine whether a service organization is meeting the quality requirements of ISO 9000, since service quality can be more difficult to measure than the quality of hardware, processed materials, or software products. After all, the best measurement of service quality is, "Are your customers satisfied?" and "Is there measurable evidence of this?"

SERVICES NEED TO BE DESIGNED

"Another key point [emphasized by ISO 9000] is that services need to be designed," says Marquardt. "The design steps are the same as those applied to a hardware product, except that some of the emphases need to be different." Why do services need to be designed?

- To meet the needs of your customers.
- To make sure that your services are performed properly.
- To make sure that your services are actually provided consistently day after day, month after month.
- To make sure that your services can be properly supported.

"In designing services, people often talk about a 'service brief,' " says Marquardt. "This is a document that describes what the service will be like, how it will be carried out, how to interact with the customer, and so forth. That is equivalent to the design documents written when designing a piece of hardware.

"The Phase 1 revisions of ISO 9001 and ISO 9002 very explicitly have subparagraphs and subclauses on design review and design validation. There is a very close analogy here. The processes were put there to help the service industry. In the revised standard, it talks about 'design review' and 'design validation,' which apply for a service product."

➤ *Design review* is done during specific parts of the design process, Marquardt explains. At these times, everyone involved with the design makes sure it is proceeding according to the prescribed specifications to meet the goals set for it.

➤ *Design validation* takes place at the end of the design process. The purpose is to check with typical customers to see whether the design really meets their needs and expectations.

"These are exactly the same things that are expected when designing a hardware product," Marquardt points out. "Also, as with a hardware product, you have a production process for a service. This involves setting service quality standards and having forms and procedures that should be checked and documented."

PHASE TWO REVISIONS

Looking beyond Phase 1 to the Phase 2 revisions to ISO 9000, which are expected to take place sometime in the late 1990s, Marquardt hints that this revision will include a rewrite of ISO 9004 Part 2, the comprehensive standard that deals with all facets of providing a service. He believes that this revision will make ISO 9000 even more user-friendly for service organizations, as well as for other types of organizations.

---■---

10 TIPS ON WRITING FOR ISO 9000*
by Gary Blake, Ph.D.

1. While preparing to meet ISO 9000 standards, write an action plan listing every activity that must be accomplished along the way.

Before starting to pursue ISO 9001, the quality manager of Symbol Technologies wrote an action plan of 267 steps—that was just for creating the quality manual. The plan listed every task, the people responsible for it and an estimated time to complete the task. The first task, "List all procedures that are associated with each clause," was estimated to take a week.

This type of global thinking is also exemplified by the quality manager at Dynepco, who sent out a long memo to his staff about achieving certification for ISO 9002. The memo, part strategy and part pep talk, listed 16 steps toward achieving certification. The first four are:

- Obtain management commitment.

- Appoint a management representative to lead the process.

- Form a steering committee or team that includes hourly people and has all areas represented.

- Educate the team about the ISO 9000 registration process.

2. Write ISO 9000 procedures that are specific but do not handcuff your people in completing their work.

If you were writing, for example, a procedure on how a report was to be bound, you might write: "Put all sheets in a 'Clear-Vue' see-through report cover and thread a black spine over the left side of the cover to bind the report."

But what if you run out of "Clear-Vue" covers? Are others just as good? And what about those black spines? Would a green one make a big difference? Perhaps you could write: "Put all sheets in a see-through report cover and thread a spine over the left side of the cover to bind the report."

3. If any of those who must write ISO 9000 procedures are inexperienced writers, have them create flowcharts describing their tasks.

While flowcharts are not a substitute for narrative in an ISO 9000 procedure, they can help procedure writers explain what they do. Many engineers think visually and it's easier for them to do a flowchart than to construct a paragraph or even a series of bullet points.

Flowcharts should be easy to read and contain less than eight steps. Try to fashion a set of procedures based on the flowchart.

Streamline procedures by bulleting parallel items, especially those that start with verbs. Often, there's no need to put procedures in paragraph form. For example, instead of a paragraph filled with items separated by commas or semicolons, break out of the paragraph by putting in a colon after that announces a break from the prose; then put in a series of bullet points to line up the thoughts for the reader.

4. Keep your ISO 9000 quality policy manual to less than 40 pages.

The quality policy manual is sometimes thought of as pointing to or referencing lower-level documents. The quality manual is not the place to go into detail about who does what or how things are done. It is a place to set policy.

The quality manual should contain no proprietary material. In fact, it should be written as if it were to be given to customers and, in some cases, competitors. If the manual has more than 40 pages, it's probably going into more depth than necessary or is redundant. At that point, the manual will start to resemble a list of procedures or work instructions.

5. Model your quality manual after the ISO 9000 standards.

The topic order in the ISO 9000 standard should guide you in organizing your quality policy manual. Even if you have a manual partially written, it's best to start again, mirroring

---

*For information about Dr. Blake's on-site seminar, "Writing for ISO 9000," please call (516) 767-9590.

the topics and order of the particular ISO 9000 standard for which your company is trying to become certified. By making the manual's topics the same as the standard's, you help potential auditors follow your thoughts and make sure you've covered the required topics.

6. Make quality manuals easily auditable and maintainable.

Making a quality manual auditable means making it easy to read, easy to reference and easy to reread. By reflecting the ISO 9000 standards, the manual becomes easier to audit quickly.

Other format issues to consider include wide margins (a lot of white space makes reading easy on the eyes); consistent spacing (helps highlight what's important); consistent numbering (shows readers which topics are subsets of others); large, serif typefaces (helps readability, save italics for emphasis only); correct capitalization; and title blocks that include the company name, document name, revision or signature line, page number and document number.

Title blocks help you maintain your manual by making it easy to see where revised pages fit and by telling you the last time a document was revised.

7. Keep documentation concise.

Don't throw in the kitchen sink. Like every other type of writing, documentation is selective and should contain the minimum amount necessary to convey the idea.

Avoid redundancies like, "All quality systems, current and new, used. . ." Knock out "current and new." Here's another redundancy: "The sales division will completely document all the processes that affect the customer-supplier relationship between Acme and its customers." Leave out "customer-supplier."

Avoid wordy expressions (e.g., "on an annual basis") and the obvious (e.g., "all staff reporting directly or indirectly will support this policy.")

Avoid clichés and puffery such as, "Quality is the basis of our corporate culture" or "We will produce perfect products and services every time, on time."

8. Make documentation self-explanatory and authoritative.

Ralph Waldo Emerson once said you should write not just so that you'll be understood but so that you cannot be misunderstood.

To do this, you must delete any hedging. Get rid of words like "basically," "perhaps," "under certain circumstances" and "in most cases."

Here's a vague and weak purpose statement: "To assign the responsibilities and authorities of the various departments within the company."

Here's the sharper, more authoritative version: "To assure individual department compliance with quality management system guidelines for managing responsibilities."

9. Use hierarchical, easy-to-follow numbering systems for sections and subsections.

Stay consistent:

1.0 PURPOSE
2.0 SCOPE
3.0 DEFINITIONS

The headings are all capital. Subtopics are indented and line up underneath the headings:

3.0 DEFINITIONS
   3.1   Document—The original media that conveys information or proof of an activity, task or procedure.
      3.2   Standard Operating Procedure
      3.3   Process Sheet

10. When trying to explain your tasks to a layperson, ask yourself, "How would I explain this to a very bright child?"

When talking to children, you automatically know to boil down difficult-to-grasp concepts. The same idea should apply when circulating documents to people who are not versed in your technical field. Don't expect that they "know it." They may not. They often need help from you in forming a mental image of the product or process you are trying to describe.

Avoid vague phrases such as, "To ensure that the requirements between ACME Co. and its customers are effectively communicated. . . ."

Which requirements? Contractual? Procedures? Don't make the reader guess. "Use the correct word and not," as Mark Twain once said, "its second cousin."

■

REVISITING AN ISO 9000-CERTIFIED COMPANY*
by Maureen Fischer

A year ago, the July/August 1994 issue of The FABRICATOR® described the steps a software company took to achieve ISO certification. Now a year later, this article revisits that company to look at the pros and cons of certification one year after the fact. Has business increased? Were the effort and expense worth it? Would they do it over again?

As of second quarter 1995, 6,366 companies have achieved certification.[1] That is up from 3,968 second quarter 1994. More than 600 of those certified are manufacturers within SIC 3400.

The Big Three automakers announced last year that they are adopting their QS-9000 standard, based on the most stringent of the registration certificates (9001), plus additional requirements.[2]

They have issued an edict to their estimated 13,000 first-tier suppliers that they must comply to QS-9000. In early 1995, the Big Three unveiled another ISO 9000-based quality standard—TE-9000—which will affect all non-production parts suppliers. The planned release is for the third quarter of 1995 and is expected to affect as many as 50,000 manufacturers, including third-tier suppliers such as fabrication shops and stampers.

ISO can expand the market for a manufacturer's products and services and help them compete domestically and worldwide. Its discipline and procedures translate into increased efficiency, less rework, cost savings, and respect within the industry. Here is what a software company had to say about it one year after certification.

ONE YEAR AFTER CERTIFICATION

JobBOSS Software, a provider of shop floor control software, started the certification process in January 1993. The company knew certification would provide a marketing competitive advantage, but discovered that ISO also shortened the time to market for new product. For example, the company recently did in seven months what in the past took three years to accomplish.

It took 18 months and about $25,000 for the company to achieve registration to ISO 9001, 9000-3, and TickIT (the European standard for software).

A year later, Lori Sweningson, president, believes ISO certification dramatically expanded their competitiveness. ISO's discipline and procedures provide the company with a quality discipline. She says, "We spend much more time in the design specification stage, making sure we know exactly what we need to do to satisfy the needs of our customers; much effort is placed in designing quality into the process."

MORE RESPECT

The software company sells mainly to U.S. companies, specifically job shops, including fabricators, stampers, mold makers, and machine shops.

In 1993, few of its customers were undertaking ISO certification, much less demanding that the software company become certified. Nevertheless, top management felt an urgency to become certified to gain a competitive edge among software companies. In July 1994, it became one of only nine application software companies to have achieved certification.

A year later, the company believes ISO gives it added credibility. Marlene Walsten, vice president and ISO project leader, says because so many software companies are here today, gone tomorrow, ISO sets them apart. "Anybody who understands the standards and requirements of certification knows ISO demands good procedures and diligence to maintain. It brings credibility and respect."

As a certified vendor, the software company's preventive action and problem-solving processes are part of the quality standards.

---

*Reprinted with permission from *The Fabricator,* October 1995. Copyright 1995 by The Croydon Group, Ltd.

THE REWARDS OF QUALITY

At the software company, the effects of ISO on productivity have been good. Documenting procedures has resulted in greater efficiency. "The whole company is more productive because we have been able to identify all our procedures," says Walsten. "When that is done, it is really easier to teach people, to make sure everyone is going in the same direction and keeps the company cohesive."

The biggest advantage, however, came from the requirement of maintaining management indicators. These monthly statistics monitor key processes to ensure quality objectives are being met. They include major indicators such as revenue, returns, customer response indicators, lead generation, and length of sales cycle. Watching these indicators closely signals where, when, and how quality standards and functions may need revising or updating.

DAILY DOCUMENTATION

Once certified, all procedures are still subject to change and need to be updated and documented so everyone is aware of the latest revisions. The software company chose to handle its documentation on-line rather than on paper.

Walsten recommends documentation on-line whenever possible because it eliminates the need for hard copy of all quality documents. If the business is small and lacks a computer network doing the job manually makes sense.

MAINTENANCE, TIME, AND COST

This year at the software company Walsten began doing studies to track time spent by her ISO team. Until those results are in, she estimates that laborpower investment for two surveillance audits a year is about 500 hours spread over five or six people.

"That is time-specific to being ISO certified," says Walsten. "I'm not counting time that people spend updating procedures. That's just good business. At $18 an hour, she estimates ISO costs at about $9,000 to $10,000 a year for in-house time. For six-month surveillance audits, auditors cost $1,500 a day plus expenses, which amounts to another $3,000 to $5,000 annually. The total is $13,000 to $15,000 a year.

Though the software company used a consultant part-time at the beginning of the process; they are now totally self-sufficient. The company has a team of six people who attended internal auditor training and lead auditor training—two-day seminars run by the Minnesota Technology Center.

When selecting an auditor, the software company knew customer perceptions mattered, so they consulted with customers before choosing an auditor. Walsten recommends that if the purpose of getting certified is to have a certificate you can tout and that third-part auditor lends the credibility, then choose one your customers believe in. As a U.S. company, they made sure they hold accreditation from a U.S. company.

SIX-MONTH AUDITS

Six-month audits can be a frightening experience if a company decides to tighten up procedures just before the auditor plans to visit and disregards them the rest of the time.

The software company went through its first six-month audit in January 1995. It was inundated with procedure changes shortly before the audit and the surveillance audit was a tense two days.

Certification is such a major push that many companies tend to settle into a relaxed mode immediately afterwards. "Then, all of a sudden, it is time for your first audit," admits Walsten, "and you have to get all sorts of things done. Our second audit in late June went much more smoothly. We were like a fine-tuned race car, stopping for a routine check rather than major repairs." Fortunately too, the auditor gives advance notice of where they are going to focus.

Management review, change documentation, and corrective action are areas tested every audit. As for recertification, the software company has five more six-month audits before recertification and has not started planning for it yet.

THE BIG THREE AND THE DEPARTMENT OF DEFENSE

Not only have the Big Three automakers embraced ISO, but the U.S. Department of Defense has now decided to cancel the longtime military quality standard MIL-Q-9858. There is little doubt that military contractors will be transitioning to ISO 9000.

According to experts at the CEEM (Center for Energy and Environmental Management) Information Services, which maintains the ISO 9000 Registered Company Database for the U.S. and Canada, during the coming year, many contractors will choose to become ISO 9000-compliant before undertaking registration.

While the standard is a baseline quality standard, manufacturers are finding the hardest part is understanding the requirements of the standard and documenting what they do. The CEEM has found that most shops are about 80 percent in compliance, and for many, the only need is to document their processes.

SMALL MANUFACTURERS

Walsten believes that small manufacturers can achieve certification just as easily if not more so than big companies. One of the keys is to invest money to educate someone internally rather than relying solely on consultants.

She and three other of the software company employees attended lead auditor training early on in the process. This group keeps documentation updated and prepares the company for each of its six-month audits with weekly

company-wide communication regarding ISO and one-on-one refresher training sessions, if needed.

Several of the software company's customers have earned their ISO certification, including a 15-person machine shop in Louisiana that achieved certification in six months. The process can be easier for a small shop because there is less to clean up. Picture a General Motors assembly plant with 6,000 employees going for its ISO certification versus a fabricator with 30 people.

CONCLUSION

If you are thinking of starting certification, a good first step is to network with other ISO-certified shops and learn all you can about the process before plunging in, hiring a consultant, and incurring major expenses.

Perhaps, the right time to earn your ISO certification depends on your customers, your competition, and your resources. Most of all, it depends on desire. At the software company, top management wanted certification badly, despite the big push it required during a very busy period. When that time comes at your shop, you will know it.

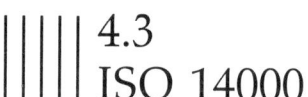 4.3
ISO 14000

ISO 14001—SPECIFICATIONS FOR AN EMS*
by Richard B. Clements

Last month we examined ISO 14000, the general guidelines to developing an environmental management system (EMS). This month we want to look at the current working document proposed for ISO 14001, the actual requirements to which you may someday have to conform.

Please keep in mind we are discussing drafts that are still in transition. However, these working documents will become draft standards this year and fully approved standards most likely at the end of 1996. By looking at them now, you can get a rough idea of what to expect. Even more

*Reprinted with permission from *Continuous Improvement*, February 1995. Richard B. Clements is president of Solution Specialists in Alto, MI.

importantly, you will discover that the ISO 9000 systems laid into place at your company will help you to dovetail in the 14000 series of standards.

THE STANDARD PROPOSED

Many companies today conduct environmental audits of their facilities to see if they conform to local, state, and federal regulations. However, these audits by themselves will not guarantee continuous improvement or future conformance. Only a well established environmental management system can do that. The thrust of ISO 14001 is to give you the minimal structure for such a system.

A key point to remember when discussing ISO 14001 is that it shares an important characteristic with ISO 9001—it won't produce an environmentally friendly company by itself. In the same way that ISO 9001 will not make the quality of your product automatically improve, ISO 14001 only lays out the system. It is up to your management to set the level of environmental impact to obtain and then seek those targets.

A second key point to remember is the draft working document says specifically that an ISO 9000 system can be used as the model for a single management system that addresses both quality and environmental issues. We would like to point out that your health and safety issues can also be wrapped into the same system.

Finally, you can use the proposed ISO 14001 for any of several purposes, such as
   —creating an EMS
   —auditing your EMS
   —seeking third-party certification
   —seeking customer recognition of your EMS
   —declaring your EMS to the general public.

THE REQUIREMENTS

"The organization shall establish and maintain an EMS. . ." begins section four of ISO 14001. Just like ISO 9000, section four contains all the requirements you must meet. And also like ISO 9000, the word "shall" means you must take this action. You must have a well documented EMS that can be demonstrable to an auditor as being in conformance and effective.

ENVIRONMENTAL POLICY

Your top management must write, and make known, a company-wide policy on environmental issues. Remember, this is not environmentalism. We are talking about anything that has an impact on your surrounding environment, such as noise, quality of work life, discharge, scrap, disposal of products, neighborhood aesthetics, and so on.

Your environmental policy will have to be relevant to the size and nature of your company and the impact it has on its environment. You must state continuous improvement is one of your strategic goals. You must say you will comply with all relevant regulations and how and when you will review your system, including your stated targets and objectives. All employees have to be aware of your policy and it has to be made available to the public.

That last requirement is what is causing all of the trouble with this proposed standard in the United States. If environmental policies are made available to the public, it also means they can be used in a court of law.

PLANNING

Planning begins by defining where your company can control the environmental results of its operations, products, and services. Then you have to compile an up-to-date list of environmental regulations and requirements that apply to your company. Using this information, begin setting your targets and objectives.

Targets and objectives have to be readily measurable. In addition, you have to consider what impacts your company has that can be controlled economically. Also, the concerns of other outside parties must be considered. At the same time, you have to stay true to your original environmental policy.

Each target and objective is then assigned to a specific job title for control and continuous improvement. A specific time frame must be created. As new projects or production methods are adopted, the EMS plan will have to be changed or expand to include these developments.

IMPLEMENTATION AND OPERATION

Just like ISO 9000, you have to define lines of responsibility and then provide the people and resources to get the job done. You must also have top management assign a manager as the official EMS coordinator. This coordinator is responsible for ensuring implementation, regularly reviewing the EMS, and reporting to management. All of this has to be documented.

All employees having a significant impact on the environment will need training to meet identified levels of skills and knowledge. This is very similar to the training requirement of ISO 9000.

In addition, you must train all employees on the importance of conformance to your environmental policies and procedures, the type of impacts your company has, who has responsibility for controlling which impacts, and the potential damage from non-conformance.

Internal communication concerning environmental issues shall be documented. You will also need a formal system for recording and acting on communications received from external sources, i.e. customers, regulators, environmental groups, etc. Likewise you need a formal procedure for releasing environmental information to the public.

Naturally, document control plays a central role in your EMS. A written procedure is required. We recommend that the Level II document created to meet the document control requirement from ISO 9000 be used to meet this same requirement.

An environmental control plan must be developed for daily operations. Such a plan would be very similar to the quality control plans required in the 1994 version of ISO 9000. You would use a flow chart of your process to identify points where environmental control is required. Each of these points would be listed on the plan along with the criteria to be met and how to react if they are not met. In addition, you should include how you communicate your requirements to suppliers and contractors.

Unique to ISO 14001 is the need for a procedure to cover emergencies. If you suffer a spill or accidental impact, how will you prevent further environmental damage while also correcting the situation? After any accident or emergency is corrected, the management should review what happened and decide how to prevent reoccurrence and whether the procedure should be changed.

CHECKING AND CORRECTIVE ACTION

Once you have identified what will be monitored and where it will happen, you will have to write a procedure on exactly how this is done. First, set up a system where key evironmental characteristics are measured and recorded. These are done in a fashion similar to an SPC system, that is, a regularly scheduled activity assigned to specific people. Then the written data has to be handled, analyzed, and stored under your ISO 9000 procedure for quality records. In addition, any measurement equipment will come under your ISO 9000 procedure for the maintenance and calibration measuring devices.

Just like ISO 9000 you will need a corrective action procedure identifying when to react, who responds, and what actions are taken. The ISO 9000 version of this can be used to meet this requirement.

At least annually you should perform an internal audit of your complete EMS. The procedure for this will be identical to those required under ISO 9000. The key difference is that the internal auditors will need to have knowledge, experience, and/or training in environmental assessment. They need to understand why a particular characteristic is being checked and what potential impacts it could create. ISO 9000 internal auditor training or lead assessor training is recommended, followed by a seminar on environmental assessments.

MANAGEMENT REVIEW

At regular intervals, usually at least once a year, your top management needs to review the complete EMS for completeness and effectiveness. This review should consist of the results of internal audits, reports on new requirements and regulations, and management's discussion of the strategic plan for the company. Then upper management decides whether to modify or change the existing EMS to better meet their changing needs and targets. All of this must be documented.

CONCLUSION

As you can see, the five basic requirements of an EMS really are a combination of environmental concerns and ISO 9000 requirements. In fact, the most widely used national standard for EMS, BS 7750, is extremely similar to ISO 14001. It would be fair to say a company that has ISO 9000 in place and has studied BS 7750 would be well on its way to conforming with ISO 14001.

An interesting aspect of ISO 14001 is the proposed idea of written targets and objectives. This would make conformance and improvement obvious to anyone who took the time to look at a series of charts. Employees would gather regular readings of environmental impacts. These could be charted and posted for everyone to see. The target for each chart would be noted. By doing this, continuous improvement would be a regular part of the EMS system.

Finally, a warning. ISO 14001 will not help you when auditors come from organizations like the Environmental Protection Agency (EPA) or OSHA. Conformance to ISO 14001 will not guarantee conformance to regulations. It is up to the management of a company to set targets and objectives to ensure such continuous conformance.

In regulatory situations, ISO 14001 will be a double-edged sword. On one hand, you will be able to easily demonstrate your efforts to maintain conformance. On the other hand, the system will leave a paper trail that can be easily followed and used in court if you flagrantly violate the law.

ISO 14010—ENVIRONMENTAL AUDITING*
by Richard B. Clements

Three standards actually cover the topic of environmental auditing. They are:

ISO 14010—Guidelines for Environmental Auditing—General Principles of Environmental Auditing.

ISO 14011/1—Guidelines for Environmental Auditing—Audit Procedures-Part 1: Auditing of Environmental Management Systems.

ISO 14012—Guidelines for Environmental Auditing—Qualification Criteria for Environmental Auditors.

Other related standards are expected to be developed at a later time. For right now, we only need to examine these three guideline standards for ISO 14001 to gain a basic understanding of how an environmental management system (EMS) will be audited.

INSIDE 14010

ISO 14010 is the general principles of environmental audits. It is comparable to ISO 9000-1 and ISO 9004-1. It also refers to the yet unpublished ISO 14050—Environmental Management—Vocabulary. It calls for a clearly written plan of the scope of the audit and the people responsible for its execution. It also calls for the dedication of the needed and proper resources for the audit activity. Without these, it says that an audit should not be attempted.

This standard is intended to be used for either EMS, environmental statement, or compliance audits. Activities such as environmental impact studies and other related procedures can work with or without the use of ISO 14010.

Because the standard tries to cover any type of environmental audit, it speaks in very general terms. For example, the scope of the audit is left up to the client. In general, the ISO 14010 standard lays out simple guidelines for auditing.

1. Auditors should be objective, independent, and competent. (See ISO 14012).

2. The auditors should act with professionalism, confidentiality, and discretion under the orders of the client.

3. ISO 14011 should be followed with a strict and systematic audit procedure.

---

*Reprinted with permission from *Continuous Improvement,* February 1995. Richard B. Clements is president of Solution Specialists in Alto, MI.

4. Audit criteria should be established before the audit, evidence collected to compare to the criteria, and findings written up based on this comparison.

5. The level of assurance and risk in the findings should be established.

6. A written report should be submitted to the client.

As you can see, this is a very general approach to laying out principles for auditing. Never does the standard stray from the conventions established in ISO 10011.

INSIDE ISO 14011 PART 1

Thanks to the growing scope of world trade and the general agreements on international trade, companies are finding they need a common way to demonstrate their environmental conformance to an international audience. Many nations already have national programs for this purpose. The intent of ISO 14001 is to give companies the specific requirements for an international scheme of conformance. It is ISO 14011 Part 1 that follows up by laying out how to audit for ISO 14001.

ISO 14011 Part 1 is intended primarily for EMS audits. It follows closely the format laid out in ISO 10011 for auditing quality management systems. The primary difference lies in the extensive knowledge an environmental auditor must possess to control an audit. This is at least true in the United States where countless regulations and local codes have to be known, tracked, and complied with.

Under ISO 14001, you establish your own relevant criteria for your EMS. One purpose of auditing is to examine the level of conformance in your plant against these criteria. The audit is for both conformance and effectiveness, just like the ISO 9000 audits. Nonconformance and opportunities for improvement are two primary targets of the audit. However, an EMS audit can also be used by an outside customer to assess the adequacy of your EMS for contractual purposes.

Just like ISO 9000 audits, a lead auditor is specially trained and placed in charge of the entire audit. The lead auditor bears the responsibilities of the audit team and its activities. The lead auditor also selects the audit team based on the auditors' qualifications and the needs of the

audit scope. For example, if two languages are used in the plant, then one auditor must be proficient in both.

Also like ISO 9000, the auditor will collect evidence, make sound judgements, protect documents collected, prepare working documents, interview people, and verify conformance and effectiveness of the EMS.

At this point it is easy to speculate on the nature of ISO 14001 audits. It seems likely that ISO 9000 registrars with qualified environmental specialists will quickly take up the task of conducting EMS audits. It is also likely that corporations might train their environmental specialists to audit suppliers. What is not certain is whether registrars or other similar organizations will be created solely for ISO 14001 audits.

Either way, the audits for registration will most likely follow the pattern established by ISO 9000. That is, an initial document review will take place to assure that a Level 1 document exists addressing all points of ISO 14001. It is fairly easy to incorporate this with the ISO 9000 system's Level 1 documentation.

After that, an audit team will be selected by the registrar and approved by the customer. Check lists and other working documents will be prepared. Assignments will be made to each auditor. Of course, a formal, written audit plan will be prepared by the lead auditor. With an audit scope established, the team will schedule the actual registration audit. The audit will point out critical nonconformances immediately and report on all major and minor nonconformances in a written report and in a closing meeting at the end of the audit. Corrective actions, if needed, will be planned and executed by the customer. The lead auditor will confirm all corrective actions. After that, you should be eligible for registration.

For internal audits, your management has several tasks:

- notify employees of the audit and its scope

- provide necessary resources

- appoint the audit team

- assure the proper training of the team

- give the auditors full access to facilities and people

- cooperate and communicate with the audit team to ensure a completed, successful audit.

Whether an internal audit or a registration audit, a key document will be the final written report. ISO 14011 Part 1 lays out the elements for any final report.

1. The date of the audit, name of the audited company, the auditors, and any other representatives.

2. The audit plan, including the scope and objectives of the audit.

3. A list of the critical criteria of the EMS under audit.

4. Summary of the audit process.

5. A list of findings on conformance, effectiveness, and management review of each element of ISO 14001 is adequate.

6. A distribution list for the report.

7. A statement on the confidentiality of the data within the report.

As usual for any audit, the audit is only considered closed when the report is completed, signed off, and the lead auditor has confirmed all corrective actions. Your company is responsible for assuring that corrective actions are taken in a timely manner.

A note of caution for companies conducting EMS audits is in order. Since environmental lawsuits are fairly common, remember that your audit reports can be used as evidence in a court of law. Therefore, careful control of the documents, quick reaction to nonconformance, and sign offs on all paperwork is critical. Also remember that the purpose of a good EMS is to keep a company in constant conformance. When successfully implemented, a good EMS should be more helpful to your company in a court of law. A poorly operated EMS will only add to your troubles during litigation.

INSIDE ISO 14012

This leaves us with one more issue to discuss—how to select the proper people to be EMS auditors. Much like ISO 10011 for ISO 9000 audits, ISO 14012 establishes the basic criteria for qualified auditors.

As stated within ISO 14012, a qualified auditor possesses the following:

- A college degree and two years work experience in an environmentally related job.

- Training in methods of auditing, environmental regulations, environmental processes, environmental impacts, and EMS standards.

- Participation as a trainee in at least four audits for not less than 20 total days of duration under the guidance of a lead auditor.

- Demonstrate competency in auditing.

- Strong communication skills, interpersonal skills, objectivity, and organization.

A lead auditor must have all of this and three additional audits for a total of 15 days as a fully qualified auditor, and also demonstrated the skills of leadership. All types of auditors have to maintain their level of skill and knowledge at all times. This is accomplished through constant monitoring of new regulations or updates, refresher training, more technical or skill training, and constant audit experience. Naturally, the auditor should maintain a written record of all of these accomplishments.

At this time it is not clear who, if anyone, will establish a nationally recognized method of accrediting EMS auditors. There are other accreditation programs in existence for environmental specialists. The question is whether governmental, voluntary, or professional organizations will take on this task. Annex B of ISO 14012 calls for someone to take on this task and lays out the first rough criteria.

Finally, ISO 14012 ends by repeating the need for due professional care in an audit. This point cannot be stressed enough. High emotions are involved with environmental issues. However, ISO 14012 also ends with an unusual paragraph not found in ISO 10011. It repeats the need for all audit team members being able to communicate effectively in the languages used by customers.

For the company facing the need to conduct ISO 14001 audits or other EMS audits, ISO 14012 is very helpful for selecting auditors. However, it does not specify all points. For example, it leaves open the question of how an auditor in training demonstrates competency or how to evaluate the leadership skills of an auditor.

Annex A of ISO 14012 attempts to address this by giving further guidance on evaluation methods. They cite techniques such as interviews with candidates, written assessments, oral tests, review of previous work, role playing, peer review, and so on. However, the standard still leaves the final form of this system up to you. Therefore, you should design your selection criteria and method based on the best practices for your particular industry. For example, if your environmental people have to obtain accreditation from their professional societies to be promoted, then this can be incorporated into your selection criteria.

mum flexibility in forming an EMS system, including the methods for internal audits. Design your EMS and auditing system for your maximum benefit. The standards give you the minimal base upon which to build a system. Only add to this base with the criteria and extra procedures necessary to achieve your company's strategic environmental goals.

CONCLUSION

ISO 14010, 14011, and 14012 are left to general description so that your company has the maxi-

---

■

ISO 14001 STANDARD ON ITS WAY*

Oslo, Norway—With a spontaneous burst of applause, an international committee ended two years of intense debate last month, putting the finishing touches on a global standard for environmental management that is likely to become a condition for doing business, much like the ISO 9000 series standards.

Meeting in this Scandinavian capital June 26–July 1, a key subcommittee of International Organization for Standardization (ISO) Technical Committee 207, charged with creating the ISO 14000 series of standards on environmental management, voted to elevate the sole registration standard in the series—ISO 14001: Environmental Management Systems—Specification with Guidance for Use—to the status of a draft international standard (DIS) (see Exhibit 1).

Such a designation means the document will undergo a series of ballotings by ISO member bodies and then publication as an international standard, a process that could be completed as early as mid 1996 barring any significant opposition. Only changes considered editorial in nature may take place at the DIS level under ISO rules.

The widely-anticipated publication of the DIS is likely to signal the start of yet another

EXHIBIT 1.—KEY DATES IN THE EVOLUTION OF TC 207

Strategic Advisory Group on the Environment (SAGE) Established	June 1991
SAGE Recommendations to ISO Technical Management Board (TMB)	December 1992
ISO TMB Decision to Establish TC 207	January 1993
Canada Awarded Secretariat	March 1993
First TC 207 Plenary; Toronto, Canada; Work Begins	June 1993
Second TC 207 Plenary; Brisbane, Australia	May 1994
Third TC 207 Plenary; Oslo, Norway	June 1995

registration boon in North America, Europe and elsewhere as companies jockey to be among the first in their industry or geographic region to earn an ISO 14001 registration certificate.

"I think use of 14001 will tell the world at large . . . that the company has a concern about the environment and environmental performance, and how they affect and are effected by the environment around them," explained Oswald Dodds, chairman of TC 207's subcommittee 1, which drafted ISO 14001.

---

*Reprinted with permission from *Quality Systems Update*, July 1995. Published by IRWIN Professional Publishing, Fairfax, VA.

"It will also tell those stakeholders or interested parties that they have a system in place to try and identify the impacts, the aspects of their business that might interact with the environment, and how those aspects actually interact with the environment.

Unlike the ISO 9000 series, which have spawned well over an estimated 100,000 registration certificates throughout the world since their initial publication in 1987, there does not yet appear to be a clear business reason for US companies to seek registration to the environmental management standard.

But many experts believe it is only a matter of time before major overseas and domestic purchasers begin encouraging suppliers to seek registration to ISO 14001.

If and when that occurs, the experts say companies registered to ISO 9000 will have a clear advantage in meeting the requirements of the new standard.

The draft environmental management document shares common management system principles with ISO 9001. It requires companies to have a general policy providing the framework for setting and reviewing environmental objectives and targets.

It also requires that companies perform a management review and have procedures in place to address corrective and preventive actions and training.

"It should be understood, however, that the application of various elements of the management system may differ due to different purposes and 'different interested parties," the document warns.

"While quality management systems deal with customer needs, environmental management systems address the needs of a broad range of interested parties and the evolving needs of society for environmental protection."

The general approach of the two documents is similar. Just as the ISO 9000 series does not ensure product quality, the environmental management standard will not guarantee regulatory compliance or improved environmental performance.

It will provide assurances that the company has an environmental policy in place that addresses, among other things, compliance with all relevant laws and regulations, including prevention of pollution; a management system to achieve its objectives and targets; and a structure to help it improve the management system.

"I think US industry is going to begin to get ready for registraton but I don't think US industry is going to jump onto the registration bandwagon," explained Joe Cascio, who heads the US delegation to TC 207 (see Exhibit 2).

"The registration is only going to take off in the states when it becomes a marketing reality, when in fact the marketplace begins to demand it and when it makes a difference," he told *QSU* in an interview. "I don't think companies are going to do this" without some external pressure.

Christopher Bell, an attorney in the Environmental Practice Group of the law firm Sidley and Austin in Washington, DC, agreed that companies should approach the question of third-party registration with caution.

"I think most companies should have environmental management systems because it makes it more likely that they will identify their obligations and meet their obligations," said Bell, a key US delegate to TC 207.

"Whether or not you go the extra . . . step of third-party certification is going to depend upon a lot of things. It's going to depend on your industrial sector and what your customers want."

Some foreign governments already are considering the acceptance of third-party registration to ISO 14001 as an optional way of demonstrating compliance with environmental permitting requirements, according to Bell.

And in some cases, purchasers may look to third-party registraton as one indication of a supplier's commitment to environmental excellence.

"There's obviously a growing interest by purchasers to have confidence that their suppliers are environmental good actors," Bell said. "Some buyers might find it a useful shortcut. On the other hand, it's always going to be important for the buyer to remember that the key issue shouldn't be whether or not they have certification."

The ISO 14001 document makes clear that standards writers make a distinction between environmental management and environmental performance (see Exhibit 3).

"The adoption and implementation of a range of environmental management techniques in a systematic manner can contribute to optimal outcomes for all interested parties," the document states. "However, adoption of this specification will not in itself guarantee optimal environmental outcomes."

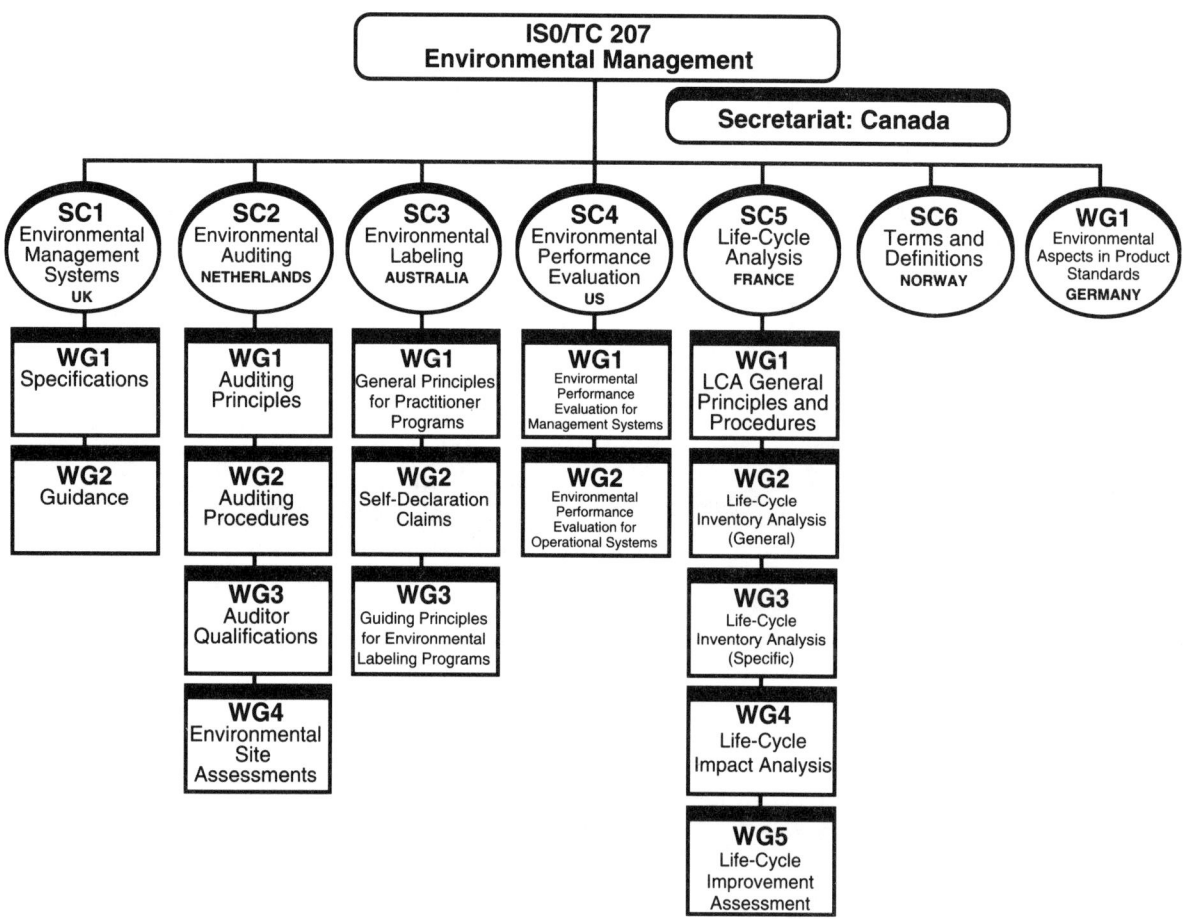

EXHIBIT 2.—ISO/TC 207 SUBCOMMITTEES AND WORKING GROUPS

The degree that the document focuses on environmental performance has been among the most tempestuous issues in the standards-writing process. Europeans, seeking to have the document approved by the European Union (EU) as acceptable for demonstrating compliance with the EU's Eco-Management and Audit Scheme (EMAS) voluntary regulation, have pressed for the incorporation of more performance-oriented requirements (see Exhibit 4).

The US and other delegations have been successful in minimizing performance-oriented requirements. The US also has been successful in persuading other delegations to accept a conservative approach to continual improvement.

The US position stems from a belief that ISO is not the appropriate venue for developing internationally accepted performance standards. The US believes that the management system standard focuses on a framework that allows companies to identify, manage and meet performance obligations.

"I think the Europeans were very forceful in making their points about the needs for EMAS and I think we were all very fortunate that some compromise could be made that seemed to be able to satisfy the needs," Cascio explained.

If ISO 14001 is accepted by the EU, it will probably hasten the spread of the standard among European companies because all conflicting or overlapping standards at national levels would be replaced by the international standard. This would include the United Kingdom's BS 7750 standard on environmental management, which has been used by a number of companies throughout Europe for registration purposes in the absence of an international standard.

Companies that are already registered to BS 7750 also are expected to find the transition to ISO 14001 relatively painless. European companies might eventually require ISO 14001 registration of their suppliers.

EXHIBIT 3.—ISO 14000 SERIES STANDARDS—DOCUMENT STATUS (CONT.)

SC	WG	STATUS	DOCUMENT NAME/PROGRESS
3	2	Other	**ISO 14022 Environmental Labeling—Symbols** Preliminary work has started on this item but the WG will not continue until the ISO 14021 advances to a CD.
3	2	Other	**ISO 14023 Environmental Labeling—Testing and Verification Methodologies** This is the third proposed document. No work on this yet.
3	3	CD	**ISO 14020 Goals and Principles of All Environmental Labeling** The 6th Draft Working Document has been approved to a CD and will be issued by late summer, 1995.
4	1	WD	**ISO 14031.2 Evaluation of the Environmental Performance of the Management System and Its Relationship to the Environment** Another draft will be produced by December, 1995, as a CD for comment. Drafting committees are revising the annexes. A CD for voting is expected by June, 1996. Between June 1996 and February 1998, the CD version will undergo a pilot test.
4	2	WD	**Evaluation of the Envoronmental Performance of the Operational System and Its Relationship to the Environment** This involves work on that part of the ISO 14031 standards that deals with environmental performance indicators.
5	1	CD	**ISO 14040.2 Environmental Management—Life Cycle Assessment—General Principles and Guidelines** This will be revised and issued as another CD for ballot by November, 1995.
5	2	WD	**ISO 14041 Life Cycle Assessment—Inventory Analysis** This will be revised and issued as a CD for comment by November, 1995 (WG2 and 3).
5	4	WD	**ISO 14041 Life Cycle Assessment—Impact Assessment** WG4 is developing an outline for a working draft document.
5	5	WD	**ISO 14041 Life Cycle Assessment—Improvement Assessment** This item will be modified to Interpretation, since it is an application of LCA methodology, not a part of it. WG5 is reviewing its scope of work and may join WGI to develop the scope of work.
6	1	WD	**ISO 14050—Terms and Definitions** This working document will compile all definitions and move forward to a CD by late fall, 1995. DIS may be issued by September, 1996.

KEY: CD = Committee Draft; DIS = Draft International Standard; IS = International Standard; NWI = New Work Item;
      WD = Working Draft

"Acceptance of 14000 in Europe will promote more acceptance of 14000 in the United States," according to Cascio.

Dodds, of the UK, who is also on the committee that will be asked to rule on the merits of ISO 14001 for satisfying the European requirement, said he believes the document will be acceptable.

"I think at this point in time the document can be accepted, but I think there are some differences in the language that might need to be addressed by CEN in order to meet the EMAS requirements," he said.

CEN, the Committee for European Standardization, hs been given the responsibility of reviewing the acceptability of ISO 14001 and related auditing documents. It has the option of creating additional requirements as part of a so-called "bridge document" to make ISO 14001 acceptable in meeting the requirements of EMAS.

The development of ISO 14001 is consistent with a general trend in business to focus on management systems, according to George Connell, international chairman of TC 207. He said companies may find advantages in third-party registration to ISO 14001, particularly in the case of companies that have the choice of complying with national requirements or the international standard.

"I'm sure they are going to find over time that it is much simpler to cope with what could otherwise be seen as technical barriers to trade if they are part of the worldwide harmonized approach," he said.

EXHIBIT 4.—DIFFERENCES BETWEEN TC 207/CD 14001 AND EMAS

TC 207/CD 14001	EMAS
A draft standard	An EU legislative instrument, i.e., a regulation
Applies to the international arena	Applies across the whole of the EU
Can apply to the whole organization or part of an organization	Applies to sites only
Applicable to an organization's activities, products and services in any sector	Restricted to site-specific industrial activities
Applicable to non-industrial activities, e.g., transport and local government	Non-industrial activities can only be included on an experimental basis
Focuses on organizations implementing environmental management systems; indirect link to environmental improvements emerging from the system	Direct focuses on environmental performance improvements at a size and the provision of information to the public
Review (identification of environmental aspects) suggested in annex 4.2.1 but not a specification of the draft standard	Initial environmental review essential
Environmental policy commitment to continuous improvement of environmental management system and compliance with relevant environmental legislation	Environmental policy commitment to continuous improvement of environmental performance and compliance with relevant environmental legislation
Environmental management audits concerned with the assessment of environmental management systems only	Environmental audit assesses management systems, processes, factual data and environmental performance
Frequency of audits not specified	Maximum audit frequency specified at 3 years
Only the environmental policy must be publicly available	A description of the environmental policy, program and management system made publicly available in the statement
Public statement not required, consideration must be given to external communication (subclause 4.3.3) but left up to management as to how much information to disclose	Public environmental statement and annual simplified statement including factual data essential
Document is more clearly structured	Confusing arrangement (a lot of cross-references)

—■—

COMBINED AUDITS LIKELY FOR QUALITY AND ENVIRONMENTAL MANAGEMENT SYSTEMS*

Oslo, Norway—Now that an international registration standard for environmental management systems is one step closer to reality, many ISO 9000 registered companies are wondering if a single audit will suffice for both quality and the environment.

The answer is yes, according to officials of International Organization for Standardization (ISO) Technical Committee 207, charged with developing the ISO 14000 series standards on environmental management.

"There is no threshold against integrating audits," explained John C. Stans, a Netherlands delegate who chairs the subcommittee charged with developing auditing documents for the ISO 14000 series.

*Reprinted with permission from *Quality Systems Update,* July 1995. Published by IRWIN Professional Publishing, Fairfax, VA.

"There is no problem in doing that as long as you are sure that you have the right people on the (audit) team," Stans said. "That means you should have people qualified as quality auditors and people qualified as environmental auditors."

Stans said it not likely that many ISO 9000 auditors will hold dual certification as environmental management and quality system auditors.

"What you need is real experience dealing with environmental aspects and technology in companies" to become an environmental management system auditor, according to Stans.

Draft auditing standards for auditors of environmental management systems are similar to the three-part ISO 10011 Guidelines for Auditing Quality Systems, however the documents differ in one respect.

"ISO 10011 does have a similar document on procedures and it also has a document on qualification criteria but it does not have a document on general principles," Stans observed, noting that planned revisions to ISO 10011 consider the addition of a document on general principles.

Overall "the documents are quite in agreement with each other," he noted. "The only difference is that I think in environmental auditing you have to take very well into account that . . . you have identified the main priority areas of a company so that you are really sure that your audit concentrates on the high priority areas . . . and the areas where there is a risk of environmental impacts."

The most significant difference among environmental management and quality system auditors will be work experience, Stans said.

"What you really need is . . . enough knowledge and ability to perform environmental audits," he explained. "In my appreciation that boils down to that you should have appropriate work experience."

In the Netherlands, which has had experience in implementing the UK's BS 7750 standard on environmental management, registrars have opted to use auditors with backgrounds in environmental management systems as opposed to quality systems, Stans said.

"They could not use their already existing quality auditors," he said of the registrars. "You need qualified people in order to be accredited as an environmental management system certification body."

Stans said he can foresee a time when environmental management and quality systems auditing documents are merged, but he said that probably won't happen in the immediate future.

"We have been discussing the merits of an overarching document that would cover the general auditing principles," said Stans. He said that such a document might contain separate modules for quality audits, environmental audits and yet-to-be-defined types of audits.

INTEREST IN ISO 14000 STANDARDS*
by Dave Hadlet

INTRODUCTION

In April 1995, Lloyd's Register Quality Assurance (LRQA) conducted a survey of its US clients to determine their level of awareness and plans with respect to the developing ISO 14000 standards. The primary purpose of the survey was to collect market information for our internal purposes. Consequently, much of the information obtained from the survey is confidential and/or has significant commercial value. Nevertheless, we are pleased to share some of the more general findings. The results are believed to be generally representative of the US ISO 9000 registered company base and will be of interest to any company considering ISO 14000 within the management framework of their business.

---

*Reprinted with permission from *Quality Systems Update,* August 1995. Published by IRWIN Professional Publishing, Fairfax, VA. Dave Hadlet is director of business development with Lloyd's Register Quality Assurance Ltd. (LRQA).

THE SURVEY

The survey questionnaire was mailed to 500 US organizations under contract with LRQA for ISO 9000 registration. Although the questionnaires were addressed to the ISO 9000 representative, recipients were encouraged to coordinate with their environmental colleagues in preparing a response. Accompanying the survey was a copy of LRQA's EMS newsletter. The newsletter provided an overview of the ISO 14000 and other EMS standards and discussed some of the issues surrounding their development and application.

We received 123 completed questionnaires for a response rate of approximately 25 percent. In several instances, multiple organizations within the same company combined their response. Each of these was treated as a single response in the survey analysis even though they represented more than one of the 500 survey recipients. Because of this factor, a more accurate response rate would be closer to 40 percent.

The 500 organizations invited to participate were a representative cross section of the LRQA client base, which in turn is generally representative of the US ISO 9000 registered company base.

Of the 123 organizations responding, three asked to remain anonymous. Of the remaining 120, 107 had attained ISO 9000 registration and 13 were still undergoing the registration process. The response rate for those registered was significantly higher than for those organizations that were still in the implementation phase.

ANALYSIS AND RESULTS

Companies responding to the survey were identified to their primary industry sector using a standard industrial classification (SIC) code label. A breakdown by SIC code of the respondents is shown at the end of the article. In most, if not all, sectors the number of respondents was considered too small to provide confidence that the results were truly representative of the sector as a whole. For this reason the results of the survey were broken down more broadly into manufacturing industries (SIC 3400/3500/3600), process industries (SIC 2000/2600/2800/3300), and all respondents combined (all SIC codes). Differences between the industry sectors were relatively small and are only presented where believed to be significant.

Survey recipients were initially questioned on their level of 14000 awareness, the status of their environmental compliance systems and their plans in respect to implementing a formal EMS. Those respondents indicating no intention to implement an EMS (numbering 15 to 20 percent) did not complete the remainder of the questionnaire and were therefore excluded from the subsequent statistical analysis.

The results of the analysis are as follows:

ISO 14000 AWARENESS

The level of awareness of ISO 14000 was relatively low. Sixty-four percent of respondents were unaware or had little awareness of the development of the new standards. In considering this result, it is important to recognize that the survey was directed specifically toward companies directly involved in, and knowledgeable of, the ISO 9000 registration process. As such, it can be reasonably expected that the level of ISO 14000 awareness across industry at large will be significantly lower.

Companies in the process sector indicated a marginally greater awareness. Forty-one percent were at least reasonably aware compared to only 30 percent in the manufacturing sector.

STATUS OF ENVIRONMENTAL MANAGEMENT SYSTEMS

When questioned whether a formal system was used to manage environmental regulatory compliance, 77 percent of respondents replied in the affirmative. Of the 77 percent, however, almost half stated that their environmental management systems were less formal than their systems for managing quality.

The most significant difference between the process and manufacturing sectors was the degree to which companies had integrated their environmental and quality management systems. Seventeen percent of respondents in the manufacturing sector had integrated their EMS with either their ISO 9000 or TQM programs. This figure compared with only 5 percent in the process sector.

ESTIMATED TIME TO EMS IMPLEMENTATION

Twenty-seven respondents had already commenced EMS implementation or were planning to start within the next 12 months. The manufacturing sector appeared somewhat more proactive in this respect, within 33 percent of respondents falling into this category, compared to only 18 percent in the process sector.

The largest single survey grouping was the 39 percent indicting a 12- to 36-month time frame prior to commencing EMS implementation. A further 34 percent appear to be adopting a wait-and-see attitude, with no plans to implement for at least three years if at all. Interestingly, the 13 percent stating no intention to implement an EMS were represented across most industry sectors. The one sector indicating universal non-acceptance was the computer software industry. Three software companies participated in the survey.

ESTIMATED TIME TO EMS CERTIFICATION

In general, EMS certification was seen to be a medium- to long-term project. Of those companies implementing an EMS, 39 percent did not anticipate certification for at least three years. Fifty percent were planning for certification in the one- to three-year time frame. A significant number (8 percent) planned to start the certification process within 12 months. It is assumed these companies are implementing or developing systems based on BS 7750 or the ISO 14001 draft.

Encouraging news for the registration community was the very high percentage of respondents intending to pursue certification at some stage. Of those implementing an EMS, 96 percent intend to go through the certification process.

FUNCTIONAL RESPONSIBILITY FOR EMS COORDINATION

Companies were divided on the question of whether their ISO 14000 programs would be coordinated by functions presently responsible for quality or those presently responsible for environmental compliance.

Fifty percent of respondents favored the environmental compliance function over a sepa-

rate quality function for coordination of the ISO 14000 program. Of the remainder, 31 percent favored a single function with responsibility for both programs and 14 percent favored the quality function over a separate environmental function for their ISO 14000 coordination. Five percent were either undecided or favored the creation of a new position or department within the organization.

The process sector, with 57 percent of respondents, leant more towards assigning the ISO 14000 coordination role to a separate environmental compliance function. This figure compared to only 47 percent in the manufacturing sector.

INFLUENCES BEHIND THE DECISION TO IMPLEMENT AN EMS

Not surprisingly, for most companies senior management was seen as the primary driving force behind the decision to implement an EMS.

As to the factors influencing the senior management decision, several are expected to come into play. Internal benefits, pursuit of market leadership, pressure from customers and pressure from regulators were each cited by between 47 percent and 56 percent of respondents as major influencing factors. Pressure from shareholders was seen to be by far the smallest influence of the factors rated, although there was a wide divergence in responses. Twenty-one percent considered shareholders to be a major influence whereas 38 percent viewed them as having to influence at all.

CRITERIA FOR EMS REGISTRAR SELECTION

Survey recipients were asked to compare the most frequently stated registrar selection criteria for QMS (ISO 9000), with equivalent criteria for EMS. Overwhelmingly, as a group the respondents saw little difference in relative importance. This result might be viewed as somewhat surprising given the broader focus of EMS, which will require consideration of the expectations of a much wider constituency of interested parties. Nevertheless, as might have been anticipated, experience, reputation and accreditation were the criteria most frequently cited as being more important for EMS than for QMS.

||||| 4.4
MALCOLM BALDRIGE NATIONAL QUALITY AWARD

■

HOW DO PEOPLE USE THE BALDRIGE AWARD CRITERIA?*
by Karen Bernowski and Brad Stratton

Almost 1 million copies of the Malcolm Baldrige National Quality Award (MBNQA) criteria have been distributed. Yet, in the seven years that the award has been given, only 546 companies have applied for the award.[1] What happened to the other 99,000 or so copies? Have companies or individuals used them? Were they pitched into the "circular file," never to be seen again?

To find out how the MBNQA criteria are being used, *Quality Progress* conducted a survey of those who have requested a free, single copy or have purchased bulk copies of the criteria between 1992 and 1995. A randomly selected sample of 3,000 people worldwide were sent surveys. (For more on the survey methodology, see the sidebar "The Survey Specifics.") The answers of the 840 who responded shed light on previously unknown areas.

Three findings are worth highlighting:

- The criteria are being used primarily to obtain information on how to achieve business excellence.

- The criteria's usefulness, overall, has met or exceeded users' expectations.

- The criteria know no boundaries when it comes to who uses them. They are used by the management of a broad range of industries several times a year.

"We have always regarded the Baldrige Award as primarily a national education program," said Curt Reimann, director of the National Institute of Standards and Technology (NIST), the organization that manages the award. "The award criteria are the centerpiece of the education process as they provide the best way to capture and disseminate lessons learned to a mass audience. The *Quality Progress* survey confirms most of our beliefs about wide use, multiple uses, use in all sectors of the economy, and copying of the criteria by other organizations."

FINDING NO. 1: THE CRITERIA'S PRIMARY USE

While 18.4% of the respondents indicated that neither they nor their companies used the MBNQA criteria (the aforementioned circular file), the majority used them at least once. What did they primarily use them for?

The survey respondents were asked to indicate whether they didn't use, have used, or plan to use the criteria in 15 areas:

- As a tool to apply for an award (company, state, or national award)

- As a written self-assessment tool for an entire company

- As a written self-assessment tool for a department or division

- As an informal self-assessment tool for an entire company

- As an informal self-assessment tool for a department or division

*Reprinted with permission from *Quality Progress*, May 1995.

- As a tool to set up quality processes in an entire company
- As a tool to set up quality processes in a department or division
- As a tool to improve existing quality processes in an entire company
- As a tool to improve existing quality processes in a department or division
- As a common language to communicate with others inside a company (e.g. other departments or divisions)
- As a common language to communicate with outside business partners (e.g., suppliers)
- As a common language to communicate with other companies
- As a common language to communicate with public-sector institutions (e.g., education or health care organizations)
- As part of the curriculum for a course, seminar, or workshop
- As a source of information on how to achieve business excellence

As Exhibit 1 shows, the criteria were overwhelmingly used as a source of information on how to achieve business excellence. More than seven out of 10 respondents used them this way. Other common uses were applying the criteria as a tool to set up quality processes in an entire company (48.8%) and as a common language to communicate with others inside a company (48.7%).

While about half of the respondents use the criteria as a common language within their companies, they did not use them to communicate with those on the outside. As Exhibit 2 shows, the criteria were infrequently used as a tool to communicate with business partners (53.2% didn't use them for this purpose), other companies (54.7%), and public-sector institutions (68.9%).

About one-quarter of the survey respondents said they used the criteria to apply for awards. So while relatively few companies have applied for the Baldrige award, the criteria have likely been used to apply for company, supplier, local, and state awards. Many of the latter awards are based on the MBNQA criteria.[2]

Not many respondents were planning to use the criteria in the future (see Exhibit 3). For those respondents who foresaw future use, the top six plans involved using the criteria to set up quality processes, improve quality processes, or perform informal self-assessments in their departments, divisions, or companies.

FINDING NO. 2: THE CRITERIA'S USEFULNESS

In the survey, respondents were asked to indicate whether the criteria were "more useful than expected," "about as useful as expected," or "less useful than expected" for each of the 15 applications. They also had the option of indicating that they had no opinion (if they hadn't used the ap-

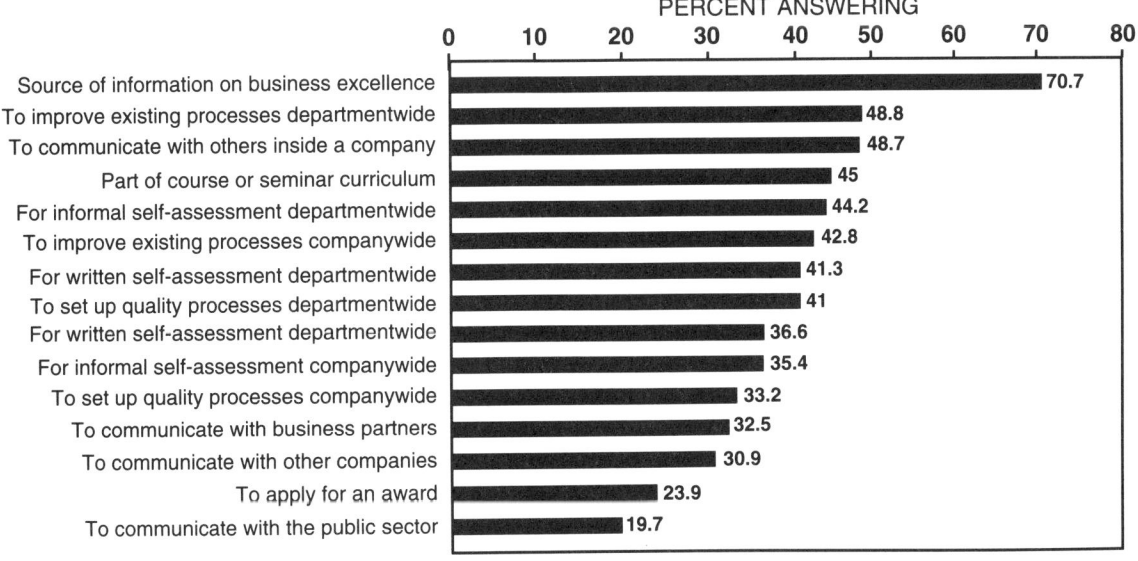

EXHIBIT 1.—RESPONDENTS WHO USED THE CRITERIA

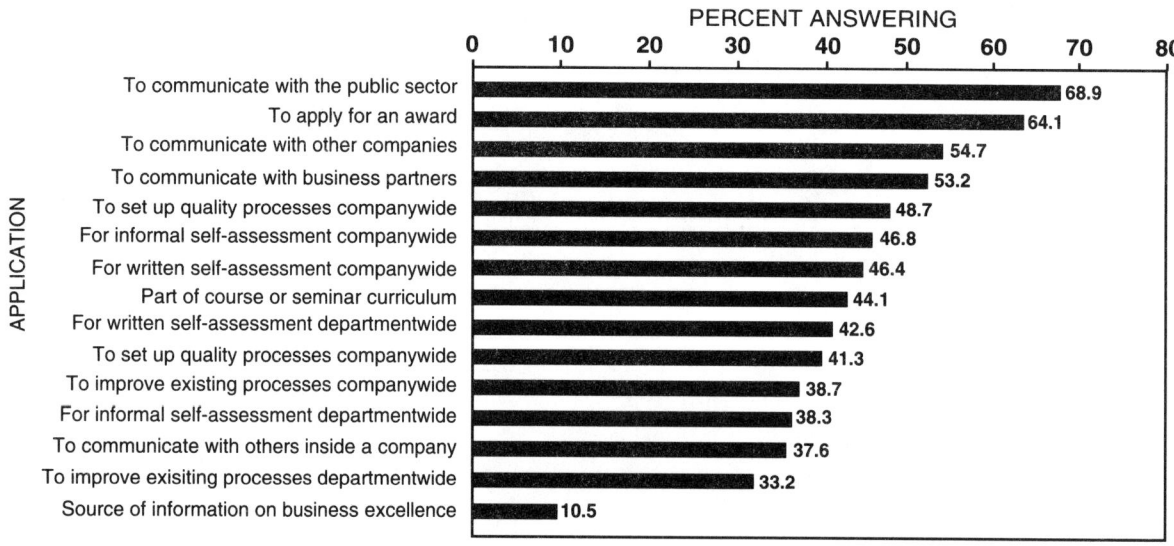

PERCENT ANSWERING

APPLICATION

To communicate with the public sector	68.9
To apply for an award	64.1
To communicate with other companies	54.7
To communicate with business partners	53.2
To set up quality processes companywide	48.7
For informal self-assessment companywide	46.8
For written self-assessment companywide	46.4
Part of course or seminar curriculum	44.1
For written self-assessment departmentwide	42.6
To set up quality processes companywide	41.3
To improve existing processes companywide	38.7
For informal self-assessment departmentwide	38.3
To communicate with others inside a company	37.6
To improve exisiting processes departmentwide	33.2
Source of information on business excellence	10.5

EXHIBIT 2.—RESPONDENTS WHO DIDN'T USE THE CRITERIA

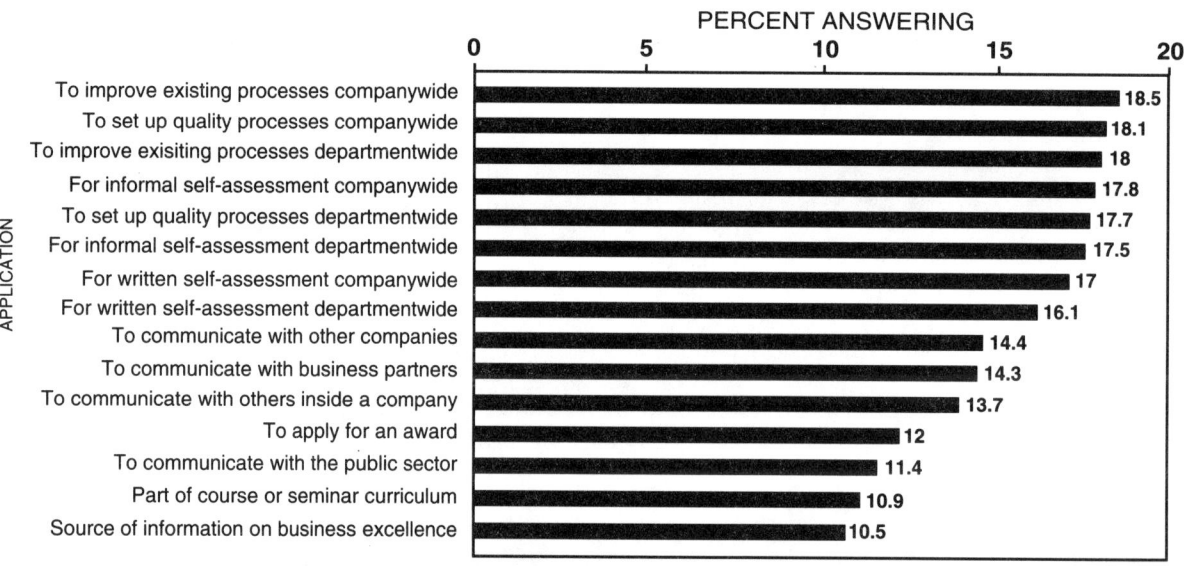

PERCENT ANSWERING

APPLICATION

To improve existing processes companywide	18.5
To set up quality processes companywide	18.1
To improve exisiting processes departmentwide	18
For informal self-assessment companywide	17.8
To set up quality processes departmentwide	17.7
For informal self-assessment departmentwide	17.5
For written self-assessment companywide	17
For written self-assessment departmentwide	16.1
To communicate with other companies	14.4
To communicate with business partners	14.3
To communicate with others inside a company	13.7
To apply for an award	12
To communicate with the public sector	11.4
Part of course or seminar curriculum	10.9
Source of information on business excellence	10.5

EXHIBIT 3.—RESPONDENTS PLANNING TO USE THE CRITERIA

plication or could not make a judgment). As Exhibit 4 shows, the majority of the respondents indicated that the criteria's usefulness met or exceeded their expectations.

The one application that most exceeded respondents' expectations was the criteria's use as a source of information on business excellence, as indicated by 31.4% of the respondents. This is 60% higher than the next runner up: a tool to improve existing processes in a company.

Although there was no one application that completely failed to meet users' expectations, the criteria's use as a tool to set up quality processes did not fare as well as other applications. Al-

most 15% of the respondents said the criteria did not meet their expectations when setting up processes in departments or divisions, and 12.4% indicated that their expectations were not met when setting up processes companywide.

By comparing the results in Exhibit 4 against those on how the criteria was used, a correlation can be seen. Exhibit 5 shows, the criteria generally exceeded users' expectations in applications for which they were used more often. This should serve as validating information to NIST. It indicates that, in areas in which the criteria are more heavily used, they are perceived as quite useful. It should also encourage NIST to

PERCENT ANSWERING

- More useful than expected
- As useful as expected
- Less useful than expected

APPLICATION	More useful than expected	As useful as expected	Less useful than expected
Source of information on business excellence	31.4	46.2	9.5
To improve existing processes companywide	19.6	38.8	8.3
Part of course or seminar curriculum	19.3	35.9	8.3
To communicate with other companies	18.9	41.8	8.7
For informal self-assessment departmentwide	17.4	43.1	8.5
To improve exisiting processes departmentwide	17	43.2	10.7
For informal self-assessment companywide	16.1	38.9	6.9
To set up quality processes departmentwide	15.3	38.9	14.5
For written self-assessment departmentwide	15.2	41.8	10
For written self-assessment companywide	15.1	39.6	8.5
To set up quality processes companywide	15	35.7	12.4
To communicate with business partners	13.9	34.5	9.5
To communicate with other companies	13.8	35.5	8
To apply for an award	9.8	37.3	5.4
To communicate with the public sector	9.3	26	10

EXHIBIT 4.—HOW THE CRITERIA MET RESPONDENTS' EXPECTATIONS

continue to focus on improving those areas perceived as not useful. In fact NIST plans to review the survey's findings, including respondents' comments on how the criteria could be improved.

FINDING NO. 3: HOW OFTEN THE CRITERIA ARE BEING USED AND BY WHOM

While 18.4% of the respondents said that neither they nor their companies used the criteria,

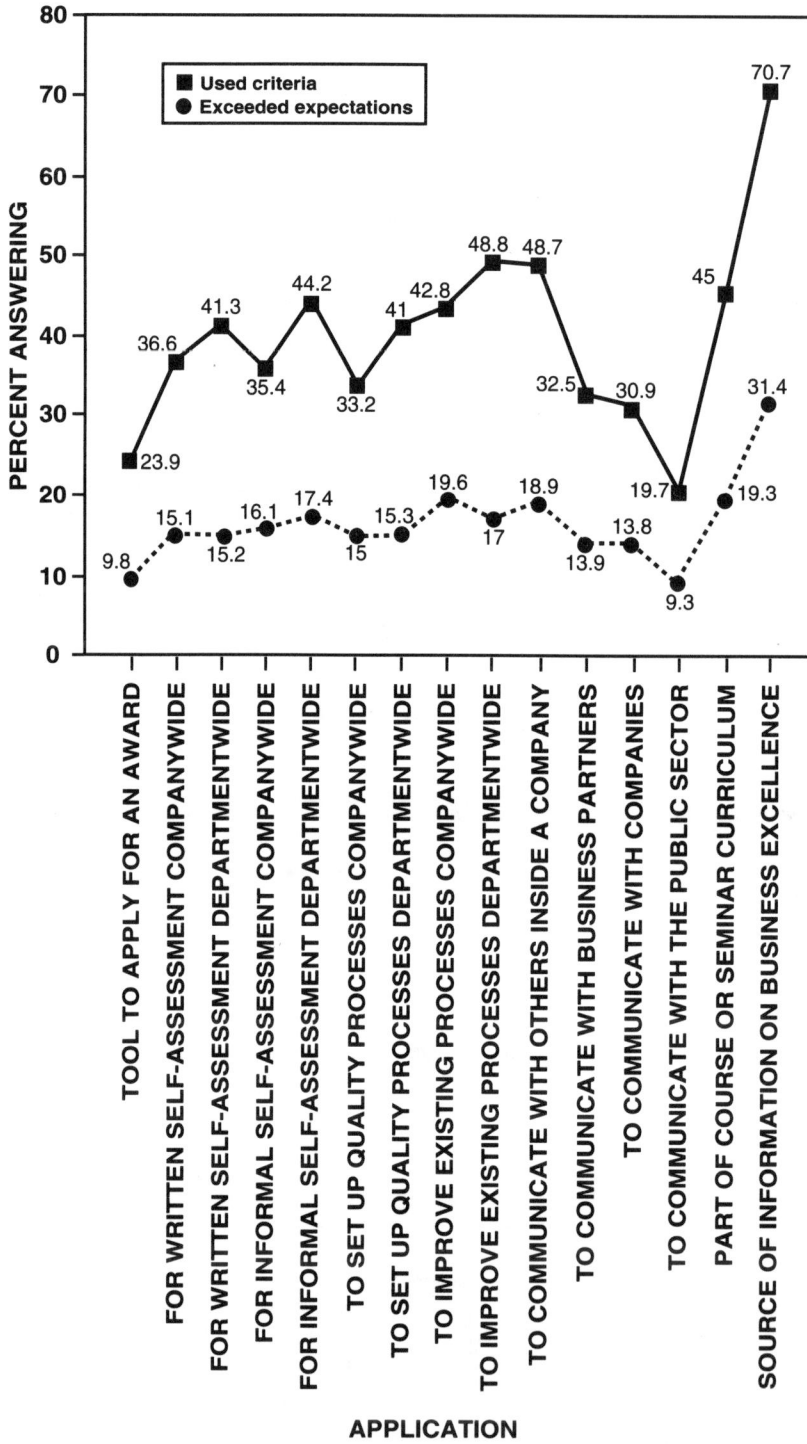

EXHIBIT 5.—COMPARISON OF USAGE AND EXPECTATION LEVELS

21.7% indicated that they had used them at least once a week in the past 12 months. Most respondents, however, were between the two extremes (see Exhibit 6).

More than three-quarters of the respondents (79.8%) primarily used the criteria in their com-

panies rather than for personal use. The industries represented by the respondents' companies cover a broad spectrum, from manufacturing and service industries to health care, education, and government institutions. Even industries such as agricultural production, oil and gas extraction,

The Survey Specifics

The survey on how the Malcolm Baldrige National Quality Award (MBNQA) criteria are being used began in January 1995 when *Quality Progress* staff brainstormed with members of ASQC's Market Research and MBNQA departments about the feasibility and logistics of the survey. They determined that to accurately represent those people who request the criteria, two populations needed to be surveyed:

- People who ordered a single, free copy of the criteria from the National Institute of Standards and Technology (NIST)
- People who purchased bulk copies (10 or more) of the criteria from ASQC

To ensure that the more recent versions of the MBNQA criteria were being critiqued by respondents, the populations were narrowed to those who ordered or purchased copies between 1992 and 1995. A sample of 1,500 randomly selected people was the chosen from each population, for a total of 3,000 people worldwide.

With input from NIST officials, the survey questions were developed. In addition to the nine questions concerning the use of and satisfaction with the criteria, two optional, open-ended questions were included:

- If informal or written assessments have been conducted, how have the results been used?
- How might the Baldrige Award criteria be improved?

The answers to these questions, along with the survey results, will be sent to NIST officials for feedback purposes.

Survey packets were mailed to the 3,000 randomly selected people. The packet included a postage-paid return envelope. For those people who were from the bulk-order population, the return envelope had an order number on it. When one of those surveys was returned, the order number was noted and that person's name was removed from the mailing list for a second survey. The survey was then separated from the envelope to guarantee each respondent's anonymity. This process could not be instituted for the people from the single-copy population. Thus, they all received a second survey, regardless of whether they returned the first one.

A week after the first mailing, everyone was sent a postcard reminding them to complete the survey if they hadn't already done so. The postcard also told them to contact ASQC headquarters to request another survey if they hadn't received the first one.

Two weeks after the postcard was mailed, the second survey packet was mailed. The second packet included a postage-paid return envelope, but none of the envelopes had order numbers on them. A week later, another reminder postcard was mailed.

Although the surveys were sent to 3,000 people, not all were deliverable nor were all surveys returned in time to be part of the data base. Thus, two calculations were made. First, it was determined that no more than 2,936 surveys should have been mailed; some surveys were incorrectly mailed to people who had changed their addresses or their jobs. Comparing those 2,936 surveys to the total number of responses, 893, produced a gross response rate of 30.4% (893/2,936). The surveys that were returned too late, however, had to be accounted for, so a second calculation was made. Of the 2,936 surveys that could have been returned, 840 were usable. Therefore, the usable response rate was 28.6% (840/2,936), giving a statistical significance of ±3.4% and a confidence interval of 95%.

---

and real estate were represented. Overall, more than two-thirds (67.1%) of the Standard Industrial Classification codes (two-digit breakdown) were represented by the respondents' companies.[3]

Both small companies (defined as those with 500 or fewer employees) and large companies (those with more than 500 employees) were represented by the respondents. Forty-two percent of the respondents worked for small companies, while 57% worked for large organizations (about 1% were uncertain). The findings that the respondents were from companies of all sizes and from a wide variety of industries confirm that people perceive the MBNQA criteria as applicable to any organization.

The survey also revealed that those who requested the criteria were usually in managerial positions. Seventy-seven percent were in managerial positions: 29.9% were midlevel managers, 23.2% were senior managers, 18.6% were executives, and 5.3% were supervisors. The remainder were nonmanagerial employees (12.9%) and outside consultants (10.1%).

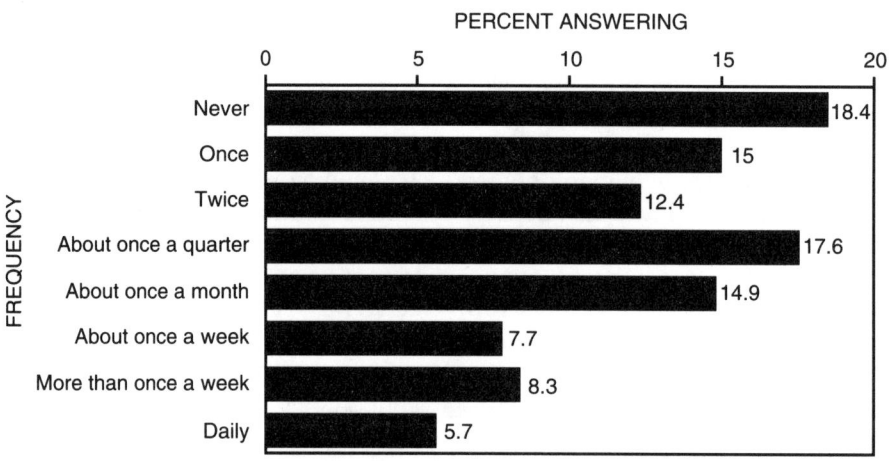

EXHIBIT 6.—HOW OFTEN THE CRITERIA WERE USED

CRITERIA MEET STATED PURPOSES

In NIST's *1995 Award Criteria* booklet, the purposes of the criteria are outlined. In addition to being the basis for giving awards and feedback to applicants, the criteria's purposes are:

- "To help improve performance practices and capabilities;
- "To facilitate communication and sharing of best practices information among and within organizations of all types based upon a common understanding of the key performance requirements; and
- "To serve as a working tool for managing performance, planning, training, and assessment."[4]

Based on the survey's results, the criteria appear to be strong in most of these areas. Most respondents indicated that they were satisfied with the criteria's usefulness in improving existing processes, conducting courses or seminars (i.e., training), performing self-assessments, and communicating with others in their companies. The one area that appears to represent an opportunity for improvement is in facilitating and sharing best practices information among organizations. This is evidenced by the finding that the criteria were infrequently used to communicate with outside organizations, whether they be business partners, other companies, or public-sector institutions.

"The survey provides us with new and valuable insights regarding improvements we need to

make as we continue to refine the criteria and publicize their uses," said Reimann. "For example, we believe that more should be done to emphasize that the Baldrige Award criteria are about overall performance management and organization learning. Product and service quality are essential parts of performance, but performance includes productivity, speed, new product development, and many other factors. These factors are addressed in the 1995 criteria.

"The survey also shows us that more needs to be done to foster criteria used in communication among organizations," said Reimann. "Also, we need to do more to ensure that organizations know that the Baldrige Award criteria focus on improving overall organizational competitiveness and effectiveness. Everything needed to win the award is highly relevant to organizational success, whether or not the organization is interested in applying for an award. For this reason, *all* organizations should find value and uses for the Baldrige Award criteria. The survey shows that we still have much work to do. Overall, the survey adds appreciably to the store of knowledge regarding national-level learning."

EVIDENCE NOW EXISTS

Based on *Quality Progress'* survey findings, people now have an idea as to what happened to the other 999,000 or so copies of the MBNQA criteria. While about 180,000 were thrown into the circular file, the other 819,000 have been used at least once, most likely for information on how to achieve business excellence.

Acknowledgment

We wish to thank Vince Hope and Karen Krsticevic of ASQC's Market Research Department; Regina Robinson-Stokes and Cheryll Parker of ASQC's MBNQA Department; and Curt Reimann, Harry Hertz, Dan Barton, and Lauren Kubacki of NIST for their help in conducting this survey.

REFERENCES

1. Based on data provided from the National Institute of Standards and Technology for the years 1988-1994.

2. Karen Bemowski, "State of the States," *Quality Progress*, May 1993, pp. 27-36.

3. The Standard Industrial Classification (SIC) code is a commonly used classification system for U.S. industries. Depending on the detail desired, the codes can be broken into one-, two-, or four-digit numbers. For the purposes of the survey, two-digit SIC codes were used. Of the possible 82 two-digit SIC codes, 55 were indicated by respondents.

4. *1995 Award Criteria*, U.S. Department of Commerce, Technology Administration, National Institute of Standards and Technology, Gaithersburg, MD.

HOW CONTINUOUS IMPROVEMENT AND TEAMWORK WON THE BALDRIGE*

In 1981, when the automotive industry was losing its market share to the Japanese, General Motors called 400 of its approximately 50,000 suppliers together. This group was told that they were considered GM's preferred suppliers.

Among the suppliers attending that meeting was Don Wainwright, Chairman and CEO of Wainwright Industries (St. Peters, MO), a small, family-owned manufacturer of component parts for the automotive, aerospace, and information industries.

Wainwright and his fellow suppliers were asked to institute Statistical Process Control (SPC) and to stop their lines if the products did not meet GM specifications. In making the request, GM was asking these suppliers for a radical change. In the early '80s, most companies rarely stopped their production lines.

"We were shocked," recalls Wainwright of the GM request. "If GM, our main customer, was losing its market, it meant that we were losing ours, too. So, we started using SPC tools.

"Before you knew it, our customers and all our associates (employees) and the leadership at Wainwright Industries were working together as

a team," Wainwright continues. "We found that we needed one another to make this thing happen. We didn't know it then, but this was our introduction to Total Quality Management."

The company also didn't realize back then that this marked the beginning of the journey that would culminate in its becoming the sole 1994 winner of the Malcolm Baldrige National Quality Award in the small business category.

EVENTS SET TONE FOR QUALITY JOURNEY

In 1984, after several years of teamwork, the company decertified the 27-year-incumbent union by a six-to-one vote. "At that point, Wainwright says, "we all became partners and associates."

In fact, the team spirit aspect caught on so quickly at Wainwright that very employee—from the CEO to the associate working on the loading dock—began to wear Team Wainwright uniforms while at work as a symbol of their team spirit. The shirts are black and white striped with *Team Wainwright* and the associate's name on the front. Men wear black pants while women have a choice of black pants or skirts.

"The associates came up with this idea," says Wainwright, "so they were surprised when management came out wearing them and said, 'We want to join the team too.' But that was logical. After all, quality is everyone's responsibility."

Around 1987, General Motors initiated its "Targets for Excellence" (TFE) Program, a Baldrige-like program for certifying its suppliers. TFE assesses and grades suppliers in five areas, including management and quality. In 1990 Wainwright Industries became the one hundred twenty-sixth supplier to achieve that certification. During that period, the company also received Ford Ql Preferred Certification, and won IBM Rochester Division's outstanding supplier award—one of only three quality awards presented by IBM in 23 years.

During these years, the company was using Baldrige criteria to guide its business, along with studying best practices of past Baldrige winners. So it was only natural that in 1992, when the company helped start a state program called the Missouri Quality Award, it was closely modeled after the Baldrige.

A year later, Wainwright officially submitted applications for both the Missouri Quality Award and the National Baldrige Award. Dave Robbins, the Executive Vice President, wrote the initial Baldrige application, with input from teams in the various areas.

The first draft of the Baldrige application was 110 pages long. The team found it difficult to edit the information down to the allowed maximum of 75 pages allotted for the Baldrige application. So, the company didn't apply that year.

Wainwright applied the following year, but it didn't reach the third step, a site visit. However, the company received an extensive four-day site visit from Missouri Quality Award examiners. The result: Wainwright won the 1993 Missouri Quality Award.

Buoyed by the state win, the company submitted a second Baldrige application (trimmed to 63 pages) in 1994. When the six assessors left after the site visit, Wainwright called the associates together and told them, "We have reached the summit of the mountain. Whether or not we win the trophy is really not important because your interaction during the site visit was fantastic, and we are so proud of everyone."

As it turned out, there *was* nothing to worry about. The company brought home the Baldrige.

CONTINUOUS IMPROVEMENT LED THE WAY

There are many reasons Wainwright Industries won the award, but continuous improvement in all areas of the company led the way. Here are two major examples:

■ *Customer Satisfaction.* The company's commitment to listening to its customers is evidenced by the process it has set up to monitor customer feedback.

In the process, customers grade Wainwright in the areas of quality, delivery, communication, and responsiveness.

Each month customers phone, fax, or mail their grades. The grades are then averaged to come up with a final number. These averages are plotted on a Customer Satisfaction Index (CSI).

Most customers are obviously happy with what Wainwright is doing. The company received high marks last year—95 percent customer satisfaction (up from 84 percent in 1992). Its goal is to reach 98 percent this year.

■ *Continuous Improvement Process (CIP).* This is a world-class suggestion system (benchmarked by Toyota) that emphasizes on ongoing flow of improvement ideas from employees.

"Last year, each associate averaged 54.7 implemented continuous improvement ideas," says Wainwright. "This translates into a 5 or 6 percent annual cost reduction. Our goal is for every associate to implement 1.25 improvements per week."

The associate not only makes the suggestion but drives the improvement until it is finished. The philosophy behind this is *A thousand raindrops make an ocean.* "We're not looking for home runs—although if we get one, we'll take it," says Wainwright. "We want those base hits and those stolen bases to win the game."

RESULTS SHOW MANY GAINS

Considering the Baldrige win, teamwork and the continuous improvement process have obviously fared well at Wainwright. In addition to the dramatic rise in customer satisfaction, other results since 1990 tell more of the success story:

Sales have improved from $18 million to $30 million. And this in spite of some of the most chal-

lenging automotive and engineering market years on record.

Company profit has held at 2 percent after taxes and profit sharing.

Accidents have decreased by 72 percent.

Lost time due to accidents has decreased by 85 percent.

Lost work days are down by 87 percent.

INGREDIENTS BRING SUCCESS AND RECOGNITION

What, then, are the ingredients that will lift a company to success and high-level recognition? If Wainwright Industries' successful bid for the Baldrige is any indication, perseverance, teamwork, and continuous improvement figure prominently.

Blending those ingredients with an overall attitude that quality is everyone's responsibility is a sure-fire recipe for creating a four-star operation.

‖‖‖ 4.5 THE DEMING PRIZE

■

AN INSIDE LOOK AT JAPAN'S DEMING PRIZE*
by Doni Chamberlain

Writing about the Deming Prize for *Quarterly Digest* is like defining a spark plug for *Car and Driver*. It's one of those terms so generous that if you're the least bit cognizant of the business, you'll recognize the words. And in the quality business, W. Edwards Deming—the man, the teachings, the Prize—is a quality-thinking staple. And, although Deming is gone, the union of Japanese Scientists and Engineers continues its 44-year tradition of announcing Deming Prize winners—its proclamation of the cream of the international quality crop.

AN AMERICAN FIGURE—A JAPANESE PRIZE

While revered with near god-like admiration in Japan, Deming remained relatively unknown in the United States until the 1980s. Even after his popularity rose in the United States, the prize that bears his name remains relatively unknown. Only two U.S. companies have won the Deming Prize: Florida Power & Light and a division of AT&T.

In contrast, the Deming Prize is pursued by Japanese-based corporations with almost the intensity of Sir Gawain pursuing the Holy Grail, says Robert C. Christopher, author of *Second to None*.

Many people have tried to explain Deming's impact on the Japanese. His long-time assistant and secretary, Cecilia S. Kilian, perhaps knew him best.

"Dr. Deming's invitation to Japan in 1950 by the Union of Japanese Scientists and Engineers gave him the opportunity to teach leaders of Japanese industry about the use of statistical analysis to improve productivity," writes Kilian in *The World of W. Edwards Deming*. " 'What I saw was a magnificent work force, unsurpassed management and the best statistical ability in the world.' Deming said of the Japanese, 'and it seemed to me that those three forces could be put together, and I put them together, so that Japanese quality, instead of being shoddy, became known as the standard within a few years. In less than four years,

---

*Reprinted with permission from *Quality Digest*, April 1995, © 1995 QCI International.

manufacturers all over the world were scream-
ing for protection.' "

During deming's repeated visits to Japan, he
not only taught statistical methods but counseled top managers, says Mary Walton, author of
Deming Management at Work. "What he taught
in Japan did not exist in America," she writes,
"He taught a new system—his product. Japanese managers and engineers listened and
learned, and put into practice what he taught."

However, not everyone thinks that the Japanese should credit Deming for their quality success. Some analysts say that the Japanese were
self-taught. "Much of what is now called the
Deming method . . . are not ideas that Deming
taught the Japanese, but principles that he
learned while watching the Japanese develop,"
says Robert E. Cole, professor of sociology and
business administration at the University of
California at Berkeley. "If there had been no Dr.
Deming, the Japanese would have successfully
developed their quality-improvement strategy all
the same."

The debate about whether the Japanese actually needed Deming to succeed will undoubtedly continue for some time. However, JUSE
reached its own conclusion, and in 1951, its board
of directors established Japan's highest industrial award, the Deming Prize, " . . . to commemo-
rate Deming's contribution and friendship in a
way that would last a long time and to further
promote the continued development of quality
control."

Since the Deming Prize's inception, it has
gained a reputation for being an international
measure of quality excellence. Companies and
individuals world-wide challenge the prize to
promote companywide quality control.

THE PRIZE PROCESS

Applying for the Deming Prize might be compared to the children's game, "Mother May I?"
Companies or individuals may apply, but they
must ask for JUSE's permission and consultation before progressing to each step. The process
starts with the applicant's submission of a Description of Quality Control Practice and a business prospectus. Before applying, however, prospective applicants are advised to hold
preliminary consultations with the Deming Prize
Committee secretariat before completing and
submitting the application.

If Deming Prize hopefuls pass that stage,
they may then move on to the examination process. All examination costs—including JUSE reviewers' expenses, process correspondence fees
and interpreter costs—are incurred by the applicant. Naturally, there's no refund for companies that don't pass the first level.

The on-site examination is the next step.
*The Reports of Statistical Application Research,
JUSE* (Vol. 37, 1990–1991—"Special Issue: The
Deming Prize") perhaps best describes the pro-
cess:

"An examination is conducted by the Deming Prize for Corporate TQC Implementation
Subcommittee, beginning with a review of
the contents of the "Description of QC Practices.'

"If the Description of QC Practices is approved, the applicant is subjected to on-site examination. If the applicant passes this on-site examination, the Deming Prize Committee decides
to award a prize to the applicant, and the winner receives the Deming Medal with an accompanying certificate of merit."

Sound simple? Ask two U.S. Deming-Prize
winners: 1989 recipient Florida Power & Light
and 1994 recipient AT&T Power Systems.

FLORIDA POWER & LIGHT: THE TRAIL BLAZER

In 1989, FPL had the distinction of being the
first non-Japanese company—and the first U.S.
company—to receive the Deming Prize. An award
won six years ago may sound like yesterday's
news. Not necessarily. For FPL, winning the
Deming Prize was just the beginning. Since acquiring the prize, FPL has increased its customer base by 3.5 million (more than doubling its
1989 level), its current electric rates are lower
than its 1984 rates, and it has one of the highest employee-safety ratings among electric utili-
ties.

J. Michael Adams, manager of quality services at FPL, has a clear recollection of life during the Deming Prize application process.

"As an advisor to one of the examination
units, I can say firsthand that the preparation
was intense," remembers Adams. "We challenged
each other, mapped processes, solved problems
and strengthened plans."

Deming Prize Structure

The Deming Prize Categories include: the Deming Prize for Individuals, the Deming Application Prize and the Quality Control Award for Factories. JUSE's Deming Prize Committee classifies the categories as follows:

* *The Deming Prize for Individuals* is given to those who have made outstanding contributions in the study and/or dissemination of companywide quality control using statistical methods or in the study and/or dissemination of statistical companywide quality control methods.

* *The Deming Application Prize* is awarded to companies or to divisions of companies that have achieved distinctive performance improvement through the application of companywide quality control using statistical methods.

* *The Deming Application Prize* for small- or medium-sized companies is called the *Deming Application Prize for Small Companies*, while the prize awarded to a division of a company is called the *Deming Application Prize for Divisions.*

* *The Deming Control Award for Factories* is awarded to factories or plants that have achieved distinctive performance improvement through the application of quality control/ management in the pursuit of companywide quality control.

The Deming Prize Committee determines award winners based upon the candidates' application, the subcommittees' recommendations, and examination feedback and reports.

JUSE, in conformance with the Deming Prize regulations, carries out all Deming Prize Committee administrative work.

Overseas companies

Initially, non-Japanese companies were restricted from the Deming Prize because the prize's original purpose was to encourage quality control development in Japan. However, after many non-Japanese companies expressed strong interest in the Deming Prize, JUSE altered its administrative regulations for the first time in 1984, allowing non-Japanese companies to challenge the Deming Prize Application Prize.

It's noteworthy that the Deming Prize for Individuals, the Quality Control Award for Factories and the Japan Quality Control Medal are still open only to Japanese candidates. Japanese companies may apply for the Japan Quality Control Medal five or more years after winning the Deming Application Prize. To win the Japan Quality Control Medal, recipients must show that their companies' companywide quality control implementation has improved substantially beyond the level when they won the Deming Application Prize.

Source: The Deming Prize Committee, Union of Japanese Scientists and Engineers, 5-10-11 Sandageya. Shibuya-ku, Tokyo 151, Japan.

Adams says that the "real-time" examination sessions were a series of "Show-mes:" "Show me the process. Show me how this links to corporate policy. Show me how this satisfies the customer. Show me with data and facts."

Hindsight being what it is, Adams says that the actual examination process, including preparation, was much more difficult and all-encompassing than FPL had anticipated. but he also attributes the ultimate process' success to FPL's teamwork.

"From the area's vice president, down to the meter readers, I can say the team really had it together," recalls Adams. "When our examiners were giving us their closing remarks, I can to this day recall their excitement courtesies, encouragement and smiles that have left a lasting historic memory."

AT&T POWER SYSTEMS

When AT&T Power Systems won a 1994 Deming Prize, it became the first U.S.-based *manufacturing* company to be honored by JUSE. And although AT&T's Consumer Long-Distance unit went after (and won) the 1994 Malcolm Baldrige National Quality Award, the Power Systems unit chose the Deming Prize as its goal. Why choose the Deming Prize over the Baldrige Award?

Andy Guarriello, AT&T Power Systems' vice president and chief operating officer, says that pursuing the Deming Prize seemed the obvious choice for his unit. "In the business I'm in, the Deming Prize is recognized around the world as a standard of excellence," he says. He also points out that the company's most formidable competition is outside the United States, lying primarily along the Pacific rim.

"To be competitive, we really had to be the best we could be to compete with those people [outside the United States] because they're paying a lot less for labor than we are," explains Guarriello.

Guarriello says the difference between the Deming Prize and the Baldrige Award goes beyond merely keeping score. "With the Baldrige, you add up the score: with the Deming Prize, there is no such thing as a score," he explains. "What the examiners are looking for is not only how well you're doing in TQM, but have you something to advance the base of TQM? They're not looking for you to install a system that's exactly the same as someone else's, they're looking for what you've done that's different from someone else—better than someone else—that they could point to and say, "These folks have done a little bit better in this area than the rest of the prize winners.""

THE CATEGORIES

There are 10 examination items within the Deming Application Prize. Each category item contains between four to seven subcategories. Each category is based upon the prize's primary objective: companywide quality control, which is based on statistical quality control. The following are the examination items:

- Policies
- The organization and its operations
- Education and dissemination
- Information gathering, communication and its utilization
- Analysis
- Standardization
- Control/management
- Quality assurance
- Effects
- Future plans

There are three basic Deming Prize categories: the Deming Prize for Individuals, the Deming Application Prize and the Quality Control Award for Factories. JUSE awards prizes to public or private organizations, with subcategories

classified as small enterprises, divisions of large corporations and overseas companies. According to JUSE, the prize's objective is simple: "To award prizes to those companies that are recognized as having successfully applied companywide quality control based on satistical quality control and are likely to keep up with it in the future."

That definition alone prompts confirmations from some who say that the Deming Prize focuses more on paper, less on customer satisfaction.

But AT&T's Guarriello disagrees. "There is no question that the Deming Prize places great emphasis on customer satisfaction," he says. "But, in addition to that, I think that emphasis is also placed on asking companies, 'Are you growing the business? Do you have a profitable business?'

"In other words, are you doing the kinds of things throughout the total business that make it a good solid business, instead of just focusing on customer satisfaction? You could focus on customer satisfaction by *giving* the product away, but you don't stay in business that way."

FPL'S POST-DEMING PRIZE REVIEW

FPL has moved on, saying that it's doing better than ever. And although the Japan Quality Control Medal (awarded by JUSE to worthy recipients—former Deming Prize winners—five years later) is open only to Japanese companies, in September of 1994 FPL requested and received JUSE's post-Deming Prize review.

For Japanese comapnies that have already won, the JUSE post-Deming Prize review is mandatory. It's optional for overseas winners. Initially, FPL intended to request the review in 1992, but the effects of Huricane Andrew and a cost-reduction initiative sidetracked the company's review request until January 1994.

Two of the original JUSE FPL 1989 reviewers also conducted the 1994 FPL review. They asked to return to the locations they had visited during the Deming Prize application process. Although FPL sees winning the Deming Prize as a forward-moving, positive experience, it also recognizes that the prize was not the end-all corporate success solution.

FPL addressed these post-prize concerns in its February 1994 in-house publication. "A Status Report on FPL's Improvement Activities Four Years After Receiving the Deming Prize." The report says that although winning the Deming Prize was a source of great company pride and honor, a number of FPL employees felt that their quality-improvement program, initially intensified by the Deming challenge, had not become mechanical and inflexible.

One strategy change included FPL's shift in focus. After winning the Deming Prize, the company's emphasis centered on "doing things right"—primarily by encouraging employees to do things better within the existing business environment. "Doing things right" continues, but now FPL's stragety has broadened to include organizational restructuring and creating success strategies within the entire competitive market.

TIPS FROM THE WINNERS

FPL's Adams has some sage advice for Deming Prize novices.

"The drawback of the process, particularly in 1989, is that it interrupted life as we knew it," recalls Adams. "Of course, on such a rigorous path, there was little time for deviation from plan, so accommodating some normal activities like vacation, sickness, having babies and summer storms were a challenge."

Another drawback was paperwork—and a lot of it, says Adams. But each piece was necessary for showing process, data, information, results, plans, etc.

The process helped Adams to stay humble and in a learning mode, he says. "I recall the praise that was pointed out to us repeatedly, 'You don't know what you don't know,'" says Adams. "Therefore, we remain in a seek-and-improve mode in this continuous journey and aspire to those that have better-in-class performance in the functions they perform."

SECTION

Five

THE STATE OF THE QUALITY PROFESSION

The state of the profession for a quality professional has been improving steadily since the 1980s. Today, experienced consultants and managers in quality assurance command their highest salaries ever. As the following survey indicates, the current level of status and pay for various quality related job titles has increased. When you use this table to compare your own situation to the averages, keep in mind that higher wages are paid to those professionals in larger corporations and in higher cost-of-living areas. If you are thinking of hiring a quality professional, this survey will give you benchmarks to use to set the salary range.

1995 QUALITY SALARY SURVEY*

We would like to thank the more than 1,000 readers who responded to *Quality Digest's* 1995 Salary Survey. We hope that these results are useful. Survey results are based on 848 valid responses received by the due date. Averages are based on responses from the continental United States.

Since more than half of survey responses were from managers or executives, the salary chart provides a regional breakdown for people in those categories (see Exhibit 1). The chart is further broken down by gender. The charts on the following pages give you a breakdown of average salaries of the top 10 job categories (about two-thirds of our respondents). We have also included several useful bar charts that provide overall regional averages, overall averages for particular job titles, comparisons between male and female salaries, and more.

TRENDS

This year, as last year, an important trend to watch was the relationship between male and female salaries for comparable positions. We were pleased to note that although men and women have not yet reached parity when it comes to salaries, the gap for those with 11 or more years' experience has closed considerably since our 1993 survey. In that year, a comparison of executive and manager salaries for men and women with 11 or more years' experience revealed a gap of 10 percent to about 25 percent.

This year, the same group is seeing a gap of 5 percent to 13 percent. Women's salaries surpassed men in the 16- to 20-years' experience range. The bad news is that the gap for executive and management men and women increased for those with 10 years or less experience.

The ratio of women holding executive positions compared to men decreased markedly from the 1993 survey. In that survey, male executives outnumbered female executives 10-to-1. This year that ratio dropped to 7-to-1—a considerable improvement. For management positions, the ratio remained constant at 6-to-1, men over women. Compare these figures to an overall male/female ratio of 4-to-1 for all survey respondents.

Looking at average salaries between regions, we see that Western and Northeastern companies still tend to pay more than their

EXHIBIT 1.—REGIONS HAVE BEEN DIVIDED AS FOLLOWS:			
Western	**North Central**	**Southern**	**Northeastern**
Arizona	Illinois	Alabama	Connecticut
California	Indiana	Arkansas	Delaware
Colorado	Iowa	Georgia	Maine
Idaho	Kansas	Kentucky	Maryland
Montana	Michigan	Florida	Massachusetts
Nevada	Minnesota	Louisiana	New Hampshire
New Mexico	Missouri	Mississippi	New Jersey
Oregon	Nebraska	North Carolina	New York
Utah	North Dakota	Oklahoma	Pennsylvania
Washington	Ohio	South Carolina	Rhode Island
Wyoming	South Dakota	Tennessee	Vermont
	Wisconsin	Texas	
		Virginia	
		West Virginia	

*Reprinted with permission from *Quality Digest*, June 1995. © 1995 QCI International.

Quality Executives' and Managers' Salaries by Years' Experience

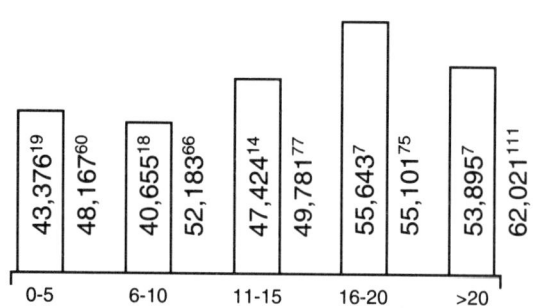

	0-5	6-10	11-15	16-20	>20
	43,376[19]	40,655[18]	47,424[14]	55,643[7]	53,895[7]
	48,167[60]	52,183[66]	49,781[77]	55,101[75]	62,021[111]

Male/female salary gap

Last year's gap %	6	11	10	27	22
This year's gap %	10	22	5	1*	13

*Women's salaries exceeded men's salaries.

Quality Executive and Manager Salaries by Industry

	Female	Male
Manufacturing	43,390[49]	53,904[365]
Service	54,220[9]	67,170[14]
Government	61,125[4]	46,950[7]
Health Care	46,333[3]	62,856[3]

Quality Technical Salaries by Region
(Includes engineers, specialists, technicians)

Western	37,933[7]
Southern	33,728[12]
North Central	39,266[18]
Northeastern	43,613[5]

Quality Supervisor Salaries by Region

Western	38,651[5]
Southern	36,388[16]
North Central	36,427[18]
Northeastern	50,363[3]

Southern or North Central counterparts. In additio, salaries in the Western states have re-

mained about the same or decreased since 1993. Could this be due to cuts in defense spending that have affected many large West Coast defense contractors?

Not too surprisingly, education is a key player in determining an employee's salary. Employees with four-year degrees can expect to earn anywhere from 20 percent to 33 percent more than those with high school or vocational/technical degrees in the same positions. We found that two-thirds of executives and managers have at least a four-year degree (but 10 percent of executives only have a high school or vocational/technical degree). The message here is clear—higher education equals higher pay.

METHODOLOGY

The *Quality Digest* 1995 salary survey questionnaire appeared in the April 1995 issue. This year we asked respondents to supply their answers on a computer-scanned form, which allowed us to input the data into our spreadsheet program more accurately and in about 10 percent of the time.

We asked readers to supply data on their current salary, job description, job location, age, sex and the number of years' employment and experience. Respondents returned the questionnaires by postage-paid mail.

The magazine received 1,050 responses from the 38,000 people who received the issue, a response rate of 2.8 percent. This figure is about half the rate of our previous survey, which we attribute to two factors—the newness of using a computer form for answers and a somewhat daunting initial set of questions. Live and learn. We promise that the next survey using a computer form will be less confusing.

Of the 1,050 surveys received, about 200 arrived too late to be included in the results. Of the 848 valid responses, 122 (14%) were quality/QA/QC executives, 332 (39%) were quality/QA/QC managers, and 84 (10%) were supervisors or technical personnel involved in quality/QA/QC functions.

Combined Averaged Salaries for Executives
(The number of respondents is in superscript)

	Western F	Western M	Southern F	Southern M	North Central F	North Central M	Northeastern F	Northeastern M	Overall Averages by Category
Age									
<30	$31,845^3$	—	$29,533^3$	$36,333^3$	$27,416^2$	$38,045^8$	$37,500^1$	$37,000^2$	$34,557^{22}$
30–39	$30,333^3$	$47,975^{14}$	$39,633^8$	$51,677^{29}$	$41,658^9$	$47,620^{52}$	$53,632^3$	$52,467^{12}$	$47,505^{130}$
40–49	$49,500^2$	$53,040^{26}$	$41,300^6$	$58,463^{44}$	$60,867^{11}$	$55,429^{69}$	$80,086^7$	$55,350^{24}$	$55,912^{190}$
50–60	$61,000^1$	$57,313^{19}$	$57,500^1$	$65,479^{33}$	$34,400^2$	$60,538^{27}$	$23,483^2$	$60,088^{15}$	$60,159^{100}$
>60	—	$57,375^4$	$36,500^1$	$61,250^2$	—	$48,250^2$	—	$50,114^3$	$52,584^{12}$
Years at company									
0–2	$43,312^3$	$48,255^{14}$	$35,420^5$	$53,250^{27}$	$38,000^2$	$52,943^{35}$	$84,250^2$	$50,651^{10}$	$50,359^{99}$
3–5	$19,600^1$	$54,119^{19}$	$37,800^6$	$48,255^{27}$	$45,990^5$	$50,547^{47}$	$28,588^3$	$53,359^{14}$	$48,828^{122}$
6–10	$43,000^3$	$54,540^9$	$42,593^6$	$57,478^{17}$	$41,422^8$	$53,434^{30}$	$66,199^2$	$57,255^{13}$	$52,941^{88}$
11–20	$34,000^2$	$53,067^{14}$	$44,000^2$	$63,164^{19}$	$64,034^7$	$50,715^{34}$	$68,260^5$	$52,175^{10}$	$54,673^{93}$
>20	—	$72,496^7$	—	$71,884^{21}$	$35,400^2$	$63,354^{12}$	$78,000^1$	$70,005^9$	$67,181^{52}$
Years' experience									
0–5	$30,884^4$	$49,672^7$	$30,727^6$	$47,646^{20}$	$58,958^5$	$48,343^{24}$	$67,325^4$	$55,787^9$	$47,026^{79}$
6–10	$23,000^1$	$59,085^7$	$42,125^4$	$61,725^{18}$	$38,306^{10}$	$45,994^{32}$	$49,566^3$	$57,443^9$	$49,287^{84}$
11–15	$47,500^2$	$51,667^{17}$	$46,350^6$	$53,104^{19}$	$39,328^3$	$46,910^{30}$	$62,333^1$	$51,046^{10}$	$49,274^{91}$
16–20	$52,500^2$	$50,701^{11}$	$40,000^2$	$55,668^{17}$	$76,750^2$	$56,662^{35}$	$51,000^1$	$55,724^{12}$	$55,237^{82}$
>20	—	$59,326^{21}$	$36,500^1$	$64,995^{37}$	$47,700^4$	$62,750^{37}$	$74,983^2$	$57,514^{16}$	$61,482^{118}$
Employees supervised									
0	$27,900^4$	$48,400^5$	$34,350^2$	$54,584^{16}$	$52,592^6$	$48,404^{19}$	$44,822^3$	$63,993^8$	$49,611^{63}$
1–5	$49,500^2$	$51,544^{26}$	$36,700^{10}$	$54,375^{43}$	$48,983^7$	$50,887^{74}$	$61,500^7$	$50,003^{21}$	$50,967^{190}$
6–15	$34,935^1$	$52,274^{19}$	$39,932^5$	$57,240^{31}$	$44,241^8$	$53,553^{48}$	$51,000^1$	$55,094^{22}$	$53,010^{136}$
16–50	$61,000^1$	$66,313^9$	$40,000^1$	$66,178^{17}$	$37,000^2$	$56,156^{11}$	$95,000^2$	$60,780^5$	$61,288^{48}$
>50	$40,000^1$	$57,440^4$	$57,500^1$	$72,850^4$	$70,000^1$	$88,257^6$	—	—	$69,013^{17}$
Overall regional average	$38,504^9$	$53,154^{63}$	$38,792^{19}$	$57,777^{111}$	$47,211^{24}$	$52,574^{158}$	$59,636^{13}$	$54,569^{56}$	

*Includes presidents/CEOs, vice-presidents or directors directly responsible for quality management, QA/QC or inspection.

Quality Executive Salaries by Region
(Includes president/CEO, vice-president, directors)

Western	$69,628^{17}$
Southern	$67,772^{36}$
North Central	$65,044^{50}$
Northeastern	$72,062^{19}$

Quality Manager Salaries by Region

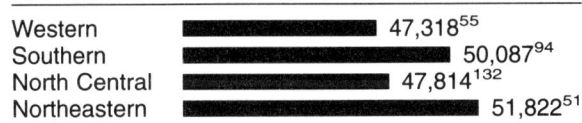

Western	$47,318^{55}$
Southern	$50,087^{94}$
North Central	$47,814^{132}$
Northeastern	$51,822^{51}$

Except for the Western region, managers' salaries have increased by about 8 percent. Western salaries remain stagnant (or have decreased) for both managers and executives.

Average Salaries for Top Two-Thirds of Survey Respondents
(The number of respondents is in superscript)

	Western		Southern		North Central		Northeastern		Average	≤10 yrs' Experience	>10 yrs' Experience
	F	M	F	M	F	M	F	M			
Quality Manager	45,800[5]	50,733[31]	39,513[10]	56,761[57]	45,194[15]	49,482[78]	49,161[6]	52,657[28]	50,951[230]	47,614[125]	54,835[105]
QA/QC VP	32,645[3]	45,577[13]	32,432[5]	44,591[22]	48,948[4]	44,354[34]	38,800[1]	50,664[15]	44,808[98]	42,533[68]	50,173[30]
Quality Director	19,600[1]	73,053[10]	40,350[2]	69,822[21]	57,813[4]	66,756[25]	90,575[4]	68,383[8]	67,268[75]	63,438[38]	70,894[37]
Manager	64,433[3]	66,853[4]	71,300[1]	50,005[10]	41,975[4]	54,747[18]	56,500[1]	56,740[5]	54,661[46]	51,460[25]	58,753[21]
QA/QC Supervisor	34,500[1]	43,000[3]	35,567[3]	34,793[11]	29,257[5]	37,650[8]	—	45,250[2]	35,747[33]	33,750[20]	40,061[13]
Mfg. Manager	51,300[1]	48,100[4]	30,800[3]	46,213[6]	25,800[1]	54,321[11]	—	—	47,307[26]	47,942[16]	46,910[10]
QA/QC Director	—	76,750[2]	42,500[1]	64,584[8]	50,000[1]	48,889[9]	50,897[1]	63,700[3]	57,292[25]	47,000[12]	66,485[13]
QA/QC Coordinator	—	34,420[3]	35,750[4]	54,850[4]	27,500[2]	37,556[8]	—	48,600[1]	38,134[22]	34,772[16]	49,483[6]
QA/QC Engineer	41,925[2]	36,045[4]	48,000[1]	36,953[3]	43,210[2]	41,230[6]	55,236[1]	47,000[1]	40,892[20]	39,824[15]	44,519[5]
Quality VP	—	68,167[3]	66,000[1]	106,833[3]	—	88,050[8]	—	95,000[2]	86,360[17]	80,786[7]	91,238[10]

Average Salaries by Education
(The number of respondents is in superscript)

	No High School	Vocational/ Technical	2-Year Degree	4-Year Degree	Master's Degree	Doctorate
All	41,922[7]	40,750[156]	44,967[126]	51,671[359]	61,158[172]	69,116[19]
Technical	36,500[1]	32,504[9]	33,980[7]	40,006[21]	44,857[6]	—
Managers	—	42,077[69]	44,127[57]	50,140[155]	59,392[49]	65,750[3]
Executives	—	51,908[12]	62,700[15]	66,468[62]	77,346[29]	76,938[4]
Supervisors	—	31,475[12]	34,375[7]	42,000[20]	55,500[2]	28,200[1]

The relationship between education and salary is quite evident—the higher the education, the higher the pay. The difference in pay between a person with a technical degree vs. four-year degree can be as high as 33 percent. Note that the majority of respondents have four-year degrees. This table indicates that it might be worth the extra year required to get a two-year degree as opposed to a vocational/technical certificate.

Six

CHECKLISTS

Today, the modern quality professional has to be able to evaluate the state of management within his own company. This is a task of enormous size, complexity, and importance. Standards like ISO 9000 and ISO 14000 make this task an annual event. Therefore, checklists are valuable tools to assist you and to help train your audit team. What follows are a few useful checklists you can use for your own company. It is strongly recommended that you modify these lists to match your particular situation and scope of your audit.

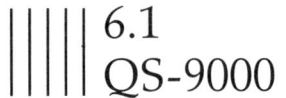
---■---

QS 9000 AUDITOR/'S CHECK LIST*
by Richard B. Clements

What follows is the actual checklist used by a QS 9000 auditor. This does not represent an exhaustive list of questions, nor does it represent the actual questions you may be asked. Instead, it is presented as a preview of the type of questions to expect. In addition, you can use this information to evaluate your internal readiness for QS 9000 registration. You can also use a copy of the QS 9000 to create your own check list.

4.1 MANAGEMENT RESPONSIBILITY

1. How do you assure your quality policy is widely known and understood?

2. Can I see your organizational chart?

3. How do you delegate authority to manage your quality system?

4. What multi-disciplinary, problem-solving method do you use?

5. How often do you review the effectiveness of the quality management system?

6. Can I see those meeting notes?

7. How do you assure qualified people are in support positions?

8. Who is responsible for QS 9000 implementation?

9. Can I see a business plan showing QS 9000 as a part of the plan?

10. Do you use benchmarking for quality, production, and operation efficiency?

11. Can I see the data?

12. How do you measure customer satisfaction? Is it a formal plan?

13. Do you use multi-functional teams for advanced quality planning?

4.2 QUALITY SYSTEM

1. Show me your Level II quality manual.
    *Examine the manual to assure all document requirements of QS 9000 as shown in the standard have been addressed.

2. Does the quality planning process parallel the Level II manual description and Level III procedures for the following?
    A. product program plan preparation
    B. resource acquisition
    C. design and process capability studies
    D. updating and maintenance of quality control and inspection methods
    E. control plan development
    F. review of standards and specifications

3. Do you conduct design feasibility reviews? Can I see the results for products x, y and z?

4. Did this design review also encompass the statistical capabilities?

5. To what level do you develop plans?

6. Do the control plans include all special characteristics? How do you know?

7. When do you revise a control plan?

8. Do control plans cover all three phases of production?

---

* Reprinted with permission from Continuous Improvement, February 1995. Richard B. Clements is president of Solution Specialists, located in Alto, MI.

9. Do FMEAs consider special characteristics?

4.3 CONTRACT REVIEW

1. How do you define a contract?

2. Is that in writing?

3. Do you require QS 9000 of your subcontractors?

4. Can I see where you acquire compliance (how notified)?

5. How do you change customer requirements under a current contract when requested to do so by a customer?

6. How are contracts reviewed?

7. Can I see those records?

4.4 DESIGN CONTROL

1. Who is responsible for product design? How are the design plans established?

2. How do you know that people assigned to a project have the necessary skills?

3. What are applicable regulation standards? How are they identified?

4. Do you use CAD/CAE? If you subcontract, how did you select the suppliers?

5. Can I see records of project/product design reviews?

6. Can those design outputs be verified?

7. Does the design output meet customer input requirements?

8. How do you cross reference?

9. Does you design output process include any of the following:

    A. GDT and other design techniques as listed in 4.4.2

    B. customer performance risk trade off analysis

    C. testing—production and field

    D. design FMEA?

10. Can I see your performance testing results?

11. Can I see your prototype program results?

12. Do you validate designs as part of the quality planning process?

13. Can I see your engineering change procedure?

14. Show me how the Engineering Change Notice (ECN) accommodates customer initiated change.

4.5 DOCUMENT CONTROL

1. Show me a master list of controlled documents

2. Show me how customer-initiated changes are controlled.

3. Can I see all your reference documents?

4. Describe your document control process to me.

5. How do you control documents resident in software?

6. What special characteristics do you use?

7. Do you have a procedure for controlling customer engineering specifications?

4.6 PURCHASING

1. Do your subcontractors meet the same standards you do?

2. How do you survey subcontractors?

3. Can I see those records?

4. Can I see a copy of your approved vendor list?

5. How do you unapprove a vendor?

6. How do you decide to monitor a vendor?

7. Are you developing subcontractors to the requirements of QS 9000?

8. Can you verify quality on site?

9. Can you show me purchase orders? (Use this question to evaluate "completeness" of purchasing requirements section.)

4.7 PURCHASER SUPPLIED PRODUCT

1. Do you inspect product supplied by your customer at receiving and then periodically to assure its condition?

2. Show me the procedure you use.

4.8 PRODUCT ID AND TRACEABILITY

1. How do you identify product at each stage?
2. Show me how I could take product "X" from shipping and trace it backward through the production system.
3. Do your customers require part or component traceability?
4. Show me how you maintain traceability.

4.9 PROCESS CONTROL

1. How do you develop job instructions?
2. Are they complete with respect to accessibility, full communication of requirements, required tooling and gages, statistical process control, and all the other requirements of 4.9.1?
3. Can we follow 3 or 4 jobs on the shop floor to assure process control?
4. Do you have a preventive maintenance and predicted maintenance plan?
5. What process do you use to ensure that all regulatory safeguards are followed? Are there certificates? Can I see them?
6. What are your process controls for items designated appearance items?

4.10 INSPECTION AND TESTING

1. How do you control purchased material?
2. Do you require your suppliers to send you statistical data?
3. Can I see it?
4. Describe your defect prevention methods.
5. Can I follow products x, y, and z through your production process to verify your documented inspection?
6. How do you verify that product will not ship until all inspection and test procedures are complete?

7. Show me your layout and functional test records.
8. Are records maintained for production cycle plus one year?

4.11 INSPECTION, MEASURING, TEST EQUIPMENT

1. Do you use the Measurement System Analysis (MSA) manual guidelines to determine accuracy/precision?
2. Is the MSA noted on the central plan?
3. Do you use an outside calibration service?
4. Is the appropriate calibration standard noted on the proper outside service?
5. How is each piece of inspection measurement and test equipment identified?
6. How do you control or calibrate employee-acquired equipment?
7. If you drop a pair of calipers, what do you do?
8. How do you know how to use those micrometers?
9. Do you recalibrate after engineering changes?
10. How and where do you store calibration standards?
11. How can you use a gage if the calibration sticker is missing?
12. How do you identify inspection and test status throughout the production process?

4.12 INSPECTION AND TEST STATUS

1. How does a person on the line know the product they receive has been properly inspected or tested?
2. How do you mark the inspection and test status on your production parts?
3. May I randomly sample such parts to confirm this?

4. Are you required to have early launch controls or other identification requirements by your customer?

4.13 CONTROL NONCONFORMING PRODUCT

1. Do you have segregated hold areas?
2. Do you have a Material Review Board (MRB) or related procedure?
3. Can I see the last six months MRB history?
4. What are suspect products?
5. How do you control those?
6. What do you do with nonconforming and suspect parts?
7. Do you research parts?
8. How do you trace customer approved deviations?
9. Do you record nonconformances? How?
10. Do you reinspect reworked product?
11. Show me rework and repair instructions.
12. Do you maintain records of customer-approved deviations and authorized quantities?

4.14 CORRECTIVE ACTION

1. What problem-solving method do you use?
2. Do you verify effectiveness of corrective actions?
3. What do you feel are appropriate corrective actions?
4. Do you analyze returned parts to develop corrective actions?
5. Do you use nonconformance reports to develop corrective actions?
6. Is upper management part of the review process?
7. Show me.

4.15 HANDLING, STORAGE, ETC.

1. Do you check or rotate stock?
2. Show me your packaging procedures.

3. Do you have customer packaging specifications? Can I see them?
4. Do you have a target of 100% ontime delivery?
5. What do you do when product is damaged in the plant?
6. Are material handling methods appropriate for the product?

4.16 QUALITY RECORDS

1. Show me copies of your subcontractor development records.
2. Are records accessible on site?
3. How do you prevent deterioration of electronic records?
4. Are records retained for the following time periods at a minimum?
    a. production plus one (1) year
    b. charts and other Level IV documents one (1) year

4.17 INTERNAL QUALITY AUDITS

1. Show me the last six (6) months of internal audit reports
2. Are corrective actions initiated from the internal audits?
3. Are auditors independent from the department/function being audited?
4. How do you schedule and prioritize audits?
5. Is upper management part of the review process?

4.18 TRAINING

1. How did employees receive qualification/training in each aspect of their job?
2. Is the training effectiveness verified?
3. Do you perform a training needs analysis?
4. If supervisors are qualified to sign off on training, where did they become qualified?
5. Can I see your training records?

6. How did you learn to set up this machine?

7. How did you learn to assemble this job?

4.19 SERVICING

1. Show me your service reports, internal and field, for the last six (6) months.

2. Tell me how service data is communicated to the other levels of the organization.

4.20 STATISTICAL TECHNIQUES

1. What do you do when the dots on the chart are above or below the control limits?

2. What do you do when the line is trending up or down?

3. Does advanced quality planning develop the appropriate statistical techniques?

4. Are special techniques established and used per the guidelines of the AIAG manual?

‖‖‖ 6.2
‖‖‖ ISO 9001

---■---

ISO 9000 AND WORKPLACE SAFETY*
by Bob Kozak and Rick Clements

ISO 9000 is now a strong reality in the manufacturing community. With the adoption of ISO 9001 into the automotive industry supplier quality assurance standard (QS-9000) and the U.S. Department of Defense, the standard series has made a significant impact. Soon to follow will be a standard for environmental management (ISO 14000) and eventually another for safety in the workplace.

As various industries incorporate ISO 9000-based quality-management systems, the question arises whether other management-based programs can be fully incorporated into the ISO 9000 management model. As we have seen in past articles, the answer for total quality management and environmental management is yes. In addition, workplace safety programs can also be incorporated into the ISO 9000 management model.

The heart of an ISO 9000 system is a documented quality manual, which is a collection of management policies on quality-related topics. The system also includes a standard operating procedures manual and related work instructions. Top management endorses these documents.

Thus, if you already have an ISO 9000-based system of policies, procedures and work instruc-

tions, you can easily incorporate new documents to cover your workplace safety program. If you are getting ready to implement an ISO 9000 system, then you can add the safety needs to the implementation process (see Exhibit 1).

THE LINK

In ISO 9000-1, the guidelines for the selection and use of the ISO 9000 standards family, it specifically states that you must comply with all applicable safety regulations. Also note that the ISO 9000 standards frequently use the terms "safety," "health," "liability" and "environment." For example, the ISO 9000 standards address product safety through its requirements for design control and design verification. In addition, element 4.9, Process Control, specifies a "suitable working environment." This is widely understood to include suitable environment, health and safety.

If we examine each element in section four of ISO 9001, we can see where most workplace

* Reprinted with permission from *Quality Digest*, May 1995. © 1995 QCI International. Bob Korzak, CQA, CSP, is certification manager for Entela Inc., Quality Systems Registration Division in Grand Rapids, MI. Rick Clements is president of Solution Specialist, located in Alto, MI.

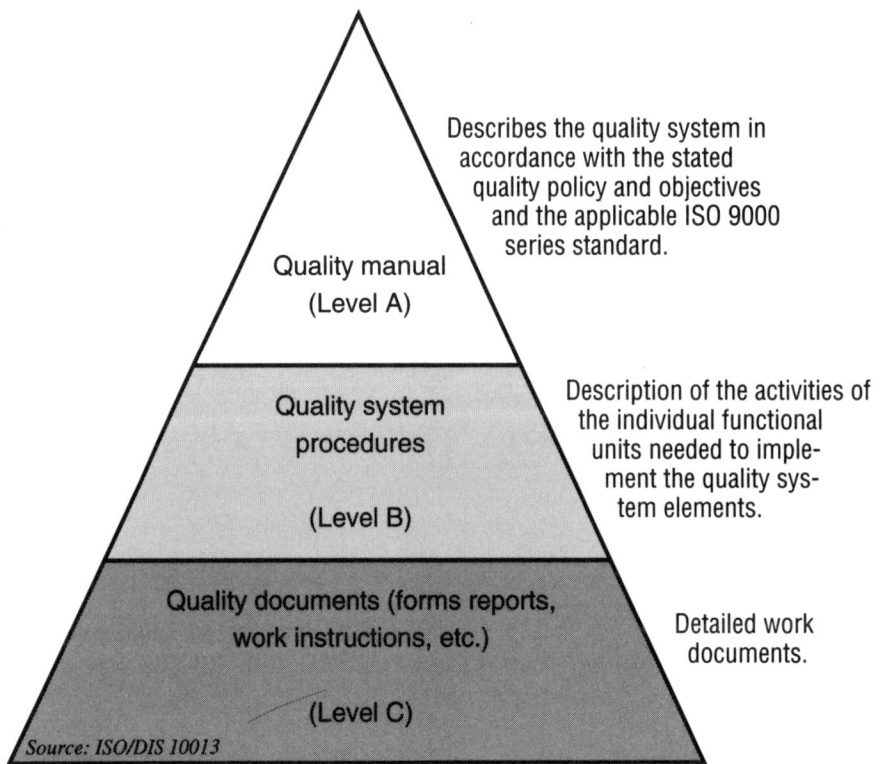

Note: Any document level in this hierarchy may be separate, used with cross-references or combined.

EXHIBIT 1.—TYPICAL QUALITY SYSTEM DOCUMENT HIERARCHY

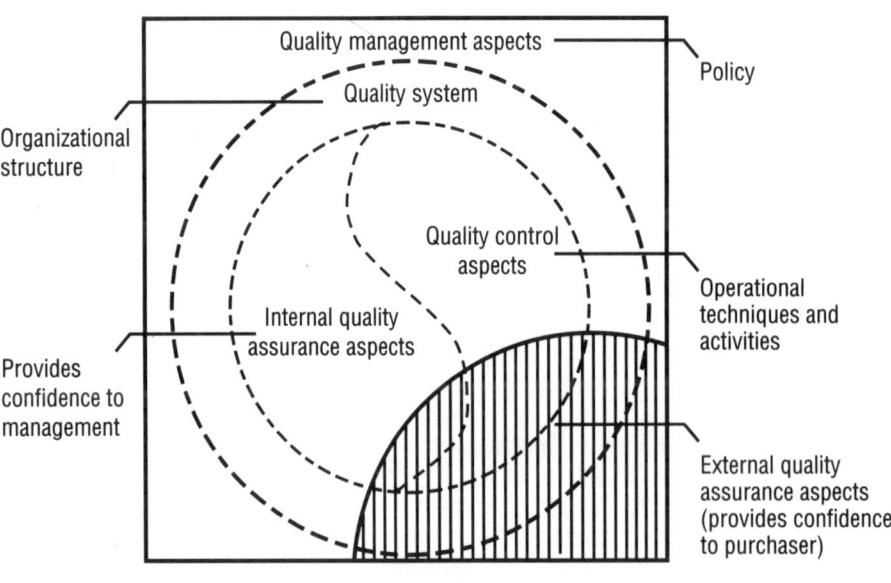

Source: ISO 9000: 1987 (E)

EXHIBIT 2.—DOCUMENTATION STRUCTURE

safety programs can be easily incorporated into the normal implementation plan for a quality-management system (see Exhibits 2 and 3).

LOOKING TO ISO 9001

To see how to implement a workplace safety program at the same time as an ISO 9000 model of quality-management system, let's look at the affected elements in the 1994 edition of ISO 9001.

4.1   Management Responsibility—This section of ISO 9001 establishes the lines of responsibility and the dedication of resources.

When developing organizational charts showing lines of responsibility, incorporate safety responsibilities as well. Include resources for verification of the safety program. As part of the management-review process, look at measurable safety data such as incident rates, site surveys, accident data and the like. Set written goals for compliance and establish continuous improvement.

And make sure to set a regular schedule for reviewing the entire system. Typically, this will take the form of an internal audit that is reported to top management. Top management, in turn, must respond to the finding and improve the management system to move beyond compliance or encourage continuous improvement (see Exhibit 2).

4.2   Quality System— This establishes the overall management system for quality, including procedures and work instructions.

An integral part of a quality system is quality planning. This is where you determine the points in a process for verifying your products' critical characteristics. You could also perform preliminary hazard analysis here. In addition, you could include your safety, health, environment and employee manuals as part of your documentation structure. The level 1 document (policy) for element 4.2 should note this. Establish operational procedure format and work instructions that cover safety precautions (see Exhibit 3).

4.3   Contract Review— The examination of a customer's contract for its implied and stated needs and requirements.

Where customer-supplied material is used to build products, packaging may require specific methods of handling, such as material safety data sheet enclosures and labeling, and Department of Transportation regulations. Some customers may have other safety-related requirements such as nondestructive testing, transportation, in-field set-up and testing. You will need a documented system for handling

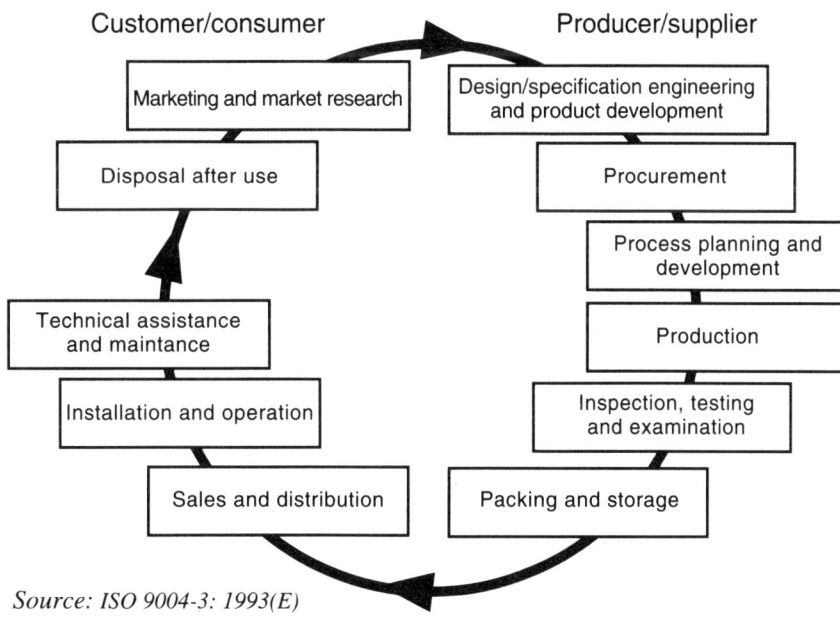

Source: ISO 9004-3: 1993(E)

EXHIBIT 3.—CONTINUOUS IMPROVEMENT CYCLE

these requirements. Such systems should identify potential hazards and preventative measures prior to shipment or commencing work.

4.4 Design Control—The review of the design process for completeness.

You may find that many design requirements include safety standards specific to the product. At this point in the process, you should specify engineering controls and warning labels to be used in the manufacturing process and on the specific product. Such labeling should point out specific product hazards, environmental considerations and safe working methods.

The design review should also include a review of product instructions, catalogs, brochures, legal documents and a quality control plan that includes safety characteristics. In addition, it should include methods such as failure mode-and-effects analysis or fault tree analysis. Be sure to note potential sources of failure and the corrective actions and preventative measures to take.

Next, create and monitor cross-functional teams to address the question of safety and manufacturability. In addition to the product-safety aspects already required, examine possible areas to address involving preliminary hazard analysis for in-plant activities such as stress testing, processing, material incompatibilities, packaging, handling and end-use recyclability or disposal.

4.5 Document and Data Control— The written procedure for authorizing new documents, updating existing documents and ensuring that the right document is in the right place at the proper time.

The same controls for documentation expected in ISO 9001 should also apply to your safety manual's procedures and work instructions. All documentation related to controlling your safety program should be reviewed, approved, signed and dated. A master list of the controlled documents is required. You must know that everyone who needs safety instructions has them at their work site. In addition, you must be able to review changes in standards and regulations, and immediately update all copies of related documents.

4.6 Purchasing— Material MSDS should be considered as a purchase order requirement and treated according to the requirements in section 4.6.

New machinery requirements for ergonomics, safety mechanisms, manuals, test runs, guarding, nationally recognized test lab listing and so on could also be made part of the purchase order requirement. In-plant services purchased from outside suppliers should require specific purchase order data clearly describing the service required and contractor safety requirements.

4.7 Control of Customer-Supplied Product —Goods provided by the customer to be used to create the products sold back to the customer. This includes materials, fixtures, dunnage, tools and measurement equipment from a customer. See 4.3 for how to handle this.

4.8 Product Identification and Traceability—A system must be in place to ensure that all material and product is adequately labeled during processing so that each stage of manufacturing can quickly tell if they have the right materials for a particular job. All flammable and explosive materials should be properly identified as well with UN, DOT or NFPA hazard labels. Routing slips, color codes, sign-off sheets and other methods have been used to meet this requirement. Include process labels, warnings (where applicable) and color coding for issues or as right-to-know regulations. Shelf life is an important consideration because some materials become more reactive or explosive as they deteriorate.

4.9 Process Control—Maintaining a documented system for ensuring the successful processing of materials.

When designing the process system, be sure to include ergonomic factors and to list safety-related requirements, such as improved human factors output, quality of work and efficiencies. When a process is changed, another preliminary hazard analysis may be required. The process safety standard as applied to certain chemical industries requires this activity to be documented and effectively implemented. Also specify your preventive maintenance and predictive maintenance programs.

4.10 and 4.11 Inspection and Testing —When establishing calibration schedules for measurement and test equipment, add to the list items such as fume hoods, fire-protection devices, dB meters and other equipment/ engineering controls used to measure safety-related characteristics. When one of these devices is found to be out of tolerance or in nonconformance, then you must have a written plan to uncover why it happened and how to prevent it from recurring, and an examination of what effects might have happened since the last check. Test software must be controlled and verified prior to use. Many process control/robotics software programs incorporate safety-related hazard potentials.

4.12 Inspection and Test Status—The current test status of a product must be noted so that each stage of production knows that all verification from previous stages has been conducted. Critical safety characteristics/devices should be treated like critical quality characteristics. Each verification should be noted along with the inspector's signature.

4.13 Control of Nonconforming Product—Just like the situation where a quality characteristic is found nonconforming, a nonconforming safety item must be clearly identified and documented. Establish a single method of investigating the cause in advance, with the goal of finding the root cause to prevent recurrence. Problems such as co-mingling of wastes, defective engineering controls or nonconforming raw materials are all potential root causes. Report any root cause to management, and change the safety-management system to prevent a recurrence. Examples include defective personal protective equipment, fire extinguishers, valves and detectors.

4.14 Corrective and Preventive Action—Behavioral studies, near-miss investigations, accident reports, safety audits, surveys and other mechanisms can all prevent safety problems before they occur. Always practice corrective action, tracking and prevention where safety is concerned. In addition, ISO 9001 makes it clear that top management has the ultimate responsibility to make sure that employees take these steps. The responsible area should be in charge of corrective action, and the implement function responsible for verifying effective corrections.

4.15 Handling, Storage, Packaging, Preservation and Delivery—Here, safety measures are more obvious than their cousins, the quality characteristics. Use safety methods such as ergonomics, grounding, stacking heights, safe-handling instructions, environmental-protection equipment and engineering controls where required. Departmental procedures and instructions should specify potential hazards to precautions.

4.16 Control of Quality Records—In the same way quality records must be retained for set periods of time and be retrievable, safety records must also be carefully stored. This includes records such as OSHA 200, safety-audit reports, accident investigations, safety-device inspection, maintenance, corrective-action reports

for safety items and other similar documents. Your level II document (procedure) should specify storage conditions and retention times.

4.17 Internal Quality Audits—Internal safety audits should be conducted at least annually. You can easily incorporate them into the quality-system audit required by ISO 9001. Checklists and questions related to workplace safety can be easily attached to the audit sheets used for internal ISO 9000 audits.

The same key managers interviewed by the ISO 9000 audit team may be required for a safety audit. This holds true for the procedures and records to check: they should be under the same system of control. The only notable difference is that the auditors must have knowledge and/or experience in identifying safety hazards.

4.18 Training—Anyone with a direct relationship to the quality of your product must be trained to the skill and knowledge levels your company's quality plan requires. You can easily include safety criteria to these lists. Specifically, these include training related to right-to-know, lockout tagout, ergonomics, lifting techniques, respirator use and so on. Your training department should analyze the needs and create a list of skills, knowledge and attitudes each person should demonstrate by job title.

4.19 Servicing—Servicing plans for your product should include specific contractor safety procedures, PPE, road-travel restrictions and emergency plans for off-site employees. In addition, installation instructions should include hazard notifications.

4.20 Statistical Techniques—Since your original safety policy and plan noted specific targets and objectives, monitor this data with statistical methods such as control charts, trend analysis, bar charts, correlation studies and designed experiments.

PROACTIVE SAFETY

By utilizing the current drive to implement ISO 9000 across entire industries, safety and quality professionals can incorporate proactive safety programs into their management systems. This could result in several possible benefits, such as:

- Lower insurance rates
- Lower personnel costs
- Higher productivity
- Higher quality

- Reduced worker dissatisfaction
- Increased customer satisfaction
- Reduced exposure to law suits
- Smoother audits with regulatory agencies.

To fully understand the philosophy and implementation of ISO 9000, additional study is required. However, those professionals who strive to gain knowledge of safety-management systems and quality-management systems should succeed in breaking down the barriers perceived to exist between the two disciplines.

Remember that quality cannot exist without safety.

6.3
ISO 14000

CHECKLIST FOR ISO 14001 COMPLIANCE
by Richard B. Clements

The following is a checklist for ISO 14001 compliance to be used as a guide when performing an environmental management system audit.

Audit Checklist (environmental management system)

ISO 14000 Item	Checklist question
4.1 Policy	Is a written environmental policy in existence?
	Was the policy produced and distributed by top management?
	Is the environmental policy appropriate to the nature, scale, and environmental impacts of the company?
	Does the policy contain commitments to the prevention of pollution and does it support continuous improvement?
	Does the policy support a commitment to complying to environmental regulations and customer requirements related to the environment?
	Is there a framework for setting environmental objectives and targets?
	Is there a framework for monitoring environmental objectives and targets?
	Has the policy been implemented, maintained, and communicated to all employees?
	Is the policy available to the public?
4.2 Planning	Does the company have a procedure for identifying the environmental aspects of its activities and product?
	Examine the company's list of environmental aspects.
	Do the environmental objectives of the company match the level of risks related to the list of environmental aspects?
	Is the list of environmental aspects and objectives up to date?
	Is there a procedure to identify and have access to the legal environmental considerations related to the company's activity and products?
	Does each significant level of the company have environmental objectives and targets at appropriate locations?
	Are all environmental objectives and targets consistent with the environmental policy?
	For each objective and target are specific responsibilities documented at every level in the organization? Does this include the means and time frame for completion?
	Are new products or processes and their development included in the environmental management system?

Audit Checklist (environmental management system)

ISO 14000 Item	Checklist question
4.3 Operation and Implementation	Does an organizational chart exist showing roles, responsibilities, and authorities of the environmental management system?
	Are there adequate resources to support the environmental management system?
	Has a management representative been appointed?
	Is there written evidence that the management representative is able to assure the establishment, implementation, and maintenance of requirements related to the environmental system?
	Does the management representative regularly report on the performance of the environmental management system to top management?
	Are training needs identified?
	Are personnel having a job with environmental impacts required to attend appropriate training? Is there a written record of such training? Is there a training schedule?
	Does training emphasize the importance of compliance with the environmental policy and procedures? Are employees aware of the environmental impact of their job function? Are the employees aware that their personal performance can have positive environmental benefits?
	Is emergency preparedness and response part of the required training? Are the employees aware of the consequences of departures from environmental procedures?
	Are there job descriptions outlining the education, training, and experience required for performing tasks that can cause significant environmental impacts?
	Is there a procedure for internal communication between various levels and functions?
	Is there a written procedure for receiving, documenting, and responding to relevant communication from external parties regarding environmental matters?
	Does the company have a procedure for transmitting communications to external parties concerning environmental matters?
	Does the company have a level 1 environmental management manual? Does a level 2 manual exist?
	Is there a written procedure for the control of key documents within the environmental management system?
	Does this procedure for document control include a list of where controlled documents can be located, that the documents are periodically reviewed for adequacy, the current version of a document is in the appropriate locations, obsolete documents are quickly removed from the system, and that some obsolete documents can be retained for legal or reference purposes?
	Looking at a sample of controlled documents, are they legible, correctly dated, readily identifiable, maintained in an orderly manner, and retained for a designated period of time?
	Are the procedures and responsibilities for the establishment and maintenance of new or revised documents established?
	Is there a documented list of operations and activities directly related with the environmental impacts identified by the company? Do these operations and activities fall within the scope of the company's environmental policy, objectives and targets?
	Are these operations and activities planned and maintained with procedures and work instruction to insure that there are no deviations from the environmental policies, objectives, and targets? Is there a stipulated operating criteria in the written procedures and work instruction for operations?
	Has the company established a written procedure for identifying the significant environmental aspects of the goods and services used by the organization (i.e. life-cycle assessment)? Are these environmental aspects also communicated to suppliers and contractors?
	Has the company identified any situation where there is a potential for accidents or emergency situations creating significant environmental impacts? Is there a written procedure for emergency preparedness and response?
	Does the company review its emergency preparedness and response procedures regularly? After an accident or emergency, does the company perform a review of the emergency preparedness and response procedure? Is this procedure ever tested?

Audit Checklist (environmental management system)

ISO 14000 Item	Checklist question
4.4 Checking and corrective action	Does the company have a written procedure for monitoring and measuring key characteristics which have significant impacts on the environment? Are the measurements recorded and compared to objectives and targets?
	Is the monitoring equipment maintained and calibrated? Are records kept for equipment maintenance and calibration?
	Is there a procedure for evaluating compliance with relevant environmental regulations?
	Is there a procedure for investigating non-conformance and taking actions to mitigate the environmental impacts that could result? Has a single job title been identified as the ultimate authority for this procedure?
	Are corrective and preventive actions taken appropriate to the size of the problem and the level of risk involved? Is there a written record of the corrective and preventive actions?
	Does the company change its procedures and processes based on corrective and preventive recommendations? Are these changes documented?
	Is there a written procedure for the identification, maintenance, and disposal of environmental records? Are the environmental records legible, identifiable, and traceable to their related activity, product, or service? Are the environmental records stored to prevent deterioration or loss? Is there an established retention time?
	Is there a written procedure to establish and maintain a system of internal auditing of the environmental management system? Does the procedure establish an internal auditing system to assure the environmental management system conforms to planned activities, has been properly implemented, is properly maintained, and are these findings reported to management?
	Is there a written audit schedule to which the company conforms to completely?
	Does the internal audit procedure document the method for establishing the audit scope, audit frequency, the methodologies to use, how to report results, and the responsibilities of the audit team?
4.5 Management review	Does the company's management regularly review the entire environmental management system? Is the environmental management system checked for its suitability, adequacy, and effectiveness?
	Is the management review documented? Did previous management reviews consider changes in policies or objectives based on audit results, changing circumstance, or the need for continuous improvement?

Appendices

The following appendices represent a collection of information of great value to any quality professional. Here you will find numerous sources of further information, resources, and events. All of this is designed to help you develop yourself and your quality department.

Specifically, the following information is presented to help you locate new information, knowledge, skills, resources, and other colleagues with which you can communicate. The competitive quality manager needs to network with professional societies, consultants, registrars, and other quality professionals to keep in touch with the latest developments in this field.

As mentioned at the beginning of this book, you can also interact directly with the authors. We have provided several ways for you to communicate with us. In return, we are providing computer based services that will update the information presented in the following appendices. In that way, you can always be up to date.

In addition, if you discover an omission, or need for a correction, please feel free to forward that information to our attention.

Our internet e-mail address is: isogroup@cris.com

Our World Wide Web Page is located at: http://www.cris.com/~isogroup

Our fax number is: (616) 891-9114

Our computer bulletin board system can be reached at: (616) 891-9433 [please set your communication software to 8 data bits, no parity, 1 stop bit and set your terminal emulation to ANSI]

APPENDIX A - UPCOMING EVENTS

The following is a list of upcoming conferences and events related to quality.

Please contact the following organizations by phone, mail, or FAX to confirm the location, dates, and other particulars of a conference. If the date of the conference has already passed, you can still contact the sponsor to obtain information on next year's event.

10th Annual Quality Conference

Location: Rockford, IL
Date: February 22 - 24, 1996

Sponsor: ASQC Section 1205
ASQC Conference and Exhibits Department
PO Box 3005
Milwaukee, WI 53201-9402

Registration Phone: (800) 248-1946
Contact Person: Roy Ervin, Dolores Ford, Dom Vitale

12th Annual International Strategic Management Conference

Location: Atlanta, GA
Date: April 28 through May 1, 1996

Sponsor: Intl. Society for Strategic Mgt. and Planning
The Strategic Leadership Forum
P.O. Box 70
Oxford, OH 45056-0070
USA

Registration Phone: (312) 644-0829
Contact Person: Jenny

12th Annual Productivity-Quality Conference

Location: Dayton, OH
Date: October 23 & 24

Sponsor: PQ Systems
PO Box 10
Dayton, OH 45475-0010

Registration Phone: 800-777-3020
Registration FAX: 513-885-2252

16th Aerospace Testing Seminar

Location: Manhattan Beach, California
Date: March 12 - 13, 1996

Sponsor: Institute of Environmental Sciences
Institute of Environmental Sciences
940 E Northwest Highway
Mount Prospect, IL 60056

Registration Phone: 708-255-1561
Registration FAX: 708-255-1699

16th Annual Conference on Control, Audit, and Security of Information Systems

Location: Boston, MA
Date: October 14 - 18, 1996

Sponsor: MIS Training Institute
498 Concord Street
Framingham, MA 01701-2357

Registration Phone: 508-879-7999
Registration FAX: 508-872-1153
Contact Person: Pam Bissett

1996 Annual Meeting of the Psychometric Society

Location: Baniff, Alberta, Canada
Date: June 27 - 30, 1996

252 Bloor Street West
Toronto, Ontario M5S 1V6
Canada

Registration FAX: 416-926-4725
Contact Person: Shizuhiko Nishisatom OISE

1996 Joint Statistical Meetings

Location: Chicago, IL
Date: August 4 - 8, 1996

Sponsor: ASA, IMS, ENAR, and WNAR
1429 Duke Street
Alexandria, VA 22314-3402

Registration Phone: 703-684-1221
Registration FAX: 703-684-2037

1996 Quality Conference

Location: New York City, New York
Date: March 19 & 20, 1996

Sponsor: National Institute of Standards and Technology
The Conference Board, Inc.
PO Box 4026 Church Street Station
New York, NY 10261-7014

Registration Phone: 212-759-0900
Registration FAX: 212-980-7014

19th Space Simulation Conference

Location: Baltimore, Maryland
Date: October 28 - 31, 1996

Sponsor: Institute of Environmental Sciences
Institute of Environmental Sciences
940 E. Northwest Highway
Mount Prospect, IL 60056

Registration Phone: 708-255-1561
Registration FAX: 708-255-1699

28e journees de statistique de Association pour la statistique et ses utilisations

Location: Quebec City, Quebec, Canada
Date: May 27 - 30, 1996

Sponsor: Bureau de la statistique du Quebec,
Statistique Canada
Societe statisique de France, Societe statistique
du Canada
Department de mathematiques et de statistique
Universite Laval
Sainte-Foy, Quebec G1K 7P4
Canada

Registration Phone: 418-656-5280
Registration FAX: 418-656-2817
Contact Person: Christian Genest

40th EOQ Annual Congress

Location: Berlin, Germany
Date: September 9-13, 1996

Sponsor: European Organization for Quality
Deutsche Gesselschaft fur Qualitat e.V.
August-Schanz-Strasse 21A
Frankfurt am Main, D-60433
Germany

Contact Person: Secretariat of Congress

42nd Annual Technical Meeting & Exposition

Location: Orlando, Florida
Date: May 12 - 17, 1996

Sponsor: Institute of Environmental Sciences
Institute of Environmental Sciences
940 E. Northwest Highway
Mount Prospect, IL 60056

Registration Phone: 708-255-1561
Registration FAX: 708-255-1699

50th Annual Quality Congress & Exposition (AQC)

Location: Chicago, IL
Date: May 13 - 15, 1996

Sponsor: ASQC
ASQC Conference and Exhibits Department
PO Box 3005
Milwaukee, WI 53201-9402

Registration Phone: (800) 248-1946
Contact Person: ASQC Headquarters

7th Annual Super Strategies

Location: Atlanta, GA
Date: April 22 -26, 1996

Sponsor: MIS Training Institute
498 Concord Street
Framingham, MA 01701-2357

Registration Phone: 508-879-7999
Registration FAX: 508-872-1153
Contact Person: Pam Bissett

7th Annual TPM Conference & Exposition

Location: Nashville, TN
Date: September 24 - 26, 1996

Sponsor: Productivity
101 Merritt
7 Corporate Park
Norwalk, CT 06851

Registration Phone: 203-846-3777
Registration FAX: 203-846-6883

9th Annual Software Technology Conference

Location: Salt Lake City, Utah
Date: April 27 - May 3, 1996

Sponsor: Society for Software Quality
PO Box 86958
San Diego, CA 92138-6958

AAAS Conference

Location: Baltimore, MD
Date: February 8 - 13, 1996

Sponsor: American Association for the Advancement of Science
A AAS Meetings Office
1333 H Street NW
Washington, DC 20005

Registration Phone: 202-326-6450
Registration FAX: 202-289-4021

Air Force Quality Symposium 1996

Location: Montgomery, Alabama
Date: To be determined

Communications Events, Inc.
40 Richards Avenue
Norwalk, CT 06854

Registration Phone: 203-855-3000
Registration FAX: 203-855-3003
Contact Person: John W. Goeller

American Industrial Hygiene Conf & Expo

Location: Washington, D.C.
Date: May 18 - 24, 1996

Registration Phone: 703-849-8888
Registration FAX: 703-207-3561

American Productivity & Quality Center Conference

Location: Denver, CO
Date: July 15 - 19, 1996 (tentative)

Sponsor: American Productivity & Quality Center
International Benchmarking Clearinghouse
123 North Post Oak Lane 3rd Floor
Houston, TX 77024-7797

Registration Phone: 713-685-4666
Registration FAX: 713-681-5321
Contact Person: Carla Murray-Wolfe

American Productivity & Quality Center Conference

Location: Houston, TX
Date: Oct 28 - Nov 1, 1996 (tentative)

Sponsor: American Productivity & Quality Center
International Benchmarking Clearinghouse
123 North Post Oak Lane 3rd Floor
Houston, TX 77024-7797

Registration Phone: 713-685-4666
Registration FAX: 713-681-5321
Contact Person: Carla Murray-Wolfe

American Productivity & Quality Center Conference

Location: Houston, TX
Date: April 1 - 5, 1996 (tentative)

Sponsor: American Productivity & Quality Center
International Benchmarking Clearinghouse
123 North Post Oak Lane   3rd Floor
Houston, TX 77024-7797

Registration Phone: 713-685-4666
Registration FAX: 713-681-5321
Contact Person: Carla Murray-Wolfe

Auditmation

Location: Chicago, IL
Date: June 23 - 26, 1996

Sponsor: MIS Training Institute
498 Concord Street
Framingham, MA 01701-2357

Registration Phone: 508-879-7999
Registration FAX: 508-872-1153
Contact Person: Pam Bissett

Automated Manufacturing 96

Location: Greenville, SC
Date: April 23 to 25, 1996

Sponsor: Automated Manufacturing
South Carolina Board for Tech. and Comprehensive Ed.
111 Executive Center Dr.
Columbia, SC 29210
USA

Contact Person: Sam Jenkins

AutoTech

Location: Cobo Hall, Detroit, Michigan
Date: September 17 - 19, 1996

Sponsor: Automotive Industry Action Group
26200 Lahser Road
Suite 200
Southfield, MI 48034

Registration Phone: 810-358-3570
Registration FAX: 810-358-3253

COMPSTAT 96 - XII Symposium on Computational Statistics

Location: Barcelona, Spain
Date: August 26-30, 1996

Sponsor: International Assoc. for Statistical Computing
Dept of Statistics
Avada. Diagonal 647

Barcelona, 08028
Spain

Contact Person: Prof. Albert Prat

Conference on Applied Statistics in Agriculture

Location: Manhattan, Kansas
Date: April 28 - 30, 1996

Sponsor: Kansas State University
Kansas State University Dickens Hall
Department of Statistics
Manhattan, KS 66506-0802

Registration Phone: 913-532-6883
Registration FAX: 913-532-7736
Contact Person: James R. Schwenke or George
A. Milliken

Conference on Highly Structured Stochastic Systems

Location: Rebild, Denmark
Date: May 19 -24, 1996

Sponsor: European Science Foundation's
Network on Highly Structured
Stochastic Systems Steffen Lauritzen
Aalborg University
Denmark

Conference on Software Engineering Education (CSEE)

Location: Daytona Beach, FL
Date: April 22 -24, 1996

Sponsor: Carnegie Mellon University
Software Engineering Institute
4500 Fifth Avenue
Pittsburgh, PA 15213

Registration Phone: 412-268-6467
Registration FAX: 412-268-5758
Contact Person: Rhonda Green

Conference Software Engineering Process Group (SEPG)

Location: Atlantic City, NJ
Date: May 20 - 23. 1996

Sponsor: Carnegie Mellon University
Software Engineering Institute
4500 Fifth Avenue
Pittsburgh, PA 15213

Registration Phone: 412-268-6467
Registration FAX: 4122-268-5758
Contact Person: Rhonda Green

EDMS/PDM Spring 96

Location: Houston, Texas
Date: February 26 - 29, 1996

Kalthoff International
8260 Northcreek Drive
Suite 250, Cincinnati OH
45236

Registration Phone: 513-794-3367

Eighth Annual National Forum on Quality Improvement in Healthcare

Location: New Orleans, LA
Date: December 4 to 7, 1996

Sponsor: Institute for Healthcare Improvement
One Exeter Plaza
Ninth Floor
Boston, MA 02116
USA

Emergency Management Conference

Location: Washington, D.C.
Date: June 6 - 13, 1996

Sponsor: MIS Training Institute
498 Concord Street
Framingham, MA 01701-2357

Registration Phone: 508-879-7999
Registration FAX: 508-872-1153
Contact Person: Pam Bissett

Euro-Star 96

Location: Dublin, Ireland
Date: November 25 to 28, 1996

Sponsor: SQE
Contact Person: Wayne Middleton

FABTECH Conference & Exposition

Location: Rosemont, Illinois
Date: October 6 - 9, 1997

Sponsor: Society of Manufacturing Engineers &
Fabricators & Manufactures Association, Int.
833 Featherstone Road
Rockford, IL 61107-9909

Registration FAX: 815-399-8618
Contact Person: Mark Hoper

FABTECH East 96

Location: Philadelphia, PA
Date: April 23 - 25, 1996

Sponsor: Fabricators & Manufacturers
Association International
833 Featherstone Road
Rockford, IL 61107-9909

Registration Phone: 815-399-8700
Registration FAX: 815-399-7279
Contact Person: Mark Hoper

FABTECH West 96

Location: San Jose, California
Date: October 29 - 31, 1996

Sponsor:
Fabricators & Manufacturers Association
International
833 Featherstone Road
Rockford, IL 61107-9909

Registration Phone: 815-399-8700
Registration FAX: 815-399-7279
Contact Person: Mark Hoper

Fifth Annual Service Quality Conference

Location: New Orleans, LA
Date: April 1996

Sponsor: ASQC
ASQC Conference and Exhibits Department
PO Box 3005
Milwaukee, WI 53201-9402

Registration Phone: (800) 248-1946

Fifth Islamic Countries Conference on Statistical Science (ICCS-V)

Location: Malang, Indonesia
Date: August 24 - 29, 1996

Brawijaya Universtiy
Jl. Majen Haryono No. 169
Malang, Indonesia 65145
Indonesia

Registration Phone: 62-341-51611
Registration FAX: 62-341-82124/65420
Contact Person: Dr. Waego Hadi Nugroho

Fifty-Second Deming Conference on Applied Statistics

Location: Atlantic City, NJ
Date: December 8 - 14, 1996

Sponsor: ASQC
Metropolitan Section, ASQC
42 Whitewood Drive
Morris Plains, NJ 07950-3329

Registration Phone: 908-820-6904
Contact Person: Jenny Wong

GEMI 96

Location: Arlington, Virginia
Date: March 20 - 21, 1996

Sponsor: Global Environmental Management
Initiative
1000 Connecticut Avenue NW
Suite 802
Washington, DC 30036

Registration Phone: 202-429-0776
Registration FAX: 202-466-8554
Contact Person: Carlene Bahler

Hannover Messe 96

Location: Hannover, Germany
Date: April 22 - 27, 1996

Sponsor: Hannover Fairs USA, Inc.
103 Carnegie Center
Princeton, NJ 08540

Registration Phone: 609-987-1202
Registration FAX: 609-987-0092

Instrument Society of America Conference 96

Location: Chicago, IL
Date: October 7-10, 1996

Sponsor: ISA
67 Alexander Dr.
P.O. Box 12277
Research Triangle Park, NC 27709
USA

International Biometric Society (ENAR) Spring Meeting

Location: Richmond, VA
Date: March 17 - 20, 1996

Sponsor: Eastern North American Region of the
International Biometric Society
Dept of Biostatistics, Box 32
Medical College of Virginia
Richmond, VA 23298-0032

Registration Phone: 804-828-9824
Registration FAX: 804-828-9000
Contact Person: Chris Gennings

International Conference on Applied Statistics in Business and Economics

Location: Moscow, Russia
Date: To be determined

Sponsor:
39 Myasnitskaya Str
Moscow, Russia 103450
Russia

Registration Phone: 095-207-48-51
Registration FAX: 095-207-45-92
Contact Person: Professor M. Korolev

International Conference on Problems of Statistical Education

Location: St. Petersburg, Russia
Date: July 21 - 23, 1996

Sponsor:
St. Petersburg University of Economics and
Finance
30/32 Griboedov Kanal
St Petersburg, Russia 191023
Russia

Registration Phone: 812-110-55-94
Registration FAX: 812-247-30-45
Contact Person: Professor I. Elisseeva

Intl. Conference on Probablistic Safety Assessment and Management

Location: Crete, Greece
Date: June 24-28, 1996

Sponsor: IAPSAM
Commission of the European Communities, Joint
Research Centre
Institute for Systems Engineering and Informatics
Ispra (VA), I-21020
Italy

Contact Person: Dr. P. Carlo Cacciabue

ISA/96 International Conference and Exhibition

Location: Chicago, IL
Date: October 7 - 10, 1996

Sponsor: International Society for Measurement
and Control ISA

67 Alexander Drive
P.O. Box 12277
Researach Triangle Park, NC 27709

Registration Phone: 919-549-8411
Registration FAX: 919-549-8288

Kullback Memorial Research Conference

Location: Washington, D.C.
Date: May 24 - 25, 1996

Sponsor: George Washington University
Department of Statistics
Funger Hall
Washington, DC

Registration Phone: 202-994-6350
Registration FAX: 202-994-6917

Maintenance Miracle (Master Series)

Location: Milwaukee, OR
Date: February 13 - 16, 1996

Sponsor: Productivity
101 Merritt
7 Corporate Park
Norwalk, CT 06851

Registration Phone: 203-846-3777
Registration FAX: 203-846-6883

Measurement Science Conference

Location: Anaheim, California
Date: January 25 - 26, 1996

Sponsor: ASQC Measurement Quality Division
Contact Person: Ray Vurpillant

Medical Design & Manufacturing

Location: Minneapolis, Minnesota
Date: October 30 - 31, 1996

Sponsor: Canon Communications, Inc.
3340 Ocean Park Blvd Suite 1000
Santa Monica, CA 90405-3216

Registration Phone: 310-392-5509
Registration FAX: 310-392-1557
Contact Person: Mary Gordon

Medical Design & Manufacturing

Location: New York, New York
Date: June 4 - 6, 1996

Sponsor: Canon Communications Inc
3340 Ocean Park Blvd Suite 1000
Santa Monica, CA 90405-3216

Registration Phone: 310-392-5509
Registration FAX: 310-392-1557
Contact Person: Mary Gordon

Minnesota Quality Conference

Location: Minneapolis, Minnesota
Date: March 7 - 8, 1996

Sponsor: ASQC Section 1203

Registration Phone: (800) 248-1946
Contact Person: Minnesota Section

Minnesota Quality Conference - Exploring Quality

Location: Minneapolis, Minnesota
Date: March 5 - 6, 1995

Sponsor: ASQC
Minnesota Section - ASQC
PO Box 9370
North St. Paul, MN 55109-0370

Contact Person: Minnesota Section - Region 12

Ninth International Software Quality Week

Location: San Francisco, CA
Date: May 21-24, 1996

Sponsor: Software Research Institute
625 Third Street
San Francisco, CA 94107-1997
USA

Registration Phone: (415) 957-1441
Contact Person: Rita Bral

Open Systems

Location: Orlando, FL
Date: March 3 - 7, 1996

Sponsor: MIS Training Institute
498 Concord Street
Framingham, MA 01701-2357

Registration Phone: 508-879-7999
Registration FAX: 508-872-1153
Contact Person: Pam Bissett

QS-9000 Conference

Location: To be determined
Date: February 27 - 29, 1996

Sponsor: Global Business Research

Registration Phone: 212-645-4226
Registration FAX: 212-645-4490
Contact Person: Ann Healey

Quality Council of Alberta - Second Annual Conference

Location: Edmonton, Alberta, Canada
Date: August 21 - 23, 1996

Sponsor: Quality Council of Alberta
1531, 10060 Jasper Avenue
Edmonton, Alberta T5J 3R8
Canada

Registration Phone: 403-423-6878
Registration FAX: 403-426-1509
Contact Person: Kari Taylor

Reliability and Maintainability Symposium

Location: Las Vegas, Nevada
Date: January 22 - 25, 1996

Sponsor: AIAA, ASQC, IEEE, IES, IIE, SAE, SOLE, SRE, SSS
Institute of Environmental Sciences
940 E. Northwest Highway
Mount Prospect, IL 60056

Registration Phone: 708-255-1561
Registration FAX: 708-255-1699
Contact Person: Carol San Filippo

Risk Conference

Location: To be determined
Date: (date has not been determined yet)

Sponsor: Carnegie Mellon University
Software Engineering Institute
4500 Fifth Avenue
Pittsburgh, PA 15213

Registration Phone: 412-268-6467
Registration FAX: 412-268-5758
Contact Person: Rhonda Green

Saturn Corporation

Location: Spring Hill, TN
Date: January 23 - 25, 1996

Sponsor: Productivity
101 Merritt
7 Corporate Park
Norwalk, CT 06851

Registration Phone: 203-846-3777
Registration FAX: 203-846-6883

Scanning 96

Location: Monterey, CA
Date: April 9 to 12, 1996

Sponsor: Foundation for Advances in Med. and Sci.
P.O. Box 832
Mahwah, NJ 07430-0832
USA

Contact Person: Mary Sullivan

Second International Symposium on Spatial Accuracy Assessment in Natural Resources and Environmental Sciences

Location: Fort Collins, CO
Date: May 21 - 23, 1996

Sponsor: Colorado State University

Southwest Annual Resource Management Conference

Location: Arlington, TX
Date: May 22 -23, 1996

Sponsor: APICS; Greater Fort Worth Area Chapter, Automation and Robotics Research Institute, University of Texas at Arlington
Automation and Robotics Research Institute
7300 Jack Newell Blvd South
Forth Worth, TX 76118

Registration Phone: 817-273-3530
Registration FAX: 817-794-5801
Contact Person: Professor Joseph Sarkis, PhD., CPIM

Stat expo Centre des congres, Cite des Sciences et de industrie

Location: La Villette, Paris, France
Date: April 10 - 12, 1996

Sponsor: EUROSTAT
DSI
51, rue ledru Rollin
Irvy sur Seine, France 94853
France

Registration Phone: 33 1 46709868
Registration FAX: 33 1 46709780
Contact Person: Elodie Creuzet

Statistical Challenges in Modern Astronomy II

Location: University Park, Pennsylvania
Date: June 2 - 5, 1996

Sponsor: Pennsylvania State University
Pennsylvania State University
319 Classroom Building
Universtiy Park, PA 16802

Registration Phone: 814-863-2837
Registration FAX: 814-863-7114
Contact Person: Gutti Jogesh Babu

The 18th International Biometric Conference

Location: Amsterdam, The Netherlands
Date: July 1 - 5, 1996

Sponsor: International Biometric Society
808 - 17th Street NW
Suite 200
Washington, DC 20006

Registration Phone: 202-223-9669
Registration FAX: 202-223-9569

The 32nd Annual Meeting of the Drug Information Association

Location: San Diego, CA
Date: June 6 - 12, 1996

Sponsor: Drug Information Association
Drug Information Association
PO Box 3113
Maple Glen, PA 19002

Registration Phone: 215-628-2288

The Census Bureau's 1996 Annual Research Conference (ARC 1996)

Location: Arlington, Virginia
Date: March 17 - 21, 1996

Sponsor: ARC Conference
Office of the Director
Bureau of the Census
Washington, DC 20233

Registration Phone: 301-457-3408
Registration FAX: 301-457-3682
Contact Person: Ms. Maxine Anderson-Brown

Training 96 Conference & Expo

Location: Atlanta, GA
Date: January 28 - February 1, 1996

Sponsor: Lakewood Conferences
50 South Ninth Street
Minneapolis, MN 55402

Registration Phone: 800-707-7792
Registration FAX: 612-340-4819

Training Directors' Forum Conference

Location: Phoenix, Arizona
Date: May 5 - 8, 1996

Sponsor: Lakewood Conferences
50 South Ninth Street
Minneapolis, MN 55402

Registration Phone: 1-800-707-7792
Registration FAX: 612-340-4819

University of Minnesota Conference on Inference and Applications Honoring the 25th Year of the School of Statistics

Location: Minneapolis, Minnesota
Date: June 22 & 23, 1996

Sponsor: School of Statistics
University of Minnesota

Registration Phone: 612-625-7030
Contact Person: Frank B. Martin

Month to month Calendar of Quality Conferences

The following is the same listing of conferences related to quality, organized by month. If you have some time in a given month, perhaps there will be a conference in a location near you.

January

Reliability and Maintainability Symposium

Location: Las Vegas, Nevada
Date: January 22 - 25, 1996

Sponsor: AIAA, ASQC, IEEE, IES, IIE, SAE, SOLE, SRE, SSS
Institute of Environmental Sciences
940 E. Northwest Highway
Mount Prospect, IL 60056

Registration Phone: 708-255-1561
Registration FAX: 708-255-1699
Contact Person: Carol San Filippo

Saturn Corporation

Location: Spring Hill, TN
Date: January 23 - 25, 1996

Sponsor: Productivity
101 Merritt
7 Corporate Park
Norwalk, CT 06851

Registration Phone: 203-846-3777
Registration FAX: 203-846-6883

Measurement Science Conference

Location: Anaheim, California
Date: January 25 - 26, 1996

Sponsor: ASQC Measurement Quality Division
Contact Person: Ray Vurpillant

Training 96 Conference & Expo

Location: Atlanta, GA
Date: January 28 - February 1, 1996

Sponsor: Lakewood Conferences
50 South Ninth Street
Minneapolis, MN 55402

Registration Phone: 800-707-7792
Registration FAX: 612-340-4819

February

AAAS Conference

Location: Baltimore, MD
Date: February 8 - 13, 1996

Sponsor: American Association for the Advancement of Science
A AAS Meetings Office
1333 H Street NW
Washington, DC 20005

Registration Phone: 202-326-6450
Registration FAX: 202-289-4021

Maintenance Miracle (Master Series)

Location: Milwaukee, OR
Date: February 13 - 16, 1996

Sponsor: Productivity
101 Merritt

7 Corporate Park
Norwalk, CT 06851

Registration Phone: 203-846-3777
Registration FAX: 203-846-6883

10th Annual Quality Conference

Location: Rockford, IL
Date: February 22 - 24, 1996

Sponsor: ASQC Section 1205
ASQC Conference and Exhibits Department
PO Box 3005
Milwaukee, WI 53201-9402

Registration Phone: (800) 248-1946
Contact Person: Roy Ervin, Dolores Ford, Dom
Vitale

EDMS/PDM Spring 96

Location: Houston, Texas
Date: February 26 - 29, 1996

Kalthoff International
8260 Northcreek Drive
Suite 250, Cincinnati OH
45236

Registration Phone: 513-794-3367

QS-9000 Conference

Location: To be determined
Date: February 27 - 29, 1996

Sponsor: Global Business Research

Registration Phone: 212-645-4226
Registration FAX: 212-645-4490
Contact Person: Ann Healey

March

Open Systems

Location: Orlando, FL
Date: March 3 - 7, 1996

Sponsor: MIS Training Institute
498 Concord Street
Framingham, MA 01701-2357

Registration Phone: 508-879-7999
Registration FAX: 508-872-1153
Contact Person: Pam Bissett

Minnesota Quality Conference - Exploring Quality

Location: Minneapolis, Minnesota
Date: March 5 - 6, 1995

Sponsor: ASQC
Minnesota Section - ASQC
PO Box 9370
North St Paul, MN 55109-0370

Contact Person: Minnesota Section - Region 12

Minnesota Quality Conference

Location: Minneapolis, Minnesota
Date: March 7 - 8, 1996

Sponsor: ASQC Section 1203

Registration Phone: (800) 248-1946
Contact Person: Minnesota Section

16th Aerospace Testing Seminar

Location: Manhattan Beach, California
Date: March 12 - 13, 1996

Sponsor: Institute of Environmental Sciences
940 E. Northwest Highway
Mount Prospect, IL 60056

Registration Phone: 708-255-1561
Registration FAX: 708-255-1699

The Census Bureau's 1996 Annual Research Conference (ARC 1996)

Location: Arlington, Virginia
Date: March 17 - 21, 1996

Sponsor: ARC Conference
Office of the Director
Bureau of the Census
Washington, DC 20233

Registration Phone: 301-457-3408
Registration FAX: 301-457-3682
Contact Person: Ms. Maxine Anderson-Brown

International Biometric Society (ENAR) Spring Meeting

Location: Richmond, VA
Date: March 17 - 20, 1996

Sponsor: Eastern North American Region of the
Internation Biometric Society

Dept of Biostatistics, Box 32
Medical College of Virginia
Richmond, VA 23298-0032

Registration Phone: 804-828-9824
Registration FAX: 804-828-9000
Contact Person: Chris Gennings

1996 Quality Conference

Location: New York City, New York
Date: March 19 & 20, 1996

Sponsor: National Institute of Standards and
Technology
The Conference Board, Inc.
PO Box 4026 Church Street Station
New York, NY 10261-7014

Registration Phone: 212-759-0900
Registration FAX: 212-980-7014

GEMI 96

Location: Arlington, Virginia
Date: March 20 -21, 1996

Sponsor: Global Environmental Management
Initiative
1000 Connecticut Avenue NW
Suite 802
Washington, DC 30036

Registration Phone: 202-429-0776
Registration FAX: 202-466-8554
Contact Person: Carlene Bahler

April

Fifth Annual Service Quality Conference

Location: New Orleans, LA
Date: April 1996

Sponsor: ASQC
ASQC Conference and Exhibits Department
PO Box 3005
Milwaukee, WI 53201-9402

Registration Phone: (800) 248-1946

American Productivity & Quality Center Conference

Location: Houston, TX
Date: April 1 - 5, 1996 (tentative)

Sponsor: American Productivity & Quality Center
International Benchmarking Clearinghouse

123 North Post Oak Lane 3rd Floor
Houston, TX 77024-7797

Registration Phone: 713-685-4666
Registration FAX: 713-681-5321
Contact Person: Carla Murray-Wolfe

Scanning 96

Location: Monterey, CA
Date: April 9-12, 1996

Sponsor: Foundation for Advances in Med. and
Sci.
P.O. Box 832
Mahwah, NJ 07430-0832
USA

Contact Person: Mary Sullivan

Stat expo Centre des congres, Cite des Sciences et de industrie

Location: La Villette, Paris, France
Date: April 10 - 12, 1996

Sponsor: EUROSTAT
DSI
51, rue ledru Rollin
Irvy sur Seine, France 94853
France

Registration Phone: 33 1 46709868
Registration FAX: 33 1 46709780
Contact Person: Elodie Creuzet

Conference on Software Engineering Education (CSEE)

Location: Daytona Beach, FL
Date: April 22 -24, 1996

Sponsor: Carnegie Mellon University
Software Engineering Institute
4500 Fifth Avenue
Pittsburgh, PA 15213

Registration Phone: 412-268-6467
Registration FAX: 4122-268-5758
Contact Person: Rhonda Green

7th Annual Super Strategies

Location: Atlanta, GA
Date: April 22 - 26, 1996

Sponsor: MIS Training Institute
498 Concord Street
Framingham, MA 01701-2357

Registration Phone: 508-879-7999
Registration FAX: 508-872-1153
Contact Person: Pam Bissett

Hannover Messe 96

Location: Hannover, Germany
Date: April 22 - 27, 1996

Sponsor: Hannover Fairs USA, Inc.
103 Carnegie Center
Princeton, NJ 08540

Registration Phone: 609-987-1202
Registration FAX: 609-987-0092

FABTECH East 96

Location: Philadelphia, PA
Date: April 23 - 25, 1996

Fabricators & Manufacturers Association International
833 Featherstone Road
Rockford, IL 61107-9909

Registration Phone: 815-399-8700
Registration FAX: 815-399-7279
Contact Person: Mark Hoper

Automated Manufacturing 96

Location: Greenville, SC
Date: April 23-25, 1996

Sponsor: Automated Manufacturing
South Carolina Board for Tech. and Comprehensive Ed.
111 Executive Center Dr.
Columbia, SC 29210
USA

Contact Person: Sam Jenkins

9th Annual Software Technology Conference

Location: Salt Lake City, Utah
Date: April 27 - May 3, 1996

Sponsor: Society for Software Quality
PO Box 86958
San Diego, CA 92138-6958

12th Annual International Strategic Management Conference

Location: Atlanta, GA
Date: April 28 through May 1, 1996

Sponsor: Intl. Society for Strategic Mgt. and Planning
The Strategic Leadership Forum
P.O. Box 70
Oxford, OH 45056-0070
USA

Registration Phone: (312) 644-0829

Conference on Applied Statistics in Agriculture

Location: Manhattan, Kansas
Date: April 28 - 30, 1996

Sponsor: Kansas State University
Kansas State University Dickens Hall
Department of Statistics
Manhattan, KS 66506-0802

Registration Phone: 913-532-6883
Registration FAX: 913-532-7736
Contact Person: James R. Schwenke or George A. Milliken

May

Training Directors' Forum Conference

Location: Phoenix, Arizonia
Date: May 5 - 8, 1996

Sponsor: Lakewood Conferences
50 South Ninth Street
Minneapolis, MN 55402

Registration Phone: 1-800-707-7792
Registration FAX: 612-340-4819

42nd Annual Technical Meeting & Exposition

Location: Orlando, Florida
Date: May 12 - 17, 1996

Sponsor: Institute of Environmental Sciences
Institute of Environmental Sciences
940 E. Northwest Highway
Mount Prospect, IL 60056

Registration Phone: 708-255-1561
Registration FAX: 708-255-1699

50th Annual Quality Congress & Exposition (AQC)

Location: Chicago, IL
Date: May 13 - 15, 1996

Sponsor: ASQC
ASQC Conference and Exhibits Department
PO Box 3005
Milwaukee, WI 53201-9402

Registration Phone: (800) 248-1946
Contact Person: ASQC Headquarters

American Industrial Hygiene Conf & Expo

Location: Washington, D.C.
Date: May 18 - 24, 1996

Registration Phone: 703-849-8888
Registration FAX: 703-207-3561

Conference on Highly Structured Stochastic Systems

Location: Rebild, Denmark
Date: May 19 - 24, 1996

Sponsor: European Science Foundation's Network on Highly Structured Stochastic Systems
Steffen Lauritzen
Aalborg University
Denmark

Conference Software Engineering Process Group (SEPG)

Location: Atlantic City, NJ
Date: May 20-23, 1996

Sponsor: Carnegie Mellon University
Software Engineering Institute
4500 Fifth Avenue
Pittsburgh, PA 15213

Registration Phone: 412-268-6467
Registration FAX: 412-268-5758
Contact Person: Rhonda Green

Second International Symposium on Spatial Accuracy Assessment in Natural Resources and Environmental Sciences

Location: Fort Collins, CO
Date: May 21-23, 1996

Sponsor: Colorado State University

Ninth International Software Quality Week

Location: San Francisco, CA
Date: May 21-24, 1996

Sponsor: Software Research Institute
625 Third Street
San Francisco, CA 94107-1997
USA

Registration Phone: (415) 957-1441
Contact Person: Rita Bral

Southwest Annual Resource Management Conference

Location: Arlington, TX
Date: May 22 - 23, 1996

Sponsor: APICS; Greater Fort Worth Area Chapter, Automation and Robotics Research Institute, University of Texas at Arlington
Automation and Robotics Research Institute
7300 Jack Newell Blvd South
Fort Worth, TX 76118

Registration Phone: 817-273-3530
Registration FAX: 817-794-5801
Contact Person: Professor Joseph Sarkis, PhD., CPIM

Kullback Memorial Research Conference

Location: Washington, D.C.
Date: May 24 - 25, 1996

Sponsor: George Washington University
Department of Statistics
Funger Hall
Washington, DC

Registration Phone: 202-994-6350
Registration FAX: 202-994-6917

28e journees de statistique de Association pour la statistique et ses utilisations

Location: Quebec City, Quebec, Canada
Date: May 27 - 30, 1996

Sponsor: Bureau de la statistique du Quebec, Statistique Canada, Societe statisique de France, Societe statistique du Canada, Department de mathematiques et de statistique
Universite Laval
Sainte-Foy, Quebec G1K 7P4
Canada

Registration Phone: 418-656-5280
Registration FAX: 418-656-2817
Contact Person: Christian Genest

June

Statistical Challenges in Modern Astronomy II

Location: University Park, Pennsylvania
Date: June 2 - 5, 1996

Sponsor: Pennsylvania State University
Pennsylvania State University
319 Classroom Building
Universtiy Park, PA 16802

Registration Phone: 814-863-2837
Registration FAX: 814-863-7114
Contact Person: Gutti Jogesh Babu

Medical Design & Manufacturing

Location: New York, New York
Date: June 4 - 6, 1996

Sponsor: Canon Communications, Inc.
3340 Ocean Park Blvd Suite 1000
Santa Monica, CA 90405-3216

Registration Phone: 310-392-5509
Registration FAX: 310-392-1557
Contact Person: Mary Gordon

Emergency Management Conference

Location: Washington, D.C.
Date: June 6 - 13,1996

Sponsor: MIS Training Institute
498 Concord Street
Framingham, MA 01701-2357

Registration Phone: 508-879-7999
Registration FAX: 508-872-1153
Contact Person: Pam Bissett

The 32nd Annual Meeting of the Drug Information Association

Location: San Diego, CA
Date: June 6 - 12, 1996

Sponsor: Drug Information Association
Drug Information Association
PO Box 3113
Maple Glen, PA 19002

Registration Phone: 215-628-2288

University of Minnesota Conference on Inference and Applications Honoring the 25th Year of the School of Statistics

Location: Minneapolis, Minnesota
Date: June 22 & 23, 1996

Sponsor: School of Statistics
University of Minnesota

Registration Phone: 612-625-7030
Contact Person: Frank B. Martin

Auditmation

Location: Chicago, IL
Date: June 23-26, 1996

Sponsor: MIS Training Institute
498 Concord Street
Framingham, MA 01701-2357

Registration Phone: 508-879-7999
Registration FAX: 508-872-1153
Contact Person: Pam Bissett

Intl. Conference on Probablistic Safety Assessment and Management

Location: Crete, Greece
Date: June 24-28, 1996

Sponsor: IAPSAM
Commission of the European Communities, Joint Research Centre
Institute for Systems Engineering and Informatics
Ispra (VA), I-21020
Italy

Contact Person: Dr. P. Carlo Cacciabue

1996 Annual Meeting of the Psychometric Society

Location: Baniff, Alberta, Canada
Date: June 27 - 30, 1996

252 Bloor Street West
Toronto, Ontario M5S 1V6
Canada

Registration FAX: 416-926-4725
Contact Person: Shizuhiko Nishisatom OISE

July

The 18th Internation Biometric Conference

Location: Amsterdam, The Netherlands
Date: July 1 - 5, 1996

Sponsor: International Biometric Society
808 - 17th Street NW
Suite 200
Washington, DC 20006

Registration Phone: 202-223-9669
Registration FAX: 202-223-9569

American Productivity & Quality Center Conference

Location: Denver, CO
Date: July 15 - 19, 1996 (tentative)

Sponsor: American Productivity & Quality Center
International Benchmarking Clearinghouse
123 North Post Oak Lane 3rd Floor
Houston, TX 77024-7797

Registration Phone: 713-685-4666
Registration FAX: 713-681-5321
Contact Person: Carla Murray-Wolfe

International Conference on Problems of Statistical Education

Location: St. Petersburg, Russia
Date: July 21 - 23, 1996

Sponsor:
St. Petersburg University of Economics and Finance
30/32 Griboedov Kanal
St Petersburg, Russia 191023
Russia

Registration Phone: 812-110-55-94
Registration FAX: 812-247-30-45
Contact Person: Professor I. Elisseeva

August

1996 Joint Statistical Meetings

Location: Chicago, IL
Date: August 4 - 8, 1996

Sponsor: ASA, IMS, ENAR, and WNAR
1429 Duke Street
Alexandria, VA 22314-3402

Registration Phone: 703-684-1221
Registration FAX: 703-684-2037

Quality Council of Alberta - Second Annual Conference

Location: Edmonton, Alberta, Canada
Date: August 21 - 23, 1996

Sponsor: Quality Council of Alberta
1531, 10060 Jasper Avenue
Edmonton, Alberta T5J 3R8
Canada

Registration Phone: 403-423-6878
Registration FAX: 403-426-1509
Contact Person: Kari Taylor

Fifth Islamic Countries Conference on Statistical Science (ICCS-V)

Location: Malang, Indonesia
Date: August 24 - 29, 1996

Brawijaya Universtiy
Jl. Majen Haryono No. 169
Malang, Indonesia 65145
Indonesia

Registration Phone: 62-341-51611
Registration FAX: 62-341-82124/65420
Contact Person: Dr. Waego Hadi Nugroho

COMPSTAT 96 - XII Symposium on Computational Statistics

Location: Barcelona, Spain
Date: August 26-30, 1996

Sponsor: International Assoc. for Statistical Computing
Dept of Statistics
Avada. Diagonal 647
Barcelona, 08028
Spain

Contact Person: Prof. Albert Prat

September

40th EOQ Annual Congress

Location: Berlin, Germany
Date: September 9-13, 1996

Sponsor: European Organization for Quality
Deutsche Gesselschaft fur Qualitat e.V.
August-Schanz-Strasse 21A
Frankfurt am Main, D-60433
Germany

Contact Person: Secretariat of Congress

AutoTech

Location: Cobo Hall, Detroit, Michigan
Date: September 17 - 19, 1996

Sponsor: Automotive Industry Action Group
26200 Lahser Road
Suite 200
Southfield, MI 48034

Registration Phone: 810-358-3570
Registration FAX: 810-358-3253

7th Annual TPM Conference & Exposition

Location: Nashville, TN
Date: September 24 - 26, 1996

Sponsor: Productivity
101 Merritt
7 Corporate Park
Norwalk, CT 06851

Registration Phone: 203-846-3777
Registration FAX: 203-846-6883

October

FABTECH Conference & Exposition

Location: Rosemont, Illinois
Date: October 6 - 9, 1997

Sponsor: Society of Manufacturing Engineers &
Fabricators & Manufactures Association, Int.
833 Featherstone Road
Rockford, IL 61107-9909

Registration FAX: 815-399-8618
Contact Person: Mark Hoper

Instrument Society of America Conference 96

Location: Chicago, IL
Date: October 7 to 10, 1996

Sponsor: ISA
67 Alexander Dr.
P.O. Box 12277
Research Triangle Park, NC 27709
USA

ISA/96 International Conference and Exhibition

Location: Chicago, IL
Date: October 7 - 10, 1996

Sponsor: International Society for Measurement
and Control
ISA
67 Alexander Drive
P.O. Box 12277
Research Triangle Park, NC 27709

Registration Phone: 919-549-8411
Registration FAX: 919-549-8288

16th Annual Conference on Control, Audit, and Security of Information Systems

Location: Boston, MA
Date: October 14 - 18, 1996

Sponsor: MIS Training Institute
498 Concord Street
Framingham, MA 01701-2357

Registration Phone: 508-879-7999
Registration FAX: 508-872-1153
Contact Person: Pam Bissett

12th Annual Productivity-Quality Conference

Location: Dayton, OH
Date: October 23 & 24

Sponsor: PQ Systems
PO Box 10
Dayton, OH 45475-0010

Registration Phone: 800-777-3020
Registration FAX: 513-885-2252

19th Space Simulation Conference

Location: Baltimore, Maryland
Date: October 28 - 31, 1996

Sponsor: Institute of Environmental Sciences
Institute of Environmental Sciences
940 E. Northwest Highway
Mount Prospect, IL 60056

Registration Phone: 708-255-1561
Registration FAX: 708-255-1699

American Productivity & Quality Center Conference

Location: Houston, TX
Date: Oct 28 - Nov 1, 1996 (tentative)

Sponsor: American Productivity & Quality Center
International Benchmarking Clearinghouse
123 North Post Oak Lane 3rd Floor
Houston, TX 77024-7797

Registration Phone: 713-685-4666
Registration FAX: 713-681-5321
Contact Person: Carla Murray-Wolfe

FABTECH West 96

Location: San Jose, California
Date: October 29 - 31, 1996

Sponsor:
Fabricators & Manufacturers Association International
833 Featherstone Road
Rockford, IL 61107-9909

Registration Phone: 815-399-8700
Registration FAX: 815-399-7279
Contact Person: Mark Hoper

Medical Design & Manufacturing

Location: Minneapolis, Minnesota
Date: October 30 - 31, 1996

Sponsor: Canon Communications, Inc.
3340 Ocean Park Blvd Suite 1000
Santa Monica, CA 90405-3216

Registration Phone: 310-392-5509
Registration FAX: 310-392-1557
Contact Person: Mary Gordon

November

Euro-Star 96

Location: Dublin, Ireland
Date: November 25 to 28, 1996

Sponsor: SQE
Contact Person: Wayne Middleton

December

Eighth Annual National Forum on Quality Improvement in Healthcare

Location: New Orleans, LA
Date: December 4 to 7, 1996

Sponsor: Institute for Healthcare Improvement
One Exeter Plaza
Ninth Floor
Boston, MA 02116
USA

Fifty-Second Deming Conference on Applied Statistics

Location: Atlantic City, NJ
Date: December 8 - 14, 1996

Sponsor: ASQC
Metropolitan Section, ASQC

42 Whitewood Drive
Morris Plains, NJ 07950-3329

Registration Phone: 908-820-6904
Contact Person: Jenny Wong

Dates Pending

International Conference on Applied Statistics in Business and Economics

Location: Moscow, Russia
Date: To be determined

Sponsor:
39 Myasnitskaya Str
Moscow, Russia 103450
Russia

Registration Phone: 095-207-48-51
Registration FAX: 095-207-45-92
Contact Person: Professor M. Korolev

Risk Conference

Location: To be determined
Date: (date has not been determined yet)

Sponsor: Carnegie Mellon University
Software Engineering Institute
4500 Fifth Avenue
Pittsburgh, PA 15213

Registration Phone: 412-268-6467
Registration FAX: 412-268-5758
Contact Person: Rhonda Green

Air Force Quality Symposium 1996

Location: Montgomery, Alabama
Date: To be determined

Communications Events Inc
40 Richards Avenue
Norwalk, CT 06854

Registration Phone: 203-855-3000
Registration FAX: 203-855-3003
Contact Person: John W. Goeller

APPENDIX B
QUALITY-RELATED ORGANIZATIONS

Membership in a professional organization, such as the American Society for Quality Control, can help a quality manager to expand his/her base of knowledge, meet face-to-face with colleagues, and obtain certification. However, there are many organizations in the world that have quality assurance as a primary function or concern. A quality professional should look through this list and see if his/her particular industry or interest is represented. By calling or writing to the organization you can obtain a complete information package.

AACE International

c/o M. Melissa Moore
209 Prairie Avenue
Morgantown, WV 26505

Phone: 800-858-2678
FAX: 304-291-5728

Alliance for Telecommunications Industry Solutions

1200 G Street NW
Suite 500
Washington, DC 20005

Phone: 202-628-6380
FAX: 202-393-5453

American Assembly of Collegiate Schools of Business

600 Emberson Road
Suite 300
St Louis, MO 63141

Phone: 314-872-8481
FAX: 314-872-8495

American Board of Quality Assurance and Utilization Review Physicians

4890 W. Kennedy Blvd
Suite 260
Tampa, FL 33609

Phone: 813-286-4411

American College of Medical Quality

9005 Congressional Ct.
Potomac, MD 20854

Phone: 301-365-3570

American College of Physician Executives

4890 W. Kennedy Blvd
Suite 200
Tampa, FL 33609

Phone: 800-562-8088
FAX: 813-287-8993

American Council of the Blind

1155 - 15th Street NW
Suite 720
Washington, DC 20005

Phone: 800-424-8666
FAX: 202-467-5085

American Marketing Association

250 S. Wacker Drive
Suite 200
Chicago, IL 06060

Phone: 312-648-0536
FAX: 312-993-7542

American Medical Peer Review Association

1140 Conneticut Ave NE
Suite 1050
Washington, DC 20036
Phone: 202-331-5790

American Productivity & Quality Center

123 N. Post Oak Lane
Suite 300
Houston, TX 77024-7797

Phone: 713-681-4020

FAX: 713-681-8578

American Society for Quality Control

611 E. Wisconsin Avenue
PO Box 3005
Milwaukee, WI 53201-3005

Phone: 414-272-8575

American Subacute Care Association

PO Box 5445939
Surfside, FL 33154

Phone: 305-864-0396
FAX: 305-868-0905

American Supplier Institute

17333 Federal Drive
Suite 220
Allen Park, MI 48101

Phone: 313-336-8877
FAX: 313-336-3187

Association for Quality and Participation

801 - B West 8th Street
Suite 501
Cincinnati, OH 45203-1601

Phone: 800-733-3310

Association of Image Consultants International

1000 Connecticut Ave NW
Suite 9
Washington, DC 20036-5032

Phone: 301-371-9021
FAX: 301-317-8847

Association of Researh Libraries

21 Dupont Circle NW
Washington, DC 20036

Phone: 202-296-2296
FAX: 202-872-0884

Association of State & Interstate Water Pollution Control Administrators

750 - 1st Street NE
Suite 910
Washington, DC 20002

Phone: 202-898-0905
FAX: 202-898-0929

Automotive Service Association of Arizona

PO Box 10584
Glendale, AZ 85318

Phone: 602-867-6792
FAX: 602-561-8233

Awards and Recognition Association

36 S. State Street
Suite 1212
Chicago, IL 60603

Phone: 312-782-5252

Business Espionage Controls & Counter-measures Association

PO Box 55582
Seattle, WA 98155

Phone: 206-364-4672

Center for Human Services

7200 Wisconsin Avenue
Suite 600
Bethesda, MD 20814

Phone: 301-654-8338

Chamber of Commerce of the United States—U.S. Chamber

1615 H Street NW
Washington, DC 20062

Phone: 202-659-6000
FAX: 202-463-5836

China Quality Control Association

12 Zhongjing Jidao
Xicheng District
Beijing, People's Republic of China 100032
China

Phone: 1-6021408
FAX: 1-6017824

Convenient Automotive Services Institute

PO Box 34595
Bethesda, MD 20827

Phone: 301-897-3191

Engineering and Science Network on Thinking

154 Hamilton Blvd.
Struthers, OH 44471-1446

Phone: 216-755-2710
FAX: 216-750-9400

EuroCity

Postbus 2025
Utrecht, Netherlands NL - 3500 HA
Netherlands

Phone: 30 354883
FAX: 30 357736

European Federation of Chemical Engineering (EFCE)

c/o DECHEMA eV
Theodor-Heuss-Allee 25 Postfach 15 01 04
Frankfurt, Germany 60486
Germany

Phone: 69 7564149
FAX: 69 7564201

European Safety, Reliability, and Data Association (ESReDA)

JRC Ispra ISEI/IE
TP210
Ispra, Varese 21020
Italy

EUROTEST

Van Rijswijcklaan
213-B17
B-2020 Antwerp, Belgium B-2020
Belgium

Phone: 3-2483953
FAX: 3-2483941

Federation of Hong Kong Industries (FHKI)

Hankow Centre 4th Floor
5 - 15 Hankow Road Tsim Sha Tsui
Kowloon, Hong Kong
Hong Kong

Phone: 3 7230818
FAX: 852 7213494

French Society of Automotive Engineers (FSAE)

3, ave. du President Wilson
Paris, France F-75116
France

Phone: 1 47209323
FAX: 1 47204873

Healthcare Information and Management Systems Society

230 E Ohio Street
Suite 600
Chicago, IL 60611

Phone: 312-664-4467
FAX: 312-664-6143

Home Builders Association of Brevard

1500A W. Eau Gallie Blvd
Melbourne, FL 32935-5336

Phone: 407-254-3700
FAX: 407-259-9504

Institut fuer Naehtechnik (IFN)

Krefelder Strasse 147
Aachen, Germany 52070

Phone: 241 153562
FAX: 241 154402

Institute of HeartMath

PO Box 1463
14700 W Park Avenue
Boulder Creek, CA 95006

Phone: 408-338-8700
FAX: 408-338-9861

International Academy for Quallity (IAQ)

Postfach 50 07 63
60395 Frankfurt, Germany
Germany

Phone: 69-954240
FAX: 69-95424133

International Association on Water Quality (IAWQ)

1 Queen Anne's Gate
London, England SW1H 9BT
England

Phone: 171 2223848
FAX: 171 2331197

International Commission for the Protection of the Moseolle Against Pollution (ICPMP)

c/o M. Herfeldt
Bundesministerium fuur Umwelt
Postfach , Bonn 1 54295
Germany

Phone: 228-3052310
FAX: 228-3053854

International Federation of Consulting Engineers (FIDIC)

BP 86
Lausanne 12
Switzerland CH-1000

Phone: 21 6535003
FAX: 21 6535432

International Motor Vehicle Inspection Committee (IMVIC)

21 - 25, rue de la Technologie
Brussels, Belgium 1080
Belgium

Phone: 2 4690900
FAX: 2 4690795

International Organization for Standardization (ISO)

1, fuue de Varembe
Postale 56
Geneva 20, Switzerland CH-1211
Switzerland

Phone: 22 7490111
FAX: 22 7333430

Manufacturers Alliance for Productivity & Innovation

1525 Wilson Blvd.
Suite 900
Arlington, VA 22209

Phone: 703-841-9000
FAX: 202-331-7160

Manufacturers' Agents National Association

PO Box 3467
Luguna Hills, CA 92654

Phone: 714-859-4040
FAX: 714-855-2973

National Association for Healthcare Quality

5700 Old Orchard Road
1st Floor
Skokie, IL 60077

Phone: 708-965-2776

National Association of Emergency Medical Service Physicians

230 McKee Place
Suite 500
Pittsburgh, PA 15213

Phone: 800-228-3677
FAX: 412-578-3241

National Committee for Quality Assurance

1350 New York Avenue NW
Suite 700
Washington, DC 20005

Phone: 202-955-3500

National Prevention Network

444 N. Capitol Street NW
Suite 642
Washington, DC 20001

Phone: 202-783-6868
FAX: 202-783-2704

National Roofing Contractors Association

10255 W Higgins Road
Suite 600
Rosemont, IL 60018-5607

Phone: 708-299-9070
FAX: 708-299-1183

New Jersey Society of Certified Public Accountants

425 Eagle Rock Ave
Roseland, NJ 07068

Phone: 201-226-4494
FAX: 201-226-7425

Pennsylvania Society of Public Accountants (PSPA)

232 State Street
Harrisburg, PA 17101

Phone: 717-234-4129
FAX: 717-232-5905

Professional Standards Review Council of America

200 Madison Avenue
Suite 1910
New York, NY 10016

Phone: 212-686-9147

Quality and Productivity Management Association

300 N. Martingale Road
Suite 230
Schaumburg, IL 60173

Phone: 708-619-2909
FAX: 708-619-3383

Research & Development Associates for Military Food & Packaging Systems

16607 Blanco Road
San Antonio, TX 78232

Phone: 210-493-8024
FAX: 210-493-8036

Society for Software Quality

PO Box 86958
San Diego, CA 92138-6958

Phone: 619-297-1544

Standards Association of Australia (SAA)

PO Box 1055
Strathfield, NSW, Australia 2135
Australia

Phone: 2 74464700

State and Territorial Air Pollution Program Administrators

444 N. Capitol Street NW
Suite 307
Washington, DC 20001

Phone: 202-624-7864

Statistical Process Control Society

PO Box 1203
Avon, CT 06001

Phone: 203-676-8890

Urban Initiatives

530 West 25th Street
New York, NY 10001

Phone: 212-620-9773
FAX: 212-727-9894

Valve Manufacturers Association of America

1050 - 17th Street NW
Suite 701
Washington, DC 20036

Phone: 202-331-8105
FAX: 202-296-0378

Washington Independent Telephone Association (WITA)

2405 Evergreen Park Drive SW
Suite B1
Olympia, WA 98502

Phone: 206-352-5453
FAX: 206-352-8886

APPENDIX C
INTERNET AND OTHER
COMPUTER RESOURCES

A wide variety of resources are available to the quality professional through a computer and a phone modem. In fact, the phone modem is perhaps one of the most important tools now available for a quality manager that wants to keep up to date on developments in the field or who which to discuss quality issues with colleagues around the world.

Computer Bulletin Board Services (BBSs)

Computer bulletin board services are locally operated services that usually focus on a highly specialized topic. Below is a sample of such BBSs. These should be investigated if the topic of interest applies directly to your job. Many of these BBSs also have list of additional BBSs on similar topics. The phone numbers given are the ones the phone modem should dial.

DMSA BBS (800) 252-1366

Information from the Division of Small Manufacturers Assistance.

FDA BBS (800) 252-1366

Information from the Food and Drug Adminstration.

FDA Online (800) 222-0185

BBS for obtaining information from the U.S. Food and Drug Administration.

National ISO 9000 Support Group

Support and discussion of companies trying to get ISO 9000 registered. BBS is at (616) 891-9433. Fax on Demand at (616) 891-0161.

Quality Online

Quality resources and other internet connections. You have to call them to get the special software needed for contact with a modem. Voice phone: (913) 379-5590.

The Benchmarking Exchange

Benchmarking discussions. Call at (408) 662-9814.

TQM BBS (301) 585-1164

TQM discussions.

The Internet

The internet represents one of the greatest expansions of information exchange for quality managers in history. Constructed as a network of networks, the internet allows a quality professional to send e-mail around the world, participate in discussions, view current information, and obtain software files with just a few strokes of the keyboard. Every quality manager needs to investigate the use of an internet account. Popular services providing internet connections include Prodigy, CompuServe, America OnLine, Pipeline, and others. Direct internet connections are also available for individuals and local area networks.

Gophers

Gophers are menu driven search devices that walk you through a variety of information on a particular topic. Most can be accessed with web browsers (see below).

gopher.babson.edu

TQM sites, many related topics.

gopher://gopher.adp.wisc.edu/11/.facstf./.tqm

IBM TQM partnership with universities.

Mailing Lists

To participate in a group discussion of a topic with up to thousands of people from around the world, you join a mailing list. These are automated programs that receive discussions from participants and then resend them to all parties on the mailing list. Thus, you receive dozens of messages each week in your e-mail.

To join a mailing list you need to send an e-mail to the addresses listed below along with a command in the message. Typically, subscribing to a list involves a message such as JOIN or SUBSCRIBE followed by your first and last name. You can also send HELP to get the users guide for the list, which usually includes additional commands for activities such as retrieving archives of past discussions.

Be careful to only join one or two lists at first. More than that will result in possibly hundreds of e-mails being sent to you each week.

listproc@cornell.edu

Environmental quality engineering information. Send INFORMATION CEE351-L.

listpro@cornell.edu

1993 Total quality business and education partnerships program. Send INFORMATION QUALPART-L.

listserv@admin.humberc.on.ca

TQM in education discussion. Send REVIEW TQMEDU-L.

listservahearn.nic.surfnet.nl

Information exchange for people involved in the quality field. Send REVIEW VSNUQA-L.

listservanetcom.com

Discussion of Goldratt's theory of constraints. Send SUBSCRIBE TOC-L.

listservaukcc.uky.edu

Discussion of quality in education. Send REVIEW BGEDU-L.

listservaumab.umd.edu

UMAB's quality council. Send REVIEW QCUMAB.

listservaumab.umd.edu

TQM facilitator's support group. Send REVIEW TQMFSG.

listservayorkvm1.bitnet

Discussion of quality control for distance learning. Send REVIEW CREAD-D.

mailbaseamailbase.ac.uk

Quality management discussion. Send JOIN QUALITY-MANAGEMENT [first name] [last name].

mailbaseamailbase.ac.uk

Business process reengineering discussion group. Send JOIN BRP [first name] [last name] [your organization].

majordomoapogo.wv.tek.com

GPID quality assurance. Send INFO QA.

majordomoaquality.org

Quality in design and construction disucssions. Send SUBSCRIBE ASQC-DCD.

majordomoaquality.org

Quality in health care disucssions. Send SUBSCRIBE QP-HEALTH.

qpi@brameur.u-net.com

European benchmarking club and ESSI project mast. Send simple message requesting further information.

quasaraspice.crim.ca

Discussion of ISO 9000 and software. Send HELP QUASAR.

sbrigham@cni.org

Quality in higher education. Send HELP.

tqmnetauwyo.edu

Acedemy of Management's discussion of TQM. Send SUBSCRIBE TQMNET-L.

listprocagmu.edu

Reinventing government. Send SUBSCRIBE REGO-L [first name] [last name] for general discussion of reinventing government.

listprocagmu.edu

Reinventing government. Send SUBSCRIBE REGO-QUAL [first name] [last name] for the discussion of quality leadership in government.

listprocagmu.edu

Reinventing government. Send SUBSCRIBE REGO-DOD [first name] [last name] for discussion about the Department of Defense.

listprocagmu.edu

Reinventing government. Send SUBSCRIBE REGO-EOP [first name] [last name] for discussion of the reinventing the office of the President.

listprocagmu.edu

Reinventing government. Send SUBSCRIBE REGO-ORG [first name] [last name] for discussion on how to transform organizations.

listservais.twi.tudelft.nl

Business process reengineering discussion. Send SUBSCRIBE BPR-L [first name] [last name].

listservamr.net

Quality improvement in higher education. Subscribe to CQI-L.

listservamsu.edu

Best practices in manufacturing. Send SUBSCRIBE MFG-INFO [first name] [last name].

listservapucc.princeton.edu

TQM in manufacturing and services. Send REVIEW QUALITY.

listservaukanvm.cc.ukans.edu

Quality improvement team leaders and facilitators. Send REVIEW TEAMS-L.

listservaukanvm.cc.ukans.edu

TQM in higher education. Send SUBSCRIBE TQM-I [first name] [last name].

listservavm1.nodak.edu

ISO 9000 discussion. Send INFO ISO9000.

roquemoraterrill.unt.edu

Center for the study of work teams. Send e-mail to this address asking to subscribe.

UseNet Groups

UseNet groups are also discussion areas, except you have to log into them to read through the most recent discussions. To reach these groups you need to use your UseNet reader on your internet service to subscribe and to read through discussions.

bit.listserv.quality

General discussion group on quality topics.

misc.industry.quality

Usenet discussion group on quality topics.

bit.listserv.quality

Quality discussion newsgroup.

bit.listserv.iso9000

ISO 9000 postings and archieves of previous discussions.

World-Wide Web

Perhaps the most interesting feature of the internet to use is the World-Wide Web (WWW). In 1995 it was the fastest growing business on earth, expanding in usage by 1800%. The web is made up of home pages created by individuals, businesses, and organizations. Each page is a combination of graphics, text, audio, and movies. The power of the web lies in the use of hypertext that allows you to link pages together from around the world. For example, you could be reading through a discussion of total quality, see a reference to a group in Japan, and with a click of a mouse key be switched to the pages in Japan.

Most popular online services provide web browsers. Individuals with direct internet connections via SLIP or PPP or T1 can use programs such as NetScape and Mosaic to browse the web. The following addresses are called URLs and are entered in a line on the browser to activate the connection.

http://www.quality.co.uk/quality/certbody.htm

List of registrars around the world.

http://138.81.2.245/9000e/forum.html

ISO 9000 forum home page.

http://204.7.246.6

Center for International Project and Program Management. Also try http://www.iol.ie/~mattewar.

http://deming.eng.clemson.edu

TQM and quality discussions. Some ISO 9000 material.

http://www.digimark.net/1/educ

Resources on quality in education.

http://fytqm.uafadm.alaska.edu/

University of Alaska's TQM Web site.

http://quality.org/pub/qc

Large collection of QC and ISO 9000 information

http://quality.org/qc

Site of the online publications Global Strategic Systems Newsletter and Quality Systems Behavior Newsletters.

http://stdsbss.ieee.org

IEEE's site for standards.

http://vaxmsx.babson.edu

Babson college's web page for quality related files.

http://vector.casti.com/qc

Quality Resources Online. Source of information on local ASQC sections online and agile manufacturing.

http://www.ansi.org

Home page of the American National Standards Institute, source of many ISO standards for use in the U.S. and national quality standards.

http://www.apqc.org

Web homepage for the American Productivity and Quality Center.

http://www.asqc.org

Home page of the American Society for Quality Control.

http://www.aztec.com/aztec/iso9000

ISO 9000 information.

http://www.benchnet.com

Homepage for the Benchmark Exchange, a fee-based resource.

http://www.care.panam.edu

UTPA Center for applied research in education.

http://www.cc.emory.edu/ITD/tqm.html

Emory University's TQM web site.

http://www.creacon.com

Newsletter on quality issues.

http://www.cybernetics.net/users/RAinfo/

Regulatory affairs discussions.

http://www.dbainc.com/dba

TQM site maintained by David Butler Associates.

http://www.exit109.com

ISO 9000 information.

http://www.hci.com.au/management/

Discussion of management, quality, and ISO 9000.

http://www.industry.net

Home page for the Association for Manufacturing Excellence.

http://www.iso.ch/welcome.html

ISO headquarters in Geneva, Switzerland.

http://www.lia.co.za/users/johannh/index.html

A South African site on business process reengineering and project management.

http://www.netview.com/qualinet

Discussions for quality professionals.

http://www.netview.com/qualinet/

Qualinet's home page.

http://www.nist.gov

Home page for the National Institute for Standards and Technology (U.S.).

http://www.nist.gov.8102/

The quality program at NIST.

http://www.ornl.gov/orcmt/

Results of the Navy's best manufacturing practices survey.

http://www.quality.org/qc

Quality Resources Online.

http://www.sei.cmu.edu

Software Engineering Institute's web page.

http://www.semi.org

Information on the semiconductor manufacturing.

http://www.sirim.my/

Malaysian standards group.

http://www.topometrix.com

Information on scanning probe microscopicity.

ftpatqm.permanet.org

The TQM BBS FTP address.

http://www.xnet.com/˜creacon/Q4Q

Extensive source of quality information and links to other groups.

APPENDIX D
EDUCATIONAL OPPORTUNITIES*

In addition to reading magazines and journals and attending seminars and conferences, college courses are an excellent way to gain knowledge and insight into the vast subject area of quality. Courses covering such topics as implementing quality practices in administration, engineering technology, quality management, statistics, quality control, education, and others are offered at colleges and universities in every state. The following list provides (alphabetically according to state) the names of the schools, their addresses, and the contact people at each institution.

COLLEGES AND UNIVERSITIES

ALABAMA

Alabama, Birmingham (University of)
School of Business
Birmingham, AL 35294
(205) 934-8830
fax (205) 975-6234
Contact: Joseph G. Van Matre, professor,
   School of Business

Alabama, Tuscaloosa (University of)
Department of Industrial Engineering
Tuscaloosa, AL 35487-0288
(205) 348-1609
fax (205) 348-8573
Contact: Robert G. Batson, professor,
   Department of Industrial Engineering

Auburn University
209 Samford Hall
Auburn University, AL 36849-5108
(205) 844-2000
fax (205) 844-2001
Contact: Betty B. Burkhalter, assistant provost
   for assessment and quality improvement

Jacksonville State University
Department of Technology
217 Self Hall
Jacksonville, AL 36265
(205) 782-5294
fax (205) 782-5355
Contact: Stanley G. Aman, head, Department
   of Technology

Samford University
800 Lakeshore Dr.

Birmingham, AL 35229
(205) 870-2674
fax (205) 870-2908
Contact: John Harris, assistant to the provost
   for quality assessment

South Alabama (University of)
College of Business and Management Studies
Mobile, AL 36688
(205) 460-6715
fax (205) 460-6529
Contact: Edward L. Harrison, chair,
   Department of Management

Troy State University at Dothan
P.O. Box 8368
Dothan, AL 36304
(205) 983-6556, ext. 273
fax (205) 983-6322
Contact: William Borders, associate professor
   and assistant dean, School of Business

ALASKA

Alaska, Fairbanks (University of)
VCAS-TQM
P.O. Box 757900
Fairbanks, AK 99775-7900
(907) 474-7516
fax (907) 474-5674
Contact: V. Janene McMahan, program
   development coordinator, VCAS-TQM

ARIZONA

Arizona State University
College of Business
Tempe, AZ 85287-4206
(602) 965-5439

---

*Reprinted with permission from *Quality Progress*, September 1994.

fax (602) 965-5539
Contact: Richard K. Burdick, Decision and
    Information Systems Department

Arizona (University of)
Continuous Organizational Renewal (CORe)
McClelland Hall 417
Tucson, AZ 85721
(602) 621-2394
fax (602) 621-8105
Contact: Ron Petersen, director, CORe

ARKANSAS

Central Arkansas (University of)
College of Business Administration
Conway, AR 72035
(501) 450-3106
fax (501) 450-5302
Contact: Peter Lorenzi, dean

Harding University
P.O. Box 762
Searcy, AR 72149-0001
(501) 279-4497
fax (501) 279-4865
Contact: Bob Reely, professor of management

CALIFORNIA

California Polytechnic State University, San
    Luis Obispo
College of Business
San Luis Obispo, CA 93407
(805) 756-1418
fax (805) 756-1473
Contact: Ramon Haynes, professor of
    management and engineering management

California State Polytechnic University,
    Pomona
3801 W. Temple
Pomona, CA 91768
(909) 869-2555
fax (909) 869-4370
Contact: Phil Rosenkrantz, chair, Industrial
    and Manufacturing Engineering Department

California State University, Dominguez Hills
Master of Science in Quality Assurance Office
    (MSQA)
1000 E. Victoria St.
Carson, CA 90747
(310) 516-3880
Contact: Eugene Watson, chair, MSQA

California State University, Long Beach
1250 Bellflower Blvd.
Long Beach, CA 90840
(310) 985-7509
fax (310) 985-7561
Contact: Thomas L. Robinson, professor,
    Engineering Technology Department

California State University, Sacramento
School of Business Administration
Sacramento, CA 95819-6088
(916) 278-6992
fax (916) 278-5437
Contact: Joseph L. Orsini, professor of quality
    management and marketing

California State University, Stanislaus
801 Monte Vista
Turlock, CA 95382
(209) 667-3149
fax (209) 667-3333
Contact: Nael Aly, professor and chair,
    Management, Operations, and Marketing
    Department

Phoenix, Fountain Valley (University of)
10540 Talbert Ave.
Fountain Valley, CA 92708
(714) 968-2299
fax (714) 964-7429
Contact: Robert Venti, Center for Professional
    Education

San Francisco State University
1600 Holloway Ave.
San Francisco, CA 94132
(415) 338-1701
fax (415) 338-6237
Contact: Al Schainblatt, College of Business

San Francisco (University of)
2130 Fulton Ave.
San Francisco, CA 94556
(415) 666-6628
fax (415) 666-2502
Contact: Stephen J. Huxley, professor of
    decision sciences, McLaren School of
    Business

San Jose State University
1 Washington Square
San Jose, CA 95192-0061
(408) 924-3194
fax (408) 924-3198

Contact: Ali M. Zargar, associate professor,
Division of Technology

COLORADO

Colorado, Boulder (University of)
1511 University Ave.
Campus Box 467
Boulder, CO 80309
(303) 492-4968
fax (303) 492-4693
Contact: Susan R. Gressett, total quality
specialist, Employee Development
Department

Colorado Tech
4435 North Chestnut St.
Colorado Springs, CO 80907-3896
(719) 598-0200
fax (719) 598-3740
Contact: Robert G. Stein, dean, Management
Department

Southern Colorado (University of)
2200 Bonforte Blvd.
Pueblo, CO 81001
(719) 549-2880
fax (719) 549-2909
Contact: Peter Billington, professor, School of
Business

CONNECTICUT

Hartford (University of)
200 Bloomfield Ave.
W. Hartford, CT 06002
(203) 768-4962
fax (203) 768-4732
Contact: Mark Borzi, manager, Staff
Organizational Development and Human
Resources Department

Western Connecticut State University
181 White St.
Danbury, CT 06810
(203) 837-8650
fax (203) 837-8339
Contact: Ronald Benson, professor

FLORIDA

Central Florida (University of)
P.O. Box 160020 / P.O. Box 162450

Orlando, FL 32816
(407) 823-3452 / (407) 823-5306
fax (407) 823-5533 / (407) 823-3413
Contact: Janice Dossey Terrell, director of
quality management, or William W. Swart,
chair and professor, Department of
Industrial Engineering and Management
Systems, and A. Elshennawy, Department of
Industrial Engineering and Management
Systems

Florida State University
Department of Statistics
Tallahassee, FL 32306-3033
(904) 644-3218
fax (904) 644-5271
Contact: Duane Meeter, chair, Department of
Statistics

Florida (University of)
103 Griffin-Floyd Hall
P.O. Box 118454 / 303 Weil St.
Gainesville, FL 32611
(904) 392-1441, ext. 204 / (904) 392-1464
fax (904) 392-5175 / (904) 392-3537
Contact: Geoff Vining, associate professor,
Statistics Department, or D. Jack Elzinga,
Industrial and Systems Engineering
Department

Miami (University of)
School of Business Administration
Jenkins Bldg., Rm. 417A
Coral Gables, FL 33146
(305) 661-4425
fax (305) 661-4908
Contact: Howard S. Gitlow, executive director,
Institute for the Study of Quality

South Florida (University of)
4202 E. Fowler Ave.
Tampa, FL 33620
(813) 974-2154
fax (813) 974-5093
Contact: John S. Hodgson, vice-provost,
Academic Affairs Department

Tampa (University of)
401 West Kennedy Blvd.
Tampa, FL 33606-1490
(813) 258-7420
fax (813) 258-7408
Contact: Al C. Endres, Center for Quality

GEORGIA

Albany State College
504 College Dr.
Albany, GA 31705
(912) 430-4662
fax (912) 430-3935
Contact: Betty J. Washington, director,
 Institutional Research and Planning
 Department

DeVry Institute
250 N. Arcadia Ave.
Decatur, GA 30030
(404) 292-7900
fax (404) 292-2321
Contact: L. Bowman, chair of business
 operations

Georgia College
Department of Management
Campus Box 11
Milledgeville, GA 31061
(12) 453-4324
fax (912) 453-5249
Contact: Bob Craft, total quality coordinator

Georgia Institute of Technology
225 N. Ave. N.W.
Carnegie Bldg.
Atlanta, GA 30332-0325
(404) 894-1099 / (404) 894-9455
fax (404) 853-9163
Contact: Hal Irvin, director, Office of
 Continuous Quality Improvement, or Joseph
 E. Gilmour Jr., vice-president of strategic
 planning

Georgia Southern University
Landrum Box 8152
Statesboro, GA 30460
(912) 681-5087
fax (912) 681-0292
Contact: U.S. Knotts, professor, Management
 Department

Georgia State University
University Plaza
Altanta, GA 30303-3083
(404) 651-4061
fax (404) 651-2708
Contact: Harvey Brightman, Decision Sciences

Georgia (University of)
Terry College of Business

Athens, GA 30602
(706) 542-3701
fax (706) 542-3743
Contact: James P. Gilbert, associate professor,
 Management Department

Southern College of Technology
1100 South Marietta Pkwy.
Marietta, GA 30060
(404) 528-7242
fax (404) 528-4991
Contact: Larry Aft, professor, Industrial
 Engineering Technology Department

IDAHO

Boise State University
College of Business
1910 University Dr.
Boise, ID 83725
(208) 385-3786
fax (208) 385-3637
Contact: Patrick Shannon, professor, Computer
 Information Systems and Production
 Management

ILLINOIS

Bradley University
Industrial Engineering Department
Peoria, IL 61625
(309) 677-2744
fax (309) 677-2853
Contact: K.S. Krishnamoorthi, professor,
 Industrial Engineering Department

Chicago (University of)
Graduate School of Business
1101 E. 58th St.
Chicago, IL 60637
(312) 702-7317
fax (312) 702-0458
Contact: William Youser, associate dean

De Paul University
1 E. Jackson Blvd.
Chicago, IL 60056
(312) 362-8382
fax (312) 362-6973
Contact: James Belohlav, associate professor,
 Management Department

Eastern Illinois University
101 Klehm Hall
Charleston, IL 61920

(217) 581-6267
fax (217) 581-6607
Contact: Ping Liu, associate professor of
    technology

Illinois Benedictine College
5700 College Rd.
Lisle, IL 60532-0900
(708) 960-1500, ext. 4890
fax (708) 960-1126
Contact: Peter F. Soresen Jr., director,
    Management and Organizational Behavior
    Department

Illinois, Chicago (University of)
601 S. Morgan St.
M/C 104, Rm. 2715 UH
Chicago, IL 60607
(312) 413-3600
fax (312) 413-3606
Contact: Robert S. Winter, associate chancellor
    for quality advancement

Illinois Institute of Technology
565 W. Adams St., Rm. 430C
Chicago, IL 60661-3691
(312) 906-6515
fax (312) 906-6549
Contact: Zia Hassan, dean, Stuart School of
    Business

Loyola University, Chicago
820 N. Michigan Ave.
Chicago, IL 60611
(312) 915-7517
fax (312) 915-6231
Contact: Kathleen Goeppinger, director, Center
    for Organizational Development

Northern Illinois University
101 Still Hall
DeKalb, IL 60115
(815) 753-1350
fax (815) 753-3602
Contact: James R. Stewart, assistant professor,
    Technology Department

Southern Illinois University, Carbondale
Mail Code 6603
Carbondale, IL 62901
(618) 536-3396
fax (618) 453-7455
Contact: Thomas Velasco, assistant professor,
    Technology Department

Western Illinois University
President's Office
Sherman Hall
Macomb, IL 61455
(309) 298-2674
fax (309) 298-2089
Contact: Lowell Lueck, total quality
    management coordinator

INDIANA

Huntington College
2303 College Ave.
Huntington, IN 46750
(219) 356-6000, ext. 2032
fax (219) 356-9448
Contact: Robert Boozer, assistant to the
    president for planning and assessment

Indiana University-Purdue University,
    Indianapolis
355 N. Lansing St., A0140
Indianapolis, IN 46202-2896
(317) 274-4111
fax (317) 274-4651
Contact: Trudy W. Banta, vice-chancellor for
    planning and institutional improvement

Purdue University
Krannert Graduate School of Management
1310 Krannert Bldg.
West Lafayette, IN 47907-1310
(317) 494-4413
fax (317) 494-9658
Contact: Tom Brady, assistant director, Center
    for the Management of Manufacturing
    Enterprises

Rose-Hulman Institute of Technology
5500 Wabash Ave.
Terre Haute, IN 47803
(812) 877-8390
fax (812) 877-3198
Contact: John Kinney, professor, Mathematics
    Department

IOWA

Iowa State University
102 Snedecor Hall / 125 Beardshear Hall
Ames, IA 50011
(515) 294-3440 / (515) 294-8437
fax (515) 294-4040 / (515) 294-1621
Contact: Dean Isaacson, professor and head,
    Statistics Department, or Peter Hetland,

quality manager, Business and Finance
Department

KANSAS

Friends University
2100 University
Wichita, KS 67213
(316) 261-5882
fax (316) 292-5516
Contact: Frank Patton, associate dean of
continuing education

Kansas Newman College
3100 McCormick Ave.
Wichita, KS 67213-2097
(316) 942-4291
fax (316) 942-4483
Contact: Anna McLeod, total quality
management program director

Kansas State University
101 Calvin Hall
Manhattan, KS 66502
(913) 532-4358
fax (913) 532-7024
Contact: Cynthia McCahon, associate professor
of management

Kansas (University of)
P.O. Box 505
Lawrence, KS 66044-0505
(913) 864-4412
fax (913) 864-5324
Contact: Shery Stump, quality improvement
coordinator, Office of Institutional Research
and Planning

Mid America Nazarene College
2030 E. College Way
Olathe, KS 66062-1899
(913) 791-3276
fax (913) 791-3409
Contact: Dan Croy, director, Graduate Studies
in Management

Wichita State University
1845 N. Fairmount
Wichita, KS 67260-0035
(316) 689-3425
fax (316) 689-3742
Contact: Ming C. Lui, assistant professor

KENTUCKY

Eastern Kentucky University
307 Whalin Complex
Richmond, KY 40475-3115
(606) 622-1194
fax (606) 622-6274
Contact: M.I. Lifland, associate professor,
Technology Department

LOUISIANA

Louisiana Technical University
P.O. Box 10348
Ruston, LA 71272
(318) 257-4647
fax (318) 257-2562
Contact: Barry A. Benedict, dean, College of
Engineering

Loyola University, New Orleans
6363 St. Charles Ave.
New Orleans, LA 70118
(504) 865-3544
fax (504) 865-3496
Contact: Caroline M. Fisher, director of
graduate programs, College of Business

McNeece State University
P.O. Box 92940
Lake Charles, LA 70609-2940
(318) 475-5593
fax (318) 475-5189
Contact: Ben Harlow

New Orleans (University of)
Department of Management
New Orleans, LA 70148
(504) 286-6481
fax (504) 286-3951
Contact: William P. Galle Jr., professor and
continuous quality improvement coordinator

MAINE

Southern Maine (University of)
37 College Ave.
Gorham, ME 04038
(207) 780-5440
fax (207) 780-5129
Contact: Greg P. Bazinet, director, Applied
Technology Department

MARYLAND

Maryland, College Park (University of)
1131E Engineering Classroom Bldg.
College Park, MD 20742
(301) 405-3866
fax (301) 314-9867
Contact: George Dieter, director, Office for
  Continuous Quality Improvement

MASSACHUSETTS

Babson College
Office of Quality
Park Manor South
Babson Park, MA 02157-0310
(617) 239-5017
fax (617) 239-5089
Contact: Susan West Engelkemeyer, director of
  quality and assistant professor of
  management

Boston University
621 Commonwealth Ave.
Boston, MA 02215
(617) 353-2919
fax (617) 353-4098
Contact: Janelle Heineke, assistant professor,
  Operations Management Department

Harvard University
1350 Massachusetts Ave., Rm. 814
Cambridge, MA 02138
(617) 495-2936
fax (617) 495-5800
Contact: Connie Towler, program director,
  Harvard Quality Process

Massachusetts, Amherst (University of)
Marston Hall
Amherst, MA 01002
(413) 545-0646
fax (413) 545-0724
Contact: Richard J. Giglio, head, Industrial
  Engineering and Operations Research
  Department

Massachusetts, Dartmouth (University of)
Old Westport Rd.
North Dartmouth, MA 02747
(508) 999-8428
fax (508) 999-8776
Contact: Richard D. Legault, professor,
  Management Department

Massachusetts, Lowell (University of)
1 University Ave.
Lowell, MA 01854
(508) 934-2595
fax (508) 458-8289
Contact: Paul Kales, associate professor,
  Engineering Technology Department

Western New England College
1215 Wilbraham Rd.
Springfield, MA 01119
(413) 782-1727
fax (413) 782-1746
Contact: John Maleyeff, associate professor,
  Industrial Engineering Department

MICHIGAN

Cleary College
2170 Washtenaw / 3750 Cleary Dr.
Ypsilanti, MI 48197 / Howell, MI 48843
(313) 483-4400 / (517) 548-3670
fax (313) 483-0090 / (517) 548-2170
Contact: Thomas Sullivan, president and
  corporate executive officer, or Vince Linder,
  vice-president, Academic Affairs Department

Eastern Michigan University
118 Sill Hall
Ypsilanti, MI 48917
(313) 478-2040
fax (313) 487-8755
Contact: Daniel J. Fields, quality program
  coordinator, Industrial Technology
  Department

Ferris State University
Swan 107
Big Rapids, MI 49307
(616) 592-2959
fax (616) 592-2407
Contact: William Winchell, associate professor,
  Manufacturing Engineering Technology
  Department

GMI Engineering & Management Institute
W. 17th Ave.
Flint, MI 48504
(810) 762-7949
fax (810) 762-9836
Contact: John Lorenz, provost and vice-
  president of academic affairs

Hope College
Department of Economics and Business
   Administration
P.O. Box 9000
Holland, MI 49422-9000
(616) 394-7979
Contact: Thomas Smith, assistant professor,
   Business Administration

Michigan State University
Department of Statistics and Probability
East Lansing, MI 48824-1027
(517) 353-7820
fax (517) 336-1405
Contact: Dennis Gilliland, professor,
   Department of Statistics and Probability

Michigan Technological University
1400 Townsend Dr.
Houghton, MI 49931-1295
(906) 487-2416
fax (906) 487-2935
Contact: Rebecca Christianson, manager,
   Quality Service Education/Total Quality
   Education

Michigan (University of)
College of Engineering
North Campus
Ann Arbor, MI 48109
(313) 936-3045
fax (313) 763-9487
Contact: Michael G. Parsons, associate dean
   for undergraduate education, College of
   Engineering

Oakland University
417 Varner Hall
Rochester, MI 48309-4401
(810) 370-3286
fax (810) 370-4275
Contact: George E. Stevens, dean, School of
   Business Administration

Western Michigan University
3070 Seibert Administration Bldg.
Kalamazoo, MI 49008
(616) 387-3655
fax (616) 387-2355
Contact: Barbara S. Liggett, associate vice-
   president and executive advisor for quality

MINNESOTA

Minnesota (University of)
1313 5th St. S.E. #108
Minneapolis, MN 55414
(612) 627-4277
fax (612) 627-4280
Contact: Judith A. Gaston, coordinator, Quality
   Improvement Department

St. Thomas (University of)
The Management Center
1000 LaSalle Ave. MPL166
Minneapolis, MN 55403-2005
(612) 962-4612
fax (612) 962-4610
Contact: Mike Fedock, program manager,
   Quality/Productivity Institute

Winona State University
Stark Hall
Winona, MN 55987
(507) 457-5585
fax (507) 457-5681
Contact: Dennis N. Nielsen, dean, College of
   Science and Engineering

MISSISSIPPI

Mississippi (University of)
School of Education
Oxford, MS 38677
(601) 232-5016
fax (601) 232-7249
Contact: Julie E. Horine, Department of
   Educational Leadership

MISSOURI

Missouri, Kansas City (University of)
Bloch School
5110 Cherry St.
Kansas City, MO 64110
(816) 235-2324
fax (816) 235-2312
Contact: F. Dean Booth, assistant professor,
   Bloch School

Missouri, Rolla (University of)
Engineering Management Department
Rolla, MO 65401
(314) 341-4579

fax (314) 341-6567
Contact: Henry Wiebe, professor, Engineering
    Management Department

Missouri Southern State College
3950 E. Newman Rd.
Joplin, MO 64801
(417) 625-9507
fax (417) 625-9782
Contact: Terry Marion, coordinator, Quality
    Resource Center

Northeast Missouri State University
Normal St.
Kirksville, MO 63501
(816) 785-4228
fax (816) 785-7460
Contact: Dennis Peacock, director of
    assessment and testing

Northwest Missouri State University
800 University Dr.
Maryville, MO 64468
(816) 562-1277
fax (816) 562-1484
Contact: Ron DeYoung, dean, College of
    Business, Government, and Computer
    Science

NEW HAMPSHIRE

New Hampshire (University of)
Whittemore School of Business
McConnell Hall
Durham, NH 03824
(603) 862-3355
fax (603) 862-4468
Contact: Craig H. Wood, assistant professor of
    operations management

Rivier College
420 S. Main St.
Nashua, NH 03060-5086
(603) 888-1311, ext. 8537
Contact: George E. Shagory, chair, Graduate
    Business Department

NEW JERSEY

Bloomfield College
Bloomfield, NJ 07003
(201) 748-9000, ext. 292
fax (201) 429-3507
Contact: Alfonso A. Roman, assistant to the
    president for planning

Ramapo College
505 Ramapo Valley Rd.
Mahwah, NJ 07430
(201) 529-7442
fax (201) 529-7508
Contact: Dorothy Echols Tobe, assistant vice-
    president, Administration and Finance
    Department

Rider University
2083 Lawrenceville Rd.
Lawrenceville, NJ 08648-3099
(609) 895-5532
fax (609) 896-5304
Contact: Stan Temkin, associate professor,
    Management Sciences Department, or
    Cengiz Haksever, associate professor,
    Management Sciences Department

Rutgers University, Piscataway
P.O. Box 909
Piscataway, NJ 08855
(908) 445-2238
fax (908) 445-5467
Contact: Susan L. Albin, professor, Department
    of Industrial Engineering

Stevens Institute of Technology
Castle Point
Hoboken, NJ 07030
(201) 216-5229
fax (201) 216-8326
Contact: Joseph J. Moeller Jr., vice-president,
    Graduate School and Research

NEW MEXICO

New Mexico State University
Box 30001, Dept. 3449
Las Cruces, NM 88003
(505) 646-2912
fax (505) 646-3549
Contact: J. Eldon Steelman, associate dean of
    engineering

NEW YORK

Albany, (University at), State University of
    New York
135 Western Ave.
Albany, NY 12222
(518) 442-5700
fax (518) 442-5768

Contact: Thomas Kinney, director, Professional
  Development Program and chair, Quality
  Forum

Binghamton University
School of Management
Binghamton, NY 13902
(607) 777-2673
fax (607) 777-4422
Contact: Gary M. Roodman, professor School of
  Management

Buffalo State College, State University College
  of New York
Upton Hall #314
1300 Elmwood Ave.
Buffalo, NY 14222
(716) 878-4220
fax (710) 878-3033
Contact: Deborah Rindfuss Ellis, assistant
  professor, Technology Department

Cornell University
317 Day Hall
Ithaca, NY 14853
(607) 255-3759
fax (607) 255-9412
Contact: James E. Horley Jr., senior vice-
  president

Dominican College
470 Western Hwy.
Orangeburg, NY 10962
(914) 359-7800
fax (914) 359-2313
Contact: Lorraine Bousard, director of
  institutional research and planning

Dowling College
Idle Hour Blvd.
Oakdale, NY 11769
(516) 244-3355
fax (516) 589-6644
Contact: Michael A. Mogavero, dean, School of
  Business

Fordham University
Graduate School of Business
113 West 60th St.
New York, NY 10023
(212) 636-6219
fax (212) 765-5573
Contact: Joyce Nilsson Orsini, director Deming
  Scholars Program and Management
  Department

Marist College
290 North Rd.
Poughkeepsie, NY 12601-1387
(914) 575-3000
Contact: Eugene H. Melan, professor of
  management studies

New York, Farmingdale (State University of)
Whitman Hall, Rte. 110
Farmingdale, NY 11735
(516) 420-2189
fax (516) 420-2689
Contact: Daniel S. Marrone, director of
  management technology

Rensselaer Polytechnic Institute
Decision Science and Engineering Systems
  Department
Troy, NY 12180
(518) 276-2962
fax (518) 276-8227
Contact: M. Raghavachari, professor, Decision
  Science and Engineering Systems
  Department

Rochester Institute of Technology
98 Lomb Memorial Dr.
Rochester, NY 14623-5604
(716) 475-6129
fax (716) 475-5959
Contact: Edward G. Schilling, director, Center
  for Quality and Applied Statistics

Rochester (University of)
William E. Simon Graduate School of Business
  Administration
Rochester, NY 14627
(716) 275-8177
fax (716) 271-3907
Contact: Faith D. Diehl, director, Student
  Affairs Department

St. John Fisher College
3690 East Ave.
Rochester, NY 14618
(716) 385-8015
fax (716) 385-8029
Contact: Dennis W. Crowley, assistant to the
  president for quality leadership

Union College
Graduate Management Institute
Bailey Hall 300A
Schenectady, NY 12308
(518) 388-6248

fax (518) 388-6686
Contact: Josef Schmee, professor, Graduate
　Management Institute

NORTH CAROLINA

Duke University
711 Iredell St.
Durham, NC 27708
(919) 684-6412
Contact: Jane W. Tucker, director,
　Development and Services Department

North Carolina, Charlotte (University of)
Precision Engineering
Charlotte, NC 28223
(704) 547-4370
fax (704) 547-3246
Contact: J. William Shelnutt, associate
　professor, Engineering Technology
　Department

North Carolina State University
College of Engineering
Page Hall
P.O. Box 7101 / P.O. Box 8109 /
P.O. Box 7902
Raleigh, NC 27695
(919) 515-1871 / (919) 515-4620 / (919) 515-
　3940
fax (919) 515-7685 / (919) 515-1794 / (919) 515-
　6159
Contact: Thomas H. Brown Jr., quality
　facilitator, Dean's Office; Tom Johnson,
　quality facilitator; or Margaret O'Brien,
　quality facilitator

Western Carolina University
Belk Bldg.
Cullowhee, NC 28723
(704) 227-7272
fax (704) 227-7705
Contact: Jerry Cook, professor, Industrial and
　Engineering Technology

NORTH DAKOTA

Mayville State University
Mayville, ND 58257
(701) 786-2301
fax (701) 786-4748
Contact: Ray Genszewski, vice-president for
　student affairs

North Dakota (University of)
P.O. Box 7136
University Station
Grand Forks, ND 58202
(701) 777-4419 or (612) 559-2410
fax (701) 777-3650
Contact: James H. Larson, director of special
　projects and professor

Valley City State University
101 College St. S.W.
Valley City, ND 58072
(701) 845-7100
fax (701) 845-7245
Contact: Ellen Earle Chaffee, president

OHIO

Cincinnati (University of)
College of Business Administration / College of
　Engineering
P.O. Box 210130 / 651 Baldwin
Cincinnati, OH 45221
(513) 556-7152 / (513) 556-2933
fax (513) 556-4891 / (513) 556-3626
Contact: James R. Evans, professor and
　director, Total Quality Management Center,
　or Constantine Papadakis, dean of
　engineering

Cleveland State University
2501 Euclid Ave.
Cleveland, OH 44115
(216) 687-4665
fax (216) 687-9260
Contact: Fred Schoenig, Department of
　Industrial Engineering

Marietta College
Fifth and Putnam
Marietta, OH 45750
(614) 376-4702
fax (614) 376-4703
Contact: Alice Warner, special assistant to the
　president and director of total quality
　management

Mount St. Joseph (College of)
Department of Business
Administration
5701 Delhi Rd.
Cincinnati, OH 45233
(513) 244-4918
fax (513) 244-4270

Contact: Gerry Polesky, coordinator and
    assistant professor

Ohio University
116 Stocker Center
Athens, OH 45701
(614) 593-0258
Contact: Peter Klein, assistant professor,
    Department of Industrial Technology

OKLAHOMA

Oklahoma State University
School of Industrial Engineering
Stillwater, OK 74078-0540
(405) 744-6055
fax (405) 744-6187
Contact: Kenneth E. Case, regents professor,
    School of Industrial Engineering

OREGON

Oregon Institute of Technology
3201 Campus Dr.
Klamath Falls, OR 97601
(503) 885-1902
fax (503) 885-1687
Contact: Errol Roy, chair, Business
    Technologies Department

Oregon State University
Administrative Services A638
Corvallis, OR 97331-2128
(503) 737-0548
fax (503) 737-3033
Contact: Nancy Lee Howard, quality manager,
    Office of Quality and Continuous
    Improvement

Oregon (University of)
College of Business Administration
Eugene, OR 97403
(503) 346-1593
fax (503) 346-3341
Contact: Kenneth D. Ramsing, professor,
    College of Business Administration

Portland State University
P.O. Box 751
Portland, OR 97207
(503) 725-3722
fax (503) 725-5850
Contact: A.J. Arriolo, Finance and
    Administration Department, or Ed L. Grubb,

associate dean, School of Business
Administration

PENNSYLVANIA

Drexel University
College of Business and Administration
32nd and Chestnut Sts.
Philadelphia, PA 19104
(215) 895-6996
fax (215) 895-2907
Contact: Hazem D. Maragah, Department of
    Quantitative Methods

Duquesne University
709 Rockwell Hall
Pittsburgh, PA 15282
(412) 396-6269
fax (412) 396-4764
Contact: William D. Presutti Jr., associate
    dean, Graduate School of Business

Eastern College
10 Fairview Dr.
St. Davids, PA 19087-3696
(610) 341-1459
fax (610) 341-1569
Contact: David King, director of human
    resources

Edinboro University of Pennsylvania
Mathematics and Computer Science
    Department
Edinboro, PA 16444
(814) 734-1185
Contact: William D. Etling, associate professor,
    Mathematics and Computer Science
    Department

Grove City College
100 Campus Dr.
P.O. Box 2661
Grove City, PA 16127-2104
(412) 458-2027
Contact: Bruce W. Ketler, chair, Department of
    Industrial Management

Lehigh University
200 W. Packer Ave.
Bethlehem, PA 18015-1582
(610) 758-4032
fax (610) 758-4886
Contact: John W. Adams associate professor,
    Industrial Engineering Department

Pennsylvania College of Technology
1 College Ave.
Williamsport, PA 17701
(717) 326-3761
Contact: William R. Thompson, professor of
  manufacturing

Pennsylvania State University
201 Old Main
University Park, PA 16802
(814) 863-8721
fax (814) 863-8685
Contact: Louise Sandmeyer, executive director,
  Continuous Quality Improvement Center

Pittsburgh (University of)
1048 Benedum Hall
Pittsburgh, PA 15261
(412) 624-9830
fax (412) 624-9831
Contact: Harvey Wolfe, chair, Department of
  Industrial Engineering

Scranton (University of)
School of Management
Scranton, PA 18510-4602
(717) 941-7782
fax (717) 941-4201
Contact: Len Tischler, assistant professor of
  management

Temple University
309 Speakman Hall
Philadelphia, PA 19122
(215) 204-8130
fax (215) 204-5698
Contact: Mark Gershon, chair, MSOM
  Department

Villanova University
800 Lancaster Ave.
Villanova, PA 19085-1699
(610) 519-4835
fax (610) 519-7162
Contact: John M. Kelley, director, Office of
  Planning and Institutional Research

PUERTO RICO

Inter American University of Puerto Rico
P.O. Box 363255
San Juan, PR 00936-3255
(809) 763-4633

fax (809) 751-2190
Contact: Ileana Iruine, institutional quality
  coordinator

Puerto Rico (University of)
P.O. Box 5000
Mayaguez, PR 00681-5000
(809) 832-4040, ext. 2006
fax (809) 265-3819
Contact: Noel Artiles-Leon, director, Industrial
  Engineering Department

SOUTH CAROLINA

Anderson College
316 Boulevard St.
Anderson, SC 29621
(803) 231-2160
fax (803) 231-2004
Contact: Carol Karnes, professor of
  management Department of Business

Central Wesleyan College
1 Wesleyan Dr.
Central, SC 29630
(803) 639-2453
fax (803) 639-0826
Contact: W. Jim Mahony, chair, Social Sciences
  Division

Clemson University
223 Poole Agricultural Center
Clemson, SC 29634-0371
(803) 656-2786
fax (803) 656-0331
Contact: John G. Surak, professor, Department
  of Food Science

South Carolina, Columbia (University of)
Department of Statistics
Columbia, SC 29208
(803) 777-7800
fax (803) 777-4048
Contact: James Lynch, professor, Department
  of Statistics

South Carolina, Spartanburg (University of)
490 Rifle Rd.
Spartanburg, SC 29303-6254
(803) 599-0205
fax (803) 599-9720
Contact: R.J. Garrison Jr., executive director,
  Quality Institute

SOUTH DAKOTA

South Dakota State University
Department of Math and Statistics
Brookings, SD 57007
(605) 688-6196
fax (605) 688-5880
Contact: Robert Lacher, professor, Department
of Math and Statistics

TENNESSEE

Belmont University
1900 Belmont Blvd.
Nashville, TN 37212
(615) 386-4460
fax (615) 386-4593
Contact: Susan G. Hillenmeyer, vice-president
for quality and professional development

David Lipscomb University
3901 Granny White Pike
Nashville, TN 37204-3951
(615) 269-1000, ext. 2487
fax (615) 269-1818
Contact: Hugh Daniel, associate professor of
management

East Tennessee State University
P.O. Box 70553, ETSU
Johnson City, TN 37614-0553
(615) 929-4465
fax (615) 929-5743
Contact: James A. Hales, dean, College of
Applied Science and Technology

Memphis (University of)
Department of Engineering Technology
Memphis, TN 38152
(901) 678-3296
fax (901) 678-4180
Contact: Robert E. Magowan, professor,
Department of Engineering Technology

Middle Tennessee State University
P.O. Box 19
Murfreesboro, TN 37132
(615) 898-2776
fax (615) 898-5697
Contact: Richard H. Gould, chair, Industrial
Studies Department

Tennessee, Chattanooga (University of)
247 Grote Hall / 615 McCallie Ave.
Chattanooga, TN 37403

(615) 755-4718
fax (615) 755-5229
Contact: Greg Sedrick, or Larry Ettkin,
director, Engineering Management

Tennessee, Knoxville (University of)
111 Student Service Bldg.
Knoxville, TN 37996-0211
(615) 974-6613
fax (615) 974-6171
Contact: Francis M. Gross, associate vice-
president for management services

Tennessee Technological University
P.O. Box 5011
Cookeville, TN 38505
(615) 372-3959
fax (615) 372-6172
Contact: James R. Smith, professor, Industrial
Engineering Department

TEXAS

Dallas Baptist University
3000 Mountain Creek Pkwy.
Dallas, TX 75211
(214) 333-5239
fax (214) 333-5579
Contact: Richard S. Weintraub, executive
director, College of Business

Dallas (University of)
Graduate School of Management
1845 E. Northgate
Irving, TX 75062
(214) 721-5046
fax (214) 721-5130
Contact: Richard Peregoy, associate professor

East Texas Baptist University
1209 W. Grove
Marshall, TX 25670
(903) 935-7963, ext. 353
fax (903) 922-4448
Contact: Ward Walker, vice-president, Spiritual
Affairs Department

Houston (University of)
4800 Calhoun
Houston, TX 77204-6283
(713) 743-4600
fax (713) 743-4622
Contact: Tom Duening, assistant dean, College
of Business Administration

Lamar University, Beaumont
P.O. Box 10032, LUS
Beaumont, TX 77710
(409) 880-8804
fax (409) 880-8121
Contact: Victor Zaloom, chair, Industrial
   Engineering Department

North Texas (University of)
College of Business Administration
Denton, TX 76203-3677
(817) 565-4767
fax (817) 565-4935
Contact: Victor R. Prybutok, director, Center
   for Quality and Productivity, Business
   Computer Information Systems Department

Texas A&M University, Kingsville
Campus Box 172
Kingsville, TX 78363-8201
(512) 595-2235
fax (512) 595-3409
Contact: Margaret Land, professor,
   Mathematics Department

Texas, Austin (University of)
P.O. Box 7459
Austin, TX 78713
(512) 471-9970
fax (512) 471-1063
Contact: Michelle O'Reilly, associate director,
   Quality Center

Texas, Houston (University of)
Health Science Center
P.O. Box 20036
Houston, TX 77225
(713) 792-5307
fax (713) 792-5625
Contact: Alan L. Austin Jr., assistant vice-
   president, Continuous Quality Improvement
   Department

Texas, San Antonio (University of)
6900 Loop 1604 N.W.
San Antonio, TX 78249-0664
(210) 691-5552
fax (210) 691-4439
Contact: Youn-Min Chou, professor, Division of
   Mathematics, Computer Science, and
   Statistics

Texas Tech University
P.O. Box 42015
Lubbock, TX 79409-2015

(806) 742-0530
fax (806) 742-2241
Contact: Kerry Billingsley, director, Office of
   Quality Service

UTAH

Brigham Young University
Department of Statistics
203 TMCB
Provo, UT 84602
(801) 378-4505
fax (801) 378-5722
Contact: Lee Hendrix, professor and chair,
   Department of Statistics

Phoenix, Salt Lake City (University of)
5251 Green St.
Salt Lake City, UT 84123
(801) 263-1444, ext. 110
fax (801) 269-9766
Contact: Craig Swenson, vice-president and
   director

Weber State University
Ogden, UT 84408-1006
(801) 626-6389
fax (801) 626-7922
Contact: Carol V. Gaskill, director, Budget and
   Institutional Research Department

VERMONT

Vermont (University of)
16 Colchester Ave.
Burlington, VT 05401-1455
(802) 656-4350
fax (802) 656-2552
Contact: Larry D. Haugh, director, Statistics
   Program

VIRGINIA

Marymount University
2807 N. Glebe Rd.
Arlington, VA 22207
(703) 284-1622
fax (703) 284-1693
Contact: John P. Fry, associate dean, Human
   Resource Programs

Virginia Commonwealth University
P.O. Box 844000
Richmond, VA 23284-4000
(804) 828-1479

fax (804) 828-8884
Contact: Kim Melton, assistant professor,
    School of Business

Virginia Tech
333 Norris Hall
Blacksburg, VA 24061-0217
(703) 231-9764
fax (703) 231-3031
Contact: Pamela Kurstedt, assistant dean,
    College of Engineering

WASHINGTON

Washington State University
Pullman, WA 99164
(509) 335-5595 / (509) 335-1870 or (509) 335-
    7527
fax (509) 335-3818 / (509) 335-7736
Contact: E. Ray Ladd, Engineering
    Management Program, or Min-Chiang Wang,
    Department of Management and Systems

Washington (University of)
Mackenzie Hall DJ-10
Seattle, WA 98195
(206) 543-4369
fax (206) 658-9392
Contacts: Douglas L. MacLachlan, professor,
    Marketing and International Behavior
    Department

WASHINGTON, DC

George Washington University
Continuing Engineering Education Programs
801 22nd St., Rm. 308
Washington, DC 20052
(202) 994-6106
fax (202) 872-0645
Contact: John Davis Rohrbough, director of
    quality and productivity programs

WEST VIRGINIA

Marshall University
1050 Fourth Ave.
Huntington, WV 25755
(304) 696-3093
fax (304) 696-6280
Contact: Larry Kyle, director, Business
    Development and Training Department

West Virginia University, Morgantown
College of Engineering

P.O. Box 6107
Morgantown, WV 26506-6107
(304) 293-4607, ext. 706
fax (304) 293-4970
Contact: Rashpal S. Ahluwalia, professor,
    Industrial Engineering Department

West Virginia University, Parkersburg
Rte. 5, Box 167A
Parkersburg, WV 26101
(304) 424-8271
fax (304) 424-8315
Contact: Robert A. Thorne, director of training
    and development

WISCONSIN

Alverno College
3401 S. 39th St.
P.O. Box 343922
Milwaukee, WI 53234
(414) 382-6238
fax (414) 382-6354
Contact: William McEachern, dean, Business
    and Management School

Keller Graduate School of Management
100 E. Wisconsin Ave.
Milwaukee, WI 53202
(414) 278-7677
fax (414) 278-0137
Contact: Mike Wegmann, curriculum
    coordinator

Marian College
45 S. National Ave.
Fond du Lac, WI 54935
(414) 923-8149
fax (414) 923-7154
Contact: Rodolfo Ledesma, chair, Business
    Administration Division

Milwaukee School of Engineering
1025 N. Broadway St.
Milwaukee, WI 53202-3109
(414) 277-7324
fax (414) 277-7477
Contact: Thomas W. Davis, dean and senior
    vice-president of academics

Northland College
1411 Ellis Ave.
Ashland, WI 54806
(715) 682-1226
fax (715) 682-1308

Contact: Marianne E. Inman, vice-president
  and dean

Wisconsin, Madison (University of)
90 Bascom Hall
Madison, WI 53706
(608) 262-6843
Contact: Maury Cotter, acting director, Office
  of Quality Improvement

Wisconsin, Milwaukee (University of)
P.O. Box 742
Milwaukee, WI 53201
(414) 229-5274
fax (414) 229-6957
Contact: Ronald L. Heilmann, director, Center
  for Quality, Productivity, and Economic
  Development

Wisconsin, Stout (University of)
Menomonie, WI 54751-0790
(715) 232-1145
fax (715) 232-1105
Contact: Wallace Carlsone, professor,
  Industrial Management Department

Wisconsin, Whitewater (University of)
Whitewater, WI 53190
(414) 472-5473
fax (414) 472-4863
Contact: Mete Sirvanci, professor, Marketing
  Department

WYOMING

Wyoming (University of)
P.O. Box 3413
Laramie, WY 82071
(307) 766-2760
fax (307) 766-2800
Contact: Janet R. Costin Guest, project
  director, Division of Administration and
  Finance

CANADA

Jonquiere (Cegep de), (College of Jon Quiere)
2525 St. Hubert
Jonquiere, Quebec
Canada G7X 7W2
(418) 547-3672
fax (418) 547-6765
Contact: Lise T. Barrette, Service de
  l'education Permanente, or Stanley
  McLeffen, Service de l'education Permanente

Mohawk College of Applied Arts and
  Technology
P.O. Box 2034
Hamilton, Ontario
Canada L8N 3T2
(905) 575-1212, ext. 3091
Contact: Hank Verspagen, professor, Industrial
  Management

Quebec (University of)
Ecole de Technologie Superieure
4750 Henri-Julien
Montreal, Quebec
Canada H2T 2C8
(514) 289-8860
fax (514) 289-8755
Contact: Youssef A. Youssef, professor of
  quality engineering, Mechanical Engineering
  Department

Sherbrooke (University of)
2500 University Blvd.
Sherbrooke, Quebec
Canada J1K 2R1
(819) 821-7152
fax (819) 821-7163
Contact: Bruno-Marie Bechard, professor,
  Engineering Department

DENMARK

Engineering Academy of Denmark
Bldg. 451
DK-2800 Lyngby, Denmark
45 42 88 30 22
fax 45 42 88 02 86
Contact: Jorgen Moltoft, professor, Electronic
  and Electrical Engineering Department

MEXICO

Monterrey Institute of Technology (ITESM
  Campus Monterrey)
Sucursal de Correos "J"
Monterrey, NL 64849
Mexico
(528) 358-2000, ext. 3326
fax (528) 358-4555
Contact: Daniel Meade, coordinator,
  Continuous Quality Improvement Program

Monterrey (Universidad de)
4500 Morones Prieto Pte.
Garza Garcia, NL 66238
Mexico

(528) 338-5050 / (528) 338-5504
fax (528) 336-4202
Contact: Eduardo Garcia Luna, director of
planning, or Calidad Intergrad, direccion de
ingenieria

SCOTLAND

Stirling (University of)
Scottish Quality Management Centre
Stirling, Scotland FK9 4LA
44 786 43 73 72
fax 44 786 46 73 59
Contact: Ian W. Hannah, director of programs

COMMUNITY COLLEGES

ARIZONA

Maricopa Community College District
2411 W. 14th St.
Tempe, AZ 85281
(602) 731-8206
fax (602) 731-8210
Contact: Tricia Euen, occupational program
specialist

Rio Salado Community College
640 N. First Ave.
Phoenix, AZ 85003
(602) 223-4000
Contact: Sharon Koberna, total quality
management coordinator

CALIFORNIA

American River College
4700 College Oak Blvd.
Sacramento, CA 95841
(916) 484-8162
fax (916) 484-8673
Contact: Del Nelson, chair Management
Department

DeAnza College
21250 Stevens Creek Blvd.
Cupertino, CA 95014
(408) 864-8673
Contact: Short Courses Department

El Camino Community College
16007 Crenshaw Blvd.
Torrance, CA 90506

(310) 715-3129
fax (310) 715-7818
Contact: Donna Manno, staff development
coordinator, Staff Development Department

Glendale Community College
520 N. Central Ave., Ste. 270
Glendale, CA 91203
(818) 545-0196
fax (818) 246-6019
Contact: Marc R. Striegel, manager,
Continuous Improvement Services
Department

Palomar College
1140 W. Mission Rd.
San Marcos, CA 92069
(619) 744-1150, ext. 2286
fax (619) 591-9108
Contact: Robert Kuretich, director of vocational
programs

Solano Community College
4000 Suisun Valley Rd.
Suisun, CA 94585
(707) 864-7000, ext. 374
fax (707) 864-0361
Contact: Charles R. Shatzer, Business
Administration Department

COLORADO

Aims Community College
P.O. Box 69
Greeley, CO 80632
(303) 330-8008, ext. 222
fax (303) 339-6666
Contact: Richard Wood, director, Continuing
Education Department

Lamar Community College
2401 S. Main
Lamar, CO 81052
(719) 336-2248, ext. 30
fax (719) 336-2448
Contact: Marvin E. Lane, president

CONNECTICUT

Naugatuck Valley Community-Technical
College
750 Chase Pkwy.
Waterbury, CT 06708
(203) 575-8089
fax (203) 575-8096

Contact: Stephen M. Colwell, dean of technical
    education

FLORIDA

Brevard Community College
250 Grassland Rd. S.E.
Palm Bay, FL 32909
(407) 951-1060, ext. 2038
fax (407) 723-4674
Contact: Don Tate, coordinator, ISO 9000
    Computer Integrated Manufacturing
    Program

George Stone Area Voc-Tech Center
2400 Longleaf Dr.
Pensacola, FL 32526
(904) 944-1424
fax (904) 944-9560
Contact: Robert Lindner, director

GEORGIA

Savannah Technical Institute
Main Campus
5717 White Bluff Rd.
Savannah, GA 31499
(912) 351-4404
fax (912) 352-4362
Contact: Don Stewart, assistant
    superintendent

ILLINOIS

Rock Valley College
3301 N. Mulford Rd.
Rockford, IL 61114
(815) 654-5511
fax (815) 654-4459
Contact: Don P. Williams, director, Technology
    Division

Triton College
2000 Fifth Ave.
River Grove, IL 60171
(708) 456-0300
fax (708) 456-0049
Contact: Tom Bondi, dean, Technology
    Department

INDIANA

Indiana Vocational Technical College, Central
    Indiana
P.O. Box 1763
Indianapolis, IN 46206-1763

(317) 921-4967
fax (317) 921-4753
Contact: Thomas C. Cooke, dean of
    instructional affairs

IOWA

Eastern Iowa Community College District
306 W. River Dr.
Davenport, IA 52801-1221
(319) 322-5015
fax (319) 322-3956
Contact: George W. Varchola, director of
    continuous quality improvement

Hawkeye Community College
P.O. Box 8015
Waterloo, IA 50704
(319) 296-2320
fax (319) 296-2874
Contact: Debra J. Corson, coordinator, Quality
    Improvement Services Department

North Iowa Area Community College
500 College Dr.
Mason City, IA 50401
(515) 421-4210
fax (515) 423-1711
Contact: Michael C. Morrison, vice-president
    for academic affairs

KANSAS

Cowley County Community College and Area
    Vocational Technical School
125 S. Second St.
Arkansas City, KS 67005
(316) 442-0430
fax (316)441-5350
Contact: Jim Miesner or Wayne Short, Total
    Quality Management Program

Fort Scott Community College
2108 S. Horton
Fort Scott, KS 66701
(316) 223-2700
fax (316) 223-4927
Contact: Dennis Hauswirth, total quality
    management coordinator

Hutchinson Community College
1300 N. Plum
Hutchinson, KS 67501
(316) 665-3506
fax (316) 665-3310
Contact: Ed Berger, president

KENTUCKY

Elizabethtown Community College
600 College Street Rd.
Elizabethtown, KY 42701
(502) 769-2371, ext. 215
fax (502) 769-0736
Contact: Shannon Whelan, business and
industry liaison

MARYLAND

Prince George's Community College (PGCC)
Department of Engineering Technology and
Quality Assurance
301 Largo Rd., Mail Stop L217
Largo, MD 20772
(301) 322-0760
Contact: Charles Hendrickson, professor, NASA
Goddard PGCC Space and Technology Institute

MASSACHUSETTS

Northern Essex Community College
Elliott Way
Haverhill, MA 01830
(508) 374-3814
fax (508) 374-3723
Contact: Sandra Roberts, business
development director, Center for Business
and Industry

Quinsigamond Community College
670 W. Boylston St.
Worcester, MA 01606
(508) 854-4435
fax (508) 856-0395
Contact: Stanton Rome, dean, Center for
Education and Training

Springfield Technical Community College
One Armory Sq.
Springfield, MA 01101-9000
(413) 781-7822
fax (413) 746-4569
Contact: James J. Dowd, assistant to the
president

MICHIGAN

Jackson Community College
2111 Emmons Rd.
Jackson, MI 49201
(517) 787-0800
fax (517) 787-1630
Contact: Carole J. Schwinn, assistant to the
president, President's Office

Lansing Community College
Technology Careers-36
P.O. Box 40010
Lansing, MI 48901-7210
(517) 483-1318
fax (517) 483-9619
Contact: Jane Muzi, Quality Assurance
Department

Macomb Community College
14500 E. Twelve Mile Rd.
Warren, MI 48093
(810) 445-7472 or (810) 445-7411
fax (810) 445-7887
Contact: Ben S. Selleck Jr., professor, Division
of Mechanical Technology

St. Clair County Community College
P.O. Box 5015
323 Erie St.
Port Huron, MI 48061-5015
(810) 989-5621
fax (810) 984-4730
Contact: John P. Borris, chair, Industrial
Technology Department

West Shore Community College
3000 N. Stiles Rd.
Scottville, MI 49454
(616) 845-6211
fax (616) 845-0207
Contact: Gerald Svendor, chair, Business
Division

MINNESOTA

Alexandria Technical College
1601 Jefferson St.
Alexandria, MN 56308
(612) 762-0221
fax (612) 762-4501
Contact: David Trites, quality coordinator

MISSOURI

St. Louis Community College at Florissant
Valley
Engineering Department
3400 Pershall Rd.
Ferguson, MO 63135-1499
(314) 595-4308
fax (314) 595-4544
Contact: Bob Deufel, adjunct faculty and chair,
Advisory Committee and Quality Technology
Department

NEW JERSEY

Mercer County Community College
1200 Old Trenton Rd.
Trenton, NJ 08690
(609) 586-4800, ext. 485
fax (609) 890-6338
Contact: Jacqueline B. Sanders, academic
division dean, Business Division

NEW YORK

Broome Community College
P.O. Box 1017
Binghamton, NY 13902
(607) 778-5318
fax (607) 778-5345
Contact: Gregory E. Sliwa, assistant professor,
Mathematics Department

Drake Business Schools, Inc.
36-09 Main St.
Flushing, NY 11354
(718) 353-3535
Contact: Lois A. Citron, academic dean

Monroe Community College
1000 E. Henrietta Rd.
Rochester, NY 14623-5780
(716) 292-2000 / (716) 292-2696
fax (716)427-2749
Contact: Edgar Whitcomb, Mechanical/Quality
Control Technology Department, or Donald
E. Day, chair of integrated technologies

NORTH CAROLINA

Asheville-Buncombe Technical Community
College
340 Victoria Rd.
Asheville, NC 28801
(704) 254-1921
fax (704) 251-6355
Contact: Deborah Porto, Total Quality Program

Catawba Valley Community College
2550 Highway 70 S.E.
Hickory, NC 28601
(704) 327-7000
fax (704) 327-7276
Contact: Thomas C. Lavender, professor,
Industrial Engineering Technology
Department

Central Carolina Community College
1105 Kelly Dr.

Sanford, NC 27330
(919) 775-5401
fax (919) 775-1221
Contact: Paul C. Harris, quality assurance
instructor

Western Piedmont Community College
1001 Burkemont Ave.
Morganton, NC 28655
(704) 438-6165
fax (704) 438-6015
Contact: Jane B. Carswell, associate dean,
Business Technologies Department

NORTH DAKOTA

Bismark State College
1500 Edwards Ave.
Bismark, ND 58501
(701) 224-5462
fax (701) 224-5550
Contact: Greg Bach, associate professor,
Management Department

OHIO

Cincinnati Technical College
3520 Central Pkwy.
Cincinnati, OH 45223
(513) 569-1715
fax (513) 569-1463
Contact: Terrence L. Huge, instructor of
applied statistics

Miami University Middletown
4200 E. University Blvd.
Middletown, OH 45042
(513) 424-4444
fax (513) 424-4632
Contact: Rob Speckert, chair, Engineering
Technology Department

Owens Community College
P.O. Box 10,000
Toledo, OH 43699
(419) 661-7458
Contact: George MacRitchie, chair, Quality
Engineering Technology Department

Sinclair Community College
444 W. Third St.
Dayton, OH 45402
(513) 226-3050
fax (513) 226-3080
Contact: Steve Jonas, vice-president for
administration

Terra Community College
2830 Napolean Rd.
Fremont, OH 43420-9670
(419) 334-8400
fax (419) 334-2300
Contact: Lyn Sullivan, assistant professor,
Quality Control Department

OKLAHOMA

Oklahoma State University
900 N. Portland, ET300
Oklahoma City, OK 73107
(405) 545-8619
Contact: Dan L. Johnson, coordinator, Total
Quality Initiatives Department

PENNSYLVANIA

Delaware County Community College
901 S. Media Line Rd.
Media, PA 19063
(215) 359-5325
fax (215) 359-5343
Contact: Susanna B. Stass, quality coordinator,
Total Quality Department

Peirce College
1420 Pine St.
Philadelphia, PA 19102
(215) 545-6400
fax (215) 545-2517
Contact: Helen Rosenfeld, chief quality officer,
QSM and Institutional Research Department

TENNESSEE

Knoxville Business College
720 N. Fifth Ave.
Knoxville, TN 37917
(615) 524-3034
fax (615) 637-0127
Contact: Joseph C. Fields, academic dean

Roane State Community College
276 Patton Ln.
Harriman, TN 37748-5011
(615) 882-4612
fax (615) 882-8179
Contact: Jim Clauson, director of quality
training, Total Quality Management Center

State Technical Institute at Memphis
5983 Macon Cove
Memphis, TN 38134
(901) 383-4112

fax (901) 383-4503
Contact: James Willis, assistant director,
Business, Industry, and Government
Training Department

Walters State Community College
500 S. Davy Crockett Pkwy.
Morristown, TN 37813
(615) 585-6897
fax (615) 585-6853
Contact: Gary Skolits, director of planning,
Research and Assessment Department

TEXAS

Austin Community College
11928 Stonehollow Dr.
Austin, TX 78758
(512) 823-4800
fax (512) 823-4867
Contact: Thomas N. Colbath, head, Quality
Assurance Department

Brazosport College
500 College
Lake Jackson, TX 77566
(409) 266-3256 / (409) 266-3203
fax (409) 265-2944 / (409) 265-2944
Contact: David L. Preston, director,
Institutional Research, Planning, and
Administration Computer Services, or John
Ray, vice-president

Collin County Community College
2200 W. University
McKinney, TX 75070
(214) 548-6606
fax (214) 548-0464
Contact: Martha M. Ellis, director of staff,
program, and organization development

San Antonio College
1300 San Pedro
San Antonio, TX 78212
(210) 733-2652
fax (210) 733-2634
Contact: Raymond Blythe, program manager,
Institute of Quality Improvement

Texas State Technical College
Harlingen, TX 78550-3697
(210) 425-0640
fax (210) 425-0799
Contact: Terry H. Brattin, director, Industrial
Effectiveness Department

VERMONT

Vermont (Community College of)
119 Pearl St.
Burlington, VT 05404
(802) 655-2396
fax (802) 865-3323
Contact: David Ellis, coordinator

VIRGINIA

Central Virginia Community College
3506 Wards Rd.
Lynchburg, VA 24502
(804) 386-4666
fax (804) 386-4681
Contact: Tom McGrath, Engineering/
   Technology Department

WASHINGTON

Lake Washington Technical College
11605 132nd Ave. N.E.
Kirkland, WA 98034
(206) 828-5643
fax (206) 828-5648
Contact: Lupe Reyes Jr., vice-president,
   Training and Continuing Education

South Seattle Community College
6000 16th Ave. S.W., Rm. TC140
Seattle, WA 98106-1499
(206) 764-5390 or (206) 764-5339
fax (206) 763-5156 or (206) 764-7949
Contact: Bill Walker, quality assurance
   coordinator and instructor Technical
   Education Division

Yakima Valley Community College
P.O. Box 1647
Yakima, WA 98907
(509) 575-2355
fax (509) 575-2461
Contact: Phil Tullar, president

WISCONSIN

Chippewa Valley Technical College
620 W. Clairemont Ave.
Eau Claire, WI 54701
(715) 835-1910
fax (715) 833-6470
Contact: Larry Doyle, business coordinator

Fox Valley Technical College
5 Systems Dr.

Appleton, WI 54913
(414) 735-5707 / (414) 735-4772
fax (414) 735-4771
Contact: Callie Zilinsky, consultant/trainer,
   FVTC Quality Academy, or Rick Miech,
   instructor/coordinator, QIPS Program

Mid-State Technical College
2600 W. Fifth St.
Marshfield, WI 54449
(715) 387-2538
fax (715) 389-2864
Contact: Dennis Wessel, supervisor, Business
   Department

Milwaukee Area Technical College
700 W. State St.
Milwaukee, WI 53233
(414) 297-7806
fax (414) 297-7764
Contact: James B. Rieley, director, Center for
   Continuous Quality Improvement

Moraine Park Technical College
235 N. National Ave.
P.O. Box 1940
Fond du Lac, WI 54936-1940
(414) 924-3298
fax (414) 929-2478
Contact: John Horvath and Paul Morin,
   Technical Division

Northeast Wisconsin Technical College
2740 W. Mason St.
Green Bay, WI 54307
(414) 498-5484
fax (414) 498-6313
Contact: Melvin K. Buckmaster, associate
   dean, Center for Business and Industry

Waukesha County Technical College
800 Main St.
Pewaukee, WI 53072
(414) 691-5566
fax (414) 691-5593
Contact: Liane A. Dolezar, quality advisor

Wisconsin Indianhead Technical College
505 Pine Ridge Dr., HCR 69/1900 College Dr.
Shell Lake, WI 54871 / Rice Lake, WI 54868
(715) 468-2815 / (715) 234-7082
fax (715) 468-2819 / (715) 234-5172
Contact: David Hildebrand, president, or
   Michael W. Boyle, quality assurance
   instructor

Appendix E
ISO 9000 Registrars Worldwide

Registrars are third-party organizations that will vouch for the compliance of your company to various international standards. The registrars listed below all handle ISO 9000. Some also handle QS-9000 and ISO 14000 as well as other system and product standards. The accreditations listed were current as of December 1995. The RvC is now known by the accronym RvA. The NACCB is now known as the UKAS.

ABS Quality Evaluations, Inc.

ABS Plaza
16855 Northchase Dr.
Houston, TX 77060-6008

Phone: (713) 873-9400
FAX: (713) 874-9564

Accredited by: RvC, RAB, INMETRO, ANSI-RAB

AENOR

Fernandez de la Hoz, 52
Madrid, 28010
SPAIN

Phone: +34 1 410 4851
FAX: +34 1 410 4976

Accredited by: Recognition by Spanish Government

AGA Quality

1425 Grand Vista Avenue
Los Angles, CA 90023

Phone: 213-261-8161
FAX: 213-261-3369

AIB - VINCOTTE (AV QUALITE)

2900 Wilcrest
Suite 300
Houston, TX 77042

Phone: (713) 465-2850
FAX: (713) 465-1182

Accredited by: NAC-QS, RvC

AIB Registration Services

1213 Bakers Way
Manhattan, KS 66502

Phone: 913-537-4750
FAX: 913-537-1493

American Assoc. for Lab Accred. (A2L2)

656 Quince Orchard Road #620
Gaithersburg, MD 20878-1409

Phone: (301) 670-1377
FAX: (301) 869-1495

Note: This registrar does not issue ISO 9000 certificates, instead it accredits labs to ISO standards.

American European Services

1054 31st Street NW
Suite 120
Washington, DC 20007

Phone: (202) 337-3214
FAX: (202) 337-3709

American Quality Assessors

1200 Main Street
Suite M107
Columbia, SC 29201

Phone: (803) 779-8150
FAX: (803) 779-8109

American Software Quality Assurance

3187 Blue Rock Rd.
Cincinnati, OH 45239

Phone: 513-385-8210; 513-259-4048
FAX: 513-385-2571

AOQC, Inc

650 N. Sam Houston Pkwy
Suite 228
Houston, TX 77060

Phone: 713-591-7882
FAX: 713-448-1401

AQSR (See OMNEX)

Ascert USA, Inc.

1054 - 31st Street NW
Suite 120
Washington, DC 20007

Phone: 202-337-3214
FAX: 202-337-3709

ASME

345 East 47th Street
New York, NY 10017

Phone: 212-705-8590
FAX: 212-705-8599

Accredited by: RAB, RVC, ANSI-RAB

*AT&T Quality Registrar (Call DNV)

1945 Chaussee de Wavre
Brussels, Belgium 1160

Phone: 322-676-3596
FAX: 322-676-3812

*AT&T Quality Registrar (Call DNV)

2600 San Tomas Expressway
Santa Clara, CA 95051

Phone: 800-521-3399
FAX: 408-522-4436

Accredited by: ANSI-RAB

*AT&T Quality Registrars (Call DNV)

650 Liberty Ave.
Union, NJ 07083

Phone: 800-550-9001
FAX: 908-851-3360

Accredited by: ANSI-RAB

Automotive Quality Systems Registrar, Inc.

P.O. Box 15019
Ann Arbor, MI 48106

Phone: 313-480-9940
FAX: 313-480-9941

BQS

110 Summit Ave.
P.O. Box 460
Montvale, NJ 07645

Phone: (800) 624-5892

BSI Quality Assurance

P.O. Box 375
Milton Keynes, MK14 6LL
United Kingdom

Phone: 0908-220-908
FAX: 0908-220-671

Accredited by: NACCB, RvC

BSI Quality Assurance

Tysons Corner
8000 Towers Crescent Dr., Suite 1350
Vienna, VA 22182
USA

Phone: 703-760-7828
FAX: 703-761-2770

Accredited by: NACCB & RvC

Bureau De Normalisation Du Quebec

70, rue
Dalhousie, bureau 220
Quebec, Quebec GIK 4B2
Canada

Phone: (418) 643-5813
FAX: (418) 646-3315

Accredited by: SCC (Canada)

BVQI

North American Central Offices
509 North Main Street
Jamestown, NY 14701

Phone: (716) 484-9002
FAX: (716) 484-9003

Accredited by: ANSI-RAB, NACCB, RvC,
NAC-QS

BVQI

Suite G1
Norton Centre Pnynernook Road
Aberdeen, Scotland AS1 2RN
Scotland

Phone: 44 224 212 838
FAX: 44 224 210 924

---

*Det Norsk Veritas (DNV) has recently purchased these offices.

BVQI

223 Wolverhampton Street
Dudley, West Midlands DY1 1EF
United Kingdom

Phone: 44 384 459 546
FAX: 44 384 238 741

BVQI

Huyssennallee 5
Essen, Germany D-45128

Phone: 49 201 810 7614
FAX: 49 201 810 762

BVQI

Sachsenfeld 4 Haus 5
Hansa Carree
Postfach 100940, Hamburg 1 D20006
Germany

Phone: 49 201 810 7614
FAX: 49 201 810 7620

BVQI

14 Challenge House
Sherwood Drive
Bletchley, Milton Keynes MK3 6DP
United Kingdom

Phone: 44 224 212 838
FAX: 44 224 210 924

BVQI (NA)—East Coast Office

50 Park Row West
Providence, RI 02903

Phone: 401-273-7810
FAX: 401-273-7812

BVQI (NA)—West Coast Office

1245 Oakmead Parkway
Suite 105
Sunnyvale, CA 94086

Phone: 408-730-9001 or 800-900-0476
FAX: 408-739-9003

BVQI France

925665 Rueil-Maimaison
10, Rue Jacques Daguerre
Cedex, France
France

Phone: 33 1 47 14 43 30
FAX: 33 1 47 14 43 25

BVQI Ltd

London Central Office
70 Borough High Street
London, England SE1 1XF
England

Phone: 44 71 378 8113
FAX: 44 71 378 8014

BVQI Quality Assurance

PO Box 375
Milton Keynes MK14 6LL
United Kingdom

Phone: 01908-22 908
FAX: 01908-220671

BVQI Sweden

Stora Badhusgatan 20
Gotenborg, Sweden S-411 21

Phone: 46 3117 14 15
FAX: 46 3113 39 73

Canadian Gas Association

55 Scardale Road
Don Mills, Ontario M3B 2R3
Canada

Phone: (416) 447-6468
FAX: (416) 447-7076

Accredited by: SCC (Canada)

Canadian General Standars Board

222 Queen Street
Suite 1402
Ottawa, Quebec K1A 1G6
Canada

Phone: (613) 941-8709
FAX: (819) 941-8706

Accredited by: SCC (Canada)

Centerlor Registration Services

300 Madison Avenue
Toledo, OH 43652

Phone: 419-249-5001
FAX: 419-249-4126

Ceramic Industry Certification Scheme (CICS)

Queens Road
Penkhull, Stoke-on-Trent ST4 7LQ
United Kingdom

Phone: 44-1782-411008
FAX: 44-1782-412331

CSC Professional Services Group

1340 Ashton Rd
Suite I
Hanover, MD 21076

Phone: 410-350-5411
FAX: 410-859-2859

Accredited by: Has applied for RvC accreditation

Davy Registrar Services, Inc. (DRS)

One Oliver Plaza
Pittsburgh, PA 15222-2604

Phone: 412-566-3086
FAX: 412-566-5290

Accredited by: ANSI-RAB

Defense Electronic Supply Center (DESC)

Sourcing and Qualifications Division
1507 Wilmington Pike
Dayton, OH 45444-5764

Phone: 513-296-6272
FAX: 513-296-6112

Det Norsk Veritas Certification, Inc.

16340 Park Ten Place
Suite 100
Houston, TX 77084

Phone: (713) 579-9003
FAX: (713) 579-1360

Det Norsk Veritas QA Limited

Palace House
3 Cathedral Street
London, England SE1 9DE
England

Phone: 0171-357-6080
FAX: 0171-357-6048

DLS Quality Tech. Assoc., Inc.

108 Hallmore Dr.
Camillus, NY 13031

Phone: 315-468-5811
FAX: 315-699-6332

Accredited by: ANSI-RAB

Electronic Ind Assoc. Quality Registry

2001 Pennsylvania Ave. NW
Washington, DC 20006

Phone: (202) 457-4970
FAX: (202) 457-4985

Accredited by: RvC

Entela

3033 Madison Ave. SE
Grand Rapids, MI 49548

Phone: (616) 247-0515
FAX: (616) 247-7527

Accredited by: RvC, ANSI-RAB

ETL Testing Laboratories/Inchcape Testing Services Co.

3933 U. S. Route 11
Cortland, NY 13045

Phone: 607-753-6711
FAX: (607) 756-9891

Accredited by: RvC (Netherlands), ANSI-RAB

French Association for Quality Assurance (AFAQ)

116 avenue Aristede Briand
BP No 40
Bagneus Cedex, France F-92224
France

Phone: 33-1-46-11-3713
FAX: 33-1-46-11-3710

GBJD Registrars, Ltd.

32 Clerissa Dr.
Suite 822
Richmond Hill, Ontario L4C 9R6
Canada

Phone: 905-508-9417
FAX: 905-471-0822

Accredited by: NACCB

Global Certification

The Old School
Leicester Road
Groby, Leicester LE6 6DQ

Phone: 01162-977700
FAX: 01162-878337

Global Registrars, Inc.

4700 Clairton Blvd.
Pittsburgh, PA 15236

Phone: (412) 884-2290
FAX: (412) 884-2268

Accredited by: ANSI-RAB, RvC

Hartford Steam Boiler Inspection & Insurance Corp

One State Street
Hartford, CT 06102-3001

Phone: 203-722-5294
FAX: 203-722-5530

Hong Kong AT&T Registrar

23rd Floor, 3 Exchange Square
8 Connaught Place
Central Hong Kong, Hong Kong
Hong Kong

Phone: 852-846-2823
FAX: 852-810-0564

Inscape Testing Services (Intertek Services Corp)

9900 Main Street
Suite 500
Fairfax, VA 22031-3969

Phone: 703-ISO-9000 x3011
FAX: (703) 273-4124 or 703-273-2895

Accredited by: RvC

Instituto Mexicano de Normalizacion y Certificacion, A.C. (IMNC)

Manuel Marie Contreras No. 133 pisol, col.
Cuauhtemoc C. P., Mexico D.F. 06470
Mexica

Phone: 703-2591 X179

Intertek Services Corporation

9900 Main Street
Suite 500
Fairfax, VA 22031

Phone: (703) ISO-9000 x 3011
FAX: (703) 273-2895

ISOQAR, Inc.

One World Trade Center
Suite 7967
New York, NY 10048

Phone: 212-432-5900
FAX: 212-524-0745

ISOQAR Limited

Suite 7—Metropolitan House
City Park Business Village
Cornbrook, Manchester M16 9HQ
United Kingdom

Phone: 01618776914
FAX: 01618776915

Kema Registered Quality (KRQ)

4379 County Line Road
Chalfont, PA 18914

Phone: (215) 822-4258
FAX: (215) 822-4285

Accredited by: RvC, ANSI-RAB

KPMG Quality Registrars

150 John F. Kennedy Pkwy
Short Hills, NJ 07078-2778

Phone: 800-716-5595
FAX: 201-912-6050

Accredited by: ANSI-RAB, RvC

Lloyd's Register Quality Assurance Ltd. (LRQA)

33-41 Newark Street
Riverview Historical Plaza
Hoboken, NJ 07030

Phone: (201) 963-1111
FAX: (201) 963-3299

Accredited by: NACCB, RvC, DAR, RAB-ANSI, JAS-ANZ

Lloyds Register Quality Assurance

Norfolk House
Wellesley Road
Croydon, CR9 2DT
United Kingdom

Phone: 01816886882
FAX: 01816818146

Loss Prevention Certification Board

Melrose Avenue
Borehamwood, Hertfordshire WD6 2BJ
England

Phone: 0181-207-2345
FAX: 0181-207-6305

LRQA Training Services

Siskin Drive
Middlemarch Office Village
Hiramford, Coventry CV34FJ
United Kingdom

Phone: 01213639660
FAX: 01203639493

MGQA

57 Simcoe Street
Oshawa, Ontario L1H 4G3
Canada

Phone: 905-433-2418
FAX: 905-436-6835

Moody International Quality Assurance Registrar

350 McKnight Plaza Building
105 Braunlich Dr.
Pittsburgh, PA 14237

Phone: (412) 366-5567
FAX: (412) 366-5571

Accredited by: Pursuing accreditation from RAB

National Quality Assurance, USA

1146 Massachusetts Ave.
Boxborough, MA 01719

Phone: (508) 635-9256
FAX: (508) 266-1073

Accredited by: NACCB. ANSI-RAB

National Standards Authority of Ireland (NSAI)

5 Medallion Center
Greenley Street
Merrimack, NH 03054

Phone: 603-424-7070
FAX: 603-429-1427

NQA—Northern Ireland

The Courtyard
Galgorm Castle
Ballymena, Northern Ireland BT42 1HL

Phone: 01266-44699
FAX: 01266-44977

NQA—Northern Region (of UK)

152/154 Tower Street
Brunswick Business Park
Liverpool, England L3 4BJ
England

Phone: 01517-087227
FAX: 01517-089788

NQA—Southern Region (of UK)

5 Cotswold Business Park
Caddington, Bedfordshire LU1 4AR
England

Phone: 01582-841144
FAX: 01582-841288

NQA—Wales & SW England

The QED Centre
Treforest Industial Estate
Pontypridd, CF37 5YR
England

Phone: 0144-3844321
FAX: 0144-3844345

NQA, USA

1146 Massachusetts Ave
Boxborough, MA 01719

Phone: 508-635-9256
FAX: 508-266-1073

Accredited by: NAACB, RAB

NSAI

39159 Paseo Padre Pkwy
Suite 232
Fremont, CA 94538

Phone: (510) 713-0292
FAX: (510) 713-0294

NSAI

5 Medallion Center
Greeley Street
Merrimack, NH 03054

Phone: (603) 424-7070
FAX: (603) 429-1427 / 429-1234

Accredited by: Directly by Irish Government

NSF International

3475 Plymouth Road
P.O. Box 130140
Ann Arbor, MI 48113-0140

Phone: 313-769-6728
FAX: 313-769-0109

Accredited by: RvC, ANSI-RAB

OMNEX

880 South Grove
Ypsilanti, MI 48198

Phone: (313) 480-9940
FAX: (313) 480-9941

Accredited by: RAB

Performance Review Institute Registrar (PRI)

163 Thornhill
Warrendale, PA 15086-7527

Phone: 412-772-1616
FAX: 412-772-1699

Perry Johnson Registrars, Inc. (PJR)

3000 Town Center
Suite 408
Southfield, MI 48075

Phone: 800-800-7910
FAX: 313 358-0882

Accredited by: ANSI-RAB, RvC

Professional Environmental Caring and Services QA

Resource House
144 High Street
Rayleigh, Essex SS6 7RU
England

Phone: 01268-770135
FAX: 01268-774436

Quality Certification Bureau, Inc.

Advanced Tech Center
Suite 208, 9650-20 Ave
Edmonton, Alberta T6N 1G1
Canada

Phone: 1-800-268-7321
FAX: 403-496-2464

Accredited by: RvC, SCC

Quality Control Systems and Services

P.O. Box 4417
San Clemente, CA 92672

Phone: (800) 423-8060

Quality Management Institute

Mississauga Exec. Center Suite 800
2 Robert Speck Parkway
Mississauga, Ontario L4Z 1H8
Canada

Phone: (416) 272-3920
FAX: (416) 272-3942

Accredited by: RvC, SCC

Quality Systems Management, Inc.

P.O. Box 58431
Los Angeles, CA 90058
USA

Phone: 805-722-5347
FAX: 805-722-5347

Accredited by: IQA/RAB

Quality Systems Registrars, Inc.

13873 Park Center Road
Suite 217
Herndon, VA 22071-3279

Phone: (703) 478-0241
FAX: (703) 478-0645

Accredited by: RvC, RAB

Quebec Quality Certification Group (GQCQ)

700, rue Dalhousie
Bureau 220
Quebec City, Quebec G1K 4B2
CANADA

Phone: (418) 643-5813
FAX: (418) 646-3315

Accredited by: SCC

RAYTHEON QUALITY REGISTAR

2 Wayside Road
Burlington, MA 01803

Phone: 617-238-2900
FAX: 617-238-3200

Accredited by: RvC

RTi/TUV Essen

1032 Elwell Ct.
Suite 222
Palo Alto, CA 94303

Phone: 415-961-0521
FAX: 415-961-9119

S A Bureau Veritas Quality International NV

Place Bara 26 Bte 17/19
Brussels, Belgium B-1070

Phone: 32 2 520 2090
FAX: 32 2 520 2030

Scott Technical Service

PO Box 812296
Wellesley, MA 02181-0016

Phone: 508-358-3470
FAX: 508-358-6119

SGS Internationai Certification Services Canada, Inc.

90 Gough Rd
Unit 4

Markham, Ontario L3R 5V5
Canada

Phone: 905-479-1160
FAX: 905-479-9452

Accredited by: NACCB, RVC, SCC, RAB, DAR, OFF-MET, SINCERT, JAS-ANZ, NAC-QS

SGS International Certification Services, Inc

Meadows Office Complex
301 Route 17 North
Rutherford, PA 07070

Phone: 201-935-1500
FAX: 201-935-4555

Accredited by: ANSI-RAB, Other Accreditations through SGS network, NACCB, SCC, NAC-QS, RVC, JAS-ANZ, ORMET, DAR/TGA

SGS Yarsley

Trowers Way
Redhill, Surrey RH1 2JN
England

Phone: 01737-768445
FAX: 01737-761229

Small Business Certification

Garfield House
165 - 167 High Street
Rayleigh, Essex SS6 7QA
England

Phone: 01268774430
FAX: 01268741493

Smithers Quality Assessment, Inc.

425 W. Market Street
Akron, OH 44303-2099

Phone: 216-762-4231
FAX: 216-762-7447

Accredited by: RVC

Southwest Research Inststite

P.O. Drawer 28510
6220 Culbra Road
San Antonio, TX 78288-0510

Phone: 210-522-2942
FAX: 210-522-3692

SRI Quality Registrar

2000 Corporate Drive
Suite 450
Wexford, PA 15090

Phone: (412) 935-2844
FAX: (412) 935-6825

Accredited by: RAB and RvC (Netherlands)

TRA Certication

700 E. Beardsley Ave.
P.O. Box 1081
Elkhart, IN 46515

Phone. 219-264-0745
FAX: 219-264-0740

Accredited by: ANSI-RAB, RvC

TUEV Rheinland e.V. Quality Mangement

Am Grauen Stein
Koeln, Germany 51105

Phone: 49 221 806 2250
FAX: 49 221 806 1754

TUV America

5 Cherry Hill Drive
Danvers, MA 01923

Phone: (508) 777-7999
FAX: (508) 777-8414

Accredited by: DAR

TUV Essen

1032 Elwell Ct.
Suite 222
Palo Alto, CA 94303

Phone: 415-961-0521
FAX: 415-961-9119

TUV Rheinland of North America

12 Commerce Road
Newtown, CT 06470

Phone: (203) 426-0888
FAX: (203) 270-8883

Accredited by: RvC, DAR

Underwriters Laboratories, Inc.

333 Pfingsten Road
Northbrook, IL 60062-2096

Phone: 708-272-8800
FAX: 708-272-8129

Underwriters Laboratories, Inc.

Quality & Reliability Dept.
1285 Walt Whitman Road
Melville, NY 11747-3081

Phone: 516-271-6200 x500
FAX: 516-271-6242

Accredited by: RvC, SCC, ANSI-RAB

United Registrar of Systems Ltd.

8 Chertsey Road
Woking, Surrey GU21 5AB
England

Phone: 01483-755003
FAX: 01483-755302

Vincotte, USA

10497 Town & Country Way
Suite 900
Houston, TX 77024

Phone: (713) 465-2850
FAX: (713) 465-1182

Wamock Hersey Prof. Services Ltd.

8810 Elmslie Street
LaSalle, Quebec H8R 1V8
Canada

Phone: 514-366-3100
FAX: 514-366-5350

Accredited by: SCC

Wamock Hersey Professional Services

8431 Murphy Dr.
P.O. Box 735
Middleton, WI 53562

Phone: 1-800-888-8431

Accredited by: SCC (Canada)

APPENDIX F
SOURCES OF THE ARTICLES
APPEARING IN THE *YEARBOOK*

The following is an alphabetical listing of the periodics that graciously granted us permission to reprint some of their articles. Where noted, subscription information is also listed.

17th Annual Spring Conference and Resource 1995 Proceedings

A Q P
801—B West Eighth Street
Cincinnati, OH 45203

Phone: 513-381-1959
FAX: 513-381-0070

ASQC *Quality Management Journal*

ASQC
PO BOX 3005
Milwaukee, WI 53201-3005

Phone: 414-272-8575

Best's Review

A M Best Road
Oldwick, NJ 08858-9999

Buying Quality

Purchasing Magazine
PO Box 497 New Town Branch
Boston, MA 02258

Phone: 617-964-3030

BYTE

One Phoenix Mill Lane
Peterborough, NH 03458

Phone: 603-924-2525
FAX: 603-924-2602

Continuous Improvement

8460 Dygert Drive
Alto, MI 49302

Phone: 616-891-9114
FAX: 616-891-9114

Continuous Journey

American Productivity & Quality Center
123 North Post Oak Lane Suite 300
Houston, TX 77024-7797

Phone: 713-685-4642

Executive Excellence

Institute for Principle-Centered Leadership
1 East Center Street Suite 303
Provo, UT 84606-3154

Phone: 801-375-4014
FAX: 801-377-5960

The Fabricator

The Groydon Group Ltd
833 Featherstone Road
Rockford, IL 61107-6302

Phone: 815-399-8700
FAX: 815-399-7279

F-D-C Reports

5550 Friendship Blvd
Suite One
Chevy Chase, MD 20815-7278

Phone: 301-657-9830 x 225
FAX: 301-656-3094

FDA Consumer

Folio

6 River Place
Stamford, CT 06907-1426

Forbes

60 Fifth Avenue
New York, NY 10011

Phone: 212-620-2200

H R Magazine

606 North Washington Street
Alexandria, VA 22314

Phone: 703-548-3440 X5310
FAX: 703-836-0367

Journal of the Society for Software Quality

PQR Group
190 North Mountain Avenue
Upland, CA 91786

Phone: 909-949-0857
FAX: 909-949-2968

Journal of Quality Technology

611 E. Wisconsin Avenue
P.O. Box 3005
Milwaukee, WI 53201-3005

Phone: 414-272-8575
FAX: 414-272-1734

Manufacturing Engineering

P.O. Box 930
Dearborn, MI 48121

Phone: 313-271-1500
FAX: 313-271-2861

Mechanical Engineering

345 East 47th Street
New York, NY 10017-2330

Phone: 212-705-7782
FAX: 212-705-7841

Mortgage Banking

Mortgage Bankers Association of America
1125—15th Street NW
Washington, DC 20005

Phone: 202-861-6500

Personnel Journal

245 Fischer Ave
B-2
Costa Mesa, CA 92626

Phone: 714-751-1883
FAX: 714-751-4106

Production

6600 Clough Pike
Cincinnati, OH 45244-4090

Phone: 513-231-8020
FAX: 513-231-2818

Production and Inventory Management Journal

APICS Headquarters
500 West Annandale Road
Falls Church, VA 22046-4274

Phone: 703-237-8344
FAX: 703-237-4316

Progressive Grocer

4 Stamford Forum
Stamford, CT 06901-3218

Purchasing

275 Washington Street
Newton, MA 02158-1630

Quality

191 S. Gary Avenue
Carol Stream, IL 60188

Phone: 708-665-1000
FAX: 708-462-2225

Quality Assurance Bulletin

24 Rope Ferry Road
Waterford, CT 06386

Phone: 203-442-4365

Quality At Work

24 Rope Ferry Road
Waterford, CT 06386

Phone: 800-876-9105

Quality Digest

PO Box 882
Red Bluff, CA 96080

Phone: 916-527-8875
FAX: 916-527-6983

Quality Management

24 Rope Ferry Road
Waterford, CT 06386-0001

Phone: 800-243-0876

Quality Progress

611 E. Wisconsin Avenue
PO Box 3005
Milwaukee, WI 53201-3005

Phone: 414-272-8575
FAX: 414-272-1734

Quality Solutions

24 Rope Ferry Road
Waterford, CT 06386

Phone: 203-442-4365

Quality Systems Update

Irwin Publishing
11150 Main Street
Fairfax, VA 22030

Phone: 703-591-9008
FAX: 703-591-0971

Risk Management

655 Third Avenue
New York, NY 10017-5637

Phone: 212-286-9364 x 248
FAX: 212-922-0716

Target

Association for Manufacturing Excellence
380 West Palatine Road
Wheeling, IL 60090-5863

Phone: 317-839-9829
FAX: 317-839-2979

Ward's Auto World

Ward's Communications
3000 Towne Centre Suite 2750
Southfield, MI 48075

Phone: 810-357-0800
FAX: 810-357-0810

INDEX

Butler Gas Products Co., FDA product
  seizure, 1-15–1-16
BYK Gardner, 3-210

C

CADEYES system, 3-242–3-243
Caldata Systems, 3-206
Calender, Doug, 3-206
Calibration, of artifacts, 3-199–3-201
California Eureka Award, 3-253
Caltabiano, John, 3-222
Campanizzi-Mook, Jane, 3-17, 3-21
Campbell, Mike, 3-119
Camp, Robert C., 3-264
Canada, trade outlook, 4-30
Cannizzaro, Michael N., 2-56
Canonical analysis, 3-167–3-171
  eigenanalysis, 3-168
  eigenangle, 3-167, 3-168–3-170
  eigenvectors, 3-169, 3-171
  nonstandard example of, 3-167
  numerical example, 3-168–3-169
  standard example of, 3-167
Capacitance method, non-contact
  measurement, 3-237, 3-243
Carl Zeiss, 3-210–3-211
Carrots and sticks approach, 3-152
Carter, Charles, 3-209
Caterpillar, 3-190, 3-192
Cause diagrams, 3-155
Center for Drug Evaluation and
  Research, 2-69
Center for Energy and Environmental
  Management (CEEM), 4-38
Center Line Flex-Plugs, 3-215
Certification
  of auditors, 3-235–3-237
  for employees, 2-21
Chappell, Robert T., 2-46
Chemical/process industry (CPI),
  supplier quality in, 3-226–3-228
China
  economic reform, 3-70
  and ISO 9000, 3-73
  and total quality management
    (TQM), 3-71–3-74
  trademark protection, 3-73–3-74
  trading volume of, 3-70
Choi, I.S., 3-138
Christensen, Robert, 3-210
Christopher, Robert C., 4-61
Chrysler, 4-17
Ciba-Geigy, 2-69
CIMNET Folders MICS, 3-117
City Kitchen, 2-26–2-27
Clapper, Allen R., 2-101
Clark, Greg, 3-67–3-69
Clarkson, Mark, 2-4
Cleary, Barbara A., 3-121
Clements, Richard B., 4-6, 4-11, 4-20,
  4-38, 6-7

Clinton, Bill, 2-36, 2-42, 3-161
CMI International, 3-205
C-mode scanning acoustic microscope
  (C-SAM), 3-207
Cohen, Dan, 3-239
Cole, Robert E., 4-62
Colicci, Michael, 3-192
Commare, Don, 3-204
Committee for European
  Standardization (CEN), 4-47
Competition, and cross-functional
  teams, 3-107
Composite materials
  ultrasonic inspection, 3-207–3-208
  x-ray inspection, 3-208
Computers
  man-machine interface (MMI), 2-6–
    2-9
  SCADA (supervisory control and
    data acquisition), 2-8
  structured query language (SQL),
    2-7–2-8
  Windows, 2-7, 2-8
  See also Software
Cone & vee design measure, 3-213
Cone, Beth, 3-190, 3-192
Conrail, quality goals, 2-103
Continuous quality improvement, BCS
  Richland, Inc., 3-87–3-88
Cookie Store, 3-281–3-282
Corrective action-oriented audit
  checklist, 3-229, 3-231
Costigan, Robert D., 3-52
Cost of quality
  appraisal costs, 3-152
  evaluation costs, 3-150–151
  failure costs, 3-151
  general ledger baseline assessment,
    3-154
  implementation team, 3-154
  low costs, caution about, 3-151–3-
    152
  prevention costs, 3-150, 3-152–3-153
  and process reengineering, 3-153–3-
    155
Crandall, R. L., 2-103
Crane, L. Stanley, 2-103
Creativity, and growth, 3-78–3-79
Creedon, Lawrence P., 3-70
CRISP (Continuous Rapid
  Improvement System of
  Production), 3-268
Crosby, M.D., 2-11
Crosby, Phil, 3-150
Cross-functional teams, 3-103–3-108,
  3-85–3-86
  awareness of impact of, 3-106
  barriers to, 3-108
  and boundary management, 3-104,
    3-106, 3-107
  communicating information about,
    3-107
  and competition, 3-107

credibility of, 3-108
customer interaction, 3-105
and differentiation, 3-107
functional department manager, role
  of, 3-104
compared to functional teams, 3-104
information requirements for, 3-105
and process reengineering, 3-154
resource needs of, 3-106
and senior management, 3-105
support and assistance for, 3-105,
  3-106
Cross-function management, 1-8–1-10
  concepts of, 1-8, 1-9
  cross-function committees, 1-8–1-10
  effectiveness of, 1-10
  problems with, 1-9–1-10
C-SAM, 3-204
CSX Corp., quality process, 2-103
Cummins Engine Co., 3-209
Currier, James H., 3-222
Curtis-Wright Flight Systems, 3-117
Cushing, Barry, 3-271
Customer feedback
  as energy boost, 3-90
  listening to customers, elements of,
    3-88–3-94
  and quality, 3-31
  quality feedback, 2-35
  recipients of, 3-90
  satisfaction as quality measure,
    3-269
  tools for, 3-91–3-94
  use of customer information, 3-90
  value conversations, 3-92–3-93
Customer retention, 2-28–2-31
  and customer complaints, 2-29–2-30
  improvement process, 2-29–2-31
  predictive model of, 2-29, 2-30
  problems related to, 2-28–2-29
Customers
  consumer orientation approach,
    1-4–5
  customer retention, 2-28–2-31
  Customer Satisfaction Management
    (CSM), 2-16–2-19
Customer Satisfaction Management
  (CSM), 2-16–2-19
  basic steps ink, 2-16
  employee participation, 2-17–2-18
  and middle management, 2-17
  necessity of, 2-18
  satisfaction goal setting, 2-18–2-19
  and senior management, 2-16–2-17
Customer satisfaction surveys, 3-84–
  3-85
Customer service, and process
  mapping, 3-278
Customer-service initiative, national
  Performance Review, 2-38–2-39
Customs Service, improvement of, 2-39
CUSUM, 3-132–3-136
CyberOptics Corp., 3-238